Herzog, Johann Jacob, Schaff, Philip; Hauck Albert

The new Schaff-Herzog encyclopedia of religious knowledge

Vol. 10

Herzog, Johann Jacob, Schaff, Philip; Hauck Albert

The new Schaff-Herzog encyclopedia of religious knowledge

Vol. 10

Inktank publishing, 2018

www.inktank-publishing.com

ISBN/EAN: 9783747768426

THE NEW
SCHAFF-HERZOG ENCYCLOPEDIA
OF
RELIGIOUS KNOWLEDGE

EDITED BY

SAMUEL MACAULEY JACKSON, D.D., LL.D.
(*Editor-in-Chief*)

WITH THE SOLE ASSISTANCE, AFTER VOLUME VI., OF

GEORGE WILLIAM GILMORE, M.A.
(*Associate Editor*)

AND THE FOLLOWING DEPARTMENT EDITORS

CLARENCE AUGUSTINE BECKWITH, D.D.
(*Department of Systematic Theology*)

HENRY KING CARROLL, LL.D.
(*Department of Minor Denominations*)

JAMES FRANCIS DRISCOLL, D.D.
(*Department of Liturgics and Religious Orders*)

JAMES FREDERIC McCURDY, PH.D., LL.D.
(*Department of the Old Testament*)

HENRY SYLVESTER NASH, D.D.
(*Department of the New Testament*)

ALBERT HENRY NEWMAN, D.D., LL.D.
(*Department of Church History*)

FRANK HORACE VIZETELLY, F.S.A.
(*Department of Pronunciation and Typography*)

VOLUME X
REUSCH — SON OF GOD

FUNK AND WAGNALLS COMPANY
NEW YORK AND LONDON

EDITORS

SAMUEL MACAULEY JACKSON, D.D., LL.D.
(EDITOR-IN-CHIEF.)
Professor of Church History, New York University.

GEORGE WILLIAM GILMORE, M.A.
(ASSOCIATE EDITOR.)
New York,
Formerly Professor of Biblical History and Lecturer on Comparative Religion, Bangor Theological Seminary.

DEPARTMENT EDITORS, VOLUME X

CLARENCE AUGUSTINE BECKWITH, D.D.,
(Department of Systematic Theology.)
Professor of Systematic Theology, Chicago Theological Seminary.

HENRY KING CARROLL, LL.D.,
(Department of Minor Denominations.)
Secretary of Executive Committee of the Western Section for the Fourth Ecumenical Methodist Conference.

JAMES FRANCIS DRISCOLL, D.D.,
(Department of Liturgics and Religious Orders.)
Rector of St. Gabriel's, New Rochelle, N. Y.

JAMES FREDERICK McCURDY, Ph.D., LL.D.,
(Department of the Old Testament.)
Professor of Oriental Languages, University College, Toronto.

HENRY SYLVESTER NASH, D.D.,
(Department of the New Testament.)
Professor of the Literature and Interpretation of the New Testament, Episcopal Theological School, Cambridge, Mass.

ALBERT HENRY NEWMAN, D.D., LL.D.,
(Department of Church History.)
Professor of Church History, Southwestern Baptist Theological Seminary, Fort Worth, Tex.

FRANK HORACE VIZETELLY, F.S.A.,
(Department of Pronunciation and Typography.)
Managing Editor of the STANDARD DICTIONARY, etc., New York City.

CONTRIBUTORS AND COLLABORATORS, VOLUME X

JUSTIN EDWARDS ABBOTT, D.D.,
Missionary in Bombay, India.

HANS ACHELIS, Th.D.,
Professor of Church History, University of Halle.

FRANKLIN CARL ARNOLD, Ph.D., Th.D.,
Professor of Church History, University of Breslau.

BRUNO BAENTSCH (†), Ph.D., Th.D.,
Late Professor, University of Jena.

FERENCZ BALOGH, D.D.,
Professor of Church History, Reformed Theological Academy, Debrecsen, Hungary.

HERMANN GEORG JULIUS BECK,
Consistorial Councilor and First Preacher, Bayreuth.

CLARENCE AUGUSTINE BECKWITH, D.D.,
Professor of Systematic Theology, Chicago Theological Seminary.

KARL BENRATH, Ph.D., Th.D.,
Professor of Church History, University of Königsberg.

IMMANUEL GUSTAV ADOLF BENZINGER, Ph.D., Th.Lic.,
German Orientalist and Vice-Consul for Holland in Jerusalem.

CARL BERTHEAU (†), Th.D.,
Late Pastor at St. Michael's, Hamburg.

EDWIN MUNSELL BLISS, D.D.,
Author of Books on Missions, Washington, D. C.

AMY GASTON CHARLES AUGUSTE BONET-MAURY, D.D., LL.D.,
Professor of Church History, Independent School of Divinity, Paris.

GOTTLIEB NATHANAEL BONWETSCH, Th.D.,
Professor of Church History, University of Göttingen.

GUSTAV BOSSERT, Ph.D., Th.D.,
Retired Pastor, Stuttgart.

JOHANN FRANZ WILHELM BOUSSET, Th.D.,
Professor of New Testament Exegesis, University of Göttingen.

FRIEDRICH HEINRICH BRANDES, Th.D.,
Reformed Minister and Chaplain at Bückeburg, Schaumburg-Lippe.

KARL BURGER (†), Th.D.,
Late Supreme Consistorial Councilor, Munich.

JOHN CAIRNS,
Clergyman of the United Free Church of Scotland, Dumfries, Scotland.

PAOLO CALVINO,
Pastor at Lugano, Switzerland.

HENRY KING CARROLL, LL.D.,
Secretary of the Executive Committee of the Western Section for the Fourth Ecumenical Methodist Conference.

JOHN FLEMING CARSON, D.D.,
Pastor of the Central Presbyterian Church, Brooklyn, New York.

JAMES CARTER,
Professor of Church History and Sociology, Lincoln University, Pa.

PAUL CHRIST (†), Th.D.,
Late Professor of Theology, University of Zurich.

FERDINAND COHRS, Th.Lic.,
Consistorial Councilor, Ilfeld, Germany.

WILLIAM HENRY COX,
Editor-in-Chief for the Salvation Army.

SAMUEL CRAMER, Th.D.,
Professor of the History of Christianity, University of Amsterdam, and Professor of Practical Theology, Mennonite Theological Seminary, Amsterdam.

AUGUST HERMANN CREMER (†), Th.D.,
Late Professor of Systematic Theology, University of Greifswald.

SAMUEL MARTIN DEUTSCH (†), Th.D.,
Late Professor of Church History, University of Berlin.

FRANZ WILHELM DIBELIUS, Ph.D., Th.D.,
Supreme Consistorial Councilor, City Superintendent, and Pastor of the Kreuzkirche, Dresden.

ERNST VON DOBSCHUETZ, Th.D.,
Professor of New Testament Exegesis, University of Breslau.

RICHARD WILHELM DOVE (†), Ph.D., Th.D.,
Late Professor of Ecclesiastical Law, University of Göttingen.

PAUL GOTTFRIED DREWS, Th.D.,
Professor of Theology, University of Berlin.

JAMES FRANCIS DRISCOLL, D.D.,
Pastor of St. Gabriel's, New Rochelle, New York.

SIMEON BILLINGHAM DUNN, D.D.,
Of the Editorial Staff of the New York *Observer*.

EMIL EGLI (†), Th.D.,
Late Professor of Church History, University of Zurich.

CHRISTIAN FRIEDRICH DAVID ERDMANN (†), Ph.D., Th.D.,
Late Honorary Professor of Church History, University of Breslau.

JOHN OLUF EVJEN, Ph.D.,
Professor of Theology, Augsburg Seminary, Minneapolis, Minn.

E. FABIAN, Ph.D.,
Gymnasial Professor in Zwickau, Saxony.

CHRISTIAN THEODOR FICKER, Ph.D.,
Emeritus Pastor at Eythra, near Leipsic.

FRITZ FLIEDNER (†), M.D.,
Late German Evangelist in Spain.

FRANK HUGH FOSTER, Ph.D., D.D.,
Professor of History, Olivet College, Michigan.

FRANZ HERMANN FRANK (†), Ph.D., Th.D.,
Late Professor of Theology, University of Erlangen.

GUSTAV WILHELM FRANK (†), Th.D.,
Late Professor of Dogmatics, Symbolics, and Christian Ethics, University of Vienna.

ALBERT FREYBE, Ph.D., Th.D.,
Emeritus Gymnasial Professor, Parchim, Mecklenburg.

GEORG FROBOESS,
Director for the Evangelical Lutheran Church in Prussia.

WILHELM GASS (†), Ph.D., Th.D.,
Late Professor of Theology, University of Heidelberg.

DAVID PERCY GILMORE, B.A.,
Specialist in Germanics, Brooklyn, N. Y.

GEORGE WILLIAM GILMORE, M.A.,
Formerly Lecturer on Comparative Religion, Bangor Theological Seminary, Associate Editor of The New Schaff-Herzog Encyclopedia of Religious Knowledge.

WASHINGTON GLADDEN, D.D., LL.D.,
Pastor of the First Congregational Church, Columbus, Ohio.

FRANZ GOERRES, Ph.D.,
Assistant Librarian, University of Bonn.

LEOPOLD KARL GOETZ, Ph.D., Th.D.,
Professor of Philosophy, University of Bonn.

WILHELM GOETZ (†), Ph.D.,
Late Honorary Professor of Geography, Technical High School, and Professor, Military Academy, Munich.

GWILYM OSWALD GRIFFITH,
Pastor of the Sixth Avenue Baptist Church, Brooklyn, N. Y.

GEORG GRUETZMACHER, Ph.D., Th.Lic.,
Extraordinary Professor of Church History, University of Heidelberg.

HERMANN GUTHE, Th.D.,
Professor of Old Testament Exegesis, University of Leipsic.

WILHELM HADORN, Th.Lic.,
Pastor in Bern and Lecturer on New Testament Exegesis, University of Bern.

ARTHUR CRAWSHAY ALLISTON HALL, D.D., LL.D.,
Protestant Episcopal Bishop of Vermont.

JULIUS HAMBURGER (†), Ph.D., Th.D.,
Late Professor of Theology, University of Munich.

ADOLF HARNACK, Ph.D., Th.D., Dr. Jur., M.D.,
General Director of the Royal Library, Berlin.

EDWIN FRANCIS HATFIELD (†), D.D.,
Late Stated Clerk of the Presbyterian General Assembly, New School.

ALBERT HAUCK, Ph.D., Th.D., Dr.Jur.,
Professor of Church History, University of Leipsic, Editor-in-Chief of the Hauck-Herzog *Realencyklopädie*.

CARL FRIEDRICH GEORG HEINRICI, Ph.D., Th.D.,
Professor of New Testament Exegesis, University of Leipsic.

HEINRICH HERMELINK, Ph.D., Th.Lic.,
Privat-docent in Church History, University of Leipsic.

JOHANN CHRISTOPH FRANZ MAX HEROLD, Th.D.,
Ecclesiastical Councilor, Dean and City Preacher, Neustadt-an-der-Aisch, Bavaria.

JOHANN JAKOB HERZOG (†), Ph.D., Th.D.,
Late Professor of Reformed Theology, University of Erlangen.

PAUL HINSCHIUS (†), Th.D., Dr.Jur.,
Late Professor of Ecclesiastical Law, University of Berlin.

OSWALD HOLDER-EGGER, Ph.D.,
Professor at Berlin and Director for the Publication of the *Monumenta Germaniæ Historica*.

KARL HOLL, Ph.D., Th.D.,
Professor of Church History, University of Berlin.

HENRY SCOTT HOLLAND, D.D.,
Canon of St. Paul's Cathedral, London.

GEORG HOLZ, Ph.D.,
Professor of German Language and Literature, University of Leipsic.

JOHN HORSCH,
Pastor at Scottdale, Pa.

CARL BERNHARD HUNDESHAGEN (†), Th.D.,
Late Professor of New Testament Exegesis at Bonn.

GEORGE McPHERSON HUNTER,
Secretary of the American Seamen's Friend Society.

KARL JOHANNES HERMANN JACOBY, Th.D.,
Professor of Homiletics, University of Königsberg.

MARTIN KAEHLER, Th.D.,
Professor of Dogmatics and New Testament Exegesis, University of Halle.

ADOLF HERMANN HEINRICH KAMP-HAUSEN (†), Th.D.,
Late Professor of Old Testament Exegesis, University of Bonn.

FERDINAND FRIEDRICH WILHELM KATTENBUSCH, Ph.D., Th.D.,
Professor of Dogmatics, University of Halle.

EMIL FRIEDRICH KAUTZSCH, Ph.D., Th.D.,
Professor of Old Testament Exegesis, University of Halle.

PETER GUSTAV KAWERAU, Th.D.,
Supreme Consistorial Councilor, Provost of St. Peter's, Berlin, and Honorary Professor, University of Berlin.

GOTTLOB KIRCHHOFER,
Minister at Schaffhausen, Switzerland.

OTTO KIRN, Ph.D., Th.D.,
Professor of Dogmatics, University of Leipsic.

RUDOLF KITTEL, Ph.D., Th.D.,
Professor of Old Testament Exegesis, University of Leipsic.

GEORG HEINRICH KLIPPEL (†), Ph.D.,
Late Rector at Verden, Prussia.

HEINRICH ADOLF KOESTLIN (†), Ph.D., Th.D.,
Late Privy Councilor in Cannstadt, formerly Professor of Theology, University of Giessen.

THEODOR FRIEDRICH HERMANN KOLDE, Ph.D., Th.D.,
Professor of Church History, University of Erlangen.

HERMANN GUSTAV EDUARD KRUEGER, Ph.D., Th.D.,
Professor of Church History, University of Giessen.

ERNST KUEHN, Th.D.,
Supreme Consistorial Councilor, Dresden.

ABRAHAM KUENEN (†), D.D.,
Late Professor of Theology, University of Leyden.

EUGEN LACHENMANN,
City Pastor, Leonberg, Württemberg.

GEORG RITTER VON LAUBMANN (†), Ph.D.,
Late Director of the Royal Library, Munich.

LUDWIG LEMME, Th.D.,
Professor of Systematic Theology, University of Heidelberg.

C. H. d'E. LEPPINGTON,
Fellow of the Royal Economic Society, England.

ORLANDO FAULKLAND LEWIS,
General Secretary of the Prison Association of New York.

E. LEYRER (†),
Late Pastor in Plochingen, Württemberg.

RUDOLF LIECHTENHAN, Th.Lic.,
Pastor at Buch, Canton of Zurich, Switzerland.

PAUL LOBSTEIN, Th.D.,
Professor of Dogmatics in the Evangelical Theological Faculty, University of Strasburg.

GERHARD LOESCHKE, Th. Lic.,
Privat-docent in Church History, University of Bonn.

FRIEDRICH ARMIN LOOFS, Ph.D., Th.D.,
Professor of Church History, University of Halle.

WILHELM PHILIPP FRIEDRICH FERDINAND LOTZ, Ph.D., Th.D.,
Professor of Old Testament Exegesis, University of Erlangen.

CHARLES HALLAN McCARTHY, Ph.D.,
Professor of American History in the Catholic University, Washington, D. C.

HERMANN MALLET (†),
Late Pastor in Bremen.

PHILIPP MEYER, Th.D.,
Supreme Consistorial Councilor, Hanover.

GEROLD MEYER VON KNONAU, Ph.D., Th.D.,
Professor of History, University of Zurich.

ALEXANDER MICHELSEN (†), Ph.D.,
Late Pastor at Lübeck.

CARL THEODOR MIRBT, Th.D.,
Professor of Church History, University of Marburg.

ERNST FRIEDRICH KARL MUELLER, Th.D.,
Professor of Reformed Theology, University of Erlangen.

GEORG MUELLER, Ph.D., Th.D.,
Inspector of Schools, Leipsic.

CHRISTOF EBERHARD NESTLE, Ph.D., Th.D.,
Professor in the Theological Seminary, Maulbronn, Württemberg.

ALBERT HENRY NEWMAN, D.D., LL.D.,
Professor of Church History, Southwestern Baptist Theological Seminary, Fort Worth, Texas.

THEODOR JULIUS NEY, Th.D.,
Supreme Consistorial Councilor, Speyer, Bavaria.

JAN JACOB VAN OOSTERZEE (†), Ph.D., Th.D.,
Late Professor of Theology, University of Utrecht.

CONRAD VON ORELLI, Ph.D., Th.D.,
Professor of Old Testament Exegesis and History of Religion, University of Basel.

KARL HERMANN PAHNCKE,
Ecclesiastical Inspector, Public Schools, Pforta, Prussia.

ANTON FRIEDRICH LUDWIG PELT (†), Ph.D., Th.D.,
Late Superintendent in Kemnitz.

CARL PETER (†), Th.D.,
Late Consistorial Councilor, Jena.

CARL PFENDER,
Pastor of St. Paul's Evangelical Lutheran Church, Paris.

EDUARD CHARLES PLATZHOFF-LEJEUNE, Ph.D.,
Formerly Privat-docent in Philosophy at Geneva.

LYMAN PIERSON POWELL,
Rector of St. John's, Northampton, Mass.

WALDO SELDEN PRATT, Mus.D.,
Professor of Music and Hymnology, Hartford Theological Seminary, Conn.

ERWIN PREUSCHEN, Ph.D., Th.D.,
Pastor at Hirschhorn-on-the-Neckar, Germany.

EDUARD GUILLAUME EUGÈNE REUSS (†), Ph.D., Th.D.,
Late Professor of Theology, University of Strasburg.

OTTO KARL ALBRECHT RITSCHL, Th.D.,
Professor of Systematic Theology in the Evangelical Theological Faculty, Bonn.

RUDOLF ROCHOLL (†), Th.D.,
Late Ecclesiastical Councilor, Düsseldorf.

GUSTAV RUDLOFF (†), Th.D.,
Late Superintendent in Wangenheim.

KARL HEINRICH SACK (†), Ph.D., Th.D.,
Late Professor of Theology at Bonn.

DAVID SCHLEY SCHAFF, D.D.,
Professor of Church History, Western Theological Seminary, Pittsburg, Pa.

PHILIP SCHAFF (†), D.D., LL.D.,
Late Professor of Church History, Union Theological Seminary, New York, and Editor of the Original SCHAFF-HERZOG ENCYCLOPÆDIA.

CHRISTOF GOTTLOB VON SCHEURL (†), Ph.D., Th.D.,
Late Professor in Nuremberg.

CARL SCHMIDT (†), Th.D.,
Late Professor of Theology, University of Strasburg.

EDMUND SCHMIDT,
Pastor in Krappitz, Prussia.

OSWALD SCHMIDT (†),
Late Superintendent in Werdau, Saxony.

JOHANNES SCHNEIDER,
Emeritus Pastor, Darmstadt.

CARL WILHELM SCHOELL (†), Ph.D., D.D.,
Late Pastor of the Savoy Church, London.

KARL SCHORNBAUM, Ph.D.,
Pastor in Alfeld, Prussia.

MAXIMILIAN VICTOR SCHULTZE, Th.D.,
Professor of Church History and Christian Archeology, University of Greifswald.

LUDWIG THEODOR SCHULZE, Ph.D., Th.D.,
Retired Professor of Systematic Theology, University of Rostock.

REINHOLD SEEBERG, Th.D.,
Professor of Systematic Theology, University of Berlin.

EMIL SEHLING, Dr.Jur.,
Professor of Ecclesiastical and Commercial Law, University of Erlangen.

WILLIAM AMBROSE SHEDD, D.D.,
Missionary, Urumia, Persia.

FRIEDRICH ANTON EMIL SIEFFERT, Ph.D., Th.D.,
Professor of New Testament Exegesis, University of Bonn.

ERNEST GOTTLIEB SIHLER, Ph.D.,
Professor of Latin, New York University.

EDUARD SIMONS, Th.D.,
Extraordinary Professor of Practical Theology, University of Berlin.

PHILIPP FRIEDRICH ADOLPH THEODOR SPAETH (†), D.D., LL.D.,
Late Professor in the Lutheran Theological Seminary, Mt. Airy, Philadelphia.

ANTHONY ANASTASIOU STAMOULI,
Formerly Member of the Editorial Staff of *Atlantis*, New York.

CHARLES JANEWAY STILLÉ (†), LL.D.,
Late Professor of History, University of Pennsylvania.

HERMANN LEBERECHT STRACK, Ph.D., Th.D.,
Extraordinary Professor of Old Testament Exegesis and Semitic Languages, University of Berlin.

LEWIS CLINTON STRANG,
Author and Christian Science Practitioner, Boston, Mass.

RUDOLF STUEBE, Ph.D.,
Head Master, Nicolai Gymnasium, Leipsic.

JAMES WESTFALL THOMPSON, Ph.D.,
Associate Professor of History, University of Chicago.

CRAWFORD HOWELL TOY, LL.D.,
Emeritus Professor of Hebrew, Harvard University.

PAUL TSCHACKERT, Ph.D., Th.D.,
Professor of Church History University of Göttingen.

JOHANN GERHARD WILHELM UHLHORN (†), Th.D.,
Late Abbot of Lokkum, Germany.

EBERHARD VISCHER, Th.D.,
Professor of Theology, University of Basel.

WILHELM VOGT, Ph.D.,
Gymnasial Rector, Nuremberg.

HENRI VUILLEUMIER, Th.D.,
Professor of Hebrew and Old Testament Exegesis, University of Lausanne.

JULIUS AUGUST WAGENMANN (†), Th.D.,
Late Consistorial Councilor, Göttingen.

HANS WAITZ, Th.D.,
Pastor in Darmstadt.

CARL HEINRICH VON WEIZSAECKER (†), Ph.D., Th.D.,
Late Professor of Theology, University of Tübingen.

JOHANN JAKOB WERNER,
Privat-docent in Medieval Philology, Zurich.

FRANCIS METHERALL WHITLOCK,
Pastor of the Bethlehem Congregational Church, Cleveland, Ohio.

AUGUST WUENSCHE, Ph.D., Th.D.,
Retired Titular Professor, Dresden.

RUDOLF ZEHNPFUND, Ph.D.,
Pastor in Oranienbaum.

OTTO ZOECKLER (†), Ph.D., Th.D.,
Late Professor of Church History and Apologetics, University of Greifswald.

RICHARD OTTO ZOEPFFEL (†), Ph.D., Th.D.,
Late Professor of Theology, University of Strasburg.

BIBLIOGRAPHICAL APPENDIX—VOLS. I—X

The following list of books is supplementary to the bibliographies given at the end of the articles contained in vols. I.-X., and brings the literature down to Feb. 20, 1911. In this list each title entry is printed in capital letters. It is to be noted that, throughout the work, in the articles as a rule only first editions are given. In the bibliographies the aim is to give either the best or the latest edition, and in case the book is published both in America and in some other country, the American place of issue is usually given the preference.

ABBOTT, E. A.: *The Son of Man: or, Contributions to the Study of the Thoughts of Jesus*, London, 1910.

AFRICA: R. E. Dennett, *Nigerian Studies; the religious and political System of Yoruba*, New York, 1910.

ALEXANDRIA: *CSCO*, vol. IX., fasc. II., contains Severus Ben el Mogaffa: *Historia Patriarcharum Alexandrinorum*, vol. I., fasc. II., ed. C. F. Seybold, Vienna, 1910.

APOCRYPHA: J. Müller, *Beiträge zur Erklärung und Kritik des Buches Tobit*, in *Revue de l'orient chrétien*, 1910.

APOLOGETICS: J. F. Love, *The Unique Message and the Universality of Christianity*, New York and Chicago, 1910.
W. D. Mackenzie, *The Final Faith; a Statement of the Nature and Authority of Christianity as the Religion of the World*, New York, 1910.

ARMENIA: T. E. Dowling, *The Armenian Church*, London, 1910.
M. Ormanian, *L'Église arménienne. Son histoire, sa doctrine, son régime, sa discipline, sa littérature, son présent*, Paris, 1910.

ASYLUM: J. C. Cox, *The Sanctuaries and Sanctuary Seekers of Mediæval England*, London, 1910.

ATONEMENT: J. B. Champion, *The Living Atonement*, Philadelphia, 1910.
C. C. Morgan, *A Lawyer's Brief on the Atonement*, Boston, 1911.

AUGUSTINE: W. J. S. Simpson, *St. Augustine and African Church Divisions*, London, 1910.
Sancti Aurelii Augustini episcopi de civitate dei libri XXII., ed. E. Hoffmann, vol. I., libri i.-xiii., Vienna, 1910.

BABYLONIA: C. Fossey, *L'Assyriologie en 1907. Généralités. Explorations et fouilles. Langues sumérienne et assyrienne. Geographie et histoire, religion, droit, vie privée, astronomie, météorologie, littérature, varia, archéologie, influences babyloniennes*, Paris, 1910.
R. F. Harper, *Assyrian and Babylonian Letters belonging to the Kouyunjik Collections of the British Museum*, vol. ix., Chicago, 1910.
H. Schneider, *Kultur und Denker der Babylonier und Juden*, 2 vols., Leipsic, 1910.

BACON, F.: G. W. Steeves, *Francis Bacon: a Sketch of his Life, Works, Literary Friends*, etc., London, 1910.

BERNARD OF CLAIRVAUX: *St. Bernard, Abbot of Clairvaux. Selections from his Letters, Meditations, etc., rendered into English by H. Grimley*, London, 1910.

BIBLE TEXT: *Der Cambridger Psalter*, Hamburg, 1911.
H. A. Sanders, *The Old Testament Manuscript in the Freer Collection*. Part I.: *The Washington Manuscript of Deuteronomy and Joshua*, New York, 1910.
A. Souter, *Novum Testamentum Græce*, London, 1910.
H. J. Vogels, *Die Harmonistik im Evangeliumtext des Codex Cantabrigiensis. Ein Beitrag zur neutestamentlichen Textkritik*, Leipsic, 1910.

BIBLE VERSIONS: J. O. Bevan, *Our English Bible: The History and Its Development*, London, 1911.
W. J. Heaton, *Our Own English Bible: its Translators and their Work*, London, 1910; *The Bible of the Reformation*, London, 1910.
J. P. Hentz, *Hist. of Lutheran Versions of the Bible*, Columbus, Ohio, 1910.
W. Muir, *Our Grand Old Bible. Being the Story of the Authorized Version of the English Bible, Told for the Tercentenary Celebration*, London, 1910.
Fourteenth Century English Bible Versions, ed. A. C. Pauis, Cambridge, 1904.

BIBLICAL CRITICISM: F. C. Conybeare, *History of New Testament Criticism*, London, 1910.
R. Kittel, *The Scientific Study of the Old Testament. Its Principal Results, and their Bearing upon Religious Instruction*, London, 1910.

BIBLICAL THEOLOGY: T. K. Cheyne, *The Two Religions of Israel. With a Re-examination of the Prophetic Narratives and Utterances*, London, 1910.
M. Dibelius, *Die Geisterwelt im Glauben des Paulus*, Göttingen, 1909.
P. C. Purves, *The Gospel according to Hosea and the Master's Gospel*, London, 1910.
H. C. Sheldon, *New Testament Theology*, new rev. ed., New York, 1911.
J. Weiss, *Paulus und Jesus*, Berlin, 1909.

BLAURER, T.: *Briefwechsel der Brüder Ambrosius und Thomas Blaurer, 1509–1548. Herausgegeben von der badischen historischen Kommission*, ed. Traugott Schiess. Vol. i.: *1509 bis Juni 1538*. Vol. ii., *August 1538 bis Ende 1548*, Freiburg, 1908–10.

BOSSUET, J. B.: E. Longuemare, *Bossuet et la société française sous le règne de Louis XIV.*, Paris, 1910.

BOURIGNON, A.: A. R. Macewen, *Antoinette Bourignon, Quietist; her Life and Doctrines*, New York, 1910.

BOWNE, B. P.: C. B. Pyle, *The Philosophy of Borden Parker Bowne and its Application to the Religious Problem*, Columbus, O., 1910.

BROOKS, P.: J. Gregory, *Phillips Brooks: A Study for Present-day Preachers*, London, 1911.

BRAHMANISM: H. Brunnhofer, *Das Buch der hundert Pfade (Catapatha Brahmana), die älteste Quelle der Ritualwissenschaft*, Bern, 1910.

BUDDHISM: T. Richard, *The New Testament of Higher Buddhism*, New York, 1911.
J. Wettha Sinha, *The Singularity of Buddhism, with Introduction and Notes by F. L. Woodward*, London, 1910.

BURKITT, F. C.: *The Earliest Sources for the Life of Jesus*, London, 1910.

BURMA: R. T. Kelly, *Burma; the Land and the People*, Boston, 1911.

CATHARINUS, AMBROSIUS: J. Schweiser, *Ambrosius Catharinus Politus (1484–1553), ein Theologe des Reformationszeitalters. Sein Leben und seine Schriften*, Münster, 1910.

CHARLES V.: E. Armstrong, *The Emperor Charles V.*, 2 vols., new ed., London, 1910.

CHINA: A. Little, *Gleanings from Fifty Years in China. Revised by Mrs. A. Little*, London, 1910.
E. H. Parker, *Studies in Chinese Religion*, New York, 1910.

CHRISTOLOGY: W. Olschewski, *Die Würzeln der paulinischen Christologie*, Königsberg, 1909.

CHURCH HISTORY: H. Appel, *Kurzgefasste Kirchengeschichte für Studierende.* Part 1. *Alte Kirchengeschichte*, 1909. Part 2. *Kirchengeschichte des Mittelalters*, Leipsic, 1910.
B. W. Bacon, *The Founding of the Church*, London, 1910.
F. W. Butler, *The Permanent Element in Christianity*, London, 1909.
L. David and P. Lorette, *Histoire de l'église*, Paris, 1910.
S. M. Deutsch, *Lehrbuch der Kirchengeschichte*, Bonn, 1909.
E. A. Edgehill, *The Spirit of Power, as seen in the Christian Church in the Second Century*, London, 1910.
Canon E. E. Holmes, *The Church; her Books and her Sacraments*, New York, 1910.
W. Köhler, *Idee und Persönlichkeit in der Kirchengeschichte*, Tübingen, 1910.
M. Manitius, *Geschichte der lateinischen Literatur des Mittelalters*, I. Teil: *Von Justinian bis zur Mitte des 10. Jahrhundert*, Munich, 1910.
C. Platts, *Pioneers of Faith*, London, 1910.
Sir W. M. Ramsay, *Pictures of the Apostolic Church, its Life and Thought*, Philadelphia, 1910.
K. Sell, *Christenthum und Weltgeschichte bis zur Reformation*, Leipsic, 1910.

CLEMENT OF ROME: *Bruchstücke des ersten Clemensbriefes*, ed. F. Rösch, Strasburg, 1910.

COMENIUS, J. A.: *The Great Didactic. Translated into English and edited with biographical, historical and critical Introductions by M. W. Keatinge*, part 1, London, 1910.

COMMON PRAYER, BOOK OF: J. H. Benton, *The Book of Common Prayer and Books Connected with its Origins and Growth; Catalogue of the Collection of Josiah Henry Benton*, Boston, 1910.

COMPARATIVE RELIGION: A. Churchward, *The Signs and Symbols of Primordial Man. Being an Explanation of the Evolution of Religious Doctrines from the Eschatology of the ancient Egyptians*, London, 1910.
F. B. Jevons, *The Idea of God in Early Religions*, London, 1910.

CONSCIENCE: T. H. Lipscomb, *Conscience and its Culture; or through Conscience to Christ*, Nashville, Tenn., 1910.

COOKE, G. A.: *The Progress of Revelation. Sermons chiefly on the Old Testament*, Edinburgh, 1910.

CREATION, BABYLONIAN ACCOUNTS OF THE: A. Kirchner, *Die babylonische Kosmogonie und der biblische Schöpfungsbericht. Ein Beitrag zur Apologie des biblischen Gottesbegriffes*, Münster, 1910.

DANIEL: E. Hertlein, *Der Daniel der Römerzeit*, Leipsic, 1908.

DANTE: R. W. Church, *Dante*, new ed., London, 1910.
F. Flamini, *Introduction to the Study of the Divine Comedy*, Boston, 1910.

DENMARK: A. Krarup and J. Lindbæk, *Acta Pontificum Danica*, vol. iv., *1471–92*, Copenhagen, 1910.

DIONYSIUS: A. B. Sharpe, *Mysticism, its true Nature and Value. With a Translation of the mystical Theology of Dionysius and of the Letters of Carus and Dorotheus*, London, 1910.

DISEASES AND THE HEALING ART: L. Kotelmann, *Die Opthalmologie bei den alten Hebräern. Aus den alt- und neutestamentlichen Schriften mit Berücksichtigung des Talmuds dargestellt*, Hamburg, 1910.

DIVORCE: H. J. Wilkens, *The History of Divorce and Remarriage. Compiled from Holy Scripture, Church Councils, and Authoritative Writers*, London, 1910.

DOBSCHUETZ, E. VON: *The Apostolic Age*, New York, 1910; *The Eschatology of the Gospels*, London, 1910.

DOCTRINE, HISTORY OF: G. N. Bonwetsch, *Grundriss der Dogmengeschichte*, Munich, 1909.
A. Humbert, *Les Origines de la theologie moderne.* I. *La Renaissance de l'antiquité chrétienne (1450–1520)*, Paris, 1910.

DODS, M.: *Early Letters of Marcus Dods*, London, 1911.

DOGMA, DOGMATICS: See below, LOBSTEIN.
J. H. Snowden, *The Basal Beliefs of Christianity*, New York, 1911.

EGYPT: E. A. W. Budge, *Facsimiles of Egyptian Hieratic Papyri in the British Museum*, British Museum, 1911.

EGYPTIAN EXPLORATION FUND: E. Naville, *The Eleventh Dynasty. Temple at Deir-el-Bahari.* Part II. *With Architectural Descriptions by Somers Clark. 13th Memoir of the Egyptian Exploration Fund*, 1911.

ENGLAND, CHURCH OF: J. F. Kendall, *A Short History of the Church of England*, New York, 1911.
F. J. Kinsman, *Principles of Anglicanism* London, 1911.

EPIPHANIUS: K. Holl, *Die handschriftliche Ueberlieferung des Epiphanius (Ancoratus und Panarion)*, Leipsic, 1910.

EPISCOPACY: D. Stone, *Episcopacy and Valid Orders in the Primitive Orders in the Primitive Church. A Statement of Evidence*, New York, 1910.

ESCHATOLOGY: See above, DOBSCHUETZ.

ETHICS: T. C. Hall, *History of Ethics within Organized Christianity*, London, 1910.

EUSEBIUS OF CÆSAREA: *Eusebii Hieronymi epistulæ.* Pars I. *Epistulæ I.-LXX.*, ed. I. Hilberg, Vienna, 1910.

EXORCISM: F. J. Dölger, *Der Exorzismus im altchristlichen Taufritual. Eine religionsgeschichtliche Studie*, Paderborn, 1909.

EZRA-NEHEMIAH: J. Theis, *Geschichtliche und literarkritische Fragen in Esra i.-vi.*, in *Abhandlungen, alttestamentliche*, vol. ii., part 4, Münster, 1910.

FAITH: J. G. W. Herrmann, *Faith and Morals.* 1. *Faith as Ritschl defined it;* 2, *The Moral Law as understood in Romanism and Protestantism*, London, 1910.
J. Lindsay, *The Psychology of Belief*, London, 1910.

GARVIE, A. E.: *The Christian Certainty amid the Modern Perplexity*, London, 1910.

GEIGER, A.: L. Geiger, *Abraham Geiger, Leben und Lebenswerk*, Berlin, 1910.

GERMANY: W. Konen, *Germanenbekehrung.* Part I. *Die Heidenpredigt und der Germanenbekehrung*, Düsseldorf, 1910.

GOSPELS: W. M. F. Petrie, *The Growth of the Gospels as Shown by Structural Criticism*, New York, 1910.
T. J. Thoburn, *The Resurrection Narratives and Modern Criticism. A Critique of Prof. Schmiedel's Article in the Encyclopædia Biblica*, London, 1910.
J. M. Wilson, *Studies in the Origins and Aims of the Four Gospels*, London, 1910.

HALL, F. J.: *The Trinity (Dogmatic Theology*, vol. iv.), New York and London, 1911.

HEBREWS, EPISTLE TO THE: F. Dibelius, *Der Verfasser des Hebräerbriefes. Eine Untersuchung zur Geschichte des Urchristentums*, Strasburg, 1910.

HEGEL, G. W. F.: *The Phenomenology of Mind*, 2 vols., *Transl., with Introduction and Notes by J. B. Baillie*, London, 1910.

HERRMANN, J. G. W.: See FAITH, above.

HEXATEUCH: See below under NAVILLE.
H. M. Wiener, *The Origin of the Pentateuch*, Oberlin, O., 1910.

HINDUISM: Brahm Sankar Misra, *Discourses on Radhasoami Faith. An Exposition of the Principles of the New Religious Order*, Benares, 1910.

HOLY SPIRIT: W. E. Biederwolf, *A Help to the Study of the Holy Spirit*, New York and Chicago, 1911.

HUGUENOTS: J. Bloundelle-Burton, *The Fate of Henry of Navarre*, London, 1910.

HUTTEN, U. VON: D. S. Jordan, *Ulrich von Hutten "Knight of the Order of Poets,"* Boston, 1910.

INNOCENT XI.: F. de Bojani, *Innocent XI. Sa correspondance avec ses nonces 21 Septembre 1676–31 Décembre 1679*, Rome, 1910.

ISAIAH: M. Glasebrook, *Studies in the Book of Isaiah*, New York, 1910.

ISRAEL, HISTORY OF: D. Chwolson, *Beiträge zur Entwickelung des Judentums*, Leipsic, 1910.
S. Daiches, *The Jews in Babylonia in the Time of Nehemiah according to Babylonian Inscriptions*, London, 1910.
A. Loisy, *The Religion of Israel*, New York, 1910.
L. Lucas, *Zur Geschichte der Juden im 4. Jahrhundert*, Berlin, 1910.
D. Neumark, *Geschichte der jüdischen Philosophie des Mittelalters nach Problemen dargestellt.* Vol. II., part 1. *Die Grundprinzipien;* part 3: *Attributenlehre*, 1st half: *Altertum*, Berlin, 1910.
N. Peters, *Die jüdische Gemeinde von Elephantine-Syene und ihr Tempel im 5. Jahrhundert vor Christi*, Freiburg, 1910.
W. M. F. Petrie, *Egypt and Israel*, London, 1910.

ITALY: G. Buschbell, *Reformation und Inquisition in Italien um die Mitte des XVI. Jahrhunderts*, Paderborn, 1910.
P. Villari, *Mediæval Italy from Charlemagne to Henry VII.*, London, 1910.

JAINISM: Nyâyâvatara: *The Earliest Jaina Work on Pure Logic*, by Siddha Sena Divakara, Calcutta, 1909.

JESUS CHRIST: C. M. Bishop, *Jesus the Worker; Studies in the Ethical Leadership of the Son of Man*, London, 1910.
A. Drews, *The Christ Myth. Translated from the Third Edition (revised and enlarged) by C. Burns*, Chicago and London, 1910.
F. H. Dudden, *Christ and Christ's Religion*, Edinburgh, 1910.
F. R. M. Hitchcock, *Christ and His Critics. Studies in the Person and Problems of Jesus*, London, 1910.
A. Niemojewski, *Gott Jesus im Lichte fremder und eigener Forschungen samt Darstellung der evangelischen Astralstoffe, Astralszenen und Astralsysteme*, 2 vols., Munich, 1910.

JOB: N. Schmidt, *The Message of the Poets; the Book of Job and Canticles and some Minor Poems in the Old Testament*, New York, 1911.

JOHN THE APOSTLE: E. H. Askwith, *The Historical Value of the Fourth Gospel*, London, 1910.
P. Ferguson, *A Month with the Apostle John. A Study of his First Epistle*, London, 1910.
G. T. Jowett, *The Apocalypse of St. John; a brief Contribution to the Controversy as to Date and Authority thereof with a short History of its interpretation*, New York, 1910.

KANT: F. Pinski, *Der höchste Standpunkt der Tranzendental Philosophie. Versuch einer Vervollständigung und systematischen Darstellung der letzten Gedanken Immanuel Kants*, Halle, 1911.
R. M. Wenley, *Kant and his Philosophical Revolution*, Edinburgh, 1910.

KEMPIS, T. À.: R. Storr, *Concordance to the Latin Original of De imitatione Christi*, New York, 1910.

KNOX, G. W.: *The Gospel of Jesus, the Son of God. An Interpretation for the Modern Man*, London, 1910.

LEIGHTON, R.: *Archbishop Leighton's Practise of the Presence of God: a Tercentenary Volume with Biographical Introduction by D. Butler*, London, 1911.

LITURGY: F. C. Eeles, *Traditional Ceremonial and Customs Connected with the Scottish Liturgy*, New York, 1910.
T. Schermann, *Der liturgische Papyrus von der Balyzeh. Eine Abendmahlsliturgie des Ostermorgens*, Leipsic, 1910.

LOBSTEIN, P.: *An Introduction to Protestant Dogmatics*, Chicago, 1910.

LUKE: B. S. Easton, *Linguistic Evidence for the Lucan Source L*, in *JBL*, xxix (1910), 139–180.

LUTHERANS: E. Weber, *Der Einfluss der protestantischen Schulphilosophie auf die orthodoxlutherische Dogmatik*, Leipsic, 1908.

MCCABE, J.: *The Evolution of Mind*, London, 1910.

MAGIC: T. de Cauzons, *La Magie et la sorcellerie en France*, Paris, 1910.

MANNING: V. de Marolles, *Kardinal Manning*, Mains, 1911.

MARY: S. Beissel, *Geschichte der Verehrung Marias im 16. und 17. Jahrhundert*, Freiburg, 1910.

MISSIONS: W. O. Carver, *Missions and Modern Thought*, New York, 1910.
J. Jackson, *Lepers: Thirty-six Years' Work Among Them. Being the History of the Mission to Lepers in India and the East, 1874–1910*, new ed., London, 1910.
H. F. Williams, *In Four Continents; a Sketch of the Foreign Missions of the Presbyterian Church, U. S.*, Richmond, Va., 1910.
W. T. Coppin, *John Martin; Pioneer, Missionary, Hero, and Saint*, London, 1911.
J. P. Jones, *The Modern Missionary Challenge; a Study of the Present Day World Missionary Enterprise; its Problems and Results*, New York and Chicago, 1910.
H. C. Mabie, *The Task worth while; or, the divine Philosophy of Missions*, Boston, 1910.
Alexander Tomory: *Indian Missionary*, Edinburgh, 1910.

METHODISTS: G. Alexander, *The Doctrines and Discipline of the Methodist Episcopal Church, South*, Nashville, Tenn., 1910.
W. J. Townsend, H. B. Workman, and G. E. Ayres, *New History of Methodism*, 2 vols., London, 1910.

MOHAMMED, MOHAMMEDANISM: M. Bromhall, *Islam in China. A Neglected Problem*, London, 1910.
J. Strzygowski, *Beiträge zur Kunstgeschichte des Mittelalters von Nordmesopotamien*, in *Materiaux pour l'épigraphie et l'histoire musulmanes du Diyar-Bekr par M. van Berchem*, Heidelberg and Paris, 1910.

MONASTICISM: M. Dix, *Instructions on the Religious Life. Given to the Sisters of St. Mary*, New York and London, 1910.

MORALITY, MORAL LAW: See FAITH, above.
E. Westermarck, *Ursprung und Entwickelung der Moralbegriffe*, vol. ii., Leipsic, 1909.

MYTHOLOGY: W. Schmidt, *Die Mythologie der austronesischen Völker*, Vienna, 1909; idem, *Grundlinien einer Vergleichung der Religionen und Mythologien der austronesischen Völker*, Vienna, 1910.

NAVILLE, E.: *La Découverte de la loi sous le Roi Josias. Une Interprétation égyptienne d'un texte biblique*, Paris, 1910, Eng. transl., *The Discovery of the Book of the Law under King Josiah*, London, 1910.

NESTORIANS: W. A. Wigram, *An Introduction to the History of the Assyrian Church; or the Church of the Sassinid Persian Empire, 100–640, A.D.*, London, 1910.

NESTORIUS: *Le Livre d'Heraclide de Dumas. Traduit en français par F. Nau, avec le concurs du R. P. Bedjan et de M. Brière. Suivi de texte grèc des trois homélies de Nestorius sur les tentations de Notre-Seigneur et de trois appendices: Lettre à Cosme, Presents envoyés d'Alexandrie, Lettre de Nestorius aux habitants de Constantinople*, Paris, 1910.

NICÆA: E. A. W. Budge, *Texts Relating to Saint Mêna of Egypt and Canons of Nicæa in a Nubian Dialect*, London, 1910.

NIETZSCHE, F.: S. Friedländer, *Friedrich Nietzsche: Eine intellektuelle Biographie*, Leipsic, 1911.
D. Halevy, *The Life of Friedrich Nietzsche*. Translated by J. M. Hone, London, 1911.
A. M. Ludovici, *Nietzsche*, London, 1910.
Works, vols. vii.–ix., New York, 1911.

NON-CONFORMISTS: J. Ritson, *The Romance of Nonconformity*, London, 1910.

NORTH AFRICAN CHURCH: F. Martroye, *Genseric. La Conquête vandale en Afrique et le destruction de l'empire d'occident*, Paris, 1907.
W. J. S. Simpson, *St. Augustine and African Church Divisions*, New York, 1910.

OESTERLEY, W. O. E., *The Psalms in the Jewish Church*, London, 1910.

ORDINATION: T. A. Lacey, *A Roman Diary and other Documents Relating to the Papal Inquiry into English Ordinations*, London, 1910.

ORGANIZATION: C. G. A. Harnack, *Constitution and Law of the Church in the First Two Centuries*, New York, 1910.

ORR, J.: *The Faith of a Modern Christian*, London, 1910.

PALESTINE: W. Harvey and Others, *The Church of the Nativity at Bethlehem*, London, 1911.

PARABLES: L. G. Broughton, *The Kingdom Parables and their Teaching*, New York and Chicago, 1910.

PASCAL: A. Grazier, *Les Derniers Jours de Blaise Pascal. Étude historique et critique*, Paris, 1911.

PASTORAL THEOLOGY: W. J. Davies, *The Minister at Work*, London, 1910.

PAUL THE APOSTLE: R. J. Fletcher, *A Study of the Conversion of St. Paul*, London, 1910.
M. Jones, *St. Paul the Orator*, London, 1910.
R. Knopf, *Paulus*, Leipsic, 1909.
E. Vischer, *Der Apostel Paulus und sein Werk*, Leipsic, 1910.

PAUL IV.: L. Riess, *Die Politik Pauls IV. und seiner Nepoten*, Berlin, 1909.

PERSECUTIONS: J. Visser, *Der Christenvervolgingen in de eerste eeuwen na Christus*, Kempen, 1910.

PERSIA: V. Bérard, *Révolutions de la Perse. Les Provinces, les peuples, et le governement du roi des rois*, Paris, 1910.
Ella C. Sykes, *Persia and its People*, New York, 1910.

PERU: C. R. Markham, *The Incas of Peru*, London, 1910.

PESSIMISM: A. Vögele, *Der Pessimismus und das Tragische in Kunst und Leben*, Freiburg, 1910.

PETRIE, W. M. F.: see above, ISRAEL, HISTORY OF.

PFLEIDERER, O.: *Primitive Christianity; Its Writings and Teachings in their Historical Connections*, vol. 3, London, 1910.

PHILIP OF HESSE: P. Wappler, *Die Stellung Kursachsens und des Landgrafen Philipp von Hessen zur Tauferbewegung*, Münster, 1910.

PHILO: E. Bréhier, *Philon, Commentaire allegorique des Saintes Lois*, Greek Text with French Translation, Paris, 1909.

PIERSON, A. T.: *Knowing the Scriptures; Rules and Methods of Bible Study*, London, 1910.

PLATONISM: N. Hartmann, *Platos Logik des Seins*, Giessen, 1909.

POPE, PAPACY: W. E. Beet, *The Rise of the Papacy*, London, 1910.
H. K. Mann, *The Lives of the Popes in Middle Ages*, vols. v.–viii., London, 1910.
L. Pastor, *History of the Popes from the close of the Middle Ages*, vol. x., London, 1911.
Regesta Pontificum Romanorum. Iubente regia societate Gottingensi congessit Paulus Fridolinus Kehr. Vol. i., *Italia pontificia sive repertorium privilegiorum et litterarum a Romanis pontificibus ante annum MCLXXXXVIII. Italiæ ecclesiis, monasteriis, concessorum singulisque personis concessorum*, vol. iii., *Etruria*, Berlin, 1908.

PRAGMATISM: J. M. MacEachran, *Pragmatismus, eine neue Richtung der Philosophie*, Leipsic, 1910.
A. W. Moore, *Pragmatism and its Critics*, Chicago, 1910.

PROPERTY, ECCLESIASTICAL: A. Hauck, *Die Entstehung der geistlichen Territorien*, Leipsic, 1909.

PSALMS: See above, OESTERLEY.

PSYCHOTHERAPY: R. M. Lawrence, *Primitive Psycho-Therapy and Quackery*, Boston and London, 1910.

PUNISHMENT, ETERNAL: C. K. Irwin, *Eternal Punishment. The Teaching of the Church and Holy Scripture upon the Doctrine*, London, 1910.

PUNISHMENT, FUTURE: Add to bibliography: W. Jackson, *The Doctrine of Retribution, philosophically Considered* (Bampton lectures), 1875.

REFORMATION: F. Thudichum, *Die deutsche Reformation 1517 bis 1537*, vol. ii., *1525–37*, Leipsic, 1909.

RELIGION, PHILOSOPHY OF: H. E. Warner, *The Psychology of the Christian Life*, London, 1911.

RITUALISM: F. G. Henke, *A Study of the Psychology of Ritualism*, Chicago, 1910.

ROBINSON, C. S.: Add to list of his writings: *Annotations upon Popular Hymns: for Use in Praise-Meetings* (New York, 1893).

SABBATH: Add to bibliography: G. Schiaparelli, *Astronomy in the O. T.*, chap. ix., Oxford, 1905.
A. T. Clay, *Amurru, the Home of the Northern Semites*, pp. 55 sqq., Philadelphia, 1909.

SANCTIFICATION: P. Fleisch, *Zur Geschichte der Heiligungsbewegung*. I Heft. *Die Heiligungsbewegung von Wesley bis Boardman*, Leipsic, 1910.

SAVONAROLA, G.: T. Sardi, *Girolamo Savonarola giudicato da un suo contemporaneo. Documenti inediti publicati da A. Bianconi*, Rome, 1911.

SOCIAL SERVICE: W. F. Crafts, *A Quarter Century of . . . Legislation . . . Relating to Moral and Social Reforms*, Washington, D. C., 1911.

BIOGRAPHICAL ADDENDA

Atwill, E. R.: d. at Kansas City Jan. 24, 1911.

Bertheau, C.: d. at Hamburg Dec. 19, 1910.

Bradford, A. H.: d. at Montclair, N. J., Feb. 18, 1911.

Dawson, W. J.: Accepted call to First Presbyterian Church, Newark, N. J., 1911.

Ferris, J. M.: d. at Flatbush, L. I., Jan. 30, 1911.

Funcke, O.: d. at Bremen Dec. 26, 1910.

Hastings, T. S.: d. at New York Apr. 2, 1911.

Klostermann, E.: called to Strasburg as ordinary professor of N. T. theology.

Krieg, K.: d. at Freiburg Jan. 24, 1911.

Mead, C. M.: d. at New Haven Feb. 15, 1911.

Paret, W.: d. at Baltimore Jan. 18, 1911.

ADDENDA ET CORRIGENDA

Vol. vii., p. 251, col. 2, lines 7 and 6 from bottom: Read " Doniso . . . Domniso " for " Donisone . . . Domnisone."

Vol. viii., p. 143, col. 2, line 14: Read " Odhner " for " Odlmer."

Vol. viii., p. 162, col. 1, line 17, first word: Read " *Papacy* " for " *Popes*."

Vol. viii., p. 236, col. 1, line 21 from bottom: Read " Nagot " for " Magot."

Vol. viii., p. 487, col. 2, line 40: Read " S. D. F." for " G. D. F."

Vol. ix., p. 120, col. 1, article Polycrates: Insert after line 2 " by his controversy with Pope Victor on the cele-."

Vol. ix., p. 122, col. 1, line 14 from bottom: Read " *den Ursprung* " for " *den Alter*."

Vol. ix., p. 132, col. 2, line 9 from bottom: Read " Giesebrecht " for " Gieselbrecht."

Vol. ix., p. 143, col. 2: Read " Hölscher " in signature.

Vol. ix., p. 163, col. 2, lines 18–17 from bottom: Read " Jan van Ruysbroeck " for " Henry Ruysbroek."

Vol. ix., p. 174, col. 1, line 17: Remove " (q.v.)."

Vol. ix., p. 175, col. 1, line 1: Read " I. F. E." for " J. E. F."

Vol. ix., p. 289, col. 1, line 21: Read " Batterson " for " Patterson "; line 24: Read " E. E." for " R. E."; line 47: Read " J. W." for " J. A."; line 53: Read " F. N." for " F. W."

Vol. ix., p. 337, col. 1, line 20: Read " 1723 " for " 1743 "; line 21: Read " Vlis " for " Blis "; line 10 from bottom: Read " Gunkel " for " Gunkelchen."

Vol. ix., p. 338, col. 1, line 21 from bottom: Read " *Apocryphæ* " for " *Apocryphi* "; line 19 from bottom: Read " Beloved of God."

Vol. ix., p. 339, col. 1, line 6 from bottom: Read " *Abrahæ* " for " *Abrahamæ* "; line 4 from bottom: Read " Vassilyew " for " Bassilyew."

Vol. ix., p. 340, col. 1, line 20: Read " B. Beer " for " G. Beer."

Vol. ix., p. 342, col. 1, line 2 from bottom: Read " Bousset " for " Bossuet "; col. 2, line 6: Read " Couard " for " Conrad."

Vol. ix., p. 479, col. 1, line 11 from bottom: Read " 1911 . . . $101,000 " for " 1908 . . . $65,000."

Vol. ix., p. 422, col. 2, line 37: Read " 1570 " for " 1557 "; line 39: Read " Bocskai " for " Bocskag."

Vol. x., p. 19, col. 2: In signature read " G. E." for " D."

Vol. x., p. 38, col. 2, line 3 from bottom: Change signature to " H. Cremer."

LIST OF ABBREVIATIONS

Abbreviations in common use or self-evident are not included here. For additional information concerning the works listed, see vol. i., pp. viii.–xx., and the appropriate articles in the body of the work.

ADB	*Allgemeine deutsche Biographie*, Leipsic, 1875 sqq., vol. 53, 1907
Adv	*adversus*, "against"
AJP	*American Journal of Philology*, Baltimore, 1880 sqq.
AJT	*American Journal of Theology*, Chicago, 1897 sqq.
AKR	*Archiv für katholisches Kirchenrecht*, Innsbruck, 1857–61, Mainz, 1872 sqq.
ALKG	*Archiv für Litteratur- und Kirchengeschichte des Mittelalters*, Freiburg, 1885 sqq.
Am	American
AMA	*Abhandlungen der Münchener Akademie*, Munich, 1763 sqq.
ANF	*Ante-Nicene Fathers*, American edition by A. Cleveland Coxe, 8 vols. and index, Buffalo, 1887; vol. ix., ed. Allan Menzies, New York, 1897
Apoc	Apocrypha, apocryphal
Apol	*Apologia, Apology*
Arab	Arabic
Aram	Aramaic
art	article
Art. Schmal	Schmalkald Articles
ASB	*Acta sanctorum*, ed. J. Bolland and others, Antwerp, 1643 sqq.
ASM	*Acta sanctorum ordinis S. Benedicti*, ed. J. Mabillon, 9 vols., Paris, 1668–1701
Assyr	Assyrian
A. T.	*Altes Testament*, "Old Testament"
Augs. Con	Augsburg Confession
A. V	Authorized Version (of the English Bible)
Baldwin, *Dictionary*	J. M. Baldwin, *Dictionary of Philosophy and Psychology*, 3 vols. in 4, New York, 1901–05
Bardenhewer, *Geschichte*	O. Bardenhewer, *Geschichte der altkirchlichen Litteratur*, 2 vols., Freiburg, 1902
Bardenhewer, *Patrologie*	O. Bardenhewer, *Patrologie*, 2d ed., Freiburg, 1901
Bayle, *Dictionary*	*The Dictionary Historical and Critical of Mr. Peter Bayle*, 2d ed., 5 vols., London, 1734–38
Benzinger, *Archäologie*	I. Benzinger, *Hebräische Archäologie*, 2d ed., Freiburg, 1907
Bingham, *Origines*	J. Bingham, *Origines ecclesiasticæ*, 10 vols., London, 1708–22; new ed., Oxford, 1855
Bouquet, *Recueil*	M. Bouquet, *Recueil des historiens des Gaules et de la France*, continued by various hands, 23 vols., Paris, 1738–76
Bower, *Popes*	Archibald Bower, *History of the Popes . . . to 1758, continued by S. H. Cox*, 3 vols., Philadelphia, 1845–47
BQR	*Baptist Quarterly Review*, Philadelphia, 1867 sqq.
BRG	See Jaffé
Cant	Canticles, Song of Solomon
cap	*caput*, "chapter"
Ceillier, *Auteurs sacrés*	R. Ceillier, *Histoire des auteurs sacrés et ecclésiastiques*, 16 vols. in 17, Paris, 1858–69
Chron	*Chronicon*, "Chronicle"
I Chron	I Chronicles
II Chron	II Chronicles
CIG	*Corpus inscriptionum Græcarum*, Berlin, 1825 sqq.
CIL	*Corpus inscriptionum Latinarum*, Berlin, 1863 sqq.
CIS	*Corpus inscriptionum Semiticarum*, Paris, 1881 sqq.
cod	codex
cod. Theod	*codex Theodosianus*
Col	Epistle to the Colossians
col., cols	column, columns
Conf	*Confessiones*, "Confessions"
I Cor	First Epistle to the Corinthians
II Cor	Second Epistle to the Corinthians
COT	See Schrader
CQR	*The Church Quarterly Review*, London, 1875 sqq.
CR	*Corpus reformatorum*, begun at Halle, 1834, vol. lxxxix., Berlin and Leipsic, 1905 sqq.
Creighton, *Papacy*	M. Creighton, *A History of the Papacy from the Great Schism to the Sack of Rome*, new ed., 6 vols., New York and London, 1897
CSCO	*Corpus scriptorum Christianorum orientalium*, ed. J. B. Chabot, I. Guidi, and others, Paris and Leipsic, 1903 sqq.
CSEL	*Corpus scriptorum ecclesiasticorum Latinorum*, Vienna, 1867 sqq.
CSHB	*Corpus scriptorum historiæ Byzantinæ*, 49 vols., Bonn, 1828–78
Currier, *Religious Orders*	C. W. Currier, *History of Religious Orders*, New York, 1896
D	Deuteronomist
Dan	Daniel
DB	J. Hastings, *Dictionary of the Bible*, 4 vols. and extra vol., Edinburgh and New York, 1898–1904
DCA	W. Smith and S. Cheetham, *Dictionary of Christian Antiquities*, 2 vols., London, 1875–80
DCB	W. Smith and H. Wace, *Dictionary of Christian Biography*, 4 vols., Boston, 1877–87
DCG	J. Hastings, J. A. Selbie, and J. C. Lambert, *A Dictionary of Christ and the Gospels*, 2 vols., Edinburgh and New York, 1906–1908
Deut	Deuteronomy
De vir. ill	*De viris illustribus*
DGQ	See Wattenbach
DNB	L. Stephen and S. Lee, *Dictionary of National Biography*, 63 vols. and supplement 3 vols., London, 1885–1901
Driver, *Introduction*	S. R. Driver, *Introduction to the Literature of the Old Testament*, 10th ed., New York, 1910
E	Elohist
EB	T. K. Cheyne and J. S. Black, *Encyclopædia Biblica*, 4 vols., London and New York, 1899–1903
Eccl	*Ecclesia*, "Church"; *ecclesiasticus*, "ecclesiastical"
Eccles	Ecclesiastes
Ecclus	Ecclesiasticus
ed	edition; *edidit*, "edited by"
Eph	Epistle to the Ephesians
Epist	*Epistola, Epistolæ*, "Epistle," "Epistles"
Ersch and Gruber, *Encyklopädie*	J. S. Ersch and J. G. Gruber, *Allgemeine Encyklopädie der Wissenschaften und Künste*, Leipsic, 1818 sqq.
E. V	English versions (of the Bible)
Ex	Exodus
Ezek	Ezekiel
fasc	fasciculus
Fr	French
Friedrich, *KD*	J. Friedrich, *Kirchengeschichte Deutschlands*, 2 vols., Bamberg, 1867–69
Gal	Epistle to the Galatians
Gams, *Series episcoporum*	P. B. Gams, *Series episcoporum ecclesiæ Catholicæ*, Regensburg, 1873, and supplement, 1886
Gee and Hardy, *Documents*	H. Gee and W. J. Hardy, *Documents Illustrative of English Church History*, London, 1896
Germ	German
GGA	*Göttingische Gelehrte Anzeigen*, Göttingen, 1824 sqq.
Gibbon, *Decline and Fall*	E. Gibbon, *History of the Decline and Fall of the Roman Empire*, ed. J. B. Bury, 7 vols., London, 1896–1900
Gk	Greek
Gross, *Sources*	C. Gross, *The Sources and Literature of English History . . . to 1485*, London, 1900
Hab	Habakkuk
Haddan and Stubbs, *Councils*	A. W. Haddan and W. Stubbs, *Councils and Ecclesiastical Documents Relating to Great Britain and Ireland*, 3 vols., Oxford, 1869–78

Hær	Refers to patristic works on heresies or heretics, Tertullian's *De præscriptione*, the *Pros haireseis* of Irenæus, the *Panarion* of Epiphanius, etc.
Hag	Haggai
Harduin, *Concilia*	J. Harduin, *Conciliorum collectio regia maxima*, 12 vols., Paris, 1715
Harnack, *Dogma*	A. Harnack, *History of Dogma . . . from the 3d German edition*, 7 vols., Boston, 1895–1900
Harnack, *Litteratur*	A. Harnack, *Geschichte der altchristlichen Litteratur bis Eusebius*, 2 vols. in 3, Leipsic, 1893–1904
Hauck, *KD*	A. Hauck, *Kirchengeschichte Deutschlands*, vol. i., Leipsic, 1904; vol. ii., 1900; vol. iii., 1906; vol. iv., 1903
Hauck-Herzog, *RE*	*Realencyklopädie für protestantische Theologie und Kirche*, founded by J. J. Herzog, 3d ed. by A. Hauck, Leipsic, 1896–1909
Heb	Epistle to the Hebrews
Hebr	Hebrew
Hefele, *Conciliengeschichte*	C. J. von Hefele, *Conciliengeschichte*, continued by J. Hergenröther, vols. i.–vi., viii.–ix., Freiburg, 1883–93
Heimbucher, *Orden und Kongregationen*	M. Heimbucher, *Die Orden und Kongregationen der katholischen Kirche*, 2d ed. 3 vols., Paderborn, 1907
Helyot, *Ordres monastiques*	P. Helyot, *Histoire des ordres monastiques, religieux et militaires*, 8 vols., Paris, 1714–19; new ed., 1839–42
Henderson, *Documents*	E. F. Henderson, *Select Historical Documents of the Middle Ages*, London, 1892
Hist	History, *histoire*, *historia*
Hist. eccl	*Historia ecclesiastica, ecclesiæ*, "Church History"
Hom	*Homilia, homiliai*, "homily, homilies"
Hos	Hosea
Isa	Isaiah
Ital	Italian
J	Jahvist (Yahwist)
JA	*Journal Asiatique*, Paris, 1822 sqq.
Jacobus, *Dictionary*	*A Standard Bible Dictionary*, ed. M. W. Jacobus, . . . E. E. Nourse, . . . and A. C. Zenos, New York and London, 1909
Jaffé, *BRG*	P. Jaffé, *Bibliotheca rerum Germanicarum*, 6 vols., Berlin, 1864–73
Jaffé, *Regesta*	P. Jaffé, *Regesta pontificum Romanorum . . . ad annum 1198*, Berlin, 1851; 2d ed., Leipsic, 1881–88
JAOS	*Journal of the American Oriental Society*, New Haven, 1849 sqq.
JBL	*Journal of Biblical Literature and Exegesis*, first appeared as *Journal of the Society of Biblical Literature and Exegesis*, Middletown, 1882–88, then Boston, 1890 sqq.
JE	*The Jewish Encyclopedia*, 12 vols., New York, 1901–06
JE	The combined narrative of the Jahvist (Yahwist) and Elohist
Jer	Jeremiah
Josephus, *Ant*	Flavius Josephus, "Antiquities of the Jews"
Josephus, *Apion*	Flavius Josephus, "Against Apion"
Josephus, *Life*	Life of Flavius Josephus
Josephus, *War*	Flavius Josephus, "The Jewish War"
Josh	Joshua
JPT	*Jahrbücher für protestantische Theologie*, Leipsic, 1875 sqq.
JQR	*The Jewish Quarterly Review*, London, 1888 sqq.
JRAS	*Journal of the Royal Asiatic Society*, London, 1834 sqq.
JTS	*Journal of Theological Studies*, London, 1899 sqq.
Julian, *Hymnology*	J. Julian, *A Dictionary of Hymnology*, revised edition, London, 1907
KAT	See Schrader
KB	See Schrader
KD	See Friedrich, Hauck, Rettberg
KL	*Wetzer und Welte's Kirchenlexikon*, 2d ed., by J. Hergenröther and F. Kaulen, 12 vols., Freiburg, 1882–1903
Krüger, *History*	G. Krüger, *History of Early Christian Literature in the First Three Centuries*, New York, 1897
Krumbacher, *Geschichte*	K. Krumbacher, *Geschichte der byzantinischen Litteratur*, 2d ed., Munich, 1897
Labbe, *Concilia*	P. Labbe, *Sacrorum conciliorum nova et amplissima collectio*, 31 vols., Florence and Venice, 1759–98
Lam	Lamentations
Lanigan, *Eccl. Hist*	J. Lanigan, *Ecclesiastical History of Ireland to the 13th Century*, 4 vols., Dublin, 1829
Lat	Latin, Latinized
Leg	*Leges, Legum*
Lev	Leviticus
Lichtenberger, *ESR*	F. Lichtenberger, *Encyclopédie des sciences religieuses*, 13 vols., Paris, 1877–1882
Lorenz, *DGQ*	O. Lorenz, *Deutschlands Geschichtsquellen im Mittelalter*, 3d ed., Berlin, 1887
LXX	The Septuagint
I Macc	I Maccabees
II Macc	II Maccabees
Mai, *Nova collectio*	A. Mai, *Scriptorum veterum nova collectio*, 10 vols., Rome, 1825–38
Mal	Malachi
Mann, *Popes*	R. C. Mann, *Lives of the Popes in the Early Middle Ages*, London, 1902 sqq.
Mansi, *Concilia*	G. D. Mansi, *Sanctorum conciliorum collectio nova*, 31 vols., Florence and Venice, 1728
Matt	Matthew
MGH	*Monumenta Germaniæ historica*, ed. G. H. Pertz and others, Hanover and Berlin, 1826 sqq. The following abbreviations are used for the sections and subsections of this work: *Ant.*, *Antiquitates*, "Antiquities"; *Auct. ant.*, *Auctores antiquissimi*, "Oldest Writers"; *Chron. min.*, *Chronica minora*, "Lesser Chronicles"; *Dip.*, *Diplomata*, "Diplomas, Documents"; *Epist.*, *Epistolæ*, "Letters"; *Gest. pont. Rom.*, *Gesta pontificum Romanorum*, "Deeds of the Popes of Rome"; *Leg.*, *Leges*, "Laws"; *Lib. de lite*, *Libelli de lite inter regnum et sacerdotium sæculorum xi. et xii. conscripti*, "Books concerning the Strife between the Civil and Ecclesiastical Authorities in the Eleventh and Twelfth Centuries"; *Nec.*, *Necrologia Germaniæ*, "Necrology of Germany"; *Poet. Lat. ævi Car.*, *Poetæ Latini ævi Carolini*, "Latin Poets of the Caroline Time"; *Poet. Lat. med. ævi*, *Poetæ Latini medii ævi*, "Latin Poets of the Middle Ages"; *Script.*, *Scriptores*, "Writers"; *Script. rer. Germ.*, *Scriptores rerum Germanicarum*, "Writers on German Subjects"; *Script. rer. Langob.*, *Scriptores rerum Langobardicarum et Italicarum*, "Writers on Lombard and Italian Subjects"; *Script. rer. Merov.*, *Scriptores rerum Merovingicarum*, "Writers on Merovingian Subjects"
Mic	Micah
Milman, *Latin Christianity*	H. H. Milman, *History of Latin Christianity, Including that of the Popes to . . . Nicholas V.*, 8 vols., London, 1860–61
Mirbt, *Quellen*	C. Mirbt, *Quellen zur Geschichte des Papsttums und des römischen Katholicismus*, Tübingen, 1901
MPG	J. P. Migne, *Patrologiæ cursus completus, series Græca*, 162 vols., Paris, 1857–66
MPL	J. P. Migne, *Patrologiæ cursus completus, series Latina*, 221 vols., Paris, 1844–64
MS., MSS.	Manuscript, Manuscripts
Muratori, *Scriptores*	L. A. Muratori, *Rerum Italicarum scriptores*, 28 vols., 1723–51
NA	*Neues Archiv der Gesellschaft für ältere deutsche Geschichtskunde*, Hanover, 1876 sqq.
Nah	Nahum
n.d.	no date of publication
Neander, *Christian Church*	A. Neander, *General History of the Christian Religion and Church*, 6 vols., and index, Boston, 1872–81
Neh	Nehemiah
Niceron, *Mémoires*	R. P. Niceron, *Mémoires pour servir à l'histoire des hommes illustrés* . . . , 43 vols., Paris, 1729–45
Nielsen, *Papacy*	F. K. Nielsen, *History of the Papacy in the Nineteenth Century*, 2 vols., New York, 1906
Nippold, *Papacy*	F. Nippold, *The Papacy in the Nineteenth Century*, New York, 1900
NKZ	*Neue kirchliche Zeitschrift*, Leipsic, 1890 sqq.
Nowack, *Archäologie*	W. Nowack, *Lehrbuch der hebräischen Archäologie*, 2 vols., Freiburg, 1894
n.p.	no place of publication
NPNF	*The Nicene and Post-Nicene Fathers*, 1st series, 14 vols., New York, 1887–92; 2d series, 14 vols., New York, 1890–1900
N. T.	New Testament, *Novum Testamentum*, *Nouveau Testament*, *Neues Testament*
Num	Numbers
Ob	Obadiah

O. S. B. — *Ordo sancti Benedicti*, "Order of St. Benedict"

O. T. — Old Testament

OTJC — See Smith

P — Priestly document

Pastor, *Popes* — L. Pastor, *The History of the Popes from the Close of the Middle Ages*, 8 vols., London, 1891–1908

PEA — *Patres ecclesiæ Anglicanæ*, ed. J. A. Giles, 34 vols., London, 1838–46

PEF — Palestine Exploration Fund

I Pet — First Epistle of Peter

II Pet — Second Epistle of Peter

Platina, *Popes* — B. Platina, *Lives of the Popes from . . . Gregory VII. to . . . Paul II.*, 2 vols., London, n.d.

Pliny, *Hist. nat.* — Pliny, *Historia naturalis*

Potthast, *Wegweiser* — A. Potthast, *Bibliotheca historica medii ævi, Wegweiser durch die Geschichtswerke*, Berlin, 1896

Prov — Proverbs

Ps — Psalms

PSBA — *Proceedings of the Society of Biblical Archæology*, London, 1880 sqq.

q.v., qq.v — *quod (quæ) vide*, "which see"

Ranke, *Popes* — L. von Ranke, *History of the Popes*, 3 vols., London, 1906

RDM — *Revue des deux mondes*, Paris, 1831 sqq.

RE — See Hauck-Herzog

Reich, *Documents* — E. Reich, *Select Documents Illustrating Mediæval and Modern History*, London, 1905

REJ — *Revue des études juives*, Paris, 1880 sqq.

Rettberg, *KD* — F. W. Rettberg, *Kirchengeschichte Deutschlands*, 2 vols., Göttingen, 1846–48

Rev — Book of Revelation

RHR — *Revue de l'histoire des religions*, Paris, 1880 sqq.

Richardson, *Encyclopaedia* — E. C. Richardson, *Alphabetical Subject Index and Index Encyclopaedia to Periodical Articles on Religion, 1890–99*, New York, 1907

Richter, *Kirchenrecht* — A. L. Richter, *Lehrbuch des katholischen und evangelischen Kirchenrechts*, 8th ed. by W. Kahl, Leipsic, 1886

Robinson, *Researches*, and *Later Researches* — E. Robinson, *Biblical Researches in Palestine*, Boston, 1841, and *Later Biblical Researches in Palestine*, 3d ed. of the whole, 3 vols., 1867

Robinson, *European History* — J. H. Robinson, *Readings in European History*, 2 vols., Boston, 1904–06

Robinson and Beard, *Modern Europe* — J. H. Robinson, and C. A. Beard, *Development of Modern Europe*, 2 vols., Boston, 1907

Rom — Epistle to the Romans

RTP — *Revue de théologie et de philosophie*, Lausanne, 1873

R. V — Revised Version (of the English Bible)

sæc — *sæculum*, "century"

I Sam — I Samuel

II Sam — II Samuel

SBA — *Sitzungsberichte der Berliner Akademie*, Berlin, 1882 sqq.

SBE — F. Max Müller and others, *The Sacred Books of the East*, Oxford, 1879 sqq., vol. xlviii., 1904

SBOT — *Sacred Books of the Old Testament* ("Rainbow Bible"), Leipsic, London, and Baltimore, 1894 sqq.

Schaff, *Christian Church* — P. Schaff, *History of the Christian Church*, vols. i.–iv., vi., vii., New York, 1882–92, vol. v., 2 parts, by D. S. Schaff, 1907–10

Schaff, *Creeds* — P. Schaff, *The Creeds of Christendom*, 3 vols., New York, 1877–84

Schrader, *COT* — E. Schrader, *Cuneiform Inscriptions and the Old Testament*, 2 vols., London, 1885–88

Schrader, *KAT* — E. Schrader, *Die Keilinschriften und das Alte Testament*, 2 vols., Berlin, 1902–03

Schrader, *KB* — E. Schrader, *Keilinschriftliche Bibliothek*, 6 vols., Berlin, 1889–1901

Schürer, *Geschichte* — E. Schürer, *Geschichte des jüdischen Volkes im Zeitalter Jesu Christi*, 4th ed., 3 vols., Leipsic, 1902 sqq.; Eng. transl., 5 vols., New York, 1891

Script — *Scriptores*, "writers"

Scrivener, *Introduction* — F. H. A. Scrivener, *Introduction to New Testament Criticism*, 4th ed., London, 1894

Sent — *Sententia*, "Sentences"

S. J. — *Societas Jesu*, "Society of Jesus"

SMA — *Sitzungsberichte der Münchener Akademie*, Munich, 1860 sqq.

Smith, *Kinship* — W. R. Smith, *Kinship and Marriage in Early Arabia*, London, 1903

Smith, *OTJC* — W. R. Smith, *The Old Testament in the Jewish Church*, London, 1892

Smith, *Prophets* — W. R. Smith, *Prophets of Israel . . . to the Eighth Century*, London, 1895

Smith, *Rel. of Sem* — W. R. Smith, *Religion of the Semites*, London, 1894

S. P. C. K — Society for the Promotion of Christian Knowledge

S. P. G — Society for the Propagation of the Gospel in Foreign Parts

sqq — and following

Strom — *Stromata*, "Miscellanies"

s.v — sub voce, or sub verbo

Swete, *Introduction* — H. B. Swete, *Introduction to the Old Testament in Greek*, London, 1900

Syr — Syriac

Thatcher and McNeal, *Source Book* — O. J. Thatcher and E. H. McNeal, *A Source Book for Mediæval History*, New York, 1905

I Thess — First Epistle to the Thessalonians

II Thess — Second Epistle to the Thessalonians

ThT — *Theologische Tijdschrift*, Amsterdam and Leyden, 1867 sqq.

Tillemont, *Mémoires* — L. S. le Nain de Tillemont, *Mémoires . . . ecclésiastiques des six premiers siècles*, 16 vols., Paris, 1693–1712

I Tim — First Epistle to Timothy

II Tim — Second Epistle to Timothy

TJB — *Theologischer Jahresbericht*, Leipsic, 1882–1887, Freiburg, 1888, Brunswick, 1889–1897, Berlin, 1898 sqq.

Tob — Tobit

TQ — *Theologische Quartalschrift*, Tübingen, 1819 sqq.

TS — J. A. Robinson, *Texts and Studies*, Cambridge, 1891 sqq.

TSBA — *Transactions of the Society of Biblical Archæology*, London, 1872 sqq.

TSK — *Theologische Studien und Kritiken*, Hamburg, 1826 sqq.

TU — *Texte und Untersuchungen zur Geschichte der altchristlichen Litteratur*, ed. O. von Gebhardt and A. Harnack, Leipsic, 1882 sqq.

Ugolini, *Thesaurus* — B. Ugolinus, *Thesaurus antiquitatum sacrarum*, 34 vols., Venice, 1744–69

V. T — *Vetus Testamentum, Vieux Testament*, "Old Testament"

Wattenbach, *DGQ* — W. Wattenbach, *Deutschlands Geschichtsquellen*, 5th ed., 2 vols., Berlin, 1885; 6th ed., 1893–94; 7th ed., 1904 sqq.

Wellhausen, *Heidentum* — J. Wellhausen, *Reste arabischen Heidentums*, Berlin, 1887

Wellhausen, *Prolegomena* — J. Wellhausen, *Prolegomena zur Geschichte Israels*, 6th ed., Berlin, 1905, Eng. transl., Edinburgh, 1885

ZA — *Zeitschrift für Assyriologie*, Leipsic, 1886–88, Berlin, 1889 sqq.

Zahn, *Einleitung* — T. Zahn, *Einleitung in das Neue Testament*, 3d ed., Leipsic, 1907; Eng. transl., *Introduction to the New Testament*, 3 vols., Edinburgh, 1909

Zahn, *Kanon* — T. Zahn, *Geschichte des neutestamentlichen Kanons*, 2 vols., Leipsic, 1888–92

ZATW — *Zeitschrift für die alttestamentliche Wissenschaft*, Giessen, 1881 sqq.

ZDAL — *Zeitschrift für deutsches Alterthum und deutsche Literatur*, Berlin, 1876 sqq.

ZDMG — *Zeitschrift der deutschen morgenländischen Gesellschaft*, Leipsic, 1847 sqq.

ZDP — *Zeitschrift für deutsche Philologie*, Halle, 1869 sqq.

ZDPV — *Zeitschrift des deutschen Palästina-Vereins*, Leipsic, 1878 sqq.

Zech — Zechariah

Zeph — Zephaniah

ZHT — *Zeitschrift für die historische Theologie*, published successively at Leipsic, Hamburg, and Gotha, 1832–75

ZKG — *Zeitschrift für Kirchengeschichte*, Gotha, 1876 sqq.

ZKR — *Zeitschrift für Kirchenrecht*, Berlin, Tübingen, Freiburg, 1861 sqq.

ZKT — *Zeitschrift für katholische Theologie*, Innsbruck, 1877 sqq.

ZKW — *Zeitschrift für kirchliche Wissenschaft und kirchliches Leben*, Leipsic, 1880–89

ZNTW — *Zeitschrift für die neutestamentliche Wissenschaft*, Giessen, 1900 sqq.

ZPK — *Zeitschrift für Protestantismus und Kirche*, Erlangen, 1838–76

ZWT — *Zeitschrift für wissenschaftliche Theologie*, Jena, 1858–60, Halle, 1861–67, Leipsic, 1868 sqq.

SYSTEM OF TRANSLITERATION

The following system of transliteration has been used for Hebrew:

א = ' or omitted at the beginning of a word.	ז = z	ע = '
בּ = b	ח = ḥ	פּ = p
ב = bh or b	ט = ṭ	פ = ph or p
גּ = g	י = y	צ = ẓ
ג = gh or g	כּ = k	ק = ḳ
דּ = d	כ = kh or k	ר = r
ד = dh or d	ל = l	שׂ = s
ה = h	מ = m	שׁ = sh
ו = w	נ = n	תּ = t
	ס = s	ת = th or t

The vowels are transcribed by a, e, i, o, u, without attempt to indicate quantity or quality. Arabic and other Semitic languages are transliterated according to the same system as Hebrew. Greek is written with Roman characters, the common equivalents being used.

KEY TO PRONUNCIATION

When the pronunciation is self-evident the titles are not respelled; when by mere division and accentuation it can be shown sufficiently clearly the titles have been divided into syllables, and the accented syllables indicated.

a as in *sofa*	o as in not	iu as in duration
ä " " *arm*	ô " " nor	c = k " " cat
a " " *at*	u " " full[2]	ch " " *church*
â " " *fare*	ū " " rule	cw = qu as in *queen*
e " " pen[1]	ʊ " " but	dh (*th*) " " *the*
ē " " *fate*	ʊ̄ " " burn	f " " *fancy*
i " " *tin*	ai " " pine	g (hard) " " *go*
ī " " machine	au " " *out*	H " " loch (Scotch)
o " " *obey*	ei " " oil	hw (*wh*) " " *why*
ō " " *no*	iū " " few	j " " *jaw*

[1] In accented syllables only; in unaccented syllables it approximates the sound of e in over. The letter ṇ, with a dot beneath it, indicates the sound of n as in ink. Nasal n (as in French words) is rendered n.

[2] In German and French names ū approximates the sound of u in dune.

THE NEW SCHAFF-HERZOG ENCYCLOPEDIA OF RELIGIOUS KNOWLEDGE

REUSCH, reish, **FRANZ HEINRICH:** German Old Catholic; b. at Brilon (78 m. n.e. of Cologne) Dec. 4, 1825; d. at Bonn Mar. 3, 1900. He was educated at the universities of Bonn (1843–45), Tübingen, and Munich (1845–47), and the seminary of Cologne (1848–49); he was ordained to the priesthood in 1849, chaplain of St. Alban's at Cologne until 1853, when he returned to Bonn as lecturer in the theological seminary there, and in 1854 became privat-docent in the Roman Catholic theological faculty of the university of the same city. In 1858 he was appointed associate professor of Old-Testament exegesis, and three years later became full professor, while in 1873–74 he was rector of the university. The Vatican Council of 1870 marked an epoch in the life of Reusch, after he had already written his commentaries on Tobit (1857) and Ecclesiasticus (1861), as well as a *Lehrbuch der Einleitung in das Alte Testament* (1859) and *Bibel und Natur, Vorlesungen über die mosaische Urgeschichte und ihr Verhältnis zu den Ergebnissen der Naturforschung* (1862). As a theologian he had taken a position with the liberal wing of the Roman Catholics, as evidenced by his editorship of the *Theologisches Litteraturblatt* from 1866 to 1877. His refusal to subscribe to the declaration of papal infallibility, however, caused him to be suspended and excommunicated, and he then took an active part in organizing the Old Catholic Church, being made general vicar by Reinkens, and also acting as pastor of the Old Catholic congregation at Bonn. With the abolition of the requirement of celibacy in his denomination in 1878, Reusch resigned his offices, though he continued to give instruction in religion, as well as to conduct occasional services and to hear confessions.

His change of confession turned Reusch from Old-Testament exegesis to the history of the Roman Catholic Church after the Reformation. Here belong, accordingly, his *Luis de Leon und die spanische Inquisition* (1873), *Der Prozess Galileis und die Jesuiten* (1879), and, above all, his *Index der verbotenen Bücher* (2 vols., 1883–85). Together with J. J. I. von Döllinger (q.v.) he published the *Selbstbiographie des Kardinals Bellarmin* (1887) and the *Geschichte der Moralstreitigkeiten in der römisch-katholischen Kirche seit dem sechzehnten Jahrhundert* (2 vols., 1889), and after Döllinger's death he edited his *Briefe und Erklärungen über die vatikanischen Dekrete* (1890) and *Kleinere Schriften* (1890). During this latter period of his life Reusch also wrote, besides numerous briefer contributions, *Die deutschen Bischöfe und der Aberglaube* (1879) and *Beiträge zur Geschichte des Jesuitenordens* (1894), while his last work was his *Briefe an Bunsen von römischen Kardinälen und Prälaten (1818–87) mit Erläuterungen* (1897). (L. K. Goetz.)

Bibliography: L. K. Goetz, *Franz Heinrich Reusch 1825–1900*, Gotha, 1901; J. F. von Schulte, *Der Altkatholicismus*, Giessen, 1887; J. Mayor, *Franz Heinrich Reusch*, Cambridge, 1901; Vigouroux, *Dictionnaire*, fasc. xxxiv. 1078–79.

REUSS, rois, **EDUARD GUILLAUME EUGÈNE:** Biblical scholar; b. at Strasburg July 18, 1804; d. there Apr. 15, 1891. His preliminary studies were pursued at the gymnasium of his native city, during which his bent was developed for accurate scholarship; he continued work first at the University of Strasburg, where his dissertation *De statu literarum theologicarum per sæcula VII. et VIII.* was written (1825), after which he went to Göttingen and later to Halle and Jena, and finally to Paris, where he worked under Sylvestre de Sacy. In 1828 he became privat-docent in the Protestant seminary at Strasburg, in 1829 licentiate in theology with the thesis *De libris Veteris Testamenti apocryphis*, extraordinary professor in 1834, professor in 1836, and he entered the theological faculty in 1838. During the rest of his activity there he held many offices of importance and influence.

Reuss did not permit himself to engage in a wide field of research, and had no interest in either dogmatic or practical theology, while he preached only three times. Philosophic speculation also had no attraction for him, and he confined his efforts to Biblical science, in which he evinced the talents of a historical investigator, showing patience in pursuing details and diligence in collecting facts. An illustration of this is the fact that he projected his work on the history of the Old Testament as early as 1834 but issued it only in 1881 (*Geschichte der heiligen Schriften des Alten Testaments*, Brunswick). Graf was one of his students and was influenced by him in the line of work carried on by himself and further developed by Kuenen and Wellhausen. A like importance attaches to his work on the New Testament, his original edition of *Die Geschichte der heiligen Schriften Neuen Testaments* appearing in Brunswick, 1842 (6th ed., 1887; Eng. transl., *Hist. of the Sacred Scriptures of the N. T.*, Edinburgh,

1884), in subsequent editions growing greatly in size, comprehensiveness, and completeness. His general attitude had some connections with the Tübingen school, but was much more conservative. His *Bibliotheca Novi Testamenti Græci* (1872) is the result of twenty years of unremitting toil. His work as a teacher was no less effective than his literary labors, fitting his teachings to the needs of his students, and eschewing the merely pedantic, and he lectured in both French and German. The results of his first lectures in French was a demand for the printing of his work, and this ended in his *Hist. de la théologie chrétienne au siècle apostolique* (2 vols., Strasburg, 1852; Eng. transl., *Hist. of Christian Theology in the Apostolic Age*, 2 vols., London, 1872–74). Other works which may be noted are *Die johanneische Theologie* (Jena, 1847); *Hist. du canon des saintes écritures dans l'église chrétienne* (Paris, 1863; Eng. transl., *Hist. of the Canon of the Holy Scriptures in the Christian Church*, Edinburgh, 1884); *La Bible, traduction nouvelle avec introductions et commentaires* (16 vols., Paris, 1874–81); *Notitia codicis quatuor evangeliorum Græci* (Cambridge, 1889); and a large number of luminous contributions to the *Revue de théologie* (1850–67) and to other periodicals. He also collaborated in the complete edition of Calvin's works (see CALVIN, JOHN, Bibliography), for which he furnished the prolegomena.

(P. LOBSTEIN.)

BIBLIOGRAPHY: Reuss' correspondence, ed. K. Budde and H. J. Holtzmann, appeared at Giessen, 1904. Consult: T. Gerold, *Eduard Reuss, 1804–91*, Strasburg, 1892; idem, *Edouard Reuss. Notice biographique*, Paris, 1897; A. Grotz, in *Vie chrétienne*, May, 1891; H. Holtzmann, in *Protestantische Kirchenzeitung*, 1891, pp. 385–393; P. Lobstein, in *Evangile et liberté*, 1891, nos. 20–23; idem, in *Revue chrétienne*, viii (1891), 481–487; J. H. W. Stuckenberg, in *Homiletic Review*, xxiii (1892), 81–82; C. A. Briggs, *General Introduction to the Study of Holy Scripture*, passim, New York, 1899; Vigouroux, *Dictionnaire*, fasc. xxxiv. 1079–1080.

REUTER, rei'ter, **HERMANN FERDINAND:** German Lutheran; b. at Hildesheim Aug. 30, 1817; d. at Kreiensen (35 m. s.w. of Brunswick) Sept. 17, 1889. He was educated at the universities of Göttingen (1837–38) and Berlin (1838–40), and in 1843, after having published his *De erroribus qui ætate media doctrinam christianam de sancta eucharistia turpaverunt* (Berlin, 1840) and *Johannes von Salisbury: zur Geschichte der christlichen Wissenschaft* (1842), he began as privat-docent his lectures at Berlin, which were eventually to range over the entire domain of the historical theology of the time. In 1845 he published at Berlin the first volume of his *Geschichte Alexander des Dritten und seiner Zeit*, which he later entirely rewrote (3 vols., Berlin, 1860–64). In 1852 he became associate professor at Breslau, where he lectured primarily on church history, though he also gave courses in systematic theology. During this period, besides editing the *Allgemeines Repertorium für die theologische Litteratur*, of which he was the head from 1845 to 1860, he published his *Abhandlungen zur systematischen Theologie* (Berlin, 1855). Immediately after the publication of this collection Reuter was called to Greifswald as professor of theology. He now began to restrict himself more and more to symbolics, the results being shown in his *Ueber die Eigenthümlichkeit der sittlichen Tendenz des Protestantismus im Verhältnis zum Katholizismus* (Greifswald, 1869).

In 1866 Reuter returned to Breslau as professor of church history. Pursuing the theme already begun in his history of Alexander III., he wrote his *Geschichte der religiösen Aufklärung im Mittelalter vom Ende des achten Jahrhunderts bis zum Anfang des vierzehnten* (2 vols., Berlin, 1875–77). In 1876 he was called to Göttingen as the successor of Duncker. Here he was appointed abbot of Bursfelde in 1881, having been a consistorial councilor at Breslau since 1869. In 1887 he issued his *Augustinische Studien* (Gotha, 1887), and in the same year received, in honor of his seventieth birthday, the *Kirchengeschichtliche Studien* of T. Brieger, P. Tschackert, T. Kolde, F. Loofs, K. Mirbt, and his son, A. Reuter (Leipsic, 1888). Reuter also contributed largely to theological periodicals, especially to the *ZKG*, of which he was one of the founders.

(T. KOLDE.)

BIBLIOGRAPHY: *Worte gesprochen an dem Sarge des Professors Hermann Reuter*, Gotha, 1889; T. Brieger, in *ZKG*, vol. xi.

REUTER, QUIRINUS: German Reformed; b. at Mosbach (20 m. e. of Heidelberg) Sept. 27, 1558; d. at Heidelberg Mar. 22, 1613. He was educated at the Sapienzkollegium, a theological institution in Heidelberg, and when the Reformed were dismissed from it in 1577 by the Lutheran Louis VI., he received a scholarship at the Dionysianum, an institute for indigent scholars. In the following year (1578) he accepted a call to Neustadt. In 1580 he went to Breslau as the tutor of the eldest son of Andreas Dudith, whom he succeeded in winning over completely to Reformed views. He quickly became the confidant of Dudith, whose *Orationes* he published posthumously (Offenbach, 1590). During his residence in Breslau, Reuter is said to have written his *De significatione cometarum*, but early in 1582 he was recalled by John Casimir to Neustadt. He did not, however, leave Breslau until the end of Mar., 1583. His teacher Ursinus had died on the sixth of the same month, and at the suggestion of Dudith Reuter edited the works of Ursinus (3 vols., Heidelberg, 1612).

Reuter's initial duties in Neustadt were teaching and preaching. He was soon appointed third pastor at Neustadt, and in 1584 was the opponent of Jakob Grynæus in the disputation between the Lutherans and Reformed. Soon after he became teacher at the Pædagogium, and in the same year was made pastor at Bensheim, while in 1587 he was called to the pastorate of Neuhausen near Worms. Three years later he was appointed second teacher at the Sapienzkollegium, but in 1593 became the pastor of the Reformed church in Speyer. In 1598 he succeeded Pareus as ephor of the Sapienzkollegium. Four years later he was appointed professor of Old-Testament theology at Heidelberg, a position which he retained until his death. Reuter was the author of *Censura catecheseos Heidelbergensis diatriba de ubiquitate; Tractatus de ecclesia; Aphorismi theologici de vera religione; De cultu Dei naturali; De lege morali non abrogata; Utrum inter ecclesiam Lutheranam et pontificiam sit speranda conjunctio; De reformatione ecclesiæ;* and a commentary on Obadiah. (J. Schneider.)

Bibliography: The original source is an oration by Simon Stenius issued in 1613. Dependent upon this are: P. Freber, *Theatrum virorum clarorum*, 2 vols., Nuremberg, 1688; M. Adam, *Vitæ clarorum virorum*, pp. 390 sqq., Frankfort, 1706; C. G. Jöcher, *Gelehrten-Lexikon*, 10 vols., Bremen, 1750–87; J. Schwab, *Quatuor seculorum rectorum in academia*, Heidelberg, 1786; *ADB*, xxxviii. 328–329.

REUTERDAHL, rei'ter-dūl, **HENRIK:** Swedish archbishop; b. at Malmö (20 m. s.e. of Copenhagen) Sept. 10, 1795; d. at Upsala June 29, 1870. After completing his education at the University of Lund, he became, in 1817, docent at the theological seminary at the same city, associate adjunct in the theological faculty in 1824, and prefect of the seminary in 1826. Several years later he was made first adjunct of theology, was appointed chief librarian of the university in 1838, full professor of theology in 1844. With all his duties Reuterdahl found time for literary pursuits. Together with J. H. Thomander, Bergquist, and others, he founded the "Theological Quarterly" in 1827, and in 1838 published the first volume of his *Svenska kyrkans historia* (3 vols., Lund, 1838–63), a work in which the ecclesiastical material is obscured by details of secular politics, though its author's careful investigation of original sources renders it important for future investigators. In 1844 Reuterdahl was elected deputy to the diet for the theological seminary, and was repeatedly reelected, even after being appointed provost of the cathedral at Lund in 1845. He was minister of religion, 1852–55, and in this capacity sought forcibly to prevent any defections from the Swedish church through sectarian movements, thus arousing considerable opposition. In 1855 Reuterdahl was chosen bishop of Lund, and in the following year was appointed archbishop by the king, as well as prochancellor of the University of Upsala. During his administration sweeping reforms were carried out by Charles XV. in 1865, whereby the clergy ceased to form an estate in the diet. Reuterdahl, reluctantly acquiescing, held the first general synod under the new order of affairs in Sept., 1868. In the winter of 1869 severe illness put an end to his public career.

(A. Michelsen†.)

REVEL, ALBERT: Waldensian; b. at Torre Pellice (21 m. s.w. of Turin), Italy, Jan. 2, 1837; d. at Florence Nov. —, 1888. He was educated at the Waldensian college of his native place, at the theological school at Florence, and in the New College (Free Church), Edinburgh; was ordained in 1861; became professor of Latin and Greek literature in the Waldensian college at Torre Pellice, 1861, and professor of Biblical literature and exegesis to the Waldensian Church, Florence, 1870. He was the author of *L'Epistola di S. Jacobo* (Florence, 1868); *L'Epistola di S. Clemente Romano à Corinti* (1869); *Antichita bibliche* (1872); *Teoria del culto* (1875); *Le origini del Papato* (1875); *Cento lezioni sulla vita di Gesu* (1875); *Storia letteraria dell' antico Testamento* (Poggibonsi, 1879); *Manuale par lo studio della lingua ebraica* (Florence, 1879); *I Salmi; verzione e commento sopra i Salmi i.–xl.* (1880); *Il Nuovo Testamento, tradotto sul testo originale* (1881); *Le sette chiese dell' Asia Minore* (1886); *Enciclopedia delle scienze teologiche* (1886); *Letteratura ebraica* (2 vols., Milan, 1888); and *I sette suggelli* (*Apoc.* IV.–VII.; Florence, 1890).

REVELATION.

Origin and Meaning (§ 1).
Biblical History (§ 2).
Dogmatic History (§ 3).
Modern Method (§ 4).
Subjectivism (§ 5).
Depreciation of the Historical and Personal (§ 6).
Theory Based on the Bible and Positivism (§ 7).
The Doctrine of the Word of God (§ 8).
Philosophic Adjustment of this View (§ 9).

1. Origin and Meaning.

Revelation is the act of God in disclosing or communicating truth to the human soul. The concept here becomes a subject of theological discussion as a scientific technical expression. Doubtless it comes from the Greek Bible (*apokalyptein, phaneroun, dēloun, gnorizein*), where the variety of representation indicates that, as later in the language of prayer and hymn, no fixedness of idea had yet been reached. The idea embodied in the later technical term was distinctly that of an act of God, direct or indirect. Ecclesiastical Latin first provided definite form by laying down the term *revelare*, with *manifestare* for narrower usage. With the Christian era philosophy ceased to employ itself exclusively with the concept of God; so religious phenomena, and consequently also the idea of revelation, were taken under consideration, especially after the advent of the genus-concept of *religio*, which is not found in the Bible. With increasing measure *religio* and *revelare* become twin-thoughts; the idea of revelation became estranged from its original historical ground and both were subjected to comparative generalization and lifted to the rare atmosphere of abstraction. The utmost content comprehended in these conceptions may be denoted as that which constitutes the ground of religion. The variety of meanings is not improbably due to subservience to expediency in theological system-building. Fundamental to all views is a making or becoming manifest, whether the object enter within the horizon for the first time (either existing previously or coming into existence simultaneously), or the removing of an impediment to its realization (either without or within the recipient). By this the conveyance of the description, originally received by sensible appreciation, to the spiritual realization is for the most part effected, if this also mediates through sense. The process of revelation presupposes consciousness for its object, and through taking possession of intuition for the sphere of religion, there fall to revelation, as its content, the actual or possible subjects of a religious character.

2. Biblical History.

Thought on these points originated in connection with the historical monotheism of the Bible. God is represented as opening intercourse with men by various means. Theophany or the appearance of angels alternates or combines with speech. Miraculous events assume the value of signs. Decisive experiences of the people or of divinely appointed persons are conceived as specially designed dispensations of God. Prophecy comes to the front, retiring what resembles oracle (Urim and Thummin; q.v.), and by the prophets God now speaks directly to the people. Thus the word coming from God takes its authoritative place. In the immediate pre-Christian period, under the impression that prophecy has been silenced, apocalyptic revelation takes its place. Instead of continuous intercourse with God there arises tradition with the dogma of sacred Scripture and its inspiration, more and more extraordinary, in representation. Dependence upon Hellenism introduced the allegorical method of interpretation. This dogma of Old-Testament Scripture was carried over for the estimation and treatment of the New, with two points of difference. First, the Jewish representation dealt with reflection upon events in the past; the New arose under the sense of a living intercourse with God. Second, and more significant, Judaism directs its inquiry to the transcendent God who controls the world; the New Testament realizes more intimately than in olden time the relation with God, and this through the presence of the Holy Spirit. In the fellowship of the risen Christ all are in the most direct communion, as were the prophets. This assurance is dependent on the knowledge of the person of him who was sent by the only true God (John xvii. 3). Jesus is more than prophet; he not only speaks the word of God, but this was made a human person in him, manifesting the invisible God. What this person represents historically, is transmitted and interpreted by the Spirit of God and Christ in the hearts of believers. In this Christ are all the treasures of wisdom but not their acquirement, for redemption is the instrumental good.

Two elements, more distinct in thought than in life, are contained in the New-Testament idea of the Spirit of Christ in Christianity: the distinctive significance of the historical fact named Christ; and the immediate contact of every Christian with God through his Spirit. The conception of the former is identified with the received account of it, and subsequently with the Bible. With the completion of the double canon of Scripture, the other element, conscious possession, either had to lose itself in the confirmation of crystallizing tradition, or aim to sustain its independence by new productivity, which it did in Montanism (q.v.) and Ecstasy (q.v.), or in eclectic Biblicism or mysticism. In the next place, the Church in awe of traditionalism fell a victim to the confusion of dogma and revelation. This, together with the native equipment and training of the Greek theologians, resulted in positing the operation of revelation as the advancement of knowledge, and the validity of such knowledge was to be deduced from the idea of the supernatural mode of transmission. In support was adduced, in dependence upon Scripture, the proof of the Spirit and power evidenced by the accordance of prophecy with fulfilment and by miracle. This resulted, in the course of the Middle Ages, in the problem of the relation of the reason to the materials of traditional thought (see SCHOLASTICISM). Previously an observation of far-reaching consequence comes into view. The mission to the Greeks was fond of falling back upon the philosophic and popular monotheism for a basis of connection, and for a counterpart to revelation. This gave rise to the assumption of a revelation in all religions, even in the ethical, and the claim was made for these remnants or rays of light, in behalf of the revealer or *Logos*. The Reformation planting itself on the Bible destroyed irremediably the assurance that church doctrine and revelation coincide. Protestant orthodoxy in the interest of dogmatism followed with the reenforcing dogma of the inspiration of an infallible text. The strain of attack drew out, on the part of reason, the theory of an original revelation, of the innate ideas, and of the two books of nature and conscience. The period of the Enlightenment (q.v.) brought forth the idea of a supernatural instruction as a supplement to a rational foundation given in and with creation. A philosophic followed by a literary criticism demolished the dogma of a miraculously constructed text. The supernatural instruction was said either to be substantially corroborated by reason (Wolff), or to be a temporary episode until rational knowledge was ripe and self-sufficient (Semler, Lessing). Finally, the possibility itself of such a revelation comes to be challenged (Reimarus), and ordinary rationalism presumes, on the basis of deism, to have done with revelation as superfluous, impossible, and unreal. Meanwhile, earnest treatment of Scripture turns from the validity of dogma to the unity of Biblical history. Romanticism (q.v.) instilled a reaction as to the value and origin of religion. The mystical infusion is not to be disregarded after Schleiermacher. To this influence of psychological and anthropological empiricism only one more point of view has been added, which may be termed ethnological empiricism. Under its banner, Comparative Religion (q.v.) is prosecuted, which is a statistic of religions with retrospect of their origin and growth, which again in respect of the study of the sources is denominated history of religion, and on the basis of the evolutionary hypothesis is elaborated into a philosophy of religion.

3. Dogmatic History.

During the long period of orthodox thought the concept of revelation served to insure an otherwise inaccessible content. To remain certain that this was received intact, the representation of the communication was wrought out without regard to the facts of historical and individual personal life. Ecstasy as the intermission of personal life is valid in the strictest sense, and miracle as interruption is a mark for the recognition of revelation, particularly in rationalistic supernaturalism (see RATIONALISM AND SUPERNATURALISM), at the risk of losing a content, however, otherwise inaccessible. In straining the point of the mode, the content was neglected, with which, however, revelation originally started out. The resulting modern movement has, in all its variations, the observation of the human phenomenal form of revelation in the forefront. The problem presents itself in the relation of human autonomy to divine operation, and further in tense ethical subjectivism. This is most evident in the consideration of prophecy. The matter of content, however, readily recedes into the background, while the problem becomes epistemological because

4. Modern Method.

the content whose form of transmission is under examination is itself spiritual. Within this anthropocentric, exclusively earthly horizon two fundamentally distinct series of observation have found room: one, the historical empiricism from Bengel to Hegel, to the modern science of religion; the other, the psychological, proceeding from "the inner testimony of the Holy Spirit," through Schleiermacher, to the agnostic mysticism of the religion of the indeterminate or blank religiousness.

According to Aristotle (see RELIGION, PHILOSOPHY OF), the practical activity of reason consists in the judgments of formal thought, from which results the overestimation of coordinating abstractions and of empty universal formal concepts.

5. Subjectivism.

Such a fate also befalls the consideration of the religious life from which depends the understanding of revelation. Employed by the universal concept of religion, revelation is either not universal and then not essential to religion, or else remains as an inseparable accompaniment. Theology presumes to find in revelation the cause of religion, and the term offers itself conveniently to denote that unknown quantity through the effective entrance of which into the soul-processes the appearance of religion in the inner household may be explained. The points of connection with the ideas of natural religion and revelation lie already at hand for the correlation of these ideas. The axiom is assumed: no revelation, no religion, whether in history or in personal life. What, however, is thus thought of as revelation is compared throughout with the prevalent idea of religion according to psychological determination. In this collation immediacy of the religious relation or the original capacity for religious experience in every human being coalesces with revelation. R. A. Lipsius emphatically pronounces mystical experience to be the vital center in religion and the essential in revelation. This experience, however, is not a disclosure, since it gives rise to a feeling never fully tangible to apprehension. Turning the thought around, it appears evident that religion, so far as its content is concerned, would never get beyond the speaking of tongues. But the fundamental perception is everywhere at hand, wherever the fact of religion is found in universal religiousness fundamentally independent of history. In case this religiousness is found in connection with an atheistic philosophy, it affords revelation even without deity. The transfer of the ecclesiastical technical expression to formal analogies observed in other departments of life affords means for closer comparison. Discoveries have been made, whether by search or fortuitously, which have been designated revelations. The ingenious conception of the thinker (especially of the artist), or vision, offers itself as analogous to the flash of the religious spark. If thought be not reinforced by conviction, with reference to the content of religion, from elsewhere, namely, from the more securely grounded ethical consciousness, or if the pious only experiences himself and the self-assigned relation to the non-ego, then the fear arises that such revelation may be no more than self-deception of the imagination, or possibly a universal strained representation, without foundation in fact (Feuerbach). Against such a subjectivistic dissection of the generalized concept of revelation recourse from the abstract theory of religion to comparative religion affords no relief. There is, indeed, no little mention, in such presentations, of revelation underlying all religions, without going into the concept of it. Nevertheless it is admitted (Thiele) that a class of religions of revelation is to be abstracted; namely, those conscious of the possession of revelations. Meanwhile there remains for this consciousness, so long as religion is assumed to be nothing else than becoming inwardly aware of an inevitable superior power, nothing but the verdict that it is an imagery of the fancy pertaining to psychological movements otherwise explainable. If it is only a matter of influences and their psychological exercise, then the specially religious lies either in the content, or perhaps on the side of the elaborating soul and its mode of apprehension. In either case the special mediation of religious operations drops out and with this also the occasion for applying the notion of revelation. If not set aside, its universalized use serves to generalize the Biblical religions with the others, by presenting them merely as particularly shaded modes of the universal concept of religion.

This entire point of view is guilty of a depreciation of the historical. Schleiermacher was aware of this when he declared ethics to be the book of forms for history, and history to be the book of illustrations for ethics; only it is to be borne

6. Depreciation of the Historical and Personal.

in mind that by ethics he meant the formulation of the natural laws of social life. The uniform laws, therefore, are essential; the variations of phenomena are secondary. So also as regards the religious; they are varieties similar in kind to the species of a genus. So far, however, the introduction of the historical treatment of religion does not alter the case. For if the steps of religious movement are deduced not from what is characteristic in religion, but from the progress of mental culture, the illumination of ethical views, or the repletion of philosophical thought—in short, from influences whose representations are independent of religion—then religion and its line of development remain the same, namely, the ever fundamentally invariable religiousness. Only its reflex imagery in consciousness and its spiritual elaboration vary. Consequently the standard for judging these influences lies outside of the religious, according to this position. In this connection also appears, with some logical consequence, a departure in the use of the concept of revelation. Originally denoting an impulse giving rise to the fact of religion, its given historical connection leads to the observation that religiousness in the strongly exercised becomes itself revealing upon the passively susceptible. As these transmissions must fulfil themselves in the active appropriation of impulses, and their use is determined by influences from without, these mediations must ultimately be of indifferent importance or must act as inhibitions, just as soon as religiousness becomes first-hand or original. Inasmuch as this form of revelation again removes itself from the field, all thought of a religious content communicated thereby can no longer be entertained, or the unvarying consciousness of dependence continues to hold the ground, remaining fundamentally awry with respect to all individual or historical supplementing. The concept of revelation is consumed by the naked idea of causation. The reason is that the phenomena dealt with are taken from the observation of things in general without respect to the peculiarity of personal life; except that it is impossible to banish reflex imagery from consciousness, although this receives treatment only in accordance with the nature of those phenomena. The main matter is not altered by substituting for the differentiation of the class in varieties the series of necessary development, i.e., for things coexistent things in succession. The resultant ever remains the exercise of the unvarying basis in religious consciousness. If this is as a matter of fact once conceded, its practical elaboration or "revelation," just as readily on an atheistic as a pantheistic hypothesis, is of itself understood.

7. Theory Based on the Bible and Positivism.

In this way, the idea of revelation has become a mere adjunct to that of religion, and with doubtful advantage; for it serves partly to make prominent the nativity of religion in every individual, and partly to describe in a vacillating manner the religion's reciprocal activity. In contrast, the idea has been positively remanded to its original field; i.e., for the historical life. This has taken place in the name of the Bible, on the part of the later Biblicists, and on the ground that religion exists only in historical positivism (Ritschl). History is the department of those facts which pertain to acting persons, their practical conduct, and its effects. Here the setting of aims or ends is a matter of fact. Room is afforded for the transactions of God apart from his universal activity according to law. It may find play in events, in the formal complexity of things, or in the appointment of particular persons. Such transaction invades effectively the whole; for the receptive mind it is at the same time presentation. It is to be called revelation by manifestation. In reaction to the self-analyzing intellectualistic conception, revelation by divine act merely has obtained acceptance (Hofmann). The question then occurs, What raises a fact or group of facts in their revealing value above doubt? Two answers are possible: the one points to the unity of universal design; the other to the admission that the revealing fact may not be satisfactorily deduced from historical conditions. These considerations may mutually support or may oppose each other. Both result in recognizing in Jesus Christ the focus of historical revelation. That is to say, they will admit, as real revelation, only history determined through him. Another path leads to this point. If the personal life be held in view, its ethical quality looms up as important, and so also, in connection with the Bible, the fact of human sin. It throws light upon the necessity of a special revelation, productive of the view that it is to be regarded as one phase of the redemptive activity of God (Krauss). As redemption appears to generalizing thought in the aspect of a particular form of revelation, so here this appears as an instrumental effort of divine activity for the conquest of evil wrought by sin. Its unique position within the comprehensive divine activity becomes self-evident as well as characteristic. However forcefully this special activity of God in the manifestation of Christ is set forth, it yet falls subject, so far as it is presentative, to the conceptual appropriation of man. Then the old question reappears—whence comes the warrant for the corresponding conception and a reliable transmission, if even this presentation constitutes an indispensable part of the redeeming act. Further, how is certainty to be gained that God is acting and making revelation in any other way than in his universal world-activity? Does not special history dissolve on every hand into the stream of human evolution in conformity with law? Within this, the merely negative marks of an undeducible content of the fact or uniqueness of the personal manifestation of Christ will not submit to proof. The transcendence above nature and the revelation value of the fact has become questionable. Here the most recent critical movement has applied the fruits of oriental study to the Old Testament.

8. The Doctrine of the Word of God.

The Bible places the word foremost among the instruments of revelation. Word and act are not exclusive in simple meaning or in human life. Word is not without act; it may be a most forceful act, but wordless act is never revelation. Revelation has not to do with an all-working power that must be provided with the word by the contemplation of its impression on man who has fallen under its influence; but it knows the speaking God. God avails himself of human thought and speech to make himself known and his speech intelligible, so far as knowledge of him is requisite for sinners to overcome by it sin and death. How much, according to the Biblical mode of thought, the divine act, for the sake of continuing disclosure, is in need of the opening of the mind to conceive and of the understanding to explain, is shown in that the incarnate Word attains only to effective revelation by the aid of the Paraclete. As indispensable as this instructive disclosing activity may be, so positive is this effected Word of revelation; it is not merely the inadequate expression of what is, according to its nature, ineffable. Without hesitation this intuition so obtained is regarded even to its very form of statement as that designed and imparted by God concerning himself and his will (I Cor. ii. 9–10). The operation of God by his Spirit upon men is not limited to the generation of his Word; for it is the comprehensive challenge, which calls forth the relation to him in all phenomenal forms: but the formation of words belongs to it essentially. Such influence of the Holy Spirit restricts itself not to impulse and feeling; it makes requisition upon all the forms of thought. The indwelling Spirit is not thought of as a power operating externally upon the conscious activities which mediate through the senses. The characteristic figure within the horizon of this circle is not the genius who founds sects, but the prophet prepared for martyrdom; the messenger of the word which laid a task upon him.

This statement concerning a process which interrelates manifestation and inspiration, the permanent result of which is the word of God (C. J. Nitzsch; Rothe), produces itself as the expression of present experience. Just as soon as the thread of continuity is broken, as among the Jews after the exile and in the post-Apostolic Church, perception becomes readily darkened. That, however, not merely its *caput mortuum* is present, is proved by the experience that this word may by proxy represent the manifestation more effectively than the manifestation itself, where there is a thorough activity of the Spirit. This statement of the self-revelation of God does not explain how religion originated on the whole or primarily. The knowledge concerning God, who may then be sought and rediscovered in his world-activity, is presupposed in all revealing action; the Bible knows nothing concerning a monotheism discovered only in late times. The fact of religion is presupposed for all men, and not until the state of religious necessity appears does revelation come under observation. Revelation is fundamentally always the self-evidencing of God for the recognition of him, and only subsequently does it extend itself also to the correlative. Wherefore, the knowledge of God has just the opposite force, within these limits, of humanly found and humanly conditioned thoughts concerning the divine. For it no simpler or more absolute testimony can be given than that of the first petition of the Lord's Prayer. Neither are the depths of deity exhausted in every dimension nor are the means provided for the impenetration of the universe in detail (theosophy); only the reality and verity of the acquaintance with the self-revealing God are assured.

9. Philosophic Adjustment of this View.

It has already become clear that the historicity of revelation is not alone to be proved in the fact that it fulfils itself in actuality that must first be understood in order to be described; much rather the emphasis rests upon the complex happening, evidently in fulfilment of a purpose, in which the indicating word is involved in a corresponding onward movement. So it may well be said of revelation, that it generates a development; in a certain sense also that it develops in its results. Only that such revelation must not be taken as analogous to the process in nature, but is to be conceived as the manifestation of a training according to design; for otherwise there would be a becoming manifest by means of, but not a revelation to, human consciousness. If abstract metaphysics, to the extent of deism, has assumed too disparate a conception of the highest being for alternative activity with the finite, then modern anthropology takes too disparate a conception of the subjectivity of persons to get any farther with respect to influence upon them than a stimulus to self-propulsion. Both exclude such a revealing operation of God, which is something else than a condition of the well-ordering of the whole. Therefore the God-man must be, apart from the ethical, a cosmic ordering and with him and in him is revelation (Dorner). At this point comes to view the dependence of the various forms of the conception of revelation upon cosmology. Something of this kind seems to be unavoidably bound up with the solution of the problem of the natural or the supernatural character of revelation through the generalizing of this idea, which is really indigenous only to the circle of New-Testament religions. Therefore, it is advisable, in its theological treatment, not to overlook how, in its origins, revelation serves, not only to weigh the knowledge of God afforded by it over against other representations; but, much more, to distinguish it as the true over against the deceptions; and not to forget how positively revelation is identified in thought, not merely with the reality of contact with God, but above all with the truth of the knowledge of God. In the restriction of the concept to this one side of the comprehensive activity of God, by which he founds the new life and within it the perfect religion, it preserves its peculiar significance, and is indispensable for the maintenance of the understanding of the religious relation on the high level of personal life, be it in the form of religiousness or of positive religion.

(M. Kähler.)

Bibliography: For the Biblical side consult the literature named in and under Biblical Theology; and for the dogmatic side the works on systematic theology named in and under Apologetics; Dogma, Dogmatics; Doctrine, History of; and Inspiration. Consult further: R. Seeberg, *Revelation and Inspiration*, New York, 1910; J. Leland, *The Advantage and Necessity of Christian Revelation, shown from the State of Religion in the Ancient Heathen World*, 2 vols., London, 1768, Philadelphia, 1818; H. Alford, *Consistency of the Divine Conduct in Revealing the Doctrines of Redemption*, 2 vols., London, 1842; F. D. Maurice, *What is Revelation? A Series of Sermons on the Epiphany*, ib. 1859; idem, *Sequel, to the Inquiry, "What is Revelation?" Letters in Reply to Mansel's Examination of Strictures on the Bampton Lectures*, ib. 1860; K. A. Auberlen, *Die göttliche Offenbarung*, Basel, 1861, Eng. transl., *The Divine Revelation*, Edinburgh, 1867; E. Krauss, *Die Lehre von der Offenbarung*, Gotha, 1868; A. B. Bruce, *The Chief End of Revelation*, London, 1881, new ed. 1887; R. W. Dale, *Epistle to the Ephesians, its Doctrine and Ethics*, lecture viii., ib. 1882; G. T. Ladd, *The Doctrine of Sacred Scripture*, 2 vols., New York, 1883; J. Robson, *The Bible: its Revelation . . . .*, London, 1883; C. A. Row, *Revelation and Modern Theology*, ib. 1883; J. H. A. Ewald, *Revelation: its Nature and Record*, Edinburgh, 1884; H. Rogers, *The Superhuman Origin of the Bible*, London, 1884; W. W. Olssen, *Revelation, Universal and Special*, New York, 1885; S. J. Andrews, *God's Revelations of Himself to Men as successively made in the Patriarchal, Jewish, and Christian Dispensations and in the Messianic Kingdom*, ib. 1886; R. H. Hutton, *Essays Theological and Literary*, 2 vols., London, 1888; J. F. Weir, *The Way, the Nature, and the Means of Revelation*, Edinburgh, 1889; G. P. Fisher, *The Nature and Method of Revelation*, New York, 1890; E. Cowley, *The Writers of Genesis and Related Topics, Illustrating Divine Revelation*, ib. 1890; W. D. Thomson, *Revelation and the Bible. A popular Exposition for the Times*, London, 1890; R. F. Horton, *Revelation and the Bible. An Attempt at Reconstruction*, ib., New York, 1892; E. R. Palmer, *Development of Revelation*, London, 1892; D. Van Horne, *Religion and Revelation*, Dayton, Ohio, 1892; J. Macgregor, *Revelation and the Record*, London, 1893; S. J. Andrews, *God's Revelations of Himself to Men*, New York, 1901; C. B. Brewster, *Aspects of Revelation*, London, 1901; J. R. Illingworth, *Reason and Revelation*, ib. 1902, new ed., 1908; T. Simon, *Entwicklung und Offenbarung*, Berlin, 1907; H. Bavinck, *The Philosophy of Revelation*, New York, 1909; J. Wilson, *How God has spoken. Or, Divine Revelation in Nature, in Man, in Hebrew History and in Jesus Christ*, Edinburgh, 1909; J. Orr, *Revelation and Inspiration*, London, 1910; G. Henderson, *The Bible a Revelation from God*, Edinburgh, 1910; *DCG*, ii. 520–526; Vigouroux, *Dictionnaire*, fasc. xxxiv. 1080–83.

RÉVÉSZ, IMRE: Hungarian Reformed; b. at Debreczin (116 m. e. of Budapest) Jan. 14, 1826; d. there Feb. 13, 1881. He was educated at Debreczin (1841–51), and after completing his studies at Vienna, Berlin, and in Switzerland, became, in 1856, pastor at Debreczin. In 1861 he was elected to the Reichstag, though he resigned a few months later to devote himself exclusively to pastoral and literary labors. He distinguished himself in the defense of his church, when, in 1856, Leo Thun, the Austrian minister of public worship, drafted a new system of government for the Hungarian Protestants which completely destroyed consistorial independence. Three years later an imperial patent was issued directing the Hungarian Lutherans and Reformed to organize in accordance with the royal charter. Both churches protested, while Révész presented arguments from history to show that the autonomy of the Protestant bodies could not be changed without the consent of their own synods. He likewise addressed a memorial to the foreign powers, which was presented, in English translation, to the British ambassador and printed in *The Edinburgh Review* (1860). He was a member of the Protestant deputation which unsuccessfully sought to gain audience with Francis Joseph I. in Jan., 1860, and after his return he drew up and published a program for passive resistance to the execution of the obnoxious patent. The program was, however, confiscated by the government, and Révész, among others, was summoned to appear before the civil courts. He now wrote his "Defense of the Hungarian Protestant Church" (Sárospatak, 1862; which appeared in its essential parts in German in the *Protestantische Kirchenzeitung*, 1861). In 1860 the obnoxious patent was withdrawn, and the suits against Révész and other Protestants were quashed.

In 1870 Révész founded the monthly *Figyelmező*, which he conducted for nine years, and in this he combated the German Protestant Union (see PROTESTANT UNION, GERMAN). Among his numerous works, all of them in Hungarian, special mention may be made of the following: "Basal Principles of Protestant Church Organization" (Szarvas, 1856); "Jan Erdösi, the Hungarian Reformer" (Budapest, 1859); "Life and Works of the first Hungarian Reformer, Mathias Biró of Déva" (1863); "Calvin's Life and Calvinism" (1864); and a Hungarian translation of the sermons of Frederick William Robertson (3 vols., 1864–69).

F. BALOGH.

BIBLIOGRAPHY: F. Balogh, in *The Catholic Presbyterian*, London, 1881, pp. 418–427; K. Kuzmani, *Urkundenbuch zum österreichischen evangelischen Kirchenrecht*, Vienna, 1856.

RÉVILLE, ré-vil', ALBERT: French Protestant: b. at Dieppe Nov. 4, 1826; d. at Paris Oct. 25, 1906. He was educated in his native city and at the universities of Geneva and Strasburg; was assistant pastor at Nîmes in 1847–48; pastor at Luneray in 1848–51; and of the Walloon church at Rotterdam, 1851–73; professor of the history of religions in the Collège de France, Paris, 1880–1906, as well as president of the section in the École pratique des hautes études for religious sciences in the same city after 1884. He translated J. H. Scholten's *Geschiedenis der godsdienst en wijsbegeerte* (Leyden, 1853) under the title *Manuel d'histoire comparée de la philosophie et de la religion* (Paris, 1861); and wrote *L'Authenticité du Nouveau Testament* (1851); *De la rédemption* (1860); *Essais de critique religieuse* (1860); *Études critiques sur l'évangile selon Saint Matthieu* (Leyden, 1862); *Manuel d'instruction religieuse* (1863; Eng. transl., London, 1864); *Théodore Parker, sa vie et ses œuvres* (1865; Eng. transl., London, 1865); *Histoire du dogme de la divinité de Jésus-Christ* (1869; 5th ed., 1906; Eng. transl., *History of the Doctrine of the Deity of Jesus Christ*, London, 1870; revised, 1905); *Histoire du diable, ses origines, sa grandeur et sa décadence* (Strasburg, 1870; Eng. transl., *The Devil, his Origin, Greatness, and Decadence*, London, 1871); *Prolégomènes de l'histoire des religions* (1881; Eng. transl., London, 1884); *Les Religions des peuples non-civilisés* (2 vols., 1883); *The Origin and Growth of Religion as illustrated by the Native Religions of Mexico and Peru* (Hibbert lectures, London, 1884; French transl., Paris, 1885); *La Religion chinoise* (2 vols., Paris, 1888); and *Jésus de Nazareth* (2 vols., 1897).

BIBLIOGRAPHY: *Polybiblion*, 1897, pp. 199–203; P. Alphandéry, in *RHR*, 1906, pp. 401–423; *Revue chrétienne*, 1906, pp. 416–417; Vigouroux, *Dictionnaire*, fasc. xxxiv. 1083–1084.

RÉVILLE, JEAN: French Protestant, son of the preceding; b. at Rotterdam, Holland, Nov. 6, 1854; d. at Paris May 6, 1908. He was educated at the universities of Geneva, Paris, Berlin, and Heidelberg; was pastor at Sainte-Suzanne (1880–83); teacher of the Evangelical religion in the Lycée Henri Quatre, Paris (1884–86); instructor in church history in the École pratique des hautes études, Paris (1886–94); and professor of patristics in the Protestant theological faculty of the University of Paris (1894–1907); succeeded his father as professor of the history of religions in the Collège de France. He was also editor of the *Revue de l'histoire des religions* after 1884. Among his numerous works special mention may be made of *La Religion à Rome sous les Sévères* (Paris, 1884); *Les Origines de l'épiscopat* (1894); *Paroles d'un libre croyant* (1898); *Le Quatrième Évangile, son origine et sa valeur historique* (1900); *Le Protestantisme libéral, ses origines, sa nature, sa mission* (1903; Eng. transl., *Liberal Christianity, its Origin, Nature, and Mission*, London, 1903); and *Le Prophétisme hébreu; esquisse de son hist. et de ses destinées* (Paris, 1906).

BIBLIOGRAPHY: W. Sanday, *Criticism of the Fourth Gospel*, pp. 2, 28, 31, 200, 256, Oxford, 1905; *Journal de Genève*, May 8, 1908; A. Reyss, in *Le Protestant, journal des chrétiens libéraux*, 1908, pp. 155–156; *RHR*, June–July, 1908; Vigouroux, *Dictionnaire*, fasc. xxxiv. 1084.

REVIUS, ré'vi-us, JACOBUS: Dutch theologian; b. at Deventer (8 m. n. of Zutphen) Nov., 1586; d. at Leyden Nov. 15, 1658. He was educated at Leyden (1604–07) and Franeker (1607–10), and in 1610–1612 visited various foreign universities, particularly Saumur, Montauban, and Orléans. Returning to Holland, he held brief pastorates at Zeddam, Winterswijk, and Aalten in 1613, and by Oct., 1614, had become pastor in his native city, where he remained twenty-seven years. In 1618 he was appointed librarian of the Fraterhuis, and in the same year the Synod of Dort assigned him a part in the new revision of the Dutch translation of the Old Testament. The committee of translators and revisers, which convened at Leyden in 1633–34, made Revius secretary. He likewise took an active part in the establishment of the Athenæum at Deventer in 1630, and was influential in calling the first professors. In 1641 he accepted a call to Leyden as regent of the state college, and held this position for the remainder of his life. His closing years were embittered by the rise of Cartesianism, to which he was intensely opposed. A rare Hebrew scholar, Revius was also a prolific writer. He showed, however, a domineering disposition and exercised a vehement polemic, as shown in his struggle with Cartesianism and the Remonstrants. Against the latter he wrote, *Schriftuurlijk tegen Bericht van de Leere der Gereformeerde Kerken aengaende de goddelijke Predestinatie ende andere aen-clevende Poincten* (Deventer, 1617); against the former he wrote especially his *Statera philosophiæ Cartesianæ* (Leyden, 1650); and *Theke, hoc est levitas defensionis Cartesianæ* (Briel, 1653). The rights of the Church he defended in his *Examen . . . seu de potestate magistratuum reformatorum circa res ecclesiasticas* (Amsterdam, 1642), and his *Uittreksels . . . over de macht der overheid in het afzetten van predikanten* (Leyden, 1650). While endeavoring to avoid the contemporary controversy whether men might wear long hair, he was obliged to defend his moderate position in his *Libertas Christiana circa usum capillitii defensa* (1647).

While he was regent, no less than 576 disputations took place at Leyden. In 1623 Revius published at Leyden his own Greek and Latin translation of the Belgic Confession, a revised and enlarged edition appearing four years later as *Belgicarum ecclesiarum doctrina et ordo*. Copies of this were widely circulated among the Orthodox Greeks and won the approval of Cyril Lucar (q.v.), whose own "Confession" may thus have been materially influenced by the Belgic Confession. Revius also conferred a considerable service on science by editing 300 letters of the famous Joseph Juste Scaliger (q.v.) under the title *Epistres françoises des personnages illustres et doctes à M. Joseph Juste de la Scala* (Harderwijk, 1624). His main work entitled him to prominence among historical writers, *Daventriæ illustratæ, sive historiæ urbis Daventriensis libri sex* (Leyden, 1651). Revius was also one of the best poets of his time, publishing *Over-Ysselsche Sangen en Dichten* (Deventer, 1630; enlarged ed., Leyden, 1634), and *De CL Psalmen Davids . . . in sin en de rijmen gebetert* (Deventer, 1640).

(S. D. van Veen.)

Bibliography: Sources are his own sketch in his *Daventriæ illustratæ*, ut sup., pp. 725–728; and J. Hoornbeek, *Miscellanea sacra*, pp. 575–591, Utrecht, 1676. Consult: J. van Vloten, *Het Leven en de uitgelezen sangen en dichten van Jacobus Revius*, Schiedam, 1863; E. J. W. Posthumus Meyjes, *Jacobus Revius, zijn Leven en Werken*, Amsterdam, 1895.

REVIVALS OF RELIGION.

The phrase "revivals of religion" is ordinarily applied to the spiritual condition of a Christian community, more or less limited in extent, in which a special interest is very generally felt in respect to religious concerns, accompanied with a marked manifestation of divine power and grace in the quickening of believers, the reclaiming of backsliders, and the awakening, conviction, and conversion of the unregenerate.

I. Theory of Revivals: The progress of Christianity in the world has rarely, for any length of time, been uniform. Its growth in the individual and in the community is characterized by very obvious fluctuations. Like all things temporal, it is subject to constant change, exposed to influences the most varied and antagonistic. Now it makes rapid advances in its conflict with sinful propensities and developments; again it is subjected to obstructions and reverses that effectually check its onward course, and result in spiritual declensions. Growth in grace is attainable only by ceaseless vigilance, untiring diligence, unremitting conflict, and a faithful improvement of the opportunities and means of spiritual advancement. Any relaxation in the strife with moral evil tends to spiritual retardation: the evil gets the advantage over the good; the religious fervor abates; the soul becomes lukewarm, cold, dead. As with the individual believer, so is it with the community. A church, a sisterhood of churches covering a large section of country, by reason of the predominating influence of some worldly interests—the greed of gain in a season of great commercial prosperity, the strife of party during a highly excited political campaign, the prevalence of a martial spirit in time of war, or the lust of pleasure in a time of general worldly gaiety and festivity, or any absorbing passion for mere temporal good—may be so diverted from the direct pursuit of holiness, and the prosecution of the work of advancing the kingdom of Christ, as to lose, to a considerable extent, the power, if not the life, of godliness. The spiritual and eternal become subordinate to the worldly and temporal. The blight of spiritual declension settles down and attaches itself with increasing persistency year by year. Such has been the history of Christian churches everywhere. This being the testimony of universal experience to the proneness of human nature to decline from the spirit and the power of godliness, how, it is asked, is this tendency to be checked? Obviously the true and only effective and appropriate remedy for a season of spiritual declension is a season of spiritual revival. Such a season, by whatever agencies or instrumentalities brought about, by whatever adjuncts of questionable propriety it may be accompanied, and of greater or less extent, may properly be termed "a revival of religion." These manifestations, moreover, are to be regarded as a result of a special and peculiar effusion of the Holy Spirit. All spiritual life, all progress in the divine life, whether in the individual or in the community, in the church or in the nation, is the Spirit of God. The whole period of grace, from the Day of Pentecost to the final judgment, is properly termed "the dispensation of the Holy Spirit." Every true convert is begotten of the Spirit, and so becomes a child of God. The Spirit is always in and with the Church, carrying forward the work of redemption.

II. Early Revivals: Mention, moreover, is made in the Scriptures of special dispensations of the Holy Spirit, of copious effusions of the Spirit of particular times of refreshing from the presence of the Lord: "It shall come to pass afterward, that I will pour out my spirit upon all flesh." The fulfilment of this prediction of the prophet Joel began, as the Apostle Peter testifies, on the Day of Pentecost next following the crucifixion of our Lord. So great and so efficacious was this outpouring of the Spirit, that about 3,000 souls were that day made partakers of the divine nature by regeneration. And this was only the initial of a marvelous dispensation and display of divine grace in the renewal and sanctification of a great multitude of souls extending through a continued series of years, whereby the Christian Church was planted, took root, and filled the land of Israel with its blessed fruits. It was a great and glorious revival of religion. This was but the first great revival in the history of the Christian Church. Times without number, at particular periods, in peculiar exigencies God has interposed for the redemption of the Church and for the triumphant advancement of the Gospel of Christ. After a season of spiritual declension, when iniquity had come in, and rolled over the whole land like a desolating flood, a wave of renewing and sanctifying grace has spread itself over a whole region of country, whereby the attention of the multitude has been aroused, great numbers of the careless and thoughtless have been brought under saving conviction, and converts by thousands have been brought into the Church of such as should be saved. Marvelous changes have thus been wrought in the aspect of large communities, affecting most favorably the character and the results of the preaching of the Word, the devotions of the closet, the family, and the sanctuary, and the interest taken by the multitude in spiritual and external concerns, resulting in an extraordinary quickening of religious affections, a general stimulus of Christian graces, and the divine renewal of souls that were dead in trespasses and sins. Not only at Jerusalem, but everywhere in all the region round about where the apostles and apostolic men preached in those days, and far away among the Gentiles, such scenes were witnessed. So many and so mighty were those special manifestations of divine power and grace in the Gospel, by reason of such effusions of the Holy Spirit, that Tertullian could say at the beginning of the third century, in his appeal to the civil authorities, "We have filled all places of your dominions,—cities, islands, corporations, councils, armies, tribes, the senate, the palace, the court of judicature." "So mightily grew the work of God, and prevailed."

1. In Biblical Times.

Passing over the intervening centuries, it may well be asked, What was the Protestant Reformation, that, beginning in the fourteenth century under Wyclif, and continuing under Huss in the fifteenth, at length culminated in the sixteenth under Luther and Calvin and a host of kindred spirits? It was a special dispensation of the Spirit, whereby the minds of men everywhere in Christian lands were turned toward the utterances of the divine word, the errors of the papacy were discovered and renounced, the truth as it is in Jesus was apprehended and embraced by multitudes, and the churches were built up in the faith of the Gospel. It was a great and general revival of religion, whereby converts by tens of thousands were born of the Spirit of God. So thorough and wide-spread were those conversions, that the fires of persecution were kindled in vain. In spite of princes and prelates, converts to the pure faith of the Gospel were made all over Germany, Switzerland, France, Holland, and Great Britain, and not a few in Spain and Italy. It was the greatest revival of religion that the world had witnessed, and the Church enjoyed, since the days of Constantine. From that day, all along the centuries, the annals of the Church abound in testimonies to the reality and efficacy of these special effusions of the Spirit. The Church of Scotland was born anew in the great revival under Knox and his brethren. "The whole nation," says Kirkton, "was converted by lump." Near the close of the sixteenth century, under the ministry of such divines as Wishart, Cooper, and Welsh, all Scotland was visited by an extraordinary effusion of the Holy Spirit. So mightily were men affected, that the whole general assembly, 400 ministers and elders, while renewing their solemn league and covenant, with sighs and groans and tears, were swayed by the Spirit, as the leaves of the forest by the "rushing of the wind" of the driving tempest. Similar scenes were further witnessed in Scotland, beginning in 1625, at Stewarton, extending through the land and into the north of Ireland, and eventuating in that remarkable display of divine grace in the Kirk of Scotland, where in June, 1630, under the preaching of Bruce and Livingston, "near 500"

2. Protestant Revivals.

souls in one day were brought under deep conviction of sin, and presently into the light and liberty of the Gospel. So, too, in 1638, on the occasion of signing the covenant, the whole country was stirred as by the mighty hand of God. Such was the preparation in Scotland, and in England, also, for the great reformation that issued in the commonwealth under Cromwell and the prevalence of Puritanism in the Church of England.

Like importance attaches to what is known as the Evangelical revival under the Wesleys in Great Britain, which spread also to America under Francis Asbury (q.v.) and Philip Embury (q.v.), resulting in the foundation and upbuilding of Methodism (see METHODISTS). E. F. HATFIELD†.

III. In America.—1. Revivals under Edwards: The earliest period of New England history was a period of almost constant revival, for religion was the chief interest of the Pilgrim and Puritan churches, and revivals of a less continuous type were not infrequent in the later years of their first century and the beginning of the next. Increase Mather was a powerful revival preacher. Both the father and the grandfather (Solomon Stoddard, q.v.) of Jonathan Edwards had revivals in their parishes. But the history of American revivals, as a distinct element of the religious life, begins properly in 1734 with the preaching of a series of sermons by Edwards, at Northampton, upon justification by faith. There had at this date been no considerable additions to the village church for a long time. The religious condition of the church had become low, and that of the community around it worse. Interest began among the young and spread to the old. Five or six persons were converted; and then, all at once, the community as a whole began to manifest an absorbing interest in personal religion. Religious meetings became thronged. In half a year about 300 persons were converted, embracing nearly all the town above sixteen years of age. The revival was not limited to Northampton, but spread, partly with the active cooperation of Edwards, to most of the towns about, then into Connecticut, and even into New Jersey. The means taken to extend the revival were the simple and ordinary services of the house of God, special meetings for a lecture by the minister, followed by meetings for prayer, group meetings of young and of old, and private interviews by the pastor with persons specially concerned. The sermons upon justification were upon the traditional lines of Calvinistic theology, and great emphasis was laid upon what "justice" would demand in God's treatment of men, and upon the utter lack of claim that any sinner had upon God for favorable treatment. And the sovereignty of God was so emphasized as to give the impression that, even after the sinner has repented, it may be entirely uncertain whether God will forgive him or not! Still, Edwards took occasion to encourage the diffident with the assurance of the goodness of God, and that it is his "manner" to give success to diligence. The great motive employed was, however, fear. It was Edwards' purpose to produce conviction of sin and a sense of the great danger in which the soul stood of suffering the torments of an eternal hell.

1. Revival of 1734-35.

In the spring of 1740 the spirit of revival was again present. The same increasing seriousness as had ushered in the former revival was observed. Some conversions occurred. And in October George Whitefield (q.v.), who had come to New England from Georgia, and was preaching from place to place with great power, to immense assemblies of people, arrived in Northampton. While his coming does not seem to have had a revolutionary influence, he was largely instrumental in producing the general prevalence of a revival which was limited to no part of the country, and enlisted the active cooperation of a large number of effective preachers. Of these one of the most famous was Gilbert Tennent (q.v.). Edwards himself joined in the itinerant work in which Whitefield took the lead. In this revival, as in the former, the great appeal was to fear. It was at this time that the famous sermon of Edwards upon *Sinners in the Hands of an Angry God* was preached at Enfield, Conn. "Before the sermon was ended, the assembly appeared deeply impressed and bowed down with an awful conviction of their sin and danger. There were such manifestations of distress and weeping that the preacher was obliged to speak to the people and desire silence that he might be heard. This was the beginning of the same great and prevailing concern in that place with which the colony in general was visited."

2. Great Awakening, 1740.

Had the revival been confined to places under the influence of Edwards and his more immediate associates, it may be that comparatively little criticism would have been called forth. It is necessary here to call attention to certain phemonena which arose in the newly compacted Presbyterian church of New Jersey. This was composed of a Scotch-Irish element, attached to the forms and methods of an established church, and making little inquiry into the evidence of regeneration among professing Christians, and a New England Congregational element, with whom the reality of the experience of regeneration was the great prerequisite for church membership as well as the great essential of the religious life. William Tennent (q.v.), of the New England side, had founded a college in his parish to educate men for the ministry, upon which the Scotch looked with some suspicion; and when his son, Gilbert Tennent (q.v.), inveighed against an "unconverted ministry" and went about preaching the Gospel to all whom he could gather, the criticism was still stronger. Tennent and his friends were thus brought into the parishes of many men who had no sympathy with their doctrines or their methods. And so at the synod of 1741 a "protestation" was made which objected to their "anarchical principles," their "irregular irruptions upon the congregation to which they have no immediate relation," "their principles and practise of rash judging and condemning all who do not fall in with their measures, both ministers and people," their doctrine of the necessity of an inward divine call to the ministry, "their preaching the terrors of

3. Revival under Criticism.

the law," and their doctrine of conscious religious experience. It was natural that Tennent's preaching in New England should arouse strong criticism from men of like mind with the "Old Side" of his own church.

The first and chief difficulty in New England was, however, connected with James Davenport, of Southold, L. I. The news of Whitefield's successes had led him in 1740 to begin special exhortation of his people, and in the following year he began an itinerary at Easthampton which carried him through

4. James Davenport.

Connecticut, and finally as far as Boston. While his piety was genuine, it is not to be doubted that he was laboring under a mental aberration which increased during his itinerant ministry. He indulged in caustic criticism of most of the ministers whom he met. In New Haven the final outcome of his work was the formation of a separate church. Even the legislature at Hartford took notice of his excesses and sent him home as a man of disordered mind. In June, 1742, he appeared in Boston, and here began in consequence that opposition to the revival which long continued and greatly affected the entire later history not only of that city but of all America. The association of ministers issued a declaration in which they gave generous recognition to Davenport's excellencies, but on account of his irregularities, they judged it their "present duty not to invite Mr. Davenport into our places of public worship." The result of this declaration was that there were preachings upon the common, a great deal of controversy and disturbance, and finally a presentment before the general court, upon which Davenport was discharged as not guilty because *non compos mentis*. After a while Davenport departed for home. On his arrival, and with the mending of his health, he saw his errors and published "retractations" in which he withdrew his statements and explicitly recognized his errors. It is upon such a background that the history of Whitefield's revival movements in New England is painted. He was charged with being an "enthusiast," i.e., one who acted on stimuli furnished by dreams and sudden impulses which he mistook for inspiration, with disorderly methods, censoriousness, slander, and with deluding the people.

Edwards' defense of the revival did not ignore "imprudences," "irregularities," "indiscreet zeal," nor "outcries, agitations, and faintings of the body"; but he defended the revival, nevertheless,

5. Edwards' Defense; Statistics.

because it had produced "a remarkable and general alteration in the face of New England" in matters pertaining to religion and common morals. He defends the evangelists in respect to many things for which they had been unjustly blamed, as he thought, and maintains that there is a proper address to the emotions, and that the preaching of terror is justifiable, for the state of unrepentant man is indeed terrible. Neither did he refuse to see in physical effects of preaching "probable tokens of God's presence." Edwards left quite complete and very significant data as to the numbers affected by this revival, and their ages, from which the following table is compiled, in which no distinction is made between males and females, who were converted, according to Edwards' explicit statement, in about equal numbers.

Age.	Number.	Age.	Number.
4	1	20	10
9	2	21	7
12	30	22	3
13	21	23	4
14	24	24	2
15	25	25	5
16	35	45	50
17	22	55	20
18	11	65	10
19	17	70	2

It will serve the purposes of confirmation of the Edwardean table as normal and valuable, if the following table of a revival in an Iowa town, about ten years since, be given. It was conducted by a Congregational minister.

Age.	Number.	Age.	Number.
7	1	32	2
11	1	33	6
12	4	34	1
13	6	36	1
14	4	37	2
15	1	38	1
16	3	39	1
17	7	40	7
18	5	44	1
19	6	45	1
20	6	46	1
21	2	48	1
23	2	50	1
24	1	54	2
25	7	55	2
27	1	56	1
28	1	58	1
29	2	64	1
30	2	67	1
31	1		

The numerical results of the revival in the country at large can be estimated upon the basis of only partial information; a conservative estimate puts the number of additions to the New England churches in consequence of the revival at 25,000, which, as there seem to have been then about 250,000 population in New England, makes the proportion of conversions to the population at least ten per cent. This does not, however, completely cover the number of conversions, for a large number were already within the churches by the operation of the Half Way Covenant (q.v.), who needed conversion, and actually were converted. The whole number of conversions, therefore, when these dead church-members are included in the enumeration, must have been nearly 50,000. One hundred and fifty Congregational churches were formed in less than twenty years, most of which can be credited to the revival. A considerable number of separatist churches were formed, many of which contributed powerfully to the influence of practical religion; while Baptist and Presbyterian forces were largely increased. Thus, when a broad review of the numerical results is taken, it is evident at once that the reenforcement of the religious forces of the country was very great.

2. Revivals About the Year 1800: From the close of the "Great Awakening," as the revival just sketched was called, there were no general revivals in America till about the year 1800. It was the period of war, with the consequent demoralization.

But as the new century drew near, isolated revivals occurred in a number of places. In 1781 there was a revival in Dartmouth College, extending into the towns twenty miles around; in 1783 in Yale College, which increased the membership of the college church to a point to which it had never before attained. Twelve years later, however, its visible effects had departed. Princeton College was in a condition quite similar to Yale. From 1778 to 1787 there had been a revival, under the lead of a layman, Joseph Patterson, in western Pennsylvania, and more than 1,000 persons professed conversion. In the winter of 1798 there was a great revival in western New York, and in 1796–1798 in western Connecticut and Massachusetts. But in eastern Massachusetts there was no revival from 1745 till long after 1800. The most important center of this revival was Yale College under Timothy Dwight. When he came to the presidency in 1795 he found infidelity very prevalent among the students, while the college church was almost extinct. Dwight began by discussing the fundamentals of theology with the senior students, and soon open infidelity passed away. But the "revival" proper did not break out in Yale College till 1802. A student destined to play a large part in later revivals, Lyman Beecher, was converted in 1795–96, but it was a case of solitary religious interest, beginning at home in consequence of a chance remark of his mother, but kept in progress largely by the sermons of Dwight in the college pulpit, and gradually developing into fixity of purpose to serve God. There were other solitary cases, but the college for some time went backward rather than forward. In 1799 only four or five undergraduates were members of the college church. But in 1801 desire for a revival began to be manifested, and in the spring of 1802 the work developed until seventy-five out of 230 students had been converted, of whom about one-half became ministers. There were later revivals in 1808, in 1812–13 with twenty converts; in 1815 with eighty; in 1831, and so on, so that up to 1837 there were seventeen distinct revivals in Yale College.

1. College Revivals; Timothy Dwight.

What Dwight was as a revivalist may be still more clearly seen from the work of his pupil, Lyman Beecher (q.v.). Settled in Easthampton in 1799, his activity in revivals began at once. Interest was awakened that spring, and in 1800 a marked revival, continuing six weeks, resulted in the conversion of eighty and the addition of fifty to the church. But the revival of 1807–08 brought out the principles upon which Beecher always conducted such work and showed what manner of man he was. From the general assembly at Newark he returned with "fire in his heart," and began with the young people; but when nothing "would take hold," he planned a series of sermons on election. He preached "cut and thrust, hip and thigh," but it was a new doctrine of election that he taught, under the influence of Dwight and Taylor, by which its eminent reasonableness was emphasized. The doctrine of eternal punishment was also so preached as to present "the kingdom of darkness . . . as nothing but the prison of the universe . . . and small compared to the realms of light and glory." It was the emancipation of the congregation from the domination of the instinctive emotion of overpowering fear.

2. Lyman Beecher.

While this early revival at Yale was proceeding quietly, avoiding excesses of every kind, in Kentucky in the year 1800 there was proceeding a revival which illustrated the dangers which attend the supreme appeal to fear in a population of a low grade of intellectual life. The Scotch-Irish immigration into America had brought into the mountains of Kentucky and Tennessee a population which had degenerated in the seclusion of these remote regions. Religion had lost its hold upon them. The "inhibitions" of both the intellectual and the moral natures were largely removed, and at the same time a condition of unstable equilibrium had been set up in the nervous system. They had to be ever upon the alert against the savages. Thus they lived in an environment of apprehension, the power of "latent fear" was therefore very great, and excessive emotional manifestations might be counted upon. This mountain population sent out numbers of emigrants as time went on, and about the year 1800 there had gathered in Logan County, in southwestern Kentucky, on the Tennessee border, a large population of this people, intermixed with numbers of violent and hardened criminals. An irregular government had been established in the interest of law and order, and a miniature civil war had been waged till finally the better elements had got the upper hand. The ministry of James McGready, who came to this region in 1796, was from the first attended with great power. His preaching seems to have resembled that of Edwards. "He would so array hell before the wicked," it was said, "that they would tremble and quake, imagining a lake of fire and brimstone yawning to overwhelm them and the hand of the Almighty thrusting them down the horrible abyss." In 1799 he was holding a meeting at Red River for the purpose of observing the sacrament when violent physical demonstrations began in the audience so that people fell from their seats to the floor. This was the beginning of a great epoch of nervous excitement in connection with revivals. The work spread to Pennsylvania and Ohio, and violent physical phenomena called "the jerks" prevailed. Great camp-meetings were gathered, and, like a contagion, excitement would run through the crowds assembled. People would continue for hours in an apparently breathless and motionless state; about one in every six would fall helpless to the earth, and one man jerked so violently as to snap his neck and die. It was not till the summer of 1803 that an end came to such manifestations.

3. Kentucky Revival.

3. Theology of these Revivals: Theology had passed through a regular development since the time of Edwards. The treatise upon the freedom of the will, in which the great leader had pronounced for determinism, had led to a constant discussion of the whole psychology of revivals, and while this was conducted upon the universal plan of that day, the consultation of the individual consciousness, it had led to a gradual modification of determinism in favor of a true freedom, till in Nathaniel William Taylor's teaching the will has always, in every case of actual choice, a "power to the contrary" (for the history see New England Theology). As the outcome of the development of this theology, the preacher in these revivals felt that he was actually and powerfully influencing his hearers to repentance, and they felt that upon them alone lay the responsibility of choosing or refusing the service of God, since they possessed a perfect ability to choose or refuse; and yet preacher and convert praised the grace of God as efficient agent and divine benefactor in every man's salvation (cf. F. H. Foster's *Genetic History of the New England Theology*, Chicago, 1907).

4. Later Revivals: Among Congregationalists and associated denominations revivals went forward up to the point now reached without the help of any one who was exclusively devoted to this work. The period of professional revivalists had not set in. The early educational advantages of Asahel Nettleton (q.v.) were small, and, as his parents were not professing Christians, it was not till his eighteenth year that he became a Christian. Inclined first to the foreign missionary work, he was gradually drawn into revival labors, and was never able to extricate himself from the responsibilities thus incurred. He traversed a large part of Connecticut, with frequent labors in Massachusetts and New York, and in the South his journeys carried him as far as Charleston, S. C. For about twenty-three years he was one of the most active and conspicuous figures in the service of the churches through the conduct of revivals. Of his special preparation for his work, gained by experience in the work itself, his observers frequently speak. Because of his familiarity with the experiences of many different men in many different places, he often seemed to be describing the experience of his auditors as if he were personally acquainted with their innermost thoughts. "When he commenced his labors in any place, he first attempted to impress the people with the fact that their help must come from above, and that they must place no dependence upon an arm of flesh." So earnest was he in this feeling, that if he thought they were depending too much upon him, he would suddenly leave them for a time. He began his work by seeking to deepen the earnestness of the church and the sense of responsibility. He would preach upon the sins of Christians, and by his searching and personal methods of application seek to carry conviction home to them first. Then he was ready to preach to sinners. His style was simple and impressive. He did not seek to awaken great emotion, but preferred a quiet revival. Preaching earnestly, following this with familiar addresses in the lecture room, and adding to these faithful private conversation and personal labor, he gathered the fruit "by hand," as some one has felicitously described the personal method of labor. His conversation with such was, however, usually brief, and partook somewhat of the nature of a physician's prescriptions. One duty and one only did he press upon anxious inquirers, that of immediate repentance. He urged this upon them because they could do nothing short of it which would in any way improve their condition. Thus he fell in with the best line of New England teaching. In one respect these revivals were very defective. To the end, the peculiar path which Nettleton had had to tread when he came into the kingdom continued to exercise an influence upon him and upon the religious experience of his converts. There was a long period of distress through which most of them had to pass, and a great degree of dimness and mystery and uncertainty about the act of conversion itself. It was the result of bad teaching, just as was the supreme (and successful!) effort which one of Edwards' young people went through with, to repent of her sin in Adam! Nowhere is it possible to find a clear explanation of the nature of faith in his sermons. Nowhere does he tell a sinner exactly what he is to do in terms which possess clearness because resting upon a clear psychology of repentance and faith. The day for all this had not come. He produced true faith because he so powerfully presented the motives under which it arises; but just what happened at the decisive moment in his soul, neither the sinner nor his teacher really knew.

1. Asahel Nettleton.

Charles Grandison Finney (q.v.), living in Central New York, then a frontier country, was brought up with meager advantages as to education, and with religious advantages yet more deficient; so he grew to young manhood, studied law and entered upon its practise, in Adams, N. Y., without any real acquaintance with the Gospel. He had had some educational opportunities in his later youth, having spent a brief time in a high school in Connecticut; but the religious privileges which he then enjoyed had brought little light to his mind. He says of himself, when he began the study of law, that he was "almost as ignorant of religion as a heathen." His first Bible was purchased because of the references to it which he found in his law books. There was a new element in the revival work which Finney's conversion led him to undertake which goes back to his own mental processes and spiritual experiences. The day he was converted he gained a new idea of the nature of faith. He had held it to be an intellectual belief, but now he understood that it was a voluntary trust. This he put forth by the direct act of his will, and upon this his conversion followed, though he did not at once understand that he was converted, in this particular rehearsing the experiences of many converts from the time of Edwards down. But the application of this principle to the philosophy and the methods of revivals could not long remain hid from him, nor his own mode of procedure remain unaffected by it. The out-working of this principle manifested itself first in the realm of theology. Finney was a born theologian. He possessed the interest in abstract truth, the power of analytical thought, and the love of cogent proof, which united make the theologian, and constitute him, at the same time, an original, investigating, and advancing theologian. He was therefore soon engaged in further discussions with his pastor, and was led step by step to substantially the same positions taken by Nathaniel William

2. Charles Grandison Finney.

Taylor (see NEW ENGLAND THEOLOGY, V., § 1), with whom he afterward had some brief association. He was soon licensed to preach by the local presbytery and subsequently ordained, though not without much criticism of his peculiar views. His labors had, however, been too fruitful to permit of refusing him ordination. After his work at Adams, Finney went to Evans' Mills and began that long series of revival meetings by which he wrought more powerfully and over a greater territory than any man of his generation. The story is fascinating as repeated by himself in his *Memoirs*, replete with striking incidents and with remarkable successes. From the first he was apparently fully prepared and entirely mature. His eloquence was astonishing, his methods were original and effective, his personal power was extraordinary, the results were unmatched. The open secret of his skill in handling men was the perfect clearness with which he apprehended the nature of conversion and the nature of man. His perfect confidence also in the main doctrines of the Evangelical scheme and the startling vividness with which he presented them led to the most profound self-examination and personal consecration. Through it all ran the vein of rationality, for Finney was always explaining and defending doctrines, and had the art of making them appear self-evident and their contradictories inconceivable. It is to be doubted if anywhere, at any period in the history of the Christian church, there were more profound experiences or a firmer and more intelligent grasp of the essentials of the process of making one's peace with God.

Opposition was early felt in various ways, but it was to those features of Finney's methods which would to-day be regarded as his principal merits, to his use of homely illustrations, his avoidance of a stilted rhetorical style, and his extemporaneous address.

3. Criticism of Finney's Methods.

They were the very reasons of his success, and had he listened to the directions of those about him, he would have become as ineffective as they were. But there was no opposition from those that knew the work because of any irregularities, such as were soon to raise the antagonism of the brethren in New England and involve Asahel Nettleton. Nettleton's objections to Finney's methods were to the "irreverence" displayed in prayer, to "the spirit of denunciation" exhibited, especially against ministers, "the practise of females praying in promiscuous assemblies," the creation of discord in churches, and "praying for people by name." In his own letters nothing is said against the practise of asking inquirers to come forward to anxious seats; but this is one of the new measures against which Nettleton's biographer, Bennet Tyler, represents him as objecting. On the whole, it appears that Tyler's representation of the matter is somewhat exaggerated, and that he did not have correct sources of information; Nettleton also seems to have obtained his information largely indirectly, and it appears exaggerated and incorrect. Finney's work was not open to the charges which both of these men made so freely against it. The antagonism between Finney and Nettleton was a matter of temperament, for the one was as contained as the other was unrestrained. It was partly a matter of civilization—the settled and staid East against the newer West; partly a matter of party—conservative New England against a man who reproduced in the West the Taylorism against which Tyler and Nettleton were contending in the East. But at bottom it was an antagonism of ideas, excited by the inability of Nettleton and others to think their way through the consequences and implications of a new theory of the will.

Finney's revivals covered a wide and interesting field, which included Philadelphia, New York (where he founded the Broadway Tabernacle, and made the acquaintance of the men who sustained him at Oberlin), Oberlin itself and the intense and wonderful history of its early years, London, England, and back again among American towns of greater or less celebrity. The revivals at Rochester were among his greatest, and long left their mark upon that city. That in the year 1842 was chiefly among the lawyers of the city, a large number of whom were converted. The preaching was argumentative and covered the range of Christian doctrine. That Finney should have gained men is not strange when it is remembered that men are gained preeminently by the ideal, by convictions as to duty, and rational fear. Were exact statistics present, they would probably show something like those of Edwards' revival of 1734–35, the culmination of conversions lying about the years of a man's prime, viz., about forty-five.

For the work of Dwight Lyman Moody see the article on him. The philosophy of revivals under which this laborer worked was, for the most part, the philosophy of common sense. He believed in large assemblies of people, and was anxious to have

4. Dwight Lyman Moody.

Christian people in great numbers. He knew the dangers of a crowd, and promptly suppressed everything like undue excitement. To preach the Gospel as wisely as he could, to gather the interested together for special instruction and encouragement, to rely greatly upon prayer, to busy converted men in various Christian work, these constituted all the method Mr. Moody had. Perhaps a greater change from the methods of his predecessors was to be found in his preaching than anywhere else. His doctrine was of the old Evangelical type, and he taught as an essential part of it the eternal future punishment of the wicked. This position gave strenuousness to his efforts for the salvation of men; but it did not fix that salvation as consisting primarily in rescue from punishment. He preached the doctrine of atonement by the substitution of Christ for the sinner before the face of justice; but this did not make the salvation which Christ brought an external and merely forensic affair which left the innermost man untouched. Both of these doctrines were transfigured by the conception of the awfulness of sin as alienation from God, and the glory of salvation as the restoration of personal and loving relations between the sinful child and the heavenly Father. The doctrine of the divine love had at last come to its rights. Moody urged predominantly the love of God as the great reason for repentance. It was preeminently reasonable that the child should return to his Father, to be away from him could be nothing but misery, the love of God constituted a claim upon the man which could not be ignored—all of which considerations Moody urged with great power and pathos, guided by the instincts of a great heart, aflame with love to God. He preached particularly to despairing sinners, sinners who knew they were such and who could not believe that the grace of God was meant for them. Probably his greatest sermons were upon this general topic.

5. General View of the Nineteenth and Twentieth Centuries: Besides the revivals of the year 1800 and the years immediately following, it should be noted that the period of the Unitarian controversy in New England (1819 sqq.) was also one of revival. During the first thirty years of the century the Presbyterians increased fourfold in membership, chiefly by revivals, the Congregationalists twofold, the Baptists threefold, and the Methodists sevenfold. In the six years from 1826 to 1832 it is estimated that 200,000 people united with the leading Evangelical churches, of whom 60,000 were young men. The financial panics of 1837 and 1857 were followed by revivals, the latter of great power. The Millerite excitement of 1843 (see ADVENTISTS) produced a reaction unfavorable to revivals. But after 1857, for two years there was a general revival all over the country, conducted for the most part by pastors through their regular ministrations, having its chief expression in prayer-meetings, which brought in about 300,000 into the churches. The period of the Civil War was unfavorable to revivals; and it was not till 1874 that the current was reversed in connection with the great revivals under Moody, George Frederick Pentecost (q.v.), and others. The decade from 1870 to 1880 saw an increase of 3,392,567 communicants in Evangelical churches, among the best in the history of American Christianity. Nothing is more remarkable in the whole history than the revivals in colleges. Among recent prominent revivalists are to be mentioned B. Fay Mills, Sam Jones, and Sam Small, William A. Sunday, R. A. Torrey, and J. Wilbur Chapman (qq.v.).

1. In General.

F. H. FOSTER.

In the perspective of revival history during the close of the nineteenth and beginning of the twentieth century, three persons, Benjamin Fay Mills, Reuben Archer Torrey, and J Wilbur Chapman (qq.v.), all clergymen, appear as leaders in a movement especially noted for the prominent part taken in it by the laity. They all owe their stimulus in their special work to Dwight L. Moody (q.v., and see above), with whom they were early brought into close touch. They borrowed from him their message—plain, Scriptural, urgent, made effective by a fiery conviction, feathered by anecdote, incident, and experience, and unfettered by labored argumentation or the embellishments of rhetoric.

The first of these, Benjamin Fay Mills (q.v.), was a classmate at Lake Forest University, Ill., of Chapman, with whom also for a time later he was associated with marked success in revival campaigns. He began his evangelistic work in 1886, and for ten years continued in it uninterruptedly, visiting many of the principal centers of population in the United States and Canada. His main and immediate dependence was a popular address to the masses assembled, in which he was a master; but back of that, Mills may be said to have been the first to have "organized success." His one outstanding method was his "district combination plan" by which cities were divided into sections over which a network of services was spread. He was systematic, taking time and pains to prepare by arousing interest, enlisting support, and forming and multiplying prayer-circles. And then when the blow was struck in his Gospel appeal he drew the net by his card-signing device, which he was the first to introduce, thereby securing immediate decision. For the time in which Benjamin Fay Mills gave his fine talents to the work of soul-saving, few men have been more honored of God.

2. Benjamin Fay Mills.

Next to him, an evangelist of commanding personality is Reuben Archer Torrey (q.v.). The rise of Torrey goes back to the founding in 1889 at Chicago of the Moody Bible Institute, the purpose of it being a thorough and practical study of the English Bible. His close, personal connection with Moody in this Bible work made him, like Moody himself, a "Bible-man." Torrey is distinguished above both Mills and Chapman by a thorough mastery and use in revival work of the Bible in the vernacular. That Bible Institute, under Moody, Torrey, and others, became a veritable "powerhouse" in the great World's Fair campaign in Chicago in 1893. And since then, out from its Bible atmosphere Torrey himself has gone forth on many a revival enterprise, notably in the instance of his recent English mission which was marked by such intense interest, not, however, without much antagonism on the part of some non-conforming clergymen who took exception to his hyper-orthodoxy.

3. Reuben Archer Torrey.

But the foremost of the three named is J Wilbur Chapman (q.v.). He is the product of a wider environment, and therefore reaches out in influence to a larger periphery. He was early associated with Moody both as vice-president of the Bible Institute and in evangelistic work. His pastorates were a gymnasium where he was put in training for the noblest athletics, that of bringing sinners to God—in Albany, N. Y., where in one revival he harvested more than 100 souls, including some of the leading men of the city; and later in a steady revival fire, gathering in more than 500 converts in five years; in Philadelphia, adding 1,100 to the membership of the church in three years; and in New York, when he resigned the pastorate, in 1902, to become head of the Evangelistic Committee of the General Assembly of the Presbyterian Church in the United States of America.

4. J Wilbur Chapman.

His subsequent record is brilliant. His famous Boston campaign, for magnitude, power, and permanence of results, is without a parallel in this country. Early in 1910 he returned from evangelistic journey around the world, in which he visited eleven countries, spoke in sixty cities—in Australia, China, Japan, and England. Late in the winter of 1910–11 he resumed work in Brooklyn, N. Y.

The period of Mills, Torrey, and Chapman has been the most fruitful in the history of revivals in American Christianity. Those named have had as associates and imitators men like A. C. Dixon, H. M. Wharton, Major Whittle, J. Arthur Smith, and others; and so their methods have been adopted in many places with greater or less effect.

S. B. DUNN.

IV. The Welsh Revival of 1904–1906: Wales is well known as the land of revivals. Owing to the intense national spirit of the Welsh people these awakenings possess characteristics which distinguish them from the general religious movements of Great Britain as a whole. Through the long centuries of Saxon domination the inhabitants of Wales—who number, all told, less than one-half of the population of London—have preserved their independence in language, literature, and national consciousness. A fiery and imaginative race of mountaineers, imbued with a strong religious spirit, they have from time to time experienced great spiritual upheavals which have proved epochal in the life of the nation. Thus the revival of the eighteenth century under Daniel Rowlands and Howel Harris was a national renaissance which liberated the forces of Christian democracy in the principality and introduced a new era of progress and education.

1. The Welsh People.

The religious movement known as "The Great Welsh Revival" is the latest and most widely known of these national awakenings. This revival covers a period of two years—from the early part of 1904 to the beginning of 1906. During that time it is estimated that over 100,000 professed conversion. Of this number some 60,000 can be accounted for as being in 1910 members in good standing in the Protestant churches of Wales. The immediate ethical results of the movement were remarkable. A great wave of sobriety overswept the country so that the liquor trade suffered enormous financial losses; the decrease in criminal cases was no less remarkable; hundreds of outlawed debts were settled; goods stolen fifteen or twenty years before were returned to their owners; a phenomenal increase was recorded in the demand for good literature; feuds of long standing were healed; and sectarianism, a great curse of Welsh national life, was softened by a larger charity and a deeper consciousness of an underlying unity. The movement must not be confused with the organized missions that were held about this time in various parts of Great Britain. The genius of the Welsh revival was quite distinct from that of any of these missions. It was spontaneous, unconventional, and without organization of any sort. None of its "leaders" was over thirty years of age, and none was a great preacher. Most of the workers were from the humble walks of life and were comparatively uneducated. Some of the most successful were young girls, under twenty, who assisted at the meetings with exhortation and song. In method—or its absence—the services have been termed a triumph for Quakerism; "obedience to the Spirit" was the only condition insisted upon. Only very rarely was a sermon attempted; the meetings were devoted to prayer, song, testimony, and exhortation, and seldom concluded before the small hours of the morning. They were characterized by far less violent demonstrations than previous revivals in the principality. The burden of the revival-message was the love of God. As is usually the case in Wales, there were many apparently occult phenomena—visions, voices, and signs in the heavens (see § 6, below).

2. The Revival Described.

So far as the origin of the movement can be traced at all, it appears to have begun in Feb., 1904, in New Quay, Carmarthenshire, South Wales. Revival manifestations were first noticed in the local Calvinistic Methodist Church, of which Joseph Jenkins was pastor. Later, a convention was held in Blaenanerch where there were many indications of a spiritual awakening. This convention was attended by a young man who was to be known later as the "leader" of the revival—Evan John Roberts, at that time a candidate for the Welsh Presbyterian ministry and student in a preparatory school in Newcastle Emlyn, South Wales. In the autumn of the same year the revival flame that had been flickering obscurely in New Quay and other places, burst forth and quickly spread over the country, sweeping upward from the South to the mountainous extremities of northern Wales and subduing all before it. The remarkable scenes witnessed were reported in the English press and presently aroused the interest of the entire civilized world. By this time Evan Roberts had become the central figure of the awakening; still, to designate him the "leader" of the revival is to contradict the real genius of the movement, which, throughout, was without organization or executive direction. The revival was really begun before Roberts started upon his apostolate; but undoubtedly he became the chief and most honored representative of the movement.

3. Its Origin.

Evan John Roberts was born on July 8, 1878. He is of humble parentage and is the ninth of a family of fourteen children; of these, two sisters are living in the United States. His birthplace is Bwlchymynydd, Loughor, South Wales, a small mining town of 3,000 or 4,000 inhabitants. He was brought up in the Welsh Calvinistic Methodist Church (see PRESBYTERIANS, IV.), of which his parents are members and which he himself joined at the age of thirteen. When eleven years old Roberts left school and went to work as door-boy in a local coal mine where his father also labored. Here he narrowly escaped death in a coal-truck accident, and, later on, in a colliery explosion. A third narrow escape happened toward the end of the revival when, a few yards from a steep precipice, he was thrown from a carriage drawn by a runaway team. At twenty-four Evan Roberts left the mines and apprenticed himself to the trade of his uncle, Evan Edwards, a blacksmith. A year later he was accepted as candidate for the Welsh

4. Evan John Roberts; Early Life.

X.—2

Presbyterian ministry and in 1904 entered a preparatory school in Newcastle Emlyn, South Wales. Before this he had become subject to mystical experiences of a trance-like nature. He devoted many hours each day to prayer. He heard " voices " and saw " visions " and felt himself caught up above the limitations of time and sense into the immediate presence of God. This last experience came to him twice a day at regular hours and continued for some time. He found himself unable to pursue his studies to his own satisfaction in Newcastle Emlyn. His text-books would seem, as he has expressed it, to be aflame in his hand, and he would be seized with violent physical pain until he would drop the book and take up his Bible. His friends feared for his mental condition. On Sept. 29, 1904, in Blaenanerch Calvinistic Methodist Chapel he passed through a spiritual crisis, in which, to use his own words, " Living Force " entered him with almost physical violence, imparting to him intense joy, bodily strength, and mental illumination, as well as spiritual earnestness and power.

5. Work in the Revival.

On Oct. 31 he returned to his home in Loughor and began his work as revivalist—first among his own family and then in the church of which he was a member. At the beginning he was regarded with suspicion and considered demented, but the power of his meetings was irresistible and he quickly became a national figure as the torch-bearer of the revival. In his meetings he confined himself almost exclusively to the Welsh language. He sometimes gave addresses of an hour or an hour and a half in duration, but usually he spoke for less than ten minutes at a time. His style was pithy and epigrammatic, abounding in quaint metaphor and homely illustration. He was ready-witted and often in the meetings indulged in dialogue and quick repartee. He is possessed of clairvoyant and clairaudient powers, and occasionally these were exercised in the meetings. Toward the close of the revival he cloistered himself in the home of a friend and observed a seven-days' silence, shutting himself away from the outside world, and refusing to communicate with any one except by writing. This he did, as he believed, in obedience to the divine voice. He emerged from this strange experience much stronger physically and in a state of great mental and spiritual exaltation. His only mission outside Wales was in Liverpool (where he was accorded a public banquet by the lord mayor, Apr. 7, 1905). In this mission he addressed himself mainly to the Welsh people and rarely spoke in English. When in Liverpool, in order to silence adverse criticism which had raised the question of his sanity, he was examined by five English specialists who issued a certificate of his mental soundness. In 1906, at the end of the revival, Roberts suffered a severe nervous collapse. He passed into retirement in the home of friends residing in Leicestershire, England, where, until Nov., 1910, he remained in comparative seclusion. His health has improved. From his retirement he has written one or two articles for the religious press, but they lack the brilliance of his extempore revival addresses. He is a good musician and a poet of some ability. Before the revival he acquired an elementary knowledge of Greek and Latin and took up as a diversion the study of astronomy and some of the occult sciences.

The religious awakening has brought about in Wales a quickening of national spirit which is seeking expression in progressive legislation and general reform, and in this way it is still fulfilling itself. It has undoubtedly contributed to the movement for the political independence of Wales—the granting of a measure of autonomy by which the idealism of Welsh democracy can be given an adequate organ of expression.

6. Occult Phenomena.

Concerning the so-called occult phenomena of the revival much could be written. In almost every village within the revival zone testimony was given to the experience of mysterious psychical experiences. In Evan Roberts himself, the occult faculties are strongly developed (see § 4 above). He is (or was) subject to trance-like ecstasies. He claimed to be able to hear the prayers offered for him in far-distant places; he was quick to detect any spirit of opposition or skepticism in his meetings and to trace it to its source; he was continually hearing " voices " and seeing visions. It must be added that in these matters the self-restraint of the revivalist was as remarkable as the experiences themselves. They came to him unsought and were consistently subordinated to his Evangelical message. The Rev. H. Elvet Lewis in his chronicles of the awakening (*With Christ among the Miners*, London, 1906) narrates many instances of signs and visions, the most noteworthy being the case of Mrs. Jones, a peasant woman of Egryn, Merionethshire, whose evangelistic work during the revival was largely influenced by the appearance of phenomenal lights (a record of her experiences is to be found in the *Transactions* of the British Psychical Research Society for Dec., 1905). Mr. Lewis thus describes his meeting with her: " She made no reference to the signs until my friend and I asked her. She answered us simply as if she were speaking about the fire on the hearth, that she had seen, almost from the first, each evening a fire or light between her and the hills which rise from the marshy shore—a quickly vibrating light, ' as though full of eyes,' so another described it. It had revealed to her what to expect at the meetings? Yes, without fail. One evening she had interpreted the sign to mean four converts. But only three responded when the test was made in the crowded little chapel. ' But there must be four,' she said. No, there could not be; all the rest, except the three who had declared themselves that night, were already members. ' But there ought to be four to-night,' she repeated. No fourth could be found, until the door of the little vestibule was opened and one stood there halting between two opinions. The opening of the door and a kindly word of invitation brought the inquirer inside. And the four was completed. She had seen the light hovering over some houses on the hilltops; she was puzzled, for she thought there was no one in those houses unconverted, or at least out of church membership. But one day she was told by the Wesleyan minister at Barmouth and another friend who visited her, that there was one old woman in one of the houses, not now on Christ's side. 'Ah, that must be it,' she said. The two friends went up—found the woman in concern for her soul. Mrs. Jones herself visited her; she became one of the fifty-one [converts] in that marvelous fortnight.

"She had visited several villages near her home during the dark nights. The light, she said, had frequently accompanied her—not a terrifying light, but gentle and calm, just showing her way as she walked." "The problem," concludes Mr. Lewis, "still remains unsolved. But there can be no reasonable doubt of the appearance of these lights, at the time and place. Afterward they grew, no doubt, into a sort of foolish cult. Some, from mischief, made lights appear where Mrs. Jones went to conduct missions; at other times natural lights were taken to be extraordinary. But the earlier phenomena stand by themselves—possibly natural, but in any case abnormal. There still remain to be explained their association with her movements and their alleged clairvoyant signs."

It must be said that these phenomena have in some quarters been exaggerated out of all proportion to their importance in the revival. The part that they played was comparatively insignificant. GWILYM OSWALD GRIFFITH.

V. The Roman Catholic Mission: "Mission" is a term applied by Roman Catholics to efforts which are the equivalent of the Protestant "revival," consisting of efforts directed to reclaiming those within the territory of the Church who have been estranged from religious observances. There was no need for this sort of work until, with the establishment of Christianity as the state religion, large numbers of pagans came in, and, with the conversion of the Teutonic races, the Church was further increased by multitudes who were only superficially affected by the Christian spirit. The earlier penitential institutions no longer sufficed. When, in 1215, the duty of confession was made universal, the idea of legal satisfaction, made prominent by the hierarchical tendency, was a hindrance to real pastoral work, and neither the monks nor even the friars found the right road to successful pastoral influence. Only small communities, like the Brothers of the Common Life (see COMMON LIFE, BRETHREN OF THE) at the end of the Middle Ages, devoted themselves with real thoroughness and love to the cultivation of an inner spirit of Christian piety. It was the Reformation which stirred the Roman Catholic Church to make strong efforts to confirm the wavering and reclaim the wanderers. The Jesuits (q.v.) were the most zealous instruments of this movement for restoration among the upper classes, and the Capuchins (q.v.) among the lower. The movement first gained strength in France, where the bishops had kept up a tradition of personal acquaintance with the spiritual state of their dioceses. It was furthered by Vincent de Paul, who, in 1616, began his work in behalf of the galley-slaves, and at Folleville in the next year preached the desirability of general confession with such fervor that he was obliged to call in the Jesuits from Amiens to help him with the crowds who came. Ultimately he founded the Congregation of the Mission, or Lazarist order (see LAZARISTS), to promote not only education and missions among the heathen but also similar efforts in Christian lands. A new impulse was given by the congregation of mission-priests founded in 1815 by the Abbé Legris-Duval, expressly devoted to this particular work. After the upheaval of 1848 the German episcopate made frequent use of missions to reclaim the estranged masses; they were usually preached by Jesuits and Redemptorists (qq.v.), sometimes by Capuchins and Franciscans (qq.v.), and by the two latter orders from 1872 to 1894, when the two former were excluded from the Empire. [In the United States missions have become a regular part of the ecclesiastical machinery, held at intervals in most of the larger parishes, by Jesuits, Augustinians, Dominicans, Passionists, Paulists (qq.v.), and other orders.] They last two or three weeks, after careful preparation of the ground by the parochial clergy, and consist largely of frequent stirring sermons on sin, repentance, judgment, and Christian duties, leading to the reception of the sacraments of penance and communion, and closing with the solemn renewal of the baptismal vow by the whole congregation. There can be no difference of view between Protestants and Roman Catholics as to the duty of the Church to preach the Gospel not only to the heathen but also to lukewarm and nominal Christians. But there may well be a question as to whether this rapid succession of exciting sermons, accompanied by appeals to the emotions in external ways, is really calculated to produce lasting fruits rather than simply to bring the people into obedience to ecclesiastical precepts, especially confession. It is doubtful whether the constant striving after effect, the rhetorical declamation, the exaggerated pictures drawn of the evils and the punishment of sin, and the appeal to fear can well be productive of real moral renewal.

(D. STEITZ†.)

BIBLIOGRAPHY: To be taken into account are (1) the articles in this work on the men named as revivalists in the text, especially those of Edwards, Lyman Beecher, Tyler, Finney, Spring, Taylor, Wesley, Whitefield, Moody, Torrey, and others; (2) the works by those men which deal with the subject (e.g., Edwards' *Thoughts concerning the Present Revival of Religion*, and *Narrative of the Work of God in Northampton*); and (3) the literature under the articles on these men, which often discusses the revival activities of the subjects.

Treatises on the general history of revivals are: W. B. Sprague, *Lectures on Revivals of Religion*, New York, 1833; C. G. Finney, *Lectures on Revivals of Religion*, Boston, 1835, new ed., London, 1910; J. Gillies, *Historical Collections Relating to Remarkable Periods of Success of the Gospel. Preface by H. Bonar*, London, 1845; B. Tyler, *New England Revivals, as they Existed at the Close of the 18th and the Beginning of the 19th Centuries*, Boston, 1846; E. Porter, *Letters on the Religious Revivals which Prevailed about the Beginning of the Present Century*, Boston, 1858; H. Humphrey, *Revival Sketches and Manual*, New York, 1859; W. Gibson, *The Year of Grace: a Hist. of the Revival in Ireland, 1859 A.D.*, Boston, 1860; J. H. Vincent, *Hist. of the Camp Meeting and Grounds at Wesleyan Grove*, Boston, 1869; Mrs. M. N. Van Cott, *The Harvest and the Reaper: Reminiscences of Revival Work*, New York, 1876; C. L. Thompson, *Times of Refreshing: Hist. of American Revivals*, Chicago, 1877; W. W. Bennett, *Narrative of the Great Revival in the Southern Armies during the Civil War*, Philadelphia, 1877; J. Porter, *Revivals of Religion*, New York, 1878; S. C. Swallow, *Camp Meetings: their Origin, Hist., and Utility; also their Perversion*, New York, 1878; H. Bushnell, *Building Eras in Religion*, New York, 1881; C. F. Jones, *From the Forecastle to the Pulpit; fifty Years among Sailors; containing an Account of a wonderful Revival upon the Sea; with an Introduction by W. P. Strickland*, New York, 1884; S. B. Halliday and D. S. Gregory, *The Church in America and its Baptisms of Fire*, London and Toronto, 1896; A. Sims, *Remarkable Narratives, or Records of Powerful Revivals*, Kingston, Ont., 1896; H. Johnson, *Stories of Great Revivals*, London, 1900; A. T. Pierson, *Forward Movements of the Last Half Century*, New York, 1900; G. C. Morgan, *Evangelism: a Study of Need and Opportunity*, London, 1904; W. A. Candler, *Great Revivals and the Great Republic*, Atlanta, Ga., 1904; F. G. Beardsley, *Hist. of American Revivals*, New York, 1904; J. Page, *Great Evangelists and how God has used them*, London, 1905; J. Burns, *Revivals; their Laws and Leaders*, London, 1909.

On the "Great Awakening" consult: J. Tracy, *The Great Awakening: a Hist. of the Revival of Religion in the Time of Edwards and Whitefield*, Boston, 1842 (a classic); E. P. Hood, *Vignettes of the Great Revival of the 18th Century*, London, 1880, reissued *With a supplemental Description of the Revival in America*, Philadelphia, 1882; J. H. Overton, *Evangelical Revival in the 18th Century*, New York, 1886.

On special recent revivals: D. L. Moody and I. D. Sankey, *Narrative of Labors in Great Britain and Ireland; with Addresses and Lectures*, New York, 1875; R. W. Clark, *The Work of God in Great Britain under Messrs. Moody and Sankey in 1873–75*, New York, 1875; *Christian Convention of the Northwest. . . . Union Revival Meetings conducted by B. F. Mills and J. W. Chapman*, Minneapolis, 1893; R. Harkness, *With the Torrey-Alexander Mission round the World*, London, 1904; J. K. Maclean, *Triumphant Evangelism: the three Years' Missions of Torrey and Alexander in Great Britain*, London, 1905; G. T. B. Davis, *Torrey and Alexander; the Story of a World-wide Revival*, London, 1905; T. R. Williams, *The True Revival versus Torreyism*, London, 1905.

On the Welsh revival: W. T. Stead, *The Coming Revival. What I have seen and hope to see*, London, 1905; idem, *The Revival in the West*, ib. 1905; Awstin (pseud.), *The Religious Revival in Wales, 1904*, Cardiff, 1905; I. W. Charlton, *The Revival in Wales*, London, 1905; J. P. Lewis, *The Awakening in Wales and Some of the Hidden Springs*, London, 1905; H. Elvet Lewis, *With Christ among the Miners*, ib., 1907; J. V. Morgan, *The Welsh Religious Revival 1904 05; a Retrospect and a Criticism*, London, 1909; *The Welsh Revival*, in *Cambridge Modern History*, vi. 81 sqq., New York, 1909.

On the psychology of revivals: E. D. Starbuck, *Psychology of Religion; an empirical Study of the Growth of religious Consciousness*, New York, 1899; G. A. Coe, *Spiritual Life, Studies in the Science of Religion*, New York, 1900; W. James, *Varieties of Religious Experience*, New York, 1902; F. M. Davenport, *Primitive Traits in Religious Revivals*, New York, 1905; Henke, in *AJT*, 1909, pp. 193 sqq.

On the theory and practise consult: J. W. Alexander, *The Revival and its Lessons*, New York, 1861; L. T. Townsend, *The Supernatural Factor in Religious Revivals*, Boston, 1877; W. W. Newell, *Revivals: how and when*, New York, 1882; W. P. Doe, editor, *Revivals; how to promote them*, New York, 1884; G. W. Hervey, *Manual of Revivals*, New York, 1884; J. O. Peck, *The Revival and the Pastor*, New York, 1894; J. E. W. Ditchfield, *Fishers of Men, or how to win the Men*, London, 1899; J. W. Chapman, *Revivals and Missions*, New York, 1900; idem, *Present-Day Evangelism*, ib., 1903; J. P. Brushingham, *Catching Men: Studies in vital Evangelism*, Cincinnati, 1906; R. A. Torrey, *How to Conduct and Promote a Successful Revival*, Chicago, 1906; J. V. Coombs, *Christian Evangelism*, Cincinnati, 1907; C. LeR. Goodell, *Pastoral and Personal Evangelism*, New York, 1907; W. Hamilton, *Sane Evangelism*, Philadelphia, 1909; J. Burns, *Revivals, their Laws and Leaders*, London, 1909; O. O. Green, *Normal Evangelism*, New York, 1910.

REWARD: That which is given in recognition of merit or work performed, or in requital of good or evil. The Bible frequently employs the conception of reward to express the certainty that God guarantees the ultimate success and happiness of those who obey his law. Such expressions, however, raise two serious questions: Does not the promise of a reward vitiate the motive of ethical conduct by introducing into it an egoistic element, and does it not contradict the doctrine of salvation through God's grace as taught by Paul?

On closer examination it will be seen that both questions can be answered in the negative. In private life reward is an economic conception, representing proportionate compensation for work accomplished. Here the reward is usually the sole motive for action. In public life the case may be quite different. Here altruistic motives come into play, and reward, in the sense of remuneration, may cease to form a motive for action, since the service rendered, the good done the community, may be its own reward. However, the public official who neglects his private affairs to serve the community may reasonably expect to be provided for. Similarly the Christian in the service of God. Since his work in the moral vineyard leaves mere personal interest out of account, it, too, can be regarded as a service rendered to the community, or to the divine power that presides over the moral order; and it carries with it naturally the expectation of recompense for the personal sacrifice entailed. Here there is no thought of an equivalent for service rendered, as in the case of a laborer in private life, for the reward has not been the sole motive to action. If reward be taken in the strictest sense, it is clear that no one can make demand of God for recompense. The expectation of a reward, therefore, becomes a matter of faith, and the reward itself a matter of grace. In the last analysis human service itself is a gift of grace, since it is accomplished through the spirit of God (Phil. i. 6, ii. 13). In this view the objections urged by many modern ethical writers (most strongly by Eduard von Hartmann and Nietzsche, qq.v.) against reward as a motive become irrelevant. Both Jesus and Paul taught expressly that the Christian-ethical life does not spring from any thought of reward, but from the grace of God in us and from the love toward God and our neighbors which it awakens. In the New Testament the conception of reward is not employed as a motive for conversion, but as an encouragement to perseverance in the Christian life; and in the religious view of the world it serves to express the certainty that the moral order is not merely a human but a divine affair.

The idea that God not only gives the law but also sees to its fulfilment is inseparable from the religious view of the world. According to the prophets it is an inviolable rule that the righteous are rewarded and the wicked punished (Isa. iii. 10–11; Amos v. 14–27; Hos. iv. 1–3). A decision between obedience and disobedience toward God is a choice between blessing and curse, between life and death (Deut. xxviii. 1–68, xxx. 15–20; Lev. xxvi. 3–45; Josh. xxiii. 14–16). In numerous sayings and parables Jesus promises the goods of his kingdom, or eternal life, as the reward of his disciples (Matt. v. 2–10, xix. 29, xxiv. 45–51, xxv. 34–46; Luke vi. 22–35, xii. 33–44, xiv. 12–14); but it is clear that he did not make the expectation of reward the chief motive of Christian life. In fact, the man who seeks to gain the reward by his own efforts forfeits it (cf. Matt. vi. 1–6, 16, xviii. 1–4; Mark viii. 35). It is duty done without expectation of reward that is rewarded (cf. Luke xvii. 10). In the writings of Paul the idea of reward is subordinated to the doctrine of salvation by grace. Eternal life is a gift of God (Rom. vi. 23), which can not be demanded as a right (cf. Rom. iv. 4–5); and the basis of ethical conduct is not the hope of reward, but a realization of the mercy of God (Rom. xii. 1), love toward Christ and a desire to obey him (II Cor. viii. 8, x. 5–7), and the desire to live in the spirit (Gal. v. 25; Rom. viii. 13–17). While Paul does not always reconcile the idea of reward with the doctrine of salvation by grace, on the whole he teaches that any divine requital of human activity is a manifestation of grace; and that such activity itself can not be dissolved into a series of separate deeds meriting reward. Rather, Christian conduct presents itself as a uniform manifestation of faith working itself out ethically.

The Biblical conception of reward has been explained away in mysticism, which sees in it a relic of egoism; or it has been rejected in non-religious systems of ethics, which, regarding ethical conduct as a human affair, find that the idea of an eternal reward obscures ethical insight; or it has been coarsened and formalized in legal conceptions of religion, where the basis of Christian-ethical conduct is laid in arbitrary statutes. Here the striving for a reward, which was only an accessory motive in the Biblical view, becomes the chief motive.

From the view of Augustine that to cling to God is both virtue and the reward of virtue (*Epist.*, clv. 12) was developed in the Middle Ages that mystical love of God in which the self is forgotten. Bernard of Clairvaux gave this mysticism its classic expression in his doctrine of the four gradations of love. It may be added that Melanchthon, in the "Apology" of the Augsburg Confession (*CR*, xxvii. 275 sqq.), opposes the obscuring of the Pauline doctrine of grace by the conception of reward. Similarly, the Council of Trent (*Session VI., cap.* xi.) characterized the expectation of an eternal reward as a subsidiary motive beside the chief motive, viz., the glorification of God, though Canon XXXI. seems to make expectation of reward alone a sufficient motive (Schaff, *Creeds*, ii. 117). While in modern philosophical ethics reward as a motive has been severely criticized and generally rejected, it may be said that any system of ethics which rejects the idea of an ultimate divine recompense is incomplete, in that it neglects to emphasise the dominant position of the good in the world.

(O. Kirn.)

Bibliography: R. W. Hamilton, *The Revealed Doctrine of Rewards and Punishments*, London, 1853; P. Mehlhorn, in *Jahrbücher für protestantische Theologie*, 1876; R. Neumeister, *Die neutestamentliche Lehre vom Lohn*, Halle, 1880; W. G. T. Shedd, *Dogmatic Theology*, i. 369, New York, 1889; H. Schultz, in *TSK*, 1890, 1894; A. Juncker, *Das Ich und die Motivation des Willens im Christenthum*, Halle, 1891; H. P. Liddon, *Sermons on Some Words of Christ*, London, 1892; H. H. Wendt, *Die Lehre Jesu*, pp. 166 sqq., 2d ed., Göttingen, 1901, Eng. transl. of 1st ed., *The Teaching of Jesus*, 2 vols., London, 1892; E. Ehrhardt, *Der Grundcharakter der Ethik Jesu*, Freiburg, 1895; K. Thieme, *Die sittliche Triebkraft des Glaubens*, Leipsic, 1895; A. Titius, *Die neutestamentliche Lehre von der Seligkeit*, parts i.–iv., Tübingen, 1895–1900; H. Jacoby, *Neutestamentliche Ethik*, Königsberg, 1899; H. Cremer, *Die paulinische Rechtfertigungslehre*, pp. 359–368, Gütersloh, 1900; C. A. Briggs, *Ethical Teaching of Jesus*, pp. 206, 240, New York, 1904; *DCG*, ii. 528.

REYNOLDS, ren'els, **EDWARD:** Church of England bishop; b. at Southampton Nov., 1599; d. at Norwich Jan. 16, 1676. He was educated at Merton College, Oxford (B.A., 1618; fellow, 1620; M.A., 1624; D.D., 1648); became preacher at Lincoln's Inn in 1622 and served as royal chaplain; became vicar of All Saints, Northamptonshire, 1628, and rector of Bramston, 1631. At the breaking out of the civil war he was a moderate Anglican, was a member of the Westminster Assembly, 1643, but did not take the covenant till 1644. He was one of the committee of twenty-two to examine and approve ministers, was vicar of St. Lawrence Jewry, London, 1645–62; dean of Christ Church, 1648–50 and again in 1659; was chosen vice-chancellor in 1648, but ejected from Christ Church in 1659 for not taking the "engagement." At the Restoration Reynolds conformed, was made warden of Merton College and canon of Worcester in 1660, and bishop of Norwich in 1661. In the same year he took part in the Savoy Conference (q.v.).

He carried his Puritanic principles into practise even while a bishop, and lived only for his diocese. His *Works* were first collected and published in 1658; best edition, with *Life*, by A. Chalmers, 6 vols. (London, 1826).

Bibliography: Besides the *Life* by A. Chalmers, ut sup., consult: A. à Wood, *Athenæ Oxonienses*, ed. P. Bliss, iii. 1083, and *Fasti Oxonienses*, ii. 115, 120, 355, 4 vols., London, 1813–20; *DNB*, xlviii. 40–41.

REYNOLDS, HENRY ROBERT: Congregationalist; b. at Romsey (7 m. n.w. of Southampton), Hampshire, England, Feb. 26, 1825; d. at Broxbourne (16 m. n.n.e. of London), Hertfordshire, Sept. 10, 1896. He was educated at Coward College and University College, London (B.A., 1848); became pastor at Halsted, Essex, 1846; at Leeds, 1849; president of Countess of Huntingdon's College, Cheshunt, Herts, 1860, from which he retired in 1894. He was author of *Beginnings of the Divine Life* (London, 1859); *Notes of the Christian Life* (1865); *John the Baptist*, Congregational Union lectures for 1874 (1874); *Philosophy of Prayer, and other Essays* (1881); commentary on *Hosea* and *Amos* (1884), in C. J. Ellicott's *Old-Testament Commentary* (1882–84); of exposition, commentary, and introduction to the *Gospel of John* (1887–88; in the *Pulpit Commentary*); *Athanasius: his Life and Life Work* (1889); *Light and Peace. Sermons and Addresses* (1892); and *Lamps of the Temple, and other Addresses to Young Men* (1895). He was also joint editor and compiler of *Psalms, Hymns, and Passages of Scripture for Christian Worship* (1853); editor of *Ecclesia: Church Problems*, 2 series (1870–71); *Athanasius* (1889); and was coeditor of the *British Quarterly Review* (1866–74), and of *The Evangelical Magazine* (1877–82).

Bibliography: A memoir is prefixed to one of his publications not named above, *Who say ye that I am*, London, 1896; *H. R. Reynolds, His Life and Letters*, ed. by his sisters, ib. 1898.

REYNOLDS (RAINOLDS), JOHN: Puritan divine; b. at Pinhoe (4 m. n.e. of Exeter), Devonshire, 1549; d. at Oxford May 21, 1607. He probably entered Merton College, Oxford, but in 1563 received a scholarship at Corpus Christi (probationary fellow, 1566; full fellow, and B.A., 1568); he there became tutor to Richard Hooker (q.v.), Greek reader (an important office), 1572-73-78; resigned his fellowship in 1586; was then appointed to a temporary lectureship; became dean of Lincoln, 1593; and president of Corpus Christi, 1598. He was one of four Puritan representatives (and the chief one) at the Hampton Court Conference (q.v.), at which he is credited with suggesting to King James the desirability of a new translation of the Bible (see BIBLE VERSIONS, B, IV., 6). Of this work he was made a participant, being one of the committee which had in charge the translation of the prophets, but he did not live to see the completion of the task. He was celebrated for his great learning, remarkable memory, sound judgment, lofty character, uprightness, piety, and regard for his students. Among the works published by him are: *Sex theses de sacra Scriptura et ecclesia* (London, 1580); *The Summe of the Conference between John Rainolds and John Hart touching the Head and the Faith of the Church* (1584); *De Romanæ ecclesiæ idolatria* (1596); *The Overthrow of Stage-Players* (1599). The following were issued after his death: *Defence of the Judgment of the Reformed Churches that a Man may lawfullie not onlie put awaie his Wife for her Adulterie but also marry another* (1609); *Censura librorum Apocryphorum Veteris Testamenti* (1611); *The Prophecie of Obadiah opened and explained* (1613); *The Judgment of Doctor Reignolds concerning Episcopacy, whether it be God's Ordinance* (1641); and *Sermons on the Prophecies of Haggai* (1648).

BIBLIOGRAPHY: R. Crackanthorpe, *Defensio ecclesiæ Anglicanæ*, chap. lxix., London, 1625; D. Neal, *Hist. of the Puritans*, i. 252, ed. J. Toulmin, Bath, 1793; W. H. Frere, *The English Church (1558-1625)*, pp. 296 sqq., ib. 1904; R. G. Usher, *The Reconstruction of the English Church*, New York, 1910; *DNB*, xlvii. 180-182.

RHABANUS MAURUS. See RABANUS MAURUS.

RHEES, rîs, RUSH: Baptist; b. at Chicago Feb. 8, 1860. He was educated at Amherst (A.B., 1883), where he was Walker instructor in mathematics in 1883-85, and at Hartford Theological Seminary, from which he was graduated in 1888. After being pastor of the Middle Street Baptist Church, Portsmouth (1889-92), he was associate professor of New-Testament interpretation at Newton Theological Institution (1892-94); professor of the same subject (1894-1900); and president of the University of Rochester since 1900. He has written *The Life of Jesus of Nazareth: A Study* (New York, 1900).

RHEGIUS, rî'ji-us (RIEGER), URBANUS: German Reformer; b. at Langenargen (17 m. e. of Constance) in the latter half of May, 1489; d. at Celle (23 m. n.e. of Hanover) May 27, 1541. He received his first education at Lindau, whence he went to Freiburg, where he came under strong humanistic influence, also associating much with Eck, the subsequent opponent of Luther. When Eck was called to a professorship at Ingolstadt in 1510, Rhegius followed him. After 1512 he devoted increased attention to theology, still under Eck's guidance, and in 1518, while visiting Constance, he wrote his first theological treatise, the *De dignitate sacerdotum*, from a strictly orthodox Roman Catholic point of view. In 1519 he was ordained to the priesthood at Constance, and at the beginning of the controversy between Luther and Eck took the side of his teacher. By Mar., 1520, however, his position had for some unknown reason so veered that he could be termed a friend of Luther. He can not, however, at that time have changed his attitude decidedly, for in the same year he was called to Augsburg as cathedral preacher in place of Œcolampadius, who had entered the monastery of St. Brigitta. He was forced to leave late in 1521 for openly supporting Luther, and he then lived at Argen and Tetnang, and preached for a time at Hall in the valley of the Inn. In 1524 he published his *Ob das new testament yetz recht verteutscht sey*, in reply to the attack of Hieronymus Emser (q.v.) against Luther's translation of the Bible in his *Auss was grund vnnd ursach Luther's dolmatschung . . . dem gemeinen man billig vorbotten sey* (Leipsic, 1523), and in the same year returned to Augsburg as a private citizen. During his absence friction between the old faith and the new movement had led to riot and even to conspiracy, until the demands laid on the vacillating city council forced it to take a firm stand and finally to check the uprising. Rhegius now became pastor of St. Anne's; on Christmas Day, 1524, he administered the Lord's Supper under both kinds; and in 1526 he married. In the eucharistic controversy, except for a brief period of practical subscription to Zwinglianism, Rhegius adhered to the position of Luther, swayed, no doubt, by fear of the dangerous radicalism of the Anabaptist movement, which both he and his colleagues vainly sought to check. His feeble efforts to effect a mediation between Lutheranism and Zwinglianism were equally fruitless; religious dissension of all kinds steadily increased, and the civil authorities were timid and wavering.

The diet of 1530 ended the career of Rhegius at Augsburg. On the day after his arrival (June 17) the emperor demanded that all Protestant preaching cease at once, and Rhegius was dismissed with the other preachers. Toward the end of August he accepted the invitation of Ernest the Confessor (q.v.), duke of Lüneburg, to become pastor at Celle, and, after having brought about a conference between Melanchthon and Butzer, he took with him a series of articles to be submitted to Luther, whom he met at Coburg in an interview which made a deep impression upon him. In the territory of Lüneburg, though it was already won for the Lutheran cause with the exception of the capital, much remained to be done by Rhegius, who was appointed superintendent in 1531. In this same year he preached at Lüneburg and issued a church order, though it was not firmly established until Sept., 1532. As superintendent Rhegius took special pains to provide the congregations with efficient preachers and to rouse those already in office to the proper discharge of their duties. His activity extended even beyond the duchy of Lüneburg, especially after the monasteries had been reformed by his untiring activity. The city of Hanover owes to him the renovation of its religious life after the victory of the Reformation, for in 1536 he drew up for it the church order which is still in force. He was also active in the reformation of the cities of Minden, Soest, and Lemgo, and he strenuously opposed the Anabaptists who found warm sympathizers throughout northern Germany. As the adviser of Duke Ernest, Rhegius was an important factor in securing the acceptance of the Formula of Concord. His last public appearance was at the conference of Hagenau in 1540. Among his writings special mention may be made of the following: *De dignitate sacerdotum* (Augsburg, 1519); *Underricht, Wie ain Christenmensch Got seinem herren teglich beichten soll* (1521); *Wider den newen irrsal Doctors Andres von Carlstadt des Sacraments halb warnung* (n.p., 1524); *Von leybeygenschafft oder Knechtheyt* (n.p., 1525); *Warnung wider den neuen Tauforden* (1527); and *Formulæ caute loquendi* (Wittenberg, 1535; Germ. ed., 1536, Celle, 1880). The works of Rhegius, both Latin and German, were almost completely edited by his son, E. Rhegius (2 vols., Nuremberg, 1561–62).

[Rhegius also wrote the following works which were translated into English: *Novæ doctrinæ ad veterem collatio* (Augsburg, 1526 [?]), transl. by W. Turner, *A Comparison betwene the Olde learnynge and the Newe* (Southwark, 1557); *Ain Summa christlicher leer* (Augsburg, 1527), transl. by W. Lynne, *A declaration of the twelve articles of the christen faythe* (London, 1548); and *Doctrina certissima* (Frankfort, 1545), transl. by J. Fox, *An instruccyon of Christen fayth* (London, 1550 [?]); as well as sermons on Matt. ix. 16–26 (transl. by W. Lynne, London, 1548), Luke xxiv. (transl. by W. Hilton, London, 1578), and Matt. xviii. 10 (transl. by R. Robinson, London, 1590), and an exposition of Ps. lxxxvii. (transl. by R. Robinson, London, 1594).] (PAUL TSCHACKERT.)

BIBLIOGRAPHY: H. C. Heimburger, *Urbanus Rhegius*, Gotha, 1851; G. Uhlhorn, *Urbanus Rhegius, Leben und ausgewählte Schriften*, Elberfeld, 1862; O. Seitz, *Die theologische Entwickelung des Urbanus Rhegius*, Gotha, 1898; and literature under LUTHER, MARTIN; and ZWINGLI, HULDREICH.

RHEIMS NEW TESTAMENT. See BIBLE VERSIONS, B, IV., § 5.

RHODES. See ASIA MINOR, V.

RHODES, KNIGHTS OF. See JOHN, SAINT, ORDER OF HOSPITALLERS OF.

RHODON, rō'don: Greek author of the second century. The sole source of information concerning him is Eusebius (*Hist. eccl.*, V., xiii.), who states that he was born in Asia and educated at Rome by Tatian, so that he would seem to have been converted between 165 and 172. Rhodon, however, never broke with the Church. According to Eusebius, he was the author of a work against Marcion, and the citations preserved by Eusebius are important for a knowledge of Apelles and his doctrine, as well as other Marcionists. Eusebius likewise states that Rhodon wrote a commentary on the hexaemeron, and that he designed a polemic against an otherwise unknown work of Tatian entitled "Problems," in which all difficult passages of the Bible had been collected. Whether Rhodon ever wrote this refutation and explained the problems thus posited is unknown. At Rome Rhodon held a disputation with Apelles, and as the latter died about 180, while Rhodon wrote his anti-Marcionistic treatise during the lifetime of Apelles, the composition of the work must have been between 170 and 180. It has been suggested, though without foundation, that Rhodon was the author of the Canon of Muratori (q.v.; Harnack, *Litteratur*, i. 599) and of the anti-Montanistic treatise excerpted by Epiphanius (*Hist. eccl.*, xlviii. 2–13; H. G. Voigt, *Eine verschollene Urkunde des antimontanistischen Kampfes*, pp. 224 sqq., Leipsic, 1891).

(ERWIN PREUSCHEN.)

BIBLIOGRAPHY: The fragments are collected, with notes, in M. J. Routh, *Reliquiæ sacræ*, i. 435–446, Oxford, 1846; *MPG*, v. 1331–38; Eng. transl. in *ANF*, viii. 766. Consult: A. Gallandi, *Bibliotheca veterum patrum*, ii., pp. xvii., 144–145, Venice, 1765; P. Caspari, *Ungedruckte . . . Quellen zur Geschichte des Taufsymbols*, iii. 315, 340–341, 364–365, Christiania, 1871; A. Hilgenfeld, *Die Ketzergeschichte des Urchristenthums*, 532–533, Leipsic, 1884; Bardenhewer, *Patrologie*, pp. 105, 110–111, Eng. transl., St. Louis, 1908; idem, *Geschichte*, i. 490–491; Krüger, *History*, pp. 143–144; Harnack, *Litteratur*, i. 599, ii. 1, pp. 313–314; *DCB*, iv. 545.

RICCI, CATHERINE DE. See CATHERINE DE RICCI.

RICCI, rit'chi, **LORENZO:** General of the Jesuits; b. at Florence Aug. 2, 1703; d. at Rome Nov. 24, 1775. He entered the order of the Jesuits in 1718, and became its general in 1758. He was of an amiable yet inflexible disposition, and was unalterably attached to the tenet of obedience. To all propositions to change the constitution of the order, emanating either from the pope or from the Roman Catholic princes, he answered "*Sint ut sunt, aut non sint.*" ("Let them [the Jesuits] be as they are or let them cease to exist"). The consequence was that the pope dissolved the order by the bull *Dominus ac redemptor noster*, July 21, 1773. Ricci protested emphatically against the action and was confined in the castle of St. Angelo for the rest of his life.

BIBLIOGRAPHY: J. J. I. von Döllinger, *Beiträge zur politischen, kirchlichen, und Culturgeschichte*, iii. 1–74, Vienna, 1882; *A Circumstantial Account of the Death of Abbé Laurence Ricci. To which is annexed a Copy of the Protestation which he left at his Death*, London, 1776; A. Carayon, *Documents inédits concernant la compagnie de Jésus*, vol. xvii., Paris, 1869; L. A. de Caraccioli, *Vita dell' Abati Lorenzo Ricci*, n.p., n.d.; Ranke, *Popes*, ii. 446–447; *KL*, x. 1170–72.

RICCI, MATTEO: Roman Catholic missionary and astronomer; b. at Macerata (120 m. e.s.e. of Florence), Italy, Oct. 6, 1553; d. at Peking, China, May 11, 1610. He first studied law, but, going to Rome in 1571, entered the Society of Jesus and gave especial attention to the study of astronomy; he was sent to India as a missionary in 1577, and there completed his theological studies and was made priest; thence he was called to Macao, where he gained the favor of the viceroy of the province of Kwantung both by his personal characteristics and by his acquaintance with the Chinese language. Under the new viceroy he was compelled to leave

Macao, but had permission to settle at Shaotsao in the same province, 1590. He had as his object, which he kept steadily in mind, a mission to Peking; this he brought about in 1600, where his astronomical instruments aroused the curiosity of the emperor; permission to remain was not definitely gained, however, until 1605, when he was enabled to gain a settled residence. His further religious activities were carried on there, looking to the conversion of the Chinese; and no less devoted were his services to astronomy and mathematics, which, however, he made use of as an introduction to the truths of Christianity. The esteem which he won at court paved the way for the success of Roman Catholic missions in China, and his work was carried on by his successors. He did much in the way of writing in the Chinese language, producing works not only in theology, but also in mathematics and geometry. See CHINA, II., 2, § 2.

BIBLIOGRAPHY: Biographies have been written by Père D'Orleans, Paris, 1693; C. Sainte-Foi, ib., 1859; A. Werfer, Regensburg, 1870; and L. Nocentini, in the "Acts" of the fourth international congress of orientalists, ii. 273 sqq., Florence, 1881.

RICCI, SCIPIONE DE': Bishop of Pistoja and one of the few representatives of the Enlightenment within the Roman Catholic Church in Italy; b. at Florence Jan. 9, 1741; d. at Rignano (11 m. e.s.e. of Florence) Jan. 27, 1810. At the age of fifteen he was placed in a Jesuit school at Rome, but was recalled on manifesting a tendency to enter the order, and completed his theological studies at Pisa and Florence. He was ordained to the priesthood in 1766, and in 1775 became vicar-general to the archbishop of Florence. Five years later, on the death of the bishop of Pistoja, Ricci was nominated as his successor by Leopold, grand duke of Tuscany, who deemed him capable of carrying out proposed reforms in the training of the clergy, the improvement of moral conditions, and the introduction of the Jansenistic "Colbert catechism." Ricci was duly consecrated, only to be confronted by almost insuperable difficulties in his diocese. Evil conditions in the monasteries could be remedied only by abrogating their exemption and placing them under episcopal jurisdiction; and other reform measures contemplated the improvement of the cure of souls and of preaching, the protection of the secular against the regular clergy, the enforcement of the rules on fasting, the introduction and diffusion of enlightening literature; the purification of religious ideals, and the diminution of the cult of saints and relics and of the Sacred Heart. To these the synod convened by Ricci at Pistoja in 1786 added the holding of annual synods, improvement of the breviary, encouragement of Bible reading, and the strengthening of episcopal power against the Curia. Only two bishops, however, besides Ricci, took the decisions of the synod seriously, although the sessions were attended by 233 parish priests and thirteen regular clergy. Every effort was made to obviate the charges of Jansenism already made against the leaders by stressing the articles on sin and original sin transmitted by the faculty of Louvain to Innocent XI. and recognized as orthodox. It was also affirmed that even the Church had no power to posit new rules of faith, her sole duty being to preserve in original purity what had been given her by Christ and the apostles. Indulgences, moreover, were declared to be simply the remission of the discipline of the Church; parallel forms for the liturgy in the vernacular were demanded; processions were restricted; the number of saints' days was decreased, and a decree on the life of the clergy and the conferring of ecclesiastical offices formed the conclusion. A letter was likewise addressed to the grand duke, containing additional proposed reforms, and asking that a national council be convened.

With the express sanction of Leopold, the council was convened at Florence on Apr. 23, 1787, only to reject most decidedly the fifty-seven propositions of the grand duke. The canonists and theologians deputed to present them were silenced by the episcopal authority of the assembled bishops, who, with the exception of Ricci and the bishops of Chiusi and Colle, voted unanimously against each of Leopold's proposed reforms. This overwhelming opposition rendered it impossible for the grand duke to carry out the changes which he desired, although, as long as he remained in Italy, he supported Ricci against the efforts of his opponents to render it impossible for him to remain in Pistoja. When, however, Leopold succeeded his brother, Joseph II., as emperor of Austria in 1790, Ricci's enemies, aided by a feeble regency, attained their object, and the bishop, resigning from his see, retired to private life. The resolutions of the Synod of Pistoja were condemned by the bull *Auctorem fidei* (Aug. 28, 1794), which also rejected eighty-five statements in it as heretical and erroneous, a decision to which Ricci formally submitted before Pius VII., when the pontiff was returning from Paris in 1805. Ricci was the author of a number of episcopal charges as well as of *Istruzione cristiana sopra il sacramento della confermazione* (3d ed., Pistoja, 1783), a volume of sermons (1788), and the posthumous *Memorie di Scipione de' Ricci, vescovo di Prato e Pistoja* (ed. A. Gelli, 2 vols., Florence, 1865) and *Alcune lettere inedite di Scipione de' Ricci ad Antonio Marini* (ed. C. Guasti, Prato, 1857). K. BENRATH.

BIBLIOGRAPHY: The sources are the *Memorie* and *Alcune lettere* noted above. Based on these is L. J. A. de Potter's *Vie de Scipion de Ricci*, 3 vols., Brussels, 1825, which was put on the Index. Consult further: A. von Reumont, *Geschichte Toscanas*, ii. 148 sqq., Gotha, 1877; *KL*, x. 34 sqq.; Lichtenberger, *ESR*, xi. 230–231.

RICE, EDWIN WILBUR: Congregationalist; b. at Kingsborough, N. Y., July 24, 1831. He was graduated from Union College (A.B., 1854) and Union Theological Seminary, New York (1857). He has been associated with the American Sunday School Union since 1859, in which he has been a missionary (1859–64), superintendent of missions (1864–70), assistant secretary of missions (1870–1879), and editor of the periodicals and other publications of the organization (since 1879). He has prepared the *Scholar's Handbooks on the International School Lessons* from 1873 to 1889 and written popular commentaries on Matthew (Philadelphia, 1886; 6th ed., 1910); Luke (1889); John (1891), and Acts (1896; 4th ed., 1909), as well as *Organization and Classification of Sunday Schools* (1881); *The Origin of Sunday Schools* (1886); *Stories of Great Painters: or, Religion in Art* (1887); *Our Sixty-Six*

Sacred Books: How they came to us and What they are (1892); *Handy Helps for Busy Workers* (1899); *The Heavenly City* (1899); *A Century of Sunday School Progress* (1899); and *A Short History of the International Lesson System* (1902).

RICE, LUTHER: Baptist; b. at Northborough, Mass., Mar. 25, 1783; d. at Edgefield, S. C., Sept. 25, 1836. Converted in his youth, he united with the Northborough Congregational church in Mar., 1802. As a student in Williams College he manifested a deep interest in missions to the heathen and in association with other students was instrumental in bringing about the organization of the American Board of Commissioners for Foreign Missions (see CONGREGATIONALISTS, I., 4, § 11; cf. JUDSON, ADONIRAM). He offered himself as a missionary along with Judson, Nott, Mills, and Richards (1811). The number of applicants being thought too great, his appointment was made conditional on his first raising the money for outfit and passage. He accomplished this in a few days and was ready to go with the rest (Feb. 6, 1812). He followed Judson and his wife in adopting Baptist views and was immersed in India by the English Baptist missionary William Ward, Nov. 1, 1812. He returned to America (Sept., 1813) to adjust relations with the American Board and to interest and organize the Baptists for the support of the Burman mission which Judson proceeded to inaugurate. Through his untiring efforts funds were raised for the immediate need, local missionary societies were organized in many places, and in 1814 the Triennial Convention was formed as a national Baptist society for the support of missions. Largely through his efforts a theological seminary in Philadelphia was established in 1818, and Columbian University in Washington in 1822. Under his leadership the Triennial Convention undertook home mission work (from 1817), for which a separate society was later constituted. In 1816 he began the publication of a religious quarterly (*Latter Day Luminary*) and in 1822 he began to issue the first Baptist weekly, *The Columbian Star*. His multifarious denominational enterprises soon outgrew the income that he was able to secure and financial worries probably shortened his days. A. H. NEWMAN.

BIBLIOGRAPHY: T. Armitage, *Hist. of the Baptists*, pp. 434, 464, 502, New York, 1893; A. H. Newman, in *American Church History Series*, ii., 390, 392, 399, 405, 427, ib., 1894; H. C. Vedder, *The Baptists*, pp. 163–164, ib., 1902.

RICE, NATHAN LEWIS: Presbyterian; b. in Garrard County, Ky., Dec. 29, 1807; d. at Chatham, Bracken County, Ky., June 11, 1877. He studied at Center College, Danville, Ky., and at Princeton Theological Seminary, 1829; and was pastor at Bardstown, Ky., 1833–41, where he also established an academy and a newspaper, the *Western Protestant*, afterward merged in the Louisville *Presbyterian Herald*. He preached at Paris, Ky., 1841–1844; was pastor at Cincinnati, 1845–53; at St. Louis, Mo., 1853–58, where he edited the *St. Louis Presbyterian;* was pastor at Chicago, 1857–61; professor of theology at the Chicago Theological Seminary, 1859–61; pastor of the Fifth Avenue Presbyterian Church, New York, 1861–67; president of Westminster College, Fulton, Mo., 1869–74; and professor of theology at Danville, Ky., 1874–77. An able debater and preacher, he engaged in several memorable discussions: namely, with Alexander Campbell (q.v.) at Lexington, Ky., in 1843, on baptism; with J. A. Blanchard in 1845, on slavery; with E. Pingree the same year, on universal salvation; and with J. B. Purcell (q.v.) in 1851, on Romanism. His publications, besides the debates already referred to, include *God Sovereign, and Man Free* (Philadelphia); *Romanism not Christianity* (New York, 1847); *Baptism, the Design, Mode, and Subjects* (St. Louis, 1855); and *Immortality* (Philadelphia, 1871).

RICH, EDMUND. See EDMUND, SAINT, OF CANTERBURY.

RICHARD FITZRALPH: Archbishop of Armagh and primate of Ireland; b. at Dundalh (50 m. n. of Dublin), County of Louth, Ireland, probably in the last years of the thirteenth century; d. at Avignon, France, probably Nov. 16, 1360. He was fellow of Balliol College, Oxford; became chancellor of the University of Oxford in 1333; chancellor of Lincoln cathedral, 1334; soon after archdeacon of Chester; dean of Lichfield in 1337; and in July, 1347, archbishop of Armagh, from which he was called "Armachanus." When negotiations were going on between the Armenians and Pope Boniface XII., and two of their number, Nerses, archbishop of Melaggert, and John, bishop-elect of Khilát, appeared at Avignon, Richard, who happened to be on a mission at the papal court, upon their request, wrote a treatise in nineteen books, *Summa in quæstionibus Armenorum* (Paris, 1511), in which he examined their doctrines and refuted their heresies. This work won him widespread fame as defender of Roman orthodoxy. His visit to Avignon in 1349 marked the opening of a conflict with the mendicant friars which lasted all his lifetime. A memorial to the pope, presented in July, 1350, he later elaborated and published as *De pauperie salvatoris* in seven books. His attacks upon mendicancy occasioned great agitation in the orders which were quietly supported by the pope. Richard was summoned to appear at Avignon and there defended himself in a discourse, Nov. 8, 1357, later published as *Defensio curatorum* (Lyons, 1496; also in *Fasciculus rerum expetendarum et fugiendarum*, ed. E. Brown, ii. 466–487, London, 1690).

BIBLIOGRAPHY: J. Ware, *De præsulibus Hiberniæ*, Dublin, 1665; J. Prince, *Worthies of Devon*, Exeter, 1701; H. Cotton, *Fasti ecclesiæ Hibernicæ*, 5 vols., Dublin, 1845–1860; T. Netter, *Fasciculi Zizaniorum*, ed. W. E. Shirley, pp. xiii., liii., 284, 346, 355, London, 1858; G. Lechler, *John Wiclif and his English Precursors*, i. 75–88, 117–118, London, 1878; W. W. Capes, *English Church in 14th and 15th Centuries*, London, 1900; G. M. Trevelyan, *England in the Age of Wycliffe*, pp. 139, 143, 172, London, 1900.

RICHARD OF ST. VICTOR: French Augustinian; b. probably in Scotland; d. at St. Victor 1173 (probably Mar. 10). At an early age he went to Paris and entered the monastery of canons regular at St. Victor several years before the death of Hugo of St. Victor (q.v.), whose pupil he was. In 1159 he was subprior and in 1162 became prior, although the incapacity of the abbot caused double responsibility to devolve on Richard. Richard was an important figure in the struggle of Thomas à Becket with Henry II. of England. Together with a certain abbot of St. Augustine he recommended Thomas' cause to the pope, and, with Abbot Ervisius, sharply admonished Robert of Melun, bishop of Hereford, who had deserted his patron Thomas for the king.

Like his teacher Hugo, Richard was one of the theologians who sought to save traditional dogmas, imperilled by the dialectic methods of Aristotelian logic, by recourse to mysticism. Holding the objects of belief to be partly in accord with reason, partly transcending reason, and partly contradictory to reason, he taught that truth could be attained only by him who should immerse himself in them in believing mysticism, so that where reason failed, meditation and contemplation might lead to the truth. These views he advanced especially in his *Benjamin minor*, or *De præparatione animi ad contemplationem*, and the *Benjamin major*, or *De gratia contemplationis*, with the appendix *Allegoria tabernaculi fœderis*. These sources are supplemented by his *De exterminatione mali et promotione boni*, *De statu interioris hominis*, *De eruditione interioris hominis*, and *De gradibus caritatis*, as well as by his interpretations of Ezekiel and the Apocalypse, the *Explicatio aliquorum passuum difficilium (Pauli) apostoli*, *Declarationes nonnullarum difficultatum scripturæ*, *De Emmanuele*, *De superexcellenti baptismo Christi*, *Mysticæ adnotationes in Psalmos*, *Expositio cantici Habacuc*, *In cantica canticorum*, *Quomodo Christus ponitur in signum populorum*, and the Easter sermon *De missione Spiritus Sancti*.

In the *Benjamin minor* Richard traces the psychological development of man from his first dim longings for purer knowledge to the highest contemplation by an allegorical exegesis of the family of Jacob (Gen. xxix. 16 sqq.). The wives of Jacob represent the basal powers of the soul, Leah typifying affection and Rachel reason, the two operating through their handmaids sensuality and imagination (Zilpah and Bilhah). The births in Jacob's house symbolize the progress of the soul to contemplation, Leah bearing first because the primal impulse comes from affection. Reuben, the "son of vision," typifies the fear arising from careful consideration of faults; while the grief following fear wherein man is heard, is symbolized by Simeon, "hearing." To fear and grief are added the hope (represented by Levi, "addition") which leads to forgiveness. The hope gained from fear and grief results in loving praises of God (Judah, "confessing"). Lest, however, one should now think himself at his goal, Leah, or affection, now ceases to bear, and Rachel, or reason, longs for offspring, since reason is unable to think through mere intelligence, but begins with imagination. Bilhah, or imagination, accordingly bears two sons, Dan typifying the formation of a mental image on the basis of visible objects, and Naphthali symbolizing the endeavor to rise from the visible to a knowledge of the invisible. The success of reason now rekindles affection, and when Leah sees that Rachel bears children by her handmaid, she could not rest until Zilpah also bore, and from sensuality thus controlled proceeded temperate life (Gad) and patience in adversity (Asher). The way is thus prepared for new affection and Leah herself again bears. After departing from false joys and idle commotions, affection gives rise to true joy (Issachar), on which follows hatred of all evil (Zebulon). The series of virtues is completed by shame (Dinah), which proceeds from abhorrence of sin.

All these affections can not bring man to his goal, for virtues become vices unless controlled by meditation. God accordingly gives fertility to Rachel, since only through the interposition of divine grace can man realize his capabilities. Thus Joseph and Benjamin typify meditation and contemplation. But the birth of contemplation is accompanied by the extremest pangs, yet reason, though knowing that this birth transcends her powers, is insatiable in her longing. After the birth of contemplation, therefore, reason must die. Thus the goal is gained, but the soul must still press on until at the last all darkness shall vanish and eternal truth shall be revealed.

In the *Benjamin major* Richard, restricting himself to the intellectual factors, distinguished six grades of contemplation: imagination alone; imagination according to reason; reason according to imagination; reason alone; above, but not contrary to, reason; and above, and apparently contrary to, reason. The three first grades can not dispense with the imaginative faculty, though they gradually weaken it, so that in the second grade imagination receives reason, and in the third reason rises to an equality with imagination. The fourth stage is pure reason, which in the sixth is entirely transcended by true wisdom.

Richard appears in an absolutely different light in a series of writings on the Trinity: *De Trinitate* with its appendix, *De tribus appropriatis personis in Trinitate; De Verbo incarnato;* and *Quomodo Spiritus Sanctus est amor Patris et Filii*. The argument of the six books *De Trinitate* is conventionally scholastic, but there seems to be no reason to doubt its authenticity. In the philosophy and theology of the Middle Ages Richard exercised considerable influence, as on Alexander of Hales, Bonaventura, and Peter of Ailli (qq.v.), as well as on much later German mysticism. He is also interesting for culture history, as in his accounts of contemporary philosophy and monastic life. (FERDINAND COHRS.)

BIBLIOGRAPHY: The best edition of the *Opera* is by J. Berthelin, Rouen, 1650, reproduced in *MPL*, cxcvi. Earlier eds. were Venice, 1506, 1592, Paris, 1518, 1550, Lyon, 1534, Cologne, 1621.

A *Vita* is given in the ed. of Berthelin. Consult further: *Hist. littéraire de la France*, xiii. 472–488; C. T. A. Liebner, *Richardi a S. Victore de contemplatione doctrina*, 2 parts, Göttingen, 1837–39; J. G. V. Engelhardt, *Richard von St. Victor und Johann Ruysbroek*, Erlangen, 1838; M. Laforet, *Coup d'œil sur l'hist. de la theologie dogmatique*, Louvain, 1851; W. Kaulich, *Die Lehren des Hugo und Richard von St. Victor*, Prague, 1864; W. Preger, *Geschichte der deutschen Mystik im Mittelalter*, i. 241 sqq., Leipsic, 1874; J. Bach, *Dogmengeschichte des Mittelalters*, ii. 367 sqq., Vienna, 1875; L. Stein, in *Archiv für die Geschichte der Philosophie*, ii (1889), 193–245; B. Hauréau, *Hist. de la philosophie scolastique*, i. 509–514, Paris, 1872; idem, *Notices et extraits*, iv. 256–259, ib. 1892; Harnack, *Dogma*, vi. 100, 103, 179, 182; the works on the history of philosophy, e.g., by J. E. Erdmann, 3 vols., London, 1893, and W. W. Windelband, ib. 1893; Schaff, *Christian Church*, v. 1, pp. 647–648; *DNB*, xlviii. 188–190.

RICHARD, FRANÇOIS MARIE BENJAMIN: Cardinal; b. at Nantes Mar. 9, 1819; d. at Paris Jan. 28, 1908. He was educated at the château of Lavergne and at the Seminary of St. Sulpice, Paris, and from 1849 to 1869 was vicar general of Nantes. In 1871 he was consecrated bishop of Belley, and four years later was made titular archbishop of Larissa and coadjutor of the archbishop of Paris, with the right of succession. In 1886 he succeeded to this dignity, and in 1889 was created cardinal-priest of Santa Maria in Via. He wrote *Vie de la bienheureuse Françoise d'Amboise, duchesse de Bretagne et religieuse carmélite* (2 vols., Nantes, 1865), and *Les Saints de l'église de Nantes* (1873).

RICHARD, TIMOTHY: Baptist missionary and educator; b. at Ffaldybrenin, Carmarthenshire, Wales, Oct. 10, 1845. He received his education at Swansea Normal School and Haverfordwest College; went out as missionary for the Baptist Missionary Society to China in 1869, very early traveling in Manchuria and in Korea; he was located for eight years in the province of Shantung, then for the same length of time in Shansi; was in Peking and Tientsin, 1889–90; in 1890 he was chosen by the missionaries on the field to make a presentation of Christianity to the Chinese government, and in the same year became editor of a daily and a weekly paper in Chinese, both of which were influential in wide circles; became secretary in 1891 for The Society for the Diffusion of Christian and General Knowledge among the Chinese, now the Christian Literature Society for China; in 1877–78 he was chief almoner of the fund raised to relieve the great famine in China; in 1901 he was called in to aid in the negotiations for settling the indemnity for the massacre of missionaries in Shansi, and through him a university, of which he was made chancellor, was established in the capital of the province, the example of which led to a decree for like colleges in each of the capitals of the separate provinces; in 1901 he was appointed religious adviser to the Chinese government; in 1904 he assumed, in addition to his other duties, the position of secretary to the International Red Cross Society in Shanghai; he is in charge of the work for his denomination of disseminating Christian literature among the Chinese, and is president of the Educational Association of China. His theological position is stated in the words that he "desires to promote everything which God has revealed or man discovered for the progress of the human race in all departments." He "believes that God has left none of the great nations without light from Heaven, that those who divide the religions of the world into true and false, and go in for destructive criticism and attacks on the native religions, do incalculable harm." Most of his literary work has been done in Chinese (the number of works rendered by him into Chinese numbers over fifty), and his labors have been recognized by the Chinese government by an appointment as mandarin of the first rank and religious adviser. In English he has written *Historical Evidences of Christianity; Conversion by the Million* (2 vols., published in the East); *Guide to Buddahood: being a standard Manual of Chinese Buddhism, translated from the Chinese* (London, 1908); and *The New Testament of Higher Buddhism* (Edinburgh, 1910).

RICHARDS, WILLIAM ROGERS: Presbyterian; b. at Boston Dec. 20, 1853; d. in New York City Jan. 7, 1910. He studied at Yale University (B.A., 1875), Columbia Law School (1875–76), and Andover Theological Seminary (graduated, 1879); was pastor of the Central Congregational Church, Bath, Me., 1879–84; of the Crescent Avenue Presbyterian Church, Plainfield, N. J., 1884–1902; and also of the Brick Presbyterian Church, New York City, after 1902. He served on the Board of Foreign Missions of his denomination, on the Board of Directors of Union Theological Seminary, New York, and on the Council of the University of the City of New York. He wrote: *Ways of Wisdom* (New York, 1886); *For Whom Christ died* (Philadelphia, 1902; sermons); *God's Choice of Men: a Study of Scripture* (New York, 1905); *The Apostles' Creed in Modern Worship* (1906); and *A Study of the Lord's Prayer* (1910).

RICHARDSON, ERNEST CUSHING: Congregationalist; b. at Woburn, Mass., Feb. 9, 1860. He was graduated from Amherst College (B.A., 1880) and Hartford Theological Seminary (1883). He was librarian of Hartford Theological Seminary (1883–90); and associate professor (1885–90), and since 1890 has been librarian of Princeton University. He is prominent in library work, especially in the American Library Association, in which he has held many offices. He has also been chairman of the bibliographical committee of the American Historical Association since 1901 and vice-president of the Bibliographical Society of America since 1906. In theology he describes himself as "scientific, independent, Biblical, Congregational," and as holding "the deity of Christ, the Virgin birth, the organic evolution of the Bible, regeneration by the Word, the survival of the fittest for eternal life, and the climax of the evolutionary progress of the universe in the social and material headship of Jesus Christ in a substantial resurrected universe." He has revised the translation of Eusebius' "Life of Constantine" for the *NPNF* (New York, 1890) and the "Lives of Illustrious Men" of Jerome and Gennadius for the same series (1892), edited the same in Latin (Leipsic, 1896); prepared *Bibliographical Synopsis of the Ante-Nicene Fathers* (New York, 1887) and *An Alphabetical Subject Index and Index Encyclopædia to Periodical Articles on Religion (1890–99)* (1908); and has written *Classification, Theoretical and Practical* (1901).

RICHELIEU, rish-lyū' or rish'e-lū.

Youth; Call to Public Office (§ 1).
Conflict with the Protestants (§ 2).
Struggle against Conspiracy (§ 3).
Constructive Policy (§ 4).
Achievements for Marine, Industry, and Commerce (§ 5).
Foreign Policy (§ 6).
Foreign Alliances (§ 7).
Characterization (§ 8).

Armand-Jean Duplessis, duc de Richelieu, French cardinal and statesman, was born at Paris Sept. 5, 1585, and died there Dec. 4, 1642. He was the fourth son of a petty noble of Poitou. At first he was intended for the army, but his eldest brother, who was bishop of Luçon, having resigned his dignity in order to enter a monastery, Richelieu entered the Church in order to preserve this bishopric in the family.

1. Youth; Call to Public Office. He was educated at the Sorbonne and then returned, as he said, "to the poorest bishopric in France." In 1614 he was elected a deputy of the clergy of Niort to the States-General, where he attracted the attention of the queen-mother, Marie de Medici, who made him almoner to the young queen, Anne of Austria, in 1616. In the mazes of intrigue that prevailed at court Richelieu displayed from the first a keen knowledge of men and great capacity for dissimulation. Physically half an invalid, his energy of mind and body was astonishing. It is said that he required eleven hours' sleep. Nevertheless he was capable of great physical endurance, as before La Rochelle in 1628, and in 1630 in the war against the duke of Savoy. The weakness of Louis XIII. was Richelieu's opportunity, but the fondness of Marie de Medici for him was also a factor. In 1622 he was made cardinal and soon after entered the king's council as secretary of state, of war, and of foreign affairs (Apr., 1624), becoming prime minister in Nov., 1629. In assuming office Richelieu had a clear idea of his own purposes and the needs of France. As he said: "When your Majesty resolved to give me, at the same time, both entrance into your council and a great part of your confidence in the government of affairs, I can truthfully say that the Huguenots divided France with you; that the nobles conducted themselves as if they were not subjects, and the powerful provincial governors as though they were sovereigns in their offices. . . . I promised your Majesty to employ all my industry and all authority that might be given me to ruin the Huguenot party, to abase the pride of the nobles, to reduce all subjects to duty, and to raise your name among foreign nations to the point where it ought to be." To the execution of these purposes Richelieu brought an inflexible and fierce energy justified, in his eyes, by the grandeur of the purposes to be attained. At the beginning of his ministry Richelieu summoned an assembly of fifty-five prelates, nobles, magistrates, financial officials, and others, in Dec., 1626. Fifteen propositions were laid before them dealing with the means to suppress corruption in the army, with the development of commerce, the navy, and the suppression of crimes against the safety of the state.

Richelieu was the enemy of the factional Huguenots because, as he said, they tended "to form a state within a state," and set himself "to ruin the Huguenot party." It was accomplished in two wars.

2. Conflict with the Protestants. In 1625 difficulties in connection with the execution of the Treaty of Montpellier provoked a rising of the Huguenots in Brittany, Poitou, and Languedoc. At the head of the movement were Henri, duke of Rohan (see ROHAN, HENRI), and his brother Soubise. The latter seized the Isle of Oleron. Richelieu sent troops into Brittany and Poitou and obtained ships and seamen from Holland and England. Oleron was taken; Soubise fled to England. But the cardinal was threatened by court intrigues and did not follow up his advantage, renewing the settlement of Montpellier (February, 1626). The Protestant refugees in England resumed the conflict with the aid of Buckingham, the favorite of Charles I. An English fleet disembarked a force on the Island of Ré in July, 1627. Richelieu displayed a prodigious activity in collecting vessels of war, munitions, and provisions, and forced the English to withdraw. Then began the protracted siege of La Rochelle, the stronghold of the Huguenots. Rochelle was not an easy place to take; on the land side it was protected by marshes and formidable fortifications, and its harbor enabled it to reach the open sea. Among the famous Huguenot leaders within the city were the mayor Guiton, the admiral of the Protestant fleet, the pastor Salbert, and the intrepid dowager duchess of Rohan, who despite her eighty years displayed amazing resolution and activity. Richelieu, with a force of 25,000 men, blockaded the place and threw up a line of entrenchments. The greatest difficulty was to close the port to outside assistance. In spite of the winter storms a tremendous mole over 1,400 paces long was built across the harbor. Two English relief fleets were unable to force this colossal barrier. When all hope of deliverance failed and the city was reduced to starvation, Rochelle surrendered, on Oct. 28, 1628. The historic city was condemned to lose its municipal privileges and franchises and to have its walls rased. The war continued in the Cévennes, where Henri Rohan for a time held out with the mountaineer Calvinists and the aid of Spain—a most anomalous alliance. The Edict of Nimes (q.v.) fixed anew the situation of the Huguenots. The Edict of Nantes (q.v.) was maintained in so far as it guaranteed liberty of conscience and liberty of worship, but the Huguenot strongholds were surrendered and their political assemblies forbidden. The Protestants as a political party ceased to exist.

Since the death of Henry IV. in 1610 the chief obstacle to the regular exercise of the royal authority had been the factions and the hopes of the noblesse. The whole ministry of Richelieu was filled with the conflict against them.

3. Struggle Against Conspiracy. The cardinal has been accused of having been a bitter enemy of the privileged order, but this is a mistake. "It is necessary to consider the noblesse as one of the chief sinews of the state," he wrote in his "Political Testament." What he did exact was obedience and the abandonment of political activity by the nobles. Most of the intrigues and plots against Richelieu were hatched at court, and the instigators or accomplices were often members of the royal family. Gaston of Orléans, who for a long time had cherished the hope of succeeding his brother, was the soul of all these conspiracies; another was the queen-mother, Marie de Medici, who became an implacable enemy of the cardinal after his elevation. A third was the queen herself, Anne of Austria, whose secret correspondence with Spain Richelieu stopped. Mother, wife, and brother brought all the pressure they could upon Louis XIII. to dismiss his minister.

The first important conspiracy was that in which the count of Chalais and Marshal Ornano were the chief outward factors. It culminated in the death of both of them. Nov. 11, 1630, was the famous "Day of Dupes." The king, who never liked, but who feared the cardinal, had been persuaded to close his private cabinet to the minister. For a moment Richelieu thought himself lost. But the duke of St. Simon, father of the great writer, brought about an interview between the king and Richelieu at Versailles, where Louis XIII. had a shooting box. The great palace was not yet built. In the presence of the cardinal, Louis XIII.'s opposition oozed away. Richelieu's enemies paid dear for their short triumph. Chancellor Marillac was deprived of office; his brother, Marshal Marillac, was arrested in Italy at the head of his command, tried before a commission which sat in the cardinal's own house, and put to death. Marie de Medici, exiled from court, fled to Brussels, became a wanderer in Flanders and England, and died miserably poor and despised at Cologne. Gaston fled to Duke Charles IV. of Lorraine, whose sister he married. He attempted, with a small army, to reenter France and join the duke of Montmorency, governor of Languedoc, who had espoused his cause, but the royal army defeated the rebels under the walls of Castelnaudary, Sept. 1, 1632. In spite of his wonderful popularity in the country the duke was executed at Toulouse. Less important plots were crushed in the ensuing years. The most important of them was the conspiracy of Cinq-Mars in 1642.

Similarly, the provincial governors who behaved like sovereigns in their governments were rigorously crushed; e.g., the duke of Vendôme in Brittany, Marshal Vitry in Provence, the duke of Epernon in Guyenne. Richelieu reduced the governors to mere military commandants and took from them the administration of justice and the finances. The offices of constable and grand admiral, to which was attached a power which might be dangerous, were suppressed. Two edicts abolished some inveterate abuses; the first, the practise of dueling, which was remorselessly enforced; the second required the destruction of the fortifications of towns, castles, and fortresses, unless situated upon the frontier. A final step in the destructive policy of Richelieu was the overcoming of the provincial parlements, the historic opposition of which was crushed by an edict of 1641, which required them to register all acts sent to them without deliberation and without change.

4. Constructive Policy.

In his conflict with the Huguenots and the nobles Richelieu was not content to destroy; he also built up. In the theory of the law the royal authority was absolute; Richelieu made it so in fact. Administration had become loose during the wars of religion and the troubles of the regency. Richelieu resumed the unfinished monarchical policy of Francis I. and Henry II. The council of state had acquired a great importance during the sixteenth century, but during the regency its organization fell into confusion. A series of regulations rendered during the ministry of Richelieu fixed its rank in the administrative hierarchy, its competence, its composition. It became the center of all administration. The councilors of state no longer purchased their seats like the officials of justice and finance. They were chosen and held office at the pleasure of the king. The secretaries of state, who executed the decisions of the council, became the agents of the cardinal and lost much of their independence. Under Louis XIII. a permanent division began to be made in their attributes. After 1619 general affairs of war and correspondence with commanders of the army corps were entrusted to a single secretary of state. The same change was made in the administration of foreign affairs in 1626. Before that time the foreign affairs of each important country had had each its particular secretary. In order to execute the king's will in the provinces, Richelieu made great use of agents chosen from among the masters of requests (maîtres des requêtes), ordinarily known as intendants. Richelieu was not, as was once almost universally supposed, the creator of the intendants. They first appeared in the middle of the sixteenth century as special commissioners of the crown in designated provinces, but they did not then become a regular institution, and recourse to them was only occasional. Such as it was the institution went to pieces during the Huguenot wars and was revived and made universal for France by the cardinal. The intendants were employed, sometimes in the *généralités* (revenue districts), sometimes in the armies, where they were responsible for the commissariat, the ambulance corps, and the pay of the soldiers, and were required to suppress pillage and mutiny. Richelieu found in these functionaries, who were revocable at will, devoted agents of his policies. Those who were permanently established in the *généralités* took the title of intendants of justice, police, and finance, and concentrated in their hands a large part of the provincial administration. Under Louis XIV. the intendants became the regular and omnipotent agents of the absolute monarchy.

5. Achievements for Marine, Industry, and Commerce.

Every part of the state was the object of Richelieu's activity. He is one of the creators of the French navy. In his "Political Testament" he says: "The sea is the heritage over which all sovereigns claim sovereignty," but that "one must be powerful to claim such a heritage." Again he says: "It seems that nature has wished to offer the empire of the sea to France when we regard the position of its two coasts, equally provided with harbors on two seas, the Atlantic and the Mediterranean." Richelieu sought to profit by the natural advantages of the country to establish ports and arsenals, construct vessels, recruit sailors. He improved the harbors of Havre and Toulon; he created those of Brest and Brouage, south of La Rochelle. He made the French navy a material fact. The king, who in 1621 and in 1626 had been obliged to purchase or to hire vessels from the Dutch in order to combat the Huguenots, in 1642 possessed sixty-three vessels of war and twenty-two galleys. The French fleets, commanded by the archbishop of Bordeaux, d'Escoubeau de Sourdis, met victoriously those of Spain. In regard to commerce and industry Richelieu was the forerunner and model of Colbert. He outlined his project in his "Political Testament." He wanted to develop the national industry to such a point that the French might become an export nation for cloth, velvet, taffetas, and silks. His numerous occupations, his continual conflicts against enemies within and without, the importance of the foreign politics of France, prevented Richelieu from realizing all these projects. But at least he attempted much for French commerce. He was an advocate of great commercial companies, such as those of England and Holland. "In order to become master of the sea," he said, "it is necessary for us, like our neighbors, to form great companies, to compel the merchants to enter into them, to give them great privileges." In conformity with this idea Richelieu created and favored various trading companies, notably those of Morbihan, of the West Indies (1628), of the American Isles (1635), and of Africa. They were not successful during his life, and failed after his death. Nevertheless Richelieu was the founder of the French colonial empire. He created Canada by sending out Champlain.

In 1624 Richelieu came into power with a well-formed design "of raising the name of the king among foreign nations to the point at which it ought to be." It was shortly after the beginning of the Thirty-Years' War (q.v.). He found the emperor in conflict with the king of Denmark and some of the German Protestant princes, but he could not at once profit by the op- **6. Foreign Policy.** portunity to revive the policy of Henry IV. to debase the house of Austria because of the troubles at home with the great nobles, and especially with the Huguenots. Nevertheless, he attentively followed events in Germany and sustained with French subsidies the enemies of the emperor—Mansfeld, the king of Denmark, Gustavus Adolphus, and the Swedes after Lützen. On two different occasions he went to war to protect the interests of France. When he came to power the Valteline, that is to say, the upper valley of the Adda, had revolted against the Grisons, and was occupied by papal troops in alliance with Spain. It was important not to let the Spaniards, who were masters of the Milanais, seize the communications between the upper Adda and the Tyrol, which belonged to Austria. Richelieu threw an army into the region, which drove out the papal troops and Spaniards from the Valteline, and put the country again under the domination of the Grisons (1626). Some years later he intervened in upper Italy in the matter of the succession to the duchy of Mantua. The duke of Savoy, the Spaniards, and Emperor Ferdinand sought to prevent the legitimate claimant, the duke of Nevers, who was a French prince, from entering into his heritage. Louis XIII., accompanied by Richelieu, forced the Alps through the Pass of Susa (1629). The territories of the duke of Savoy were occupied by a French army and the Spaniards beaten. At the same time the famous Jesuit diplomat, Père Joseph, was sent by Richelieu to the diet of Regensburg, and succeeded in altering the policy of the emperor. The duke of Nevers acquired the duchy of Mantua and France retained the important fortress of Pignerol on the eastern side of the Alps (Treaty of Cherasco, 1631).

At the moment of intervening in Germany after the death of Gustavus Adolphus in 1632, Richelieu concluded alliances with the states of Germany threatened by the fanaticism and ambition of the house of Austria. To the German **7. Foreign Alliances.** princes in alliance against the emperor he promised men and money, conditional upon the acquirement of Alsace by France and imperial confirmation of French possession of the "Three Bishoprics," which France had possessed since 1552, but which the empire had never confirmed. In 1635 he concluded a treaty with the Dutch Republic for the partition of the Spanish Netherlands; with the Swiss and the dukes of Parma and Mantua, for the partition of the Milanais, which Spain possessed. The alliance formed with Gustavus Adolphus was renewed with Oxenstierna, the Swedish chancellor. Finally Richelieu took into the pay of France the most famous general of the Protestants after the death of Gustavus, the brilliant Bernard of Saxe-Weimar. In pursuing these negotiations Richelieu revived the policy originated by Francis I., actually begun by Henry II., long interrupted by the wars of religion, revived by Henry IV., and abandoned by Marie de Medici. The general characteristics of this policy consist (1) in the alliance of France, though a Roman Catholic power, with the Protestant powers, as Holland, Sweden, England, and with the German Protestant princes and cities. Though a cardinal of the Roman Church, a zealous Roman Catholic, and victor over the Huguenots in France, Richelieu had no scruples in making common cause with Protestant powers when the interests of the State demanded it. He did not confuse spiritual and temporal interests. (2) In the protection accorded by France to the petty states of Germany and Italy, oppressed by Austria and Spain. It was not for conquest that France intervened in Germany, except in so far as she might realize her "natural frontiers," that is to say, the Rhine, the Alps, and the Pyrenees. The realization of these purposes, in so far as they were realized, is a part of the history of the Thirty-Years' War, and the consummation of them came after Richelieu's death.

No better characterization of Richelieu has ever been made than that of Montesquieu: "He made his master the first man in Europe and the second man in France." Richelieu kept the promise made to Louis XIII. when he became minister. **8. Characterization.** He left the king master within, powerful and feared without. The Huguenot party was ruined, the nobles and provincial governors obedient, the parlements reduced to silence. Abroad the two branches of the house of Hapsburg had been reduced, and the French armies occupied Artois, Alsace, and Roussillon. In spite of his immense services to the king and to the State, Richelieu was hated by his contemporaries, and has been judged too severely by posterity. It is true that he was harsh and hypocritical, but though he may be criticized for the means and methods he used, the verdict of history is clear as to the value of the results he achieved. It is not to be forgotten that in the seventeenth century the French nobility had long ceased to fulfil the duties corresponding to their privileges; that the conduct of officials was too often influenced by narrow self-interest; that the position of France both at home and abroad was a perilous one. The evils of the later monarchy are not to be laid to his charge. In fine, Richelieu's great policy was to unite France at home and make it powerful and feared abroad. More than any of its kings, he was the founder of the French monarchy.

JAMES WESTFALL THOMPSON.

BIBLIOGRAPHY: The first place in authority will be taken by *Mémoires du Cardinal de Richelieu, Publiés d'après les manuscrits originaux pour la société de l'histoire de France, sous les auspices de l'académie française*, vol. i., Paris, 1907. Consult further: M. Topin, *Louis XIII. et Richelieu*, Paris, 1876; W. Robson, *Life of Richelieu*, London, 1878; H. Cinget, *Le Cardinal de Richelieu et son ministère*, St. Denis, 1879; E. de Monzie, *Le Cardinal de Richelieu*, Tours, 1879; G. Masson, *Richelieu*, London, 1884; G. d'Avenel, *Richelieu et la monarchie absolue*, 4 vols., Paris, 1884–90; idem, *La Noblesse française sous Richelieu*, ib. 1901; L. Dussieux, *Le Cardinal de Richelieu*, ib. 1885; J. B. Perkins, *France under Mazarin, with a Review of the Administration of Richelieu*, 2 vols., New York, 1886; idem, *Richelieu and the Growth of French Power*, ib. 1900; A. Pellisier, *L'Apogée de la monarchie française. Études historiques sur Richelieu et Louis XIV.*, Paris, 1889; J. Michelet, *Richelieu et la Fronde*, in vol. xi. of his *Œuvres complètes*, ib. 1893–99; G. Hanotaux, *Histoire du Cardinal de Richelieu*, vols. i.–ii., ib. 1893–1903; G. Fagniez, *Le Père Joseph et Richelieu (1577–1638)*, 2 vols., ib. 1894 (crowned by the Academy); R. Lodge, *Richelieu*, London, 1896; L. Lacroix, *Richelieu à Luçon; sa jeunesse, son épiscopat*, new ed., Paris, 1898; J. B. Perkins, *Richelieu, Growth of French Power*, New York, 1900; Comte de Beauchamp, *Louis XIII., d'après sa correspondance avec le cardinal de Richelieu (1622–42)*, ib. 1902; L. Dedouvres, *Le Père Joseph et le siège de la Rochelle*, ib. 1904; G. Pasmot, *Pancan et Richelieu, le problème protestant sous Louis XIII.*, ib. 1904; *Cambridge Modern History*, vol. iv., chap. iv., New York, 1906; J. McCabe, *The Iron Cardinal. The Romance of Richelieu*, ib. 1909.

RICHER, EDMOND: French Roman Catholic and advocate of Gallicanism; b. at Chource, a village of Champagne, 1560; d. at Paris 1631. After completing his education in 1590, he was a parish priest for four years, and was then made president of the college of Cardinal Lemoine. Shortly afterward, he became a censor of the university, where he was also professor in the theological faculty. In 1607 he published in three volumes at Paris, after some opposition, an edition of the writings of J. Gerson, and in the following year he was chosen syndic of the theological faculty, in this capacity opposing theses in defense of papal infallibility. In 1611 the brief summary of his *De ecclesiastica et politica potestate* (2 vols., Cologne, 1629), defending the superiority of councils over the pope and maintaining the independence of the secular government in things temporal, brought a storm of attack upon him. His doctrines were condemned by several provincial synods and the Curia, he was deposed from office, and was saved from imprisonment and being sent to Rome only by the appeal of the university. In 1627, after years of struggle, he made a forced recantation. Among his works, special mention may be made of the posthumous *Apologia pro J. Gersonio* (Leyden, 1674). (C. SCHMIDT†.)

BIBLIOGRAPHY: A. Baillet, *La Vie d'Edmond Richer, docteur de Sorbonne*, Amsterdam, 1715; E. Puyol, *E. Richer. Étude historique et critique sur la renovation du gallicanisme . . . du xvii. siècle*, 2 vols., Paris, 1876.

RICHMOND, LEGH: Church of England; b. at Liverpool Jan. 29, 1772; d. at Turvey (50 m. n.w. of London), Bedfordshire, May 8, 1827. He was graduated at Trinity College, Cambridge, 1704 (M.A., 1797). In the latter year he became a curate on the Isle of Wight, and in 1805 rector of Turvey. While a child he was lamed for life. He edited *The Fathers of the English Church* (8 vols., London, 1807–12); and wrote *Domestic Portraiture, or the Successful Application of Religious Principle in the Education of a Family, exemplified in the Memoirs of Three of the Deceased Children of the Rev. Legh Richmond* (9th ed., 1861). But the work by which he is best known is *The Annals of the Poor*, 2 vols., 1814, which contains the immortal tracts: *The Dairyman's Daughter*, *The Negro Servant*, and *The Young Cottager*, previously published separately, of the first of which millions of copies have been circulated in nineteen languages.

BIBLIOGRAPHY: T. S. Grimshawe, *Memoir of the Rev. Leigh Richmond*, London, 1828 (many eds. during the first year of publication); G. T. Bedell, *Life of Legh Richmond*, Philadelphia, 1829; T. Fry and E. Bickersteth, *Domestic Portraiture*, London, 1833; G. F. U. Munby and T. Wright, *Turvey and Legh Richmond, with an Account of the Mordaunts*, Olney, 1894; *DNB*, xlviii. 258–259.

RICHTER, rιн'ter, ÆMILIUS LUDWIG: Protestant canonist; b. at Stolpen (2 m. e. of Dresden) Feb. 15, 1808; d. at Berlin May 8, 1864. He entered the University of Leipsic in 1826, studied law, became privat-docent and associate professor in 1835; and in 1839 regular professor of canon law and civil procedure at Marburg. His first publication was *Corpus juris canonici* (Leipsic, 1833–39), followed by *Lehrbuch des katholischen und evangelischen Kirchenrechts mit besonderer Rücksicht auf deutsche Zustände* (1842; 8th ed., 1886). Fundamental in importance was *Die evangelischen Kirchenordnungen des 16. Jahrhunderts* (2 vols., Weimar, 1846). In 1846 he went to Berlin, where he continued as teacher in the high school and author, serving in the mean time in various ecclesiastical positions, and displaying in all his tasks a deep spirituality, devotion to the Evangelical church, erudition, conscientious exercise of duty, and an irenic reserve. His knowledge and counsel were in demand in all Germany and Austria, and he served no less Roman Catholics, by whom his standpoint was often acknowledged to be liberal and unbiased. He recognized in the historical churches certain ethical quantities distinct from the State, to be conducted by organs of their own, unhindered by the sovereign State in the exercise of its function of securing to the church associations autonomy within legitimate spheres and defining its limits. He denied the doctrine of state omnipotence and vindicated for the Roman Catholic Church autonomy and self-administration, without, however, acceding to the pretension of that church to an *imperium in imperio*. Of much concern to him were the conditions of laissez-faire that arose in Prussia and continued until 1873, in relation to the Roman Catholic Church, when a delimitation of Church and State was attempted by constitutional compliance with the Concordat and the necessary supplementary legislation was delayed. Richter insisted upon the necessity of enforcing by repressive means the right of state supervision, whereby the State insured its own safety, so that the churches in their functions would confine themselves within their limits; and, especially, upon the necessity of defining by statute the right of state self-preservation.

In relation to the canonical sources are the following works: *Beiträge zur Kenntnis der Quellen des canonischen Rechts* (3 parts, Leipsic, 1834), and *De inedita decretalium* (1836). In relation to the particular sources of the Roman Catholic canon law must be mentioned above all Richter and J. F. Schulte's edition of *Canones et decreta concilii Tridentini ex editione Romana ab 1834 repetiti* (1853). The special value of this work is the treatment of the subject in its historic development. *Die evangelischen Kirchenordnungen des 16. Jahrhunderts* (ut sup.) has become an indispensable basis for the study of Evangelical canon law. Its advantage consists in the comprehensive appropriation of source-material from the century of the Reformation. Richter was imbued with the historical spirit, and offered a prospective history of the canonical sources. His labors in this connection are characterized by a profounder basis, elaborate particularistic development, and a broad grasp of the inner connection. He falls back upon the cardinal principles of the Reformation in his fundamental constructions, having in mind to offset the fatal conditions due not only to the territorial system (see TERRITORIALISM) of Christian Thomasius (q.v.), but to the neglect of church organization during the Reformation period. He none the less objected to church government in the hands of the educationals using the sovereigns as their mere agents. While declaring, in 1848, church government by the sovereign ruler, as then constituted, to be incompatible with a constitutional monarchy, he opposed the error that they were irreconcilable. He countenanced a representative synod as an extreme necessity on extraordinary occasions. The recognition of the right of self-administration was to be followed by the gradual formation of an ascending organization of congregations and synods to represent the development of the church constitution, without infringing upon the historical right of the relation of the king to the Church. Later he foresaw that the general synod must occupy a larger sphere; for it became evident to him that in the conflicts between Church and State and between different churches, the constitutional monarch could not occupy the same position in the forefront as the former land sovereign. Other works were, *Beiträge zur Geschichte des Ehescheidungsrechts in der evangelischen Kirche* (Berlin, 1858); *Geschichte der evangelischen Kirchenverfassung in Deutschland* (Leipsic, 1851); and *Der Staat und die Deutschkatholiken* (1846). (R. W. DOVE†.)

BIBLIOGRAPHY: P. Hinschius, in *Zeitschrift für Kirchengeschichte*, iv (1864), 351 sqq.; J. F. Schulte, in *ZKR*, v (1865), 250 sqq.; R. W. Dove, in *ZKR*, vii (1867), 273 sqq.

RICHTER, GREGOR: German Roman Catholic; b. at Grüsselbach (a village near Cassel) Apr. 29, 1874. He was educated at the philosophical and theological institute of Fulda and the University of Freiburg, and after the completion of his studies was ordained to the priesthood and was city chaplain at Fulda until 1899. Since the latter year he has been professor of church history and canon law at the philosophical and theological institute in the same city. In addition to editing the *Fuldaer Geschichtsblätter* and *Quellen und Abhandlungen zur Geschichte der Abtei und der Diözese Fulda* since 1904, he has written *Die ersten Anfänge der Bau- und Kunstthätigkeit des Klosters Fulda* (Fulda, 1900) and *Statuta majoris ecclesiæ Fuldensis, ungedruckte Quellen zur kirchlichen Rechts- und Verfassungsgeschichte der Benediktinerabtei Fulda* (1904).

RICKARD, HERBERT: Church of England; b. at Derby Feb. 23, 1867. He received his education at Derby School, King's College School, London, and Jesus College, Oxford (B.A., 1886; M.A., 1889); was made deacon, 1888, and priest, 1889; was curate of St. Paul Loséll, Birmingham, 1888–90; assistant organizing secretary of the Assistant Curates Society, 1890–92; curate of Christ Church, Epsom, 1892–97; vice-principal of Chichester Theological College, 1897–99; principal in 1899; perpetual curate of Sennicotts, 1897–1906; rector of St. Peter's the Less, Chichester, 1903; and prebendary of Chichester, 1905.

RIDDLE, JOSEPH ESMOND: Church of England; b. at Bristol Apr. 7, 1804; d. at Cheltenham Aug. 27, 1859. He was educated at Oxford (B.A., 1828; M.A., 1831); was ordained priest, 1832, and was incumbent of Leckhampton, near Cheltenham, 1840–59. In 1852 he was Bampton lecturer. He is best known for his *Latin-English Dictionary*, founded on W. Freund (London, 1849), and (with T. K. Arnold) *English-Latin Lexicon* (1849); he also wrote a commentary on I Peter (1834); *Luther and his Times* (1837); *Sermons Doctrinal and Practical* (1838); the valuable *Manual of Christian Antiquities* (London, 1839); *Ecclesiastical Chronology* (1840); *Churchman's Guide to the Use of the English Liturgy* (1848); *Natural History of Infidelity* (Bampton lectures, 1852); *History of the Papacy to the Period of the Reformation* (1854); *Manual of Scripture History* (1857); and *Household Prayers* (1857).

BIBLIOGRAPHY: *DNB*, xlviii. 274.

RIDDLE, MATTHEW BROWN: Presbyterian; b. at Pittsburg, Pa., Oct. 17, 1836. He was graduated from Jefferson College, Canonsburg, Pa. (A.B., 1852), and New Brunswick Theological Seminary, New Brunswick, N. J. (1859). He was adjunct professor of Greek in Jefferson College in 1857–58 and chaplain of the Second New Jersey Volunteers in the Army of the Potomac in 1861. He then held Dutch Reformed pastorates in Hoboken, N. J. (1862–65), and at Newark, N. J. (1865–1869), and spent two years (1869–71) in travel and study in Europe. He was professor of New-Testament exegesis in Hartford Theological Seminary (1871–87), and since 1887 has filled a similar position in the Western Theological Seminary, Allegheny, Pa. He was a member of the American Company of New-Testament revisers, and for many years was an editor of the American standard edition of the Revised Version of the Bible, besides being a member of the general assembly's committee to revise the proofs of the Westminster Standards. He translated and edited the sections on Romans (except chaps. i.-v.), Galatians, Ephesians, and Colossians for the American edition of J. P. Lange's commentary (New York, 1869-70); contributed (in collaboration with P. Schaff) the portions on Matthew, Mark, and Luke (1879), Romans (1882), and Ephesians and Colossians (1882; these two independently) to P. Schaff's *Illustrated Popular Commentary;* and the volumes on Mark (1881), Luke (1883), and Romans (1884) to the same scholar's *International Revision Commentary;* edited Mark and Luke in the American edition of H. A. W. Meyer's *Commentary on the New Testament* (New York, 1884); revised E. Robinson's *Harmony of the Four Gospels in Greek* (Boston, 1885), *Harmony of the Four Gospels in English* (1886); and revised the Didache, II Clement, Pseudo-Clementine Literature, and the New-Testament Apocrypha for the American edition of *The Ante-Nicene Fathers* (New York, 1886-1888), as well as Chrysostom's "Homilies on Matthew" and Augustine's "Harmony of the Gospels" for the first series of *The Nicene and Post-Nicene Fathers* (1888); and wrote *Story of the Revised New Testament, American Standard Edition* (Philadelphia, 1908).

RIDGEWAY, CHARLES JOHN: Church of England bishop of Chichester; b. at High Roding, near Dunmow (32 m. n.e. of London), July 14, 1841. He received his education at Trinity College, Cambridge (B.A., 1863; M.A., 1884; D.D., 1905); was curate of Christ Church, Tunbridge Wells, 1866-1868; vicar of North Malvern, 1868-75; rector of Buckhurst Hill, 1875-80, being also diocesan inspector at St. Albans, 1876-80; rector of St. Paul's, Edinburgh, 1880-84; vicar of Christ Church, Lancaster Gate, 1884-1905, serving also as select preacher at Cambridge in 1893, to which office he was again called in 1905; Golden lecturer at St. Margaret's, Lothbury, 1896-1905; prebendary of St. Paul's, 1899-1905; rural dean of Paddington, 1901-05; commissioner to the archbishop of Capetown, 1900-1905, to the bishop of North China, 1901-05, and to the bishop of Shantung, 1904-05; dean of Carlisle, 1905-08; and was consecrated bishop of Chichester, 1908. He is the author of: *Foundation Truths: a Course of Instructions* (Edinburgh, 1884); *Holy Communion. Instructions and Devotions* (London, 1887); *The Mountain of Blessedness* (1888); *Is not this the Christ? A Course of Sermons* (1889); *Confirmation; or, the Laying on of Hands* (1898); *What does the Church of England Say?* (1899); *In Paradise* (1904); *Story of the Prayer Book* (1906); *The King and his Kingdom, and Other Sermons* (1906); *Social Life* (1907); and *Short Family Prayers* (1908).

RIDLEY, NICHOLAS: English Reformer and martyr; b. near Willimontswyke (30 m. w. of Newcastle), Northumberland, early in the sixteenth century (1500?); d. at the stake at Oxford Oct. 16, 1555. After studying at the grammar-school at Newcastle-upon-Tyne, he entered Pembroke Hall, Cambridge, 1518, where he later became fellow. In 1527 he took orders and went for further study to the Sorbonne, Paris, and to Louvain. Returning to England, he rose to the position of senior proctor at Cambridge, 1533. As proctor he signed the decree against the papal supremacy, 1534. He was already much sought after as a preacher. Cranmer made him his domestic chaplain and vicar of Herne, East Kent. In 1540 he was appointed king's chaplain and master of Pembroke Hall, in 1541 canon of Canterbury, in 1545 canon of Westminster, and in 1547 bishop of Rochester. During the reign of Edward VI., Ridley was active in promulgating the new views. In 1545, and partly in consequence of the perusal of Ratramnus' *De corpore et sanguine Domini* (Eng. transl., *The Book of Bertram the Priest Concerning the Body and Blood of Christ in the Sacrament*, London (1549, 1686, and often, latest, 1880) he publicly renounced the doctrine of transubstantiation. He was deputed to set forth the Reformed views in York, Durham, and other dioceses, and in 1549 to place Protestantism on a firm basis at Cambridge. He sat on the commission that deposed Bonner, bishop of London, and Gardiner, bishop of Winchester, and in 1550 was promoted to Bonner's place. Foxe instances, as a sign of his goodness, that for months he entertained Bonner's mother at his palace, assigning to her the place of prominence at the table, and contrasts Ridley's spirit with the severity of Bonner. His deep interest in the unfavored classes led him to make suggestions to King Edward which found ultimate expression in the foundation of three hospitals in London, St. Thomas, Christ, and Bethlehem. Ridley's name is indissolubly associated with the names of Cranmer and Latimer as a foremost leader and a martyr of English Protestantism. Mary, who had taken offense at a visit Ridley had made her and his offer to preach in her presence, on her accession to the throne quickly ordered his deposition, reinstating Bonner as bishop of London, July 20, 1553. Ridley was committed to the Tower from which he was removed to Oxford, where he was held a prisoner in Bocardo jail and the mayor's house. On Apr. 17, 1554, he was called upon to stand trial in the Divinity School, Oxford, and was declared a heretic. The Spanish friar, Soto, labored in vain to turn him back to the old faith. After the passage of the new statutes on heresy, the prisoner was summoned again, Sept. 30, 1555, by Archbishop Pole, and was convicted and condemned to the flames. In company with Latimer, he was burned in "the ditch" over against Balliol Hall. The night before his execution he said to some friends with whom he supped: "I mean to go to bed, and, by God's will, to sleep as quietly as ever I did in my life." Arrived at the stake, he ran to Latimer, embraced him, and kissed him. A "scant sermon, in all a quarter of an hour," as Foxe puts it, was preached by Dr. Smith, which Latimer and Ridley were both ready to answer but they were denied the opportunity. Promised life, if he would recant, Ridley replied, "So long as breath is in my body, I will never deny my Lord Christ and his known truth." He gave his clothes to the bystanders, and was bound to the stake by an iron chain. When the faggots were being lighted, Latimer spoke to Ridley the famous words, "Be of good comfort, Master Ridley. Play the man. We shall this day light such a candle, by God's grace, in England, as I trust shall never be put out." The flames were slow in doing their work. Again and again the martyr cried, "Let the fire come unto me. I can not burn." His lower members were first consumed, and the end came when the fire reached a bag of gunpowder which Ridley's brother-in-law had tied at his neck. Foxe has given the best account of Ridley's life and martyrdom, and describes him as "a man beautified with excellent qualities so ghostly inspired and godly learned and now written, doubtless, in the Book of Life." In his account of Ridley's administration of the episcopal office, this writer emphasizes his attention to prayer, as well as his constant industry, relieved after dinner and supper by a game of chess. His most famous saying is the one recorded during his interview with Mary before she became queen. When the Reformer expressed the hope that she would not refuse God's Word, the princess replied, "I can not tell what ye call God's Word. That is not God's Word now that was God's Word in my father's days." To this Ridley answered: "God's Word is one at all times, but hath been better understood and practised in some ages than in others." Mary in her response declared, "As for your new books, I thank God I never read any of them. I never did, nor ever will do." The few writings Ridley left behind him have been published by the Religious Tract Society, *Treatise and Letters of Dr. Nicholas Ridley* (London, 1830?), and by the Parker Society, *Works of Nicholas Ridley, D.D.* (ed. H. Christmas, London, 1841). Among the writings are a *Brief Declaration against Transubstantiation*, a *Treatise against Image Worship*, and *A Piteous Lamentation of the Miserable Estate of the Church in England in the Time of the Late Revolt from the Gospel.* The Parker Society volume also contains an account of his disputations at Oxford prior to his death and a reprint of Fox's account of his martyrdom. An avenue in the yard of Pembroke Hall is still known as Ridley's Walk. Quarles has a poem on Ridley in which are the lines:

"Rome thundered death, but Ridley's dauntless eye
Star'd in Death's face, and scorned Death standing bye.
In spite of Rome, for England's faith he stood
And in the flames, he sealed it with his blood."

David S. Schaff.

In 1839 there was erected at Oxford a "Martyrs Memorial," with statues of Cranmer, Latimer, and Ridley, partly by way of protest against the Tractarian Movement (see Tractarianism), one of the characteristics of which was hostility to the Reformation. A. H. N.

Bibliography: The original source is J. Fox's *Actes and Monuments* (for editions see under Fox, John). An excellent memoir appears in H. Moule's ed. of the *Brief Declaration of the Lordes Supper*, London, 1895. Consult further: G. Ridley, *Life of Dr. Nicholas Ridley, sometime Bishop of London*, London, 1763; the memoir in the volume on Ridley in L. Richmond's *Fathers of the English Church*, 8 vols., London, 1807–12; G. T. Ridlon, *Hist. of the Ancient Ryedales and their Descendants*, pp. 419–424, Manchester, N. H., 1884; W. Clark, *The Anglican Reformation*, New York, 1897; J. Gairdner, *English Church in the 16th Century*, passim, London, 1903; *DNB*, xlviii. 286–289; and, in general, the works on the history of the period, secular and ecclesiastical.

RIEGER, rî'ger, **GEORG KONRAD:** Pietistic preacher; b. at Cannstadt (4 m. n.e. of Stuttgart) Mar. 7, 1687; d. at Stuttgart Apr. 16, 1743. After studying theology he was private tutor at Tübingen, 1713–15; city vicar at Stuttgart and deacon at Urach, 1715–31; and from that time continued in educational and ministerial work at Stuttgart. He was one of the most gifted preachers in the Evangelical Church of Germany, and was of the school of J. A. Bengel (q.v.). He excelled all other Pietists in eloquence, emotional power, and freshness. He knew how to employ simple colloquialisms without losing in dignity and force. His preaching was marked by clearness, interest, and fluency. His imagination served him well in using illustrations. Dogmatic subjects frequently received painstaking treatment, though without pedantry. He placed himself in immediate touch with his hearers, never losing the thread of his discourse. He published collections of sermons as follows: *Herzenspostille* (Züllichau, 1742; Stuttgart, 1853–54); *Herz- und Hand-Postille* (1746; Berlin, 1852); *De cura minimorum in regno gratiæ* (Stuttgart, 1733); and *Richtiger und leichter Weg zum Himmel* (Stuttgart, 1744, 1844, and after). He published also *Die Kraft der Gottseligkeit* (1732–36). (Hermann Beck.)

Bibliography: Biographic material is contained in Rieger's *Richtiger und leichter Weg* (Stuttgart, 1844); C. G. Schmidt, *Geschichte der Predigt in der evangelischen Kirche Deutschlands*, pp. 196 sqq., Gotha, 1872; H. C. Stuckenberg, *Lutheran Quarterly Review*, xix (1889), 564 sqq.

RIEGER, KARL HEINRICH: Son of the preceding; b. at Stuttgart June 16, 1726; d. there Jan. 15, 1791. After studying theology, he was domestic tutor at Augsburg, 1747–49; vicar, 1749–50; tutor at Tübingen, 1750; deacon at Ludwigsburg, 1754–57; and until his death preacher at Stuttgart. He left the impression of a strong, firm character; and represented the traditional teaching of the Lutheran Church in opposition to the new rationalism. Through his influence the revision of the hymnal was moderate, and of the old catechism (of 1681 and 1696) conservative. He was an active member of the Christenthumsgesellschaft, founded by J. A. Urlsperger (q.v.). As a preacher, he was less spirited and forceful than his father, but possessed rare penetration, emphasis, and spirituality, moral earnestness, a quiet, clear thoughtfulness, and ease, with true Christian wisdom, and a winning grace and mildness; but his form and presentation were clumsy and awkward. After his death appeared *Predigten und Betrachtungen* (Stuttgart, 1794); *Betrachtungen über das Neue Testament* (4 vols., 1828; 1875); and *Betrachtungen über die Psalmen und die zwölf kleinen Propheten* (1835; 1859). (Hermann Beck.)

Bibliography: *Christen-Bote*, ed. J. C. F. Burk, i (1832), 105 sqq.; C. Grosse, *Die alten Tröster. Wegweiser in die Erbauungslitteratur der evangelisch-lutherischen Kirche des 16. bis 18. Jahrhunderts*, pp. 495 sqq., Hermannsburg, 1900.

RIEHM, rîm, **EDWARD KARL AUGUST:** Biblical scholar; b. at Diersburg, near Offenburg (17 m. s.s.w. of Carlsruhe), Baden, Dec. 20, 1830; d. at Halle Apr. 5, 1888. He studied theology and philology at Heidelberg, 1848–50; and at Halle,

1850–52; and again at Heidelberg, 1852; was admitted to the ministry in 1853; vicar at Durlach, 1853–54; and garrison chaplain at Mannheim after 1855. In 1858 he entered the theological faculty at Heidelberg, where he was associate professor, 1861–62; and, 1862–66, associate professor of Old-Testament exegesis at Halle, and professor, 1866–1888. He was the author of: *Die Gesetzgebung Mosis im Lande Moab* (Gotha, 1854); *Der Lehrbegriff des Hebräerbriefs* (Ludwigsburg, 1858–59); *Die besondere Bedeutung des A. T. für die religiöse Erkenntnis und das religiöse Leben der christlichen Gemeinde* (Halle, 1864); *Die messianische Weissagung* (Gotha, 1875); *Der Begriff der Sühne im Alten Testament* (1877); and *Handwörterbuch des biblischen Altertums* (Bielefeld, 1875–84, and others). After his death appeared *Einleitung in das Alte Testament* (Halle, 1889); and *Alttestamentliche Theologie* (1889). A pupil and afterward colleague of H. Hupfeld at Halle, he revised the latter's commentary on Psalms (Gotha, 1867–71); was one of the editors of the *TSK* (Gotha), 1866–88; and was a member of the commission for the revision of Luther's translation of the Bible, 1865–88. In his exegetical work he was scientific, thorough, and impartial, and emphasized the religion of the Old Testament as one of revelation.

(K. H. Pahncke.)

RIESSLER, ris'ler, **PAUL:** Old-Testament scholar; b. at Stuttgart Sept. 16, 1865. He received his elementary education at Stuttgart and Rottweil, and his advanced training at the University of Tübingen and the theological seminary at Rottenburg; was vicar at Mergentheim and Ellwangen, 1889–1892; taught in the higher gymnasium at Ehingen, 1892–98; was city preacher at Blaubeuren, 1889–1907; became professor of Old-Testament exegesis at Tübingen in the Roman Catholic theological faculty, 1907. He has written a critical commentary on Daniel (Stuttgart, 1899), and another on the same book in the *Kurzgefasster wissenschaftlicher Kommentar* (Vienna, 1902).

RIETSCHEL, rit'shel, **CHRISTIAN GEORG:** German Protestant, son of the sculptor of the famous Luther monument at Worms; b. at Dresden May 10, 1842. He was educated at the universities of Erlangen, Berlin, and Leipsic from 1860 to 1864, and after being a member of the Domkandidatenstift at Berlin in 1864–65 and of St. Paul's seminary for preachers at Leipsic in 1866–67, was pastor at Rüdigsdorf, Saxony, in 1868–74, head pastor at Zittau in 1874–78, second director of the preachers' seminary at Wittenberg in 1878–84, and first director of the same institution in 1884–87, superintendent and district inspector of schools in 1878–87, and pastor of St. Matthew's, Leipsic, in 1887–89. Since 1889 he has been professor of practical theology in the University of Leipsic, and also first university preacher and director of St. Paul's seminary for preachers in the same city, while in 1904–05 he was rector of the university. He has written *Die Gewährung der Abendmahlsgemeinschaft an Reformierte und Unierte* (Leipsic, 1868); *Martin Luther und Ignatius von Loyola, eine vergleichende Charakteristik ihrer inneren Entwicklung* (Wittenberg, 1879); *Abschnitt vierzehn der Kirchen- und Synodal-Ordnung* (1885); *Luther und sein Haus* (Halle, 1888); *Luther und die Ordination* (Wittenberg, 1889); *Das Wort vom Glauben* (sermons; Leipsic, 1892); *Die Aufgabe der Orgel im Gottesdienst bis ins achtzehnte Jahrhundert* (1893); *Der evangelische Gottesdienst unter dem Gesichtspunkt der Anbetung im Geist und in der Wahrheit* (Halle, 1894); *Die Frage des Zusammenschlusses der deutschen evangelischen Landeskirchen zur Wahrung und Förderung ihrer gemeinsamen Angelegenheiten* (Leipsic, 1900); *Lehrbuch der Liturgik* (2 vols., Berlin, 1900–08); *Weihnachten in Kirche, Kunst und Volksleben* (Bielefeld, 1901); *Die evangelische Kirche und die soziale Frage* (Leipsic, 1904); and *Zur Reform des Religionsunterrichts in der Volksschule* (Berlin, 1909).

RIGG, JAMES HARRISON: English Wesleyan Methodist; b. at Newcastle-on-Tyne Jan. 16, 1821; d. at London Apr. 17, 1909. He was educated at Old Kingswood School, and, after being a teacher from 1835 to 1845, entered the Wesleyan ministry. In 1866 he was elected a member of the "Hundred" (see Methodists, I., 1, § 6) and two years later became principal of the Wesleyan Training College for Day School Teachers, Westminster, London, a position which he retained until 1903. He was president of the Wesleyan Methodist Conference, and in this capacity was instrumental in securing the admission of laymen to that body in 1878. For fifteen years he was editor of *The London Quarterly Review* and was also on its editorial staff for several years longer. He edited E. A. Rumbold's *Vindication of the Character and Administration of Sir T. Rumbold, Bart., Governor of Madras in 1778–80* (London, 1868), and was the author of: *The Principles of Wesleyan Methodism* (London, 1850); *Congregational Independency and Wesleyan Connexionalism Contrasted* (1851); *Modern Anglican Theology* (1857); *Essays for the Times on Ecclesiastical and Social Subjects* (1866); *The Sabbath and the Sabbath Law before and after Christ* (1869); *The Churchmanship of John Wesley* (1868); *National Education, English and Foreign* (1873); *The Living Wesley as he was in his Youth and in his Prime* (1875); *Connexional Economy of Wesleyan Methodism* (1879); *Discourses and Addresses on Leading Truths of Religion and Philosophy* (1880); *The Character and Life-Work of Dr. Pusey* (1883); *Was Wesley a High Churchman, and is Modern Methodism Wesleyan Methodism? or, John Wesley, the Church of England, and Wesleyan Methodism* (1883); *A Comparative View of Church Organisms, Primitive and Protestant* (1887); *Oxford High Anglicanism and its Leaders* (1895); *Scenes and Studies in the Ministry of Our Lord, with Thoughts on Preaching* (1902); and *Reminiscences Sixty Years ago* (1904).

Bibliography: J. Telford, *The Life of James Harrison Rigg, 1821–1909*, London, 1909.

RIGGENBACH, rig'en-bāɦ, **CHRISTOPH JOHANNES:** Swiss Protestant theologian; b. at Basel Oct. 8, 1818; d. there Sept. 5, 1890. He pursued his studies at Basel, Berlin, and Bonn under Peterman, Nitzsch, Bleek, Sack, and others. He was ordained in 1842, became pastor in Bennwyl, where his affiliations were at first with the radical school of theology. His position later on became more moderate. In 1850, he was called to the theological faculty at the University of Basel, teaching New Testament, pastoral theology, giving popular lectures on the life of Jesus, and engaging also in the study of church music and hymnology. He became an earnest opponent of theological radicalism, combated the leaders of the modern school, and helped to found the *Kirchenfreund* as the organ of the conservative group. Even in this polemical atmosphere, he never lost the personal friendship of his opponents. He was one of the founders of the Evangelisch-kirchlicher Verein, which worked in conservative interests, and was interested in the Evangelical Alliance. He was also a leader in the extension of missionary work, becoming president of the Basel missions committee in 1878. He published: *Vorlesungen über das Leben Jesu* (Basel, 1858); *Die mosaische Stiftshütte* (1862); *Die Zeugnisse für das Evangelium Johannis* (1866); *Der Kirchengesang in Basel seit der Reformation* (1870); *Hieronymus Annoni* (1870); *Der sogenannte Brief des Barnabas* (1873); *Eine Reise nach Palästina* (1873); and the commentary upon I and II Thessalonians in Lange's commentary.

Bibliography: *Deutsch-evangelische Kirchenzeitung*, iv (1890), 494–498; P. Wurm, in *Allgemeine Missionszeitschrift*, xvii (1890), 560–565; Oeri, in *Basler Kirchenfreund*, 1893, nos. 2–5, cf. 1890, no. 19.

RIGGS, ALEXANDER BROWN: Presbyterian; b. at Portsmouth, O., June 21, 1842. He was educated at Jefferson College, Pa. (A.B., 1863), and after teaching mathematics at Western University, Pittsburg, Pa., for a year, was admitted to the Pennsylvania bar. He had practised only two years, however, when, giving up law, he entered Auburn Theological Seminary, where he spent two years, and completed his theological training at Union Theological Seminary (1870), after which he held pastorates at the Reformed Church, Fort Plain, N. Y. (1870–76), the Presbyterian Church, Waterford, N. Y. (1876–90), and the Seventh Presbyterian Church, Cincinnati (1891–1902). From 1894 to 1897 he was instructor in Greek in Lane Theological Seminary, Cincinnati, and since 1897 has been professor of New-Testament exegesis and introduction in the same institution.

RIGGS, EDWARD: Presbyterian; b. at Smyrna, Turkey, June 30, 1844. He was graduated from Princeton College (A.B., 1865) and Union Theological Seminary, New York City (1869). In 1869 he was appointed a missionary of the American Board of Commissioners for Foreign Missions and went at once to Sivas, Asia Minor, where he remained seven years. Since 1876 he has been stationed at Marsovan, Turkey, where he has been chiefly associated with the Theological Seminary of the Western Turkey Mission, having been professor of systematic theology for a number of years and president since 1903. He has also been a manager of Anatolia College, Marsovan, since its organization in 1886, and has given instruction in various departments as a missionary. In theology he describes himself as "a broad, progressive conservative, holding to the main tenets of the traditional evangelical theology, adhering strictly to the Scriptures of the Old and New Testaments, but subjecting everything to the most rigid tests of genuine and careful scholarly examination." He likewise holds "that an honest application of the most searching criticism results in maintaining the sound orthodox beliefs in all their essential points." He prepared the chapter on *The Christian Forces at Work in the Turkish Empire* for W. D. Grant's *Christendom Anno Domini MDCCCCI* (New York, 1902).

RIGGS, ELIAS: American missionary in Turkey; b. at New Providence, N. J., Nov. 19, 1810; d. at Constantinople Jan. 17, 1901. He graduated at Amherst College, Mass., 1829, and at Andover Theological Seminary, Mass., 1832; was missionary of the American Board at Athens and Argos, Greece, 1832–38; later at Smyrna, Asia Minor; and at Constantinople 1853–1901. He visited his native country once, in 1856, and taught Hebrew in the Union Theological Seminary, New York, 1857–58. He was a remarkable philologist, having early applied himself to a mastery of the Semitic languages and Greek. In 1844 he was assigned to the Armenian branch of the Turkish mission and was engaged in translating the Scriptures into Armenian, 1845–52. He was one of a committee engaged in 1873 by the American and the British and Foreign Bible Societies to translate the Bible into Turkish; and, as a result, the entire Bible was published both in Armenian and Arabic characters in 1878. He participated also in a revision of the same issued in 1886. He is said to have had a working knowledge of twenty languages and the mastery of twelve, and to have produced either as originals or translations no less than 478 hymns in the Bulgarian language alone. He was the author of *A Manual of the Chaldee Language containing a Grammar, Chrestomathy, and a Vocabulary* (Andover, 1832; revised ed., New York, 1858); *Grammar of the Modern Armenian Language, with a Vocabulary* (Smyrna, 1847); *Grammar of the Turkish Language as written in the Armenian Character* (Constantinople, 1856); and *Translation of the Scriptures into the Bulgarian Language*, completed with the aid of native scholars (Constantinople, 1871); *Suggested Emendations of the A. V. of the Old Testament* (Andover, 1873); *Suggested Modifications of the R. V. of the New Testament* (1883); and *Notes on Difficult Passages of the New Testament* (Boston, 1889).

RIGGS, JAMES FORSYTH: Presbyterian; b. at Bournabat (a village near Smyrna), Turkey, Oct. 4, 1852. He was graduated from Princeton College (A.B., 1872), where he was Boudinot fellow in history in 1872–73, and from Union Theological Seminary, New York City (1878). He was then pastor of the Presbyterian church at Cranford, N. J., in 1878–84, and of the Dutch Reformed church at Bergen Point, N. J., in 1884–92; professor of New-Testament Greek in the New Brunswick Theological Seminary (1892–98), and during that time delivered lectures on historical subjects under the auspices of the Rutgers College University Extension system. Since 1898 he has been pastor of the Brick Presbyterian Church, East Orange, N. J. In theology he is a moderate Calvinist and has no sympathy with revolutionary ideas in Biblical criticism.

RIGGS, JAMES STEVENSON: Presbyterian; b. at New York July 16, 1853; graduated at the College of New Jersey, Princeton, 1874; studied at Leipsic, 1875; graduated at Auburn Theological Seminary, N. Y., 1880; was pastor at Fulton, N. Y., 1880–84; adjunct professor of Biblical Greek in Auburn Theological Seminary, 1884–87; and professor since 1887. He is author of a *History of the Jewish People: Maccabean and Roman Periods* (New York, 1899), and *Messages of Jesus according to the Gospel of John* (1907).

RIGGS, STEPHEN RETURN: Presbyterian missionary to the Indians; b. at Steubenville, O., Mar. 23, 1812; d. at Beloit, Wis., Aug. 24, 1883. He was graduated at Jefferson College, 1834; studied for a year in the Western Theological Seminary, Allegheny, Pa.; was licensed in 1836; and was from 1837 till 1883 a missionary among the Dakotas. He mastered their language and reduced it to writing and into it translated nearly the entire New Testament, and also portions of the Old. He also prepared a dictionary of the language and other aids for its acquisition. He was the author of many translations into it. In English he wrote his autobiography, *Mary and I. Forty years with the Sioux*, Chicago, 1880; also *Tah-koo Wah-kan; or, the Gospel among the Dakotas*, Boston, 1869.

RIGHTEOUSNESS, ORIGINAL.

1. Doctrinal Development till Augustine.

The older Protestant theologians designated by the term *justitia originalis*, the Latin equivalent of original righteousness, the condition of man as made in the image of God, and before the fall. It is found for the first time in the writings of the Schoolmen, but the development of the doctrine was begun by Augustine, who uses the term *prima justitia*, "first righteousness" (*De peccatorum meritis et remissione*, II., xxxvii.). While a condition of original integrity of man, and of a subsequent breach of harmony and depravation, was generally presupposed in Christian belief, Augustine was the first to bring this condition into intimate connection with man's creation in the divine image, and he arrived at a higher valuation of both. Irenæus, Theophylact, Justin, and Clement of Alexandria spoke of the first state as one of childlike simplicity and innocence, but Athanasius developed the doctrine (*De trinitate*, iii. 16): "those who mortify the deeds of the body and have put on the new man which is created after God are after his image; for such was Adam before his disobedience." The first state was not treated in its relation to the essential nature of man; prominence was given, not to what he originally was, but to what he was by nature, and the image of God was sought chiefly in man's spiritual endowment with reason and freedom, through which he is enabled to attain perfection. Thus moral perfection was denied for the first state, though nothing was said of the actual condition therein, of a "superadded gift," or of the "equilibrium" of Pelagianism. With Augustine the image of God is the inalienable "rational soul." This includes the will, with a positive inclination to holiness, though even the first man needed the assistance of grace in order to reach "full righteousness." At first man willed not to sin, and by supernatural grace he was able not to sin. It might seem as if the will not to sin was not true righteousness, but "good will" in the first man constituted righteousness in the same degree as concupiscence in man after his fall constitutes original sin. At the fall the concupiscence of the flesh took the place of the "good will" and is itself sin.

2. The Scholastic Doctrine.

After Augustine's death, semi-Pelagianism prevailed in the Church. Its opposition to Augustine directed itself, indeed, against his doctrine of predestination, but not on the basis of the conception of sin and salvation. It was really an opposition to inexorable severity in the valuation of natural corruption. In this respect, semi-Pelagianism was successful at the Synod of Orange, in 529, which asserted that "by the sin of Adam the free will was so inclined and attenuated that no one was afterwards able to love God as he should, to believe in God, or to be influenced concerning God, unless the prevenient grace of the divine mercy acted upon him." Scholastic theologians went further. They dated the discord between flesh and spirit before the fall. It is true, "original righteousness" as well as a sinful state resulting from the fall would be impossible in this case, if Augustine had not offered a way of escape in the thought that divine grace subjected the flesh to the spirit in the case of Adam, and thus a harmony was effected which is not inherent in man *per se*. But this harmony or subjection of concupiscence to reason or the will of God is "original righteousness" which consequently is a "superadded gift." The proof was found in the alleged difference between "likeness" and "image" (Gen. i. 26). The essential attributes of the divine image were reason and will. By the accidents which belong to it but do not constitute it, and are added as a gift of grace, man is enabled to acquire eternal life. Thus man after his fall is still in his first pure state with the modification that his senses and lusts are no longer held in check by the assistant grace, and thus a state of disorder has taken the place of subjection to reason. Then original sin becomes a lack of "original righteousness"; it is not, however, sin in the positive sense of Augustine, but only in a negative sense.

3. Teaching of Reformers and Roman Catholics.

The Reformers, with their deep sense of the grossness of sin, were utterly unable to assume a naturally pure condition; for nature was impure. Original sin is a real and true sin, and not simply a deficiency or infirmity, but such a sin as condemns and eternally separates from God all men that proceed from Adam (cf. *Augsburg Confession*, ii.), and thus the first state of man must have included an opposite operation of the good. But as this operation is an essential condition of life for him, it can not be regarded as a mere accident, it must be something that originally and necessarily belongs to man. The Formula of Concord, therefore, in accordance with the view of the Reformers, designated original righteousness not simply as "concreate righteousness," but as the essential fact of having been created in the image of God. Thus the Lutheran Church, as well as the Reformed, advanced a step beyond Augustine. Scholasticism had left a number of questions unsettled, such as whether original righteousness was a "grace making acceptable" (Thomas Aquinas) or a "grace given to those acceptable" like the *charismata* (Duns Scotus). The Council of Trent avoided pronouncing on this point, and affirmed that Adam, "when he had transgressed God's commandment in Paradise, immediately lost the holiness and righteousness in which he had been placed," with the apparent intention of excluding not scholastic deductions but the doctrine of the Reformers. Bellarmine developed the Roman Catholic doctrine in this opposition clearly and adroitly. The Lutherans, according to him, agree with the Pelagians because they deprive the first man of supernatural gifts, adding the further error that after the fall man lacks "a natural attribute" —free will. In contrast to this doctrine, according to him, the Roman Catholic Church distinguishes between "image" and "likeness." The former refers to nature, the latter to the supernatural, and denotes some "ornaments of wisdom and righteousness" which man received in creation but lacks now. As man came forth from the creator's hand, he consisted of flesh and spirit, and stood related both to the animals and to the angels. On the latter side he had intelligence and will; on the former, senses and appetites. A conflict arose, and from the conflict "a terrible difficulty in doing well." This was the "disease of nature" which inheres in matter, hence God added the gift of original righteousness. It was this perfection of the divine image, and not the image itself, which man lost at the fall.

Among later Protestant theologians, the rationalists did not essentially change the doctrine concerning the first state. Since the time of Schleiermacher a certain necessity of original nature has been attached to sin. Schleiermacher expressly states that an incapacity for good works was in human nature before the fall, located in the flesh, that is, "the totality of the lower faculties of the soul," and that consequently the sin which was transmitted to his descendants was originally in the first man. Sin, according to him, is not the first actual condition; with the awakening of the consciousness of God it was preceded by a state of perfection which was not without consequences perceptible even after the fall. Subsequently, however, a time was bound to come in which sensuousness increased in some direction. Lipsius transformed the "state of original perfection" as taught by Schleiermacher into the "primitive form of ethical religion," that is, into the immediate, but unconscious and only relative, communion with God which from the consciousness of its opposite appears as a lost paradise. Rothe considers man the union of two elements of opposite qualities, bound to strive after the right proportion between his ego and his material nature, thus transposing man's likeness to the image of God into the future. Biedermann sees the basis of sin in the sensual nature of man, which was created by God intentionally in order to realize and develop his redeeming grace in the history of salvation. Ritschl agrees with Biedermann so far as to hold that the doctrine of the first state should be replaced by that of the destiny of man.

4. Later Protestant Views.

All these views correctly presuppose the identity of the present substance of man with the original substance, but they err in identifying man's present condition with his original condition. It is an improbable assumption that anything lost by sin must be "superadded" unless the condition is considered something "superadded" to the substance. A substance must have its corresponding state or condition, it must have attributes; but the question is whether man's present condition corresponds to the human substance. Lutheran theologians teach that the human essence does not now possess that condition which it requires; that man's actual condition is not merely in a state of imperfect development, it is opposed to the essence. The next question is, whether man began with a state of absolute moral perfection. Against this view, Julius Müller properly brings the objection that it excludes the possibility of the fall. But neither Luther, the other Reformers, nor the Lutheran confessions teach a state of absolute moral perfection. It should be asked rather, whether man might have begun with goodness, and this question must be answered in the affirmative; for it is the conviction of every justified person that the moral condition must be good before any good action can be done. The moral condition must in the first man lie at the basis of his conduct, and can exist only as an effect wrought by God in the same way as in the justified and regenerate. In this respect there is no difference between the primitive state of innocence and the restoration of innocence in justification. The difference between the first state and that of the redeemed lies rather in the fact that the latter has reached the point where the first man should have stood after his temptation; but the moral quality imparted by God has nothing to do with this. The assumption of an original indifference presupposes a will without content or aim and at the same time a preponderating capacity for goodness; thus there would be a capacity which in its quality would be superior to the will; such an instinctive desire for goodness, overpowering the will, would make sinning impossible. Moreover, indifference annuls freedom; for indifference is not freedom, but constraint of will; freedom is rather the capacity for unhampered normal self-activity. Man's original condition was not without positive inclination to goodness. His will had this disposition; but while it was in harmony with God's will, it might sin, and in the possibility of sinning consisted its freedom. It was man's duty to preserve his rectitude by voluntary choice, thus confirming God's work. (H. T. CREMER†.)

5. Conclusion.

BIBLIOGRAPHY: The pertinent literature is quite fully given under IMAGE OF GOD. The earlier discussions are well represented by Augustine's "City of God," XII., i.-ix., xxiii.; Anselm, *De casu diaboli*, xii.; Aquinas, *Summa*, II., xciii.-xcvii.; Z. Ursinus, *Summe of Christian Religion*, Ques. 6, London, 1587; J. Edwards, *Doctrine of Original Sin Defended*, II., i., in his *Works*, New York, 1808-09; J. Howe, *Oracles of God*, lectures xvi.-xix., in his *Works*, vols. vii.-viii., London, 1822. The subject is usually discussed under Anthropology in the systems of theology (see in and under DOGMA, DOGMATICS), e.g., W. G. T. Shedd, *Dogmatic Theology*, ii. 95-114, cf. the citations from earlier authorities in iii. 288-302, New York, 1889-94, cf. also his *Hist. of Doctrine*, ii. 54-65, 8th ed., ib. 1884; C. Hodge, *Systematic Theology*, ii. 92-115, New York, 1871-73; H. B. Smith, *Systematic Theology*, pp. 252-259, New York, 1884; A. H. Strong, *Systematic Theology*, pp. 262-268, Rochester, 1886; H. E. Jacobs, *The Book of Concord*, consult index under "Man," Philadelphia, 1893.

RIMING OFFICES: Liturgical offices in which not only the hymns, but also all antiphons, responsories, versicles, etc., are in rime and meter, the only prose being the Psalms and lessons. Since the antiphons and responsories originally were concerned with the history of a feast or a saint, these offices were called *historiæ rhythmicæ*. Some 900 of these offices, only a small portion of the original number, have been edited by Clemens Blume and Guido Maria Dreves in their *Analecta hymnica medii ævi*, v., xiii., xiv. *b*, xvii., xviii., xxiv., xxv., xxvi., xxviii., xli. *a*, xlv. *a* (Leipsic, 1889-1904). First appearing in the ninth and tenth centuries, the riming offices reached their zenith between the middle of the twelfth and the middle of the fourteenth centuries, though specimens are known as late as the seventeenth century. This rich development finds its explanation in the liturgical liberty allowed in the Middle Ages, while the distinctly local character of the riming offices is shown by the fact that the chief sources are the breviaries of individual dioceses and orders. On the other hand, wider circulation was enjoyed by the offices contained in the breviaries of such orders as the Franciscans and Dominicans; if a riming office was incorporated in the Roman Breviary, its wide use was assured; and the popularity of the saint honored by a particular office, as well as the literary merit of the office in question, was yet another factor in the extension of its use. The present Breviary (q.v.) contains no complete riming office.

From a literary point of view the riming offices run the entire gamut from perfunctory doggerel to flights of genuine poetry. Among the best-known are the offices in honor of Gregory the Great (*Analecta hymnica*, v. No. 64), Saints Anne (xxv. No. 18), Benedict (xxv. No. 52), Elizabeth (xxv. No. 90), James (xxvi. No. 42) Peter (xxvi. No. 48), and Catharine (xxvi. No. 69), and the Virgin (xxiv. Nos. 25, 29, 30). The authorship of offices is known in only a few cases, among these writers being Alfanus, archbishop of Salerno (d. 1085); Goswin of Bossut (d. after 1229); Origo Scaccabarozzi of Milan (d. 1293); John Peckham, archbishop of Canterbury (d. 1292); Brinolph I., bishop of Scara (d. 1317); Christian of Lilienfeld (d. before 1332); Birger, archbishop of Upsala (d. 1383); and Lippold of Steinberg (d. 1415). (P. DREWS.)

BIBLIOGRAPHY: Consult the introductions to the offices printed in the *Analecta hymnica medii ævi*, ut sup.; S. Bäumer, *Geschichte des Breviers*, pp. 356-364, Freiburg, 1895; *Julian's von Speir liturgische Reimofficien*, ed. H. Felder, Freiburg in Switzerland, 1901.

RIMMON, rim'on.

Rimmon is the name given to a deity and to several places named in the Old Testament.

I. The Deity: According to II Kings v. 18, Rimmon was a Syrian deity who possessed a temple almost certainly located in Damascus; the name occurs as an element in the personal name Tabrimmon, father of Benhadad (I Kings xv. 18); cf. also HADADRIMMON. The pronunciation indicated by the Masoretic pointing is certainly mistaken. This is suggested (1) by the variant readings of the texts of the Septuagint (*Remman*, *Reeman*, *Remmath*, with similar forms for the element in Tabrimmon); (2) by the Syriac reading *Ramun;* (3) by the fact that a god Ramman, who is especially identified in the cuneiform writings with the "Westland" (Syria), is known to have been worshiped in Assyria and Babylonia from an early period; (4) by the form *Raman* used by Philo Byblius as preserved in a fragment (C. and T. Müller, *Fragmenta historicorum Græcorum*, iii. 575, Paris, 1841); (5) the Masoretic pointing is easily accounted for by the fact that *rimmon* is the Hebrew for "pomegranate," which (a) is common in Palestine, probably giving rise to a number of place names (see below, II.), and (b) has an important position in religious symbolism (being an emblem of fertility) and ornamentation (cf. Ex. xxviii., xxxix.; I Kings vii.; II Chron. iii. 16, iv. 13), and this pronunciation might easily be transferred to a deity by those who fixed the pointing of the text.

1. The Name; Extent of the Cult.

Assuming *Ramman* as the proper vocalization of the name (derived probably not from *râm* or *ramam*, "to be high," but from *rammanu*, "to thunder"), it appears that the ideograph used in the cuneiform records is *IM*, and that this ideograph represents also a deity Hadad (Adad, Addu, Daddu, Dada; cf. Pinches in *PSBA*, 1883, pp. 71-73; Bezold, in *PSBA*, 1887, pp. 174 sqq.) whose provenience is the "Westland," i.e., Syria. It then appears that Ramman and Hadad are the same deity, that his cult was wide-spread, and that other designations are Ragimu (from *ragam*, "to cry aloud"), Mer and Bur (these names being possibly those of earlier or local deities whose personality and functions Ramman absorbed and appropriated), Martu (from the name for "Westland"), and many others; one list alone is said to apply to him forty-one names. The worship of this deity can by many references in the cuneiform documents be traced in Babylonia and Assyria, also in Syria and Palestine through the Amarna Tablets (q.v.) and through the discoveries at Taanach (cf. Sellin in the publications of the Vienna Academy, 1904, pp. 113, 118, 119; Macrobius, *Saturnalia*, I., xxiii. 18, makes him chief deity of the Assyrians), also in Arabia (*CIS*, ii. 117 gives an inscription from North Arabia of fourth or fifth century in which appears *Rmnnthn*, "Rammon has given"—cf. the Hebrew Jonathan, "Yahweh has given"; *CIS*, iv. 140 gives an inscription of c. 24 B.C. which knows a deity *Rmn* who is "Lord of Alman"; *CIS*, ii. 73 gives a reading *ṣdḳrmn*, "Ramman is just" or "Ramman justifies," cf. the Hebrew names Zedekiah and Jehozadak). Attempts to find this deity in the Avesta are as yet doubtful in their results. The *Rama* of Vendidad i. 1; Sirozah i. 7, 16, ii. 7, etc., can be better accounted for on Indo-Aryan grounds; moreover the extent of the indebtedness of Zoroastrianism to Babylonian religion has not been made out. Hence it can not be asserted categorically that this Rama is equivalent to the Ramman of Syria, Assyria, and Babylonia.

2. Ramman in Babylonia.

In Babylonia about Hammurabi's time Ramman was associated, in a hymn which may be earlier than Hammurabi, with Bel (not Marduk), Sin, Ninib, Ishtar, and Shamash. In Babylonia the ideograph already referred to is generally used; possibly the deity was known also as Immeru (cf. the name Mer); but Ramman is well authenticated for Babylonia, especially in the region of Shirpurla (Telloh). Ramman seems to have come into prominence in the south in the time of the king named, and after that period increased in popularity (with some vicissitudes), especially under the Kasshites and later under Nebuchadrezzar I. An inscription from the Kasshite period calls him "lord of justice," and in this function he was associated with Shamash, with whom he was also consulted as an oracle god. He was a storm-deity, a syllabary designates him the god of thunder, and he carries the thunderbolt and ax (cf. with this the expression in no. 149 of the Amarna Tablets, Winckler's numbering: "he who thunders in the heavens like Addu, so that the whole land trembles at his voice"); in the omen tablets he is called the withholder and the sender of rain. His connection with the rain is distinct from that with justice; he has a twofold aspect, he sends rain to fertilize the fields and produce crops in order to reward virtue, also to destroy crops and thus to punish the sin of the impious. In this latter relation he is brought into causative connection with the deluge, this being due to his anger. He is also described as making weeds to grow and so punishing the wicked. In the pictorial representations Ramman-Hadad is often accompanied by a bull, and he at times wears the horns of that animal. The eleventh month (January-February) was sacred to him. His consort was Shala ("woman," "wife"), whose part, however, is insignificant, like that of goddesses generally in the Semitic world.

3. In Assyria and Syria.

That in Assyria this deity was early of importance is shown by the name of the king of c. 1825 B.C. which may be read either Shamshi-Ramman or Shamshi-Hadad (see ASSYRIA, VI., 3, §1). For it is now known that in at least some cases the element in Assyrian royal names which has been transcribed Ramman must be read Hadad (cf., e.g., the *Sitzungsberichte* of the Berlin Academy, 1899, p. 118). It is demonstrable that in Assyria Hadad and Ramman were current as names for this deity along with other designations as in Babylonia. He appears to have been more popular in Assyria than in the south. He shared with Anu in Asshur a temple dedicated to him alone by Shamshi-Ramman, so that the connection with Anu seems later than the dedication, Anu being received as a sort of guest. The statues of Ramman and Shala were carried away from Ekallate (a city—or temple?—represented as in the south of Assyria) and restored by Sennacherib. Tiglath-Pileser I. calls this god Martu, and the connection with storms is still held, his weapons being lightning, hunger, and death. For Syria and Palestine the worship is indicated by the personal names (probably not by the names of places; see below, II.) compounded with Hadad. Biblical passages are: (1) I Kings xv. 18, 20; II Chron. xvi. 2, 4, Benhadad a king of Syria contemporary with Asa; (2) I Kings xx.; II Kings vi. 24, viii. 7, 9, another king of the same name contemporary with Ahab; (3) II Kings xiii. 3, 24, 25, a son of Hazael; probably Amos i. 4 and Jer. xlix. 27 use the name as a title of the Syrian kings. The name Adadi-rimani appears in an inscription of the seventh century in Haran. The forms Addu and the like occur frequently in the Amarna Tablets.

4. Place of Origen.

The origin of Ramman is still a matter of doubt. Incidental expressions in the cuneiform records, such as that which names him Martu, seem to indicate that the Assyrians assigned to him an Aramean origin. The resulting supposition long was that contact of Assyria with Aram brought the god into the Assyrian pantheon, and that Aramean immigration carried him also into Babylonia, the result being his adoption by the priests and people of the two regions. But the early evidence of his worship in both Babylonia and Assyria, his mention under the ideograph *IM*, and a multiplicity of minor items have raised at least the possibility that he was of Sumerian origin, emerging into prominence only in the period named. His character as a storm-god is general and uniform. Dr. William Hayes Ward presents the theory that Hadad was the prototype out of which Yahweh developed. A Hittite deity carried the same emblems as Hadad-Ramman, as did Jupiter Dolichenus; in these cases the probability is in favor of a borrowing.

II. As a Place Name: In this sense Rimmon occurs frequently in the Old Testament: (1) a city in Judah or Simeon (Josh. xv. 32; Zech. xiv. 10), probably to be read En-rimmon (Neh. xi. 29), the present Um al-Ramamim; (2) a rock in Benjamin (Judges xx. 45, 47, xxi. 13), the modern Rammun, four miles east of Bethel; (3) a city in Simeon possibly identical with (1) above (I Chron. iv. 32); (4) a city in Zebulon (I Chron. vi. 77; cf. Josh. xix. 13 R.V.), the modern Rummaneh, north of Nazareth; (5) a station on the exodus, Rimmon-parez (Num. xxxiii. 19-20); (6) Gath-rimmon, a city of Dan (Josh. xix. 45; cf. the *Giti-rimmu* of the Amarna Tablets, no. 164 in Winckler's edition). In these cases the probability is against any connection with the deity, the name being better taken from *rimmon*, "pomegranate." GEO. W. GILMORE.

BIBLIOGRAPHY: Consult, besides the references given in the text, the literature on the religion given under Assyria and Babylonia, especially: M. Jastrow, Jr., *Religion of Babylonia and Assyria*, Boston, 1889, Germ. ed., Giessen, 1905 (best); W. von Baudissin, *Studien zur semitischen Religionsgeschichte*, i. 294 sqq., 306, sqq., Leipsic, 1876;

P. Scholtz, *Götzendienst und Zauberwesen bei den alten Hebräern*, pp. 244–247, Regensburg, 1877; J. Halévy, in *Mélanges de critique et histoire*, p. 424, Paris, 1883; F. Baethgen, *Beiträge zur semitischen Religionsgeschichte*, pp. 69, 75, 84, 255, Berlin 1880; P. D. Chantepie de la Saussaye, *Religionsgeschichte*, i. 287–288, Tübingen, 1905. For epigraphic and other illustrative material consult: H. C. Rawlinson, *Inscriptions*, iv. 28, no. 2, London, 1861; E. Glaser, *Die Abessinier in Arabien*, p. 35, Munich, 1889; P. Jensen, *Kosmologie der Babylonier*, pp. 488–489, Strassburg, 1890; idem, *Die Hittiter und Armenier*, pp. 171–173, ib. 1898; A. H. Sayce, *Higher Criticism and the Verdict of the Monuments*, London, 1894; H. Winckler, *Tel-el-Amarna Letters*, New York, 1896; idem, *Der Thontafelfund*, Berlin, 1898; C. W. H. Johns, *Doomsday Book*, Leipsic, 1901; idem, *Babylonian and Assyrian Laws, Contracts, and Letters*, Edinburgh, 1904; and the following magazine literature: *ZDMG*, xxix (1875), 237 sqq., xxxi (1877), 734–736; *Gazette archéologique*, ii (1876), 78–82; *ZA*, ii (1887), 331–332, ix (1894), 310–314; *JA*, 1887, p. 461, 1895, p. 386; *American Journal of Semitic Languages*, xii (1895–96), 159–162.

RINALDI, ri-nal'di, **ODORICO (ODERICUS RAYNALDUS)**: Italian Oratorian and church historian; b. at Treviso (18 m. n. by w. of Venice) 1595; d. at Rome Jan. 22, 1671. He was educated in his native city, the Jesuit college at Parma, and Padua; and in 1618 went to Rome, where he entered the Oratorian order, of which he was twice general superior. A diligent Thomist, such was his learning that he was chosen by his order to continue the annals of Cæsar Baronius (q.v.), beginning with 1198. Taking as his sources the notes of his predecessor and the documents contained in the archives and libraries of Rome, he completed a history of the Church from the pontificate of Innocent III. to the Reformation. His work is the best of all the continuations of Baronius, though not free from errors and prejudices. His history, the last volume edited and supplemented after his death by other Oratorians, appeared under the title *Annales ecclesiastici ab anno 1198 . . . ad annum 1565* (9 vols., Rome, 1646–77), and he also made an abridgment of both Baronius' annals and his own in Latin (3 vols., Rome, 1667) and Italian (3 vols., 1670). In recognition of his services Innocent X. offered to place him at the head of the Vatican library, but Rinaldi declined the honor. A complete edition of the annals of Baronius and Rinaldi was edited by J. D. and D. G. Mansi (38 vols., Lucca, 1738–59), and, with the continuation of Giacomo Laderchi and an extension to modern times, by A. Theiner (23 vols., Bar-le-Duc, 1864–73). (O. Zöckler†.)

Bibliography: The preface to Mansi's ed. of the *Annales*, vol. i., Lucca, 1747; G. Tiraboschi, *Storia della Letteratura Italiana*, vol. viii., 10 vols., Rome, 1782–97; H. Laemmer, *De Cæsaris Baronii literarum commercio*, Freiburg, 1903; *KL*, x. 842–843.

RINCKART (RINKART), rink'ärt, **MARTIN**: German dramatist and hymnist; b. at Eilenburg (12 m. n.w. of Leipsic) Apr. 24, 1586; d. there Dec. 8, 1649. He was educated at the University of Leipsic (1608–10), and in 1610-11 taught at Mansfeld, besides being choirmaster at the church of St. Nicholas. He was then called to be deacon of St. Ann's at Eisleben, and there wrote in 1613 the Luther drama *Der eislebische christliche Ritter*, in which the fable of the three rings, later used by Lessing, is used to typify the contest of the three confessions for the inheritance of Immanuel. In the same year Rinckart was called to the pastorate of Erdeborn, where he remained four years and wrote his second drama, *Lutherus desideratus*, in which he treated the concepts and tendencies to reform which prevailed from 1300 to 1500. A third drama, the *Indulgentiarius confusus*, was written to celebrate the jubilee of the Reformation, forming the third part of the author's intended heptalogy on Luther. In 1617 Rinckart was called to his native city as archdeacon, and there until his death he delivered weekly sermons on the catechism, the result being his *Die Katechismuswohlthaten* (Leipsic, 1645). In 1621 he wrote his fourth drama, of which the manuscript is lost, entitled *Lutherus magnanimus*. This was followed in 1624 by the fifth drama, *Monetarius seditiosus oder der müntzerische Bauernkrieg*. During this period, when the land was devastated by the hosts of Tilly, Wallenstein, and Gustavus Adolphus, and when Rinckart himself was afflicted with domestic grief, he wrote *Jobs christliche, wirkliche und wunderbare Kreuzschule* (1619), *Christbeschreibung an die herzliebste Mutter* (1619), and the brief *Kreuz-Schule*. Never losing courage, however, he wrote in 1628 the comforting *Der evangelischen Pilgrim güldener Wanderstab*. This was preceded in 1627 by the *Novantiqua Eilenbergica*, a history of Eilenburg in Latin and German verse from its foundation to 1545. To the same period of exile belongs his *Zehnfacher biblischer Lokal- und Gedenkring oder Gedenkzirkel*.

In 1630 Rinckart wrote the sixth drama of his heptalogy, *Lutherus Augustus*, based on the prophecy of Cardinal Cusanus that in 1630 John the Baptist would rise again and show the lamb of God to all the world. To this same period belong Rinckart's four "parodies," or remodelings of older poems. The first of these is the song of the "Lutheran Deborah" of 1636; the second the "extract from Martin Rinckart's jubilee comedy" of 1630, the third the Latin-German poem *Fera arundinis / ferarum ferocissimarum ferocissima*, and the fourth the hymn by which Rinckart is best known, the "Nun danket alle Gott," apparently written in its briefer form in 1630 and expanded in its author's *Jesu Herzbüchlein* (Leipsic, 1636). This hymn has been called, not inaptly, "the German Te Deum." The melody also is by Rinckart, who derived it from an older composition by Lucas Maurentius, master of the chapel at Rome (1581–99). During the famine of 1638 Rinckart composed the *Deutscher Jeremias und sein geist- und leibliches Hungerlied aus dem vierzehnten und fünfzehnten Kapitel*.

With the meeting of the envoys of the powers at Münster and Osnabrück in 1643 came hopes of peace, marked by Rinckart in his *Des teutschen Friedens-Herolden güldenes Pacem und überschönes Freuden-Kleinod* (written about 1644). Rinckart himself, the ardent lover of peace, was fortunately spared to enjoy for a brief space the Peace of Westphalia. (A. Freybe.)

Bibliography: The biographical work which uses in especially full and worthful manner a wealth of sources is W. Büchting, *Martin Rinckart, ein Lebensbild*, Göttingen, 1903. Other noteworthy sketches are: L. Plato, *Martin Rinckart nach seinem äusseren Leben und Wirken*, Leipsic, 1830; J. D. Vörkel, *Martin Rinckart, ein evangelisches Bild aus der Zeit des 30-jährigen Krieges*, Eilenburg, 1857; J. Linke, *M. Rinckarts Geistliche Lieder nebst einer Darstellung des Lebens und der Werke des Dichters*, Gotha,

1886; Graubner, *Ein Beitrag zur Lebensgeschichte M. Rinckarts. Inauguraldissertation*, Halle, 1887. Consult also: C. Müller, *Der Eislebische Ritter, ein Reformationsspiel*, Halle, 1884; S. W. Duffield, *English Hymns*, pp. 393–394, New York, 1886; E. Michael, *Martin Rinckart als Dramatiker*, Leipsic, 1894; W. Nelle, *Martin Rinckart*, Hamburg, 1904; Julian, *Hymnology*, pp. 962–963.

RING, EPISCOPAL. See VESTMENTS AND INSIGNIA, ECCLESIASTICAL.

RINGS. See DRESS AND ORNAMENT, HEBREW.

RINK, MELCHIOR: German Anabaptist; b. in Hesse in 1493 or 1494; d. after 1540. He matriculated at the University of Leipsic in 1516, and in 1523 was teaching in a school at Hersfeld, where he helped introduce the Reformation, taking an open stand in its favor in 1524. Soon afterward he came under the influence of Thomas Münzer (q.v.) and removed to Thuringia, where he labored first at Oberhausen (near Eisenach) and later at Eckardthausen. He took part in the Peasants' War, acting as leader in the battle near Frankenhausen. Neither the defeat of the Anabaptists in this engagement nor the death of Münzer could change his course; and he now proceeded to work for the propagation of Anabaptist tenets, and henceforth led the life of a wanderer. In 1527 he was at Worms, where, with other Anabaptists, he challenged the Evangelical clergy to a debate. In the following year he was again in Hesse, where he gathered some adherents in the vicinity of Hersfeld and attracted the attention of the authorities. Landgrave Philip, though enforcing no coercive measures, directed the theological faculty of Marburg to confer with Rink, but the negotiations, which were held on Aug. 17–18, 1528, led to no result, and the landgrave merely disciplined Rink with public ecclesiastical penance.

It was not until this period of his career that Rink's ability as an agitator was fully developed. He now formed small communities in Hesse and Thuringia, and saturated them so thoroughly with Anabaptist doctrines that only in rare instances do they seem to have recanted when brought to trial for their beliefs before the civil magistracy. In 1531, Rink and twelve other Anabaptists gathered for worship were discovered in the course of a domiciliary visit at the village of Vacha on the Werra. Henceforth the Anabaptist leader seems to have been held in custody. Butzer interceded with the landgrave in his behalf (Mar. 17, 1540), but since he refused to recant, he probably did not recover his freedom. The year of his death is unknown.

Rink was an opponent of infant baptism, and of the doctrines of original sin, the real presence, and the vicarious atonement, as well as of the literal interpretation of Scripture; and stood for a mystical and spiritualistic type of Christianity. At the outset, like Münzer, he contested the legitimacy of civil authority; but after the Peasants' War he restricted himself to denying the Christian's right to occupy a civil position and to demanding that the churches have authority to elect civil magistrates. The propaganda for these ideas met with great success. Rink personally evinced the courage to stand loyal to his convictions amid the gravest obstacles; while his strict morality and his learning were acknowledged.

CARL MIRBT.

BIBLIOGRAPHY: B. N. Krohn, *Geschichte der fanatischen und enthusiastischen Wiedertäufer*, pp. 18 sqq., Leipsic, 1758; J. Hast, *Geschichte der Wiedertäufer*, pp. 254–255, Münster, 1836; K. W. H. Hochhuth, in *ZHT*, xxviii (1858), 541–553, xxx (1860), 272; L. Keller, *Geschichte der Wiedertäufer und ihres Reichs zu Münster*, pp. 127–128, Münster, 1880; M. Lenz, *Briefwechsel Landgraf Philipps des Grossmütigen von Hesse mit Bucer*, i. 156, 161, 164, 325, Leipsic, 1880; F. H. Reusch, *Der Index der verbotenen Bücher*, p. 120, Bonn, 1883; F. O. zur Linden, *Melchior Hofmann*, pp. 171–185, Leipsic, 1885; A. H. Newman, *Hist. of Anti-Pedobaptism*, pp. 274–276, Philadelphia, 1897; K. Rembert, *Die "Wiedertäufer" im Herzogtum Jülich*, pp. 170, 196, 453, Berlin, 1899; O. Clemen, in *Monatsschrift der Comenius-Gesellschaft*, ix. 113–116, ib. 1900.

RIPHATH. See TABLE OF THE NATIONS, § 4.

RIPPON, JOHN: English Baptist hymnologist; b. at Tiverton (47 m. n.e. of Plymouth), Devon, Apr. 29, 1751; d. at London Dec. 17, 1836. He was pastor at London, 1773–1836; and he edited the *Baptist Annual Register*, 1790–1802. He is best known as the compiler of *Selections of Hymns from the Best Authors* (London, 1787; new ed. after the 30th, 1840; *Comprehensive Edition*, known as "The Comprehensive Rippon," 1844). The earliest edition was intended as an appendix to Isaac Watts' *Psalms and Hymns*. His final work has stood as one of the first half-dozen of hymn-books of historical importance, as a basis for subsequent compilation, and through its immense sale is said to have gained wealth for him. Among the few hymns of his own was, "The day has dawned, Jehovah comes."

BIBLIOGRAPHY: J. Ivimey, *Hist. of English Baptists*, iii. 452, 4 vols., London, 1811–30; J. A. Jones, *Bunhill Memorials*, pp. 232–236, ib. 1849; Julian, *Hymnology*, pp. 963–964; *DNB*, xlviii. 318–319.

RISHELL, CHARLES WESLEY: Methodist Episcopalian; b. near Williamsport, Pa., Mar. 9, 1850; d. at Newburyport, Mass., Sept. 27, 1908. He was educated at Drew Theological Seminary (1874–1875), Wittenberg College, Springfield, Ill. (A.B., 1876), and the University of Berlin (1889–91). In 1876 he entered the ministry of his denomination and held Ohio pastorates at Finley Church, Cincinnati (1876–78), Winton Place (1878–80), Delhi (1880–83), Avondale (1883–86), First Church, Urbana (1886–89), Asbury Church, Cincinnati (1891–1894), and Central Church, Springfield (1894–95). After 1895 he was professor of historical theology in the School of Theology of Boston University and assistant dean after 1904. In theology he was a progressive conservative. He wrote *A History of Christianity* (Chicago, 1891; based on R. Sohm's *Kirchengeschichte*); *The Higher Criticism* (1892); *The Official Recognition of Women in the Church* (1894); *The Foundations of the Christian Faith* (New York, 1899); and *The Child as God's Child* (1905).

RIST, JOHANN: German hymnist and dramatist; b. at Ottensen, a suburb of Hamburg, Mar. 8, 1607; d. at Wedel (13 m. w. of Hamburg), Aug. 31, 1667. He was educated at the universities of Rinteln and Rostock, and is also said to have studied at Leyden, Utrecht, and Leipsic, though during this latter period he seems actually to have lived at Hamburg and Ottensen. In 1633–35 he was private tutor at Heide, but in 1635 accepted the pastorate of Wedel, where he spent the remainder of his life.

Here he lived quietly, beloved by his people, and attending to their physical ills by his knowledge of medicine, until 1643, when Wedel was sacked by Torstenson in the Thirty Years' War. These melancholy events he described in his *Holsteina Klag- und Jammerlied;* another poem addressed to the emperor in the following year, when the peace envoys convened at Münster, gained him the laureateship. In 1653 he received a patent of nobility, and later the title of imperial court- and palsgrave, thus having the right to crown poets and to create doctors, licentiates, masters, and bachelors. In 1656 he founded the Elb-Schwanenorden, and also enjoyed the favor of princes, especially of Duke Christian of Mecklenburg, who created him ecclesiastical and consistorial councilor. Shortly before his death he composed his *Christliche Sterbekunst* (Hamburg, 1667) and *Alleredelste Zeitverkurzung* (1667).

Rist published his hymns, which number 659, in ten collections from 1642 to 1664. Though some of the hymns are mechanical and of inordinate length, Rist still remains, next to P. Gebhardt, both the most prolific German writer of hymns and the one who has done most for Lutheran hymnology. At the same time, he designed his compositions to serve for private worship as well as for public services. The faults of tediousness and pedantry appear prominently in his "historical poems" and his eulogies. The former he collected in his *Musa Teutonica* (1634) and *Poetischer Lustgarten.* His short lyrics are in higher vein, being conceived with true depth of feeling, though not entirely free from mythological pedantry.

As a dramatist Rist is also important. He himself states that he wrote more than thirty dramas, though only five were ever printed. These are as follows: *Irenaromachia, oder Friede und Krieg* (published under the name of his friend Stapel, 1630); *Perseus* (1634); *Das Friedewünschende Teutschland* (1647, and often); *Das friedejauchtzende Teutschland* (1653); and *Dispositio Cornuti typographici* (1654, and often). Rist likewise states that he published a tragedy entitled, *Herodes.* The *Friedejauchtzendes Teutschland* is written entirely in High German, but the other four dramas are of value for a knowledge of Low German, especially in their comic interludes, as well as for contemporary records of the period. At the same time he made a plea for pure German in his *Rettung der edlen teutschen Hauptsprache* (Hamburg, 1642). (A. FREYBE.)

Among English translations of parts of his hymns may be named "Lord Jesus Christ, the living bread," by A. T. Russell; "Praise and thanks to thee be sung," by Miss Winkworth; "O Jesu! welcome, gracious name!" by A. T. Russell; "Now God be praised, and God alone," by Miss Winkworth; and "Rise, O Salem, rise and shine," also by Miss Winkworth.

BIBLIOGRAPHY: T. Hansen, *Johann Rist und seine Zeit,* Halle, 1872; K. Goedeke and J. Tittmann, *Deutsche Dichter des 17. Jahrhunderts,* vol. xv., Leipsic, 1885 (the introduction valuable, corrects Hansen); K. T. Gaederts, in *Jahrbuch des Vereins für niederdeutsche Sprachforschung,* vii (1881), 104 sqq. Less important are H. A. Fick, *Johann Rist, der Pfarrer von Wedel,* Hamburg, 1907; and Julian, *Hymnology,* pp. 964–966.

RITSCHL, ritsh'l, **ALBRECHT BENJAMIN.**

I. **Life:** Albrecht Benjamin Ritschl, one of the foremost German Protestant theologians of the nineteenth century, was born at Berlin Mar. 25, 1822; d. at Göttingen Mar. 20, 1889. He was educated at the universities of Bonn (1839–41) and Halle (1841–43), and during this period gradually passed from Biblical supranaturalism to a critical and speculative position, to the distress of his father, Georg Karl Benjamin Ritschl (q.v.). Meanwhile he had also become interested in Hegelianism and in the study of the doctrine of the atonement, and his dissertation for the doctorate bore the title *Expositio doctrinæ Augustini de creatione mundi, peccato, gratia* (Halle, 1843). After leaving Halle, Ritschl passed the winter in Berlin and then spent almost a year with his parents at Stettin. Desiring, however, to fit himself for the career of a teacher, he studied for six months at Heidelberg in 1845, and then went to Tübingen, where he became an enthusiastic follower of Ferdinand Christian Baur (q.v.), seeking to prove that the apocryphal gospel of Marcion, mentioned by Tertullian, was the source of Luke, this theory being advanced in his *Das Evangelium Marcions und das kanonische Evangelium des Lukas* (Tübingen, 1846).

In 1846 Ritschl became privat-docent for New-Testament theology at Bonn. Here independent study led him further and further from the position of the Tübingen school, although his monograph entitled *Die Entstehung der altkatholischen Kirche* (Bonn, 1850) as yet marked no decisive break. Soon, however, he rejected his own theory concerning Luke, now maintaining the priority of Mark over the other Synoptic Gospels; and in 1856 came the open breach between him and Baur. In the following year Ritschl issued a complete revision of his history of the early Church, in which he denied the hypotheses of the Tübingen school, and maintained that the alleged delimitation between Paul and the original apostles (who were not to be considered Jewish Christians) was non-existent. He likewise held that Jewish Christianity was not a factor in the development of the early Church, but that, on the contrary, it was a specifically determined phase of gentile Christianity, which must, however, be distinguished from the system of Paul. In 1852 Ritschl, whose theological development was bringing him back to close intellectual sympathy with his father, was appointed associate professor, his work now including systematic theology, even as he had already been permitted to lecture on church history and the history of dogma since 1848.

In 1859 Ritschl was promoted to a full professorship at Bonn, but in 1864 accepted a call to the University of Göttingen. Here he lectured not only on the New Testament, but also on all branches of systematic theology, and here, after years of preliminary study and writing, he produced his great work, *Die christliche Lehre von der Rechtfertigung und Versöhnung* (3 vols., Bonn, 1870–74; 4th ed., 1895–1902; Eng. transl. of vol. i., *Critical History of the Christian Doctrine of Justification and Reconciliation*, Edinburgh, 1872, of vol. iii., *The Christian Doctrine of Justification and Reconciliation*, New York, 1900). A brief summary of the basal concepts of this work was given by Ritschl in *Ueber die christliche Volkommenheit* (Göttingen, 1874; 3d ed., 1902); his judgment of the theological tendencies of the nineteenth century was set forth in *Schleiermachers Reden über die Religion und ihre Nachwirkungen auf die evangelische Kirche Deutschlands* (Bonn, 1874); and he prepared a compend of his theological system in *Unterricht in der christlichen Religion* (1875; 6th ed., 1903). His only important later contribution to systematic theology was the *Theologie und Metaphysik* (Bonn, 1881; 3d ed., 1902). After 1876 he turned again to historical problems, as in the *Geschichte des Pietismus* (3 vols., Bonn, 1880–86).

Between 1870 and 1874 Ritschl declined a call to Strasburg and four calls to Berlin, as well as an invitation to become a member of the supreme ecclesiastical council of the State Church of Prussia. In 1876–77 and in 1886–87 he was prorector of the university, and in 1878 was elected a member of the national consistory of Hanover, although he seldom attended its sessions. After his death his briefer contributions were collected under the title of *Gesammelte Aufsätze* (Freiburg, 1893).

1. Attitude toward Dogmatics and Philosophy.

II. Theology: Although Ritschl exercised a profound influence at Bonn, the so-called "Ritschlian school" did not rise till nearly a decade after he had gone to Göttingen; and the movement was led less by his students than by those who had been impressed by his writings, especially by his study of the atonement. Ritschl himself, however, was opposed to all forms of partisanship, nor did he construct a formal system of dogmatics, the nearest approach to this being the *Unterricht* mentioned above. At the same time, in the middle portion of the third volume of his work on the atonement he found himself compelled to give an almost complete outline of dogmatics to furnish the setting for the cardinal doctrine of Protestant Christianity, though he felt himself at liberty to omit some topics and to treat others briefly. To the latter category belong the questions of general methodology and of the principles of dogmatics, which border on the sphere of philosophy. Later, however, in the *Theologie und Metaphysik* he devoted attention to the problems of epistemology as expounded by Kant and Lotze, in so far as they were pertinent to theology, although the science of epistemology always remained to him one of subordinate importance. This very attitude, however, led to many misinterpretations of his system. Since he appealed to epistemology, he was charged with making his dogmatics depend on the solution of problems involved in the theory of knowledge; and since in his later years he held that religious knowledge finds expression in inde- [illegible]dent or direct value-judgments, some of his [illegible] accused him of constructing a quasi-Feuerbachian theology. As a matter of fact, however, Ritschl's "direct or independent value-judgment" meant nothing more than that theoretical religious knowledge is differentiated from the theoretical knowledge of science simply by the fact that the former is conditioned by the inherent practical interests of the soul rather than by the impersonal endeavor to offer an objective explanation of the problem of existence. It is, therefore, entirely incorrect to charge Ritschl with the constructive use of a philosophy which he excluded on principle. His entire system of thought was centered in, and conditioned by, Christian revelation; and it applied the interpretation of a distinctively Christian religion to all the great phenomena of the soul and of the history of Christianity. It was quite characteristic, then, that, in his work on the atonement, Ritschl should proceed from the history of the development of the dogma in question back to the Biblical teachings on the theme, thus reversing the customary procedure. Maintaining that the final revelation of God was given in the person and works of Christ, and at the same time postulating the inadequacy of the mere facts recorded concerning him in the New Testament, Ritschl held that the foundation of theological doctrines must be sought in the primal consciousness of the Christian community, the sole source here being the New Testament.

2. Theological Position and Biblical Theory.

While the position just outlined implies that Ritschl was essentially a Biblicist, his attitude was materially conditioned by the ecclesiastical character which he ascribed to dogmatics. Like Luther, moreover, he held that the Bible is the word of God only in so far as it emphasizes Christ, so that, while all ordinances and beliefs of primitive Christianity are not binding on Christian theology and on the Christian Church, every doctrine of the salvation won through Christ must be based in substance on the Bible. In addition, he maintained that the Pauline doctrine of justification by faith was binding on theology; and, unlike most modern theologians, who stress the new and distinctive character of New-Testament concepts, he maintained that, unless there is direct proof to the contrary, the Biblical writers must be supposed to be capable of expressing their thoughts in orderly and methodical fashion. This theory, however, presupposed an essentially modern type of interpretation, which excluded sympathy with the ancient modes of thought and feeling that are evidently present in the New Testament; and Ritschl's Biblical theology, developed early in his career and changed but little in the course of his life, represents the point of view of the middle of the nineteenth century, and has been in great part superseded by the results of the historical studies of primitive Christianity. In addition to all this, Ritschl came to appeal more and more to the ideal of life of the Reformers and to the creeds of Lutheranism, ascribing more importance to the latter than to the symbols of the early Church, which he valued only in so far as they maintained religious positions, especially the divinity of Christ. The authority of the Protestant concept of religion consisted, in his opinion, in its maintenance of the doctrine of justification by faith, lacking in the Eastern Church, but established in the West by Augustine and defended by the medieval representatives of classical Roman Catholicism. On the other hand, this very position led him to depreciate the work of the "Reformers before the Reformation" and of the mediating theology. Like the Reformers, Ritschl made justification and atonement the cardinal doctrines of Christianity, and this fact is the key to his chief theological teachings. So strongly, moreover, did he consider that the sole basis for a knowledge of God is in the divine revelation in the works and person of Christ, that he rejected all natural theology and ignored its proofs for God's existence. Since, however, such an estimate of Christ presupposes Christian belief, and since this belief can arise in the Christian community only through experience of justification and atonement, religious comprehension of God and Christ necessarily has as its sole foundation the personal faith which arises through justification. In accordance with this position, he reversed the usual method, and placed the subjective elements of Christianity first, disregarding the ontology of the object of faith as a basis of a religiously conditioned theological knowledge. It thus becomes clear that Ritschl's concept of the Bible was not one of a mere external standard, but rather implied that the revelation of God in Christ, in so far as drawn from the New Testament, possesses the character of revelation only for a faith which comprehends and recognizes it as such.

Faith, according to Ritschl, is not a mere passive service of man, but an active trust in God and divine providence, directly displayed in humility, patience, and prayer, and influencing the development of the moral life. The reconciliation of this religious and ethical independence of the Christian with his sense of absolute dependence on God was the cardinal problem of Ritschl's theory of justification and atonement. To solve the difficulty Ritschl advanced the theory that the sinner who becomes a believer is first passively placed by God in a state of justification, justification in turn being practically realized in the atonement which perfects it, and the atonement constituting the basis of Christian activity. Justification, which is synonymous with forgiveness of sins, frees the sinner from the guilt that separates him from God; the mistrust of God arising from consciousness of sin vanishes before the promise of divine grace; and the old active opposition to the divine will gives place to an equally active obedience to the commandments of God. Though good works may be imperfect even when the will of man has been renewed, yet, on the whole, the exercise of trust, humility, patience, and prayer, and the fulfilment of moral requirements in the spirit of Christian love, constitute what was understood and required by the New Testament and by the Reformers as Christian perfection, though this must be understood qualitatively, not quantitatively. Justification and atonement lay the foundation for the transformed sinner's new status as a child of God; but at the same time justification, which finds its practical realization in the atonement, is a creative act of the divine will, conditioned by no human merits or circumstances, but due to the fact that the sinner who comes to believe is held by God to be righteous despite his sin, so that the Father takes the initiative by establishing religious fellowship between himself and man, the basis of this being, not the sinner, but the work of Christ and its efficacy.

3. Faith's Relation to Justification and Atonement.

Like Luther, Ritschl made the concept of the religious community bear directly upon his theory of justification, this religious community in question connoting, not the Church as a visible organization, but the complex of all justified believers and the permanent result of its lord and founder, Christ, whose influence it ever preserves and perpetuates. The agency which produces belief in justification in the individual, and thus leads to regeneration and divine sonship, is preaching; and through this proclamation of the word of God or of the Gospel the religious community comes to be the mother of the individual believers. Thus Ritschl was able to avoid the sectarian theory of the Church as a voluntary association of individual believers; and he could, on the contrary, maintain that the Church traces her origin back to her founder Christ, and that her members receive from a preexisting organization those powers of the Holy Ghost within her which call forth their faith and influence their subsequent lives. To establish the genetic bond between individual believers within the Church and Christ as its head, Ritschl maintained that the Church, which is not subject to the limitations of empiricism or time, is an organic whole which, though visibly existing only in its parts, logically posits the preexistence of the whole. Accordingly, the Church was the object of divine love before the individuals who belong to it. At the same time, the experience of justification and atonement is individual, not collective; especially as the consciousness of guilt and the mistrust of God, which are removed by justification, are considered by him to be individual defects. These empirical personal experiences, however, do not conflict with the logical construction of the ideal relation of the Church to Christ (who founded it for the salvation of its individual members) and God (who chose it as the body of all future believers and as the means for the realization of his kingdom on earth). Only thus could he establish the priority of justification, as a supratemporal creative act of God, to regeneration, as a personal experience of the believer.

4. Theory of the Church.

In conformity with this theory of the Church Ritschl construed the work of Christ under the two aspects of royal prophet and royal priest, the royalty of both phases being derived from the spiritual kingship exercised by Christ throughout his life. The prophetic office of Christ is exercised from God to man, the priestly from man to God. In the priestly function, which logically presupposes the achievement of his prophetic mission, is found the essential reason why, for Christ's sake, God grants regeneration to sinners—the fact that

5. The Work of Christ.

through faith they are united with Christ as members of his Church. Christ does not, however, represent the believer in a juristic sense which separates his righteousness from himself to impute it to the believer, but in an inclusive sense, so that, without being himself dispensed from the obligation of righteousness, the believer has imputed to him the relation of Christ to the love of God. From this estimate of the work of Christ Ritschl sought to deduce his view of the person of Christ. He taught an ideal preexistence of Christ as the fulfiller of the divine plan of salvation in a world which, like mankind, had been created for this very end; and although the earthly Christ lacks the traits of divine omnipotence, omniscience, and omnipresence, he is recognized and honored as God by the faithful.

Ritschl's Christology forms the transition to his doctrine of God, who must be known not from metaphysical speculations of natural religion or theology but solely in religious faith from the works and the person of Christ. Accordingly, God can be conceived only as the Father, whose essence is love, the quality which all other divine qualities serve merely to prove. Only those who sin against the Holy Ghost by obstinately opposing the good which God desires for them are doomed to final destruction. All others are objects of the fatherly training of God, so that the punishments which he visits upon them are intended solely for their correction and religious progress. All evil, however, is not to be considered divine punishment of sin, for the concept of evil is not theological and is subjectively conditioned in each specific case. The Christian must, through his faith in divine providence, transform into good the evils which beset him, regarding them as means whereby God advances what is really best for him. The true punishment of sin is guilt, which is removed by justification, or the forgiveness of sins. From the divine point of view sin is ignorance, but from the human point of view it is guilt and rebellion against God. The doctrine of original sin is, therefore, to be rejected for the theory of a kingdom of sin which impedes the freedom of the individual toward good, and which is strengthened by the evil-doing of each one. It is impossible to prove the general necessity of sin, but its empirical probability is self-evident. The kingdom of sin is, however, opposed by the kingdom of God, which is distinguished from the Church in that it promotes the moral welfare of the believer, while the Church furthers his capacity for worship. From this point of view Ritschl draws an antithesis between the ethical duties of the Church (prayer, profession of faith, and teaching) and her religious functions (preaching and the sacraments), the visible organization of the Church being but a means to these ends. In this the concept of the kingdom of God has no immediate part, but it enters vitally into Ritschl's interpretation of the Christian ideal of life, which embraces, on the one hand, all Christian duties and virtues, and, on the other, the obligation to mutual love, to be manifested in the conscientious discharge of the moral calling.

6. Doctrine of God and Sin.

(O. Ritschl.)

Bibliography: The one biography is by O. Ritschl, 2 vols., Freiburg, 1892–96. On the theology consult: E. Luthardt, in *Zeitschrift für kirchliche Wissenschaft und Leben*, 1881, pp. 617–643; H. Weiss, in *TSK*, 1881, pp. 377–417; G. A. Fricke, *Metaphysik und Dogmatik in ihren gegenseitigen Verhältnisse, unter besond. Beziehung auf die Ritschl'sche Theologie*, Leipsic, 1882; L. Haug, *Darstellung und Beurtheilung der Ritschl'schen Theologie*, Ludwigsburg, 1885; O. Flügel, *A. Ritschl's philosophische Ansichten*, Langensalza, 1886; M. Reischle, *Ein Wort zur Kontroverse über die Mystik in der Theologie*, Freiburg, 1886; J. Thikötter, *Darstellung und Beurtheilung der Theologie Albrecht Ritschls*, 2d ed., Bonn, 1887; F. H. R. Frank, *Ueber die kirchliche Bedeutung der Theologie Albrecht Ritschls*, Leipsic, 1888; T. Häring, *Zu Ritschl's Versöhnungslehre*, Zurich, 1888; F. Lichtenberger, *German Theology in the 19th Century*, Edinburgh, 1889; E. Bertrand, *Une Nouvelle Conception de la rédemption. La doctrine . . . dans le système théologique de Ritschl*, Paris, 1891; O. Pfleiderer, *Die Ritschl'sche Theologie kritisch beleuchtet*, Brunswick, 1891; H. Schoen, *Les Origines historiques de la théologie de Ritschl*, Paris, 1893; R. Favre, *Les Principes philosophiques de la théologie de Ritschl*, ib. 1894; G. Mielke, *Das System Albrecht Ritschls*, Bonn, 1894; G. Ecke, *Die theologische Schule A. Ritschls und die evangelische Kirche der Gegenwart*, 2 vols., Berlin, 1897–1904; R. Wegener, *Albrecht Ritschls Idee des Reiches Gottes im Licht der Geschichte*, Leipsic, 1897; A. E. Garvie, *The Ritschlian Theology*, Edinburgh, 1899; J. Wendland, *Albrecht Ritschl und seine Schüler*, Berlin, 1899; F. Nippold, *Handbuch der neuesten Theologie*, iii. 439 sqq., ib. 1901; A. T. Swing, *The Theology of Albert Ritschl*, New York, 1901; F. Kattenbusch, *Von Schleiermacher zu Ritschl*, 3d ed., Giessen, 1903; C. von Kügelgen, *Grundriss der Ritschl'schen Dogmatik*, 2d ed., Göttingen, 1903; J. Orr, *Ritschlianism: Exposition and critical Essays*, London, 1903; W Herrmann, *Faith and Morals*, London and New York, 1904; C. Stange, *Der dogmatische Ertrag der Ritschl'schen Theologie nach Julius Kaftan*, Leipsic, 1906; C. Fabricius, *Die Entwicklung in Albrecht Ritschls Theologie von 1874 bis 1889 nach Werke dargestellt und beurteilt*, Tübingen, 1909; J. K. Mozley, *Ritschlianism: An Essay*, London, 1909; and C. Fabricius, *Die Entwicklung in A. Ritschls Theologie, 1874–89*, Tübingen, 1909; E. A. Edghill, *Faith and Fact; a Study of Ritschlianism*, London and New York, 1910. An important periodical literature is indicated in Richardson, *Encyclopaedia*, pp. 939–940.

RITSCHL, GEORG KARL BENJAMIN: German Lutheran, father of the preceding; b. at Erfurt Nov. 1, 1783; d. at Berlin June 18, 1858. He was educated at the universities of Erfurt (1799–1801) and Jena (1801–02), where he came under rationalistic influences, though later he returned to positive Christianity. In 1804 he settled in Berlin as a private tutor, also acting as an instructor at the Gymnasium zum grauen Kloster, where he gradually rose to be subrector. He also preached after 1807, and in 1810 was chosen third pastor of St. Mary's, Berlin, where his simple and direct style of preaching, based on the Bible only, made a deep impression on all classes. On the reestablishment of the consistories in the Prussian provinces in 1816, Ritschl was appointed assessor for Brandenburg, and in the following year was made a councilor. Here his duties were practically restricted to the examination of theological candidates, but in 1818 he collaborated in the preparation of the Berlin hymnal which appeared in 1829. In 1827 he was appointed bishop of the Evangelical Church, general superintendent of Pomerania, director of the consistory, and first preacher at the castle church of Stettin. These positions he filled for many years, his service being interrupted only in 1829–30, when he was sent to St. Petersburg to collaborate on the agenda for the Russian Lutherans which was published in 1832. As general superintendent Ritschl had to encounter much less opposition than as a member of the consistory, although his coming had been the signal for a general improvement in religious and ecclesiastical conditions throughout Pomerania. After 1847 he had new problems to confront, for while he was in sympathy with the introduction of the union into his province, the measure had resulted in the separatistic movement of Old Lutheranism (see LUTHERANS, II.), the difficulty being complicated by the revival sermons of individual preachers. The attempt to obviate schism brought about the counter-evil of Neo-Lutheranism, which determinedly resisted union, especially after 1848. These troubles embittered the closing years of Ritschl's administration, despite his marked success as general superintendent. Feeling himself unable to cope, by reason of his age, with the new questions which were now arising, he resigned his offices in 1852 and retired to Berlin, and there he passed the remainder of his life. In 1855 he was made an honorary member of the supreme ecclesiastical council, where his ripe experience proved to be of the greatest value. (O. RITSCHL.)

BIBLIOGRAPHY: O. Ritschl, *Albrecht Ritschls Leben*, chaps. i.-ix. et passim, 2 vols., Freiburg, 1892-96; idem, *Die Sendung des Bischofs Ritschl nach Petersburg im Jahre 1829*, Bonn, 1890; H. Dalton, *Zur Geschichte der evangelischen Kirche in Russland*, pp. 1-35, Leipsic, 1893.

RITSCHL, OTTO KARL ALBRECHT: German Protestant; b. at Bonn June 26, 1860. He was educated at the universities of Göttingen, Bonn, and Giessen from 1878 to 1884 (lic. theol., Halle, 1885), and in 1885 became privat-docent for church history at the University of Halle. Four years later he was called to Kiel as associate professor, whence he went, in 1894, to Bonn in a similar capacity, where he became full professor of systematic theology in 1897. He has written: *De epistulis Cyprianicis* (Halle, 1885); *Cyprian von Karthago und die Verfassung der Kirche* (Göttingen, 1885); *Schleiermachers Stellung zum Christentum in seinen Reden über die Religion* (Gotha, 1888); *Das christliche Lebensideal in Luthers Auffassung* (Halle, 1889); *Albrecht Ritschls Leben* (2 vols., Freiburg, 1892-96); *Ueber Werturteile* (1895); *Nietzsches Welt- und Lebensanschauung in ihrer Entstehung und Entwicklung* (1897); *Die Causalbetrachtung in der Geisteswissenschaft* (Bonn, 1901); *Wissenschaftliche Ethik und moralische Gesetzgebung* (Tübingen, 1903); *Die freie Wissenschaft und der Idealismus auf den deutschen Universitäten* (Bonn, 1905); *System und systematische Methode in der Geschichte des wissenschaftlichen Sprachgebrauchs und der philosophischen Methodologie* (1906); and *Dogmengeschichte des Protestantismus*, vol. i., *Prolegomena, Biblicismus und Traditionalismus in der altprotestantischen Theologie* (Leipsic, 1908).

RITTER, ERASMUS: Reformer; d. at Bern Aug. 1, 1546. The place and date of his birth, like the details of his education, are unknown. He had, however, acquired distinction as a preacher at Rottweil, and in 1523 was invited to Schaffhausen to counteract the influence of the Franciscan Sebastian Hofmeister (q.v.), whom Zwingli had converted to Reformed doctrines. Though received with great honor and made preacher at the Benedictine abbey of All Saints, he met with no success, and becoming convinced that he must meet Hofmeister on his own ground, he began the studies which resulted in his own conversion to Protestantism. This remarkable change conspicuously advanced the Protestant cause, and Ritter and Hofmeister were delegated by the council to accompany the Baden deputation in 1526 and ably seconded Œcolampadius. In 1524, moreover, Michael Eggenstorfer, the last abbot of All Saints, changed the abbey into a provostship and applied its revenues to education and charity, as well as to the payment of the clergy.

In 1525, however, conditions changed. In consequence of a petty insurrection, Hofmeister was dismissed, and his place was taken by the Roman Catholic Gallus Steiger. The position of Ritter now became more difficult. Though the nascent Reformation was not forcibly suppressed, extreme caution became necessary. Nevertheless, the friends of Ritter, who was ably counseled by Zwingli, steadily increased in the great council, and they were aided by the council of Zurich. With the triumph of Protestantism in Bern (1528) and Basel (1529), all opposition vanished, and in 1529 an embassy from Zurich, Bern, Basel, and St. Gall, coming to Schaffhausen at Ritter's instigation, was cordially welcomed, so that on Sept. 29 both councils unanimously voted to accept the Reformation. With the abolition of the mass celibacy was renounced, and within the year Ritter had married an ex-nun, the sister of Michael Eggenstorfer.

The years following were unfavorable to the furtherance of the work. Ritter was involved in futile controversies with the Anabaptists, and, as an adherent of Zwingli's views, he was in open conflict with his colleague, Benedikt Burgauer of St. Gall, who was as pronouncedly Lutheran in his eucharistic doctrines. The struggle between the two dragged on, nor could either the appeal of Œcolampadius to Burgauer or the envoys from Zurich, Bern, and Basel to the council produce any lasting peace. Equally futile was the appointment of a committee of three in Dec., 1530, to hear both sides, for though Burgauer expressed himself as in error, and though both he and Ritter signed a formula drawn up by Butzer and agreed to keep peace, Burgauer's word was quickly broken. Ritter desired to found a theological school and advised the council to secure Leo Jud as instructor, but the appointment was never made, probably because Jud was from the suspected city of Zurich. Burgauer and Ritter were accordingly obliged, despite their differences, to combine in their Biblical lectures for the instruction of the young, Ritter interpreting the Old Testament, and Burgauer the New.

In view of the complications arising from the retention of certain usages of the old faith, and in consideration of the decay of moral discipline, the clergy, in 1532, presented to the council a memorial, probably drawn up by Ritter, urging the necessity of action. Burgauer alone refused to sign the memorial, which was without result. In the following year, with the arrival of new assistance in the person of Beat Gerung, the clergy of Schaffhausen determined to introduce a uniform liturgy, and their unanimous outline for such a liturgy was approved by the council. Burgauer now objected to some unessential details and refused to yield, even when urged by Bullinger and Blaurer. The clergy, wearied by his obstinacy, finally requested the council to remove him from his position; and the council, after some hesitation, acquiesced. Burgauer's partisans, in their turn, insisted on Ritter's dismissal, and on Whitsunday, 1536, both received their congé.

On May 8, 1536, Ritter was called to Bern, where he soon became chief dean. Yet here again he was involved in controversy. The rigid Zwinglianism which had formerly prevailed in Bern had been disturbed by the call to the city of two advocates of the union urged by Butser, Peter Kuns, and Sebastian Meyer. The unionistic faction was now headed by Kuns and the Zwinglians by Kaspar Megander (q.v.). In the following year, however, Megander left Bern on account of certain changes made without his knowledge by Butser in a catechism which he had been commissioned by the council to frame, Butser seeing in the original draft obstacles to the union between the Lutherans and the Reformed. Ritter, having taken no active part in the affair, felt able to obey the command of the council to subscribe to the catechism under pain of dismissal, but Megander, deeply offended by the successful opposition of Butser, left Bern for Zurich, soon followed by his friend Johannes Müller (Rhellicanus). The compliance of Ritter, though sincere, especially in view of the needs of the church at Bern, was disapproved by his partisans; and clerical dissatisfaction with the action and attitude of the council led to violent demonstrations. At this crisis Ritter labored successfully to secure peace, and at the same time regained the confidence he had forfeited.

In Mar., 1538, Ritter and Kuns were delegates to the Synod at Lausanne, where the former formed ties of friendship with Calvin, Farel, and Viret. He was the only one of the Bernese clergy to welcome the exiles from Geneva, later accompanying them to Zurich, where their case was to be considered in May; and when the council of Bern sent a delegation to Geneva to bring the exiles back, Ritter was one of the number at the special request of Calvin.

The places of Megander and Rhellicanus at Bern were filled by the unionistic Thomas Grynæus and Simon Sulzer, but Ritter, though now the only Zwinglian among the city clergy, rapidly regained his wonted sure footing, especially as he was supported by the majority of the dissatisfied clergy of the countryside, and until his death he held his position, unwearied in his polemics.

(G. Kirchhofer.)

Bibliography: J. Strickler, *Aktensammlung zur schweizerischen Reformationsgeschichte*, Zurich, 1878–84; M. Kirchhofer, *Sebastian Hofmeister*, ib. 1809; idem, *Schaffhauserische Jahrbücher 1519–29*, Frauenfeld, 1838; C. B. Hundeshagen, *Die Konflikte des Zwinglianismus, Luthertums und Calvinismus in der bernischen Landeskirche 1532–58*, Bern, 1842; J. J. Mezger, *Geschichte der deutschen Bibelübersetzungen in der schweizerisch-reformierten Kirche*, pp. 169 sqq., Basel, 1876; K. Schweizer, in *Theologische Zeitschrift aus der Schweiz*, 1891; E. Blösch, *Geschichte der schweizerisch-reformierten Kirche*, vol. i., Bern, 1898.

RITTER, KARL: German geographer; b. at Quedlinburg (31 m. s.w. of Magdeburg) Aug. 7, 1779; d. at Berlin Sept. 28, 1859. He received his education at Halle; served as private tutor; became professor of history in the Gymnasium at Frankfort, 1819; and was appointed professor of geography in the University of Berlin in 1820, and gave a new and powerful impulse to that branch of study. Those of his works which are of interest for the student of the Bible are *Der Jordan und die Beschiffung des Todten Meeres* (Berlin, 1850); *Ein Blick auf Palästina* (Berlin, 1852); and *Die Erdkunde* in nineteen parts (1822–59; in part translated by W. L. Gage and entitled *The Comparative Geography of Palestine and the Sinaitic Peninsula*, 4 vols., Edinburgh, 1866).

Bibliography: W. L. Gage, *The Life of Carl Ritter*, 1867; A. Guyot, *Carl Ritter*, Princeton, N. J., 1860; G. Kramer, *Carl Ritter, Ein Lebensbild*, Halle, 1875; F. Marthe, *Was bedeutet Carl Ritter für die Geographie?* Berlin, 1880; F. Ratzel, *Beitrag zu K. Ritters 100-jährigen Geburtstage*, in *Kleine Schriften*, vol. i., Munich, 1906.

RITUAL: A form of worship or other solemn service, prescribed and established by law, precept, or custom, in contrast with a more or less extemporaneous mode of worship that depends on the discretion of the leader or the impulse of the worshipers. Also the office-book of a ritualistic body. See Ritualism.

RITUAL-EXAMINATION (*Gebetsverhör*). From the time when the Christian Church first developed into an objective organized institution, certain proofs of a knowledge of the faith have been exacted from those accepted into its membership. The Church has endeavored to guard, confirm, and cherish the Christian life of its members, by preaching, instruction, and the other instrumentalities of the care of souls, but also by formal tests, and admission to its honors and privileges, and even participation in the sacraments have been conditioned upon the result of such examination. Thus during the Middle Ages sponsors had to show that they knew at least the creed and the Lord's Prayer. People gathered for confession before the Holy Communion were examined, and even bride and bridegroom had to undergo a test (*Brautexamen;* see Wedding Customs). The Protestant church rituals of the second half of the sixteenth century prescribe a public examination for all young people and servants, which was in no way identical with the catechetical tests for confirmation. The Pomeranian church ritual of 1593 appointed one Sunday afternoon in each quarter for this purpose. Similar orders and regulations are contained in the Brandenburg ecclesiastical order (1572) and in that of the electorate of Saxony (1580). The Thirty Years' War abolished these catechetical institutions, and it was not easy to restore them after the return of peace. But with the advent of Pietism (q.v.) under Spener they were revived.

These catechetical institutions underwent a peculiar development in Sweden and East Prussia. The Swedish ecclesiastical order of 1686 appointed examinations on a large scale. There was (1) an examination on the sermon on Sundays when the Holy Communion was not celebrated; (2) of persons engaged to be married, covering the smaller catechism of Luther; (3) church examinations consisting of questions on the catechism and in the season of Lent on the passion of Christ; (4) in the home, in which the entire family participated, and lasting for from five to eight hours. The subject was usually the catechism, some passages of the Bible, or the conduct of the people present. At the end a simple meal was served. These home-examinations were highly appreciated by the peasants, while in the cities they were not always well attended, the well-to-do especially keeping aloof. In East Prussia the development of catechetical examination underwent several phases. The first is characterized by the order of Margrave Albert (1543), according to which it was the duty of every pastor to examine and instruct all his parishioners in every place of his parish at least once a quarter. The order of 1633 marks a second phase according to which the examination was to take place once a year in the home of the burgomaster or village mayor. In the course of time the institution was frequently dropped altogether or maintained itself only sporadically. After the middle of the nineteenth century these examinations again came into vogue. The pastor visited once a year, usually in the fall, every village and hamlet of his parish. The parishioners provided for his conveyance and paid other expenses. Each family had the conference held in the home in turn and provided for a common meal. The pastor also usually received a contribution in money and products of the field. Later the people began to refuse to provide the pastor with the facilities for travel, and the conferences sometimes degenerated into carousals. So they have in large part taken the form of church services in places where there is no church. (H. JACOBY.)

BIBLIOGRAPHY: H. F. Jakobson, in *Deutsche Zeitschrift für christliche Wissenschaft und christliches Leben*, vi (1855), nos. 43–45; idem, *Das evangelische Kirchenrecht des preussischen Staates*, ii. 508, Halle, 1866.

RITUALE ROMANUM: A Roman Catholic liturgical book containing the prayers and forms for the administration of the sacraments, together with directions for pastoral care, compiled for the special assistance of parish priests. Books of this type were drawn up as early as the twelfth century, primarily for the monasteries, the secular clergy having none until the fourteenth century. There were at first no diocesan ritualia, but each parish priest might compile his own according to local usage. A book of the type in question was called *Manuale* in the thirteenth century, *Rituale* or *Liber benedictionum* in the fourteenth, and *Agenda*, *Liber obsequiorum*, *Parochiale*, *Pastorale*, etc., in the fifteenth. The name Rituale, however, came into general use through the introduction of the *Rituale Romanum*, when the attempt was made to obviate the wide divergencies of local usages and at least to secure harmony in each diocese. It was not, however, until the Council of Trent that real headway was made in securing liturgical uniformity; and even then, though the Roman breviary, missal, pontifical, and ceremonial were officially sanctioned, there was no single rituale. Paul V. (1605–21), however, appointed a committee of cardinals who, on the basis of the rituale of Cardinal Sanctorio (1584), the *Sacerdotale Romanum* of the Dominican Castellani (1537), and the *Sacerdotale* of the Lateran canon Samarino (1579), drew up the *Rituale Romanum*, which was officially confirmed by the constitution *Apostolicæ sedis* of Paul V. (June 17, 1614). So great, however, was the tenacity of local usages that this rituale, based on the Roman use, made slow progress, though it ultimately prevailed.

The *Rituale Romanum* of Paul V. was revised in 1752 by Benedict XIV., who added two formularies for the papal blessing, and Leo XIII. had a definite edition prepared (Regensburg, 1884). It is divided into ten "titles," subdivided into chapters. The first title contains general directions for the administration of the sacraments; the second treats of baptism; the third of penance; the fourth of the Eucharist (the liturgy for which is given in the missal); the fifth of extreme unction and all pastoral care of the sick and dying; the sixth of burial; the seventh of marriage and churching; the eighth of the various benedictions; the ninth of processions; and the tenth of exorcism, and the keeping of parish records; the whole being concluded by an appendix containing instructions for missionaries with various benedictions. (P. DREWS.)

BIBLIOGRAPHY: On ritualia in general consult A. Franz, *Das Rituale von St. Florian aus dem 12. Jahrhundert*, pp. 3–12, Freiburg, 1904 (contains useful bibliography). On the Roman Rituale consult: G. Catalani, *Rituale Romanum . . . perpetuis commentariis exornatum*, Rome, 1757; H. Baruffaldi, *Ad rituale Romanum commentarii*, Venice, 1731; V. Thalhofer, *Handbuch der katholischen Liturgik*, ed. A. Ebner, i. 1, pp. 51–52, 59–60, Freiburg, 1894; *KL*, x. 1217–18.

RITUALISM, ANGLICAN.

Origin in Tractarianism (§ 1).
Logical Character of Transition (§ 2).
Parallel Movements (§ 3).
Legal Questions and the Source (§ 4).
Decision Favorable to Ritualism (§ 5).
Decision Adverse to Ritualism (§ 6).
Attempts to Relieve the Stress (§ 7).
The Work of the Commission (§ 8).
The Archbishop's Decision (§ 9).
Definitive Settlement not yet Reached (§ 10).
The New Commission's Report (§ 11).
Results; Present Status (§ 12).

"Ritualism" is used as a popular catchword to describe the second stage of that movement in the English Church which in its earlier condition had been named Tractarianism (q.v.). The name first appears, probably, in connection with the riots in London at St. George's-in-the-East in 1859 (cf. quotation from *East London Observer* of May, 1859, in Bryan King, *Sacrilege and its Encouragement . . . a Letter . . . to the Lord Bishop of London*, London, 1860).

1. Origin in Tractarianism.

The revival of interest in Roman dogma, effected by the Oxford writers of the *Tracts for the Times*, was naturally succeeded by a revival of interest in Roman observances. This practical revival carried the movement into novel circumstances and situations; for the earlier detection and exhibition of that sacerdotal structure of the church which had been secured to it by struggles of the Elizabethan divines, was carried on, of necessity, in the intellectual, academic region. The claim asserted had, first, to make good its doctrinal status: it had to begin by working its way into the mind and the imagination. The Tractarian writers recognized this necessary order; they anxiously held aloof from precipitating those effects, which they, nevertheless, distinctly anticipated from this teaching. "We the old Tractarians," wrote Dr. Pusey in the *Daily Express*, May 21, 1877, "deliberately abstained from innovating in externals." "We understood the 'Ornaments Rubric' in its most obvious meaning,—that certain ornaments were to be used which were used in the second year of King Edward VI.; we were fully conscious that we were disobeying it; but we were employed in teaching the faith to a forgetful generation, and we thought it injurious to distract men's minds by questions about externals. We left it for the church to revive" (Letter of Dr. Pusey to English Church Union). Also, Letter to the *Times*, Mar. 28, 1874: "There was a contemporary movement for a very moderate ritual in a London congregation. We (the Tractarians) were united with it in friendship, but the movements were unconnected."

As soon as their teaching had secured believers, it set itself to apply its principles in action; and this active application of recovered belief in a sacerdotal church inevitably took the form of recovering and reasserting that liturgical structure which still underlay the Book of Common Prayer. The movement, in making this fresh effort, passed from the study to the street; it became practical, missionary, evangelistic. It insisted that its work upon the masses, in their dreary poverty, demanded the bright attraction and relief of outward ornament and the effective teaching of the eye. This change from the university to the town was signalized by the establishment of, e.g., St. Saviour's, Leeds (to which the Tractarian leaders lent all their authority), and of the Margaret Street Chapel, under F. Oakeley, a devoted companion of J. H. Newman.

2. Logical Character of Transition.

The transition to ritual was not only a practical expediency, it was also the logical outcome of the new position; for the doctrinal revival lay in its emphatic assertion of the conception of mediation, of mediatorial offering. This mediation was, it taught, effected by the taking of flesh; i.e., of the outward to become the offering, the instrument of worship. The body of the Lord was the one acceptable offering, sanctified by the Spirit; and in and through that mediatorial body all human nature won its right to sanctification, to holy use. The spirit needs, according to this teaching, an outward expression to symbolize its inward devotion. Its natural mode of approach to God is through sacramental signs; and the use of special sacraments justifies, of necessity, the general use of visible symbols. If grace comes through outward pledges, then devotion will obviously be right in using for its realization forms and signs and gestures; love will be right in showing itself through beauty; and prayer and praise will instinctively resort to ceremonial.

Nor was the pressure toward ritual merely doctrinal. The double movement in the church had its parallel in the secular world. The spiritual revival of Wordsworth had its reflex in the emotional revival of Walter Scott. The set of things was running counter to Puritan bareness. The force and reality of imagination in the shaping of life's interests were recognized with the glad welcome of a recovered joy. A touch of kindliness repeopled the earth with fancies and suggestions, and visions and dreams. This world was no longer a naked factory, housing the machinery of a precise and unyielding dogma; nor was it the bare and square hall in which reason lectured on the perils of a morbid enthusiasm; it was a garden once more, rich with juicy life, and warm with color. This literary warmth mixed itself in with the doctrinal movement toward the enrichment of the churches. The emotions were making new demands upon outward things; they required more satisfaction. They had been taught by the novelists to turn to the past, whether of cavaliers with plumes and chivalry, or of the Middle Ages with wild castles and belted knights, and praying monks and cloistered nuns. All this world of strange mystery and artistic charm had become alive again to them, and the revival made them discontented with the prosy flatness of common life. The churches were responding to a real and wide need when they offered a refuge and a relief to the distressed imagination. Everywhere began the Gothic revival. The restoration of the disgraced and destitute parish churches, which had become practically necessary, was taken up by men full of admiration for the architecture which had first built them. They were passionately set on bringing them back as far as possible into their original condition. The architects thus were, indirectly, ardent workers on the side of the ecclesiastical revival. They eagerly studied liturgical correctness in restoring the beauty of the chancels, in placing the altar at its proper height and distance, in arranging the screen and the stalls, the altar-rails and credence-table. This combination of ecclesiastical and architectural sentiment was greatly furthered by the Cambridge Ecclesiological Society, which did much to foster antiquarian exactness, and to promote active efforts at restoration (A. J. B. Hope, *Worship in the Church of England*, London, 1874). This architectural movement, which dated its earliest impulses from J. H. Newman's church, built at Littlemore amid much ferment and anxiety, culminated in the vast achievements of Gilbert Scott and George Street, whose handiwork has been left in restored churches throughout the length and breadth of England. [Worthy of mention here is the new Roman Catholic cathedral of London, consecrated 1910. Even though it does not belong to the Anglicans, it emanates from the same source as that named in the text and the aim was to make it primitive Byzantine in style.] This general restoration of order and fairness into the public services, which ran level with the renewal of church fabrics, roused much popular hostility, which made itself known in riotous disturbances, chiefly directed against the use of the surplice in the pulpit, following a direction for its use given in a charge by Bishop Blomfield in 1842.

3. Parallel Movements.

4. Legal Questions, and the Source.

But just as the artistic movement deepened from the external ornamentation of the Waverley novels into the impassioned mysticism of Dante Gabriel Rossetti and the pre-Raffaelite brothers, so the architectural revival deepened into the symbolism of a more rapt sacramentalism. This it was which produced the historical crisis; and this crisis became yet more critical by forcing into sharp antagonism the civil and ecclesiastical jurisdictions which were called upon to deal with the renovating ministers. The story of the movements turns around the various legal judgments given to determine the sense of the "Ornaments Rubric," i.e., the rubric inserted, in its first form, into the Prayer-Book of Elizabeth, and reinserted, in a slightly changed form, in the Prayer-Book of the Restoration, prescribing the ornaments of the minister and of the chancel during all offices (see ORNAMENTS). The aim of the Elizabethan divines had been to secure the main work of the Reformation, and yet to protect the liturgy from the "loose and licentious handling" of the more eager of the Marian exiles. They had therefore accepted, with some important alterations, the second of the two Prayer-Books of Edward VI. as the standard of the Reformed services; but, owing to the strong pressure of the queen, they refused to adopt it also as the standard of the ornaments; and for this they went back to an earlier date, the second year of King Edward VI., when much ritual remained which the first Prayer-Book of Edward VI. had accepted, but which the second book had rejected. There is no doubt that this included and intended chasubles and copes, albs and tunicles (see VESTMENTS AND INSIGNIA, ECCLESIASTICAL), with other details of altar furniture. The question that arose was as to how far this rubric, when reenacted in the Act of Uniformity (see UNIFORMITY, ACTS OF), was intended by the divines of the Restoration to retain its full original sense. In its earlier form it was prescribed "until the queen should take further order." Was that "further order" ever taken; and, if so, does the later condition of the rubric, in omitting any reference to this "further order," assume that order, or ignore it? If it ignored it, why was it never acted upon? For certainly these ornaments have never been in full use. But, if it assumed it, how was it possible not to define what the "order" was, or to prescribe still the second year of Edward VI. as the standard, without a hint of any qualification? Around this main issue a swarm of complicated historical, legal, and liturgical arguments arose; and who was to decide among them? Here started up a new difficulty.

The juridical relations between Church and State were the result of a long and intricate history, which at the Reformation had finally assumed this general form. The old machinery of ecclesiastical courts remained entire—consisting of the bishop's courts of first instance, in which the bishop's chancellor adjudicated; and the archbishop's court of appeal, in which the dean of arches gave judgment, as the embodiment of the archbishop. But from this, again, there was to be an appeal to the king; and for hearing such appeals a composite court had been erected by Henry VIII., the court of delegates, the exact jurisdiction of which had never been clearly defined. This had continued, rarely used, dimly considered, until, without anybody's notice, a great legal reform, carried out by Lord Brougham, was discovered to have transferred, without intending it, all the power of this court of delegates to a certain committee of privy council, composed and defined for other general purposes. When suddenly there was need of a final adjudication on anxious and agitating spiritual questions, it was this committee of privy council which the rival parties found themselves facing. It dealt with the question of baptism, in the case of George Cornelius Gorham (see GORHAM CASE); and Bishop Blomfield of London had in consequence, speaking in the house of lords, protested against the nature and character of the committee as a court of final appeal in ecclesiastical questions. No change, however, had been effected; and in Mar., 1857, the question of ritual was brought before it, on appeal, in the case of "Westerton vs. Liddell," in which case the ritualistic practises of St. Barnabas, Pimlico, had been condemned in the consistory court of London and in the court of arches. Amid great excitement, the committee pronounced that the rubric permitted generally the use of those articles which were prescribed under the first Prayer-Book, and therefore sanctioned the use of credence-table, altar-cross, altar-lights, colored altar-cloths, etc. From that moment the Ritualists have acted steadily in the belief that this legal decision was but affirming that which is the plain, historical sense of the words in the rubric, and have pressed, often with rashness, sometimes with insolence, for the revival of all the ritual which this interpretation justified. In accomplishing this, they have been aided, advised, and sustained by the elaborate organization of the English Church Union, numbering now over 20,000 members, formed for the defense and protection of those who, in carrying out the rubric so understood, were menaced by perils and penalties. For however favorable single congregations might be, yet the work of revival had to be carried on, (1) in defiance of the long unbroken usage, which had never attempted anything beyond that simpler ritual which had been adopted and allowed as the practicable minimum under Elizabeth and Charles II.; (2) in defiance of the bishops, whose paternal authority was generally exercised to suppress, by any pressure in their power, any sharp conflict with this common custom; (3) in defiance of fierce popular suspicion, roused by dread of Romish uses, such as broke out, e.g., in the hideous rioting at St. George's-in-the-East (1858–60), which the weakness of the bishop of London and the apathy of the government allowed to continue for months, and finally to succeed in expelling the rector, Bryan King, and in wrecking his service; (4) in defiance of the court of final appeal, which in a series of fluctuating, doubtful, and conflicting judgments, had created a deep distrust of its capacity to decide judicially questions so rife with agitated feelings and popular prejudices.

This distrust—strongly roused by the Mackonochie judgment (1868) and the Purchas judgment (see PURCHAS, JOHN), in which it was supposed, in spite of obvious paradox, that everything not mentioned in the Prayer-Book was disallowed and illegal —culminated in the Ridsdale judgment (1877), in which it was declared that the "further order" allowed by the queen had been taken in the issuing of the advertisements under Archbishop Parker (see ADVERTISEMENTS OF ELIZABETH), and that the divines of Charles II. therefore, when they permitted the ritual of the second year of Edward VI., really intended only so much of it as was required in the Elizabethan advertisements. This startling decision the main block of High-church clergy found it impossible to respect or accept; and this repudiation of its verdict brought to a head the protest that had been made ever since the Gorham judgment against the validity of the court itself as an ecclesiastical tribunal. This last problem had been made critical by the famous Public-Worship Regulation Act (1874), introduced in the house of lords by the archbishop of Canterbury, in disregard of the protests of the lower house of convocation, and declared in the house of commons to be a "bill to put down ritualism" by Disraeli, then prime-minister, who, in spite of Gladstone's impetuous opposition, carried it, amid intense excitement, in an almost unanimous house. This bill swept away all the process in the diocesan courts; it allowed any three aggrieved parishioners to lodge a complaint, which, unless stayed by the bishop's veto, was carried before an officer nominated normally by the two archbishops to succeed to the post of dean of arches on its next vacancy. From him the appeal would be, as before, to the privy council. Thus the scanty fragments of ecclesiastical jurisdiction, which, under existent conditions, might be supposed to balance the civil character of the court of appeal, were all but wholly abolished. The attempt to enforce this bill by the bishops was met by absolute resistance, ending, after being challenged at every turn by technical objections, in the imprisonment of four priests. In this collision with the courts, the Ritualists had the steady support of the mass of High-church clergy, who had held aloof from their more advanced and dubious ritual. This support evidenced itself in the "Declaration" of over 4,000 clergy, headed by the deans of St. Paul's, York, Durham, Manchester, and others (1881).

6. Decision Adverse to Ritualism.

The condition of things had become intolerable; and in 1881 a royal commission was issued to consider the whole position of ecclesiastical jurisdiction. A similar mode of relief had been attempted in 1867, when a royal commission on ritual had been appointed, which under the chairmanship of Archbishop Longley,—after taking an immense mass of evidence, and after prolonged discussions—had issued a report on the crucial point of the "Ornaments Rubric," which recommended the "restraint" of the use of vestments, "by providing some effectual process for complaint and redress," but which, by the use of the word "restrain," declined to declare their illegality, and then had found itself unable to attain anything like unanimous agreement on the nature of the legal process which it proposed to recommend. The inner history of the commission will be found in A. R. Ashwell and R. G. Wilberforce, *Life of . . . S. Wilberforce*, vol. iii. (London, 1882). No legislation on the main subject followed this divided report. But convocation in 1879, and the Pan-Anglican Synod in 1880, had come to resolutions more or less in accord with the commissioners' report, in the sense of recommending a prohibitory discretion to the bishop in any case where a change of vesture was attempted. Such a recommendation seemed naturally to allow and assume the abstract legality of the change. Yet the courts of law had finally decreed vestments illegal, and the majority of bishops were prepared to accept their interpretation; and, as long as they did so, no terms of peace could be found on the basis of the proposal in convocation. For even though the bishops were willing to abstain, in favorable cases, from pressing the legal decisions, they were forced to set the law in motion by the action of a society called the "Church Association," which exerted itself to assert and support the rights of any parishioners who might be aggrieved by the ritual used in any church. Thus the exercise of discretion was made all but impossible to a bishop, who could only veto proceedings brought against a clergyman by giving a valid reason, and yet was forbidden to offer as a valid reason the possible legality of the vestments.

7. Attempts to Relieve the Stress.

The commission on ritual, therefore, had left the conflict still severe and unappeased. Only the signal to relieve its stress had been given. For the last act of Archbishop Tait, on his death-bed, was to suggest a truce to the fierce legal prosecutions which had embittered the long controversy, by bringing about an arrangement which would terminate the historic case of Martin vs. Mackonochie, round which the contest had turned for eighteen years. Thus the tension slackened; the possibility of peace seemed to have become conceivable. The question had widened from the consideration of ritual to the problem of the permanent adjustment of Church and State. A wiser temper had come over the public, which had, by the appointment of the commission, allowed that the problem of ecclesiastical jurisdiction was open to historical examination. Bishop Temple had come to London and was determined to avoid all legal measures. A time for consideration was then secured, pending the report of the commission. It did not report until 1883. The report included the historic papers prepared by Bishop Stubbs and Dean Church. Under the weight of their authority it decided against retaining the existing judicial committee of privy council as the court of final appeal. It proposed a reconstructed court which should obviously exhibit its primary character, as a court of the crown and not of the church, while, on all matters affecting doctrine and discipline, it should act on the advise of the spirituality, which for this purpose is represented by the bishops. No action was taken on the recommendation of this report—a fatal in-

8. The Work of the Commission.

action, for the report had decisively confirmed the protest of churchmen against the jurisdiction of the privy council. The existing judgments, which constituted the actual law, now, therefore, lost all moral authority. No one could expect them to be obeyed, when the case against the authority which promulgated them had been formally justified. This is the heart of all the difficulties that followed. The appeal to the bishops to make the law obeyed and the appeal to the clerical conscience to repudiate breaches of law lost all force when once it was allowed that the law itself was the chief matter in question.

9. The Archbishop's Decision.

It was obvious that the bishops must secure obedience by other methods than prosecution in court. They must discover some basis of agreement other than that provided by privy council judgment. At the crisis, providence gave them the opportunity of finding such a basis—an opportunity bravely seized by the chief authority concerned. In 1888, the Church Association instituted legal proceedings against Dr. King, Bishop of Lincoln, in order to test the legality of certain usages. The archbishop, after prolonged discussion as to the legitimacy of his action, decided to hear the case himself with the episcopal assessors. He gave his judgment Nov. 29, 1890, sanctioning under defined conditions the use of the mixed chalice, of altar lights, the adoption of the eastward position, and the singing of the Agnus Dei; and he forbade the signing of the cross in giving the absolution and the benediction. An appeal was made to the privy council, but that judicial body was far too wise to traverse a judgment of such intrinsic weight backed by knowledge superior to their own. They confirmed it, even where it was against their former decision.

10. Definitive Settlement not yet Reached.

Here, then, was a basis provided, on which a general conciliation could take effect. The judgment stood on its own merits as an ecclesiastical pronouncement delivered by the highest authority in the church. The clergy could afford to accept it, if the bishops would limit their claims within its lines. Under the broad assumption of these terms, ten years followed of steady peace. Bishop Temple had resolutely used his power of veto to prohibit legal measures being taken against the reredos of St. Paul's cathedral, and had been supported in his right by the highest court of appeal. It was understood that he had set his face against any appeal to force. He honored good pastoral work in whatever form he found it; and he trusted to his own personal influence to do the rest. It was a noble hope, and indeed it ought to have been met by a spontaneous determination not to take advantage of his confidence. But a great diocese like London can not, ultimately, be expected to work on delicate understandings of this kind. New men come in who have had no part in the understanding. The extreme pressure of local work compels even the best men to concentrate upon its immediate needs, as they feel them, without regard to the wider political situation. The situation develops of itself without anyone exactly intending it. So it was that while Bishop Temple absorbed himself in the labors of the diocese and left his clergy to themselves over ritual, trusting to their honor to keep the terms, a very wide license was gradually taken, and the individual divergences of use became perilous and alarming. The leaders of the movement themselves became aware that things were getting out of hand; and, at a sudden crisis over some practises in a city church, they refused to defend them, drew up a statement which recognised the necessity for a stricter supervision of special services, and expressed their desire for a greater measure of submission to authority as the first principle of catholicism. The bishops were prepared to take action, and they met with signs of loyal response. Unluckily a storm broke out, and swept away the opportunity for conciliatory action. A Protestant speaker of the name of Kensit aroused the passion of the crowd against illicit practises, and Sir William Harcourt kindled the flame in parliament by letters to *The Times* in the summer of 1898. From this moment reasonable treatment of a delicate and complicated situation became impossible. In 1899 Archbishop Temple made one notable attempt to rescue the cause of reason and peace from the welter of passion. He requested the bishop of London to bring before him as supreme ordinary certain vexed questions about the use of the incense, of portable lights, of the practise of reservation, that he might give them a "hearing"; not as before a court, but as a matter for "an opinion." He and the archbishop of York delivered a joint "opinion" on the first two points and concurred in forbidding any form of reservation of the consecrated elements. This "opinion" failed to secure complete compliance. The archbishop, who had been driven back on the law, which he had done his utmost to avoid, took a singularly limited and unelastic view of what the law was; and in the mean time Mr. Kensit, in town and country, and Sir William Harcourt, in parliament, had made a peaceable solution impossible. A series of church discipline bills introduced by Mr. McArthur in the house of commons, even though they never got beyond second readings, and not always so far as that, nevertheless, raised the ultimate issues between Church and State; and these issues had to be met. The result was a new royal commission on ecclesiastical discipline, very strongly manned, which was authorized to "inquire into the alleged prevalence of breaches or neglect of the law, relating to the conduct of divine service, and to the ornaments and fittings of the churches; and to consider the existing power and procedure applicable to such irregularities." It was appointed in Apr., 1904, and reported in 1906. It will be noticed that it was to consider "neglect" as well as disorder, and also to report on the problem of the jurisdiction of the courts. By including the last point it confessed that the key to the ritual disorder lay in the doubtful condition of the authoritative law. Obedience to the law is possible only when moral confidence in the law had first been secured.

The commission was faithful to its conception of the task committed to it, and after taking an enormous amount of evidence dealing with neglect and omissions, as well as with the excesses and irregularities, it accepted the verdict given by the earlier commission on the con-

11. The New Commission's Report.

stitution of the present court of final appeal. It declared that "the present structure of the ecclesiastical jurisdiction is, in our view, one chief cause of the growth of ritual irregularities." It pronounced the present court of final appeal to be a civil court of the crown, not exercising any authority from the church. It desires this character to be made clear in a newly constituted court, which should be obviously secular, and should be required to refer any matter of doctrine or discipline to the spirituality, in the persons of the bishops. Until this new court of appeal has been secured, with its correspondent church courts, it considers it inexpedient to press for coercive measures, excepting in certain specified cases of special gravity, which are inconsistent with the teaching of the Church, and the illegality of which can not be held to depend upon judgments of the privy council. These include reservation of the sacrament, with a view to its adoration; benediction with the sacrament; hymns, prayers, etc., involving invocation of the Blessed Virgin; the observance of the festival of the Assumption of the Virgin; the veneration of images and roods. These practises are to receive no toleration. But for the other matters it is pronounced desirable "to postpone proceedings until the reforms recommended in connection with the final court of appeal and the diocesan and provincial courts can be carried into effect." The commission, therefore, admits the case against the courts, on which the ritualists have insisted. But it considers that certain specified acts can be dealt with as illegal because their illegality is separable from any judgment of the existing court of appeal.

But the commission did more. It recognized frankly the impossibility and the inexpediency of the rigid uniformity of worship implied under the Elizabethan settlement. Such a uniformity has never been actually carried out in practise. It belongs as an ideal to a time when the ideas of religious liberty and toleration in Church

12. Results; Present Status.

and State were unknown. "In Church and State alike, these ideas have now seen their way to undisputed prevalence. It is incongruous that the precise and uniform requirements which were in harmony with the Elizabethan ideas of administration should still stand as the rule for the public worship of the Church under altered conditions and amid altered ways of thought." "A large comprehensiveness in matters of doctrine has grown up, while it is sought to maintain a severe rigidity in rites and ceremonies." This is inconsistent and inconceivable. "It has proved impracticable to obtain complete obedience to the acts of uniformity in one direction, because it is not now, and never has been, demanded in other directions." By these pronouncements the commission has opened a new era. It has abandoned the ideal of Elizabethan uniformity, on which an appeal to coercion had rested. It asks for elasticity or variety within the limits of the church order, and under the direction of the ordinary. It advises that letters of business be issued to the convocations to consider (a) a new rubric regulating the vesture of the ministers, and (b) to frame modifications in the existing law which will secure greater elasticity in the conduct of divine service. It would give the bishops power to authorize special services, etc. So the verdict stands. The letters of business have been issued, the convocations are engaged in the task of revision. No action has as yet been taken on the matter of the final court of appeal. Until this is done the ritual details under dispute (other than the specified illegalities singled out for independent condemnation) should, according to the report, be held over in suspended judgment. On these lines a conciliatory policy is made possible, and it is this which the bishops are now attempting to work. If they are hurried into immediate coercive measures by popular passion, at this juncture, they will be defying the serious and wise conclusion of this powerful commission. This consideration of the evidence leads to two conclusions: first, the law of public worship is too narrow for the religious life of the present generation. Secondly, the machinery for discipline has broken down.

HENRY SCOTT HOLLAND.

BIBLIOGRAPHY: W. H. Frere, *The Principles of Religious Ceremonial*, London, 1906; *History of Ritualism*, by Vox Clamantis, London, 1907; P. Martin, *Anglican-Ritualism as seen by a Catholic and a Foreigner*, ib. 1881; J. G. Norton, *A Plea for the Toleration of Ritualists*, ib. 1881; S. D. White, *Ritualism*, ib. 1881; C. Wordsworth, *On the Present Disquietude in the Church*, ib. 1881; Oxoniensis, *Romanism, Protestantism, Anglicanism*, ib. 1882; Z. H. Turton, *High Churchmen and their Church*, ib. 1888; W. Nicholas, *Ritualism*, ib. 1890; J. C. Ryle, *The Present Crisis*, London, 1892; *Romanism and the Ritualism in Great Britain and Ireland*, Edinburgh, 1895; W. M. Sinclair, *Words to the Laity on Contemporary Ecclesiastical Controversy*, London, 1895; Père Ragey, *La Crise religieuse en Angleterre*, Paris, 1896; F. Peek, *The English Church and the Altar*, London, 1897; J. Brown, *The Present Crisis in the Church of England*, ib. 1899; H. W. Clarke, *Romanism without the Pope in the Church of England*, Beckenham, 1899; P. T. Forsyth, *Rome, Reform and Reaction; four Lectures*, London, 1899; K. Ireton, *Ritualism Abandoned: or, a Priest redeemed*, ib. 1899; A. W. Joliffe *What is Ritualism? and who are Ritualists?* Shanklin, 1899; J. Meldrum, *Lawbreaks in the Church*, Singapore, 1899; H. H. Henson, *Church Problems. A View of modern Anglicanism*, London, 1900; F. Meyrick, *Old Anglicanism and Modern Ritualism*, ib. 1901; V. Staley, *Studies in Ceremonial*, Oxford, 1901; J. Wenn, *The Priestly Letters: or, the Priest that is the Enemy*, London, 1902; L. Heitland, *Ritualism in Town and Country*, ib. 1903; E. W. Leachman, *The Church's Object Lessons. Lessons on the Structure, Symbolism, and outward Worship of the Church*, Oxford, 1904; F. Meyrick, *An Appeal from the Twentieth to the Sixteenth and Seventeenth Centuries*, London, 1905; W. P. Swain, *History and Meaning of the Ornaments Rubric*, Bath, 1905; H. Wace, *An Appeal to the First Six Centuries*, London, 1905; J. Warren, *Ritualism, its Leading Tenets*, ib. 1906; C. Walker, *The Ritual Reason why*, ed. T. I. Ball, London, 1908; W. Preston, *Anti-Ritualism. A Catechism for Protestant Communicants*, new ed., by C. Neil, ib. 1910.

RIVER BRETHREN: A denomination of Mennonite origin and peculiarities, dating from a revival in Pennsylvania in 1770. The name is supposed to be due to the fact that the original members were baptized in the Susquehanna River, or, because living near that stream, came to be known to others as the "Brethren by the River." Jacob Engle, the first minister among them, came with thirty Mennonite families from Canton Basel, Switzerland, on account of long persecution. The voyage was disastrous, one of the ships with the goods of the emigrants being lost. One company, including Jacob Engle and his brother John, settled near the Susquehanna River in the southeastern part of Lancaster County, Pa. A revival in 1770, conducted by Lutherans, Mennonites, and Baptists, including Philip William Otterbein (q.v.), Boehm, and the Engles, resulted in many conversions. Differences arose among the converts respecting the mode of baptism and separate movements were the result. The Engles held to trine immersion and those who were of the same mind formed the denomination known simply as the River Brethren, which gradually spread to Ohio, Indiana, Kansas, New York, and other states, and to Canada. In 1862 the denomination sought a legal status as a body holding to the principle of non-resistance. Some of its members had been drafted for the army in the Civil War, and a legal status was needed to protect them from a violation of their principles. At the same time they adopted the name "Brethren in Christ," which is also claimed by a small Mennonite body. The River Brethren have suffered division. Differences on minor points led to the withdrawal of the Yorker Brethren in 1843 and in 1852 of the "Brinsers" or United Zion's Children.

The River Brethren have no formulated creed. They accept the doctrines known as Evangelical, and hold to Trine Immersion (q.v.) as the only proper form of baptism, to confession of sins to God and man, and to the ceremony of foot-washing in connection with the eucharist. Non-resistance is one of their cardinal principles. There are bishops, ministers, and deacons. The deacons have charge of the business of the churches, serve at the communion table, and do some pastoral visiting. Ministers are the teaching body, do parish work, and in the absence of the bishop administer the communion. The bishops preside at all council meetings and exercise all the functions of the ministry. District councils and the general conference are composed of ministers and laymen. The latter meets annually and has charge of the missionary work of the Church. The denominational headquarters are at Harrisburg, Pa.

The differences between the three bodies are slight. In the United Zion's Children in the ceremony of foot-washing one person both washes and wipes; in the other branches one person washes and another wipes. The three bodies in 1908 reported 201 ministers, 98 churches, and 4,114 communicants. The Brethren in Christ, the main body, has 174 ministers, 65 churches, and 3,675 communicants.

H. K. Carroll.

Bibliography: Consult the literature under Mennonites.

RIVET, ri-vé', ANDRÉ (ANDREAS RIVETUS): Huguenot; b. at Maixent (27 m. s.w. of Poitiers), France, Aug., 1572; d. at Breda (28 m. s.e. of Rotterdam), Holland, Jan. 7, 1651. After completing his education at Bern, he studied theology privately at Bern and La Rochelle, and from 1595 to 1620 was at Thouars, first as chaplain of the duke of La Trémouille and later as pastor; in 1617 he was elected president of the Synod at Vitré; and in 1620 he was called to Leyden as professor of theology. In 1632 Frederick Henry appointed Rivet tutor of his son, later William II., while the university made him honorary professor. In 1641 he attended the prince on his visit to England, and in 1646 was appointed curator of the educational institution in Breda, where he passed the remainder of his life.

A rigid Calvinist and an uncompromising enemy of the Roman Catholic Church, Rivet was in his day the most influential member of the theological faculty of Leyden; and together with his colleagues he drew up, in 1625, the *Synopsis purioris theologiæ*, which discussed the entire field of Reformed dogmatics in fifty-two disputations. At Leyden Rivet labored also in Old-Testament exegesis. His numerous writings are divided among the provinces of polemics, exegesis, dogmatics, and edification. They were collected in three volumes (Rotterdam, 1651–53), the most important being the *Isagoge ad scripturam sacram Veteris et Novi Testamenti* (Dort, 1616).

(S. D. van Veen.)

Bibliography: J. Meursius, *Athenæ Batavæ*, pp. 315 sqq., Leyden, 1625; *Les Dernières Heures de M. Rivet*, Delft, 1651, Eng. transl., *The Last Houers of . . . Andrew Rivet*, The Hague, 1652; B. Clasius, *Godgeleerd Nederland*, iii. 180–186, 's Hertogenbosch, 1851–56; E. and E. Haag, *La France protestante*, ed. H. L. Bordier, viii. 444–449, Paris, 1877 sqq.; Lichtenberger, *ESR*, xi. 238–241.

RIVIUS, riv'i-us, JOHANNES: German humanist and theologian; b. at Attendorn (42 m. n.e. of Cologne) Aug. 1, 1500; d. at Meissen (15 m. n.w. of Dresden) Jan. 1, 1553. In 1516 he entered the University of Cologne, and later, after studying manuscripts in Rhenish monasteries, went to Leipsic, where he found friendly reception with Kaspar Borner. After teaching at Zwickau for a short time, he went to Annaberg, Marienberg, and Schneeberg, and in 1537 was called to Freiberg as director of the Latin school and tutor to Duke August. With the latter, in 1540, he visited the University of Leipsic, and he also accompanied his pupil to Dresden after the death of Duke Henry. In the latter city Rivius was employed in church and school administration, and when Duke Maurice departed for the Turkish war in 1542, he was made a member of the bureau of spiritual affairs. In 1544 he was appointed inspector of schools at Meissen, where he evinced excellent administrative gifts. In 1545 he was made assessor in the newly established consistory of Meissen, and occupied this position until his death.

The literary activity of Rivius was directed primarily to the humanistic sphere. Here belong collections of notes on Terence, Cicero, and Sallust, and an edition of the last-named, as well as the long popular *De iis disciplinis quæ de sermone agunt, ut sunt grammatica, dialectica, rhetorica libri duodeviginti* (Leipsic, 1539). Far more important, however, were his theological writings, in which the elegant diction, Biblical and ecclesiastical learning, and hilosophic training make him appear a pupil of Erasmus. He was sometimes regarded with suspicion by Luther. His polemic writings in behalf of the new doctrines show an honorable and exact mode of discussion of the problems involved, and he did not hesitate to quote from his opponents in the course of his arguments. To this class of works belong his *De instaurata et renovata doctrina eccle-*

siastica (Leipsic, 1541); *De abusibus ecclesiasticis sive erroribus pontificiorum* (1546); *De admirabili Dei consilio in celando mysterio redemptionis humanæ* (Basel, 1545); *De fiducia salutis propter Christum* (1552); and *De religione et quo pacto se in hisce dissidiis gerere juventus debeat.* Some of his ethical works are still worth reading, among them *De conscientia bonæ mentis* (Leipsic, 1541); *De perpetuo in terris gaudio piorum* (Basel, 1550); *De vita et moribus Christianorum* (1552); and *De stultitia mortalium in procrastinanda vitæ correctione* (n.d.; Eng. transl. by J. Bankes, London [1550?], and T. Rogers, London [1582]). To the department of practical theology, finally, belong his *De consolandis ægrotantibus* (Basel, 1546) and *De officio pastorali* (1549). One of his writings was translated into English by W. G(ace) as *A Guide unto Godlinesse, moste worthy to bee followed of all true Christians* (London, 1579).

GEORG MÜLLER.

BIBLIOGRAPHY: The *Opera*, vol. i., pp. a[8] to b[8], contain a *Vita* by Georg Fabricius, Basel, 1562, new ed., 1614, and this was often printed separately, e.g., Meissen, 1843. Consult further: K. Kirchner, *Adam Siber*, pp. 9–19, 39, 67, 151–164, Chemnitz, 1887; *ADB*, xxviii. 709–713.

ROBBER COUNCIL. See EUTYCHIANISM, § 3.

ROBBINS, WILFORD LASH: Protestant Episcopalian; b. at Boston Aug. 7, 1859. He was graduated from Amherst College (A.B., 1881) and the Cambridge Episcopal Theological School (1884). He was ordered deacon in the same year and priested in 1885. He was rector of the Church of Our Redeemer, Lexington, Mass. (1883–87), and dean of All Saints' Cathedral, Albany, N. Y. (1887–1903). Since 1903 he has been dean of the General Theological Seminary, New York City. He has written *An Essay toward Faith* (New York, 1900) and *A Christian Apologetic* (1902).

ROBERT D' ARBISSEL. See FONTÉVRAULT, ORDER OF.

ROBERT OF CÎTEAUX. See CISTERCIANS, § 1.

ROBERTS, WILLIAM HENRY: Presbyterian; b. at Holyhead (67 m. w. of Liverpool), Wales, Jan. 31, 1844. He was educated at the College of the City of New York (A.B., 1863); was statistician in the United States Treasury Department (1863–1865) and assistant librarian of Congress, Washington, D. C. (1866–71); graduated from Princeton Theological Seminary (1873). He was then pastor of the Presbyterian church at Cranford, N. J. (1873–1877); librarian at Princeton Theological Seminary (1878–86); professor of practical theology at Lane Theological Seminary, Cincinnati, O. (1886–93); acting pastor of the Fourth Presbyterian Church, Trenton, N. J. (1895–1900); and since 1884 stated clerk and treasurer of the General Assembly of the Presbyterian Church in the United States of America. He has been American secretary of the Alliance of the Reformed Churches throughout the World since 1888, chairman of the Committee on Church Cooperation and Union of the General Assembly since 1903, and secretary of the Inter-Church Conference on Marriage and Divorce since the same year. In addition to editing the *Minutes of the General Assembly* (27 vols., Philadelphia, 1884–1910) and *Addresses at the Two Hundred and Fiftieth Anniversary of the Westminster Assembly* (1898), he has written, *History of the Presbyterian Church* (Philadelphia, 1888); *The Presbyterian System* (1895); *Laws relating to Religious Corporations* (1896); and *Manual for Ruling Elders* (1897).

ROBERTSON, ALEXANDER: Presbyterian; b. at Edinburgh, Scotland, Nov. 30, 1846. He was educated at the University of Edinburgh and has held pastorates at South Ronaldshay, Orkney (1875–81), San Remo, Italy (1881–90), and Venice, Italy (since 1890). He has lectured extensively in Great Britain on the religious condition of Italy, the ancient republic of Venice, and similar topics, and has written *Count Campobello and Catholic Reform in Italy* (London, 1891); *Fra Paolo Sarpi, the Greatest of the Venetians* (1894); *Through the Dolomites from Venice to Toblach* (1896); *The Bible of St. Mark: St. Mark's Church, the Altar and Throne of Venice* (1898); *The Roman Catholic Church in Italy* (1902); *Venetian Sermons* (1905); and *The Papal Conquest: Italy's Warning—"Wake up, John Bull"* (1909).

ROBERTSON, ARCHIBALD: Church of England, bishop of Exeter; b. at Sywell (6 m. n.e. of Northampton), Northamptonshire, June 29, 1853. He was educated at Trinity College, Oxford (B.A., 1876), where he was fellow from 1876 to 1886 and dean from 1879 to 1883, and honorary fellow since 1903. He was ordered deacon in 1878 and ordained priest in 1882. He was principal of Bishop Hatfield's Hall, Durham (1883–97); principal of King's College, London (1897–1903); fellow of the same institution after 1899; member of the Senate of the University of London (1899–1903); and vice-chancellor of the same (1902–03). In 1903 he was consecrated bishop of Exeter. He was examining chaplain to the bishop of Bristol in 1897, Boyle lecturer in 1900, and Bampton lecturer in the following year. Besides performing his duties as editor of *Handbooks of Theology* from 1896 to 1903, he has edited and translated the *De Incarnatione* of Athanasius (2 vols., London, 1884–93); prepared *Select Works of St. Athanasius* for *The Nicene and Post-Nicene Fathers*, 2d series, vii. (London, 1892); and written *Regnum Dei* (Bampton lectures; 1901) and *The Roman Claims to Supremacy* (1902).

ROBERTSON, ARCHIBALD THOMAS: Baptist; b. near Chatham, Va., Nov. 6, 1863. He was educated at Wake Forest College, Wake Forest, N. C. (A.M., 1885), and Southern Baptist Theological Seminary, Louisville, Ky. (Th.M., 1888). Since 1888 he has been connected with the latter institution, where he has been instructor in New-Testament interpretation (1888–92), professor of Biblical introduction (1892–95), and professor of New-Testament interpretation (since 1895). He has written *Critical Notes to Broadus's Harmony of the Gospels* (New York, 1893); *Life and Letters of John A. Broadus* (Philadelphia, 1900); *Syllabus of New Testament Greek Syntax* (Louisville, 1900); *Bibliography of New Testament Greek* (1903); *Teaching of Jesus concerning God the Father* (New York, 1904); *Students' Chronological New Testament* (1904); *Keywords in the Teaching of Jesus* (Philadelphia, 1906); *Syllabus for New Testament Study* (Louisville, 1906);

Epochs in the Life of Jesus (New York, 1907); *Short Grammar of the Greek New Testament* (1908; 2d ed., 1909); and *Epochs in the Life of Paul; A Study of Development in St. Paul's Career* (1909).

ROBERTSON, FREDERICK WILLIAM: English preacher; b. at London Feb. 3, 1816; d. at Brighton Aug. 15, 1853. He was the descendant of a family of soldiers whose traditions afterward became of decisive influence upon his inner life. He was brought up under the strong Evangelical impressions of his home, then studied at Beverley grammar-school, the gymnasium of Tours, the New Academy of Edinburgh, and the university of the same place. His father had intended him for the ministry, but he himself desired to become a soldier. He was finally articled to a solicitor, but the sedentary habits of his calling broke down his health. He was then placed upon the list of dragoons in India and prepared himself for that service in the usual manner, but as he had to wait more than two years for a call, the desires of his father became urgent so that with self-sacrifice—a characteristic trait—he entered, in 1837, Brasenose College, Oxford (B.A., 1841; M.A., 1844), to study theology. He occupied himself for a time with Platonic metaphysics and Aristotle. As a theologian he clung at that time to the Evangelical party in its strict Calvinistic expression. The theological ferment at Oxford impelled him to the study of the Bible, especially of the Greek New Testament, the most important portions of which he memorized. In 1840 he took orders and the curacy of the parish of St. Mary Kalendar, Winchester. Breaking down under the pressure of hard work and nervous affection, he was compelled in 1841 to seek relaxation, and went to Switzerland, meeting there Helen, a daughter of Sir William Denys, whom he married the same year. After his return to England he accepted, in 1843, a position as curate at Christ Church, Cheltenham. Discouraged by ill success in his official life, he resigned his position and in 1846 sought rest in Heidelberg. After a short rest he accepted the charge at St. Ebbe's in Oxford, and, in 1847, the incumbency of Trinity Chapel, Brighton, which he held until his death.

Robertson's character was marked by great intensity of feeling, which led him into an emphasis of expression that sometimes partook of over-statement. He was broad in his feelings, realizing something in each of the schools of theology in the Anglican communion with which he was in sympathy. He was especially successful in winning the confidence of the working classes. His usefulness was limited and his own life shortened by the absolute seriousness of his temperament, which did not permit the soothing and quieting influences of humor to have their effect in the bearing of petty annoyances. He was one of the foremost pulpit orators of his people, excelling less in depth and learning than in the power of his pathos, warm feeling, dignity, and beauty of language. Most of his published works, principally sermons, were issued posthumously. The most important are: *Sermons preached at Trinity Chapel, Brighton* (5 series, London, 1855–74, often reprinted, e.g., 1906, in the later editions with sketch of the life prefixed. This is one of the most remarkable and influential series of sermons ever issued, and is marked by a fresh, strenuous, and burning piety and a hunger for souls. They were written out after delivery, and are much condensed); *Literary Remains* (1876) among them *Lectures on the Influence of Poetry on the Working Classes*. Less influential were *Expository Lectures on St. Paul's Epistles to the Corinthians* (1859), and *Notes on Genesis* (1877).

Bibliography: S. A. Brooke, *Life and Letters of F. W. Robertson*, new ed., 2 vols., London, 1873 (thorough, sympathetic); W. Sawyer, *Memoir of Rev. F. W. Robertson*, Brighton, 1853; G. Sutton, *Faith and Science, and a Critique upon Mr. Robertson of Brighton*, London, 1868; F. A. Noble, *A Lecture on F. W. Robertson*, ib. 1872; G. MacCrie, *The Religion of our Literature*, ib. 1875; F. Arnold, *Robertson of Brighton, with some Notices of his Times and Contemporaries*, ib. 1886 (contains many interesting notices of friends of Robertson); J. P. Edgar, *Robertson of Brighton*, Edinburgh, 1887; L. Dumas, *Un prédicateur anglais*, Montauban, 1894; *DNB*, xlviii. 404–407; and the list of literature in Richardson, *Encyclopaedia*, p. 941.

ROBERTSON, JAMES: The name of three Presbyterian divines.

1. Church of Scotland; b. at Ardlaw (36 m. n. of Aberdeen), Aberdeenshire, Jan. 2, 1803; d. in Edinburgh Dec. 2, 1860. After a brilliant career at Aberdeen University (M.A., 1820) and study in the divinity hall there from 1821 to 1824, he was licensed by the presbytery of Deer and appointed schoolmaster of Pitsligo, 1825, tutor and librarian at Gordon Castle, the seat of the duke of Gordon, headmaster of Gordon's hospital in Aberdeen, 1829, and at last given a parochial charge, that of Ellon, 1832. In the troubles preceding the disruption of the Church of Scotland, he took a prominent part on the side of the moderates who opposed the rupture. He also sided with the ministers of Strathbogie presbytery who had been deposed by the general assembly because they, constituting the majority of presbytery, had acted contrary to the order of the assembly in taking a presentee on trial, 1842. When the disruption came the next year he stayed in the Kirk, and was made professor of divinity and church history in the University of Edinburgh, and so remained till his death. In 1844 he demitted his parochial charge.

He is remembered for two things, that in 1841 he advised the farmers, in accordance with Liebig's suggestion, to use bones dissolved in sulphuric acid as a manure; and second, that he was the remarkably efficient chairman of the committee in the Kirk on the endowment of chapels of ease. In recognition of his services he was elected moderator of the general assembly in 1856.

His publications embrace *Exposition of the Principles, Operation, and Prospects of the Church of Scotland's Indian Mission* (Edinburgh, 1835); *On the Power of the Civil Magistrate in Matters of Religion* (1835); *Observations on the Veto Act* (1840); *Statement for the Presbytery of Strathbogie* (London, 1841); *Answers to the Remonstrance* (1841); *Appeal for the Advancement of Female Education in India* (Edinburgh, 1846); *Remarks and Suggestions relative to the Proposed Endowment Scheme* (1846); *Letters to the Editor of the Northern Standard* (1854); *Old Truths and Modern Speculations* (1860).

2. Canadian Presbyterian; b. at Dull (25 m. n.w. of Perth), Scotland, Apr. 24, 1839; d. in Toronto, Canada, Jan. 4, 1902. He was born in poverty, attended the school at Dull, but in 1855 removed to East Oxford, Ontario, Canada, with the family and then attended school at Woodstock, a neighboring village; passed the teacher's examination and returned to teach at Woodstock (1857), later near Innerskip (1859), but in 1863 he matriculated at the University of Toronto, from which he passed to Princeton Theological Seminary in 1866 and after two years entered Union Theological Seminary, New York City, whence he graduated in 1869. For the next six years he was pastor of Norwich, Windham, and East Oxford in the Presbyterian Church of Canada; in 1874 he became pastor of Knox Church, Winnipeg, Manitoba, and in 1877 lecturer in Manitoba college in the same place. In 1881 he became superintendent of missions of his church for Manitoba and the Northwest, and so continued till his death. In 1895 he was moderator of the general assembly.

While a student in the university he belonged to the Queen's Rifles and saw service in connection with the Fenian raid of 1866. Thus early did he show his courage and his fidelity to duty. When his church called him to watch over and promote her missions in the wilds of Canada he addressed himself to his task with a skill, devotion, boldness, and tact which have seldom been equalled, and so he passes into history as one of the master missionaries. Those who would know what kind of a life he led have but to read the tales of Ralph Connor (Charles William Gordon, q.v.) for he was the "sky pilot" who moves through them as the great friend of God and man.

3. Church of Scotland; b. at Alyth (14 m. n.w. of Dundee), Perthshire, Mar. 2, 1840. He was educated at University and King's College, Aberdeen (M.A., 1859), and St. Mary's College, St. Andrews; was a missionary of the Church of Scotland at Constantinople in 1862–64 and at Beirut in 1864–75; minister of Mayfield Church, Edinburgh (1875–77); and since 1877 has been professor of Hebrew and Semitic languages in the University of Glasgow. In 1904 he was Murtle lecturer at the University of Aberdeen. Theologically he is "Calvinistic by temperament, and generally described (by others) as a conservative theologian or conservative critic." He prefers, however, "to be regarded as a critic of the modern school of Old-Testament criticism." He has edited *Sabbath School Teachers' Book, Third Grade* (Edinburgh, 1890), translated the syntactic portion of A. Müller's *Hebräische Schulgrammatik* (Halle, 1878) under the title *Outlines of Hebrew Syntax* (London, 1882); and written *The Early Religion of Israel* (Edinburgh, 1892); *The Old Testament and its Contents* (1893); *The Poetry and the Religion of the Psalms* (1898); *The First and Second Books of the Kings in the Temple Bible* (London, 1902); and *Fire and Twenty Years in a Hebrew Chair* (Edinburgh, 1903).

BIBLIOGRAPHY: On 1: A. H. Charteris, *Life of Rev. James Robertson, Professor of Divinity*, London, 1863; idem, *A Faithful Churchman: Sketch of the Life and Work of Professor James Robertson*, ib. 1897; *DNB*, xlviii. 410–411. On 2: C. W. Gordon (Ralph Connor), *The Life of James Robertson, Missionary Superintendent in the Northwest Territories*, New York, 1908.

ROBERTSON, JAMES CRAIGIE: Church of England; b. at Aberdeen 1813; d. at Canterbury July 9, 1882. He was graduated at Trinity College, Cambridge (B.A., 1834; M.A., 1838); was vicar of Beckesbourne, near Canterbury, 1846–59; canon of Canterbury, 1859–82; and professor of ecclesiastical history, Kings College, London, 1864–74. His historical works take high rank. He wrote: *How shall we Conform to the Liturgy of the Church of England?* (London, 1843); *History of the Christian Church to the Reformation* (4 vols., 1854–73; new ed., 8 vols., 1874–75); *Sketches of Church History* (1855–78); *Becket, Archbishop of Canterbury* (1859); and *Plain Lectures on the Growth of the Papal Power* (1876). He edited P. Heylyn's *History of the Reformation* (2 vols., 1849); John Bargrave's *Alexander VII. and his Cardinals* (1867); and *Materials for the History of Thomas Becket*, in the *Rolls Series* (8 vols., 1875–83).

BIBLIOGRAPHY: *DNB*, xlviii. 412–413.

ROBERTSON, WILLIAM: Church of Scotland; b. at Borthwick (10 m. s.s.e. of Edinburgh) Sept. 19, 1721; d. in Edinburgh June 11, 1793. After studying at the University of Edinburgh, he was licensed and settled at Gladsmuir, 1743; was settled over Lady Yester's Chapel, Edinburgh, 1758; was translated to the Old Grayfriars Church, 1761. He was reputed the most eloquent preacher in Scotland, but he published only one sermon, the one he preached before the Society in Scotland for Propagating Christian Knowledge, upon the state of the world at the coming of Christ (1755). From 1763 till 1780 he was moderator of the general assembly; from 1762 till 1792 principal of Edinburgh University. His fame with posterity does not come from his pulpit or administrative ability, but from three historical works which are now superseded because later writers have had access to much better information than he, but are noteworthy for their style and their impartiality: *The History of Scotland during the Reigns of Queen Mary and of King James VI. till his Accession to the Crown of England. With a Review of the Scotch History previous to that Period, and an Appendix containing original Papers* (London, 2 vols., 1758–59); *The History of the Reign of the Emperor Charles V., with a View of the Progress of Society in Europe from the Subversion of the Roman Empire to the Beginning of the Sixteenth Century* (3 vols., 1769); and *The History of America* (4 vols., 1777–96, going down to 1652 for Virginia and to 1688 for New England). There are numerous collected editions of his *Works* (most of them containing the *Life* by Dugald Stewart), e.g., 11 vols., London, 1800–02, 12 vols., 1812; 6 vols., Edinburgh, 1813; best, 8 vols., Oxford, 1825, reprints often, e.g., 1865.

BIBLIOGRAPHY: Besides the life by Stewart, ut sup., there is *An Account of the Life and Writings of William Robertson*, by G. Gleig, Edinburgh, 1812; and one in Lord Brougham's *Lives of Men of Letters and Science*, 2 vols., London, 1845–46. References to scattered notices are given in *DNB*, xlviii. 425–430.

ROBINS, HENRY EPHRAIM: Baptist; b. at Hartford, Conn., Sept. 30, 1827. He was educated at the Literary Institute, Suffield, Conn., Fairmount Theological Seminary, and Newton Theological Institution, from which he was graduated in 1861. He held Baptist pastorates at the Central Baptist Church, Newport, R. I. (1861–67), and the First Baptist Church, Rochester, N. Y. (1867–73); was president of Colby University (1873–82); and professor of Christian ethics in Rochester Theological Seminary (1882–1904). He has written *Harmony of Ethics with Theology* (New York, 1891); *The Christian Idea of Education as distinguished from Secular Education* (Philadelphia, 1895); and *Ethics in Christian Life* (1904).

ROBINSON, CHARLES HENRY: Church of England; b. at Keynsham (5 m. s.e. of Bristol), Somerset, Feb. 27, 1861. He was educated at Trinity College, Cambridge (B.A., 1883), and was ordered deacon in 1884 and ordained priest in 1885. He was curate of Pateley Bridge, Yorkshire (1884–86) and of St. Johns, Darlinghurst, Sydney, N. S. W. (1886–1887). He became fellow and tutor of St. Augustine's College, Canterbury (1889), and was vice-chancellor of Truro Cathedral and vice-principal of the Chancellor's School at Truro (1890–93). In 1892 he visited Armenia to report to the archbishop of Canterbury on the condition of the Armenian Church. He was engaged in a first expedition to Kano, the commercial capital of central Soudan (1893–95), and since 1896 has been lecturer in Hausa in the University of Cambridge, honorary canon of Ripon since 1897, and in 1902 was made editorial secretary to the Society for the Propagation of the Gospel. He has written *The Church and her Teaching* (London, 1893); *Hausaland: or, Fifteen Hundred Miles through the Central Soudan* (1896); *Specimens of Hausa Literature* (Cambridge, 1896); *Grammar of the Hausa Language* (London, 1897); *Mohammedanism, has it any Future?* (1897); *Dictionary of the Hausa Language* (in collaboration with W. H. Brooks; 2 vols., London, 1899); *Studies in the Character of Christ* (1900); *Nigeria, our latest Protectorate* (1900); *Human Nature a Revelation of the Divine* (1902); *Studies in Christian Worship* (1908); and *Studies in the Resurrection of Christ* (1909).

ROBINSON, CHARLES SEYMOUR: Presbyterian; b. at Bennington, Vt., Mar. 31, 1829; d. at New York Feb. 1, 1899. He graduated at Williams College, 1849; studied at Union (New York) and Princeton Theological Seminaries; was pastor at Troy, N. Y., 1855–60; Brooklyn, N. Y., 1860–68; the American Chapel at Paris, France, 1868–71; Madison Ave. Church, New York, 1871–88; and of other churches at New York, 1890–92, and after. He has published volumes of sermons entitled, *Christian Work* (New York, 1874) and *Bethel and Penuel* (1874); *Studies of Neglected Texts* (1883); *Sermons in Songs* (1885); and *Simon Peter: His Early Life and Times* (2 vols., 1889). He is especially famous as the compiler of books of hymns and tunes, some of which are, *Songs of the Church* (New York, 1862); *Songs for the Sanctuary* (1865, 1889); *Psalms, Hymns, and Spiritual Songs* (1874); and *Laudes Domini* (1884–90).

BIBLIOGRAPHY: S. W. Duffield, *English Hymns*, pp. 472–473, New York, 1886; Julian, *Hymnology*, p. 969.

ROBINSON, EDWARD: Biblical scholar, and pioneer in modern explorations in Palestine; b. at Southington, Conn., Apr. 10, 1794; d. in New York City Jan. 27, 1863. He was graduated from Hamilton College (1816), and after studying law at Hudson, N. Y., returned to his alma mater as tutor in mathematics and Greek (1817–18). In 1818, he married Miss Eliza Kirkland, daughter of the Oneida missionary, who died the next year. From his marriage until 1821, he worked his wife's farm, but also pursued his studies. In 1821 he went to Andover to superintend the printing of his edition of part of the *Iliad* (bks. i.–ix., xviii., xxii.), which appeared in 1822, and while there, under Moses Stuart's influence, began his career as a Biblical scholar and teacher. From 1823 to 1826 he was instructor in the Hebrew language and literature at Andover Theological Seminary, meanwhile being busily occupied with literary labors. He assisted Professor Stuart in the 2d ed. of his *Hebrew Grammar* (Andover, 1823, 1st ed., 1813), and in his translation of Winer's *Grammar of the New-Testament Greek* (1825), and alone translated Wahl's *Clavis philologica Novi Testamenti* (1825). In 1826 he went to Europe, and studied at Göttingen, Halle, and Berlin, making the acquaintance, and winning the praises, of Gesenius, Tholuck, and Rödiger in Halle, and Neander and Ritter in Berlin. In 1828 he married the youngest daughter of L. A. von Jacob, professor of philosophy and political science at the university of Halle, a highly gifted woman of thorough culture, well known before her marriage by her pseudonym of "Talvi." In 1830 he returned to America, and from 1830 to 1833 was professor-extraordinary of Biblical literature, and librarian at Andover. In 1831 he founded the *Biblical Repository*, subsequently (1851) united with the *Bibliotheca Sacra*, to which he contributed numerous translations and original articles. In 1832 he issued an improved edition of Taylor's translation of Calmet's *Dictionary of the Bible*, and in 1833 a smaller *Dictionary of the Holy Bible*, and a translation of Buttmann's *Greek Grammar* (extensively used as a text-book). In 1833 ill-health, induced by his severe labors, compelled him to resign his professorship, and he removed to Boston. In 1834 he brought out a revised edition of Newcome's *Greek Harmony of the Gospels;* in 1836, a translation of Gesenius' *Hebrew Lexicon* (5th edition, the last in which Robinson made any changes, 1854), and the independent *Greek and English Lexicon of the New Testament* (revised ed., 1850). In 1837 he was called to be professor of Biblical literature in Union Theological Seminary, New York City. Prior to entering upon his duties, he sailed in July, 1837, for the Holy Land, and in conjunction with Rev. Dr. Eli Smith, the accomplished Arabic scholar and faithful missionary of the American Board in Syria, explored all the important places in Palestine and Syria. In Oct., 1838, he returned to Berlin; and there for two years worked upon his *Biblical Researches in Palestine, Mount Sinai, and Arabia Petræa.* This great work, which at once established the author's reputation as a geographer and Biblical student of the first rank, appeared simultaneously in London, Boston, and in a German translation carefully revised by Mrs. Robinson, and carried through the press in Halle by Professor Rödiger (3 vols., 1841). In recognition of his eminent services, he received in 1842 the Patron's Gold Medal from the Royal Geographical Society of London, and the degree of D.D. from the university of Halle, while in 1844 Yale College gave him that of LL.D. In 1852 he visited Palestine again, and published the results of this second visit in 1856, in the second edition of his *Biblical Researches*, and in a supplemental volume, *Later Biblical Researches in Palestine and the Adjacent Regions* (3d. ed. of the whole work, 3 vols., 1867). Dr. Robinson regarded the work as only a preparation for a complete physical, historical, and topographical geography of the Holy Land. But repeated attacks of illness undermined his constitution and an incurable disease of the eyes obliged him in 1862 to lay down his pen. After his death, the first part of the projected work, the *Physical Geography of the Holy Land*, which was all he had prepared, was published in English (London and Boston, 1865) and in German translation by his wife (Berlin). He also prepared a *Greek Harmony of the Gospels* (1845), which was far superior to anything of the kind which had then appeared, and in 1846 an *English Harmony*.

In May, 1862, he made his fifth and last visit to Europe, but failed to receive any permanent benefit to his eyesight. In Nov. he returned, and resumed his lectures, but died after a brief illness.

Dr. Robinson was a man of athletic form and imposing figure, though somewhat bent in later years; of strong, sound, good sense; reserved, though when in congenial company often entertaining and humorous. He was thorough and indefatigable in his investigations, skeptical of all monastic legends, reverent to God's revelation. Outwardly cold, his heart was warm, and his sympathies tender. He is probably the most distinguished Biblical scholar whom America has produced, indeed, one of the most distinguished of the nineteenth century. The original manuscript of Dr. Robinson's *Biblical Researches* and a part of his library are in the possession of the Union Theological Seminary.

P. Schaff†. D. S. Schaff.

Bibliography: The memorial addresses by R. D. Hitchcock and H. B. Smith are in *Life, Writings, and Character of Edward Robinson*, New York, 1863; A. P. Stanley, *Addresses and Sermons in America*, pp. 23-34, ib. 1879; G. L. Prentiss, *The Union Theological Seminary in the City o New York*, pp. 243-254 et passim, ib. 1889.

ROBINSON, GEORGE LIVINGSTONE: Presbyterian; b. at West Hebron, N. Y., Aug. 19, 1864. He was graduated from Princeton College (A.B., 1887), Princeton Theological Seminary (1893), and studied at the universities of Berlin (1893-94) and Leipsic (Ph.D., 1895). He was an instructor in the Syrian Protestant College, Beirut, Syria (1887-90); pastor of the Presbyterian church at Roxbury, Mass. (1896); professor of Old-Testament literature and exegesis at Knox College, Toronto (1896-98); held a similar position in McCormick Theological Seminary, Chicago (1898-1906); and was appointed professor in the American School of Archeology at Jerusalem (1906). He has made extensive explorations in Palestine, particularly in the peninsula of Sinai and Kadesh-Barnea. In theology he is a conservative liberal. He has written *The Origin and Date of Zechariah ix.-xiv.* (Chicago, 1896); *The Biblical Doctrine of Holiness* (1904); and *Leaders of Israel: History of the Hebrews from the Earliest Times to the Downfall of Jerusalem, A.D. 70* (New York, 1906).

ROBINSON, HENRY DOUGLAS: Protestant Episcopal missionary bishop of Nevada; b. at Lowell, Mass., Mar. 15, 1860. He was educated at Racine College (B.A., 1884), and was assistant rector of the grammar-school of the same institution in 1884-85, and instructor in mathematics in San Mateo Military Academy, San Mateo, Cal., in 1885-89. Having been ordered deacon in 1886 and priested in 1888, he was also curate of St. Matthew's in the same city until 1889, after which he was rector (1889-99) and warden (1899-1908) of the grammar-school of Racine College. In 1908 he was consecrated missionary bishop of Nevada.

ROBINSON, JOHN: English Separatist, the minister of the Pilgrim Fathers; b. probably at Lincoln, about 1575; d. at Leyden Mar. 1, 1625. He entered Corpus Christi (or Benet) College, Cambridge, in 1592 (B.A., 1596; fellow, 1598; M.A., 1599); was curate of St. Andrew's, Norwich, 1602; married 1604; was compelled to leave his charge because he had criticised prelacy and the ceremonies of the Church of England, 1606; then is heard of in many places anxiously endeavoring to find out his duty as to leaving the church. Finally he decided to leave and in 1606 became an officer of the Separatist congregation meeting at William Brewster's house, Scrooby, Nottinghamshire; he went with the congregation to Amsterdam in 1608, and in May, 1609, settled in Leyden, where he was publicly ordained as pastor and Brewster became ruling elder. In Jan., 1611, Robinson and three others bought a house for 8,000 guilders, but, probably owing to difficulty in raising the money, did not obtain possession till May, 1612; the building was then used as a church and dwelling, and a score of small houses were erected on the property for the poorer members. In Sept., 1615, Robinson was admitted a member of the university as a student of theology and attended the lectures of Episcopius and Polyander (Jan Kerckhoven). He is said to have entered actively into the Arminian controversies, taking the Calvinistic side. The determination to emigrate to America was formed as early as 1617, when John Carver, a deacon, and Robert Cushman, a man of business experience, were sent to London to negotiate with the London-Virginia Company, carrying with them seven articles of belief subscribed by Robinson and Brewster as evidence of their orthodoxy and loyalty. The first company of emigrants crossed the Atlantic in the *Mayflower* and landed at Plymouth, Dec. 21, 1620, under Brewster's guidance. Robinson remained in Holland with the majority of the congregation, who chose to defer their departure, and he died before he was able to unite his divided flock. He was buried Mar. 4, 1625, in St. Peter's Church, Leyden. His congregation was broken up, some going to New England and others to Amsterdam. In 1865 a marble slab was placed on the building occupying the site of Robinson's house in Leyden (taken down about 1650), and in 1891 a bronze tablet was dedicated on St. Peter's Church. Robinson was a man of amiable character, of sound judgment and good sense, and exercised a good influence over all the English in Holland. See CONGREGATIONALISTS, I., 1, §§ 5–7. His *Works* (nearly complete), with memoir by Robert Ashton, appeared in 3 vols., London, 1851. The most important are *A Justification of Separation from the Church of England* (Leyden, 1610); *Of Religious Comunion, Private and Public* (1614), a reply to Thomas Helwys and John Smyth; *Apologia justa et necessaria quorumdam Christianorum dictorum Brownistarum sive Barrowistarum* (1619; in Eng., 1625); *Observations, Divine and Moral*, essays on moral and religious topics (1625; 1628; 1638).

BIBLIOGRAPHY: The first source for a life is Robinson's own writings, and next to that is W. Bradford, *Hist. of Plymouth Plantation*, in *Collections of Massachusetts Historical Society*, 4 series, vol. iii., 1856, cf. A. Young, *Chronicles of the Pilgrim Fathers*, 2d ed., Boston, 1844. The principal external sources are conveniently and compactly brought together by E. Arber in *The Story of the Pilgrim Fathers 1606–23 . . . as Told by themselves, their Friends, and their Enemies*, London, 1897. Consult further: O. S. Davis, *John Robinson, the Pilgrim Pastor*, Boston, 1903; H. M. Dexter, *Congregationalism of the Last Three Hundred Years*, pp. 357–410 et passim, New York, 1880; D. Campbell, *The Puritan in Holland, England, and America*, ii. 240 sqq., ib. 1893; W. Walker, in *American Church History Series*, iii. 57–72, ib. 1894; idem, *Ten New England Leaders*, pp. 17–29 et passim, ib. 1901; A. E. Dunning, *Congregationalists in America*, ib. 1894; John Brown, *The Pilgrim Fathers of New England and their Puritan Successors*, ib. 1897; C. Burrage, *New Facts concerning John Robinson, Pastor of the Pilgrim Fathers*, Oxford, 1910 (used in the foregoing sketch); *DNB*, xlix. 18–22 (where reference is made to scattering notices). Much of the literature cited under PURITANS, PURITANISM will be found to contain material on the subject.

ROBINSON, JOHN EDWARD: Methodist Episcopal bishop in Southern Asia; b. at Gort (28 m. n. of Limerick), County Galway, Ireland, Feb. 12, 1849. He was graduated at Drew Theological Seminary (1874), and in that year went to India as a missionary. He was presiding elder of the Burmah District (1884–88), the Bombay District (1888-1896), the Asansol District (1896-1900), and the Calcutta District (1900–04). He was elected bishop in 1904. In theology he is a liberal evangelical. In addition to editing the *Burmah Evangelist* from 1884 to 1887 and the *Indian Witness* from 1896 to 1904, he has written *Apostolic Succession Refuted* (Rangoon, 1884) and *The Rise and Progress of Methodism* (1899).

ROBINSON, JOSEPH ARMITAGE: Church of England; b. at Keynsham (5 m. s.e. of Bristol), Somerset, Jan. 9, 1858. He was educated at Christ's College, Cambridge (B.A., 1881), and was ordered deacon in 1881 and advanced to the priesthood in the following year. He was then domestic chaplain to the bishop of Durham (1883–84), curate of Great St. Mary's, Cambridge (1885–86), Cambridge Whitehall preacher (1886–88), vicar of All Saints', Cambridge (1888–92), Norrisian professor of divinity at Cambridge (1893–99), and canon of Westminster (1899-1902). Since 1902 he has been dean of Westminster. He was likewise fellow of his college in 1881–99, of which he has been honorary fellow since 1904, and was dean of the same college in 1884–90. He was examining chaplain to the bishop of Bath and Wells in 1888–92, a prebendary in Wells Cathedral in 1894–99, select preacher at Oxford in 1899, and rector of St. Margaret's, Westminster, in 1899–1900, while since 1902 he has been a chaplain-in-ordinary to the king. He prepared the English translation, with a preface and appendices, of S. Lampros's *Collation of the Athos Codex of the Shepherd of Hermas* (Cambridge, 1888); and edited the larger portion of the Greek text of the "Apology" of Aristides for J. R. Harris's edition of the Syriac version of the same document (1891); *The Passion of Saint Perpetua* (1891); and *The Philocalia of Origen* (1893); besides editing *Texts and Studies: Contributions to Biblical and Patristic Literature* (Cambridge, 1891 sqq.); and *An Unrecognized Westminster Chronicler, 1381–1394* (1907). As independent works he has written *The Gospel according to Peter and the Revelation of Peter* (Cambridge, 1892; in collaboration with M. R. James); *Euthaliana: Studies of Euthalius* (1895); *Unity in Christ, and other Sermons* (London, 1901); *Study of the Gospels* (1902); *Some Thoughts on the Incarnation* (1903); *St. Paul's Epistle to the Ephesians: Revised Text and Translation, with Exposition and Notes* (1903); *Some Thoughts on Inspiration* (1905); *Some Thoughts on the Athanasian Creed* (1905); *The Vision of Unity* (1908; sermons); *The Historical Character of St. John's Gospel* (1908); *St. Paul's Epistle to the Ephesians, an Exposition* (1909); *The Manuscripts of Westminster Abbey* (1909; with M. R. James).

ROBINSON, ROBERT: Baptist; b. at Swaffham (25 m. w. of Norfolk), Norfolk, Sept. 27, 1735; d. at Birmingham June 8, 1790. From 1761 he was pastor of a society at Cambridge, acquired considerable land, and engaged at the same time in business as a corn and coal merchant; and, besides preaching on Sundays at Cambridge, did Evangelical work in as many as fifteen neighboring stations during week-days. In his *Plea for the Divinity of our Lord Jesus Christ* (Cambridge 1776; new ed., 1813) he represented Sabellian views, was influenced by Joseph Priestley (q.v.), and in a letter (1788) scouted the idea of the doctrine of the Trinity and of the personality of the Spirit. Deficient in training, he taught himself four or five languages, possessed great powers of speech, and his *History of Baptism* (London, 1790) was strongly written, minute in learning, and abounding in rustic witticism. His *Posthumous Works* were issued in 1792; a volume of *Sermons* in 1804; his *Miscellaneous Works*, ed. B. Flower, in 4 vols., in 1807; and *Select Works*, ed. W. Robinson, 1861. He wrote the two popular hymns "Come thou Fount of every blessing" (1758) and "Mighty God, while angels bless thee" (1774).

BIBLIOGRAPHY: The funeral sermons by Joseph Priestley, Abraham Rees, and Joshua Toulmin were all published in 1790. The monograph is by G. Dyer, *Memoirs of the Life and Writings of Robert Robinson*, London, 1796. *Memoirs* by the editors were prefixed to the *Miscellaneous Works* and *Select Works*, ut sup. Consult further: S. W. Duffield, *English Hymns*, pp. 116–117, 352–357, New York, 1886; Julian, *Hymnology*, pp. 969–970.

ROBINSON, STUART: Presbyterian; b. at Strabane (13 m. s.s.w. of Londonderry), Ireland, Nov. 26, 1816; d. at Louisville, Ky., Oct. 5, 1881. He was graduated at Amherst College, 1836; studied theology at Union Theological Seminary, Va., and at Princeton; was ordained, 1842; pastor at Kanawha Salines, W. Va., 1841–47; at Frankfort, Ky., 1847–52; at Baltimore, 1852–56; was professor of church polity and pastoral theology in the Presbyterian theological seminary at Danville, Ky., 1856–57; and pastor at Louisville, Ky., 1858–81. He was one of the most prominent clergymen of the South, and published *The True Presbyterian;* but, his loyalty being doubted, the paper was suppressed by the military in 1862, and he removed to Canada, preaching at Toronto. In 1866 he returned to his pastorate at Louisville and resumed his journal under the title *Free Christian Commonwealth.* Expelled from the general assembly in 1866 for signing the "Declaration and Testimony" (a protest against political deliverances by the official bodies of the church), he induced the synod of Kentucky to unite with the general assembly of the Southern Presbyterian Church in 1869. Among his published works are, *The Church of God an Essential Element of the Gospel* (Philadelphia, 1858); *Slavery as Recognized by the Mosaic Law* (Toronto, 1865); and *Discourses of Redemption* (New York, 1866; Edinburgh, 1869).

ROBSON, GEORGE: United Free Church of Scotland; b. at Glasgow May 8, 1842. He was educated at the university of his native city (M.A., 1861), the universities of Erlangen, Berlin, Tübingen, and Geneva (1862–65), and United Presbyterian Hall, Edinburgh (1866). In 1866 he was ordained minister of Union Street Church, Inverness, where he remained until 1895, when he accepted a call to the pastorate of Bridgend Church, Perth. He retired from the active ministry in 1903, and since that time has resided in Edinburgh, although he still remains senior pastor of Bridgend. He has taken a prominent part in educational movements and was one of the founders of the Northern Counties Institute for the Blind. In 1874 he visited Norway to investigate recent religious movements in that country, and fifteen years later paid a similar visit to the Church missions in the West Indies. He has been the editor of *The Missionary Record* since 1891. His theological position is essentially conservative, and he has a strong desire for union among evangelical churches and for their cooperation in evangelistic work. In addition to translating and editing the first volume of the English version of I. A. Dorner's *Geschichte der protestantischen Theologie, besonders in Deutschland* (Munich, 1867) under the title *History of Protestant Theology, particularly in Germany* (Edinburgh, 1871) and preparing the English translation of the seventh edition of G. A. Warneck's *Abriss einer Geschichte der protestantischen Missionen von der Reformation bis auf die Gegenwart* under the title *Outline of the History of Protestant Missions* (Edinburgh, 1901), he has written *The Story of the Jamaica Mission* (Edinburgh, 1894).

ROCHELLE: A city on the west coast of France in the department of the Charente-Inférieure, having a population of about 28,000. It is a suffragan bishopric of Bordeaux and a fortress of the first class. Its origin dates from the tenth century when the town grew up around a feudal castle built upon a rocky escarpment (*Rupella, Rochella*) in the midst of the marshes of the lower Charente. In the twelfth century it became the chief place of the feudal county of Aunis. The city and territory passed to England with the marriage of Eleanor of Aquitaine to Henry II. (1151), and remained under English rule until 1224 when it was captured by Louis VIII. During the Hundred Years' War, it was taken by the English and formally ceded by France in the Treaty of Brétigny (1360). But it continued to remain French in spirit. In 1372 the Rochellois refused to help the fleet of the Earl of Pembroke which was destroyed by a Castilian fleet in the service of France in the Bay of Biscay. In recognition of this service Charles V. confirmed anew the city's ancient municipal privileges. Its harbor became an important roadstead of the French marine and it was from Rochelle that the French discoverer Bethencourt sailed in 1402 for the conquest of the Canary Isles. The chief interest in La Rochelle, however, is religious, in connection with the Huguenot wars. About 1534 Calvinism acquired an important following in the region round about, and when the wars of religion began in 1562, Rochelle became an important Protestant stronghold in the west of France, rivaling Montauban and Montpellier in the south. Its peculiar importance lay in the fact that it was open to the sea and had ready communication with its coreligionists in England and Holland. During the third civil war (1572–74), which was precipitated by the Massacre of St. Bartholomew, Rochelle was ineffectually besieged by the Roman Catholic forces under command of the duke of Anjou, brother of Charles IX. The peace which terminated this war had an important part in shaping the ultimate settlement of the Huguenot question by the Edict of Nantes. In 1624, when the Huguenot troubles broke out anew, but under radically changed conditions (see RICHELIEU), Rochelle again was their chief stronghold. The situation was all the more dangerous to France because the Huguenots were operating in connection with the English under the duke of Buckingham, whose fleet had captured the Island of Ré. Fortunately for the king Cardinal Richelieu was at the helm. On Aug. 15, 1627, the royal army invested the city. The difficulties of the siege were great. The walls were so strong that with the means which siegecraft possessed at that time it seemed impossible to force them. The chief difficulty, however, was the ready assistance of England. Richelieu did not lay siege to the place in regular form at once. He attempted one or two surprises, but sapping and mining were not effective and no assault was made. Instead a long line of redouts, some three leagues in length and connected by forts, was thrown up from one side of the bay to the other. It was then decided to close the bay. In accordance with the plans of an Italian engineer and a Parisian architect, an enormous dike was built. The work was begun at the end of November, with a spur of masonry from each side of the bay, which when completed was over 1,400 paces long. By May, 1628, the construction of the mole was so well advanced that an English relief fleet was unable to enter the harbor. Meantime Rochelle was famishing. Everything edible was devoured, even boiled parchment. Finally, on Oct. 28, 1628, the city surrendered. Its privileges were abolished, its property was attached to the royal domain, its walls were leveled, and the Roman Catholic religion was restored within it. But Richelieu's opposition had been purely political. Freedom of worship was still left to the Protestants.

Under the active commercial policy of Colbert Rochelle shared with all the Huguenots of France in the prosperity of the times. It had important commercial connection with the French colonies in America, with Santo Domingo, and the West African coast. But the revocation of the Edict of Nantes (q.v.; also see NÎMES, EDICT OF) in 1685 was a blow from which it never recovered. It is estimated then to have lost 5,000 inhabitants. So low did it sink that even during the French Revolution and Napoleonic wars it had almost no history. To-day it is a dull provincial town engaged in the fisheries and having some South American trade. See HUGUENOTS; RICHELIEU; and ROHAN, HENRI, DUC DE.

JAMES WESTFALL THOMPSON.

BIBLIOGRAPHY: J. W. Thompson, *Wars of Religion in France, 1559–76*, Chicago, 1909 (with extensive bibliography; relates to the siege of 1573–74); A. Barbot, *Hist. de la Rochelle*, Paris, 1886; T. E. Kemmerer, *Hist. de l'île de Ré*, La Rochelle, 1888; G. Musset, *La Rochelle et ses ports*, ib. 1890; P. Suzanne, *La Rochelle pittoresque*, ib. 1903; *Cambridge Modern History*, iii. 10–11, 20–25, 32, New York, 1905; and the literature under HUGUENOTS; RICHELIEU; and ROHAN, HENRI.

ROCHET. See VESTMENTS AND INSIGNIA, ECCLESIASTICAL.

ROCK, DANIEL: Roman Catholic; b. at Liverpool Aug. 31, 1799; d. at Kensington, London, Nov. 28, 1871. He was educated in the English College, Rome; was ordained priest in 1824; served at St. Mary's, Moorfields, London, 1825–26, then at the Bavarian Chapel in Warwick St., 1826–27; was domestic chaplain to the earl of Shrewsbury, 1827–1840; then pastor at Buckland, near Farringdon; and, on the reintroduction of the Roman Catholic hierarchy, canon of Southwark, 1852–54. He was an eminent antiquarian, and wrote, *Hierurgia, or the Sacrifice of the Mass Expounded* (2 vols., London, 1833); *Did the Early Church in Ireland acknowledge the Pope's Supremacy?* (1844); and *The Church of our Fathers, as seen in St. Osmund's Rite for the Cathedral of Salisbury* (3 vols., 1849–54).

BIBLIOGRAPHY: J. Gillow, *Literary and Biographical History . . . of English Catholics*, v. 436–437, London and New York, n.d.; *DNB*, xlix. 75–76.

ROCK, JOHANN FRIEDRICH. See INSPIRED, THE.

RODANIM. See DODANIM.

RODE, rō'de, **HINNE (JOHANNES RHODIUS):** B. in Friesland c. 1490; d. in East Friesland c. 1535. He belonged to the Brethren of the Common Life (see COMMON LIFE, BRETHREN OF THE) as their most eminent member and the most conspicuous personal force, and was connected with the school they had established under the patronage of St. Jerome. Nothing is known of his early life, neither the exact time nor place of his birth. He first comes into public note as rector of the school named above, and was held in high esteem for piety and learning. He was no stranger to humanistic efforts, nor to the movements that preceded the Reformation, especially as exemplified by Wessel. Whether Rode made the acquaintance of Wessel, who died in 1489, and so received some incitation from him directly, is not ascertainable. At all events he was acquainted with Wessel's widely diffused, much read and esteemed, influential writings. In this situation Luther's advent was hailed with joy. His theses were circulating in that region as early as 1518, while his books found ready sale despite of or perhaps because of much vehement zeal on the opposing side (Erasmus, *Epist.*, cccxvii., May 18). The contest was also greatly reinforced by Luther's pupils, as by Henry of Zütphen (see MOLLER, HEINRICH).

The Lutheran movement at Utrecht had begun in 1520, through the efforts of a Dominican, Worte (Walther), who preached in Delft against the indulgence bestowed by the pope in favor of St. Lawrence's Church at Rotterdam. He was joined by Master Friedrich Hondebeke (Canirivus); Georgius Saganus, a scholastically cultivated man, with whom Rode subsequently journeyed to Germany; and the youthful Johannes Sartorius, or Snijders. Their most important fellow-combatant was Cornelis Henriks (Hinrichson) Hoen (Honius), advocate in the court of justice at The Hague; but Rode was the movement's leading spirit. Hoen objected to the Roman doctrine, deviating, however, from Wessel in construing the words of institution, which Hoen explained: "this is a pledge, the symbol of my body; it signifies my body." On all sides, however, there was a desire for Luther's view, upon which rested all decisions as to Scripture. Rode was sent to ask from Luther a decision upon this matter and to request him to edit the writings of Wessel. In spite of all researches, there is still debate as to the year when Rode was at Wittenberg. The majority favor 1520–21; Möller and Loofs, 1522. After visiting Luther, Rode made a journey by way of Basel to Zurich, to confer with Zwingli. In 1522 he was condemned at home on the ground of his Lutheran doctrine.

Leaving the Netherlands, Rode returned to Basel some time before Sept. 1, 1522, his immediate purpose being to supervise the issue of Wessel's *Farrago*, which appeared in Sept., 1522. Rode could not continue at home by reason of the hostile state of mind there. So early as 1523, two Augustinians were executed; also two young lads, Henricus Voes and Johannes Esch. The new bishop, Henry of Bavaria, continued the persecution with greater vehemence. Johannes Pistorius, a pupil of Rode's, was executed Sept. 8, 1525.

At this period Rode was in Strasburg with Butzer, as witness the latter's letter to Martin Frecht, a document of much significance in connection with Butzer's attitude toward Rode and with the controversy over the Lord's Supper. In this the following passage occurs:

"Meanwhile, after Carlstadt's tract had appeared, presenting his revised interpretation down to 1524, . . . there came to me a strange man, Joh. Rodius, a heart so devout, so illumined in deeds and words, that I know of no one, not even excepting Luther, . . . whom I could prefer to this man in insight and judgment. . . . He is a native of the Netherlands, where he follows the same calling as Paul among the Greeks. Although recognising Luther as his teacher, he owes more, in certain articles, to Wessel. Moreover, I can note ease wondering that we profit so little by this man. This Rodius was my guest (in the autumn of 1524); and, Bible in hand, he conversed at much length with me on the question of the Lord's Supper, wherein I defended Luther's opinion against him with all my might. But I then discerned that I was no peer to this man's mind, nor equal to all his arguments; and that one can not consistently maintain, by the Scripture, what I desired to affirm. I had to waive the corporeal presence of Christ in the bread; albeit I still hesitated concerning the certain explanation of the words."

The foregoing sketch by a contemporary discloses the significance of Rode, and likewise his influence upon the Swiss Reformed theology. The Eucharistic dispute emanated from Rode; Luther gaged him correctly, and hence Luther's vigorous opposition. Just as the Strasburg and Swiss theologians proved susceptible to Rode's influence in the doctrine as to the Lord's Supper, it was also due to him that the Netherlands Church, and afterward the East Frisian Church, became estranged from the Lutheran trend. Rode later returned to Deventer, in his home country, where Gerhard Geldenhauer (Noviomagus) met him in 1525. From data concerning Rode in the letters of Butser and Capito, dated July 9 and Sept. 26, 1526, it appears that he married in 1526. This was why, to escape constant persecutions, he accepted a teacher's position at Norden, in Ostfriesland. Owing to Rode's aggressive intervention in the East Frisian movement, the previously Lutheran sentiment now took on a Reformed complexion. Rode, when deposed on account of his opposition to Luther, went to Wolfhusen, protected by Count Enno.

Rode's widow died in 1557; the year of his own death is not known. While nothing is certainly extant in the way of his writings, that he produced none is hardly probable; it is not beyond reason to suppose Rode the possible author of a work with the title *Œconomia Christiana*. Rode is still mentioned along with Gnapheus and Honius in connection with the translation of Luther's New Testament into Dutch (Amsterdam, 1525). Yet there are serious doubts in the matter. L. Schulze.

Bibliography: The first source is the Doesburg Chronicle, in part published by W. Moll, in *Kerkhistorisch Archief*, iii. 108–115, Amsterdam, 1862; then A. R. Hardenberg's *Vita Wesselii*, prefixed to the *Opera* of Wessel, Groningen, 1614 (cf. the literature under Wessel); and D. Gerdes, *Introductio in hist. Evangelii seculo XVI.*, i. 228–331, Groningen, 1744. Consult A. J. Van der Aa, *Biographisch Woordenboek van der Nederlanden*, xvi. 302, Haarlem, 1852 sqq.; W. Moll, *Kerkgeschiedenis van Nederland*, 2 vols., Arnhem and Utrecht, 1864–71; J. G. de Hoop-Scheffer, *Geschiedenis der Kerkhervorming in Nederland*, pp. 30, 90–91, 105–106, 263, 316 et passim, Amsterdam, 1873; T. Kolde, *Martin Luther*, ii. 557–578, Gotha, 1884; O. Clemen, *Hinne Rode in Wittenberg, Basel, Zürich*, . . . , in *ZKG*, xviii (1898), 346 sqq.; J. Köstlin, *Martin Luther*, ed. Kawerau, Berlin, 1903; *ADB*, vol. xxix.

RODGERS, JOHN: Presbyterian; b. at Boston Aug. 5, 1727; d. at New York May 7, 1811. He received his education under Samuel Blair and Gilbert Tennent (qq.v.); was licensed Oct., 1747; pastor at St. George's, Del., 1749–65; and at New York, 1765–76, and from the the close of the Revolutionary War till his death. In 1789 he was elected moderator of the first general assembly of the Presbyterian Church, at Philadelphia. He was a stanch patriot during the Revolution, and served as chaplain in the continental army in 1776, of the provincial congress of New York, of the council of safety, and of the first legislature in 1777. He was a prominent character in church and city life.

Bibliography: S. Miller, *Memoirs of the Rev. J. Rodgers, Late Pastor of the Wall Street and Brick Churches in the City of New York*, New York, 1813; W. B. Sprague, *Annals of the American Pulpit*, iii. 154–165, ib. 1858; E. H. Gillett, *Hist. of the Presbyterian Church*, vol. i. passim, Philadelphia, 1864; R. E. Thompson, in *American Church History Series*, vol. vi. passim, New York, 1895.

ROEHM, rōm, JOHANN BAPTIST: German Roman Catholic; b. at Lauingen (26 m. n.e. of Ulm) Jan. 6, 1841. He was educated at the University of Munich, after which he was curate in Ettringen, Thannhausen, and Oettingen in the diocese of Augsburg, and then an instructor in religion at Augsburg, and curate and professor at the royal theological seminary in Munich. Since 1899 he has been canon of the cathedral at Passau.

He has written: *Ausgewählte Reden des heiligen Gregor von Nazianz* (Kempten, 1874); *Ausgewählte Schriften des Origenes* (1876); *Predigten auf dem Feste der Heiligen* (Augsburg, 1876); *Das Glaubensprinzip der katholischen Kirche* (Vienna, 1877); *Predigten auf dem Feste der seligsten Jungfrau* (Passau, 1879); *Aufgabe der protestantischen Theologen* (Augsburg, 1882); *Gedanken über die Union* (Hildesheim, 1883); *Confessionelle Lehrgegensätze* (1883); *Grobe Unwahrheiten von und über Luther* (1884); *Der erste Brief an die Thessaloniker* (Passau, 1885); *Ein Wort über die deutsche protestantische Schule* (5 parts, Hildesheim, 1887); *Zur Charakteristik der protestantischen Polemik der Gegenwart* (1889); *Zur Tetzellegende* (1889); *Protestantische Lehre vom Antichrist* (1891); *Zur Charakteristik des Protestantismus in Vergangenheit und Gegenwart* (1892); *Sendschreiben eines katholischen an einen orthodoxen Theologen* (Augsburg, 1895); *Der Protestantismus unserer Tage* (Munich, 1897); *Die Wiedervereinigung der christlichen Konfessionen* (Mainz, 1900).

ROEHR, rūr, JOHANN FRIEDRICH: German Lutheran of the rationalistic school; b. at Rossbach (24 m. s.w. of Leipsic) July 30, 1777; d. at Weimar June 15, 1848. After completing his education at the University of Leipsic, he was appointed assistant preacher at the university church of the same city, and then taught for two years at Pforta (1802–04). He was then pastor at Ostrau, near Zeitz, until 1820, when he was called to become chief pastor at Weimar, where he passed the remainder of his life. He was likewise chief court preacher, supreme consistorial and ecclesiastical councilor, and general superintendent for the principality of Weimar.

The importance of Röhr lies in his defense of popular rationalism, a position first consciously set forth in his *Briefe über den Rationalismus* (Aachen, 1813). This system was essentially the blending of two religious truths, revealed and non-revealed (reason), the final end of religion being pure morality; the divinity of Christ was categorically denied. Röhr's views were received with so little favor that in the second and third editions of his *Grund- und Glaubenssätze der evangelisch-protestantischen Kirche* (Neustadt-on-the-Oder, 1834, 1844) he was forced to modify the radicalism of his theories. He continued his advocacy of rationalism in the journal published by him under the successive names of *Predigerlitteratur* (1810–14), *Neue und neueste Predigerlitteratur* (1815–19), and *Kritische Prediger-Bibliothek* (1820–48). He was at the same time involved in polemics with all who differed from him, until the untenability of the position of popular rationalism was effectually shown by Hase after a bitter controversy. Röhr likewise savagely assailed the school of Scheiermacher after the death of its founder. The character of Röhr, both as a theologian and as a man, is mirrored in his sermons, which appeared in several collections, as in his *Christologische Predigten* (2 vols., Weimar, 1831–37), as well as in the *Magazin für christliche Prediger*, which he edited after 1828. He also wrote *Lehrbuch der Anthropologie für Volksschulen und den Selbstunterricht* (Zeitz, 1815); *Palästina oder historisch-geographische Beschreibung des jüdischen Landes zur Zeit Jesu* (1816); *Luthers Leben und Wirken* (1818); *Kleine theologische Schriften* (Schleusingen, 1841); and *Die gute Sache des Protestantismus* (Leipsic, 1842).

(G. Frank†.)

Bibliography: B. Hain, *Neue Nekrolog der Deutschen*, xxvi. 1 (1848), 431; G. Frank, *Geschichte der protestantischen Theologie*, iii. 368, Leipsic, 1875; *ADB*, xxx. 92.

ROËLL, rōl, HERMANN ALEXANDER: Dutch Reformed; b. at Dolbergh, Westphalia, 1653; d. at Amsterdam July 12, 1718. He was educated at Hamm (1669–70), Utrecht (1670–71), and Groningen (1671–72), but he was forced by the siege to leave the latter city, and remained in Germany and Switzerland until 1674, when he resumed his studies at Hamm (1674–75), completing them at Utrecht. He then lived for a time at Leyden, after which he was chaplain of the Princess Palatine Elizabeth (1679–80) and of Albertina Agnes, widow of William Frederick, stadtholder of Friesland (1680–82). For four years he was pastor at Deventer, but in 1686 was appointed professor of theology at Franeker, where he remained until 1704, when he accepted a similar appointment at Utrecht. Toward the end of his life he resided in Amsterdam. Roëll belonged to the school of Coccejus and Descartes, and as a rigid critic, holding that reason could not be in conflict with revelation, he sought to harmonize the two, maintaining that revelation had been given to supplement the inadequacy of reason. Working along the lines of his inaugural address at Franeker, *De religione naturali* (Franeker, 1686), Roëll became the object of severe criticism, particularly from the rigidly Calvinistic Ulrich Huber, professor of jurisprudence. Before the controversy was ended by the command of the estates of Friesland, Roëll, who was supported by his Franeker colleagues J. van der Waeyen and R. ab Andala, had written, in reply to the critiques of Huber, his *Kort onderzoek over de twaalf stellingen van Ulr. Huber* (Franeker, 1687) and *Vindiciæ examinis brevis duodecim positionum Ulr. Huberi* (1687). Meanwhile his deference to the importance of reason and his non-Calvinistic views on the eternal generation of the Son had aroused suspicion. He taught that "generation" here implied merely that the second person of the Trinity possessed the same nature and essence as the first, coexisting with the Father from eternity, appearing in the flesh, and revealing the glory of the Father in his works. The terms "Father" and "Son," moreover, connoted simply an extremely close association of the two, the relation between the divine sender and the divine envoy. He also taught that the earthly death of the righteous satisfies divine justice and is sufficient to obtain forgiveness; and at the same time he was suspected of entertaining heretical views on the eternity of the divine decree and the divine obligation to punish sin, as well as on satisfaction, justification, and other doctrines.

These views were assailed by Roëll's colleague, C. Vitringa, in 1689, whereupon Roëll defended a series of *Theses theologicæ de generatione Filii et morte fidelium* (Franeker, 1689), following this up with the publication of his own two dissertations *De generatione Filii* (1689) in answer to the strictures of Vitringa. The controversy was finally ended in 1691 and Roëll, to prevent any further misunderstanding, wrote the *Kort en eenvoudig berigt van het verschil over de geboorte des Soons* (Amsterdam, 1691), while the senate forbade all professors, pastors, and ecclesiastical bodies to occupy themselves longer with the matter. Despite all this, the Synod of South Holland condemned the teachings of Roëll in 1691, similar courses being pursued by the synods of North Holland, Utrecht, and Groningen. Even with Roëll's death bitterness against him did not disappear, for until the end of the eighteenth century some synods issued an annual warning against his doctrines. At the same time, though condemned by his church, Roëll enjoyed the support of the civil authorities, and, thanks to his gentle disposition, had an honorable career as a teacher. Among his works not already mentioned, special allusion may be made to his *De theologiæ et theologiæ supranaturalis præ naturali præstantia* (Utrecht, 1704); *Commentarius in epistolam ad Ephesios* (2 parts, 1715–31); and *Explicatio cathecheseos Heidelbergensis* (1728), as well as to his editions of the writings of A. Gulichius, A. Rouse, and T. Nemethi.

(S. D. van Veen.)

Bibliography: A *Vita* is in *Bibliotheca Bremensis*, Class II., pp. 707–723, Bremen, 1760–66; the *Judicium ecclesiasticum* was published at Leyden, 1723; B. Glasius, *Godgeleerd Nederland*, iii. 189–197, Bois-le-Duc, 1851–1856; W. B. S. Boeles, *Frieslands Hoogeschool en het Rijks Athenæum te Franeker*, ii. 309–318, Leeuwarden, 1889.

ROERDAM, rōr′dām, THOMAS SKAT: Danish bishop; b. at Laastrup (15 m. n. of Viborg) Feb. 11, 1832; d. at Copenhagen Sept. 25, 1909. Having acquired the degree of B.A. in 1848, he continued study under his father and at the University of Copenhagen (candidate in theology, 1855), specializing in the Semitic languages; as a result he published Paul of Tella's Judges and Ruth in the Syriac from the Septuagint (*Libri Judicum et Ruth secundum versionem Syriaco-Hexaplarem*, Copenhagen, 1859–61), with Greek translation, notes, and dissertation. During 1858–69 he resided in Copenhagen, studying and teaching, in 1866 publishing *Historisk Oplysning om den hellige Skrift*, and in 1868 *Den kristelige Lære fremstillet i Sammenhæng*. He was minister in Sönderup and Nordrup (1869–73), in Rönnebæk and Olstrup (1873–80), at Helligaandskirken in Copenhagen (1880–86); provost at Holmen (1885–95); and in 1895 was appointed bishop of Zealand, being *primus inter pares* among the Danish bishops, and having after 1900 the title of Ordensbiskop. As a preacher his influence was wide, especially among the younger clergy, and his sermons are widely read. As bishop he worked indefatigably for the building of churches, did much for the hymnal, and also influenced legal provisions for Denmark. He translated the New Testament, with explanatory notes (1887–1892).

JOHN O. EVJEN.

ROEUBLI, WILHELM. See REUBLIN.

ROGATION DAYS: Days appointed for public supplication to God for a blessing on the fruits of the earth and other benefits. Such special supplications, known as *litaniæ rogationes*, are found in the Church at an early period (Sozomen, *Hist. eccl.*, viii. 8). Processions with litanies of two kinds took place, the regular on St. Mark's Day (April 25) and in the week before Ascension Day, and others on special occasions for extraordinary needs. Sidonius describes the solemnities as consisting of fasting, preaching, singing, and weeping. In the Frankish kingdom the rogations before Ascension Day were made of universal obligation by the first Synod of Orléans (511); in Spain there were peculiar observances (second Synod of Braga, 563, can. xvi., cf. Hefele, *Conciliengeschichte*, iii. 17–18, Eng. transl., iv. 383–384, Fr. transl., iii. 1, p. 178; fifth of Toledo, can. i., cf. Hefele, ut sup., iii. 88, Eng. transl., iv. 459, Fr. transl., iii. 1, pp. 277–278; sixth, can. ii., Hefele, ut sup., iii. 90 [merely reaffirms the finding of the fifth synod]). Those who took part in the St. Mark's Day procession in Rome were divided, according to the pattern set by Gregory the Great, into seven classes, clergy, laymen, monks, virgins, married women, widows, the poor, and children, and from this arose the "sevenfold litany." The seventeenth Council of Toledo, 694 (can. vi.), decreed monthly rogations for the Visigothic kingdom, and the same were ordered by the Lateran Council under Innocent III. for the deliverance of the Holy Land. In the Evangelical Lutheran Church the ancient "week of prayer" before Pentecost has been retained in a number of places, sometimes with the processions, as in Pomerania and Brandenburg. Even to-day solemn processions are made through the fields for a blessing on the fruits of the earth in the month of May or at other times, on which occasions the ancient solemn litanies (the *Litania communis*) in responsive form are usually used. [In the Anglican communion the Monday, Tuesday, and Wednesday before Ascension Day are counted as fast-days, "on which the Church requires such a measure of abstinence as is more especially suited to extraordinary acts and exercises of devotion."]

M. HEROLD.

BIBLIOGRAPHY: Bingham, *Origines*, XIII., i. 10, XXI., ii. 8; A. J. Binterim, *Denkwürdigkeiten*, iv. 555 sqq., Mainz, 1827; J. C. W. Augusti, *Denkwürdigkeiten*, x. 7–72, Leipsic, 1829; T. F. D. Kliefoth, *Liturgische Abhandlungen*, vi. 155, 8 vols., 2d ed., Schwerin, 1858–60; F. Procter and W. H. Frere, *New Hist. of the Book of Common Prayer*, passim, London, 1905; J. H. Blunt, *Annotated Book of Common Prayer*, pp. 221–222, 296–298, New York, 1908; *KL*, ii. 894–897.

ROGERS, HENRY: Essayist and apologist; b. at St. Albans (19 m. n.n.w. of London) Oct. 18, 1806; d. at Pennal Tower, Machynlleth (53 m. n.e. of Cardigan), North Wales, Aug. 20, 1877. He was educated at Highbury College, 1826–29; was Independent minister at Poole, Dorset, 1829–32; lecturer on rhetoric and logic at Highbury College, 1832–36; professor of the English language and literature, University College, London, 1836–39; of English literature and language, mathematics, and mental philosophy, Spring Hill College, Birmingham, 1839–1858; and principal of the Independent College, Manchester, from 1858 until a few years before his death. An incurable throat trouble compelled him to abandon preaching so that he devoted himself to literary pursuits. From 1839 to 1859 he was connected with the *Edinburgh Review*, in the columns of which he published much of his best work. He particularly distinguished himself by his opposition to the Tractarian movement. His reputation mainly rests upon his *Eclipse of Faith, or a Visit to a religious Sceptic* (London, 1852) and *Defence* (1854). His other writings embrace, *Essay on the Life and Genius of Jonathan Edwards* (prefaced to Edwards's Works, 1834); *Life of John Howe* (1836); *Essays from the Edinburgh Review* (3 vols., 1850–55); *Essay on the Life and Genius of Thomas Fuller* (1856); *Selections from the Correspondence of R. E. H. Greyson*, the name Greyson being an anagram for Rogers (2 vols., 1857); and *The Superhuman Origin of the Bible inferred from itself*, Congregational Lectures (1873).

BIBLIOGRAPHY: A *Memoir* by R. W. Dale prefaces the 8th ed. of *The Superhuman Origin of the Bible*, 1893; *Congregational Year Book*, 1878, p. 347; *DNB*, xlix. 121–123.

ROGERS, JOHN: 1. English Protestant martyr; b. at Deritend in the parish of Aston (2 m. n. of Birmingham) about 1500; burned at Smithfield, London, Feb. 4, 1555. He was graduated at Cambridge (B.A., 1526); received an invitation to Christ Church, Oxford; about 1534 became chaplain to the Merchant Adventurers at Antwerp, and there made the acquaintance of Tyndale and became a Protestant. In 1537 he issued (probably at Wittenberg), under the pseudonym of "Thomas Matthewe," a skilful combination of the Bible translation of Tyndale and Coverdale with preface and notes, which has since been known as Matthew's Bible. (See BIBLE VERSIONS, B, IV., § 4.) He removed to Wittenberg, where he was pastor until the accession of Edward VI., when he returned to England (1548). He was in 1550 provided by Bishop Ridley with settlements in London, and in 1551 made prebendary of St. Paul's. On the succession of Queen Mary (1553) he was arrested for his vigorous denunciation of Romanism, and after months of imprisonment was burnt—the first Marian martyr.

BIBLIOGRAPHY: J. L. Chester, *John Rogers, the Compiler of the First Authorised English Bible*, London, 1861; C. Anderson, *Annals of the English Bible*, ed. Hugh Anderson, pp. 268, 294, 295, 429–438, ib. 1862; J. I. Mombert, *Hand-Book to the English Versions of the Bible*, pp. 176 sqq., New York, 1883; H. W. Hoare, *Evolution of the English Bible*, pp. 180–183, ib. 1902; I. M. Price, *Ancestry of our English Bible*, pp. 250–253, 262, Philadelphia, 1907.

2. English Fifth-monarchy man; b. at Messing (43 m. n.e. of London) in 1627; d. probably in London in 1665. His father Nehemiah was a devout Anglican minister, loyal to Charles I. and Archbishop Laud. Religiously awakened when ten years of age by the terrific preaching of the Puritan William Fenner and later by Stephen Marshall, one of the Presbyterian preachers to the Long Parliament, and by the reading of H. Drexelius' *Considerations upon Eternity* (in Latin, Cologne, 1631), his reason was dethroned so that he had to be tied hand and foot in bed where his continuous cry was, "I am damned! I am damned! I am sure I can not be saved! It is impossible! Oh, hell! hell! fire about me! The devils are at me!" As dreams of torment drove him mad, so a dream of heavenly mercy and comfort restored his reason. After he had associated himself with the Roundheads (1642), his father cast him off in the midst of winter. He made his way by begging to Cambridge, where he had studied for awhile before, hoping to support himself by labor or to secure a scholarship. Failing in this he came near starving, subsisting for some time on refuse, and even eating leather, feathers, and grass. He was sorely tempted to eat his own flesh and to commit suicide. Just in the nick of time a position as tutor in a gentleman's family was offered him (1643). Soon afterward he felt called to preach and realized that he possessed the necessary gifts and graces in multiplied abundance. He was ordained as a Presbyterian minister (1647 or 1648) and became rector of Burleigh. In less than a year he renounced Presbyterianism and became Independent lecturer at St. Thomas Apostle's in London. In 1650 he was chosen by parliament one of six ministers to preach in Dublin at a salary of £200 a year. Christ Church cathedral was assigned to him and Governor Hewson was a member of his congregation. He did not hesitate to join with Hewson in military service when there was need. His ministerial work was seriously disturbed by Thomas Patient, also a parliamentary preacher, who convinced many of Rogers' parishioners of the unscripturalness of infant baptism and the duty of believers' baptism. Rogers' defense of infant baptism alienated half of his constituents and his advocacy of toleration and the rights of women the other half. His position having thus become untenable he returned to London after six months in Dublin and resumed his lectureship. In his *Bethshemish: Epistle to the Churches* (London, 1653) he gives a highly colored account of the annoyances and persecutions that he suffered in Dublin and reveals much of the spirit of his ministry. He also polemizes sharply against the Presbyterian clergy, whom he compares with Romanist priests in point of bigotry and intolerance. In his *Sagrir: or Domesday Drawing Nigh, with Thunder and Lightning to Lawyers* (1654), he denounces the lawyers as the archenemies of true Christianity and sets forth his views respecting the approaching end of the Fourth Monarchy with its laws and lawyers and the inauguration of the Fifth Monarchy "with those godly laws, officers, and ordinances that belong to the legislative power of the Lord Jesus." The *Sagrir* contains a letter "to the Right Honorable the Lord General Cromwell, the People's Victorious Champion in England, Ireland, and Scotland." He seeks to convince Cromwell that he has been chosen by the Lord to lead the hosts of the redeemed against the Roman Catholic and Protestant persecutors of the continent, "to break in pieces the oppressor and to deliver the poor and needy." In the "Epistle to the Reader" he declares himself the champion of Christ against Antichrist and polemizes fiercely against the tithing-law and any connection of Church and State. He claims recently to have been treated contemptuously and violently by a committee of parliament while presenting his objections to tithing and State-Churchism. He predicts that the Fifth Monarchy, "where Christ and his saints shall rule the world," will begin in 1656. "As in Noah's flood, after the doors were shut up there was no mercy, though they came wading middle-deep, so let this be an alarum to all men to make haste while the door of the ark is open. In a few years they will find it shut, and then though they wade through and through much danger, whether Parliament men, Army men, Merchant men, Clergy men, Lawyers, or others, they may find it too late." His demand was that Cromwell first of all lead an English army into France for the overthrow of the Bourbon dynasty and the relief of the persecuted Huguenots. Germany and Austria were to be conquered by the English with the help of the Huguenots and the persecuted in those countries. Last of all Rome should be taken and the hierarchy destroyed. He assures the English army and statesmen that "if they will not take their work abroad they shall have it at home, as sure as God lives and is righteous. For when the kingdom of Christ comes there is no such thing as bounds, or limits, or rivers, or seas, that shall cap up or confine the fervent zeal and flaming affections of an Army, Representative, or People spirited for the work of Christ." His exhortations are based upon the most sanguinary passages in the Old Testament and the Apocalypse. The forcible dissolution of the Barebones Parliament by Cromwell (Dec., 1653) because of its abolition of tithes and of the court of chancery and other radical measures infuriated the Fifth-monarchy men, one of whose leaders, Major-general Harrison, was highly influential in this legislation. Harrison, Rich, and Carew, lay members of the party, were imprisoned or sent into involuntary retirement. Rogers, Feak, Vavasor Powell, and Simpson, Fifth-monarchy preachers, violently denounced Cromwell and his supporters and were one by one on various pretexts imprisoned, Rogers at Lambeth in July, 1654. In February preceding he had published his *Fifth Epistle to Cromwell*, entitled *Mene, Tekel, Peres: or a Little Appearance of the Handwriting . . . against the Powers and Apostles of the Times*. While in prison at Lambeth Rogers published *Morning Beams: or the Vision of the Prison Pathmos* (1654). This writing throws much light on the spirit of the Fifth-monarchy movement. An interview with Cromwell Feb. 6, 1655, resulted in no better understanding. Two months later he was removed to Windsor Castle. His sufferings at Windsor he recorded in *Jagar Sahadutha: An Oiled Pillar*. Released in Jan., 1657, he returned to Lon-

don and soon became involved in a Fifth-monarchy conspiracy against Cromwell's government and was sent with Harrison and others to the Tower. Cromwell died the following September and was succeeded by his son Richard. Rogers and other Fifth-monarchy men cooperated with Sir Henry Vane for the overthrow of Richard Cromwell and enjoyed great favor under the restored Long Parliament. At the restoration of the Stuart dynasty (1660) Rogers retired to Holland and studied medicine at Leyden and Utrecht, proceeding to the degree of M.D. in the University of Utrecht Oct. 17, 1662. Returning to England soon afterward he practised medicine at Bermondsey and was admitted *ad eundem gradum* at Oxford June 13, 1664. He published medical theses in 1662 and 1664, in connection with the receiving of his degree. He seems to have taken no further interest in religious questions after he became interested in medicine. He is lost sight of after 1665 and probably died of the plague that prevailed in London and its suburbs that year. See FIFTH-MONARCHY MEN. A. H. NEWMAN.

BIBLIOGRAPHY: E. Rogers, *Some Account of the Life and Opinions of a Fifth-Monarchy-Man. Chiefly extracted from the Writings of John Rogers, Preacher*, London, 1867. J. L. Chester, *The Life of John Rogers, the Compiler of the first Authorized English Bible*, ib., 1861 (contains sketch of the Fifth-monarchy man, who according to family tradition was a descendant of the martyr); *DNB*, xlix. 130-132.

ROGERS, ROBERT WILLIAM: Methodist Episcopal, orientalist; b. at Philadelphia Feb. 14, 1864. He studied at the high school of his native city, the University of Pennsylvania (1882-84), Johns Hopkins University, Baltimore (graduated, 1887), where he took post-graduate courses, the University of Leipsic (Ph.D., 1895), and Haverford College, Pa. (Ph.D., 1890); was instructor in Hebrew in Haverford College, 1890; professor of English Bible and Semitic History, Dickinson College, Pa., 1890-92; and has been professor of Hebrew and Old-Testament exegesis in Drew Theological Seminary since 1893, also non-resident lecturer at the Woman's College, Baltimore, 1896-1900. In the interest of oriental studies he attended the congresses of orientalists at London in 1892, where he was honorary secretary, Geneva in 1894, Paris in 1897, Hamburg in 1902, and Copenhagen in 1908. He has prepared *Two Texts of Esarhaddon* (Cambridge, Eng., 1889); *Catalogue of Manuscripts, chiefly Oriental* (1890); *Inscriptions of Sennacherib* (London, 1893); *Outlines of the History of Early Babylonia* (Leipsic, 1895); *History of Babylonia and Assyria* (2 vols., New York, 1900); and *Religion of Babylonia and Assyria, especially in its Relation to Israel* (1909).

ROGGE, rog'e, **BERNARD FRIEDRICH WILHELM:** German Protestant; b. at Grosstinz (a village near Liegnitz, 40 m. w.n.w. of Breslau), Silesia, Oct. 22, 1831. He was educated at the universities of Halle and Bonn, after which he was a teacher in a high school for girls at Coblenz and a vicar in Vollenden in 1854-56, a pastor at Stollberg near Aachen in 1856-59, and a divisional pastor at Coblenz in 1859-62. Since 1862 he has been court chaplain at Potsdam, serving also as army chaplain in the campaigns of 1866 and 1870-71. In theology he belongs to the mediating school of Lutheranism. Among his numerous writings, special mention may be made of his *Die evangelischen Geistlichen im Feldzug von 1866* (Berlin, 1867; Eng. transl., *The Chaplain in the Field of War*, London, 1870); *Die evangelischen Feld- und Lazarethgeistlichen der königlichen preussischen Armee im Feldzuge von 1870-71* (1872); *Gott war mit uns, Predigten und Reden im Feldzuge von 1870-71* (1872); *Lutherbüchlein* (Leipsic, 1883); *Feldmarschall Prinz Friedrich Carl* (Berlin, 1885); *Kaiserbüchlein zur Erinnerung an Deutschlands Heldenkaiser Wilhelm I.* (1888); *Friedrich III., deutscher Kaiser* (1888); *Kaiser Wilhelm der Siegreiche* (Bielefeld, 1889); *Allezeit im Herrn* (collected hymns and poems; Leipsic, 1890; new ed., 1909); *Christliche Charakterbilder aus dem Hause Hohenzollern* (Hanover, 1890); *Vom Kurhut zur Kaiserkrone* (2 vols., 1891-92); *Generalfeldmarschall Graf Moltke* (Wittenberg, 1891); *Theodor Körner* (1891); *Pförtnerleben* (Leipsic, 1893); *Fürst Bismark* (Hanover, 1895); *Sedanbüchlein* (Dresden, 1895); *Bei der Garde, Erinnerungen aus dem Feldzuge 1870-71* (Hanover, 1895), *Aus sieben Jahrzehnten* (autobiography; 2 vols., Hanover, 1895-99); *Eine Osterreise nach Jerusalem* (1896); *Illustrierte Geschichte der Reformation in Deutschland* (Leipsic, 1899); *Johann Friedrich der Grossmütige* (Halle, 1902); *Generalfeldmarschall Roon* (Hanover, 1903); and *Unser Kaiserpaar* (Goslar, 1906); *Bildersaal der christlichen Welt* (1907 qq.); *Religiöse Charaktere aus dem 19. Jahrhundert* (1908); and *Das Evangelium in der Verfolgung. Bilder aus den Zeiten der Gegenreformation* (Cologne, 1910).

ROHAN, rō"ān', **HENRI, DUC DE:** Huguenot leader; b. at the château of Blain (23 m. n.w. of Nantes) Aug. 21, 1579; d. on the battlefield of Rheinfelden (10 m. e. of Basel) Feb. 28, 1638. He belonged to a famous Breton family which espoused Protestantism in the sixteenth century, of which he and his brother Benjamin, prince of Soubise, were the most celebrated members. Each owed his abilities to his mother, Catherine de Parthenay, who educated them. At the age of sixteen under Henry IV. Henri fought against the Spaniards and was present at the siege of Amiens (1597). In the years following he traveled through Italy, Germany, Holland, England, and Scotland. He married a daughter of Sully, the great minister of Henry IV. When the troubles of the Huguenots (q.v.) broke out early in the reign of Louis XIII., Rohan became their leader. He commanded their forces in Upper Languedoc and Upper Guienne, and checkmated Marshal Luynes at Montauban. As a result of the peace of Oct. 9, 1623, in which the Edict of Nantes (q.v.) was confirmed, Rohan was made a marshal of France and invested with the governments of Nîmes and Usès, with a compensation of 800,000 livres for the loss of the government of Poitou and St. Jean d'Angély. This peace was merely a truce, and in 1627 the Huguenots, rebelling anew, made their last stand at La Rochelle, in the defense of which Rohan and his brother took part (see ROCHELLE). With the fall of the Huguenot power in France Henri retired to Italy, where he wrote his celebrated *Le parfaict Capitaine* (1636; Eng. transl., *The Complete Captain*, London, 1640). But Richelieu was loath to lose his abilities, and in 1633 he took part in the war in the Valteline (see RICHELIEU). He was also made commander of the Swiss mercenaries in France, but the cardinal, growing suspicious of his influence with the Protestants, sent him into exile, and he retired to Baden. Again he returned to France and for a time fought against the Spaniards in the Alpine passes, but soon fell out with the cardinal and offered his sword to Bernard of Saxe-Weimar, the greatest Protestant leader in the Thirty Years' War (q.v.) after the death of Gustavus Adolphus. He fell in the first engagement (at Rheinfelden) in which he took part. Among other works he wrote *Mémoires sur les choses advenues en France depuis la mort de Henri IV jusqu'à la paix de Juin, 1629* (Paris 1630; 8th ed., 2 vols., Amsterdam, 1756; Eng. transl., London, 1660); and *Mémoires et lettres sur la guerre de la Valteline*, ed. Zurlauben (3 vols., Geneva, 1758). JAMES WESTFALL THOMPSON.

BIBLIOGRAPHY: Fauvelet du Tor, *Hist. de Henry Duc de Rohan*, Paris, 1667; A. Laugel, in *Revue des deux mondes*, 1879; idem, *Henry de Rohan, son rôle politique et militaire sous Louis XIII.*, ib. 1889; M. G. Schybergson, *Le Duc de Rohan et la chute du parti protestant en France*, ib. 1880; H. de La Garde, *Le Duc de Rohan et les protestants sous Louis XIII.*, ib. 1884; J. Bühring, *Venedig, Gustaf Adolf, und Rohan*, Halle, 1885; F. Guillermet, *Rohan et les Genevois*, Paris, 1891; J. de Bouffard-Madiane, *Mémoires sur les guerres civiles du duc de Rohan, 1610–29*, ed. C. Pradel, ib. 1889; F. Pieth, *Die Feldzüge des Herzogs Rohan in Veltlin und in Graubünden*, Bern, 1905; Lichtenberger, *ESR*, xi. 255–257.

ROHR, rōr, IGNATZ: German Roman Catholic; b. at Hochmössingen (a village near Oberndorf, 43 m. s.w. of Stuttgart) June 29, 1866. He was educated at the University of Tübingen (Ph.D., 1894; D.D., 1899), where he was a lecturer on philosophy from 1894 to 1899 and on dogmatics from 1899 to 1903. In 1903 he was appointed professor of New-Testament exegesis at the University of Breslau, where he remained until 1906, when he went in a similar capacity to Strasburg. He assists in editing *Biblische Zeitfragen* (Münster, 1908 sqq.); and has written *Paulus und die Gemeinde von Corinth auf Grund der beiden Corintherbriefe* (Freiburg, 1899); *Der Vernichtungskampf gegen das biblische Christusbild* (Münster, 1908); and *Die Glaubwürdigkeit des Markusevangeliums* (1909).

ROIJAARDS, roy'yärds, HERMAN JOHAN: Dutch Reformed; b. at Utrecht Oct. 3, 1794; d. there Jan. 2, 1854. After completing his education at the University of Utrecht in 1818, he became pastor of the church at Meerkerk, and in 1823 was appointed professor of theology at Utrecht. He was one of the founders in 1839 of the *Archief voor kerkelijke Geschiedenis*, a journal, in which he began his history of the Church in Holland, by an account of the Reformation in Utrecht (1845). He published *Invoering en vestiging van het Christendom in Nederland* (Utrecht, 1842), which was supplemented by *Geschiedenis van het gevestigde Christendom en de christelijke kerk in Nederland gedurende de middeleeuwen* (2 parts, 1849–53), which as a principal work is of permanent value. He also furthered the study of canon law in Holland, by his *Hedendaagsch Kerkregt bij de Hervormden in Nederland* (2 parts, 1834–37). (J. J. VAN OOSTERZEE†.)

ROKYCANA, roc''is-ā'nā, JOHN: Bohemian priest, who was the central figure in the ecclesiastical history of Bohemia, 1430–70; d. 1471. He first became prominent in 1427, by denouncing, in a sermon, the policy of Sigismund Korybut, who was attempting to bring about a reconciliation between Bohemia and the pope, which led to the expulsion of Korybut. After a temporary success at arms, Bohemia was induced, from exhaustion, to enter the negotiations of the Council of Basel (q.v.), which ended in the acceptance of the compacts by the Bohemians, Rokycana taking a chief part. Before the compacts were signed (1435), the Bohemians secretly elected Rokycana archbishop of Prague, with two suffragans; but Sigismund did not recognize him as archbishop without the consent of the council of Basel. The Roman Catholic reaction in 1437 obliged Rokycana to flee from Prague, but he resumed his office when the influence of George of Podiebrad (q.v.) became supreme, in 1444.

BIBLIOGRAPHY: *Monumenta conciliorum generalium seculi*, xv., vol. i., Vienna, 1857; F. Palacky, *Beiträge zur Geschichte des Hussitenkrieges*, 2 vols., Prague, 1872–73; Creighton, *Papacy*, ii. 189, 238–246, 255 et passim, iii. 130, iv. 35–38; Hefele, *Conciliengeschichte*, vol. vii. passim; and the literature under BASEL, COUNCIL OF; HUSS, JOHN, HUSSITES; and PODIEBRAD AND KUNSTATT, GEORGE OF.

ROLLS. See CANON OF SCRIPTURE, I., 6.

ROMAINE, ro-mēn', WILLIAM: English Evangelical divine; b. at Hartlepool (17 m. s.e. of Durham), England, Sept. 25, 1714; d. at London July 26, 1795. He was educated at Hart Hall and Christ Church, Oxford (B.A., 1734; M.A., 1737); was ordained deacon, 1736, and priest, 1738; and was curate for many years at Baustead, Surrey, and Horton, Middlesex. While yet a deacon he made an attack upon William Warburton's *Divine Legation*, pursuing the subject in his first two sermons at the University of Oxford (1739, 1741). To critical study he made the contribution of a Hebrew Concordance, 1747–48, being an edition of that of Marius de Calasso. Drawn into the Evangelical revival, he first adhered to John Wesley, but in 1755 passed to the side of George Whitefield; and remained the ablest exponent among the Evangelicals of the highest Calvinistic doctrine. He was appointed to a lectureship at the united parishes of St. George's, Botolph's Lane, and St. Botolph's, Billingsgate, London, 1748; and to a double lectureship at St. Dunstan's-in-the-West, 1749, in addition to which he became morning preacher at St. George's, Hanover Square. His extreme Calvinism and radical manner, though popular with the masses, resulted in turbulence; and he was limited to an evening service at St. Dunstan's and deprived of St. George's. In 1756 he became curate at St. Olave's, Southwark; of St. Bartholomew the Great, in 1759; and at Westminster Chapel, 1761. After a turbulent career, he obtained the living at St. Anne's, Blackfriars, and St. Andrew of the Wardrobe in 1764, where he continued as a great popular attraction till his death. As a preacher he exercised great power, and his theology and views on the spiritual life are best contained in the long-popular works: *The Life of Faith* (London, 1764); *The*

Walk of Faith (1771); and *The Triumph of Faith* (1795).

BIBLIOGRAPHY: W. B. Cadogan, *Life of W. Romaine*, prefixed to Romaine's *Works*, 8 vols., London, 1796; C. E. De Coetlogon, *Life of the Just Exemplified in the Character of . . . W. Romaine*, ib. 1795; T. Haweis, *Life of W. Romaine*, ib. 1797; J. C. Ryle, *Christian Leaders of the Last Century*, ib. 1868; G. T. Fox, *Life and Doctrine of Romaine*, ib. 1876; *DNB*, xlix. 175–177.

ROMAN CATHOLICS.

I. In General: The Roman Catholic Church is the largest of the three grand divisions of Christendom (Greek, Latin, and Protestant), and in its own estimation the only church founded by Christ on earth. Bellarmin, one of its standard divines, defines the Church as consisting of all who (1) profess the true faith, (2) partake of the true sacraments, and (3) are subject to the rule of the pope as the head of the Church. The first mark excludes all heretics, as well as Jews, heathen, and Mohammedans; the second excludes the catechumens and the excommunicated; the third, the schismatics (i.e., the Greeks and Oriental Christians, who hold substantially "the true faith" and the seven sacraments, but refuse obedience to the pope). The Protestants, without distinction, are excluded as being both heretical and schismatical. The members of the Anglican communion and of the Protestant Episcopal Church of the United States also belong in this category of heretics by the decision of Leo XIII., in an Apostolical Letter of Sept. 13, 1896, pronouncing Anglican orders invalid (Eng. transl. is given in *The Great Encyclical Letters of Pope Leo XIII.*, New York, 1903). But all who hold those three points belong to the church militant on earth, without regard to their moral character (*etiamsi reprobi, scelesti et impii sint*), though only the good members will be saved. Thus defined, the Church, says Bellarmin, is as visible and palpable as the (*quondam*) republic of Venice or the (*quondam*) kingdom of France. He denies the distinction between the visible and invisible Church altogether.* A recent Roman Catholic writer on canon law, Philipp Hergenröther (*Lehrbuch des katholischen Rechts*, p. 2, Freiburg, 1905), defines the Church as "the communion of those who are united under one Head, Christ, and his visible vicegerent for the confession of one faith and the participation in the same means of grace." One of the fundamental qualities of the Church is visibility (p. 22). The full name of the Roman communion is the "Holy, Catholic, Apostolic, and Roman Church." It numbers over two hundred millions of souls, or about one-half of the entire Christian population of the globe.* It is found in all continents and among all nations, but is strongest in southern countries, and among the Latin and Celtic races in Italy, Spain, France, Austria, Ireland, and South America. It agrees in all essential doctrines and usages with the Greek Church (except the papacy), but has more vitality and energy; while it is behind the Protestant communions in general culture, intelligence, and freedom. The Roman Church has a rich and most remarkable history, and still exercises a greater power over the masses of the people than any other body of Christians. It stretches in unbroken succession back to the palmy days of heathen Rome, has outlived all the governments of Europe, and is likely to live when Macaulay's New-Zealander, "in the midst of a vast solitude, shall take his stand on a broken arch of London Bridge to sketch the ruins of St. Paul's."

1. Doctrine: The Roman Catholic system of doctrine is contained in the ecumenical creeds (the Apostles', the Nicene with the *Filioque*, and the Athanasian, qq.v., and also see SYMBOLICS), in the dogmatic decisions of the ecumenical councils (twenty in number, from 325 to 1870), and in the *ex cathedra* deliverances of the popes. The principal authorities are the canons and decrees of the Council of Trent (see TRENT, COUNCIL OF), the Profession of the Tridentine Faith, commonly called the "Creed of Pius IV." (see TRIDENTINE PROFESSION OF FAITH), the Roman Catechism (1566), the decree of the immaculate conception (1854), and the Vatican decrees on the Catholic faith and the infallibility of the pope (1870). A thesaurus of decisions on all sorts of doctrinal and disciplinary questions is af-

* *De conciliis et ecclesia*, lib. iii. c. 2: "*Professio veræ fidei, sacramentorum communio, et subjectio ad legitimum pastorem Romanum pontificem. . . . Ecclesia est cœtus hominum ita visibilis et palpabilis, ut est cœtus populi Romani, vel Regnum Galliæ aut Respublica Venetorum*" (the text is given by Mirbt, *Quellen*, pp. 274 sqq.).

* According to the statistics of 1907, the proportion stood thus:

Roman Catholics	230,866,533
Protestants	143,237,625
Greeks	98,016,000

The number of Roman Catholics assigned to the United States is 10,879,950, the enumeration being of the total Catholic constituency, while the Protestant denominations count only their communicants.

forded in the books of the canon law beginning with the "Concordance" of Evatian (c. 1150), but this has never been pronounced a final authority. The best summary of the leading articles of the Roman faith is contained in the Creed of Pius IV., which is binding upon all priests and public teachers, and which must be confessed by all converts. It consists of the Nicene Creed and eleven articles. To these must now be added the two additional Vatican dogmas of the Immaculate Conception (q.v.), of the Virgin Mary and the Infallibility of the Pope (q.v.). The Roman Catholic system of doctrine was prepared as to matter by the Fathers (especially Irenæus, Cyprian, Augustine, Jerome, Leo I., Gregory I., qq.v.), logically analyzed, defined, and defended by the medieval schoolmen (Anselm, Alexander Hales, Peter the Lombard, Thomas Aquinas, Duns Scotus, qq.v.), and vindicated, in opposition to Protestantism, by Bellarmin, Bossuet, and Möhler (qq.v.), and completed in the Vatican dogma of papal infallibility, which excludes all possibility of doctrinal reformation. A question once settled by infallible authority is settled forever, and can not be reopened. But the same authority may add new dogmas, such as the assumption of the Virgin Mary, which still remains only a "pious opinion" of a large number of Catholics, as the immaculate conception was before 1854.

2. Government and Discipline: The Roman Church has reared up the grandest governmental fabric known in history. It is an absolute spiritual monarchy, culminating in the pope, who claims to be the successor of Peter, and the vicar of Christ and God on earth, and hence the supreme and infallible head of the Church. The laity are excluded from all participation even in matters of temporal administration; they must obey the priest; the priests must obey the bishop; and the bishops, the pope, to whom they are bound by the most solemn oath. This system is the growth of ages, and reached its final statement at the Vatican Council (q.v.). The claim of the bishop of Rome to universal dominion over the Christian Church, and even over the temporal kingdoms professing the Roman Catholic faith, goes back to the days of Leo I. (440–461), and was renewed by Nicholas I., Gregory VII., Innocent III., Boniface VIII., Leo X., and by other less prominent pontiffs. But this claim has always been resisted by the Greek Church, which has claimed equal rights for the Eastern patriarchs, and by the German emperors and other princes, who were jealous of the independent rights of their sovereignty. The conflict between the pope and the emperor, between priestcraft and statecraft, runs through the whole Middle Ages, and was revived under a new aspect by the papal syllabus of 1864, which reasserted the most extravagant claims of the medieval papacy, and provoked the so-called *Kulturkampf* in Germany and France (see ULTRAMONTANISM), and the recent movements in France (q.v.) culminating in the complete separation of Church and State.

The pope is aided in the exercise of his functions by a college of cardinals limited to seventy. Archbishop McCloskey (q.v.) of New York was the first American cardinal, appointed in 1875, and Archbishop Gibbons (q.v.) of Baltimore the second (1882). The pope was at first chosen by the Roman clergy and people; but since the time of Gregory VII. he has been elected by the cardinals (for method of election see POPE, PAPACY, PAPAL SYSTEM, II.). The pope with the cardinals together form the Consistory (q.v.). The various departments of administration are assigned to Congregations (q.v.), under the presidency of a cardinal, such as the Congregation of the Index librorum prohibitorum, the Congregation of Sacred Rites, the Congregation of Indulgences, and the Congregation de propaganda fide. The pope has regular nuncios in the principal Roman Catholic capitals of Europe except Paris, namely, in Munich, Vienna, Lisbon, Madrid, and Brussels. The greatest public display of the Roman hierarchy was made in the Lateran Council of 1214 under Innocent III., and in the Vatican Council of 1870 under Pius IX.

3. Worship and Ceremonies: These are embodied in the Roman Missal, the Roman Breviary, and other liturgical books for public and private devotion (see BREVIARY; MISSAL). The Roman Church accompanies its members from the cradle to the grave, receiving them into life by baptism, dismissing them into the other world by extreme unction, and consecrating all their important acts by the sacramental mysteries and blessings. The worship is a most elaborate system of ritualism, which addresses itself chiefly to the eye and the ear, and draws all the fine arts into its service. Cathedrals, altars, crucifixes, madonnas, pictures, statues, and relics of saints, rich decorations, solemn processions, operatic music, combine to lend to it great attractions for the common people and for cultured persons of prevailing esthetic tastes, especially among the Latin races. Yet it must be noted that converts from Rome often swing to the opposite extreme of utmost simplicity. In this communion every day of the calendar is devoted to the memory of one or more saints. The leading festivals are Christmas, Easter, Pentecost, the feast of the Immaculate Conception, the Annunciation (Mar. 25), Purification (Feb. 2), Assumption of the Virgin Mary, All Saints, and All Souls (Nov. 1, 2; see FEASTS AND FESTIVALS). The weekly Sabbath is not nearly as strictly observed in Roman Catholic countries as in Great Britain and the United States. Roman Catholic worship is the same all over the world, even in language, the Latin being its sacred organ, and the vernacular being used only for sermons, which are subordinate. Its throne is the altar, not the pulpit (which is usually built at one side). It centers in the Mass (q.v.), and this is regarded as a real though unbloody repetition of the atoning sacrifice of Christ on the cross. At the moment when the officiating priest pronounces the words, "This is my body," the elements of bread and wine are believed to be changed into the very substance of the body and blood of our Savior; and these are offered to God the Father for the sins of the living and the dead in purgatory. The Reformers saw in the mass a relapse into Judaism, a refined form of idolatry, and a virtual denial of the one sacrifice of Christ, who, "by one offering hath perfected forever them that are sanctified" (Heb.

x. 14). But Roman Catholics deny the charge, and reverently regard the mass as a dramatic commemoration and renewed application of the great mystery of redemption, and the daily food of the devout believer (on the Roman Catholic worship, cf. the literature under BREVIARY; MASS; and MISSAL).

4. History. The earliest record of a Christian Church in Rome is given in Paul's Epistle to the Romans (58 A.D). Though not founded by Peter or Paul, it may possibly be traced to those " strangers of Rome, Jews, and proselytes," who witnessed the Pentecostal miracle on the birthday of the Christian Church (Acts ii. 10). It is probably the oldest church in the West, and acquired great distinction by the martyrdom of Peter and Paul. The Vatican Hill, where the chief of the apostles was crucified, became the Calvary, and Rome the Jerusalem, of Latin Christendom. The Roman martyrdom of Paul is universally conceded. The sojourn of Peter in Rome has been doubted by eminent Protestant scholars, and it can not be proved from the New Testament (unless " Babylon " in I Pet. v. 13 be understood figuratively of Rome); but it is so generally attested by the early Fathers, Greek as well as Latin, that it must be admitted as a historical fact, though Peter probably did not reach Rome before 63 A.D., as there is no mention made of him in the Epistle to the Romans, or in Paul's Epistles of the Roman captivity, written between 61 and 63. The metropolitan position of the city, whose very name means " power," and which for so many centuries had been the mistress of the world, together with the wide-spread belief that Christ (Matt. xvi. 18) had instituted a perpetual primacy of the Church in the person of Peter and his successors in office, supposed to be the bishops of Rome, are the chief secondary causes of the rapid growth of that congregation to the highest influence. It inherited the ambition and prestige of empire, and simply substituted the cross for the sword as the symbol of power. For fifteen centuries the fortunes of Western Christendom were bound up with the Roman Church; and even now, in its old age, it is full of activity everywhere, but especially in Protestant countries, where it is stimulated by opposition. Three stages may be distinguished in the development of Roman Catholicism.

1. The Foundation.

The age of ancient Greco-Latin Catholicism, from the second to the eighth century, before the final rupture of the Greek and Latin communions. This is the common inheritance of all churches. It is the age of the Fathers, of the ecumenical creeds and councils, and of Christian emperors. Many of the leading features of Roman Catholicism, as distinct from Protestantism, are already found in the second and third centuries, and have their roots in the Judaising tendencies combated by St. Paul. The spirit of traditionalism, sacerdotalism, prelacy, m. asceticism, monasticism, was power- the East and the West, in the Niages, and produced most of institutions which are to Greek and Roman churches. There are few dogmas and usages of Romanism which may not be traced in embryo to the Greek and Latin Fathers: hence the close resemblance of the Greek and Roman churches, notwithstanding their rivalry and antagonism. But, alongside of these Romanizing tendencies, there are found also, in the school of St. Augustine, the Evangelical doctrines of sin and grace, which were, next to the Bible, the chief propelling force of the Reformation.

2. Greco-Latin Catholicism.

The age of Medieval Latin Catholicism, as distinct and separated from the Greek, extends from Gregory I. (or from Charlemagne) to the Reformation (590–1517). It is the missionary age of Catholicism among the Celtic and Teutonic races in northern and central Europe. Here belong the conversion of the barbarians of Europe, under the fostering care of the bishops of Rome; the growth of papal absolutism, though in constant conflict with the secular power, especially the German empire; the scholastic theology, culminating in the discussions of Anselm and the system of Thomas Aquinas, and also the various forms of mysticism, represented by St. Bernard, Richard and Hugo of St. Victor (qq.v.), and Eckhart, Tauler (qq.v.), and other German mystics (see MYSTICISM); an imposing theocracy, binding all the nations of Europe together, yet with strong elements of opposition in its own communion, urging forward toward a reformation in head and members. Here occurred the Crusades (q.v.), lasting for two hundred years (1096–1292), and here was born the Gothic type of architecture and were reared the imposing cathedrals of the continent and Great Britain. In this period belongs the revival of monasticism in the rise of the mendicant orders, with Francis of Assisi and Dominic of Spain (qq.v.) as their founders; and also the papal schism with rival popes reigning in Rome and Avignon (1377–1417). The Middle Ages cradled the Protestant Reformation as well as the papal Counter-Reformation. Wyclif in England, Hus in Bohemia, Wessel in Germany, Savonarola in Italy, the Waldenses, the Bohemian Brethren, the Councils of Pisa, Constance, and Basel (qq.v.), and the revival of letters (see HUMANISM), prepared the way for the great movement of the sixteenth century, which emancipated Christendom from the spiritual bondage of Rome.

3. Medieval Latin Christendom.

The age of modern Romanism, dating from the Reformation, or from the Council of Trent (1563). This is Roman Catholicism, in opposition not only to the Greek Church, but to Evangelical Protestantism. In some respects it was an advance upon the Middle Ages, and experienced great benefit from the Reformation. No Alexander VI., who was a monster of wickedness, nor Julius II., who preferred the sword to the staff, nor Leo X., who had more interest in classical literature and art than in the Church, could now be elected to the chair of St. Peter. No such scandal as the papal schism, with two or three rival popes cursing and excommunicating each other, has disgraced the Church since the sixteenth century. On the other hand, the papacy has given

4. Modern Romanism.

formal sanction to those scholastic theories and ecclesiastical traditions against which the Reformers protested. It has also again and again expressly condemned their doctrines, and, by claiming to be infallible, made itself doctrinally irreformable. In 1816 the first condemnation of Bible societies was issued by Pius VII., who declared them "a most subtle invention for the destruction of the very foundations of religion" (Mirbt, *Quellen*, p. 347). Pius IV. in 1564 expressly condemned all versions of the Scriptures by heretical authors, i.e., Lutherans, Zwinglians, Calvinists, and the like.

In modern Romanism, again, two periods must be distinguished, which are divided by the reign of Pope Pius IX. (*a*) Tridentine Romanism is directed against the principles of the Protestant Reformation, and fixed the dogmas of the rule of faith (Scripture and tradition), original sin, justification by faith and works, the seven sacraments, the sacrifice of the mass, purgatory, invocation of saints, the veneration of relics, and indulgences. The "Old Catholics" (q.v.), who seceded in 1870 and were excommunicated, took their stand first on the Council of Trent, in opposition to the Council of the Vatican, and charged the latter with apostasy and corruption; although in fact, and as viewed from the Protestant standpoint, the one is only a legitimate, logical development of the other. (*b*) Vatican Romanism is directed against modern infidelity (rationalism), and against liberal Catholicism (Gallicanism) within the Roman Church itself. It created, or rather brought to full maturity and exclusive authority, two new dogmas and two corresponding heresies,—concerning the Virgin Mary, and the power and infallibility of the Roman pontiff, questions left unsettled by the Council of Trent. Gallicanism flourished in France during the golden age of its literature, and was formulated by Bossuet in the famous articles of Gallican liberties; but, since the restoration of the order of Jesuits in 1814, the Ultramontane school, which defends papal absolutism, has gradually gained the ascendency, and secured a complete triumph—first in 1854, when Pius IX. proclaimed the immaculate conception of the Virgin Mary to be a dogma of faith; and in the Vatican Council in 1870, which declared the pope to be infallible. The same pope, in 1864, issued the "Syllabus of Errors,"—an infallible official document, which arrays the papacy in open war against modern civilization and civil and religious freedom.

5. Tridentine and Vatican Romanism.

The reign of Pius IX. (q.v.) was very eventful in the history of the papacy: it marked the height of its pretensions and the logical completion of its doctrinal system, but also the loss of its temporal power. On the very day after the passage of the papal infallibility dogma (July 18, 1870), Napoleon III., the chief political and military supporter of the pope, declared war against Protestant Prussia (July 19), withdrew his troops from Rome, and brought upon imperial France utter defeat and contributed to the rise of the new German Empire with a Protestant head, and the downfall of the temporal power of the papacy. Victor Emmanuel, supported by the vote of the people, marched into Rome, fulfilled the dream of centuries by making it the capital of free and united Italy, and confined the pope to the Vatican and to a purely ecclesiastical jurisdiction (Sept. 20, 1870). History has never seen a more sudden and remarkable revulsion. The rule of Pius IX., lasting thirty-one years, broke the tradition that no pontificate would exceed that of Peter, said to have lasted twenty-five years. His successor, Leo XIII. (q.v.), who gained the respect of all Western Christendom by his culture and character, walked in the way of his predecessors in again denouncing Protestantism as the "Lutheran rebellion, whose evil virus goes wandering about in almost all the nations" (Encyclical, Aug. 1, 1897) and in exalting the scholastic theology by formally pronouncing Thomas Aquinas the standard theologian of the Roman Catholic Church and the patron of Roman Catholic schools (*Æterni patris*, Aug. 4, 1879). He also took an almost impossible position against Biblical scholarship in pronouncing the passage about the three witnesses, I John v. 7, genuine (Jan. 15, 1897). His successor, Pius X. (q.v.), in his encyclical *Pascendi gregis*, 1907, has taken a position against all freedom of Biblical and theological discussion by condemning Modernism (q.v.), forbidding all meetings of the clergy for theological discussion except in rarest cases and under severe restrictions, and ordering the appointment of "councils of vigilance" in every diocese to condemn, without giving reasons, all writings and teachings containing the scent of "Modernism." He has also shown his retrograde policy by forbidding women to sing in churches and limiting church music to the Gregorian chant. Both these popes have been as emphatic as was Pius IX., who made Alphonso da Liguori a doctor of the Church, in ascribing to the invocation of Mary infinite efficacy, and in calling upon the Roman Catholic world to pray to her.

6. Pius IX.; Leo XIII.; Pius X.

The history of the Roman Church during the nineteenth century shows the remarkable fact that it has lost on its own ground, especially in Italy, France, and Spain, but gained large accessions on foreign soil, especially in England, by the secession of Cardinal Newman, Cardinal Manning, and 400 Anglican clergymen, and, by immigration, from Ireland, in the United States, and, to mention a small district, Geneva. Pius IX. reestablished the Roman Catholic hierarchy in England in 1850 and in Holland in 1853, and Leo XIII. in Scotland, 1878. On the other hand, this gain has been more than neutralized by the Old Catholic secession in Germany and Switzerland, under the lead of Drs. Döllinger, Reinkens, and von Schulte, and other eminent Catholic scholars, whose learning and conscience did not permit them to submit to the Vatican decrees of 1870 (see Old Catholics), and the *Los von Rom* (q.v.) movement in Austria, and by a growing spirit of enlightened Biblical discussion within the church by such men as Loisy of France and Father Tyrrell of England.

P. Schaff†. D. S. Schaff.

For the Roman Catholic Church in different lands apart from the United States and the Uniates (for which see below) see the articles on the separate countries.

II. Uniate Churches.—1. In General: Rome has been successful in winning away from all the churches of the orient greater or (more generally) smaller fragments and subjecting them to obedience to itself.

1. Bases of Union.

In corporate form, though in individual cases under circumstances which it is not profitable to follow out in detail, native churches in Europe, Asia, and Africa have submitted to affiliation with Rome, and so in the peculiar sense which that church attaches to the word "Catholic" have gained the right to apply the term to themselves. Officially these churches are spoken of as having their own "rite." As opposed to the "Latin" rite the rites of the Uniates are said to be four in number, the Greek, Armenian, Syrian, and Coptic. But there are within these divisions, apart from the Armenian, subdivisions which are made partly upon national grounds and partly upon the bases of customs of cultus or of speech. The term "rite" is according to Latin usage broader than in common acceptation. Commonly the word denotes the form of cultus, the usages of the church in its celebrations, while the Latin sense includes every kind of ecclesiastical custom and also descent or derivation. Everywhere it may be said that a rite is "introduced," so that a "rite" may spring up anywhere; but ecclesiastically a rite must represent a tradition. The expression is akin to that conveyed by "discipline," and so may include the idea of organization, but must exclude that of theory. The Roman Church distinguishes between ordinances of divine right and those of human right. What is not of divine right is freer in its nature, over it the Church exercises jurisdiction. To the sphere of divine right belong dogma and the sacrament. Hence every dogmatic teaching, everything that belongs to the "essentials," must be taken into recognition where the "Catholic" church is. "Rite" includes the external usages, customs, ordinances, and institutions which are in the sphere of "human right" and are consequently not necessarily uniform throughout the Church. Even in the sacrament what is not of its essence is "rite." Hence Rome suffers as a condition of affiliation, where insistence upon the Latin rite would raise serious opposition, the waiving of externals, provided that submission is made to its dogma and "all" the sacraments are admitted. Since 1870 one of the requirements is acceptance of papal infallibility. In the orient dogma lives in the celebration; what is not liturgically expressed is dogmatically irrelevant; conversely, there is seen in the permission of individual mysterious usages a cheapening of the customary special teachings. The oriental churches are generally ready to grant that other churches may have a charism. Their demands in the matter [illegible] propaganda and union are small. Having due [illegible] the protection of their forms of cultus, [illegible] able to make approach to other [illegible] therefrom receive leadership. Forms [illegible] vary among oriental Christians. [illegible] which established "divine eccle- [illegible] nised as ecumenical in the [illegible] churches even concede a [illegible] bishop, according to their own definition of it. Hence a sort of superiority may be conceded by the orientals to the Latin Church, which the latter may wield in a way not to displease. Again, the latter may waive the Latin rite in virtue of its own reception as ruler and of the pope as the highest "regent." Until 1870 illusions might be cherished respecting the character of the Roman primacy. Since then no union has been effected, nor is any likely to occur.

A certain measure of theological, though not of juristic, importance attaches still to the confession of faith submitted, in accordance with the proposal of Clement VI. in 1267, to Gregory X. (q.v.) at the Council of Lyons in 1274 by the Emperor Michael Palæologus (cf. H. Denzinger, *Enchiridion symbolorum et definitionum . . .*, no. LIX., Würzburg, 1900).

2. Acts of Union, 1267-1596.

It agreed to the *filioque*, the Roman doctrine of the sacraments and purgatory, and, above all, in blunt form, to the papal primacy. Over against this document is to be noted the reservation of the *Decretum unionis* of Florence in 1439, proclaimed in the bull *Lætentur cœli* of Eugenius IV. In this latter there appears as assured to the Roman Church only the recognition of the "right" of its dogmatic position, particularly so far as liturgical forms were concerned; the *filioque* was recognised as lawfully and rationally added to the creed, but the Greeks were not obligated to embody it; transubstantiation was practically admitted, though not in explicit terms, and the controversy over leavened or unleavened bread was regarded as dealing with non-essentials, each church being permitted to follow its own custom. The matter of purgatory and of the value of masses for the dead was "defined," as was the papal power of ruling and governing the whole Church universal (Denzinger, ut sup., no. LXXIII.; A. Hefele, *Conciliengeschichte*, vii. 724; see also FERRARA-FLORENCE, COUNCIL OF). With the bull *Lætentur cœli* as the basis of the expected union of the whole Greek Church, or at least of certain fragments of it, Eugenius could issue two further decrees of union, the *Exultate Deo* of 1439 having reference to the Armenians, and the *Cantate Domino* concerning the Jacobites (Denzinger, ut sup., LXXIII., B and C). The result of these last was only partial success, as in the case of the Greeks. A brief of Leo X. (q.v.) issued in 1521 confirmed to the Greeks not only their cultic forms and usages, but also their hierarchy. The bull *Magnus Dominus* of 1595 of Clement VIII. simply renewed the formula of Ferrara-Florence and laid the basis for the Ruthenian union, and the bull *Decet Romanos pontifices* of 1596 followed, having relation to the hierarchy of the new church.

The relation of Benedict XIV. to union is of especial importance; through the bull *Etsi pastoralis* of 1742 he regulated the connection of the so-called Italo-Greeks in Italy, and through the bull *Demandatam cœlitus* he dealt with the patriarchs and bishops of the Melchites (q.v.).

3. Acts of Union after 1596.

By the bull *Inter plures* of 1744 he extended the conditions of the preceding bull to the Ruthenians, a process carried still farther, to the "oriental Church," by Leo XIII. in the bull *Orientalium dignitas* of Nov., 1894. In 1755 Benedict XIV. confirmed formally the correctness of certain "rites." Pius IX. also has significance here because of his two briefs of 1862, *Romani pontifices* and *Amantissimus*, creating a central institution to deal with the churches of the oriental rite, viz., the Congregatio de propaganda fide pro negotiis ritus orientalis. He thought it time to go farther into the matter of introducing "reforms" and organic changes in the hierarchical relations of the oriental churches; hence there issued the bull *Reversurus* in 1867 referring to the Armenians and the *Cum ecclesiastica* of 1869 to the "Chaldeans." But of all the popes Leo XIII. was most earnest in his efforts for union. He wooed the orientals incessantly, and employed to the full measures of organization in order to strengthen the Uniate churches and to enlarge them by accessions (cf. L. K. Goetz, *Leo XIII.*, pp. 221 sqq., Gotha, 1899). He followed the example of certain of his predecessors in establishing colleges for the education of the priesthood to serve among the Uniates, carrying this movement out not only in Rome but also in Constantinople and Athens. Among the subjects which appeared in the encyclical *Præclara gratulationis*, issued at his episcopal jubilee in 1894, which he said lay near to his heart, appeared that of union. He promised the orientals both for himself and his successors that there should be no deduction from the rights, patriarchal privileges, or the ritual customs of each church, and this was in legal form confirmed by the bull *Orientalium dignitas* already mentioned. He listened with patience to the complaints of the orientals concerning the persecutions which they had suffered, notwithstanding the consideration due them because of their long-established freedom. He was clever enough and great enough to censure the attempts at Latinization which were made; while he did not recall the Latin patriarchates of the orient, he limited the zeal which was being exercised in making "Latins" of the orientals.

Were these intentions carried out fully in papal policy, the essential aspect of the Uniates would by no means be that of Roman Catholicism. It is well remarked by Loofs (*Symbolik*, vol. i., Tübingen, 1902) that the non-use of Latin is not the only privilege left to the Uniates. They have their own liturgies and a series of festivals peculiar to themselves; while they must recognize the saints of the Roman Church they do not celebrate the days sacred to these saints, and of the celebrations of the Western Church they have actually taken in only Corpus Christi; their monasticism has not the great diversity of that of the West, there being in most regions only the Basilian and the Antonian orders, to which may be added that of the Mekhitarists (q.v.) in Venice and Vienna; and above all they retain in slightly modified form their own ecclesiastical law and church discipline. Indeed, it may be said that the Western-Roman type of piety could not in any case be made to grow in these churches; for eastern piety is dependent upon other factors than sheer dogma and external connection with Rome.

2. The Individual Uniate Churches: The entire number of Uniates may amount to five and a half millions. Varied groupings may be made according to the principle employed. One method has already been given above (1, § 1), depending upon the "rite." Another is based upon the method of organization, resulting in three groups: (1) those which have their own "rite" only in a subordinate sense, and have not a separate hierarchy, being under Latin bishops, of whom are the Greeks in Italy, the few Bulgarians and Abyssinians, a part of the Armenians, and the so-called Thomas Christians (see NESTORIANS); (2) those which have their own bishops and sometimes a metropolitan, especially in Austria-Hungary; (3) the patriarchates of the East. It must always be borne in mind that there is a difference in the conception of ecclesiastical law in the Roman Church as applied to "provinces of the apostolic see" and "mission lands," making it necessary to have in mind the organization in force in the latter. The details regarding the Uniate churches are under the Congregation de propaganda fide. A practical method which will be followed in this article is to consider the churches in their geographical order.

1. In Europe; Ruthenians, Rumanians, Armenians.

In Europe the Uniate churches are oldest in their connection with the Roman Catholic Church and have attained the closest union. The **Italo-Greeks** (cf. *KL*, vi. 1133–41) consist of isolated groups scattered throughout the kingdom. There are more compact groups in Calabria and Sicily, and the total number is about 50,000. A source of knowledge is the bull *Etsi pastoralis*, referred to above. Though these Greeks are under Latin bishops as ordinaries, yet there are special bishops who administer consecration to the priests. The Uniate churches of Austria-Hungary include Ruthenians, Rumanians, and Armenians. The first two belong to the Greek rite. Of the **Ruthenians** there are now only remnants, comparatively speaking, though they are still the most numerous of all the Uniates, three millions in Galicia and half a million in Hungary. The churches which use the Old Slavic have a complete independent organization in Galicia with archbishopric (established 1807), with Halicz as see city, and two suffragan bishoprics, Przemysl and Stanislau. In Hungary there are two bishoprics, Munkacs and Eperies, these being under the Latin primate, the archbishop of Gran. There is also an affiliated Servian bishopric in Hungary, that of Kreutz in Croatia under the Latin archbishop of Agram, representing about 25,000. This was an independent eparchy under Maria Theresa. It may be classed under the Ruthenians, since all the Slavic churches use the same ecclesiastical language, and the Uniates use this written in the same alphabet, the Glagolitic; the "Orthodox," or, as the Roman Catholics express it, the non-Catholic or "schismatic" churches use this language, but written with a different alphabet called the Cyrillian. The Ruthenians are among the peoples who have not yet come into their rights in history. They first bore the name "Russian," and in Kief possessed the first metropolis of the East Slavs; even yet in Russia they are known as

Ukrains or Little Russians, and altogether they number about 30,000,000. After the Tatar invasion in the thirteenth century, their land fell partly to the Poles and partly to the Lithuanians, and after the union of the two kingdoms (1385) to the Poles. They were an unsafe element in this kingdom so long as they remained "orthodox." Particularly after "Great Russia" had won in Moscow, by the elevation of the metropolitanate into a patriarchate, a new center and new éclat, there existed a great danger for the Poles. So there arose from political motives a movement for a union between the Ruthenians and Rome. The metropolitan of Kief, Michael Rahosa (Ragoza), found them only externally pliant; his successors, Hypatius Pociej (1600–13) and Velamin Rutski (1613–37), were the more eager; though in fact the negotiations had been completed at the Synod of Brest in 1596, yet actual union did not eventuate till the middle of the seventeenth century, the dioceses of Lemberg and Luzk, however, not coming in till 1700 and 1702. This union affected essentially that part of the kingdom which eventually fell to Austria. The Ruthenians have often complained of what they have had to endure at the hands of Latin bishops, and in Galicia complaints continue on both political and ecclesiastical grounds. Even in Russia the Ruthenians suffer under disabilities as a separate nationality, and consequently the Orthodox Church has little real attraction for them.

The church of the **Rumanians** exists only in Hungary, especially in Transylvania, and it may be traced back into the seventeenth century. The incidents of its changing history are not without interest. It was in connection with the Rumanians that the idea of "personal dioceses" first arose, under which it is possible to have several bishops (for the separate "rites") at the same place, and of course the occasion was the existence in the same region of churches having separate rites, etc. This church came to possess its own ecclesiastical language first in the seventeenth century. At present it possesses an independent metropolitan at Fogaras in Transylvania, and three suffragans at Lugos, Grosswardein, and Szamos-Ujvar, and its adherents number about a million. For the church of the **Armenians** there is an archbishopric at Lemberg, and a very large community at Vienna, and the Armenians of Venice belong in this communion also. The adherents number only about 5,000. The Mekhitarists (q.v.) are an important order of this branch.

2. In Russia and Turkey.

The changes in fortune in the Ruthenian Church were, as already seen, closely connected with the Polish kingdom. At times it seemed as though this church would be coextensive with the kingdom. The Polish Latin clergy was exceedingly zealous to transform the union into annexation and to reduce the independent hierar[...] dependence; on the other [...]
litically too strong t[...]
independence a[...]
established a[...]
"Orthodox" [...]
as 1620, a[...]
not hinde[...]

series of bishops, the most noted of whom was Petrus Mogilas (q.v.). After a great part of the region had been absorbed by Russia, Kief remaining in Poland but becoming ecclesiastically insignificant, this place was established firmly as a Uniate metropolitanate. Meanwhile, in 1775, 1793, 1795, and 1815 successive parts of Poland were incorporated in Russia, and in Prussia there was absorbed the Uniate diocese of Suprasl (1807). It became a settled policy of Russia to recover the Ruthenians for the Greek Church; the measures of Catharine II. were direct and restrained by no scruples, and she endeavored to have the see of Kief done away with entirely. It is reported that she recovered for the Greek Church no less than 8,000,000 Ruthenians, though she still suffered the archbishopric of Polotsk to continue. The next rulers, Paul I. and Alexander I., were in comparison tolerant, and the Uniates, especially in the northern Lithuanian districts, were reorganized. But Nicholas I. resumed the policy of Catharine, and by 1839 brought it about that the Uniates in Russia proper "voluntarily" asked to be received into the Greek Church. In 1875 the relatively small diocese of Chelm, which until then remained in the ranks of the Uniates, was also received into the national church, and this ended the existence of a Uniate Church in Russia. The "Easter decree" of 1905 issued by Nicholas II., which proclaimed freedom as to worship in the empire, apparently put it within the power of those who have secretly remained Uniates in sentiment to go over to Rome; but as yet there is no recognition of a Roman Catholic Church with the Greek rite in Russia. There are, however, scattered Uniates in Russia, belonging to the Armenian rite, and these are under a Latin vicariate.

The only Uniates to be considered in Turkey in Europe are those in the Balkan peninsula, and they are in small groups, considered as belonging to the "missions." There appeared to be hope for union so long as they were politically under an alien government and ecclesiastically dependent upon the ecumenical patriarchate. In 1860 a movement toward union was begun, but it was too energetically pushed by Pius IX., and it died out, especially after the foundation of the "Bulgarian exarchate" in 1872. Bulgarians have been ever since their conversion (see BULGARIANS, CONVERSION OF THE) an object of hope to the Roman Catholic Church, and as continually a disappointment. Leo XIII. in 1883 divided the "United Church of the Bulgarians" into three apostolic vicariates; but the adherents do not exceed in number 15,000. In Constantinople there are a number of Uniate Armenians and Melchites.

3. In Asia and [Af]rica.

The Uniate churches in Asia and Africa have especial historical and legal interest owing to the fact that they are organized as patriarchates. But the measure of independence of the Uniate patriarchs with reference to the pope lies in obscurity. The Roman Church is prepared to protect the [ec]clesiastical rank and rights in definite meas[ure so f]ar as they are involved in the title of patri[arch. T]he chief characteristic of this ecclesiastical [...] that the patriarchs have the right to name their suffragans and may call specific synods (cf. P. Hinschius, *Das Kirchenrecht*, i. 538 sqq., 562 sqq., Berlin, 1869). There are six Uniate patriarchates as follows: (1) **Patriarchatus Ciliciæ Armenorum.** This has had its home in Constantinople since 1862, and claims fourteen churches and about 16,000 adherents; the Armenian-Catholic communities in Russian Armenia and in the non-European dominions of the Sultan belong to this patriarchate. The title indicates the origin of the church among Cilician and Syrian Armenians (until 1867 the patriarch resided in the Lebanon). Under the patriarch are nineteen dioceses, but the total number of souls in his jurisdiction can not much exceed 100,000. (2) There are three Antiochian patriarchates: (a) **Patriarchatus Antiochenus Græco-Melchitarum.** This includes the Uniate Greek nationals of the Turkish empire. The largest number are in Syria. The Melchites are organized in fifteen dioceses and number about 120,000 souls. (b) **Patriarchatus Antiochenus Syro-Maronitarum.** This represents the most compact Uniate church of the orient, most of its adherents living in Lebanon. It is organized with eight or nine dioceses, and the number of adherents is about 250,000. (c) The **Patriarchatus Antiochenus Syrorum** consists of a fragment of the Jacobites (q.v.). The patriarch resides in Mardin (near Diarbekr on the upper Tigris), and governs nine dioceses with perhaps 20,000 adherents. The inclusion of the name of Antioch in the title of these three patriarchates probably indicates a historical tradition of connection with that city. (3) The **Patriarchatus Chaldæorum Babylonensis** represents a Uniate church won from the Nestorians (q.v.). The patriarch, with Mosul as see city, is at the head of eleven dioceses, and the estimates of adherents range from 40,000 to 70,000. They present an attractive subject for the historian on account of their past. The erection of a sixth Uniate patriarchate is due to the measures of Leo XIII., and is known as **Patriarchatus Alexandrinus Coptorum.** The seat of the patriarch is Cairo, and he has two dioceses; the number of adherents is in doubt, but does not exceed 21,000. In addition to the foregoing there are to be taken into account the Abyssinians and Thomas Christians (see NESTORIANS). The number of the first who are in affiliation with Rome is very small and they are under a resident vicar. Leo XIII. in 1887 established for the Thomas Christians three **Vicariatus apostolici Syro-Malabarorum,** the vicars using the Syrian rite, and the vicar-general having a council from the people to act as his advisers. The number of Thomas Christians involved here is about 100,000. (F. KATTENBUSCH.)

III. In America: By the conversion of the inhabitants of Greenland early in the eleventh century (see EGEDE, HANS, § 2), Christianity was first established in the western hemisphere. To the people of Iceland (q.v.), which is situated in both hemispheres, the Gospel had been preached long before. The first incumbent of the bishopric of Gardar, in Greenland, was appointed in the year 1112, and thereafter, until 1492, there was a succession of bishops of Greenland and Vineland (cf. Gams, *Series episcoporum*, p. 334).

1. Early Work in Greenland and Iceland.

As shown by the sagas, one of those ecclesiastics, Bishop Eric, sailed in quest of Vineland in the year 1121, but of his having found it there is no mention. In the sagas now extant there is no evidence that any church was ever built in Vineland. It is only known that the Norsemen who visited that country were Christians. It is almost certain that the region in which they traded for centuries was within the present limits of the Atlantic States. No memorials of Norse activity have ever been found in America, and the discovery of any is hardly to be expected, for those intrepid mariners were simply traders or at most but the sojourners of a few seasons. The skraelings or natives appear not to have been influenced by the religion or the civilization of their visitors. In the very year that Columbus discovered America, Pope Alexander VI. confirmed the last bishop appointed to the see of Gardar. After a long struggle for existence that lonely outpost of Christianity was abandoned.

2. In Brazil.

When Spain discovered the New World, her population, diminished by centuries of warfare, could not have exceeded 6,500,000. Nevertheless, she endeavored to achieve what no nation has ever attempted. Amid the wildernesses of mighty continents and in vast archipelagos the Spaniards sought to civilize innumerable races of whom even the most advanced had scarcely attained to the upper stages of barbarism. In Brazil (q.v.), where the Jesuits and other Portuguese missionaries engaged in work similar to that undertaken by the Spanish friars, the aborigines were, if possible, still more degraded. In many parts of that vast country the practise of cannibalism was common. It was on this foundation that the first Christian missionaries were compelled to begin the civilization of two continents. For more than 2,000 miles along the Brazilian coast all the natives were brought under the superintendence of missionaries. They were taught to know God, to comprehend something of the universal laws of morality, and in many other ways prepared for civilization. Joseph Anchieta, who labored among them for forty-four years, composed a Brazilian grammar and also a dictionary of that dialect. The canticles prepared by him replaced the indecent songs of the natives. Antonio Vieyra, an author and statesman, continued in the succeeding century the splendid work of Anchieta. In districts from which Portuguese soldiers had been expelled the zealous missionaries established themselves. In this noble work the Franciscans and the Dominicans were also engaged. At one time the Jesuits in South America numbered 1,700. Their number is not to be ascribed, however, to the pleasures of an apostolic career. In his *History of Brazil* (part I., 2d ed., pp. 320, 321, London, 1810), Robert Southey states that in the year 1570 sixty-nine missionaries set sail for South America in Portuguese vessels, and encountered the British and French (Huguenot) pirates off the coast of Brazil and were put to death. Missionaries had also been attacked by the Dutch. Even Portuguese merchants, with whose slave-trade they interfered, misrepresented the missionaries in Lisbon and in 1573 hundreds of them were deported and for eighteen years were allowed to languish in Portuguese prisons. After the expulsion of the missionaries the industries established by them were soon in ruins. The prosperity of the country was destroyed, slavery was easily revived, and vice and drunkenness became general. Notwithstanding this succession of calamities it was estimated that in 1856 there were 800,000 domesticated Indians in Brazil.

With some modifications this outline of missionary activity in Brazil will serve for a sketch of early Spanish America. Everywhere there was the same apostolic zeal, the same enlightened missionary methods, the same miraculous success, and the same fatal interference by government. In the Cordilleras, where no Spanish army had ever penetrated, a successful college was established by the missionaries. Indeed, the educational progress of Spanish America was remarkable. The late Prof. Edward Gaylord Bourne, of Yale, says that the efficiency of Spanish colonial academies in the sixteenth century was not equaled in the United States until the nineteenth century was well advanced (*Spain in America*, p. 310, New York, 1906). Long before the humane Quakers, of Pennsylvania, began their agitation for the abolition of slavery a South American Jesuit had denounced it. When guilty traders brought their human cargoes from Guinea or Angola, Blessed Peter Claver consoled the wretched negroes on their arrival in Cartagena. From the experience of Brazil the Duc de Choiseul had learned nothing. He, too, attempted to get along without missionaries and endeavored to develop Guiana along economic lines of his own. Perhaps no political philosopher has ever surpassed this particular act in stupidity. When he had banished the priests, the Indians fled to the forests and his colony was practically destroyed. Prosperity returned with the restoration of the missionaries. The economist Rae, quoted by John Stuart Mill, gives an interesting account of the celebrated Jesuit missions of Paraguay. For winning savages to the ways of civilization they appear to have been ideal, but, like those established elsewhere in South America, they, too, were destroyed by government interference. After the conqueror came the missionary. Everywhere civilization was sustained by the priests, and when they were expelled it began everywhere to decline. The political science of a later day seems to have regarded as antiquated the custom of adopting an enlightened system of taxation to obtain a revenue for government and instead to have relied chiefly upon confiscation. From the effects of this new system of economics and from the selfish opposition to religion many parts of South America have never completely recovered. In favored regions, however, it is even now in the vanguard of civilization, and almost everywhere there are evidences of improvement. So rapid is the succession of changes in that part of the globe that descriptions written a decade ago are no longer correct.

3. In Other Parts of South America.

It has already been stated that the contact of Norse Roman Catholics with the natives of Vineland had no lasting consequences. Roman Catholics did not revisit that country until 1497, when John Cabot's expedition traced the eastern outline of North America. In the knowledge of the New World brought to Europe by these Englishmen there is something of the vagueness of the sagas. When England resumed the work of exploration, her rulers had become Protestant. Her claims to this continent were based, however, upon the discovery and exploration encouraged by Henry VII., her last great Roman Catholic king. After the Cabots the Spanish navigators explored the Atlantic seaboard from Nova Scotia to Cape Horn and from Magellan's Strait northward to the Oregon country. They also explored Mexico and much of what is now the southwestern part of the United States. In the extension of geographical knowledge the Portuguese had few rivals; even in the New World they were distinguished explorers. The French, too, were interested in discovery, exploration, and settlement. That nation, however, confined its activity chiefly to the country of the St. Lawrence, the region of the Great Lakes, and the great basin of the Mississippi.

4. Exploration.

From the preceding it is clear that with the discovery and the larger exploration of America, the Protestant states of Europe had nothing whatever to do. With the settlement and development of the northern continent the matter is quite different. In the territory now comprised in the United States so great was the activity and success of the people of non-Catholic nations that Roman Catholics are not popularly regarded as having been among the founders of this republic.

Of those colonies that were destined to form the United States, Maryland alone was settled by Roman Catholics. Though they were in a minority at the outset and in every later stage of its development, they shaped its policy as completely as if they had been the only people in that part of our planet. From the beginning all its inhabitants enjoyed religious liberty. It was not, however, until Apr., 1649, that there was passed the famous act of toleration. William Claiborne had already invaded the province and it then seemed necessary to enact into law the objective fact of freedom of worship. When religious strife had once begun, it was not easy to restore tranquillity. Indeed, until the era of independence Roman Catholics were the victims of gross discrimination. On the subject of the first establishment of religious toleration in the United States, controversy may wax and wane, but it is not probable that there will ever be found for that honor any person with a title so clear as that of George Calvert. In Pennsylvania and in other communities Roman Catholics were also to be found. However, they formed only a very small part of the population, and the chronicles of the time tell little concerning their numbers, their social status, or their contributions to the intellectual life of the colonies. It has been estimated that at the time of the Revolution they numbered about 25,000. Though the Roman Catholic population of the United States was small at the time of the War of the Revolution, members of that faith were numerous on all its borders and everywhere

5. The Colonies of North America.

they were either neutral or friendly. When Colonel George Rogers Clark was engaged in the winning of the West, two Roman Catholic companies from the Illinois country joined his gallant battalion of Virginians; a priest, Pierre Gibault, acted as his recruiting officer at Kaskaskia and his treasury was strengthened by the loan of one François Vigo. In case of disaster Clark knew that he could find a haven of refuge with the Spaniards beyond the Mississippi. The Spaniards of New Orleans, too, were friendly from the beginning of the war for independence. This friendship was confirmed when, in 1779, Spain declared an independent war on England. Though the policy of Spain seemed hesitant, she finally loaned a considerable sum to the young republic. In the United Provinces were elements friendly to America, but none more so than the Roman Catholics. The friendship of Spain and of the United Provinces, however, was completely overshadowed by the generous assistance of France. So much so, indeed, that their services are not popularly known. A very few Roman Catholics took sides with England, but there was probably no Christian church unrepresented in the ranks of the American loyalists. Roman Catholics were to be found in the army, in the navy, and in the halls of legislation. In all the later wars they have not been less loyal than in the struggle for independence. Those who were not qualified for military or naval service, the faithful and patient sisters, rendered services not less useful in a multitude of hospitals. In vain might one scan the pages of our history for any complete narrative of the nurses of the Civil War. The veterans of that conflict, however, cherish a vivid recollection of the fine services of those gentle heroines.

6. Accession by Immigration.

At an early date the Roman Catholic Church in the United States began to receive accessions from immigration. These came chiefly from Europe and because of the operation of a variety of causes. Multitudes have come from Germany, Ireland, Poland, Austria, Italy, Portugal, and Canada. In some instances they were driven hither by oppressive laws; in others they came to escape religious discrimination, and in many cases to avoid military service. The expectation of enjoying political liberty and industrial prosperity was not the least powerful of the causes that have attracted settlers to this favored nation. In shaping these multitudes for citizenship many forces have operated. One of the most important agencies in making homogeneous this variety of ethnical elements has been the Roman Catholic Church. To this end the influence of priests and prelates has tended constantly. The services in this field of such leaders as Archbishops Carroll and Hughes, Bishop England and Father Hecker, Archbishop Ireland and Cardinal Gibbons (qq.v.), is a matter of common knowledge. The list of patriotic clergymen, from the Revolution to the Civil War, could be extended indefinitely. Only typical examples will be given.

To the political institutions that they assisted in founding, Roman Catholics have been zealously attached. Indeed, Charles Carroll of Carrollton, the public representative of their faith whom they hold in highest esteem, was an honored signer of the Declaration of Independence. They also cherish the memory of Daniel Carroll, one of the framers of the Constitution. Of that instrument Chief Justice Taney was one of the ablest expounders. In a democracy an exponent of social authority is needed, and the Roman Catholic Church supplies that need. To regard Roman Catholicism as a sort of police power, however, is puerile. It is infinitely more than that.

7. Services to Indians and Negroes.

It is greatly to be regretted that, as yet, no satisfactory narrative exists of the services rendered by the Roman Catholic Church to the Indians of the United States. In its nature that work is not spectacular and many a noble deed has passed without observation. This is a phase of activity for which it will never be necessary to apologize and a theme that is likely some day to attract some competent historical scholar. Few achievements of the Roman Catholic Church or, for that matter, of any other church, are more praiseworthy than the services to the Indians. The Roman Catholic Church has been criticized for alleged indifference to the negro. Doubtless more could have been done for him. Nevertheless, the negro had friends among Roman Catholics, and a scrutiny of the list of anti-slavery men would discover the name of an occasional priest. In the Nashville diocese, situated in the very heart of the slave states, Bishop Whalen and, except the poet, Father Ryan, all his priests were anti-slavery men. Notwithstanding the existence of the "black code," Roman Catholic masters very commonly taught their negroes to read the catechism and the prayer-book. Macaulay affirms that in Roman Catholic countries slavery has always worn a milder aspect than elsewhere. It should be remembered that in the South, where slavery was established, Roman Catholics were and still are few in numbers. The utmost activity on their part could have accomplished little in the way of changing public opinion in communities where they were themselves only tolerated.

8. Attitude of the American Government and People.

Toward the Roman Catholic Church the Federal government has always maintained a friendly attitude. In the beginning this was demanded both by the sentiments of gratitude and the teachings of political science. However, after the republic became great and powerful, it continued and thereby proved the sincerity of its friendship. It has not always been so with the American people. In the long intervals of peace there have been a few anti-Roman Catholic outbreaks. In the early thirties the opposition to Roman Catholicism was marked; again, in 1844, and thereafter till the Civil War, the Know-Nothing party (see KNOW-NOTHING MOVEMENT) developed considerable strength. The latest of these agitations was that organized by those who were popularly known as A. P. A.'s. Notwithstanding these symptoms of religious intolerance, the American people are the most tolerant and the most fair-minded on the globe. The constant stream of Roman Catholic immigrants is sufficient proof of this statement, if, indeed, any proof is required.

9. Charities, Architecture, and Schools. The charity work of this church is immense. Hospitals, orphan asylums, houses of the Good Shepherd, and similar eleemosynary institutions cover the face of the continent, and their administration is both efficient and enlightened. For the general absence of beauty in their ecclesiastical structures American Roman Catholics have been criticised with severity. From this general censure, it is true, certain cathedrals, which are triumphs of architectural skill, are commonly excepted. In contrasting Protestant Episcopal churches with Roman Catholic churches it should be remembered that many entire Roman Catholic congregations are composed of the industrial classes. The nature of their employments leaves little leisure for the cultivation of esthetics. Though American Roman Catholics are in advance of European Roman Catholics in many things, it may be admitted that in music, painting, sculpture, and architecture their triumphs are yet to come.

One of the grandest achievements of American Roman Catholics is the fine system of parochial schools (see ROMAN CATHOLIC PAROCHIAL SCHOOLS) that they have established. In good part this has been accomplished during the past thirty years and, of course, without assistance from any of the states, as the latter have public schools of their own. In these schools the instruction is even now efficient, and when their organization and unification are further perfected, it will be still more so. From the earliest times academies, ecclesiastical seminaries, and colleges have been in existence, and these have long been sending forth cultured men and women. The demand for higher education led later to the establishment of a number of universities. These are already doing scholarly work and are contributing rapidly to improve both secondary and primary education. The appearance of Roman Catholic pedagogical journals, the establishment of summer courses, and the institution of normal and other schools for the training of teachers are the present evidences of Roman Catholic activity in this important field.

10. Achievements of Roman Catholics. What has been said of apostolic labors in South America is equally true of the northern continent. There was scarcely an achievement of Brazil or Paraguay that was not paralleled by the Jesuits of North America. The nature of the task was the same and the training of those who attempted it was similar. In those vivid narratives known as the *Jesuit Relations* (see bibliography) there exists an early and an exceedingly valuable contribution to American scholarship. As historical documents they have great worth. There is also contained in them a vast mass of facts of the highest linguistic and anthropological value. Indeed, there were few phases of human activity untouched by those trained observers. Since the seventeenth century American Roman Catholics have been contributors to pure as well as applied literature. In the literature of power they are creditably represented in poetry, fiction, oratory, and criticism. It is true that there have been among them no great poets. Indeed, in this country there have been none of the first class among the members of any creed. For the entertainment of the reader, and that is a legitimate object for the poet, John Boyle O'Reilly, Father Ryan, Maurice Francis Egan, Father Tabb, Miss Eleanor Donnelly, and Miss Guiney take high rank. As in the case of poets, there have been no American Roman Catholics in the first class among orators. A few, such as Daniel Dougherty and William Bourke Cockran, have been successful in political oratory, and many, like the late Archbishop Ryan, were pulpit orators of rare eloquence. In essay writing and in criticism Roman Catholic names are familiar. In this department are found Richard Malcom Johnston, Agnes Repplier, and Bishop John Lancaster Spalding (q.v.). Except to say that he was a prose writer of ability it is not easy to classify the convert Orestes Brownson. He was active in many fields. In the literature of knowledge Roman Catholics have been creditably represented. To say nothing of historical essays and monographs, of which many of excellence have appeared, Hughes, Shahan, and Shea rank with the first historians of America. On the subject of law, Dr. W. C. Robinson is an authority of considerable reputation, and Dr. Murphy is not unknown in the science of medicine. In economics Roman Catholics have been interested from the days of Matthew Carey to the time of Rev. John A. Ryan, the author of *A Living Wage*. Perhaps the best notion of the standing of Roman Catholics in applied literature will be obtained from an examination of *The Catholic Encyclopedia*, a publication covering, if not the entire realm of knowledge, at least many of its important provinces. In didactic literature also American Roman Catholics are well represented. In the ranks of translators and prose stylists there are authors of the type of Rev. Dr. Hugh T. Henry. There is not space even to enumerate those who have been distinguished in journalism. Many Roman Catholics may be found in the medical and in the legal professions. In a word, they are very rapidly rising into those classes that may be considered the natural leaders of society.

11. Administration. In the United States the affairs of the Roman Catholic Church are administered by an apostolic delegate, by fourteen archbishops, of whom one has the rank of cardinal, and by upwards of eighty bishops. These ecclesiastical superiors, acting in perfect harmony with the Holy See, are assisted by more than 16,550 priests in attending to the spiritual needs of, perhaps, 15,000,000 Roman Catholics. Frequent reports furnish the Holy See with accurate information concerning American conditions and needs. If Rome were not very exactly acquainted with the institutions of America, Pope Leo XIII. could never have obtained so firm a grasp of its current problems and he never could have manifested for the entire American nation so enlightened and so profound a sympathy. His affection for this republic will be evident to even a casual reader of his great encyclicals. The attitude of his illustrious successor is the same.

In the minds of many non-Catholic Americans there exists a distrust of Catholicism, but for this suspicion there is no foundation in American history; it was imported, and it is about as old as the Reformation in England. The privilege of living in an enlightened state under a constitution of government such as the world has never seen, is appreciated by Roman Catholics as fully as it is by men of other creeds, and that fact begets as high a degree of loyalty. If our Federal state is ever menaced by socialism, one of its greatest resources will be found in the patriotism of its millions of Roman Catholics.

CHARLES H. MCCARTHY.

BIBLIOGRAPHY: The literature on the Roman Catholic Church prior to the Reformation is that on the Church at large apart from that on the oriental churches, and the works which stand out are cited in the article CHURCH HISTORY. Much relevant material is to be found in the bibliographies to the articles to which cross reference is made in the text, as well as in the articles on the popes and the various notables and ecclesiastics found throughout this work, as well as under such articles as CURIA; POPE, PAPACY, PAPAL SYSTEM; ULTRAMONTANISM, and the like. A reference list in certain important departments is given in this work in vol. i., pp. xxii.–xxiv. The literature, historical, apologetic, and polemic, is so vast that only a comparatively small selection can be given here. The history, dogma, and apologetics of the church in all their branches are set forth in the *KL*, and in *The Catholic Encyclopedia*, New York, 1907 sqq. A very large list of books is given in G. K. Fortescue's *Subject Index . . . of the British Museum*, under "Roman Catholics," London, 1903–06. Other lists of literature are: J. M. Finotti, *Bibliographia Catholica Americana; List of Works by Catholics Authors and Publishers in the U. S., 1784–1820*, New York, 1872; D. Gla, *Systematisch geordnetes Repertorium der katholisch-theologischen Litteratur . . . 1700–1900*, 2 vols., Paderborn, 1895–1904; *A Complete Catalogue of Catholic Literature; containing all Catholic Books published in the United States together with a Selection from the Catalogues of the Catholic Publishers of England and Ireland*, Boston, 1910.

Among works to be named on Roman Catholic apologetics and dogmatics is the fullest repository of Roman Catholic theological learning, viz., Migne's *Nouvelle encyclopédie théologique*, 52 vols., Paris, 1850 sqq., to which are to be added the *KL*, and the *Catholic Encyclopedia*, ut sup. Consult further: R. F. R. Bellarmin, *Disputationes de controversiis Christianæ fidei*, 4 vols., Ingolstadt, 1581–1593 (standard; often republished); J. B. Bossuet, *Exposition de la doctrine de l'église catholique sur les matières de controverse*, Paris, 1671 (standard); B. J. Hilgers, *Symbolische Theologie oder die Lehrgegensätze des Katholicismus und Protestantismus*, Bonn, 1841; J. L. Balmes, *El Protestantismo comparado con el Catolicismo en sus relaciones con la civilizacion Europea*, 2d ed., 4 vols., Barcelona, 1844–45, Eng. transl., *Protestantism and Catholicity Compared in their Effects on the Civilization of Europe*, London, 1849, 10th ed., Baltimore, 1868; J. J. I. von Döllinger, *Kirche und Kirchen, Papstthum und Kirchenstaat*, Munich, 1861; J. Gibbons (cardinal), *The Faith of our Fathers*, New York, 1871, Baltimore, 1890, and often (the circulation has run up into the hundreds of thousands); J. Perrone, *Prælectiones theologicæ*, 36th ed., Regensburg, 1881; R. Soeder, *Der Begriff der Katholicität der Kirche*, Würzburg, 1881; J. P. Gury, *Compendium theologiæ moralis*, New York, 1884; N. A. Perujo, *El Apologista católico*, 2 vols., Valencia, 1884; E. Sala, *La Religione cattolica esposta ai fedeli*, Milano, 1884; G. Baluffi, *The Charity of the Church a Proof of her Divinity*, Dublin, 1885; *Faith of Catholics: confirmed by Scripture and attested by the Fathers of the First Five Centuries of the Church*, 3 vols., New York, 1885, 4th ed., 1910 (J. Berington and J. Kirk, compilers); J. J. Moriarty, *The Keys of the Kingdom; or, the unfailing Promise*, ib. 1885; C. F. B. Allnatt, *The Church and the Sects*, 2 ser., London, 1887–1890; P. Schanz, *Christian Apology*, 3 vols., New York, 1891; W. Byrne, *The Catholic Doctrine of Faith and Morals*, Boston, 1892; D. Lyons, *Christianity and Infallibility; both or neither*, London and New York, 1892; J. D. G. Shea and R. H. Clarke, *Our Faith and its Defenders*, New York, 1892; J. A. Möhler, *Symbolik oder Darstellung der dogmatischen Gegensätze der Katholiken und Protestanten*, 9th ed., Regensburg, 1894, Eng. transl., *Symbolism; or, Exposition of the doctrinal Differences between Catholics and Protestants as evidenced in their symbolical Writings*, 5th ed., London, 1906 (standard); L. Rivington, *The Primitive Church and the See of Peter*, New York, 1894; C. Pesch, *Prælectiones Dogmaticæ*, 9 vols., St. Louis, 1895–99; P. Bold, *Catholic Doctrine and Discipline simply Explained*, London, 1896; W. W. Pounch, *The Catholic Church. An Explanation of her Faith, her Ministry and her Sacraments*, New York, 1896; G. Tyrrell, *External Religion; its Use and Abuse*, St. Louis, 1899; A. de Salas y Gilavert, *Influence of Catholicism on the Sciences and Arts*, St. Louis, 1901; A. Ehrhard, *Der Katholizismus und das zwanzigste Jahrhundert im Lichte der kirchlichen Entwickelung der Neuzeit*, 12th ed., Stuttgart, 1902; W. Devivier, *Christian Apologetics; Defense of the Catholic Faith*, 2 vols., New York, 1903; R. Merry del Val, *Truth of the Papal Claims*, St. Louis, 1903; M. J. Scheeben, *Handbuch der katholischen Dogmatik*, 4 vols., Freiburg, 1903; C. M. Schneider, *Die fundamentale Glaubenslehre der katholischen Kirche. Aus den päpstlichen Kundgebungen*, Paderborn, 1903; J. Burg, *Kontroverslexikon. Die konfessionellen Streitfragen zwischen Katholiken und Protestanten*, Esslingen, 1905 (combats Kohlschmidt); J. Chapman, *Bishop Gore and the Catholic Claims*, London, 1905; M. Hébert, *L'Evolution de la foi catholique*, Paris, 1905; J. H. Newman, *Addresses to Cardinal Newman with his Replies, 1879–81*, London, 1905; G. Reinhold, *Der alte und der neue Glaube. Ein Beitrag zur Verteidigung des katholischen Christentums gegen seine modernen Gegner*, Vienna, 1908; H. E. Sampson, *Progressive Redemption. The Catholic Church, its Functions and Office in the World*, London, 1909; especially the works of Cardinals Newman and Wiseman (named in the articles on them).

Some examples of anti-Roman polemics are: M. Chemnitz, *Examen concilii Tridentini, 1565–73*, new ed., by E. Preuss, Berlin, 1861, there was an Eng. transl., London, 1582 (damaging to papal claims); I. Barrow, *Treatise on the Pope's Supremacy*, ib. 1680, new ed., 1881; P. K. Marheineke, *Das System des Katholicismus*, 3 vols., Heidelberg, 1810–13; R. Whately, *The Errors of Romanism Traced to their Origin in Human Nature*, London 1830; F. C. Baur, *Der Gegensatz des Katholicismus und Protestantismus*, Tübingen, 1836 (against Möhler); P. Schaff, *Das Princip des Protestantismus*, Chambersburg, Pa., 1845; idem, *Creeds*, i. 83–191, ii. 77–274; C. Wordsworth, *Letters to Mr. Gordon on the Destructive Character of the Church of Rome, both in Religion and Policy*, London, 1847; J. Bragden, *Catholic Safeguards against the Errors, Corruptions, and Novelties of the Church of Rome; being Discourses and Tracts selected from the Writing of Divines . . . who lived during the Seventeenth Century*, 3 vols., ib. 1849–51; C. Elliott, *Delineation of Romanism Drawn from the Authentic and Acknowledged Standards of the Church of Rome*, 2 vols., New York, 1851; F. D. Maurice, *The Religion of Rome and its Influence on Modern Civilization*, London, 1855; J. C. Hare, *The Contest with Rome*, ib. 1856; J. Cairns, *Romanism and Rationalism as Opposed to Pure Christianity*, ib. 1863; E. B. Pusey, *Irenicon*, 3 parts, Oxford, 1856–70; H. L. Martensen, *Katholicismus und Protestantismus*, Gütersloh, 1874; *Proceedings of the Evangelical Alliance Conference of 1873*, pp. 449–488, New York, 1874; J. Delitzsch, *Das Lehrsystem der römischen Kirche*, Gotha, 1875; W. E. Gladstone, *Rome and the Newest Fashions in Religion*, London, 1875; E. de Laveleye, *Protestantism and Catholicism in their Bearings upon the Liberty and Prosperity of Nations*, ib. 1875; S. W. Barnum, *Romanism as it is; an Exposition of the Roman Catholic System for the Use of the American People*, new ed., Hartford, 1876; R. W. Thompson, *The Papacy and the Civil Power*, New York, 1876; C. A. Hase, *Handbuch der protestantischen Polemik gegen die römisch-katholische Kirche*, 4th ed., Leipsic 1878, Eng. transl., *Handbook to the Controversy with Rome*, London, 1906, rev. ed., 1909; R. Jenkins, *Romanism, a Doctrinal and Historical Exam-*

ination of the Creed of Pius IV., ib. 1882; P. Tschackert, *Evangelische Polemik gegen die römische Kirche*, Gotha, 1885, 2d ed., 1888; E. Eisele, *Jesuitismus und Katholicismus*, Halle, 1888; S. S. Wynell-Mayow, *The Light of Reason*, London, 1889; R. F. Littledale, *Plain Reasons against Joining the Church of Rome*, ib. 1880; T. Moore, *Anglican Brief against Roman Claims*, ib. 1895; Graf P. von Hoensbroech, *Das Papsttum in seiner sozialkulturellen Wirksamkeit*, vol. i., Leipsic, 1900; D. H. Falconer, *The Errors of the Roman Catholic Faith*, ib. 1901; J. MacLaughlin, *The Divine Plan of the Church*, ib. 1901; A. H. Galton, *The Church's Outlook, Our Attitude toward English Roman Catholics and the Papal Court*, ib. 1902; J. B. Nichols, *Evangelical Belief. Its Contrast with Rome*, ib. 1903; J. M. Logan, *Six Anti-Papal Studies*, ib. 1904; *Kontrovers-Lexikon, Die konfessionellen Streitfragen zwischen Katholiken und Protestanten*, Essen, 1904–05; O. Hermens and O. Kohlschmidt, *Protestantisches Taschenbuch*, Leipsic, 1904; C. Gore, *Roman Catholic Claims*, London, 1905; K. Sell, *Katholizismus und Protestantismus in Geschichte, Religion, Politik, Kultur*, Leipsic, 1908.

On the unfolding of worship and law consult: L. P. Guéranger, *L'Année liturgique*, 16 vols., Paris, 1841 sqq., Eng. transl., London, 1867 sqq.; R. von Liliencron, *Ueber den Inhalt der allgemeinen Bildung in der Zeit der Scholastik*, Munich, 1876; B. Thalhofer, *Handbuch der katholischen Liturgik*, 2 vols., Freiburg, 1883–93; H. von Eicken, *Geschichte und System der mittelalterlichen Weltanschauung*, Stuttgart, 1887; J. J. I. von Döllinger and F. H. Reusch, *Geschichte der Moralstreitigkeiten in der römisch-katholischen Kirche seit dem 16. Jahrhundert*, 2 vols., ib, 1889; J. Dippel, *Das katholische Kirchenjahr*, 6 vols., Regensburg, 1889–93; S. Bäumer, *Geschichte des Breviers*, St. Louis, 1895; P. Batiffol, *Hist. of the Roman Breviary*, London, 1898; K. A. H. Kellner, *Heortologie oder das Kirchenjahr und die Heiligenfeste in ihrer geschichtlichen Entwickelung*, Freiburg, 1901; F. Fleiner, *Entwickelung des katholischen Kirchenrechts im 19. Jahrhundert*, Tübingen, 1902; F. von Tessen-Wesierski, *Der Autoritätsbegriff in den Hauptphasen seiner historischen Entwicklung*, Paderborn, 1907; F. Acin, *La iglesia catolica, su constitucion interna y relaciones externas*, Huesca, 1910.

For the general history of the church consult: The *Annales* of Baronius (for bibliographical details see BARONIUS); J. J. I. von Döllinger, *Lehrbuch der Kirchengeschichte*, Regensburg, 1833–38, 2d ed., 2 vols., 1843, Eng. transl., *Hist. of the Church*, 4 vols., London, 1840–1842; J. A. Möhler, *Kirchengeschichte*, ed. P. B. Gams, 3 vols., Regensburg, 1867–70; F. X. Kraus, *Lehrbuch der Kirchengeschichte*, 4 vols., Treves, 1872–76; J. B. Alzog, *Universalgeschichte der christlichen Kirche*, 10th ed., 2 vols., Mainz, 1882, Eng. transl. of 9th ed., 3 vols., Cincinnati, 1874–78, new ed., 1903; E. Renan, *Lectures on the Influence of Rome on Christianity* (Hibbert Lectures), new ed., New York, 1898; R. F. Rohrbacher, *Hist. universelle de l'église catholique*, 9th ed., 15 vols., Paris, 1899–1900; F. Nippold, *Handbuch der neuesten Kirchengeschichte*, 4 vols, Berlin, 1901; C. Bouglé, *L'Église romaine. Drame historique de xx. siècles*, Paris, 1902; H. Brück, *Geschichte der katholischen Kirche im 19 Jahrhundert*, 2d ed., 2 vols., Mainz, 1902; E. Pardo-Bazan, *Por la Europa catolica*, Madrid, 1902; B. W. Ascher, *Characteristics of the Roman Church*, London, 1904; J. P. Kirsch and V. Luksch, *Illustrierte Geschichte der katholischen Kirche*, Munich, (1905); A. Baudrillart, *The Catholic Church, the Renaissance and Protestantism*, London, 1908; MacCaffrey, *Hist. of the Catholic Church in the 19th Century*, 2 vols., Dublin, 1909.

The literature on the history of the church in different lands is to be looked for under the articles on those lands, the following works being merely supplementary except in the cases of Great Britain and the United States. On the history of the Roman Catholic Church in **Great Britain and colonies** consult: J. Forbes, *L'Église catholique en Écosse à la fin du xvi. siècle*, Paris, 1885; W. F. Leith, *Narratives of Scottish Catholics under Mary and James VI.*, Edinburgh, 1885, A. Bellesheim, *Geschichte der katholischen Kirche in Schottland*, 2 vols., Mainz, 1883, Eng. transl., *History of the Catholic Church in Scotland*, 4 vols., Edinburgh, 1887–90, W. J. Amherst, *History of Catholic Emancipation and Progress of the Church, 1771–1820*, 2 vols., London, 1886; Kenny, *History of Catholicity in Australia to 1840*, Sydney, 1886; T. D. Ingram, *England and Rome: History of the Relations between the Papacy and the English State*, London, 1892; G. Grabinski (Count), *La Renaissance catholique en Angleterre et le Cardinal Newman*, Lyon, 1893; W. Ward, *W. G. Ward and the Catholic Revival*, London, 1893; De Madaune, *Histoire de la renaissance du catholicisme en Angleterre au xix. siècle*, Paris, 1896; Alexis, *Histoire de la province ecclesiastique d'Ottawa*, 2 vols., Ottawa, 1879; P. F. Moran, *History of the Catholic Church in Australasia*, Sydney, 1897; idem, *The Catholics in Ireland under the Penal Laws in the Eighteenth Century*, London, 1899; P. Thureau-Dangin, *La Renaissance catholique en Angleterre au xix. siècle*, Paris, 1899; P. H. Fitzgerald, *Fifty Years of Catholic Life under Cardinals Wiseman, Manning, Vaughan and Newman*, 2 vols., London, 1901; J. Forbes, *L'Église catholique en Écosse à la fin du xvi. siècle*, Paris, 1901; S. J. Jones, *England and the Holy See*, London, 1902; M. J. F. McCarthy, *Priests and People in Ireland*, Dublin, 1902; idem, *Five Years in Ireland, 1895–1900*, London, 1903; idem, *Rome in Ireland*, ib. 1904; M. O'Riordan, *Catholicity and Progress in Ireland*, ib. 1905; J. B. Willington, *Dark Pages of English History. Being a short Account of the penal Laws against Catholics from Henry VIII. to George IV.*, ib. 1902; F. A. Gasquet, *Short History of the Catholic Church in England*, ib. 1903; J. B. Nichols, *The Advance of Romanism in England*, ib. 1904; D. Williamson, *Roman Catholic Orders in Great Britain*, ib. 1904; Mrs. Bryan Stapelton, *History of the Post-Reformation Catholic Missions in Oxfordshire*, ib. 1905; J. A. Bain, *The New Reformation. Recent Evangelical Movements in the Roman Catholic Church*, Edinburgh, 1906; idem, *The Developments of Roman Catholicism*, London, 1908; W. Forbes-Leith, *Historical Letters and Memoirs of Scottish Catholics*, 2 vols., London and New York, 1908; B. Ward, *The Dawn of the Catholic Revival in England, 1781–1803*, 2 vols., London, 1909; *Report of the 19th Eucharistic Congress, held at Westminster, Sept. 9–13, 1908*, ib. 1909. For **France**, beside the literature under that article and GALLICANISM, consult: J. de Magdeleine, *La France catholique et la France juive*, 2 vols., Paris, 1888; J. B. Jeannin, *L'Église et la fin de siècle*, ib. 1891; P. Boyle, *The Irish College in Paris, 1578–1901*, London, 1901; L. Bourgain, *L'Église de France et l'état au dix-neuvième siècle*, 2 vols., Paris, 1901; M. P. Imbart, *L'Église Catholique, La Crise et La Renaissance*, ib. 1909. On **Germany** use: F. W. Woker, *Aus norddeutschen Missionen des 17. und 18. Jahrhunderts*, Cologne, 1884; Michel, *Die römische Kirche, ihre Einwirkung auf die germanischen Stämme*, Halle, 1889; J. May, *Geschichte der Generalversammlungen der Katholiken Deutschlands, 1848–1902*, Cologne, 1903; R. Seeberg, *Die Kirche Deutschlands im neunzehnten Jahrhundert*, Leipsic, 1903; H. A. Krose, *Konfessionsstatistik Deutschlands*, Freiburg, 1904; G. Gayau, *L'Allemagne religieuse. Le Catholicisme, 1800–1848*, 2 vols., Paris, 1905. For **Italy** consult: Letino Carbonelli, *La Chiesa, la proprieta, lo stato*, Naples, 1884; S. Muens, *Aus Quirinal und Vatikan*, Berlin, 1891; R. Murri, *Battaglie d'oggi*, 3 vols., Rome, 1901; A. Robertson, *The Roman Catholic Church in Italy*, London, 1903; R. de Cesare, *The Last Days of Papal Rome, 1850–1870*, ib. 1909. On the church in the **United States** consult: J. J. O'Connell, *Catholicity in the Carolinas and Georgia . . . , 1820–78*, New York, 1879; B. J. Webb, *Centenary of Catholicity in Kentucky*, Louisville, 1884; J. G. Shea, *History of the Catholic Church in the U. S. A.*, 2 vols., New York, 1886; idem, *The Catholic Church in Colonial Days, 1521–1763*, ib. 1887; H. H. Heming, *Catholic Church in Wisconsin*, Milwaukee, 1897; T. O'Gorman, in *American Church History Series*, vol. ix., New York, 1897; *Hist. of the Catholic Church in the New England States*, 2 vols., Boston, 1899; J. O'K. Murray, *Catholic Pioneers of America*, new ed., Philadelphia, 1901; G. F. Houck, *Hist. of Catholicity in Northern Ohio*, 2 vols., Cleveland, 1903; J. M. Flynn, *Catholic Church in New Jersey*, Morristown, N. J., 1904; A. Houtin, *L'Americanisme*, Paris, 1904; W. P. Tracy, *Old Catholic Maryland and its Early Jesuit Missionaries*, Baltimore, 1906; *The Catholic church in the United States of America*, vol. i., *The religious Communities*, vol. ii., *Province of Baltimore*, New York, 1908 sqq.; W. H. Bennett, *Catholic Footsteps in Old New York; a Chronicle of Catholicity in New York, 1524–1808*, ib. 1909, J. P. Conway, *The Question of the Hour: a Survey of the Position and Influence of the Catholic Church in the*

U. S., ib. 1909; J. L. Kirlin, *Catholicity in Philadelphia from the Earliest Missionaries down to the Present Time*, Philadelphia, 1909; F. T. Morton, *The Roman Catholic Church and its Relation to the Federal Government*, Boston, 1909; *The Catholic Church in the United States*, New York, 1908 sqq. On **Other Countries** consult: B. Wolferstan, *The Catholic Church in China 1860–1907*, London, 1909; P. Pierling, *La Russie et le Saint-Siège. Études diplomatiques*, Paris, 1896–1901; L. Lescœur, *L'Église catholique et le gouvernement russe*, ib. 1903; P. H. Zaebers, *Geschiedenis van het Herstel der Hierarchie in die Nederlanden*, 2 vols., Nijmegen, 1903–04; G. Verspeyen, *Le Parti catholique belge*, Ghent, 1893; F. Deschamps, *Catholiques actuels. Nos littéraires*, Louvain, 1893; L. Schmitt, *Die Verteidigung der katholischen Kirche in Dänemark gegen die Religionsneuerung im 16. Jahrhundert*, Paderborn, 1899; J. P. Restrepo, *La Iglesia y el Estado en Colombia*, London, 1885.

On the Uniate churches consult: L. Allatius, *De ecclesiæ occidentalis atque orientalis perpetua consensione*, Cologne, 1648; P. P. Rodotà, *Del Origine . . . del rito Greco in Italia*, Rome, 1758–63; A. Theiner, *Die neuesten Zustände der katholischen Kirchen beider Ritus in Polen und Russland seit Katharina II.*, Augsburg, 1841; O. Mejer, *Die Propaganda, ihre Provinzen und ihr Recht*, 2 parts, Göttingen, 1852–53; L. Lescœur, *L'Église catholique en Pologne*, Paris, 1860; J. Lelewel, *Hist. de la Lithuanie et de la Ruthénie*, Paris, 1861; M. von Malinowski, *Die Kirchen- und Staatsatzungen bezüglich des griechisch-katholischen Ritus der Ruthenen in Galizien*, Lemberg, 1861; J. Hergenröther, *Die Rechtsverhältnisse der verschiedenen Riten*, in *Archiv für katholisches Kirchenrecht*, vols. vii.–viii., 1862; L. Tolstoi, *Le Catholicisme romain en Russie*, Paris, 1863; A. Pichler, *Geschichte der kirchlichen Trennung zwischen dem Orient und Occident*, 2 vols., Munich, 1864–65; J. B. Pitra, *Juris ecclesiastici Græcorum historia et monumenta*, 2 vols., Rome, 1864–68; A. Theiner and F. Miklosich, *Monumenta spectantia ad unionem ecclesiarum Græcæ et Romanæ*, Vienna, 1872; J. Pelesz, *Geschichte der Union der ruthenischen Kirche mit Rom*, 2 vols., Vienna, 1878–80; N. Nilles, *Kalendarium manuale utriusque ecclesiæ*, 4 vols., Innsbruck, 1879–85, 2d ed. of vols. i.–ii., 1896–97; E. Likowski, *Geschichte des allgemeinen Verfalls der unierten ruthenischen Kirche im 18. und 19. Jahrhundert*, 2 vols., Posen, 1885–87; O. Werner, *Orbis terrarum catholicus sive totius ecclesiæ catholicæ . . . conspectus geographicus et statisticus*, Freiburg, 1890; F. Kattenbusch, *Vergleichende Konfessionskunde*, Leipsic, 1892; G. M. Rae, *The Syrian Church in India*, London, 1892; A. Arndt, *Die gegenseitigen Rechtsverhältnisse der Riten in der katholischen Kirche*, in *Archiv für katholisches Kirchenrecht*, lxxi (1894); W. Köhler, *Die katholischen Kirchen des Morgenlands*, Darmstadt, 1896 (very thorough); H. Denzinger, *Ritus orientalium*, 2 vols., Würzburg, 1863–64, 9th ed., 1900; M. Fowler, *Christian Egypt*, London, 1901; K. Beth, *Die orientalische Christenheit der Mittelmeerländer*, Berlin, 1902; Cotroneo, *Il Rito Greco in Calabria*, Reggio, 1902; F. Loofs, *Symbolik*, i. 393 sqq., Tübingen, 1902; E. Likowski, *Die ruthenisch-römische Kirchenvereinigung, genannt Union zu Brest*, Cracow, 1904; A. Silbernagl, *Verfassung und gegenwärtiger Bestand sämtlicher Kirchen des Orients*, 2d ed., ed. J. Schnitzer, Regensburg, 1904; Prince Max, Duke of Saxony, *Vorlesungen über die orientalische Kirchenfrage*, Freiburg-in-Switzerland, 1907; Sesostris Sidarouss, *Des Patriarcats. Les Patriarcats dans l'empire ottoman et spécialement en Égypte*, Paris, 1907; Charon, *Le quinzième centenaire de S. Jean Chrysostome*, pp. 258–284, Rome, 1909; *KL*, iii. 41–45, vi. 428–446, 1133–41, x. 1418–20; Hübner-Juraschek, *Geographisch-statistische Tabellen aller Länder* (an annual); *La Gerarchia Cattolica* (an annual).

ROMAN CATHOLIC EUCHARISTIC CONGRESSES: Name given to assemblies of ecclesiastics and laymen convened for the purpose of glorifying the Eucharist, and of devising means to promote knowledge and love thereof among the faithful. Because of the constant traditional doctrine of the real presence (see LORD'S SUPPER; and TRANSUBSTANTIATION), the Eucharist has always been considered as the most precious treasure bestowed by Christ upon his Church, and for long centuries it has been the center of Roman Catholic worship, the chief source of Christian piety. The latter half of the nineteenth century was marked by a general movement among Roman Catholics in the direction of an increase of devotion toward the Eucharist; confraternities of the Blessed Sacrament were organised, and works of adoration and the practise of frequent communion became more wide-spread (see PERPETUAL ADORATION OF THE BLESSED SACRAMENT). Of this general movement Eucharistic Congresses became an important and stimulating factor. The first of these gatherings was convened at the instance of Bishop Gaston de Ségur and was held at Lille, France, in June, 1881. It was a local event with a small attendance, but the idea rapidly gained favor and from the year 1885 when the fourth congress was held in Freiburg, Switzerland, under the direction of Mgr. Mermillod, bishop of Lausanne, the assemblies began to assume an international character. The eighth congress was held in Jerusalem (May 14–21, 1893) and was presided over by Cardinal Langénieux, archbishop of Reims, who acted as papal delegate sent by Leo XIII. In the mean time there had grown up, in all countries where Roman Catholics were numerous, local gatherings of the Eucharistic leagues, and these too became potent factors in the spread of the devotion. The nineteenth congress was held in London Sept. 9–13, 1908. It was attended by a vast number of ecclesiastics and laymen from all parts of the world, and it was considered to be in many respects the most important congress yet held. Besides great numbers of bishops and priests, there were present seven cardinals, among whom was Cardinal Vincenzo Vanutelli, who presided as special delegate of Pius X. It had been planned to carry the host in triumphal procession through the streets, but on account of violent opposition on the part of many English non-Catholics the project was abandoned after a request to that effect had been addressed by Premier Asquith to Archbishop Bourne of Westminster. The twentieth congress was held in Montreal, Canada, Sept. 7–11, 1910. It was the first held in America, and in point of enthusiasm and attendance on the part of the faithful it surpassed all previous gatherings of the kind. Three cardinals were present, one of them being Cardinal Vincenzo Vanutelli, who again presided as papal delegate. Among the salient features of the congress were a monster procession in the streets, and an open-air mass celebrated on the southeastern slope of Mount Royal at which 40,000 persons assisted.

JAMES F. DRISCOLL.

BIBLIOGRAPHY: Thomas F. Meehan, in *Catholic Encyclopedia*, v. 593–594, New York, 1909; official *Reports* of the different congresses; *The Narrative of the Eucharistic Congress*, Montreal, 1910; A. Ségur, *Biographie nouvelle de Mgr. De Ségur*, Paris, 1885.

ROMAN CATHOLIC PAROCHIAL SCHOOLS: Name given to the private schools maintained in the United States chiefly by Roman Catholics independently of support from the State. The reason for the existence of such schools outside and independent of the otherwise excellent public school system of this country is simply a matter of religious principle. No fault is found with the equipment or efficiency of the public schools on the score of secular instruction or ethical standing, but the contention of Roman Catholics, and of some other religious bodies as well, is that these schools are wanting in an important respect, that they lack an essential factor in the training of youth, viz., the element of religious instruction and influence, and for Roman Catholics, of course, religious influence means the specific influence of the Roman Catholic religion. Hence throughout the period of the rapid growth of Catholicism in the United States the school question has always been a matter of concern and frequently of controversy. The practical impossibility of giving religious instruction in the public schools, frequented as they are by pupils representing the various Christian denominations and the Hebrew faith, is recognized by Roman Catholics and Protestants alike, and though it has been sometimes suggested that a general knowledge of Christian truth might be imparted without giving offense to the adherents of any of the sects, the idea has been opposed especially by Roman Catholics who contend that all religious instruction, to be of any value or even safe, must be positive and doctrinal, and consequently denominational in character. But the zeal of Roman Catholics for the establishment and maintenance of parochial schools is not determined solely or even primarily by the desire to secure for their children proper religious instruction. This need can be, and often has to be, provided for in other ways. Of still greater importance in their esteem is what may be termed the religious atmosphere of the Roman Catholic school, with its multifarious subtile influences, all tending to foster reverence and love for the Church and all things pertaining thereto. The schools are organized under the immediate direction of the parish clergy, and are for the most part in charge of teaching brothers and nuns whose lives, being models of devotedness and self-sacrifice, can not fail to make a deep and lasting impression on the minds of the children. These and other influences create in the parochial schools a feeling and attitude toward religion and things religious which is rarely, if ever, met with in the public schools. The same secular instruction is given as in these latter, but it is permeated throughout with a religious spirit, and Roman Catholic ideals and practises are commended by word and example. Doubtless Roman Catholics are not alone in advocating the importance and need of the religious element in the education of our American youth. Like views have often been proclaimed by representatives of other religious bodies, and within the last few years an important movement in this direction has been inaugurated by an association of eminent educators, but it is among Roman Catholics that the principle of religious education has been most widely and consistently carried out especially as regards the elementary schools.

The origin of the parochial schools in the United States dates from the early days of the Maryland colony, about the middle of the seventeenth century, and the growth of the system ever since has been intimately connected with the growth and organization of Catholicism in the country. For more than a century development was very slow, but the American Revolution, by bringing about a relatively greater freedom for Roman Catholics than they had previously enjoyed, gave an impetus to the cause of Roman Catholic education which was later on powerfully aided by the great influx of Roman Catholic immigrants with whom came also many members of the various teaching orders. Passing over in this connection the early work of the Benedictines (see Benedict of Nursia), Dominicans (see Dominic, Saint), Franciscans (see Francis, Saint, of Assisi), and Jesuits (q.v.), who generally combined educational activities with their missionary labors, mention should be made of the Christian Brothers (q.v.), and particularly of the orders of women, for it is chiefly through their zeal that the rapid development of the parochial system has been made possible. As early as 1727 the Ursuline Sisters (see Ursulines) established the first sisters' school in the then French-speaking colony of New Orleans. In 1799 the founders of what was destined to become the American branch of the Visitation order (see Visitation, Nuns of the) opened at Georgetown the first free school in the District of Columbia, and by the year 1850 branch houses and schools under the control of this center had been established in Baltimore, Washington, St. Louis, Mobile, and Kaskaskia, Ill. Of still greater importance was the work begun by Mrs. Elizabeth Ann Seton (q.v.), who, being a convert to the Roman Catholic Church, founded in Baltimore (1812) the American branch of the Sisters of Charity of St. Vincent de Paul (see Charity, Sisters of, 1). This foundation proved remarkably successful, and in 1908 the community, together with the branches connected with it, comprised about 5,500 sisters with over 120,000 pupils—being about one-tenth of the total Roman Catholic school attendance in the United States. Among the other orders which have rendered important services in the cause of parochial school education are the Sisters of Mercy (see Mercy, Sisters of), the Sisters of St. Benedict, the Franciscan Sisters, the Sisters of St. Dominic, the Sisters of St. Joseph, and many others (see Teaching Orders). Because of the great expenditure involved in the establishment and support of the parochial schools, the Roman Catholics of this country have frequently sought to obtain state recognition for their educational work and thus be relieved of the burden of taxes imposed for the maintenance of the public school system which for religious reasons they do not find satisfactory.

A notable effort in this direction was made in 1840 by the Roman Catholics of New York under the leadership of Archbishop John Hughes (q.v.). It was argued in a petition to the aldermen of the city and to the state legislature that if the same quality of secular instruction was given in the parochial as in the public schools—a point of fact to be controlled by state inspection and examinations—the former were in justice entitled to a pro rata share in the public funds set apart for school purposes. But the proposal was bitterly assailed by Protestants generally, and the project failed, as have also all subsequent efforts on the part of

Roman Catholics to bring about a compromise in the matter such as obtains in England and Canada. Local concessions and arrangements have been sometimes made, as, for instance, in Poughkeepsie, and at Faribault, Minn., in the early nineties, but they have been of short duration, and have generally failed to satisfy either party to the controversy. In the mean time the Roman Catholics have gone on building and equipping their schools, and according to the official statistics of the year 1908 the total number of such schools in the United States was 4,443, the number of pupils 1,136,906, and the number of professional teachers, lay and religious, 20,755. The amount of property invested was estimated to be over $100,000,000, with an annual expenditure for school purposes of about $15,000,000. A few years previous to this date an important movement was inaugurated for the better organization and unification of the system throughout the country. This is a part of the work undertaken by the Catholic Educational Association which aims at carrying out a similar aim for all the Roman Catholic educational establishments in the United States, theological seminaries, colleges, academies, and high schools, under the general supervision of the Catholic University of America located in Washington, D. C. To aid in the accomplishment of this general purpose the professors of the latter institution have begun the publication of a Catholic Educational Review. JAMES F. DRISCOLL.

BIBLIOGRAPHY: J. A. Burns, *The Catholic School System in the United States, its Principles, Origin and Establishment*, New York, 1908; *Annual Reports* of the Catholic Educational Association, 1903 sqq., Columbus, Ohio; *The Official Catholic Directory*, published yearly by the M. H. Wiltzius Co., Milwaukee and New York.

ROMAN CATHOLIC POSITION ON THE BIBLE IN THE PUBLIC SCHOOLS: This topic has frequently been a matter of controversy between Protestants and Roman Catholics, particularly in the United States. The custom of reading the Bible as a part of the regular school exercises is doubtless a survival from the earlier days when educational institutions were in the main denominational, and consistently imparted religious as well as secular instruction. The attitude of Roman Catholics toward the practise is determined not by hostility to Bible-reading as such, but by certain considerations of principle. In the first place, they are not convinced of the utility or expediency of indiscriminate Bible-reading especially for young children, unless it be accompanied by suitable explanation, and consequently this mode of imparting Scriptural knowledge is rarely employed in Roman Catholic elementary schools. It is judged preferable to reduce the voluminous and often bewildering narrative portions of the Bible to the simpler form of Bible histories, while its dogmatic, ethical, and religious teaching finds expression in catechisms and religious instruction. If it be proposed as an alternative to have the Bible-reading in the public schools accompanied by commentary on the part of the teachers, Roman Catholics object, not only because they question the authority of these exponents and their competency for such a task, but also because such commentary is liable to be tinged with sectarian bias.

Furthermore, Bible-reading in the schools is sometimes connected with the recitation of prayers and the singing of hymns, thus taking on the character of a religious service. All these elements may be very good in themselves and free from any inherent denominational tendencies, but Roman Catholics consistently, with that exclusiveness which is traditional in their church, refuse to take part in a non-Roman Catholic (or, as they claim) heterodox act of public religious worship. This prohibitive principle, logically reducible to what the theologians term *communicatio in divinis*, obtained originally in most of the Protestant denominations as well as among the older branches of Christianity, but of late, and for obvious reasons, it has been rapidly disappearing from the various forms of Protestantism, and though among Roman Catholics it is now less acutely emphasized than formerly, it is nevertheless maintained as an integral element of the Roman Catholic position—a principle which can not consistently be sacrificed.

Exception has also been taken by Roman Catholics to the fact that the Bible read in the public schools was the "Protestant" or King James version, whereas a long-standing decree of ecclesiastical authority had made it obligatory for lay Roman Catholics (unless otherwise permitted) to use currently only those vernacular translations of Holy Writ which had received the approbation of their church, and were provided with suitable notes for the proper understanding of certain passages. This objection flows logically from the general Roman Catholic principle according to which the Church is held to be the divinely appointed guardian of the Scriptures and their sole authoritative interpreter. The prohibition in question, which is as old as the Council of Trent, was based on the assumed danger (now doubtless more remote than in the sixteenth century) which, especially in those troubled times, might result for the faith of Catholics from an indiscriminate use of the various unauthorized translations then in vogue. It was assumed—and not entirely without cause—that doctrinal bias had influenced the rendering of certain passages supposed to have a bearing on the religious differences between Protestants and Roman Catholics. As instances of this Bishop Kenrick (*Theologia Dogmatica*, i. 427 sqq., Philadelphia, 1839) calls attention to such passages in the Authorized Version as Matt. ix. 11; I Cor. vii. 9, ix. 5, xi. 27; Heb. x. 38, etc., as being erroneous dogmatic renderings due to polemical preoccupation. In this connection Roman Catholics quote also the words of Robert Gell, the chaplain to George Abbot (q.v.), Protestant archbishop of Canterbury (one of the translators), who says: "Dogmatic interests were in some cases allowed to bias the translation, and the Calvinism of one party, the prelatic views of another, were both represented at the expense of accuracy." To this may be added a recent Protestant admission, viz., that of Bishop Ellicott: "In spite of the very common assumption to the contrary, there are many passages (in the version of 1611) from which erroneous doctrinal inferences have been drawn, but where the inference comes from the translation, and not the original" (*Considerations on the Revision of the English Version of the New Testament*, p. 89, cf. also p. 88, London, 1870). Be that as it may, it is certain, on the other hand, that this phase of the objection to the Protestant Bible has now lost much of its interest and cogency. It is not here the place to discuss the relative merits of the "Authorised" and of the Douay version, which through episcopal authority has become the accepted translation for the use of English-speaking Roman Catholics. Each has its points of superiority and its defects. It is worthy of note, however, that some of the alleged faulty renderings mentioned above have been emendated by the revisers of 1881.

A further and more serious objection on the part of Roman Catholics to the use of the Protestant Bible is based on the difference as regards the Scriptural canon. The so-called "apocryphal" or deutero-canonical books, which Roman Catholics (on the authority of the Church) accept as having the same divine authority as the other portions of Holy Writ, have been excluded from the King James version since the edition of 1826, whence arises the Roman Catholic contention that the Protestant Bible is a truncated version and materially incomplete. Apart from the question of authority which finally determines the Roman Catholic position in such matters, it is pertinent to note that such an eminent and independent scholar as Charles A. Briggs (*General Introduction to the Study of Holy Scripture*, chap. v., "The Canon of Scripture," New York, 1899) is inclined to accept the larger traditional canon as defined by the Council of Trent. But whatever the scientific merits of the controversy, this and the above-mentioned reasons may serve to render intelligible the attitude of Roman Catholics who have opposed the reading of the Bible in the public schools. JAMES F. DRISCOLL.

ROMAN CATHOLIC RESTRICTION OF BIBLE-READING BY THE LAITY: The traditional and official attitude of the Roman Catholic Church toward Sacred Scripture and its use was formulated in the fourth session of the Council of Trent (Apr. 8, 1546) the main enactments of which were reaffirmed by the Vatican Council (q.v.). After declaring the substance of divine revelation to be contained in Holy Writ and in the unwritten (i.e., non-inspired) ecclesiastical traditions (*in libris scriptis, et sine scripto traditionibus*), the council formally accepted the traditionally received books of the Old and New Testaments with all their parts as contained in the Latin Vulgate (decreeing at the same time that a new, and as far as possible accurate, edition of the same be prepared; see BIBLE VERSIONS, A, II., 2, § 5), and further enacted that this version, which was declared a substantially correct translation of the original Scriptures, should henceforth be considered as the official text to be appealed to in all theological discussions, and for general use in the Church. At that time, as for centuries before, Latin was the official and liturgical language of the Church, and the Fathers of the council, in thus making the Vulgate the standard text, had no intention of declaring a preference for it over the original Hebrew or Greek, but wished simply to affirm its substantial conformity with the latter, and to confer upon it for practical purposes an official authority with reference to the other existing Latin translations. Underlying these and similar enactments is the fundamental Roman Catholic doctrine that the authority of the living Church—not the letter of Scripture—is the proximate rule of belief, and that the Church is the divinely appointed custodian of Holy Writ, the sole authoritative interpreter of its meaning in all matters pertaining to faith or morals. In her capacity of guardian the Church assumes the duty of preserving the substantial purity of the original text, and likewise claims the right of supervision and direction whenever it is question of translating the Scriptures into any of the modern languages. As these vernacular versions formed an important factor of the controversies and the disturbed religious conditions of the sixteenth century, it was decreed by the Council of Trent that no such translation might be used by the laity unless it had the sanction of ecclesiastical authority, and were provided with suitable notes for the proper understanding of difficult and disputed passages. This restrictive legislation still retains force of law, though the reasons justifying it are obviously less cogent now than in the days of early Protestantism when so much stress was laid by the Reformers on the right of private interpretation. The Latin Vulgate is still retained as the basis of all authorised translations, though free recourse may be had to the Hebrew and Greek by way of comparison and elucidation. In this as in similar matters, Roman Catholic authority, while professing due respect for the conclusions of critical scholars, seeks above all to maintain the consensus of Christian tradition. See BIBLE-READING BY THE LAITY, RESTRICTIONS ON. JAMES F. DRISCOLL.

BIBLIOGRAPHY: *Acta et Decreta Concilii Tridentini, Sessio IV.*; H. Denzinger, *Enchiridion Symbolorum*, Freiburg, 1908; *The Catholic Church and the Bible*, London, 1906.

ROMANS, EPISTLE TO THE. See PAUL THE APOSTLE, II., 3, §§ 5–7.

ROMANTICISM: The name of a movement which especially affected literature, art, religion, and theology in the last half of the eighteenth and the first half of the nineteenth century. It arose on a background of three other movements which had much in common with one another, Classicism, Humanism, and the Enlightenment. (1) Classicism, which has retained its place ever since the revival of learning, has adhered to those forms of expression which prevailed in the creative periods of Greece and Rome. It was an attitude of mind, a method of literary and artistic activity formed on the severe models of ancient thought, characterised by energy, freshness, purity, proportion, restraint, objectivity, i.e., subserviency to nature, and reverence for the authority of long-established types. (2) Humanism (q.v.)—another name for the Renaissance in Italy, 1350–1425—turned away from metaphysics, from scholastic logical formulas as defined by the Church, from the despotism of the Church as claiming exclusive right to absorb human interests, from the division of knowledge into that of the "Two ways"—supernatural and natural, re-

The Background.

ligious and scientific (see ALBERTUS MAGNUS). It studied afresh the literature of classic Rome; through the revival of Platonism, Neoplatonism, and Aristotelianism the freshness and freedom of the Greek spirit were reawakened; and the ancient Greek cosmology, doctrines of nature, philosophical skepticism, and the eclectic mixture of incongruous elements all came to life again. Owing to the new scientific spirit discoveries and inventions of great magnitude were on the threshold. With the rediscovery of many splendid examples of Greek statuary there was quickened the illimitable sense of beauty and wonder associated especially with the human form as the most perfect embodiment of the ideal. In a word, Humanism drew attention once more to man himself as a rational being with capacities of inexhaustible richness, susceptible of infinite culture (cf. J. A. Symonds, *Renaissance in Italy*, 5 vols., new ed., New York, 1885). (3) The Enlightenment (q.v., 1650–1800; also see RATIONALISM AND SUPERNATURALISM). More than two centuries after the decline of Humanism and when the Protestant Reformation was well under way, interest was again directed to man, this time centering in his rational nature and its capacities as such. The movement may be summarized as the sufficiency of the human reason for all the problems of life. Humanism had indeed implied this, but it had not proceeded far enough to become self-conscious, to reflect upon what would be required to justify its attitude and activity, and to offer a rational defense for the entire movement. The Enlightenment was, however, the spirit of Humanism come to life again in the English, French, and German consciousness. Like Humanism it eschewed metaphysics; it continued the investigation into the inner nature of man always from the side of experience, the validity of his knowledge of the world, and the meaning of human life both individual and social; and it allied itself with the culture and literary activity of the period. Yet it was conscious of having awakened in a new world, no longer that of the church or of Greece and Rome, but of new discoveries, a new scientific method, new economic and social values, a new psychology, and new historical postulates. In the process of working out its essential principle, however, there were disclosed its inevitable limitations, and also its inadequacy to answer to one large element in man's nature—the poetic and imaginative and the more definitely personal. In its abstract superficial intellectualism, its individualistic and social utilitarianism, its denial of personal freedom, and its elimination of mystery it paved the way for a profound reaction of consciousness in which neglected regions of personality should reassert their abiding worth. The time was therefore ripe for a movement in which intellect and theoretic culture should give place to the esthetic side of man's nature wherein this should find authentic and luxuriant expression.

In a description of Romanticism the following features require attention: (1) Subjectivity. J. G. Fichte (q.v.) held that self-consciousness is determined by nothing outside of itself, and that everything exists only by the activity of the Ego. According to F. W. Schelling (q.v.) nature is the Ego in process of becoming. In English thought nature was conceived as an analogon of spirit so that nature and spirit answer to one another (cf. S. T. Coleridge, *Aids to Reflection*, London, 1825, and often, e.g., ed. T. Fenby, 1873; H. Bushnell, *God in Christ*, "Dissertation on Language," New York, 1849, and often).

Special Features.

Besides this philosophical basis, there was a profound feeling that the soul itself was a mine of exhaustless treasure as yet scarcely explored. Nor was this limited to the normal consciousness, but in certain of the German romanticists the weird, fantastic, capricious, and morbid were developed to extreme proportions (cf. Novalis, i.e., Baron F. L. von Hardenberg, d. Mar. 25, 1801; and E. T. A. Hoffmann, d. July 24, 1822). (2) Not so much the rational as the esthetic aspect of the world and human life absorbed interest. Thus appeal was made to imagination and fancy. Duty was determined by feeling, and even religion was resolved into the feeling of absolute dependence (cf. Schleiermacher, q.v.). (3) Closely associated with the esthetic element was the sense of beauty, not indeed that of standards derived from Greece and Rome or even of the Middle Ages, except in Scott. There was first the beauty of the natural world which, slumbering for centuries, awoke in the romantic spirit—not alone the beauty of great mountains, of quiet or tumultuous seas, but clouds, sunsets, moonlight, flowers. The search became a passion. It was found in out-of-the-way places, in outcast and neglected persons, in common and trivial events. On the other hand the most extravagant situations were created, the personality subjected itself to the most extraordinary experiences in order to discover and extract a quintessence of beauty never before distilled. (4) Mystery arising not only from the unfathomed depths of the soul, from the infinite aspects of being, but also from an inner and insatiate longing for the unexperienced and the unknown. For Novalis philosophy is homesickness—the wish to find one's home in the Absolute. Johann Ludwig Tieck was consumed with longing for something which transcended the finite. Schelling thought of beauty as the infinite appearing in finite form. Wordsworth was haunted by the strangeness of nature, which only reflected a deeper strangeness in his own soul. (5) The relation of the inner to the outer world is presented from two points of view. First, so far as the outer world is a copy of the inner world, this may be due to an idealizing pantheism. For either the harmony of the external world is the creation of the Ego, or both are partial expressions of the infinite and all-pervading Unity (Novalis, *Lehrlinge zu Sais*). Or, secondly, the inner world of individual consciousness is first depicted with entire disregard of outer social conventions, wherein two types of life are allowed to coexist side by side, one, of untrammeled development of those who are gifted with genius, the other, the conventional order of such as have not the strength or courage to assert the independent freedom of self-realization. The first type is regarded as the highest human ideal, and the actual world is judged by its degree of correspondence with this "unchartered freedom." In like manner by a process of ideal selection even the natural world is conceived as the seat of marvelous forces which rarely come to manifestation. (6) The free unfolding of each personality according to its genius involved recognition and obedience of all individual impulses, inclinations, and even idiosyncrasies. Various were the outward conditions in which the great romanticists developed their genius—Wordsworth in solitude, Scott in historical study of medieval life, Byron in wanderings and heroic devotion to the cause of liberty, Schelling and Schlegel in speculative philosophy, most of the French and German writers in more or less indifference to social conventions. The theory constantly reiterated is, that the genius must be free to follow his star so as to give his artistic powers free play. Not only must no constraint be permitted, but only in the pathway of perfect liberty can the individual reach the goal of self-realization. Instead of turning back to Greece and Rome or to the Middle Ages for their material, they isolate single aspects of their own experience and develop these as if they were in truth of universal validity. Whatever is vital in their writings is autobiographic. Each one felt that he must himself first live the romantic life, since only then was he able by subtle analysis and unsparing self-revelation of his inmost consciousness to portray his ideal. Accordingly he renounced conventions in his writings as he had already done in his life, he wrote as he felt and as he thought, and dipped his metal white hot from the seething cauldron of his own heart. (7) The romantic writings are all with scarcely an exception tinged with pantheism and mysticism. Philosophy, ethics, religion, no less than conceptions of nature and human love, so far as these are self-conscious, are frankly pantheistic. The infinite is not fully realised save as every possible form of consciousness and action and human relation finds expression. If the English pantheism was on the whole more sober and naturalistic than that of the German and French, this may be referred to the quieter temperament and severer restraint of the English mind. As related to mysticism, not all mystics are romanticists, and not all romanticists are mystics, but the two are commonly associated in the same person. The romanticists believe that reality is revealed not by rational thought, but through feeling, immediate experience, spiritual illumination. Accordingly a part of the meaning of life eludes analysis. Any portrayal of it, however concrete and vivid, is at best partial and suggestive rather than complete and final. On the other hand, in romantic experience ecstasy is never far away. The secret of gaining truth is less by searching than by brooding, by listening to the inner voices, by interpreting what is "given" in moments of rare and exalted feeling (see WORDSWORTH, WILLIAM).

Authorities are not agreed as to the exact beginnings of romanticism. One may, however, hold that, in literature, the earlier traces of the movement in Great Britain after Spenser, Shakespeare, and Milton are in the eighteenth century found in Thomas Gray, d. 1771, and William Blake, d. 1827 (cf. Arthur Symonds, *The Romantic Movement in English Poetry*, New York, 1909); in France in J. J. Rousseau, d. 1778; and in Germany in Herder (q.v.). In philosophy, its ultimate vindication is to be referred to Kant's (q.v.) primacy of the will, reaching its metaphysical exposition in the doctrine of Schopenhauer (q.v.) that the essence of man and world is will. In theology, one goes to Fichte and Schleiermacher (qq.v.) for the subjective and esthetic elements respectively.

Beginnings.

The spirit of Romanticism has been active in other fields than those described above: in music, F. P. Schubert (d. 1828), F. F. Chopin (d. 1849), and R. Schumann (d. 1856); in painting, J. M. W. Turner (d. 1851), and F. V. E. Delacroix (d. 1863); in travel, the inspiring motive of which since the latter part of the eighteenth century has been to quicken the feeling of beauty and sublimity in the presence of impressive natural scenery; in social experiment, as the Brook Farm episode, 1841–47, which sought to put into practise the system of association or phalanstery proposed by F. M. C. Fourier (d. 1837); and, finally, in appeal to the chivalrous and heroic in ministry to the suffering on the field of battle (Florence Nightingale, q.v., in the Crimea, 1854–1856) and in great cities (William Booth, q.v.).

Spirit.

The literature of Romanticism is of extraordinary brilliancy—tales, poems, dramas, essays, psychology, ethics, religion, and theology. Only a tithe of this output can be here referred to. In Great Britain: Lord Byron (d. 1824); William Blake (d. 1826); S. T. Coleridge (q.v.); W. Wordsworth (q.v.). In Germany: Novalis (d. 1801), *Die Lehrlinge zu Sais*, and *Heinrich von Ofterdingen* in *Werke* (Leipsic, 1898), and, in Eng. transl., *Hymns and Thoughts on Religion* (Edinburgh, 1888); H. von Kliest (d. 1811), *Werke* (Berlin, 1826); E. T. A. Hoffmann (d. 1822), *Werke* (Leipsic, 1899); J. P. F. Richter, "Jean Paul" (d. 1825), *Titan* (Berlin, 1800–03; Eng. transl., London, 1863; cf. T. Carlyle, *Essays*, vols. i. and iii., ib. 1887); F. von Schlegel (d. 1829), *Lucinde*, in *Athenäum*, 1798–1800, cf. also *Esthetic and Miscellaneous Works* (London, 1875); F. D. E. Schleiermacher (q.v.), *Reden ueber die Religion* (Berlin, 1799; Eng. transl., *On Religion*, London, 1893); A. W. von Schlegel (d. 1845), *Vorlesungen ueber dramatische Kunst und Litteratur* (Heidelberg, 1805–11; Eng. transl., *Lectures on Dramatic Art and Literature*, London, 1861); Ludwig Tieck (d. 1853), "William Lovell," *Die Verkehrte Welt*, in collected works published in Berlin from 1828 to 1854 (for Eng. transl. of several stories, cf. *Translations from Musæus, Tieck, and Richter*, London, 1889). In France: Madame de Staël (d. 1817), *De l'Allemagne* (London, 1813, Eng. transl., *Germany*, 2 vols., New York, 1871; cf. H. Heine, *Romantische Schule*, Hamburg, 1836); Théophile Gautier (d. 1872), *Mademoiselle de Maupin* (Paris, 1835; Eng. transl., London, 1887), *Fortunio* (Paris, 1837); Alfred de Musset (d. 1857), *La Confession d'un enfant du siècle* (Paris, 1836); George Sand (d. 1876), *Indiana* (Paris, 1831), *Lélia* (ib. 1833), *Jacques* (ib. 1834), *Lucrezia Floriani* (ib. 1846; Eng. transl. of *Consuelo*, London, 1847, and *Little Fadette*, b. 1849); Victor Hugo (d. 1885), *Hernani* (Paris, 1830; Eng. transl. in idem,

Literature.

Dramas, London, 1888), *Les Misérables* (Paris, 1862; Eng. transl., London, 1862). C. A. Beckwith.

Bibliography: T. Carlyle, *Critical and Miscellaneous Essays*, Boston, n.d.; J. A. Symonds, *Renaissance in Italy: The Revival of Learning*, New York, 1885; W. Pater, *Appreciations*, London, 1889; H. H. Boyesen, *Essays in German Literature*, "The Romantic School in Germany," New York, 1892; George Brandes, *Main Currents in Nineteenth Century Literature*; "The Romantic School in Germany," vol. ii.; "Naturalism in England," vol. iv.; "The Romantic School in France," vol. v., New York, 1902; D. G. Mason, *The Romantic Composers*, ib., 1906; *Cambridge Modern History*, vi. 822–837, ib., 1909; R. Eucken, *The Problem of Human Life*, pp. 308–336, 345, 418, 447–482, ib. 1910; I. Babbitt, *The New Laokoon*, Boston, 1910.

ROMANUS, ro-mē'nus: Pope, 897. Formerly cardinal priest of St. Peter ad Vincula, he was raised to the papal throne in the autumn of 897 on the murder of Stephen VII. His pontificate lasted only four months, during which he confirmed the possessions of the Spanish churches of Elna and Gerona at the request of their bishops.

(R. Zöpffel†.)

Bibliography: *Liber pontificalis*, ed. L. Duchesne, ii. 230, Paris, 1892; Jaffé, *Regesta*, pp. 303 sqq.; Mann, *Popes*, iv. 86–87; Hefele, *Conciliengeschichte*, iv. 566; Bower, *Popes*, ii. 301; Platina, *Popes*, i. 239.

ROMANUS: Byzantine religious poet; b. at Miseani (according to the Bollandists, at Emesa), Syria; d. at Constantinople in the sixth century. After being deacon at the church of St. Anastasia at Berytus, he came to Constantinople during the reign of Anastasius (probably in the last decade of the fifth century), where he was attached to the church of St. Mary's *en tois Kyrou*. Either here or in the Blachernian church he received from the Virgin in a vision the gift of poetry, and forthwith composed his famous Christmas hymn, which was followed by a thousand other hymns for various feasts. According to Nicephorus Callistus, the Greek Church later discarded the hymns of Romanus, with the exception of one for each feast; while Metrophanes Critopulus (*De vocibus*) states that in his time only four hundred of the thousand hymns survived. The scanty details concerning the poet are practically restricted to a brief *synaxarium* (ed. most conveniently in the *Analecta Bollandiana*, 1894, pp. 440–442).

The titles of all the hymns of Romanus are known. They contain no allusion that would imply a later date than the reign of Justinian (527–65), the period assigned Romanus by the author of the *Synaxarium*. Thus, the passage in the first hymn to the ten virgins, with its phrase, "Lo, the Assyrians, and the Ishmaelites before them, have led us captive," needs not refer to successive inroads by the Omayads of Damascus and the Abbasids of Bagdad, thus referring to the eighth century, but may equally well allude to the Persians and Saracens who menaced Byzantium in the reign of Anastasius I. Nor do the doctrinal references in the hymns imply a later date than Justinian's reign, for though Mary is termed "ever virgin," her freedom from original sin is not taught, though great reverence is shown her and she is regarded as a mediator between God and Christ for mankind—concepts which were held in the Justinian period. Again, the Christology of Romanus seems to allude to docetic theories, to Arius, to Apollinarius of Laodicea, and to the theopaschitic controversy in the reign of Anastasius, but of references to the monothelite heresy, for example, there is no clear evidence. There are likewise probable allusions to the Chalcedonian Creed. The question of the date of the poet, who would thus seem to be no later than the reign of Justinian, though some have sought to place him in the period of Anastasius II. (713–716), is of importance in that on its solution depends the setting of the acme of Byzantine religious poetry in the sixth or the eighth century.

Until the second third of the nineteenth century the poems of Romanus were scarcely known in the West, and occidental knowledge of them was introduced by Cardinal J. B. Pitra's edition of twenty-eight hymns and four sticharia in his *Analecta Solesmensia*, i. 1–241 (Paris, 1876). A faulty edition was later prepared by the archimandrite Amphilochius in his *Kondakarion* (2 vols., Moscow, 1879), but chief knowledge concerning Romanus and his work is due to four studies of K. Krumbacher in the *Sitzungsberichte der Münchener Akademie* (*phil.-phil. Klasse*, 1898, ii. 69–268, 1899, ii. 1–156, 1901, pp. 693–766, 1903, pp. 551–691). The material of the poems is drawn chiefly from the Bible, especially from the great events of salvation such as Christ's nativity, epiphany, passion, crucifixion, resurrection, and ascension, and the outpouring of the Holy Ghost. Romanus was likewise attracted by Biblical accounts of the Virgin and by leading events in the lives of the apostles, such as the denial of Peter and the conversion of Thomas. Beautiful parables, as that of the ten virgins, afforded welcome material to the poet. Some fifty of his poems are concerned with Biblical themes, thirty with the saints, while the remainder are penitential hymns and the like. In his exegesis he showed the influence of Chrysostom and Ephraem, and in his hymns to the saints he followed well-known lives. The purpose of his poems Romanus expressly states to be didactic. Strangely enough, his hymns were almost totally abandoned by his church some centuries later, when, in the ninth century, the Greek liturgies were remodeled and the canons took the place of the hymns. Only a few of the poems of Romanus were then retained, such as the Christmas hymn and the so-called requiem. Of the other hymns only single stanzas were retained in the liturgies, chiefly introductory and closing verses of general character.

The beauty of the poems of Romanus is evident even in their external form. In Byzantine poetry rhythm took the place of the classical metrical scheme, thus giving a characteristic form with peculiar rhythmic melody. After one or more proems follows the poem proper, which may have more than twenty stanzas. Each strophe closes with a refrain which repeats the chief thoughts of the poem, and the name of the author is usually given in an acrostic. This form of poetry was developed to its perfection by Romanus, the greatest hymn-writer of the Greek church. His verse is easy and euphonious, and varied by antitheses, assonances, paronomasias, and rime plays. The refrain is used by Romanus with admirable effect. The poems are preponderatingly dramatic in form, consisting of conversations between the characters introduced, as in the dialogue between Satan and Hades, when they learn that the cross of Golgotha is destined to crush their power. On the other hand, Romanus occasionally becomes unnecessarily dogmatizing, moralizing, and prolix.

Romanus was a noble poet in matter as well as in form, beautifully expressing the spirit of the Gospel and seeking to lead man to believe that for him personally salvation exists. He frequently praises the free grace of God and Christ, declaring that the reward which the Lord shall give in the life to come is the reward of grace. Through sin mankind falls, but rises through righteousness and faith, and is saved through grace. Above asceticism and orthodoxy Romanus ranks love of man, though he praises asceticism highly. He likewise lauds celibacy, but at the same time does not unduly depreciate marriage. Finally it may be noted that his view of life was strongly eschatological, some of his most beautiful poems being devoted to the last judgment and to the life to come. In him Byzantine poetry comes to its fullest bloom.

(PHILIPP MEYER.)

BIBLIOGRAPHY: A complete edition of the works is promised by Krumbacher. Twenty-nine poems, ed. J. B. Pitra, are in *Analecta Sacra*, i (1876), 1–241; three others, in *Sanctus Romanus veterum melodorum princeps*, Rome, 1888; a prayer, ed. Papadopulos Kerameus, in *Analekta Ierosolumitikês*, i (1891), 390–392. Consult: Krumbacher, *Geschichte*, pp. 663–671; idem, in the *Sitzungsberichte* of the Bavarian Academy, philologic-philosophical and historical class, 1898, vol. ii. 69–268, 1899, vol. ii. 1–156, 1901, pp. 693–766, 1903, pp. 551–691; idem, *Miscellen zu Romanos*, Munich, 1907; J. B. Pitra, *Hymnographie de l'église grecque*, Rome, 1867; idem, *Analecta sacra spicilegium*, i. 1–241, Paris, 1876; idem, *Al Sommo Pontifice Leone XIII. omaggio giubilare della Biblioteca Vaticana*, Rome, 1888; W. Christ and M. Paranikas, *Anthologia Græca*, Leipsic, 1871; Jacobi, in *ZKG*, 1882, pp. 177–250; W. Meyer, in the *Abhandlungen* of the Bavarian Academy, philosophic-historical class, 1886, pp. 268–449; H. Gelzer, in the *Abhandlungen* of the Saxon Academy, xviii. no. 5, p. 76; *Byzantinische Zeitschrift*, 1893, pp. 559–605 (by Papadopulos Kerameus), 1900, pp. 633–640 (by De Boor), 1903, pp. 153–166 (by Van den Ben), 1902, pp. 358–369 (by S. Pétrides), 1906, pp. 1–44, 337, 1907, pp. 257, 565–587, and 1910. 285–306 (all by P. Maas); Vailhé, in *Echos d'orient*, 1902, pp. 207–212; T. M. Wehofer, *Untersuchungen zum Lied des Romanos auf der Wiederkunft des Herrn*, ed. A. Erhard and P. Maas, Vienna, 1907.

ROMESTIN, AUGUST HENRY EUGENE DE: Church of England; b. at Paris May 9, 1830; d. at London May 18, 1900. He was a scholar of Winchester College, 1843–48; of St. John's College, Oxford (B.A., 1852; M.A., 1854); was ordained deacon 1852, and priest 1854; was curate of Mells, Somerset, 1853–54; of St. Thomas Martyr, Oxford, 1854–1855; English chaplain at Freiburg-im-Breisgau, 1863–65; and at Baden-Baden, 1865–68; chaplain of Woolland, Dorset, 1868–69; perpetual curate of Freeland, Oxford, 1874–85; rural dean of Woodstock, 1879–85; vicar of Stony Stratford, Buckinghamshire, 1885; warden of House of Mercy, Great Maplestead, Essex, 1885–91; rector of Tiptree, 1891–96; and vicar of Sledmere, 1896–1900. His theological standpoint was that of the school of E. B. Pusey. He was the author or editor of *Teaching of the Twelve Apostles, Text, with Introduction, Translation, and Notes* (London, 1884); *Saint Augustine, On Instructing the Unlearned; Concerning Faith of Things Unseen; On the Advantages of Believing; The Encheiridion to Laurentius;* and *Concerning Faith, Hope and Charity*, Latin and English (1885); *The Five Lectures of Saint Cyril on the Mysteries* (1887); *An Inquiry into the Belief of the Church from the Beginning until Now as to the Limitation of Our Lord's Knowledge* (1891); and *Saint Ambrose* in the *Select Library of the Nicene and Post Nicene Fathers* (1895).

ROMUALD, SAINT. See CAMALDOLITES.

RONGE, JOHANNES. See GERMAN CATHOLICISM, §§ 1, 6.

RONSDORF, rens'dorf, **SECT:** A chiliastic and communistic sect founded at Elberfeld in 1726 by Elias Eller and the Reformed pastor Schleiermacher. Eller (b. at Ronsdorf, 5 m. s.e. of Elberfeld, early in the eighteenth century; d. there May 16, 1750) went, while still a lad, to the neighboring city of Elberfeld, where he became foreman of a factory for a rich widow named Bolckhaus. Pietistic, chiliastic, and communistic influences had been rampant in the district, and with these Eller came in contact. He began to read the Bible and all accessible writings of the enthusiasts and pietists, and evolved an apocalyptic, chiliastic system of his own, blending it with communistic elements. The reception accorded his teachings attracted the attention of Frau Bolckhaus, whom he soon converted to his tenets and married, thus becoming a man of wealth. Eller now came in contact with Schleiermacher, and the pair held frequent meetings of the faithful, who called themselves the awakened and the elect. Among their number was a certain Anna van Buchel, the daughter of an Elberfeld baker, a girl of remarkable beauty. She was converted by Eller, who instructed her how to undergo ecstasies and receive revelations from heaven, taught her the Apocalypse, and inspired her with chiliastic ideas. Somewhat later, accordingly, she was seized with religious ecstasy, prophesying and describing in glowing colors the coming of the chiliastic kingdom in 1730, also declaring that the Lord had frequently appeared to and spoken with her. Henceforth Anna van Buchel was regarded as a prophetess. Before long, Eller's wife died, and he soon married Anna van Buchel with whom he had maintained for some time illicit relations; as he alleged, to protect her innocence. He now resolved to advance his doctrines more openly. His wife's visions became still more frequent. She and her husband were of the tribe of Judah and the lineage of David; and were to found the New Jerusalem. Kings and princes were to descend from them; they were the two witnesses (Rev. xi.), she was the woman clothed with the sun (xii.), the tabernacle of God among men (xxi. 3), and thebri de of the lamb (Cant.). These revelations being received with trust and awe, Eller now declared that God had revealed to his wife that she was the mother of Zion who should give birth to the savior of the world a second time, who would be the king of the chiliastic reign. Unfortunately Anna gave birth to a daughter. Eller, however, explained this by the fact that sufficient faith had not been shown him and the mother of Zion, and bade his followers wait in patience. In 1733 the mother of Zion gave birth to a son, who was baptized as Benjamin, on the basis of Ps. lxviii. 27. The child was reverenced in his cradle as the future great prophet and savior of the world, and Eller declared that his children were divinely begotten, and consequently born without sin.

By this time the number of his adherents had so increased that Eller could think of establishing a church. He accordingly divided his adherents into three classes; those of the court, the threshold, and the temple. Only the initiate were allowed to receive the complete doctrine, and they must first swear to maintain inviolable secrecy. The distinctive tenets were as follows: (1) the fulness of the Godhead dwells in Eller alone; (2) though the Bible is the Word of God, the divine annunciation to the mother of Zion that a new epoch is to begin necessitates a new revelation, this being in the booklet called *Hirtentasche* which was granted in secret to the select alone; (3) not only will the saints appear again on earth, but the Savior must be born again; (4) Eller is the counterpart of Abraham, but greater than he. The person of the Father is in Abraham, of the Son in Isaac, and of the Holy Ghost in Sarah; but in Eller is the fulness of the Godhead. Hence, except through him there is no blessing or happiness from above, and those who do not follow him must face the wrath of God; (5) Eller, circumcised by God, must bear sickness and pain for the sins of the world; (6) Moses and Elijah were not only prototypes of Christ, but also of Eller, as were David and Solomon; (7) the children of Eller are begotten directly of God. Eller now sent apostles throughout Germany, Switzerland, and the northern countries; but somewhat to the detriment of his doctrine "little Benjamin" died when barely a year old. Though able to restore the confidence of his followers, the practises of his community attracted suspicion and silent investigation by the consistory from 1735, so that in 1737 he left Elberfeld, which he declared to be a second Sodom and Gomorrah; and removed to Ronsdorf, where God had bidden the mother of Zion to build the New Jerusalem. Many of his adherents followed him, so that soon fifty houses had been erected, all facing the East toward Zion, which, as the tabernacle, was Eller's house, and his wife was the ark, the Urim and Thummim. So many funds poured in from various portions of Germany, as well as from Holland, England, and Switzerland, that not only could a new church be built at Ronsdorf, but in 1741 the Reformed preacher Schleiermacher was called from Elberfeld to be the preacher of the sect. Schleiermacher and Eller worked in harmony, and when the mother of Zion again bore a daughter, instead of the prophesied Benjamin, it was Schleiermacher who held the doubting believers together, until Eller had assembled the chief members of the sect and informed them that God had revealed to the mother of Zion that her daughter was called to do masculine deeds. Hardly had this child reached the age of two, before it received divine homage.

Meanwhile the growth of the sect in Ronsdorf rendered it possible for Eller to gain absolute control of the government; and the most unlimited license held sway in connection with the rites of the sacraments or on birthdays, Eller justifying himself boldly by the transgressions of the patriarchs, David, and Solomon. In 1744 the mother of Zion died mysteriously, after giving birth to another daughter; and Eller now declared that all which had previously applied to his wife must henceforth be understood as referring to himself, the prophet, high priest, and king. Schleiermacher, however, becoming suspicious of Eller, and horrified at his licentiousness, finally was convinced of his leader's vileness. In bitter repentance, he acknowledged his errors openly, charged Eller with wilful deceit, and sought in his sermons to undo the mischief he had wrought. Eller, in alarm, unsuccessfully forbade attendance at Schleiermacher's addresses; and then called one of his fieriest adherents, Wülfing of Solingen, to Ronsdorf as second preacher. For a time Wülfing and Schleiermacher remained on peaceable terms, but in 1749 the latter was forced to leave Ronsdorf. Rudenhaus of Ratingen was chosen in his stead, at the instance of Eller to whom he, like Wülfing, rendered blind submission. At Eller's death the sect began to decline. Wülfing vainly endeavored to carry on Eller's practise, aided by Johannes Bolckhaus, the son of Eller's first wife. Shortly afterward, however, Wülfing himself died, and the great majority of the villagers of Ronsdorf quickly returned to the Evangelical faith.

(G. H. Klippel†.)

Bibliography: Sources are: J. W. Knevel, *Gräuel der Verwüstung an heiligen Stätte, oder die Geheimnisse der Bosheit der Ronsdorfer Sekte*, Frankfort, 1750; P. Wülfing, *Ronsdorffischer Katechismus*, Düsseldorf, 1756; idem, *Ronsdorffs silberne Trompete oder Kirchenbuch*, ib. 1761; J. Bolckhaus, *Ronsdorfs gerechte Sache*, ib. 1757; P. Wülfing and J. Bolckhaus, *Das jubilierende Ronsdorf*, Mühlheim, 1751. Consult: J. A. Engels, *Versuch einer Geschichte der religiösen Schwärmerei in . . . Herzogtum Berg*, Schwelm, 1826.

ROOS, rōs, **MAGNUS FRIEDRICH**: German Lutheran and devotional writer; b. at Sulz (40 m. s.w. of Stuttgart) Sept. 6, 1727; d. at Anhausen (about 20 m. s.e. of Tübingen) Mar. 19, 1803. He was educated at Tübingen, and in 1767 became pastor at Lustnau and dean of the diocese of Bebenhausen, also lecturing on theology at Tübingen. He was later transferred, in accordance with his own wish, to Anhausen, where he could have more leisure for writing. In 1788–97 he was also a member of the national committee of Württemberg. Theologically Roos was a moderate Pietist and essentially a pupil of Johann Albrecht Bengel both in his life and his writings. Among the latter, which were very numerous, special mention may be made not only of his commentaries on Daniel, Galatians, Romans, the Johannine Epistles, etc., but also of his *Einleitung in die biblischen Geschichten* (Tübingen, 1774; Stuttgart, 1876) and *Christliche Glaubenslehre* (Stuttgart, 1786; Basel, 1867). He likewise wrote much on eschatology, as *Beleuchtung der gegenwärtigen grossen Begebenheiten durch das prophetische Wort Gottes* (Tübingen, 1779) and *Prüfung der gegenwärtigen Zeit nach der Offenbarung Johannis* (Stuttgart, 1786); while his strictly devotional works include his *Christliches Hausbuch* (2 parts, Stuttgart, 1790;

1871); *Kreuzschule* (1799; 8th ed., 1896), and *Beicht- und Kommunionbuch* (4th ed., 1805).

(Hermann Beck.)

Bibliography: An autobiography with notes by his son and his grandson is contained in the *Einleitung*, ut sup., ed. of 1876. Consult: *Christenbote*, 1831, pp. 1 sqq., 1832, pp. 53 sqq.; C. Grosse, *Die alten Tröster*, pp. 484 sqq., Hermannsburg, 1900.

ROOTS, LOGAN HERBERT: Protestant Episcopal missionary bishop of Hankow, China; b. near Tamaroa, Ill., July 27, 1870. He was educated at Harvard (A.B., 1891), and, after a year as graduate secretary of the Harvard Christian Association and traveling secretary of the college department of the Y. M. C. A., entered the Episcopal Divinity School, Cambridge, Mass., from which he was graduated in 1896. He was ordered deacon in the same year and was advanced to the priesthood in 1898. In 1896 he went to China, and, after studying at Wuchang until 1898, was stationed as a missionary at Hankow until 1904, when he was consecrated (second) missionary bishop of Hankow.

ROPES, CHARLES JOSEPH HARDY: Congregationalist; b. in St. Petersburg, Russia, Dec. 7, 1851. He was educated at the City of London School (1862-67), the gymnasium of Arnstadt, Germany (1868-69), the Sorbonne, Paris (1869), Yale College (A.B., 1872), the University of Tübingen (1872-73), Andover Theological Seminary (1873-75; resident licentiate, 1875-76), and Union Theological Seminary (1876-77). He was pastor at Ellsworth, Me. (1877-1881); and professor of New-Testament language and literature in Bangor Theological Seminary (1881-1908). He was also librarian of the same institution from 1887-1901, and resumed this office in 1906. He has written *The Morality of the Greeks as shown by their Literature, Art, and Life* (New York, 1872), and has translated G. Uhlhorn's *Conflict of Christianity with Heathenism* (in collaboration with E. C. Smyth; 1879).

ROPES, JAMES HARDY: Congregationalist; b. at Salem, Mass., Sept. 3, 1866. He was graduated from Harvard (A.B., 1889), Andover Theological Seminary (1893), and studied at the universities of Kiel, Halle, and Berlin (1893-95). He was instructor in New-Testament criticism and exegesis at Harvard (1895-1903), and has been Bussey professor of the same subjects since 1903, as well as Dexter lecturer on Biblical literature since 1904. He has written *Die Sprüche Jesu die in den kanonischen Evangelien nicht überliefert sind* (Leipsic 1896).

ROSARY: A string of beads, each eleventh one larger than the rest, used in the Roman Catholic Church to aid in the reciting of a fixed number of Our Father's and Hail Marys; also the devotion in which such a string of beads is employed. Quasi-analogues may be traced in non-Christian religions, as among the Tibetan Buddhists, who use strings of beads, generally 108 in number, and made of jewels, sandal-wood, mussel-shells, and the like, according to the status of their owners; while the Mohammedans, in like manner, have a *tasbih*, or string of thirty-three, sixty-six, or ninety-nine beads, to be counted as the corresponding names of Allah in the Koran are recited.

Origin and History.

The custom of repeatedly reciting the Our Father arose in the monastic life of Egypt at an early time, being recorded by Palladius and Sozomen. The Hail Mary, or Ave Maria, on the other hand, first became a regular prayer in the second half of the eleventh century, though it was not until about the thirteenth that it was generally adopted. The addition of the words of Elizabeth, "blessed is the fruit of thy womb, Jesus" (Luke i. 42), to the Angelical Salutation, "Hail, Mary, full of grace; the Lord is with thee; blessed art thou among women" (Luke i. 28), is first mentioned about 1130; but Bishop Odo of Paris (1196-1208) requires the recitation of the Hail Mary together with the Our Father and the Creed as a regular Christian custom. The closing petition, "Holy Mary, Mother of God, pray for us sinners, now and at the hour of our death," developed gradually in the sixteenth century, and was regarded even by the Council of Besançon (1571) as a superfluous but pious custom. These facts show that the traditions which ascribe the invention of the rosary to Benedict of Nursia, Bede, or Peter the Hermit are untrustworthy, and the same statement holds of the Dominican tradition which makes Dominic receive a vision of the Virgin commanding him to introduce the use of the rosary. At the same time, the rosary was originally an essentially Dominican mode of devotion, though first arising long after the death of the founder of the order; but while some influence may have been exercised by the acquaintance of oriental Christians with the Mohammedan *tasbih*, all the characteristics of the recitation of the Our Father, like the meditations connected with it, can be explained only from the operation of specifically Christian ideas.

Chief Types and Derivation of Name.

The devotions of the rosary are some twenty in number, of which the most important now call for consideration. The complete, or Dominican, rosary discovered, according to tradition, by Dominic about 1208, consists of fifteen decades of small beads (Hail Marys), each separated by a large bead (Our Father). This is also called the rosary (or psalter) of the Blessed Virgin Mary, the alternative title implying that the 150 Psalms may likewise be regarded as so many prayers to the Virgin. The ordinary rosary, traditionally ascribed to Peter of Amiens about 1090, contains five decades of Hail Marys and five Our Fathers, the former shaped (toward the end of the Middle Ages) like white lilies to symbolize the purity of the Virgin, and the latter like red roses to typify the five wounds of Christ. The rosary of St. Bridget consists of sixty-three Hail Marys, representing the traditional number of years of the Virgin's life (or seventy-two among the Franciscans), and seven Our Fathers. The Crown of our Savior is a rosary traditionally ascribed to a Camaldolite monk of the early sixteenth century, and consists of thirty-three Our Fathers (representing the thirty-three years of the life of Christ) and five Hail Marys (typifying the five wounds of Christ). A similar devotion is the "little rosary," with three decades of Hail Marys and three Our Fathers; and the angelical rosary likewise has thirty-three beads. In the latter, however, the Hail Mary is recited only at the first bead of each decade, the *Sanctus*, followed by the lesser doxology, being repeated at each of the nine others.

The origin of the name rosary for an object bearing no resemblance whatever to a garland of roses is problematical. Some Roman Catholic authors derive the term from the Virgin's appellation of "mystic rose" in the Church; or from St. Rosalie (twelfth century), who is represented sometimes with a string of beads and sometimes with a crown of gold and roses; or from the roses which, legend says, bloomed on the lips of those who paid true homage to the Virgin and the Angelical Salutation, and which she plucked and twined into a garland about their brows. It is more probable, however, that, in the spirit of the mystic piety of the Middle Ages, the devotion itself was conceived as a garden of roses, each of which, as a separate prayer, unfolded in honor of the Blessed Virgin, especially as this corresponds in meaning with the English "chaplet," Lat. *corona* ("crown"), etc., as a designation of the rosary or of separate decades of it.

Mode of Recitation.

On beginning the rosary the sign of the cross is made, the small cross attached to the center of the string of beads is held, and the Creed, one Our Father, three Hail Marys, and one Gloria are recited, as they also are on the completion of the devotion. The recitation of the rosary also involves meditation on the five joyful, the five sorrowful, and the five glorious mysteries. The five joyful mysteries are the annunciation, the visitation, the nativity, the presentation, and the finding of Jesus in the Temple; the five sorrowful mysteries are the agony and bloody sweat of Christ in the garden, the scourging, the crown of thorns, Christ carrying his cross, and the crucifixion; the five glorious mysteries are the resurrection, the ascension, the coming of the Holy Ghost, the assumption of the Virgin, and the coronation of the Virgin. The joys, sorrows, and glories of Mary are thus linked in an ascending scale with the great facts of redemption. The rosary is generally connected with a single group of the mysteries at a time: the joyful mysteries on Mondays and Thursdays, and the Sundays of Advent and from Epiphany to Lent; the sorrowful mysteries on Tuesdays and Fridays, and the Sundays in Lent; and the glorious mysteries on Wednesdays and Saturdays, and the Sundays from Easter to Advent. A tradition of the Church, first fully developed in the nineteenth century, grants indulgences for the recitation of the rosary. The indulgence attaches, moreover, to individual beads as well as to the entire rosary, and only when more than half are lost at the same time, or when the medal with the picture of the Virgin is mutilated or become unrecognizable, does the indulgence become invalid.

Confraternity of the Holy Rosary.

The Confraternity of the Holy Rosary was founded at Cologne by the famous Dominican Jakob Sprenger in 1475, and was privileged by Sixtus IV. on condition that the rosary be recited on the five great feasts of the Virgin (Purification [Feb. 2]; Annunciation [Mar. 25]; Visitation [July 2]; Assumption [Aug. 15]; and Nativity [Sept. 8]), as well as on other days, each time with an indulgence of 100 days. Succeeding pontiffs extended the confraternity and its privileges, and its prestige was increased during the Turkish wars of the sixteenth century. The success of the Christian arms at the battle of Lepanto (Oct. 7, 1571; the first Sunday in October) was attributed to the intercession of the Virgin for the prayers of the confraternity, and Pius V. accordingly made that day the feast of Our Lady of the Rosary (transferred by Gregory XIII. in 1583 to its present place, the first Sunday in October). The limitation of the feast, by Gregory XIII., to churches containing a chapel or altar in honor of the rosary was gradually extended by his successors until the Austrian victory at Temesvar on the feast of Our Lady of the Snows (Aug. 5) and the raising of the Turkish siege of Corfu on the feast of the Assumption of the Blessed Virgin Mary (Aug. 15) were deemed such conclusive proofs of her power of intercession that Clement XI., in the following year, commanded that the feast be observed throughout Christendom. The members of the Confraternity of the Holy Rosary are bound to recite the rosary at least once daily. Recently, however, there has been a tendency to form "Living Rosaries," each of fifteen members, each reciting a decade daily. These fifteen members constitute a "rose," fifteen "roses" a "tree of God," and fifteen "trees of God" a "divine garden of the Blessed Virgin." Leo XIII. was an especially fervent promoter of the devotion of the rosary, no less than eight of his encyclicals touching upon it.

The monks of the Greek Church, particularly on Mount Athos, have a quasi-analogue to the rosary in their *kombologion* or *komboschoinion*, a cord with a hundred knots, each of which, when told, must be accompanied with the sign of the cross. Some of the monks of Athos are required to repeat this office twelve times daily, accompanying these 1,200 prayers with 120 genuflections. (O. ZÖCKLER†.)

BIBLIOGRAPHY: H. Alt, *Das Kirchenjahr des christlichen Morgen- und Abendlandes*, pp. 72 sqq., Berlin, 1860; V. Morassi, *Il Rosario della B. V. Maria*, Casalis, 1867; M. Chéry, *La Théologie du saint rosaire*, 2 vols., Paris, 1869; K. Martin, *Die Schönheiten des Rosenkranzes*, Mainz, 1876; H. Duffant, *Une hypothèse sur la date et le lieu de l'institution du rosaire*, Freiburg, 1878; M. Plues, *Chats about the Rosary*, London, 1881; T. Leikes, *Rosa aurea*, Dülmen, 1886; L. C. Gay, *Entretiens sur le rosaire*, 2 vols., Paris, 1887; W. Lescher, *The Rosary, its Hist. and Indulgences*, London, 1888; idem, *St. Dominic and the Rosary*, Leicester, 1901; T. Esser, *Unserer lieben Frauen Rosenkranz*, Paderborn, 1889; A. König, *Officium des heiligen Rosenkranzes*, Breslau, 1890; *Acta sanctæ sedis . . . pro societate s. rosarii*, 4 vols., Leyden, 1891; T. Esser, in *Katholik*, 1897, pp. 346 sqq., 409 sqq., 515 sqq.; O. Zöckler, *Askese und Mönchtum*, passim, Frankfort, 1897; S. Knoll, *Maria die Königin des Rosenkranzes, oder vollständige Erklärung der heiligen Rosenkranz Geheimnisse*, Regensburg, n.d.; *Manual of Prayers for the Use of the Catholic Laity*, pp. 368–382, New York, n.d. (gives English prayers, meditations, etc.); J. J. Roche, *Short Explanation of the Rosary*, London (Duffy and Co.), n.d.; Canon Ryan, *The Holy Rosary*, in vol. iv. of *Collected Publications*, Catholic Truth Society, London, n.d.; Graf Hoensbroech, *Das Papsttum in seiner social-kulturellen Wirksamkeit*, i. 277–283, Leipsic, 1901; J. Procter, *Rosary Guide for Priests and People*, London, 1901; D. Dahm, *Die Brüderschaft vom heiligen Rosenkranz*, Treves, 1902; H. Holzapfel, *St.*

Dominikus und der Rosenkrans, Munich, 1903; W. Schmitz, *Das Rosenkransgebet im 15. und im Anfange des 16. Jahrhunderts*, Freiburg, 1903; K. D. Beste, *Rosa mystica; the Mysteries of the Rosary*, London, 1904; *ASB*, Aug., i. 422–437; *DCB*, ii. 1819–20; *KL*, x. 1275–80. For ethnic rosaries consult: Monier Williams, in *Athenæum*, Feb. 9, 1878; I. M. Casanowicz, *The Collection of Rosaries in the U. S. National Museum* (Washington Gov't Pub.), 1909.

ROSCELINUS, ros-e-lai'nus (**ROSCELLINUS, ROZELINUS, RUCELINUS**), **JOHANNES**: Nominalist and tritheist of the eleventh century; b. in northern France, probably in the diocese of Soissons. Of his life almost nothing is known, and it is difficult to define his theological and philosophical views. He received his education at Soissons and **Life.** Reims, and then taught at Tours and at Locmenach near Vannes in Brittany. Shortly before 1092 he was canon at Compiègne, but since he taught views on the Trinity that seemed heretical, and since he appealed to Lanfranc and Anselm as supporting his position, the latter addressed a letter of complaint to Bishop Fulco of Beauvais immediately before the synod of Soissons (1092). The synod bade Roscelinus to recant, and as not only the members of the synod, but apparently the whole people, had been aroused against him, he obeyed from fear. The form of recantation, which seems to have been merely an abjuration of tritheism, must have enabled him to adhere to his doctrine without directly violating his word, for he was soon once more defending his old opinions. He lost his canonry and sought refuge in England where, as an opponent of Anselm, he expected a favorable reception from William Rufus. He was compelled to leave, however, after the reconciliation of the king with Anselm, especially as he had attacked Anselm's teaching concerning the incarnation. He returned to France and became canon of Tours and Besançon. While at Locmenach he had been the first teacher of Abelard, but the pupil came to despise his master, and in his *De trinitate* (1119) Abelard very emphatically defended the unity of God in the trinity of persons, with unmistakable reference to the opinions of Roscelinus which had been condemned at Soissons. Roscelinus determined to charge his pupil with heresy in regard to the Trinity before Bishop Gisbert of Paris, whereupon Abelard addressed a letter to the bishop, defending himself and offering to hold a disputation with Roscelinus, at the same time making a sharp attack on his errors and his private life. The letter in which Roscelinus replied to Abelard is the sole product of his pen which is now extant (ed. J. A. Schmeller, in *AMA*, philosophisch-philologische Klasse, 5 ser., iii. 189–210, 1849; also in Abelard's *Opera*, ed. V. Cousin, ii. 792–803, Paris, 1859). In this letter he haughtily ignored the attacks upon his character, but referred to Abelard's career, and expressed himself cautiously but clearly on the theological points in controversy. He reveals himself as ready to submit to the authority of both the Bible and the Church, and as fully recognizing the prestige of such a theological opponent as Anselm. After this episode Roscelinus disappears from history.

In considering the doctrine of Roscelinus, his deviation from the orthodox doctrine of the Trinity may first be discussed, then his nominalism, and finally the connection between the two. He regarded the three persons of the Trinity as "three self-existent beings," who, however, are united by unity of power and will, thus endeavoring to avoid the deductions that in the Son the Father and the Holy Ghost were also incarnate. Anselm, in his **Trinitarian Doctrine.** polemic against Roscelinus, asked what he meant by the expression "three self-existent beings"; if he referred simply to the relations by which the Father and the Son are distinguished in God, his doctrine would not be in disagreement with the doctrines of the Church which teaches that the Father as Father is not the Son, and the Son as Son is not the Father. This, however, in his judgment, could not be the opinion of Roscelinus, since he says that the three Persons are "three essentially separate beings," which would imply a stronger distinction, the assumption of three different Gods. This was likewise evident, according to Anselm, from Roscelinus' comparison of the Trinity with three angels or three souls, these evidently being three substances, and not merely three relations of one and the same being, whereas the Church teaches that the three persons of the Trinity are not three substances (i.e., three Gods), but one God. Furthermore, if the "three beings" bore the name of God in virtue of one and the same power and will, as three men bear the name of king, God would not be something substantial, but accidental, and the "three beings" would then be three Gods as certainly as three men could not be one king. If Roscelinus divides the whole God into three individuals, he would have to extend the incarnation, according to Anselm, to all three persons if this is to be true and perfect. The doctrine of the Church, however, is not compelled to assume this because it sees in the one being, which is God, three distinct persons, so that it sees the same God in the Father as in the Son, only in another relation, and is, accordingly, not forced to ascribe to the Father everything that belongs to God in the Son, e.g., the incarnation. Anselm derived the error of Roscelinus from his excessive stress on the concept of personality in reference to God. When he states that Roscelinus "either wished to set up three gods or did not know what he did mean," he was half right and half wrong. Roscelinus posited three gods in so far as he clearly perceived the difficulty of simultaneously conceiving of numerical unity and triple and true personality in the Trinity; but he was no tritheist in the heretical sense of the term, and he thought that tritheism was fully avoided by his union of the persons in power and will. Herein he was wrong, and the rigid dialectics of Anselm clearly proved how inevitably his phraseology led to tritheistic conclusions.

In philosophy Roscelinus was a nominalist, maintaining that universals are not real and self-existent, but are mere abstract names which exist in and for thought. He, therefore, taught that a whole cannot have parts in the sense that the whole really exists while the parts proceed from it; on the contrary, only the parts are real, their synthesis forming a whole that can be distinguished

Nominalistic Foundation.

as a unit from them only logically, not really. If, now, the whole, or "thing," comprised parts, then, since the whole is nothing but the parts, the part would be part both of itself and of the other parts; and again, since each part is necessarily prior to the whole, this whole, if it is comprised of parts, must be prior to them, so that the part is prior to itself. This paradox is solved by the fact that Roscelinus attached to "whole" (or "thing") the connotation of a concrete and existent individual, which is consciously delimited from other objects, and ceases to be itself when one of its elements is withdrawn. The heresy of Roscelinus condemned by the Synod of Soissons was not based ostensibly upon his nominalism; but it is probably incorrect to argue that he proceeded from a theological to a nominalistic point of view in order to reconcile philosophy and theology, for he was primarily a dialectician, and considered theological problems from his philosophical standpoint. Regarding the universal as a mere logical, nominal abstraction of particulars, he could conceive God to exist only as an individual, and could construe the "three beings" only as three individuals, not as "one being" in the realistic sense, so that the unity of the three could consist only in their common power and will. In reaching this conclusion he seems to have concealed his nominalistic basis, lest, from its use in advancing a theological innovation, he should bring both theory and basis into discredit. According to Anselm, Roscelinus declared that "we must defend the Christian faith." On the surface this implies a purely apologetic interest, but it has also been construed as a plea for dialectic elucidation of the faith, and even for relative freedom of reason in the interpretation and development of ecclesiastical doctrine, especially as nominalism was generally associated with a more rationalistic tendency than was realism. The data are, however, too scanty to pronounce a decision. (A. HAUCK.)

BIBLIOGRAPHY: Anselm, *De fide trinitatis, contra blasphemias Roscellini*, in *MPL*, clviii.; F. Picavet, *Roscelin, philosophe et théologien*, Paris, 1896; *Histoire littéraire de la France*, ix. 358 sqq.; J. M. Chladen, *De vita et hæresi Roscellini*, Erlangen, 1756; J. M. de Gerando, *Hist. comparée des systèmes de philosophie*, ii. 446, Paris, 1804; V. Cousin, *Fragments de philosophie scolastique*, pp. 119 sqq., Paris, 1840; H. Bouchitté, *Le Rationalisme chrétien à la fin du onzième siècle*, Paris, 1842; C. de Rémusat, *Abélard*, 2 vols., Paris, 1845; B. Hauréau, *De la philosophie scolastique*, i. 175–179, Paris, 1850; C. Prantl, *Geschichte der Logik im Abendlande*, ii. 77 sqq., Leipsic, 1861; A. Stöckl, *Geschichte der Philosophie des Mittelalters*, i. 135 sqq., Mainz, 1864; C. S. Barach, *Zur Geschichte des Nominalismus*, in *Kleine philosophische Schriften*, Vienna, 1878; F. Ueberweg, *Geschichte der Philosophie*, ed. M. Heinze, vol. ii., Berlin, 1905, Eng. transl. of earlier ed., i. 364, 372–376, 380, New York, 1874; Schaff, *Christian Church*, v. 1, pp. 592, 600, 613; Neander, *Christian Church*, vol. iv. passim; *KL*, x. 1272–73; Harnack, *Dogma*, vi. 34, 151–162, 182; the works on the history of philosophy by J. E. Erdmann, 3 vols., London, 1892–98, and W. Windelband, New York, 1893.

ROSE, THE GOLDEN. See GOLDEN ROSE.

ROSE, HENRY JOHN: Church of England; b. at Uckfield (15 m. n.e. of Brighton) Jan. 3, 1800; d. at Bedford Jan. 31, 1873. He was graduated from St. John's College, Cambridge (B.A., 1821; M.A., 1824; B.D., 1831; fellow, 1824–38); rector of Houghton Conquest, Bedfordshire, 1837–73; and archdeacon of Bedford, 1866–73. He was joint editor of the *Encyclopedia Metropolitana* (London, 1817–45) from 1839, from which he reprinted, with additions, his *History of the Christian Church from 1700 to 1858* (1858). He was a member of the English Old-Testament company of revisers, and wrote in part the notes on Daniel in *The Bible Commentary* (London, 1872–82). He was author of *The Law of Moses in Connection with the History and Character of the Jews*, Hulsean lectures, 1833 (Cambridge, 1834); and *Answer to the Case of Dissenters* (1834). He was a conservative churchman, an indefatigable collector of books, and a voluminous miscellaneous editor and writer.

BIBLIOGRAPHY: J. W. Burgon, *The Lives of Twelve Good Men*, pp. 284–295 et passim, 2 vols., London, 1888; E. M. Goulburn, *John W. Burgon: a Biography*, 2 vols., London, 1891; *DNB*, xlix. 232–233.

ROSE, HUGH JAMES: Church of England, brother of the preceding; b. at Little Horsted (14 m. n.e. of Brighton) June 9, 1795; d. at Florence, Italy, Dec. 22, 1838. He was graduated at Trinity College, Cambridge, 1817; was vicar of Horsham, 1822–30; prebendary of Chichester, 1827–33; Christian Advocate in the University of Cambridge, 1829–1833; rector of Hadley, Suffolk, 1830–33; incumbent of Fairsted, Essex, 1834–37, and of St. Thomas, Southwark, 1835–38; professor of divinity at the University of Durham, 1833; and principal of King's College, London, 1836. He was a very learned man, and a High-churchman of the most pronounced type. He early established relations with J. H. Newman and others of the Oxford movement, and the celebrated Hadleigh conference, which bore fruit later in crystallizing that movement, was held at his rectory, although later Rose took but little part (see TRACTARIANISM). He founded the *British Magazine and Monthly Register of Religious and Ecclesiastical Information*, 1832; was editor of the *Encyclopedia Metropolitana* (29 vols., London, 1817–45) in 1836–38; and projected the *New General Biographical Dictionary* (12 vols., London, 1848). He published *Christianity always Progressive* (London, 1829); and *The Gospel an Abiding System* (1832).

BIBLIOGRAPHY: J. W. Burgon, *The Lives of Twelve Good Men*, 2 vols., London, 1888; J. H. Newman, *Apologia pro vita sua*, chap. ii., ib. 1864; H. P. Liddon, *Life of Edward Bouverie Pusey*, passim, 3 vols., ib. 1893–94; *DNB*, xlix. 240–242; and literature under TRACTARIANISM.

ROSENIUS, KARL OLOF. See BORNHOLMERS.

ROSENMUELLER, rō′zen-mül″ler, **ERNST FRIEDRICH KARL:** German Lutheran and orientalist; b. at Hessberg (a village near Hildburghausen, 17 m. s.e. of Meiningen) Dec. 10, 1768; d. at Leipsic Sept. 17, 1835. He was educated at the University of Leipsic, where he was privat-docent (1792–96), associate professor of Arabic (1796–1813), and full professor of oriental languages (1813–1835). His life was the uneventful one of a quiet, earnest student. Besides reediting S. Bochart's *Hierozoicon* (3 vols., Leipsic, 1793–96), he wrote *Scholia in Vetus Testamentum* (16 parts, 1788–1817; excerpted in five parts, 1828–35); *Handbuch für die Litteratur der biblischen Kritik und Exegese* (4 parts,

Göttingen, 1797–1800); *Institutiones ad fundamenta linguæ Arabicæ* (Leipsic, 1818); *Das alte und neue Morgenland, oder Erläuterungen der heiligen Schrift aus der natürlichen Beschaffenheit, den Sagen, Sitten und Gebräuchen des Morgenlandes* (6 vols., 1818–20); *Handbuch der biblischen Altertumskunde* (4 vols., 1823–31); and *Analecta Arabica* (1824). Portions of his *Handbuch* were translated by N. Morren under the titles *Biblical Geography of Asia Minor, Phenicia, and Arabia* (Edinburgh, 1836), and *Biblical Geography of Central Asia* (2 vols., 1836–37), and by N. Morren and T. G. Repp under the title *Mineralogy and Botany of the Bible* (Edinburgh, 1840). (G. Frank†.)

Bibliography: *Neuer Nekrolog der Deutschen*, XIII., ii. 766–769; *ADB*, xxix. 215.

ROSENMUELLER, JOHANN GEORG: German Lutheran, father of the preceding; b. at Ummerstädt, near Hildburghausen (17 m. s.e. of Meiningen), Dec. 18, 1736; d. at Leipsic Mar. 14, 1815. After completing his education at the University of Altdorf, he was for several years a private tutor and teacher; then pastor at Hildburghausen (1767–1768), Hessberg (1768–72), and Königsberg in Franconia (1772–75); professor of theology at Erlangen (1775–83); first professor of the same at Giessen (1783–85); and professor of theology, pastor of St. Thomas', and superintendent at Leipsic (1785–1815). In theology he was an opponent of the Kantian exegesis and an adherent of the mediating school, regarding the principles of the unbiased reason to be as authoritative as the clear expressions of Scripture. The fruit of his activity as teacher and preacher appeared in writings on exegesis, hermeneutics, practical theology, and, above all, in books of edification. Special mention may be made of his *Scholia in Novum Testamentum* (6th ed., 6 vols., Nuremberg, 1815–31); *Historia interpretationis librorum sacrorum in ecclesia Christiana* (5 vols., Hildburghausen, 1795–1814); *Morgen- und Abendandachten* (1799); *Betrachtungen über die vornehmsten Wahrheiten der Religion auf alle Tage des Jahres* (4 vols., Leipsic, 1801); *Auserlesenes Beicht- und Kommunionbuch* (1799); and *Christliches Lehrbuch für die Jugend* (1809). (G. Frank†.)

Bibliography: *Notizen aus Rosenmüller's Leben*, Leipsic, 1815; J. C. Dols, *Rosenmüllers Leben*, ib. 1816; G. Frank, *Geschichte der protestantischen Theologie*, iii. 102, ib. 1875; *ADB*, xxix. 219.

ROSENZWEIG, rō'zen-tsvaig, ADOLF: German rabbi; b. at Turdossin (52 m. s.s.w. of Cracow), Hungary, Oct. 20, 1850. He was educated at the rabbinical seminary at Pressburg, the Lehranstalt für die Wissenschaft des Judentums, Berlin, and the University of Berlin. In 1874 he became rabbi at Pasewalk, Pomerania, whence he was called, a few years later, to Birnbaum, Posen, where he remained until 1879. From 1879 to 1887 he was rabbi at Teplitz, Bohemia, and since 1887 has been rabbi and preacher of the Jewish community at Berlin. He has written *Zur Einleitung in die Bücher Esra und Nehemia* (Berlin, 1875); *Zum hunderten Geburtstage des Nathan der Weise* (Posen, 1878); *Das Jahrhundert nach dem babylonischen Exile mit besonderer Rücksicht auf die religiöse Entwicklung des Judentums* (Berlin, 1885); *Künstler und Jugendbilder* (Neuhaus, 1886); *Der politische und religiöse Charakter des Josephus Flavius* (Berlin, 1889); *Jerusalem und Caesarea* (1890); *Das Auge in Bibel und Talmud* (1892); *Geselligkeit und Geselligkeitsfreuden in Bibel und Talmud* (1895); and *Kleidung und Schmuck im biblischen und talmudischen Schriften* (1905).

ROSETTA STONE. See Egypt, I., 6, § 1; Inscriptions, I., § 3.

ROSICRUCIANS: An alleged mystical order of the early seventeenth century, whose origin is supposed to be given in the *Allgemeine vnd General Reformation, der gantzen weiten Welt. Beneben der Fama Fraternitatis, dess Löblichen Ordens des Rosenkreutzes . . . Auch einer kurtzen Responsion, von dem Herrn Haselmeyer gestellet, welcher desswegen von den Jesuitern ist gefänglich eingezogen, vnd auff eine Galleren geschmiedet* (Cassel, 1614).

The Apocryphal Sources.

The *Fama* is the most important section of the work, the *General Reformation* being a satire on crazy reforms translated from an Italian original, and the *Responsion* (which had been printed separately two years previously) likewise deviating widely from the style of the *Fama*. The alleged author of the *Responsion*, Adam Haselmeyer, is described as a notary of the archduke or an ordinary imperial judge in a Tyrolese village near Hall, but how far these assertions are authentic is unknown. The *Fama* professes to give information concerning a secret society founded some two centuries before, by a German of noble birth called Fr. R. C. (=*Frater roseæ crucis*, or "brother of the rosy cross"), who, placed in a monastery at the age of five, had started on a pilgrimage to the Holy Sepulcher. At Damascus he had become acquainted with the lore of the Arabs, and there he had translated into Latin "the book and the book M" (=*mundi*). After three years he was sent by his hosts to Egypt and Fez, but in the latter city he learned the superiority of his own faith and that man is a microcosm. Two years later he sought to promulgate his new wisdom in Spain, but to no purpose, and finally he returned to Germany. Here, in a special "house of the Holy Spirit," he formed a little band who were to go into all lands, wearing no special habit, freely healing the sick, reporting annually in person or by letter to their founder, seeking worthy successors, having as their seal and symbol "R. C." (=*Rosea Crux*, "Rosy Cross"), and concealing the existence of the fraternity for a hundred years. A hundred and twenty years after the death of the founder, a secret door was discovered in the "house of the Holy Spirit," behind which was a vault with an altar covering the uncorrupted body of the founder, who held in his hand a little parchment book with letters of gold. This discovery showed that the Rosicrucians could now publicly proclaim themselves; the *Fama* was published in five languages; the learned were invited to test it; and the hope was expressed that some might be led to join the fraternity. The Rosicrucians explicitly declared their belief in Christ, also implying that they were Protestants, and particularly disavowing all connection with heretics, sectarians, and false prophets. Their philosophy was to be "Jesus on every side." They opposed the accursed transmutation of metals as a petty thing in comparison with the real glory of the true philosopher, who is able to see the heavens open and the angels of God ascending and descending, and to know that his name is written in the book of life. The *Fama* was supplemented in 1615 by the *Confessio fraternitatis R. C. ad eruditos Europæ*, printed at Cassel, both in Latin and German. While in general harmony with the *Fama*, it is more strongly apocalyptic and opposed to Roman Catholicism; and it suggests positive reforms and advocates a practical Biblical piety which would transcend the denominational barriers of Protestantism. Its fanciful history occupies a minor place, but at the same time it states that the name of the founder of the Rosicrucians was Christianus Rosenkreutz, and that he was born in 1378 (d., according to the Rosicrucian system, 1484).

These two works, the *Fama* and the *Confessio*, are the sole original sources for the Rosicrucians. They both had a phenomenal popularity, and evoked a flood of writings on, for, and against them. Some doubted the very existence of the fraternity, and Descartes and Leibnitz vainly sought to make the acquaintance of a real Rosicrucian. From Germany the Rosicrucian excitement spread to England, France, and Italy; they were identified with the Spanish Alombrados (q.v.); under the pseudonyms of Irenæus Agnostus and Menapius a pretended adept (probably really named Friedrich Grick) wrote again and again in pretended defense of the Rosicrucians, though really in mockery of them; and Johann Valentin Andreä added his serious warnings against them. Finally the outbreak of the Thirty Years' War centered attention on other matters, and more discerning minds at least perceived that the whole fraternity was nothing but a gigantic hoax. Henceforth the name Rosicrucian proved an attraction for secret societies and many sorts of impostures, and a century after its origin Rosicrucianism underwent a recrudescence in connection with freemasonry, which not only deemed Rosicrucianism genuine, but even borrowed usages and customs from the writings of those who had satirized the fraternity.

Sensational Results.

The *Fama* and *Confessio* have been ascribed to the most divergent sources, including Luther and Tauler, but it is now generally agreed that the real author was Johann Valentin Andreä (q.v.). Though intended externally as a satire, the underlying motive of the works was, as in most satires, serious; and though later Andreä saw himself forced to attack the unruly spirits he had unwittingly unloosed, he never denied his authorship of the two writings in question. Moreover he criticized with equal severity his own *Chymische Hochzeit Christiani Rosencreutz* (Strassburg, 1616), which is analogous in style, phrase, and content (even to the name of the hero) with the *Fama* and the *Confessio*. According to his own statement, the *Hochzeit* was written about 1603, and was, therefore, Andreä's first essay in that development of the Rosicrucian hoax which was to lead to results so unwelcome to its author. The fantastic elements were drawn from romances of knighthood and travel, and from cycles of alchemistic legend, and were designed to arouse interest in the serious portions. The very name of the hero contains allusions to the author, "Christian" obviously referring to Andreä's *Reipublicæ christianopolitanæ descriptio*, and "Rosenkreutz" to his coat of arms, a St. Andrew's cross, gules, between four roses, gules, shadowed by two wings, argent. Under all this fantasy lay, as already noted, the most serious purposes: the combating of alchemy and Roman Catholicism, and the promotion of Christian truth as revealed in the Bible and the maintenance of the principles of the Reformation. The intermingling of jest and earnest finds its parallel in Andreä's own *Menippus*, which appeared in 1618. As early as 1617, however, Andreä was obliged to attack his creation in his *Invitatio ad fraternitatem Christi ad amoris candidatos*, but his attempt to found a Christian brotherhood, together with his introduction of Calvinistic elements into his own church, aroused suspicions of his orthodoxy on the part of strict Lutherans, especially when it became known that he was the author of the *Hochzeit*. In his own defense he pleaded that he was not a Rosicrucian in the accepted sense of the term, but his peculiar position in the Church of Württemberg, as well as his personal vicissitudes, forbade him either to deny or to admit the authorship of the *Fama* and *Confessio*, the first of which seems to have been in his mind as early as 1604 and was in manuscript by 1610, or about the time when the *Confessio* appears to have been taking shape. (H. Hermelink.)

Authorship and Motive of the Fraud.

Bibliography: For lists of the older literature consult: G. Kloss, *Bibliographie der Freimaurer*, pp. 174 sqq., Frankfort, 1844; and F. Katsch, *Die Entstehung und der wahre Endzweck der Freimaurerei*, pp. 116 sqq., Berlin, 1897. Consult: A. E. Waite, *The Real History of the Rosicrucians*, London, 1887; G. Arnold, *Unparteiische Kirchen- und Ketzerhistorie*, part II., chap. xviii., Frankfort, 1729; J. S. Semler, *Unparteiische Sammlungen zur Historie der Rosenkreuzer*, Leipsic, 1786–88; C. G. de Murr, *Ueber den wahren Ursprung der Rosenkreuzer und Freimaurer*, Sulzbach, 1803; J. G. Buhle, *Ueber den Ursprung und die vornehmsten Schicksale der Orden der Rosenkreuzer und Freimaurer*, Göttingen, 1806; G. E. Guhrauer, in *ZHT*, 1852, pp. 298–315; F. C. Baur, *Geschichte der christlichen Kirche*, iv. 351 sqq., Leipsic, 1863; E. Sierke, *Schwärmer und Schwindler zu Ende des 18. Jahrhunderts*, Leipsic, 1874; J. G. Herder, *Sämtliche Werke*, xv. 57 sqq., xvi. 298 sqq., 591 sqq., Berlin, 1877–99; H. Kopp, *Die Alchemie*, 2 vols., Heidelberg, 1886; F. Hartmann, *The Secret Symbols of the Rosicrucians*, London, 1888; idem, *Among the Rosicrucians*, ib. 1888; idem, *In the Pronaos of the Temple of Wisdom*, ib. 1890; idem, *With the Adepts*, ib. 1900; W. Begemann, in *Monatshefte der Comeniusgesellschaft*, viii (1899), 145 sqq.; J. Kvaçala, in *Acta et commentationes imperialis universitatis Jurievienis*, Dorpat, 1899; F. B. Dowd, *The Temple of the Rosy Cross*, Salem, 1906; R. S. Clymer, *The Fraternity of the Rosicrucians; their Teachings and Mysteries according to the Manifestoes issued at various Times*, Allentown, 1906; H. Jennings, *Rosicrucians, their Rites and Mysteries*, 1870, 4th ed., London and New York, 1907; *KL*, x. 1283–90; literature under Andreä, Johann Valentin.

ROSIN BIBLE. See Bible Versions, B, IV., § 9.

ROSKOFF, GEORG GUSTAV: German Protestant; b. at Pressburg Aug. 31, 1814; d. at Obertressen, near Aussee (40 m. s.e. of Salzburg), Styria, Oct. 20, 1889. He was educated at the University of Halle and the Evangelical theological faculty at Vienna (1839–46); and was privat-docent of Old-Testament exegesis in the latter institution (1846–1850); and professor from 1850. He was the author of *Die hebräischen Altertümer in Briefen* (Vienna, 1857); *Die Simsonssage und der Heraclesmythus* (Leipsic, 1860); *Die Geschichte des Teufels* (2 vols., 1869); and *Das Religionswesen der rohesten Naturvölker* (1880). (G. Frank†.)

Bibliography: *Evangelische Kirchenzeitung für Oesterreich*, 1885, no. 3, 1889, no. 21; *Protestantische Kirchenzeitung*, 1889, no. 45.

ROSMINI-SERBATI, ros-mî'nî-sār-bā'tî, **ANTONIO**: Italian Roman Catholic and philosopher, and founder of the Institute of Charity, or Congregation of Rosminians; b. at Roveredo (13 m. s.w. of Trent), Tyrol, Mar. 25, 1797; d. at Stresa (3 m. s. of Pallanza), Italy, July 1, 1855. He was educated at the University of Padua and was ordained to the priesthood in 1820, after having already pursued the studies in mathematics and philosophy which were later to result in his *Nuovo saggio sull' origine delle idee* (3 vols., Rome, 1830; Eng. transl., *Origin of Ideas*, 3 vols., London, 1883–1886). He now took up his residence at Milan, where he became acquainted with the French missionary, J. B. Löwenbrück, and with him established at Domodossola, on the road from Lago Maggiore to the Simplon, the Instituto di carità as a center for a congregation of clergy who would devote themselves both to learning and to practical Christian piety. At Rome, in 1628, Rosmini was cordially welcomed by Cardinal Bartolommeo Alberto Capellari (afterward Pope Gregory XVI.), although the Jesuits were later to oppose him with the weapons placed in their hands by his own *Cinque piaghe della santa chiesa* (Lugano, 1848; abridged Eng. transl., *Five Wounds of the Holy Church*, London, 1883). Nevertheless, the years immediately following were devoted by Rosmini to the elaboration of his epistemology. As a genuine realist, he held that ideal being is the ultimate cause behind phenomena, and maintained that such being is cognoscible through immediate perception; but while thus opposing the prevailing sensationalistic philosophy, he diverged equally from the pantheism of Vincenzo Gioberti, who based perception on purely natural grounds, thus positing a natural intuition of God. In the literary controversy which ensued the Jesuit Joseph Aloysius Dmowski shifted the issue to theology and charged Rosmini with Jansenistic errors, so that in 1843 Gregory XVI. found himself obliged to command both parties to be silent. Rosmini now restricted himself to practical duties, especially as the Institute of Charity had spread widely, particularly in England and Ireland. Rosmini himself went in 1837 to Stresa, where he labored for some years in his college for novices until he saw himself involved in the excitement which pervaded all classes in Italy at the accession of Pius IX. He submitted to the new pontiff an outline of a constitution for the States of the Church, but it was unheeded, and he then published the *Cinque piaghe*, which he had written sixteen years before, the "five wounds" in question being declared to be the suppression of the vernacular in the liturgy, the false training of the clergy, the false position of the bishops, the exclusion of the lower clergy and the laity from the election of the popes, and the arbitrary use of the property of the Church. The work evoked bitter opposition from the ultramontanes and was naturally placed upon the Index, whereupon Rosmini made his submission. The attempt was also made to condemn Rosmini's other writings, but the Congregation of the Index, in 1854, officially declared that they might be read. Nevertheless, opposition to them was still maintained, and by a decree of 1887 Leo XIII. expressly condemned forty propositions of Rosmini. The institutions founded by him, however, still exist both in England and in Italy.

A collection of Rosmini's works, although not absolutely complete, has appeared under the title *Opere edite e inedite dell' abbate A. Rosmini-Serbati* (31 vols., Milan and Turin, 1837–57). Among these special mention may be made of the following, all of which have been translated into English: *Massime di perfezione cristiana* (13th ed., Milan, 1883; Eng. transl., *Maxims of Christian Perfection*, London, 1849); *Catechismo disposto secondo l'ordine delle idee* (latest ed., Rome, 1898; Eng. transl., *Catholic Catechism, methodically Arranged*, by W. S. Agar London [1849]); *Psicologia* (2 vols., Novara, 1846–1848; Eng. transl., *Psychology*, 3 vols., London, 1884–88); *Sistema filosofico* (Lucca, 1853; Eng. transl., *Philosophical System of Antonio Rosmini Serbati*, London, 1882); and the posthumous *Del Principio supremo della metodica e di alcune sue applicazioni in servigio dell' umana educazione* (Turin, 1857; Eng. transl., *The Ruling Principle of Method applied to Education*, by Mrs. W. Grey, Boston, 1887) and *Schizzo sulla filosofia moderna* (Turin, 1881; Eng. transl., *Short Sketch of Modern Philosophies*, London, 1882). A number of his letters have also been translated by D. Gazzola under the title *Letters on Religious Subjects* (London, 1901).

K. Benrath.

Bibliography: On the life consult: W. Lockhardt, *Life of Antonio Rosmini-Serbati*, 2 vols., 2d ed., London, 1886; V. Garelli, *Biografia di Antonio Rosmini*, Turin, 1861; F. Angeleri, *Antonio Rosmini*, Treves, 1871; E. H. Dering, *The Philosopher of Rovereto*, London, 1874; T. Davidson, *The Philosophical System of A. Rosmini-Serbati, with Sketch of Author's Life*, etc., London, 1882; G. S. Macwalter, *Life of A. Rosmini-Serbati*, London, 1883; S. E. Jarvis, *Rosmini, a Christian Philosopher*, Market Weighton, 1888; A. Dyroff, *Rosmini*, Mainz, 1906; G. B. Pagani, *Life of Antonio Rosmini-Serbati*, London and New York, 1907.

On his philosophy consult: G. Ferrari, *Essai sur le principe et les limites de la philosophie de l'histoire*, pp. 184–202, Paris, 1843; A. Pestalozza, *Le Dottrine di Rosmini*, 2 vols., Milan, 1851–53; idem, *La Mente di Rosmini*, ib. 1855; T. Roberti, *Della Spirito filosofico di A. Rosmini*, Bassano, 1855; G. Bertazzi, *Sistema ideologico di Antonio Rosmini*, Verona, 1858; M. Debrit, *Histoire des doctrines philosophiques dans l'Italie contemporaine*, Paris, 1859; C. M. Ferré, *Esposizione del Principio filosofiro di Antonio Rosmini*, Verona, 1859; J. Bernardi, *Giovane età e primi Studii di Antonio Rosminii*, Pinerolo, 1860; S. Frati, *A Rosmini: cenni sull' Immortalita dell' Anima*, Parma, 1861; L. Ferri, *Essai sur l'histoire de la philosophie en Italie*, Paris, 1869; V. Lilla, *Kant e Rosmini*, Turin, 1869; L. Palatini, *Del Principio filosofico di Antonio Rosmini*, Verona, 1869; G. Buroni, *Rosmini e S. Tommaso*, Turin, 1878; idem, *Antonio Rosmini e La Civiltà Cattolica*, ib. 1880; G. Petri, *A. Rosmini e i Neo-Scolastici*, Rome, 1878; K. Werner, *A. Rosmini's Stellung in der Geschichte der neueren Philosophie*, Vienna, 1884; idem, *Die italienische Philosophie des 19. Jahrhunderts*, Vienna, 1884; E. Avogadro, *La Filosofia dell' Abbate Antonio Rosmini esaminata*, Napoli, 1885; F. H. Reusch, *Index der verbotenen Bücher*, ii. 1139 sqq., Bonn, 1885; F. X. Kraus, in *Deutsche Rundschau*, 1888; P. Montagnani, *Rosmini, San Tommaso, e la Logica*, Bologna, 1890; G. Vidari, *Rosmini e Spencer*, Milan, 1890; F. de Sarlo, *La Logica di A. Rosmini*, Rome, 1893; idem, *Le Basi della Psicologia e della Biologia secondo il Rosmini*, ib. 1893; H. C. Sheldon, in *Papers of the American Society of Church History*, first series, viii. 41–66, New York, 1897; G. Gentile, *Rosmini e Gioberti*, Pisa, 1898; C. Calzi, *Rosmini nella presente Quistione sociale*, Turin, 1899.

On the order: Heimbucher, *Orden und Kongregationen*, iii. 522.

ROSS, JOHN: Presbyterian missionary to China; b. at Easter Rarichie, Nigg (138 m. n. of Glasgow), Scotland, Aug. 6, 1842. He received his education at the village school at Nigg, through private instruction, at Glasgow University, and at the United Presbyterian Theological Hall, Edinburgh; and has been a missionary in Manchuria since 1872, during recent years serving also as principal of the Theological Hall for Manchuria. In 1873 he visited the Korean Gate, at that time the only place where Koreans could come into contact with foreigners, and he became in this way a pioneer in the work of introducing Protestant Christianity into the Korean peninsula. He states his theological position as follows: "Mankind, being alienated from the unselfish goodness which is the character of God, has brought loss and misery unlimited upon itself. God being the All-loving as he is the All-righteous, it is reasonable that he should by abnormal means reveal this his character to his handiwork man, such revelation being beyond the normal. Jesus in his life, by word and deed culminating in the cross, revealed the fact that God pities man, desires his salvation from the state of alienation, and pleads with the alienated to become reconciled and thus eradicate the cause of his misery. By this reconciliation and imitation of the unselfish good-doing of God, the reign of peace for which Jesus came will be established on earth." By his writings he has contributed to the success of missions, enabling later comers to the field to acquire through his works acquaintance with the languages of the parts adjacent to Manchuria. Of his works mention may be made of: *Mandarin Primer* (Shanghai, 1876); *Corean Primer* (1877); *History of Corea, Ancient and Modern* (Paisley, 1879); *The Manchus, or the Reigning Dynasty of China* (1880); *Old Wang, the First Chinese Evangelist in Manchuria* (London, 1889); *Mission Methods in Manchuria* (1903); and *The Original Religion of China* (Edinburgh, 1909). He also translated the New Testament into Korean (Mukden, 1882–84); and was a member of the committee to provide a commentary on the Bible in Chinese, in connection with which he furnished the parts on Isaiah i.–xxxix., Job, the latter half of Matthew, and James.

ROSSI, rös'sî, GIOVANNI BATTISTA DE: Roman Catholic archeologist; b. at Rome Feb. 23, 1822; d. there Sept. 20, 1894. He was educated at the Collegium Romanum. Under the impulse from the Jesuit Marchi he devoted himself to archeology, particularly the catacombs, laying the foundation of his work by collecting antiquities in Italy, Switzerland, France, Germany, and England. In this department he became the chief by universal acknowledgment and the founder of Christian archeology. In 1854 he became one of the collaborators of the *Inscriptiones urbis Romæ Latinæ* for the Berlin Academy of Sciences, *Corpus inscriptorum*, vol. vi (Berlin, 1863 and after). In the *Spicilegium Solesmense* of J. B. Pitra were published *De christianis monumentis ichthun exhibentibus*, vol. iii (Paris, 1855), and *De christianis titulis Carthaginiensibus* (1858). His great work, which he began in 1843, was *Inscriptiones christianæ urbis Romæ septimo sæculo antiquiores* (vols. i. and ii., Rome, 1861–1888). This was followed by the *Roma sotteranea christiana* (3 vols., 1864–77; Eng. adaptation, London, 1869), leaving the materials for vol. iv. almost complete. He made the *Bulletino di archælogia sacra*, which he issued quarterly, 1863–94, a treasure store of material from the excavations of catacombs and archeology in general. He succeeded, during forty years, in investigating the most important cemeteries, relocating most of the martyrs' tombs, and bringing them to light. From 1872–1894, he published the *Musaici cristiani* with its chromo-lithographic plates (Spithoever ed., Rome, 1872–1900). For fifty years secretary at the Vatican, he published with copious notes *Index codicum latinorum Bibliothecæ Vaticanæ*, vols. x.–xiii (1886, and after), treating over 2,600 codices; and, with other scholars, issued the *Œuvres complètes de Bartolomeo Borghesi* (9 vols., 1862, and after). Rossi was professor at the University at Rome and after 1851 a member of the Accademia pontificia di archæologia, and before his death its president. He promoted a common bond between Roman Catholic and other archeologists, and passed the influence of his spirit to a school of successors.

Bibliography: F. B. Leitner, *Leben des . . . Johannes Baptista de Rossi*, Regensburg, 1899. A valuable periodical literature is indicated in Richardson, *Encyclopaedia*, p. 958.

ROSWEYDE, ros-vai'de, HÉRIBERT: Jesuit hagiographer, originator of the idea afterward carried out by Bolland and his associates in the *Acta Sanctorum Bollandistarum* (see Bolland, Jan, Bollandists); b. at Utrecht Jan. 21, 1570; d. at Antwerp Oct. 4, 1629. He entered the Society of Jesus in 1588, and was ordained priest in 1598. He was professor of rhetoric at Brussels, 1592–95, of philosophy 1598–1600, and of controversial theology 1605–07, then for four years head of the colleges of Courtray and Antwerp. From about 1614 he devoted himself with increasing exclusiveness to historical studies, especially the lives of the saints, for which the Belgian abbeys offered a vast mass of manuscript material. He formed the plan of a comprehensive collection of such lives which should surpass the existing ones in extent and critical accuracy; but official duties and the controversies in which he became engaged with Scaliger, Casaubon, and others took up too much of his time for him to do more than begin the vast labor. He published the *Martyrologium parvum Romanum* which he had discovered, together with that of Ado (Antwerp, 1613); the first edition of the Windesheim Chronicle of Johann Busch (1621); an edition of the "Imitation of Christ" (1617); and one of the *Vitæ patrum* (1615). His faithfulness to duty was no less admirable than his scholarly activity, and his last illness was due to disease contracted at the bedside of the dying.

Bibliography: *ASB*, Jan., i., preface, § 6, and Mar., i., preface to the life of J. Bolland, § 4; [V. de Buck], in *Analectes pour servir à l'histoire ecclésiastique de la Belgique*, v (1868), 261–270; *KL*, x. 1314–15; Lichtenberger, *ESR*, xi. 301–302.

ROSWITHA, ros-vī'tā (**ROSWITH, HROSWITHA, HROTSUIT**): Nun of Gandersheim in the duchy of Saxony in the last third of the tenth century; the years of her birth and death are not known. Her abbess Gerberga (959–1001) asked her to write a heroic poem in honor of the Emperor Otho I. It was finished in 968 and is entitled *Hrotsuithæ carmen de gestis Oddonis I. imperatoris*, but is not preserved entire. As the authoress drew her material from members of the imperial family, diplomatic considerations influenced her work; yet her representation is an important source of history. Later she wrote the history of her monastery, *De primordiis cœnobii Gandersheimensis*, and also composed many poems on saints. Her Christian comedies, modeled after those of Terence, are well known. Ebert has disputed with good reason the earlier view that these plays were written with the intention of suppressing the immoral plays of Terence.

(A. Hauck.)

Bibliography: Roswitha's works were edited by K. A. Barack, Nuremberg, 1858; and K. Strecker, Leipsic, 1906; and are in *MPL*, cxxxvii. 971–1196. The two historical poems are in *MGH*, *Script.*, iv (1841), 302–335. There are German translations of the Otto by W. Gundlach, Innsbruck, 1894, and others. Consult A. Ebert, *Litteratur des Mittelalters*, iii. 285 sqq., Leipsic, 1887; A. H. Hoffmann, *De Roswithæ vita et scriptis*, Wratislaw, 1839; O. Rommel, in *Forschungen zur deutschen Geschichte*, iv (1864), 123–158; R. Kopke, *Hrotsuit von Gandersheim*, Berlin, 1869; idem, *Die älteste deutsche Dichterin. Kulturgeschichtliches Bild aus dem 10. Jahrhundert*, ib. 1869; R. Steinhoff, in *Zeitschrift des Harzvereins für Geschichte und Alterthumskunde*, xv (1882), 116–140; a notable series of contributions by O. Grashof are to be found in *Studien und Mittheilungen aus den Benediktiner- und Cistercienser-Orden*, 1884–88; Wattenbach, *DGQ*, i (1885), 4, 313–316, i (1893), 334–336; W. H. Hudson, in *English Historical Review*, 1888, pp. 431–457; *ADB*, xxix. 283–294; Mary Reed, in *Free Review*, i. 260–282, London, 1893–94; Hauck, *KD*, iii. 301 sqq.

ROTA ROMANA. See Curia, § 3.

ROTH, rōt, **KARL JOHANN FRIEDRICH**: German Lutheran; b. at Vaihingen (5 m. s.w. of Stuttgart), Württemberg, Jan. 23, 1780; d. at Munich Jan. 21, 1852. He studied law at the University of Tübingen (1797–1801), and was then consul for Nuremberg at Paris, Vienna, and Berlin. When Nuremberg came under Bavarian control, Roth entered the service of the state, first as financial counselor for the circle of Pegnitz at Nuremberg, then (1810) as chief financial counselor at Munich, and finally (1817) as ministerial counselor in the royal ministry of finances. His *De bello Borussico commentarius* (1809) proved his unusual scholarship. Meanwhile he had passed from the point of view of Voltaire and Rousseau to orthodoxy, as was shown by his selections from Luther's writings, *Die Weisheit Dr. Martin Luthers* (1817), and his editions of the works of J. G. Hamann (Leipsic 1821–25). As president of the supreme consistory of Bavaria (1828–48) he exercised rare tact and administrative skill, in guiding the Church through the troublous reaction against rationalism, in cultivating the personal acquaintance of the clergy, and in executing the existing order, thus elevating the moral and the intellectual status of the clergy. He established a stated supervision of theological students at Erlangen, which was soon given up, and a seminary for the training of the Evangelical clergy at Munich, which was soon obliged to reduce its number of students from eight to six annually. During the period 1837–48, the Roman Catholics were in the ascendency with the government, and Roth was blamed for being remiss in not insisting upon the Protestant claims, though, perhaps, without justice. Nevertheless, in 1848 he was retired in order to allay the agitation against him. Soon after, he was made a member of the council of state, in which he continued almost till his death.

(Karl Burger†.)

ROTHE, rō'te, **RICHARD**: Theologian; b. at Posen (100 m. e. of Frankfort-on-the-Oder) Jan. 28, 1799; d. at Heidelberg Aug. 20, 1867. His father was characterized by strong fidelity to duty and patriotic devotion; his mother by fervent piety. The latter was of a rationalistic type, as was also the wretched religious instruction obtained from the side of the school and the Church. However, he was led into a supernatural vein of thought by the imaginative works of Novalis and other leaders in the Romantic movement, and by his own reading of the Bible. He thus acquired a living Christianity. Accordingly, against his parents' inclination, he resolved to study theology, and, at Easter, 1817, betook himself to Heidelberg. Here he was influenced anew by Romanticism, so that he came to entertain warm sympathies with Roman Catholicism. At Berlin, whither he removed in 1819, there prevailed, in part, a Pietistic type of religion, together with a very conservative spirit in matters of State and Church, and a preference for the Hegelian philosophy. Rothe listened to Hegel's lectures on natural law and political science with enthusiasm, and was but little attracted by Schleiermacher's lectures and sermons. He acquired growing reverence for August Neander (q.v.), through whose good offices he found entrance to the circle that gathered about Baron von Kottwitz. Yet he felt not at all content, but tired of academic life and yearned for home. Cheered and refreshed by a brief visit to his parents, he went to the Theological Seminary at Wittenberg in the autumn of 1819. Most influential over him here was the third director H. L. Heubner (q.v.); nevertheless Rothe aimed to preserve his individuality and mental freedom. He also here, as formerly at Berlin, at first vigorously withstood the attempts of the new seminary adjunct Rudolf Stier and of Baron von Kottwitz and the licentiate Tholuck on a visit from Berlin to win him over to a Pietistic form of religion; but before long his sensitive temperament yielded. On May 9, 1821, he reports of the inward

Early Life and Education.

change produced in him, as though it were the entrance of a new spiritual spring. For a considerable time thereafter his letters were couched in the unnatural mode of utterance in vogue among Pietists, and abounded in the bluntest expressions respecting everybody of a different opinion and all worldly pursuits. He even condemned all scientific treatment of theology. The Evangelical attempts in the cause of church union merely aroused his abhorrence, and served only to enhance his inclination toward Roman Catholicism. He manifested special predilection for the quietistic mysticism of the extravagant Francis of Sales (q.v.). Although he then assured his distressed parents that he had won inward rest and blessedness, he nevertheless later admitted in retrospect that he had not been a happy Pietist, but had been without joy. Gradually he felt the lack of satisfying, solid work at the Wittenberg Seminary, though he had often preached and studied much there, and, in the autumn of 1822, he left Wittenberg, not without satisfaction, to return home. Here, thanks to the good offices of Heubner, he was called to be chaplain to the Prussian embassy at Rome. He now passed his second theological examination, was ordained at Berlin, married Louise von Bruck, a sister-in-law of Heubner, and journeyed with her to Italy.

He reached Rome early in 1824. What usually attracted people he regarded with indifference, desiring simply to serve his congregation faithfully, and thereby the kingdom of God. But

Career.

owing to the peculiar constituency of that body, the conscientious execution of this task was bound to enlarge his field of vision. The nucleus of the Prussian congregation at Rome comprised some finely cultivated Evangelical families of the embassy, and a number of artists of idealistic taste. He soon discerned that Christianity was not to be presented before these circles in the form of a narrow-minded Pietism. Not a few of the members, above all the highly talented, eager personality of Josias Bunsen (q.v.), counselor of the legation, evinced by their combination of a vital Christian intelligence with political, scientific, artistic, and other spiritual and secular interests, that the two do not exclude each other. Hence the Pietistic forms, foreign as they always were to Rothe's individuality, fell gradually away from his habit of life and thought. In his modesty, his inner devoutness, his fellowship with Christ, his preference for quiet, he had much in common with Pietism, and these he retained enduringly. His style of correspondence now became more natural, and his judgment of Pietism more and more critical. At the same time, being at the very center of Roman Catholicism, he was radically cured of his predilection for that system, and perceived that a stanch ecclesiasticism still affords no warrant of Christian piety. Thus his own Christianity grew more liberal toward the world, and, stimulated by his official activity, he awakened more keenly to the need of scientific studies. Before conferences of cultivated members of his congregation, in response to the request of some artists, he discussed topics in ecclesiastical history. This Roman sojourn, however, had also its dark sides. Rothe's wife appeared unable to bear the climate. Then the frequent changes in the constituency of the Prussian congregation rendered the fruits of his activity insecure. With increasing diffidence toward publicly disclosing his inmost mind, he began to doubt his qualification for a practical church career, and his desire for active scholarship grew apace. Under the circumstances a call to be professor at the theological seminary at Wittenberg in 1828 was gladly accepted, and this was followed by the appointment to be second director and ephor, 1832. In 1837 he became university preacher, and professor and director of the new seminary at Heidelberg. To be released from the latter office he accepted a call to Bonn in 1849. Feeling too much weighed down by the practical duties of preaching in connection with the public worship of the university, he returned to Heidelberg, 1854, where he now lectured on ecclesiastical history, exegesis, systematic theology, the life of Christ, encyclopedia, and, occasionally, on practical theology till his death.

From the beginning of his independent theological research, his deepest interest turned to the scientific knowledge of the ideal truth of Christianity. But in distinction from the dialectics of Schleiermacher, which seemed to him too formal and abstract, he strove after a more replete speculation, rendering more justice to the realities

Work in Exegesis and History.

of the world and of historical Christianity. Hence his theological studies were applied, first, to Biblical exegesis and ecclesiastical history. His exegetical studies were taken up at Rome, and pursued with special zeal during the later period of his sojourn there, since Biblical writings formed the topics of discussion in the conferences of cultivated church-members. This gave rise to Rothe's first literary publication, his monograph on Rom. v. 12-21, prepared at Ischia, and published under the title, *Neuer Versuch einer Auslegung der Paulinischen Stelle Römer V., 12-21* (Wittenberg, 1836). However, purely exegetical interest was not very lively with him, and he published nothing further in scientific exegesis. Still, his official tasks at Wittenberg led him to produce edifying elucidations of Scripture; and his exposition of I John is one of the best of its kind, *Der erste Brief Johannis* (Wittenberg, 1878). His studies next turned to the historical field. Already at Breslau, after Neander had inspired him at Berlin to the academic vocation, he had devoted himself to studies in ecclesiastical history. At Rome association with the versatile and scholarly Bunsen gave him new impetus. Coincident with his own interest the Roman artists besought him for information on the history of Roman Catholicism. The reaction which then took place in his critical estimation of Romanism also occasioned the need of some independent historical examination on this topic. His deep study of the sources thus prepared him for the course of lectures on "Church Life" that he was pledged to deliver at Wittenberg, in which he treated the nature and history of the Christian religion and Church. Another fruit of this labor was his much-noted work, *Die Anfänge der christlichen Kirche und ihrer Ver-*

fassung (1837). Inherent in the nature of all religions, he asserts, there is the radical impulse of self-expression. In the Christian religion, the process of such manifestations has for its goal the consummation of the kingdom of God on earth, as promised by Christ. But the State, as the most comprehensive structure wrought by mind into matter, is the actual realization of all moral life, which, in its final perfection, must immanently involve religion. In contrast, the Church, by virtue of its intrinsic character, shall ever serve purely religious ends. Therefore the kingdom of God on earth can present itself only in the form of a perfected state or organism of states, wherefore the Church becomes gradually superfluous. For the present, however, the Church still has a lofty significance. The idea of the Church sprang from an internal necessity, and began to achieve its fulfilment. As a matter of fact, the formation of the Church followed soon after the destruction of Jerusalem, when the surviving apostles instituted the episcopate as an organic expedient for the outward unity of Christian fellowship. Incipiently, the idea of the Church was vaguely identified with this empirical Church. As all sorts of contingencies arose to make this identification less congruous, there developed, over against the heresies, with increasing certainty, the recognition of the papal Church of Rome. This fiction, however, was bound ere long to give rise to a contradiction resting fundamentally upon the fact that the Church, as a whole, is not the form of the Christian life in correspondence with it. For the first time was the question fundamentally involving the transition from Apostolic Christianity to the hierarchical Roman Catholic Church so definitely raised. In comparison with Neander's treatment of church history, whereby the inner life of the individual Christian personalities received a one-sided emphasis, there was a distinct advance with Rothe, when he placed due importance upon the general development of Christianity in its social forms. A reciprocal defect appeared, however, in that, according to Rothe, the idea of the Church realized itself essentially only by the adoption of constitutional forms; and that this abstraction of a constitution did not appear to be evolved from the inner life of the Church, but was externally instituted by the apostles. In this view a reaction from his earlier admiration of Roman Catholicism can not be mistaken, while his thought of a gradual resolution of the Church into the State becomes clear in the light of his impressions in childhood, and his subsequent transition from narrow Pietism to the wider sphere of life at Rome. Rothe did not publish any further historical development of this view, and his lectures were published in fragmentary form, *Vorlesungen über Kirchengeschichte* (2 vols., Heidelberg, 1875–76).

Rothe's first production in church history impelled him to a purely systematic work. Only then did he approach the task for which he was best fitted, by which he most amply developed his gifts. He sought to arrive at an explanation of his views on Christianity, Church, and State on the basis of the clear representation of the relation between the religious and the ethical. This was the purpose of his ethics. While he assigned dogmatics to historical theology, ethics, as the conclusive part of speculative theology, was to unfold its subject only in accordance with the law of logical thought. It was to take its point of departure from the consciousness of God; and this, contrary to Schleiermacher, from its objective content. Rothe thus proceeds deductively from God to the creation of the world as the necessary means whereby he is distinguishable, and from the infinite process of creation to its continuation in the ethical process, which subsists in the unity, fixed in the human mind, of personality and material nature. Inasmuch as this concept of the ethical appears in the threefold form of moral good, virtue, and duty, Rothe's ethics falls under three main heads. The first sets forth the ethical process, namely, the original unity of morality and religion; its disturbance by the evil which subsists in the predominance of the nature of sense over personality; the redemption from evil through the second Adam; the primarily religious, then moral efficacy of this redemption upon individual men, through the kingdom of God, first resolved in the form of a church and finally fulfilled in a Christian state organism; and the end of all things. Compared with this comprehensive thought outline of the first part, all else in his ethics, although containing many beautiful details, is like a superfluous appendix.

Theological Ethics.

Concerning the fundamental views of his religious-ethical system in the first part, his effort to derive the entire organism of Christian truth by logical deduction from a single concept can not be upheld. It proved itself incapable of logical conclusion, and led to the tendency of a pantheistic confusion of God and the world; of conceiving the divine and the moral in natural terms; of thinking of the spiritual as a mere product of matter; and of denying, in determinist fashion, all freedom of divine and human action. Yet this tendency was contradicted by Rothe's strong ethical and theistic temperament, as well as by his positive supernaturalism, such as he exhibited in his admirable *Zur Dogmatik* (Gotha, 1863). This inconsistency occasioned many palpable contradictions and defects in his system. His identification of religion with morality, whence emanated his evidently erroneous ideas on the relation of Church and State, was also involved with a pantheistic inclination. A practical consequence of these views was his mode of participation during his closing years in the affairs of the State Church of Baden. In the liberation of culture and of its exponents from domination by the Church, he saw nothing short of an operation by his Savior. Therefore he believed that he was serving him best when he cooperated in the plan of introducing the congregational principle in constitutional polity, whereby cultivated laymen, with their "unconscious Christianity," were to be associated in congregational autonomy, and when by the "Protestant Union" (q.v.) Christianity became effectually emancipated from its ecclesiastical restrictions, offensive as these were to the cultured. Thus Rothe, though abhorring all partisan tactics, himself proved a partisan. Finally,

Estimation.

it should be borne in mind that the defects in Rothe's ethics are, to some extent, involved with insoluble antinomies, and they are compensated in his work by superior merits; such as his dialectical adaptability and his skill in the grouping of his matter, let alone his affluence of significant and useful ideas, even of elements of truth in his most vulnerable representations. F. SIEFFERT.

BIBLIOGRAPHY: F. Nippold, *Richard Rothe*, 2 vols., Wittenberg, 1873–74; A. Hausrath, *Richard Rothe und seine Freunde*, 2 vols., Berlin, 1902–06; J. Cropp, in *Protestantische Monatshefte*, 1897, 1899; E. Achelis, *Dr. Richard Rothe*, Gotha, 1869; W. Hönig, *Richard Rothe. Charakter, Leben und Denken*, Berlin, 1898; H. Bassermann, *Richard Rothe als praktischer Theologe*, Freiburg, 1899; O. Flügel, *Richard Rothe als spekulativer Theologe*, Langensalza, 1899; P. Mezger, *Richard Rothe. Ein theologisches Charakterbild*, Berlin, 1899; K. Sell, in *Theologische Rundschau*, 1899; H. Spörri, *Zur Erinnerung an Richard Rothe*, Hamburg, 1899; E. Troeltsch, *Richard Rothe. Gedächtnisrede*, Freiburg, 1899; R. Kern, *Dr. Richard Rothe*, Cassel, 1904; L. Witte, *Richard Rothe über Jesus als Wunderthäter*, Halle, 1907; J. Happel, *Richard Rothes Lehre von der Kirche*, Leipsic, 1909.

ROTHMANN (ROTTMANN), BERNHARD. See MUENSTER, ANABAPTISTS IN.

ROTHSTEIN, röt'stdin, **JOHANN WILHELM:** German Protestant; b. at Puhl, a village of Rhenish Prussia, Mar. 19, 1853. He was educated at the universities of Bonn (Ph.D., 1877; lic. theol., 1878) and Halle, where he devoted himself to theology and Semitics (1872–78). He was a teacher in the gymnasium at Elberfeld until 1884 and at the girls' high school in Halle until 1889, when he was appointed associate professor of Old-Testament exegesis at the University of Halle, and in 1910 became professor in the same branch at Breslau. Theologically he bases his work on a belief in Biblical revelation, and, though favoring earnest historical criticism, is opposed to rationalistic interpretations of the Old and New Testaments from the point of view of comparative religion. He has written: *De chronographo Arabe anonymo qui codice Berolinensi Sprengeriano tricesimo continetur* (Bonn, 1877); *Das Bundesbuch und die religionsgeschichtliche Entwicklung Israels* (Halle, 1888); *Das Hohe Lied* (1893); *Der Gottesglaube im alten Israel und die religionsgeschichtliche Kritik* (1900); *Bilder aus der Geschichte des alten Bundes in gemeinverständlicher Form*, vol. i. (Erlangen, 1901); *Die Genealogie des Königs von Juda Jojachin und seiner Nachkommenschaft in I Chron. iii. 17–24* (Berlin, 1902); *Geschichte und Offenbarung mit Bezug auf Israels Religion* (Stuttgart, 1903); *Juden und Samaritaner. Die grundlegende Scheidung von Judentum und Heidentum. Eine kritische Studie zum Buche Haggai und zur jüdischen Geschichte im ersten nachexilischen Jahrhundert* (Leipsic, 1908); *Grundzüge des hebräischen Rhythmus und seiner Formenbildung, nebst lyrischen Texten mit kritischem Kommentar* (1909); *Psalmentexte und der Text des Hohen Liedes* (1909; reprinted from the *Grundzüge des . . . Rhythmus*); and *Die Nachgesichte des Sacharya* (1910). He has translated into German W. R. Smith's *The Old Testament in the Jewish Church* (Freiburg, 1894) and S. R. Driver's *Introduction to the Literature of the Old Testament* (Berlin, 1896), and contributed Jeremiah and Zephaniah to E. Kautzsch's *Das Alte Testament* (Freiburg, 1894; in the 3d ed., 1910, Jeremiah, Ezekiel, and Chronicles), the apocryphal portions of Daniel, as well as Baruch and the Epistle of Jeremiah to the same scholar's *Apokryphen und Pseudepigraphen des Alten Testaments* (1900), and Jeremiah and Ezekiel to R. Kittel's *Biblia Hebraica* (Leipsic, 1906).

ROUS, raus, **FRANCIS:** Puritan; b. at Dittisham (25 m. e. of Plymouth) in 1579; d. at Acton (7 m. w. of London) Jan., 1658–59. He was educated at Oxford (B.A., 1596–97), and the University of Leyden (1598–99); was a member of parliament during the reign of Charles I., of the Long Parliament, and others (1625–56); was appointed lord of parliament by Cromwell (1657); and became provost of Eton (1643–44). The Westminster Assembly appointed him one of its lay assessors (1643); and he was chairman of the committee for ordination of ministers after its organization (1643–44). In 1649 Rous went over to the Independents and served on the committee for the propagation of the Gospel, which framed an abortive scheme for a state church on the Congregational plan, revived without success by the Little Parliament of which he was speaker (1653). When that body dissolved itself, he was sworn on the protector's council of state. He was placed on the committee for the approbation of public preachers 1653–54, and with Cromwell on that of discussion of the kingship (1656). He was author of *Psalms Translated into English Metre* (1643; 1646), a version approved by the Westminster Assembly, authorised by parliament for general use, and adopted by the committee of estates in Scotland, where its popular use has continued till the present day. During a period of retirement from the Middle Temple to Landrake, Cornwall (1601–25), he wrote *Meditations of Instruction, of Exhortation, of Reproof* (London, 1616); *The Arte of Happiness* (1619); *Diseases of the Time* (1622); and *Oyl of Scorpions* (1623). His piety was of an intensely subjective kind, as illustrated in *Mystical Marriage* (1635), and *Heavenly Academie* (1638). A number of his works were collectively republished in *Treatises and Meditations* (London, 1656–57).

BIBLIOGRAPHY: A. à Wood, *Athenæ Oxonienses*, ed. P. Bliss, iii. 467, 4 vols., London, 1813–20; D. Neal, *Hist. of the Puritans*, ed. J. Toulmin, 5 vols., Bath, 1793–97; J. A. Alexander, *Lives of the Speakers of the House of Commons*, London, 1850; S. W. Duffield, *English Hymns*, p. 533, New York, 1886; W. A. Shaw, *History of the English Church . . . 1640–60*, 2 vols., London, 1900; Julian, *Hymnology*, pp. 918, 979, 1023; *DNB*, xlix. 316–317 (where many scattering references are given).

ROUSSEAU, rus"sō', **JEAN JACQUES:** French deistic philosopher and author; b. at Geneva June 28, 1712; d. at Ermenonville (28 m. n.e. of Paris) July 2, 1778. His mother died at his birth, and his father, a dissipated and violent-tempered man, paid little attention to the son's training, and finally deserted him. The latter developed a passion for reading, with a special fondness for Plutarch's Lives. Apprenticed first to a notary and then to a coppersmith, he ran away (1728) to escape the rigid discipline, and, after wandering for several days, he fell in with Roman Catholic priests at Consignon in Savoy, who turned him over to Madame de

Warens at Annecy, and she sent him to an educational institution at Turin. Here he duly abjured Protestantism, and next served in various households, in one of which he was charged with theft. After more wanderings he was at Chambéry (1730), whither Madame de Warens had removed. In her household he spent eight years diverting himself in the enjoyment of nature, the study of music, the reading of the English, German, and French philosophers and chemistry, pursuing the study of mathematics and Latin, and enjoying the play-house and opera. He next spent eighteen months at Venice as secretary of the French ambassador, Comte de Montaignu (1744–45). Up to this time, when he was thirty-nine, his life, the details of which he publishes in his *Confessions* (Geneva, 1782; Eng. transl., *The Confessions of J. J. Rousseau*, London, 1891), may be styled as subterranean. He now returned to Paris, where his opera *Les Muses galantes* failed, copied music, and was secretary of Madame Dupin. Here he came into association with Diderot, Grimm, D'Alembert, Holbach, and Madame d'Épinay, and was admitted as a contributor to the *Encyclopédie* (see ENCYCLOPEDISTS); and his brilliant gifts of entertainment, reckless manner, and boundless vanity attracted attention. With the *Discours sur le sciences et les arts* (Paris, 1750), a prize essay in which he set forth the paradox of the superiority of the savage state, he proclaimed his gospel of "back to nature." His operetta *Devin du village* (1752) met with great success. His second sensational writing appeared: *Discours sur l'inégalité parmi les hommes* (1753), against the inequalities of society. His fame was then assured. In 1754 he revisited Geneva, was received with great acclamation, and called himself henceforth "citizen of Geneva." In 1756, upon invitation of Madame d'Épinay, he retired to a cottage (afterward "The Hermitage") in the woods of Montmorency, where in the quiet of nature he expected to spend his life; but domestic troubles, his violent passion for Countess d'Houdetot, and his morbid mistrust and nervous excitability, which lost him his friends, induced him to change his residence to a château in the park of the duke of Luxembourg, Montmorency (1758–62). His famous works appeared during this period: *Lettre à d'Alembert* (Amsterdam, 1758); *Julie ou la nouvelle Heloïse* (1761); *Du contrat social* (Amsterdam, 1762; Paris, 1795; Eng. transl., *The Social Contract*, 2 vols., New York, 1893, new transl., 1902); and *Émile ou de l'education* (Amsterdam, 1762; Eng. transl., *Emilius; or an Essay on Education*, 2 vols., London, 1763, and again, 1895). The last-named work was ordered to be burned by the French parliament and his arrest was ordered; but he fled to Neuchâtel, then within the jurisdiction of Prussia. Here he wrote his *Lettres écrites de la Montagne* (Amsterdam, 1762), in which, with reference to the Geneva constitution, he advocated the freedom of religion against the Church and police. Driven thence by peasant attacks (Sept., 1765), he returned to the Isle St. Pierre in the Lake of Bienne. The government of Berne ordered him out of its territory, and he accepted the asylum offered him by David Hume in England (Jan., 1766). But his morbid misanthropy, now goaded to an insane sense of being persecuted, made him suspicious of plots, and led him to quarrel with his friends for not making his opponents their own enemies, and he fled to France (1767). After wandering about and depending on friends he was permitted to return to Paris (1770), where he finished the *Confessions* begun in England, and produced many of his best stories. Here he copied notes, and studied music and botany. His dread of secret enemies grew upon his imagination, until he was glad to accept an invitation to retire to Ermenonville (1778), where his death came suddenly.

Rousseau was possessed with an overmastering love of nature, and reacted against the artificiality and corruption of the social customs and institutions of the time. He was a keen thinker, and was equipped with the weapons of the philosophical century and with an inspiring eloquence. To these qualities were added a pronounced egotism, self-seeking, and an arrogance that led to bitter antagonism against his revolutionary views and sensitive personality, the reaction against which resulted in a growing misanthropy. Error and prejudice in the name of philosophy, according to him, had stifled reason and nature, and culture, as he found it, had corrupted morals. In *Émile* he presents the ideal citizen and the means of training the child for the State in accordance with nature, even to a sense of God. This "nature gospel" of education, as Goethe called it, was the inspiration, beginning with Pestalozzi, of world-wide pedagogical methods. The most admirable part in this is the creed of the vicar of Savoy, in which, in happy phrase, Rousseau shows a true, natural susceptibility to religion and to God, whose omnipotence and greatness are published anew every day. The *Social Contract*, on the text that all men are born free and equal, regards the State as a contract in which individuals surrender none of their natural rights, but rather agree for the protection of them. Most remarkable in this projected republic was the provision to banish aliens to the state religion and to punish dissenters with death. The *Social Contract* became the text-book of the French Revolution, and Rousseau's theories as protests bore fruit in the frenzied bloody orgies of the Commune as well as in the rejuvenation of France and the history of the entire Western world. Among many editions of Rousseau's complete works are those by P. A. Du Peyron (35 vols., Geneva and Paris, 1782) followed by *Œuvres posthumes* (12 vols., 1782–83); and by V. D. Musset-Pathay, with biography and notes (26 vols., Paris, 1823–27). His *Lettres inédites*, ed. H. de Rothschild, appeared Paris, 1892. Also see DEISM, II., § 4.

BIBLIOGRAPHY: Recent issues of some of the works of Rousseau in English are: *Emile; or, Treatise on Education*, London, 1895; *The Social Contract; or, Principles of Political Right*, ib. 1902; *Confessions*, 2 vols., ib. 1907; *Morals*, ib. 1908; *Humane Philosophy, Maxims and Principles, selected . . . by Frederika Macdonald*, ib. 1908.

Studies of Rousseau's life and works are: J. Morley, *J. J. Rousseau*, 2 vols., London, 1888; A. J. Barruel-Beauvert, *Vie de J. J. Rousseau*, ib. 1789; V. D. Musset-Pathay, *Histoire de la vie et des ouvrages de J. J. Rousseau*, 2 vols., Paris, 1822; M. G. Streckeisen, *J. J. Rousseau, ses amis et ses ennemis*, 2 vols., ib. 1865; F. Brockerhoff, *J. J. Rousseau, sein Leben und seine Werke*, 3 vols., Leipsic, 1863–74; T. Vogt, *J. J. Rousseau's Leben*, Vienna, 1870; H. Beaudouin, *La Vie et les œuvres de Jean Jacques Rousseau*, 2 vols., Paris, 1872; A. Chuquet, *Jean Jacques Rousseau*, ib. 1893; Saint-Marc-Girardin, *J. J. Rousseau, sa vie et ses ouvrages*, ib. 1875; A. Meylan, *Jean-Jacques Rousseau, sa vie et ses œuvres*, ib. 1878; H. Gehrig, *Jean Jacques Rousseau, sein Leben und seine pädagogische Bedeutung*, Neuweid, 1879; H. G. Graham, *Rousseau*, London, 1882; A. Bougeault, *Étude sur l'état mental de J. J. Rousseau*, Paris, 1883; L. Ducros, *J. J. Rousseau*, ib. 1888; R. Wahrenbolts, *Jean-Jacques Rousseau: Leben, Geistesentwicklung und Hauptwerke*, Leipsic, 1889; idem, *Jean Jacques Rousseau*, New York, 1907; E. Asse, *J. J. Rousseau*, Paris, 1900; J. Lemaitre, *Jean Jacques Rousseau*, ib. 1907, Eng. transl., London, 1908.

On the philosophy and ideas of Rousseau consult: E. v. Hohenhausen, *Rousseau . . . ein kritisch-literarischer Umriss*, Cassel, 1847; L. Moreau, *J. J. Rousseau et le siècle philosophique*, Paris, 1870; C. Borgeaud, *J. J. Rousseau's Religionsphilosophie*, Leipsic, 1883; G. Maugras, *Querelles de philosophes Voltaire et J. J. Rousseau*, Paris, 1886; O. Schmidt, *Rousseau und Byron*, Leipsic, 1890; A. Spitzner, *Natur und Naturgemässheit bei J. J. Rousseau*, Leipsic, 1892; L. Claritte, *J. J. Rousseau*, Paris, 1896; H. Höffding, *Rousseau und seine Philosophie*, Stuttgart, 1897; T. Davidson, *Rousseau and Education according to Nature*, New York, 1898; E. Fährmann, *Rousseau's Naturanschauung*, Leipsic, 1901; W. H. Hudson, *Rousseau and Naturalism in Life and Thought*, Edinburgh, 1903; Frederika Macdonald, *Jean Jacques Rousseau, a New Criticism*, 2 vols., London and New York, 1907(?); G. Compayré, *Jean Jacques Rousseau and Education from Nature*, London, 1908.

ROUSSEL, rū-sel′, **GÉRARD (GERARDUS RUFUS or TOLNINUS)**: French Roman Catholic; b. at Vaquerie (a village near Amiens) about 1500; d. at Mauléon (25 m. s.w. of Pau) in the early part of 1550. At the age of twenty he went to Pau, where he attended the lectures of Jacobus Faber Stapulensis (see FABER, STAPULENSIS, JACOBUS); but his teacher was suspected of heresy by the Sorbonne, and Roussel accordingly followed him to Meaux, where they found refuge with Bishop Guillaume Briçonnet (q.v.). Under this prelate's patronage Roussel was appointed vicar of St. Saintain, later becoming canon and treasurer of the cathedral of Meaux, where for some months he preached without interference. Though he held that the time had not yet come to break with the Roman Catholic Church, nevertheless, on Dec. 13, 1524, Bishop Briçonnet, alarmed by the warning that he might be summoned before parliament, suspended Roussel, who, at the instigation of Farel, endeavored to set up a printing-office at Meaux for the publication of Protestant tracts, but was forced to take refuge in Strasburg, where the new teachings had become supreme. At the invitation of Francis I., he went, in 1535, to Paris, where he delivered sermons of a Protestant character at the Louvre, but was forbidden by the Sorbonne to continue. Nevertheless, he enjoyed the patronage of Margaret of Navarre, and in 1536 was consecrated bishop of Oleron.

Roussel's dream was the reformation of the Church without breaking with it. He preached three and four times daily, administered the Eucharist in both kinds, and his clergy were required to recite each Sunday in the vernacular the Ten Commandments, the Lord's Prayer, and the Apostles' Creed. His two main doctrines were that God can be known only through the study of the Bible and that salvation is won only through grace. The dialogue in which he set forth these views, the *Familière exposition du symbole, de la loi et de l'oraison dominicale*, was, however, condemned by the Sorbonne and was never published, although it is preserved in manuscript in the Bibliothèque Nationale, together with its continuation, the *Forme de visites de diocèse*. Before this action on the part of the Sorbonne had become known to him, the bishop died from injuries received while preaching at Mauléon, where a fanatic had hacked away the pulpit with an ax. The only works of Roussel, besides those just noted, were editions of the *Arithmetica* of Boethius (Paris, 1521) and of the *Moralia magna* of Aristotle (1522). G. BONET-MAURY.

BIBLIOGRAPHY: Sources are: Beza's *Hist. ecclésiastique des églises reformées*, 1580, new ed. by J. W. Baum and A. E. Cunitz, 3 vols., Paris, 1883–89, also, ed. P. Vesson, 2 vols., Paris, 1882–83; and A. L. Herminjard, *Correspondance des Réformateurs*, vols. i., iii., v.–vii., ix (consult index), Geneva, 1878–97. Consult: C. Schmidt, *Gérard Roussel*, Strasburg, 1845; Toussaint du Plessis, *Hist. de l'église de Meaux*, vol. i., Paris, 1731; H. Graf, *Essai sur la vie et les écrits de Lefèvre d'Etaples*, Strasburg, 1842; E. and É. Haag, *La France protestante*, ed. H. L. Bordier, Paris, 1877 sqq.; E. Doumergue, *Jean Calvin*, Lausanne, 1899; L. Delisle, *Notices et extraits de la Bibliothèque nationale*, vol. xxxvi., Paris, 1899; G. Kawerau, in *TSK*, 1902 (on the letters of Sturm to Butzer); V. L. Bourilly and N. Weiss, in *Bulletin du protestantisme français*, 1903 (on the Protestants and the Sorbonne); cf. also the *Bulletin*, xiv., p. cli., and 2 ser., x. 415; Lichtenberger, *ESR*, xi. 334–35.

ROUTH, routh, **MARTIN JOSEPH**: Church of England; b. at South Elmham (90 m. n.e. of London), Suffolk, Sept. 18, 1755; d. at Oxford Dec. 22, 1854. He was educated at Oxford (B.A., 1771; M.A., 1776; B.D., 1786). In 1791 he succeeded to the presidency of Magdalen College, Oxford. He published the *Reliquiæ sacræ*, fragments of the lost Christian authors of the second and third centuries, one of the most important and useful works upon patristic literature, revealing the finest English scholarship (4 vols., Oxford, 1814–18; 2d ed., 1846, supplementary vol., 1848); and *Scriptorum ecclesiasticorum opuscula* (2 vols., 1832); and edited *Bishop Burnet's History of his Own Time* (7 vols., 1823).

BIBLIOGRAPHY: J. W. Burgon, *Lives of Twelve Good Men*, 2 vols., London, 1888; T. Mozley, *Reminiscences, chiefly of Oriel and the Oxford Movement*, 2 vols., ib. 1882; *DNB*, xlix. 324–326.

ROW, THOMAS: English Baptist hymnist; b. in 1786; d. at Little Grausden, Cambridgeshire, Jan. 3, 1864. He was pastor at Hadleigh, Suffolk, and, after 1838, at Little Grausden. He published *Concise Spiritual Poems* (London, 1817), containing 529 hymns; and *Original and Evangelical Hymns* (1822), containing 543 hymns. They are Calvinistic in type, and possess little poetic merit, but some have found their way into well-known collections.

BIBLIOGRAPHY: Julian, *Hymnology*, p. 979; *DNB*, xlix. 331.

ROWE, HENRY KALLOCH: Baptist; b. at Dorchester, Mass., Nov. 30, 1869. He was educated at Brown University (A.B., 1892; A.M., 1895), Harvard (1892–93), and Boston University (Ph.D., 1905). From 1893 to 1903 he was a teacher in academies and private schools, after which he was instructor in history in Boston University until 1906, since when he has been assistant professor of church history in Newton Theological Institution, Newton Center, Mass.

ROWE, PETER TRIMBLE: Protestant Episcopal missionary bishop of Alaska; b. at Meadowville, Ont., Nov. 20, 1856. He was educated at Trinity University, Toronto (B.A., 1878); was a missionary at Garden River, Ont. (1876–82); a missionary at Sault Ste. Marie, Mich. (1882–95); and a commissioner of schools in Chippewa County, Mich. (1890–94). In 1895 he was consecrated bishop of the newly created missionary diocese of Alaska.

ROWLANDS, DANIEL: Welsh Methodist; b. at Pantybeudy, parish of Nautcwnlle (40 m. n.n.w. of Swansea), Cardiganshire, Wales, in 1713; d. at Llangeitho (41 m. n.w. of Swansea) Oct. 16, 1790. Of his youth and early manhood nothing is known, except that he studied at the grammar-school of Hereford. Ordained deacon in London, 1733, whither he traveled on foot, and priest in 1735, he became curate to his brother at Llangeitho. Some time before 1736 he became curate at Ystrad Ffin, Carmarthenshire, and presently began to organize Calvinistic Methodist societies. His Methodistic zeal cost him his curacy of Ystrad Ffin, but he received instead that of Llanddewi Brefi, Cardiganshire. In 1763 Bishop Squire suspended him from clerical functions, and henceforth he preached in an improvised building at Llangeitho, thronged for twenty-five years by pilgrims from all parts of Wales in addition to his congregation. He exercised an immense power as a preacher, ranking next to George Whitefield. Once in his history a revival began with his reading of the litany of the Church of England. At the words, "By thine agony and bloody sweat, good Lord, deliver us," the congregation began to weep loudly. Eight *Sermons*, translated from the Welsh, were published (London, 1774); and *Three Sermons* (1778; new ed. in Welsh, 1876, with memoir).

Bibliography: The best memoir is that in the 1876 ed. of the *Sermons* (ut sup.) in Welsh. Consult further: J. Owen, *Memoir of the Rev. Daniel Rowlands*, London, 1840; E. Morgan, *Ministerial Records; or, brief Account of the great Progress of Religion under . . . D. Rowlands . . . .*, London, 1840; J. C. Ryle, *Christian Leaders of the Last Century*, London, 1869; Owen Jones, *Some of the Great Preachers of Wales*, London, 1885; *DNB*, xlix. 350–351.

ROWLANDS, DAVID: Welsh Congregationalist; b. at Geufron, Rhosybol, Anglesea, Mar. 4, 1836. He was educated at the Independent College, Bala, New College, London (B.A., University of London, 1860), and the Congregational Memorial College, Brecon. He was ordained in 1861, and held Congregational pastorates at the Welsh church in Llanbrynmair, Montgomeryshire (1861–67), and the English churches in Welshpool, Montgomeryshire (1867–71), and Carmarthen (1871–72). Since 1872 he has been connected with the Congregational Memorial College, Brecon, Wales, where he has been professor of mathematics (1872–82), professor of Greek Testament exegesis and church history (1882–96), and principal and professor of Greek Testament exegesis and practical theology (since 1896). He has been for many years adjudicator in poetry and prose at the National Eisteddfod, and has also been a member of the Gorsedd of the Bards of the Isle of Britain, with the degrees of Druid and Bard under the pseudonym of Dewi Mon, since 1863, and a member of the Honorable Society of Cymmrodorion since 1874. In theology he is a liberal conservative. He was associate editor of *Yr Annibynwr* ("The Independent"); *Y Dysgedydd* ("The Instructor"; the monthly journal of the Welsh Congregationalists); *Cambrian Minstrelsie*, a collection of Welsh airs, to which he contributed the notes and most of the Welsh and English lyrics (6 vols., Edinburgh, 1893); and *Caniedydd yr Ysgol Sul* ("Sunday School Songster"), to which he contributed many hymns (1898); and also edited *Telyn Tudno* ("Tudno's Harp"), the poetical works of Tudno (Wrexham, 1897). In addition to twelve volumes of sermons and his *Men and Women of the Old and New Testaments* (6 vols., Manchester, 1904), special mention may be made of his *Caniadau Serch* ("Songs of the Affections," Bala, 1854); *Sermons on Historical Subjects* (London, 1870); *Gramadeg Cymraeg* ("Welsh Grammar"; Wrexham 1874); *Gwersi mewn Gramadeg* ("Lessons in Grammar"; Dolgelly, 1876); the librettos of the late Joseph Parry's *Emmanuel, Arianwen, Blodwen, Joseph*, and *Paul;* and the notes on I and II Thessalonians in the *Bibl y Teulu* ("Bible for the Family"; Denbigh, 1906).

ROYCE, JOSIAH: Layman, philosopher; b. at Grass Valley, Nevada Co., Cal., Nov. 20, 1855. He was graduated from the University of California (1875); was instructor in English literature and logic in the same institution, 1878–82; instructor and assistant professor at Harvard University, 1882–92; and has been professor of the history of philosophy there since 1892. He is the author of: *Religious Aspect of Philosophy: Critique of the Bases of Conduct and of Faith* (Boston, 1885); *California, from the Conquest of 1846 to the Second Vigilance Committee in San Francisco* (1886); *Spirit of Modern Philosophy* (1892); *Conception of God: philosophical Discussion concerning the Nature of the Divine Idea as a demonstrable Reality* (in collaboration with others; New York, 1897); *Studies of Good and Evil: Essays upon Problems of Philosophy and of Life* (1898); *Conception of Immortality* (1900); *The World and the Individual* (2 series, Gifford lectures; London and New York, 1900–01); *Outlines of Psychology* (1903); *Herbert Spencer; an Estimate and a Review* (New York, 1904); *Philosophy of Loyalty* (1908); and *Race Questions, Provincialism, and Other American Questions* (1908).

ROYSTON, PETER SORENSON: Church of England; b. in London June 6, 1830. He was educated at St. Paul's School, London, and at Trinity College, Cambridge (B.A., 1853; M.A., 1861; D.D., 1872); was resident tutor in the Church Missionary College, London, 1853–55; corresponding secretary for the Church Missionary Society and incumbent of that society's church at Madras, India, 1855–62 and 1866–71, during the same period editing the *Madras Church Missionary Record;* fellow of Madras University, 1858–73; incumbent of St. Thomas', Mauritius, 1865; was chosen bishop of Mauritius, 1872, resigning because of ill-health in 1891; was assistant bishop to the bishop of Liverpool, 1891–1905; vicar of Childwall, 1896–1903, and rural dean of Childwall, 1896–1903. He was also one of the editors of the *Proceedings of the South Indian Missionary Conference* held in 1858.

RUBRICS (Lat. *rubrica*, from *ruber*, "red"): In the ecclesiastical sense, the directions in service books which show how, when, and where the various parts of the liturgy should be performed. The name was derived from the fact that rubrics were originally written in red, a custom which is now almost obsolete. The word was borrowed from the legal usage, according to which it was applied to the titles or headings of chapters in certain law-books.

RUCHAT, rü-shā', ABRAHAM: Historian of the Reformation in French Switzerland; b. at Grandcour (28 m. n.n.e. of Lausanne) Sept. 15, 1678; d. at Lausanne Sept. 29, 1750. He was educated at Lausanne, and after being ordained in 1702 was for several years a teacher in Bern. In 1705 he secured a scholarship which enabled him to travel, and he accordingly studied for a time in Berlin, and still longer in Leyden, during this period preparing his *Grammatica Hebraica facili methodo digesta* (Leyden, 1707). Returning to Switzerland, he made his first essay in what was to prove his future field in his *Abrégé de l'histoire ecclésiastique du pays de Vaud depuis l'établissement du christianisme jusqu'à notre temps* (Bern, 1707; Lausanne, 1838). After being vicar in his native district, he was appointed minister at Aubonne in 1709, and in 1716 was called to the pastorate of Rolle, where he remained more than twelve years. The sole production of his pen during this period was his *Délices de la Suisse* (4 vols., Leyden, 1714), a work which won high praise and evoked equally strong opposition. In 1721 Ruchat was appointed professor of eloquence at Lausanne, a position which carried with it the rectorate of the Latin school. The success which his own talents should have gained was, however, frustrated by the theological animosities of the time, and he accordingly plunged into the historical studies for which he had been collecting materials for two decades. He now published the first half (1516–36) of his *Histoire de la réformation en Suisse* (6 vols., Geneva, 1727–28); but political conditions forbade the publication of the entire work, which extended to 1566, until a century later, when the complete history was edited by L. Vulliemin (7 vols., Lausanne, 1835–38; abridged Eng. transl. by J. Collinson, London, 1845). In 1733 Ruchat became second professor of theology, and was promoted to the first professorship fifteen years later. During this period of his career his writings were mainly theological and in the domains of polemics and Old-Testament theology. To the former category belong his *Examen de l'origénisme* (Lausanne, 1733) and the anti-Roman Catholic *Lettres et monuments de trois pères apostoliques* (2 vols., Leyden, 1738; translations of the epistles of Clement, Ignatius, and Polycarp and the martyrdoms of the two latter, with excursuses attacking the Roman Catholic Church); to the latter, among others, his *Traité des poids, des mesures et des monnoyes dont il est parlé dans l'écriture sainte* (Lausanne, 1743). He took an active interest in missions to the Jews, while his leisure was devoted to studies in Swiss history, especially of the medieval period, the results being contained in manuscript in the libraries of Bern and Lausanne. Ruchat's *Délices de la Suisse* and *Histoire de la réformation en Suisse* were placed on the Index, and two unnamed Jesuits sought, in 1724, formally to refute his history of the Reformation in Vaud. In addition to the works already noted, mention may be made of his anonymous French translations from the English and Spanish of works of J. Beeverell and J. Alvarez de Colmenar under the respective titles *Délices de la Grande Bretagne et de l'Irlande* (8 vols., Leyden, 1707) and *Délices de l'Espagne et du Portugal* (5 vols., 1707).

(H. Vuilleumier.)

Bibliography: Bridel, in *Conservateur suisse*, vol. xiv (1828); the sketch by L. Vulliemin in his ed. of the *Hist. de la réforme de la Suisse*, vii. 423–448, 1838; E. Secretan, *Galerie suisse*, i. 586–590, Lausanne, 1874; P. Godet, *Hist. littéraire de la Suisse françoise*, pp. 178–179, Paris, 1889; V. Rossel, *Hist. littéraire de la Suisse romande*, ii. 53 sqq., ib. 1890; Lichtenberger, *ESR*, xi. 342–346.

RUCHRATH, JOHANN. See Wesel, John of.

RUDELBACH, rū'del-bāH, ANDREAS GOTTLOB: Dano-German Lutheran; b. at Copenhagen Sept. 29, 1792; d. at Slagelse (50 m. s.w. of Copenhagen), Zealand, Mar. 3, 1862. He was educated at the university of his native city, where he became privat-docent. During this period he edited, in collaboration with N. F. S. Grundtvig, the *Theologisk Maanedskrift* (13 vols., 1825 sqq.), and in 1829 was called to the pastorate of Glauchau, Saxony, where he powerfully aided religious awakening and revolt against the rationalism of the period, though at the same time he opposed any formal separation from the Lutheran Church. In 1830 he aided in founding the Muldenthal pastoral conference, but opposition gradually developed against him, largely on account of his uncompromising Lutheranism, and in 1845 he gladly resigned his pastorate and returned to Denmark. From 1846 to 1848 he lectured at the University of Copenhagen on dogmatics and introduction, but the death of his royal patron in the latter year exposed him to the attacks of those who regarded him as a German and a traitor. He accordingly accepted a call to the pastorate of Slagelse, where he passed the remainder of his life.

He edited the *Zeitschrift für die gesammte lutherische Theologie und Kirche* (in collaboration with H. E. F. Guericke, Leipsic, 1839 sqq.) and *Christliche Biographie*, i (1849), and wrote, in addition to the works already mentioned and several volumes of sermons: *Hieronymus Savonarola und seine Zeit* (Hamburg, 1835); *Reformation, Luthertum und Union* (Leipsic, 1839); *Historische-kritische Einleitung in die Augsburgische Konfession* (Dresden, 1841); *Amtliches Gutachten über die Wiedereinführung der Katechismus-Examina im Königreich Sachsen, nebst historischer Erörterung der Katechismus-Anstalten in der evangelisch-lutherischen Kirche Deutschlands* (1841); and *Om Psalme-Literaturen og Psalmebogs-Sagen, historisk-kritiske Undersögelser* (Copenhagen, 1856). (Oswald Schmidt†.)

Bibliography: An autobiography was projected, and its publication as "Confessions" begun in the *Zeitschrift für lutherische Theologie und Kirche*, 1861, i. 1 sqq., ii. 601

sqq., 1862, iii. 401 sqq., and continued (ed. C. R. Kaiser from author's manuscript) in *NKZ*, 1902, pp. 163–180, 522–545 (goes to end of university period). Consult: C. R. Kaiser, *Andreas Gottlob Rudelbach*, Leipsic, 1892; J. R. Stockholm, in *Kirkelig Kalendar for Norge*, pp. 38–230, Christiania, 1877 (in Norwegian); and for a list of the writings, E. A. Zuchold, *Bibliotheca Zuchold*, ii. 1094–1095, Göttingen, 1864.

RUDIN, ERIC GEORG VALDEMAR NAPOLEON: Swedish Lutheran; b. at Oesterryd, Oestergötland, July 20, 1833. He was educated at the University of Upsala, being graduated from the philosophical course in 1857 and from the theological two years later. He was then secretary of the National Evangelical Society at Stockholm (1859–62), and director of the Foreign Missionary Society in the same city (1862–69), after which he was vice-chaplain of St. Clara's, Stockholm, until 1872. In 1872 he became privat-docent at the University of Upsala, where he was made adjunct in theology in 1875; was associate professor of exegetical theology (1877–93), and from 1893 until his retirement as professor emeritus in 1900 was full professor of the same subject. He was appointed court preacher in 1873 and in 1886 was made provost. In 1883 he became a member of the committee for the revision of the Swedish translation of the Old Testament. In theology he is a moderate Lutheran, friendly to the Biblical theology of Beck and to the mystics. He has written "Intimations of Eternity" (Stockholm, 1872); "Biblical Psychology," i (Upsala, 1875); "Life of Sören Kierkegaard" (1880); "Synopsis of the Gospels" (1881); "Gospel of Mark" (1883); "Introduction to Old Testament Prophecy" (1884); "Commentary on the Minor Prophets" (1884); "Discussions on Theological and Ecclesiastical Subjects" (2 parts, 1885–1886); and "Survey of the Scriptural History of the Old Testament" (1886).

RUDOLF OF EMS: German poet and writer of the thirteenth century. The details of his life are unknown, except that he was probably a Swiss by birth and that his death occurred between 1250 and 1254 at some place unknown while he was in the company of Emperor Conrad IV. He was, however, one of the most fruitful poets of his period, and also entered the field of historical writing, besides working in the field of Biblical history (see HISTORICAL BIBLES). Among his poems are *Der gute Gerhard* (ed. M. Haupt, Leipsic, 1840; Germ. transl. by Lersch, Bonn, 1847, and K. Simrock, 2d ed., Stuttgart, 1864), which exalts the grace of Christian humility; and *Baarlaam und Josaphat* (ed. F. K. Köpke, Berlin, 1818, and F. Pfeiffer, Leipsic, 1843), a retelling of that story (see BAARLAAM AND JOSAPHAT for analysis and literature). Of his historical works the two of interest are Wilehalm von Orlens (ed. V. Junk, Berlin, 1905), and *Weltchronik*, dedicated to Conrad IV. (only fragments have been published for this—for a list of these cf. Potthast, *Wegweiser*, pp. 986–987), which told the story of the Old Testament as far as the death of Solomon. This was much used for a time, but was combined with the much poorer work of an unknown writer to its own detriment.

BIBLIOGRAPHY: A. F. C. Valmar, *Die zwei Recensionen und Handschriftenfamilien der Weltchronik Rudolphs von Ems*, Marburg, 1839; Zacher, in *Zeitschrift für deutsche Philologie*, ix (1877), 461–471; O. Doberentz, in the same, xii (1880), 257–301, 387–454, xiii (1881), 29–67, 165–223; V. Zeidler, *Die Quellen von Rudolfs von Ems Wilhelm von Orlens*, Berlin, 1894.

RUDOLPH, ROBERT LIVINGSTON: Reformed Episcopal bishop-coadjutor of the New York and Philadelphia Synod; b. in New York City Dec. 29, 1865. He was educated at New York University (B.A., 1892) and the Reformed Episcopal Theological Seminary, Philadelphia, from which he was graduated in 1894, also taking a post-graduate course at Princeton Theological Seminary, and later studying at Erlangen. He became assistant pastor of the First Reformed Episcopal Church, New York City, in 1895, and in 1903 was appointed professor of systematic theology and Christian ethics in the Reformed Episcopal Theological Seminary, Philadelphia, still retaining his pastorate. In 1896 he was made secretary of the New York and Philadelphia Synod and held this position until 1908, when, without resigning his professorship, he was made bishop of the same synod.

RUECKERT, rüc'kert, **KARL THEODOR:** German Roman Catholic; b. at Beckstein (a village near Königshofen, 17 m. s.e. of Wertheim), Baden, Feb. 2, 1840; d. at Freiburg Nov. 8, 1907. He was educated at the University of Freiburg from 1859 to 1862 (D.D., 1865), and, after being engaged in pastoral and state duties from 1863, was a professor at the gymnasia of Tauberbischofsheim and Freiburg until 1880, when he became privat-docent at the University of Freiburg, still retaining his gymnasial professorship, however, until 1890, when he was appointed associate professor of New-Testament literature at the University, where he was promoted to a full professorship of the same subject in 1895. He wrote *Die Quellen der Apostelgeschichte* (Freiburg, 1865); *Die Religion vom apologetischen Standpunkt* (Tübingen, 1874); *Nach Palästina und über Libanon* (Mainz, 1881); *Nach Nordafrika* (Würzburg, 1898); and *Die Lage des Berges Sion* (Freiburg, 1898).

RUECKERT, LEOPOLD IMMANUEL: German Lutheran; b. at Grosshennersdorf (a village near Herrnhut) Feb. 1, 1797; d. at Jena Apr. 9, 1871. His first education was received from the Moravians and was completed at Leipsic (1814–17). After being a private tutor in Niederlausitz and Juterbog, and after preaching at Berlin, he became deacon of his native village in 1819. He earnestly desired an academic position, but as this was impossible for the time being, he set forth his ideals of a teacher in a series of works which included *Christliche Philosophie, oder Philosophie, Geschichte und Bibel nach ihren wahren Beziehungen zu einander* (2 vols., Leipsic, 1825). In 1825 Rückert was appointed a teacher in the gymnasium at Zittau. There he taught Hebrew, French, history, mathematics, and science, and studied not only Plato, whose *Symposium* he edited (Leipsic, 1828), but also the New Testament, especially the Pauline writings, publishing commentaries on Romans, Galatians, Ephesians, and Corinthians (5 vols., Leipsic, 1831–37). After having been suggested, but not accepted, as a professor in Erlangen in 1832 and at Greifswald in 1836, he became the successor of F. L. O. Baumgarten-Crusius at Jena in 1844. Here, besides his academic duties, he preached frequently, some of his sermons being collected in his *Sechs Zeitpredigten in den Jahren 1848 und 1849 gehalten* (Jena, 1850) and *Kleine Aufsätze für christliche Belehrung und Erbauung* (Berlin, 1861). After the stormy year of 1848 Rückert wrote his *Theologie* (2 parts, Leipsic, 1851), which was essentially a scientific picture of the ideal life, practical life, and the life revealed and rendered possible to man through Christ, and not the conventional dogmatic or ethical theological treatise. Certain portions of this work were further elucidated in his *Das Abendmahl, sein Wesen und seine Geschichte in der alten Kirche* (Leipsic, 1856), and his *Büchlein von der Kirche* (Jena, 1857). His theological point of view receives its full expression in his *Der Rationalismus* (Leipsic, 1859). It should also be noted that in his *Luthers Verhältnis zum augsburgischen Bekenntnis* (Jena, 1854) he sought to prove that the Augsburg Confession could not truly be called Luther's.

Rückert held in exegesis that a prime factor was the ability of the scholar so to identify himself with his subject as to have no idea of his own which should diverge from the subject in question; he denied the existence of any evidence beyond the sphere of morals; and he regarded Christ merely as a man of surpassing goodness who gave his life for the moral regeneration of his race. His rationalism, however, was regarded by him as ethical, or Christian, and as opposed to the older empirical system. He deemed it to consist solely in search for facts and their truths, and to be hindered by no authority from clinging to the truths thus ascertained. He accordingly advocated a critical process of simple investigation, neither believing nor denying, but accepting what seemed to be credible and rejecting all else. Portions of Rückert's commentary on I Cor. were translated into English by B. B. Edwards in the *Selections from German Literature* prepared by him and E. A. Park (Andover, 1839). (G. Frank†.)

Bibliography: H. Doering, *Jenaischer Universitäts-Almanach*, p. 64, Jena, 1845; J. Günther, *Lebensskizzen der Professoren der Universität Jena*, p. 42, ib. 1858; G. Frank, *Die jenaische Theologie*, p. 125, Leipsic, 1858; C. Schwarz, *Zur Geschichte der neuesten Theologie*, p. 482, ib. 1869.

RUEDINGER (RUEDIGER), rü'ding-er, ESROM: German Protestant theologian and educator; b. at Bamberg May 19, 1523; d. at Nuremberg Jan. 2, 1590. He was educated at Leipsic, and after being tutor to the children of Joachim Camerarius (q.v.) was privat-docent at Leipsic in 1546–47 and second teacher at Schulpforta in 1547–48, reassuming his position at Leipsic that he might marry the eldest daughter of Camerarius. From 1549 to 1557 he was rector of the school at Zwickau, but his theological position as a firm Philippist brought him into conflict with strict Lutherans, especially as he taught the necessity of good works. It was a welcome change, therefore, when he was called in 1557 to be professor of physics at Wittenberg, where he also lectured on ethics and the interpretation of Latin authors. In 1570 he became professor of Greek, and was dean of the philosophical faculty in 1559 and 1570 and rector in 1562. He became involved, however, in the eucharistic controversy between the Lutherans and the Philippists in 1574, and was imprisoned for a short time at Torgau for refusing to sign the "Torgau Articles." He was permitted to return to Wittenberg, and then, though forbidden to leave the city, he fled to Berlin. Declining offers from Basel and Heidelberg, he accepted the rectorate of a school newly erected at Eibenschitz (12 m. s.w. of Brünn) for young nobles of the Bohemian Brethren and Moravians. The school finally became offensive to the nascent Roman Catholic reaction, and though in 1578 an imperial command to close the institution was disregarded, a sharper order, issued on Jan. 22, 1583, directing that Rüdinger be arrested and placed in the custody of the bishop of Olmütz, caused him to take refuge with Frederick of Zerotin. There he remained until 1588, when his widowed sister invited him to spend the remainder of his life with her at Nuremberg.

Rüdinger's principal theological works were the following: *Libri Psalmorum paraphrasis Latina* (Görlitz, 1581); *Endexion, tunica funebris ex tela Paradisi ad dextram crucis Christi* (Nuremberg, 1591); *De origine ubiquitatis pii et eruditi cujusdam viri tractatio* (Geneva, 1597); and *De fratrum orthodoxorum in Bohemia et Moravia ecclesiolis narratiuncula*, in the *Historica narratio de fratrum orthodoxorum ecclesiis in Bohemia, Moravia et Polonia* of J. Camerarius (Heidelberg, 1605). A number of theological works (especially on predestination, the "Torgau Articles," and the *De Jesu Christo martyre*) are contained in the Collectio Cameraria in the Royal Library at Munich. (E. Fabian.)

Bibliography: A. Strobel, *Neue Beiträge zur Litteratur des 16. Jahrhunderts*, vol. ii., part 1, 5 vols., Nuremberg, 1790–94; M. Adamus, *Vita Germanorum philosophorum*, pp. 372–373, Heidelberg, 1615; J. F. Köhler, in *Dresdener Gelehrten Anzeigen*, 1790, parts xxv.–xxviii.; J. F. A. Gillet, *Crato von Crafftheim*, 2 vols., Frankfort, 1860; H. Ball, *Das Schulwesen der böhmischen Brüder*, Berlin, 1898.

RUEETSCHI, rüet'shi, RUDOLF: Swiss Protestant; b. at Bern Dec. 3, 1820; d. there 1903. He was educated at the universities of Bern, Berlin, and Tübingen; and in 1842 became vicar, first in the country and later at Bern. In 1845 he became privat-docent for Old-Testament theology at the university of his native city; and during this period edited the *Biblische Dogmatik* of his teacher, J. L. S. Lutz (Pforzheim, 1847). Next, Rüetschi was pastor at Trub (1848–53), Kirchberg in Oberaargau (1853–67), and at the Cathedral of Bern (1867–97). As a theologian he belonged to the intermediate party, midway between the extremes of conservatism and rationalism. In 1878 he received an honorary professorship at Bern, where he lectured on Semitics, and on the history of Israel from the exile to the time of Christ. He took an active part in a Swiss translation of the Bible, of which only the New Testament appeared, and translated Ecclesiastes for E. Kautzsch's *Die heilige Schrift des Alten Testaments* (Freiburg-im-Breisgau, 1892–94). He retired from active life in 1897. (W. Hadorn.)

RUET, rū-ét', FRANCISCO DE PAULA: Spanish Protestant; b. at Barcelona Oct. 28, 1826; d. at Madrid Nov. 18, 1878. After a meager education he became a strolling player, and about 1841 abandoned Roman Catholicism for Waldensian teachings at Turin, where he prepared himself for the ministry. The revolution in 1855 rendered it possible for Ruet to reenter Spain, and he preached for a month at Barcelona. He was imprisoned, first by the governor, and again by the captain general, and the political reaction a few weeks later rendered it possible for the bishop of Barcelona to cite him before the spiritual court, which, after he had been in prison seven months, sentenced him to the stake for heresy. As such a sentence could no longer be executed in Spain, it was changed, Sept. 18, 1856, to perpetual banishment. Forming a small Protestant community among the Spaniards at Gibraltar, where Ruet was ordained by a Waldensian committee, he made it a center for the dissemination of Protestantism in Spain. Intercepted by the rigid watch on the Spanish border, Ruet left, and first preached to his countrymen during the London exposition, and later went under the auspices of a French committee to Algiers, working among the thousands of Spaniards there, as well as in Blidah and Oran. At the liberation of Spain in 1868–69, he returned and founded the Protestant church at Madrid. The French committee being no longer able to assist him after 1870, Ruet entered the service of the German missionary society and labored zealously in a chapel purchased for him in 1874 by German friends. (FRITZ FLIEDNER†.)

RUFINUS, ru-fai'nus, TYRANNIUS: Latin ecclesiastical writer; b. near Aquileia, in Venetia, at the head of the Adriatic, about 345; d. in Sicily about 410. He seems to have obtained his education at Rome, and in 370 or 371 received baptism in a monastery at his native place; at this time he was a friend of Jerome. He left Aquileia probably in 373 for Egypt bent on the practise of asceticism, and, some think, in company with a certain Melania, a rich Roman lady, who, enamored of the ascetic life, devoted her property to the service of the saints of Christ. He visited the celebrated hermits of the Scetic and Nitrian deserts and was there during the time of persecution under Lucius, the Arian bishop, opponent of the Alexandrian Patriarch Peter, meanwhile studying under Didymus the Blind of Alexandria (q.v.). Possibly in 379 he went to Palestine and settled on the Mount of Olives and devoted himself to ministrations to the pilgrims to the place. Not long before 394 he was made presbyter by Bishop John of Jerusalem. In the dissension between John of Jerusalem and Epiphanius of Salamis, Rufinus took the side of John, an action which interrupted his friendship with Jerome, though this was once more cemented. When he returned home again, it is not impossible that Melania was again in his company, though the expression in a letter of Paulinus of Nola (in *CSEL*, xxix. 246, 1), in which Rufinus is called "attendant on the spiritual journey of Melania," is susceptible of another interpretation. Rufinus appears next at the cloister of Pinetum near Terracina, where at the wish of the Abbot Ursacius he adapted the rules of Basil in Latin for the monks. A certain Macarius desired him to translate the works of Origen. He translated the first book of the Apology (for Origen) by Pamphilus, and followed this with a translation of Origen's *Peri archōn*, the first draft of which he completed in 398 or 399. Rufinus saw that this engagement with the works of Origen might bring him into disrepute, especially at a time when Origen was not in favor; yet at the urgency of Macarius, he carried the work through. The unfinished manuscript, according to the report of Rufinus, was purloined and sent to Jerome by some friends of the latter, who at once set to work on a translation which should show the inadequacy of that of Rufinus, accompanying the transmission of this with a long letter (no. lxxxiv., Eng. transl. in *NPNF*, 2 ser., vi. 175–181); Jerome also wrote a letter to Rufinus (no. lxxi., Eng. transl., ut sup., p. 170), which was suppressed by the false friend, who took advantage of the absence of Rufinus; meanwhile Rufinus was under deep suspicion on account of his supposed leaning toward Origenism. Rufinus learned of Jerome's letter and wrote to a friend at Rome, Apronianus, not for publication, however, in sharp terms against Jerome; Pammachius and Marcella, the friends of Jerome, learned enough of it to send a report of the writing to Jerome. The latter then wrote the first two books of his "Apology" answered by a letter to Jerome, who then wrote the third book of the "Apology." Rufinus spent most of the remaining years of his life in Aquileia, and added new friends to the old who still stood by him, to some of whom he dedicated further labors in translation and original work. With old age he desired to visit again the holy places, but got no farther than Sicily when he died.

The dispute with Jerome brought a shadow upon Rufinus' life in the Church. Pope Gelasius held that while Rufinus' books contained much good, Jerome's estimate must stand (*MPL*, lix. 75); but Gennadius praised him (*De vir. ill.*, xvii.) and his Latin. Of independent works may be named, besides the two books against Origen's "Apology," the continuation of Eusebius' "Church History," covering the period 324–395, which is valuable in spite of its defects; *Commentarius in symbolum apostolorum*, the earliest treatment of assured date in Latin dealing with exposition of the symbol, but dependent upon Cyril of Jerusalem; *De benedictionibus patriarcharum*, in which the mystical interpretation rules, written at the request of a Paulinus, probably not Paulinus of Nola. Concerning the translations made by Rufinus it is to be remembered that he never strove to give an exact rendering. He translated numerous exegetical works of Origen (Homilies on Gen.–Num., Josh., Judges, Psalms, and the Song, and the commentary on Romans); he saved for us the *Peri archōn;* the "Apology" of Pamphilus he called *De adulteratione librorum Origenis*, really the title of the preface, screening himself with the suspicion that the heretics had interpolated or changed Origen's statements. In the translation of the *Dialogus de recta fide* he is adjudged more faithful to his text than in the other works of Origen. Greater congeniality seems manifested in the rendering of the "Church History" of Eusebius in nine (not ten) books; and the translation is of value for text-critical purposes in spite of the freedom occasionally allowed himself by the translator. He felt no satisfaction in rendering the Clementine Recognitions. Out of Basil's *Instituta monachorum* he translated a series of homilies, also rendering some homilies of Gregory Nazianzen, some *Sententiæ* of Evagrius Ponticus (possibly the *Liber centum sententiarum*). He put into Latin the *Sententiæ ad eos qui in cœnobiis et xenodochiis habitant fratres* and the *Sententiæ ad virgines*. The "Sentences of Sixtus" mentioned by Origen and used by Porphyry were also translated by him, with the addition of a prologue, and attributed to Sixtus II. of Rome, though they were the product of a Pythagorean philosopher (cf. F. C. Conybeare, *The Ring of Pope Xystus, together with the Prologue of Rufinus, now first rendered into English, with an historical and critical Commentary*, London, 1910). For this he was severely handled by Jerome. It is a long-standing cause of debate whether the *Historia monachorum* is Rufinus' own or a translation from a Greek work, with the probabilities now tending in favor of the second alternative, though the translation is unquestionably by Rufinus. Still an open question is whether the old Latin rendering of Josephus' "War of the Jews" is to be attributed to Rufinus. Works not by him, but in the list of his works, are *Commentarius in lxxv Davidis psalmos* (probably by the Gallic Presbyter Vincentius of the second half of the fifth century); *Commentarius in prophetas . . . Osee, Joel et Amos*; *Vita sanctæ Eugeniæ virginis ac martyris*; and two writings entitled *De fide*. (G. Krüger.)

Bibliography: The complete works of Rufinus have never been published. Parts were edited by L. de la Barre, Paris, 1580; a fuller edition is by D. Vallarsi, Verona, 1745, this being taken into *MPL*, xxi., with the *Vita* of J. Fontanini (originally published Rome, 1742) and that by C. T. G. Schoenemann (Leipsic, 1792). A critical edition of the Latin translation of Eusebius is by T. Mommsen, vol. i., Leipsic, 1903; one of the *Commentarius in symbolum apostolorum, with Notes by C. Whittaker*, also *Translation*, 2 parts, London, 1908. Translations into English of selected works are in *NPNF*, 2 ser., iii. 405–568.

Sources for a life are Rufinus' own works; Jerome's "Apology against Rufinus," Eng. transl. in *NPNF*, 2 ser., iii. 482–540, and his Epistles (nos. 3–5, 51, 57, 80–84, 97, 125, 133); Augustine, *Epist.*, lxiii., clvi.; Gennadius, *De scriptoribus ecclesiasticis*, xvii., Eng. transl. in *NPNF*, 2 ser., iii. 389. Consult further: A. Ebert, *Allgemeine Geschichte der Litteratur des Mittelalters*, i. 321–327, Leipsic, 1889; J. F. B. M. de Rubeis, *Dissertationes duæ*, pp. 1–160, Venice, 1754; H. Bruell, *De Tyrannii Rufini . . . Commentario in symbolum apostolorum*, Düren, 1872–79; F. Kattenbusch, *Beiträge zur Geschichte des altkirchlichen Taufsymbols*, pp. 27–32, Giessen, 1892; B. Czapla, *Gennadius als Litterarhistoriker*, pp. 27–28, 44 sqq., 95, Münster, 1898; C. Schmidt, in *GGA*, clxi (1899), 7–27; P. Reinelt, *Studien über die Briefe des . . . Paulinus von Nola*, Breslau, 1904; M. Schanz, *Geschichte der römischen Litteratur*, iv. 1, pp. 371–387, Munich, 1904; Bardenhewer, *Patrologie*, pp. 397–400, Eng. transl., St. Louis, 1908; Krüger, *History*, passim; *DCB*, iv. 555–561; *KL*, x. 1353–56; Ceillier, *Auteurs sacrés*, vii. 448–484, et passim; Harnack, *Dogma*, vols. iii.–iv. passim; Schaff, *Christian Church*, iii. 701, 884, 984 note; Neander, *Christian Church*, vols. i.–iii. passim.

RUINART, rwi'nar, THIERRI: French Benedictine; b. at Reims June 10, 1657; d. at the monastery of Hautvilliers, near Reims, Sept. 27, 1709. He entered the Benedictine abbey of St. Remy in 1674, made his profession in 1675, and in 1682 was called to the great Maurist center of learning, St. Germain-des-Prés, at the instance of Jean Mabillon (q.v.), to whom he was pupil, co-worker, and biographer. His life was a quiet one, broken only by two journeys—to Alsace in 1696 and to Champagne in 1709—for material for his works. The first of these was the *Acta primorum martyrum sincera et selecta* (Paris, 1689; 2d revised ed., Amsterdam, 1713), which was followed by the *Historia persecutionis Vandalicæ* (1694) and the *Gregorii episcopi Turonensis opera omnia necnon Fredegarii scholastici epitome et chronicum* (1699). Ruinart collaborated with J. Mabillon in the eighth and ninth volumes of the *Acta sanctorum ordinis sancti Benedicti* (1701), and also prepared the second edition of Mabillon's *De re diplomatica* (1709), which he had previously defended in his *Ecclesia Parisiensis vindicata* (1706). He likewise wrote an admirable *Abrégé de la vie de D. Jean Mabillon* (1709); but his intention of editing the fifth volume of the *Annales ordinis Sancti Benedicti* was frustrated by his death. The work was prepared by René Massuet (Paris, 1713), who placed Ruinart's biography in the preface. An interesting diary of Ruinart's on the history of the Benedictine edition of Augustine has been edited by A. M. P. Ingold as an appendix to his *Histoire de l'édition Bénédictine de S. Augustin* (pp. 154–193, 1903). Ruinart wrote also *Apologie de la mission de S. Maur, apostre des Bénédictins en France* (1702), as well as three treatises: *Disquisitio historica de pallio archiepiscopali; Vita beati Urbani papæ II.*; and *Iter litterarium in Alsatiam et Lotharingiam*, all in *Ouvrages posthumes de Mabillon et de Ruinart*, vols. ii.–iii. (1724); and many letters, edited by E. Gigas, *Lettres des bénédictins de Saint-Maur* (2 vols., Copenhagen, 1892–93), also in *Correspondance inédite de Mabillon et de Montfaucon* (3 vols., Paris, 1846). (G. Laubmann†.)

Bibliography: A life by R. Massuet is in the *Annales de l'ordre de S. Bennoit*, vol. v. Consult further: G. Loriquet, *Le Cardinal de Bouillon . . . et T. Ruinart dans l'affaire de l'hist. générale de la maison d'Auvergne*, Reims, 1870; H. Jadart, *Dom Thierry Ruinart*, ib. 1886; E. de Broglie, *Mabillon et la société de Saint-Germain des Prés*, 2 vols., Paris, 1888; J. B. Vanel, *Les Bénédictines de Saint-Maur*, pp. 87–90, ib. 1896; Lichtenberger, *ESR*, xi. 348–350.

RULE OF FAITH. See Regula Fidei.

RULING ELDERS. See Laity; and Presbyterians, x., 2, § 2 (4).

RULMAN MERSWIN. See Friends of God.

RUMANIA: A kingdom (after 1881) in southeastern Europe, between Russia on the north and Bulgaria on the south, and the Black Sea and Russia on the east and Austria-Hungary and Servia on the west; area, 50,720 square miles; population (1907), 6,684,265. Not including the Russian sect of the Lipovanians and the Roman Catholics, each numbering about 140,000 to 150,000, the Christian population is of the Orthodox Greek Church, which is the State Church. Art. 7 of the Constitution of 1866 provides that variance in religious confession shall constitute no hindrance to civil and political rights; and art. 20 assures freedom of all religions, in so far as their exercise does not violate public order or good morals. Further, it is provided that the Orthodox Church is independent of all foreign supervision, while thoroughly maintaining the unity with the ecumenical Church of the East in the sphere of doctrine. As early as 1864, subordination to the patriarchate of Constantinople was declared to be abolished, and the church of the land to be independent, national, and autocephalous, this in order to avert outside political influence and unforeseen protection. For purposes of self-government the holy synod was organized, whose constituent members are the metropolitan primate of Hungary-Wallachia, or the archbishop of Bucharest; the metropolitan of Moldavia and Susava, or the archbishop of Jassy; the three episcopal eparchs of Wallachia, respectively Rimnic-Valcei, Buzeu, and Arjish; and those of Moldavia, respectively, Roman, Galatz, and Hush. The synod convenes twice a year, with the minister of worship in attendance. These eight dioceses embrace 3,670 parishes, 370 of which are in the cities. In round numbers there are 8,000 priests. The clergy also comprises about 600 monks, distributed in four notable cloisters of Moldavia and five in Wallachia, in addition to which there are 160 small cenobitical abodes with two to four inmates to each. The education of the clergy is provided by six seminaries with a curriculum of four years and by the theological faculty of the University of Bucharest. The other university, at Jassy, makes no such provision. The archbishops are elected by popular representatives and the boyars (privileged classes) of the first class; and the bishops are appointed by the archbishops. By action of the synod in agreement with the state government, each diocese also receives a titular bishop as an alternate to the highest dignitary. Although the State, in 1864, sequestered most of the cloistral estates, it contributes only small amounts for the support of the bishops, and the parish clergy depend exclusively on the proceeds of the parochial real estate and the surplice fees.

The Roman Catholic Church, influential, especially in Moldavia, till after the Middle Ages, lost the bulk of its following; but by immigration in the nineteenth century it has entered a more marked development. By 1818 Jassy had become the seat of a papal vicariate, and in 1884 of a bishopric embracing 26 parishes, most of which are in the southern part of the diocese, and are supplied mainly with Minorite pastors. This bishopric has about 90,000 Roman Catholics. The bishopric of Wallachia did not originate until 1883, when it was detached from that of Nicopolis in Bulgaria and erected into an archbishopric; although there are only 18 parishes and somewhat above 50,000 members. Evangelical Christians are much scattered, especially in Moldavia. Their number is estimated at 25,000 to 26,000, including about 8,000 Magyar Calvinists. There are from 15,000 to 16,000 German Evangelicals, and a small number of Methodists, Anglicans, and Presbyterians, principally at Bucharest and Galatz. Owing to the immigration from Transylvania, the German Protestants have a congregation in Bucharest of about 8,000, whose formal constitution, together with the school establishments, was confirmed by the German and Austrian consuls-general. Other congregations in Wallachia are at Crajova, Turnu-Severin, Rimnic, and Braila. There has been one at Jassy, Moldavia, since 1754, now including six branch congregations, and there is one equal in size at Galatz. There are three congregations in the Dobrudja district (east of the Danube), among them, that of the port Constantsa. There is no synodical bond between these church communities. Excepting Bucharest, they have subjoined themselves to the superior church council of Berlin (see PRUSSIA, III., 1, §1), and are related with the pastors of Rumelia and Bulgaria through conferences. The Jews, in spite of much emigration to the United States, number about 260,000. In 1878 they obtained an equality of status with the Christians, but can acquire no real estate before the end of a naturalization term of ten years. There are from 44,000 to 45,000 Mohammedans in the country (43,470 in 1900), mostly in the Dobrudja, where they have many mosques. Armenians (16,598 in 1900) have a few small congregations in the two capitals and the ports of the Danube. (WILHELM GÖTZ†).

BIBLIOGRAPHY: J. Samuelson, *Roumania Past and Present*, London, 1882; J. H. A. Ubicini, *Les Origines de l'hist. roumaine*, Paris, 1886; R. Bergner, *Rumänien*, Breslau, 1887; T. Tamm, *Ueber den Ursprung der Rumänen*, Bonn, 1891; W. Miller, *The Balkans: Roumania*, London and New York, 1896; G. Benger, *Rumänien im Jahre 1900*, Stuttgart, 1900; F. Damé, *Hist. de la Roumanie contemporaine, 1822–1900*, Paris, 1900; Stourdza, *La Terre et la race roumaines*, Paris, 1904; A. Bellesort, *La Roumanie contemporaine*, Paris, 1905; N. Jorga, "Hist. of the Rumanian Church and of the Religious Life of the Rumanians," Valenii-de Munte, 1909 (in Rumanian); J. Gherghel, *Zur Frage der Urheimat der Rumänen*, Vienna, 1910.

RUMANIAN ORTHODOX CHURCH IN THE UNITED STATES AND CANADA: In the year 1900 Rumanian immigration from Transylvania, in Hungary, began to flow toward the United States, and later followed immigration from Rumania itself. At present there are about 60,000 Rumanians in the United States and Canada. Of these about 35,000 are Uniates (Roman Catholic) from Transylvania and 25,000 Orthodox. Of these last about half come from Rumania and half from Transylvania, and for this reason of the six Orthodox congregations three are under the jurisdiction of the primate of Rumania and three under that of the metropolitan of Hermannstadt in Transylvania. The first congregation of the Orthodox was organized in 1904 at Cleveland, Ohio; other congregations are in East Chicago, Ill.; Lawyer, N. D.; and Regina, Canada. The first congregation of the Rumanian Uniates was also founded in 1904, at Cleveland, Ohio, only a little before the Orthodox congregation of that place. Rumanian Uniate churches are at present located at Scalp Level, Pa.; Aurora, Ill.; Youngstown, Ohio; and New York City. The relations between the Orthodox and Uniate Rumanians are very friendly.

A. A. STAMOULI.

RUNZE, run'tse, **GEORG AUGUST WILHELM:** German Lutheran; b. at Woltersdorf, Pomerania, Feb. 13, 1852. He was educated at the universities of Greifswald and Berlin (1870–74), and after being private tutor in a nobleman's family in Curland, Russia (1874–76), adjunct of the Domkandidatenstift, Berlin (1876–77), and senior in the Studentenkonvikt Johanneum (1878–80), became privat-docent for systematic theology and the philosophy of religion at the University of Berlin in 1880. In 1885 he was made a teacher at the Falk real-gymnasium in Berlin, and since 1890 has been associate professor of systematic theology and the philosophy of religion at the University of Berlin, and instructor in the Lessinghochschule in the same city since 1902. Besides preparing the sixth and seventh editions of C. G. J. Deter's *Abriss der Geschichte der Philosophie* (Berlin, 1898–1901, and 1906), he has written *Schleiermachers Glaubenslehre in ihrer Abhängigkeit von seiner Philosophie* (Berlin, 1877); *Der ontologische Gottesbeweis, kritische Darstellung seiner Geschichte seit Anselm bis auf die Gegenwart* (Halle, 1881); *Grundriss der evangelischen Glaubens- und Sittenlehre* (2 vols., Berlin, 1883–84); *Studien zur vergleichenden Religionswissenschaft* (3 vols., 1889–97); *Praktische Ethik* (1891); *Die akademische Laufbahn und ihre ökonomische Regelung* (anonymous; 1895); *Friedrich Nietzsche als Theolog und als Antichrist* (1896); *Katechismus der Dogmatik* (Leipsic, 1897); *Religionsphilosophie* (1901); and *Metaphysik* (1905); *F. F. Calos Leben und Wirken* (Berlin, 1907; prefixed to Calo's *Photinissa Chrysopulos*); *Der Religionsunterricht eine Gewissensfrage* (Osterwieck, 1908); and *Religion und Geschlechtsliebe* (Halle, 1909).

RUPERT OF DEUTZ.

Rupert of Deutz, an important medieval theologian and abbot of Deutz, was born, probably in Germany, about the middle of the eleventh century; d. at Deutz (now part of Cologne) Mar. 4, 1135. While a child he was brought by St. Laurence to the Benedictine monastery at Liége, his slow talents, he affirmed, being quickened by the special favor of the Virgin; but he refused to receive ordination since the investiture controversy was then raging in Liége (see INVESTITURE). During this early period of his life Rupert composed some hymns, including one, now lost, on the incarnation, a lost work *De diversis scripturarum sententiis*, the fragment of the *Chronicon Sancti Laurentii Leodiensis*, and biographies of Augustine and St. Odilia. On the death of Bishop Waso of Liége, Abbot Berengar was removed from his monastery, and with him, in 1092, Rupert and other Cluniac monks sought refuge in the monastery of St. Hubert in the Ardennes. It was at this time that Rupert wrote his *Libellus hymnorum*, which in its thirteen poems gives a faithful picture of the condition of the Church as it appeared to the eyes of a faithful Ultramontane. A commentary to these hymns is afforded by the chronicle of the monastery, which must have been completed before Aug. 9, 1095, when Berengar and his companions returned to

1. Early Life and Writings.

X.—8

Liége. He now received the ordination which he had refused to accept from the schismatic of Liége, probably after 1106. During this time, moreover, besides his undoubted study of Hebrew, he read deeply in Plato, Plotinus, Dionysius the Areopagite, Aristotle, Heraclitus, Augustine, Jerome, Hilary, Arius, Sabellius, Symmachus, Aquila, Theodotion, and Gregory the Great. In 1111 Rupert wrote his twelve books *De divinis officiis*, which explains the mystical meaning of the priestly office, beginning with the hours, vigils, bells, service of the altar, and vestments. The third book proceeds to the church year, the lessons, and the services on individual feasts, all the rites being explained by an astonishing abundance of symbolical exegeses of Scripture. At the same time he held that unworthy communicants received only the outward forms in the sacrament; and that Christ gives in the Eucharist only his spiritual, not his physical, body.

Rupert was still at Liége when he wrote the *Super Hiob commentarius*, based on the *Moralia* of Gregory the Great. The allegorical method of his predecessor is followed with extreme closeness, Job, for instance, allegorically representing the Savior. But his views had excited some suspicion, and Berengar, anxious to provide for Rupert's safety, recommended him to Abbot Cuno of Siegburg and gained him a patron in Archbishop Frederick of Cologne. Rupert went to Siegburg apparently in 1113, but was soon recalled, and within the year, or at most in 1114, wrote his *De voluntate Dei* to defend himself against the attacks of Anselm's pupils at the cathedral of Laon. The work is in twenty-six chapters and is a critique against the teaching at Laon and Chalons that God's will concerning evil was twofold, one permitting evil deeds and the other approving them, to the end that ultimate good might result. Rupert, on the other hand, maintained that the divine permission of evil by no means implied approval of it, but only divine patience concerning it. In his effort to escape the predestinationalism of William of Champeaux and Anselm, Rupert approximated the position of Johannes Scotus Erigena (q.v.), who regarded evil as in itself non-existent, and as merely the shadow of the substance. Like thoughts filled the twenty-seven chapters of the *De omnipotentia Dei*, the tenth chapter of which establishes the thesis that God desires the salvation of all mankind. The Laon theologians were angered, and Anselm himself complained to Berengar's successor, Heribrand, as though Rupert were still a monk at Liége. Heribrand actually cited Rupert to appear at Liége, where he was acquitted. The opposition still continued, however, and he now assumed the offensive. In 1117 he went to Laon and then disputed at Chalons. Charge after charge was brought against him, only to be refuted with ease. In the midst of the controversy, the course of events changed and Rupert was called from Liége to Cologne, thus returning to his monastery of Siegburg. Here he planned to write on the majesty and the honor of Christ; but from this task he was called by Cuno to prepare a work *In regulam Sancti Benedicti*. The first book tells of its author's learned controversies, the

2. Controversies on the Nature of God.

second of the arrangement of vigils, and the third of the order of the service of the altar, while the fourth deals with the dispute concerning the preeminence of Augustine or Benedict. Still under the patronage of Cuno, Rupert wrote his *In evangelium sancti Joannis commentarius*. This work, which is distinctly allegorical in character, is divided into fourteen books, and was probably written before 1117. After its completion, Rupert finished his *De trinitate et operibus ejus*, which he had begun in 1114. This is the most important of all his writings, and falls into three main portions: the work of the Father, from the beginning of creation to the fall of man; the work of the Son, from the fall to the passion; the work of the Spirit, from the passion to the resurrection at the last day. The major part of the *De trinitate* is occupied with the Old Testament, with the mystical interpretation of its entire ceremonial law and sacrificial ritual. Like Augustine in his "City of God," and like Irenæus, Hilary, Justin, and Hugo of St. Victor, Rupert regards the six ages of the world as embracing the entire history of the earth, the sixth day of history corresponding to the sixth day of creation, as well as to the spirit of fear of Isa. xi. 2, and beginning with the birth of the Son of man. The third part of the entire work now opens, and the four Gospels show the glory of the kingdom in which are developed the gifts of the Holy Ghost, the liberal arts, music, etc.

3. Allegorical, Biographical, and Practical Works.

The *De trinitate* was followed by the *In apocalypsim Joannis apostoli libri duodecim*. Here the seven churches of Asia are compared with the seven women that take hold of one man in Isa. iv. 1, and the glassy sea of Rev. iv. 6 is explained as baptism, through which man passes to the throne of grace as Israel passed through the Red Sea. The serpent that cast water out of his mouth after the woman (Rev. xii. 15–16) typifies Arius with his attack upon the Church. The number 666 is that of man, who was created on the sixth day, without entering the divine heptad. The triple hexad is ruled by Satan, and not only can not, but will not, become a heptad, being triply augmented in its opposition to God. Abbot Cuno was likewise the inspiration of Rupert's *In cantica canticorum commentarius*, also called *De incarnatione Domini*, a work naturally composed in the allegorical exegesis of the period. To this time may belong the charge brought against Rupert that he taught that the Holy Ghost was incarnate in the Virgin. Norbert was the first to make the accusation, and it has been conjectured that Rupert's reply may be embodied in the *Conflictus Ruperti cum Norberto*, which is preserved in two manuscripts at Lobkow and Weissenau. In the *Altercatio monachi et clerici* the controversy between secular and regular priests is discussed, the decision being that a monk may preach after receiving ordination. A like opinion was later expressed by Rupert in his *Epistola ad Everardum* (the abbot of Brauweiler), and his *Epistola ad Liezelinum canonem* on the dignity of monasticism may belong to the same period. It was probably at the request of the abbot of St. Martin in Cologne that Rupert wrote the *Vita Sancti Eliphii*, and about 1120 he also composed his *Vita Sancti Heriberti*. Toward the end of the same year he was chosen tenth abbot of Deutz, and is said to have built a dormitory and the chapel of St. Laurence before the castle doors. To his literary controversies were now added troubles with squatters in the old castle, who were later guilty of burning both the castle and the monastery. In 1120 Abbot Wibald of Stablo wrote Rupert asking whether, in his opinion, self-pollution involved so grave a breach of chastity as to forbid ordination, and Rupert's reply, the *De læsione virginitatis*, constitutes a noteworthy chapter of clerical discipline. If the unique manuscript of the *De vita vere apostolica*, now preserved in the monastery of Grafschaft, is to be ascribed to Rupert, there are here five dialogues essentially on the old question of the relative position of seculars and regulars. Rupert, writing to Canon Liezelin, ranked the monks far above the secular clergy, the regulars being both priests and monks.

4. The Writings of his Later Years.

About this time Rupert wrote his *Commentarius in duodecim prophetas minores*, which seems to have been completed about 1124. It contains little which is especially noteworthy, however, and when Archbishop Cuno interrupted the work, Rupert turned to his *De victoria Verbi Dei*, based on the conversations between the author and his patron during the latter's visits to Deutz, and picturing, in thirteen books, the victory of the Son of God over Satan. After a brief preface, Rupert passes to the names of the fiend, and then the battle breaks out in heaven, rolls over the earth, blazing most fiercely when Christ and Satan enter on the stage of earth, and lasts until the dragon is slain by the Lord. On the completion of this work, Rupert resumed his commentary on the prophets, and at Christmas of the same year (1124) was present at the enthronization of Pope Honorius at Rome. He then visited Monte Cassino, but within the year was one of the signers of a diploma at the monastery of Grafschaft. Shortly after his return to Deutz, Rupert must have begun his *De gloria et honore filii hominis*, a free exegesis of Matthew in thirteen books. He begins with the vision of Ezek. i. 5 sqq., the four cherubim typifying Christ: four, since he is at once God and man, king and priest; man, since he was born in Zion; an ox, since as a priest he offered himself in sacrifice; a lion, since he conquered death and rose from the dead; an eagle, since God ascends above all the heavens. For almost every word of Matthew the Old Testament is cited by Rupert, but in the last book he returns to a philosophical consideration of the necessity of the incarnation. The work can not have been completed before 1126, but it was ready by 1127, and together with it the abbot had written his commentary on the books of Kings. About the same time, moreover, he wrote his *Dialogus inter Christianum et Judæum*, a work of minor importance, except as showing his vast knowledge of the Old Testament and his skill in devising exegetical arguments. On Aug. 25, or Sept. 1, 1128, Deutz was consumed by fire, and Rupert, an eye-witness of the disaster, describes it in his *De incendio oppidi Tuitii*. Soon afterward he composed his *De glori-*

ficatione sanctæ trinitatis et processu Spiritus Sancti, quickly followed by the *De meditatione mortis*. In the latter he holds that the word of God which forbade Adam to eat of the tree of life was a word of the highest grace, in that through the death of the body man is freed from the death of the soul in the death of Christ. About 1130 Rupert also wrote his *In librum Ecclesiastes commentarius*, the method of exegesis being the same as in his other works. Rupert likewise wrote a *De glorioso rege David*, which is no longer extant. The *De glorificatione*, however, was his last important work, and in his later years the infirmities of age seem to have prevented him from continuing his literary labors.

5. Rupert's Theological System.

Essentially an allegorical exegete and a poet, Rupert of Deutz can scarcely be said to possess a formal dogmatic system. Dogmatic problems, indeed, are touched on only in the course of his exegesis, and receive varying answers, in consequence of the varying context; and thus it became possible for the most divergent views to be held concerning his actual position. On the other hand, he appealed constantly to the Bible, and to it alone, so that his view of the universe and his concepts of God and of the world must be drawn from his exegesis. He regarded the Bible in all three senses: literal, allegorical, and moral. In each point of his interpretation the Scriptures were present to his vision as a whole, forming for him a single sentence of many clauses, each word, each syllable, each letter of and for the one thought. The whole system of his interpretation centers about Christology. At the creation the incarnation was already provided for, and the divine command that man should multiply was designed to fill the city of God. In his Christology, moreover, Rupert strongly insisted on the perfect blending of the human and divine natures in Christ; and from his Christology his views concerning the means of grace, especially the Eucharist, become plain. Of the Eucharist he writes (*De divinis officiis*, II., 11): "The body of Christ, which before the passion was the body of the Word alone, so increased through the passion, was so spread abroad, so filled all the world, that by the new diffusion of this sacrament it makes into one Church all the elect that have been from the beginning of the world, or that shall be to the last one chosen at the end of the ages," that the Redeemer may say, when he gives the Church to God, "This is now bone of my bones, and flesh of my flesh." At the same time, there has been much question whether the eucharistic doctrine of Rupert was orthodox or not, his editor, J. Cochlæus, followed by the Maurists, affirming it, while Bellarmine denied it. In the first place, since he regarded the Church as essentially the mystery of the body of Christ, little room was left for the Eucharist. His views on the problem can scarcely be reduced on a definite formula, and passages may be cited from his writings which seem, at first blush, to imply that he taught that the elements merely represented the body and blood of Christ. It is clear, however, that, as a matter of fact, he postulated the reality of the presence, and it is equally evident that he held the doctrine of transubstantiation. The truth is that Rupert, impelled by his general point of view, was involuntarily led to phrases and similes which exposed him to suspicion. Again, while some passages would imply that he taught that unbelievers received only the outward signs of the Eucharist, there is too little evidence on this score to assert positively that such was his doctrine. Thirdly, it would seem that he would have inclined toward the doctrine of impanation, had this been sanctioned by the Church. There is, however, nothing to prove, as is sometimes alleged, that Rupert taught not only consubstantial impanation, but also hypostatic impanation, holding that Christ was united with the bread and wine in the same sense that his divine and human natures were hypostatically united.

The deviations and the inconsistencies of Rupert were those of his age, nor can he be judged by a norm suited neither to him nor his period. It is far more important to know that he was, in his teachings, a mirror of the Church of the twelfth century. In philosophy he was a Platonizing mystic, a follower of Augustine, Johannes Scotus Erigena, Bernard of Chartres, and Odo of Cambray. He was, therefore, essentially opposed to Aristotelianism. By his side in Germany were Gerhoh and Arno of Reichersberg and Honorius of Autun (qq.v.), all Platonizing mystics, in their opposition to Nestorianism almost approximating Eutychianism in their Christology. (R. Rocholl†.)

Bibliography: Frequent editions of the *Opera* were issued from Cologne—by Cochlæus in 1526, 1527, 1528, by Melchior Novesianus in 1539, 1540, 1542, 1577, 1602; an enlarged ed. was put forth by Hermann Mylius at Mainz, 1631; Chastelain's ed. was issued at Paris, 1638; the Benedictine ed. appeared in 1751, and they are in *MPL*, clxvii.–clxx. Parts of the *De incendio* and of the *De gloria et honore Filii hominis* are in *MGH*, *Script.*, xii (1856).

Consult: R. Rocholl, *Rupert von Deutz*, Gütersloh, 1886; idem, in *ZKG*, xxiv. 1 (1903); *ASM*, vol. v.; Jaffe, *BRG*, vol. v.; *Hist. littéraire de la France*, xi. 422–587; J. Bach, *Dogmengeschichte des Mittelalters*, vol. ii., Vienna, 1875; F. W. E. Roth, in *Die katholische Bewegung in unseren Tagen*, vol. xx., parts 16–18, Würzburg, 1887; J. Müller, *Ueber Rupert von Deutz und dessen Vita S. Heriberti*, Cologne, 1888; Wattenbach, *DGQ*, ii (1886), 123, 136, 137, 237, 347, ii (1894), 137, 150–152, 194, 382. Schaff, *Christian Church*, v. 1, pp. 714, 719; Neander, *Christian Church*, iv. 79, 337–338, 411; Hauck, *KD*, iv. 319–320; Vigouroux, *Dictionnaire*, fasc. xxxv., col. 1272.

RUPERT, rū'pert, SAINT: The apostle of the Bavarians; d. at Salzburg early in the eighth century. His biography exists in three recensions: the oldest (between 790 and 800), the *Gesta sancti Hrodberti confessoris* (ed. F. M. Mayer, *Archiv für österreichische Geschichte*, lxiii. 606 sqq., Vienna, 1882); the *Vita primigenia*, the first part of the ninth century *De conversione Bagoariorum et Carantanorum* (*MGH*, *Script.*, xi. 1854, 4–5); and the version in *ASB*, Mar., iii. 702 sqq. According to the *Gesta*, he was a kinsman of the Merovingians and in the second year of Childebert III. (695–711) was bishop of Worms. His fame led to his invitation to Bavaria by Duke Theodo II., and he accordingly went to Regensburg. Urged by his patron to select a see city, Rupert visited Lorch, but did not remain there; and later founded St. Peter's on the Wallersee (Seekirchen in Upper Austria). There he heard of the Roman ruins at Salzach, and received from the duke a grant of four square miles. He then founded at Salzburg the church of St. Peter, a monastery, and also a nunnery for Erindruda of Worms. The *Gesta* thus present the picture of a man laboring in a land only nominally Christian, and seeking primarily to revive a dead faith. It is likewise noteworthy that the *Notitia Arnonis* of 790 (*Salzburger Urkundenbuch*, ed. W. Hauthaler, i. 3 sqq., Salzburg, 1898) represents him simply as a mitred abbot, thus casting doubt on his being called to Bavaria by Theodo, as well as on the entire previous history of his life. Immediate pupils of his and monks invested by him are mentioned in the ninth century *Breves notitiæ Salzburgenses* (viii. 13, ed. G. Kains, Munich, 1869). (A. HAUCK.)

BIBLIOGRAPHY: A very full list of editions of sources and of literature is given in Potthast, *Wegweiser*, pp. 1557-58. Consult, besides the sources named in the text: *ASM*, iii. 1, pp. 340-346; *Hist. littéraire de la France*, iii. 448 sqq.; J. Friedrich, *Das wahre Zeitalter des heiligen Rupert, Apostels der Bayern*, Bamberg, 1866; W. Wattenbach, *Beiträge zur Geschichte der christlichen Kirche in Mähren und Böhmen*, Vienna, 1849; J. G. von Koch-Sternfeld, *Ueber das wahre Zeitalter des heiligen Rupert*, in *Archiv für Kunde österreichischer Geschichtsquellen*, v (1850), 385-497; R. Mittermüller, *Das Zeitalter des heiligen Rupert*, Metten, 1857; P. Heber, *Die vorkarolingischen christlichen Glaubenshelden am Rhein*, pp. 140-148, Frankfort, 1858; A. Huber, *Das Grab des heiligen Rupert*, Vienna, 1869; S. Riezler, *Geschichte Baierns*, vol. i., Gotha, 1878; W. Hauthaler, *Die dem heiligen Rupertus . . . geweihten Kirchen und Kapellen*, Salzburg, 1885; F. von Pichl, *Kritische Abhandlungen über die älteste Geschichte Salzburgs*, Innsbruck, 1889; Rettberg, *KD*, ii. 193 sqq.; Hauck, *KD*, i. 372 sqq.; *DCB*, iv. 562-563.

RUPPRECHT, rū'preHt, **GOTTLIEB FRIEDRICH EDUARD:** German Lutheran; b. at Atzendorf (15 m. s.s.w. of Magdeburg) Mar. 2, 1837. He was educated at the University of Erlangen (1855-59); was a teacher of Latin at Münchberg (1859-61); *vicar* at Fürth, Middle Franconia (1862-64); he was so seriously ill as to be incapacitated for any active life (1864-70), but in 1870 became pastor at Wallesau, Middle Franconia, where he remained eight years. Since 1878 he has been pastor at Sausenhofen, Middle Franconia. In theology he adheres to the system of Thomasius and Hofmann as set forth by the Iowa and Ohio synods of the Lutheran Church; in regard to the Old Testament, however, he is an adherent of Hengstenberg and Keil. He has written: *Was ist Wahrheit* (3 parts, Sagan and Gütersloh, 1875-77); *Die Anschauung der kritischen Schule Wellhausen vom Pentateuch, ein wissenschaftlich begründetes Glaubenszeugnis an die Gegenwart* (Leipsic, 1893); *Der Pseudodaniel und Pseudojesaja der modernen Kritik, ein neues Glaubenszeugnis vor dem Forum des christlichen Glaubens, der Moral und Wissenschaft* (1894); *Das Ende dieses Weltlaufes, zur Einführung in die neutestamentliche Weissagung* (Munich, 1894); *Das Rätsel des Fünfbuches Mose und seine falsche Lösung* (Gütersloh, 1894); *Des Rätsels Lösung, oder Beiträge zur richtigen Lösung des Pentateuchrätsels* (3 vols., 1895-97); *Die Kritik nach ihrem Recht und Unrecht* (1897); *Wissenschaftliches Handbuch der Einführung in das Alte Testament* (1898); *Erklärte deutsche Volksbibel* (Hanover, 1900); and *Das Christentum von D. Adolf Harnack nach dessen sechzehn Vorlesungen* (Gütersloh, 1901).

BIBLIOGRAPHY: E. Timotheus, *Licht im Dunkel, Skizzen aus dem Leben eines süddeutschen Theologen in Novellenform*, Sagan, 1897.

RURAL DEAN. See DEAN (4).

RURER, rū'rer, **JOHANN:** First Protestant pastor of Ansbach; b. at Bamberg; d. at Ansbach about Whitsuntide, 1542. His university career is unknown, but about 1505 he was in Brandenburg, and by 1512 had attained such reputation that he was appointed vicar of St. Catherine's at Ansbach. He soon became chaplain to Margrave Casimir, who later placed him in full control of the parish, where, already an adherent of the teachings of Luther, he was able to exercise a powerful influence on the religious fortunes of the margravate. On Palm Sunday, 1525, he held the first German services at Ansbach, and was soon opposing the margrave, who, for political reasons, saw that he had gone too far toward the Lutheran side. Finding that he could make no impression on Casimir and fearful of arrest, Rurer fled, in Feb., 1527, to Liegnitz, where Duke Frederick sought to secure him for his "Christian school." Before long, however, Rurer was recalled to Ansbach by George, the successor of Casimir, and was made preacher at the collegiate church, a position which he retained until his death. He was one of those appointed to draw up new church regulations for the margravate; he took a prominent part in the conference at Schwabach on June 15, 1528; and was a factor in the three conferences on the Nuremberg proposals in February, May, and December, 1531. Meanwhile he had accompanied the margrave to the Diet of Augsburg in 1530, where, though at first hopeful that an understanding might be reached between Roman Catholics and Protestants, he opposed the compliance of Melanchthon; yet he was one of the clergymen who, dreading the responsibility of resistance to the emperor, advised George not to join the Schmalkald League. Rurer was likewise active in the introduction of the Brandenburg-Nuremberg agenda of 1533, which was a potent weapon in the struggle against Roman Catholics and Anabaptists, although he deprecated the use of violent measures against adherents of the ancient faith. His services to the Protestant cause, including the winning over of the aged Margrave Frederick, were rewarded by George with the income belonging to the dean of the cathedral, L. Keller. Toward the end of his life Rurer was a delegate to a number of diets, but died shortly after the Conference of Regensburg in 1541. (KARL SCHORNBAUM.)

BIBLIOGRAPHY: F. J. Beyschlag, *Sylloge variorum opusculorum*, i. 787 sqq., 864 sqq., 996, ii. 184 sqq., Hall, 1727-1731; C. F. Jacobi, *Geschichte der Stadt Feuchtwangen*, pp. 69-70, Nuremberg, 1833; T. Kolde, *Andreas Althamer*, Erlangen, 1895; K. Schornbaum, *Die Stellung des Markgrafen Kasimir*, Nuremberg, 1900; F. Cohrs, *Die evangelischen Katechismusversuche*, iii. 3 sqq., Berlin, 1901.

RUSHBROOKE, WILLIAM GEORGE: Church of England layman; b. at Ampthill (8 m. s. of Bedford) Jan. 21, 1849. He prepared for the university at the City of London School, 1862-68; became a scholar at St. John's College, Cambridge, 1868, and graduated, taking degrees both in Cambridge and

London University; became senior classical master at the City of London School, 1872; fellow of St. John's College, Cambridge, 1879; and headmaster of St. Olave's Grammar School, 1893. He has issued: *First Greek Reader* (London, 1878); *Synopticon. An Exposition of the common Matter of the Synoptic Gospels* (1880); and *The Common Tradition of the Synoptic Gospels* (in collaboration with E. A. Abbott; 1884).

RUSSELL, CHARLES TAZE. See MILLENNIAL DAWN.

RUSSELL, CHARLES WILLIAM: Roman Catholic; b. at Killough (27 m. s.w. of Belfast), Ireland, May 14, 1812; d. at Dublin Feb. 26, 1880. He received his education at Drogheda, Downpatrick, and at Maynooth College, becoming a Dunboyne student at the latter in 1832; he was made professor of humanity in 1835; was selected for the apostolic vicariate of Ceylon in 1845, became professor of ecclesiastical history at Maynooth in 1845, and president in 1857. His significance lies in two directions; his influence on the Tractarian movement (Newman attributes to him the major influence in his own conversion to Roman Catholicism), and his scholarship in antiquarian matters. He was appointed to the Historical Manuscripts Commission in 1869; published *A Report on the Carte MSS. in the Bodleian Library* (8 vols., Oxford, 1871), in collaboration with John Patrick Prendergast; and compiled the *Calendar of Irish State Papers during the Reign of James I.* (4 vols., 1872–77). He was the author of *The Life of Cardinal Mezzofanti* (1858); and, with M. Kelly, translated from the German of Christian Heinrich Schmid the *Catholic Tales* (3 vols., London, 1846), and also Leibnitz's *System of Theology* (1850).

BIBLIOGRAPHY: *DNB*, xlix. 438–439.

RUSSIA.

I. Early History of the Orthodox Greek Church: The existence of Christianity in Russia as early as the tenth century is shown by the treaty between the Greeks and the Varyags of Kief made in 944, the Christian Varyags being especially obligated to maintain the peace, being called upon at its conclusion to take the oath in the churches of St. Elias, "for," says the annalist, "many Varyages were Christians." A few years later Olga, the widow of Igor, embraced Christianity; and the annals state that Vladimir accepted the faith after listening to the arguments of envoys of the Mohammedan Bulgars, the pope, the Jewish Ḫazars, and a Greek philosopher, his baptism taking place after the capture of Korsun. The scanty account of the monk Jacob (1070) represents that he adopted Christianity of his own accord and through the example of his grandmother Olga, and that he was baptized three years before reducing Korsun. The Christianization of Russia, which was almost contemporaneous with the conversion of Hungary and Poland, was closely connected with Vladimir's alliance with the hard-pressed Byzantine emperors and his marriage with their sister. At Kief the idols were thrown into the river, and the people were driven in throngs to be baptized in the Dnieper. At Novgorod baptism does not seem to have been received without resistance, and Murom and Ryazan were not converted until the end of the eleventh century. It was only in the latter part of the twelfth century that Russia could be considered Christian. Vladimir (d. 1015), Yaroslaw, and Vladimir Monomach (d. 1125) sought to make provision for schools and the training of clergy; and the bishops and metropolitans—the latter, until the Mongol invasion, all Greeks with two exceptions—brought with them a certain degree of culture. But the almost ceaseless wars were unfavorable to the development of clerical life; and theology amounted to little more than polemics against the Latins, with a few ascetic writings, accounts of pilgrimages, annals, and legends. The writings on canon law, however, give glimpses of the civilization of the time. Religious life and culture centered at the eremitic monastery at Kief, founded by a certain Antonius, but influenced more by its second abbot, Theodosius, who introduced the Studite rule. The ideals of the monastery, which was filled chiefly with members of the higher classes, were those of Greek monasticism; but ignorance prevailed, and the cloister exerted influence only over the more cultured grades of society. The masses were openly pagan and utterly ignorant.

1. Beginnings.

The Mongol invasion was a blow to the Church as well as to the kingdom; the metropolitan was either killed or forced to flee, and the same fortunes befell the most of the bishops. After the establishment of Mongol rule, however, the Russian Church shared in the religious toleration of Genghis Khan. The worship, laws, judgments, and property of the Church were undisturbed; and the clergy were exempt from taxation and could exercise jurisdiction over their people in civil and criminal matters. The Russians themselves preferred to bow before the Mongols rather than to submit to Rome. The metropolitans were no longer exclusively Constantinopolitan Greeks, but also numbered native Russians. Meanwhile the grand dukes of Moscow had contrived to enlist the cooperation of the metropolitans as well as the favor of the

2. From the Mongol Invasion.

Mongol khans. The metropolitans imposed upon the opponents of the grand duke bans and interdicts and helped them to unite Russia. Especially is this true of the two most distinguished ones, Peter (d. 1326) who designated Moscow for his burial-place, and Alexei. When Vladimir became the second metropolitan late in 1354, it was to the advantage of Moscow. The relation of the metropolitans to the patriarch was changed by the fall of Constantinople, shortly before the expulsion of the Mongols from Russia. In 1436 the metropolitan Isidore sent from Constantinople to Moscow was imprisoned by the grand duke because he had accepted the Florentine union. The next metropolitan, Jonas, was appointed without confirmation from the patriarch, and Gennadius of Constantinople even granted the Russian Church the right to choose and consecrate its own metropolitans. This practically meant, however, the subjugation of the church to the grand dukes, and no less than eight metropolitans were removed by these princes between the consecration of Jonas and the erection of the Russian patriarchate. During the reign of Ivan IV., "the Terrible," the wilful caprice of that prince dominated the church and the metropolitan Daniel was compelled to validate his fourth marriage. In consequence of this dependence of the metropolitans on the grand dukes, the church of Lithuania separated from that of Moscow and received a metropolitan of its own at Kief. Moscow now retained the archdioceses of Novgorod, Kazan, and Rostov, and the dioceses of Susdal, Ryasan, Tver, Sarai, Kolomna, Smolensk, and Perm. The grand duke of Moscow regarded himself as the real protector of the orthodox faith, and Moscow became a third Rome. It was during this period that Christianity first took deep root in Russia. Monasteries multiplied, among them being that of St. Sergius of Radonesh (d. 1391), where communal monastic life was adopted, as it was at the Cyrillic monastery on the White Sea and at Joseph Sanin's cloister at Volokalamsk. Nil Sorski (1433–1508), on the other hand, defended the ideal of the sketists (see ATHOS), even combining with his pupil Vassian and the grand duke in an unsuccessful attempt to secure the secularization of monastic property at the Moscow Synod of 1503. The sole heresies reported at this period were the "Jewish sect" and the Strigolniki at Novgorod. The latter, about 1375, represented essentially a protest against simoniacal priests, and were soon suppressed. The "Jewish sect" is said to have been founded at Novgorod about a century later by a Jew named Skhariyah (Zachariah), its tenets including denial of the Virgin, icons, crosses, sacraments, fasting, and holy days. Archbishop Gennadius of Novgorod instituted stern measures against them, despite the influence they had obtained over Ivan III.; and after about 1520 nothing more is heard of the sect. Far more important than the Moscow Synod of 1503 was the "Synod of a Hundred Chapters," at Stoglav in 1551, which sought to preserve genuine tradition and to improve moral conditions. Its measures were later disavowed, however, as sanctioning the shibboleth of the Raskolniki (q.v.); the sign of the cross with two fingers, and the double Halleluiah, the triple Halleluiah, and shaving the beard being rejected as Latin heresies. Gennadius of Novgorod now sought, about 1493, to unite the Slavic translations of the Bible, while Macarius prepared Russian lectionaries for the entire year (1541, 1552). But despite the growth of a literature in which translations were still more important than original productions, even the Russian bishops remained ignorant, and Protestant travelers in the land considered Christianity almost non-existent.

3. From the Patriarchate.

In 1589 Job was consecrated independent patriarch of Russia, as one of the four of the Orthodox Greek Church. The Patriarch Hermogen, aided by hatred of and aversion to the Latin Church, prevented the Poles from becoming masters of Moscow during the period of chaos. When Michael Romanoff ascended the throne, his father was made patriarch and virtual regent (1619), and similar power was enjoyed for a time by his third successor, Nikon (q.v.). The latter, in 1667, carried through a reform of the liturgy, thus leading to the great schism of the Raskolniki. In 1654 the metropolitanate of Kief was reunited, after long preliminary negotiations, with Moscow. At Kief, moreover, contact with the West and polemics with the Roman Catholic Church had resulted in the growth of a type of scholastic learning, and in 1631 Petrus Mogilas (q.v.) had founded a college in the city. From this school proceeded many distinguished men—Silvester Medviedeff, who began the controversy over the instant of the transformation of the bread in the Eucharist, in which for the first time the methods of Western theology were employed; Dimitri, metropolitan of Rostov (1651–1709); Stephan Yavorski (d. 1722), patriarch and the assistant of Peter the Great, who founded the holy synod to take the place of the patriarch; and Theophanes Prokopovich (d. 1736), archbishop of Novgorod, ecclesiastical adviser of Peter, and for a century the authority in dogmatics and pulpit oratory. In 1764 the monasteries were secularized under Peter III. and Catharine II. The early part of the reign of Alexander I., like the rule of Catharine, favored the Enlightenment, but gradually the czar turned toward mysticism. In 1812 a Bible society was established, but in 1824 the orthodox archimandrite Photius of Novgorod changed the course of events. The Bible society and the Protestant mission in Transcaucasia were suppressed under Nicholas I., and in 1835 with Protassoff began the series of conservative chief procurators of the Holy Synod, later ably represented by Pobiedonostsev (q.v.), a firm opponent of Protestantism. The dogmatic theology of Russia during the nineteenth century was likewise predominantly anti-Protestant, until Yanisheff brought on a more favorable reaction. At the present time notable services are rendered, especially in the department of church history. The theological seminaries in St. Petersburg, Moscow, Kief, and Kazan have their own journals; the first three have published translations of the Church Fathers and the last a translation of the ecumenical councils.

II. Statistics: According to the census of 1897, published in 1905, the population of European and Asiatic Russia, numbering 125,640,021 (not including Finland; see below), was distributed as follows: Orthodox Greek including the United Greek Church, 87,123,604; dissidents, including the Old Believers, 2,204,596; Roman Catholics, who form 74 per cent of the population of Russian Poland, 11,506,809; Lutherans, mostly in the Baltic provinces, 3,572,653; Armenian Gregorians, 1,179,241; Armenian Catholics, 38,840; Reformed, 85,400; Mennonites, 66,564; Baptists, 38,139; Church of England, 4,183; other Christians, 3,952; Mohammedans, 13,906,972; Jews, 5,215,805; Buddhists, 433,863; Karaites, 12,894; and other non-Christians, 285,321.

1. The Orthodox Greek Church: According to the representation of the procurator of the holy synod the gain was from 79,115,820 in 1898 to 86,259,732 in 1902. In 1902 there were 49,703 churches, including 723 cathedrals, 46,827 priests, and 58,529 cantors. A parish is normally inherited by the son-in-law of the previous incumbent. In 1898 the official income of the Orthodox Church was about 60,000,000 rubles (ruble, 51 cents), 40,000,000 from the State and 10,000,000 direct gifts, while the budget of the holy synod in 1900 was 24,000,000 rubles, and the imperial budget for 1906 was 29,126,000 rubles for the Orthodox Church, and 1,752,000 for others. The czar is the head of the Russian Church and the directing power is the holy synod, which, by the ukase of 1763, must include six clerical members, among them the three metropolitans and the exarch of Georgia; and now includes seven bishops and a proto-presbyter, the confessor of the czar. The presiding officer is the metropolitan of St. Petersburg, and the rank of a clerical member is held by the chief procurator, who is a minister of state. There are three metropolitans (St. Petersburg, Moscow, and Kief) and fourteen archbishops, though these have no actual superiority in rank. The exarch of Grusia, or Georgia, alone has jurisdiction over his bishops. Each bishop is aided by a consistory, whose members are appointed by the synod at his nomination; and the supervision of religious instruction and censorship are especially under his control. The eparchies, or dioceses, generally correspond to the provinces, and there are sixty-six, nearly fifty in European Russia. The bishops frequently rise through a series of dioceses. The monasteries number 862, of which only the most famous have many inmates; among these are the cave-monastery, and the monastery of St. Sergius, of Alexander Nevski at St. Petersburg (the three lauras besides the one at Potchaiev in Volhynia), and of Solovetski on the White Sea. In 1902 the monks numbered 8,455 with 8,090 aspirants, and the nuns 10,082 with 31,533 aspirants. The higher clergy are drawn from the monks, but they are such only as a transient stage in their promotion. The real monks guard relics and icons, collect alms, and by singing increase the dignity of the service. Of the half-million white or secular clergy, barely 35,000 were priests (" popes ") in 1887, the remainder being deacons or psalmodists, sacristans, sextons, and bell-ringers. The theological seminaries and academies are more for the education of the sons of priests than of the future clergy. In 1899 there were 58 seminaries with 19,642 students; 4 academies with 930 students; and 185 secondary schools. The clergy have no fixed income, except in the western provinces, where they must protect the Orthodox Church against Roman Catholicism and Protestantism. They are accordingly obliged to use their sacred calling as a means of gain, and possess scant educational influence. They enjoy little respect except when conducting services, which they make full of pomp. To many Russians worship is chiefly reverence of the icons by crossing themselves, lighting candles, prostrations, and genuflexions. Sermons are rare. The chief saint, next to the Virgin, is St. Nicholas. The rigorous fasting, for which the Russians were long famous, seems to have been mitigated in recent years. In 1905 freedom of worship was granted to the Old Believers, but reclamation from schism, as well as the conversion of the non-faithful, has always formed a prominent activity of the Russian Church with the aid of the State. Between 1840 and 1890 there were 1,172,758 conversions, including 580,000 Greek Uniates, Roman Catholics, and Protestants. The average annual converts from Judaism number 936, from Mohammedanism 1,315, and from paganism 3,104. In Japan Russian missionary efforts are phenomenally successful.

2. The Evangelical Church: The Protestants in Russia, including Poland but excluding Finland, numbered (1897) 3,762,756; of whom there were 1,790,489 Germans, 1,435,937 Letts, 1,002,738 Esthonians, and 351,169 Finns (in Russia). Of

1. Lutherans in Russia Proper. these 3,322,242 were Lutherans: 799,748 in the consistorial district of St. Petersburg; 454,912 in Moscow; 659,291 in Courland; and 1,156,083 in Livonia. The confession of the Lutheran Church in Russia is that of the Book of Concord, and of all the Russian Protestants the Lutherans of the Baltic provinces are the most prominent. Livonia sympathised with Lutheranism from the first, but it was unable to withstand the armies of Ivan IV. When, in 1561, it submitted to Poland, protection was promised to Lutheranism. At the same time an Evangelical Church was organised in Courland. Attempts at a Roman Catholic propaganda in Livonia were frustrated by the invasion of Gustavus Adolphus, which assured the continuance of the existing state of affairs. Even when the country came under Russian control, the Augsburg Confession remained supreme, though freedom of worship was guaranteed for the Greek Church. In the reorganization of the church after the war between Russia and Sweden the pietism of Halle found welcome in Livonia, as did the doctrines of Herrnhut (1729–43, 1764). On the other hand, rationalism was disseminated from Riga throughout Livonia, at first finding a foothold even in the new center of spiritual life created by the establishment of the University of Dorpat in 1802. In 1849 the schools were placed under the control of the nobility and clergy, and were raised by the aid of the Church to a standard approximating that of the Germans. In 1832 the Lutheran Church of the Baltic provinces was united with the remainder of the denomination in the interior of the empire by means of a general consistory, meeting at St. Petersburg. This consistory is composed of a lay president and clerical vice-president (appointed by the czar), and of two clerical and two lay delegates serving for three years each. Administratively it is under the control of the minister of the interior, judicially it is subject in general to the senate. Until 1890 the consistories of Riga, Reval, and Oesel, each with a superintendent at the head, were retained side by side with those of Courland, Livonia, and Esthonia; but in the latter year they were merged in their provincial consistories. In 1794 the order for the training of children of mixed marriages was made applicable to Esthonia, and in 1857 all penal jurisdiction in provinces claimed by the State Church was extended to the Baltic provinces. This was of the utmost importance, in that, 1845–48, a tenth of the population of Livonia had been led to enter the Russian Church, and then a considerable number returned to their former faith. By an oral declaration of Alexander II. the penalty was removed from receiving of such reconverts, and about 30,000 returned to the Lutheran Church. When, however, Pobiedonostzeff assumed control, the Russian Church claimed these members, and the resisting Lutheran clergy of Livonia were prosecuted and disciplined. It was not until the accession of Nicholas II. that affairs were at all ameliorated, and the first real assistance was afforded by the proclamation of religious toleration at Easter in 1905. The consistorial district of Courland had (1904) 129 parishes with 117 clergy, and an outlying diaspora of 19 churches, 42 chapels, and 23 clergy in the provostship of Vilna, and the governments of Kovno, Grodno, Vilna, Minsk, Mohileff, and Vitebsk. The district of Livonia has 154 parishes and 180 clergy; and that of Esthonia, 57 parishes and 69 clergy. In Livonia the Unity of the Brethren and Baptists are decreasing, but the latter gained a solid footing in Courland in 1857. In 1882 they numbered in these provinces, 5,884, with 10 churches and as many missionaries. The Lutherans in the interior of the Russian Empire are divided into two widely extended consistorial districts. The consistory of St. Petersburg stretches over eighteen governments from the Gulf of Finland and the White Sea to the Black Sea and the Sea of Azov. The consistory of St. Petersburg reported in 1910 641,000 Lutherans, of whom 390,000 were Germans, 133,000 Finns, 84,000 Esthonians, 26,800 Letts, 6,200 Swedes, and 1,000 belonged to other nationalities. The city of St. Petersburg lies at the heart of a district with 22 German colonies and many congregations in cities, besides 19 Finnish churches; and itself has 13 Lutheran congregations, with (1904) about 105,000 members. The number shows a marked diminution, due in great measure to the law that the children of mixed marriages must be brought up in the Orthodox Greek faith. In Kief the Lutheran community, founded in 1767, numbers about 5,500. The Lutheran colonies in the government of Kief are now mostly combined into the independent parish of Radomysl, with between 8,000 and 9,000 members in some 40 places. In the government of Volhynia, where the first colonies were formed in 1816, there were some 75,000 Evangelicals by 1885, scattered abroad among the dissident Methodist or Baptist propaganda. In the governments of Bessarabia, Cherson, Taurien, Yekaterinoslaf, and the southwest district of the Don Cossacks, many Lutherans are scattered in thirty-four parishes. The community of Odessa, founded in 1804, had in 1905 about 7,000 members. Swabian colonies in this part of Russia are noteworthy for their spiritual zeal, and show tendencies that expose them to Baptist proselyting. A separate community was founded by immigrants from Württemberg at Hoffnungsthal in 1817, and in 1881 numbered 2,009. Far larger than the St. Petersburg consistory is that of Moscow, under a general superintendent, which embraces all eastern Russia in Europe, as well as the Caucasus, Transcaspia, and Siberia. In 1910 the consistory contained 459,000 Lutherans, of whom 411,000 were Germans, 22,000 Letts, 3,000 Finns, 600 Swedes, 1,000 Armenians, and 400 others. In the diaspora covering the eighteen governments from Tver to Astrakhan, outside of Saratof and Samara, there is only the colonial community of Kharkof of 3,500 members; the isolated Lutherans almost inevitably give up their denomination, and even in the oldest Lutheran communities of the Empire no family remains Evangelical for more than a century in consequence of the law governing mixed marriages. A compact Lutheran population is found in the colonies of the governments of Saratof and Samara, which also includes the Unity of the Brethren community of Sarepta, founded in 1764. Over 25,000 colonists, mostly from central Germany, accepted the invitation of Catharine II. in 1763, and reached the Volga in 1767. Their privileges were annulled in 1872, and their schools were placed under state control. They now number 406,170, despite extensive emigration; and are divided into 32 parishes. Their interest in religion, however, is keen, and they possess five hospitals, four orphan asylums, and a deaf and dumb asylum. Three parishes are Reformed. A number of colonists migrated from the Volga to Stavropol and Piatigorsk north of the Caucasus, where at Karas a Scotch mission has been active since about 1820. Chiliastic hopes and opposition to rationalism led many to emigrate from Württemberg to Georgia in 1817, where they were served for a time by missionaries from Basel. They have recently been included in the consistory of Moscow, and have ten congregations with twelve pastors. The congregation at Tiflis includes about 3,000 members. Transcaspia forms a single parish, with but one pastor. In Siberia, from the Ural to the Pacific, there were, in 1880, about 6,650 Lutherans, about 5,000 being in the colonies of exiles at Omsk and Yeniseisk, about 1,400 in the cities, and the remainder in penal institutions. They now possess eight parishes with eight pastors.

2. Lutherans in Finland and Poland. The grand duchy of Finland had, in 1900, a population of 2,673,200, of whom 48,812 were Orthodox, 560 Roman Catholics, 2,620,891 Lutherans, 2,630 Baptists, and 317 Methodists. The Lutheran clericals number 758 in 512 parishes; and are controlled administratively by four bishops (the bishop of Abo being also archbishop of Finland) and by the cathedral chapter, while the legislative body is the general synod, two-fifths of the members being clerical. The supreme control of the Church, however, devolves on the department for spiritual affairs in the Finnish senate. The laws proposed by the synod must, on the one hand, be approved by the diet and confirmed by the emperor; and, on the other hand, laws may be proposed by the priest diets, which, when affecting the liturgy, must be sanctioned by the congregations. The pastors nominate the provosts, canons, and three candidates for the bishopric, of whom the emperor selects one. The congregations are free to choose their pastors and officers. Since 1868 only religious instruction has been left officially to the Church; but as a matter of fact the majority of the presidents of the school boards are Lutheran clergymen, and all the principal teachers of the secondary schools must be Lutherans. At the University of Helsingfors there are four professors of theology, and the entire school system of the grand duchy is well organized. For the Finnish Bible Society, see BIBLE SOCIETIES, II., § 5. Since 1859 Finland has had its own missionary society which works, in collaboration with the Rhenish mission, in the Ovambo district, West Africa, having five stations and thirteen missionaries. Finnish missionary activity likewise endeavors to reclaim the Lapps of the far north, who have almost fallen back into paganism because of the constant lack of preachers (see LAPPS). In the spiritual life of the Finnish Church two opposing tendencies may be distinguished: one pietistic, laying all its stress on repentance and sanctification, and the other emphasizing forgiveness of sins by grace and joy in the perfected atonement. Also a Biblical stands in contrast with an ecclesiastical tendency. See FINLAND, CHRISTIANIZATION OF. The ten governments of the former kingdom of Poland had, in 1871, a population of 6,026,421, of whom 4,596,956 were Roman Catholics, and 327,845 were Protestants. The Lutheran parishes number sixty-five. At the time of dismemberment only two Lutheran parishes remained, those of Warsaw and Vengrov. The others have sprung from German immigration since. The control of the Polish Lutherans is vested in the Evangelical Augsburg Consistory at Warsaw, which has been subject to the ministry of the interior from 1867. The lay president is appointed by the emperor, and the clerical president, who is at the same time general superintendent, by the minister. Five superintendents (at Warsaw, Kalish, Augustovo, Petrikau, and Plock) are under the control of the general superintendent. The pastors are chosen by the congregations and confirmed by the consistory. They are members of the church boards which, in every congregation, not only administer the secular side of the church, but also supervise the pastors and other officials and provide for the poor. The schools are now withdrawn from Evangelical control. German Lutherans have migrated in large numbers from the Polish to the Russian provinces of the empire in recent decades, and it is only of late years that the Polish Evangelicals have thrown off the influence of rationalism.

The Reformed Church in Russia enjoys greater freedom than the Lutheran in the control of its property and the conduct of its services. On the other hand, it lacks the bond of a common creed and is less consolidated. It consists of two large bodies, the synod of Lithuania and the consistory of Warsaw. The other nine communities are controlled by the independent "Reformed sessions" coordinated with the Lutheran consistories at St. Petersburg, Moscow, Riga, and Mitau, and composed of the secular members of the Lutheran consistories, the Reformed pastors, and one or two elders. Their powers are limited to marriage, the examination and ordination of pastors, discipline of their clergy, and the presentation of candidates for approval to the minister of the interior, under whose jurisdiction they stand. In the consistorial session of St. Petersburg there are the French and German congregations in the capital, and churches at Odessa, Chabag, Neudorf, and Rohrbach. The German Reformed at St. Petersburg number about 3,000, and are active not only in religion, but also in philanthropy and education. At Riga there were, in 1881, 1,843 Reformed; 118 in the smaller cities of Livonia; and 88 in Reval. The Reformed community at Moscow numbered about 2,000 in 1882, and at Mitau about 400. The Reformed Church in Lithuania is controlled by the Lithuanian synod, to which each member of the congregation belongs. The decisive vote, however, rests in the *synedrium*, a committee composed of the *curatores nati*, the superintendent, and elected lay "curators." The executive body, under the supervision of the minister of the interior, is the Reformed *collegium* at Vilna, composed of four clerical and four lay members. The synod comprises three districts: the Samogitian with four Lithuanian communities and 10,600 members (1881), and two Polish congregations with about 300 Poles and Germans in the government of Kovno; the district of Vilna with four congregations in the government of Vilna; and the district of White Russia with five congregations in the governments of Grodno and Minsk. The schools formerly controlled by the Reformed Church in the Samogitian district were closed by the State in 1869, and replaced by state schools. The Reformed Church of the former kingdom of Poland is governed by a synod and a consistory. The former, in which only delegates of the individual churches are now allowed to vote, rules on general matters concerning the church; while the consistory, chosen from the synod, proposes new measures, carries out the resolutions of the synod, and decides questions concerning marriage. The individual congregations are represented by presbyteries, to which the pastor belongs. This consistorial district embraces six pastoral congregations, of which that of Warsaw is the largest with (1887) 2,700 members; three branch congregations with 7,659 pastoral members and 3,957 communicants; the Reformed in Lodz; and a number of scattered representatives of the denomination. The denomination controls several schools, but is compelled to support the elementary crown schools. The small embassy churches are entirely independent, these being the Dutch in St. Petersburg; six Church of England, in St. Petersburg, Kronstadt, Odessa, Moscow, and Riga; and an Anglo-American Congregational church at St. Petersburg. In Archangel the Lutherans and Reformed united in 1818. The Unity of the Brethren congregation at St. Petersburg numbers about 45. The Mennonites, who settled in the governments of Tauris, Yekaterinoslaf, and Samara after 1784 and 1804, numbered 34,217 in 1860, while in 1903 there were in Samara 1,218 Mennonites in 10 congregations. Since 1880 the Baptists have been officially recognized.

III. Sectarianism in Russia: The stress laid by the Eastern Church on the forms of worship as a means of grace, with consequent insistence on the abrogation of all innovations and opposition to any alleged emendation, however slight, became the cause of Russian sectarianism when, in the seventeenth century, the attempt was made to revise the liturgy. In the course of time deviations in ritual had naturally developed, but in 1551 the "Synod of the Hundred Chapters" had definitely sanctioned the liturgy then observed. When the task of printing the ritual began, the uncertainties of the text became painfully evident, and while stern measures were adopted to prevent emendations, the double halleluiah was substituted for the triple (1610) and the sign of the cross with two fingers was adopted (1641) —the principal matters of the subsequent controversy. When Nikon (q.v.) became patriarch, he energetically undertook the emendation of the rituals and had them sanctioned by the synods of 1654–56. The form of the Greek and old Slavonic books was made the norm, and the approbation of the patriarchs of Antioch, Servia, and Constantinople was secured. Reforms of so sweeping a character naturally evoked opposition, but the vigorous policy of Nikon prevailed, and the synod of 1656 pronounced the anathema over the adherents of the old uses. His enemies gradually gained strength, however, but even while the synod of 1666–67 condemned Nikon, it confirmed his reform, and thus became the starting-point of the great schism which still exists in the Russian Church. In the north it was the monastery of Solovetskii on the White Sea that formed the center of the opposition. It was treacherously surrendered in 1676, after a seven years' siege, and 400 of its inmates were put to death. Yet this, and other stern measures, failed to crush the "ancient faith." The new ritual was regarded by its opponents as the doctrine of Antichrist. The making of the sign of the cross with three fingers instead of two, the pronunciation Iisus instead of Isus ("Jesus"), the threefold halleluiah instead of the twofold during mass, the four-armed cross instead of the eight-armed, celebration with seven "prosphers" instead of with five, procession in a direction contrary to the apparent course of the sun, the omission of "very" (instead of "Lord") as applied to the Holy Ghost in the Nicene Creed, and the prayer "Jesus Christ, our God" instead of "Jesus Christ, Son of God" were all considered essential heresies of Antichrist. Later still numerous other heresies were alleged against the State Church, especially all innovations of Peter the Great and the entire infiltration of occidentalism.

1. Origin.

Within the schism itself the dying-out of priests ordained before the separation from the State Church led to a distinction between the "Priestly" (*Popovshchina*) and "Priestless" (*Bezpopovshchina*), since the lack of any bishop rendered it necessary either to have all sacraments administered by priests who had renounced the State Church, or entirely to surrender the sacraments excepting baptism, which, in case of necessity, might be performed by a layman. The *Popovshchina*, as the less radical sectaries, were the more successful in founding a new church. Their chief center at the end of the seventeenth century was on the island of Vietka in one of the tributaries of the Dnieper, in the government of Moghilef, where more than 30,000 gathered. Two attacks, in 1735 and 1764, destroyed their possessions, and many of them were exiled, chiefly to Siberia. While Nijni-Novgorod was a favorite residence of the *Skiti*, a sub-sect of the *Popovshchina*, the center of the latter became Starodub in the government of Chernigof. Since 1771, except for an interruption of a few years, the Rogoshski cemetery at Moscow has been the center of the *Popovshchina*, as the Preobradshenski cemetery has been for the *Bezpopovshchina*. The question of reanointing priests who had become converts from the State Church led, in 1779, to a loss of the prestige of the *Popovshchina*, who were forbidden in 1832 to receive priests from the Russian Church. A few years later, however, they received priests ordained by a deposed Bosnian patriarch, though they were long obliged to officiate in secret. A variety of liturgical and other questions have caused more or less serious divisions among the *Popovshchina;* while the permission of the Synod (1800) for priests to officiate according to the ancient rite resulted in the reconciliation of many *Popovshchina* with the Church—the *Yedinovyeretzi*, or "Coreligionists." The monasteries of the *Yedinovyeretzi* are recognized by the State, but they have not been able to obtain an independent hierarchy. The number of this sect scarcely exceeds a million; in 1886 it possessed 244 churches.

2. The Popovshchina.

The *Bezpopovshchina*, who number between two and three million, are much more radical than the *Popovshchina*, and are split into a greater number of minor sects. Their chief home is between Lakes Ladoga and Onega and the White Sea, so that they are termed *Pomoryane*, or "Sea-Dwellers." Since all priests ordained before the time of Nikon had died, these sectaries declared that the time of Antichrist had come, in which all sacraments except baptism were abrogated. Instead of ordained priests they had only elders and readers, who expounded the Scriptures, heard confessions, and baptized, the mode of baptizing being the cause of many divisions. They observe the fasts of the Russian Church, venerate icons and relics, and avoid tobacco, sugar, and certain sorts of food. Their formal organization was begun in 1691, and their monastery on the River Vyga long formed their center. After the time of Peter the Great they enjoyed a certain degree of toleration;

3. The Bezpopovshchina.

but when, in 1738, some of them were willing, for political reasons, to include intercession for the czar and his family in their prayers, the majority proved recalcitrant, and the two sub-sects (both named from their founders) of "Philipists" and "Feodosians" were consequently formed, refusing to have any fellowship with their former comrades. The most difficult problem for the *Bezpopovshchina* was that of marriage. Their quasi-monastic ideals proving impracticable, some renounced religious marriage, others rejected its indissolubility, and others still would not tolerate marriage at all, so that their level of morality proved inferior to that of the orthodox. The abolition of marriage could not be carried out; the *novoshennye* ("newly wedded") were married by priests of the State Church and then did penance. From the Filipovtzi, toward the end of the eighteenth century, arose the "Pilgrims" (*Stranniki*) or "Fugitives" (*Byeguny*), who, in supposed conformity with Matt. x. 37–38, forsook their homes and families, rejected legal marriage and the certificate of naturalization with the seal of "Antichrist," and ate no food from the vessels of strangers. A sub-sect of the "Pilgrims" intentionally postponed their vow of wandering until toward the end of their lives, but occupied a less honored position. From the loss of a hierarchy others of the "priestless" Russian sectaries inferred that the sacraments and public worship were altogether abrogated, as by several divisions of the Netovtzi ("Deniers"). The "Non-Prayers" respected only the prayer of the heart, and even regarded all prayer as an affront to the divine omniscience, and explained all Christian doctrine as allegorical; the Molchalniki ("Silent") refused to speak, even under torture; others used raisins instead of wine in the Eucharist; and the tenets of others are still unknown.

Besides these sects there are a number of others which did not originate from the schism of 1667, which is called the *raskol* ("schism") *par excellence*, whence its adherents are known as Raskolniks ("Schismatics"). Among them mention should first be made of certain mystics who are not separated externally from the Orthodox Church, but frequently seem to be her most zealous members. These are the "People of God," or Khlysty ("Flagellants"), probably a corruption of Khristy ("Christs"). According to their account, God descended in 1645 on Mount Gorodin in the government of Vladimir, and took up his abode in the peasant Daniel Philippov, who chose as his son, "Christ," the peasant Ivan Suslov, who in turn chose a "Mother of God" and twelve apostles. Suslov is said to have been twice crucified, to have risen and been manifested to his followers, and to have lived until 1716. Since that time the Khlysty have had many "Christs" (including Peter III.; see § 5). Each member of the sect is expected to endeavor to become a "Christ" or a "Mother of God" by mortification of the flesh and prayer. The "ships" in which the Khlysty gather are directed by a prophet or angel, aided by a prophetess, and the commands of these prophets are the law of their adherents. The twelve commands of Philippov are

4. The Khlysty.

also still in force, including abstinence from intoxicating liquors and all carnal indulgence. They hold that the essential baptism is that of the Spirit, and they celebrate the Eucharist with the triturated Easter prospher and the water blessed at the feast of the Epiphany. Dancing and singing form the principal parts of their religious exercises, the men in the center and the women on the outside circling round with frantic gestures (supposed to imitate the flying of the angels) until exhausted and even unconscious (cf. ECSTASY); while the incoherent phrases which they utter are taken to be prophecies. The secrecy attaching to the Khlysty enhances their prestige, but much of the scandal popularly ascribed to them seems apocryphal. The exact relation of the Skakuny ("Jumpers") to the Khlysty is problematical.

5. The Skoptzi.

An offshoot of the Khlysty is formed by the Skoptzi ("Self-Castrators"). They were founded by a certain Selivanov (whose real name is unknown), who, about 1770, declared himself to be Peter III. and a son of God. Banished to Siberia, he was permitted to return by Paul I., but was confined as insane until released by Alexander I. He then enjoyed quasi-divine honor in St. Petersburg, but in 1820 he was again placed in confinement in the monastery of Suzdal, where he died in 1832, a centenarian. In opposition to the licentiousness of some Khlysty, Selivanov laid all stress on Matt. xix. 12, xviii. 8–9, distinguishing between the "royal seal" and "second purity" (partial castration). Women usually have the breasts amputated. Many Skoptzi are "white doves" or "pure spirits" only after they have begotten children, and others are nominally married. Selivanov is considered the perfect redeemer. The Skoptzi, who on principle deny that they belong to the sect, carry on an active propaganda, and all measures to suppress them have failed. Their number is estimated at between two and three thousand, many of them emigrants to Rumania.

6. The Molokani.

Opposition to the ceremonial of the Orthodox Church is embodied in the Molokani ("Milk Drinkers") and Dukhobors (q.v.), who reject the sacraments and are officially designated as rationalistic sects. Scorning ceremonial, a special priesthood, and the veneration of icons, they maintain that the only worship of God is in spirit and that the heart of man is the sole true temple of God. Instead of baptism by water they demand the baptism of the Spirit, instead of confession to a priest confession to each of the brethren, and instead of the Eucharist meditation on the words of Christ. The origin of the Molokani is obscure, nor are they officially mentioned until 1765. They claim that the Bible is their sole foundation, and though they explain it allegorically, they do not reject the historical elements in the Gospel. They refuse to eat pork, but in general their doctrines are vague, so that much diversity of opinion prevails among them. Their congregations meet in private houses, each body having a presbyter and two assistants conspicuous for uprightness of life. Their devotions consist of prayer, the singing of hymns and reading of the Bible, and conversations on religious themes. Their morality is high, and their readiness to assist one another has led to frequent experiments in communism. Theoretically they hold that earthly rulers are only for the worldly, so that many of them refuse to pay taxes, take oaths, or perform military service, but practically they are, as a rule, loyal and peaceful subjects. Large inroads have been made in their numbers by the Baptists and Stundists. The Molokani are also held by some investigators to include the Subotniki ("Sabbatarians"), who, though having no affinities with Judaism, observe Saturday as the Sabbath, practise circumcision, and observe the dietary laws.

There are many minor mystic and rationalistic Russian sects, such as the "Sighers," "Spiritual Brethren," "Nameless," etc. The most important development of Russian sectarianism, however, is that of the Stundists, who arose about 1864, primarily in southern Russia. They seem to have originated from devotional "hours" (Germ. *Stunden*) held in the German colony of Rohrbach and visited by Russians. Under Baptist influence Stundism assumed a position of hostility toward the ritual, sacraments, and icons of the Orthodox Church, and at the same time incurred the suspicions of the government for supposed German tendencies. Stundism seems no longer connected with the Baptist denomination, but it has developed the sub-sect of Malovantsi (named from its founder, the peasant Kondrat Malovani, who is supposed to be the Messiah), who resemble the Khlysty.

7. The Stundists.

The number of Russian sectaries is too vague to be stated even approximately, the figures assigned ranging from 3,000,000 to 15,000,000.

(N. Bonwetsch.)

Bibliography: For the background in the history of the people, country, literature, and civilization consult: W. K. Kelly, *Hist. of Russia*, London, 1854; A. von Haxthausen, *The Russian Empire: its People, Institutions, and Resources*, 2 vols., London, 1856; A. Rambaud, *Hist. of Russia*, 3 vols., London, 1887; H. H. Howorth, *Hist. of the Mongols*, 3 vols., London, 1888; D. M. Wallace, *Russia*, new ed., London, 1905; A. Brückner, *Geschichte Russlands bis zur Ende des 18. Jahrhunderts*, Gotha, 1896; S. Wolkonsky, *Pictures of Russian History and Russian Literature*, Boston, 1897; A. Leroy-Beaulieu, *L'Empire des tsars et les russes*, 4th ed., 3 vols., Paris, 1897–98; P. Milukow, *Skizzen russischer Kulturgeschichte*, 2 vols., Leipsic, 1898–1901; K. Waliszewski, *Hist. of Russian Literature*, New York, 1900; W. K. Morfill, *Hist. of Russia from Peter the Great to Alexander II.*, New York, 1901; F. H. E. Palmer, *Russian Life in Town and Country*, New York, 1903; R. U. Bain, *The First Romanovs (1613–1725): Hist. of the Muscovite Civilization*, New York, 1905; A. Ular, *Russia from Within*, New York, 1905; Jeremiah Curtin, *The Mongols in Russia*, Boston, 1908; A. Brückner *Russlands geistliche Entwicklung im Spiegel seiner schönen Literatur*. Tübingen, 1908; T. H. Pantenius, *Geschichte Russlands von der Entstehung des russischen Reiches bis zur Gegenwart*, Leipsic 1908; D'Abnour, *Hist. abrégée des peuples de la Russe*. Paris 1910.

For the history of the church nearly all the literature under Eastern Church is pertinent, and the most important entries are cited there in classified form. The literature under Nikon, Photius, and Platon is also to be consulted. P. Strahl, *Beiträge zur russischen Kirchengeschichte*, Halle, 1827; idem, *Geschichte der russischen Kirche*, vol. i., ib. 1830; A. N. Mouravieff *Hist. of the Church of Russia*, London, 1842; H. Lutteroth *Russia and the Jesuits, from 1772 to 1820*, ib. 1858; H. Dalton, *Geschichte der reformierten Kirche in Russland*. Gotha, 1865; idem, *Beiträge zur Geschichte der evangelischen Kirche in Russland*, 4 vols., ib. 1887–1905; idem, *Die russische Kirche*, Leipsic, 1892; Gayarin, *Russian Clergy*, London, 1872; Philaret, *Geschichte der Kirche Russlands*, 2 vols., Frankfort, 1872; *The Patriarch and the Tsar, from the Russian by William Palmer*, 3 vols., London, 1871–73; M. Kostomorov, *Russische Geschichte in Biographien*, Leipsic, 1889; F. Nippold, *Handbuch der neuesten Kirchengeschichte*, ii. 247 sqq., Berlin, 1901; F. Kattenbusch, in W. D. Grant, *Christendom anno Domini 1901*, i. 388 sqq., New York, 1902; L. K. Götz, *Das Kiewer Höhlenkloster als Kulturzentrum des vormongolischen Russland*, Passau, 1904; idem, *Kirchenrechtliche und Kulturgeschichtliche Denkmäler Altrusslands*, Stuttgart, 1905; idem, *Staat und Kirche in Altrussland. Kiewer Periode 988 bis 1240*, Berlin, 1908; A. Malvy, *La Réforme de l'église russe*, Paris, 1906; *Service Book of the Holy Orthodox-Catholic Apostolic (Greco-Russian) Church, compared, translated and arranged for the Old Church-Slavonic Service Books of the Russian Church and collated with the Service Books of the Greek Church*, by Isabel F. Hapgood, Boston, 1906; J. Wilbois, *L'Avenir de l'église russe*, Paris, 1907; A. Palmieri, *La Chiesa Russa. Le sue odierne condizioni e il suo riformismo dottrinale*, Florence, 1908. Treatises in Russian on the church history of Russia are by Makarij, 12 vols., St. Petersburg, 1868–83, E. Golubinsky, 2 vols. in 3, Moscow, 1900–02.

For the history of Russian dissent and the sects consult: K. K. Grass, *Die russischen Sekten*, Leipsic, 1905–09; E. Pelikan, *Geschichtlich-medizinische Untersuchungen über das Skopzentum in Russland*, Giessen, 1876; T. Pech, *Die Molokanen*, in *Historisches Taschenbuch*, 5 ser., viii. 203 sqq., Leipsic, 1878; N. von Gerbel-Embach, *Russische Sektierer*, in *Zeitfragen der Christlichen Volkslebens*, vol. viii., part 4, Heilbronn, 1883; A. F. Heard, *The Russian Church and Russian Dissent; comprising Orthodoxy, Dissent, and Erratic Sects*, London, 1887; N. Tsakni, *La Russie sectaire*, Paris, 1888; V. Frank, *Russische Selbstzeugnisse. Russisches Christentum*, Paderborn, 1889; A. Roschdestwenskij, *Der südrussische Stundismus*, St. Petersburg, 1889; D. Dan, *Die Lippowaner in der Bukowina*, Czernowitz, 1890; F. Kattenbusch, *Lehrbuch der vergleichenden Konfessionskunde*, i. 234 sqq., 542 sqq., Freiburg, 1892; F. Kale, *Die russisch-schismatische Kirche*, Graz, 1894; H. Dalton, ut sup., pp. 57 sqq.; idem, *Der Stundismus in Russland*, Güterloh, 1896; Hesba Stretton, *Highway of Sorrow at the Close of the 19th Century*, London, 1897; P. Birukoff, J. Treguboff, and W. Tschertkoff, *Christenverfolgung in Russland*, Munich, 1898; J. Gehring, *Die Sekten der russischen Kirche*, Leipsic, 1898; F. Loofs, *Symbolik*, i. 169 sqq., Tübingen, 1902; S. Margaritow, *Geschichte der russischen rationalistischen und mystischen Sekten*, Kishinew, 1902; K. K. Grass, *Die geheime heilige Schrift der Skopzen*, Leipsic, 1904; J. B. Sévérac, *La Secte russe des hommes de Dieu*, Paris, 1906; P. Strahl, *Beiträge*, ut sup., i. 250 sqq.; and literature under Dukhobors.

RUST, GEORGE: English theologian, usually reckoned among the Cambridge Platonists (q.v.); b. at Cambridge; d. at Dromore (15 m. s.w. of Belfast), Ireland, Dec., 1670. He was educated at St. Catharine's Hall, Cambridge (B.A., 1647; M.A., 1650), and was elected fellow of Christ College in 1649. He resigned his fellowship in 1659, and soon after the Restoration was invited by Jeremy Taylor to Ireland, was ordained deacon and priest May 7, 1661, becoming dean of Connor in August, and in 1664 was rector of Lisburn. In 1667 he succeeded Taylor as bishop of Dromore, which was now again separated from Down and Connor, and died three years later. He was the intimate friend of Henry More and Joseph Glanvill (qq.v.), and wrote two works whose subjects and spirit connect him with their school: *Discourse of Truth* (London, 1677; ed. Glanvill); and a *Discourse of the Use of Reason in Matters of Religion* (ed. H. Hallywell, 1683). The former, by which he is chiefly known, shows an enlightened mind, but no largeness of grasp, while its line of thought is a weaker echo of Cudworth.

His *Remains* were edited by H. Hallywell (1686).

BIBLIOGRAPHY: Besides the literature under CAMBRIDGE PLATONISTS, consult: C. H. Cooper, *Annals of Cambridge*, iii. 545–546, 5 vols., Cambridge, 1842–53; idem, *Memorials of Cambridge*, new ed., 2 vols., ib. 1858–60; J. Ware, *Antiquities and Hist. of Ireland*, 9 parts, London, 1704–05; H. Cotton, *Fasti ecclesiæ Hibernicæ*, vol. iii., 5 vols., Dublin, 1845–60; J. Worthington, *Diary and Correspondence*, ed. J. Crossley for Chetham Society, Manchester, 1847 sqq.; *DNB*, l. 1–2.

RUST, ISAAK: German Evangelical; b. at Mussbach (59 m. n.w. of Stuttgart) Oct. 14, 1796; d. at Munich Dec. 14, 1862. He was educated at the University of Heidelberg (1815–17); and was first vicar, then teacher at the progymnasium at Speyer (1817–20), where he also lectured for a term on philosophy at the Lyceum. In 1820 he became pastor at Ungstein, where he wrote his *Philosophie und Christentum, oder Wissen und Glauben* (Mannheim, 1825), in which, from a rationalistic point of view, he traced the intellectual and religious development of mankind in parallels through three stages: paganism, the stage of feeling; Judaism, of understanding; and Christianity, of reason. Similar views were maintained in his *De nonnullis quæ in theologia nostræ ætatis dogmatica desiderantur* (Erlangen, 1828), a polemic against Schleiermacher. In 1827 Rust was called to Erlangen as pastor of the French Reformed church; and, in 1830, was appointed associate professor of theology, and full professor in 1831. His *Geist aus Luthers Schriften, oder Concordanz der Ansichten und Urteile des grossen Reformators* (in collaboration with F. W. Lomler, E. Zimmermann, and others; 4 vols., Darmstadt, 1827–31), and *Stimmen der Reformation und der Reformatoren an die Fürsten und Völker dieser Zeit* (Erlangen, 1832), indicate his change to orthodoxy. In 1833 Rust was appointed director of the consistory of Erlangen in place of a pronounced rationalist. His arbitrary spirit and zeal for the Palatine union and against the rationalistic element raised such opposition that, in 1836, the supreme consistory sent two councilors to the Palatinate, where they held ineffectual conferences with clerical and lay members of the synod. Rust remained in the consistory, however, where he exercised a reactionary influence on theological education, Biblical instruction, and missions, and on the synods. Opposition to him and his measures continued, until, in 1846, he was appointed to the supreme consistory at Munich. In the stormy year of 1848, however, his removal was repeatedly demanded, and the separation of the unionistic Palatinate Church from the consistory was urged again and again. This took place in 1849, to avert which Rust had meantime been retired from the supreme consistory, but continued to be court chaplain, and in 1850 was appointed ministerial councilor and referee for Palatine ecclesiastical affairs in the ministry of worship. Henceforth his influence on the church was not such as to evoke opposition, and in 1861 he retired from active life.

(J. SCHNEIDER.)

BIBLIOGRAPHY: H. E. G. Paulus, *Die protestantisch-evangelisch-unierte Kirche in der baierischen Pfalz*, Heidelberg, 1840; G. F. Kolb, *Kurze Geschichte der vereinigten protestantisch-evangelisch-christlichen Kirche der baierischen Pfalz*, Speyer, 1847; E. F. H. Medicus, *Geschichte der evangelischen Kirche im Königreich Bayern*, supplement vol., Erlangen, 1865; F. W. Laurier, *Die evangelisch-protestantische Kirche der Pfalz*, Kaiserslautern, 1868.

RUSTON, WILLIAM OTIS: Presbyterian; b. in New York City Dec. 6, 1852. He was graduated from the College of the City of New York (B.A., 1872), and from Union Theological Seminary, New York City (1875); was pastor at Fairmount, N. J., 1875–77; at West Union, Ia., 1877–86; at Dubuque, Ia., 1886–1903; professor of sacred languages and literature in the German Presbyterian Theological School of the Northwest, since 1903; and president of the same, 1904–08.

RUTH, BOOK OF: A book of the Old Testament placed in the English canon between Judges and I Samuel. It is a narrative of events which purport to have taken place in the period of the Judges, about the Moabitess Ruth, who, through a series of singular incidents, became the ancestress of David. Elimelech, a Bethlehemite, driven by famine, emigrated, with his wife, Naomi, and his two sons, Mahlon and Chilion, to the land of Moab, where he and his two sons died after these had taken Moabitish wives, Ruth and Orpah. After remaining ten years in Moab, Naomi decided to return to her native land and advised her daughters-in-law to leave her; but Ruth, with filial attachment, followed her back to Judah. There, while gleaning in a field belonging to Boaz, a kinsman, she was well treated by him. Naomi instructed her to offer herself in marriage to her well-to-do kinsman, he being, to a certain extent, bound to take the childless widow and "to raise up the name of the dead upon his inheritance." Boaz accepted the obligation, after a nearer relative, to whom he gave the opportunity of redeeming the land of Elimelech and taking Ruth, had declined. The son of Boaz and Ruth became the grandfather of David.

The grace and freshness of the narrative have always been admired. It bears internal evidence of its truth, for it is not likely that a fiction would have ascribed a Moabitish ancestress to David. However, it has an especial spiritual significance; it indicates that God's people was ordained to draw fresh strength from a heathen source. Ruth is mentioned as an ancestress of the Messiah in Matt. i., beside Tamar and Rahab. Tamar, mother of Phares (Gen. xxxviii.), of the same genealogy, is also mentioned by the narrator of Ruth as a source of divine blessing (iv. 12); not only as a foreigner, but as the mother of the offspring from a marriage based on the obligations of kinship, which Judah unknowingly and involuntarily had to fulfil. Still, in spite of the inner significance of this mixture of Jewish with foreign blood, in the house of David, it seems clear that it could not have been the invention of a didactic "tendency." Just as little could the story have been conceived for the sake of commending the levirate marriage, since that is taken for granted and not especially urged. Political and mythological motives have been ascribed to the book, but on insufficient grounds. The book presents a historically faithful picture of ancient customs and traditions. It is not certain to what period of the era of the Judges Ruth belongs. According to the genealogy of Ruth (iv. 18 sqq.), she lived about 100 years before David. The history of David's family could have been of general interest only after his accession to the throne. Philological evidence points to a much later date of the writing of the book of Ruth, probably after the exile.

If the matter was derived from an oral family tradition of the house of David and the present is a redaction of an earlier text (E. König), the fact would be admissible that the editor introduced also didactic motives with the reproduction; but the principal thing is not to contend for a certain "tendency," but to throw light on the origin of the house of David. Some (e.g., A. Bertholet) think that he wrote in the Ezra-Nehemiah period to combat the exclusion of foreigners from the connubium. Such a polemic intention is too faintly brought out to make its existence probable. As to integrity it is not improbable that iv. 18–22 was a later addition. The position of the Book of Ruth differs in the Hebrew canon and in the Septuagint. The latter placed it after Judges; and Josephus, following this, combines it with Judges as one book. Many have assumed that it once formed the third appendix of Judges and was later separated. It was counted among the five rolls to be read at the five feasts. (C. VON ORELLI.)

BIBLIOGRAPHY: Commentaries are by: S. H. Tyng, *The Rich Kinsman*, New York, 1855; Metzger, Tübingen, 1857; C. F. Keil and F. Delitzsch, Eng. transl., Edinburgh, 1865; A. Raabe, *Das Buch Ruth und das Hohelied im Urtext*, Leipsic, 1879; C. Hamann, *Annotationes criticæ et exegeticæ in librum Ruth*, Marburg, 1871; H. Zschokke, *Biblische Frauen*, pp. 208–225, Freiburg, 1882; E. Bertheau, 2d ed., Leipsic, 1883; H. F. Kohlbrügge, Utrecht, 1886; R. Brown, *Gleanings from the Book of Ruth; or, the Book of Ruth opened out by Comparison with other Parts of Scripture*, London, 1887; F. de Hummelauer, Paris, 1888; S. Oettli and J. Meinhold, in *Die geschichtlichen Hagiographien*, Munich, 1889; M. C. Horine, Philadelphia, 1892; A. Bertholet and G. Wildeboer, Tübingen, 1898; W. Nowack, Göttingen, 1900; A. Black, *Ruth, a Hebrew Idyl*, London, 1906. The Midrash *Ruth Rabba* is in A. Wünsche, *Bibliotheca rabbinica*, Leipsic, 1883, cf. the *Collegium rabbinico-biblicum in librum Ruth*, ed. J. B. Carpzov, ib. 1703.

On questions of introduction, teaching, and text consult the works on O. T. theology, on introduction to the O. T., and on the history of Israel under AHAB; and ISRAEL, HISTORY OF; F. W. C. Umbreit, in *TSK*, 1834, pp. 305–308; Auberlen, *Die drei Anhänge des Buches der Richter*, in *TSK*, 1860, pp. 536–568; C. H. H. Wright, *Book of Ruth in Hebrew, . . . Text, Readings, Critical Commentary*, London, 1864; R. W. Bush, *Popular Introduction to . . . Ruth*, London, 1883; K. Budde, in *ZATW*, xii (1892), 37–51; *DB*, iv. 316; *EB*, iv. 4166–72 (important); *JE*, x. 576–578; Vigouroux, *Dictionnaire*, fasc. xxxv., cols. 1273–82.

RUTHENIAN CATHOLICS: See ROMAN CATHOLICS, II., 2, § 1.

RUTHERFORD, ruth'er-ferd, **SAMUEL:** Scotch Covenanter; b. in Nisbet Parish, now part of Crailing (42 m. s.e. of Edinburgh) about 1600; d. at St. Andrews (11 m. s.e. of Dundee), Roxburgshire, Mar. 20, 1661. He graduated from Edinburgh (M.A., 1621); was regent of humanity, 1623–25; began the study of theology, 1626; was pastor of Anworth, Galloway, 1627–36, when he issued *Exercitationes apologeticæ pro divina gratia* (1636), a work in defense of the doctrine of grace against the Arminians which attracted wide attention and elicited a call to the chair of theology at Utrecht and also to that at Hardewyk. On July 27, 1636, he was cited before the high commission court to answer for his non-conformity to the Acts of Episcopacy, and his work against the Arminians. Deprived of his living at Anworth, he was banished to Aberdeen. When the Covenant was again triumphant, in 1638, he returned to Anworth, and in 1639 was made professor of divinity at St. Mary's, at St. Andrews. In 1643 he was chosen one of the Scotch commissioners to the Westminster Assembly (q.v.), and during his four years of service in that capacity wrote *The Due Right of Presbyteries* (London, 1644); *Lex, rex; the Law and the Prince* (1644); *The Tryal and Triumph of Faith* (1645); and *The Divine Right of Church Government and Excommunication* (1646). Soon after, he became principal of St. Mary's, and in 1651 rector of the University of St. Andrews. His *Free Disputation against Pretended Liberty of Conscience* (1649) was pronounced by Bishop Heber "perhaps the most elaborate defense of persecution which has ever appeared in a Protestant country." Joining with the western remonstrants in their protest to the assembly in 1651, the schism was opened which, ten years later, resulted in the restoration of episcopacy. These ten years were filled with acrimonious controversy both with the sectarians and with his colleagues at St. Andrews, where, on account of strife, the communion was suspended for six years. Possessed of high ability, honesty, and unselfishness, Rutherford was called the "true saint of the covenant"; yet by his narrow, bitter, and scurrilous antagonism, he helped to degrade and destroy presbyterianism, which he aimed to serve. The *Lex, rex* was ordered to be burned; he was deprived of his offices, and summoned to answer to a charge of treason by parliament, in 1661; but severe illness which resulted in his death prevented his appearance. He published further: *The Covenant of Life Opened* (1655); *Survey of the Survey of Church Discipline by T. Hooker* (1658); and *Influences of the Life of Grace* (1659). Rutherford's letters are specially interesting and edifying, published under the title *Joshua Redivivus* (1664; or *Letters of Samuel Rutherford, with Sketch of his Life*, by A. A. Bonar, New York, 1851; 5th ed., London, 1906).

BIBLIOGRAPHY: Besides the *Letters*, ut sup., consult: *Manna Crumbs, . . . being Excerpts from the Letters of Samuel Rutherford, Gathered by W. P. Breed*, Philadelphia, 1865; T. Murray, *The Life of Samuel Rutherford*, Edinburgh, 1828; Hew Scott, *Fasti ecclesiæ Scoticanæ*, 6 vols., Edinburgh, 1866–71; A. P. Stanley, *The Church of Scotland*, pp. 100–108, London, 1872; A. B. Grosart, *Representative Nonconformists*, London, 1879; A. F. Mitchell, *The Westminster Assembly*, London, 1883; *Scottish Divines: 1505–1872* (St. Giles Lectures), Edinburgh, 1883; A. T. Innes, *Samuel Rutherford*, Edinburgh, 1884; A. Thomson, *Samuel Rutherford*, London, 1884; A. Whyte, *Samuel Rutherford and some of his Correspondents*, Edinburgh, 1894; *The Upward Way. A Book of Extracts from the Letters of Samuel Rutherford. Written chiefly from his Prison at Aberdeen, 1636–38*, ed. Eleanor C. Gregory, London, 1908; and the literature under PRESBYTERIANS relating to Rutherford's period, and that under WESTMINSTER ASSEMBLY.

RUYSBROECK, reis'broн, **(RUUSBROEC, RUYSBROEK), JAN VAN:** Dutch mystic; b. at Ruysbroeck (4 m. s.w. of Brussels) 1294; d. at the

Augustinian monastery of Groenendael (2 m. s.e. of Brussels) Dec. 2, 1381. Inclined, even as a child, to the religious life, he left home at the age of eleven and went to his uncle, canon of St. Gudula at Brussels. Here he studied diligently for four years, and then determined to renounce all secular learning for theology. At the age of twenty-four he became a priest and vicar of St. Gudula's. Of his career here little is known, though he seems to have devoted himself more and more to the contemplative life. Mild and charitable, he was yet stern to all forms of vice and error, and associated much with other mystics. In order to give his undivided thoughts to contemplation he retired from the secular priesthood at the age of sixty to the newly established monastery of Groenendael, of which he became the first prior. Dividing his time between a reform of his order and meditation, he became a model of monastic sanctity, and received visitors from far and wide, among them Johannes Tauler and Geert Groote (qq.v.). Soon after his death legend gathered around his name; and, at an early date, he was styled *doctor ecstaticus*.

Biography.

The writings of Ruysbroeck show a marked similarity to those of Meister Eckart (q.v.), by which they may well have been influenced, especially as the works of the older mystic were certainly read in the vicinity of Groenendael, and he may have heard Eckart at Cologne. Ruysbroeck, the best prose writer of the Netherlands in the Middle Ages, wrote entirely in Dutch, in a style mostly quiet and simple, but capable, under the stress of feeling and imagination, of rising to lofty heights. On the other hand, despite the precision with which he was able to express the profoundest thoughts, he is frequently obscure through his allegories, similies, repetitions, digressions, and subtile (though often illogical) divisions. His works were soon translated into Latin by his pupils Willem Jordaens and Groote, and translations into the dialects of Gelderland, Cologne, the Upper Rhine, and High German are extant. The first printed treatise of Ruysbroeck was the *Brulocht*, which appeared under the title *De ornatu spiritualium nuptiarum* (Paris, 1512), while later L. Surius published the *Rusbrochii opera* (Cologne, 1552). From the latter text, which is paraphrastic and often incorrect, Ruysbroeck's writings were translated into German by "G. J. C." (ed. G. Arnold, Offenbach, 1701). The Gelder and Cologne versions of four tractates have been edited by A. von Arnswaldt under the title *Vier Schriften von Johann Rusbroek in niederdeutscher Sprache* (Hanover, 1848). The chief edition, however, is the complete one prepared, under the auspices of the Flemish Academy of Bibliophiles, by J. B. David, *Werken van J. van Ruusbroec* (6 vols., Ghent, 1858–69). This contains twelve treatises: (1) *Chierheit der gheesteleker Brulocht*, sent in 1530 to the friends of God at Strasburg, and consisting of three books treating respectively of the active, the inward, and the contemplative life; (2) *Dat Boec van den Gheesteleken Tabernacule* is a long allegorical interpretation of the ark of the covenant as the type of the mystical life, based on the *Historia scholastica* of Peter Comestor (q.v.); (3) *Dat Boec van den Twaelf Dogheden*, more ethical than mystical, is a development of Christian virtue, whose foundation is humility; (4) the *Spieghel der ewigher Salicheit*, written for the Poor Clares in 1359, is an application of the three grades of the mystical life, respectively, to monasticism and to the Eucharist, the work being mostly devoted to the author's views on the sacrament; (5) the *Van den Kerstenen Ghelove* is a short exposition of the Athanasian Creed; (6) *Dat Boec van seven trappen in den groet der gheesteliker minnen*, on the three grades; (7) *Tractaet van seven sloten* was written for the Poor Clares and describes the duties of the nunnery, with special stress on the necessity of inward meditation; (8) *Tractaet van den Rike der Ghelieven* is written largely in rime of little poetic value; (9) *Dat Boec van den vier Becoringhen* combats the chief errors in the author's time; (10) *Dat Boec van den twaelf Beghinen*, on contemplation, though often disturbed in context, is of much importance for a knowledge of Ruysbroeck's mysticism; (11) *Vingherlinc, of het blickende Steentje*, on the "white stone" of Rev. ii. 17 (Christ, who is given to the man of meditation), is also devoted to the three grades, especially the last; (12) *Samuel, of dat Boec der hoechster Waerheit*, is an apology for the author's mysticism.

Writings.

Ruysbroeck proceeds, in his mystical system, from God, descends to man, and finally returns to God. God is simple unity, the supernal essence of all, himself immovable, and yet the motive source of things. The Son is wisdom, the uncreated image of the Father; and the Holy Ghost, proceeding from and returning to both, is love, which unites the Father and the Son. In the persons God is eternal activity, in his essence eternal rest. All creatures are thoughts of God before creation. In man soul and spirit are to be distinguished, the former the principle of the life of the creature, and the latter the principle of divine life. The soul has three qualities: memory, reason, and will. Higher than these are, the essential simplicity and formlessness of the spirit which render it like the Father; the intelligence which receives eternal Wisdom (the Son); and the *synderesis* (or spark of the soul) which strives back to the origin, and unites man with the divine unity by means of love through the Holy Ghost. These three qualities, being inseparable, constitute the simple substance of the spirit. Obscured by sin they must be transported by grace, or wisdom incarnate, above nature to God through the three grades of the active, inward, and contemplative life. The first consists in conquering sin and approaching God by outward acts and good works. The second (*vita affectiva*), in which asceticism is of minor importance, is characterised by ecstacy and visions, by reentrance into self, by indifference to everything that is not God and the defacing of all mental pictures, striving toward God with mystical love and feasting upon him, and by the interpretation of the divine spirit and the spirit of man. In the third stage (*vita vitalis*), the Christian rises above hope, faith, and all the virtues, even grace, to plunge into the abyss of the divine essence; it

Doctrines.

is an immediate sense and possession of God without knowledge or bounds. It means the dying and annihilation of self, in order to behold the absolute and eternal essence. This life, a gift of grace, renewed in the inner secrecy of the Spirit through love, comes to its reality in the quiet contemplation of God and in the absolute submission to his operation. From this repose of the Spirit is developed the superessentia, a supraessential contemplation of the means of differentiation of the Trinity, an indescribable feeling and state of bliss. The ultimate differences in consciousness between God and creature, between thing and nothing, disappear. This is the bridal flight of Christ with the human spirit; the Word is continually reborn in the eternal present, in which God is self-producing in the highest excellence of the spirit. This proceeds from light to light until the clearness by which it sees, the clearness which it sees, and itself are one and the same. Consciousness of supraessential being and unity of essence in God are attained. Here Ruysbroeck arrives on the border of pantheism. Yet he ever endeavored to distinguish between the eternal spirit and the created; and in the union with God he held that only the difference of will and thought vanished, not the difference of personality. However, so delicate was the line that in his phraseology he often overstepped it; and, though he was in reality in thorough accord with orthodoxy, and he continually antagonized the Brethren of the Free Spirit and the Beghards (see FREE SPIRIT, BRETHREN OF THE; BEGHARDS AND BEGUINES), yet in his writings he roused grave suspicions among some more cautious minds, among whom was J. C. Gerson (q.v.). The influence of Ruysbroeck on theological and philosophical thought in the Netherlands was relatively slight, and the mystical writings of his immediate pupils were either ascetic or repetitions of his own thoughts. This was doubtless due in part to his obscurity and the liability of his phraseology to misinterpretation and also to the fear of the Flemish heretical pantheistic mysticism of the Beghards. Ruysbroeck's activity, indeed, lay rather in the power of his personality and in the influence he exerted on kindred minds. It was his pupil Groote who founded the Brethren of the Common Life (see COMMON LIFE, BRETHREN OF THE), who also very probably drew his inspiration from Ruysbroeck himself.

(S. D. VAN VEEN.)

BIBLIOGRAPHY: In addition to the editions noted in the text F. A. Lambert edited *Die Zierde, Vom glanzenden Stein*, and *Das Buch von . . . Wahrheit*, Leipsic (1901). In English there is *Reflections from the Mirror of a Mystic, being Gleanings from the Works of John Ruysbroek ("Doctor Ecstaticus"), a Mystic of the XIVth Century, translated by Earle Baillie*, London, 1905 (contains sixteen chapters of the choicest thoughts of the great mystic). Besides the literature under MYSTICISM, and under the articles to which reference is made in the text, especially COMMON LIFE, BRETHREN OF THE, consult: M. Maeterlinck, *Ruysbroeck and the Mystics, with Selections from Ruysbroeck*, London, 1894, new ed., 1908; J. G. V. Engelhardt, *Richard von St. Victor und Johannes Ruysbroeck. Zur Geschichte der mystischen Theologie*, Erlangen, 1838; C. Schmidt, *Études sur le mysticisme allemand au quatorzième siècle*, Strasburg, 1845; F. Böhringer, *Die Deutschen Mystiker des 14. und 15. Jahrhunderts*, pp. 442–611, Zurich, 1855; C. C. Schmidt, *Étude sur Jean Ruysbroeck, . . . sa vie, ses écrits, et sa doctrine*, Strasburg, 1859; A. Jundt, *Hist. du panthéisme populaire au moyen âge*, Paris, 1875; C. Ullmann, *Reformers before the Reformation*, ii. 31–55, Edinburgh, 1877; A. Auger, *De doctrina et meritis Joannis van Ruysbroeck*, Louvain, 1892; W. L. de Brosse, *Bijdrage tot de Kennis van het Leven en de Werken van J. van Ruusbroec*, Ghent, 1896; A. A. van Otterloo, *Johannes Ruysbroeck. Een Bijdrage tot de Kennis van den Ontwikkelingsgang der Mystiek*, 2d ed. by J. C. van Slee, The Hague, 1896; V. Sully, *Short Account of the Life and Writings of the Blessed John Ruysbroeck*, London, 1910; Schaff, *Christian Church*, v. 2, pp. 273–278; Lichtenberger, *ESR*, xi. 363–366.

RYAN, PATRICK JOHN: Roman Catholic archbishop of Philadelphia; b. at Thurles (21 m. n.e. of Tipperary), County Tipperary, Ireland, Feb. 20, 1831; d. at Philadelphia Feb. 11, 1911. He was educated at Carlow College, Ireland (from which he was graduated in 1852), and, leaving Ireland for the United States, was attached to the clergy staff of the Roman Catholic cathedral in St. Louis, of which he became rector in 1856. Later he was appointed rector of St. John the Evangelist's in the same city, and rose to be vicar-general of the diocese. During the Civil War he was chaplain of the Gratiot Street Military Prison and Hospital, St. Louis, and in 1868 accompanied the archbishop of St. Louis to Rome, where he preached the English Lenten sermons. Four years later (1872) he was consecrated titular bishop of Tricomia and appointed bishop-coadjutor of St. Louis, with the right of succession. He was again in Rome in 1883 as one of the United States prelates to represent the interests of religion, and in 1884 was created titular archbishop of Salamis. Within the year he became archbishop of Philadelphia. He wrote *Some of the Causes of Modern Religious Scepticism* (St. Louis, 1895).

RYDBERG, rid'berg, **ABRAHAM VIKTOR:** Swedish author and educator; b. at Jönköping (80 m. e. of Gothenburg), province of Småland, Sweden, Dec. 18, 1828; d. at Stockholm Sept. 21, 1895. He studied philosophy at the University of Lund, 1848–52; was literary editor of *Göteborgs Handelstidning*, 1854–76; lay representative at the church congress of the Swedish State Church, 1868; member of the lower house of the Swedish Parliament as representative of the city of Gothenburg, 1870–72; and professor at the high school of Stockholm from 1884. His service to Sweden was in the dissemination of liberal thought. He was author of "The Doctrine of the Bible on Christ" (Gothenburg, 1862); "The Jehovah Worship among the Hebrews before the Babylonian Captivity" (1864); "Magic of the Middle Ages" (Stockholm, 1865; English transl., New York, 1879); "On the Preexistence of Man" (1868); "Church and Priesthood" (1868); "Genealogy of the Patriarchs in Genesis and the Chronology of the Septuagint" (Gothenburg, 1870); "Roman Legends about St. Paul and St. Peter" (Stockholm, 1874); "Roman Days" (1877; Eng. transl., including "Roman Legends," New York, 1879); and "The Ultimate Things" (1880). In his romances he strives for freedom, tolerance, and knowledge: "The Pirate of the Baltic" (Gothenburg, 1857); "Singoalla" (1857); and "The Last Athenian" (1859; Eng. transl., Philadelphia, 1869). His scientific works are: *Segersvärdet* (1884); *Undersökningar i germansk Mythologi* (2 vols., 1886–90; Eng. transl., *Teutonic Mythology*, Aberdeen, 1889); and *Om Ting och fenomen ur empirisk synpunkt* (1890). Complete works, *Skrifter*, were issued by Carl Warburg (15 vols., Stockholm, 1896–1900).

RYDER, WILLIAM HENRY: Congregationalist; b. at Elyria, O., July 24, 1842. He was graduated from Oberlin College, Oberlin, O. (A.B., 1866), and Andover Theological Seminary (1869). After being pastor of the Congregational church at Watertown, N. Y. (1869–70), he was professor of Greek at Oberlin until 1877, and was then pastor of the First Congregational Church at Ann Arbor, Mich., until 1888; then became professor of New-Testament interpretation at Andover Theological Seminary. He served throughout the Civil War in the Union Army and was promoted second lieutenant.

RYERSON, rai'er-sun, **ADOLPHUS EGERTON:** Canadian Methodist; b. at Charlotteville, Norfolk County, Ontario, Mar. 24, 1803; d. at Toronto Feb. 19, 1882. His father was an American loyalist from New Jersey. The son entered the Methodist ministry in 1826; became editor of the *Christian Guardian* in 1829; was first president of Victoria College, 1841–44; and superintendent of education in Upper Canada, 1844–76. As a preacher he was eloquent and effective, and in representative missions for his church he was able and commanding. His main work was in organizing education; the act which he drafted in 1850 is the one under which the schools of Ontario have since been maintained. He published *Epochs of Canadian Methodism* (1882), and *The Loyalists of America and their Times: 1620–1816* (1880).

RYLAND, JOHN: Baptist; b. at Warwick (20 m. s.e. of Birmingham) Jan. 29, 1753; d. at Bristol May 25, 1825. He was exceedingly precocious as a child, learning Hebrew when only five years of age, and Greek when nine; when fifteen he began to teach at Northampton in the school of his father (who was also a pastor); he began to preach to Baptist congregations in 1769, and was admitted to the ministry in 1771; he continued to teach till 1778, and became assistant pastor with his father in 1781 and sole pastor in 1786; in 1793 he took charge of the Broadmead chapel at Bristol and became president of the Baptist college there, holding both positions till his death. He was one of the founders of the Baptist Missionary Society in 1792, and its secretary from 1815 till his death. He was also a hymnist of some note, and a few of his hymns continue in use, including "In all my Lord's appointed ways." Among his works may be noted: *Serious Essays on the Truths of the Glorious Gospel* (London, 1771; 121 pieces in verse, including some hymns); *The Divine Inspiration and Authority of the Holy Scriptures Asserted and Proved* (1772); *Compendious View of the Principal Truths of the Glorious Gospel of Christ* (Salisbury, 1774); *A Candid Statement of the Reasons which induce the Baptists to differ in Opinion and Practice from their Christian Brethren* (London, 1827); *Memoir of the Rev. Andrew Fuller* (1816); *Serious Remarks on the Different Representations of Evangelical Doctrine by the Professed Friends of the Gospel* (2 parts, Bristol, 1817–18); *Pastoral Memorials; with a Memoir of the Author* (2 vols., 1826–28); and *Hymns and Verses on Sacred Subjects, with a biographical Sketch* (1862).

Bibliography: Besides the sketches as noted above consult: the memorial sermon by Robert Hall, in the latter's *Works*, i. 369–414, London, 1832; F. A. Cox, *Hist. of the Baptist Missionary Society*, i. 1–290, ib. 1842; F. L. Colvile, *Worthies of Warwickshire*, pp. 623–625, ib. 1870; J. B. Meyers, *Centenary Volume of the Baptist Missionary Society*, ib. 1893; S. W. Duffield, *English Hymns*, p. 259, New York, 1886; Julian, *Hymnology*, pp. 983–984; *DNB*, l. 55–56.

RYLE, rail, **HERBERT EDWARD:** Church of England, bishop of Winchester; b. in London May 25, 1856. He was educated at King's College, Cambridge (B.A., 1879; M.A., 1882), of which he was fellow (1881–1901). He was ordered deacon (1882), and ordained priest (1883); was divinity lecturer at Emmanuel College, Cambridge (1881–84) and at King's College (1882–86). He was principal of St. David's College (1886–88); Hulsean professor of divinity in the University of Cambridge (1887–1901); president of Queen's College, Cambridge (1896–1901); examining chaplain to his father the bishop of Liverpool (1883–87), to the bishop of St. Asaph (1887–89), and to the bishop of Ripon (1889–1901); select preacher at Cambridge in 1889, 1892, 1895, 1899, and 1902, and at Oxford in 1901–03; Warburton lecturer at Lincoln's Inn and chaplain in ordinary of the same body in 1898–1901; honorary canon of Ripon and commissary of Wellington (1895–1901); honorary chaplain to the queen (1896–98), and chaplain in ordinary (1898–1901). In 1901 he was consecrated bishop of Exeter, and in 1903 was translated to his present see of Winchester. He has edited *The Psalms of the Pharisees* (in collaboration with M. R. James; Cambridge, 1891), and has written *The Canon of the Old Testament* (London, 1892); *The Early Narratives of Genesis* (1892); *Commentary on Ezra and Nehemiah* (Cambridge, 1893); *Philo: Quotations from the Old Testament* (London, 1895); *On the Church of England* (1904); and *On Holy Scripture and Criticism* (1904).

RYLE, JOHN CHARLES: Church of England; b. at Macclesfield (30 m. e.s.e. of Liverpool) May 10, 1816; d. at Liverpool June 10, 1900. He was educated at Eton and at Christ Church, Oxford (B.A., 1838; M.A., 1871). He became curate of Exbury, Hampshire, 1841; rector of St. Thomas, Winchester, 1843; of Helmingham, Suffolk, 1844; vicar of Stradbroke, Suffolk, 1861; rural dean of Hoxne, 1869; honorary canon of Norwich, 1872; select preacher at Cambridge, 1873–74; at Oxford, 1874–1876, 1879, 1880; dean designate of Salisbury, 1880; and was bishop of Liverpool, 1880–1900. He was an Evangelical in type, and in an uncommonly pure and expressive style wrote more than a hundred tracts on doctrinal and practical subjects, of which more than two millions have been circulated, and many have been translated into foreign languages. He was also author of *The Bishop, the Pastor, and the Preacher, being biographical Lectures on Latimer,*

Baxter, and Whitefield (Ipswich, 1854); *Bishops and Clergy of Other Days* (London, 1868); *The Christian Leaders of the Last Century* (1869); *Expository Thoughts on the Gospels* (7 vols., 1856–73; new ed., 4 vols., 1900); *Hymns for the Church on Earth* (1860), being 300 hymns and spiritual songs; *Practical Religion* (1874–80); *Knots Untied* (1874); *Holiness* (1879); and *Light from Old Times* (1891).

BIBLIOGRAPHY: J. C. MacDonnell, *Life and Correspondence of William Connor Magee*, 2 vols., London, 1896; A. C. Benson, *Life of E. W. Benson*, 2 vols., ib. 1899; *DNB*, Supplement iii. 334–335.

RYSWICK, ris'wic, **CLAUSE:** A stipulation introduced by the French representative into the peace of Ryswick. The French had installed Roman Catholic worship and diverted Evangelical church properties to Roman Catholic use in many German places of which Louis XIV. had taken possession under pretext of the reunion of Nimeguen (1679). These were now to be restored by the peace of Ryswick. The final draft was already being prepared when shortly before midnight of Oct. 29, 1697, the French representative insisted upon adding to the fourth article the clause, "nevertheless the Roman Catholic religion shall remain in the same status in which it now is in the places so restored"; and he threatened that the French king would break off negotiations immediately and resume the war against those offering impediments. The representatives of the emperor and the Roman Catholic estates, the imperial deputation, and the delegates of Württemberg, of the counts of Wetterau, and the imperial city of Frankfort attached their signatures; and for want of a vigorous support from the English and Dutch representatives and the Swedish mediator, the remonstrances of the remaining Evangelicals were in vain. The emperor, however, unconditionally ratified the peace, and thus the diet consented that the matter should rest, although 1,922 places were affected by a change of their religious relation. Specially, the Elector Palatinate Johann Wilhelm, under Jesuitic influence, employed the clause for despoiling the Evangelicals.

(C. T. G. VON SCHEURL†.)

BIBLIOGRAPHY: J. S. Pütter, *Historische Entwickelung der heutigen Staatsverfassung des deutschen Reichs*, ii. 300 sqq., Göttingen, 1787; J. C. Neuhaus, *Der Friede von Ryswick und die Abtretung Strassburgs an Frankreich 1697*, Freiburg, 1874. The background in the other treaties mentioned is given in brief in *Cambridge Modern History*, vol. v. passim, New York, 1908.

S

SAADIA, sā-ā'dī-ā, **BEN JOSEPH (SA'ID AL FAYYUMI):** Jewish rabbi; b. at Dilas in Upper Egypt, 892; d. at Sura (100 m. s. of Bagdad), Babylonia, 942. In 915 he went to Palestine, and in 928 became gaon, or head teacher, of the ancient academy of Sura; but on account of strife was compelled to retire to Bagdad, 930-937. He is distinguished for his Arabic translation of the Pentateuch, Job, Psalms, Canticles, and other books of the Bible, with brief annotations; his grammatical and lexical works; and, above all, for his "Book of Articles of Faith and Doctrines of Dogma" in Arabic, completed in 933; known only in the Hebrew translation of Judah ibn Tibbon, *Sefer emunot we-de'ot* (Constantinople, 1562; Germ. transl., by Julius Fuerst, *Glaubenslehre und Philosophie von Saadja Fajjumi*, Leipsic, 1845, in *Die jüdischen Religionsphilosophen des Mittelalters*, vol. i.). Saadia was a representative of the *peshat*, or literal interpretation, a creator of Hebrew philology, and the promoter of a new school of exegesis characterized by a rational investigation of the contents and a scientific knowledge of the text. His work was characterized by treating each book as a whole and the contents as a unity, and by minuteness of exegesis; and his style, in translation and authorship, aimed at simple form and pure vocabulary. In his philosophy he surveyed the entire field of doctrine, ranging from the idea of God to ethics, in the light of reason and revelation.

BIBLIOGRAPHY: *JE*. x. 578–586 (excellent; contains very full list of literature); S. Munk, *Notice sur R. Saadia Gaon*, Paris, 1838; A. Geiger, in *Jüdische Zeitschrift für Wissenschaft und Leben*, v. 267–316; J. Guttmann, *Die Religionsphilosophie des Saadia*, Göttingen, 1882; A. Harkavy, *Studien und Mittheilungen*, vol. v., Berlin, 1891; idem, in *JQR*, xiii. 655–668; W. Engelkemper, *De Saadiæ Gaonis vita*, Münster, 1897; M. Friedländer, in *JQR*, v. 177–199; S. Poznanski, in *JQR*, viii. 684–691, x. 238–276.

SAALSCHUETZ, sāl'shüts, **JOSEPH LEVIN:** German rabbi and archeologist; b. at Königsberg Mar. 15, 1801; d. there Aug. 23, 1863. He studied in the university of Königsberg (Ph.D., 1824); held positions as rabbi and teacher in Berlin, 1825–29, and in Vienna 1829–35; became rabbi at Königsberg, after 1835; in 1847 he became privatdocent in Hebrew archeology, and afterward professor extraordinary. He was the author, among other works, of *Forschungen im Gebiete der hebräisch-ägyptischen Archäologie*, three parts (Königsberg, 1838–51); *Form und Geist der biblisch-hebräischen Poesie* (1853); and *Archäologie der Hebräer*, in twelve parts (1855–56). He also edited a new edition of J. D. Michaelis' *Das mosäische Recht mit Berücksichtigung des spätern Jüdischen*, in two parts (Berlin, 1846–48).

BIBLIOGRAPHY: S. Carpin, in *Allgemeine Zeitschrift des Judentums*, Oct. 18, 1901; *JE*, x. 586.

SABAOTH, sab'ē-eth or sā-bā'-ōth: A term used twice in the New Testament (Rom. ix. 29; Jas. v. 4) as a title of God, but in the English Old Testament translated "hosts."

From I Sam. i. 3, throughout the Old Testament the Hebr. *ẓebaoth*, "hosts," appears constantly as an element in the attributes ascribed to the God of Israel. The word is used with or without the article in various combinations, such as "Yahweh God of hosts," "Adonai Yahweh of hosts," "Adonai Yahweh God of hosts," "the Lord Adonai of hosts," with variants even from these several forms (cf. Isa. i. 24, x. 23, 24; Hos. xii. 5; Amos. iii. 13, v. 16; II Sam. v. 10, and many times).

Use and Distribution of the Term.

In many of these combinations Adonai is a reading in the margin intended to displace Yahweh; in other cases, particularly in the second and third books of Psalms, Elohim displaces an original Yahweh. The formula "Yahweh God of hosts" is comparatively rare, while "Yahweh of hosts" occurs 234 times, and the presupposition is that the latter is the original form, which may, however, have implied the fuller formula, unless it be supposed that Yahweh is a later substitution for an earlier "El," another form for "God." The distribution of the expression "of hosts" may be set forth something like this: in the books of Samuel, eleven times; in the books of Kings, five times; in I Chron., in parallels to Samuel, three times; in the prophetic books 247 (248) times, of which fifty-five occurrences are in Isa. i.-xxxix., and six times in Isa. xliv.-liv.; while fifteen occurrences are in Psalms, of which fourteen are in the second and third books. It is omitted from the Hexateuch, Judges, Ezekiel, Joel, Obadiah, Jonah, and the whole of the Hagiographa except Psalms and Chronicles. It often occurs in the text of the Septuagint where it is not in the Hebrew, and vice versa. In the books of Samuel in five of the eleven cases it is used in connection with the ark or with war, and this is to be remembered in relation with the fact that the root *ẓaba'* is broadly Semitic and deals with war. Whether the hosts of which Yahweh was God were those of heaven—the angels and stars—or of Israel seems to be decided by the fact that the use of the word in the plural is generally in connection with the armies of Israel (cf. Ex. vii. 4); in Ps. lxviii. 13; Jer. iii. 19 the reference is to the armies of the nations (when the heavenly hosts are meant, the singular is everywhere used, cf. Ps. ciii. 21, cxlviii. 2 amended text).

Earlier Usage; Israel's War Hosts.

This conclusion is supported by I Sam. xvii. 45, cf. verses 26, 36; by the fact that Israel's wars are Yahweh's (Num. xxi. 14; I Sam. xxv. 28); and by the fact that Yahweh is the leader of the Israelitic armies (II Sam. v. 24; Isa. xiii. 4; in Joel iv. 11 it is doubtful whether the reference is to heavenly armies). A question of interpretation is raised by Ps. xxiv. 10, cf. verse 8 and I Sam. xvii. 45; the fact that verses 7-10 were chanted on the occasion of the bringing of the ark into the sanctuary makes it preferable to construe "the Lord of hosts" of this passage also with reference to the Hebrew armies. A similar line of reasoning is reached in connection with I Sam. i. 3, iv. 3 sqq., where the ark is designated as belonging to "the Lord of hosts"; of especial weight in this relation is II Sam. vi. 2. In this last case the formula in the latter part of the verse simply shows that the person or thing mentioned is in a relation of subordination to the person bearing the name (cf. Isa. iv. 1, lxiii. 19), which subordination involves the claim to protection (Jer. xiv. 9). As the name of Yahweh is "called" over Jerusalem (Jer. xxv. 29) and the temple (I Kings viii. 43) to indicate the closeness of relations with Yahweh, so the ark in II Sam. vi. 2 is called by Yahweh's name to show its close connection with him. The same relationship of the ark with Yahweh as the leader of the hosts of Israel appears in the early passage Num. x. 35-36; cf. xiv. 44; Josh. vi. 4 sqq.; II Sam. xi. 11, xv. 24 sqq. The general tenor of the passages considered is to show that the expression "Lord of hosts" recalled Yahweh as the leader of the Israelitic battle array.

While this is so and while it appears to be the consistent usage in the Old Testament, it is a question whether it represents the original usage.

Objections.

An examination is the more necessary in view of the absence of the article in some cases and of the use of the plural. It was advanced by Delitzsch as an objection to the view here stated that in this case the expression would have been expected in the Pentateuch inasmuch as in twenty cases the formula "hosts of Israel" is found. But it was pointed out by A. Klostermann (*Geschichte des Volkes Israel*, p. 76, Munich, 1896) that "Lord of hosts" was evidently cast out of Joshua in the process of editing (in Josh. vi. 17 the Septuagint still reads it, and Josh. xi. 11, 13 probably had it) at a time when the formula recalled the hosts of heaven (as objects of idolatry). Borchert attempted to show that *ẓaba'* did not designate "hosts of war" but mere population; in this he overlooked that in P at least (Num. ii.) the conception is that of a warlike host from which the Levites were excluded as not subject to warlike levies. A more difficult objection to meet is the one that if "Lord of hosts" originally designated the war god as the leader of Israel's hosts, this expression should be more frequent in this sense in the earlier prophecies. Passages which raise a doubt are Amos iii. 13, v. 16, 27, vi. 8, 14 where the "Lord of hosts" threatens Israel, and Isa. i. 24, ii. 1, 12, 15, and the like, where classes or individuals are under menace. Another class of passages is that in which the idea of world rulership is inherent, such as II Kings xix. 31; Isa. ix. 7, x. 16, 24, 26, 33, and similar passages. Sometimes the phrase denotes simply "the sublime" and is equivalent to "the Holy One" (Isa. vi. 5, viii. 13, xviii. 7, li. 15; Amos. iv. 13). But since the activities of the divine absoluteness or holiness are related to his plans for Israel, *Yahweh ẓebaoth*, "Yahweh of hosts," may designate without special emphasis Israel's God and king, as is shown by the numerous cases in which the expression is found either in apposition or parallelism with "God of Israel" or like expressions. The opposition between prophetic usage and the fundamental thought of the idea of God as leader in battle is by many commentators set aside by the conception of a transformation in the course of centuries; i.e., the earthly hosts give way in the enlarging conceptions to heavenly hosts, whether of stars or angels or other heavenly powers. The transformation of the idea of hosts from heaven to earth is evident; but the passages give ground for debate whether the heavenly hosts were angels or stars. For the former make such passages as Josh. v. 13 sqq.; II Kings vi. 17; Isa. xxiv. 21; I Kings xxii. 19; Dan. vii. 10. Yet frequently "host of heaven" represents in part the objects of idolatrous worship (Deut. iv. 19; II Kings xvii. 16; Jer. viii. 2;

Zeph. i. 5), in part the monuments of God's creative omnipotence (Gen. ii. 1; Isa. xxxiv. 4; Jer. xxxiii. 22). In this line of reasoning the mistake has been made sometimes of noting the fact of the use of the singular "host of heaven" and ignoring the use of *zebaoth* (plural) to designate earthly hosts where "of heaven" is omitted. Another difficulty is that if *Yahweh zebaoth* originally designated the war god of Israel as represented by the ark, this connection could not have been so wholly forgotten by the time of Isaiah as to be entirely absent.

Solution Indicated by Isaiah.

It is not a chance that just this designation is used by Isaiah in the trisagion (Isa. vi. 3). Though Isaiah was still conscious of the connection of *Yahweh zebaoth* with the ark, yet the reference of *zebaoth* to the hosts of Israel alone was still inconceivable. The solution of these difficulties has been sought by considering that the phrase as referring to the God represented by the ark had also another designation than "earthly hosts," a meaning to us unknown but of which the prophets had a clear consciousness. The expression may have been transferred from some other deity to Yahweh, the original sense lost, and the epithet avoided by the older writers. But Isaiah, e.g., could not have used the phrase so purposely and with such solemnity without a definite conception of its content, and this, too, as warranted by its original meaning, even though he deepened and extended this. And this latter would be helped by the fact that since Solomon's time the ark had receded from observation by remaining in the Holy of Holies, and had come to be regarded as something fearful, unapproachable, and supremely holy. After Isaiah had so stamped the usage as extended to a transcendental or heavenly host, there could be no reason why another, such as Jeremiah, should not employ it for special emphasis. As the original meaning of the phrase receded in memory, the more would the conception of Yahweh as leader of angel hosts appear in expression, and the same would apply to the connection of *zebaoth* with the stars. Thus "Yahweh of hosts" came to designate the world creator and world ruler. A proof of the transformation of the word is found in the varied and successive translations of the Septuagint, where there appear *kurios* (*ho theos*) *Sabaoth*, *kurios* (*ho theos*) *tōn dynameōn* (in other translators, *kurios tōn stratiōn*), *ho theos ho pantokratōr* or *kurios pantokratōr*. "Sabaoth" stands alone as a designation of God in the Sibylline Books, i. 304, while the Ophitic Gnostics made Sabaoth one of the planet spirits.

(E. Kautzsch.)

Bibliography: F. Delitzsch, in *Zeitschrift für lutherische Theologie und Kirche*, 1874, pp. 217 sqq.; E. Schrader, in *Jahrbücher für protestantische Theologie*, 1875, pp. 316 sqq.; W. von Baudissin, *Studien zur semitischen Religionsgeschichte*, i. 119, Leipsic, 1876; W. H. Kosters, in *TAT.*, x (1876), 53 sqq.; H. Schultz, *Old Testament Theology*, 2 vols., London, 1892; A. Dillmann, *Handbuch der alttestamentlichen Theologie*, pp. 220 sqq., Leipsic, 1895; Borchert, in *TSK*, 1896, pp. 619 sqq.; R. Smend, *Lehrbuch der alttestamentlichen Religionsgeschichte*, pp. 201 sqq., Freiburg, 1899; M. Lohr, *Untersuchungen zum Buch Amos*, pp. 38 sqq., Giessen, 1901; F. Schwally, *Semitische Kriegsaltertümer*, i. 4 sqq., Leipsic, 1901; B. F. Westcott, *The Historic Faith*, pp. 21 sqq., London, 1904; H. Gressmann, *Der Ursprung der israelitisch-jüdischen Eschatologie*, pp. 72 sqq., Göttingen, 1905; W. Hammann, *Erklärung von Ps. 24*, pp. 81 sqq., Darmstadt, 1905; B. Stade, *Biblische Theologie des A. T.*, i. 73–74, Tübingen, 1905; G. Westphal, in *Orientalische Studien zum 70. Geburtstag T. Nöldekes*, ii. 717 sqq., Giessen, 1906; K. Marti, *Geschichte der israelitischen Religion*, pp. 157 sqq., Strassburg, 1907; Zimmern, in Schrader, *KAT*, pp. 421, 456; *DB*, ii. 203, iii. 137–138, extra vol., pp. 636–637; *EB*, iii. 3328–3330; Vigouroux, *Dictionnaire*, fasc. xxxv. 1288–1289.

SABAS, sā'bās: Name of several saints.

1. Palestinian hermit and abbot, and founder of the order of Sabaites; b. at Mutalasca (Mutala) near Cæsarea, Cappadocia, 439; d. near Jerusalem, probably on Dec. 5, 531 or 532. At the age of five his parents took him to Alexandria; at eight, he renounced the world and entered a monastery; and at eighteen he began to live as a hermit on the southern course of the Kedron near the northwest end of the Dead Sea (the site of the present monastery of Mar Sabba). There he remained five years, being a favorite disciple of the abbot Euthymius (d. 473). With the spread of his fame for holiness, he succeeded in founding a laura with the rule of St. Basil, which was the first of many. In 491 Sabas was ordained priest and made exarch of all hermits in southern Palestine. Such was the honor in which he was held by the Emperor Anastasius, that his intercession in behalf of Elias, bishop of Jerusalem, was received. Though Elias was forced into exile in 517, his successor, Johannes, was induced by Sabas to anathematize all opponents of the Council of Chalcedon, especially the Origenistic monks.

In art Sabas is represented with an apple, since he refused to eat that fruit on account of its part in the fall of man. He is likewise sometimes represented with lions, in allusion to his hermit life in a cave. His order, the Sabaites, never spread beyond Palestine. Their habit was a yellowish-brown mantle, with a black scapular.

2. Gothic martyr; drowned in the Musaeus (a tributary of the Danube) about 372. He is said to have been horribly tortured by the Visigothic King Athanaric (or Athanarid), and the account of his death is contained in a letter from the Christian Goths to the Church of Cappadocia, to which the Roman prefect Soranus is said to have sent his remains at the request of Basil the Great.

3. Gothic martyr, put to death at Rome during the reign of Aurelian (270–275), together with some seventy other Christians.

4. Bishop of Paltus in Syria, and an orthodox delegate to the synods of Constantinople (448) and Chalcedon (451).

5. The surname of a hermit named Julianus, who lived in the fourth century in a cave near Edessa, and was distinguished for his anti-Arian orthodoxy and for his miracles.

(O. Zöckler†.)

Bibliography: On 1: the *Vita* by Cyril of Scythopolis, in J. B. Cotelerius, *Monumenta ecclesiæ Græcæ*, iii. 220–376, Paris, 1686; A. H. Hore, *Eighteen Centuries of the Orthodox Greek Church*, pp. 285–286, New York, 1899; F. Diekamp, *Die origenistischen Streitigkeiten im 6. Jahrhundert*, pp. 5 sqq., Münster, 1899; Ceillier, *Auteurs sacrés*, x. 750, xi. 274–277, 882, xiv. 268; Neander, *Christian Church*, ii. 271, 764; *DCB*, iv. 566–567. On 2: *ASB*, April. ii. 88–90; Tomaschek, in the *Sitzungsberichte* of the Vienna Academy, 1881–82, pp. 437–492; C. A. Scott, *Ulfilas, Apostle of the Goths*, p. 90, London, 1885. On 3: *ASB*,

Apr., iii. 261. On 4: M. Le Quien, *Oriens Christianus*, ii. 799, Paris, 1740; Harduin, *Concilia*, ii. 138, 170, 370. On 5: *ASB.*, Oct. 18.

SABATIER, sā-bā-tyê', CHARLES PAUL MARIE: French Protestant; b. at St. Michael-de-Chabrillanoux, a village in the department of Ardèche, Aug. 3, 1858. He was educated at the lyceums of Besançon and Lille and in the theological department of the University of Paris, from which he was graduated in 1885. He was then vicar of the Protestant Church of St. Nicholas at Strasburg, but was expelled from Germany because he declined to accept a position which would oblige him to become a German citizen. He then returned to France and was for five years (1889–94) pastor at St. Cierge-la-Serre, Ardèche, when he was obliged by ill-health to retire from the ministry. After that time he devoted himself entirely to historical and theological studies. In 1902 he founded at Assisi, Italy, the Société internationale des études franciscaines. In 1898 he was created an honorary citizen of Assisi in recognition of his studies of the life of St. Francis of Assisi (an honor previously conferred only on Garibaldi) and in the following year was elected a member of the Accademia dei Lincei, Rome. He has edited *La Didachè des douze apôtres* (Paris, 1885); *Speculum perfectionis, seu Sancti Francisci Assisiensis legenda antiquissima, auctore fratre Leone* (1898); *Fratris Francisci Bartholdi de Assisio tractatus de Indulgentia Sanctæ Mariæ de Portiuncula* (1900); *Actus Sancti Francisci et seniorum ejus* (1902); *Floretum Sancti Francisci Assisiensis, liber aureus qui Italice dicitur, I. Fioretti di San Francesco*, and the periodical *Opuscules de critique historique*, which he founded in 1904. He discovered in May, 1901, at Capestrane in the Abruzzi the long-lost manuscript of the Franciscan *Regula antiqua tertii ordinis*, which he edited at Paris in 1901. As independent works he has written *Vie de St. François d'Assise* (Paris, 1893; Eng. transl. by L. S. Houghton, New York, 1894; this work has been translated into the principal European languages); *À propos de la séparation des églises et de l'état* (1905; Eng. transl., *Disestablishment in France*, by Robert Dell, London, 1906); *Lettre ouverte à . . . le cardinal Gibbons . . . sur la séparation des églises et de l'état en France* (1907); *Modernism* (London, 1908; Jowett Lectures); and *Les Modernistes, Notes d'histoire religieuse contemporaine* (Paris, 1909).

SABATIER, LOUIS AUGUST: French Protestant; b. at Vallon (95 m. n.w. of Marseilles) Oct. 22, 1839; d. at Paris Apr. 12, 1901. He was educated at the college of Montpellier and at Montauban, and also studied for a time at Basel, Tübingen, and Heidelberg. After being an agent of the Société centrale protestante d'évangélisation at Aubenas, he was appointed, in 1870, professor of Reformed dogmatics at the University of Strasburg. On the outbreak of the Franco-Prussian war, however, he helped to organize a Protestant ambulance service which accompanied the Army of the Loire; and declining a professorship proffered him at Strasburg by the German government, and otherwise manifesting his hostility to the new régime, he was ordered to leave the city. He went to Paris, where he became secretary of the École libre des sciences religieuses, seeking meanwhile to replace Strasburg by a theological faculty to be affiliated with the Sorbonne. Declining a call to Lausanne, he supported himself chiefly by journalism; but in 1877 he saw his hopes fulfilled when the theological faculty of Strasburg was transferred to Paris and he again assumed the chair of Reformed dogmatics. Later he became associate director of the section for the history of religion at the École des hautes études, and in 1895 was made dean of the theological faculty.

The initial point of view of Sabatier was that of entire orthodoxy; but the lifelong problem which he set himself, the reconciliation of faith with science, led him further and further away from orthodox tenets. As early at 1880 he adopted the methods of historical criticism, and his conclusions were such as to lead him to abandon the teaching of the Church not only concerning the person and the work of Christ, but also with regard to the remaining positions of orthodox dogma. To Sabatier religion owed its origin to the desire of man to reconcile the antinomy between his empirical and his ideal ego, and thus became the spiritual aspect of the instinct of self-preservation. In the religious evolution of the race revelation has passed through three stages: mythological (paganism), dogmatic (Roman Catholic and Protestant), and critical or psychological, the latter alone at once satisfying the requirements of piety and criticism. Such revelation is essentially spiritual and progressive, though always subject to the limits of human subjectivity. Religious sources and standards thus need constant revision on the basis of personal experience.

The culmination of religious development, according to Sabatier, is Christianity, the cardinal principle of which is to be a child of God, historically assured to man in the person of Jesus, in whom was first realized the divine revelation which has since been repeated as the experience of the pious Christian. This principle can not be overthrown by scientific criticism, since it is raised above the means and methods of historical criticism in virtue of being personal experience. Yet theology can not dispense with criticism, the function of which is to strip temporary and chance elements from the absolute principle, and thus to render possible an ever purer realization of Christian piety. This process of continual revision is the task of dogmatics, its subject matter being primarily the creeds, which, in the evolution of religion, become obsolete, lose their practical meanings, and become mere formulas. The function of Protestant dogmatics accordingly lies in the choice of such creeds as shall correspond to the requirements of the soul and shall harmonize with the religious consciousness.

Sabatier's works, received in Germany with comparative coolness, were enthusiastically welcomed in France; a section of French Roman Catholicism received a new impulse; and his books appealed to the general Protestant public, and even to circles which had broken with all religion. He was essentially a representative of the modern type of theologian, yet free from all factionalism, and anxious to construct and reconcile rather than to destroy and alienate. In his *Religions of Authority* he declared that his object was "to reconcile all that is eternal in the Christian faith with the most rigid demands of the scientific spirit."

His principal writings are as follows: *Le Témoignage de Jésus-Christ sur sa personne* (Paris, 1863); *Essai sur les sources de la vie de Jésus* (1866); *Johannis evangelium seculo ineunte secundo in ecclesia jam adfuisse demonstratur* (1866); *Jésus de Nazareth* (1867); *L'Apôtre Paul* (1870, 3d ed., 1896; Eng. transl., *The Apostle Paul*, London, 1891); *Guillaume le taciturne* (1872); *De l'influence des femmes sur la littérature française* (1873); *Rapport sur les dangers qui menacent l'église réformée et les moyens de rétablir la paix dans son sein* (1876); *Le Canon du Nouveau Testament* (1877); *De l'esprit théologique* (1878); *Mémoir sur la notice hébraïque de l'esprit* (1879); *Les Origines littéraires de l'Apocalypse de Saint-Jean* (1888); *La Vie intime des dogmes* (1890); *Essai d'une théorie critique de la connaissance religieuse* (1893); *Esquisse d'une philosophie de la religion d'après la psychologie et l'histoire* (1897; partial Eng. transl., *Outlines of a Philosophy of Religion based on Psychology and History*, London, 1897, new ed., 1902); *La Religion et la culture moderne* (1897); *The Vitality of Christian Dogmas and their Power of Evolution: a Study in Religious Philosophy* (London, 1898); *La Critique biblique et l'histoire des religions* (Paris, 1901); *La Doctrine de l'expiation et son évolution historique* (1903; Eng. transl., *Doctrine of the Atonement and its Historical Evolution; Religion and Modern Culture*, London, 1904); and the posthumous *Les Religions d'autorité et la religion de l'esprit* (1903; Eng. transl., *Religions of Authority and Religions of the Spirit, with Memoir* . . . by Jean Réville, London, 1904).

(EUGEN LACHENMANN.)

BIBLIOGRAPHY: On Sabatier's philosophy and theology consult: E. Ménégoz, *Publications diverses sur le fidéisme et son application a l'enseignement chrétien traditionnel*, Paris, 1900; idem, *La Théologie d'Auguste Sabatier*, ib. 1901; idem, *Le Fidéisme et la notion de la foi*, ib. 1905; Riemers, *Het Symbolofideisme. Beschrijving en kritische Beschouwing*, Rotterdam, 1900; G. Lasch, *Die Theologie der Pariser Schule, Characteristik und Kritik des Symbolo-Fideismus*, Berlin, 1901 W. Ward, *Auguste Sabatier and Newman*, in *Fortnightly Review*, lxxv (1901), 808 sqq.; J. Berthoud, *Auguste Sabatier et Schleiermacher*, Geneva, 1902. On the life consult, J. Vienot, F. Puaux, J. E. Roberty, and H. Monnier *Auguste Sabatier, sa vie, sa pensée, et ses travaux*, Paris, 1903; J. Pédézert, *Souvenirs et études*, Paris, 1888; dem *Cinquante ans de souvenirs religieux et ecclésiastiques 1830–80*, ib. 1896; idem, *Auguste Sabatier, simples souvenirs*, Alençon, 1904; P. Chaponnière, *Le Professeur Auguste Sabatier*, Paris, 1902; L. S. Houghton, in *Reformed Church Review*, (1904), 523 sqq H. Dartigue, *Auguste Sabatier, critique littéraire*, Paris, 1910.

SABBATARIANS. See ADVENTISTS, § 2; BAPTISTS, II., 4 (b); COMMUNISM, II., § 5.

SABBATH: The seventh day of the week, observed as a holy day by the Jews. The command to hallow each seventh day as the sabbath of Yahweh by refraining from all work (Ex. xx. 8–11; Deut. v. 12–15) is the only one in the Decalogue which refers to ritual. The sanctity of the sabbath is stressed in the book of the covenant and the holiness code (Ex. xxiii. 12, xxxi. 13 sqq., xxxiv. 21; Lev. xix. 3, 30, xxiii. 3, xxiv. 8; cf. xxvi. 34–35, 43): and the priest code also forbids the lighting of a fire on the sabbath (Ex. xxxv. 3), while the account of the manna in Ex. xvi. 22 sqq., evidently implies that the institution of the sabbath had long been known. The necessity of hallowing the sabbath is further emphasized by the event narrated in Num. xv. 32–36. The proper offerings for the sabbath are enumerated in Num. xxviii. 9–10; and the holiness code (Lev. xxiv. 8) adds that fresh showbread was to be placed in the tabernacle on the sabbath. From II Kings iv. 23 it is evident that the pious were accustomed to visit prophets on the sabbath, doubtless'y to hear the word of God; and in the regal period two-thirds of the royal body-guard were on watch at the Temple on the sabbath, and one-third at the palace, since on that day the concourse of worshipers was especially large (II Kings xi. 5 sqq.). The meaning of the "covert for the sabbath" mentioned in II Kings xvi. 18 is unknown, neither the supposition that it was a covered way for the king to pass from the palace to the Temple nor the hypothesis that it was a covered place built in the Temple for the king to take part in the sabbath services being plausible. The last general event narrated in the Old Testament concerning the sabbath is the suppression of traffic on that day by Nehemiah (Neh. x. 32, xiii. 15 sqq.). The earlier prophets mention the sabbath three times. Amos viii. 4–5 shows that in the northern kingdom of the eighth century traffic was forbidden on the sabbath and on the days of the new moon. According to Hos. ii. 13 the sabbath was a day of rejoicing, and it is also clear from Isa. i. 13–14 that it was a festival of Yahweh, on which the people assembled at the Temple and offered sacrifices. Jeremiah's exhortation to keep the sabbath (Jer. xvii. 19 sqq.) is held by many to be a late addition, but the only basis for this assumption—the theory that such a speech could have been delivered only in the time of Nehemiah, while Jeremiah himself was opposed to all ritual—is entirely inadequate. Jeremiah certainly had the Decalogue before his eyes when he condemned the violation of the sabbath, and the sabbath laws of the Pentateuch were already ancient in Jeremiah's day. His language should be understood in the light of the utterances of his contemporary, Ezekiel, who charged Israel and Judah with having desecrated the sabbath (Ezek. xxii. 8, xxiii. 38), and also severely condemned the elders of Israel who, while wandering in the wilderness, broke the sabbath laws given by Yahweh when he led them out of Egypt (Ezek. xx. 10 sqq.). Since the Pentateuch does not record a profanation of the sabbath in the wilderness, accounts of the events during the thirty-eight years of wandering after the Israelites left Sinai would seem to have existed in the time of Jeremiah and Ezekiel which are no longer extant. Ezekiel describes the sabbath as a sign of the sanctification of Israel by Yahweh (Ezek. xx. 12, 20), a concept found by him in Ex. xxxi. 13, 17, the hypothesis that the Pentateuchal law in question is later than Ezekiel being untenable. It is also evident that by the time of Ezekiel the sabbath had long been distinctively a day of rest, and there is no reason to suppose that either he or his contemporaries made the requirements for its observation more rigid than they had previously been. The Deutero-Isaiah likewise mentions the sabbath. He is blessed who keeps the sabbath holy (Isa. lvi. 2), while one of the indispensable conditions of securing the divine favor is maintaining the sanctity of the sabbath as a day of rest and one sacred to Yahweh (Isa. lviii. 13–14): and, finally, in the

Data of the Old Testament

future reign of the Lord all flesh shall come on each sabbath and each new moon to worship Yahweh (Isa. lxvi. 23). Turning to the Hagiographa, the books of Chronicles, besides their parallel reference to II Kings xi. 5 sqq. (II Chron. xxiii. 1 sqq.), contain a number of allusions to the showbread that was to be placed in the sanctuary on sabbaths and new moons (I Chron. ix. 32, xxiii. 31; II Chron. ii. 3, viii. 13, xxxi. 3); in the Psalms the only reference to the sabbath is the heading of Ps. xcii.; and Lam. ii. 6 mourns that Yahweh has caused feast-day and sabbath to be forgotten in Zion.

Observance in Old-Testament Times.

The Old Testament frequently mentions the sabbath in connection with the new moon (Amos. viii. 5; Isa. i. 13, lxvi. 23; Ezek. xlvi. 1, 3; II Kings iv. 23; II Chron. ii. 3) and also in connection with both new moon and feast (Hos. ii. 13; Ezek. xlv. 17; Neh. x. 34), but in none of these passages is there the slightest implication that the sabbath was connected in any way with the moon, particularly (in contradistinction to the new moon) with the full moon. This statement is decisively confirmed by the commandments regarding the sabbath (Ex. xx. 9-11, xxiii. 12, xxxiv. 21; Deut. v. 12-15), especially as there is no reason to suppose the Decalogue to be later than Ezekiel, or the other sabbatical commandments to be post-exilic. The character of the day clearly remained practically the same from the time of Moses—a day of gladness, sacred to Yahweh, marked by offering of sacrifice, listening to the discourses of prophets, visiting the sanctuary, and cessation of all ordinary toil. The true reason for the collocation of sabbaths and new moons in the Old Testament seems to be that they were recurrent throughout the year, whereas the other feasts occurred but once annually. While, however, the sabbath thus retained its original character throughout the period between Moses and Christ, the views concerning its proper mode of observance apparently changed. It was indeed held that all work, except what was absolutely necessary for daily life, should cease on that day, but the precise scope of these limitations received varying interpretations. Although exact details are unobtainable, it is evident from the words of Jeremiah and Ezekiel that those Israelites who were little inclined to obey the law had almost wholly secularised the sabbath, especially in troublous times. It is equally impossible to ascertain the precise requirements laid down for the proper observance of the day, but it is at least clear that the priestly class was particularly firm in its demand for the hallowing of the sabbath and that the rules laid down gradually increased in strictness.

Origin of the Sabbath.

Two opinions as to the origin of the sabbath were formerly held—one, that God commanded man to rest as he himself had done after creating the world, and that Moses revived the still lingering observance of the command; the other, that the ordinance was originated by Moses, both views being based on the allusions to the sabbath in Ex. xvi. 22 sqq. It is now held by many that the sabbath is Babylonian in origin, though received by the Jews immediately from the Canaanites; while another hypothesis maintains that the sabbath represents a moon-feast of the nomadic ancestors of the Israelites. The Canaanitic and nomadic theories are both undemonstrable and unnecessary, but with the relation between the Jewish and the Babylonian sabbath the problem is more complex. The cuneiform inscriptions contain two equations of importance in this connection, *shabattu* = "day of appeasing the heart (of the gods)," also *shabattu* = "fifteenth day." Consequently the Babylonian sabbath was a day of penance, and the middle of the Babylonian month. It has also been held that the seventh, fourteenth, twenty-first, and twenty-eighth days of the month, designated as ill-omened, were the Babylonian sabbaths; but for this argument there is no evidence, and it must accordingly be assumed that the fifteenth day of each month was the sabbath of the Babylonians. This day was reckoned that of the full moon, but since the Hebrew sabbath was not connected with the full moon and was a day of gladness, not of penance, and since the Babylonians had no week of seven days, the assumption that the Hebrews borrowed the sabbath from the Babylonians lacks all foundation. At the same time there is a certain connection between the Hebrew sabbath and the Babylonian *shabattu*, since the root of both means "cease, end." A number of other etymologies have been proposed, as from Babylonian *shabatu*, "to strike" (the day of striking the breast), or *shapatu*, "to judge" (the day of legal decisions), as a Sumerian word, as an Arabic word *shabat*, "seat" (the alleged pause of the moon at each of its four phases), and as denoting the "perfect moon" (although *shabbath* never means "to be perfect"), but none of these is satisfactory. Both the Hebrew *shabbath* and the Babylonian *shabattu* must, therefore, mean "rest," and while there is no evidence that the Babylonian sabbath was such a day of rest, it can not be demonstrated that the Babylonian here preserved the original character of the day. The reverse would seem to be the case, especially as the Hebrew sabbath was so much more important than the Babylonian. The reason for resting on the sabbath (according to Ex. xx. 10, xxxi. 15; cf. Lev. xix. 3, 30, xxiii. 3, xxvi. 2; Deut. v. 14) is that the day belongs to Yahweh, so that men may not use it for their own purposes. Ex. xxiii. 12 extends its beneficent effects to dependents and cattle (cf. Deut. v. 14-15). The cause of the special sanctity of the sabbath is that on it Yahweh rested after the six days' work of creation (Gen. ii. 2-3; Ex. xx. 11, xxxi. 17). The association of sabbath rest with the account of creation must have been very ancient among the Hebrews, and t is noteworthy that no other Semitic peoples, even the Babylonians, have any tradition of the creation in six days. It would appear that the primitive Semites had four chief moon-days, probably the first, eighth, fifteenth, and twenty-second of each month, called sabbaths from the fact that there was a tendency to end work before them so that they might be celebrated joyfully. Among the Babylonians these seventh days through astrological conceptions became ill-omened, while the sabbath in the middle of the month was made a propitiation, and its name was construed as meaning "the day for ending the wrath of the gods." The Israelites, on the other hand, made the sabbaths the feasts of a living and holy God. The work of man became symbolic of the work of God, and human rest of divine rest, so that the sabbaths became preeminently days of rest. Since, moreover, the lunar month had twenty-nine or thirty days, the normal lapse of time between sabbaths was six days, although sometimes seven or eight; and six working days were accordingly assigned to the creation, which was to furnish a prototype for human life. The connection of the sabbath with the lunar phases, however, was discarded by the Israelites, who did not worship the moon, and the weeks were accordingly divorced from the days of the months and were made to follow in succession throughout the year, a more regular correspondence with the week of creation being thus secured. The first lunar day, however, or the day of new moon, retained, although no longer called sabbath, somewhat of its sabbatical character, so that in the Old Testament it frequently appears as a pendant of the sabbath (see FEASTS AND FESTIVALS, I., § 2; MOON, HEBREW CONCEPTIONS OF THE, § 4).

After the exile the observance of the sabbath was made extremely rigid and in the Maccabean period a large number of ultra-orthodox Jews were killed, together with their wives and children, on the sabbath day, on which they would offer no resistance (I Macc. ii. 27 sqq.; Josephus, *Ant.*, XII., vi. 2–3). Later, however, the Jews considered it lawful to defend themselves on the sabbath, though not to take the offensive (I. Macc. ii. 39–41; II. Macc. viii. 26; Josephus, *Ant.*, XIV., iv. 2). Thirty-nine principal forms of work, together with many minor varieties, came to be forbidden on the sabbath. On the other hand, the work involved in the ritual of the Temple and circumcision was permitted (Matt. xii. 5; John vii. 22–23); assistance might be given to a woman in childbirth and also to the sick if in danger of death; and Matt. xii. 11 states that it was lawful to rescue a sheep from a pit on the sabbath, though this is denied by the Talmud. On the basis of Ex. xvi. 29, combined with Num. xxxv. 5 and Josh. iii. 4, more than a "sabbath day's journey" (2,000 cubits) was forbidden on the sabbath. Nevertheless, the sabbath remained a day of joy among the Jews, and the eating of three hearty meals on that day was enjoined. The sabbath feasts of the Jews accordingly became widely known, although not without receiving mocking criticism, as from Juvenal ("Satires," xiv. 96–106), Persius (v. 184), and Martial (iv. 417), while Seneca (*Opera*, ed. F. Hasse, iii. 427, Leipsic 1863) lamented that a seventh part of life should thus be wasted. Despite this the Jews were imitated by many pagans, so that Josephus could say (*Apion*, ii. 40): "There is not any city of the Grecians, nor any of the barbarians, nor any nation whatsoever, whither our custom of resting on the seventh day hath not come."

Later Jewish Development.

(W. LOTZ.)

BIBLIOGRAPHY: J. Spencer, *De legibus Hebræorum ritualibus*, 2 vols., Cambridge, 1727; F. W. Farrar, *Life of Christ*, i. 374 sqq., 430–443, ii. 83, 118 sqq., London, 13th ed., n.d.; A. Edersheim, *Life and Times of Jesus the Messiah*, ii. 52–62, 182, 774 sqq., London, 1883; W. Lotz, *Quæstiones de historia Sabbati*, Leipsic, 1883; L. Thomas, *Le Jour du seigneur*, 2 vols., Paris, 1892–93; A. H. Sayce, *Verdict of the 'Higher Criticism' and the Monuments*, pp. 76 sqq., London, 1894; H. Gunkel, *Schöpfung und Chaos*, Göttingen, 1895; M. Jastrow, in *AJT*, 1898, pp. 315–352; C. H. W. Johns, *Assyrian Deeds and Documents*, London, 1898; C. H. Toy, in *JBL*, 1899, pp. 191–193; W. Riedel, *Alttestamentliche Untersuchungen*, pp. 74–89, Leipsic, 1902; F. Bohn, *Der Sabbat im Alten Testament*, Gütersloh, 1903; D. Nielsen, *Die altarabische Mondreligion*, pp. 63 sqq., Strasburg, 1904; Pariches, in *PSBA*, 1904, pp. 51–66; Zimmern, in *ZDMG*, 1904, pp. 199 sqq., 458 sqq.; F. Delitzsch, *Babel und Bibel*, i. 62–65, Leipsic, 1905; J. Meinhold, *Sabbat und Woche im A. T.*, Göttingen, 1905; H. Winckler, *Religionsgeschichtlicher und geschichtlicher Orient*, pp. 58 sqq., Leipsic, 1906; J. Hehn, *Siebenzahl und Sabbat bei den Babyloniern und im Alten Testament*, Leipsic, 1907; C. F. Kent, *Student's Old Testament*, iv., § 217, pp. 263–265, New York, 1907; G. Beer, *Schabbath*, Tübingen, 1908; Schürer, *Geschichte*, ii. 450–459, 470–478, 491–493 et passim, Eng. transl., II., ii. 75–83, 96–105, 120–122, et passim; Schrader, *KAT*, pp. 592–594; Nowack, *Archäologie*, ii. 140 sqq.; Benzinger, *Archäologie*, pp. 389–391; *DB*, iv. 317–323; *EB*, iv. 4173–80; *JE*, x. 587–602; *DCG*, ii. 540–542; Vigouroux, *Dictionnaire*, fasc. xxxv., cols. 1291–1306. Also cf. the literature under SUNDAY.

SABBATH DAY'S JOURNEY. See WEIGHTS AND MEASURES, HEBREW.

SABBATH LAWS. See SUNDAY, II.

SABBATICAL YEAR AND YEAR OF JUBILEE: The seventh and fiftieth year respectively, connected with the idea of the Sabbath (q.v.) among the ancient Hebrews and associated with religious usages. The Book of the Covenant directs (Ex. xxi. 2) that a slave of Hebrew descent be set free in the seventh year of his servitude, and Deut. xv. 12 extends this requirement to Hebrew female slaves as well. It is evident that this year was connected with the sabbath, although as yet there was no reference to a year which should possess a sabbatical character throughout the country. The Book of the Covenant (Ex. xxiii. 10–11) requires tillage and harvesting for six years, while in the seventh year the land was to lie fallow and what grew spontaneously was to be left for the poor and wild beasts (see also Lev. xxv. 1–7). Although the context (v. 12) clearly shows that the rest of the land should be analogous to that of the sabbath, there is no implication even here of a sabbatical year for the whole country. Deut. xv. 1 sqq. further required a release from all indebtedness of one Israelite to another every seventh year, the passage in question implying that the "year of release" was observed in the whole country (cf. also Deut. xxxi. 10). These debts were to be remitted each seventh year, not after the lapse of six years from their contraction (cf. Deut. xv. 9); but since a year was required for the release in question, although the actual remission might be made in a single day, it would seem that the "release" was not a remission of the debt but merely a cessation of requests for payment during the year. Since the Deuteronomic law for the manumission of slaves after six years of bondage immediately follows the requirements governing the "year of release," it would appear that this manumission was at least desired in the "year of release." Although it is uncertain when and why each seventh year came to be regarded as a sabbatical year, the basis would seem to have been the "year of release." According to Jer. xxxiv. 8 sqq., there was a general manumission of slaves in harmony with Deut. xv. 12 during the reign of Zedekiah, but no certain conclusions can be drawn from this passage. The sabbatical year was reckoned from autumn to autumn, since the land could not be allowed to begin to lie fallow in the spring, and this is borne out by the fact that the year of jubilee, itself in a sense a sabbatical year, was solemnly announced to begin on the tenth day of the seventh month (Lev. xxv. 9). Although in the preexilic period the sabbatical year was only imperfectly observed (Lev. xxvi. 34–35, 43; II Chron. xxxvi. 21), the Jews under Ezra and Nehemiah expressly pledged themselves to keep it (Neh. x. 31), and it was fully observed in the time of Alexander the Great, the Hasmoneans, and the Herodians (I Macc. vi. 49, 53; Josephus, *Ant.*, XI., viii. 6, XIII., viii. 1, XIV., x. 6, xvi. 2, XV., i. 2; *War*, I., ii. 4; Philo, in Eusebius, *Præparatio evangelica*, vii., Eng. transl., i. 389–391, Oxford, 1903; Tacitus, *Hist.*, v. 4). This observance must, however, have been extremely difficult, and the Talmud (*Shebhi'ith*, VI., ii. 5–6), on the basis of Lev. xxv. 2, restricted the validity of the law to Palestine.

The law of the year of jubilee follows that of the sabbatical year in Lev. xxv. 8 sqq., which enacts that at the expiration of seven sabbatical years, i.e., in each fiftieth year, a trumpet should be sounded throughout the land on the tenth day of the seventh month, i.e., on the Day of Atonement, the first day of the year of jubilee. Like the sabbatical year, the year of jubilee was to have no harvest reaped in it, but in addition it was a year of freedom for all the inhabitants of the country. Each man should return to the property which he had been obliged to sell; all lands and buildings sold outside the walled cities were to be held only until the next year of jubilee; and Israelites who had been forced to sell themselves into bondage were to be released in the year of jubilee (Lev. xxv. 39–55). There is no reason to doubt that the law of the year of jubilee is preexilic, and it is evidently a remodeling of an older enactment of uncertain nature. The precise date of its origin is equally obscure, though it may be a parallel to the Feast of Weeks. There is an obvious allusion to the year of jubilee in Ezek. xlvi. 16 sqq., and probably in Isa lxi. 1–2. Ezra and Nehemiah, on the other hand, never mention it, and there is an express Jewish tradition that after the time of Ezra the year of jubilee was no longer observed. (W. Lotz.)

Bibliography: B. Zuckermann, *Ueber Sabbathjahrcyclus und Jobelperiode*, Breslau, 1857; C. P. Caspari, *Die geschichtlichen Sabbathjahre*, in *TSK*, 1876, pp. 181–190; H. Ewald, *Antiquities of Israel*, pp. 338, 369–372, Boston, 1876; J. Fenton, *Early Hebrew Life*, pp. 66–74, London, 1880; Schürer, *Geschichte*, i. 35–37, 214, 258–259, ii. 363, iii. 104–105, Eng. transl., I., i. 41–43, 224, 274, ii. 157, II., i. 362–363, ii. 295; Nowack, *Archäologie*, ii. 163–165; Benzinger, *Archäologie*, 398; J. Meinhold, *Sabbat und Woche im Alten Testament*, pp. 21 sqq., Göttingen, 1905; C. F. Kent, *Students' Old Testament*, iv., §§ 223–224, pp. 274–276, New York, 1907; *DB*, iv. 323–326; *EB*, ii. 2614–16, *JE*, x. 605–608. Vigouroux, *Dictionnaire*, iii. 1753 and fasc. xxxv., cols. 1302–1306; the commentaries on the passages cited, and the works on the theology of the Old Testament (under Biblical Theology).

SABELLIUS, SABELLIANISM. See Monarchianism, VI.

SABIANS. See Mandeans.

SABINE, WILLIAM TUFNELL: Reformed Episcopal bishop; b. in New York City Oct. 16, 1838. He was graduated from Columbia University, (A.B., 1859) and at the General Theological Seminary, New York City (1862), being ordered deacon in the Protectant Episcopal Church in the same year and ordained priest in 1863. After being curate of St. George's, New York City (1862–63), he was rector of the Church of the Covenant, Philadelphia (1863–65), and of the Church of the Atonement, New York City (1866–74). In 1874, on the formation of the Reformed Episcopal body, he withdrew from the Protestant Episcopal Church, and from that year to 1907 was pastor of the First Reformed Episcopal Church, New York City. In 1902 he was elected bishop of the New York and Philadelphia Synod of the Reformed Episcopal Church.

SABINIAN, sa″bin'i-an: Pope 604–606. He was born at Volterra (32 m. s.w. of Florence), Italy, in the sixth century. Though only a deacon, he was elected on Sept. 13, 604, to succeed Gregory I., who had once sent him as nuncio to Byzantium. The only known events of his pontificate are his endeavors to relieve a severe famine, but even these efforts do not seem to have saved him from the hatred of the Roman populace [aroused by his avarice and cruelty to the poor]. (A. Hauck.)

Bibliography: Sources are: *Liber pontificalis*, ed. L. Duchesne, 2 vols., Paris, 1886–92, and ed. T. Mommsen, in *MGH*, *Gest. pont. Rom.*, i. 1 (1898), 163; and Paul the Deacon's *Vita Gregorii I.*, in *MPL*, lxxv. 41 sqq. Consult: R. Baxmann, *Die Politik der Päpste von Gregor I. bis auf Gregor VII.*, i. 149, Elberfeld, 1868; F. Gregorovius, *Hist. of . . . Rome in the Middle Ages*, ii. 104–105, London, 1894; Mann, *Popes*, i. 251–259; Bower, *Popes*, i. 424–425; Platina, *Popes*, i. 140–141; Milman, *Latin Christianity*, ii. 262–264.

SABTAH. See Table of the Nations, § 6.

SACCHONI, sach-o'ni, **RAINERIO:** Roman Catholic inquisitor; d. after 1262. His birthplace was Piacenza, but nothing is known of his early years. He joined the Cathari (see New Manicheans, II.) and was one of them for seventeen years, attaining the dignity of bishop. He was brought back to the faith of the Church apparently by the preaching of Peter of Verona (q.v.) and the Dominican Moneta (d. about 1235). When Peter Martyr was murdered at Como in 1252 at the instigation of the Cathari, Rainerio was appointed in his place as inquisitor in Lombardy. In 1259, the heretics succeeded in driving him out of Milan. He had induced Alexander IV. to put under the ban Uberto Pallacino, a distinguished personage of Milan, who favored the Cathari. Uberto obtained a decision of the Podesta banishing Rainerio (Muratori, *Scriptores*, xvi. 662). The last known of Rainerio is that he was summoned to Rome on July 31, 1262, by Urban IV. to consult on important matters. The year of his death is unknown. Rainerio is important for his account of the Cathari. His *Summa de Chataris et Leonistis*, obviously intended for the information of the Inquisition, is still the most important source for the history and doctrines of that obscure sect, though it no longer exists in its original form. It was first published by Gretser (*Liber contra Waldenses*, Ingolstadt, 1613), but it is doubtful whether other writings are not included with it; also in E. Martène and U. Durand, *Thesaurus novum anecdotorum*, v. 1775 sqq. (Paris, 1717). (F. COHRS.)

BIBLIOGRAPHY: J. Quétif and J. Échard, *Scriptores ordinis prædicatorum*, i. 154 sqq., ii. 817, Paris, 1719–21; A. Touron, *Hist. des hommes illustres de l'ordre de St. Dominique*, i. 313 sqq., ib. 1743; J. C. L. Gieseler, *De Rainerii summa commentatio critica*, Göttingen, 1834; A. W. Dieckhoff, *Die Waldenser im Mittelalter*, pp. 152 sqq., ib. 1851; W. Preger, *Geschichte der deutschen Mystik im Mittelalter*, i. 168 sqq., Leipsic, 1874; H. Reuter, *Geschichte der religiösen Aufklärung im Mittelalter*, ii. 317, Berlin, 1877; K. Müller, *Die Waldenser*, pp. 147–148, Gotha, 1886; *KL*, x. 1452–53; H. C. Lea, *Hist. of the Inquisition in the Middle Ages*, vol. ii. passim, New York, 1906.

SACHAU, sac'au, EDUARD: Orientalist; b. at Neumünster (36 m. n. of Hamburg) July 20, 1845. In 1869 he became extraordinary professor of Semitic languages at Vienna, and was advanced to ordinary professor in 1872; went to Berlin as professor of oriental languages, 1876; traveled in Syria and Mesopotamia, 1879–80, and 1897–98; became director of the oriental seminary at Berlin, 1887; and received civil recognition as councilor in 1906. He has written or edited: *De Aljavaligi ejusque opere* (Halle, 1867); *Theodori Mopsuesteni fragmenta Syriaca* (Leipsic, 1869); *Inedita Syriaca; eine Sammlung syrischen Uebersetzungen von Schriften griechischer Profanliteratur* (Vienna, 1870); *The Chronology of Ancient Nations. An English Version of the Arabic Text of the Athar-ul-bakiya of Albiruni* (London, 1879); *Syrisch-römisches Rechtsbuch aus dem 5. Jahrhundert* (Leipsic, 1880; in collaboration with C. G. Bruns); *Reise in Syrien und Mesopotamien* (1883); *Albiruni's India* (London, 1888); *Indo-Arabische Studien zur Aussprache und Geschichte des Indischen in der ersten Hälfte des 11. Jahrhunderts* (Berlin, 1888); *Muhammedanisches Erbrecht von Zanzibar und Ost-Afrika* (1894); *Skizze des Fellichi-Dialekts von Mosul* (1895); *Ueber die Poesie in der Volkssprache der Nestorianer* (1896); *Muhammedanisches Recht nach schafiitischer Lehre* (1897); *Am Euphrat und Tigris. Reise Notizen . . . 1897–98* (Leipsic, 1900); *Drei aramäische Papyrus-Urkunden aus Elefantine* (Berlin, 1908); and Ibn Saad's *Biographien Muhammeds* (Leyden, 1908–09); besides a considerable number of smaller brochures dealing with various inscriptions and other matters of oriental and Biblical interest.

SACHEVERELL, sa-shev'er-el, HENRY: Church of England; b. at Marlborough (70 m. w. of London), Wiltshire, about 1674; d. at The Grove (13 m. n.w. of London), Highgate, Middlesex, June 5, 1724. He was graduated at Oxford (B.A., 1693; M.A., 1695; B.D., 1707); was senior dean of arts of Magdalen College, 1708, and bursar in 1709; and was appointed preacher at St. Saviour's, Southwark, in 1705. In 1709 he preached two sermons which, on account of their political bearing, gave the gravest offense to the ministry and the majority of parliament (whigs). He was impeached for libel by the house of commons; and in 1710 he was convicted by the peers, and suspended for three years from the ministry. He was ardently supported, however, by the tories, the clergy, and the country squires; and the excitement caused by his trial contributed much to the defeat of the whigs in the general election of 1710 and the downfall of Sidney Godolphin and his colleagues. In 1713 he was made rector of St. Andrew's, Holborn, in which position he died.

BIBLIOGRAPHY: F. Madan, *A Bibliography of Dr. Henry Sacheverell*, privately printed, Oxford, 1887 (indispensable for sources); W. Bisset, *The Modern Fanatick*, London, 1710 (a violent attack); W. King, *Vindication of the Rev. Dr. Henry Sacheverell*, ib. 1710 (reply to Bisset); T. Hearne, *Remarks and Collections*, ed. C. E. Doble for Oxford Historical Society, vols. i.–iii. passim, Oxford, 1885 sqq.; C. A. Lane, *Illustrated Notes on English Church History*, pp. 205–206, London, 1892; W. H. Hutton, *The English Church . . . (1625–1714)*, pp. 260–262, ib. 1903; *DNB*, l. 80–83 (has reference to scattering notices).

SACHS, sacs, HANS: German Lutheran poet; b. at Nuremberg Nov. 5, 1494; d. there Jan. 19, 1576. After completing his education at the Latin school of his native city, he was apprenticed, at the age of fifteen, to a shoemaker, and during the two years following received his first instruction in the Meistersinger's art.

His Life.

After his "wander years" (1511–16), he returned to his native town, where he henceforth resided as a shoemaker and poet. His life falls in the period of Nuremberg's prosperity, and in this city, the home of wealth, art, and learning, he was honored as the master and patriarch of the Meistersingers. The dialect used by him is Bavarian High German. His first work as a Meistersinger was his *Bul Scheidelied* (1513), but his chief activity began after his return to Nuremberg. At the instance of his friends, he undertook a complete edition of his writings (5 vols., Nuremberg, 1558–79, reprinted, Kempten, 1612–17), which contained 1,462 poems, though he himself prepared only the first three volumes. All forms of poetry are represented—epic, lyric, didactic, and dramatic—and the themes are drawn indifferently from sacred and profane history, legend, descriptions of nature and geography, civil and domestic life, events of the author's own life or the lives of others, and from his own imagination. The sources which he expressly names are more than 120, among the more modern being Boccaccio, S. Brant, Reuchlin, Erasmus, Alberus, and Agricola.

The first volume of the Nuremberg edition of Hans Sachs is opened by his *Tragedia von der Schöpffung, Fall und Austreibung Ade auss dem Paradeiss*, a drama with eleven characters and three acts, written in 1533. This is followed by a poem on the children of Eve, based on the writings of Agricola.

Principal Poems.

The most important poem drawn from the New Testament is the tragedy of the passion with thirty-one characters and ten acts, written in 1557. The antagonism between the law and the Gospels is set forth in the tragedy of the last judgment with thirty-four characters and seven acts (1558). From the "golden legend" is drawn *Ein Comedi von dem reichen sterbenden Menschen der Hecastus genannt* (1549), which treats of a rich man called from the joys of life to the divine judgment seat, where, abandoned by his friends, he finds consolation in faith in the merits of Christ. Besides purely Biblical narratives are found legends of apostles and martyrs. In the writings which treat of virtues and vices there is found keen observation, cogent thought, and well-drawn characters, despite frequent monotony and prolixity. Here mention can only be made of *Das künstlich Frauen Lob, Fama das weitfliegend Gerücht, Die gut und bös Eigenschaft des Geldes*, and *Kampfgespräch Xenophontis Philosophi mit Frau Tugend und Frau Untugend*. It is, however, in the fables, farces, and Shrove Tuesday plays that Hans Sachs reaches the zenith of his art. In the farces, 210 in number, the devil and fools are the principal characters. The devil, however, is ridiculous rather than dangerous, while the speeches of the fools contain serious admonitions. Among these farces allusion may be made to *Der Teufel sucht ihm eine Ruhstatt auf Erden, Der eigensinnig Mönch mit dem Wasserkrug*, and *Der Einsiedel mit dem Honigkrug*. The Shrove Tuesday plays, of which the Nuremberg edition contains forty-two, are essentially dramatized farces, designed, as their author said, "only for seemly merriment and joy." The first of these plays, *Das Hofgesind Veneris* 1517), is based on the Tannhäuser cycle, and among the others are *Das bös Weib, Der fahrend Schüler im Paradeiss, Das heiss Eisen*, and *Das Weib im Brunnen*. In regard to religion and the Church, Hans Sachs was a Christian, almost a Protestant, poet. Between 1514 and 1518 he wrote eight hymns, in 1525 he issued his *Etliche geystliche in der schrifft gegrünte Lieder für die layen zu singen*, and in 1528 his *Dreytzehen Psalmen*, his entire contributions of this character numbering thirty-five. Many of these marked distinct changes from the older views, as when he modified the *Sant Christoff du heyliger man* into the *Christe warer sun Gottes fron*. To the same category belong the paraphrases of books and portions of the Bible, as of the Psalter, Ecclesiastes, Ecclesiasticus, the types of the Old Testament, and the gospels for Sundays.

Anti-Romanist Writings.

Hans Sachs was not only a poet, but a polemist, and was one of the first and most decided adherents of the Reformation in Nuremberg. Long an admirer of Luther, he himself entered the lists against the Roman Catholic Church with his poem of 700 verses, *Die Wittembergisch Nachtigall, die man yetz höret überall* (1523). In 1524 he published his *Vier Dialogen in Prosa:* the disputation between a canon and a shoemaker; an attack on the outward works and vows of the clergy; and two admonitions to the Lutherans themselves against unseemly conduct and against abuse of their freedom. He created a sensation in 1527 by publishing, together with A. Osiander, his *Eyn wunderliche weyssagung von dem Babstumb, wie es yhm biss an das endt der welt gehen sol, in Figuren oder gemäl begriffen*, a work consisting of thirty pictures and 150 verses by Hans Sachs. Luther highly approved the production, but it was suppressed at Nuremberg, and its author received a sharp warning from the authorities. Nevertheless, he expressed similar views two years later in his *Inhalt zweierlei Predigt, jede in einer kurzen Summ begriffen*, in which the Lutheran doctrine of salvation was set forth in fifty-five verses, while all the practises of the Roman Catholic Church were pictured in an equal number of strophes, the reader being invited, at the close, to make his choice. To the same category belongs his *Der gut und der bös Hirt* (1531), based on John x., in which the shepherd with the triple crown enters the house by the roof, while the good shepherd (the Lutheran pastor) comes in by the door. Of bitterly polemic character was the *Vergleichung des Babst mit Christo, jr paider leben und passion* (1551), in seventy-five verses, and equally virulent was his *Epitaphium Lutheri* (1546). Repeatedly in other poems Hans Sachs assails usages and conditions in the Roman Catholic Church of which he disapproved. His *Heiltum für das unfleissige Haushalten* was directed against relics, *Der Ketzermeister mit den viel Kesselsuppen* against luxury in monastic life, and *Der Schwank vom verlornen und redeten Gulden* against the pope and indulgences, while auricular confession, holy water, and monasticism also came in for a share of his sarcasm. In the comedy of *Die ungleichen Kinder Evä* the good children repeat the Lutheran catechism by heart and receive all earthly blessings, while the bad answer with nonsense or in terms of atheism and Roman Catholicism, and are condemned to servitude and wretchedness.

In his lifetime Hans Sachs enjoyed wide esteem. With the change in poetic structure in the early seventeenth century, he sank into oblivion, but was rescued by Goethe and Herder, and since then he has been recognized as the first poet of the sixteenth century. (G. Holz.)

Bibliography: M. S. Ranisch, *Historisch-kritische Lebensbeschreibung Hans Sachsens*, Altenburg, 1765; R. Genée, *Hans Sachs und seine Zeit*, 2d ed., Leipsic, 1902; J. L. Hoffmann, *Hans Sachs. Sein Leben und Wirken*, Nuremberg, 1847; O. Haupt, *Leben und dichterische Wirksamkeit des Hans Sachs*, Posen, 1868; F. Ahlfeld and E. Luthard, *Hans Sachs und Albrecht Dürer*, Leipsic, 1875; F. Schultheiss, *Hans Sachs in seinem Verhältnisse zu Reformation*, Leipsic, 1879; W. Kawerau, *Hans Sachs und die Reformation*, Halle, 1883; H. Nietschmann, *Hans Sachs, Ein Lebensbild*, Halle, 1889; E. Mummenhoff, *Hans Sachs*, Nuremberg, 1894; J. Nover, *Hans Sachs*, Hamburg, 1895; L. B. Suphan, *Hans Sachs, Humanitätszeit und Gegenwart*, Weimar, 1895; L. Mettetal, *Hans Sachs et la réformation*, Paris, 1895; F. Fichler, *Das Nachleben des Hans Sachs*, Leipsic, 1904; H. Holzschuher, *Hans Sachs in seiner Bedeutung für unsere Zeit*, Berlin, 1906.

SACHSSE, säc'se, **EUGEN:** German Protestant; b. at Cologne Aug. 20, 1839. He was educated at the universities of Bonn and Berlin (lic. theol., 1863), and after being pastor at Notho-on-the-Weser (1863–69), and teacher at the normal school of Hilchenbach (1869–71), was pastor at Hamm (1871–1883); director and professor of the seminary for preachers at Herborn (1883–90), and was called to his present post of professor of practical theology in the Protestant faculty of the University of Bonn in 1890. He has written *Ursprung und Wesen des Pietismus* (Wiesbaden, 1884); *Die ewige Erlösung* (sermons: 2 vols., Gütersloh, 1885–98); *Ueber die Möglichkeit Gott zu erkennen* (Giessen, 1888); *Evangelische Katechik* (Berlin, 1897), and *Der geschichtliche Wert der drei ersten Evangelien* (1904); and has published a German translation of A. Hyperius's *Homiletik und Katechik* (in collaboration with E. C. Achelis; Berlin, 1901).

SACK BRETHREN (*Fratres saccati, Saccophori, Sachetti*): An order of hermits formed early in the thirteenth century for rigid asceticism and works of mercy. They received their name from the rough garments worn by them, though they were also known as "Penitential Brethren of Jesus Christ" and *Boni Homines* (q.v.). The Sack Brethren were introduced into England by Henry III. in 1257, though they had existed in Spain in the pontificate of Innocent III., and in France and Flanders. The order seems to have been suppressed by the Council of Lyons in 1275, probably because of heretical views rife among them, whereupon the brothers entered other orders, such as the Servites. The Sack Brethren lived extremely rigorously, abstaining from the use of wine, drinking only water, and practising communism of property. By the end of the fourteenth century their name had vanished from history.

A similar order of nuns was founded by Louis IX. of France in 1261. They termed themselves the "Penitent Daughters of Jesus," and were also called, from their habit, Saccariæ or Sachettes. Though the order survived only a short time in France, where the nunneries were near St. André-des-Arcs, Sack Sisters seem to have had houses in London as late as 1357. (O. Zöckler†.)

Bibliography: Helyot, *Ordres monastiques*, iii. 175 sqq.; Heimbucher, *Orden und Kongregationen*, ii. 182; A. G. Little, in *English Historical Review*, Jan., 1894, pp. 121 sqq.

SACK, sëc, AUGUST FRIEDRICH WILHELM: German Reformed; b. at Harzgerode (50 m. s.e. of Brunswick) Feb. 4, 1703; d. at Berlin Apr. 23, 1786. He was educated at Frankfort and Leyden, after which he was a private tutor in Groningen. Returning to Germany, he became, in 1728, tutor of the hereditary prince of Hesse-Homburg, and in 1731 was called to be third minister of the German Reformed church in Magdeburg, where he founded a poorhouse and orphan asylum which still exist. In 1738 he became first minister of the same church, and consistorial councilor and inspector of the Reformed churches in the duchy of Magdeburg. From 1740 until his retirement in 1780 he was court and cathedral preacher at Berlin and member of the consistory. Theologically he was orthodox in a period of religious indifference and latitudinarianism, yet possessed of characteristic Protestant independence of thought and averse to all forms of compulsion. Though his mediating position exposed him to severe criticism from adherents of more one-sided views, he enjoyed, in general, the support of men of all parties, many of whom he counted among his personal friends and correspondents. In 1745 Sack was chosen a member of the physical section of the Berlin Academy of Sciences, and from 1751 to 1766, in addition to his other duties, he was a visitor of the Reformed Joachimsthal Gymnasium. He also directed for a time the benevolent institutions connected with the cathedral, and during the residence of the royal family at Magdeburg during the Seven Years' War was not only their chaplain, but also the religious teacher of the princes and princesses.

Sack's theological convictions may be gathered most fully from his *Vertheidigter Glaube der Christen* (Berlin, 1751), a popular presentation of apologetics and dogmatics, as well as from the notes and meditations contained in his *Lebensbeschreibung* (ed. F. S. G. Sack, 2 vols., Berlin, 1789). He was naturally under the influence of the philosophy of Leibnitz and Wolff, and consequently presupposed a natural religion based on concepts of divine perfections, the attainment of religious convictions by processes of reason, and the like. At the same time, he regarded such natural religion as inadequate for the needs of man, seeing perfection in the Bible alone, and seeking the proof of its divine inspiration in its contents and their effect on the human soul. The central point of revelation he held to be the mediation and the redemption by Christ; forgiveness and blessedness are possible only on condition of repentance and true faith in Christ the mediator. The doctrines of prevenient grace and justification by faith, on the other hand, are comparatively neglected, while regeneration is emphasized. His sermons were collected in six volumes (1735–64). (K. H. Sack†.)

Bibliography: The chief source is the *Lebensbeschreibung*, ut sup. Consult further: J. M. H. Döring, *Die deutschen Kanzelredner des 18. und 19. Jahrhunderts*, pp. 353–360, Neustadt, 1830; R. Rothe, *Geschichte der Predigt*, p. 421, Wittenberg, 1881.

SACK, FRIEDRICH SAMUEL GOTTFRIED: German Reformed; b. at Magdeburg Sept. 4, 1738; d. at Berlin Oct. 2, 1817. He was educated at the University of Frankfort (1755–57) and in England (1758–59), and was appointed, in 1769, German Reformed preacher in his native city. In 1777 he was called to Berlin as fifth court and cathedral preacher, becoming the Reformed member of the supreme consistory in 1786. He gradually rose to be first court preacher, but was chiefly active in religious instruction and in official duties. In 1804 he was made chief school councilor, and in 1814 was appointed presiding officer of the committee for the improvement of the Protestant church system; in 1816 he became a bishop of the Evangelical Church. In his theological views he was slightly semi-Pelagian, but an opponent of deism and of the speculation and pantheistic tendencies of German philosophy beginning with Fichte. In ecclesiastical administration he sought to keep the Church from too close connection with the State, and in 1788 was one of the five who protested against the officializing of orthodoxy enacted by the religious edict issued by Wöllner's ministry. He labored earnestly to revive true religion among both Lutherans and Reformed, as exemplified in his *Gutachten über die Verbesserung des Religionszustandes in den königlichen preussischen Ländern* (Berlin, 1802). He also wrote *Schriften an einen Freund den Herrn Dr. Bahrdt und sein Glaubensbekenntnis betreffend* (1779); *Ein Wort der Ermunterung an meine Mitbürger* (1807); and *Ueber die Vereinigung der beiden protestantischen Kirchenparteien in der preussischen Monarchie* (1812). (K. H. Sack†.)

Bibliography: M. S. Löwe, *Bildnisse . . . jetztlebender Berliner Gelehrten*, Berlin, 1806–07 (supplied by Sack himself); F. Theremin, *Gedächtnisspredigt auf den Bischof F. S. G. Sack*, Berlin, 1817; J. M. H. Döring, *Die deut-*

schen Kanzelredner des 18. und 19. Jahrhunderts, p. 365, Neustadt, 1830.

SACK, KARL HEINRICH: German Lutheran, son of the preceding; b. at Berlin Oct. 17, 1789; d. at Bonn Oct. 16, 1875. He was educated at the University of Göttingen, returning to Berlin in 1810. Three years later he served as a volunteer in the Napoleonic war, where he gained the Iron Cross, and in 1815 returned to the field as a chaplain. On the close of hostilities he spent a year and a half in touring Germany, Holland, and England, and on his return became privat-docent at the University of Berlin. In 1818 he was called to Bonn as professor of theology, and in the following year also became Lutheran pastor in the same city. In 1834, however, he resigned his pastorate that he might devote himself to his professorial duties. In his theology Sack was strongly influenced by Schleiermacher, as is clear from his *Idee und Entwurf der christlichen Apologetik* (Bonn, 1819), *Christliche Apologetik* (Hamburg, 1829), and *Christliche Polemik* (1838). His rigid adherence to the Bible as the foundation of the Church was evinced in his *Vom Worte Gottes* (Bonn, 1825) and *Ueber das Ansehen der heiligen Schrift* (1827; in collaboration with Nitzsch and Gottfried Christian Friedrich Lücke), while he attacked the myth-theory of Strauss in his *Das Leben Jesu von Strauss* (1836). Shortly after 1840 Sack visited Scotland, the results of his observations being embodied in his *Die Kirche von Schotland* (2 parts, Heidelberg, 1844–45). In 1847 he accepted a call to Magdeburg as consistorial councilor. Here, in the face of many difficulties, he strove faithfully to promote the cause of union, until, in 1860, he retired from active life, living henceforth first in Berlin, and later at Neuwied and Bonn. During these years of retirement he wrote his last work, *Ueber die Geschichte der Predigt von Mosheim bis Schleiermacher* (1866). (David Erdmann†.)

Bibliography: W. Beyschlag, *Karl Immanuel Nitzsch*, Berlin, 1872; *Neue evangelische Kirchenzeitung*, 1875, pp. 772–773; L. Lemme, *Heilsthatsachen und Glaubenserfahrung*, Heidelberg, 1895.

SACRAMENT.

The name sacrament is given to seven sacred Christian rites in the Roman Catholic and Eastern churches, and to two, baptism and the Lord's Supper, in the Protestant churches. The Greek word *mysterion*, "mystery," used in the Eastern Church to designate these rites, is taken from the New Testament, and contains a reference to the hidden virtue behind the outward symbol (see Mystagogical Theology).

1. Name and Early Church Theory.

The Latin word *sacramentum* means something that is consecrated, more particularly an oath, especially a military oath of allegiance to the standard; and also the sum of money deposited in court by the plaintiff and defendant previous to the trial of a case, and kept in some sacred place. The term was applied to Christian rites in the time of Tertullian, but can not be traced further back by any distinct testimony. Jerome translated the Greek work *mysterion* by *sacramentum* (Eph. i. 9, iii. 3, 9, v. 32; I Tim. iii. 16; Rev. i. 20), and from the Vulgate the word sacrament passed into the Reims Version in Eph. v. 32, where marriage is spoken of, and the translation is, "This is a great sacrament." In other cases the Reims Version retains the word "mystery."

The doctrine of the sacraments was not fully developed till the Middle Ages, and the Schoolmen did for it what the Church Fathers did for the doctrines of the Trinity and for Christology. With the exception of Augustine, none of the Fathers gave more than passing attention to the definition and doctrine of sacraments; but the Eastern Church held that there were two sacraments, baptism and the Eucharist, although later the number seven was accepted. St. Augustine has a number of passages bearing on the definition, meaning, and necessity of the sacraments. He calls baptism and the Eucharist sacraments "in an eminent sense" (*Epist. ad Januarium*, liv. 1, *MPL*, xxxiii. 2000), and he likewise applied the term sacrament to ordination to the priesthood (*Contra epist. Parmeniani*, II., xiii. 20; *MPL*, xliii. 70), to marriage (*De bono conjugali*, 21; *MPL*, xl. 394; *NPNF*, 1 ser., iii. 408), and to other rites. He assigned sacraments to the Old Testament as well as to the New, and spoke of the former as promising a Savior, and of the latter as giving salvation (On Ps. lxxiv. 1; *NPNF*, 1 ser. viii. 343). He defined a sacrament as a visible sign of a thing divine (*De catechizandis rudibus*, xxvi. 50; *NPNF*, 1 ser., iii. 312), and, commenting on John vi. 41–59, he declared: "The sacrament is one thing, the virtue of the sacrament another" (*In Joannis Evangelium Tractatus*, xxvi. 11; *NPNF*, vii. 171). He did not, however, write a connected treatise on the sacraments; this task remained for the Schoolmen.

The sacramental system was one of the inspiring constructions of the Schoolmen and engaged their most careful and profound speculation. To no other one branch of theology did they give more attention, and their conclusions determined the dogma of the Latin Church, especially when reaffirmed by the Council of Trent. The theologians most prominent in developing the sacramental system were Hugo of St. Victor, who wrote the first formal treatise on the sacraments (see Hugo of St. Victor, §§ 5–6), Peter Lombard, Alexander of Hales, and Thomas Aquinas (qq.v.).

2. Medieval Development of Sacramental Doctrine.

The last-named did little more than clearly reaffirm the views of his three predecessors, especially Alexander of Hales; and with him the development may be said to have come to an end, for though the Franciscan Duns Scotus (q.v.) modified some parts of the doctrine, his teachings were set aside by the Council of Ferrara (1439) in favor of the clearer statements of his great Dominican antagonist, Thomas Aquinas. The Schoolmen all started with the definitions of Augustine and were not conscious of having departed from him, although they did so by laying emphasis upon the *ex opere operato* theory of the efficiency of the sacraments (see Opus Operantis, Opus Operatum) and by reducing the prominence given by Augustine to the operation of grace. The number was fixed at seven, and thus the uncertainty which had been inherited from the fathers and had been felt by the earlier Schoolmen was removed, especially through the influence of Peter Lombard and Thomas Aquinas. Dionysius the Areopagite had given six sacraments—baptism, the Eucharist, unction, the ordination of priests, the ordination of monks, and burial rites. Bernard of Clairvaux spoke of many sacraments and enumerated ten, including foot-washing; Abelard named five—baptism, confirmation, the Eucharist, marriage, and extreme unction; and Robert Pulleyn (q.v.) gave the same number. Hugo of St. Victor likewise seems to recognize five in his *Summa*—baptism, confirmation, Eucharist, penance, and extreme unction—but in his *De sacramentis christianæ fidei* he enumerates thirty, taking the word sacrament in the wide sense of religious rite. In this latter work he divided the sacraments into three classes, among which, for instance, holy water and the use of ashes on Ash Wednesday belong to the second class and are distinctly called sacraments, Thomas Aquinas himself ascribing a quasi-sacramental character to such rites. Councils were equally undecided as to the number of the sacraments and the definition of the term. Thus the Third Lateran Council (1179) included the investiture of bishops and the rites of burial among the sacraments, and the Roman Catholic Church to-day makes a distinction between certain sacred rites called Sacramentals (q.v.) and the seven sacraments. Peter Lombard was not the first to give the number seven. About his time it had been given by Roland Bandinelli (afterwards Alexander III.) in his *Sententiæ*, and by Otto of Bamberg in a sermon of 1158, as reported by his biographer, Herbord. The seven sacraments are baptism, the Eucharist, confirmation, extreme unction, penance, ordination, and marriage. The number seven corresponds with the seven virtues and the seven deadly sins, and also unites the number of the deity (three) and of creation (four), thus illustrating the union of God and man. This correspondence was called the "congruity" of the sacraments, that is, their correlation to the spiritual maladies and needs of man. The sacraments were not needed in man's estate of innocence. With Augustine the Schoolmen represent the sacraments of the Old Testament as prefiguring the grace to come, and the sacraments of the New as conferring grace.

3. Nature of Sacraments. In defining a sacrament, the Schoolmen started with Augustine's definition that it is a visible symbol of an invisible grace, but went beyond him in the degree of efficiency they ascribed to it. They assert that the sacraments "contain and confer grace" and that they have a virtue inherent in themselves. The favorite figure used to describe their operation is medicine, so that Hugo of St. Victor (*De sacramentis*, I., ix. 4; *MPL*, clxxvi. 325) could term God the physician, man the invalid, the priest the minister, grace the antidote, and the sacrament the vessel. The physician gives, the minister dispenses, and the vessel contains the spiritual medicine which cures the soul. The sacraments are, however, more than channels of grace. They do more than signify. They sanctify, and they are the efficient causes of the operations of grace in the recipient. The mode of this efficacy is *ex opere operato*, the expression used by such writers as William of Auxerre and Alexander of Hales. Thomas Aquinas adopted the expression, and again and again says that the sacraments make righteous and confer grace *ex opere operato*, that is, by a virtue inherent in themselves. By this he did not mean that the religious condition of the recipient is a matter of indifference, but that the sacraments impart virtue, if need be, without the operation of active faith. The sacraments are efficacious only to those who are of a religious disposition, but they are always efficacious when properly administered.

4. Intention. The relation the priest sustains to the sacraments is vital to their efficacy, and, except in extraordinary cases (as sometimes in baptism), his ministration is essential. The priest's personal character does not affect the efficacy of the sacraments, so that an unworthy priest confers grace, provided he administers the sacrament according to the prescribed rite of the Church. To use the medieval illustration, water is conveyed through a leaden pipe as well as through a silver one. The priest acts in the name of the Church, and in uttering the words of sacramental appointment he is giving voice to the intention of the Church. This intention is sufficient for the perfect work of the sacrament and ultimately, as Augustine had said, it is Christ and not the priest who gives effect to the sacrament. [But intention is far more than merely sufficient for the validity of a sacrament; it is absolutely essential in all Roman Catholic teaching; and this intention must invariably be present on the part of the minister of the sacrament, and generally on the part of the recipient. It is possible, however, for infants and idiots to receive the sacraments validly (though such sacraments as orders would scarcely ever be given them); those who subsequently lose their reason, either permanently or temporarily (as in unconsciousness), may validly receive extreme unction. All in possession of reason, however, must have intention if they are to receive a sacrament validly. This intention again may be either "actual" or "virtual," the former being a conscious intention, and the latter an intention which influences an act, even though this act be not recognized as sacramental, as when a baptized Protestant contracts marriage and thus unwittingly receives the sacrament of marriage. If there is no intention, there is no reception of a sacrament, so that if one eats consecrated hosts to satisfy hunger, he does not receive the Eucharist.

Intention on the part of the minister is invariably required by Roman Catholic teaching, whether this minister be lay (as in the case of a midwife who baptizes a new-born infant in immediate danger of death) or clerical (as in the mass, ordination, etc.). The intention must, moreover, be in accord with the teaching of the Church, though even a heretic, if possessing proper intention, may administer a valid sacrament. While there is danger that there may be, on the part of the minister, either a lack of intention or even an intention of acting contrary to the precept of the Church (both of which render the sacrament null and void), it is maintained by Roman Catholic dogmaticians (e.g., S. J. Hunter, *Outlines of Dogmatic Theology*, iii. 208–212, New York [1896]) that the chance of such invalidation is so small as to be negligible. The "defect of intention" (see the rubric on this topic in the preface to the missal), complicated by "defect of form," forms the basis of the condemnation of Anglican orders in the bull *Apostolicæ curæ* of Leo XIII. (Sept. 13, 1896), the special ground of invalidity being sought in the failure of the Anglican ordinals to express the concept of the sacrificial aspect of the Eucharist.* Intention finds a place, of course, in every sacrament; every Protestant who maintains any form of the receptivist theory of the Lord's Supper holds the doctrine of the necessity of intention, however unwittingly, and it is equally implied in such rites as the non-sacramental Protestant ordination, etc. Intention finds its most usual application, however, in the sacrifice of the mass in the Roman Catholic Church; and it should also be noted in this connection that in the High-church school of the Anglican Church Holy Communion is frequently celebrated "with intention," as for the promotion of the unity of Christendom or some other pious purpose.]

5. Necessity of the Sacraments.

To the Schoolmen Sacraments are not all of equal necessity. Baptism alone is essential to salvation, and baptism and the Eucharist are the mightiest. Baptism, confirmation, and ordination impart an indelible character. Their mark can not be effaced, nor can they be repeated.† The other four sacraments are necessary to salvation as a horse is necessary to a journey. The Schoolmen were not agreed as to the author of all the sacraments. Peter Lombard expressly ascribed extreme unction to the apostles, while Alexander of Hales, Thomas Aquinas, and others held that they were all instituted by Christ. In regard to the precedent necessity of the sacraments, Hugo of St. Victor declared that God might have saved man without them, but now that they have been instituted, no man can be saved except through them. The history of the doctrines of the seven sacraments is given under BAPTISM, LORD'S SUPPER, etc., but a general statement belongs here. Baptism is the door to the other sacraments and to the kingdom of God; confirmation completes what baptism has begun and confers the grace of ever-increasing strength; the Eucharist confers the food of spiritual life in the very body and blood of Christ; penance deletes the guilt of actual transgressions as baptism regenerates from the guilt of original sin; extreme unction heals the soul from sin not already remitted by penance, and is also intended to heal the body; ordination empowers persons to administer the sacraments; and marriage makes the union between two persons perpetual and in harmony with the union between Christ and the Church; or, to use the comparison employed by the Schoolmen, the sacraments furnish grace for the spiritual struggle and strengthen the Christian warrior at the various stages of the conflict. Baptism equips him on entering the conflict, confirmation strengthens him in his purpose, extreme unction helps him at the close of the struggle, the Eucharist and penance renew his strength, orders introduce new recruits into the ranks, and marriage prepares men to be recruits.

6. Protestant Teaching.

The first blow against the sacramental system of the medieval Church was given by Luther in his "Babylonish Captivity," in which he declared the rights and liberties of the Christian believer to be fettered by the traditions of men. He rejected all the sacraments except baptism and the Lord's Supper, and was followed in this by all the Reformers of the continent and Great Britain. All the Protestant confessions demand active faith as a condition of the efficacy of the sacrament. Faith apprehends and appropriates the spiritual benefits accruing from them. The unanimity of the Reformers as to the number of the sacraments and the conditions of their efficacious reception did not, however, exclude differences of doctrine which became the occasion of bitter controversies that greatly injured the cause of Protestantism.

There was general harmony regarding baptism, except among the Anabaptists, who rejected infant baptism and later demanded immersion; but the doctrine of the Lord's Supper was the cause of a dispute which has retarded or prevented cordial Christian cooperation until this day. The three main types of teaching on the Lord's Supper were those of Luther, who took the view of consubstantiation; of Zwingli, who made it a simple memorial feast; and of Calvin, who insisted on the mystical presence of Christ and a spiritual feeding upon him. In England the views of Luther were first adopted, but were later replaced, generally

* "The Church does not judge about the mind and intention in so far as it is something by its nature internal; but in so far as it is manifested externally she is bound to judge concerning it. When any one has rightly and seriously made use of the due form and the matter requisite for effecting or conferring the sacrament he is considered by the very fact to do what the Church does. On this principle rests the doctrine that a sacrament is truly conferred by the ministry of one who is a heretic or unbaptized, provided the Catholic rite be employed. On the other hand, if the rite be changed, with the manifest intention of introducing another rite not approved by the Church and of rejecting what the Church does, and what by the institution of Christ belongs to the nature of the sacrament, then it is clear that not only is the necessary intention wanting to the sacrament, but that the intention is adverse to and destructive of the sacrament" (*Apostolicæ curæ*, tr. in *The Encyclical Letters of Pope Leo XIII.*, New York, 1903, pp. 403–404).

† In both the Roman and Anglican churches provision is made for "conditional baptism" if there is doubt whether a former baptism was valid, i.e., administered in the name of the Trinity. The Roman Catholic Church, not recognizing the validity of Anglican or Greek confirmation, requires the reconfirmation of all converts from those communions, and for similar reasons both the Anglican and Roman churches insist on the reordination of all clergy becoming converts to them and desiring to exercise priestly functions, the Anglican church accepting, however, the validity of Greek and Roman ordination, and hence not requiring its repetition.

speaking, by those of Calvin.* The controversy between Zwingli and Luther came to a climax at the conference held at Marburg in 1529, and the difference led to a long-lasting cleavage between the Lutheran and Reformed types of Protestantism.

Certain religious bodies, of whom the most prominent are the Quakers, reject all external celebration of the sacraments as opposed to the spiritual interpretation of religion, and hold only to an internal baptism, or regeneration, by the Spirit and an internal communion with Christ. D. S. SCHAFF.

BIBLIOGRAPHY: The primary sources are of course (1) the works of the Fathers and Schoolmen mentioned in the text—Augustine, Abelard, Hugo of St. Victor, Peter Lombard, Albertus Magnus, Thomas Aquinas, Bonaventura, Duns Scotus—all of whom are discussed in this work, and usually also with reference to the subject of this article; (2) the confessions of the various churches, including the decrees of the Council of Trent, which are collected and annotated in: Schaff, *Creeds*; and E. F. K. Müller, *Die Bekenntnisschriften der reformirten Kirche*, Leipsic, 1903. Secondary sources are also of two kinds: (1) works on dogmatics and the history of dogma, which will be found given very fully in and under the articles DOGMA, DOGMATICS, and DOCTRINE, HISTORY OF; and (2) works on the history of the Church, also very fully given in and under CHURCH HISTORY, to which should be added the works on the history of the councils (see the bibliography under COUNCILS AND SYNODS), and the literature on the Fathers and Schoolmen named above under the articles on them in this work, where many monographs will be found devoted to the subject of this article. A useful literature is that on CANON LAW (q.v.), the literature of which is noted in the article on that subject. Respecting this last it is to be said that reference to this class of books is advised only for advanced students, as the relation is neither so direct nor so obvious as of the other literature named. In addition to the foregoing, the literature on the several sacraments is to be studied as given under the articles on them in this work. Special treatises from the Protestant standpoint are: R. Whately, *The Scripture Doctrine concerning the Sacraments*, London, 1857; G. L. Hahn, *Die Lehre von den Sacramenten in ihrer geschichtlichen Entwickelung innerhalb der abendländischen Kirche bis zum Konzil von Trient*, Breslau, 1864; J. S. Stone, *The Christian Sacraments*, New York, 1866; J. H. Blunt, *The Sacraments and Sacramental Ordinances of the Church*, London, 1867; G. G. Perry, *Vox ecclesiæ Anglicanæ*, ib. 1868; S. W. Crittenden, *Sacraments of the Church*, Philadelphia, 1869; W. F. Hook, *The Church and its Ordinances*, ed. W. Hook, 2 vols., London, 1876; R. Schmidt, in *TSK*, 1879, pp. 187 sqq., 391 sqq. (on the Lutheran doctrine); G. D. Armstrong, *The Sacraments of the New Testament*, New York, 1880; R. Watson, *The Sacraments: Baptism and the Lord's Supper*, ib. 1893; M. Dix, *The Sacramental System Considered as the Extension of the Incarnation*, ib. 1893; *The Church's Ministry of Grace* (lectures), ib. 1893; G. Anrich, *Das antike Mysterienwesen in seinem Einfluss auf das Christentum*, Göttingen, 1894; G. Wobbermin, *Religionsgeschichtliche Studien zur Frage der Beeinflussung des Urchristentums durch das antike Mysterienwesen*, Berlin, 1896; J. Grill, *Die persische Mysterienreligion im römischen Reich und das Christentum*, Tübingen, 1903; J. C. Lambert, *The Sacraments in the New Testament*, Edinburgh, 1903; K. G. Goetz, *Die Abendmahlsfrage in ihrer geschichtlichen Entwickelung*, Leipsic, 1904; A. Knox, *Grace of Sacraments*, New York, 1905; J. A. Beet, *The Church, Churches, and the Sacraments*, London, 1907; H. C. Beeching, *The Bible Doctrine of the Sacraments*, ib. 1908; Hauck-Herzog, *RE*, xvii. 349–381; Schaff, *Christian Church*, v. 1, pp. 701–748.

The Roman Catholic idea is presented in: F. Probst, *Sakramente und Sakramentalien in den drei ersten christlichen Jahrhunderten*, Tübingen, 1872; P. Schanz, *Die Lehre von den Sacramenten der katholischen Kirche*, Freiburg, 1893; J. H. Oswald, *Die dogmatische Lehre von den heiligen Sacramenten der katholischen Kirche*, 5th ed., Münster, 189-; S. J. Hunter, *Outlines of Dogmatic Theology*, iii. 162 sqq., New York [1896]; J. B. Sasse, *De sacramentis ecclesiæ*, Freiburg, 1897; *KL*, x. 1481–1518.

* ... Thirty-Nine Articles of the Anglican Church ... said to teach only two sacraments, baptism ... (art. xxv.), it is maintained by many ad... ...-church school of that communion that ... article in question does not necessarily ... of seven sacraments, although, ... ptism and the Eucha... ...raments preeminent ... of this Anglo... ...s of the Roman ...

SACRAMENTALS.

"Sacramentals" is a term applied to certain benedictions and consecrations in the Greek and Roman Catholic Churches, or to the objects blessed, from a partial resemblance between their purpose and use and those of the sacraments proper (see BENEDICTION). Exorcisms, which in the name of God undertake to remove the influence of evil spirits from persons and things, are included under this head (see EXORCISM). The Roman Catholic Church, however, apart from the connection of exorcism with baptism and with certain blessings and consecrations (such as that of the sacred oil and chrism by the bishop on Maundy Thursday), employs it as an independent rite only in the supposedly possible case of the demoniacal possession of a member of the Church, and its exercise even then is frequently limited to cases where the permission of ecclesiastical superiors is given after careful investigation. The order of exorcists has long been a mere stepping-stone to the higher orders, and the function is in practise performed by priests.

1. Development of the Doctrine. Before the development of the doctrine that the sacraments are seven in number, and especially from the beginning of the eleventh century to the time of Peter Lombard, the benedictions of the kind here considered, or at least the more important of them, were loosely included among the sacraments; but with the more exact definition of the term sacrament, these spiritual operations, which, while no longer considered as sacraments proper, were yet supposed to impart some special grace to persons or things, became known as sacramentals. The development of doctrine in the West was subordinated to the desire of the Roman spiritual power for domination. As in the doctrine of the sacraments (after Peter Lombard) the Church found expression for its claim of jurisdiction over all classes of persons, so the doctrine of sacramentals expressed the relation of the Church to material objects; and from both sacrament and sacramental grew up the doctrine of Sacrilege (q.v.).

As the power of holy orders takes a dominant position in the system of the sacraments, so the full significance of the sacramentals is most clearly visible in the anointing of kings by the clergy. This practise, connected with the Old-Testament custom, occurs in the West as early as the coronation of Wamba, king of the Visigoths, in 672; Egbert, king of the Anglo-Saxons, is said to have been anointed in 789, but this is uncertain.

2. The Anointing of Kings.

The practise was not found among the Merovingian kings; in the Frankish kingdom it was first used in the case of Pepin, and among the East Franks in that of Louis the Child and Conrad I., while Henry I. refused to submit to it, its connection with the Old-Testament theocracy seeming suspicious to an ambitious temporal monarch. From Otho I., however, unction accompanied coronation in each case. The German king was anointed on the head, breast, shoulders, arms, and hands; at the imperial coronation in Rome the bishop of Ostia anointed the emperor on the right arm and between the shoulders. While Gregory the Great, like Isidore of Seville and even Peter Damian (d. 1072) and Peter of Blois (d. 1200), designated the anointing of kings and princes as a sacrament, as did the Greeks also, the degradation of this rite to a sacramental, compared with the sacrament of orders, could but serve to emphasize the subordinate position of the worldly rulers in relation to the ecclesiastical hierarchy.

3. Doctrine of Royal Consecration.

According to the view laid down in the *Pontificale Romanum*, royal dignity is first conferred in its fulness upon the king by the unction connected with the benediction; but this view was not accepted, either at its promulgation or for any long period later; nor was the coronation which in the ninth century was added to the unction believed to have greater validity for conferring regal rights in the Empire. Until the eleventh century the choice of the princes, led by the archbishop of Mainz, was understood to confer these rights, and the enthronization by the Church merely exhibited the king as in possession of them. In opposition to the principle held by Charlemagne and Louis I., it was a consequence of the dissensions within the Carolingian house that under the later Carolingians the imperial title and dignity were held to depend on coronation and unction at Rome. From Otho I. the German kings claimed the right to be thus crowned as inherent in their office—a claim which was more than once (as by Calixtus II.) admitted on the side of the Church. But from the pontificate of Gregory VII. the prevalent curialist view tended to transfer the importance of the ceremony from unction to coronation. The principle of free election won its victory with the extinction of the Hohenstaufen dynasty. Conrad III. (1138) received unction and coronation as German king, not as emperor, from the papal legate at Aachen, the first instance of the kind. The contested election of 1198 and the desuetude of the earlier constitution gave the great popes from Innocent III. on a chance to dominate the elections, while the claim of the popes to depose temporal rulers brought the latter, even as to their political functions, under the jurisdiction of the Church. By this time the election was admitted to give only a right to coronation, which was required for the full possession of the office. In the ritual act, which included unction and coronation, to which the tradition of the imperial insignia and the enthronization in the chair of Charlemagne at Aachen were added, the coronation at Aachen became of decisive importance. In the *Sachsenspiegel* the Roman view as a whole is assumed—the elevation to the imperial throne connected with the coronation at Aachen is considered effectively to confer the office. The settlement of the German kingship as purely elective in 1252 marked the complete domination of the view that the right conferred by the pope definitely established the possession of the royal dignity; though in 1338 the electors rejected the claim of the pope to investigate and confirm the election. Nevertheless, although the constitution *Licet juris* of Louis the Bavarian (1338) declared that the election as German king conferred "the plenitude of imperial power," and the *Bulla aurea* spoke of the king as elected "to be promoted to emperor," throughout the Middle Ages nothing was more firmly established than the claim of the king to the imperial crown. In 1508 Maximilian I., without papal coronation and with the assent of Julius II., assumed the title of "Roman emperor-elect." This was borne also by his successors, of whom only Charles V. (1530) was crowned by the pope, thereafter dropping the "elect." After Ferdinand I. (1558) the coronation took place no longer at Aachen but in the same place as the election, Frankfort-on-the-Main, and lost its special character as a solemn induction into the kingly office. Napoleon allowed himself to be anointed by Pius VII. in 1804, but refused to be crowned by him. In modern kingdoms, in so far as the ceremony of coronation is still preserved, the acquisition of royal dignity is no longer dependent upon the ritual ecclesiastical act of unction or coronation, but the law of the State is alone effective.

4. Sacramentals in General.

The sacramentals in general, like the sacraments, have their individual recognized matter, form, and minister; but unlike the sacraments, which are based upon the direct institution of Christ, they are derived from the authority of the Church, under a general commission given by God to bless in his name. In accordance with ancient oriental custom, anointing forms a part regularly of consecrations and sometimes of benedictions. For this olive-oil is used, either pure as in the case of that employed for catechumens and the sick, or mixed with balsam (in the Eastern Church with other spices as well), when it is known as Chrism (q.v.). The effect of consecration is the definite setting apart by the rite of unction of a person or thing for the service of God and the Church. A constant feature of these ceremonies is a solemn appeal to God to grant his grace to the person or a salutary effect to the use of the thing. Outside of the use of the simple oil in baptism and the ordination of priests, and of chrism in confirmation and the consecration of bishops, chrism is employed also in the consecration of churches, altars, patens, and chalices. A simple benediction, coupled with anointing, is given by bishops to kings. Church bells are sprinkled with holy water and anointed. The water used in baptism is blessed. Holy Water (q.v.) is used in the blessing of abbots and abbesses, pilgrims, man and wife at their marriage, and women after childbirth. Special blessings are imparted to certain objects destined for the service of God—churches, cemeteries, vestments, palls, corporals, pyxes, monstrances, crosses, images of the saints, candles, and rosaries. Particular forms of benediction are also provided for a number of things connected with the daily occupations and needs of men, as for houses, ships, locomotives, battle-flags, fields, and bread, wine, salt, and other edibles.

In the case of objects consecrated for the direct service of God, the act has both a liturgical and a legal aspect.

5. Legal Aspects.

Through consecration they are not merely prepared in a specially solemn way for their sacred purpose but made externally inviolable (*res sacræ*). The administration of the sacramentals connected with the sacraments is reserved to the person who administers the sacrament. In general, however, the spiritual power to bless and consecrate is conferred on priests at their ordination, when their hands are anointed with the prayer "that whatsoever they bless may be blessed, and whatsoever they consecrate may be consecrated and hallowed." If a priest performs consecrations reserved to bishops, they are merely irregular or illicit, but not invalid as they would be if performed by a layman. To the pope, as head of the universal Church, is reserved (apart from the imperial coronation, treated above) the blessing of the wax figures known as *Agni Dei* (see Agnus Dei), of the Pallium (q.v.) for metropolitans, of the golden roses (see Golden Rose) sent to princes or churches, and of swords for kings and princes. This reservation, however, is merely a mark of honor attached to the papal primacy. As the possessor of jurisdiction over the whole Church, the pope can perform consecration or benediction for any part or any member of it, or delegate his power to any qualified person, while the bishop's authority in such cases is limited to his own diocese. It is of practical significance in the development of the modern Roman Catholic system that there has been a marked tendency to restrict the power of delegating authority to bless or consecrate churches, altars, sacred vessels, and the like, to the pope. This power is nowadays frequently conferred on the bishops by their quinquennial faculties (see Faculties). In recent times the Congregation of Rites has assumed the power of sub-delegating certain privileges directly, such as that of blessing bells to a priest of the diocese, or sacred vessels to a mitered prelate.

It is an established principle of church law and practise that whatever is supposed to be blessed or consecrated must be; but numerous objects used in Roman Catholic worship are not

6. Occasions for Consecration.

blessed, e.g., hangings, candle-sticks, and censors. Misuse or profanation of blessed objects is subject to ecclesiastical penalties. A validly administered sacramental is not allowed to be repeated while the original conditions of its administration remain; the common blessings, however, may be repeated for the same person or thing as often as there is reasonable ground. If the object has undergone an essential change, especially if it can no longer either in fact or in law subserve its liturgical purpose, the sacramental operation of the consecration or blessing is supposed to cease; the object needs no formal desecration, but a declaration of the circumstances is made to the proper authority. A new consecration is required, as in the case of a church, where the object is destroyed so far as to affect its essential character and then restored. The shedding of blood or the commission of gross immorality in a church is held to pollute but not to desecrate it; reconciliation, not a new consecration, is required, which is accomplished with holy water by the bishop. The pollution of a church affects the churchyard as well, in which Christian burial is not supposed to take place until the church has been reconciled. The pollution of the churchyard, on the other hand, has no effect on the church.

All that has been said above applies obviously to the medieval or modern Roman Catholic Church. The Evangelical Churches know no sacramentals in the sense here discussed.

7. Protestant Teachings.

They employ neither consecration nor benediction even for the immediate instruments of divine worship, such as would impart to them any property of special sanctity, although such objects, according to Protestant church law, deserve special respect and are to be protected from profane uses. A solemn dedication is indeed usual for churches and churchyards, with a prayer of benediction. In regard to the setting apart of particular objects (pulpits, sacred vessels, organs, fonts), it has been held sufficient for the officiating clergyman, on the first occasion of their use, to address a few appropriate words to the congregation, and then to ask God's blessing upon the employment of the objects. In regard to benedictions for objects of every-day use, the older Protestant ordinances not infrequently declare expressly against them, on account of the danger of superstition. (R. W. Dove†.)

Bibliography: T. Netter, *Fasciculi zizaniorum*, ed. W. Shirley, in *Rolls Series*, no. 5, London, 1858; J. Helfert, *Rechte in Ansehung der heiligen Handlungen*, Prague, 1843; F. Probst, *Kirchliche Benedictionen und ihre Verwaltung*, Tübingen, 1857; A. L. Richter, *Lehrbuch des . . . Kirchenrechts*, ed. R. W. Dove, §§ 260, 306, Leipsic, 1871; P. I. Wapelhorst, *Compendium sacræ liturgiæ, juxta ritum Romanum*, New York, 1887; P. Hinschius, *System des . . . Kirchenrechts*, iv. 141–177, Berlin, 1888; A. A. Lambing, *Sacramentals of the Catholic Church*, New York, 1892; W. Wilmers, *Lehrbuch der Religion*, iv. §§ 97–98, Münster, 1895; F. Loofs, *Symbolik*, i. 348 sqq., Tübingen, 1902; *KL*, x. 1469 sqq.

SACRED HEART OF JESUS, DEVOTION TO.

I. History of the Devotion: The devotion to the Sacred Heart of Jesus was practically, if not absolutely, originated by the Jesuits. Under the influence of her director, the Jesuit La Colombière, Marguerite Marie Alacoque (d. 1690), a nun in the Salesian convent at Paray-le-Monial in Burgundy, practised a fervent mystical devotion to Christ which resulted in ecstasy. According to her account, on June 16, 1675, when praying before the sacrament, she saw Jesus "showing to her his heart on a flaming throne, surrounded by thorns and surmounted by a cross; and he told her it was his will that a special devotion should be offered to his Sacred Heart in reparation for irreverences committed against him in the most holy sacrament, and that the Friday after the octave of Corpus Christi should be set apart for this devotion." Further revelations confirmed this, and the convent became a seat of the devotion. Colombière and his successors Croiset and Rolin labored to spread it, and Croiset published the first book on the subject at Lyons in 1691. The new devotion was not well received in Rome; Croiset's book was put on the Index in 1704, while in 1697 the request of the Salesians for a festival of the Sacred Heart with proper office had been refused by the Congregation of Rites, a refusal which was renewed in 1707 and 1727. Meantime, through confraternities (see below) the devotion spread through German Switzerland into Germany. Languet, then bishop of Soissons and later archbishop of Sens, defended it in his biography of Marguerite Marie; and the Jesuit Gallifet published the more important *De cultu sacrosancti cordis Dei* (Rome, 1726). Miracles were claimed as a result of it; kings and queens besought the pope to grant a proper mass and office for the festival, which was at last conceded, on the express understanding that the cultus was paid to the heart of Jesus only as the symbol of his love. Determined opposition was made to the devotion under the influence of Scipione de' Ricci (q.v.), bishop of Pistoja, and of the rationalizing tendency which at the end of the eighteenth century had spread from Tuscany through a large part of Italy, and a prolonged literary warfare was carried on by the two parties.

The accession of Pius VI. in 1775 marked a turning-point. The bull *Auctorem fidei* of 1794 gave additional sanction to the devotion. The Jesuits had long pushed it vigorously, and after the restoration of the order, they continued to work, with the result that one diocese after another asked permission to celebrate the festival, and an increasing number of indulgences was attached to the devotion. Both had become practically universal when Pius IX. (Aug. 23, 1856) established the festival as a greater double for the whole Church; and the beatification of Marguerite Marie in 1864 was another step in the same direction. At the Vatican Council of 1870, the majority of the bishops asked for the elevation of the feast to the rank of a double (i.e., a feast at which the antiphon is said both before and after the psalm) of the first class (i.e., one which takes precedence in case two feasts fall on the same day) with octave (i.e., lasting through eight days, with special emphasis upon the celebration on the last day), but it was then granted only to the Jesuit order, in recognition of their services in spreading the devotion. The rank was extended to the whole Church, though without an octave, by Leo XIII. in 1889. The devotion has constantly strengthened its hold on the great body of Roman Catholics; and the cautious expressions at first used have given place to a full acceptance of the literal, material heart of Jesus as its object.

II. Societies under the Name of the Sacred Heart: The first Confraternity of the Sacred Heart was founded at Paray-le-Monial in 1693; and by 1727 there were already as many as 400. That erected by Gallifet in 1729 in the church of St. Theodore at Rome became an archconfraternity in 1732. The number of confraternities was 1,089 in 1765, 6,676 in 1865, and is now over 10,000. A special confraternity is that founded at Bourg in France in 1863, whose members are divided so that each has a particular hour set apart for the adoration of the Sacred Heart and intercessory prayer which adoration and prayer thus become continuous. The most important of the confraternities which make a point of intercessory prayer is the League of the Sacred Heart or Apostleship of Prayer, founded in 1844 at Vals in France by the Jesuit Père Gautrelet, and provided with new constitutions by Leo XIII. in 1879. In 1895 it had 50,000 branches all over the world, with more than twenty million members. The organ of the league, *The Messenger of the Sacred Heart*, is published monthly in fourteen languages. Another important society is the French Dames du sacré cœur, founded in Paris in 1800 by Madeleine Sophie Barat (d. 1865), under the influence of the Jesuit Père Varin. It serves the double purpose of venerating the Sacred Heart and the education of girls. The statutes, drawn up by Varin, are modeled on those of the Jesuits. The candidate for admission spends three to six months in the house as a postulant; then follows a two years' novitiate, and then (since 1826) the taking of simple vows, an additional vow of stability, i.e., life-long adherence to the congregation, being made. Besides the professed sisters, there are *sœurs coadjutrices* for the household duties, and *sœurs commissionaires* for the necessary intercourse with the outside world. The superior is chosen for life, and resides at the mother-house in Paris, the former Hôtel de Biron in the Rue de Varennes. A general chapter every six years watches over the strict observance of the constitutions. A peculiarity of this congregation is that the members retain their original names, with the prefix of "Madame." The costume is a black dress, a cap with a white frill, and a black veil. In 1839 they had 40 houses, in 1851, 65; in 1864, 86, with 3,500 members; in 1880, 105, with 4,700 members, divided into 18 vicariates. In 1910 the order numbered 212 houses and 7,800 members. Three vicariates or provinces are established in the United States with 39 houses and 1,140 sisters. The influence exerted by them has been of no slight importance in the revival of Roman Catholicism, especially of an ultramontane or Jesuit cast.

(T. Kolde.)

Bibliography: F. S. Hattler, *Geschichte des Festes und der Andacht zum Herzen-Jesu*, Vienna, 1875; idem, *Die bildliche Darstellung des göttlichen Herzens und der Herz-Jesu-Idee*, Innsbruck, 1894; J. de Gallifet, *Ueber die Andacht zum hochheiligen Herzen . . . Jesu Christi*, ib. 1884; H. E. Manning, *The Divine Glory of the Sacred Heart*, London, 1873; idem, *The Glories of the Sacred Heart*, ib. 1876; K. Martin, *Die Lehre und Uebung der Andacht zum göttlichen Herzen Jesu*, Cologne, 1876; N. Nilles, *De rationibus festorum sacratissimi cordis Jesu et . . . Mariæ*, 2 vols., Innsbruck, 1885; H. J. Nix, *Cultus . . . cordis Jesu*, Freiburg, 1891; H. Reusch, *Index der verbotenen Bücher*, ii. 983 sqq., Bonn, 1885; idem, *Die deutsche Bischöfe und der Aberglaube*, pp. 81 sqq., ib. 1879; Heimbucher, *Orden und Kongregationen*, vol. iii. passim; F. Beringer, *Die Ablässe, ihr Wesen und Gebrauch*, Paderborn, 1895.

SACRED HEART OF JESUS AND MARY, CONGREGATION OF. See Picpus, Congregation of.

SACRED MUSIC.

A. Hebrew: The forms of musical instruments of the Hebrews are known from imprints of instruments on Jewish coins during the insurrection against the Romans (66–70 A.D.). Moreover, trumpets are represented on the Arch of Titus. Especially valuable are the manifold designs of musical instruments on Egyptian, Babylonian, and Assyrian monuments, since from these can be inferred the form of their Hebrew parallels.

I. Stringed Instruments: In the threefold category of stringed, wind, and percussive or swaying instruments, the stringed instruments (*neghinoth*, titles of Ps. iv., vi., liv., etc.) rank first in importance in Hebrew music. Their strings (*minnim*) were made of intestines (of sheep; cf. Homer, *Odyssey*, xxi. 408), or of twisted cords. It is not known whether a particular kind of wood was used for the framework, but among Solomon's luxuries were instruments of the sandal wood that came from Ethiopia (I Kings x. 12; II Chron. ix. 11). These instruments were played either with the fingers, as by pulling and twitching, or by striking with the plectrum, a small rod of gold, ivory, or metal (*naggen*, I Sam. xvi. 16, xviii. 10; Isa. xxiii. 16; etc. In the Psalms, *zamar* is ordinarily used for both playing and singing, Ps. lxxi. 22, cxliv. 9; etc.).

Apart from the foreign *sabbekha*, "sackbut" (Dan. iii. 5, 7, 10), the Greek *sambykē*, the Old Testament mentions two instruments that are purely Israelitish: *kinnōr*, "harp," and *nebhel*, "psaltery." The Old Testament gives no indications respecting their form, save that they could be

1. The Lyre. carried and played in processions (I Sam. x. 5; II Sam. vi. 5; Isa. xxiii. 16). Hence they were relatively small; though greater sizes of the harp, for instance, may have existed collaterally. And it may be assumed that among the Israelites, as among the Egyptians, the forms, in turn, were not always, and at all periods, invariably the same. Possibly even those instruments designated by one name took different shapes. In the Septuagint *kinnōr* is usually rendered *kithara* (cf. I Cor. xiv. 7; Rev. v. 8); less frequently (5 times), *psaltērion*. It was, therefore, probably an instrument similar to the Greek cithara. The Church Fathers find a point of distinction as between this instrument and the *nebhel*, in the position of the sounding-board. The *kinnōr* has this feature below; being a rotund, hollow body, whose arched surface turns downward. The strings are stretched over the concave portion horizontally. And this arrangement quite correctly describes one class of stringed instruments (lutes, guitars, etc.) in their essential outlines. According to data transmitted by the Church Fathers, the *kinnōr*, unlike the Greek cithara, is not played in an upright position, but held horizontally. It is therefore quite similar to the generally familiar ancient lyre. Its oldest form is shown in the famous and often copied group of Bedouin immigrants into Egypt, as found in a rock sepulcher of Beni Hassan (150 m. s. of Cairo) dating from the time of the twelfth dynasty (c. 2000 B.C.). The rather bulky instrument which one of these Bedouins carries under his arm consists essentially of a quadrangular board, one foot wide and a foot and a half long, with a square excision at the upper end, or part remote from the body; so that at this end only a narrow frame of wood is left whole. Eight strings are stretched parallel and lengthwise over the board and the opening. The man plays as he walks. He carries the instrument under the left upper arm, and resting lengthwise. The perforated portion is also directed forward. The strings are on the right side. His right hand touches the strings with a plectrum about where they are stretched over the lower part of the board, the part serving as sounding-board. His left hand reaches toward the strings through the excision. The like instrument often recurs in Egyptian designs. Notably from the times of the eighteenth-twentieth dynasties, it assumed finer forms: the upper part, or frame, showing variously waving lines instead of the simple square. The lower part, originally a mere board, developed into a resonant box. The origin of this instrument is Asiatic, and is found in Assyrian and Babylonian designs. The simplest form is shown by a delineation, reproduced by Rawlinson, of three Semitic captives playing this lyre under surveillance of an Assyrian warrior. It fully resembles the lyre of the Semitic Bedouins except that the frame grows wider above. It is likewise carried under the left arm, and is played with both hands. Other designs duly indicate finer forms, just as in case of the Egyptian drawings, and, in particular, the curved frame, with more or less fantastic turns. The number of strings varies; as from five to six or eight strings. From this harmony between the Egyptian and Assyrian delineations, both in the simpler and in the more elaborate forms, a corresponding diversity of forms may be assumed for the Israelitish *kinnōr*. Neither is it anything striking and improbable if the imprints on coins exhibit a frame which in the Grecian period was fashioned according to Greek taste; corresponding now rather to the Grecian lyre, now rather to the cithara. The early Hebrew instruments, indeed, may have had simpler forms; in primitive times they probably resembled the simple Egyptian and Assyrian instruments.

In the case of the *nebhel*, it appears from the Church Fathers, who style this instrument *psalterium*, that the sounding-board was furnished by a hollow wooden body, at the upper end, as though roofing the strings; the flat surface downward, the convex arching above. The chief point is, that in this instrument the strings are not stretched athwart the sounding-board, but stand perpendicular, or else at an acute angle to the resonant surface, and run thence as uprights to their supporting arm at the other end. This arrangement applies to instruments of the harp class. The Egyptian harps, both the stationary upright and the portable, have the sounding-board below; the Babylonian and Assyrian designs exhibit it above, and the Church Fathers' account answers to the latter models. The use of the harp in Asia and Egypt goes back to primitive antiquity. The most ancient of all representations of stringed instruments, a stone from Telloh in Babylonia (c. 3000 B.C.), shows an upright stationary instrument with a box-like sounding-board, upon which rises a rude framework, while the strings, two in number, run fairly vertically from the sounding-board to the upper cross-beam. The whole instrument is rather large, about three-quarters of a man's stature, and has rough embellishments. The later Babylonian harp, carried upright, is more wieldy, as is also the similarly carried Assyrian harp. Both distinctly exhibit the characteristic features of all harps: the strings run unobstructedly from beam to beam, the frame sustaining them is not closed on all four sides, as in case of the lyre, but open on one side, and the instrument is played in a vertical position. Yet the Assyrian designs also reveal a recumbent harp; and here, too, the strings are superposed, not side by side, but stretched like tendons between two pieces of wood that form an angle. It is especially interesting to note how, from the simple beam of the Babylonian harp, that holds the strings, the Assyrian harp has developed a broad sounding apparatus, which roofs the strings in the manner of a shield. The Egyptian harp shows a great diversity of forms. The ancient monarchy has only the medium-sized harp with six or seven strings, played in a sitting or kneeling position, and the large harp, with twenty strings or upward, and as tall as a man, or still taller; in playing this harp, the player stood. All these harps distinctly show the instrument's original form; a great bow, whose harp-strings take the place of bowstrings. In this case, again, and in the course of development, the simple arching beam has expanded into a sounding-board, occasionally assuming somewhat the fashion of a wooden chest. In contrast, however, with the Assyrian harp, this Egyptian sounding apparatus is placed below, and serves at the same time as the harp's base of support. The pegs for tightening or tuning the strings are above. In the new monarchy appear also the various portable small harps, both with and without a sounding-board; now in the form of a strongly curved bow, again, angular like the Assyrian harps. They are borne before the breast, though there is also a kind that is carried on the shoulder, something between lute and harp. The manifold designs of harps of all sorts attest that this instrument was in great favor with the ancient Egyptians.

2. The Harp.

Two stringed instruments besides those already mentioned were probably not unknown to the Israelites: the lute and the psaltery. The lute is repeatedly understood within the Hebrew term *nebhel*. For this the warrant rests partly upon the bulging form which *nebhel* is supposed to indicate; since the term elsewhere denotes the leathern bottle in which wine was preserved. But again, *nebhel* is often compared with the Egyptian name for lute, and the transfer of terms then readily suggests that of the objects they signify. Be this as it may, the lute, at all events, being an Egyptian instrument originally, was there highly favored. Nevertheless it migrated even quite early to Asia, and thus into Assyria, and in essentially the same form as in Egypt—an elongated, yet more or less bulging, hollow body for sounding-board, with a decidedly long support, or handle, for holding the few strings, only one to three in number and in parallel arrangement. The player holds the body of the instrument with his upper right arm. With the right hand, the strings are set swaying just above the hollow body; the left hand, quite agreeably to our custom with violins, grasps round about the upper end of the neck, and gives different lengths to the vibrating strings by downward pressure. This instrument was hardly unknown to the Israelites. And since apart from *kinnōr* and *nebhel* there are no designations for a third stringed instrument, it must be assumed that the lute was comprised under one of these terms, hence probably under the name *nebhel*. The dulcimer is an Assyrian instrument, which the Egyptians do not appear to have possessed. According to the representations, it is played as the player walks along. It is a horizontal instrument, with a low, slightly concave box by way of sounding-board. Over this, and in parallel arrangement, ten strings are stretched, with their ends dependent across their supporting staff at the forward side. The player carries the instrument horizontally before him, with a band or belt attached to his body. With the right hand he

3. Other Stringed Instruments.

strikes the strings with a plectrum, while his left hand also seizes or touches the strings. This instrument found wide circulation. It became later transmitted to the Greeks as their *magadis* and was in use during the Middle Ages under the name of *psalterium*. The name itself is very old; cf. the Greek translation of *nebhel* by *psalterium*, and the Aramaic *pesanterin* (Dan. iii. 5). Under this name, in turn (*sanṭir*), the instrument has maintained itself among the Arabs down to to-day. As a foreign instrument, moreover, there is also mention in the Old Testament of the *sabbekha*, "sackbut" (Dan. iii. 5, 7, 10). Both name and article reached the Greeks and Romans by way of the East. The *sambykē*, indeed, was carried about in the Roman Empire by oriental courtesans, accordingly styled *sambucinæ*. The instrument is described by Strabo as a triangular contrivance of barbaric origin, with four sharp-toned strings.

II. Wind Instruments: The wind instruments mentioned in the Old Testament are of the trumpet order (horn, trumpet), or of the flute kind. Among flutes, the Old Testament mentions *'ughabh*, "organ" or "flute," and *ḥālīl*, "pipe." The Egyptians had the simple long flute of wood, which varied greatly in length, however, and in number of stops.

1. The Flute and the Pipe. There likewise occur the transverse or German flutes, which are played like modern flutes by means of a lateral hole at the upper end. Much favored are the double flutes, that is, two flutes either joined together throughout their length, or else only at the mouthpiece and then diverging. Each hand plays one flute, the stops, of course, being only few. Quite similar double flutes occur in the Assyrian designs. A distinctively Syrian instrument is understood by the small flute, a span in length, which had a sharp and wailing tone, and was played in connection with the mourning for Adonis (see TAMMUZ); though with the Athenians it was employed also at banquets and carousals. The modern Arabian flutes vary in length and are made of reeds. Even nowadays the double flutes are still in great favor, of the pattern joined throughout their length. It is probable that various types of these flutes are comprehended under the Hebrew term *ḥālīl*. It is possible, too, that *'ughabh* denotes this type of flute (Gen. iv. 21; Job xxi. 12, xxx. 31; Ps. cl. 4). And as far as tradition goes, the same term should undoubtedly cover the bagpipe as well. Perhaps, again, the latter instrument is meant in Dan. iii. 5, 7, 10, by the expression *sumponyah* (cf. the Gk. *symphōnia*). At the same time, over against this tradition it should be borne in mind that neither among the Assyrians nor among the Egyptians are there designs of this instrument or any other vouchers for its occurrence. With at least the same right, indeed, the *'ughabh* might be connected with the so-called "puff-cheek" pipe, or Pan's pipe—the *syrinx* of the Greeks, which the Septuagint recovers in the *mashroḳiha* (Dan. iii. 5, 7, 10). The syrinx consists of seven to nine reed pipes, arranged in a row, of varying length and thickness and of varying pitch. This instrument is still in use in the East, notably with shepherds.

The trumpet class of wind instruments can hardly be designated now as musical instruments in the strictest sense of the word, since both horn and trumpet have only one tone, hence no melody can be played on them. They both

2. The Horn and the Trumpet. served as signal instruments and to reinforce loud shouts and cries of exultation. As its name imports, the horn (*shophar*, also *ḳeren;* Josh. vi. 5; I Chron. xxv. 5; Dan. iii. 5) was originally nothing more than a natural horn of an ox or a ram. In later times it was also fashioned of other materials, as metal, though constantly retaining the curved form of the animal horn; a distinctive feature, again, in contrast with the straight trumpet. The Talmud knows of straight horns as well. For blowing the horn the Hebrew has two expressions: to "thrust" into the horn denotes short, spasmodic blasts; to "draw" signifies prolonged tones. The trumpet (*ḥaṣoṣerah*, Num. x. 1 sqq., xxxi. 6; II Kings xi. 14; etc.) is straight, and usually of metal. According to Josephus (*Ant.*, III., xii. 6), the thin pipes or tubes were about an ell in length, and widen below into a campanulate bell; the mouthpiece also showing a slight enlargement. Herein agree the trumpets on the Arch of Titus, which also resemble those of ancient Egypt. The trumpet designs on coins from the time of Bar Kokba (q.v.) are drawn decidedly shorter, and accordingly appear quite stocky. Directly below the broad mouthpiece they show a conical expansion, which doubtless aims to strengthen the tone.

III. Instruments of Percussion: Percussive and rattling instruments play a much greater part in the ancient and modern Oriental orchestra toward enhancing the rhythm than they do with us. The most usual of these instruments was the timbrel, tabret, or tambourine (Hebr. *toph*, Gen. xxxi. 27; Ex. xv. 20; Judges xi. 34; etc.). In the Egyptian designs it is beaten mostly by women; in the Assyrian designs, by men as well. These instruments are mostly round, less frequently quadrangular. The membrane, stretched over a wooden or metal rim, is held with one hand and beaten with the fingers of the other hand. The modern tambourines have thin metallic disks or small bells about the rim, which jingle when shaken. Another kind of drum that belongs to the orchestra appears in the Assyrian delineation of drums; it is carried from the belt, and struck with both hands. The cymbals (*ṣelṣelim*, *meṣiltayim*, II Sam. vi. 5; I Chron. xiii. 8, xv. 19; etc.) are described by Josephus (*Ant.*, VII., xii. 13) as two great broad plates of bronze, that are clashed together with both hands. They serve as metronomic or time-beating instruments in the orchestra (cf. I Chron. xxv. 1–6; II Chron. v. 12). The Assyrian designs exhibit both bell-shaped cymbals, with handles, which are struck together from above downward; and also the flat platter kind, which are struck laterally together. According to the tradition attaching to the Septuagint and the Peshito, the *shalishim* are also a kind of cymbals (I Sam. xviii. 6). On account of the name others think of triangles. Castanets, or small disks of metal, ivory, bone, or wood, that are seized between the fingers and struck together, are in great favor to-day and were also known to the ancient Egyptians. Probably the Israelites also had them, but whether the term *ẓelẓelim-shama* signifies castanets is quite uncertain. The sistra are probably meant by the term *mena'an'im* (II Sam, vi. 5). In Egypt they were notably in use in the service of Isis, and then generally in sacred rites. They are represented in the designs as consisting of a broad, oval brass frame with iron cross-bars. The latter support a number of loose metal rings. A long handle, which, in turn, supported the frame, served as motive rod, for evoking sound by agitating the rings.

IV. Uses: As touching the use of these instruments, it is obvious that neither horn and trumpets, nor the percussive and rattling instruments, can serve to accompany a vocal melody, or even to play one in the orchestra; they occur only as "noise" instruments to produce a loud stress of sound and to accentuate the rhythm.

1. For Marking Rhythm.

Horns answer preferably to secular ends, such as watchman's signals (Jer. vi. 1; Hos. viii. 1; Amos iii. 6), war signals (Judges iii. 27, vi. 34; I Sam. xiii. 3; Amos. ii. 2; etc.); and still other signals (II Sam. xv. 10; I Kings i. 34 seq.; II Kings ix. 13). They serve also to announce worship (II Sam. vi. 15; I Chron. xv. 28; etc.); and especially the new year and the year of jubilee are proclaimed by the blowing of trumpets (Lev. xxiii. 24; Num. xxix. 1). Otherwise the trumpet appears as the properly sacred instrument. Yet even in the ancient times, it also naturally served secular ends as well: war blasts and the like (II Kings xi. 14; II Chron. xxiii. 13; Hos. v. 8). At the time of the second Temple, however, the trumpet appears to have served exclusively liturgical ends; above all, the feasts and new moons are ushered in with the blare of trumpets, and the sacrifices are accompanied with trumpet blasts (Num. x. 2 seq., xxxi. 6). For this purpose, according to II Chron. v. 12, there was a temple corps of 120 trumpeters. Tambourines, or the timbrel, and cymbals, have their place chiefly in the dance and processions (Ex. xv. 20; Judges xi. 34; I Sam. xviii. 6; Jer. xxxi. 4), and with joyous festival singing (Gen. xxxi. 27; Ps. lxxxi. 3; Isa. v. 12). In the second Temple, when the timbrel ceased to be used, its place was taken by the cymbals, for beating time (I Chron. xxv. 6; II Chron. v. 12).

The proper musical instruments on which melodies could be played were the stringed instruments and the flutes, hence they are termed *kelē shīr*, "song instruments" (Amos vi. 5; Neh. xii. 36; I Chron. xvi. 42; II Chron. v. 13, etc.).

2. For Leading Melody.

In this connection the *nebhel* and *kinnōr* were played only with joyful music, never in mourning for lamentation or dirges; hence they appear at the festive banquet, at family feasts, and at popular jollifications (Isa. v. 12; Gen. xxxi. 27; Job xxi. 12). Spiritual songs, too, were accompanied with these instruments, both in the liturgical worship (I Chron. xxv. 6; Neh. xii. 27, etc.), and at religious popular feasts (I Sam. x. 5; II Sam. vi. 5). From its frequent mention, the *kinnōr* appears to have been the favorite instrument in popular use (Gen. xxxi. 27; Job xxi. 12; etc.); and it was also the instrument of the shepherd David (I Sam. xvi. 16 seq.). On the other hand, where the playing of the *nebhel* is alone in question, it was employed for liturgical purposes (Amos v. 23; Ps. cxliv. 9), or in the hands of "artists" (Amos vi. 5; Isa. xiv. 11), at all events, never at popular merry-makings, nor in the hands of the people. In mourning, both are out of place; they are "hanged upon the willows" (Ps. cxxxvii. 2; Isa. xiv. 11, xxiv. 8; Lam. v. 14; Ezek. xxvi. 13). As a distinctively wailing, or elegiac, instrument the flute was used, and in particular, the *ḥalīl* type. In like manner, among other ancient peoples (the Egyptians and Babylonians, for instance) the playing of flutes was by no means to be omitted on occasion of death dirges (Matt. ix. 23; Josephus, *War*, III., x. 15). This is not saying, however, that the flute was not used on many other occasions, as it was a very popular instrument. Flute and pipe occurred in all periods in connection with popular rejoicings such as dancing, weddings, banquets, and the like (I Kings i. 40; Job xxi. 12, xxx. 31; Isa. v. 12). The "bands" of prophets animated themselves with music of flutes (I Sam. x. 5); while festal pilgrims accompany their songs with the "pipe" (Isa. xxx. 29). On the other hand, this instrument is wanting in the music of the Temple.

V. Effects: The importance of music as affecting the popular life, and the position it occupied both in the common life and in the worship of the period before the exile, are not to be so highly appraised as with the Greeks, who constantly regarded music as an educational medium of great value. Still it may be said that the ancient Israelites loved music. It was not absent from popular feasts nor family festivals; neither from divine service nor from lamentation and mourning. At the festival of harvest, young men and maidens lead processions of dancing with song and music (Judges ix. 27. xxi. 21); whereas the same features also accompany the patriotic festivals (Judges xi. 34; I Sam. xviii. 6; I Kings i. 39 sqq.; Ps. xlv. 8 sqq.; I Macc. ix. 39). He that is a master in music and song is sure to be surrounded by a constant circle of grateful auditors (I Sam. xvi. 18; Lam. v. 14). "Men singers" and "women singers" are not lacking at the court of the king (II Sam. xix. 35; Eccles. ii. 8). Joyful song and strains of mirth adorn the banquet (Ecclus. xxxii. 5). True, the prophets have no delight in such sumptuous entertainments (Amos vi. 5; Isa. v. 12, xxiv. 8, xxiii. 16; Jer. vii. 34, xxv. 10) because the vocation of professional singers and dancers was not always followed by reputable persons (Isa. xxiii. 16). Where the religious application of music best shows its importance is in connection with the popular life. Doubtless that ancient hymn of praise in Ex. xv. was by no means the only song to Yahweh by the women of Israel at patriotic and religious festivals (II Sam. vi. 5, 14 sqq.). With the prophets music serves direct religious objects: it is amid music that they become transported into holy exaltation (I Sam. x. 5, xix. 20 sqq.; II Kings iii. 15; and see Ecstasy). With the same enchanting tones it was also customary to exorcise the evil spirit in men (I Sam. x. 5, xvi. 23). In the divine service music still retained a leading significance even in later times. A large and well-organized gild of temple musicians was active in the second Temple (I Chron. xxv. 6, xvi. 4 sqq., xxv. 1 sqq.). And if all this is traditionally referred back to David, at least so much is correct that the beautifying of the kingly temple worship with music reaches back to those ancient times. After the exile, many singers and musicians returned with Zerubbabel (Ezra ii. 41; Neh. vii. 44), a proof that the musical tradition had not been dislodged in captivity. In this matter, the blowing of the trumpets on feast days is committed to the priests in the way of a high prerogative; though even in the genealogies of Chronicles, musicians are incorporated with the tribe of Levi. From King Agrippa they later won the privilege of wearing the white, and, in its origin, priestly robe (Josephus, *Ant.* XX., ix. 6). Their sustenance is provided by special prescription under Darius (Ezra vi. 6 sqq., vii. 20 sqq.; Neh. xi. 23), which attests their importance. Their song was accompanied by the Temple orchestra consisting of eight *nebhel* players and six *kinnōr* players. The chief musician marked the time with cymbals (I Chron. xv. 19-21). In the Temple of Herod the orchestra was composed of two to six *nebhel* players, nine *kinnōr* players, and one beater of cymbals. And according to the Talmud, there were also from two to twelve flute players and two trumpeters. Most intimately connected with the entire development of the Temple music stands the composition of the Psalms (q.v.; also see PSALMODY).

VI. Harmony and Rhythm: Concerning the character of Hebrew music, a few conclusions may be reached alike from what has been said concerning the instruments and from modern oriental music. But in the first place it is necessary to remember that harmony, which is based on the triad and on the interplay and flow of consonant and dissonant tones, is of very late origin (tenth century); and that harmony, as such, is generally wanting in the ancient music. To the oriental, even to-day, what seems to us the harmonic blending of various tones in chords, is a repulsive jumble. Hence the old Hebrew music was played thoroughly in unison. Both song and instruments run unisonally together, or perhaps follow the octave, which also sounds harmonious to them (cf. II Chron. v. 13). For the distinction between men's and women's voices, and their semblance of sounding a single tone as they render the same tune, is supplied by nature itself. This being so, it may be left as a remote issue, whether the expression *'al 'alamoth*, of playing the *nebhel* (I Chron. xv. 20), is to be understood with reference to the natural pitch of the "virginal voice"; and the same as to whether the designation *'al-hasheminith* [*sheminith*], "after the eighth," is to be connected with the octave as "eighth" tone, in case of other instruments. But even apart from this, the division of the octave into a scale of seven tones is to be surely assumed. At best, detailed consideration cannot here be given to the connection between this scale and the whole philosophy of the orient, with its doctrine as to the harmony of the spheres; or the tones produced by the seven planets in their courses. In the place of harmony, rhythm plays a leading part, even at the expense of melody. Ancient songs, like the hymn of triumph in Ex. xv. 20, were sung with the timbrel alone in the way of accompaniment. The timbrels, however, simply mark the rhythm. This shows that the singing was mainly a sort of rhythmic declamation. Incipiently, indeed, this was the case with vocal music generally. Nor is this the place to set forth the process of development step by step; as from a regular variation of the tone into an actual melody. Suffice it that the Hebrew popular song stood on the plane where melody is overbalanced by rhythm. And this is still the situation in respect to Arabian song.

Two traits that are now distinctive in the rendering of oriental vocal music are nasalizing and vibration. That the former trait is ancient may be surmised on the ground of other observed qualities of agreement between ancient and modern music. On the other hand there is direct witness as to vibration of the voice, from an Assyrian design, wherein one of the singing women, quite in the manner of Arabian singers to-day, holds one hand under her chin, thus exercising a slight pressure against the throat. This is done in order to produce notably flat tones, and to impart to them a peculiar vibration, not identical, however, with our tremolo style. Sundry obscure data in the Psalms, referring presumably to the delivery, are not certainly resolvable. Some of them, perhaps, involve directions concerning the tune to be followed in singing the Psalm (titles to Ps. ix., xxii., xlv., lvi., lvii., etc.). *Selah* (occurring seventy-one times in forty Psalms) is rendered in the Septuagint by *diapsalma*, which possibly means "interlude." At all events it may be assumed that, in rendering songs, the singing was interrupted at that point, and the pause filled in by playing of the orchestra. The expression *lamenaṣeaḥ* has lately been translated "for the liturgy"; but this, too, is uncertain, though, indeed, the traditional interpretation, "To the Chief Musician," is still more questionable. Else why do just those fifty-three Psalms, and not the rest, need the like specification?

I. BENZINGER.

B. Christian.—I. Character, Purpose, and Forms: Sacred music is properly music which serves for edification, either in the general sense or in the narrower sense of edification as pertaining to divine worship. It is distinguished from secular music, which is designed to serve ends not specifically religious, such as those of art, social life, or instruction. From the distinction between religious edification in its wider sense and edification in the sanctuary arises a distinction between sacred music in the wider and in the stricter sense: that is, between what may be called spiritual music, and the music of divine worship, church music or liturgical music. To the former class belongs all music which has an edifying effect upon the feelings, which incites to devotion, which directs the im-

1. General Conception and Purpose.

agination toward the realm of the eternal and divine; such as the Biblical oratorio, the spiritual song, and serious instrumental music. The music of the sanctuary comprises only such music as according to its substance and form, object and character, harmonizes with divine worship as a homogeneous element of the same, not overstepping the sphere of divine worship but essentially complementing it and strengthening its effectiveness. The essential mark of sacred music in the stricter sense is that its artistic effect accords with the effect aimed at in worship, producing a single combined effect. This accord requires that the music heard in divine worship shall not evoke in the hearer memories and ideas that may divert from the object of reverence. It excludes transfer of compositions known to the hearer in other connections. It requires on the composer's part subordination of the artistic purpose to the end and conception of divine worship. If divine worship be regarded only as a means of converting the masses, music is employed simply for its operation upon the emotions; and nothing further is required of it than exciting power, easy access to the mind, action upon the nerves. Its esthetic value, its artistic constitution, is not essentially in question. Artistic excellence and purity must frequently be sacrificed for immediate effect and influence upon the lower stratum of the congregation. This view of church music obtains more or less where divine service is regarded exclusively from the missionary and pedagogical standpoint (e.g., among German Methodists and the Salvation Army). Where divine worship is an end in itself, either as consummating a sacred act whose value properly inheres in the strict observance of the form of its consummation (the Roman Catholic conception), or as the voluntary assembling of the congregation before God with preaching of the Gospel and prayer (the Evangelical conception), the music is, in the one instance, ecclesiastical in the sense of constituting a portion of the liturgy; in the other instance, in the degree that it animates and strengthens the presentation of the Gospel, or as it unifies the congregation's prayer in due liturgical process.

According to the Roman Catholic conception, the Church decides what belongs to the essence of divine worship; music is ecclesiastical in so far as it answers to the "will of the Church in the sphere of music." Roman Catholic church music is liturgical song as appointed by the Church and such artistic song as has been carefully examined and admitted for use in divine worship. This was expressed in no equivocal manner by the decree of the Congregation of Rites of Apr. 23 and 26, 1883. According to this decree, "only that form of Gregorian song was to be regarded as authentic and regular, which in virtue of the provisions of the Council of Trent has been approved and confirmed by His Holiness Pope Leo XIII., as likewise by the Congregation of Sacred Rites, conformably to the edition prepared at Regensburg, as the one used by the Roman Church." [This decree, however, in so far as it made the Regensburg edition "authentic" or authoritative, was reversed by Pius X., who shortly after his accession to the papal throne issued a most important *Motu Proprio* concerning the reform of abuses in church music and embodying many positive instructions. Scientific students of plain-song, especially the Benedictines, had already proved conclusively that the Regensburg "authentic" edition was very imperfect and uncritical—that it by no means represented the old traditional Gregorian melodies. A critical edition of the latter, embodying the results of long and painstaking labor on the part of eminent scholars, was prepared from a comparative study of the ancient manuscripts by the Benedictine Fathers of the monastery of Solesmes in France, but while competent and disinterested critics unanimously recognized its superiority over the Regensburg edition, the latter still retained its authoritative position in virtue of the above-mentioned decree of the Congregation of Rites. But Pius X., who took a deep, intelligent interest in the subject, cast the weight of his authority in favor of the school of Solesmes, and the undeserved monopoly hitherto enjoyed by the Regensburg editors came suddenly to an end. The pope appointed a pontificial commission to supervise the carrying-out of the instructions contained in the *Motu Proprio*, and to look after the publication of a new "authentic" edition of the liturgical plain-song, to be known as the Vatican edition. The members of this commission were all chosen from among the experts representing the Benedictine school, and the new edition (not yet completed) is based exclusively on that of Solesmes. The *Motu Proprio* deals at length and with not a little detail with the entire question of church music in its various aspects. Many abuses are pointed out and reproved, and while modern music is not excluded from use in church services, it is subjected to restrictions requiring that it be religious and ecclesiastical in character. Music of the Palestrinian style is commended, but a strong preference is expressed in favor of the traditional Gregorian or plain-song, the use of which is prescribed for all those parts of the service known as the "proper." This decree was followed by a keen revival of interest in the question of church music both in Europe and in America, and in most of the dioceses musical commissions were appointed by the bishops with a view to carry out the instructions contained in the papal document. J. F. D.] Church music is ecclesiastical according to its relation to the sanctioned choral music. Its ecclesiastical quality is not involved in the musical style of any specified epoch; or in any specified harmonic form or musical mode of expression. Music is ecclesiastical in so far as it is an artistic consummation and idealization of the liturgical song sanctioned by the Church.

2. The Roman Catholic Conception.

According to the Evangelical conception, it is essential to divine service that the word of God, the Gospel, be proclaimed, and that the congregation make its confession in prayer. Here music becomes the art which expresses emotions that strive in vain for words, as well as the art which unifies and idealizes every form of expression. As music supplements the spoken word, its tones impart a vital, apprehensible quality to the "unspeakable words" (I Cor. xii. 4) of the revelation disclosed to the human soul in the divine word, and the "groanings which can not be uttered" (Rom. viii. 26) which accompany the prayer of faith. But only to the extent that it serves to attune the proclaiming of the Gospel to its utmost impressiveness, and to harmonize the congregation's prayer by melodiously defining and rhythmically modulating the same, in accord with the fundamental principle that "all things be done decently and in order" (I Cor. xiv. 40)—that is, only as a means, and not for its own sake—has music its rightful place in divine service. It is the "tongue" of art, which edifies only where it utters "words easy to be understood" (I Cor. xiv. 9), and is made immediately intelligible by virtue of the divine word, which it aids to expound, or unto which it contributes a freely uplifting power. For in divine service, the question is not one of artistic edification; that is, of that intellectual stimulation of life which contact with the beautiful evokes, but of edification in the religious sense, or the strengthening and enhancement of the life of faith, as this is vouchsafed by the living realization of the divine means of salvation in the Gospel, and immediate contact with the same in prayer. Religious edification can be promoted only by music which strengthens the impression made by the Gospel, and fosters prayer; hence by music which directs attention steadfastly not upon itself, but upon the Gospel and prayer. Accordingly the commonplace, frivolous, and sentimental are excluded, because these contradict the dignity, the earnestness, and the sublimity of the object and the sacredness of the end; and likewise there is excluded whatever is technical and too refined artistically or professionally, because this appeals to musical interest exclusively, thus withdrawing attention from the word of God, even depreciating the same as a mere means of artistic exercise. Moreover church music must speak to the congregation; accordingly, as touching its content and style, that quality which presupposes, in order to be intelligently understood, a strictly technical education is excluded. Church music does not make its appeal to the professional musician or to the concert public. The requirement of close concentration upon the aim in view becomes restricted on the one hand to the requirement of musical self-discipline and self-limitation, divesting itself of every extraneous purpose; on the other hand, to the requirement of noble simplicity and luminous clearness in the form of composition. These fundamental requirements premised, no musical style or species of music is in itself excluded which answers to these requirements. If in many circles there is a disposition to restrict the conception of church music to the productions and style of the sixteenth and seventeenth centuries, the reason is that this was in fact a period of productiveness in classical church music, a time of concentrating the creation upon church requisitions. But the works of a Johann Sebastian Bach (q.v.) likewise bear the impress of perfect devotion to the object and end of Evangelical divine service; and the motets of the sixteenth and seventeenth centuries are not to be preferred simply because their style has become strange (see below, II., 1, b).

3. The Protestant Conception.

If, furthermore, rigid practise would exclude instrumental music from church music (the organ excepted), and limit the conception of what is ecclesiastical to the vocal choir, this inheres in the fact that the use of instruments demands a far greater degree of both foresight and restraint than the vocal choir. Choral song incites to a mood in harmony with the Church, because the very ideal roundness and detachment of the choral sound gives an impression of pureness above the prose of everyday routine. The sound of orchestral instruments easily rouses in the hearer the thought of secular occasions wherein they are employed, and for this reason orchestral music has for many people a somewhat mundane tone. But, after all, this is merely a matter of convention, and principally subjective. It is only necessary to recall Bach's employment of the orchestra—his passion music and his cantatas—to make clear that the matter turns only upon the manner of the employment. Bach knew how to devote this mighty giant of instrumentation, commanding, as it does, every harmonic effect and shade of tone, every variety of expression, and every gradation of tonic power, to the service of edification. It is not abstract principles and theories, but only practical difficulties, which oppose themselves to the employment of the orchestra for church music, and persuade most congregations to restrict themselves to the vocal choir and the organ. For the latter instrument in Evangelical church music, see ORGAN.

4. The Use of Instrumental Music.

Many people would exclude solo singing from church music for the reason that it tends to emphasize the individual, to divert the hearer's interest from divine worship, and thus interfere with edification. Yet, while this may easily happen, it does not necessarily and always follow. The right use is not abrogated by misuse. Solo song has its good title in church music, provided it be not thrust forward for its own sake, but is called for by the subject matter and the musical composition, and accords with the general design, helping to enrich and deepen the total impression. On account of human infirmity, not on abstract grounds, it is advisable, as a rule, to keep solo song somewhat subordinated. But to renounce a musical composition as unfitted for church use merely because it requires solo voices, is not Evangelical. The text holds good of the forms and kinds of Evangelical church music, "all things are yours, but ye are Christ's." All things are to be admitted provided they consecrate themselves to the sacred service. For the Church of the Gospel, congregational singing, strictly regarded, is not a constituent integral element of divine service. That is to say, the constituent elements of the Evangelical worship are, as explained above, the proclaiming of the word of God, the Gospel, and the prayer of the congregation. Whether the word of God reaches the congrega-

5. Solo Singing.

tion in the way of oral discourse, or in the manner of the Roman church chant in a melodiously graduated delivery (or intonation), or in the festival pomp of full-voiced choir music; whether the congregation merely joins in spirit in the proffered prayer, or directly expresses the same in song, as in the congregational hymn, is determined by custom and requirements, by circumstances and means, being indeed a matter of significance with reference to the practical effect and impressiveness of worship, but not, as such, a part of its essence and intrinsic value. Nevertheless, the Evangelical worship being theoretically and essentially a congregational act, this implies, of course, that the congregation as such shall take part in the same. And this it can best do in a collective way in the form of singing which groups a diversity of voices into a harmonic unity. Such singing is well established in Evangelical worship as the most suitable form for the congregation's collective activity. The congregation as a vehicle of divine service is not an indiscriminate mass of people, but consists of a variety of living individuals and groups of people, who differ in age and sex; accordingly it contains within itself a diversity of gifts and powers. Divine worship is an act or transaction of the congregation in proportion as the separate individuals actively and individually cooperate in the service; it is a congregational act in the full sense of the term according as the gifts and powers latent in the congregation come into active play and minister to the service of edification by means of a lively presentation of the Gospel. Among gifts vouchsafed to the congregation, the gift of song stands in the front rank in relation to divine worship; especially the harmonic art when viewed as a preeminent factor for enhancing the effect of the Gospel to its utmost degree of impressiveness, thus powerfully promoting edification. Viewed in this light, as an instrument of edification of singular power and effectiveness, harmonic art, and, notably, cultivated singing, has its place in Evangelical worship; while in the same service the choir has its office in the way of expressive leadership. In this worship the choir is the exponent of musical art in the divine service, being a legitimate adjunct of the same only in so far as the purpose of edification demands that this art be coordinated as a homogeneous factor within the sphere of worship. The choir is not a necessary arrangement with reference to worship, its essence and realization; all this is complete even without the choir's cooperation. In fact the employment of a choir presupposes that the congregation already contains the proper intelligence for the artistic performances of the choir, and that this intelligence has been cultivated up to a certain degree; where this is not the case, there is no need of choir singing. But choir singing is a no less powerful than blessed instrument of congregational edification; and as such it has been duly valued by the congregation from the very outset.

6. Congregation and Choir.

The Reformation coincided with the age when the art of polyphony was ripening into classical perfection. This art was quite distinctively the creation of the Church (see below II., 2, §§ 2-4); hence the Reformation found artistic choral song at its height. Attached to the larger churches were permanent choirs, whose maintenance was provided in part by the munificence of princes and magistrates, in part by means of endowments. But in case of the rising Evangelical church the primary interest was not artistic singing, but congregational singing; and for its exponent and leader in Germany, not the trained choir was in question, but the school. All effort was accordingly directed to the training of the growing congregation for the tasks devolving upon it in the divine service, by means of a zealous cultivation of singing in the school. Nevertheless the importance of artistic singing was fully valued by the Reformers. It was quite peculiarly owing to Luther that this instrument of congregational edification was retained. He urgently enjoined upon those in authority the duty of sufficient provision to this end, in cases where the congregations lacked resources and were not able to take the initiative. "Kings, princes and lords must support music, for it becomes great potentates and lords to maintain good liberal arts and the laws." Where no choir is present to serve the congregation with the glorious gift of music, then the like service devolves as an honorable duty upon the school. The princely chorister schools were expressly and positively institutes of art, and liturgical singing engaged only a part of their professional duties. Under their direction church music came to be more and more a concert performance in the divine service. The artistic mission of the school choirs, however, accorded with the other tasks which the school had in charge. Their musical tasks were planned according to the needs of the congregation in the sanctuary, approximating more closely to the average intelligence and becoming more familiar to the congregation than the performances of the professional art choirs. Thus the school choir came to serve as a musical training establishment for the whole congregation, and from it the congregation developed the ability to help itself in case of need.

7. The Churches of the Reformation.

For example, when the choral institute, to which people had been accustomed, closed its doors—as did the residential chorister school at Torgau in 1530 on account of financial considerations, musically endowed citizens of the town associated themselves in the "Torgau Chorister Society" with a view to practising and rendering, under the leadership of the princely vocal master and precentor Johann Walther, the portions devolving upon the choir. The example of Torgau was followed by other towns. At the same time the growing delight in song and music led to associations which charged themselves with the cultivation of singing and in some cases especially sacred song (as at Reutlingen in Württemberg, 1609; St. Gallen, 1620; and elsewhere). The popularity of Handel's oratorios toward the close of the eighteenth century and the rise of male singing societies in the early decades of the nineteenth century augmented the impulse to create musical associations, which gladly lent their services to the Church; these societies, however, were primarily artistic and secular. The revival of religious and ecclesiastical interest after the wars of liberation, which manifested itself particularly in the Reformation jubilee festival (1817), led to the formation of societies devoted specifically to church song. They soon extended over all Germany and their activity has steadily become wider. In 1881 the first "General Convention of the German Evangelical Church Singing Societies" met at Stuttgart, and in the year of the Luther jubilee (1883) was organized the "Evangelical Church Singing Society for Germany," which in 1905 comprised twenty-two territorial and provincial societies, and 1,996 local societies and church choirs. The management is in the hands of a central committee whose duties are defined to be: (1) To promote the cause of Evangelical church song by spoken and written means; (2) to work for cooperation of individual societies; (3) to assist societies in selecting and securing their music; (4) to call a general convention at least once every three years; (5) to represent the general interests abroad. A periodical, the *Korrespondenzblatt des evangelischen Kirchengesangvereins für Deutschland*, is published at Leipsic.

8. German Singing Societies.

II. History: The essential ground form of the Roman Catholic church song is the choral (*cantus Gregorianus*, because its regulation and systematisation is traced back to Gregory I.; *cantus planus*, "plain-song," in distinction from figured song; *cantus choralis*, because it is rendered in unison by the aggregate of singers present in the choir), or church song in the tone style of ancient music. The Evangelical church makes some use of the Gregorian song, as when it is used for the altar chanting in German churches, and when particular melodies are borrowed from it for congregational song; but its own distinctive ground form is the popular melody adapted to church use; the modern, harmoniously tuned and harmonically intelligible melodious hymn, or church hymn. Upon these basic forms are constructed the artistic forms of church music, which are proper to the particular church in so far as their expressed object is to adorn and idealize those basic forms by process of elaborated tonal art; but they are governed by their respective standards, the choral and the church hymn.

1. The Liturgical Side. a. The Choral Chant: The authentic sources of the liturgical song of the Roman Church are the official hymnaries brought out under Popes Gregory XIII. and Paul V., on the initiative of the Council of Trent, and on the basis of the revision undertaken by Giovanni Guidetti (1532–92); viz, the *Directorium chori* (1582); the *Antiphonarium*, containing the liturgical songs for the breviary (1610); the *Graduale*, with the liturgical songs for the mass (1614 and 1615); and the *Hymnarium*, which followed under Urban VIII. in 1644, after a revision undertaken by Palestrina, Guidetti's teacher. Their authentic edition, among the later ones, is held to be that of Regensburg, 1872-1882. They contain the "authentic and authorized form of Gregorian song"; that is, that manner of song "which the Roman Church uses," or has to use. Whether the melodies thus pronounced to be authentic are really those of the earlier time correctly transmitted is a matter which, in spite of careful investigations, may not at present be determined to a certainty (but see above, B, I., § 2).

1. The Authorized Roman Hymnaries.

The Gregorian choral, as distinguished from modern melody, is conditioned in point of tune and composition by the text, and is to be understood in that light; being structurally monotonic, in part mere musically graduated, stereotyped recitative, wherein the rise and fall of the vocal tone, the choice of intervals, the tonic measure, are determined not with reference to grace or expression of the melody, but simply by the textual notation; in part, again, it is real song, melody representing a musical *ensemble*, and following, for that matter, a definite rule of construction according to the tonal mode, or key, to which it belongs, but conditioned in the composition by the verbal structure of the text. The peculiarity and significance of the melody—its musical character, in a word—inheres in the manner in which the tonal movement which the [illegible] conveys progresses from the start[illegible] the initial tone through the tonal [illegible] (diatonic) scale to the closing [illegible] in this case in-

2. The Gregorian Chant.

terests the musical imagination is the feature of the tone graduations combined with singleness of effect by the melody as it glides along; and these in relation to one another, not in their relation to the basic triad of tonal values, as is the case in modern melody—in respect to their melodious juxtaposition and sequence, not in respect to their harmonic significance. This entirely corresponds to the antique theory of musical tones: Gregorian song is church song in the tone language of ancient (Greek and Roman) music. Its melodies belong to the diatonic scheme of tones; that is, they are invariably composed of the tones of the diatonic scales; these grouping themselves, in every instance, with two and three whole steps and two half-steps. Chromatic and enharmonic scales are quite debarred. The Gregorian song, in contrast with the secular music of the first Christian century, thus reflects the reform of music in the direction of noble simplicity, the reaction to classical style. The regulation and systematization of church song for the Roman and so for the entire Western Church is traditionally connected with the name of Gregory the Great (590–604); though to what extent rightly, leaves room for further elucidation.

b. The Evangelical Hymn: In contrast with the ancient melody of Gregorian song, the musical form of the church hymn, which constitutes the foundation, soul, and center of Evangelical church music, is the modern, harmoniously definite and harmonically consistent hymn tune: harmonically consistent, that is, from the relation of the tones of the melody to the basic tone, or more precisely, to the basic accord of the key to which the melody belongs, governed by the cardinal points of the tonic and dominant, and yielding a symmetrically coherent, rhythmically expressive, sonorously emotional fabric. It is the recognized musical form for the song of the congregation; for the choral prayer thereof in distinction from the choral (or liturgical) prayer of the priestly singers assembled in the choir, wherein the priestly Church has likewise its musical speech to utter. The Reformation did not create this musical form; it found the same at hand in the spiritual and secular folk-song, which had gradually wrested itself loose from the fetters of the ancient tone theory, and had developed, in the period from the thirteenth century to the fifteenth, into luxuriant blossoming. It is true, the Church of the Reformation, in order to obtain tunes for congregational singing, did not limit itself to the folk-song, but appropriated also some of the melodious treasure of Gregorian song. But what it borrowed from this for congregational singing was recast according to the folk-song pattern. Peculiar, if not essential to the folk-song, is the so-called polyrhythm, by virtue of which in one and the same melody double and triple time interchange, thus producing rhythmical combinations which can only with difficulty be conveyed in modern measures.

1. Developed from the Folk-Song.

The early period of the Reformation had plenty to do in the way of adjusting for congregational use the tunes which it borrowed from Gregorian song, from the treasure of Latin hymns, from the sequences, from the spiritual folk-song, as also from the treasure of secular folk-song. What little the Reformation period contributed to the treasure of melodies out of its own invention (Luther's *Ein' feste Burg*, for example) reflects the classical type of the church folk-tune. Toward the close of the sixteenth century there is an increase of originators of new melodies (Selnecker, 1530–1592; Philipp Nicolai, 1556–1608; Melchior Franck, c. 1573–1639; Melchior Teschner, 1614; Melchior Vulpius, c. 1560–1615; Johann Hermann Schein, 1586–1630; Michael Altenburg, 1584–1640; Matthäus Apelles von Löwenstern, 1594–1648; Johannes Crüger, 1598–1662). The seventeenth century increasingly exhibits, in the composition of melodies, the influence of the aria song which toward the end of the sixteenth century had arisen in Italy (Heinrich Albert, 1604–51; Johann Georg Ebeling, 1637–76; Jakob Hintze, 1622–1702; Johann Rudolf Ahle, 1625–73; Georg Neumark, 1621–1681; Joachim Neander, 1650–80; Adam Drese, 1620–1701). The church melody as softened down into the spiritual aria, with its sentimental or "heart's revealing" nature, stands as far removed from the compact force and the sonorous full tones of the folk-song, as pietism, whose favorite mode it becomes, from the Reformation. In evidence of the lively and zealous activity which pietism displayed in behalf of church song, there are the *Darmstädter Kantional* (1687); the *Freylinghausen'sche Gesangbuch* (1704 sqq.); the *Choralbücher* of Dretzel (1731), König (1738), and others; in evidence of the religious vitality inherent in the movement, there is a succession of hymns, which, if not betokening vernacular simplicity and primitiveness, yet indicate hymnal buoyancy.

2. The Sixteenth and Seventeenth Centuries.

The "age of enlightenment" completes the process of modernizing the church melody. It becomes a popularized art hymn, which is distinguished from the parallel secular art song only in that it dispenses with all rhythmical charm, merging into the "slowest song" that "can fairly be conceived" (Justin Heinrich Knecht, Preface of the *Choralbuch* of 1799). In only particular instances have the numerous melodies which the "age of enlightenment" produced, evinced vitality. It was a matter full of portent, that the new trend of taste "improved upon" the transmitted wealth of the Fathers. The characteristic and ever charming polyrhythm of the old tunes appeared to the modern conception of musical measure hard and unintelligible; likewise it seemed impracticable for popular use; while the rhythmical vivacity seemed incompatible with the idea then entertained of the sublimity and "dignity" of music for the divine service. The old tunes were approximated to the ideal of the "slowest song that can fairly be conceived," being divested not only of polyrhythm, but of rhythm altogether. This leveling process for the church tune, at first in the direction of isometry, then to the completely unrhythmical plain-song, was at the same time evoked and favored by means of the growing sway of the organ in Evangelical worship. The revival of religious life and the deepening of the ecclesiastical consciousness in the first decades of the nineteenth century manifested itself less in the production of new melodies (Bernhard Klein, 1793–1832; Johann Georg Frech, 1790–1864; Conrad Kocher, 1786–1872; Heinrich Carl Breidenstein, 1796–1876; Arnold Mendelssohn, b. 1856; and others) than in the growing intelligence in behalf of distinctive charm, the historical as well as ecclesiastical and esthetic justification of the original form of the transmitted melodies; and in the zealous endeavor to recover for congregational singing the rhythmical vivacity and original freshness of the Reformation period. How far this endeavor, which is thoroughly justified from the standpoint of historic fidelity, is feasible in practise, and at what point it becomes restricted by considerations as to the nature of choral song, and of the characteristic tones of the organ, still indispensable for accompaniment, are matters which even to-day are still subject to great differences of opinion. For this reason, and because of the numberless variants which have established themselves in the several church provinces through venerable custom, attempts to secure uniformity of usage in the German churches have been successful only in a limited degree.

3. The Eighteenth and Nineteenth Centuries.

2. The Artistic Side: The first ten centuries of the Christian Church knew none but homophonic song. For the non-Latin peoples who came into the Church, this was artistic song, which required expert schooling, and this was the reason why it came to be more and more exclusively assigned to the choir of singers trained specially for church song. It was rendered in a language foreign to the congregation, and in a mode of musical articulation unusual to them, viz., the antique Greco-Roman. The liturgical song was choir song. The people still had the *canticum vulgare*, the song of their native speech; and from the twelfth century onward this became more and more independently developed, and on the chief festivals, at least, was even tolerated in the liturgy of the mass (between epistle and Gospel in place of the psalm which succeeded the halleluiah; or, as the case might be, in place of the sequence, and subsequently also following the Gospel in the way of a German creedal song, either instead of the Latin *credo* or attached to the same).

1. Church Song Homophonic till the Year 1000.

From the eleventh century and continually thenceforward, out of modest, and, according to modern ideas of musical beauty, rude attempts, as they appear in the light of the fifth and octave parallels of the Benedictine monk Hucbald of St. Amand (c. 840–930), there developed itself under the fostering care of the Church, through the middle terms of the descant (principle of reciprocal harmony) and of fauxbourdon (habituation to the harmonic euphony of thirds and sixths), the composite or polyphonic choir song, which for the most part aimed to be nothing more than the artistic expansion and enrichment of the liturgical song. By the end of the fourteenth century, polyphony, the art of counterpoint, had reached its complete development (first Netherland school, c. 1380–1480: Wilhelm du Fay, Binchois, Dunstable, and others); by the end of the fifteenth century it came to its classic bloom (second Netherland school, c. 1480–1565: Ockenheim, Josquin de Prés, Lassus, and others). It had gained entrance to the papal chapel during the exile at Avignon (1309–77). The art of blending voices through the bond of musical consonance, quite distinctively the creation of the Middle Ages—the musical expression of the medieval association and gild spirit—accorded with the spirit of the Medieval Church. The creative constructive power and the wanton constructive impulse of the master composers brought matters to such a pass that the artistic product became an end in itself, and art forgot her subservient position. Not only in the luxuriant, exuberant maze of tones was the sacred text utterly lost to the verge of unintelligibility, but also the hallowed style of the choral came to be neglected. The master composers elected the tenor parts, and along these lines they built up their themes, no longer subject to the liturgical point of view, but to the purely esthetic standpoint of artistic effect, sometimes basing their masses upon favorite and often secular popular tunes. Accordingly the Roman Catholic Church, committing itself as it did at the Council of Trent to the known Roman chant, could allow full rights to the polyphonic style in divine worship only under the proviso that art should do justice to the liturgical demands of the Church. These demands were thoroughly satisfied by the masses which Palestrina (1526?–94; see PALESTRINA, GIOVANNI PIERLUIGI DA) composed at the instance of the council, and submitted to the committee appointed by the council for the regulation of church music. In this master's *Missa Papæ Marcelli* (1565), the stricter school since that time recognizes the classic type of Roman Catholic Church music. It is true, the course of development passed beyond its bounds, and Roman Church music subsequently shared in all the transformations of tonal art. The strict Palestrina style, as represented by the Roman school (Animuccia, Vittoria, Felice and Francesco Anerio, Nanini, lastly Baini) had to yield to the style which emphasized subjective pathos, over and above the beautiful style which exhibits lofty detachment and massive repose by striving toward individual expression. The Cæcilian Society (Franz Witt, 1834–88; Franz Xaver Haberl, 1840–1910) tried to reform the Roman Church music by returning to the style of Palestrina. Yet the Church itself, though actively supporting that society's efforts, has not obstructed the further development of church music; nor has it even barred from the sanctuary productions of the most modern tonal art of a Liszt and a Verdi.

2. Development of Polyphonic Song.

The Reformation coincided with the flourishing period of polyphony. Among its peculiar forms, the nascent Evangelical church could consider, for use in divine worship, only the motet, the hymn for several voices; or the madrigal. The motet (Ital. *mottetto*, diminutive of *motto*, "a word, a saying"), a musical phrase constructed upon a more or less brief refrain either borrowed from the liturgical chant or the folk-song or even freely invented, found its place in the mass, as a musical art form, as the musical setting for passages of Scripture that mark the contextual significance of the mass in the calendar. In the Evangelical worship it occurred first by way of musical setting for the sentences of the introit, the gradual, or the epistle or Gospel sentence, and in the next place as a form of choir song during the distribution of the Eucharist, as well as at marriages, funerals, and other solemnities. The word motet eventually came to signify elaborate choir song. In a narrower sense, as artistic form for the musical embodiment of a Bible sentence, that is, of the sentence in the introit or lection that indicated the day's calendar significance, the motet became the form in which tonal art participated in proclaiming the divine word in Evangelical worship. A form of motet which was cultivated with special favor was the polyphonic hymn (as elaborated in motet style). The task of the musical phrase in this case is artistically to modulate the harmonic suggestion already given in the closed melody preceding, and to comprehend it somewhat in the manner of a costly painting in elegantly carved framework. This form adapted itself quite peculiarly to the musical elaboration of the church tune, and therefore became the hymn form in superior choirs. But the choir song in Evangelical worship had now not only an artistic task, it had above all an educational mission; it was to lead the tunes for the congregation, in order to render them so familiar that the people should make them their own and themselves join in. The hymn tune, in this connection, ran traditionally in the tenor, which constituted the middle part. On practical grounds, it became advisable to assign the tune to the upper voice, the soprano. Everything, in this case, was left to the free invention of the composer, who sought simply to light upon the musical expression for the keynote of the appertaining text. The art of composition, the blending and the direction of voices, became an incidental, expression the chief thing. The tuneful motives concentrated themselves more and more upon the finished expressive melody, and this became the vocal surface of the composition. The artistic composition, the harmony proper, came to be more and more a mere means of expression, the chromatic tone. The decisive step toward transposing the melody to the soprano part was accomplished by the Württemberg Court Preacher Lucas Osiander, by his address to schoolmasters, Jan. 1, 1586 (see OSIANDER, 2), and the publication of the work: *Fünffzig geistliche Lieder und Psalmen. Mit vier Stimmen, auf Contrapunctsweise.* A succession of notable composers followed his example: Gesius, Raselius, Michael, Calvisius, Vulpius, Hassler, Michael Prätorius, Johann Eccard.

3. The Reformation. The Motet and Madrigal.

It was natural that the hymn tune, heretofore the foundation of the composition, should now become its actual object, the remaining voices receding more and more to the province of accompaniment, as they followed the melody in regular counterpoint; and the polyphonic motet style had to yield to the ambitious madrigal style of the modern harmonized melody. On the border line between the old and the new conception stand the great composers Hans Leo Hassler (1564–1612) and Johann Eccard (1553–1611); also Sethus Calvisius (1556–1615), Melchior Vulpius (d. 1615), Scandellus (1517–80), Joachim a Burgck (1541–1610), Jakob Meiland (1542–77), David Scheidemann (c. 1585, in Hamburg), Le Maistre, Dulichius, Johann Stobäus, Demantius, and others. They still stand upon the art of the Netherland masters; Eccard was a pupil of the great Lassus; but the congregational tune comes to its full rights. In Luther's time it was the leader in the dancing round of voices, where " one sings aloud a proper tune, beside which three, four, or five other voices likewise play round about, as it were with shouting; and leap, and with all sorts of sound wonderfully grace and adorn the same, and lead as it were a heavenly dancing procession, encountering one another cordially, and somehow caressing and lovingly embracing each other " (Luther in *Encomion musices*). It now becomes all-prevailing. The charming work of the polyphonic hymn yields to the merely harmonized four-voiced choral. Soon the choir's place is taken by the organ; and the four-voiced choral is succeeded by the homophonic song of the congregation with organ accompaniment. For the most part, the polyphonic hymn, as it still survives, is artistic song by the choir.

4. Development of the Modern Hymn Tune.

The tendency to emphasize distinctive expression, which came into vogue in Italy toward the end of the sixteenth century and led to the monodic style, had its influence very early upon the German Evangelical church music. Men like Rosenmüller (1610–84), Michael Prätorius (1571–1621), and above all, the greatest German harmonist before Bach, Heinrich Schütz (1585–1672), transplanted the Italian forms of the church concerto to Germany. In this way church music acquired the means for an animated musical interpretation of the divine word, such as was not achieved by the purely polyphonic motet. The barriers of the old church tones are broken through; the harmony becomes closer, fuller, more characteristic; the melody more pliant and expressive; while the harmony is reinforced by the accompaniment of distinct instruments (trombones, violins). Especially the arioso and the recitative enabled the composer to enliven dramatically the musical interpretation of the sacred text; to round out melodiously the various indicated moods; to illustrate musically the narrative events, and define musically the persons introduced. Church music, which had formerly elected to present to the congregation the word of God in the sumptuously elaborated monstrance of artistic polyphonic composition, comes to be more and more the independent interpreter of that word, by combining, in the way of arias and recitative, the motets and the polyphonic hymn into a larger comprehensive unity. The " motet " thus expands into the " spiritual dialogue " (Andreas Hammerschmidt, 1612–75); into the " spiritual conversation concerning the Gospel " for the day (Johann Rudolf Ahle, 1625–73; Wolfgang Briegel, 1626–1712); then into the " cantata," which in turn develops from a simple form into richer and richer complexity (Johann Kuhnau, 1667–1722; Johann Philipp Krieger, 1649–1725; Johann Krieger, 1652–1735; Dietrich Buxtehude, 1637–1707; Johann Christoph Bach, 1642–1703; Johann Michael Bach, 1649–1693; Georg Philipp Telemann, 1681–1767; Reinhard Keiser, 1674–1739; Gottfried Stölzel, 1690–1749, and others); and becomes complete in the cantatas of Johann Sebastian Bach (q.v.), the greatest harmonist of the Evangelical church. In this case the cantata has become divine service within the divine service, transcending the bounds of the liturgy. In connection with the cantata in its final manifestation, Evangelical church music steps outside the church door, so to speak, and as spiritual music, in the form of the oratorio, becomes a powerful witness of the Gospel before people who avoid that witness when uttered in God's house. Upon the broad stream of a powerful, robustly expansive music, which for all its musical profundity continues genuinely popular, Bach's greatest contemporary, Georg Friedrich Handel (q.v.), displays to the eye of the soul the story of divine revelation in his Biblical oratorios; his *Messiah* is the Gospel in monumental tone-speech, a most powerful heralding of the Gospel, a monumental anthem. Together with its intimate and lively relation to the congregational hymn, Bach's church music is characterized by its close union with the instrument of Evangelical worship, the organ. As he fructifies organ art (see ORGAN) through the congregational hymn, and thus devotes the same to the Church, adapting it to the religious mood, likewise his vocal compositions that are intended for the divine service are conceived and created out of the spirit of the organ. Handel, too, had his start on the organ bench, and from the organ received the polyphonic spirit which imparts colossal volume and power to his resounding choruses. But Bach's music is directly born of the organ, and for that very reason, the same as through the congregational hymn, it is inseparably connected with the divine service.

5. New Forms. The Cantata and the Oratorio.

There came the time which no longer understood either of these witnesses, for the primal notes of the Gospel had themselves become strange. What came to be " church music " in divine service in the rationalistic period, though sincerely intended music and technically " figural music," was in fact but a feeble imitation of the contemporary stage or concert music. Very capable masters devoted their best strength to the oratorio (Karl Heinrich Graun, 1701–1759; Friedrich Schneider, 1786–1853; Bernhard Klein, 1793–1832; Karl Loewe, 1796–1869; Ludwig Spohr, 1784–1859), and thus attested, in their way, the inexhaustible power and glory of the divinely revealed word; although their tone-language stood remote from that of a Handel. It was Felix Mendelssohn-Bartholdy (1809–47) who in 1829 roused Bach's Passion Music from the sleep of a hundred years, and thereby recalled the Evangelical church of Germany to its greatest musical wit-

6. The Period of Rationalism and the Nineteenth Century.

ness. His oratorios *St. Paul* and *Elijah*, wherein he makes music serve the Biblical text in masterly fashion, have become typical for a series of competent masters (Eckert, 1820–79; Reinthaler, 1822–1890; Rheinberger, and others). For the one school, which gives more study to Handel, the oratorio is the Biblical drama without stage scenery. Propriety and fidelity in the musical interpretation, force and fulness of expression, are the tasks to which the music is committed. The oratorio style is distinguished from that of the musical drama only and exclusively by the peculiar nature of the subject requirements. This theory later leads logically to the "spiritual opera" of Rubinstein. The others, who consciously or unconsciously bear the mark of Bach, are more or less overshadowed, even in the oratorio, by the relation to the congregation, to the house of God, to divine worship, whether they have the house of God expressly in view and aim at a combination of oratorio with congregational singing (as, for instance, F. Zimmer, Ludwig Meinardus, Albert Becker, Hermann Francke, Bernecker, Schwalm, Zierau, R. Succo, but above all, Heinrich von Herzogenberg, 1843–1900); or whether they allow the thought of edifying the congregation to operate only ideally upon their creation (Brahms, 1833–96; Kiel, 1821–85) without restricting themselves as musicians; or whether their musical creation seeks closer or more distant affinity with the elements of congregational edification (Felix Woyrsch; Wolfrum). Mendelssohn, again, prompted by King Frederick William IV., imparted new life to and exerted fresh influence upon Evangelical church music in its more limited sense of music for the divine service, by means of a number of compositions. And the list of serious and praiseworthy composers of extremely diverging tendencies who have placed themselves at the disposal of the German Evangelical church in later time is a long and imposing one. See also HYMNOLOGY; PSALMODY. H. A. KÖSTLIN.

3. In England and America: Church music in England has had a history peculiar to itself, usually quite distinct from that in Germany, though with obvious analogies. Although music has always been a stated feature in ecclesiastical life, its official and professional cultivation has varied greatly in quality at different periods, so that its progress has been somewhat fitful and inconsistent. It has not been surrounded by so rich and stimulating an atmosphere of popular aptitude for and interest in musical activity as in Germany. Yet, on the other hand, English church music, being a part of the liturgical practise of the national church, has had always a certain traditional dignity, and, at times when other musical fields have been but slightly emphasized, it has provided room for the artistic effort of many worthy musicians. There has naturally been a marked difference between the services of the cathedrals and those of the parish churches. The former have usually been maintained with much more elaboration than the latter. In tracing the history of English church music, then, it is almost inevitable to dwell more upon what is found in the diocesan or metropolitan centers, including the chapels of the great universities of Oxford and Cambridge, than upon the usages of the far more numerous parochial or rural churches.

1. The General Situation.

As in the Roman system of worship, much of the scope and character of Anglican church music is directly determined by the character of the liturgy of the Church of England. This liturgy is contained in the Book of Common Prayer (see COMMON PRAYER, BOOK OF), which originated about the middle of the sixteenth century. This important manual provides services for daily worship, morning and evening, for the Holy Communion, and for a variety of special rites and observances, its details being evolved with much freedom and originality from the Missal, Breviary, and other service-books of the medieval Church. The Prayer Book explicitly ordains the use of music at various points in all the principal services, and common custom has sanctioned some musical usages that are not thus prescribed. All Anglican church music, then, like that of the Roman Church, is essentially a part of the liturgical system embodied in the Prayer Book. A considerable number of formulas, especially certain canticles, etc., are fixed and invariable, recurring at every service; but to these are usually added others of different kinds that are suited to particular days or seasons, and that are not definitely prescribed.

2. Character of English Church Music.

Practically, as in other countries, English church music may be regarded as consisting of (a) choir music, including sentences, responses, canticles, etc., liturgically prescribed (and to be read, if singing is not feasible), and "anthems," which are optional additions to the liturgy; (b) congregational music, including prose canticles or psalms, usually set to brief harmonic forms known as "chants," metrical psalms and hymns, set to more elaborate forms known as "tunes," and occasionally some freer forms of the "anthem" class; and (c) organ music, usually consisting of service preludes and postludes. In theory, the liturgy of the Prayer Book is strongly congregational, that is, its exercises are conceived, as far as possible, as proceeding from the assembly, even when actually spoken through the minister or sung through the choir. The choir, therefore, is normally to be regarded as the agent of the laity, as is demanded by the whole Protestant theory of public worship, rather than as the agent of the hierarchy, as in the Roman theory. In the absence of a congregation, or in its silence, the choir performs the musical functions of the congregation. But wherever the congregation can be drawn into actual musical activity, it is assumed that the musical worship belongs to it and its action is to be encouraged. Yet, on the other hand, in cathedral services the choir is so closely associated in action with the stated clerical ministrants, usually officiating with the latter in the chancel, that the traditional rule against female officiants is enforced—all cathedral choirs consisting of men and boys only. Furthermore, in cathedral and collegiate services, and now also in many parochial services, there has been a decided tendency to work out a "full choral service," in which all or nearly all of the exercises, except, of course, the lessons and the sermon, are delivered with the singing voice—intoned, chanted, or sung in figured harmony. In such a service actual congregational participation is immaterial, and, in fact, the daily service in cathedrals is often carried forward with but few or even no persons present except the clergy and the choir. And in all cases where a choral service is much elaborated the tendency is to minimize the function of the congregation, except that of passive listening. This approximates rather closely to the practise of the Roman Church.

In the rubrics of the Prayer-Book hymns are but slightly provided for, and organ music is not mentioned. But both have been customary from the first. As manuals for congregational singing many metrical psalters have been "authorised," beginning with that of Sternhold and Hopkins ("the Old Version"; see HYMNOLOGY, IX., § 2) in 1562. There has never been an "authorised" hymnal, however, and, indeed, the use of "hymns" as distinct from "psalms" crept in somewhat gradually in the later eighteenth century, and under more or less protest. But the popularity of hymn-singing has led to a remarkable series of hymnals, of which without doubt *Hymns Ancient and Modern*, first published in 1861 and since repeatedly augmented or revised, is the most conspicuous. The earliest psalter contained the melodies of some tunes, and in the recent hymnals, at least in the fuller editions, tunes are provided for all the hymns. Associated with the more or less officially sanctioned liturgy of verse has accumulated a large and varied liturgy of congregational tunes, which is a feature of English church music analogous to the still larger treasury of German chorales.

3. Hymns and the Organ.

The status of organ music is but vaguely defined in English practise. The appointment to the post of organist and choirmaster rests with the rector or other clerical authority of the particular church or cathedral, and his work is understood to be under clerical direction. Organs are everywhere regarded as essential parts of ecclesiastical apparatus, and their utility is emphasized, not only for accompaniment to choir and congregational singing, but also for independent use before and after services.

What is here said refers especially to the musical usages of the Church of England, which is the national or "established" church not only in Great Britain, but also in all British colonial possessions, including Canada, India, South Africa, Australia, New Zealand, etc. All these have for the most part derived their habits in public worship directly from the mother country. The same is true in a more remote sense of the Protestant Episcopal Church in the United States, which became an independent church in 1789. For a very extensive section of the Protestant population of the world, therefore, the liturgical usages of the Church of England, including everything that pertains to music, have been either authoritative or exceedingly influential. Inasmuch, also, as they constitute the most consistent and definite body of usages among all the churches in English-speaking countries, their further indirect influence has been remarkably wide, affecting especially the hymnody and music of many non-episcopal communions.

For convenience, the history of the subject can be divided roughly into three main periods: (a) the sixteenth century, with a small part of the early seventeenth, during which musical practises, except in one or two particulars, were still dominated by the traditions of the time before the Reformation; (b) the seventeenth and eighteenth centuries, during which, for various reasons, church music was relatively unprogressive and feeble; and (c) the nineteenth century, during which there was gradually established a fresh line of development, resulting in a notable literature, which has great individuality and spiritual power.

4. The Sixteenth Century.

Since the English Church emerged at the Reformation without losing its sense of continuity with the medieval Church, it was natural that its new Prayer-Book should be musically treated, in part at least, in ways consonant with medieval tradition. Hence arose before 1553 plain-song settings of numerous formulas, which have been extensively retained ever since. Hence, also, came a considerable literature of contrapuntal choir music, much of which compared favorably with similar writing in both Italy and Germany, and which has often been exalted by later musicians as embodying a sort of ideal (analogous in some degree with the superiority attributed in the Roman Church to the Palestrina style). Among the composers of this period may be named Christopher Tye, c. 1510–72; Thomas Tallis, c. 1515–85; John Merbecke, 1523–85?; Robert Whyte, d. 1574; William Byrd, 1543–1623, and several writers of the madrigal era, like Thomas Morley, 1557–1602?; and Orlando Gibbons, 1583–1625. But, on the other hand, there were two musical movements of a different sort, due to the influence upon the English Church of the Reformed Church as it had developed under Calvin at Geneva and Strasburg. One of these was the introduction of psalm-singing, the tunes being either borrowed from Calvinistic sources or imitated from their style—opening a line of development in tunes analogous to that of the German chorales, though much inferior to the latter in variety and in intrinsic artistic worth. The other was the tendency for a brief period after 1560 to magnify a plain, "syllabic," uncontrapuntal method of setting canticles and other prose texts for choir use, this being a reaction in the direction of liturgical and artistic simplicity. This tendency was short-lived, though its essential principle reappeared later in a finer artistic form.

5. Seventeenth and Eighteenth Centuries.

Throughout the seventeenth century church music aroused only a fluctuating interest. The period of the Civil Wars checked all progress, not so much because the Puritans were averse to music, as because they were against the ecclesiastical system to which it belonged. After the Restoration in 1660 interest revived to some extent, though with confused results, owing in part to the heedless imitation by some of French and Italian models. At this point begins to be felt the drift toward solo singing in choir music which grows more pronounced in the eighteenth century—a drift that tended to set aside those broad choral effects that keep church music from too close similarity to secular music. During the latter part of this century became established in usage that special form of "chant" which is usually called "Anglican," a form which is doubtless historically connected with the "Psalm-tones" of the Gregorian system but has been developed along different lines from the latter. The stock of psalm tunes was also gradually augmented, though their variety was restricted by the fact that the metrical versions to which they belonged were in but a few meters. Prominent names in this period are Michael Wise, c. 1648-87; Pelham Humphrey, 1647-74; Henry Purcell, 1658-1695; John Blow, 1648-1708; and Jeremiah Clarke, d. 1707. The whole of the eighteenth century was a time of lethargy and barrenness, except for the work of a few sterling composers, like William Croft, 1678-1727; Maurice Greene, 1695-1755; and William Boyce, 1710-79. During this century, however, came the prodigious influence of Handel upon the musical life of England, which in many ways affected the whole standard of church music by magnifying the choral oratorio as a characteristic musical form. During this century, too, occurred the notable defections from the Church of England that established the Independent and Methodist forms of dissent, with some others, as influential elements in English religious life. The dissenters generally were eager for congregational hymn-singing, and it was their interest that brought about the multiplication of "hymns" as distinct from "psalms," together with the consequent multiplication of much more flexible tunes than had been earlier attempted. It is here that is to be sought the origin of that type of hymn-tune which is sometimes called the "part-song" tune, to distinguish it from the heavier "chorale," which later developed into a striking feature of English church music.

During the nineteenth century there was a steady and vigorous advance in the quality of English interest in things musical. At the outset this was promoted largely from within the Church, but later it received impetus more from without. But the effect upon the musical aspects of public worship has been continuous. With the rapid advance in methods of musical instruction of all kinds, including the foundation of many strong music-schools, and with the increase in such facilities for musical knowledge as popular choral societies, public concerts of various degree, including the opera, etc., the number of competent musicians has been greatly augmented and the whole standard of popular appreciation elevated. Even when the objects in view were not at all churchly, the gains have been unmistakable for church music.

6. Nineteenth Century.

In the field of choir music, the century begins with a serious effort on the part of certain cathedral musicians, like Thomas Attwood, 1765-1838; Samuel Wesley, 1766-1837, and others, to provide a new literature of anthems and other service music, of different degrees of elaboration, which should be at once devotional and expressed in modern musical idiom. Still more fertile was the middle portion of the century, under leaders like John Goss, 1800-80; Samuel Sebastian Wesley, 1810-76; Henry Smart, 1813-79; Frederick Arthur Gore Ouseley, 1825-89, and many more. The current style of expression during this period was strongly influenced, perhaps too much so, by the extreme popularity of Mendelssohn in England and the vogue of his concert oratorios. Almost all church composers exercised their talents in the field of oratorio-writing as well as in church music proper. In the latter part of the century the general current of production moves on with volume and momentum, but with a steadily increasing amount of attention to striking emotional effects, sometimes verging upon the theatrical and merely sensational, yet on the whole with an earnest purpose to make the resources of modern musical utterance genuinely serviceable in religious worship. Prominent composers in this time are John Bacchus Dykes, 1823-76; Joseph Barnby, 1838-96; John Stainer, 1840-1901; Arthur Seymour Sullivan, 1842-1900; and Charles Hubert Hastings Parry, b. 1848. Besides the fine list of anthems and services, of cantatas and oratorios, from these writers, many of them contributed worthily to the remarkable body of hymn-tunes for congregational use which has brought the impress of English church music to bear everywhere throughout the English-speaking world and among churches of every name. It is during this latest period, also, that the advance of English organ music has become most noticeable, bringing into view a large number of expert players, with an immense quantity of works, usually devised with special reference to effectiveness in connection with public worship.

In all this nineteenth-century development, there was less of that ideality and technical intensity which marked the greater periods of German church music, but one may fairly claim that in practical efficiency for the specific uses in view modern English music affords its finest examples of true worship-music.

WALDO S. PRATT.

BIBLIOGRAPHY: On Hebrew music consult: J. L. Saalschütz, *Geschichte und Würdigung der Musik bei den Hebräern*, Berlin, 1829; C. Engel, *Music of the Most Ancient Nations*, London, 1864; E. Hutchinson, *Music of the Bible*, Boston, 1864; F. Delitzsch, *Physiologie und Musik in ihrer Bedeutung*, Leipsic, 1868; E. David, *La Musique chez les Juifs*, Paris, 1873; F. Jacox, *Bible Music*, London and Boston, 1872, new ed., London, 1878; F. L. Cohen, *Rise and Development of Synagogue Music*, in *Anglo-Jewish Historical Papers*, pp. 80-135, London, 1888; Sir John Stainer, *The Music of the Bible*, New York, 1890; F. Consolo, *Libro dei canti d'Israele*, Florence, 1892; J. Weiss, *Die musikalischen Instrumente in den heiligen Schriften des A. T.*, Graz, 1895; E. Pauer, *Traditional Hebrew Melodies*, London, 1896; F. Vigouroux, *La Bible et les découvertes modernes*, iv. 305-322, Paris, 1896; idem, *Dictionnaire*, xxvii. 1347-60, Paris, 1906; Büchler, in *ZATW*, xix.-xx., 1899-1900; H. Gressman, *Musik und Musikinstrumente im Alten Testament*, Giessen, 1903; H. Smith, *The World's Earliest Music*, London, 1904; C. H. Cornill, *Music in the O. T.*, Chicago, 1909; C. Engel, *Music of the most Ancient Nations, particularly of the Assyrians, Egyptians, and Hebrews, with special Reference to the recent Discoveries in Western Asia and Egypt*, New York, 1910; P. Wagner, *Judaism in Music*, London, 1910; J. Wellhausen in *SBOT*, vol. on Psalms; Benzinger, *Archäologie*, pp. 237-246; *DB*, iii. 456-463; *EB*, iii. 3225-43; *JE*, ix. 118-135; the commentaries on the passages named in the text.

On II., works of an encyclopedic character are: S. Kuemmerle, *Encyclopädie der evangelischen Kirchenmusik*, 4 vols., Gütersloh, 1888-95; G. Schilling, *Universallexikon der Tonkunst*, 2d ed., 7 vols., Stuttgart, 1840-42; J. W.

Moore, *Complete Encyclopedia of Music*, Boston, 1854; F. J. Fetis, *Biographie universelle des musiciens, et bibliographie générale de la musique*, 10 vols., Paris, 1860–1851; H. Mendel and A. Reissmann, *Musikalisches Conversations-Lexikon*, 12 vols., Berlin, 1869–83; J. D. Brown, *Biographical Dictionary of Musicians*, London, 1886; J. D. Champlin and W. F. Apthorp, *Cyclopedia of Music and Musicians*, 3 vols., New York, 1888–90; J. Stainer and W. J. Barrett, *Dictionary of Musical Terms*, new ed., London, 1898; R. Eitner, *Biographisch-bibliographisches Quellen-Lexikon*, 10 vols., Leipsic, 1900–04; G. Grove, *Dictionary of Music and Musicians*, ed. J. A. F. Maitland, 5 vols., London, 1904–10; T. Baker, *Biographical Dictionary of Musicians*, 2d ed., New York, 1905; H. Riemann, *Musik-Lexikon*, 6th ed., Leipsic, 1905.

On the music of the Latin Church consult: J. Pothier, *Der gregorianische Choral*, Tournay, 1881; J. Tardif, *Méthode théorique et pratique de Plain-Chant*, Angers, 1883; Thiery, *Étude sur le chant grégorien*, Bruges, 1883; W. J. Walsh, *Grammar of Gregorian Music*, Dublin, 1885; J. N. Lemmens, *Du Chant grégorien*, Ghent, 1886; E. Burnouf, *Les Chants de l'église latine*, Paris, 1887; F. A. Gevaërt, *Le Chant liturgique dans l'église latine*, Brussels, 1889; idem, *Les Origines du chant liturgique dans l'église latine*, Ghent, 1890; V. J. Coornaert, *Traité de Plain-chant sacré*, Bruges, 1890; T. E. X. Normand, Toris, *L'Archéologie musicale et le vrai chant grégorien*, Paris, 1890; T. Nisard, *L'Archéologie musicale et le vrai chant grégorien*, Paris, 1890; L. Lootens, *La théorie musicale du chant grégorien*, Paris, 1895; P. Wagner, *Einführung in die gregorianischen Melodien. Ein Handbuch der Choralkunde*, Freiburg, 1895; A. Gastoue, *Les Origines du chant romain; l'antiphonaire grégorien*, Paris, 1908.

General works on the history of music are: F. W. Marpurg, *Historisch-kritische Beiträge zur Geschichte der Musik*, 5 vols., Berlin, 1744–62; C. Burney, *History of Music from the Earliest Ages to the Present Time*, 4 vols., London, 1776–1789; Sir John Hawkins, *History of the Science and Practice of Music*, 5 vols., London, 1776, new issue, re-edited, 1853–75; M. Gerbert, *Scriptores ecclesiastici de musica sacra*, 3 vols., St. Blasien, 1784 sqq.; J. N. Forkel, *Allgemeine Geschichte der Musik*, 2 vols., Leipsic, 1788–1801; T. Busby, *General History of Music*, 2 vols., London, 1819; J. Jebb, *Choral Service of the United Church of England and Ireland*, ib. 1843; C. von Winterfeld, *Der evangelische Kirchengesang*, 3 parts, Leipsic, 1843–47; idem, *Zur Geschichte heiligen Tonkunst*, 2 parts, ib., 1850–52; R. G. Kiesewetter, *History of the Modern Music of Western Europe*, London, 1848; N. E. Cornwall, *Music as it was and as it is*, New York, 1851; C. E. H. de Coussemaker, *Hist. de l'harmonie au moyen âge*, Paris, 1852; idem, *L'Art harmonique 12.–13. siècles*, ib. 1865; Austin Phelps, Edwards A. Park, Daniel L. Furber, *Hymns and Choirs*, Andover, 1860; J. Schlüter, *Allgemeine Geschichte der Musik*, Leipsic, 1863, Eng. transl., *General History of Music*, London, 1865; G. von Tucher, *Ueber den Gemeindegesang der evangelischen Kirche*, Leipsic, 1867; E. Naumann, *Die Tonkunst in der Kulturgeschichte*, Berlin, 1869–70; idem, *Illustrirte Musikgeschichte*, Stuttgart, 1880–85; F. J. Fétis, *Hist. générale de la musique*, 5 vols., Paris, 1859–76; F. L. Ritter, *History of Music*, 2 vols., Boston, 1874; O. Douen, *Clement Marot et le Psautier Huguenot; étude littéraire, musicale et bibliographique*, Paris, 1878–79; J. Hullah, *The Transition Period of Musical History*, London and New York, 3 vols., with supplement, 1879–1883; J. Sittard, *Compendium der Geschichte der Kirchenmusik*, Stuttgart, 1881; W. A. Barrett, *English Church Composers*, London, 1882; F. A. T. Klinkhardt, *Die Kunst, insonderheit die Tonkunst, als Dienerin im Heiligtum*, Leipsic, 1883; J. S. Curwen, *Studies in Worship Music*, 2 series, London, 1885–1888; F. M. Böhme, *Die Geschichte des Oratoriums*, Gütersloh, 1887; E. L. Taunton, *History of Church Music*, London, 1887; F. G. Edwards, *Common Praise; a practical Handbook of Nonconformist Church Music*, ib. 1887; A. W. Ambros, *Geschichte der Musik*, 3d ed., 3 vols., Leipsic, 1887–1893; Mrs. M. E. and W. A. Brown, *Musical Instruments and their Homes*, New York, 1888; P. Krutschek, *Die Kirchenmusik nach dem Willen der Kirche*, Regensburg, 1889; F. L. Humphreys, *The Evolution of Church Music*, London, 1890; P. Wulfrum, *Die Entstehung des deutschen evangelischen Kirchenliedes in musikalischen Beziehung*, Leipsic, 1890; J. Love, *Scottish Church Music*, Edinburgh, 1891 (on hymn tunes); R. B. Daniel, *Chapters on Church Music*, London, 1894; Henry Davey, *Hist. of English Music*, ib. 1895; F. Bachmann, *Grundlagen und Grundfragen zur evangelischen Kirchenmusik*, Gütersloh, 1899; H. Riemann, *Berühmte Musiker. Lebens- und Charakterbilder*, Berlin, 1900; A. A. Chapin, *Masters of Music*, London, 1901; W. S. Pratt, *Musical Ministries in the Church: Studies in History, Theory, and Administration of Sacred Music*, New York, 1901; idem, *Hist. of Music*, ib. 1907 (contains bibliography); A. Prosnis, *Compendium der Musikgeschichte*, 2d ed., Vienna, 1901 sqq.; H. E. Wooldridge, Sir C. H. H. Parry, J. A. F. Maitland, W. H. Hadow, and E. Dannreuther, *The Oxford History of Music*, 6 vols., Oxford, 1901–05; F. J. Crowest, *The Story of Music*, London, 1902; E. Dickinson, *Music in the History of the Western Church; Criticism on religious Music among primitive and ancient Peoples*, New York, 1902; F. Brendel, *Geschichte der Musik*, Leipsic, 1903; O. Keller, *Illustrierte Geschichte der Musik*, 2 vols., Munich, 1903–04; H. Riemann, *Handbuch der Musikgeschichte*, Leipsic, 1904–05; W. J. Baltzell, *A Complete History of Music*, Philadelphia, 1905; C. H. H. Parry, *The Art of Music*, 4th ed., London, 1905; E. Dickinson, *Growth and Development of Music*, ib. 1905; P. Viardot, *Histoire de la musique*, Paris, 1905; E. Walker, *Hist. of Music in England*, London, 1907; J. S. Bumpus, *Hist. of Eng. Cathedral Music, 1549–1889*, 2 vols., London, 1908; J. H. Edwards, *God and Music*, New York, 1908; E. S. Lorenz, *Practical Church Music*, ib. 1909; P. C. Lutkin, *Music in the Church*, Milwaukee, 1910.

SACRIFICATI. See Lapsed.

SACRIFICE.

1. Origin of Sacrifice. Ancient peoples generally, including the Hebrews, were convinced that worship of a deity consisted not only in words, but above all in offering something dear to the worshiper, which he denied himself in favor of his god. The sincerity and earnestness of worship were usually measured by the extent of self-denial which man was willing to make for the object of worship, particularly where the deity in question had been offended by some transgression of man, so that propitiation had become necessary. In the earlier forms of religion the gods are supposed not only to be well pleased with such sacrifices of gratitude or expiation, but actually to need them, since they are regarded as hungry and thirsty, and thus as dependent to a certain extent on man and his offerings. Even when, at later stages of development, the worthlessness of material goods to the deity is recognized, the conviction still survives that their surrender by man for the sake of his divinity is as pleasing as any other form of renunciation and self-mortification. The attempt has been made to derive all sacrifice from ancestor-worship or from the communal meal of the god and his worshipers, but both these theories are untenable and can not be brought into harmony with the data of the Old Testament. The real solution of the theory of sacrifice, the origin of which is prehistoric, must be sought in the childlike dependence of man upon the gods.

In the oldest portions of the Old Testament Yahweh is represented as at least enjoying the savor of the sacrifices (Gen. viii. 21; Lev. i. 9, 13, 17); when he becomes manifest to man, he must receive hospitality in the form of a sacrifice (Judges vi. 17

sqq., xiii. 15); and his wrath must be averted by the same means (Gen. viii. 20–21; I Sam. xxvi. 19). The whole, or burnt, offering is at least as ancient as the communal meal (e.g., Gen. xxxi. 54); and it was the custom from the earliest times to express gratitude to the divinity by both bloody and bloodless sacrifices (Gen. iv. 3–4). As early as the patriarchal period the sacrificial meal arose, sealing human organizations in the sight of the divinity and employed especially in covenants, alliances, and treaties of peace. All important undertakings were accompanied by sacrifices (Gen. xlvi. 1), and religious festivals were inconceivable without them (Ex. x. 25). Like the feasts, moreover, the sacrifices tended to become periodical. The covenant of the children of Israel at Sinai was also accompanied by a formal sacrifice (Ex. xxiv. 5 sqq.; cf. Ps. l. 5); and from the time of Moses to the exile the worship of Yahweh in Israel was never without sacrifice. The place in which sacrifice should be offered was from the very first a matter of moment, altars being erected preferably in places where there had been some divine manifestation (Gen. xxviii. 10 sqq.; Ex. xvii. 8 sqq.; Judges vi. 11 sqq.). As early as Moses the center of Israelitic sacrifice was the tabernacle of Yahweh, and Lev. xvii. 1 sqq. even forbade the killing of an animal at any other place, although Deut. xii. 10 sqq. restricted this prohibition to sacrificial victims. In Ex. xx. 24, on the other hand, a number of places of sacrifice are implied, even though Ex. xxiii. 14 sqq. (cf. xxxiv. 23 sqq.) indicates that the central sanctuary already existed. Many Canaanitic shrines were likewise transferred to the worship of Yahweh, but pagan rites were still performed at them, so that it again became necessary to restrict sacrifice to the central tabernacle. The concept of a central seat of Yahweh was never abandoned (cf. Joel iii. 16; Amos i. 2; Isa. xxviii. 16, xix. 1, xxxi. 9, xxxiii. 14), and centralizing reforms were also proclaimed by the theocratic kings Asa (II Chron. xiv. 3, but cf. xv. 17), Jehoshaphat (II Chron. xvii. 6, but cf. xx. 33), Hezekiah (II Kings xviii. 4, 22), and Josiah (II Kings xxiii. 8). This centralization of worship made sacrifice more formal and solemn at the expense of spontaneity. See ALTAR; HEXATEUCH.

2. Old-Testament Data.

The sacrifices of the Israelites were of two general types, bloody and unbloody, the former being animals and the latter the fruits of the land. Bloody sacrifices, moreover, are also classified (Ex. xx. 24) as burnt offerings and peace offerings, one object of the latter being the communal meal. Human sacrifices, permitted by the other Semites, were forbidden by the Mosaic code, although there is an obvious allusion to such a custom at an early period in the account of the contemplated sacrifice of Isaac by Abraham (Gen. xxii.; cf. Mic. vi. 7; Lev. xvii. 11; II Kings iii. 27; and see FAMILY AND MARRIAGE RELATIONS, HEBREW, § 10; GEZER; JEPHTHAH; MOLOCH). The sacrifice of animals, on the other hand, was widespread among the Israelites, although, unlike other Semites, they sacrificed only domestic animals, and of these only those which were ritually clean. The only birds that might be sacrificed were doves, these often instead of more expensive offerings in the case of the poor (Lev. v. 7, xii. 8), although any small clean birds might be used in the ceremony of cleansing a leper (Lev. xiv. 4 sqq.). The sex of the sacrificial victim, generally a male, was also prescribed in many cases; and the animal was required to be without blemish, except in the case of voluntary offerings, where slight imperfections were overlooked (Lev. xxii. 19 sqq.). The calf, lamb, or goat should be at least eight days old (Lev. xxii. 27; Ex. xxii. 30), and rabbinical authority required an age of less than three years, while in some cases the age was set at a year (Lev. ix. 3, xii. 6, xiv. 10; Num. xv. 27, xxviii. 3, 9, 11). Meal (A. V. "meat") offerings were in the form of ears of corn parched or bruised, with the addition of oil and incense (Lev. ii. 14 sqq.); or as fine flour (Lev. ii. 1 sqq.); or as unleavened cakes (Lev. ii. 4 sqq.). The use of leaven or honey (both of which undergo fermentation) was forbidden, except in the sacrifice of first-fruits and certain thank-offerings (Lev. ii. 11–12, vii. 13, xxiii. 17; II Chron. xxxi. 5). The meal offering might, however, be seasoned with salt (Lev. ii. 13), as might, according to the Septuagint of Lev. xxiv. 7, the showbread. According to some readings of Mark ix. 49, all offerings were salted, as were burnt offerings (Ezek. xliii. 24). Drink offerings are mentioned in the codes only in connection with other offerings, although there are traces of simple libations of water (I Sam. vii. 6; II Sam. xxiii. 17). The only instance of such libations in the developed ritual of the Hebrews, however, was the pouring-out of water from the Pool of Shiloah at the altar during the feast of tabernacles. Oil and wine were also important in libations (Gen. xxviii. 18, xxxv. 14; Num. xxviii. 7, 14; Ecclus. l. 15). All the materials of sacrifice proper were necessities of life, and the peace offering is accordingly even called the bread of God (Lev. iii. 11, 16, xxi. 6, 8, 17, xxii. 25; Num. xxviii. 2, 24; Ezek. xliv. 7), while the altar of burnt offering was the "table that is before the Lord" (Ezek. xli. 22; cf. Mal. i. 7, 12).

3. Bloody Sacrifices and Meal Offerings.

The ritual of the sacrifice varied according to the purpose of the offering, and in the case of sacrifice of animals a distinction must be drawn between burnt offerings and communal meals. The burnt offering, or "whole burnt offering" (Deut. xxxiii. 10; I Sam. vii. 9; Ps. li. 21), is fully described in Lev. i. 3 sqq., and constitutes a very ancient, perhaps even the most primitive, form of sacrifice, expressing in the widest sense adoration of the divinity, and in a manner including all the other and more special forms of sacrifice. This general character rendered the burnt offering the form best adapted for daily sacrifice in the name of the nation, and a yearling lamb was accordingly offered each morning and each evening (Ex. xxix. 38–42; Num. xxviii. 3–8). Even gentiles, excluded from all other sacrifices, might offer burnt offerings, though they were forbidden to be present during the ceremony. After the time of Alexander the Great the pagan rulers of

4. The Burnt Offering and Communal Meal.

the Jews had burnt offerings sacrificed for them, and when, on the outbreak of the war with Rome, Eleasar forbade any sacrifice to be accepted from a non-Jew, his prohibition marked an open breach with Roman sovereignty (Josephus, *War*, II., xvii. 2).

The second Israelitic form of animal sacrifice was the peace offering and communal meal. Regular family feasts were held on such occasions as new moons or annually (I Sam. xx. 5–6), and while these were primarily social, the code of Lev. vii. 11 sqq. recognizes a number of forms of communal meal with a distinctly religious basis: thanksgivings, vows, and freewill offerings, all comprised under the general terms of " peace offerings " or " sacrifices " (in the restricted sense of the term). Of these the first was the most important, probably serving as a thanksgiving for some special boon; the second was offered in accordance with a vow made if some specific prayer was granted; and the third seems to have been a spontaneous impulse of piety. In the last-named the strictness of the rule as to the physical perfection of the sacrificial victim was somewhat relaxed (Lev. xxii. 23); and while male victims were preferred for the communal meal (Lev. ix. 4, 18; Num. vii. 17 sqq.), female animals were not excluded (Lev. iii. 6). The communal sacrifices also included offerings of food and drink, especially in the thanksgiving offerings (Lev. vii. 12; Num. xv. 3 sqq.).

In sacrifices of this type the victim was not slaughtered on the north side of the altar, as in the burnt offering, but the chief difference between the two categories was that in the communal sacrifice the fat covering the intestines, kidneys, liver, etc. (and, in the case of sheep, the tail), alone were burned as being the choicest parts, and so most acceptable to Yahweh (Lev. iii. 3–5, 9–11, 14–16, ix. 19–20). The breast of the victim was devoted to the " wave offering " (Lev. vii. 30), in which the priest placed the object to be waved upon the hands of the sacrificer, then put his own hands under the hands of the one who brought the offering, and moved them backward and forward, thus apparently indicating the reciprocity of giving and accepting between the sacrificer and the divinity. The upper part of the right hind leg (A. V., " shoulder ") was made a " heave offering," a term originally connoting, no doubt, some sort of dedicatory gesture (Lev. vii. 32). The heave offering and the wave offering were the share of the priests, who might eat them with their families at any place ritually clean (Lev. x. 14), the priests also receiving one cake of each oblation (Lev. vii. 14) and the two lambs of the Passover peace offering (Lev. xxiii. 19–20). As a rule, however, the sacrificers ate the offering at a sacred meal celebrated by larger or smaller numbers (cf. Deut. xxvii. 7; I Kings viii. 63). To these communal meals guests, especially Levites and the poor, were also invited (Deut. xvi. 11), although only those who were ritually pure might partake (Lev. vii. 19–21). Such communal meals were essentially joyous in character. Whatever remained must be preserved from defilement. The sacrifice of thanksgiving must be eaten on the day it was offered (Lev. vii. 15; xxii. 30); all other communal meals must be consumed at latest on the second day; and on the third day all fragments remaining must be burned (Lev. vii. 16 sqq., xix. 6 sqq.), as must all sacrificial meat coming in contact with anything unclean (Lev. vii. 19).

Among special sacrifices the most important were the sin and the guilt (A.V., " trespass ") offerings, the former primarily an expiation for some ethical fault, the latter a satisfaction for the reparation of some injury. The guilt offering was especially required in case of defrauding or materially injuring the temple or private individuals. In case of defrauding the temple, restitution should be made in full, with a fine of one-fifth of the amount and a ram as the guilt offering (Lev. v. 14–16); and a similar punishment was imposed on one who had defrauded or otherwise financially injured his fellow (Lev. vi. 1–7), Num. v. 5–10 also requiring public confession on the part of the defendant and stipulating that the fine should go to the priest if the man injured should " have no kinsman to recompense the trespass unto " (Num. v. 5–10). Other forms of infringement of the rights of fellow Israelites were also to be atoned for by guilt offerings (Lev. xix. 20–22), while a leper and an unclean Nazirite, as having their capacity to worship Yahweh temporarily interrupted, were likewise obliged to offer guilt offerings (Lev. xiv. 11 sqq.; Num. vi. 12). In similar fashion Ezra required a ram as a guilt offering from those who had trespassed against Yahweh by marrying gentile wives (Ezra x. 18–19); and Lev. v. 17–19 also makes provision for a guilt offering in case of unwitting transgression of the law. The ritual of the guilt offering is given in Lev. vii. 1–7. The victim is a ram, except in the case of the leper and the Nazirite, when it is a yearling lamb (Num. vi. 12); and the laying on of hands was observed (cf. Lev. iv. 33 with vii. 7), probably with open acknowledgment of the transgression for which the sacrifice was made. Throughout the ceremony the form of the sacrifice was stressed as a debt to Yahweh and his representatives.

5. Sin and Guilt Offerings.

The underlying concept of the sin offering, on the other hand, is not so much that of paying a debt as of cleansing the sacrificer from sin, so that the chief factor is the use of the blood of the sacrificial victim. The sacrifices here are far more varied than in the guilt offering, depending both on the circumstances of the sacrificer and on his particular fault. The victim in the case of very grave sins was a young bullock, which was offered on the Day of Atonement, in case the high priest sinned in his official capacity of representative of the people, in the event of a sin committed by the people as a whole, and at the consecration of priests and Levites (Lev. xvi. 3 sqq., iv. 3 sqq., 13 sqq.; Ex. xxix. 10–14, 36; Num. vii. 8). A ram was sacrificed for the people on the Day of Atonement (Lev. xvi. 5), as well as at other feasts and new moons (e.g., Num. xxviii. 15, 22, 30, xxix. 5), and in case of unwitting sin on the part of a ruler or of the entire people (Lev. iv. 23; Num. xv. 24). A she-goat or young ewe was sufficient atonement for the sin of an ordinary Israelite (Lev. iv. 28, 32, v. 6); while a yearling ewe was required as a sin offering in cleansing a leper (Lev. xiv. 10) and at the completion of a Nazirite's vow (Num. vi. 14). Turtledoves and young pigeons were used in purifications (Lev. xii. 6, xv. 14, 29; Num. vi. 10), and also served as substitutes for a lamb (Lev. v. 7, xiv. 22); while if any could not afford even a dove, he might offer, in cases of ordinary sin, a tenth of an ephah of meal. In the sin offering the blood of the victim is not simply sprinkled on the altar, but is applied to specified places. In the offering of an individual Israelite (except the high priest), and in the consecration of a priest (probably also in the case of a Levite), some of the blood of the goat or lamb was smeared on the horns of the altar of burnt offering, and the rest was poured on the ground (Ex. xxix. 12; Lev. iv. 25, 30, 34). At sin offerings for the entire people or for the high priest (except on the Day of Atonement, q.v.) the blood of the sacrificial bullock was sprinkled seven times against the veil of the sanctuary and smeared on the horns of the altar, the remainder being poured on the ground (Lev. iv. 5 sqq., 16 sqq.). The ritual of the sin offering for the Day of Atonement is elaborately described in Lev. xvi. The flesh of the sin offering was sacrosanct, and rigid regulations were laid down where and by whom it might be eaten (Lev. vi. 25-26) or burned (Ex. xxix. 14; Lev. iv. 11-12, 21, vi. 23, xvi. 27). Any one besprinkled with the blood of a sin offering must wash in a sacred place, and special provision was protection of the flesh of the sacrificial victim against defilement (Lev. vi. 27-28), and he who burned the flesh must bathe and wash his clothes before returning to the camp (Lev. xvi. 28). The exact details concerning the sin offering of doves are uncertain; but in the meal offering of the very poor the priest was to cast a handful upon the altar, taking the residue as his share (Lev. v. 12-13).

It is evident, from Lev. xvii. 11, that the blood of the sacrificial victim was held to protect the life of the sacrificer in virtue of the animal's life in the blood. The actual slaughtering of the victim was merely to obtain the blood, not to inflict upon the victim the penalty merited by the sinner, the essential basis of the act being the forfeiture of an animal instead of a human life to the deity. In the sin offering, moreover, the blood is not merely important, as in the burnt offering and the communal meal, but the one essential; and the sin offerings are, accordingly, invariably bloody, except in the case of the very poor. It must be noted, however, that only involuntary sins are atoned for by these sacrifices (cf. Lev. iv. 2-3, 22, 27, v. 15, 18, xxii. 14; Num. xv. 25-26). Accordingly, an involuntary homicide has provision made for him in the "cities of refuge" (Num. xxxv. 11, 15; Josh. xx. 3, 9), but one who commits an intentional murder must die (Num. xv. 30).

6. Development of Israelitic Sacrifice.

The pre-exilic ritual of sacrifice passed through a process of development, Moses adapting to the worship of Yahweh rites in use among the Israelites from times immemorial. The theory is frequently advanced, however, that all ritual developments connected with the sacrifice are post-exilic, the sacrifice having previously been purely voluntary and regularly connected with joyous sacrificial meals. Accordingly, it is held that the sole distinctive feature in Israelite sacrifice was that it was offered to Yahweh instead of to Baal or Moloch; the Priest Code alone stresses the form of the rite; passages like Amos iv. 4-5, v. 21 sqq.; Hos. vi. 6, viii. 11 sqq.; Isa. i. 11 sqq.; Jer. vi. 19-20, vii. 21 sqq. show that at the time of the great prophets a ritual sacrificial code was unknown, Ezekiel (especially xl.-xlviii.) being the first to attach extreme importance to the sacrifice. But this theory ignores the fact that even in remotest antiquity the sacrifice is a rite of prime importance; and the Book of the Covenant itself contains ritual prescriptions concerning the sacrifice (Ex. xx. 24-26, xxiii. 18-19, cf. xxxiv. 25-26) which allow of no doubt either as regards the importance attached to the sacrifice or as to the previous existence of fully developed regulations governing the sacrificial ritual. Again, the passages just listed from the prophets neither presuppose the non-existence of such a ritual, nor do they polemize against either a liturgy of this character or against sacrifice in itself, but only against a false estimate of it, complicated by a refusal to render due obedience to God. The prophetic passages, therefore, like analogous ones which might readily be quoted from the Psalms, are to be explained in the spirit of I Sam. xv. 22. At the same time, even after Moses there was greater freedom in sacrificial ritual than is permitted by the Priest Code; and there was also no rigid adherence to the Mosaic regulations, but, on the one hand, a priestly development which finds its culmination in the Priest Code, and, on the other hand, popular deviations from the use of the priests at the central sanctuary. In the revision of the liturgy in Ezekiel, finally, the conscious and sovereign freedom of God as the lawgiver finds expression in contrast to the letter of the Mosaic code. There is, however, no reason to suppose, as is frequently held, that sin and guilt offerings are first mentioned by Ezekiel, for such a hypothesis finds immediate refutation in Hos. iv. 8; and it is equally idle to hold that, because frankincense is first mentioned (outside of the Torah) in Jer. vi. 20, it was in any sense an innovation.

For the ethnic concept and practise of sacrifice see COMPARATIVE RELIGION, VI., 1, d; for the Christian idea in connection with the death of Christ see ATONEMENT; and JESUS CHRIST, THREEFOLD OFFICE OF; and for Roman Catholic doctrines see MASS. (C. VON ORELLI.)

BIBLIOGRAPHY: On ethnic sacrifice, beside the literature adduced under COMPARATIVE RELIGION, consult: C. F. Nägelsbach, *Homerische Theologie*, Nuremberg, 1884; H. Zimmern, *Beiträge zur Kenntniss der babylonischen Religion*, Leipsic, 1896; L. R. Farnell, *Cults of the Greek States*, vols. i.-v., Oxford, 1896-1907; W. W. Fowler, *Roman Festivals of the Period of the Republic*, London, 1899; E. B. Tylor, *Primitive Culture*, 4th ed., ib. 1903; E. Crawley, *The Tree of Life, a Study of Religion*, ib. 1905; A. Bros, *La Religion des peuples non civilisés*, pp. 132 sqq., Paris, 1907; Jane E. Harrison, *Prolegomena to the Study of Greek Religion*, 2d ed., Cambridge, 1908; G. Foucart, *Methode comparative dans l'hist. des religions*, chap. iv., Paris, 1909; S. Reinach, *Orpheus. Hist. générale des religions*, ib. 1909, Eng. transl., *Orpheus, a General Hist. of Religions*, London and New York, 1909; A. le Roy, *La Religion des primitifs*, passim, Paris, 1909; P.

Stengel, *Opferbräuche der Griechen*, Leipsic, 1910; Wellhausen, *Heidentum*.

An important class of books on O. T. sacrifice is that which deals with O. T. theology (fully given in and under BIBLICAL THEOLOGY); the discussion of Pentateuchal origins also brought out much which had to do with sacrifice (see HEXATEUCH); besides the above, the commentaries on the Hexateuch are of course valuable. Special works are: F. Bähr, *Symbolik des mosaischen Kultus*, ii. 189 sqq., Heidelberg, 1837; J. H. Kurtz, *Der alttestamentliche Opferkultus*, Mitau, 1862, Eng. transl., *Sacrificial Worship of the O. T.*, Edinburgh, 1863; J. A. Seiss, *The Gospel in Leviticus; or, an Exposition of the Hebrew Ritual*, 3d ed., Philadelphia, 1876; A. Stewart, *The Mosaic Sacrifices*, Edinburgh, 1883; H. C. Trumbull, *The Blood Covenant*, New York, 1885; E. F. Willis, *The Worship of the Old Covenant*, London, 1887; J. G. Murphy, *Sacrifice as set forth in Scripture*, ib. 1889; A. Cave, *Scriptural Doctrine of Sacrifice*, Edinburgh, 1890; E. W. Edersheim, *The Rites and Worship of the Jews*, New York, 1891; A. Scott, *Sacrifice: its Prophecy and Fulfilment*, Edinburgh, 1894; W. L. Baxter, *Sanctuary and Sacrifice*, London, 1895; A. Kamphausen, *Das Verhältniss des Menschenopfers zur israelitischen Religion*, Bonn, 1896; K. Marti, *Geschichte der israelitischen Religion*, 3d ed., Strassburg, 1897; Hubert and Mauss, in *L'Année sociologique*, 1897–1898, pp. 29–138 (important); R. Smend, *Lehrbuch der alttestamentlichen Religionsgeschichte*, Freiburg, 1899; H. Schultz, in *AJT*, iv (1900), 257 sqq.; R. C. Moberly, *Atonement and Personality*, London, 1901; C. Mommert, *Menschenopfer bei den alten Hebräern*, Leipsic, 1905; C. F. Kent, *Students' O. T.*, iv. 227 sqq., New York, 1907; H. L. Strack, *The Jew and Human Sacrifice: Human Blood and Jewish Ritual*, ib. 1909; S. J. Smith, *Religion in the Making*, chap. ix., ib. 1910; O. Schmitz, *Die Opferanschauung des späteren Judentums und die Opferaussagen des N. T.*, Tübingen, 1910; Benzinger, *Archäologie*, pp. 362–387; Nowack, *Archäologie*, vol. ii.; Schrader, *KAT*, pp. 594 sqq.; *DB*, iv. 329–349; *EB*, iv. 4183–4233; *DCG*, ii. 542–648; *JE*, x. 615–628; Vigouroux, *Dictionnaire*, fasc. xxxv., cols. 1311–37 (a broad discussion).

SACRILEGE: In the wider sense, any injury or dishonor done to a sacred object; in the narrower and stricter sense, the theft of a sacred object (see SACRAMENTALS), without necessarily involving personal violence. The early Roman law imposed the severest penalties upon this crime ("Let him be treated as a parricide who steals or carries off aught sacred or what is entrusted to a sacred person," Cicero, *De legibus*, ii. 9); a law of Julius Cæsar, the *Lex Julia peculatus*, made more detailed provision against it, and it was later definitely distinguished from that of embezzlement, or the illegal appropriation of public funds. The Roman law, however, covered only the removal of a sacred object from a sacred place, not from any other place or that of an unconsecrated object from a sacred place. In the imperial period the penalties were graded according to the exact nature of the offense, and culminated in the most severe forms of capital punishment. The Germanic law, which punished severely violations of sanctuary, extended the Roman principle to cover all thefts of sacred objects from any place, or of any object from a sacred place; and the canon law took the same view. The penalties, besides restoration or compensation, included fines, penances, and excommunication. In the Middle Ages sacrilege was regarded as a crime against both Church and State, and might be punished by both. For example, the great ordinance issued by Charles V. in 1572 prescribed penalties varying with the offense; thus the theft of a monstrance with the host was punished by burning; that of other consecrated vessels of gold or silver, or breaking into a consecrated church, tabernacle, or sacristy with intent to steal, by death at the discretion of the court; and the theft of other hallowed objects, or unconsecrated objects from a holy place, with severer penalties than ordinary stealing. Such an attitude was adapted only to the Roman Catholic theory of an inherent sanctity in such objects; but it exercised no little influence on the Protestant state churches, although the severer penalties gradually fell into disuse. (P. HINSCHIUS†.)

BIBLIOGRAPHY: Bingham, *Origines*, VIII., x., XVI., vi. 23–25; Gregory of Tours, *De gloria martyrum*, chap. xvii (for an example of legendary treatment); W. Rein, *Das Criminalrecht der Römer*, Leipsic, 1844; K. Binding, *Lehrbuch des deutschen Strafrechts*, i. 157–158, ib. 1896; *KL*, x. 1519–21; *DCA*, ii. 1834–35 (gives list of acts classed as sacrilegious); Vigouroux, *Dictionnaire*, fasc. xxxv. 1327; *JE*, x. 628–629.

SACRISTAN, SEXTON: Two forms of what was originally the same word, differentiated in modern English so that the former designates in Roman Catholic churches especially the official who has charge of the vestments and other property kept in the sacristy, while the latter is in more general usage for one who takes care of the whole church building. The title *custos ecclesiæ* seems to occur first in the Spanish monasteries, denoting the monk who had charge of the conventual church. Thus Isidore of Seville (*Regula*, xix.) says: "It pertains to the office of the guardian of the sacristy to have the care of the church, to give the signals in the offices, to take charge of the veils, sacred vestments and vessels, books and other instruments, the oil for the sanctuary lamps, the candles, and other lights." The same term was commonly used in the Frankish church, where it is sometimes applied to the bishop or abbot or pastor of a parish church. From this usage it is found in the Carolingian period frequently used as synonymous with rector. The term was used all through the Middle Ages in cathedral and collegiate churches, but now no longer for the abbot or provost, but for the monk or canon who had the cure of souls. In the more important cathedral churches, e.g., Cologne, the cathedral *custos* took rank as a prelate. In many collegiate churches his duties included the custody of the corporate seal. In closer harmony with the definition given by Isidore is the Carolingian usage of the term *custos thesauri*, the official who had charge of the church property, or that cited from an old *Ordo Romanus* in the decretals of Gregory IX., where the *custos ecclesiæ* is mentioned as a subordinate of the archdeacon charged with such offices as Isidore describes. The modern use of the term sacristan is derived from this aspect of the functions of the *custos*, and his duties are minutely prescribed not only in the decrees of Roman Catholic provincial councils but also in numerous Reformation church constitutions, which lead up to the later German precentor and schoolmaster, as to the English parish clerk, who was such an important functionary down to the middle of the nineteenth century.

(A. HAUCK.)

BIBLIOGRAPHY: A. L. Richter, *Lehrbuch des katholischen und evangelischen Kirchenrechts*, 8th ed., by W. Kahl, p. 458, Leipsic, 1886; F. Dreising, *Das Amt des Küsters in der evangelischen Kirche*, Berlin, 1854.

SACY, LOUIS ISAAC LEMAISTRE DE. See Lemaistre de Sacy, Louis Isaac.

SADDUCEES. See Pharisees and Sadducees.

SADOLETO, sā"dō-lê'tō, JACOPO: Italian cardinal; b. at Modena 1477; d. at Rome Oct. 18, 1547. He received a humanistic training at Ferrara, which he completed at Rome during the pontificate of Alexander VI., the earliest results being the three treatises *De Cajo Curtio, De Laocoontis statua*, and *De laudibus philosophiæ*. Here, too, he was ordained to the priesthood and was soon appointed apostolic secretary by Leo X. to change the style of the papal briefs from barbarous Latinity to Ciceronian elegance. Though later raised to the episcopate of Carpentras, Sadoleto remained in Rome until after the death of Leo X., returning once more at the request of Clement VII. He was at Carpentras when Rome was sacked by the troops of Charles V. in May, 1527, but the event turned his thoughts to serious themes, evinced in his *De literis recte instituendis* (Venice, 1533) and his *Commentarius in epistolam Sancti Pauli ad Romanos* (Lyons, 1535). In 1534 he was raised to the cardinalate by Paul III., and accordingly resumed residence in Rome, where, in 1536, he took part in the preparation of the *Consilium de emendanda ecclesia* (see Paul III.), the result exposing him and his colleagues to suspicion of heresy. His commentary on Romans was forbidden as Semipelagian, although the prohibition was withdrawn after Sadoleto had appealed to the Sorbonne and had modified certain passages. On June 19, 1537, Sadoleto addressed a letter to Melanchthon urging him to be reconciled with the Roman Catholic Church, and in Mar., 1539, he wrote to the municipal council of Geneva to restore that city to the Roman Catholic faith, an act which evoked Calvin's brilliant *Responsio ad Sadoleti epistolam* (Sept. 1, 1539). Both letters are given in English in *Tracts Relating to the Reformation* by John Calvin, transl. by H. Beveridge, i. 3–71, Edinburgh, 1844.

Sadoleto was one of the number who based all hopes of the amelioration of the Church on the convening of a general council, and while, as in the sweeping inquiry into the existence of heresy at Modena in 1542, he deprecated extreme measures, he made no surrender of church doctrine. At the same time, he was no friend of the Reformation, and he was in hearty sympathy with the suppression of the Waldensians in Cabrières and Mérindol in May, 1545; and letters written by Sadoleto's nephew in the preceding year show that influence in this direction was brought to bear upon Francis I. from Sadoleto himself. In 1543 he was recalled to Rome to assist in the preparations for the Council of Trent, and remained there until his death. His principal writings, besides those already mentioned, were: *De philosophia* (Lyons, 1538); *Philosophicæ consolationes et meditationes in adversis; Ad principes populosque Germaniæ exhortatio;* and *Epistolarum libri sedecim ad Paulum Sadoletum* (Lyons, 1550). His collected works were edited at Mainz in 1607, and, more fully, at Verona in four volumes in 1737.

K. Benrath.

Bibliography: Lives are prefixed to the "Collected Works," ut supra. Notices from contemporary and later literature are given in A. Teissier, *Éloges des hommes savants*, vol. i., Leyden, 1715. Consult further: G. von Schulthess-Rechberg, *Der Kardinal Jacopo Sadoleto*, Zurich, 1909; F. Cancellieri, *Vita del Cardinal Sadoleto*, Rome, 1823; A. Péricaud, *Fragments biographiques sur J. Sadolet*, Lyons, 1849; A. Joly, *Étude sur J. Sadolet*, Caen, 1856; A. Zimmermann, *Kardinal Pole, sein Leben und seine Schriften*, p. 389, Regensburg, 1893; M. Haile, *Life of Reginald Pole*, passim, London, 1910; *KL*, x. 1524–1525; Lichtenberger, *ESR*, xi. 387–389.

SAEGMUELLER, sêg'mül-ler, JOHANNES BAPTIST: German Roman Catholic; b. at Winterreute (a village near Biberach, 23 m. s.s.w. of Ulm), Württemberg, Feb. 24, 1860. He was educated at the University of Tübingen (Ph.D., 1888) and the theological seminary at Rottenburg; was curate at Alpirsbach (1884–87); lecturer at the Wilhelmstift, Tübingen (1887–93); was appointed associate professor of history in the University of Tübingen (1893), where since 1896 he has been professor of church history and pedagogics. In addition to his work as associate editor of the *Tübinger theologische Quartalschrift* and the *Archiv für katholisches Kirchenrecht*, he has written *Die Papstwahlen und die Staaten von 1447–1555* (Tübingen, 1890); *Die Papstwahlbullen und das staatliche Recht der Exclusive* (1892); *Zur Geschichte des Kardinalats, ein Traktat des Bischofs von Feltre und Treviso Teodoro de' Lelli über das Verhältnis vom Primat und Kardinalat* (Freiburg, 1893); *Die Thätigkeit und Stellung der Kardinäle bei Papst Bonifaz VIII.* (1896); *Lehrbuch des katholischen Kirchenrechts* (1904, 2d ed., 1909); *Die kirchliche Aufklärung am Hofe Herzog Karl Eugens von Württemberg* (1906); *Die Trennung von Kirche und Staat* (Mainz, 1907); *Die Bischofswahl bei Gratian* (Cologne, 1908); and *Wissenschaft und Glaube in der kirchlichen Aufklärung* (1910).

SAGITTARIUS, sā"git-tā'ri-us (SCHUETZE), KASPAR: German Lutheran theologian and historian; b. at Lüneburg (68 m. n.n.e. of Hanover) Sept. 23, 1643; d. at Jena Mar. 9, 1694. He was educated at the University of Helmstädt, where his studies took the widest range, and after preaching at Helmstädt, Lüneburg, and elsewhere, and visiting Brunswick, Magdeburg, Halberstadt, and Copenhagen, he completed his training at Leipsic, Wittenberg, Jena, and Altdorf. In 1668 he accepted a call to Saalfeld as rector of the school there, and three years later was appointed to a professorship at Jena, being transferred to the chair of history in 1674. His energy was thenceforth devoted primarily to the history of German Protestantism, especially in Saxony and Thuringia. Sagittarius was also involved in a number of controversies, of which the most noteworthy was his defense of Pietism in and after 1691. Among his numerous writings special mention may be made of the following: *Harmonia historiæ passionis Jesu Christi* (Jena, 1671; revised edition 1684); *Historia antiquissima urbis Bardevici* (1674); *Epistola de antiquo Thuringiæ statu* (1675); *Nucleus historiæ Germanicæ* (1675); *Dissertatio de præcipius scriptoribus historiæ Germanicæ* (1675; the first attempt at a history of German historiography); *Antiquitates regni Thur* *ingici* (1684); *Antiquitates gentilismi et christianismi Thuringici* (1685); *Antiquitates Ducatus Thuringici* (1688); *Memorabilia historiæ Gothanæ* (1689); and *Theses theologiæ apologeticæ de promovendo vero Christianismo* (1692). His *Introductio in historiam ecclesiasticam et singulas ejus partes*, which he began in 1692, was continued and completed by Johann Andreas Schmid (2 vols., Jena, 1718). (Paul Tschackert.)

Bibliography: J. A. Schmid, *Commentarius de vita et scriptis Casp. Sagittarius*, Jena, 1713; M. J. C. Zeumer, *Vitæ professorum . . . in academia Jenensi*, ib. 1703–06; G. Frank, *Geschichte der protestantischen Theologie*, ii. 147, Leipsic, 1865.

SAILER, sail'er, **JOHANN MICHAEL VON**: Roman Catholic bishop of Regensburg; b. at Aresing (a village near Schrobenhausen, 16 m. s.s.w. of Ingolstadt), Upper Bavaria, Nov. 17, 1751; d. at Regensburg May 20, 1832. He was educated at the Jesuit colleges of Landsberg (1770–72) and Ingolstadt (1773–77), having entered the Society of Jesus as a novice. On Sept. 23, 1775, he was ordained to the priesthood, and in 1777 the Elector Maximilian III. appointed him lecturer on philosophy and theology at Ingolstadt. In 1782 he became second professor of dogmatics, but two years later he was retired on a pension of 240 guldens, since the new elector, Charles Theodore, diverted the funds of the college to other uses. The years immediately following were passed by Sailer at Ingolstadt as a private scholar. He had already published his *Fragment zur Reformationsgeschichte der christlichen Theologie* (Ulm, 1779) and *Theologiæ Christianæ cum philosophia nexus* (Augsburg, 1779), and he now issued his *Vollständiges Lese- und Gebetbuch für katholische Christen* (1783) and *Vernunftlehre für Menschen, wie sie sind, d. i. Anleitung zur Erkenntnis und Liebe der Wahrheit* (3 vols., Munich, 1783). In 1784 a new academic career was opened to Sailer by his appointment as professor of ethics at the reorganized University of Dillingen, where the lectures on pastoral theology were soon placed under his guidance. He contributed essentially to the progress of the institution, but the methods of teaching in vogue at Dillingen aroused the suspicions of the faculty of the College of St. Salvator at Augsburg, and in 1793 a committee of investigation decided adversely to Dillingen. In the year following Sailer was removed from his professorship, especially as he was suspected, though unjustly, of sympathy with the Enlightenment. While professor at Dillingen, he had been active as an author, writing, among other works, *Ueber den Selbstmord* (Munich, 1785); *Predigten bei verschiedenen Anlässen* (3 vols., 1790–92); *Kurzgefasste Erinnerungen an junge Prediger* (1792); *Glückseligkeitslehre aus Vernunftgründen* (2 parts, 1793); and *Vorlesungen aus der Pastoraltheologie* (2 vols., 1793–94). After being dismissed from Dillingen, Sailer took up his residence in Munich, but the attacks made upon him compromised his position with the papal nuncio, Zoglio, as with Elector Charles Theodore. Under these circumstances Sailer gladly accepted an invitation, in Jan., 1795, to the castle of Ebersberg, belonging to the Knights of Malta. In this retirement he turned again to literature, producing his *Buch von der Nachfolge Christi* (Munich, 1794) and his *Ecclesiæ catholicæ de cultu sanctorum doctrina* (1797), as well as his extremely popular *Uebungen des Geistes zur Gründung und Förderung eines heiligen Sinnes und Lebens* (Mannheim, 1799), and *Briefe aus allen Jahrhunderten der christlichen Zeitrechnung* (Munich, 1804). With the accession of Max Joseph I., in 1799, the entire situation changed. The Enlightenment was now officially adopted, and on the transfer of the reorganized University from Ingolstadt to Landshut Sailer was reappointed professor of ethics and pastoral theology. He now published his *Ueber Erziehung für Erzieher; oder Pädagogik* (Munich, 1807); *Grundlehren der Religion* (1805); and *Handbuch der christlichen Moral für künftige katholische Seelsorger* (3 vols., 1817–18).

Professional Career.

When, at the close of the Napoleonic wars, the Roman Catholic Church entered upon a phase of development most favorable for her revival, one of her most pressing tasks was the filling of the numerous vacant dioceses. In 1818 Sailer was twice offered the archbishopric of Cologne by the Prussian government, but his attachment to Bavaria led him to decline. In the following year Max Joseph proposed him as bishop of Augsburg, only to have the nomination rejected by the papal nuncio at Munich. Before long, however, this opposition vanished, and in 1821 Sailer was made a canon of the cathedral of Regensburg, and in the following year (Oct. 28, 1822) he was consecrated titular bishop of Germanicopolis as coadjutor to the aged bishop of Regensburg, with right of succession. In 1825 he added to his other duties those of dean of the cathedral, and, after having declined to be transferred to the diocese of Passau in 1826, he became full diocesan of Regensburg on Oct. 29, 1829. His health was, however, already failing, and within the year he was forced to have the assistance of a bishop-coadjutor, Georg Michael Wittmann, who succeeded him as full diocesan on his death in 1832.

Bishop of Regensburg.

The importance of Sailer in the German Roman Catholic episcopate of the nineteenth century was due preeminently to the fact that he was the representative of a definite type of Roman Catholicism which enabled the church to recover in a comparatively short time from the heavy losses she had incurred at the beginning of the century. Deeply religious and strongly contemplative in character, he was more than a mere teacher of theology or governing prelate. He sought to inspire others with his own enthusiasm and spirit, to train up a clergy who should appeal to all that was best in their parishes, and to lead the way in deeply needed practical reforms. At the same time, while manifesting a certain amount of sympathy with the mystical movement rife at the opening of the nineteenth century, and while not unfriendly to Protestants in many respects, he never forgot his consciousness of the superiority and divine mission of his own communion. Nevertheless, the orthodoxy of his theological writings was not free from the suspicion of a taint of the Enlightenment, and

Character and Influence.

opinion is still divided regarding them. Neither a statesman of the church nor a polemic theologian, Sailer's aim was rather the internal reform of his communion and the revival of confidence and faith in the Roman Catholic Church. In this he was successful, while as a prelate he manfully combated the contracting of mixed marriages, and through his influence a school of priests was trained both for Germany and for Switzerland who united theological and secular learning with deep moral earnestness. It may, in a word, be said that Sailer stands for Roman Catholicism before the rise of Ultramontanism. His collected works were edited by J. Widmer (40 vols., Sulzbach, 1830–41; supplementary volume, 1845). CARL MIRBT.

BIBLIOGRAPHY: An account of Sailer's life by himself is reprinted in his *Werke* (ut sup.), xxxix. 257 sqq., from F. J. Waitzenegger's *Gelehrten- und Schriftstellerlexikon*, ii. 189–218, Landshut, 1829. Biographies have been written by: E. von Schenk, Regensburg, 1838; F. W. Bodemann, Gotha, 1856; G. Aichinger, Freiburg, 1865; and J. A. Messmer, Mannheim, 1876. Consult further: A. Lütolf, *Leben und Bekenntnisse des J. L. Schiffmann*, Lucerne, 1860; M. Jocham, *Dr. Alois Buchner*, Augsburg, 1870; H. Schmid, *Geschichte der katholischen Kirche Deutschlands*, pp. 257–314, Munich, 1874; J. H. Reinkens, *M. von Diepenbrock*, Leipsic, 1881; F. Nielsen, *Aus dem inneren Leben der katholischen Kirche im 19. Jahrhundert*, i. 287–344, Carlsruhe, 1882; J. N. von Ringseis, *Erinnerungen*, 2 vols., Amberg, 1886; J. Friedrich, *Ignaz von Döllinger*, Munich, 1899; F. Nippold, *Handbuch der neuesten Kirchengeschichte*, i. 519 sqq., Berlin, 1901; A. Brück, *Geschichte der katholischen Kirche im 19. Jahrhundert*, 2 vols., Mainz and Münster, 1902–03; *KL*, x. 1536 sqq.; *ADB*, xxx. 178–192.

SAINT ALBANS: A town of Hertfordshire, twenty miles northwest of London, the seat of a bishopric, with a population of 16,109 (1901). It derives its name from Saint Alban of Verulam (q.v.), the Roman town of Verulamium. The cathedral was founded in 1077, and was restored in the nineteenth century. Names connected with the place are Matthew of Paris, Sir John Mandeville, Pope Adrian IV., and Lord Bacon.

BIBLIOGRAPHY: A. E. Gibbs, *Historical Records of St. Albans*, St. Albans, 1888; C. H. Ashdown, *St. Albans, Historical and Picturesque*, ib. 1896; idem, *The City of St. Albans*, London, 1907; D. W. Barrett, *Sketches of Church Life in the Diocese of St. Albans*, ib. 1902; T. Perkins, *The Cathedral Church of St. Albans*, ib. 1903.

SAINT CYRAN. See DU VERGIER, JEAN.

SAINT GALL, sênt gōl or san gōl, MONASTERY OF.

The Benedictine monastery of St. Gall, celebrated for centuries as a center of learning, and situated in the Swiss town of the same name (19 m. s.e. of Constance), took its rise from a hermitage established, probably in 613, by St. Gallus, a disciple of Columban (q.v.), with a few companions. It would seem, however, even from the legend-filled life of the founder, written toward the end of the eighth century, that his personal activity was of only secondary importance, since he is represented as an anchorite rather than as the "apostle of the Alemanni"; and the Christian element was already so strong that he had no lack of associates and support. It was but seldom that he could be induced to leave his cell, and before many years he died on Oct. 16, probably about 627. After this the hermitage continued to exist uneventfully until the first half of the eighth century, when the real history of the monastery of St. Gall began with the first abbot, Otmar (720–759), who, in 747 or 748, substituted the rule of St. Benedict for that of St. Columban, and likewise replaced the Irish monks with his own compatriots, the Rhaetians. Gifts of money and land were made from far and near; but, on the other hand, the independence of the monastery had to be surrendered, and it came under the control of the bishop of Constance, Otmar's resistance exposing him to ecclesiastical censure and the secular arm, so that he died a prisoner on the little island of Werd in the Rhine (Nov. 16, 759). In 816 the monastery was made exempt from episcopal control by Louis the Pious, and in 854 its annual payment of a tax to Constance, the last remnant of its dependence upon the see, was abolished.

1. Origin.

Abbot Gosbert, elected by the monks themselves (probably in 816), was the first of the long series of abbots of St. Gall whose interests embraced the whole intellectual culture of the period. In 830 Gosbert commenced the entire reconstruction of the monastery, beginning with a larger church to replace one erected apparently by Otmar. A plan of a great Benedictine abbey with all accessories was drawn in Italy especially for St. Gall, although the topography forbade its entire acceptance; and this plan, still preserved at St. Gall (ed. F. Keller, *Bauriss des Klosters St. Gallen vom Jahr 820*, Zurich, 1844), constitutes one of the most important documents of the early Middle Ages for architecture and culture-history. Gosbert likewise provided for the increase of the library, and under his successor, Grimald (841–872), the first catalogue, listing some 400 books, was drawn up. There was likewise a flourishing school, dating back to Otmar and now consisting of a division for the training of the future regular clergy and one for the education of secular priests and laymen. Close relations were also maintained with the institutions established by Alcuin, as well as with Fulda, and especially with Reichenau. St. Gall's rich historical literature began, during the abbacy of Gosbert, with a *Vita Sancti Galli* by the monk Wettinus, who died in 824 (ed. *MGH*, *Script.*, ii., 1829, pp. 1–21), followed by the two works, revised by Walafrid, of Gozbert's nephew, who bore the same name: *Miraculi Sancti Galli* and *Vita Sancti Otmari abbatis Sangallensis* (ed. *MGH*, *Script.*, ii., 1829, pp. 21–31, 40–47). In like manner Iso (d. 871) wrote a *Miracula Sancti Otmari* (ed. *MGH*, *Script.*, ii. 1829, pp. 47–54); and Ratpert (d. probably shortly after 884), distinguished as a teacher, a poet (even in German), and a historian, began the great history of the monastery, the *Casus Sancti Galli* (ed., with its continuations, *MGH*, *Script.*, ii., 1829, pp. 75–183). To the succeeding generation of monks belong Notker the Stammerer (see NOTKER, 1) and Tuotilo, as well as such abbots as Solomon III. (d. 920) and Hartmann (d. 925). The

2. Early Services to Learning.

first-named gave new form to the services by his systematic use of Sequences (q.v.), besides being, according to later tradition, the author of the antiphon *Media vita*, and also wrote the *Gesta Karoli Magni* (ed. *MGH*, *Script.*, ii., 1829, pp. 726–763); Tuotilo was distinguished as artist; and Solomon, like many of his monks, was conspicuous as a poet. With the death of Solomon, however, the state of the monastery changed, its steady progress being hindered by the indifference of the secular rulers, the frequent change of abbots and their inferior degree of ability, the invasion of the Hungarians in 926, the fire of 937, and the Saracen inroads. Nevertheless, in the tenth and early eleventh centuries the monastery could again number first-class men, especially Dean Ekkehard (d. 973) and his four nephews. The first-named was not only a distinguished economist, but also the author of the *Waltharius manufortis;* and among the pupils of his famous nephew Notker Labeo (see NOTKER, 4) was Ekkehard IV. (d. about 1060), the author of the *Liber benedictionum* and a busy glossator and poet, as well as one of those who continued Ratpert's *Casus Sancti Galli*. Besides history and literature, mathematics, astronomy, and medicine were cultivated at St. Gall by Notker Medicus (see NOTKER, 2). A reminiscence of the Irish origin of the monastery, moreover, may perhaps be traced in its cultivation of calligraphy and music. Waldo, who resigned the abbacy of St. Gall for that of Reichenau in 784, was remarkable for his skill in calligraphy, and the miniatures and the drawings of the Irish manuscripts of St. Gall clearly show Celtic coloring and ornamentation. These were, however, importations and exercised only a secondary influence, but when Grimald became abbot, he initiated a revival both of calligraphy and miniature painting which reached its acme in the Carolingian style and lasted far into the dynasty of the Ottos.

3. Increasing Secularization.

In 1034 St. Gall was placed by Conrad II. under the Cluniac reform, but though the monks firmly resisted the innovation, the unsuccessful attempt being terminated by the voluntary resignation of the Cluniac abbot, Nortpert, in 1072, the spiritual power of the monastery was broken. It became involved in political strife after 1077, Abbot Ulrich III. taking the side of Henry IV. against the pope, and himself being opposed by two anti-abbots. Ulrich's partizanship also brought him into conflict both with Reichenau and with Constance; the country about St. Gall was devastated; and learning in the monastery sank to a low level, even the *Casus Sancti Galli* being kept only indifferently, and its concluding portion being written in German by a layman, Christian Kuchemeister. St. Gall had been completely secularized, yet as a spiritual principality it maintained its importance, embracing the territory between Rorschach and Wil and the mountain districts of Appenzell. Among the abbots were many of ability, though more knightly than spiritual in type, such as Ulrich IV., Conrad of Bussnang, and Berchtold. Meanwhile, what in the tenth century had been the little village of St. Gall had been steadily increasing in importance, and simultaneously with the rise of Rudolph of Hapsburg, it constituted itself an imperial city, soon even attempting to effect a confederation of the Swabian cities. The closing centuries of the Middle Ages, moreover, brought the monastery of St. Gall into conflict with the Swiss confederation; and though the antithesis came to an end on the incorporation of the spiritual principality of St. Gall, as part of the German Empire, into the confederation, the abbots still maintained connection with the empire and, when they judged it to their advantage, assumed a peculiar intermediate position. Under Swiss protection the Appenzell vassals of St. Gall threw off their allegiance, but, on the other hand, the uprising of the shepherds, which for a time threatened the very existence of the monastery, was suppressed in 1408. Such was the northeastern spread of the influence of the confederation, however, that in 1451 Abbot Caspar formed an alliance with the two cities of Zurich and Lucerne, and the two cantons of Schwyz and Glarus, the city of St. Gall, which had now become entirely independent, joining this league three years later. Henceforth abbey and city, like Appenzell, which entered their confederacy in 1452, took an active part in Swiss affairs, as in the struggles against Charles the Bold, Maximilian, and the Swabian League.

4. The Reformation.

The first abbot of St. Gall not of noble birth, Ulrich Rösch (1463–91), strove indefatigably to unite all the prerogatives and possessions of his monastery, and in 1469 purchased the suzerainty of the Toggenburg from the heirs of the extinct house which had held it. He thus came into conflict with the city of St. Gall and with Appenzell, and though circumstances so favored him that he was able to crush them, a generation after his death the city seemed on the point of triumphing over the abbey. Zwingli, born in the Toggenburg, manifested special hatred of the monastery of St. Gall, and in this he was abetted by the burgomaster of the city of St. Gall, Joachim von Watt (q.v.), an enthusiastic advocate of the new doctrines. In 1529 the cloisters, deserted by the monks, were seized by the city, and Protestantism worked its will in the abbey church; while from the archives of the monastery were taken the materials which enabled Watt (Vadianus) to write his *Grössere Chronik der Aebte* and *Kleinere Chronik der Aebte* (ed. E. Götzinger, St. Gall, 1875–77). The death of Zwingli and the end of the second Cappel war in 1531 transformed the situation, and in the following year the new abbot, Diethelm Blaarer, reentered his abbey. The old faith was reembraced, except in the city of St. Gall and in the Toggenburg, and both Diethelm and his successors speedily revived the spiritual and material preeminence of St. Gall. Joachim Opfer (1577–94) was a martyr to his devotion to the sufferers from pestilence; and Bernhard Müller (1594–1630) and Pius Reher (1630–54) brought the discipline and administration of the abbey to such a point that St. Gall was justly placed at the head of the new Swiss Benedictine congregations, and lost territory was regained. Learning was revived in equal measure; the abbey had its own press after

1633; and the theological attainments of Abbot Celestine, Count Sfondrati of Milan (1687–96), were so great as to win him the cardinal's hat.

5. The Closing Struggle.

The last century of the monastery's existence opened with the stormy period of the last great civil war in Switzerland (1712), brought on mainly by the confessional divisions and the demagogic agitations among the Toggenburg vassals of the abbey. The Protestants conquered, to the detriment of the monastery, and it was only after the death of the stern Abbot Leodegar Bürgisser (1697–1717) that St. Gall had peace. But in succeeding years the abbey resumed its honored career, so that Abbot Celestine Gugger (1740–67) could carry out extensive architectural plans, not only constructing the imposing granary in Rorschach, but also rebuilding the monastery itself, especially the late renaissance church on the site of the venerable medieval structure, and the refectory. The next abbot, Beda Angehrn, sought to introduce reforms in school and prison, but weak economic administration plunged the monastery into financial difficulties, and the abbot had to encounter strong opposition from the younger monks, and later even from the older ones, though he emerged from the struggle triumphant, thanks to the aid of the Confederation. The succeeding abbacy of Pancratius Vorster was likewise marked by storm, and though the literary treasures of the monastery were saved both from the French Revolution and from the greed of the municipality, and though the abbot returned to his abbey with the victorious imperial troops in 1799, the second battle of Zurich forced him again to flee, and the doom of St. Gall was foreshadowed. The abbot fought bravely to regain his rights, but in 1805 the suppression of the monastery was decreed. Even the troublous times that came upon Switzerland after Napoleon's fall could not aid Pancratius, who died in the monastery of Muri in 1829. The plan of a diocese of St. Gall, thwarted in great part by the attitude assumed by Abbot Pancratius, was later realized; and after the existence of the double bishopric of Chur and St. Gall (1823–44), the latter received independent diocesan rank in 1844. At the suppression in 1805 the property of the foundation was divided between the whole canton and its Roman Catholic portion, the former receiving the palace as a government building, and the latter the treasures of the library and archives, which, after many vicissitudes, had been regained in 1804. The monastery itself, after being used as a spinning factory from 1801 to 1808, was made a Roman Catholic gymnasium. (G. Meyer von Knonau.)

Bibliography: The chief sources are collected in *MGH, Script.*, vols. i.–ii., and *MGH, Libri confraternitatum S. Galli* (1884). Collections of sources of especial value are to be found in the *Mittheilungen* and other publications of the St. Gall Historischer Verein, 1862 sqq. Other sources are: E. L. Dümmler, *Formelbuch des Bischofs Salomo III.*, Leipsic, 1857; H. Wartmann, *Urkundenbuch der Abtei St. Gallen*, parts i.–iii., Zurich, 1863–82. Consult: I. von Arx, *Geschichte des Cantons St. Gallen*, 3 vols., St. Gall, 1810–1813 (still the best special history on any part of Switzerland); F. Weidmann, *Geschichte . . . St. Gallen unter den zween letzten Fürstäbten*, ib. 1834; idem, *Geschichte der Bibliothek von St. Gallen*, ib. 1841 (both based on Arx); F. W. Rettberg, *Observationes ad vitam S. Galli spectantes*, Marburg, 1842; A. Schubiger, *Die Sängerschule St. Gallens*, Einsiedeln, 1858; J. H. A. Ebrard, *Iro-schottische Missions-Kirche des 6. bis 8. Jahrhunderts*, Gütersloh, 1873; J. R. Rahn, *Geschichte der bildenden Künste in der Schweiz*, Zurich, 1876; F. X. Wetzel, *Die Wissenschaft und Kunst im Kloster St. Gallen im 9. und 10. Jahrhundert*, Lindau, 1877; G. Meier, in *Jahrbuch für schweizerische Geschichte*, x (1885) (a good history of the school in the Middle Ages); J. Bächtold, *Geschichte der deutschen Litteratur in der Schweiz*, Frauenfeld, 1892; E. Egli, *Kirchengeschichte der Schweiz*, Zurich, 1893; L. Knappert, *La Vie de S. Gall et le paganisme germanique*, Paris, 1894; Ziegler, *Abt Othmar II. von St. Gallen*, St. Gall, 1896; F. L. Wetzel, *Das goldene Zeitalter des Klosters St. Gallen*, Ravensburg, 1900; H. Miles, *Die Chronik des Hermann Miles von St. Gall*, St. Gall, 1903; A. Scheiwiler, *Abt Ulrich Rösch der zweite Gründer des Klosters St. Gallen, 1463–91*, ib. 1903; *Beiträge zur St. Gallischen Geschichte*, ib. 1904; the *KD*, of Hauck, Friedrich, and Rettberg respectively; *KL*, v. 43–66.

SAINT JOHN, KNIGHTS OF. See Military Religious Orders.

SAINT-MARTIN, san-mār-tan', LOUIS CLAUDE DE: French mystic; b. at Amboise Jan. 18, 1743; d. at Paris Oct. 13, 1803. After studying law, he entered the army and at Bordeaux became acquainted with a Portuguese Jew named Martines de Pasqualis, whose freemasonry increased St. Martin's tendency to mysticism. At Lyons and Paris St. Martin communicated, in mysterious phraseology and ceremony, his "revelation" on God, the spirit world, the fall, and original sin. Among his hearers was a Count d'Hauterive, on whom St. Martin tried all sorts of experiments at Lyons (1774–76) to gain fellowship with the Logos. Meanwhile, he gradually withdrew from Pasqualis and his followers, formed a cautious friendship with Cagliostro, and read Swedenborg. At this period he published his first work, under the pseudonym of "un philosophe inc(onnu)," *Des erreurs et de la vérité, ou les hommes rappellés au principe universel de la science* (Lyons, 1775), a book which aroused the anger of Voltaire.

To propagate his views St. Martin now removed to Paris, where he moved in aristocratic circles, writing his emanational tenets in his *Tableau naturel des rapports qui existent entre Dieu, l'homme et l'univers* (Lyons [ostensibly Edinburgh], 1782). His travels gained him new acquaintances. In England he met William Law and Best; he accompanied Prince Gallitzin to Italy in 1787; in 1788 he resided in Montbéliard with Duchess Dorothea of Württemberg. Until 1791 he lived in Strasburg, where he studied the writings of Jacob Böhme, but in the latter year his father's illness forced him to return to Amboise, where his theories found little sympathy. To this period of his career belong his *L'Homme de désir* (Lyons, 1790), *Ecce homo* (Paris, 1792), and *Le Nouvel Homme* (1792).

St. Martin's last close friendship was formed with Baron Kirchberger of Bern, through whom he was kept informed of mystic movements abroad during the French Revolution. This latter upheaval was greeted by him with joy, and after being appointed tutor, with Condorcet, Sieyès, and Bernardin de St. Pierre, to the Dauphin in 1791, he became one of his jailers two years later. St. Martin himself was later imprisoned and exiled to Amboise. Before long, however, he was sent back to Paris as a teacher at the new normal school there. This position he held until his death, and during his incumbency he wrote *Lettre à un ami, considérations politiques, philosophiques et religieuses sur la révolution française* (Paris, 1795); *Éclair sur l'association humaine* (1797); *Esprit des choses ou coup d'œil philosophique sur la nature des êtres et sur l'objet de leur existence* (1800); *Ministère de l'homme esprit* (1802), besides translating a number of the works of Böhme.

St. Martin's views, a mixture of cabalistic, Gnostic, and neoplatonic doctrines on a Christian basis, can scarcely be reduced to a system. At the same time, he bitterly hated the Church, yet fell into all sorts of clairvoyance, conjuring, and juggling with numbers and the tetragrammaton. His favorite sphere was anthropology; he held it the aim of man to be still higher than Christ, the highest type of humanity; in his daily life St. Martin sought simply to live like a pious Christian. For his following see MARTINIST ORDER. (C. PFENDER.)

BIBLIOGRAPHY: *La Correspondance inédite de L. C. de Saint-Martin, . . .* ed. L. Schauer and A. Chuquet, Amsterdam, 1862, cf. *Mystical Philosophy and Spirit-Manifestations. Selections from the . . . Correspondence between . . . Saint-Martin . . . and Kirchberger*, Exeter, 1863; J. B. M. Gence, *Notice biographique sur L. C. de Saint Martin*, Paris, 1823; L. Moreau, *Réflexions sur les idées de L. C. de Saint-Martin*, ib. 1850; E. M. Caro, *Du mysticisme au xviii. siècle. Essai sur la vie et la doctrine de Saint-Martin*, ib. 1852; J. Matter, *Saint-Martin, le philosophe inconnu*, ib. 1862; A. Franck, *La Philosophie mystique en France à la fin du xviii. siècle. Saint-Martin et son maître Martinez Pasqualis*, ib. 1866.

SAINT-MAUR, san-mōr', **CONGREGATION OF:** The name of a branch of the Benedictine order, distinguished by reform in discipline and great services to learning. At the beginning of the seventeenth century the monastery of Saint-Vanne near Verdun was reformed by Didier de la Cour. Soon the famous old monastery of Moyenmoutier and others joined the movement, and Clement VIII. in 1604 confirmed the organization of a congregation within the order under the name of Congregatio SS. Vitonis et Hidulphi. In 1614 the general assembly of the French clergy expressed the wish that all the Benedictine monasteries associate themselves with this congregation; but its general chapter, fearing danger to its spirit from too large a growth, advised the formation of a second congregation, and in 1618 Dom Bénard, a monk of Saint-Vanne, was charged with the formation of such a union. It adopted the name of St. Maur, the companion of St. Benedict, and was confirmed by Gregory XV. in 1621, and again by Urban VIII. in 1627. By 1652 the new congregation numbered forty houses, and before the end of the eighteenth century it had grown to 191, divided into six provinces. The most influential was the abbey of Saint-Germain-des-Prés in Paris, the seat of the superior-general. Dom Bénard had not proposed to make the congregation predominantly a learned one; it was the first superior-general, Dom Tarisse (1630–48), who laid the foundations of the splendid edifice of learning which was gradually reared by the monks. Their activity has embraced all departments of knowledge, but especially the history of France and of the Church. Besides the general

Foundation of the Congregation.

outline given here of the long series of master-works which they produced by their indefatigable and intelligent labors, further information will be found in separate articles on the more distinguished members.

They made their own the science of paleography, or, as it was then called, diplomatics; Mabillon is regarded as its actual founder, with his *De re diplomatica* (1681) and its supplement (1704). As these works had special reference to France, Dom Tassin published a general treatise under the title *Nouveau traité de diplomatique* (6 vols., 1750–65); and what this did for Latin paleography Montfaucon attempted to do for Greek in his *Palæographia Græca* (1708). Modern scientific chronology may also be said to have taken its rise from them. Every historian knows the value of the *Art de vérifier les dates*, begun by Dantine and finished by Clémencet (1750; 1770; 1783–92; 1818 sqq.), which has been called the most noteworthy monument of eighteenth-century French scholarship. To the knowledge of antiquity a considerable contribution was made by Montfaucon's *Antiquité expliquée en figures* (10 vols., 1719). In the history of language, the congregation took part in, though it did not originate, Du Cange's great *Glossarium mediæ et infimæ Latinitatis*, which, originally published in 1687, was increased one-half by Dantine and Carpentier (6 vols., 1733–36, with a supplement by Carpentier, 4 vols., 1766; and two revised and enlarged editions, 1840 sqq. by Henschel, and 1883 sqq. by Henschel and Fabre).

Contributions to Paleography and Chronology.

The most extensive labors, however, were given to history. Colbert had sought in vain for able scholars to continue the undertaking of a collection of the sources of French history, until Chancellor d'Aguesseau persuaded the congregation of Saint-Maur to take it up. Martène and then Bouquet had charge of this branch, and their work resulted in the publication of fifteen folio volumes of *Scriptores rerum Gallicarum et Francicarum* between 1738 and 1818, since which time it has been carried on by the Académie des Inscriptions. This body has also, since 1814, taken charge of the *Histoire littéraire de la France*, begun by Dom Rivet and extending to thirteen volumes between 1733 and 1763, a collection of sources which has immense value for the literary history not only of France but of all medieval Europe. Provincial histories surpassing those of any other country are also due to the congregation. Their researches in the libraries of their own monasteries and their travels in quest of documents (especially Mabillon's journey to Italy and Montfaucon's to Germany) gave them an opportunity to bring together unpublished material of the highest importance. The most famous of their works in this department are D'Achery's *Spicilegium veterum aliquot scriptorum* (13 vols., 1653–77); the *Vetera analecta* of Mabillon (4 vols., 1675–85); Martène's *Collectio nova veterum scriptorum* (1700); the *Thesaurus novus anecdotorum* by Martène and Durand (5 vols., 1717), as well as their *Voyage littéraire de deux religieux bénédictins*

Contributions to History.

(1724); the *Diarium Italicum* of Montfaucon (1702), and his *Bibliotheca bibliothecarum manuscriptorum nova* (2 vols., 1739).

In the field of church history, their first noted work was the continuation and revision of the *Gallia christiana* originally published by a Benedictine not connected with the Maurists, Dom de Sainte-Marthe, in 1656. They carried it on from Sainte-Marthe's death in 1725 to 1785, by which time thirteen volumes had appeared, forming a model on which similar works for other countries have since been planned. The work was taken up anew in 1856 (16 vols., Paris, 1715–1865, vols. xiv.,–xvi. by B. Hauréau). The history of the martyrs was treated by Dom Ruinart in his *Acta primorum martyrum* (1689). Much was done in the way of editing primitive liturgies; the best-known works in this department are Ménard's Sacramentary of St. Gregory (1642), Mabillon's *De liturgia Gallicana* (1685), Martène's *De antiquis monachorum ritibus* (2 vols., 1700 sqq.), and *De antiquis ecclesiæ ritibus* (4 vols., 1700 sqq.). In this connection may be mentioned the *Acta sanctorum ordinis S. Benedicti*, begun by D'Achery and continued by Mabillon and Ruinart (9 vols., 1668 sqq.), and the *Annales ordinis S. Benedicti*, Mabillon's most famous work, completed by Massuet (6 vols., 1703 sqq.). The most enduring service rendered by the congregation was its editions of ecclesiastical writers of the early Church and of the Middle Ages, which are remarkable monuments of scholarship, distinguished by enlightened criticism, careful translation from the Greek, and admirable introductions and excursuses. They originally contemplated only the publication of medieval writers, principally those of their own order. The first was the *Concordia regularum* of Benedict of Aniane, edited by Ménard (1628). But the general favor shown to these editions, the wish to put thoroughly good texts into the hands of their novices, and the wealth of manuscripts accessible to them induced them to extend the plan. Augustine was the first of the Latin Fathers to be published (11 vols., 1679–1700); the choice of this author in the midst of the Jansenistic controversy is significant of the attitude of the congregation toward the vexed questions of the day, which, in fact, was one of scarcely concealed sympathy with Port-Royal, if not with Jansenism in general. The first early Greek text published was the Epistle of Barnabas by D'Achery and Ménard in 1645; but no special attention was paid to this department until near the end of the century, when Montfaucon edited Athanasius (3 vols., 1698). The work continued until the publication of the *Opera* of Gregory Nazianzen, begun by Maran in 1788, was interrupted by the Revolution. Useful work was done also on the old Bible versions; included were the *Hexapla* of Origen, ed. Montfaucon (2 vols., 1713), the *Bibliotheca divina* of Jerome, ed. Martianay (vol. i. of Jerome's works, 1693), and the *Latinæ versiones antiquæ*, ed. Sabatier, Baillard, and Vincent de la Rue (3 vols., 1743–49).

Contributions to Church History and Patristics.

Lack of space excludes detailed account of a great mass of other works, partly of an edifying nature, partly dealing with various subjects in classical literature, Hebrew, the arts, geography, and even the natural sciences. In controversy, to which they were not seldom exposed, the Maurists showed the same calm moderation and intellectual superiority that mark all their work. An attack by De Rancé, the founder of the Trappists, on devotion to mere learning among monks, called forth Mabillon's admirable *Traité des études monastiques* (1691). They were often engaged in disputes with the Jesuits, provoked especially by their edition of Augustine, and wrote not a few strong criticisms of the constitution *Unigenitus*. They exposed themselves to attack also by a tendency to follow the Cartesian philosophy, and some of their members even inclined in the latter half of the eighteenth century to fraternize with Voltaire and the Encyclopedists (qq.v.). The congregation was dispersed by the suppression of monastic orders at the Revolution; the last member, Dom Brial, died in 1828. After his death some friends of Lamennais, with the approval of the bishop of Mons, bought the abbey of Solesmes near Cambrai with a view to reviving the congregation. In 1837 it was made a regular abbey of the restored Benedictine order in France, the head of which its abbot was to be. Under Dom Guéranger (1805–75) a new start was made in the old Maurist direction; but up to the present the early excellence has not been reached. The most distinguished of Dom Guéranger's associates was Jean-Baptiste Pitra (q.v.), whose most noteworthy achievement is the *Spicilegium Solesmense*, a collection of unpublished writings of the Fathers and ecclesiastical writers (4 vols., 1852–58, followed by 8 vols. of *Analecta spicilegio Solesmensi parata*, 1876–1891, and by 2 vols. of *Analecta novissima*, 1885–1888). (O. Zöckler†.)

Other Labors.

Bibliography: Helyot, *Ordres monastiques*, vi. 286 sqq.; B. Pez, *Bibliotheca Benedicto-Mauriana*, Augsburg, 1716; P. Le Cerf, *Bibliothèque historique et critique des auteurs de la congrégation de St. Maur*, The Hague, 1726; R. P. Tassin, *Hist. littéraire de la congrégation de S. Maur*, Brussels, 1770; Herbst, in *TQS*, 1833, parts 1–3, 1834, part 1; E. C. de Malan, *Hist. de Mabillon et de la congrégation de St. Maur*, Paris, 1843; U. Robert, *Supplément à l'histoire de la congrégation de St. Maur*, Paris, 1881; C. de Lama, *Bibliothèque des écrivains de la congrégation de St. Maur*, Paris, 1882; A. Sicard, *Les Études classiques avant la révolution*, Paris, 1887; E. de Broglie, *Mabillon et la société de l'abbaye de St. Germain des Prés*, 2 vols., Paris, 1888; E. Gigas, *Lettres des bénédictins de la congrégation de St.-Maur 1741 ss.*, Copenhagen, 1893; J. B. Vanel, *Les Bénédictins de St.-Germain-des-Prés et les savants lyonnais*, Paris, 1894; idem, *Nécrologe de religieux de . . . St. Maur*, ib. 1896; idem, *Les Bénédictins de Saint-Maur*, Paris, 1896, J. A. Endres, *Korrespondenz der Mauriner mit dem Emmeramern*, Stuttgart, 1899; J. M. Besse, in *Revue des sciences ecclésiastiques*, ii (1902), 143 sqq., 230 sqq., 532 sqq.; Heimbucher, *Orden und Kongregationen*, i. 306–313.

SAINT-SIMON, san-sî"mōn or sênt-sai'mun, **CLAUDE HENRI, COUNT DE:** French socialist; b. at Paris Oct. 17, 1760; d. there May 19, 1825. He served as an officer in the American Revolution, and after many adventures was major and commandant at Metz at the age of twenty-three. Weary of military life, he traveled through Holland and Spain, and was an enthusiastic supporter of the French Revolution. In 1802, after an unhappy marriage, he resumed his scientific studies, fancying that he could accomplish his intended social renovation through an alliance of science and industry. With this end in view, he traveled in Germany and England, but found nothing to reward his pains. By this time he had lost his property. He now wrote, among other works, *Lettres d'un habitant de Genève à ses contemporains* (1802); *Introduction aux travaux scientifiques du dixneuvième siècle* (2 vols., 1808); *De la réorganisation de la société européenne* (1814); and *L'Industrie, ou discussions politiques, morales et philosophiques* (1817). His appeals for financial aid to scholars, bankers, and Napoleon himself were in vain. Cuvier alone encouraged him, while Lafitte and Ternaux helped defray the expense of publishing his writings. All his efforts to attract the attention of the public were equally fruitless, even his daring *Le Politique, l'organisateur, système industriel des Bourbons et des Stuarts* (1820). In despair he was about to commit suicide, but was prevented from so doing. Henceforth his fortunes were better, and with the help of his devoted adherent, Olinde Rodrigues, he published his *Catéchisme politique* (1823–24) and *Nouveau christianisme* (1825; Eng. transl., *New Christianity*, London, 1834).

In St. Simon's ideal society industry was to rule all. By "industry," however, he understood all labor, scientific as well as manual, so that among the working classes scholars and artists were to constitute the aristocracy. While recognising the power of the medieval Church as a factor of civilization, however, he failed to understand the basal doctrines of Christianity, holding that the principle of Christ and the apostles afforded "the quickest possible amelioration of material conditions among the poorer classes." He was equally blind to the course of history, maintaining that the gradual changes in doctrine, dogma, and mode of thought were the results of capricious interference on the part of individuals.

The teachings of St. Simon were propagated by his followers, the St. Simonists, who included Rodrigues, Auguste Comte (see POSITIVISM), Bazard, and Enfantin. Their place of meeting was closed by the government because of their radicalism, and Enfantin established at Ménilmontant, which was then a suburb of Paris, a sort of monastery, where he, as "père suprême," ruled a community in motley. But it was closed for offenses against morality, and Enfantin and his colleague, Michel Chevalier, were sentenced to a year's imprisonment, thus breaking the spirit of the entire movement. His works have been collected in *Œuvres de Saint-Simon et d'Enfantin* (47 vols., Paris, 1865–78), to which a life is prefixed. (C. PFENDER.)

BIBLIOGRAPHY: F. W. Carové, *Der Saint-Simonismus und die heutige französische Philosophie*, Leipsic, 1831. L. Stein, *Der Socialismus und Kommunismus des heutigen Frankreich*, ib. 1842; C. Des Guerrois, *Études littéraires et biographiques*, Paris, 1856; N. G. Hubbard, *Saint-Simon, sa vie, ses travaux*, ib. 1857; Marie Recourt, *Résurrection du Père Enfantin. Quelques lumières sur la doctrine de Saint-Simon*, ib. 1858; W. R. L. Reybaud, *Études sur les réformateurs contemporains*, ib. 1864; A. J. Booth, *Saint Simon, and Saint Simonism*, London, 1871; P. Janet, *Saint-Simon et le Saint-Simonisme*, Paris, 1878; O. Warschauer, *Saint-Simon und der Saint-Simonismus*, Leipsic, 1892; G. Weil, *Un Précurseur du socialisme, Saint-Simon et son œuvre*, Paris, 1894; idem, *L'École saint-simonienne, son hist., son influence jusq'à nos jours*, ib. 1896; P. Weisengruen, *Die sozialwissenschaftlichen Ideen Saint-Simons*, Basel, 1895; S. Charlety, *Hist. du Saint-Simonisme (1825–1864)*, Paris, 1896; L. Paoli, *Le Saint-Simonisme en Italie*, ib. 1898; *La Grande Encyclopédie*, vol. xxix., ib. 1901; F. Muckle, *Saint-Simon und die ökonomische Geschichtstheorie*, Jena, 1908.

SAINTS, VENERATION OF: In accordance with Old-Testament usage (e.g., Dan. vii. 18 sqq.) the name "saints" (Gk. *hagioi*, Lat., *sancti*) is applied in the New Testament to the members of the Christian community, and especially to those dwelling in Jerusalem. This use occurs as late as Hippolytus. At an early time attention was directed to individuals who by deeds and lives of extraordinary piety seemed to reveal the presence of the Spirit in exceptional fulness. Naturally this character was

Before Constantine.

ascribed to those whose lives were crowned with the glory of martyrdom, a view definitely expressed for the first time in the account rendered by the community at Smyrna of the death of Polycarp (about 155). The reproach advanced by the Jews that the Christians of Smyrna seemed desirous of adoring Polycarp in place of Christ caused the community to define their attitude toward the martyrs whom they declared they "did not worship as they did Christ the son of God, but regarded them with fond affection as witnesses and imitators of the Lord." Yet Lucian bears testimony to the reverence with which the confessors were regarded even in their lifetime. Between them, as representatives of the highest ideals of Christian saintliness, and the officials of the Church a certain measure of rivalry prevailed; on the theory that their superabundant merit might atone for the failings of others, they came to exercise to a certain extent the power of the keys.

With the conversion of Constantine and the cessation of persecution in the State the early confessors together with the prophets and apostles at-

Rise of the Cultus.

tained an unprecedented authority, and names of hitherto local vogue began to receive the veneration of the entire Church. Through the veneration of saints heathenism made its way into the Church which had supplanted it. Pagan worship of the dead became Christian martyrolatry, and the birthday feasts of the martyrs were but modifications of the banquets signalizing the pagan *parentalia* (V. Schultze, *Geschichte des Untergangs des griechisch-römischen Heidenthums*, ii. 351–353, Jena, 1892). Aphrodite became the source of legends connected with the names of Pelagia, Maria, Marina, Margaret, Anthusa, and Eugenia, and during the last years of an expiring paganism marked by the wide-spread worship of female divinities greater emphasis came to be laid on the worship of the "Mother of God." With the gods came also the heroes; the hymn to the martyr was but a substitute for the hymn to the hero, the translation of one was the deification of the other, and the pagan statue was replaced by the Christian relic, in the adoration of which such enlightened spirits as Gregory of Nyssa engaged. The host of saints, increased by the accession of a new category, that of ascetics, is addressed by Gregory Nazianzen, by Basil, and by Jerome as intercessors between man and God. Not alone their bones but their graves and their shrines are instruments of blessing; they appear to those who invoke them or are represented by angels who assume their form; and though Augustine issues a warning against the adoration of the dead and argues that the saints are to be reverenced as models, and not worshiped as gods, with him, too, the prayers for the saints at the eucharistic oblations become transformed into an appeal addressed to the saints for their intercession. Julian was in a position to reproach the Christians with having abandoned the service of the gods for that of mere men. In his time every altar had its relics and the sick were laid in the chapels of the saints as formerly they were placed in the temples of Æsculapius. The opposition of a Eunomius, a Eustathius, or a Vigilantius could not check the rapid increase of the cult. The wearing of relics as amulets became common, the aid of the saints was invoked before the inception of important measures, and formal gratitude was rendered them on the successful completion of an adventure. Particular lands and particular trades and professions adopted their patron saints.

In the Middle Ages.

The veneration of the saints was formally sanctioned by the second Nicene Council (787) which distinguished, however, between the *proskynesis* or *douleia*, the reverence due to the saints and the absolute worship, *latreia*, to be rendered to God alone (see DULIA). In the West, though the Caroline Books (q.v.) pronounced for the veneration of the saints, Charlemagne was no friend of the cult in its extreme form, and the Synod of Frankfort in 794 declared against the addition of new names to the list of those venerated. But under Louis the Pious (814–840) the translation of saints became common, and though protests against the abuses connected with the cult are found after 1104 the principle of the practise was not assailed. In the case of a Bernard or Francis of Assisi veneration was paid to a saintly character even in his lifetime. It was the voice of the people that at first bestowed the title of holiness; Ulrich of Augsburg was the first to receive the papal canonization. Scholasticism supplied the dogmatic basis for the worship of saints by describing them as friends of God and intercessors before his throne. The distinction between *douleia* and *latreia* was preserved and the saints were divided into six categories, patriarchs and prophets, apostles, martyrs, confessors, virgins, and holy women. Indeed the close of the Middle Ages was marked by the appearance of many new saints, the worship of Anna, the mother of Mary, becoming at that time the basis of a separate cult in Germany.

The Reformation and After.

The Reformation in transforming the ideal of the religious and moral life struck at the roots of saint worship. The certainty of salvation obtained through faith in Christ made the intercession of saints not only superfluous, but derogatory to the character of Christ as the sole advocate. The Augsburg Confession declares itself clearly on the point. The Apology would permit the rendering of honors to the saints though it finds no Scriptural basis for their invocation, and Luther in the Schmalkald Articles declares definitely against the practise. The Council of Trent contented itself with declaring the practise "good and useful," and decisively rejected a proposal looking to its abandonment. In fact, however, saint worship continued to be a very essential part of the religious life of the southern peoples. In the Greek Orthodox Church the saints are invoked "not as gods but as friends of God." Altars are not dedicated to them. In practise the worshiper addresses himself to his name saint after the Virgin, and the feast days of the saints have pushed the Sabbath day into the background. The Russian Church has added many saints to those it received from the Greek Church, but it knows no actual process of canonization. It considers the most important mark of sanctity to be the delay in, or the total absence of, physical decomposition following death, together with exhibition of miraculous powers. See CANONIZATION; COMMUNION OF SAINTS; and ACTA MARTYRUM AND ACTA SANCTORUM. (N. BONWETSCH.)

BIBLIOGRAPHY: The literature of first importance is given in ACTA MARTYRUM, ACTA SANCTORUM, which the student can not afford to miss. Further treatises (selected from an immense literature) of a general nature are: C. Cahier, *Caractéristiques des saints dans l'art populaire*, 2 vols., Paris, 1867; H. Usener, *Legenden der heiligen Pelagia*, Bonn, 1879; W. H. Anderdon, *Evenings with the Saints*, London, 1883; G. F. L. Du Broc, *Les Saints patrons des corporations*, 2 vols., Paris, 1887; H. Samson, *Die Schutzheiligen*, Paderborn, 1889; idem, *Die Heiligen als Kirchenpatrone*, ib. 1892; T. Trede, *Das Heidentum in der römischen Kirche. Bilder aus dem religiösen und sittlichen Leben Süditaliens*, 4 vols., Gotha, 1889–91; S. Beissel, *Die Verehrung der Heiligen und ihrer Reliquien in Deutschland*, ib. 1890; F. Kattenbusch, *Vergleichende Konfessionskunde*, i. 456 sqq., Freiburg, 1892; H. R. Percival, *The Invocation of Saints*, London, 1896; O. Pfleiderer, *Die Attribute der Heiligen*, Ulm, 1897; H. Leclercq, *Les Martyrs. Recueil de pièces authentiques sur les martyrs*, 3 vols., Paris, 1902–04; E. Hella, *Studies in Saintship*, London, 1903; H. P. Brewster, *Saints and Festivals of the Christian Church*, New York, 1904; E. A. Greene, *Saints and their Symbols*, London, 1904; J. Hahn-Hahn, *Die Märtyrer*, Regensburg, 1904; E. Lucius, *Die Anfänge des Heiligenkults in der christlichen Kirche*, Tübingen, 1904; H. Delehaye, *Les Legends hagiographiques*, Brussels, 1905; D. H. Kerler, *Die Patronate der Heiligen*, Ulm, 1905; H. Siebert, *Beiträge zur vorreformatorischen Heiligen- und Reliquienverehrung*, Freiburg, 1907.

For eastern hagiology consult: A. Ehrhardt, *Die Legendensammlungen*, Freiburg, 1896; idem, *Forschungen zur Hagiographie der griechischen Kirche*, in *RQS*, 1897, pp. 67 sqq.; L. Clugnet, *Bibliothèque hagiographique orientale*, Paris, 1901 sqq.; G. Rabeau, *Le Culte des saints dans l'Afrique chrétienne*, ib. 1903. For England: John Wilson, *The English Martyrologe, Conteyning a Summary of the Lives of the . . . Saintes of the Three Kingdomes, England, Scotland, and Ireland collected . . . into monethe after the Form of a Callendar according to every Sainte's Festivity*, London, 1608; idem, *The Roman Martyrologe, according to the Reformed Calendar*, ib. 1627; John Bowden, *Oratorian Lives of the Saints*, 4 vols., ib. 1873–75; T. Walsh, *The Church of Erin. Her Saints*, 3 parts, New York, 1885; R. Stanton, *Menology of England and Wales*, London, 1887; F. Heitemeyer, *Die Heiligen Deutschlands*, Paderborn, 1888; John Pinkerton, *Vitæ antiquæ sanctorum qui habitaverunt in ea parte Britanniæ nunc vocata Scotia vel ejus insulis*, ed. W. M. Mitcalfe, 2 vols., Paisley, 1890; *The Book of Lismore*, Oxford, 1890; F. A. Smallpiece, *The English Saints of the English Calendar*, ib. 1894; F. E. Arnold-Forster, *Studies in Church Dedications, or, England's Patron Saints*, 3 vols., London, 1899; W. Fleming, *A Complete Calendar of the English Saints*, ib. 1902; W. H. Hutton, *Influence of Chris-*

tianity upon National Character Illustrated by the Lives of the English Saints, ib. 1902. For other countries: O. Sainati, *Vite dei Santi nati nella Diocesi Pisana*, Pisa, 1884; E. Noyes, *Saints of Italy*, London, 1901; E. P. M. Sauvage, *Actes des saintes de Rouen*, Rouen, 1884 sqq.; C. A. Bernoulli, *Die Heiligen der Merowinger*, Tübingen, 1900; A. Legrand, *Les Vies des saints de la Bretagne Armorique*, Quimper, 1901; Mary Hamilton, *Greek Saints and their Festivals*, London, 1910; T. F. Macken, *The Canonization of Saints*, ib., 1910.

On the saints in art consult the literature under ART AND CHURCH; PAINTING, ILLUSTRATIVE AND DECORATIVE, CHRISTIAN; and SCULPTURE, CHRISTIAN USE OF; and the following: C. E. Clement, *The Saints in Art*, London, 1899; N. Bell, *The Saints in Christian Art*, 3 vols., ib. 1901–04; Margaret E. Tabor, *The Saints in Art; with their Attributes and Symbols alphabetically arranged*, New York, 1908.

SAKKOS. See VESTMENTS AND INSIGNIA, ECCLESIASTICAL.

SALEM WITCHCRAFT. See WITCHCRAFT.

SALES, FRANCIS DE. See FRANCIS, SAINT, OF SALES.

SALIG, sā'lig, CHRISTIAN AUGUST: German Lutheran church historian; b. at Domersleben, near Magdeburg, Apr. 6, 1692; d. at Wolfenbüttel (32 m. s.e. of Hanover) Oct. 3, 1738. He was educated at the universities of Halle (1707–10) and Jena (1710–12), and, after preaching in his native town for two years, returned to Halle, where he lectured on philology, theology, and history. Here he published his *Philosophumena veterum et recentiorum de anima et ejus immortalitate* (Halle, 1714) and took part in editing the *Neue hallische Bibliothek*. In 1717 he became associate rector of the lyceum at Wolfenbüttel, a position which he held until his death. Drawing his materials almost entirely from the great library at Wolfenbüttel, Salig wrote his *De Eutychianismo ante Eutychium* (Wolfenbüttel, 1723), a work which drew upon him the suspicion of Nestorianism, and thus inspired him to write a voluminous *Eutychianismi historia*, which was never published. He wrote also *De diptychis veterum, tam profanis quam sacris* (Halle, 1731), but his fame is chiefly due to his labors in the history of the Reformation. He began with the *Vollständige Historie der augsburgischen Konfession und derselben Apologie* (Halle, 1730). This was followed in 1733–35 by the *Vollständige Historie der augsburgischen Konfession und derselben zugethanen Kirchen* (omitting the Scandinavian churches), in which an unmistakable sympathy is shown for the followers of C. Schwenkfeld (see SCHWENKFELD VON OSSIG, CASPAR, SCHWENKFELDIANS) and V. Krautwald. The conclusion of the series appeared posthumously under the title *Vollständige Historie des tridentinischen Konziliums* (3 vols., ed. S. A. Ballenstedt and J. S. Baumgarten, Halle, 1741–45). (T. KOLDE.)

BIBLIOGRAPHY: J. A. Ballenstedt, *De vita et obitu . . . C. A. Saligii*, Helmstadt, 1738; F. K. Hirsching, *Historisch-litterarisches Handbuch*, x. 79, Leipsic, 1807; J. M. H. Döring, *Die Gelehrten Theologen Deutschlands*, iii. 692, Neustadt, 1833.

SALISBURY, sōlz'bur-i (NEW SARUM): Capital of Wiltshire, England (78 m. w.s.w. of London), the seat of a bishopric, with a population of 21,900 (1901). The cathedral, one of the best examples of early English architecture, was built 1220–58 and restored since 1868. The cloisters, of the thirteenth century, are the most perfect in England, and constitute a square with sides of 181 feet.

BIBLIOGRAPHY: W. H. R. Jones, *Documents Illustrating the Hist. of the Cathedral, City and Diocese of Salisbury in the 12th and 13th Centuries*, Salisbury, 1891; G. D. Boyle, *Salisbury Cathedral*, London, 1897; C. Wordsworth, *Ceremonies and Processions of the Cathedral Church of Salisbury*, Cambridge, 1901.

SALLE, JEAN BAPTISTE DE LA. See CHRISTIAN BROTHERS.

SALMANTICENSES, sal-man-ti-sen'sis: Two extensive scholastic compilations of the seventeenth and eighteenth centuries, prepared by Discalced Carmelites at Salamanca. The first was a presentation of Thomistic dogmatics, and the second a compend of Roman Catholic moral theology. The two were preceded by the Discalced Carmelite *Complutenses*, or *Collegium Complutense philosophicum, hoc est, artium cursus sive disputationes in Aristotelis dialecticam et philosophiam naturalem juxta angelici doctoris divi Thomæ doctrinam et ejus scholam* (5 vols., Alcala, 1624–25). The dogmatic work of the Salamanca Carmelites bore the title of *Cursus theologicus, Summam theologicam divi Thomæ doctoris angelici complectens* (9 vols., Salamanca, 1631 sqq.; 3d ed., by Palmi, Paris, 20 vols., 1871–85). The theological standpoint of the dogmatics is strictly Thomistic, frequently assailing the semi-Pelagianism of Molina, and more or less opposed to the Jesuits. The moral compend, or *Cursus theologiæ moralis* (6 vols., Salamanca, 1665 sqq.), on the other hand, is more akin to the Jesuit scholastic in its probabilism. The chief collaborators on the dogmatics were Antonius de Olivero (Antonius a Matre Dei), Dominicus a Santa Theresa, and Johannes ab Annuntiatione; and on the morals Franciscus a Jesu Maria, Andreas a Matre Dei, Sebastianus a Joachim, and Ildefonsus ab Angelis.

(O. ZÖCKLER†.)

BIBLIOGRAPHY: N. Antonius, *Bibliotheca Hispanica*, i. 113, ii. 220, Rome, 1672; K. Werner, *Thomas von Aquin*, iii. 361 sqq., Regensburg, 1859; J. J. I. von Döllinger and F. H. Reusch, *Geschichte der Moralstreitigkeiten in der römisch-katholischen Kirche*, i. 61, 410 sqq., Bonn, 1887; Heimbucher, *Orden und Kongregationen*, ii. 564; *KL*, x. 1565.

SALMASIUS, sal-mē'shi-us, CLAUDIUS (CLAUDE DE SAUMAISE): French Protestant polyhistor; b. at Semuren-Auxois (128 m. s.e. of Paris) Apr. 15, 1588; d. at Spaa (18 m. s.e. of Liége), Belgium, Sept. 3, 1653. While a student of philosophy at Paris (1604–06), he professed Calvinism, and later studied jurisprudence at Heidelberg (1606–09). Returning to France, he became an advocate at Dijon, but feeling himself impeded in such a career by his Protestantism, he turned to literature, and quickly became renowned throughout Europe. He accepted, in 1632, the offer to succeed Joseph Scaliger at Leyden. Here his scope as an author spread constantly. At the height of his fame he defended the cause of the Stuarts and Charles I. against the commonwealth, in his anonymous *Defensio regia pro Carolo I.* (Leyden, 1649), which provoked the anger of Milton, to whom he replied in his posthumous *Ad Miltonum responsio* (Divione, 1660). In 1650 he accepted the call of Christina of Sweden to

Stockholm. In the following year, however, the climate and his controversies with Isaak Vossius and Nicolaus Heinsius caused him to return to Leyden, laden with gifts and honors from the queen.

His theological works deal with exegesis, church history, and canon law. To the first category belong his editions of Nilus' *De primatu papæ Romani* and Barlaam's *Monachi* (Hanau, 1608), and to the second his *Amici ad amicum de suburbicariis regionibus et ecclesiis suburbicariis epistola* (n.p., 1619) and also his *Eucharisticon Jacobo Sirmondo*—both in defense of Jacques Sirmond (q.v.) against Jacobus Gothofredus. Salmasius published an edition of Tertullian's *De pallio* (Paris, 1622), which led Petavius to write his pseudonymous *Antonii Kerkoetii animadversorum liber*, to which Salmasius replied in the *Confutatio animadversorum Antonii Cercætii, auctore Francisco Franco* (Middelburg, 1623). In 1638 the *De usuris* (Leyden, 1638) involved its author in strife with theologians and jurists. This was followed by the *De modo usurarum* (1639), *Diatriba de mutuo* (1640), and *Dissertatio de fœnore* (1640). Petavius assailed Salmasius in his *Dissertationes ecclesiasticæ*, and Salmasius answered in the pseudonymous *Walonis Messalini de episcopis et presbyteris* (1641), and in *De primatu papæ* (1645). In like manner he wrote, under the pseudonym of Simplicius Verinus, the *De transsubstantione* (The Hague, 1646). (G. LAUBMANN†).

BIBLIOGRAPHY: *Salmasii epistolarum liber I. Accedunt de laudibus et vita ejusdem prolegomena*, ed. A. Clementio, Leyden, 1656; J. Arnd, *Exercitatio de erroribus Salmasii in theologia*, Wittenberg, 1651, reproduced in G. H. Goetze, *Elogia Germanorum theologorum*, pp. 207–231, Lübeck, 1708; A. Vorst, *Oratio in excessum Salmasii*, ib. 1654; P. Papillon, *Bibliothèque des auteurs de Bourgogne*, ii. 247–286, Dijon, 1742; A. J. von der Aa, *Biographisch Woordenboek der Nederlanden*, xvii. 33–53, Haarlem, 1852 sqq.; É. and E. Haag, *La France protestante*, ix. 149–173, 10 vols., Paris, 2d ed., 1877 sqq.; E. Egger, *L'Hellenisme en France*, i. 227, Paris, 1869.

SALMERON, säl'me-rōn", **ALPHONSO:** Jesuit; b. at Toledo Oct. 8, 1515; d. at Naples Feb. 13, 1585. He studied at Alcala and Paris; joined Ignatius Loyola, 1534, and became one of the founders and most active members of the Society of Jesus. Fanatical in his resistance to the Reformation, he visited almost every country in Europe, was present at the Council of Trent as papal theologian, and wrote commentaries on most of the books of the New Testament (16 vols., Cologne, 1602–04, and after), which are more theological than exegetical.

BIBLIOGRAPHY: The two important lives are by G. Boero, Florence, 1880 (in Italian), and I. Torre, Barcelona, 1887 (in Spanish). Consult also *KL*, x. 1555–56; Vigouroux, *Dictionnaire*, fasc. xxxv. 1378–1379; and the literature under JESUITS.

SALMON, GEORGE: Church of Ireland; b. in Dublin Sept. 25, 1819; d. there Jan. 22, 1904. He was educated at Trinity College, Dublin (B.A., 1839; M.A., 1843), and was ordered deacon in 1844 and ordained priest in the following year. He was assistant to the regius professor of divinity at Dublin University (1845–66); senior assistant to the professor of mathematics and lecturer in the same subject (1848–66); and regius professor of divinity (1866–88). He was also junior dean in 1848, examining chaplain to the archbishop of Dublin in 1852–1864 and 1885–88, university preacher in 1852–55 and 1857–65, and deputy Archbishop King's lecturer in 1862. From 1888 until his death he was provost of Trinity College, Dublin, and from 1871 was also chancellor of St. Patrick's Cathedral, Dublin. He wrote, besides several volumes of collected sermons, *Historical Introduction to the Study of the Books of the New Testament* (1885); *The Infallibility of the Church* (1888); *Some Thoughts on the Textual Criticism of the New Testament* (1897); and *The Human Element in the Gospels. A Commentary of the Synoptic Narrative*, ed. N. J. D. White, London, 1907.

SALMOND, STEWART DINGWALL FORDYCE: Free Church of Scotland; b. at Aberdeen June 22, 1838; d. there Apr. 20, 1905. He was educated at King's College and the University, Aberdeen, and at Erlangen; was assistant professor of Greek, University of Aberdeen, 1861–64; classical examiner, 1864–67; minister at Barry, Forfarshire, 1865–76; professor of systematic theology and New-Testament exegesis in the Free Church College, Aberdeen, after 1876; and principal after 1898. He translated with notes parts of vols. vi., ix., xiv., and xx. of the *ANF* (Edinburgh, 1867–71), and of vols. viii. and ix. of transl. of Augustine (1873), and was author of a Commentary on the Epistles of Peter (New York, 1883), in Philip Schaff's *Popular Commentary on the New Testament;* on the Epistle of Jude (New York, 1890) in *The Pulpit Commentary;* on the Gospel of Mark (London, 1902) in the *Century Bible;* on Ephesians (1904); and of *The Life of the Apostle Peter* (Edinburgh, 1884); *An Exposition of the Shorter Catechism* (1884); *The Parables of our Lord* (1884); *The Life of Christ* (1887); and *The Sabbath* (1894)—the last four are included in *The Bible Class Primers*. He published also *The Christian Doctrine of Immortality* (Edinburgh, 1895; 4th rev. ed., 1901). He was editor of *The Bible Class Primers; The Critical Review of Current Theological and Philosophical Literature;* and coeditor with Dr. Charles A. Briggs of *The International Theological Library*.

SALOME. See HEROD AND HIS FAMILY, I., §§ 1, 3, 5, II., §§ 3, 6; JAMES I., 1.

SALT: Important both as a condiment and as an element in the Hebrew ritual of sacrifice. The Dead Sea rendered it easy for the ancient Hebrews to obtain salt (Gen. xiv. 3; Deut. iii. 17; Josh. iii. 16), and they obtained it also from the Mediterranean. Crystals of salt were found on the shore of the Dead Sea ready for gathering (cf. Ecclus. xliii. 19), and at the southern extremity of the same sea are beds of rock salt (cf. Gen. xix. 26; Wisd. of Sol., x. 7). The marshes in the vicinity of the Dead Sea have an incrustation of coarse salt when the water recedes each year (Ezek. xlvii. 11; Zeph. ii. 9). For many thousand years the tribes about the Dead Sea have driven a thriving trade in salt. According to I Macc. x. 29, xi. 35, a tax was levied on salt, of which the temple consumed immense quantities (Ezra vi. 7); supplies of salt could be obtained in the temple market by the worshipers (Ezra vi. 9, vii. 22). According to Josephus the salt of Sodom alone was used for the temple.

There are in the Bible a few allusions to salt as a seasoning (Job vi. 6). The prophet Elisha threw salt into an unhealthy well (II Kings ii. 19 sqq.). To eat one's salt (Ezra iv. 14) was the same as to eat a person's bread, and when a guest had tasted bread and salt, he was under the protection of the tribe. Salt was accordingly used in making a treaty, possibly as a symbol of purity combined with the inviolable relation established by eating the salt of a host. The covenant of salt could not be broken (Lev. ii. 13; Num. xviii. 19; II Chron. xiii. 5). What was salted, being preserved from corruption, could be regarded as ritually pure and as worthy to be dedicated to the deity. Herein lies the explanation of the use of salt in the ban and in the sacrifice. When the ban was placed upon a district, it was sown with salt to imply that the ground in question was dedicated to the divinity. It was extremely perilous to occupy land thus devoted to God (I Kings xvi. 34; cf. Josh. vi. 26). In like manner, an animal was sprinkled with salt to make it fit to be a burnt offering to Yahweh (Ezek. xliii. 44; Mark ix. 49). Though this ceremony is not mentioned in the older portions of the Bible, it may well have been practised at a very early period. The only allusions to salted sacrifices in early times are those of the meal offering (Lev. ii. 13) and of the shewbread (Lev. xxiv. 7, LXX.). The oriental custom of rubbing the new-born child with salt must be regarded as a religious ceremony to purify the infant defiled by contact with the impurity of childbirth and to dedicate the babe to God and protect it against demonic influence.

The Bible frequently alludes figuratively to the properties of salt. When Jesus terms the disciples "the salt of the earth," he regards them as a new purifying element to counteract moral foulness. Other allusions are to be found in Mark ix. 49–50; Luke xiv. 44; Col. iv. 6. The Hebrews were likewise acquainted with the fondness of cattle for salt (Isa. xxx. 24). The salt of Palestine is inferior to that of Europe, since it contains a larger proportion of gypsum, magnesia, and other minerals.

In the Roman Catholic Church salt is used in exorcism, and as the salt of wisdom is placed on the tongue at baptism. Salt is likewise put in holy water with reference to II Kings ii. 21–22, and the salt for cattle is duly blessed. (R. Zehnpfund.)

Bibliography: The two books of most value are H. C. Trumbull, *The Covenant of Salt*, New York, 1899 (not to be overlooked); and M. J. Schleiden, *Das Salz*, pp. 73 sqq., Leipsic, 1875. Consult further: Shalders, in *Expositor*, xi (1880), 79 sqq.; H. H. Wendt, *Teaching of Jesus*, ii. 63 sqq., London, 1892; Landberg, *Arabica*, v. 134–157, Leyden, 1898; U. Wilcken, *Griechische Ostraca aus Aegypten*, i. 141 sqq., Leipsic, 1899; F. Schwally, *Semitische Kriegsaltertümer*, p. 32, ib. 1901; Smith, *Rel. of Sem.*, p. 479; Wellhausen, *Heidentum*, pp. 124, 189; Benzinger, *Archäologie*, pp. 69, 115, 377–378; *DB*, iv. 353; *EB*, iv. 4247–50; *DCG*, ii. 1838–39; *KL*, x. 1585–1586; and the commentaries on the passages cited.

SALUTATIONS, HEBREW: The Hebrew salutation is in its essence an invocation of good fortune, joy, peace, the blessing of God (Gen. xxiv. 60, xlvii. 7). In form it was often a question after one's welfare (Gen. xliii. 27), and might be given in person, by letter, or by messenger, on arrival or at departure, or at a chance meeting on a journey (I Sam. xiii. 10; II Kings x. 15; II Sam. viii. 10). At least among later orientals greetings became so ceremonious and protracted that they constituted serious interruption (II Kings iv. 29; Luke x. 4); Jews seem not to have offered greetings to Gentiles (Matt. v. 47). The simplest formula was: Is it well? (II Sam. xx. 9), or: Peace be unto thee (Judges xix. 20); on departure the expression was: Go in peace (I Sam. i. 17). Specifically Hebraic was the blessing which contained the name of Yahweh (Ps. cxxix. 8). An honorific form is: Let the king live for ever (I Kings i. 31), employed in Babylonia, Persia, Phenicia, and Carthage.

The gestures which accompanied the salutation varied according to station both in degree and in the matter of repetition, and included the bowing of the head (I Kings i. 16), deep obeisance (Gen. xviii. 2; I Sam. xxiv. 9), and prostration (Gen. xlii. 6). A horseman dismounts when meeting a superior (Gen. xxiv. 64) and greets him with honorific bowing. Other forms, expressing humility, are kissing the feet and bowing the knee (Luke vii. 38; II Kings i. 13). Salutation, especially by a man of lower degree, was often accompanied by gifts (Gen. xxxiii. 11, xliii. 11), and in return gifts were made by the superior on departure (I Kings x. 10 sqq.). Other forms were kissing the hand, the beard, and the mouth, and embracing. The kiss upon the face, mouth, neck, and eyes were signs of friendship or of the love of kinship. (E. Leyrer†.)

Bibliography: C. M. Doughty, *Travels in Arabia Deserta*, passim, 2 vols., Cambridge, 1888; G. M. Mackie, *Bible Manners and Customs*, p. 150, London, 1900; Benzinger, *Archäologie*, p. 171; *DB*, ii. 263, iv. 356–357; *EB*, iv. 4252 sqq.; *JE*, vi. 88–90; *DCG*, i. 692–693; *KL*, v. 1318–1319.

SALVADOR. See Central America.

SALVATION: In Biblical and ecclesiastical language the purpose and result of the redeeming activity of God. Of the corresponding Hebrew expressions, *yesha* and *yeshu'ah* signify help in general; *marpe*, recovery from disease, but also in a broader sense deliverance of any kind (as, for instance, Jer. viii. 15; Mal. iii. 20, E. V., iv. 2). The Greek *sōtēria* (from *sōs*, "safe") means security of personal life by protection from any injury. This expression corresponds exactly to the German *Heil*, since Gothic *hails*, Old High Germ. *heil*, Eng. "whole," means "safe, sound, intact."

In Old-Testament prophecy the salvation of Israel, which is to be effected by God's saving deed, became the comprehensive expression of hope for the future and the content of the Messianic activity (see Messiah, Messianism). It means originally deliverance from hostile oppression and realization of lasting peace and welfare, but these external acts of salvation on the part of God are conditioned by the religious and moral attitude of the people (Isa. xlv. 22, lix. 20). Thus salvation can be realized fully only by an ideal religious and moral order of life through the remission of guilt (Isa. xxxiii. 24, xliii. 25) and moral renovation (Jer. xxxi. 33 sqq.). The spiritualization of the blessing of salvation was completed in the New Testament, where salvation denotes that forgiveness of sins which is mediated by Christ's redeeming activity, saves from judgment, and admits to God's kingdom (Luke i. 77). The basis of salvation is God's love (Rom. v. 8 sqq.). The means by which God effects the individual's salvation is the Gospel of Christ (Rom. i. 16; I Cor. i. 21). The condition of reception is faith (Rom. x. 9; John iii. 16).

For the changes in the ecclesiastical conception of salvation see REDEMPTION. In dogmatic language the term *salus* was not strictly defined. The older Protestant dogmaticians used it to express the total result of Christ's activity in the sense of redemption, but also for the share of the individual in redemption. After the *Loci theologici* had made room for a more logical disposition of dogmatic material, the doctrine of salvation (soteriology) became an independent part of the Christian system of doctrines. (O. KIRN.)

BIBLIOGRAPHY: R. H. Charles, *Critical History of the Doctrine of a Future Life*, London, 1899; G. F. Oehler, *Theology of the O. T.*, i. 27, ii. 309, Edinburgh, 1875; C. A. Briggs, *Messianic Prophecy*, New York, 1902; *JE*, x. 663–664; and, for the Christian conception, the literature under DOGMA.

SALVATION ARMY: An international organization having for its purpose the uplift of the morally, spiritually, and materially destitute. Its founder was William Booth (q.v.), who in 1865 commenced holding meetings in a disused burial-ground in London belonging to the Quakers. Its first name was the Christian Mission, which was changed in 1878 to the present name, with the accompaniment of military titles, uniforms, and paraphernalia. The new title seemed to express more fittingly the purpose of the organization, and also to infuse into the workers an esprit de corps while at the same time it caught the popular ear and gained a hearing which otherwise might not have been secured. The work extended in the notorious East End of London, and conversions were made which showed that a need had been met which was not supplied through the channels of ordinary church work. The growth of the work, which in 1878 had 81 corps, 127 officers, and 1,987 workers, aroused some opposition; but the opposition was overcome and the activities were extended to other parts of the metropolis, then out into the country and to the other large cities of England, over the entire United Kingdom, gained a footing upon the continent, then in the United States and Canada, into the British colonies in general, until at the present all western Europe, Iceland, Italy, India, Ceylon, Java, Japan, Korea, Australia and New Zealand, South Africa, South America, and several of the West Indies are occupied by the organization—in all fifty-four countries in which twenty-eight languages are used in the services. In 1910 the reports indicated for the entire organization 8,574 corps and outposts, 16,244 officers, cadets, and employees, and 56,867 local officers, and 21,681 bandsmen. It has received official recognition from several of the crowned heads of Europe, while in other quarters as exalted its work has been commended.

The basis of the army doctrinally is that of orthodox Christianity without the distinctions of sect. Its object includes the betterment in all worthy respects of those whom it can reach in its various ways. It discards all distinctions except those of piety and ability, men and women work side by side; while the ordinary conventionalities employed in the usual agencies of Christian work are, if the case demands, entirely disregarded. The specific directions its work takes are first religious, aiming at the conversion of those who are either indifferent to religion or are opposed to it; second, social, aiming to reach especially the poor and destitute. In carrying out its specifically missionary work, preaching and exhorting in the vernacular of the country are carried on in the open air, and also in the halls which are provided by voluntary offerings. As a result of this work many thousands of conversions are reported yearly, converts being gathered from all classes. The social work is very varied. It includes the establishment and maintenance of food and shelter depots and cheap restaurants for the poor. In these the Army cares for many thousands yearly, furnishing food and lodging, insisting upon cleanliness in person and habit while under the care of the institutions, while religious services are held regularly for the inmates. In close connection with this class of work is the home visitation in the poorer districts of the cities, the women entering the homes, ministering to the sick, supplying medicines, washing and dressing children for school, even cleansing the house and furniture, supplying food, and on occasion preparing the dead for burial. Work among prisoners, including the providing of employment upon their release, is an important branch of the work. The Army has also established orphanages, especially in rural districts, where the training of the children is both mental and industrial. It also maintains a network of industrial homes in connection with which work is furnished and the self-respect of the beneficiaries is fostered. Salesrooms are kept in connection with these in which articles suitable for use in the household are dispensed at prices which are a boon to the poor and worthy. Those who enter these homes are encouraged and helped to obtain work outside at the earliest possible moment, and thus the idea of almsgiving is eliminated so far as the nature of individual cases permits. Farm colonies have been established which supplement the other establishments for furnishing work to the needy. One of the most successful branches of the Army's operations is the rescue work for fallen women, in which twenty-two homes are maintained. It is claimed that between eighty and ninety per cent of the rescue cases prove to be permanent. Maternity wards are a part of the equipment of these homes. The Salvation Army has also employed its organization as a means for collecting and disbursing funds in great emergencies like those of the earthquake disasters at San Francisco and Messina and environs. A recognized practise with the Army is the furnishing of Christmas dinners to the poor and unemployed, in the United States alone 350,000 were the guests on a single Christmas. Its funds in the course of a year are large, $300,000 being spent in the single item of poor relief. A careful system of bookkeeping is in vogue, the accounts are regularly audited, and yearly reports are issued and filed in accordance with the requirements of the laws under which the Army is incorporated.

[In Germany in 1911 the army reports 190 stations, with twenty-eight institutions for social betterment, including twelve homes for men, seven rescue homes for women, and three "Samaritan homes," besides kindergartens and other organized means of help.]

In the United States work was begun in 1880 by Commissioner George Railton and seven women officers. It reports 896 corps and outposts, 3,875 officers and employees, 75 workingmen's hotels, 4 women's hotels, and in these accommodation for 6,592 is furnished nightly, and 1,961,677 beds each year, 20 food depots, 107 industrial homes, 3 farm colonies with 2,000 colonised and 350 colonists; there are 20 employment bureaus which furnish work for 1,500 persons each month, 107 second-hand stores, 4 children's homes, 4 day-nurseries, and 23 slum settlements. In a single year in the United States 309,591 persons were afforded temporary relief, summer outings were given to 3,972 mothers and 24,373 children, employment was found for 65,124 men and 5,355 women, 1,593,834 pounds of ice and 4,579,788 pounds of coal were distributed. Regular visitation of prisons, workhouses, and hospitals is also carried on. At the Paris Exposition a gold medal was awarded the organization for the United States exhibit of the Salvation Army's operations among the poor. WM. H. COX.

BIBLIOGRAPHY: Besides the literature by members of the Booth family (see BOOTH, CATHERINE MUMFORD, and WILLIAM, and BOOTH TUCKER, EMMA MOSS, and FREDERICK ST. GEORGE DE LATOUR), which is currently published and obtainable at the principal Salvation Army depots, and the literature under the articles on the Booths, consult: J. E. Butler, *The Salvation Army in Switzerland*, London, 1883; T. Kolde, *Die Heilsarmee*, Erlangen, 1885; I. Pestalozzi, *Was ist die Heils-Armee*, Halle, 1886; E. R. Swift, *Drum Taps*, London, 1887; J. O. Bairstow, *Sensational Religion*, London, 1890; B. Booth, *From Ocean to Ocean; or, the Salvation Army's March from the Atlantic to the Pacific*, New York, 1891; J. Fehr, *Die Heilsarmee*, Frankfort, 1891; Sir W. Besant, *The Farm and the City. A Study of the social Work of the Salvation Army*, London, 1900; J. Page, *General Booth*, ib. 1901; G. S. Railton, *Hist. of our South American War*, ib. 1902; J. Hollins, *The Salvation Army: a Study of its Defects and Possibilities*, ib. 1903; F. St. G. de L. Booth Tucker, *The Consul: a Sketch of Emma Booth-Tucker*, ib. 1904; H. R. Haggard, *The Poor and the Land; a Report on the Salvation Army Colonies*, ib. 1905; idem, *Regeneration; being an Account of the Social Work of the Salvation Army in Great Britain*, ib. 1910; A. Goodrich, *Life and Work of General Booth; Story of the Salvation Army*, ib. 1906; J. Manson, *Salvation Army and the Public; a religious, social and financial Study*, New York, 1907 (criticises Army's methods in Great Britain); Hulda Friederichs, *The Romance of the Salvation Army*, London, 1908; G. S. Railton, *Day by Day in the Salvation Army. Being a brief Account of Salvation Army Work in various Countries*, ib. 1910; *Orders and Regulations for Field Officers*, ib. 1886; *Salvation Army Year Book*, annually published at London.

SALVIANUS, sal-vi-ē'nus: Presbyter of Marseilles; b. probably at Treves about 400; d. after 480. He came of a highly respected, and probably Christian, family, but married a pagan wife. After her conversion, the pair bound themselves to continence. Salvianus' ascetic tendencies opened the way for him to the monastic circles of southern Gaul, where he formed a close friendship with Eucherius, later bishop of Lyons. During the latter portion of his life Salvianus was a presbyter at Marseilles.

Gennadius (*De vir. ill.*, lxviii.) knew of the following writings of Salvianus: *De virginitatis bono ad Marcellum presbyterum; Adversus avaritiam; De præsenti judicio*, and *Pro eorum merito satisfactionis ad Salonium episcopum* (the latter title apparently corrupt). Of these, except for nine letters, only the *Adversus avaritiam* and the *De præsenti judicio* (usually known as the *De gubernatione Dei*) are extant (ed. C. Halm, *MGH*, *Auct. ant.*, I., i. 1877; F. Pauly, *CSEL*, viii.). The letters are fragments of a collection which was originally large. Of the other two works the *Adversus avaritiam* is the older. It appeared pseudonymously as *Timothei ad ecclesiam libri quatuor*, and contributes to knowledge of the moral ideals of monasticism in the fifth century, and of the gulf between ordinary Christians and ascetics. Stress is laid by Salvianus on poverty, i.e., on the communism of the primitive Church. The religious were urged to renounce their earthly possessions and were exhorted to leave their wealth to the Church, this being recommended for the moral effect which such action would produce. The *De gubernatione* passes judgment on contemporary conditions from the same point of view, and was written, in all probability, between 439 and 451. Gennadius, about 480, knew of only five books, but the work as now extant breaks off abruptly in the eighth book. Its purpose is to show why God, in the struggle between the Empire and the barbarians, seemed to take the side of Arians or pagans against Catholics. This was due to divine judgment on the degeneracy of the Romans, a thought ever reiterated by the author. Yet his very unworldliness freed him from many of the prejudices of his time. He could be fair to pagans, and even to heretics; and was as exempt from contempt for barbarians and slaves as he was unbiased in judgment on the Romans and the rich. He was keenly aware of the evil conditions of social and economic affairs, and in this lies the historical value of his pictures of the period. (A. HAUCK.)

BIBLIOGRAPHY: W. Zschimmer, *Salvianus, der Presbyter von Massilia, und seine Schriften*, Halle, 1875; F. X. Hirner, *Commentatio de Salviano ejusque libellis*, Freising, 1869; A. Ebert, *Allgemeine Geschichte der Literatur des Mittelalters*, i. 459 sqq., Leipsic, 1889; J. B. Ullrich, *De Salviani scripturæ sacræ versionibus*, Neustadt, 1892; A. Hämmerle, *Studien zu Salvian, Priester von Massilia*, Landshut, 1893; G. Valran, *Quare Salvianus presbyter Massiliensis magister episcoporum a Gennadio dictus sit*, Paris, 1899; F. Pauly, in the *Sitzungsberichte* of the Vienna Academy, xcviii., part 1; Bardenhewer, *Patrologie*, pp. 533–535, Eng. transl., St. Louis, 1908; *Hist. littéraire de la France*, ii. 517 sqq.; *DCB*, iv. 580; Hauck, *KD*, i. 66–71; Schaff, *Christian Church*, iii. 88–89.

SALVIUS: Name of several bishops.

1. Donatist bishop of Membresa (Membrissa, Membressa; 45 m. from Carthage) in the last decade of the fourth century. He was one of the ordainers of Maximianus and practised rebaptism (Augustine, *Contra epistolam Parmiani*, iii. 22), was deposed as a heretic, but resisted and the civil power was called in to execute the decision. Salvius was greatly beloved by his townsmen, consequently the populace of a neighboring town (Abitina) forcibly carried out the decree (398), so heaping insults and contumely as to lead Augustine strongly to condemn it (Augustine, ut sup., iii. 29). This father often refers to his case.

2. Fifth bishop of Martigny in Switzerland; flourished in the middle of the fifth century. To him Eucherius (q.v.), bishop of Lyons, addressed the history of St. Maurice (q.v.), and Salvius responded by dedicating to Eucherius his only extant work, the *Laticulus* (in part printed in *ASB*, Jan., i. 43–44, June, vii. 178 sqq.; and in *MPL*, xiii. 671 sqq.; cf. *Histoire littéraire de la France*, ii. 294–296; and Ceillier, *Auteurs sacrés*, viii. 452), a calendar of things sacred and profane.

3. Bishop of Alby; d. c. 584. He was an intimate of Gregory of Tours (q.v.), began life as an advocate, but was converted, became a monk, then abbot, and had a vision of heaven which Gregory relates (*Hist. Francorum*, vii. 1). Gregory speaks of him as a man of great sanctity and incessant charity, and the church at Nevers (as also another) was dedicated to him (*ASB*, Sept., iii. 575 sqq.).

SALZBURG, sälts'bŭrg, **ARCHDIOCESE OF:** An Austrian archbishopric, the see city of which is Salzburg, the Juvavum of the Romans, who reduced it, together with the rest of the province of Noricum, during the campaign of Tiberius and Drusus in 15 B.C. The original Celtic population was quickly Romanized, and Christianity early found entrance, doubtless from Aquileia, although there are no certain records of the new faith in the city previous to Constantine. After the withdrawal of the Romans, Salzburg, which evidently had not become an episcopal city during this period, fell into decay, nor did its medieval history begin until the time of St. Rupert (q.v.). The diocese was first formally organized by St. Boniface (q.v.) in 739, although it was not until 987 that the dignities of bishop or archbishop of Salzburg and abbot of St. Peter's were made distinct. In 798 Salzburg was elevated to archiepiscopal rank by Charlemagne, its jurisdiction embracing the sees of Regensburg, Passau, Freising, Seben, and the short-lived Neuburg. It was, accordingly, the largest German archbishopric next to Mainz, its boundaries being the Inn on the west and the Drau on the south, while on the north and east it practically coincided with the present northern boundary of Salzburg and Styria and with the eastern boundary of Styria.

(A. Hauck.)

Throughout its history the archdiocese of Salzburg remained true to the Roman Catholic Church, its rigorous treatment of Protestants exposing it to much criticism from adherents of the newer doctrines (see Salzburg, Evangelicals of). In 1802 the archdiocese was secularized, and after belonging in turn to Germany, Austria, and Bavaria, finally passed, in 1814, under the control of the latter country. The archdiocese was reerected in 1824, after having been vacant since 1812, and now exercises jurisdiction over the dioceses of Trient, Brixen, Gurk, Seckau, and Lavant. In 1909 it had a population of 263,080 Roman Catholics and 1,637 Protestants, 491 secular and 130 regular clergy, 183 parishes, and a theological faculty in the see city.

Bibliography: Sources are contained in *MGH*, *Script.*, i (1826), 86 sqq., ix (1851), 757 sqq., xi (1854), 1 sqq., 25 sqq., xiii (1881), 353 sqq.; ib. *Nec.*, ii (1890), 45 sqq.; ib. *Leg.*, II., *Cap. reg. Franc.*, i (1883), 226; *Salzburger Urkundenbuch*, ed. W. Hauthaler, Salzburg, 1898; *Regesta archiepiscoporum Salisburgensium*, ed. A. von Meiller, Vienna, 1866. Consult: M. Hansiz, *Germania sacra*, vol. ii., Augsburg, 1729; G. A. Pichler, *Salzburgs Landesgeschichte*, Salzburg, 1865; H. G. Gengler, *Beiträge zur Rechtsgeschichte Bayerns*, part 1, Erlangen, 1889; F. von Piche, *Abhandlungen über die älteste Geschichte Salzburgs*, Innsbruck, 1889; J. Loserth, *Salzburg und Steiermark im letzten Viertel des 16. Jahrhunderts*, Graz, 1905; H. Widmann, *Geschichte Salzburgs*, 2 vols., Gotha, 1907–09 (goes to 1519); Gams, *Series episcoporum*, pp. 307–327; *KL*, x. 1586–1642.

SALZBURG, EVANGELICALS OF: The name applied to several thousand Protestants expelled from the Archbishopric of Salzburg (q.v.) in the eighteenth century.

Initial Movements for Repression.

Protestantism early penetrated this region, especially the Salzachthal and its vicinity. Matthæus Lang, archbishop of Salzburg at the time of the Reformation, was at first not hostile to the new movement. He gave favorable reception to Johann von Staupitz, Paulus Speratus, Urbanus Rhegius, and Wolfgang Russ, and gained the approval of Luther. But before long he changed his attitude, in consequence of favors from the Curia. He now roused enmity between Luther and Staupitz, energetically opposed the Protestant preachers, and in 1520 obliged Speratus and Agricola (qq.v.) to flee. A certain Matthæus was captured, and an ex-Franciscan, Georg Schärer, was beheaded for contumacy. In spite of every effort on the part of Lang and his successors, Protestantism steadily increased; exile and visitation were alike in vain; many of the clergy broke their vows of celibacy. Yielding to repeated demands, Archbishop Johann Jakob granted the laity the cup, but was obliged by the Curia to retract his position. In 1588 Archbishop Wolfgang Dieterich visited Rome for instructions, and on his return issued a "Reformation mandate" in which he commanded all Protestants of the city of Salzburg either to recant or to leave the country within a month, permission being given the recalcitrant to convert their property into money. Since, however, nearly all preferred exile to recantation, a second mandate was issued confiscating their property. In consequence of these measures, many of the wealthiest inhabitants of Salzburg emigrated to Austria, Saxony, and elsewhere, while others, outwardly complying with Roman Catholicism, secretly adhered to Luther's teachings. In 1613–15 the mandates were extended by Archbishop Markus Sittich to the entire region in view of the increase of Protestantism. Throughout Pongau the churches stood empty, while the people thronged to Schladming in Styria to attend Lutheran gatherings; and in Radstadt, where the Protestants were in the majority, they demanded from the archbishop preachers of their own.

Persecution 1615–1727.

The archbishop increased the sternness of his measures to crush the Protestant movement. Capuchins sought in vain to restore the Evangelicals to the Roman Catholic Church, whereupon the Protestants were required to recant within four weeks or fourteen days, or to be banished with confiscation of their goods. At the same time, search was made for Protestant books, and imprisonment was enacted for those who circulated such writings. Finally, the Evangelicals were subjected to the dragonnade, many of whom feigned submission, though secretly maintaining Lutheran views. A considerable number went into exile and poverty, some 600 going from Radstadt and its vicinity to Austria and Moravia. Of 2,500 in the valleys and on the mountains of Gastein only about 300 promised to live and die in the Roman Catholic Church. The archbishop, however, was deceived by appearances. Public gatherings indeed ceased, but many of those who ostensibly professed the old faith secretly read Lutheran works which they had concealed. The children were instructed in Lutheran doctrines, and Protestantism spread under cover. This was especially the case under the mild Archbishop Paris Hadrian (1619–53), and after the peace of Westphalia Protestants sentenced to exile from Roman Catholic countries were allowed three years in which to dispose of their property. Nevertheless, these prerogatives were disregarded by Archbishop Maximilian Gandolf (1668–87). In 1683 Jesuits discovered a congregation of secret Lutherans, ostensibly professing Roman Catholicism, in the Tefferegg Valley on the southern boundary of the archdiocese. Attempts at conversion by Capuchin monks and judicial endeavors to suppress Lutheranism led only to a more stubborn adherence to their beliefs under the guidance of the miner Joseph Schaitberger (q.v.). The archbishop sought to prove that these Protestants did not come under the protection of the peace of Westphalia in that they were a sect adhering neither to the Augsburg nor the Reformed confession, but their representatives, when summoned to Hallein and Salzburg, boldly declared themselves Lutherans. After being imprisoned and made the objects of vain attempts at conversion by Capuchins, they were released, the archbishop requiring them to submit a written statement of their belief. Sterner measures followed without success, and the archbishop finally issued a mandate in the middle of the winter of 1685 banishing the Protestants from the country, and confiscating their property and children, some 600 in number. The exiles in bands of fifty or sixty sought refuge in Ulm, Augsburg, Nuremberg, Frankfort, and elsewhere, the total number of those banished being over 1,000. This act of the archbishop horrified all Protestant Germany, but neither the intervention of Elector Frederick William of Brandenburg nor the protests of the Evangelical estates in Regensburg were of avail. Under Archbishop Franz Anton (1709–27) the Salzburg Protestants fared better, and during this period Evangelical doctrines were strengthened in the region by reading Protestant books and the letters of Schaitberger, as well as by the religious meetings which were tolerated.

Increased Pressure 1727–31.

Under his successor, Leopold Anton (1727–44), however, affairs resumed their wonted course. Feigned conversions were extorted; their Bibles and books of edification were burned; they were charged with being dangerous inciters to riot; they were imprisoned, deprived of work, fined, dragonaded, and compelled to emigrate leaving property and children behind. Yet all this only increased the determination of the Salzburg Protestants. In Jan., 1730, the peasants Hans Lerchner and Veit Breme appealed to the Evangelical estates in Regensburg and sought for influence to be brought to bear that the exiles might be allowed to regain their wives and children. All was in vain, even the charge that the archbishop had violated the peace of Westphalia. In the following year the Protestants sent a deputation from Radstadt, Wagrein, Werffen, St. Johann, and Gastein to Regensburg with new complaints, and with the demand that either Evangelical preachers be given them and that they be permitted to worship in their own way, or that they be allowed to sell their property and emigrate with their wives and children. Again their demands were fruitless. Meanwhile the archbishop, seeking to determine how far Protestantism had spread, ordered that the complaints be tried before a committee. All Protestants were now summoned to appear before the commissioners sent out from Salzburg, whereupon they declared that they were willing to be the faithful subjects of the archbishop in all things temporal, but that in religion they desired freedom of conscience. The commissioners thereupon required within three days a list of all those who professed Lutheranism, the total, to the amazement of all, being over 20,000. The archbishop accordingly saw himself obliged to put forth his utmost endeavors, while the Protestants became still more firm in their resistance. On Aug. 5, 1731, about 300 representative Lutherans took a solemn oath in the town of Swarzach, and it was quickly resolved to send a committee to the emperor at Vienna. The envoys, having no passports, however, were arrested as rebels and brought back to Salzburg. Since no relief could be expected from either the archbishop or the emperor, the Lutheran envoys sought the intervention of their princes. Frederick William I. of Prussia accordingly threatened reprisals on his Roman Catholic subjects, but the threat was an empty one, and rigorous measures against the Salzburg Protestants were renewed. The Evangelicals again appealed to the emperor, who declared he had warned the archbishop to obey the laws of the empire. On Oct. 31, 1731, the archbishop issued an order requiring all non-householders over twelve years of age to emigrate within eight days as being disobedient and leagued to destroy the Roman Catholic faith. All others were to follow them into exile within one to three months. The plan of thus financially ruining the well-to-do and forcibly converting their dependents failed with but few exceptions.

Emigration to Prussia.

Meanwhile two Protestant delegates, Peter Heldensteiner and Nikolaus Forstreuter, had implored the aid of the king at Berlin in Nov., 1731. In February of the following year he issued a patent welcoming the exiles from Salzburg, requesting the archbishop to allow them to depart freely, and urging all princes through whose lands they should go to aid them. He himself promised each person a considerable sum daily for expenses, and at the same time threatened severe reprisals for any injury done them, being followed in the latter respect by Denmark, Sweden, and Holland. The exiles now thronged into Germany, everywhere joyfully welcomed by their fellow Protestants. The 4,000 who first came were quickly followed by several thousand more, so that from Apr. 30, 1732, to Apr. 15, 1733, no less than 14,728 passed through Berlin alone on their way to Lithuania, increasing the spirit of German Lutheranism as they went. A collection was raised for them in all Protestant countries at the instance of the king of England, which amounted to 900,000 gulden. Thus more than 20,000 exiles from Salzburg repopulated the wide Lithuanian plains devastated by a pestilence, and the Prussian king was richly repaid by the agricultural benefits received from his industrious and intelligent immigrants. (D. ERDMANN†.)

BIBLIOGRAPHY: C. F. Arnold, *Die Ausrottung des Protestantismus in Salzburg unter Erzbischof Firmian*, Halle, 2 parts, 1900–1901; idem, *Vertreibung der Salzburger Protestanten und ihre Aufnahme bei dem Glaubensgenossen*, Leipsic, 1900; S. Urlsperger, *Ausführliche Nachricht von den Salzburger Emigranten*, Halle, 1735; J. L. von Caspari, *Actenmässige Geschichte der Salzburger Emigranten*, Salzburg, 1790; J. K. F. Obstfelder, *Die evangelischen Salzburger*, Naumburg, 1857; L. Clarus, *Die Auswanderung der protestantisch-gesinnten Salzburger*, Innsbruck, 1864; T. Förster, *Die evangelischen Salzburger*, Halle, 1884; A. Hoese and H. Eichert, *Die Salzburger. Geschichte der im Jahre 1732 in Littauen eingewanderten Salzburger*, Gumbinnen, 1902; C. Blume, *Die Vertreibung der evangelischen Salzburger*, Leipsic, 1904; G. Nieritz, *Die protestantischen Salzburger und deren Vertreibung*, Constance, 1907. A bibliography is provided in E. Dannappel, *Die Literatur der Salzburger Emigration, 1732–36*, Stuttgart, 1886.

SAM (SOM, SAUM), KONRAD: Reformer of Ulm; b. at Rottenacker (15 m. s.w. of Ulm) 1483; d. at Ulm June 20, 1533. After studying at Freiburg, Tübingen, and some other university (perhaps Basel), he became parish preacher at Brackenheim in Württemberg in 1520. He was already an adherent of the Reformation, and his advocacy of the new doctrines exposed him to such hostility that only the encouragement of Luther kept him from resigning his position. In May, 1524, however, he was dismissed, ostensibly for harboring Johann Eberlin (q.v.), whereupon his stepbrother, Sebastian Fischer, secured for him an appointment at Ulm "to preach the word of God in purity without the addition of the doctrines of men, in peace and without strife." Despite his many excellent qualities, he lacked the power of organization and was both harsh and violent, and his position was complicated by his estrangement from Luther, with a corresponding attraction to Œcolampadius and Zwingli. Nevertheless, Sam soon enjoyed high favor throughout Upper Swabia, gaining entire control of the church in Ulm in 1526 and also furthering the cause of the Reformation in Memmingen. In the same year the course adopted by the Diet of Speyer encouraged the magistracy of Ulm to proceed with the work of the Reformation in their city, and private baptism and the marriage of the clergy were now permitted, Sam himself taking advantage of this opportunity to make public his union with a Bavarian woman. In 1528 the new schoolmaster, Michael Brodhag of Göppingen, published Sam's *Christenliche vnderweysung der Jungen*, a catechism based on the 130 questions of Agricola, as well as on Capito and Althamer, but omitting all discussion of the sacraments. A hymnal and a German Psalter followed in 1529, but, on the other hand, Anabaptism was rife, and the introduction of Protestant communion was forbidden as late as Feb., 1530. Meanwhile Sam was inveighing rabidly against both Roman Catholic and Lutheran eucharistic doctrine, his words incurring the opposition of the Protestant Billican and Althamer (qq.v.) and the Roman Catholic Johann Faber (q.v.), and Johann Ulrici. Johann Eck (q.v.) now demanded the removal of Sam, whom he challenged to a disputation, and the Ulm magistracy in perplexity appealed to Nuremberg, which advised that Sam be dismissed. The council, however, not only permitted Sam to attend the disputation at Bern, but remained wavering between the Swiss and Saxon types of doctrine. After the Diet of Speyer in 1529 Ulm decided to join the Schmalkald League, and at Augsburg it refused to accept either the Augsburg or the Tetrapolitan Confession. Sam, in disgust, thought of leaving Ulm, but the decision of the Diet of Augsburg (1530) brought matters to a crisis; Ulm went over to the Schmalkald League; the municipality determined to carry out the Reformation; and, at the instance of Sam, Œcolampadius was summoned from Basel, Butzer from Strasburg, and Blaurer from Constance. On June 16, 1531, mass was abolished, and exactly a month later the Lord's Supper was celebrated in Protestant fashion. On Aug. 6 a new agenda, similar to that of Basel, was promulgated, but though after Œcolampadius and Butzer returned home (Blaurer remaining to promote the Reformation in Geislingen) other men were called to Ulm to take their places, a heavy burden still rested upon Sam. The zeal of the people and of the council relaxed, the Roman Catholics and the Anabaptists redoubled their activity, it proved difficult to secure capable preachers, the magistracy ruled the Church arbitrarily, and the deaths of Œcolampadius and Zwingli were severe blows to the Protestants in Ulm. The latter now sought Lutheran support, and at a conference held at Schweinfurt in Apr., 1532, they determined, in Sam's presence, to accept the Augsburg Confession and Apology. Sam was intensely embittered, especially against Luther, but within the year he fell ill, and between March and June, 1533, had three strokes of apoplexy, succumbing to the third. Sam's catechism was reprinted, with a chapter on the sacraments and revised in a Zwinglian spirit, at Augsburg in 1540; his sermon at the disputation of Bern was printed by K. Schmid in his *Die Predigen so vonn den frömbden Predicanten . . . beschehen sind* (Bern, 1528); his three last sermons, *Davids Ehebruch, Mord, Strafe, und Busse*, appeared at Ulm in 1534; and in 1569 his communion sermon at Ulm in 1526 was reprinted by the Heidelberg theologians. G. BOSSERT.

BIBLIOGRAPHY: G. Veesenmeyer, *Nachrichten von Konrad Sams Leben*, Ulm, 1795; idem, *Versuch einer Geschichte des deutschen Kirchengesanges in der Ulmer Kirche*, ib. 1798; idem, *Denkmal der einheimischen und fremden Theologen . . . in Ulm*, ib. 1831; A. Weyermann, *Nachrichten von Gelehrten . . . aus Ulm*, Bern, 1798; T. Keim, *Die Reformation der Reichstadt Ulm*, Stuttgart, 1851; F. Dobel, *Memmingen in der Reformationszeit*, Augsburg, 1877; T. Schiess, *Briefwechsel der Brüder Ambrosius und Thomas Blaurer (1509–48)*, 2 vols., Freiburg, 1908–10; *ADB*, xxx. 304–305.

SAMARIA sa-mē'ri-a, SAMARITANS.

I. The Region: Samaria denotes both the central region of Palestine, between Judea and Galilee, and the capital of this district. From the time of Omri the city of Samaria became the capital of the northern kingdom of Israel, so that the city-name was extended to the entire country (e.g., I Kings xiii. 32; II Kings xvii. 24, 26, 28; Jer. xxxi. 5; Hos. vii. 1; Amos viii. 14).

1. Name and History.

The people dwelling in the land of Samaria were called Samaritans (II Kings xvii. 29). A similar usage is found in the Assyrian *Samerina*, connoting both the city and the land. When the city received the name of Sebaste from Herod the Great in 27 B.C., Samaria was in application restricted to the district. The Arab conquest destroyed all traces of the name, except among occidentals and in learned language. The oldest form of the name, given in the Massoretic text as *Shomeron*, seems to have *Shameran* (cf. I Kings xvi. 24, and the Assyr. *Samerina*, the Aram. *Shamerayin* of Ezra iv. 10, 17, and the Gk. *Samareia*). Originally synonymous with the kingdom of Israel, the area of Samaria varied with the fortunes of that kingdom. In 734–733 Tiglath-pileser so limited the territory that Hoshea retained only the small district from Judah to the plain of Jesreel (cf. II Kings xv. 29, xvii. 24 sqq.; Ezra iv. 10). The rapid decline of Assyria after 640 seems to have enabled Judah to extend its power over this region (cf. II Kings xxiii. 15, 19 sqq.; II Chron. xxxiv. 6–7), which it quickly lost after the battle of Megiddo (608). The Seleucid Demetrius II. detached three districts hitherto belonging to Samaria (Apherema, Lydda, and Ramathaim) and gave them to the Hasmonean Jonathan (145 B.C.). In 128 B.C. John Hyrcanus subdued the whole of Samaria and united it with the Judean kingdom; but in 63 B.C. Pompey freed Samaria and incorporated it with the new province of Syria. "Samaria" in this case means the city and the region from Judah to the plain of Jesreel, excepting Scythopolis and Carmel. In 30 B.C. Herod received Samaria from Augustus, and after the tetrarch's death it, together with Judea and Idumea, was placed under the control of his son Archelaus. In 6 A.D. these three districts formed part of the province of Syria, though they were governed by a special procurator at Cæsarea, except in 41–44, when Samaria and its vicinity were in the dominion of Agrippa. On the outbreak of the Jewish revolt, Samaria was given to Vespasian as a part of the province of Judea, and its fortunes were henceforth identical with those of Palestine.

The boundaries of Samaria to the east and west may be regarded as the Jordan and the declivities of the mountain district respectively. During the period of the dominion of Israel the mountain district was inhabited by the tribes of Ephraim and Manasseh (Josh. xvi.–xvii.); Josh. xvii. 14–18 implies that the tribe of Joseph spread to the southern region west of the Jordan.

2. Area and Roads.

Josh. xvii. 16, 18 implies another advance of the tribe of Joseph, this time to the north, possibly to the southern border of the great plain to the range of Yazid. Here lay, according to Judges i., the cities of Beth-shean, Ibleam, Taanach, Megiddo, and Dor, which later came under the sway of Israel, even though they were not actually occupied by Israelitic stocks (Josh. xvii. 11–13). According to Josh. xvii. 11, the district of Manasseh extended along the southern side of the plain of Jezreel from the Jordan (Beth-shean) to the Mediterranean (Dor), and was consequently more than thirty-six miles wide. The length of the district of Ephraim was from north to south between twenty-one and twenty-four miles and the territory embraced the richest and most fertile portions of the mountain district (Josh. xvi. 6–8, xvii. 7–10; cf. Deut. xxxiii. 13–16). The region of Ephraim, whose southern boundary has been given in the article JUDEA (q.v.), stretched eighteen miles from north to south, and thirty miles from the Jordan on the east to the plain of Sharon on the west. It was thus inferior to Manasseh both in area and in fertility. Apparently there was no strict line of demarcation between the districts of Manasseh and of Ephraim (Josh. xvi. 9, xvii. 8). Samaria was crossed by important highways. The continuation of the road to the coast cut through the northwest corner of Samaria from Megiddo in the direction of Lydda; and another branch of the same road reached Samaria by way of Jezreel near the present Janin, where it again divided. One of these latter roads reached the highway to Egypt at Kafr Kud, while the other ran southward to the cities of Samaria and Shechem. Shechem was at the junction of several important roads. From the south came the road from Judea (Jerusalem) by way of Bethel, from the southwest a road from Jaffa, and from the southeast a road from Jericho by way of the Wadi al-Ḥumr and the plain of al-Maḥnah. To the northwest, through the Wadi al-Sha'ir, a road led to Dor and later to Cæsarea, while to the northeast ran a road to Scythopolis, which was joined in the upper portion of the Wadi Far'ah by a road from the ford of the Jordan near Adama. The southern ranges of Samaria, on the other hand, were far less accessible.

The ancient center of the district was Shechem, which lay on the watershed not quite a mile east of the modern Nablus. Its pre-Israelitic inhabitants are termed Canaanites by J (Gen. xii. 6, xxxiv. 30), Amorites by E (Gen. xlviii. 22), and Hivites by P (Gen. xxxiv. 2); and many contests for its possession seem to have been waged between Israel and the Canaanites.

3. Shechem and Neighboring Cities.

The religious importance of Shechem is implied by Gen. xxxiii. 19–20, according to which Jacob there purchased ground and erected an altar to Yahweh; it was also the place of Joseph's burial (Josh. xxiv. 32). Another sacred place at Shechem seems to have been the oak mentioned in Gen. xii. 6–7, xxxv. 4; Deut. xi. 30; Josh. xxiv. 26 (possibly also Judges ix. 6, 37); while assemblies of the people gathered in its sanctuary (Josh. xxiv. 1; I Kings xii. 1; II Chron. x. 1). In the vicinity of the city was the well of Jacob (John iv. 6), the modern Bir Ya'kub at the foot of Gerizim, almost south of the village of Balaṭa. In the beginning of the historical period Shechem, though dependent on Gideon, was not occupied by Israel (Judges viii. 31, ix. 1–2). When it revolted against Abimelech, it was destroyed (Judges ix. 23 sqq.). The city then came under the control of Manasseh (Num. xxvi. 31; Josh. xvii. 2). Jeroboam I. fortified it and made it the royal seat (I Kings xii. 25), thus the city could justly be reckoned to Ephraim (Josh. xx. 7, xxi. 21; I Chron. vii. 28). The successor of the Biblical Shechem was Flavia Neapolis, founded by Vespasian in 72 A.D., the modern Nablus in the valley between Ebal and Gerizim. Sychar, the city nearest to the well of Jacob (John iv. 5–6), is usually identified with the modern village of 'Askar, a mile or two east of Nablus and over half a mile north of Jacob's well. The Gilgal of Deut. xi. 30; II Kings ii. 1, iv. 38, is frequently identified with the small ruin Ḥirbat al-Julaijil on the southern edge of the plain of al-Maḥnah, but without sufficient reason. On the road to 'Aḳrabah, two hours southeast of Nablus, lies the lofty village of al-'Aurma, perhaps identical with the Arumah of Judges ix. 41; while the little village of Far'ata, six miles west of Nablus, is doubtless the Pirathon of Judges xii. 13 sqq.; II Sam. xxiii. 30; I Chron. xxvii. 14, though scarcely the Pharathoni fortified by Bacchides c. 160 B.C. (I Macc. ix. 50). The village of Ḳaryat Jitt, three miles further north, is plainly synonymous with the Gitto (I Apol. xxvi., Eng. transl., *ANF*, i. 171) designated by Justin Martyr as the home of Simon Magus, though the name also occurs at the foot of the mountain district. About nine miles distant, on the road to Jaffa, is the site of Kafr Tilt, which has been identified with the Shalisha of I Sam. ix. 4 and II Kings iv. 42.

In the region north of Shechem the city of Samaria first deserves notice. The hill on which the city lay was connected to the northeast with the opposite heights by a narrow ridge, but was separated on all other sides by wide valleys (Isa. xxviii. 1).

4. The City Samaria.

It had easy access to all important points, such as Shechem in the southeast and the plain of Jezreel in the north. The city contained altars of Yahweh (Micah i. 5) and—after the reign of Ahab—of Baal (I Kings xvi. 32; cf. II Kings xiii. 6); and as early as Omri the Arameans of Damascus had their own quarter for trade there (I Kings xx. 34). During the reign of Ahab the city was beleaguered by the Arameans (I Kings xx. 1 sqq.; cf. II Kings vi. 24–vii. 20). Jehu, after his entry into Samaria, had the prophets and priests of Baal slain, and the idolatrous sites destroyed and desecrated (II Kings x. 1–7, 18–27; II Chron. xxii. 8–9). The last king, Hoshea, was shut up in Samaria by Shalmaneser IV. in 724 B.C. (II Kings xvii. 5, xviii. 9), though the city was reduced under Sargon. On his return from Egypt in 331, Alexander the Great Hellenized the city, but Ptolemy Lagos rased it in 312, and Demetrius Poliorcetes again destroyed it in 296. In 27 B.C. Samaria was rebuilt by Herod, who named it Sebaste, and it was the scene of the preaching of Philip (Acts viii. 5–7). Under Septimius Severus the city became a Roman colony, but it became second in importance to Neapolis, though having its own bishops. The Crusaders erected a magnificent church there in honor of John the Baptist.

The road to Janin cuts through the plain of Dothan (Gen. xxxvii. 14–17; Judith iv. 6–7, vii. 3), which is now represented by Tell Dautan. The name of Ibleam (Judges i. 27; II Kings ix. 27; located in Issachar in Josh. xvii. 11), to which corresponds the Bileam of I Chron. vi. 70 (the Belmaim of Judith vii. 3), is preserved in the

5. Other Inland Cities.

Ḥirbat and Wadi Bal'amah two miles south of Janin. On the road from Shechem to Scythopolis, in the upper part of the Wadi Far'ah, four miles northeast of Nablus, is Ṭallusah, identified by Robinson with Tirzah, the residence of the kings of Israel to the time of Omri, though Conder seeks this ancient capital in Tayasir, about twelve miles from Nablus on the road to Beth-shean. The pilgrim Brocardus (1332) mentions a Thersa three hours east of Samaria, thus pointing to noteworthy ruins in the vicinity of 'Ain al-Far'ah on the road to Beth-shean northeast of Ṭallusah. About six miles beyond Ṭallusah lies the ancient village of Ṭubas, which apparently corresponds to the Biblical Thebez (Judges ix. 50; II Sam. xi. 21). To the north lie the Ras Ibziḳ and Ḥirbat Ibziḳ, corresponding to the Bezek of I Sam. xi. 8 (cf. Judges i. 4). In the Jordan valley, 285 feet lower than the surface of the Mediterranean, is the flourishing village of Baisan, representing the Biblical Beth-shean, a city long independent of Israel, and reckoned to Manasseh, though lying in the district of Issachar (Josh. xvii. 11–13; Judges i. 27; I Chron. vii. 29). After the death of Saul, the city was taken by the Philistines (I Sam. xxxi. 7–13), but with David's subjugation of the Philistines, it came under Israelitic control, and formed part of one of the tributary districts of Solomon (I Kings iv. 12). During the Maccabean wars, Tryphon here sought to capture Jonathan (I Macc. xii. 40). In the Greco-Roman period the city was known as Scythopolis. It was one of the cities of the federation of Decapolis, was rebuilt by Gabinius, and contained many pagan inhabitants (Josephus, *War*, III., vi. 7; *Ant.*, XIV., v. 3). The "Ænon near to Salim," where John baptized (John iii. 23), was located, according to the *Onomasticon* of Eusebius, in the plain of Beth-shean, seven miles south of the city. Both Jerome and the pilgrim Sylvia record a Salem in this vicinity, and in 1852 Robinson found there the name Shaiḥ Salim. Abel-meholah, the home of Elisha (I Kings xix. 16, iv. 12), which Judges vii. 22 seems to locate south of Beth-shean, is identified by the *Onomasticon* with a village named Bethmaela or Bethaula, nine miles south of Scythopolis in the Jordan valley, thus pointing to the modern spring 'Ain al-Ḥalwah. The Gilboa of I Sam. xxviii. 4, after which the mountain range was named (II Sam. i. 21), corresponds to the modern Jalbaun on the western declivity of the Jabal Fuḳu'ah, which rises abruptly above the plain of Beth-shean. Further to the west, on the lower slopes, lies the little village of Bait Kad, which may correspond to the *Beth-'Ekedh*, "shearing house," of II Kings x. 12, 14.

Turning to the coast from the mouth of the Nahr al-'Aujah to Carmel, some twelve miles north of Jaffa is the ruined site of Arsuf, corresponding to the ancient Apollonia which was claimed by Alexander Jannæus for Judea and was rebuilt by Gabinius (Josephus, *Ant.*, XIII., xv. 4; *War*, I., viii. 4). The chief place on the Samaritan coast, however, was Cæsarea, also called Cæsarea Palæstina, Cæsarea Palæstinæ, Cæsarea ad mare, or Sebaste. It was earlier known as Cæsarea Stratonis, and as *Straton* here represents *'abd 'Astarton*, "servant of Astarte," it would seem to have been founded by the Sidonians late in the Persian period. Alexander Jannæus subjugated the city and its vicinity as far as Dor, but it was "freed" by Augustus and given to Herod, who must be regarded as the real founder of the city, which was henceforth called Cæsarea. On the deposition of Archelaus, Cæsarea became the seat of the Roman procurators of Judea (6–41 A.D.), and again after the death of Agrippa I. (44). Philip and the centurion Cornelius lived there (Acts viii. 40, x. 1 sqq., xxi. 8), there Paul was imprisoned before being taken to Rome, and there he appeared before Agrippa II. and Berenice (Acts xxiii. 23–24, xxiv. 27, xxv. 14 sqq.). Vespasian made it a Roman colony, and Alexander Severus gave it the title of a metropolis (Tacitus, *Hist.*, ii. 78). In consequence of its wide harbor, trade from Jerusalem to the Mediterranean passed through it (Acts ix. 30, xviii. 22, xxi. 8). The most famous bishop of the city was Eusebius (q.v.). The relatively smaller Cæsarea of the Crusaders was destroyed by the sultan Bibars in 1296. The site still bears the name of Ḳaiṣariyah. About nine miles north of Cæsarea are the ruins, now called Ḥirbat Ṭanṭurah, which mark the site of the ancient city of Dor, founded by the Phenicians. Although the king of Dor was conquered by Joshua (Josh. xii. 23), the city did not become tributary to Israel until the regal period (Josh. xvii. 11–12; Judges i. 27), so that I Kings iv. 11 makes the entire mountain region of Dor a tax-district of Solomon. The "height of Dor" (Josh. xii. 23, R. V.), apparently the southwestern slope of Carmel, must be distinguished from the city itself. According to the Eshmunazar inscription the Persian king gave Dor and the coast as far as Joppa to the Sidonians. In the Maccabean period Trypho was vainly besieged at Dor by Antiochus Sidetes (I Macc. xv. 10–14). Alexander Jannæus won the city from Zoilus, but in 63 B.C. Pompey made it a free city. It was, however, deserted in the days of Jerome. The Migdal Malḥa of the Talmud, the Magdihel of Jerome's *Onomasticon*, is represented by the modern Ḥirbat Maliḥah, five miles north of Ṭanṭurah. A Hebrew Migdal El was probably once situated at the present ruins of 'Atlit, the *Castellum Peregrinorum* of the Crusaders. (H. GUTHE.)

6. Cities of Western Samaria.

II. The People.—1. Origin and History: The account of the origin of the people (called in Greek *Samareitai*, *Samaritai*, and in Latin *Samaritani*) after the destruction of the northern kingdom is given in II Kings xvii. 24 sqq., according to which Sargon brought colonists from "Babylon, Cuthah, Ava, Hamath, and Sepharvaim" to take the place of the Jews who had been deported. The account continues to the effect that since these colonists did not fear Yahweh he sent lions among them; representations of the facts were then made to Sargon who had a Hebrew priest from among the captives sent to teach them how to worship Yahweh, "the god of the land." Yet each nationality made for itself gods in each place, while priests were appointed and offered sacrifice in the high places. This account, so far as the settling of colonists is concerned, is corroborated by the annals of Sargon (cf. Schrader, *KAT*, pp. 276 sqq.), which speak of two sets of colonists settled in the West; Ezra iv. 2, 10, speaks of settlements made by "Esar-haddon" and "Asnapper" (Asshurbanipal; cf. ASSYRIA, VI., 3, §§ 12–14). In view of the composite character of the population thus derived, the question has been raised how a people of such unity of character and with so pronounced a Jewish stamp could have been formed. Hengstenberg finds the answer in the tenacity with which they held to Jewish models, especially after they received the Pentateuch. Josephus (*Ant.*, IX., xiv. 3, X., ix. 7) claims a purely heathen origin for the Samaritans, and affirms that the Jews up to his time denied any relationship with them, calling them Cutheans (cf. II Kings xvii. 24). But this account must be rejected in favor of the other story told in the sources referred to above. Since the Hebrews deported numbered only 27,290, it is clear that not all the Hebrew population was carried away; the remnant left must have been strong enough to account for the bringing of the heathen settlers over to the practise of the religion of Yahweh. Very early the Samaritans called themselves "children of Israel" and descendants of Joseph. This conclusion is not contradicted by the few notices of the early centuries. For by the end of the seventh century B.C. there was rehabilitation of the Yahweh worship in the northern kingdom (II Kings xxiii. 15, 19 sqq.); in the report of the high places in Samaria there is no word of idolatry in connection with Josiah's reform. In Ezra iv. 2 the Samaritans make their appeal to Zerubbabel on the basis of their worship of the God of Israel from the days of Esar-haddon; and the Jews in their reply do not accuse them of idolatry. Ezra vi. 21 shows a trace of inclusion of a part of the Samaritans in association with the returned exiles after the building of

1. Origins.

the second Temple. The schism and the mutual hatred of Jews and Samaritans are most simply accounted for by the old standing opposition between north and south.

Preeminent in importance in accounting for the consolidation of the Samaritans were the recognition of the Pentateuch and the erection of the temple on Mt. Gerizim. Of the second matter Josephus

2. Josephus' Account.

gives an account (*Ant.*, XI., vii. 2, viii. 2 sqq.) much in need of critical investigation. According to him Darius Codomannus sent as satrap to Samaria a certain Sanaballetes, and he, to secure Jewish friendship, gave his daughter in marriage to Manasseh, brother of Jaddus, the high priest. In accordance with Ezra ix., Manasseh was ordered to give up his wife or his priesthood, and appealed to Sanballat; the latter then promised him a temple on Mt. Gerizim and the high priesthood of it. Manasseh therefore took up his residence in Samaria, whither other Jews, priests and laymen, who had heathen wives followed him and were joyously received by Sanaballetes and given means of support. While Alexander was besieging Tyre, the satrap went over to him and secured Alexander's consent to his project, after which he built the temple. After the death of Sanaballetes, the Samaritans sent a deputation to Alexander, invited him to their city, and asked immunity from taxation in the sabbatical year, asserting that they were Hebrews, though they disclaimed being Jews. Alexander postponed granting their request, but took the Samaritan soldiery with him to Egypt and settled them there as guardians of the boundary. But the temple at Gerizim became a refuge and resort of Jews who in their own land were accused of breaking the laws of Judaism. This account does not make clear how a heathen people through the shrewdness of their satrap and the accession of a fugitive Jewish priest permitted the victory over them of a new religion. Rather, Manasseh, if he acted as is related, found existing an idea of relationship to the Jews. The chronology of Josephus raises questions, when compared with Ezra ix., x. 5, and Neh. x. 31, xiii. 23 sqq. Neh. xiii. 28 seems to have the same basis as the narrative of Josephus; a son of Joiada, who was son of the high priest Eliashab, was son-in-law of Sanballat. Josephus makes Manasseh, son-in-law of Sanaballetes and brother of the high priest Jaddus, who was son of the high priest Johanan, the grandson of Joiada and great-grandson of Eliashab. That is, Josephus puts Manasseh a century too late. If Manasseh built the temple on Gerizim, he was not son or grandson of Joiada. It seems historical that the Gerizim temple was built under Alexander (cf. Josephus, *Ant.*, XIII., ix. 1). If Manasseh is identical with the son of the Joiada of Nehemiah, he may have been active among the Samaritans, but not as builder of the temple. At the cost of chronology, identity has been assumed (by Josephus) between the founder of the temple and the object of Nehemiah's anger. Reference to the Samaritan temple has been seen in the "Trito-Isaiah" (chaps. lvi.–lxvi.), as in lvii. 3 sqq., lxv. 3 sqq., lxvi. 1 sqq., 16 sqq., and with considerable reason (cf. on this A. Kuenen, *Gesammelte Abhandlungen*, pp. 229 sqq., Leipsic, 1894; T. K. Cheyne, *Introduction to the Book of Isaiah*, pp. 316–317, 363 sqq., London, 1895, and *Jewish Religious Life after the Exile*, pp. 25 sqq., ib. 1898).

When the Pentateuch was taken over by the Samaritans is entirely unknown. It can no longer be maintained that the hatred between Jews and Samaritans after the time of Nehemiah necessitates the acquisition by the Samaritans of the Pentateuch earlier than the breach at that time; nor can Josephus' account be wholly rejected, nor may the absolute completion of the Pentateuch be set between 444 and 432. The mutual hatred of the two peoples, moreover, was not so great as to hinder the Samaritans from adopting an unquestioned work of Moses, since they derived their religion from him as its founder. Moreover, in the Samaritan alphabet there are to be seen indications that it dates back to the forms of the fourth century B.C.

Under the Ptolemies and Seleucidæ the Samaritans shared the fortunes of the Jews (cf., e.g., Josephus, *Ant.*, XII., i. 1). The hatred of the two peoples manifested itself in acts of aggression

3. History to 66 A.D.

(Josephus, *Ant.*, XII., iv. 1; I Macc. iii. 10) and in epithets (Ecclus. l. 25–26). Under Antiochus Epiphanes the Samaritans denied kinship with the Jews and claimed descent from Medes and Persians (Josephus, *Ant.*, XII., v. 5) or Phenicians, while they contested with the Jews in Egypt for precedence in behalf of their own temple (Josephus, *Ant.*, XIII., iii. 4). John Hyrcanus overran Samaria and destroyed the temple at Gerizim and later the city of Samaria (Josephus, *Ant.*, XIII., ix. 1, x. 2), and under Alexander Jannæus (104–78 B.C.) the city was in the power of the Jews. In 63 B.C. it was made a free city, that is, was under the Roman governor of Syria. Under Gabinius (57–55) it was rebuilt, and in 30 adorned by Herod and named Sebaste in honor of Augustus. After the death of Herod the district came under Archelaus, but after his deposition came again under direct Roman rule, except that in 41–44 A.D. it was given by Claudius to Herod Agrippa. Testimony to the continuing hatred of and for the Jews is found in John viii. 48; Josephus, *Ant.*, XVIII., ii. 2, XX., vi. 1; *War*, II., xii. 3, in which the recurring conflicts are in part narrated while they explain such incidents as those of Luke ix. 53 and the remark in John iv. 9. John iv. shows, however, that the separation and exclusiveness were not absolute, and the circuit made by Galileans in going to Jerusalem was caused less by the hostility of the Samaritans than by the exposure to ceremonial defilement on the part of Jews. That the Samaritans in the time of Jesus were considered heathen follows neither from Matt. x. 5 nor Luke xvii. 18; note that in John iv. 12 the Samaritan woman speaks of "our father Jacob." The New Testament nowhere charges the Samaritans with idolatry. The report in the Talmud (*Chullin* 6a) that the Samaritans worshiped the image of a dove is a late invention, and that they worshiped a god Ashima arose from a misunderstanding. That worship continued on Gerizim in the time of Jesus is clear. The significance of Gerizim for the Samaritans is indicated by Josephus (*Ant.*, XVIII., iv.), according to whom in

35 A.D. a false prophet promised to show the Samaritans the sacred vessels buried by Moses upon the mountain; in consequence there was an assemblage of people at a village near by called Tirathana which Pilate attacked, slaying many, and his violence and cruelty caused his deposition. That the mutual hatred of the two peoples did not bar the Samaritans from the Gospel is shown by Jesus' employment of the Samaritan as the merciful man in Luke x. Further testimony is found in Luke xvii. 16; John iv. 39 sqq.; Acts viii. 5 sqq., 14 sqq.

On the outbreak of the Jewish war in 66 the Samaritans were undecided which of the two hated parties they should choose as enemies. In June, 67 (Josephus, *War*, III., vii. 32), an armed assemblage gathered on Gerizim, against which Vespasian sent Cerealis with 600 horse and 3,000 foot, who stormed the hill and killed 11,600 of them. After that the Samaritans dropped out of history for a time, but in 194 are heard of as partisans of Pescennius Niger against Septimius Severus. Roman laws of the end of the fourth century show Samaritan communities in Egypt, on some islands of the Red Sea, and elsewhere; and in Rome at the beginning of the sixth century they had a synagogue. Toward the end of the fifth century began the insurrections of this people which revealed their hate of the Christians and led to their suppression. The Emperor Zeno replaced their synagogue on Gerizim with a church to the Virgin, and under his successor they stormed the mountain and slew the keepers of the church. In 529 under Justinian they rebelled and crowned their leader Julian king, plundered and burned Christian villages and churches, until Justinian in a pitched battle conquered and slew many of them, and proclaimed severe laws against them. The next report concerning the Samaritans comes from Benjamin of Tudela c. 1170, who says that the "Cutheans" of Shechem, about 100 in number, celebrate their Passover festival on Gerizim, and speaks of about 900 Samaritans distributed in Cæsarea, Ascalon, and Damascus (for the latter cf. A. Musil, *Sieben samarit. Inschriften aus Damascus*, in *SWA*, xxxix., 1903, pp. 127–128). Since the end of the sixteenth century the Samaritans of Shechem and Cairo have been in communication with Christian travelers and scholars, the point of interest to the latter being the Samaritan recension of the Pentateuch. In 1853 Heinrich Petermann reported the number of Samaritans in Nablus as 122; in 1884 there were reported fifty-three men, forty-six women, thirty-six boys, and sixteen girls, while in 1904 the total number was given as 175, but there are no colonies of Samaritans outside Nablus. In Nablus this people inhabits its own quarter in the southwestern part of the city, living in great poverty, with a priest (*kohin*) who claims to be a Levite, though the Aaronic line is conceded to have been extinct since 1658. The present priest has the power, either at his own initiative or at the wish of the community, to anoint others to the office. He receives tithes from the community, and from this and an accessory source the income is about sixty-four dollars. The clothing is white with a red turban. The civil control is under a *shophet*, "judge."

4. Later History.

2. Doctrine: Their doctrine, apart from the special significance of Mt. Gerizim, is like that of the Jews. They emphasize the unity of God, and reject all kinds of image worship, anthropomorphism, and anthropopathism, though between God and man they conceive of mediating spirits. Moses was the greatest of the prophets, whose law is holy. The cultus on Gerizim they refer to Deut. xxvii. 4, where they read "Gerizim" for "Ebal." The Messiah (John iv. 25) is to come 6,000 years after the creation, and he will establish the Tabernacle, holy vessels, and manna on Gerizim, renew the worship, and convert all people to the true faith; he will live to the age of one hundred and be buried on Gerizim. The final judgment is to come at the end of 7,000 years, the result of which will be eternal, with a period of penance in hell for those whose lives have mingled good and evil. In the matter of the levirate marriage (Deut. xxv. 5 sqq.) the Samaritans construe "brother" as "nearest friend," and the levirate is not binding if the friend has two wives already (a second wife being allowed in case of sterility of the first). Marriages are contracted early, and divorce is extremely rare; the value or purchase price of a bride is from $300 to $115, which the bride receives. Circumcision is on the eighth day. The Samaritans follow for their religious festivals the calendar of Lev. xxiii., marking the three chief ones by processions to Gerizim. They regard the Hebrew (being the tongue of the Pentateuch) as the holy language, and some of them possess a passable knowledge of the text; their pronunciation in some particulars serves to correct the Jewish-Christian.

3. Language and Literature: The colloquial language of the Samaritans from the last century B.C. till the first centuries of the Mohammedan hegemony was a dialect of the West Aramaic, usually designated Samaritan; it presented few differences, apart from loan words from Hebrew, Greek, and Latin, as compared with the ordinary Palestinian Aramaic found in the Targums and in certain parts of the Talmud. The fact that c. 1100 A.D. the Samaritan Pentateuch was translated into Arabic shows that already the Samaritan had become a dead tongue; even earlier than that, the Arabic version of Saadia had been used. In their literature the Pentateuch takes first place. Among the tendencial text alterations the most noticeable is that already noted in Deut. xxvii. 4; there are also wide differences in the term of life given the patriarchs in Gen. v. and xi. It is said that the variants from the Hebrew text number 6,000. The theory that the Samaritan Pentateuch was the basis of the Septuagint version, though this is regarded as a falsified and corrupt recension of the Hebrew, was restated by S. Kohn, *De Pentateucho Samaritano* (Leipsic, 1865). Besides this work, the Samaritans possess the Samaritan Targum, a translation of the Pentateuch into the Samaritan; this the Samaritans claim to have been made between 50 and 1 B.C.; really it was made in the second or beginning of the third century A.D. Field's *Hexapla* (prolegomena, pp. lxxxii.–lxxxiii.) remarks that of forty-three readings in the Greek

1. Pentateuch, Targum, and Arabic Translations.

not less than thirty-six agree with the Samaritan Targum exactly and seven others do not invalidate the conclusion stated above as to the relation of the Greek to the Samaritan; this is, however, disputed by others (*Monatsschrift für Geschichte und Wissenschaft des Judenthums*, 1894, pp. 1-7, 49-67; *ZDMG*, xlvii., 1893, pp. 650 sqq.). The investigations of Kohn have shown that the views which have prevailed respecting the Samaritan Targum were erroneous. The grammars and lexicons hitherto have contained many false words and explanations, and what has passed as the Samaritan Targum was a poor exemplar of varied and unrelated writings, corrupted and distorted, with attempted corrections, the products of a time when Samaritan had long been disused, with interpolations from the Targum of Onkelos and with Arabisms; in short of the original Targum probably only small fragments are known. The tendencial changes represent accommodations, running through centuries, to all possible variations in views (Sadducean, Pharisaic, Syrian, and Arabic), and are the work of a number of different hands; the indications are not that a fundamental targum serves as the basis, but that by different priests partial translations were made for practical purposes. There is also a translation of the Pentateuch into Arabic, made in the eleventh or twelfth century, probably to supersede that of Saadia. The text current under the name of Abu Said is the result of two or more recensions. It does not seem to have used the Targum, though the latter may have received insertions from the translation; the Arabisms in the Targum, where they do not agree with the translation, are possibly of the time of Abu Said and rest upon another Arabic version.

3. Other Early Writings. Another piece of Samaritan literature is the Arabic Book of Joshua, perhaps of the thirteenth century, dealing with history from the death of Moses to that of Joshua in thirty-eight chapters, often in agreement with the Hebrew Joshua, but with apocryphal additions, and an appendix of nine chapters carrying the history down to the time of Alexander Severus. It is claimed that it was written in Hebrew originally, but possibly the whole work was composed in Arabic. There is, moreover, also written in Arabic, the Samaritan Chronicle of Abu'l Fatḥ, an apology for the Samaritans, based upon older works in 1355 A.D., coming down to Mohammed, and continued by another hand to the time of Harun al-Rashid. Both these works are historically worthless. There is also the so-called Neubauer Chronicle, and the recently edited Samaritan-Hebrew Chronicle issued by Adler and Seligsohn (see below, 4, § 2, end).

4. Literature on the Samaritans: The following gives the principal works dealing with the history and literature of the Samaritans.

1. On the History of the Samaritans. (1) C. Cellarius' *Collectanea historiæ Samaritanæ*, Zeitz, 1688; Idem, *Exercitatio, gentis Samaritanæ historiam et cærimonias, post ejusdem auctoris Collectanea . . . magis illustrans*, Halle, 1707 (these two books constitute the chief source); E. W. Hengstenberg, *Die Authentie des Pentateuches*, i. 1-46, Berlin, 1836 (apologetic); Robinson, *Researches*, vol. iii.; T. G. J. Juynboll, *Commentarii in historiam gentis Samaritanæ*, Leyden, 1846 (the best collection of the older material); A. Knobel, *Zur Geschichte der Samaritaner*, Giessen, 1846; J. Grimm, *Die Samariter und ihre Stellung zur Weltgeschichte*, Munich, 1854; H. Petermann, *Reisen im Orient*, i. 260-292, Leipsic, 1860; Heidenheim, in *Deutsche Vierteljahrsschrift*, i. 9 sqq., 374 sqq.; J. W. Nutt, *Sketch of Samaritan History, Dogma, and Literature*, London, 1874; A. Cowley, in *JQR*, 1896, pp. 562 sqq. [J. A. Montgomery, *The Samaritans*, Philadelphia, 1907; Jacob, Son of Aaron (high priest of the Samaritans), *The Messianic Hope of the Samaritans, transl. from the Arabic by Abdullah ben Kori, ed. with Introduction by W. E. Barton*, Chicago, 1908; J. W. Rothstein, *Juden und Samaritaner. Die grundlegende Scheidung von Judentum und Heidentum. Eine kritische Studie zum Buche Haggai und zur jüdischen Geschichte im ersten nachexilischen Jahrhundert*, Leipsic, 1908.] (2) On individual points in history: J. F. Zachariä, *De Samaritanis eorumque templo in monte Garisim*, Jena, 1723; Schulz, *De implacabili Judæorum in Samaritas odio*, Wittenberg, 1756; D. Mill, *De causis odii Judæos inter atque Samaritanos* in *Dissertationes selectæ*, Leyden, 1743; S. de Sacy, *Chrestomathie Arabe*, i. 163 sqq., ii. 177 sqq., Paris, 1806 (extract from Makrizi's "Description of Egypt"); idem, *Mémoire sur l'état actuel des Samaritains*, ib. 1812, in extended form in *Notices et extraits des manuscrits de la bibliothèque du roi*, pp. 1-39, ib. 1831 (deals especially with the dogmatics of the Samaritans); Gesenius, *De Samaritanorum theologia ex fontibus ineditis*, Halle, 1723; J. J. L. Bargès, *Les Samaritains de Naplouse*, Paris, 1855; G. H. A. von Ewald, *Geschichte des Volkes Israel*, iii. 724 sqq., iv. 129 sqq., 197 sqq., 274 sqq., Göttingen, 1864-66; M. Appel, *Quæstiones de rebus Samaritanorum sub imperio Romano peractis*, Breslau, 1874; A. Brüll, *Zur Geschichte und Litteratur der Samaritaner*, Frankfort, 1876; Geiger, in *ZDMG*, xi. 730 sqq., xii. 132 sqq., xiv. 622 sqq., xvi. 389 sqq., xx. 527 sqq.; Taglicht, *Der Kuthäer als Beobachter des Gesetzes*, Erlangen, 1888; L. Wreschner, *Samaritanische Traditionen*, Berlin, 1888 (includes materials from the twelfth century). (3) Interchange of correspondence between Samaritans and Europeans is contained in C. F. Schnurrer, *Samaritanischer Briefwechsel*, in *Repertorium für biblische und morgenländische Litteratur*, ix. 1 sqq.; S. de Sacy, *Litteræ Samaritanorum ad J. Scaligerum*, in the same, xiii. 257 sqq.; Allarius, *Epistola Samaritana Sichemitarum ad J. Ludolfum*, Zeitz, 1688; Bruns, *Epistola Samaritana Sichemitarum tertia ad J. Ludolfum*, Helmstädt, 1781; S. de Sacy, in *Notices et extraits des manuscrits de la bibliothèque du roi*, xii. 1-235, Paris, 1831; *ZDMG*, xvii. 375-376; *Deutsche Vierteljahrsschrift*, i. 78 sqq.; *ZDPV*, 1885, 149 sqq.; *JQR*, vol. xvi. no. 63; *Bibliotheca sacra*, lx. 610; and a letter in facsimile and translation to King Oscar of Sweden, Upsala, 1897.

2. On the Sacred or Semi-Sacred Books. (1) On the grammar of the language consult: F. Uhlemann, *Institutiones linguæ Samaritanæ*, Leipsic, 1837; G. J. Nicholls, *A Grammar of the Samaritan Language with Extracts and Vocabulary*, London, 1858; H. Petermann, *Brevis linguæ Samaritanæ grammatica, litteratura, chrestomathia, cum glossario*, Berlin, 1873; S. Kohn, *Zur Sprache, Literatur, und Dogmatik der Samaritaner*, Leipsic, 1876; J. Rosenberg, *Lehrbuch der samaritanischen Sprache und Literatur*, Vienna, 1901. On lexicography: Castelli, *Lexicon heptaglotton*, London, 1669; idem, *Animadversationes Samaritanæ*, in the "London Polyglot," vol. vi.; S. Kohn, *Samaritanische Studien*, Breslau, 1868. On Samaritan-Hebrew: T. Nöldeke, *Ueber einige samaritanisch-arabischen Schriften, die hebräische Sprache betreffend*, Göttingen, 1862; H. Petermann, *Versuch einer hebräischen Formenlehre nach der Aussprache der heutigen Samaritaner nebst einer danach gebildeten transskription der Genesis*, Leipsic, 1868. (2) On the Hebrew-Samaritan Pentateuch: bibliography under BIBLE TEXTS, A, IV.; the reprint by B. Blaynay, Oxford, 1790; C. F. Houbigant printed the Samaritan variants to the Hebrew text in his *Biblia Hebraica*, Paris, 1753; a collation by B. Kennicott is in his *Vetus Testamentum Hebraicum*, vol. i., Oxford, 1776, in the Bagster edition of the O. T., London, 1844, and in Petermann's *Versuch . . . Formenlehre*, ut sup., pp. 219 sqq. On the manuscripts: J. G. Eichhorn, *Einleitung ins Alte Testament*, ii. 584 sqq., Leipsic, 1803; Björnstal, in *Repertorium für biblische und morgenländische Litteratur*, iii. 84 sqq.; Rosen, in *ZDMG*, xviii. 582 sqq.; A. Harkavy, "The Samaritan Manuscripts of the Pentateuch in the Imperial Library at St. Petersburg," St. Petersburg, 1875 (in Russian); G. Margoliouth, in *JQR*, July, 1903, pp. 632 sqq.; and the literature under BIBLE VERSIONS, A., IV. Critical expositions are: W. Gesenius, *De Pentateuchi Samaritani* *indole*, Halle, 1815; F. Bleek, *Einleitung in das Alte Testament*, ed. Kamphausen, pp. 757 sqq., Berlin, 1870; W. M. L. de Wette, *Einleitung in das Alte Testament*, ed. Schrader, pp. 203 sqq., Berlin, 1869; F. Bleek, *Einleitung*, etc., ed. J. Wellhausen, pp. 570, 643, Berlin, 1878; E. W. E. Reuss, *Geschichte der heiligen Schriften des Alten Testaments*, pp. 470 sqq., Brunswick, 1881; B. Pick, in *Bibliotheca Sacra*, Jan., 1877–Apr., 1878; König, in *DB*, extra vol., pp. 68–72. On the Samaritan translations of the Pentateuch: printed texts are in the Paris and London Polyglots; an edition was begun by G. Petermann, *Pentateuchus Samaritanus*, of which he published Genesis and Exodus, Berlin, 1872–73, continued and completed by C. Vollers, 1883–91 (Petermann's part not very well done; cf. Kohn in *ZDMG*, xlvii. 626–697); A. Brüll, *Das Samaritanische Targum zum Pentateuch*, 5 parts and two appendixes, Frankfort, 1873–1876; idem, *Kritische Studien über samaritanische Fragmente ... in Oxford*, ib. 1875; S. Kohn, *Zur Sprache*, etc., ut sup., pp. 215 sqq.; M. Heidenheim, in *Bibliotheca Samaritana*, vol. i., Leipsic, 1884 (uncritical); A. Harkavy gives a collation of the St. Petersburg fragments with the polyglot text in *Katalog der hebräischen und samaritanischen Handschriften*, Leipsic, 1875; P. Kahle, in *ZA*, xvi (1901), 83 sqq., xvii (1902), 1 sqq.; Kohn in *ZDMG*, 1890, pp. 650 sqq.; P. Kahle, *Textkritische und lexikalische Bemerkungen zum samaritanischen Pentateuchtargum*, Halle, 1898; and the works on introduction ut sup. by Eichhorn, De Wette-Schrader, Bleek-Kamphausen, and König. On the Arabic version of the Pentateuch: the works on introduction by Eichhorn (ii. 284 sqq.), and De Wette-Schrader (p. 135); H. E. G. Paulus, in *Neues Repertorium*, 1791, pp. 171 sqq.; S. de Sacy, *De versione Samaritano-Arabica librorum Moysis*, in *Allgemeine Bibliothek der biblischen Litteratur*, x. 1–176, with additions, in *Mémoires de l'académie des inscriptions et belles lettres*, xlix. 1 sqq. (fundamental); A. Kuenen issued the text of the first three books, Leyden, 1851–54; J. Bloch, *Die samaritanisch-arabische Pentateuchübersetzung, Deut. i.–xi.*, Berlin, 1901 (cf. P. Kahle, in *Zeitschrift für hebräische Bibliographie*, 1902, no. 1). On the Book of Joshua: for the older literature the "Introduction" of Eichhorn, iii. 412 sqq., and of De Wette-Schrader, pp. 307 sqq.; and Juynboll, *Chronicon Samaritanum*, Leyden, 1848 (edits the only manuscript in Arabic with Samaritan letters); M. Gaster, *Das Buch Joshua in hebräisch-samaritanischer Rezension, entdeckt und zum ersten Male herausgegeben*, Leipsic, 1908. On the other chronicles: C. F. Schnurrer edited twenty pages of the text of Abu'l Fatḥ in *Neues Repertorium* (1790), 117 sqq.; E. Vilmar, *Abulfathi annales Samaritani*, Gotha, 1865 (complete); the Bodleian codex by Payne Smith in *Deutschen Vierteljahrsschrift für englisch-theologische Forschung*, ii (1863), 304 sqq., 432 sqq.; and De Wette-Schrader, ut sup., pp. 308–309. A. Neubauer edited a later manuscript, not the same as Abu'l Fatḥ's work, in *JA*, xiv (1869), 385–386; E. N. Adler and M. Seligsohn edited in *REJ*, xliv (1902)–xlvi (1903) a "new Samaritan Chronicle" (cf. Clermont-Ganneau, in *Journal des savants*, Jan., 1904, pp. 34 sqq., and *Recueil d'archéologie orientale*, vol. vi).

3. On Manuscripts and Other Works. On manuscripts of other literature: Barton in *Bibliotheca sacra*, Oct., 1903, pp. 612 sqq.; Neubauer, in *Chronique samaritaine*, pp. 467 sqq. (on MSS. in the British Museum); G. Margoliouth, *Descriptive List of Hebrew and Samaritan MSS.*, London, 1893 (on the same); for the Bodleian MSS., Neubauer, *Catalogue of Hebrew MSS.*, Oxford, 1853; for those at St. Petersburg, A. Harkavy, *Collection of Samaritan MSS. at St. Petersburg*, London, 1874. [Add R. Gottheil, in *JBL*, xxv. 1 (1906).] A general review of later publications till 1868 is given by A. Geiger, in *ZDMG*, vols. xvi.–xxii. On the liturgy: W. Gesenius, *Carmina Samaritana*, Halle, 1824; numerous examples are given by M. Heidenheim in the *Deutsches Vierteljahrsschrift*, Gotha, 1860–67; cf. idem, in *Bibliotheca Samaritana*, ii.–iv., Leipsic, 1885–87; A. Merx, *Carmina Samaritana*, Rome, 1887; A. E. Cowley, in *JQR*, vii (1894), 121 sqq.; idem, *The Samaritan Liturgy*, 2 vols., New York, 1909, London, 1910; S. Rappoport, *La Liturgie samaritaine, office du soir des fêtes*, Angers, 1900; idem, in *JA*, 9 ser., xvi. 289 sqq. On the Haggada and exegesis of the Pentateuch; here belongs the Samaritan *Markah*, in pure Aramaic, a commentary of the fourth century, copied by Petermann in 1868 from a Nablus MS., ed. H. Baneth, Berlin, 1888; cf. E. Munk, *Des Samaritaners Marqah*, Berlin, 1890; M. Heidenheim, *Der Kommentar Marqahs*, in *Bibliotheca Samaritana*, vol. iii., Weimar, 1896; L. Emmerich, *Das Siegeslied, eine Schrifterklärung des Samaritaners Marqah*, part i., Berlin, 1897; L. Hildesheimer, *Des Samaritaners Marqah Buch der Wunder*, Berlin, 1898. C. F. Schnurrer published in the *Repertorium für biblische ... Litteratur*, xvi (1785), 154 sqq., *Probe eines samarit.-biblischen Kommentars* on Gen. xlix.; Drabkin, *Fragmenta commentarii ad pentat. Samaritano-Arabici sex*, Breslau, 1875. On halacha: the chief work is the *Kitab al-kafi*, a work dated 1042 A.D., in thirty-two chapters, compiled from the work of the most esteemed Samaritans; N. Cohn edited chap. x. as *Die Zarathgesetze der Bibel ...*, Frankfort, 1899; M. Klumel, "*Mischpatim.*" *Ein samarit.-arab. Kommentar zu Ex. xxi.–xxii. 15*, Berlin, 1902; S. Hanover, *Das Festgesetz des Samaritaner ...*, ib. 1904. Literature on the *Taheb*: the earlier works are given in Schürer, *Geschichte*, ii. 522; A. Merx, *Ein samarit. Fragment über den Taeb oder Messias aus der Gothaer Handschrift*, Leyden, 1893 (cf. Hilgenfeld in *ZWT*, 1894, pp. 233 sqq., 1895, p. 156); Cowley, in *Expositor*, Mar., 1895, pp. 161 sqq.; Goldziher, in *ZDMG*, lvi (1902), 411–412. On other (secular) literature, J. Freudenthal, *Hellenistische Studien*, heft 1, Breslau, 1874.

(E. Kautzsch.)

SAMARITAN PENTATEUCH. See Bible Versions, A., IV.

SAMSON: The son of Manoah, of the tribe of Dan, and the last popular hero of the book of Judges (xiii.–xvi.), which drew upon special written sources, apparently with only a few additions. The special characteristic of Samson was his great and divinely given strength, due to the fact that before his birth he had been dedicated a lifelong Nazirite, his powers depending on his faithful observance of his vows, particularly by refraining from cutting his hair. He was, moreover, quick of wit, and full of biting irony, but he was also reckless and self-confident, so that he was finally overcome rather by the craft than by the strength of his foes. In like fashion he was unpractical, and though the spirit of Yahweh moved him against the enemies of Israel (Judges xiii. 25, xiv. 4), his prowess was manifested chiefly in deeds of mischief and in love adventures. The spirit of Yahweh which aided him, especially in time of need (Judges xiv. 6, 19, xv. 14; cf. xvi. 20), was often made to serve foolish and unworthy ends, so that even his serious battles had no unifying purpose, and his victories bore no adequate result. Only in a formal sense, to be in harmony with the accounts of his predecessors, can he be said to have "judged Israel" twenty years (Judges xv. 20, xvi. 31). He is never described as leading his people, who received but slight profit from the enterprises which he undertook for his own glory (Judges xiii. 5), and his character was marred by his excessive amorousness. Samson thus presents a dual aspect, the antithesis between divine calling and the nature of man, the theories of opposition between pagan nature myth and monotheistic reworking, or between popular account and religious revision, being inadequate explanations.

Judges xiii. records a twofold appearance of an angel of the Lord, announcing to Manoah and his barren wife the birth of a son who should be dedicated to Yahweh from his birth and should "begin to deliver Israel out of the hand of the Philistines." The first cycle of Samson's deeds centers around his wooing of and marriage with a Philistine bride living at Timnath. On his way to her he tore asunder a lion, an event which furnished him the basis for a riddle with which he puzzled the Philistine wedding guests until his bride coaxed its solution from him, whereupon he boldly slew thirty of the inhabitants of Ashkelon to obtain the garments to pay his forfeit (Judges xiv.). The marriage was abruptly broken off, but Samson still regarded his bride as his lawful wife (Judges xv. 1) and avenged the giving of her to another man by burning the fields of the Philistines. The latter thereupon destroyed both father-in-law and wife, while Samson, in his turn, slaughtered large numbers of them. Delivered into the hands of the Philistines by the men of Judah, he nevertheless slew a thousand more Philistines with the jawbone of an ass (Judges xv.). Somewhat later, when captured while enmeshed in an amour in Gaza, Samson carried off the city gates by night (Judges xvi. 1–4). He was finally destroyed, however, by his intrigue with a Philistine woman named Delilah, who prevailed upon him to reveal the true secret of his strength and then betrayed him to her compatriots, who seized and blinded him, compelling him to work as a slave in the prison at Gaza (Judges xvi. 4–21). But the hair which Delilah had shorn grew again, and with it his strength returned, whereupon, with one last mighty revenge, he destroyed both the Philistines and himself by pulling down the temple of the god Dagon (Judges xvi. 22 sqq.).

The attempt has been made to connect this story with Semitic and Indo-Germanic myths, the hero's name, as a derivative of *shemesh*, "sun," being etymologised as "little sun" or as "sunlike" (although others derive it from *shamem*, "to be laid waste," while according to Josephus, *Ant.*, V., viii. 4, it signifies "strong"), Samson being compared with the Greek Herakles, a view early current in the Church (Eusebius, *Chron.*, ed. A. Schöne, pp. 54–55, Berlin, 1875–76; Philaster, *Hær.*, viii.; Georgius Syncellus, ed. G. Dindorf, i. 309, Bonn, 1829), which derived the Greek from the Hebrew story. In accordance with this supposed resemblance, the attempt has repeatedly been made to explain the account of Samson as a sun myth, the hair wherein Samson's strength lies being interpreted as the rays of the sun, the lion of Judges xiv. 5 sqq., being the zodiacal sign of Leo, Delilah representing Omphale, and the gates of Gaza being the Pillars of Hercules, etc. A common source of the traditions concerning Samson and Heracles, or a Semitic bond of union, has been sought in the Babylonian Gilgamesh epic; but since the points of difference from the account of Samson are far stronger than the points of similarity, which are often strained, and since many details in the Hebrew story can scarcely be explained as parts of a nature myth, other scholars regard Samson as a historical personality, despite certain legendary accretions. Still others exclude the nature myth entirely, although attributing more or less scope to local tradition. The life of Samson shows strong influence of local coloring and was restricted to a limited territory (cf. Judges xiv. 1, 5, 19, xv. 17 sqq., xvi. 1, 3–4); his entire figure is genuinely Hebraic; and he was a true Nazirite, whose wonderful power, vanishing with his recreancy to his vows, is by this fact shown to have been divine in origin (cf. Gen. vi. 4) even though turned to unworthy purposes. (C. von Orelli.)

Bibliography: The most valuable treatment is given in the commentaries named under Judges, particularly those of Moore, Budde, and Nowack. For other discussions consult: G. G. Roskoff, *Die Simsonsage und der Heraklesmythus*, Leipsic, 1860; Steinthal, in I. Goldziher, *Hebrew Mythology*, pp. 392–446, London, 1877; E. Wietzke, *Der biblische Simson und der ägyptische Horus-Ra*, Wittenberg, 1888; F. Baethgen, *Beiträge zur semitischen Religionsgeschichte*, pp. 161 sqq., Berlin, 1889; Van Doorninck, in *ThT*, 1894, pp. 14–32, 1896, pp. 162–167; F. Vigouroux, *La Bible et les découvertes modernes*, iii. 172–220, Paris, 1896; idem, *Dictionnaire*, fasc. xxxv. 1434–1435; J. S. Reuser, *Die Hauptpersonen des Richterbuches in Talmud und Midrasch, I., Simson*, Berlin, 1902; A. Jeremias, *Das Alte Testament im Lichte des alten Orients*, pp. 287–288, Leipsic, 1904; D. Völter, *Aegypten und die Bibel*, pp. 107 sqq., Leyden, 1904; P. Carus, *The Story of Samson and its Place in the Religious Development of Mankind*, Chicago, 1907; H. Stahn, *Die Simsonsage*, Göttingen, 1908; *DB*, iv. 377–381; *EB*, iv. 4268–70; *JE*, xi. 1–2.

SAMSON, BERNHARDIN. See Sanson.

SAMSON, GEORGE WHITEFIELD: Baptist; b. at Harvard, Mass., Sept. 29, 1819; d. at New York Aug. 8, 1896. He was graduated from Brown University, 1839, and Newton Theological Institution, Newton Centre, Mass., 1843; was pastor of the E Street Church, Washington, D. C., 1843–50; at Jamaica Plain, Boston, Mass., 1850–52; E Street, Washington, D. C., 1853–59; president of Columbian College, Washington, D. C., 1859–71; of Rutgers Female Seminary, New York, 1871–75; pastor of First Church, Harlem, New York, 1873–81; from 1883 he was secretary in charge of Liberia College; after 1884 conducted private collegiate and theological instruction; and after 1886 was acting president of Rutgers Female College, New York. After his death Rev. Dr. Leighton Williams continued his class in theology in expanded form as the Amity Theological School, New York City. He was the author of *To daimonión, or the Spiritual Medium* (Boston, 1852; 2d ed., under title *Spiritualism Tested*, 1860); *Elements of Art Criticism* (Philadelphia, 1867); *Physical Media in Spiritual Manifestations, illustrated from Ancient and Modern Testimony* (1869); *The Atonement* (1878); *Divine Law as to Wines* (New York, 1880); *Guide to Self Education* (1886); and *Idols to Fashion and Culture* (1888).

SAMUEL.

I. The Prophet: The name Samuel is of early origin, pointing to pre-Hebraic times; its meaning is "his name is El"; in I Sam. i. 20 it is given the significance "asked of God," though strictly its meaning is "heard of God." According to I Sam. i. 1, Samuel came of Ephraimitic lineage; but it is not probable that the Ramathaim-zophim of that passage, the Ramah where Samuel was born, had his house, died, and was buried, is to be identified with the (Ephraimitic) Ramah in Benjamin two hours north of Jerusalem, the modern el-Ram, but rather with the place called in the New Testament Arimathea, perhaps the present Beit-

1. Name, Lineage, Youth.

Rima near Tibne. Against the Ephraimitic origin of Samuel, I Chron. vi. 11 sqq., 18 sqq. speaks, where unmistakably the same family-tree is given as in I Sam. i., tracing the descent from the Levite Kohath. Many regard this as an arbitrary arrangement of the Chronicler, who desired to derive the priest Samuel from the Levites according to "Mosaic" law. The arguments for the non-Levitical origin of Samuel are not absolutely conclusive. Samuel's continual residence at the sanctuary as against the ordinary term of residence of Levites is explained by his mother's vow (I Sam. i. 11); while Rama was not a Levitical city, the Levites lived in other than Levitical cities. Yet Elkanah's yearly pilgrimage to the shrine might easily find other explanation than that of Levitical duty, and I Sam. i. 1 nowhere suggests Levitical origin. But Samuel's grandson Heman, the celebrated singer, was a Levite (I Chron. xxv. 4, cf. vi. 18–19); on the other hand the boundaries between Levites and others may not have been hard and fast at that period, and men may have become Levites through a vow. Such a vow Hannah registered in beseeching a son, promising his lifelong service to God, and also that he should be a Nazirite (q.v.). This vow she fulfilled after her request had been granted and she had weaned the child, and he became an attendant at Shiloh, "girded with a linen ephod" (I Sam. ii. 18; see EPHOD). There he was speedily distinguished by being made the recipient of divine revelations, the first being that which concerned the judgment of God on Eli and his house (I Sam. iii.). After the death of Eli Samuel became the leader in Israel and that people's judge, the reformer of its religion (I Sam. vii. 3 sqq.), and by his answered prayer its savior (verses 9 sqq.).

2. Later Life; Character. Concerning his later life little appears which is striking, apart from I Sam. vii., which is contested on critical grounds (see below). But if this portion of the history be given up, attested though it is by the stone Eben-ezer (verse 12), the title of father which Samuel bears in his old age vouches for his thorough and comprehensive activity. His journeys among the people and attendance at their gatherings at Bethel, Gilgal, Mizpah, where he acted as consecrator of the offerings and as judge, tended to build up Mosaic tradition and prophetic illumination and to prepare for a better ethical-religious situation in the land. To this end the prophetic schools were a part of the means. Through his worth and eminence he contributed to the unifying of the people; and if the Philistine yoke was not altogether broken, the lot of Israelites was at least bearable. In his old age sorrow assailed him through his sons' departure from his upright course, and the people demanded a king, which he at first opposed, and then, at a higher bidding, granted (see SAUL). His work, however, was not at an end, his duty being to announce Saul's supersession and to anoint David (q.v.). While David was being persecuted by Saul, Samuel died, and Saul followed not long after. Since Moses, alongside whom he is placed (Ps. xcix. 6; Jer. xv. 1), no one had been endowed with so rich a spirit and entrusted with so high and comprehensive tasks as Samuel who gathered in himself all the theocratic offices, officiating as priest, prophet, and judge, and becoming the founder of the kingdom. His office of priest came to him not by birth but by an inner call and the external needs of the times; the external organization of the cultus is ascribed to him (I Chron. ix. 22), and his prophetic activity was thorough and comprehensive, he being possibly the founder of the prophetic schools. His ethical deliverance in I Sam. xv. 22-23 became the keynote of subsequent prophecy, while his work had bearing upon the building up of the "Torah" and upon prophetic writing. He appears as a true servant of God, who subjected his own will to that of the deity, and endeavored to lead the people to realize its higher call over against the striving for national greatness and worldly might.

II. The Books of Samuel: In the Hebrew these books were originally one (cf. Origen, in Eusebius, *Hist. eccl.*, VI., xxv.), in the Septuagint they were divided and called I and II Kings; this division into two books appeared in the Hebrew text of D.

1. Form and Contents. Bomberg's edition (Venice, 1517), but the Masoretic remarks prove the original unity, showing I Sam. xxviii. 24 to be the middle verse of the book. It bears the name of Samuel because in the first part he is the principal character, not because he is the author, as later *Baba Bathra* (14b) mistakenly declared. The contents of the books connect closely with the contents of the Book of Judges, showing how out of the confusion of those times the Hebrew kingdom arose and soon reached its highest point. They divide into three main parts: (1) history of Samuel, the last judge and the prophetic founder of the kingdom (I., i.-xii.); (2) history of Saul (I., xiii.-xxxi.); (3) history of David (II., i.-xxiv.), though the latter part is not complete, the closing days and death of David being described in I Kings. But the author surely wrote after the death of David (II Sam. v. 5), and certain signs indicate that he wrote also the history of Solomon; moreover, it is clear that he used various written sources.

2. The Text. The form of the text of the book requires special consideration, the Hebrew text being very often defective and not seldom susceptible of correction from the Septuagint. Yet in places this version follows a variant recension. Sometimes the Hebrew text is the more detailed, sometimes the Greek; the former is fullest in the story of the youth and persecution of David by Saul, and this raises the question whether the Greek translators (or the writer of their Hebrew exemplar) had in mind to simplify and harmonize the text or whether the longer Hebrew text contains insertions later than the Greek version. In the latter case, the source of the additions is sought either in a later midrash or in earlier books which threw light upon the situation. In the reconstruction of the text Klostermann is too subjective, while Thenius, Wellhausen, and Petri stress too much the Septuagint. While in many passages the Septuagint helps to the correct text, in others the Masoretic points to the better reading, the Septuagint leaning on a variant text or not being exact.

That the text is composite in its sources appears from the dissimilarities of its parts, mingling detailed narrative with brief notices of events. Thus of the elevation of Saul to the throne late critics find three narratives, I Sam. xi.; ix. 1-10, 16; viii. 10, 17-27, which should, however, be reduced to two, viz., ix. 1-10, 16, x. 27b, xi. 11, 15, and, for the second narrative, viii. 10, 17-27a, xi. 12-14. These two reports are marked by strong characteristics. According to the earliest of these Samuel shows only joy in the erection of the kingdom, while the more pessimistic account reflects either the exilic or postexilic times (Wellhausen), the time of Hosea (Kittel), or of Hezekiah (Kuenen). As a theocrat Samuel must have had gloomy forebodings over the new movement. Yet it is granted by several of the critics that this doubling of the narrative does not necessarily imply that either is false. Klostermann sees in the two accounts only apparent, not real, discrepancies. It is noteworthy that criticism sees so often in I Samuel doublets or repeated accounts of the same events. Some of these are: the rending of the kingdom from Saul, xiii. 8-14 and xv. 12 sqq.; the two accounts of the hurling of the spear at David, xviii. 10-11 (not in the Septuagint) and xix. 9-10; the double betrayal of David by the Ziphites, xxiii. 19-28 and xxvi.; the repetition of the proverb in x. 12 and xix. 24; the double sparing of Saul by David, xxiv. and xxvi.; the two flights of David to the Philistines, xxi. 10 sqq. and xxvii. 1 sqq. In most of these cases repetition of the occurrences is psychologically probable, while each story has its own characteristics. But in these books as in other historical books of the Bible the union of varied accounts gives rise to difficulties, to gaps, and to incongruities. Thus I., vii. 13-14 does not agree with ix. 16, x. 5, xiii., dealing with the control of the land by the Philistines, though the critics often press too far the content of the passage vii. 2-17. So in the history of David the separate narratives are put together without attempt to harmonize the differences (see DAVID). While II Samuel is wrought into a closer unity, circumstances of this kind are not lacking.

3. Sources and Composition.

While the Books of Kings often name their sources, reference to a source is made only once in Samuel (II., i. 18, where the book of Jasher is named, cf. Josh. x. 13). There is no reason to hold that other pieces of poetry given in Samuel are from this source, such as the Song of Hannah (I Sam. ii.), an early psalm of victory, and the lament over Abner (II Sam. iii. 33-34), which is genuine. The piece in II Sam. xxii. (= Ps. xviii.) is among the psalms best attested as Davidic; while the "last words of David" (II Sam. xxiii. 1-7) are to be regarded as genuine. For the historical contents no source is adduced. II Sam. viii. 16 first mentions a "recorder," who appears to have been a permanent official, so that annals of the reigns of David and Solomon could have been available whence such data as II Sam. xx. 23-26 might have been drawn. But the chief sources were doubtless the prophetical accounts such as those referred to in I Chron. xxix. 29, the "book of Samuel the Seer, and . . . Nathan the prophet, and . . . Gad the seer." These references can not be to the varied parts of the Books of Samuel, but are rather prophetical narratives which seem to have been accessible to the Chronicler as parts of a greater work on the kings of Israel and Judah. Whether the prophets named left historical narratives or not, some such sources were used by the author of the Books of Samuel, and the composition was governed by a divine pragmatism. Cornill divides the chief material between J. and E., though convincing proof is lacking. A Deuteronomic redaction like that of the Book of Judges is generally accepted as fact, though parts of the contents do not show the marks of this. Kittel distinguishes between an older and a later class of sources: the first includes a Jerusalemitic history of David from the time of Solomon or Rehoboam, another not much later, and a history of Saul contemporary with the second source; the later class includes an Ephraimitic history of Samuel and David from the time of Hosea; this material was worked over by the Deuteronomic redactor of Judges, while another Deuteronomist worked over the whole material. Oettli sees an earlier and a later section in the book, the earlier favorable to the kingdom and the later prophetic in its interests; the whole was edited in Deuteronomic style. Most important is the fact that contemporary sources are generally recognized.

4. Date and Value.

The time of the final composition of the book from these various sources can be only approximated. In general, it was later than the death of David (II Sam. v. 5), and subsequent to the division of the kingdom (I Sam. xxvii. 6). A considerable time had elapsed since the events described, according to the frequent use of the formula "unto this day" (e.g., I Sam. v. 5) and the reference to archeological matters such as I Sam. ix. 9; yet such a passage as I Sam. xxvii. 6 forbids a date in the exile. Schrader would place these books with other historical books shortly before the exile; the rabbis ascribed them to Jeremiah; Stähelin puts them in the time of Hezekiah, and they may be older than this. The author was no mere compiler, but had a definite plan and the prophetic standpoint in view. Critics generally grant the historical value of the work, while the Hebrew is pure and the narrative simple and lively, presenting a truthful and not a glossed history of the times and individuals.

(C. VON ORELLI.)

BIBLIOGRAPHY: On the prophet the reader is referred to the commentaries (see below) and to works on the history of the Hebrews (under AHAB; and ISRAEL, HISTORY OF). Of the following special note may be made: G. C. M. Douglas, *Samuel and his Age; Study in the Constitutional Hist. of Israel*, London, 1901; F. B. Köster, *Die Propheten des Alten und Neuen Testaments*, Altona, 1838; H. Ewald, *Geschichte des Volkes Israel*, ii. 591 sqq., iii. 1 sqq., Göttingen, 1865-66, Eng. transl., London, 1883; F. E. König, *Offenbarungsbegriff des Alten Testament*, pp. 69-70, Leipsic, 1882; J. Robertson, *Early Religion of Israel*, Edinburgh, 1892; H. Guthe, *Geschichte des Volkes Israel*, pp. 68 sqq., Tübingen, 1889; F. B. Meyer, *Samuel the Prophet*, new ed., London, 1900; H. P. Smith, *Old Testament Hist.*, New York, 1903; S. Oettli, *Geschichte Israels bis auf Alexander*, Calw, 1905; Wellhausen, *Prolegomena; DB*, iv. 381-382; *EB*, iv. 4270-73; *JE*, xi. 5-8; Vigouroux, *Dictionnaire*, fasc. xxxv. 1435-1442.

On questions of introduction and text consult the literature in and under BIBLICAL INTRODUCTION, especially Driver, Kirkpatrick, Davidson, Cornill, and McFadyen;

and the following: K. H. Graf, *De librorum Samuelis et Regum compositione*, Augsburg, 1842; G. E. Karo, *De fontibus librorum qui feruntur Samuelis*, Berlin, 1862; F. Böttcher, *Neue exegetisch-kritische Aehrenlese zum A. T.*, vol. i., Leipsic, 1863; J. Wellhausen, *Der Text der Bücher Samuel untersucht*, Göttingen, 1871; C. H. Cornill, in *ZKW*, 1885, pp. 112 sqq.; idem, *Königsberger Studien*, i. 25 sqq., Königsberg, 1888; idem, *Einleitung in das A. T.*, Freiburg, 1891, Eng. transl., 2 vols., New York, 1907; idem, in *ZATW*, x (1890), 96 sqq.; K. Budde, in *ZATW*, viii (1888), 223 sqq.; idem, *Die Bücher Richter und Samuel*, Giessen, 1890; idem, in *SBOT*, 1894; R. Kittel, *Geschichte der Hebräer*, ii. 22 sqq., Gotha, 1888–92, Eng. transl., London, 1895; idem, in *TSK*, 1892, pp. 44 sqq.; S. R. Driver, *Notes on the Hebrew Text of the Books of Samuel*, Oxford, 1890 (indispensable); A. Kuenen, *Historisch-kritische Einleitung in die Bücher des A. T.*, I., ii. 37–62, Leipsic, 1890; T. K. Cheyne, *Aids to the Devout Study of Criticism*, pp. 1–126, London, 1892; N. Peters, *Beiträge zur Text- und Litterarkritik*, Freiburg, 1899; S. A. Cook, in *American Journal of Semitic Languages*, 1900, pp. 145–177; G. Stosch, *Die Urkunden der Samuelsgeschichte*, Gütersloh, 1901; P. N. Schlögl, *Libri Samuelis*, Vienna, 1905; E. Sievers, *Metrische Studien*, part 3, Leipsic, 1907; Wellhausen, *Prolegomena*; *DB*, iv. 382–391; *EB*, iv. 4273–81; *JE*, xi. 8–13.

Commentaries are by: H. P. Smith, New York, 1899; O. Thenius, Leipsic, 1864, 3d ed. by M. Löhr, 1898 (the prefatory notes are valuable); C. F. Keil and F. Delitzsch, Edinburgh, 1876; C. F. D. Erdmann, in Lange's Commentary, New York, 1877; A. F. Kirkpatrick, in *Cambridge Bible*, 2 vols., Cambridge, 1880–8?; R. Payne Smith and others, in *Pulpit Commentary*, 2 vols., London and New York, 1880–88; T. J. Conant, Philadelphia, 1884; A. Klostermann, Nördlingen, 1887; W. G. Blaikie, in *Expositor's Bible*, 2 vols., London, 1887–88; K. Budde, Tübingen, 1902; W. Nowack, Göttingen, 1902; J. Witt, *Saul and David. Eine Erklärung der Bücher Samuelis*, Kiel, 1902; B. Neteler, Münster, 1903; P. N. Schlögl, Vienna, 1904; A. R. S. Kennedy, in *Century Bible*, London, 1905; P. Dhorme, Paris, 1909; H. L. Willett, *Studies in I. Samuel*, Chicago, 1909.

SANBALLAT, san-bal'at (Babylonian, "Sin preserves in life"): An opponent of Nehemiah, and a leader against the Jews in their attempts to restore Jerusalem after their return from the exile (Neh. ii. 10, 19–20, iii. 33 sqq., iv. 1 sqq., vi. 1 sqq., xiii. 28 sqq.). His special efforts were directed against the protection of Jerusalem by the erection of the city wall, in which he was aided by Tobiah the Ammonite, Geshem (or Gashmu) the Arabian, the Philistines of Ashdod, and the Persians in possession of Samaria. Threats that the king of Persia would regard the building of the wall as an act of rebellion failing, the opponents of Nehemiah proceeded to violence when the wall was half finished. This also proving unsuccessful, Sanballat endeavored by stratagem to get Nehemiah into his power, and thus to ruin his plans. Some of Nehemiah's partisans were actually won over, especially as Sanballat had influential kinsmen in Jerusalem (Neh. vi. 10 sqq., xiii. 28 sqq.). According to Josephus (*Ant.*, XI., vii. 2), who apparently drew from Jewish tradition, Sanballat lived in the reign of Darius Codomannus, and after marrying his daughter to the brother of the high priest Jaddua, set up the temple and worship of the Samaritans on Gerizim. Sanballat is described as a Horonite, implying that he was an Ephraimite from Beth-horon, though some scholars have sought his home in the Moabitic city of Horonaim.

(R. KITTEL.)

BIBLIOGRAPHY: H. Winckler, *Altorientalische Forschungen*, ii. 228 sqq., Leipsic, 1894; A. A. van Hoonacker, *Études sur la restauration juive après l'exil de Babylone*, Paris, 1896; T. K. Cheyne, *Jewish Religious Life after the Exile*, New York, 1898; C. F. Kent, *Hist. of the Jewish People*, 7th ed., ib. 1905; E. Sachau, *Drei aramäische Papyrusurkunden aus Elephantine*, Berlin, 1907; *DB*, iv. 371; *EB*, iv. 4281; *JE*, xi. 37; Vigouroux, *Dictionnaire*, xxxv., col. 1443; the commentaries on Ezra-Nehemiah; and the works dealing with this period of history cited under ARAB; and ISRAEL, HISTORY OF.

SANBENITO, san"bé-nî'tō: A pentitential garment the wearing of which was one of the punishments inflicted by the Inquisition (q.v.). In its final form it was "a kind of yellow tunic with a red St. Andrew's cross [on the breast and on the back]—a mark of infamy and a severe infliction, as it largely impeded the efforts of the penitent to gain a livelihood" (H. C. Lea, *Inquisition of Spain*, ii. 401, New York, 1906). Its origin is with probability to be traced to the habit of sackcloth worn by penitents in times earlier than the Inquisition. The sanbenetillo was a stage in the inquisitorial development of the sanbenito and was the device of Torquemada in 1490, consisting of black or gray cloth, eighteen inches long and nine wide, depending from the neck over breast and back, with the red cross on each part. It was worn over the outer garment and was therefore extremely conspicuous. In 1514 Ximenes ordered that the form of cross used should be that of St. Andrew; and in 1561 the "Instructions" (of the Inquisition) directed that the material be yellow (apparently in Valencia and Sicily, of green) linen or cloth, the aim being evidently to increase the conspicuousness of the object and the severity of the penalty. A variation that came into use was a half-cross or diagonal bar, used on the sanbenitos of those regarded as culpable in a less degree. Those who were to be "relaxed" wore a black sanbenito, on which were painted flames and figures of devils thrusting the heretic into hell.

The punishment of wearing the garment was at first inflicted for life. Later different periods were assigned, and the wearing was sometimes conterminous with the period of imprisonment, sometimes only during the period of the auto da fé, at other times the punishment varied with the adjudged degree of guilt or seriousness of the crime. The severity of the punishment can hardly be conceived in modern times and in Protestant environment. It proclaimed the wearer to have been guilty of that most detestable of crimes, heresy. The wearer could with extreme difficulty gain employment, he was an object of general horror and ostracism, and it is probable that many were driven to death by starvation. To discard the garment subjected the wearer to rearrest as one who had recanted his submission to Holy Church with all the penalties which that involved. This led naturally to appeals for dispensation from wearing the garment, and it came before long to the situation that dispensation was made a means of papal revenue and an instrument of exaction, as high as 1,000 florins having been paid in order to avoid the wearing of the sanbenito.

In order to increase the detestation of heresy and to deter from committing such a crime a new use of the garment was devised. The sanbenito was inscribed with the name of the wearer and other details and hung in the churches, this having in view the perpetuation of the memory of the offense.

This usage seems to have been followed with especial malignity and persistence, gaps in the series being filled from the records, and even those who had been exempted from wearing the sanbenito were represented by the article in the church. That the crime might be brought home to the family, a duplicate was sometimes made and hung in the church which was the parish home of the family. The inscriptions were renewed as they faded through time and handling. Naturally these articles were at times stolen from the depositaries, but were often replaced by the Holy Office. This exhibition was at times supplemented by lists made out and suspended separately, in order the more securely to perpetuate the memory of the heretic and his crime. During the second half of the seventeenth and the eighteenth century, the seal of the Inquisition in this natter relaxed, and there was connivance at the burial of the custom. The Cortes of Cadiz, Jan. 22, 1813, abolished the Inquisition, and a decree of the same date, citing Article 305 of the constitution, called attention to the provision that punishment was not to extend beyond the criminal, and directed that records or articles perpetuating the memory of punishment inflicted by the Inquisition be removed or destroyed within three days. The condition of Spain, however, could not ensure obedience to this order, and not for some time subsequently was the abolition of these garments completely carried out.

Bibliography: H. C. Lea, *Inquisition of Spain*, iii. 162–172, i. 258, 280, ii. 401–402, 409, iii. 103, 125, 156, 163, 164, iv. 527, New York, 1906–07.

SANCHUNIATHON, san-cū-nai'a-thon.

1. The Assumed Author.

Sanchuniathon is the name given to an assumed Phenician writer, alleged to have belonged to the city of Berytus (Beirut), the putative author of a work cited as "Phenician History" or "Things Phenician." This work Philo Byblius (q.v.) claims to have translated from the Phenician language into Greek, and it is known only by quotations from this alleged translation extant principally in Eusebius' *Præparatio Evangelica*, 32c–41d (Eng. transl., 2 vols., Oxford, 1903). The known fragments are collected elsewhere, best in C. Müller, *Fragmenta historicorum Græcorum*, iii. 560 sqq. (4 vols., Paris, 1841–51). According to Eusebius (ut sup., 31d), Philo Byblius describes Sanchuniathon as a man of great learning, given to research into universal history, and especially interested in the god Thoth (*Taautos*), the Hermes of the Greeks, whom he held to be the inventor of letters and writing, with whom the writing of history began. Eusebius (ut sup., 31a–c) cites also Porphyry, the anti-Christian polemist, as asserting that the "truest history of the affairs of the Jews" was written by this Sanchuniathon, "who received the records from Hierombalos, the priest of the god Ieuo" and dedicated his history to King Abibalus of Berytus. Porphyry adds that "the times of these men [i.e., evidently of Sanchuniathon, Hierombalos, and Abibalus] fall before the date of the Trojan war and approach nearly to the time of Moses, as shown by the succession of the kings of Phenicia [cf. Eusebius, ut sup., 484–486, where he uses these data to confirm the antiquity of Moses]. And Sanchuniathon . . . lived in the days of Semiramis, queen of the Assyrians, who is recorded as living before the Trojan war or in those very times." Porphyry further declares that his authority made "a complete collection of ancient history from the records in the various cities and from the registers in the temples, and wrote in the Phenician language with a love of truth." Porphyry adds his testimony that these works were translated into Greek by Philo of Byblos. Mention of Sanchuniathon appears to be confined to post-Christian writers, such as the grammarian Athenæus (fl. about 225 A.D.). The character and intrinsic interest of the material presented by Eusebius, the high antiquity claimed for it, and the line of transmission by which it has come down have combined to raise a number of problems which are of more than usual interest and are by no means merely academic. Renan voices a quite general opinion, justified by the amount of discussion the subject has raised, when he remarks that "few problems in the circle of Semitic studies and of ancient history . . . are of more importance" (*Mémoirs*, p. 6). The worth of the material is surpassing if it be of the antiquity claimed ; it is great if it be of a period anterior to the Christian era; it is well worth study if it reflect truly either the priestly or the popular belief of the period of the "translator"; and it is in any case worthy of study as a presentation of a theory of the origin of religion if it date no earlier than the translator himself.

2. Philo's Introduction.

According to Eusebius (ut sup., 31d), the work was by Philo divided into nine books; Porphyry (*De abstinentia*) reports that it was in eight, possibly counting the first book merely as an introduction. Eusebius makes it clear that Philo prefaced his "translation" with an introduction. This describes Sanchuniathon as given to historical research, and laying the foundation of his history with Thoth-Hermes. Philo then asserts that "the most recent" writers on religion [by whom he means apparently those near the age of Sanchuniathon] rejected facts, invented allegories and myths, employed fictitiously cosmic phenomena, and overlaid them with absurdities. But Sanchuniathon happened on the "secret writings of the Ammoneans" in the shrines, studied them, and put aside the myths and allegories. But the priests who followed him restored the mythical character of the narratives, and this was the origin of the legends and myths prevalent in the Greek world. Philo is then quoted as setting forth briefly his syncretistic theory of the origin of religion. He declares that the "most ancient barbarians," especially the Phenicians and Egyptians, who in these matters were the teachers of mankind, regarded as the greatest gods those who had discovered the necessaries of life or . . . done good to the nations," worshiped them as gods after their death, consecrated pillars and staves "after their names," applied the names of their kings to the elements, and knew no other gods than those of nature—sun, moon, and planets, so that "some of their gods were mortal and some immortal." Eusebius then asserts that Philo "begins his interpretation of Sanchuniathon by setting forth the theology of the Phenicians," and gives the following cosmogony and theogony.

The first principle was "an air dark with cloud and wind," and a "chaos dark as erebus," both boundless. The wind fell in love with its parents, and "Desire." This was the beginning of creation.

3. Pre-Hesiodic Theogony and Creation. Thus "Mot" was produced—either mud or a "putrescence of watery compound"—which contained the germs of all creation. There were certain insensate animals from which the sensate (called *Zuphasemin*, "observers of heaven") issued while Mot broke forth into light, the heavenly bodies and the constellations, sea and land became heated, causing storms of wind and clouds and floods and whirlwinds, the tumult of which awaked the intelligent animals that then began to move. All this Sanchuniathon discovered in Thoth's cosmogony and commentaries. Here Eusebius summarizes, saying that the winds Notus and Boreas and other things are called by name. Then he proceeds again to quote to the purport that these [intelligent animals? or "winds and other things"?] were the first who consecrated the productions of earth and worshiped them as gods because they were the supporters of life, making libations to them. From the wind Colpias and his wife Baau ("Night," cf. Hebr. *bohu*, "chaos") were born the men Aeon and Protogonus ("Age" and "Firstborn"); Aeon discovered foods borne by trees. Their offspring were Genos and Genea and dwelt in Phenicia, worshiping the sun, calling him Beelsamen (Hebr. *Baal shamayim*, "Lord of heaven"), the Greek Zeus. From Genos were born mortals named Light, Fire, and Flame, who discovered fire by friction. They also begat giants, whose names were applied to the mountains—Cassius, Lebanon, Antilebanon, and Brathy. These in turn begat Memrumus who is also Hypsuranius, taking their names from their mothers. He adds that intercourse between men and women in those days was free. Hypsuranius settled Tyre, and invented huts of reeds and rushes. He quarreled with his brother Ousōus, who invented clothing from skins of wild beasts, and first sailed the sea on a log, set up two pillars in his worship of fire and wind, and poured on them libations of blood from game. After the death of Ousōus and Hypsuranius, they were deified and worshiped by their descendants at yearly festivals, where cultic objects were pillars and staves. From the race of Hypsuranius sprang Agreus and Halieus, inventors of fishing and hunting, from whom sprang two brothers who discovered iron and how to work it; one was Chrysor, orator, magician, and diviner, also called Hephæstus, inventor of sailing on rafts, who is also Zeus Mellichios (cf. Jane E. Harrison, *Prolegomena to the Study of Greek Religion*, chap. i., Cambridge, 1908). Two youths of this race were Technites ("Artificer") and Geinos Autochthon ("Earth-born Aboriginal") who mixed straw with clay for bricks and invented roofs. From them came Agros and Agrueros or Agrotes, founders of agriculture, identified with the Titans; their offspring were Amynos and Magus, who developed villages and sheepfolds; next came Misor (Hebr. *mishor*, "uprightness") and Suduc (Hebr. *ẓedeḳ*, "righteousness"), who discovered salt. Misor's son was Thoth-Hermes, who invented the alphabet and writing. Suduc was the father of the first builders of ships (the Dioscuri or Cabeiri or Corybantes or Samothraci), from whom sprang the first physician. Then were born Elioun (cf. the Hebr. *Elyon*, "Most High") and the female Beruth (? Hebr. *berith*, "covenant"), who dwelt near Byblos, from whom came Epigeius or Autochthon (afterwards called Ouranos, Uranus), whose sister was Gē, "Earth." These deified their father Elioun after he had been killed by wild beasts, married, and produced Elus (Hebrew *El*, "God") or Kronos, Bætylus (Bethel, "shrine"), Dagon who is also Siton, and Atlas.

From this point on the substratum of the "history" is the Greek mythology of Hesiod and later writers. Uranus took other wives, and had a numerous progeny. This offended Gē and she reproached Uranus, who separated from her and then tried to destroy his offspring by her. Kronos, after

4. Theogony Based on the Greek. he had grown to manhood, with the help of his secretary Hermes, avenged his mother. Kronos became the father of Persephone and Athena, drove Uranus from his kingdom, and founded Byblos by building a wall around his own dwelling. Of a concubine of Uranus captured in the war between Kronos and Uranus was born in the house of Dagon the deity Demarus. The descendants of the Dioscuri at this time put together rafts and ships and made voyages, were shipwrecked near Mt. Cassius, and consecrated a temple there. The allies of Kronos in the war with Uranus were called Eloim (cf. Hebr. *Elohim*, "God" or "gods"). Kronos then became the murderer of one of his sons and one of his daughters. Meanwhile Uranus was constantly intriguing for the overthrow and death of Kronos, sending his daughters Astarte, Rhea, and Dione for this purpose. But they were captured and made the wives of Kronos and bore him the Titanides and others. One of the Titanides married Suduc and became the mother of Asclepius. In Persea Kronos had the sons Kronos the Younger, Zeus Belus, and Apollo, and issue from these were Pontus, Typhon, Nereus, Sidon (inventor of song), and Poseidon. To Demarus was born Melcathrus (Melkart). Finally Uranus was waylaid, killed, and deified. Astarte, Zeus Demarus, and Adodus (Hadad, see RIMMON) ruled the country; the first of these is by Phenicians identified with Aphrodite. Kronos gave Attica to his daughter Athena. When a pestilence occurred, he offered up his only begotten son Iedud (see below § 8) to Uranus (thus beginning the sacrifice of the firstborn) and introduced circumcision. When his son Muth (*Thanatos*, "Death," Pluto) died, he deified him. He gave Byblos to Baaltis (Beltis, Dione) and Berytus to Poseidon. Thoth had meanwhile invented portraiture and devised symbols of royalty for Kronos, and had received from him Egypt. The Cabeiri, Suduc's seven sons, reduced these things to writing. But the first Phenician hierophant, Thabion, allegorised the narrative and made myths of them, the prophets inaugurated the mysteries, while their successors diffused myths and ceremonials. The Greeks, in accordance with their genius, were most fertile in carrying this process forward, especially Hesiod and the Cyclic poets. Quotations from a work cited by Eusebius as "History of the Jews" repeat the story of Thoth's rescuing of the worship of the gods from ignorance, and proceeds to relate that the ancients used in crises to sacrifice their most beloved children with mystic rites. Kronos (Elus) was deified as Saturn, but had previously by Anobret a son Iedud, whom he sacrificed on an occasion like that mentioned in II Kings iii. 26-27. The origin of serpent worship is ascribed to Thoth, who saw in this animal and in the dragon the divine nature.

The material here presented embodies an eclectic theory of the origin of the gods, combining the Euhemeristic theory (see EUHEMERUS) with the naturalistic (deification of cosmic or stellar or natural forces). The line of transmission of the fragments is not altogether devoid of obscurity.

5. Antiquity of Material not Supported. For centuries the opinion obtained that Eusebius quoted from Porphyry; but a closer examination warrants the conclusion that Eusebius cited Porphyry only to establish the supposed antiquity of Sanchuniathon, and that for the rest he used Philo direct. The alleged antiquity is implied by Philo in his statements that the results of Sanchuniathon's researches had long before been perverted by the Greeks, and that Greek myths, which go back to Hesiod, were derived from this falsified material. Philo's task as he states it was to recover once more the facts from the perverted statement of them. But the fragments bear internal evidence that no such antiquity can be granted. The incidents with which they are made contemporary were not of the same period. Semiramis (the Assyrian queen of Greek legend is probably to be identified with Sammuramat, consort of Adad-nirari V., 812-783) was not a contemporary of the Trojan war, but considerably later. Hierombalos is evidently the Greek form for Jerubbaal (Judges ix.-x.), while by Abibalus is evidently meant the father of Hiram of Tyre who was a contemporary of Solomon (cf. Josephus, *Ant.*, VIII., v. 3); all of these are made nearly the contemporaries of Moses. Moreover the dedication of a work of history in those times is almost certainly an anachronism. It is beyond belief that Euhemerism was so old as to have become the subject of so early priestly falsification, which, moreover, reverses the course of history. When to Euhemerism is added so late a theory as the eclectic employed in this narrative, the ascription of so great an antiquity falls to the ground of its own weight.

It still remains to ask whether Philo reproduced the work of a man much later in history. It is to be noted that the processes of criticism reveal an evident complexity of sources. At least two cosmogonies are present besides the Greek (cf. Eusebius, ut sup., 33c with 34c). There are present at least three accounts of the invention of navigation

6. Complexity of Sources. —by Ousous, Chrysor-Hephæstus, and the Dioscuri. Similarly, there are triple accounts of the origin of hunting —through Agreus and Halieus, Ousous, and Agros and Agrueros, the first of whom invented clothing from the skins of wild animals he had slain. While so far this might have existed in the supposed original of Philo's work, a whole series of facts, viz., the distinct mingling of two separate lines of tradition—the Semitic and the Greek, the latter of which was not in existence at the time implied by Philo himself for the composition; the facts that the whole work is a distinct echo of Euhemerus (who claimed to have discovered his basal material in a temple; the most notable instance of Euhemerism in the assumption that Light, Fire, and Flame were the names of three men which were given to their discovery—a statement truly Spencerian in its boldness!); that the part assigned to Hermes as the adviser of the gods belongs to late post-Alexandrian theology; that a Greek play of words is found which involves the material of tradition (*astēr*, "star," Astarte); that the method of handling Greek, especially Hesiodic, theology is that of the period about the Christian era; that the forms followed in Phenician names are rarely old Phenician but rather Aramaic (cf. the form *Beelsamen* instead of the true Phenician *Baalsameme*),—all these considerations make it practically certain that Sanchuniathon was a fictitious personage upon whom Philo fathered the material which embodied his own philosophy of religion.

While there is little that is remarkable in the Greek material which Philo employed, the use of Semitic is interesting. The name Sanchuniathon reproduces a correct formation and means "(the god) Sakkun has given," and such a deity is abundantly attested in Phenician and Carthaginian environment. The deity Aion as discoverer of fruit finds a certain war-

7. Semitic Material Employed. rant in the inscription in Semitic environment on a late coin. Melcathrus is evidently Melcarth-Herakles. Muth (Semitic for "death") is punned upon. Adodos is Hadad, but Aramaic rather than Phenician. That Hebrew tradition is drawn upon is shown not only by mention of Hierombalos and Abibalus, but by the phrase "Iedud, the only begotten being" (Eusebius, ut sup., 40c; cf. *yaḥid*, "only son," Gen. xxii. 2, 12, 16, in the narrative of the tempting of Abraham). Ieuo is as clearly Yahweh; Elus is the Hebrew *El*, "God" (or the Semitic *ilu*, "god"). Is Ousous the hunter to be connected with Esau the hunter or with Usu, the cuneiform name for the mainland of Tyre? Misor and Suduc are Semitic abstracts, "equity" and "righteousness," though there may have been a Phenician deity *Ẓdḳ*. *Zophasemim* is correctly rendered "observers of heaven," Elioun and Eloim (Eusebius, 37b) have already been commented upon. The reasoning of the introduction is of a piece with the professed discussion, while the first part of the cosmogony is but the prologue to account for Greek mythology, used in the second part. Moreover the whole implies the current Greek conception of the wisdom of the Egyptians, modifying this, however, by putting on practically equal terms with the Egyptians the Phenicians from whom part of the material is obtained, and regarding them as disseminators of knowledge. This fits with what might reasonably be expected from an inquirer with a theory to support who found himself among the Phenicians, as did Philo. Thus Sanchuniathon reduces to a pseudonym, behind which Philo hides as he rationalizes the mythology of his times, against which he shows a polemic bias. GEO. W. GILMORE.

BIBLIOGRAPHY: For the earlier literature consult Fabricius-Harles, *Bibliotheca Græca*, i. 222–226, Hamburg, 1790. The best discussions of the subject are: H. Ewald, in the *Abhandlungen* of the Göttingen Scientific Society, Historical-philosophical series, v (1851–52), 3–68; idem, in *GGA*, 1859, pp. 1441–57; E. Renan, in the *Mémoires* of the French Academy of Inscriptions, xxiii. 2 (1858), 241–334; W. W. von Baudissin, *Studien zur semitischen Religionsgeschichte*, i. 1–46, Leipsic, 1876; O. Gruppe, *Die griechischen Culte und Mythen in ihren Beziehungen zu den orientalischen Religionen*, pp. 347–409, Leipsic, 1887; and R. P. Lagrange, *Études sur les religions sémitiques*, pp. 396–437, Paris, 1905. Consult further: J. G. von Herder, *Werke*, vi. 139–154, Stuttgart, 1827; F. C. Movers, *Die Phönizier*, Bonn, 1841; idem, in *Jahrbücher für Theologie und christliche Philosophie*, vii (1836), 51–94; F. L. Vibe, *Commentatio de Sanchoniathone*, Christiania, 1842; E. Röth, *Geschichte unserer abendländischen Philosophie*, i. 243–277, Mannheim, 1846; Eckstein, in *JA*, V., xiv (1859), 167–238, xv (1860), 67–92, 210–263, 399–414; C. P. Tiele, *Egyptische en Mesopotamische Godsdiensten*, pp. 440–448, Amsterdam, 1872, Fr. transl., pp. 273–279, Paris, 1882; P. Berger, *L'Ange d'Astarte*, in congratulatory volume in honor of E. Reuss, pp. 47 sqq., Paris, 1879; F. Lenormant, *Les Origines d'histoire*, i. 536–552, Paris, 1880, Eng. transl., *Beginnings of History*, London, 1883; J. Halévy, *Mélanges de critique et d'histoire*, pp. 381–388, Paris, 1883; Robiou, in *Mémoires présentés*, French Academy of Inscriptions, I., x. 2 (1897), 12–19; Ersch and Gruber, *Encyklopädie*, III., xxiv.; *Biographie universelle*, vol. xxxiv., s.v. "Philon de Byblos," and vol. xl., s.v. "Sanchoniathon."

SANCROFT, WILLIAM: Church of England; b. at Fressingfield (84 m. n.e. of London), Suffolk, Jan. 30, 1616–17; d. there Nov. 24, 1693. He graduated from Emmanuel College, Cambridge (B.A., 1637; M.A., 1641; B.D., 1648), where he obtained a fellowship in 1642, which, however, he lost in 1649 for refusing to sign the Solemn League and Covenant. On leaving Cambridge he retired to Fressingfield, where he remained nine years; went abroad in 1657; returned at the Restoration; became successively chaplain to John Cosin (q.v.), bishop of Durham, and university preacher, 1660; rector of Houghton-de-Spring, and the king's chaplain, 1661; prebendary at Durham Cathedral, and master of his college, 1662; dean of York, and of St. Paul's, 1664; archdeacon of Canterbury, 1668; and archbishop of Canterbury, 1677. He attended Charles II. on his death-bed, Feb., 1685; and crowned James II., Apr. 23, 1685. He would not act on James's ecclesiastical commission, and was one of the famous seven bishops who refused to read James's Declaration of Indulgence, and in consequence were confined in the Tower and tried, but were triumphantly acquitted. Sancroft also refused to take the oath of allegiance to William and Mary, 1688; and was deprived Feb. 1, 1691. The *Fur prædestinatus* (London, 1651; Eng. transl., *The Predestined Thief*, 1658) has been shown to have been erroneously attributed to him, and to be a translation of *Den ghepredestineerden Dieff* (The Hague, 1619–22). He left, *Modern Policies* (London, 1652); *Occasional Sermons* (1694); and *Familiar Letters* (1757).

BIBLIOGRAPHY: G. D'Oyley, *Life of Archbishop Sancroft*, 2 vols., London, 1821; J. Le Neve, *Lives, Characters . . . and . . . Benefactions of . . . Bishops of the Church of England since the Reformation*, ib. 1720; Agnes Strickland, *Lives of the Seven Bishops*, pp. 1–103, ib. 1866; J. Stoughton, *Religion in England*, 2 vols., ib. 1884; W. H. Hutton, *The English Church (1625–1714)*, pp. 228–233 et passim, ib. 1903; *DNB*, l. 244–250.

SANCTIFICATION: In common Christian usage the deliverance of the personal life from the power of sin accomplished by the faithful observance of faith, by the earnest struggle against all temptation to turn away from the living God, and by the practise of Christian piety. In technical language sanctification means the operation of the grace by which salvation is conveyed to man, enabling him to be freed and to free himself from sin, and to become like God in heart, will, and thought. The term is derived from Scripture (I Thess. iv. 3, 7; II Thess. ii. 13; Rom. vi. 19, 22). The Christian is admonished to yield himself to Christ, "who is made unto us sanctification" (I Cor. i. 30) and to prove his holiness by his conduct (I Peter i. 15, 16; cf. I Cor. vii. 24; Eph. i. 4, v. 27). The divine work of salvation is designated as sanctification especially in Hebrews (ii. 11, ix. 13, 14, x. 10, xiv. 29). But the sense of the term is not fixed with dogmatic precision; in Roman Catholic theology it is included in the conception of justification; in Protestant theology it follows justification, but in this case is usually identified with renovation and good works.

Definition.

According to the Roman Catholic doctrine, while the saving grace of God is operative in sanctification, the process neither follows logically upon Roman Catholic justification nor differs essentially from it. In accordance with the medieval and modern Roman Catholic doctrine of justification, it is sanctification which effects justification. Grace obliterates sin in man and endows him with supernatural righteousness and holiness through justification. Sanctification, therefore, considered as sanctifying grace, is the cause of justification, and the effects of sanctification form the content of justification, through which redemption from sin, as won by Christ, is imparted to man. In opposition to the Roman Catholic doctrine, the Formula of Concord regards sanctification as following justification, but scarcely differentiates it from renewal. Luther, on the contrary, in his larger catechism, considers sanctification as the office and work of the Holy Spirit, agreeing with the scholastic and Roman theology in so far as he looks upon sanctification as bestowal of salvation; though by this last he understands not the "infusion of righteousness," the bestowal of a power of virtue, but the effect of faith. The difference between Luther and the Formula of Concord, is, however, more nominal than real, since the Formula meant by the term sanctification apparently only a part of that which Luther meant by it. The doctrine of sanctification was not essentially changed in Pietism, but rationalism perverted the whole conception. While the term formerly denoted justification by faith and grace alone, rationalism understood by it the inner disposition which is to make man pleasing to God. Consequently the rationalists laid stress upon sanctification in the sense of man's efforts for his own moral perfection. In opposition to this tendency Schleiermacher once more emphasized faith as the truly religious attitude toward God and his revelation, as the condition of heart which is satisfied and feels itself strong in communion with Christ. This condition was developed by the following theologians into the germ of a new life on the basis of which man is justified. Accordingly, the subjective faith of man effects sanctification and lies at the basis of divine justification. This teaching was far removed from the doctrine of the Reformers. Ritschl and his school, however, returned to the latter, especially to that of Luther, by making sanctification dependent upon the justification of God. But according to Ritschl, man is justified only as a member of the Church, his act of conformity to which, and hence to the motives and purposes of God, constitutes the faith which justifies him. Thus here, too, sanctification, conceived as separation from sin, which takes form and accomplishes itself, is made within man and is the basis of justification.

The Reformed View.

In the Reformed Church and theology sanctification comes into the doctrine of perseverance. Man is justified, indeed, freely by grace; but the justified must perform good works, which he is enabled to do by a second act of grace, inseparably connected with justification. This is regeneration, which sanctifies him. By this regeneration or sanctification, however, man does not attain full perfection. His whole consolation rests upon the fact of justification. Sanctification is necessary for the elect and justified, in order to preserve the grace of their justification, and thus it follows justification with an inner divine necessity. Here also, as in Lutheran theology after Luther, sanctification is considered a special work of the Holy Spirit, following justification and conditioned by it. The distinction between the two is hardly more than a technical and controversial one.

Owing to influences from England and America, especially from the Methodists, Baptists, and Salvation Army and the doctrine of Pearsall Smith, a new doctrine of sanctification has become current, according to which it is not only different from, but even more important than, justification. It is considered as that act of divine grace in which the real tendency of divine revelation finds its fullest expression, while justification is secondary to it.

Conclusion.

Upon examination the view of the Lutheran as well as of the Reformed theologians, that sanctification is a special process to be distinguished from justification and following it, is seen to be unscriptural. Just as little authority in Scripture can be found for the view of the Pietists, of the modern dogmaticians (including Ritschl), and still less for that of the "practical" tendency in church life, according to which sanctification is the chief purpose of the divine plan of salvation. Formal scriptural authority can be found only for the view of Luther and that of the medieval or Roman theology, which designate the whole process of conveying salvation to man as sanctification. Of these two, again, Luther's alone is scriptural in so far as he looks upon this bestowal of salvation as the effect of faith. Bestowal of salvation is sanctification, because it delivers man from sin and brings him into communion with the God of redemption. It is to be distinguished, though not separated, from the divine sentence of justification, since it is that effect of the grace of God on man which makes him capable of faith and preserves it, which brings him into communion with God and preserves him in it; it is therefore not a single isolated operation but a continuous one. The scriptural term *hagiasmos* denotes the condition of being sanctified, the action performed on the object as a condition proceeding from and effected by the Holy Ghost who bestows salvation (I Peter i. 2; cf. II Thess. ii. 13; I Thess. iv. 7). If it be asked what is the relation of sanctification to the actuality of Christian life, it appears that man stands by faith in communion with God, and is thus placed in a position from which he is not only able but obliged to resist sin and fulfil the will of God out of love. The bestowal of grace, forgiveness, in a word justification, is actually sanctification; for there is no mightier deliverance from sin than that which is worked by the bestowal of grace or forgiveness, or by faith in the operation of its power. "Christ in us" is nothing else than "Christ for us," realized and held fast in faith. Such action as makes man a partaker of sanctification is precisely the same action as that by which he is made a partaker of justification; it is clear, accordingly, that in view of the position and meaning of the latter in the scheme of Christian doctrine, the term sanctification is non-essential, if not superfluous. (H. T. Cremer†.)

Bibliography: The subject is generally treated in the works on systematic theology (see under the article Dogma, Dogmatics), while treatises on the Holy Spirit (q.v.) necessarily deal with the topic; another class of works to be used for the Biblical side is that on Biblical Theology, especially W. Beyschlag's *N. T. Theology*, Edinburgh, 1896. Consult further: Walter Marshall, *Gospel Mystery of Sanctification*, London, 1692, often reprinted, e.g., Edinburgh, 1887 (a classic); E. G. Marsh, *The Christian Doctrine of Sanctification*, London, 1848; J. Q. Adams, *Sanctification*, new ed., New York, 1883; G. Junkin, *A Treatise on Sanctification*, Philadelphia, 1864; W. E. Boardman, *The "Higher Life" Sanctification Tried by the Word of God*, Philadelphia, 1877; J. A. Beet, *Holiness as Understood by the Writers of the Bible*, London, 1880; J. Hartley, *Chapters on Holiness*, London, 1883; J. H. Collins, *Sanctification, what it is, when it is, how it is*, Nashville, 1885; A. Murray, *Holy in Christ*, New York, 1888; J. Fraser, *A Treatise on Sanctification*, London, 1897; E. Hoare, *Sanctification*, 5th ed., ib., 1898; P. T. Forsyth, *Christian Perfection*, New York, 1899; H. W. Webb-Peploe, *Calls to Holiness*, London, 1900; A. Kuyper, *The Work of the Holy Spirit*, New York, 1902; W. R. Inge, *Faith and Knowledge*, Edinburgh, 1904; H. C. G. Moule, *Holiness by Faith*, London, 1906; A. B. O. Wilberforce, *Sanctification by the Truth*, London, 1906; E. Tobac, *Le Problème de la justification dans S. Paul*, Louvain, 1908; *DB*, iv. 391–395; *DCG*, ii. 561–566 (adds a bibliography of distinct homiletical value); Vigouroux, *Dictionnaire*, fasc. xxxv. 1443–44.

SANCTIS, sănc'tis, LUIGI DE: Italian Protestant; b. at Rome Dec. 31, 1808; d. at Florence Dec. 31, 1869. Of his youth little is known, but in 1831 he was ordained to the priesthood of the Roman Catholic Church, and three years later was appointed professor of philosophy and theology at Genoa, where he manifested great heroism in the care of the sick during an epidemic of cholera in 1835. In 1837 he received an appointment in the Holy Office, only to have his faith gradually but surely undermined by the books which his position compelled him to read. Nevertheless, he gained a high reputation as a pulpit orator, and from 1840 to 1847 was at the head of the parish of Santa Maddalena alla Rotonda in Rome; but the doubts already engendered were complicated by his sympathy with the movement for the unification of Italy and the overthrow of papal control, and in 1843 he was condemned to ten days' imprisonment in the monastery of San Eusebio. The accession of Pius IX. June 21, 1846, and the policy at first adopted by the new pontiff, filled De Sanctis with hope, which was speedily crushed by the encyclical of Nov. 9, 1846, exalting the cult of the Virgin. De Sanctis was now obliged to conceal his ever-increasing doubts, both family ties and official position combining to prevent him from openly breaking with his church. At this juncture he came in contact with a Scotch clergyman named Lowndes, then resident in Malta, who brought him greetings from the ex-monk Giovanni Giacinto Achilli, who was endeavoring to propagate Protestantism in Malta under British protection (see NEWMAN, JOHN HENRY). A second interview with Lowndes led De Sanctis to gain permission to visit Ancona, whence he surreptitiously sailed for Corfu, soon leaving that island for Malta. Refusing every inducement to return to Rome, he now passed two years preaching in an Italian church in Malta, but with the change of conditions in Italy he accepted an invitation to visit Tuscany, where he preached in Florence, Leghorn, and the vicinity of Lucca until ordered by the police to desist. He then returned to Malta, where, on Nov. 1, 1848, he began the publication of *Il Cattollico cristiano*, a sheet filled with denunciation of Roman Catholicism and defense of Protestantism. In 1849 he married, and in the same year published his *La Confessione* (Malta, 1849; Eng. transl. by M. H. G. Buckle, London, 1878), and in 1850 he accepted a call to Geneva to preach among the Italian political refugees, workmen, and ex-priests. He soon after made a tour of Italian Switzerland, meeting with special success in the Protestant Val Bregaglia. The growth of the Waldensian community in Turin (see ITALY, II., § 1), however, led to the call of De Sanctis to that city in 1853, and he was formally ordained to the Waldensian ministry on Aug. 31 of the same year. But a split soon arose among the Waldensians, one faction adhering to their original principles, and the other, supported largely by funds supplied by Baptists and Plymouth Brethren, terming themselves "Free Italian Churches" (see ITALY, II., § 2) and claiming that they would quickly turn all Italy to Protestantism. It was with this radical wing that De Sanctis threw in his fortunes, and in 1855, at the Paris conference of the Evangelical Alliance, he secured recognition and financial aid for his party. He also visited London in quest of funds and was cordially received, and after a tour of Piedmont took up his residence at Genoa, where he and his friends established a Protestant school. During this period he employed himself in writing, the chief results being his *Si può leggere la Bibia?* (3d ed., Florence, 1866); *La Religione degli avi* (1861); *La Messa* (Turin, 1862); and *Discussione pacifica* (1863). He did not, however, approve of the hostility of the "Free Church" to the Waldensians, and in 1863–64 events forced him to protest publicly against an attack on Roman Catholicism and Protestantism alike in favor of the exclusive claim of the Plymouth Brethren to true Christianity. The result was a fresh split in the "Free Church," and De Sanctis withdrew to Florence, where he was soon appointed professor of apologetic, polemic, and practical theology in the Waldensian seminary, a position which he held until his death.

The list of De Sanctis' writings is a long one. His principal productions, in addition to those already mentioned, are as follows: *Il Celibato dei preti* (n.p., 1850); *Popery and Jesuitism at Rome in the Nineteenth Century* (London, 1852); *Lettera a Pio nono, vescovo di Roma* (Turin, 1854); *Il Primato del papa* (Florence, 1861); *Osservazioni dottrinali e storiche* (1865); *Compendio di controversie tra la parola Dio è la teologia romana* (4th ed., 1870); *Il Papa non è successore di san Pietro* (4th ed., 1887); *Il Purgatorio perchè non è ammesso dagli evangelici* (1898); and the most important of all, *Roma papale* (1865). (PAOLO CALVINO.)

SANCTUARY, RIGHT OF. See ASYLUM, RIGHT OF.

SANDAY, WILLIAM: Church of England; b. at Holme Pierrepont (20 m. n.e. of Nottingham), Nottinghamshire, Aug. 1, 1843. He was educated at Balliol College, Oxford, and Corpus Christi College, Oxford (B.A., 1865), and was ordered deacon in 1867 and ordained priest two years later. He was fellow of Trinity College, Oxford (1866–73); in charge of Navestock, Romford (1869–71), lecturer of St. Nicholas, Abingdon (1871–72); vicar of Great Waltham, Chelmsford (1872–73); rector of Barton-on-the-Heath, Warwickshire (1873–76); principal of Hatfield Hall, Durham (1876–83); Dean Ireland's professor of the exegesis of Holy Scripture in the University of Oxford and tutorial fellow of Exeter College, Oxford (1883–95); and since 1895 he has been Lady Margaret professor of divinity and canon of Christ Church, Oxford. He was also examining chaplain to the bishop of Durham (1879–81), select preacher at Cambridge in 1880, 1892, and 1903, Whitehall preacher in 1889–90, and Bampton lecturer in 1893. He has been honorary fellow of Exeter College since 1898; chaplain in ordinary to the king, and a fellow of the British Academy since 1903. Besides being joint editor of the *Variorum Bible* (London, 1880); *Old Latin Biblical Texts*, ii. (in collaboration with Bishop John Wordsworth; 1886); *Studia Biblica et Ecclesiastica* (Oxford, 1891); *Commentary on the Epistle to the Romans* (in collaboration with A. C. Headlam; London, 1886; 5th ed., 1909); and editing the translation of select writings of

Hilary of Poictiers for the *Library of Nicene and Post-Nicene Fathers* (New York and Edinburgh, 1898); he has written *The Authorship and Historical Character of the Fourth Gospel* (London, 1872); *The Gospels in the Second Century* (1876); the sections on Romans and Galatians in Bishop C. J. Ellicott's *Handy Commentary* (London, 1878); *Appendices ad Novum Testamentum Stephanicum* (1889); *The Oracles of God* (1891); *Two Present Day Questions* (1892); *Inspiration* (Bampton lectures; 1893); *The Conception of Priesthood in the Early Church and in the Church of England* (1898); *An Examination of Harnack's "What is Christianity?"* (1901); *Criticism of the New Testament* (1902); *Divisions in the Church* (1902); *Sacred Sites of the Gospels* (in collaboration with P. Waterhouse; 1903); *Outlines of the Life of Christ* (Edinburgh, 1905); *The Criticism of the Fourth Gospel* (London, 1905); *The Life of Christ in Recent Research* (1907); and *Christologies, Ancient and Modern* (1910).

SANDEMANIANS, san-de-mé'ni-ans or man'i-ans **(GLASSITES):** A sect founded in Scotland c. 1730 by John Glas (q.v.). The basal idea of the founder was the restoration of the apostolic Church, realizing the complete independence of each local church from every other and from the State. Chief emphasis was laid upon the Lord's Supper, while feet-washing, the kiss of charity, the lovefeast, and a limited community of goods were introduced; games of chance, eating of blood and things strangled, and the use of the lot were forbidden, and church government was placed in the hands of bishops, elders, and teachers. The name came from the son-in-law of Glas, Robert Sandeman (b. at Perth, Scotland, 1718; d. at Danbury, Conn., Apr. 2, 1771), who was appointed an elder in the new organization, exercised his ministry at Perth, Dundee, and Edinburgh, and sailed in 1764 to America, where he founded churches. The denomination is now nearly or quite extinct.

(C. Schoell†.)

Bibliography: The *Works* of John Glas, especially his *Treatise on the Lord's Supper*, Edinburgh, 1743, reprinted, London, 1883; the literature under Glas, John; J. Bellamy, *Essay on the Nature and Glory of the Gospel of Jesus Christ*, i. 65–125, London, 1761, reprint 1841; A. Fuller, *Strictures on Sandemanianism*, in his *Complete Works*, ib. 1853; J. B. Marsden, *Hist. of Christian Churches and Sects*, ii. 297 sqq., ib. 1856; J. E. Ritchie, *Religious Life of London*, ib. 1870.

SANDER, IMMANUEL FRIEDRICH EMIL: Pulpit orator and polemist; b. in Saxony in 1797; d. at Wittenberg Apr. 28, 1859. In early life he was repelled by the current rationalism, and as a minor official of St. Paul's Church in Leipsic, in the first part of his career, he began to preach with emphasis the Gospel of the Crucified One. In 1822 he was called to Wichlinghausen in Wupperthal, where he exerted his activities in the same direction, translating into German, in collaboration with C. H. F. Bialloblotzky, Pusey's *Enquiry into the Probable Causes of the Rationalist Character lately Predominant in the Theology of Germany* (Elberfeld, 1829), and following this up with his own *Theologisches Gutachten* (Barmen, 1836), which was preceded and followed by several volumes of sermons and by *Beleuchtung* (1836) aimed at the *Prediger-Bibel* of Eduard Hülsmann (1835), which last brought him into court on charges of libel. He also attacked Droste-Vischering (q.v.) in *Ueber den Frieden unter der Kirche und den Staaten* and *Das Papstthum in seiner heutigen Gestalt, in seinen Ursprüngen und endlichen Ausgängen* (Elberfeld, 1845). To this period belongs also his treatise on Gal. iii. 20 (1840) and *Der Romanismus, seine Tendenzen und seine Methodik* (Essen, 1843). About this time he accepted the ideas of Johann Tobias Beck (q.v.), and placed the beginning of the parousia (see Millennium, Millenarianism) in 1847. In 1854 he accepted a call to Wittenberg, where he came to occupy the positions of city preacher, superintendent, and director of the preachers' seminary till his death. He continued to issue sermons, occasional and others, the most significant based upon the Revelation of John.

Bibliography: F. W. Krummacher, *Immanuel Friedrich Sander*, Cologne, 1860.

SANDERS, FRANK KNIGHT: Congregationalist; b. at Batticotta (a village near Jaffna, 190 m. n. of Colombo), Ceylon, June 5, 1861. He was educated at Ripon College, Wis. (A. B., 1882); was instructor in Jaffna College, Ceylon (1882–86), and continued his studies at Yale (1886–89). He was then successively assistant in Biblical literature (1889–90), instructor in Semitic languages (1890–91), and assistant professor of Biblical literature on the Woolsey foundation (1891–93)—all at Yale. In 1893 he was appointed Woolsey professor of Biblical literature in Yale, a position which he retained until 1901, when he resigned it to become professor of Biblical history and archeology and dean of Yale Divinity School, both which offices he held until 1905, when he became secretary of the Congregational Sunday-school and Publishing Society. He has been president of Washburn College, Topeka, Kan., since 1908. He has edited in collaboration with C. F. Kent *The Historical Series for Bible Students* (10 vols., New York, 1897–1906) and *The Messages of the Bible* (12 vols., 1898 sqq.), and together with the same scholar has written *The Messages of the Earlier Prophets* (New York, 1898) and *The Messages of the Later Prophets* (1899). He has also written *Outlines for the Study of Biblical History and Literature* (in collaboration with H. T. Fowler, New York, 1906); *A Student's Life of Christ* (1906); *Historical Notes on the Apostolic Leaders* (1907); and *Historical Notes on the Life of Christ* (1907).

SANDERSON, JOSEPH: Presbyterian; b. at Ballybay (60 m. n.w. of Dublin), County Monaghan, Ireland, May 23, 1823; graduated at the Royal College, Belfast, 1845; emigrated to America, 1846; was classical teacher in the Washington Institute, New York, 1847–49; studied theology and became pastor of the Associate Presbyterian Church, Providence, R. I., 1849; at New York, 1853–69; acting pastor of Saugatuck Congregational Church, Conn., 1872–78; assistant editor of the *Homiletic Monthly*, New York, 1881–83; editor of the *Pulpit Treasury*, New York, after 1883; and from 1895, secretary of the Church Extension and Sustentation Committee, New York Presbytery. He is the author of *Jesus on* *the Holy Mount* (New York, 1869); *Memorial Tributes* (1883); *The Story of Saint Patrick* (1895); and *Man's Seal to God's Word* (1902).

SAN DOMINGO. See West Indies.

SANDYS, EDWIN: Church of England, archbishop of York; b. near Hawkshead (24 m. n.w. of Lancaster), Lancashire, 1516; d. at York July 10, 1588. He was educated at St. John's College, Cambridge; was converted to Protestantism; elected master of Catherine Hall, 1547; became vicar of Caversham, 1548; canon of Peterborough, 1549; prebendary of Carlisle, 1552; and vice-chancellor of Cambridge, 1553. He was imprisoned in the Tower for espousing the cause of Lady Jane Grey, escaped, and went into voluntary exile until Elizabeth's accession; became bishop of Worcester, 1559; of London, 1570; and archbishop of York, 1576. He took part in the preparation of the Bishops' Bible (see Bible Versions, B, IV., § 4) in 1565; translated Hosea, Joel, Amos, and Malachi in the version of 1572; and assisted in the revision of the Liturgy, 1559. A volume of *Sermons* (London, 1585; 1616) contains in its newer issue (by T. Whitaker, 1812) a life; this volume was reedited with life for the Parker Society by J. Ayre (Cambridge, 1841).

Bibliography: William Thomas, *Survey of the Cathedral-Church of Worcester; with an Account of the Bishops*, pp. 210–214, London, 1736; C. H. and T. Cooper, *Athenæ Cantabrigienses*, ii. 24, 543, ib. 1861; F. G. Lee, *The Church under Queen Elizabeth*, ib. 1896; W. Clark, *The Anglican Reformation*, New York, 1897; W. H. Frere, *The English Church . . . (1558–1625)*, London, 1904; H. N. Birt, *The Elizabethan Religious Settlement*, ib. 1907; *DNB*, l. 283–286.

SANDYS, GEORGE: English poet and paraphrast; b. at Bishopthorpe (2 m. s. of York) Mar. 2, 1577–78; d. at Boxley (32 m. s.e. of London), Kent, Mar., 1644. He was educated at Oxford; traveled in the East, 1610–12; was in Virginia, 1621–24, as colonial treasurer; nominated to the colonial council, 1624, 1626, and 1628, building there "the first water-mill, the first iron-works, and the first ship," but, involved in quarrels and disappointed in not securing the appointment of secretary in 1631, returned to England; and was for some years an attendant of Charles I., and ended life in scholarly retirement. He published a much-valued *Relation of a Journey* (London 1615); translated Ovid's *Metamorphoses* (1626), partly at Jamestown, Va.; and G. Grotius' *Christ's Passion* (1640); and paraphrased the Psalms, Job, Canticles, Ecclesiastes, and Lamentation (1636–41). In James Montgomery's opinion "his psalms are incomparably the most poetical in the English language, and yet they are scarcely known." Fragments of one or two of them may be found in some of the hymn-books. The paraphrases were nearly inaccessible until H. J. Todd's *Selections from the Metrical Paraphrases on the Psalms and Other Portions of Holy Scripture by G. Sandys with a Memoir* (1839) appeared. *The Complete Poetical Works* (1872) was published with *Memoir* by R. Hooper in *Library of Old Authors* (London, 1856–72).

Bibliography: Besides the *Memoirs* named in the text, consult: Julian, *Hymnology*, pp. 918, 994; *DNB*, l. 290–293.

SANFORD, ELIAS BENJAMIN: Congregationalist; b. at Westbrook, Conn., June 6, 1843. He received his education at Wesleyan University (A.B., 1865; A.M., 1869) and Yale Divinity School; served as pastor at Cornwall (1869–71), Thomaston (1873–81), and Westbrook, all in Connecticut (1882–1895), during this period being a contributor to religious publications on subjects of importance; he was corresponding secretary of the Open and Institutional Church League (1895–1900); was the organizer of the National Federation of Churches (see Church Federation) and general secretary of the same since its founding (1900). At his suggestion this organization took action that secured the appointment of delegates from the highest judicatories and national conferences of thirty denominations representing the larger part of the Evangelical church membership of the United States. These delegates came together in an inter-church conference held in New York, Nov. 8–15, 1905, and adopted the plan of federation described in the article referred to above. Since 1903 Dr. Sanford as corresponding secretary has had in charge the correspondence and office details, under direction of the executive committee, of the several conferences. He is the author of *History of Connecticut* (Hartford, 1881); *Concise Cyclopedia of Religious Knowledge* (1890); *Church Federation. Report of Inter-Church Conference on Federation* (New York, 1905); and *Federal Council of the Churches. Report of the First Meeting of the Federal Council of the Churches of Christ in America* (Philadelphia, 1908).

SANHEDRIN, san'he-drin, **SANHEDRIM:** The term usually applied to the highest Jewish judicatory in Jerusalem at the time of Christ. The New Testament in the Greek usually employs the term *synedrion* to designate the court in which the judicial process against Jesus Christ was carried on (Matt. xxvi. 59; Mark xiv. 55, xv. 1; Luke xxii. 66), before which the apostles (Acts v. 21, 27, 34, 41), especially Peter and John (Acts iv. 15), Stephen (Acts vi. 12, 15), and Paul (Acts xxii. 30, xxiii. passim, xxiv. 20), had to answer for their faith in the Risen One. In John xi. 47 the term is applied to a session of this court. [In the English version the term "council" is usually applied to this court, and generally with additional phrases, such as "elders, scribes and the whole council," "elders, chief priests, and scribes," "council and senate."] In the passages cited above the reference is to one court alone. But the plural form in Matt. x. 17; Mark xiii. 9; cf. Matt. v. 22, refers to smaller judicatories. These bodies had the right to make arrests (Matt. xxvi. 47 sqq.; Mark xiv. 43 sqq.; cf. Acts v. 18, ix. 2), to pronounce decision and to punish, except that capital punishment required the confirmation of the Roman procurator, by whom it seems to have been executed (John xviii. 31); the only case of capital punishment mentioned in connection with this judicatory in the New Testament is that of Jesus. Acts ix. 2 indicates that the mandates of the great sanhedrin was recognized wherever Jews dwelt—the high priest's directions reached at any rate to Damascus. The great sanhedrin was composed of elders (see Elders in Israel), Scribes (q.v.), and the most eminent members of the high-priestly families. Joseph of Arimathea is called a counselor (Mark xv. 43; Luke xxiii. 50; Gk. *bouleutēs; boulē* occurs in Josephus, *Ant.*, XIX., iii. 3 for the council itself). The high priest Caiaphas appears as president in the process against Jesus (Matt. xxvi. 3, 57) and the high priest Ananias (Acts xxiii. 2, xxiv. 1) in the time of Paul.

The traditional Jewish view was that a supreme court was created in the time of Moses, and that the great sanhedrin was its legitimate successor; but, though learned and diligent attempts have been made in modern times to defend this view, success has not attended them. Even if Jehoshaphat erected a supreme court which lasted till the exile (a doubtful fact; II Chron. xix.), such a judicatory did not exist in the time of Ezra and Nehemiah, or it would have left some traces in the reports concerning the activities of these men. At the head of the community then were the "elders of the Jews" (Ezra v. 5, vi. 7, 14), also known as "princes" (Ezra ix. 1, 2, x. 8; Neh. ix. 38). From these "princes" was formed an aristocratic senate, at the head of which stood the hereditary high priest; and this body was known as the *gerousia* (from Gk. *gerōn*, "old man"), which appears under this name first in a writing of Antiochus the Great (Josephus, *Ant.*, XII., iii. 3). The letter of Jonathan the Maccabee to the Spartans (I Macc. xii. 6) begins: "Jonathan the high priest, and the *gerousia* (senate) of the nation," etc., while I Macc. xii. 35 speaks of "the elders of the people" as called together. But there is no testimony as to the exact significance of the *gerousia* under the Maccabean kings, though it is probable that it continued to exist. Such continuance would easily explain the division by Gabinius (57–55 B.C.) of the Jewish territory into five districts ruled by *synedria* or *synodoi* (Josephus, *Ant.*, XIV., v. 4; *War*, I., viii. 5), a division set aside by Cæsar in 47, when to the sanhedrin at Jerusalem was given general jurisdiction over the entire land (cf. Josephus, *Ant.*, XIV., ix. 3–5), before which Herod appeared and on which he afterward took bloody vengeance, although the sanhedrin continued to exist under his rule (Josephus, *Ant.*, XV., vi. 2). Under Roman rule through procurators the sanhedrin had naturally great importance, receiving recognition even from Jews not in Palestine. Because of the singular significance, after the exile, of the law for Jewish life, the importance of the sanhedrin as the highest theological and national court of justice continually increased, and before it were decided causes which affected the entire civil life of the Jews.

Jewish tradition is summarized in the Talmudic tract *Sanhedrin*, the data from which supplement well the scanty data obtainable from other sources. It makes clear that the membership was seventy-one, and it seems probable that the lesser sanhedrin had a membership of twenty-three. The place of session seems according to some reports to have been a hall inside the fore-court of the temple (*Sanhedrin*, xi. 2), but was really outside the court and to the west, as described by Josephus (below): members are called *bouleutai*, "counselors," and the body itself *boulē*, "council." Josephus calls the place of assemblage *boulē* or *bouleutērion* (*War*, V., iv. 2, VI., vi. 3). The tract *Chagiga*, ii. 2, makes two Pharisees, heads of schools, normally the president and vice-president, and J. Levy and D. Hoffmann (see bibliography) have defended this view. But the testimony of the New Testament and of Josephus is decisive that the high priest was always the presiding officer. (H. L. STRACK.)

BIBLIOGRAPHY: The Jewish sources are the tracts *Sanhedrin* and *Makkoth* in Mishna, Tosephtha, and Talmud. The Mishna text with Lat. transl. and notes is in the Amsterdam ed. by Surenhuysen, iv. 205–291, published 1702; with Germ. transl. in D. Hoffmann's *Mischnajot*, iv. 145–219, Berlin, 1898; the Palestinian form with Lat. introduction is in Ugolini, *Thesaurus*, xxv. 1–338, Fr. transl. in M. Schwad, *Le Talmud de Jérusalem*, vols. x.–xi., Paris, 1888–89; the Babylonian Talmudic tract *Sanhedrin* is in Ugolini, ut sup., xxv. 339–1102; both forms with Germ. transl. are in L. Goldschmidt, *Der babylon. Talmud*, vii. 1–610, Berlin, 1903.

Consult: A. Büchler, *Das Synedrion in Jerusalem*, Vienna, 1902; J. Selden, *De synedriis*, London, 1650–55; Ugolini, *Thesaurus*, xxv. 1103–1234; A. T. Hartmann, *Die enge Verbindung des A. Ts. mit dem Neuen*, pp. 166–225, Rostock, 1831; L. Herzfeld, *Geschichte des Volkes Israel*, ii. 380–396, Leipsic, 1855; J. Levy, in *Monatsschrift für Geschichte und Wissenschaft des Judentums*, 1855, pp. 266–274, 301–307, 339–358; J. M. Jost, *Geschichte des Judenthums*, i. 120–128, 270–285, 403 sqq., ii. 13 sqq., 25 sqq., Leipsic, 1857–58; J. Langen, in *TQ*, 1862, pp. 411–463; A. Kuenen, *Over de Samenstelling van het Sanhedrin*, Amsterdam, 1866; J. Derenbourg, *Hist. de la Palestine*, pp. 83–94, 465–468, Paris, 1867; D. Hoffmann, *Der oberste Gerichtshof in der Stadt des Heiligthums*, Berlin, 1878; Stapfer, in *Revue de théologie et de philosophie*, 1884, pp. 105–119; H. Grätz, *Geschichte der Juden*, iii. 100 sqq., Leipsic, 1888; Blum, *Le Synhedrin ou grand conseil de Jérusalem*, Strassburg, 1889; I. Jelski, *Die innere Einrichtung des grossen Synedrions zu Jerusalem*, Breslau, 1894; A. Hausrath, *Neutestamentliche Zeitgeschichte*, i. 63–72, Heidelberg, 1873, Eng. transl., *Hist. of N. T. Times*, London, 1895; M. Sulzberger, *The Am ha-Arets, the Ancient Hebrew Parliament; a Chapter in the constitutional History of ancient Israel*, Philadelphia, 1910; Schürer, *Geschichte*, ii. 188–214, Eng. transl., II., i. 163 sqq.; *DB*, iv. 397–402; *EB*, iv. 4840–44; *JE*, xi. 41–44.

SANKARACHARYA. See INDIA, I., 2, § 2.

SANKEY, IRA DAVID: Methodist lay evangelist; b. at Edinburgh, Lawrence County, Pa., Aug. 28, 1840; d. in Brooklyn Aug. 14, 1908. He entered business at New Castle, Pa., 1855–71, and was active as choir-leader, Sunday-school superintendent, and president of the Young Men's Christian Association; met D. L. Moody (q.v.) in 1870 at the international convention of that body at Indianapolis. He joined Moody in 1871 at Chicago and for years was associated with him in joint revival work in the United States and abroad, his part being singing solos, conducting the singing of the assembly, composing "Gospel hymns," and rendering assistance in the inquiry-meetings. In later years he also lectured. In 1903 he lost his eyesight. He compiled *Gospel Hymns* (1875–95), and *Sacred Songs and Solos* (London, 1873, and often), of which over 50,000,000 copies were sold; translations have been made into many languages. He composed also many popular songs, of which are "There were ninety and nine," and "When the mists have rolled away." He is author of *My Life and the Story of the Gospel Hymns and of Sacred Songs and Solos* (Philadelphia, 1907).

BIBLIOGRAPHY: The literature is to be sought under MOODY, DWIGHT LYMAN (RYTHER), as the sketches of the life of Moody invariably treat of his fellow-laborer. Note particularly E. Nason, *Lives of the Eminent American Evangelists, D. L. Moody and Ira D. Sankey*, Boston, 1877. Also see under REVIVALS.

SANMINIATELLI, san-min-yā-tel'lî, **ZABARELLA, ALESSANDRO**: Cardinal; b. at Radicondoli (14 m. s.w. of Sienna), Tuscany, Italy, Aug. 4, 1840. He was educated at the Collegio Romano and the Accademia dei nobili ecclesiastici, and was ordained to the priesthood in 1863. In 1868 he was appointed chamberlain to the pope, and in 1874 became grand almoner and titular archbishop of Tyana. In 1887 he was made auditor general of the Apostolic Chamber, and in 1899 was created cardinal priest of Santi Pietro e Marcellino.

SANSON, sān-sōn' (**SAMSON**), **BERNHARDINO**: Commissary of indulgences in Switzerland in 1518–1519. He is said to have come from Brescia. He was guardian of the Observantist Franciscans at San Angelo, Milan, when he was commissioned, in 1517, to preach indulgences in the Swiss cantons, among their confederates, and in the dioceses of Valais and Chur. His course through Lugano, Uri, Schwyz, Lucerne, Bugdorf, Bern, Solothurn, and Freiburg, June, 1518, to Jan., 1519, met with much success. In eastern Switzerland, however, he was less successful; Zwingli directed sermons against him and his practise, which in the more enlightened quarters was regarded as both ridiculous and outrageous. The bishop of Constance and his vicar, Johannes Faber (q.v.), resisted Sanson, who was forbidden to enter the churches in Aargau, Feb., 1519. In Baden he succeeded, but was refused admission at Staufberg and Brengarten. He then went to Zurich, where the diet of the federation had convened. Here he met the united hostility of Zwingli, Faber, and the bishop of Constance. The diet took recognition of the complaint, which Sanson met with his credentials and the request to ascertain his authority at Rome at his expense. The diet did not interpose any impediment and Sanson appeared at Sofingen, Apr. 18. But the diet asked the knight Felix Grebel of Zurich, who was about to journey to Rome, to lay certain grievances before the pope and make a thorough investigation. Before Grebel's arrival, the pope had appointed Sanson commissary of indulgences to the end of October, but upon taking knowledge of the missive of the diet, he revoked the commission, and the diet was privileged, if Sanson was objectionable, to request his peaceable return to Italy, to be examined and punished, if he exceeded his powers and committed errors in the announcing of indulgences. The matter of indulgences, although a factor in the rise of the Reformation in Switzerland, played a less important part than in Germany.

(EMIL EGLI†.)

BIBLIOGRAPHY: L. R. Schmidlin, *Bernhardin Sanson, der Ablassprediger in der Schweiz, 1518–19*, Solothurn, 1898; Schaff, *Christian Church*, vii. 31, 42–43.

SAPHIR, sā'fir, **ADOLPH**: Presbyterian; b. at Budapest, Hungary, Sept. 26, 1831; d. at London Apr. 3, 1891. Son of a Jewish merchant he, with the rest of his father's family, was converted to Christianity by the Jewish mission of the Church of Scotland; he studied at the Gymnasium of the Graue Kloster, Berlin, 1844–48; at Glasgow University, 1848–49 (M.A., 1854), at Marischal College, Aberdeen, 1849–51, and was a student of theology at the Free Church College, Edinburgh, 1851–54. He was licensed in 1854, and sent as missionary to the Jews at Hamburg, Germany; was German preacher at Glasgow, 1855; minister of the English Presbyterian Church, South Shields, 1856–61; at Greenwich, London, 1861–72; at Notting Hill, London, 1872–80; and of Belgrave Presbyterian Church, London, 1881–88. In later life Saphir took much interest in the efforts for the conversion of the Jews in Hungary and southern Russia, being president of the auxiliary in London, the Rabinowich Council. In theology he was Evangelical. He was the author of *From Death to Life* (Edinburgh, 1861; revised and published under the title *Conversion*, London, 1865); *Christ and the Scriptures* (1864); *Lectures on the Lord's Prayer* (1870); *Christ Crucified* (Lectures on I Cor. ii., 1873); *Expository Lectures on the Epistle to the Hebrews* (1874–76); and *The Divine Unity of Scripture* (1892); and of numerous tracts employed in the mission to the Jews.

BIBLIOGRAPHY: G. Carlyle, *Mighty in the Scriptures. A Memoir of A. Saphir*, London, 1893; *DNB*, l. 299.

SARABAITES, sār'a-baits (**SARABITES**): A class of Egyptian hermits, mentioned by Jerome (*Epist.*, xxiii. 34) under the name of Remoboth. The appellation Sarabaites is of unknown connotation, although Cassian (*Collationes patrum*, XVIII., iv. 7–8) declares it to be Egyptian, and names three classes of monks, cenobites, anchorites, and Sarabaites. After Cassian, who thoroughly disapproved of the Sarabaites, the only independent sources for a knowledge of these hermits are Benedict of Nursia (*Regula*, i.), who states that they were to be found in Italy, and possibly the *Dialogus Zachaei Christiani et Apollonii philosophi* of the late fifth century. In the Middle Ages the epithet Sarabaites (translated *Renuitæ* by Isidore of Seville, *De officiis ecclesiasticis*, ii. 15) was frequently applied to disobedient or turbulent monks, since their prototypes lived without teacher and without discipline; and they were likewise often confused with the Gyrovagi (q.v.).

The earliest sources concerning the Sarabaites are invariably prejudiced against them and desired to replace them by those following the cenobitic life. Nevertheless, the distinctive characteristics which separated them from hermits and cenobites are clear. They were generally considered monks, like whom they were celibate, fasted, sang in choir, and wore habits. On the other hand, they did not live in monasteries or deserts, but in towns or fortified places, sometimes in their own houses. Neither did they form communities like the cenobites, but lived alone or in groups of two or three without any superior; nor were they rigidly separated from the world like hermits and cenobites. Like other monks, they earned their livelihood by manual labor, but sold the products independently. In the time of Cassian the Sarabaites of Egypt equalled the cenobites in number, but in other lands were far more numerous, so that they were almost the only class of monks, a statement which also holds true for the days of Jerome. By the middle of the sixth century their number had declined in Italy.

The Sarabaites were essentially the successors of the primitive ascetics, and long maintained their existence in the West despite the spread of anchoritism and monasticism from the East, especially from Egypt, thus explaining the intense hatred felt by hermits and monks for them. Their freer mode of life doubtless gave some ground for the charges alleged against them, probably with some exaggeration, by their opponents; and in the course of time they sank before the more rigid ascetic ideals of monasticism. See MONASTICISM.

(G. GRÜTZMACHER.)

BIBLIOGRAPHY: C. W. F. Walch, in *Novi commentarii societatis . . . scientiarum Gottingensis*, vi. 1-34, Göttingen, 1776; Neander, *Christian Church*, ii. 283-284.

SARAVIA, ADRIAN: Reformed (afterward Anglican) theologian; b. at Hesdin (35 m. n. of Amiens), France, in 1531; d. at Westminster, London, Jan. 15, 1612-13. His father was a Spaniard, his mother a Fleming, and both became Protestants; he was trained for the Reformed ministry, and became pastor at Antwerp, and later formed a Walloon church at Brussels; he removed after 1560 with his family to the Channel Islands, where he first acted as schoolmaster, and then in 1564 became assistant minister of St. Peter's, Guernsey; he next became schoolmaster at Southampton, and, in 1582, professor of divinity at the University of Leyden; because of complicity in a political plot he was forced in 1587 to flee to England, where he became rector of Tattenhill, Staffordshire; his *De diversis gradibus ministrorum* (see below) in 1590 brought him honor there, and in 1591 he was made prebendary of Gloucester, in 1595 of Canterbury and vicar of Lewisham, Kent, and in 1601 of Worcester and of Westminster; he was nominated in 1607 one of the translators for the new version of the Bible; and in 1609-10 exchanged Lewisham for Great Chart, which he retained till his death. He was buried in Canterbury Cathedral. His promotion in England was no doubt due in part to his vigorous assertion and defense of episcopal church government, in his *De diversis gradibus* (London, 1590; Eng. transl., 1592, reissued 1640), in his *Defensio tractatus de . . . gradibus* (1594), and *Examen Tractatus D. Bezæ de triplici episcoporum genere* (1594), against the arguments of Theodore Beza, who sought to secure its abolition in Scotland. He is best known as the earliest modern advocate of worldwide evangelization, which most of the Reformers thought either impracticable or unauthorized. In his first work he devotes a chapter (xvii.) to establishing the thesis "that the command to preach the Gospel to all peoples is obligatory upon the Church since the Apostles were taken up into Heaven, and that for this purpose the apostolic office is needful." He maintains that the obligation to evangelize all peoples rests upon the Christians of every century to the end of the world on the ground that Christ in giving the commission promised to be with his disciples all the days to the end of the world, that the apostles left the work incomplete and provided for its extension, that after the apostolic age the Gospel was successfully preached to many new peoples, etc. He insists that it is not fanaticism but simple duty to try to carry out Christ's great commission. Beza (1592) and Gerhard (1617) sought by elaborate argumentation in opposition to Saravia to prove that the commission of Christ expired with the close of the apostolic age. In the opinion of contemporaries they succeeded and Saravia's plea made little impression. His *Treatise on the Christian Priesthood* was republished in London, 1845; and a Latin manuscript was translated and published by Denison as *Treatise on the Eucharist* (London, 1855). See MISSIONS TO THE HEATHEN, B, II., 1, § 2.

A. H. NEWMAN.

BIBLIOGRAPHY: *DNB*, l. 299-301, where are given references to scattering notices.

SARCERIUS, sār-sī'ri-us (SORCK), ERASMUS: German Lutheran; b. at Annaberg (18 m. s. of Chemnitz) probably Apr. 19, 1501; d. at Magdeburg Nov. 28, 1559. He was matriculated at Leipsic in 1522, but in 1524 seems to have migrated to Wittenberg, and in 1528 was a teacher at Lubeck and a firm supporter of Protestant tenets. He likewise taught in Graz, and apparently received his master's degree at Vienna, but was forced to leave because of his religious convictions and in 1530 was matriculated at Rostock. Finally completing his studies, he was recalled to Lubeck, where he remained until 1536, when Count William of Nassau called him to Siegen as rector of the Latin school. In the following year he was appointed superintendent and chaplain to the count, and henceforth all his energies were devoted to the cause of Lutheranism. He at once began a system of frequent visitations and regular pastoral synods according to the plan outlined in his *Dialogus . . . reddens rationem veterum synodorum . . . item visitationum* (n.p., 1539), likewise promoting his cause not only by his *Catechismus* of 1537, but also by his commentaries on Matthew (Frankfort, 1538), Mark (Basel, 1539), Luke (1539), John (1540), Acts (1540), Romans (1541), Galatians and Ephesians (1542), Corinthians (1542-44), Philippians, Colossians, and Thessalonians (1542), and Ecclesiasticus (1543), as well as by his *Methodus in præcipuos Scripturæ locos* (2 parts, Basel, 1539-40), *Nova methodus* (1546), *Expositiones in epistolas dominicales et festivales* (1540), *In evangelia dominicalia postilla* (1540), and *Conciones annuæ rhetorica dispositione conscriptæ* (4 vols., 1541). In 1541 Sarcerius was called to Dillenburg as court chaplain and preacher at the city church, besides being superintendent of the county. In Mar., 1540, he had taken part in the Schmalkald conference, and in 1542-46 he promoted the cause of the Reformation in the archdiocese of Cologne. He also came into momentary contact with the English movement against the Roman Church, this being the occasion of his *Loci aliquot communes et theologici* (Frankfort [1538]; Eng. transl., under the title *Cōmon places of scripture ordrely and after a cōpendious forme of teachyng set forth*," by R. Taverner, London, 1538).

As a distinguished theologian Sarcerius could boast that he had framed church orders for twenty-four counties, and in 1541 he was obliged to decline the invitation to become professor of theology at Leipsic. But the Interim ended his activity in Nassau in 1548, and he then went first to Annaberg, where he wrote his *Creutzbuchlein*, after which he became pastor at the Thomaskirche in Leipsic, publishing four volumes of sermons in 1551–52, and his *Von Synodis* and *Buch vom heiligen Ehestand* in 1553. In 1551 he was one of the theologians to whom the Saxon Confession was submitted for approval and subscription, and in the following year was a member of the unsuccessful delegation to the Council of Trent, which got no further than Nuremberg. In 1553 he published his *Hausbuch für die einfältigen Hausväter*, which is of interest for a history of Lutheran confirmation, and in the following year he was chosen superintendent of Eisleben as the successor of the adiaphoristic Georg Major (q.v.). He now necessarily adopted an attitude of opposition to the teachings of Melanchthon and completely accepted the tenets of the Gnesio-Lutherans, being active at the same time both in visitation and in writing a number of treatises on church government and discipline, the most of which were collected by his son, Wilhelm Sarcerius, in the second edition of his *Pastorale oder Hirtenbuch von Amt, Wesen und Disziplin der Pastoren*, published in 1562. Meanwhile the course of events was leading him further and further away from Melanchthon, and at the colloquy of Worms in 1557 he was on the side of the Weimar theologians. From Worms he hurried to Heidelberg to prevent the threatened schism in Protestantism, only to take part in the fatal protestation which broke off the conference. In the following year he was one of those called to Weimar to make the final revision of the Weimar Confutation, but his position in Mansfeld was becoming increasingly difficult and he was exposed to ceaseless official interference. Nevertheless, in 1559 he presided over a synod which formulated the interesting *Bekendnis der Prediger in der Graffschafft Mansfelt . . . wider aller Secten, Rotten und falsche Leren* (Eisleben, 1560), and almost immediately afterward he accepted a call to Magdeburg as pastor of the Johanniskirche and senior of the ministerium, but lived only long enough to deliver four sermons.

(G. KAWERAU.)

BIBLIOGRAPHY: The funeral sermon was by J. Wigand, Magdeburg, 1560, and *Piæ lamentationes* by Z. Prätorius, W. Sarcerius, and P. Spemlin, Eisleben, 1560; two monographs are A. W. Rösselmüller, *Leben und Wirken des Erasmus Sarcerius*, Annaberg, 1888, and G. Eskuche, *Sarcerius als Erzieher und Schulmann*, Siegen, 1901 (worthful). Compare further H. L. J. Heppe, *Dogmatik des deutschen Protestantismus*, i. 49 sqq., Gotha, 1857.

SARDICA, SYNOD OF: A synod held in 343–344 at Sardica (the modern Sophia, capital of Bulgaria). The date given above is not that of the historians Socrates (*Hist. eccl.*, ii. 20; *NPNF*, 2d ser. ii. 46–47) and Sozomen (*Hist. eccl.*, iii. 11–12; *NPNF*, 2d ser., ii. 289–290), who assign the year 347. But the *Historia acephala* (discovered in the eighteenth century, ed. S. Maffei in *Osservazioni litterarie*, vol. iii., Verona, 1738) showed that Athanasius returned to Alexandria from his second exile in 346 (see ATHANASIUS I., § 4) and this is corroborated by Jerome (*MPL*, xxix. 682), who places this return in the tenth year of Constantius. The "Paschal Letters" of Athanasius prove that the synod was held at least two years before his return. The synod may have met late in 343; it was in session in 344, for two envoys sent by Constans arrived in Antioch at Easter of that year (Athanasius, "Arian History," xx.; *NPNF*, 2d ser., iv. 276–277, footnote). It was summoned by Constans and Constantinus (Athanasius, "Defence against the Arians," xliv.; *NPNF*, 2d ser., iv. 123) with the threefold object of removing causes of dissension in the Church, rooting out false doctrine, and confirming the tradition of the true faith in Christ.

There is some debate as to the number of bishops who attended. Two parties were represented, Eusebians and the orthodox. The former in their synodal letter (Mansi, *Concilia*, iii. 132) claim to be eighty in number, but seventy-six is given by Socrates and Sozomen (ut sup.) and this seems to be right. Athanasius in his "Arian History" (xv.; *NPNF*, iv. 274) reckons the entire attendance at 170 "more or less," which leaves ninety-four for the orthodox party. The Eusebians were a compact party, whose principal animus was against Athanasius. When they learned that he was to be present and was expected to take part, they recognized that the logic of events would lead him to take the aggressive and to bring charges of unseemly conduct against them. They therefore demanded on the basis of the findings of the synods of Tyre and Antioch that Athanasius be excluded. The presidency of the synod, in the absence of the bishop of Rome, fell to Hosius of Cordova (q.v.) through whom negotiations were conducted. Hosius warned the Eusebians that their threat to abstain from participation might prove dangerous to them, and advised them to submit their proofs against Athanasius to him alone if they were unwilling to bring them before the synod, promising that if they were conclusive, Athanasius should be excluded. But this advice was rejected, and the Eusebians left the city by night.

The synod proceeded to investigate the charges of the Eusebians (1) against Athanasius and found them baseless; (2) against Marcellus of Ancyra (q.v.), and pronounced him orthodox; (3) against Asclephas of Gaza (whom the Eusebians at Antioch had deposed), and proved him innocent, acquitting of blame also certain minor officials who were involved in the major charges. Certain heads of the Eusebian party were deposed and excommunicated, viz., Theodore of Heraclea, Narcissus of Neronias, Acacius of Cæsarea, Ursacius of Singidunum, Valens of Murcia, Menophantes of Ephesus, and George of Laodicea. The alleged "creed of Sardica" rests upon a misunderstanding of a sketch of such a creed by Hosius which was not adopted by the synod, but came to be included in the *Acta*. The twenty canons were drawn up in Greek and Latin, were adopted by the second Trullan synod, and are usually appended to those of the council of Nicæa, though they are not recognized as ecumenical. The canons have to do with the rights and duties of bishops, with the filling of vacant bishoprics, the rights and duties of lower clergy, and make an attempt to arrange for union on the date of Easter.

BIBLIOGRAPHY: Original documents are the canons, with history of the synod and discussion, in Hefele, *Conciliengeschichte*, i. 533 sqq., Eng. transl., ii. 86 sqq., Fr. transl., i. 2, pp. 737 sqq. (especially valuable for the notes); the account of Athanasius in "Defence against the Arians," Eng. transl., *NPNF*, 2d ser., iv. 100 sqq.; three letters to the synod, summarised in Hefele, ut sup., given in Athanasius, "Defence," chap. iii., Eng. transl., ut sup., pp. 119 sqq. The documents appear also in Mansi, *Concilia*, vol. iii. (important) and Harduin, *Concilia*, vol. i. Consult further: W. Beveridge, *Synodicon*, Oxford, 1672; Z. B. van Espen, *Commentarius in canones et decreta juris veteris ac novi*, Cologne, 1755; idem, *Jus ecclesiasticum universum*, iii. 264 sqq., ib. 1777; L. T. von Spittler, *Sämmtliche Werke*, ed. K. Wächter, viii. 126 sqq., 15 vols., Stuttgart, 1827–37; F. Maassen, *Geschichte der Quellen und der Literatur des canonishen Rechts*, i. 50 sqq., Leipsic, 1870; *KL*, x. 1705–11; Schaff, *Christian Church*, iii. 310–314.

SARDIS. See ASIA MINOR, IV.

SARGON. See ASSYRIA, VI., § 11; BABYLONIA, VI., 3, § 1.

SARPI, sär'pi, PAOLO (FRA PAOLO): Venetian patriot and opponent of the Jesuits; b. at Venice Aug. 14, 1552; d. there Jan. 14, 1623. He obtained his education in his native city, and in 1566 entered the order of the Servites. After an activity of two years as teacher in Mantua he became priest, in 1579 was made provincial of his order in the republic of Venice, and subsequently became general procurator of the order with seat at Rome (1585–1588). But for a long time his mind had been growing increasingly hostile to the Jesuits, and he had consequently come under suspicion of the Inquisition. After 1606 his views found expression in the famous struggle of Venice with Pope Paul V. The pope in his blindness tried for the last time to gain supremacy over Venice by using the mightiest weapon of medievalism, the interdict. The consequence was that the Jesuits were expelled from the republic, while the remaining clergy were induced to continue the church services. This unexpected victory of the republic would have been impossible if public opinion had not been influenced in its favor by Sarpi, whom his native city had retained in its defense. Induced by patriotism and by hatred of the Jesuits, Sarpi published masterworks of polemics. The attempt to assassinate Sarpi on Oct. 5, 1607, shows that the authorities at Rome knew to whom their defeat was due. His principal work is *Istoria del concilio Tridentino di Pietro Soave Polano* (London, 1619; Eng. transl., *History of The Council of Trent*, 1676). Its hostility to the popes is extreme; it has been translated into the principal European languages. Other works of his which have been translated into English from his *Opere* or from separate publications are: *A Treatise of Matters Beneficiary* (London, 1680; later editions with slightly variant titles, 1727, 1730, 1736); *The History of the Inquisition* (1639); and *The Rights of Sovereigns and Subjects* (1722). His *Opere* were issued in 5 vols., Venice, 1677, better edition, 8 vols., "Helmstadt" (i.e., Verona), 1761; and his *Lettere* at Verona, 1673; *Lettere inedite*, 1833, and ed. S. and A. S. Contarini, Venice, 1892; and *Lettere raccolte*, Florence, 1863. An Eng. transl. of the *Letters* appeared London, 1693. (P. TSCHACKERT.)

BIBLIOGRAPHY: A. Robertson, *Fra Paoli Sarpi, the Greatest of the Venetians*, London, 1894; F. Micanzio, *La Vie du Père Paul*, Leyden, 1661; A. Bianchi-Giovini, *Biografia di Fra P. Sarpi*, 2 vols., Brussels, 1836; J. N. Brischar, *Beurteilung der Kontroversen Sarpis und Pallavicini*, 2 parts, Tübingen, 1844; J. Kraenker, *Essai sur la vie et les écrits de Fra P. Sarpi*, Strasburg, 1857; Arabella Georgina Campbell, *The Life of Fra Paolo Sarpi*, London, 1869; L. Lavi, *Fra Paolo Sarpi*, Bergamo, 1873; M. Brosch, *Geschichte des Kirchenstaates*, i. 354 sqq., Gotha, 1880; P. Balan, *Fra P. Sarpi*, Venice, 1887; A. Pascolato, *Fra P. Sarpi*, Milan, 1893; G. Rein, *Paoli Sarpi und die Protestanten*, Helsingfors, 1904; A. D. White, *Seven Great Statesmen*, New York, 1910; *KL*, x. 1720–26.

SARTORIUS, sär-tō'ri-us, ERNST WILHELM CHRISTIAN: German Lutheran; b. at Darmstadt May 10, 1797; d. at Königsberg June 13, 1859. He was educated at the University of Göttingen (1815–1818), where he became lecturer in 1818. Three years later he was called to Marburg as associate professor, being promoted to a full professorship in 1823. He had already written *Drei Abhandlungen über wichtige Gegenstände der exegetischen und systematischen Theologie* (Göttingen, 1820), which was quickly followed by his *Die lutherische Lehre vom Unvermögen des freien Willens zur höheren Sittlichkeit* (1821), a work strongly emphasizing the Augustinian concept of grace and criticizing Schleiermacher's theory of election. During his Marburg professorship he also wrote his *Ueber die Lehre der Protestanten von der heiligen Würde der weltlichen Obrigkeit* (Marburg, 1822) and *Die Religion ausserhalb der Grenzen der blossen Vernunft nach den Grundsätzen des wahren Protestantismus und gegen die eines falschen Rationalismus* (1822). In 1824 Sartorius was called to the University of Dorpat, where he remained until 1835, vigorously combating rationalism, a tendency which he also assailed in his *Beiträge zur Verteidigung der evangelischen Rechtgläubigkeit* (2 parts, Heidelberg, 1825–1826). During this period he also delivered a eulogy on the Augsburg Confession which was later revised and enlarged as the *Beiträge zur Apologie der augsburgischen Confession gegen alte und neue Gegner* (Gotha, 1853), and in 1831 he published at Hamburg his *Lehre von Christi Person und Werk* (Eng. transl., *Doctrine of the Person and Work of Christ*, London, 1838, and Boston, 1848), which led to his call as general superintendent of the province of Prussia and as first court chaplain of the castle church at Königsberg. In these capacities he strove earnestly for the defense of true Lutheran principles and sturdily opposed rationalism and kindred developments, as in his *Ueber die Notwendigkeit und Verbindlichkeit der kirchlichen Glaubensbekenntnisse* (Stuttgart, 1845). The most noteworthy work of Sartorius, however, was his *Lehre von der heiligen Liebe, oder Grundzüge der evangelisch-kirchlichen Moraltheologie* (2 parts, Stuttgart, 1840–44; Eng. transl., *Doctrine of Divine Love; or Outlines of the Moral Theology of the Evangelical Church*, Edinburgh, 1884), which was followed by his *Ueber den alt- und neutestamentlichen Cultus, insbesondere Sabbath, Priestertum, Sacrament und Opfer* (Stuttgart, 1852). The dissensions arising within his communion in the latter years of his life called forth his *Meditationen über die Offenbarung der Herrlichkeit Gottes in seiner Kirche und besonders über die

Gegenwart des verklärten Leibes und Blutes Christi im heiligen Abendmahl (Stuttgart, 1855), and his polemic attitude toward the Roman Catholic Church, particularly in regard to justification, found expression in his last work, the *Soli Deo gloria! vergleichende Würdigung evangelisch-lutherischer und römish-katholischer Lehre nach dem augsburgischen und tridentinischen Bekenntnis* (Stuttgart, 1859).

(DAVID ERDMANN†.)

BIBLIOGRAPHY: K. F. A. Kahnis, *Lutherische Dogmatik*, 3 vols., Leipsic, 1861–68; G. W. Frank, *Geschichte der protestantischen Theologie*, ib. 1862–75; A. Mücke, *Die Dogmatik des 19. Jahrhunderts*, Gotha, 1867; I. A. Dorner, *System der christlichen Glaubenslehre*, 2 vols., Berlin, 1879–81, Eng. transl., 4 vols., Edinburgh, 1880–82; M. A. von Landerer, *Neueste Dogmengeschichte*, Heilbronn, 1881.

SARUM USE: The name given to the liturgy in use in the diocese of Sarum (i.e., Salisbury) before the Reformation of the Church of England. It consists of several books, the direct or mediate work of Saint Osmund (q.v.), bishop of Salisbury, viz., the Portiforium or Breviary of Sarum (containing the Daily Services), the Sarum Missal (containing the Communion Service), and possibly the Sarum Manual (containing the Baptismal and "Occasional" Offices). The Sarum use was adopted in Salisbury in 1085, and by the middle of the thirteenth century was the form of liturgy most used in England. The Portiforium was the basis of the Book of Common Prayer (see COMMON PRAYER, BOOK OF, § 1). Other "uses" were those of Lincoln, Hereford, Durham (?), Bangor, and York.

BIBLIOGRAPHY: F. Procter and C. Wordsworth, *The Sarum Breviary*, Cambridge, 1882; F. Procter and W. H. Frere, *New Hist. of the Book of Common Prayer*, passim, London, 1905; J. H. Blunt, *Annotated Book of Common Prayer*, pp. 2–3, 361–363, et passim, New York, 1908.

SATAN. See DEVIL.

SATANAËL. See NEW MANICHEANS, I.

SATISFACTION: A doctrine which seeks to explain how the justice and the mercy of God are reconciled. The term "satisfaction" is traced to Tertullian, although its reference was to the penitence of man rather than the death of Christ. Man is "released from penalty by the compensating exchange of repentance." Origin held that God was rendered propitious by Christ's offering of himself. Gregory the Great taught that Christ assumed the penalty of sin and so appeased the wrath of God. Not until Anselm (q.v.), however, does the idea of satisfaction become a dominant principle of religious thought. According to him (*Cur Deus homo*) the honor of God, immeasurably injured, demanded satisfaction—either punishment of the sinner or an equivalent. God chose the latter alternative. Wherefore, the God-man who alone could fulfil the perfect obligation and who needed not to die for his sins, could and did die in behalf of men and thus satisfied God for their debt and merited the salvation which God offers. Thomas Aquinas (1274), with other Schoolmen in distinction from Anselm, denied that satisfaction was the *sine qua non* for the forgiveness of sins; God might have redeemed men in some other way than by the death of his Son, yet he adopted this method as more fitting. On account of the greatness of Christ's love, the dignity of his person, and the scope of his passion, the satisfaction was superabundant (*Summa*, pars. iii., qu. 46–49). Duns Scotus (d. 1308) argued that, since the merit of Christ belonged to his human nature, it was not infinite, yet it availed for as much as God was pleased to accept it ("Commentary on the Sentences of Peter Lombard," lib. iii., dist. 19–20). According to the authoritative Roman Catholic doctrine, Christ merited justification for us by his holy passion on the tree and made satisfaction to God the Father for us. This satisfaction extends, however, only to those sins committed before baptism and to those committed afterward which deserve eternal punishment. Christians themselves make satisfaction for sin as regards temporal punishment by punishments either inflicted by Christ, or voluntarily undertaken, or else enjoined by a priest according to their ability or the quality of their sins, the aim of which is to reduce the punishment which awaits the soul in Purgatory (*Decrees and Canons of the Council of Trent*, sess. VI., chap. vii., sess. XIV., chap. viii.–ix.; cf. J. S. Hunter, *Outlines of Dogmatic Theology*, iii. 334–337). Faustus Socinus (1604) and the Socinians (*Racovian Catechism*, 1605) rejected the idea of satisfaction, on the ground of the mutual contradiction involved in satisfaction and remission, of the incompatibility of punishment with debt or with sufferings of the innocent, of the personal and non-transferable nature of obedience as well as of guilt and punishment, and of redemption as not satisfaction but emancipation. The death of Christ was only an example, a confirmation of divine promises, a condition of his entering into glory. In opposition to this view, Hugo Grotius (1645), in his "Satisfaction of Christ," declared that God who was the source of the law could not let its violation go unpunished. If, however, he rigorously and exactly enforced punishment upon sinners, he would destroy mankind from the face of the earth. In order, therefore, to maintain "rectoral justice," he sets forth a penal example in which he exhibits his judgment against sin, which, for the preservation of his government, is of equal value as the punishment of the sinner and is substituted for this. By this "singular method of relaxation" God is enabled to forgive sin. According to Curcellæus (d. 1659) in *Institutio religionis Christianæ*, V., xix., and Limborch (1712) in *Theologia Christiana*, III., xxii., Christ's oblation was not a full satisfaction for sin; he did not suffer all the punishment which we deserve. Sacrifice does not liberate from debts; but God graciously estimates Christ's sacrifice as sufficient, and on this ground remits the punishment due us.

Various Theories.

The theory of penal satisfaction has had a long history. It differs from the view of Anselm in several particulars. The satisfaction was public or juridical, rather than offered to a person. The righteousness involved was the penal righteousness of God. Instead of the Anselmic alternative—satisfaction or punishment—satisfaction is by punishment. As far back as Wyclif (d. 1384) it was asserted that God's justice demanded that each trespass be punished either on earth or in hell. Calvin (d. 1564) held that Christ satisfied the justice of God by suffering the punishment of our sin. Gerhard (d. 1637) affirmed that Christ effected the perfect satisfaction by experiencing the wrath of God, the curse of the law, and the penalties of hell (*Loci theolici*, locus xvii., chap. ii. 54). Tobias Crisp (d. 1643; *Christ Made Sin*, London, 1691, new ed., ib. 1832) and John Owen (q.v.; "The Death of Death in the Death of Christ," in *Works*, vol. v., London, 1826) claimed that Christ satisfied for our sins by suffering the punishment and death our sin deserved—"ejusdem." According to Quenstedt (1688) Christ was substituted for debtors and "in his satisfaction . . . felt even the very pangs of hell, although not in hell or eternally" (*Theologia didactico-polemica*, i. 39). Jonathan Edwards (d. 1758), who marks the dividing line between the penal and the New England view of the atonement, declared that Christ made satisfaction for sin not by reason of any excellency in his sufferings, but by the fulfilment of the law in him whereby through his death the nature, design, and perfection of the law, together with the authority and truth of the law-giver, were maintained (*Works*, vii. 512–516, New York, 1830). The more recent advocates of the penal satisfaction theory are: T. J. Crawford (*The Doctrine of the Holy Scriptures Respecting the Atonement*, London, 1871), George Smeaton (*Doctrine of the Atonement as Taught by Christ Himself*, Edinburgh, 1868; and . . . *As Taught by the Apostles*, Edinburgh, 1870), Charles Hodge (*Systematic Theology*, New York, 1871–73), and W. G. T. Shedd (*Dogmatic Theology*, New York, 1889). The following characteristic features of their presentation are to be noted: (1) a technical meaning is assigned to the terms employed. Our "sins" and our "Guilt" (q.v.) were transferred to Christ by "Imputation" (q.v.); on him was inflicted the "punishment" which belonged to us. (2) The relative values given to justice and love: justice is "a principle of God's nature, not only independent of love but superior to love." (3) The satisfaction while sufficient for all is efficient for the elect only. J. McL. Campbell (d. 1872), taking a hint from Jonathan Edwards (*Works*, vii. 505), that satisfaction may be made for sin either by an adequate punishment or by an "answerable repentance," declared that Christ, the "great Penitent in humanity," made a perfect confession for human sin; hence that is accorded to divine justice which is its due and could alone satisfy it (*Nature of the Atonement*, pp. 117–118, London, 1873). The New England theory of the atonement (see ATONEMENT; NEW ENGLAND THEOLOGY) held that the sufferings of Christ satisfied the general or public, but not distributive or individualizing, justice of God (E. A. Park, *The Atonement*, Introductory Essay, Andover, 1859).

Penal Satisfaction.

Satisfaction has, however, been differently conceived. The point of view is love instead of justice. This presents love as the central principle of God, by which he both affirms his own perfection and blessedness and wills that all his creatures and especially man shall share his love in the measure of their capacity—a purpose which is perfectly disclosed in his revelation of grace in Christ. Here love is absolute and justice relative; or love and justice are regarded as complementary aspects of the same gracious will. Abelard (1142) maintained that Christ satisfied the divine benevolence by overcoming the rebellion and the guilty fear of sinners by his immeasurable love. Schleiermacher (d. 1834) conceives of Christ as our "satisfaction-making substitute" (*Der Christliche Glaube*, ii. 103 sqq., 128–129, Berlin, 1831–1832). According to Albrecht Ritschl (1889), since God's righteousness is essentially identical with his grace, satisfaction can only signify the fulfilment of his eternal purpose of love (*Rechtfertigung und Versöhnung*, p. 474, Bonn, 1888–89; Eng. transl., Edinburgh, 1900). Samuel Harris (d. 1899) presents the satisfaction of God as the normal consummation of all his revealed action rendering service in conformity with the law of love (*God, the Creator and Lord of All*, p. 375, New York, 1896). William Newton Clarke (q.v.) affirms that God is eternally satisfied with the suffering of love in behalf of sinners (*Outline of Christian Theology*, p. 348, ib., 1898). According to John Scott Lidgett, satisfaction is defined in terms of fatherhood; the fatherly is satisfied in perfecting the filial (*The Spiritual Principle of the Atonement*, p. 301, London, 1898).

Satisfaction from the View-point of Love.

In all the above-mentioned theories the interpretation of the ethical nature of God and that of satisfaction go hand in hand. The following statement contains, therefore, the truth which they endeavor to present: "the satisfaction of God's ethical nature is realised in three respects: (1) so far as there has been made in Christ an adequate expression of the divine character and of the divine love in relation to sin, as well as a disclosure of the nature of sin and of God's hostility to it; (2) not when the Father can see in another than the sinner the suffering and death which belong to sin, but when he can forgive and restore the child to his loving fellowship; (3) God will be perfectly satisfied when the divine purpose of grace manifested through the death of Christ shall have found in all souls a perfect Amen" (Isa. liii. 11; cf. II Cor. i. 20; C. A. Beckwith, *Realities of Christian Theology*, pp. 228–229, Boston, 1906). See ATONEMENT, § 10. C. A. BECKWITH.

BIBLIOGRAPHY: For the development of the doctrine readers are referred to the works named in and under DOCTRINE, HISTORY OF—e.g., Harnack, *Dogma*, vi. 54–78, 190 sqq., 257 sqq. et passim. As a theme in systematic theology the subject is discussed in the works named in and under DOGMA, DOGMATICS, e.g., W. G. T. Shedd, *Dogmatic Theology*, ii. 433–434, New York, 1889. The literature under ATONEMENT, with that already noted, gives practically all that is necessary. Special mention may be made of: F. C. Baur, *Die christliche Lehre von der Versöhnung*, Tübingen, 1838; G. B. Stevens, *The Christian Doctrine of Sacrifice*, New York, 1905; K. Staab, *Die Lehre von der stellvertretenden Genugtuung Christi*, Paderborn, 1908.

SATOLLI, sa-tō'lî, FRANCESCO DI PAOLO: Cardinal; b. at Marsciano (14 m. s.w. of Perugia), Umbria, Italy, July 21, 1839; d. in Rome Jan. 8, 1910. He was educated at the seminary of Perugia, the Roman Seminary, and the College of the Propaganda; after which he was professor, and later rector, of the Greek College, Rome, and later still president of the Accademia dei nobili ecclesiastici. Appointed domestic prelate to the pope and consecrated titular archbishop of Lepanto, Satolli was sent to the United States in 1890 as the papal representative at the dedication of the Catholic University of America, Washington, D. C., and in 1892 again visited America, where he was appointed papal delegate of the Propaganda at Washington. In 1895 he was created cardinal priest of Santa Maria in Araceli and shortly afterward returned to Rome, and was created cardinal bishop of Frascati, archpriest of the Basilica of San Giovanni in Laterano, prefect of the Congregation of Studies, and president of the Theological Academy.

SATORNILOS. See SATURNINUS.

SATTERLEE, HENRY YATES: Protestant Episcopal bishop of Washington; b. in New York City Jan. 11, 144; d. at Washington, D. C., Feb. 22, 1908. He was graduated from Columbia College (A.B., 1863) and the General Theological Seminary (1866); was ordered deacon in 1865 and advanced to the priesthood in 1867. He was assistant minister of Zion Church, Wappinger's Fall, N. Y. (1865–74), and rector (1874–82); rector of Calvary Church, New York City (1882–96); and was consecrated bishop of Washington, D. C. (1896). Among his writings special mention may be made of *A Creedless Gospel and a Gospel Creed* (New York, 1894) and *The Calling of a Christian* (1902).

SATTLER, MICHAEL: Leader of the South German Anabaptists; b. at Staufen (10 m. s.s.w. of Freiburg-im-Breisgau) about 1500; executed at Rottenburg (23 m. s.w. of Stuttgart) May 20 or 21, 1527. He apparently studied at Freiburg, and then entered the monastery of St. Peter in the vicinity of the same city. Here diligent reading of the Pauline epistles led him to conclude that true righteousness was to be attained in ways far different from those taught by the Roman Catholic Church and by monasticism, and, leaving the monastery in 1523, he went to Zurich, where he joined the Anabaptists and became a zealous proselytizer in 1525. He was banished on Nov. 18 and retired to his native town, only to be expelled by the Austrian government, whereupon he was kindly received by Capito at Strasburg. In 1526 he went with Wilhelm Reublin (q.v.) to the latter's home in the district of Hohenberg, south of Tübingen, and developed great activity in the vicinity of Horb. At Schlatt-on-the-Randen he participated, on Feb. 24, 1527, in a great meeting at which he formulated in seven articles the doctrines and the constitution of the South German Anabaptists, who were to form a holy community without association with other sects, and who were also to refrain from taking oaths, holding office, or engaging in military service, the entire scheme being one of high ideals but thoroughly impracticable. Returning to Horb, Sattler and his wife were arrested and imprisoned at Binsdorf, whence they were taken to Rottenburg and there executed, Sattler at the stake and his wife by drowning. His death created a wide-spread sensation and evoked the sympathy of both Capito and Butzer, as well as of some less well-known Protestants. The pamphlet *Wie die Gschrifft verstendiglich soll unterschieden und erklärt werden* (n.p., n.d.) has been attributed to him, as has the hymn *Als Christus mit seiner wahren Lehr*, but the latter is certainly not his work.

G. BOSSERT.

BIBLIOGRAPHY: Sources are: J. Beck, in *Fontes rerum Austriacarum*, vol. xliii., the series published at Vienna, 1849 sqq.; the *Werke* of Zwingli, iii. 357 sqq.; E. Egli, *Aktensammlung zur Geschichte der Zürcher Reformation*, Zurich, 1879; and *Ein Sendbrief Michael Sattlers an eine Gemeinde Gottes*, ed. W. Köhler, Halle, 1905. Consult: G. Bossert, in *Blätter fur württemburgische Kirchengeschichte*, 1891, passim, and 1892, pp. 1–4, 9–10; idem, in *Christliche Welt*, 1891, pp. 22 sqq.; A. H. Newman, *Hist. of Anti-Pedobaptism*, pp. 137, 243 sqq., Philadelphia, 1897; C. Gerbert, *Geschichte der Strassburger Sectenbewegung zur Zeit der Reformation*, Strasburg, 1889; idem, in W. Kohlhammer, *Beschreibung des Oberamts Rottenburg*, i. 409 sqq., Stuttgart, 1900; R. Wolkan, *Der Lieder der Wiedertäufer*, Berlin, 1903; *Flugschriften aus den ersten Jahren der Reformation*, vol. ii., part 3, Leipsic, 1908.

SATURDAY, HOLY. See HOLY WEEK, § 6.

SATURN. See REMPHAN; and STARS, II.

SATURNINUS, sa-tűr'ni-nus (SATORNILOS): The head of a Gnostic school of the second century. Little is known of his sect, but the infrequency of polemic against it and the fact that it is scarcely more than an item in the catalogue of heresies imply that it was of secondary importance. Saturninus distinguished a supreme God, or "one unknown Father," and his creations, the lower "angels, archangels, powers, and potentates," chief among whom were the seven demiurges, including the God of the Jews, who sometimes appeared as hostile to the Father and sometimes midway between him and their adversary, Satan, but whose part in the cosmic process is unclear. The sole innovation known in the system of Saturninus is his concept of the creation of man. For an instant the demiurges perceived an image of the Father from the upper world of light. This awakened their longing for the higher spheres, and they sought to preserve their memory of the vision by creating man, but though he was formed in the image of the Father, he could only crawl on the earth like a worm until the Father, taking pity on him, gave him a scintillation of life. At death this scintillation returns to its home, while the earthly components of man are resolved into their original elements.

The account of Irenæus is too meager to permit of a clear knowledge of Saturninus' soteriology. It is evident, however, that he taught that the demiurges created two sorts of men, good and bad. The latter were aided by the demons, whereupon the Savior (whose merely apparent humanity is stressed) came to render them and the demons harmless and to save the good, those who, possessing the scintillation of life, believed on him. The sect is also described as ascetic; marriage and generation were traced to Satan; and some of the school were vegetarians. Prophecy (i.e., the Old Testament) was regarded as given partly by Satan and partly by the demiurges, although this statement does not exclude the possibility that Saturninus also found divine elements in it.

The data concerning Saturninus are too scanty to trace either his sources or his influence; only a fuller knowledge of the nature of his dualism would permit even an approximate conclusion as to whether it was derived from Zoroastrianism or from Platonism or from some syncretism in which both elements had already been blended.

R. LIECHTENHAN.

BIBLIOGRAPHY: The sources are: Irenæus, *Hær.*, I., xxiv. 1-2, Eng. transl. in *ANF*, i. 348-349; Tertullian, *De anima*, xxiii., in *ANF*, iii. 203; Hippolytus, *Hær.*, VII., xvi., in *ANF*, v. 100-110; Eusebius, *Hist. eccl.*, IV., vii. 3-4, in *NPNF*, i. 178; Epiphanius, *Hær.*, xxiii. Consult further: *DCB*, iv. 587-588; and the literature under GNOSTICISM.

SATURNINUS, SAINT: Missionary and martyr of the third century. He was a native of Italy and was sent as a missionary to Gaul by Pope Fabian (c. 245). He settled at Toulouse and there labored with considerable success, becoming first bishop of the town. Later his preaching infuriated the mob, and he was martyred by being bound to a bull which was maddened by goads. He became the patron saint of Toulouse, and is commemorated on Nov. 29.

SAUER, sau'er, **JOSEPH:** German Roman Catholic; b. at Unzhurst (a village near Bühl, 25 m. s.s.w. of Carlsruhe), Baden, June 7, 1872. He was educated at University of Freiburg (1891-94, 1896-97; D.D., 1900), and, after being a parish priest and teacher at Sasbach, Baden, in 1898-99, studied in France and Italy in 1900-02, devoting himself especially to Christian archeology. In 1902 he became privat-docent for church history and archeology in the theological faculty of the University of Freiburg, where he was promoted to his present position of associate professor of the same subjects in 1905. In addition to editing the *Literarische Rundschau für das katholische Deutschland* since 1905 and preparing and editing the second part of the second volume of F. X. Kraus' *Geschichte der christlichen Kunst* (Freiburg, 1907), he has written *Symbolik des Kirchengebäudes und seiner Ausstattung in der Auffassung des Mittelalters* (1902).

SANKARACHARYA: Hindu philosopher. See INDIA, I., 2, § 2.

SAUL, sōl: First king of Israel. His dates, according to the old chronology, are 1099-1059; later chronographers bring down the end of his reign to 1017, and give much less than the forty years ascribed to him (Acts xiii. 21). His dates are in confusion; in his third year his son Jonathan was old enough to have command of a body of men (I Sam. xiii. 2); Josephus (*Ant.*, X., viii. 4) gives the length of his reign as twenty years; modern scholarship reduces even this to ten or nine years.

Saul was the son of Kish, a Benjaminite of Gibeah. The sources describe him as of unusual height and of prepossessing appearance, while in the first years of his reign he distinguished himself by his modest bearing, ability, and courage. In obedience to a divine revelation Samuel secretly anointed him king, and had this ratified at a later assembly of the people at Mizpah, where the use of the lot resulted in the choice of Saul. The latter continued for a time his residence in Gibeah, accompanied by a small volunteer guard. When the Ammonites assailed Jabesh-gilead, he summoned all Israel to the defense and utterly defeated the assailants. The kingdom was thus securely established, and Samuel retired (see SAMUEL).

Nearly the whole of Saul's reign was filled with wars, particularly against the Philistines who had attained such supremacy that the Israelites were not permitted to bear arms. Saul assembled an army of 3,000 men, 2,000 of whom he took with him to Michmash, and 1,000 he sent under Jonathan to Gibeah. Jonathan began the war by assaulting the garrison of the Philistines at Gibeah. When the Israelite army was assembled at Gilgal awaiting the appearance of Samuel, who was to offer the sacrifice, Samuel did not appear at the time he had set and Saul became impatient and himself offered the sacrifice. For this he was sternly rebuked by the prophet and the end of his reign foretold. Saul on this occasion for the first time showed his self-willed character, which was incompatible with the position which the anointed of the Lord was to take in Israel. There are some difficulties in the text, no directions appearing to have issued from Samuel before I Sam. xiii. 8 to the effect that Saul was to await him (cf. I Sam. x. 8). The most likely solution is that the latter passage has been transposed in editing and properly belongs immediately before xiii. 7. The war was continued by a bold feat of arms on the part of Jonathan, which came near costing him his life because of an imprudent oath of Saul's. Another act of disobedience to the voice of God was committed by Saul in the war with the Amalekites. This war was to be a holy war of vengeance for old acts of aggression and for new insults. Saul was victorious and took Agag prisoner, whereby Num. xxiv. 7, 20 was fulfilled; but he failed to carry out the command of extermination. Samuel met him again at Gilgal and foretold the loss of his kingdom (xv. 22-23).

After this second conflict Saul's degeneration was rapid. Samuel secretly anointed David king, and a melancholy fell upon Saul which could be dispelled only by David's playing. Driven by jealousy, Saul sought to destroy David. He refused to fulfil his promise to give him his daughter Mirab in marriage but gave him her sister Michal. David then had a narrow escape with the help of Michal from the emissaries of Saul, and Saul pursued the fugitive as far as Ramah, the home of Samuel. There, the spirit of the prophetic school that had settled in the place seized upon him as it had once before his accession to the throne. But the bitterness of Saul's spirit is shown by his slaughtering the eighty-five innocent priests of Nob. During his subsequent pursuit of David he was forced in shame to endure the latter's magnanimity, but his repentance was only transient.

Saul's end was sad. Abandoned by all good spirits, he sought out the witch of Endor to learn from the lips of the departed Samuel what his fate was to be. Hostilities had again broken out with the Philistines, and Saul learned that he and his sons were to perish the next day on the battle-field. The prophecy was fulfilled. Saul's sons were slain and he fell on his own sword. David recovered his body and buried it in the family tomb.

The personality of Saul rests on the firm basis of

history. The narrative is supported by contemporary songs like those given or suggested in I Sam. xviii. 7; II Sam. i. 17 sqq., and it is a misapprehension of its realistic character to assert (Winckler) that the name Saul is not the name of a man but of a moon-god. Cheyne's fantastic assertion (*EB.*, iv. 4305) that Saul was a Jerahmeelite is just as unfounded. Saul's reign began promisingly and remained powerful to the end. He secured Hebrew independence and fought victoriously against Philistines, Amalekites, Moabites, Ammonites, Edomites, and Aram Zoba. He also did good service in rooting out heathen practises (I Sam. xxviii. 3). His downfall was due to the loss of that humility with which he began his reign and to his growing self-will. His degeneration can be traced step by step, although he was not wanting in greatness of soul even to the end. (C. von Orelli.)

Bibliography: The commentaries and other works on I Samuel; the literature under David; and the works on that period of Hebrew history cited under Ahab; Israel, History of; and Samuel. Consult further: J. A. Miller, *Saul the First King of Israel*, London, 1866; W. J. Deane, *Samuel and Saul*, ib. 1888; T. K. Cheyne, *Aids to the Devout Study of Criticism*, pp. 1–126, ib. 1892; F. Schwally, *Semitische Kriegsaltertümer*, Leipsic, 1901; H. P. Smith, *Old Testament History*, chap. vii., New York, 1903; G. Beer, *Saul, David, Solomon*, Tübingen, 1906; S. A. Cook, *Critical Notes on O. T. History; the Traditions of Saul and David*, London, 1907; *DB*, iv. 412–415; *EB*, iv. 4302–14 (elaborate); *JE*, xi. 74–78; Vigouroux, *Dictionnaire*, fasc. xxxv. 1500–07.

SAUM, KONRAD. See Sam.

SAUMUR, sō'mur: A town of France (155 m. s.w. of Paris) on the Loire, famous as the seat of the Protestant academy founded in 1598 by the national synod of Montpellier, and suppressed by royal edict Jan. 8, 1685. The academy, which developed the first fertile school of criticism in modern theology, owed to a certain extent both its existence and its scientific character to Philippe Duplessis-Mornay, the governor of the place, who watched the young institution with great tenderness (see Du Plessis-Mornay, Philippe, § 5). The Scotchman John Cameron (q.v.) became one of its first professors, and brought with him that spirit of free and independent research which afterward characterized the academy. Three of his disciples became professors there nearly at the same time, Moïse Amyraut (q.v.), Josué de la Place (see Placeus), and Louis Cappel (see Cappel, 3). The theological significance of the school is in large part due to the theory of hypothetical universalism connected with the name of Amyraut, and the Biblical researches of Cappel.

Bibliography: A. Schweizer, *Die protestantische Centraldogmen in ihrer Entwicklung innerhalb der reformirten Kirche*, ii. 439–563, Zurich, 1856; Schaff, *Creeds*, i. 478 sqq.; Lichtenberger, *ESR*, xi. 467–472.

SAUR, CHRISTOPH. See Sower.

SAURIN, sō-ran', **JACQUES**: The greatest pulpit orator of French Protestantism; b. at Nîmes Jan. 6, 1677; d. at The Hague Dec. 30, 1730. He was educated at Geneva, to which he had been taken as a child on the revocation of the Edict of Nantes, and in 1701 was ordained to the ministry. He immediately went to England, and for four years was pastor of the Walloon congregation in London, until a position was especially created for him at The Hague in 1705, which he filled until his death. Through all these years his fame as a preacher steadily increased, and multitudes listened to his sermons, attracted not only by the diction, logic, and delivery of his addresses, but even more by the deep religious conviction and adherence to the Gospel which pervaded him. Apart from his sermons, his two chief works were his *Discours historiques, critiques, théologiques et moraux sur les événements les plus mémorables du Vieux et du Nouveau Testament* (4 vols., with 7 vols. of continuations by P. Roques and C. S. de Beausobre, Amsterdam, 1720–39; Eng. transl. of vol. i., on the Pentateuch, by I. Chamberlayne, London, 1723) and *L'État du Christianisme en France* (part i., The Hague, 1725–27). By far his most important productions, however, were his sermons, of which he himself published five volumes, and his son, Philippe Saurin, seven (best ed., The Hague, 1749; Eng. transl. by R. Robinson, H. Hunter, and J. Sutcliffe, 7 vols., Blackburn and London, 1800–06, and by S. Burder, 6 vols., London, 1824). These addresses, many of which have also been published individually and in selections, both in the original and in translation, range over the most diverse themes, from dogmatic theology to Christian social life. The underlying spirit in them all is essentially that of the French Reformed type of Biblical Christianity, though with a strongly ethical and practical, even a subjective and mystical, strain, while the apologetic element is also often present. The sermons are of great length, many of them doubtless requiring two hours to deliver; yet they are so compact that even their minutest subdivisions would frequently furnish material for a large number of sermons of ordinary preachers. On the other hand, both style and diction are often careless and hasty, and his sermons share the common fault of the time in the display of learning which burdens them, especially in the opening portions. In the exposition, however, and still more in the peroration, Saurin's genius reaches its climax, but in form and taste he is inferior to Bossuet, in delicacy and depth he falls below Bourdaloue, and in pathos he can not compare with Massillon. His worst fault, however, was lack of sympathy, despite his loftiness, his intellectuality, and his earnestness, and it was due to this deficiency that he never became popular and that he is now little read. (C. Pfender.)

Bibliography: Biographies are by: J. J. van Oosterzee, Brussels, 1856; J. P. Gaberel and Des Hours-Farel, Geneva, 1864. Consult further: C. A. Coquerel, *Hist. des églises du désert*, i. 241 sqq., Paris, 1841; P. A. Sayous, *Hist. de la littérature française*, ii. 106 sqq., Paris, 1853; C. Weiss, *Hist. des réfugées protestantes de France*, ii. 63 sqq., Paris, 1853; A. R. Vinet, *Hist. de la prédication parmi les réformes de France au 17. siècle*, pp. 597–714, Paris, 1860; E. A. Berthault, *Saurin et la prédication protestante*, Paris, 1875; E. Lambert, *Essai homilétique sur la prédication de Saurin*, Montauban, 1892; Lichtenberger, *ESR*, xi. 472–475.

SAUSSAYE, PIERRE DANIEL CHANTEPIE DE LA. See Chantepie de la Saussaye.

SAVAGE, MINOT JUDSON: Unitarian; b. at Norridgewock, Me., June 10, 1841; graduated at Bangor Theological Seminary, 1864; became Congregational home missionary in California, 1864; was pastor at Framingham, Mass., 1867–69; at Hannibal, Mo., 1869–73; Unitarian pastor in Chicago, 1873–74; of the Church of the Unity, Boston, 1874–1896; and of the Church of the Messiah, New York, 1896–1906, when he retired from the ministry on account of the failure of his health. He is the author of *Christianity the Science of Manhood* (Boston, 1873); *The Religion of Evolution* (1876); *Light on the Cloud* (1876); *Bluffton, a Story of To-Day* (1878); *Life Questions* (1879); *The Morals of Evolution* (1880); *Talks about Jesus* (1880); *Minister's Handbook* (1880); *Belief in God* (1881); *Beliefs about Man* (1882); *Poems* (1882 and 1905); *Beliefs about the Bible* (1883); *The Modern Sphinx* (1883); *Sacred Songs for Public Worship*, edited with H. M. Dow (1883); *Man, Woman, and Child* (1884); *The Religious Life* (1886); *Social Problems* (1886); *My Creed* (1887); *Life* (1890); *Four Great Questions Concerning God* (1891); *The Irrepressible Conflict between Two World Theories* (1891); *The Evolution of Christianity* (1892); *Jesus and Modern Life* (1893); *Life beyond Death* (New York, 1901); and *Life's Dark Problems* (1905).

SAVONAROLA, sā-vō″nā-rō′la, GIROLAMO (HIERONYMUS).

Life till 1491 (§ 1).
His Preaching (§ 2).
His Prophecies (§ 3).
As a Reformer of the Church (§ 4).
Lorenzo de Medici; Charles VII. (§ 5).
The Florentine Theocracy (§ 6).
Relations with Alexander VI. (§ 7).
Turn of Sentiment against Savonarola (§ 8).
The End (§ 9).
His Character and Work (§ 10).

Girolamo (or Hieronymus) Savonarola, Italian Roman Catholic, origniator and victim of an ecclesiastical-political reform, was born at Ferrara Sept. 21, 1452; d. at Florence May 23, 1498. He has been variously represented as an inspired prophet, as a precursor of the Reformation, and as an ambitious demagogue and deluded fanatic. His right place is among the fearless preachers of righteousness and moral reform at the side of Nathan, Elijah, John the Baptist, and John Knox. Destined by his parents for the study of medicine, he was led to seek a religious life in the seclusion of the convent through a deepening sense of the corruption of society and the refusal of a family of the Strozzi living in Ferrara to give him their daughter in marriage. In 1475 he secretly left the parental home and betook himself to Bologna, where he entered the Dominican convent. His subsequent letters to his parents were full of filial affection and begged forgiveness for the suddenness of his flight and his failure to make known his intention. To the usual routine of conventual life, he added the study of Augustine and the great Dominican, Thomas Aquinas, and also of the Bible, with which he became thoroughly conversant. In 1481 he was sent to Ferrara, where he discovered that a prophet may not expect honor in his own country. The same year he went to Florence and became an inmate of the convent of St. Mark's. His preaching attracted no attention in Florence, and his audiences during Lenten season in San Lorenzo were reduced to twenty-five persons. Suddenly in 1486, while preaching in Brescia, his eloquence broke forth in all its wealth. In 1489 he returned to the convent in Florence, Lorenzo de Medici, at the representation of Pico della Mirandola, urging his return. In 1491 he became prior of St. Mark's.

1. Life till 1491.

During the next nine years Florence was filled with Savonarola's personality, and he became the most conspicuous religious figure in Italy. During the first part of this period, he had conflicts with Lorenzo de Medici, the political despot of the city, and during the second part with Alexander VI., all the while seeking by his exhortations and startling prophecies to bring about the civic and moral regeneration of the city. He preached first in St. Mark's and then in the cathedral, immense audiences pressing to hear him expound the Hebrew prophets and the Book of Revelation. At the time of his greatest popularity throngs waited hours for his appearance and his biographer Villari estimates his audiences at from 10,000 to 12,000. "Your sins make me a prophet," he cried out, and from the depths of that stirring, brilliant half-pagan life which the Medicis had fostered in Florence he conjured up a stinging sense of its emptiness and desolation. His message was addressed to the clergy as well as to the people, and the flashes of his indignation often fell upon the palace of Lorenzo. In the last sermon he preached during Advent season, 1492, he portrayed a vision he had had the night before of a sword held by a hand in the heavens and bearing the inscription "Behold the sword of the Lord will descend quickly and suddenly upon the earth." He heard many voices proclaiming mercy for the good and judgment for the wicked. Then suddenly the sword was turned toward the earth, the sky was darkened, and swords, arrows, and flames rained down. The preacher was commanded to preach these things. This was one of those visions the description of which from the pulpit of the cathedral impressed and terrified the great audiences. The severity of his warnings upon the pleasure-loving city was at times so fearful that Savonarola himself shrank back from delivering them.

2. His Preaching.

To his gifts of vivid description, pure language, and fervor of heart he added as a chief element of his power unshaken confidence in his divinely appointed mission. He felt that he received communications directly from God, and he stood forth as a divinely commissioned prophet. His prophecies of future events were the amazement of Florence, though not all joined in accepting the preacher as an inspired seer. He, however, applied to these prophecies the words of Scripture that not one jot or tittle of them should fail till they were fulfilled. These prophecies were usually given to him in visions or transports of the soul. His views on prophecy in general and on his own prophetic endowment found utterance from the pulpit and also in two works, *Compendium revelationum* (1495) and *Dialogus de veritate et prophetica* (1497). Savonarola's most famous prophecy was of the coming of a new Cyrus from across the Alps who should bring about

3. His Prophecies.

the political emancipation of Florence and Italy. Most of the prophecies were in general terms and predicted times of dire chastisement for Florence, followed by a time of righteousness and extension of the Church. One of the proofs Savonarola gave for his prophetic gift was the fulfilment of his predictions. On this very point, however, there is doubt. In certain cases, his prophecies were certainly not fulfilled, such as his prediction of the speedy conversion of the Jews and Moors. As to whether other so-called prophecies were real is open to question. The Cyrus from the West came into Italy, Charles VIII. of France, but it is a question whether Savonarola's prediction was anything more than the forecast of an observer carefully watching the progress of political movements in Italy and alert to detect the signs of impending events. Certain it is that, while Charles' advent was followed by the expulsion of the Medicis from Florence, his Italian campaign ended in failure and the independence of Florence lasted but a short period. Another consideration that casts suspicion upon the prophetic nature of his predictions is that many of them concerned political events such as belong to the selfish policy of nations, as when he predicted that Florence would again secure sovereignty over Pisa. A large party in Florence held Savonarola to be a prophet. Men like Landucci, the apothecary, fully accepted his prophetic endowment. Some of the distinguished men of the age, like the Frenchman Commines, either accepted it or acknowledged their inability to account for the forecast. The judgment of most of Savonarola's recent biographers, such as Villari and Lucas, and of historians, such as Pastor and Creighton, Roman Catholic and Protestant, is that Savonarola was self-deceived. But while his prophetic claims were a delusion, he had none of the spirit of the impostor. What men moving amidst the common realities of life called dreams of fancy, Savonarola, longing with all the intensity of his being for the reformation of Florence, took for real visions of the soul. Much as he impressed his own age with the reality of his prophetic endowment, to modern times his glory consists in his being a preacher of righteousness in an age of deep dissoluteness and religious effrontery.

4. As a Reformer of the Church.

As a reformer, his vision ended with the moral reform of the city and of Italy and its adoption of righteousness in private conduct and in civil management. A radical doctrinal reform such as was achieved by Luther and Calvin was not in Savonarola's program. In all essential points of doctrine he agreed with the medieval Church. He did not call in question a single one of its dogmas (cf. Pastor, *Popes*, vi. 51). His only departure from the ecclesiastical belief of his time was his denial of the pope's infallibility and his appeal to a council as the final court of arbitrament in Christendom.

5. Lorenzo de Medici; Charles VII.

The internal history of Italian affairs in 1492 was marked by the death of Lorenzo the Magnificent (the most accomplished diplomat of his time) and the elevation of Alexander VI. to the pontifical throne. When Lorenzo knew that he was dying, he sent for Savonarola. The monk had kept at a distance from the prince, and Lorenzo had said with reference to him, "a stranger has come into my house, yet he will not stop to pay me a visit." Rich gifts sent to the convent of St. Mark's failed to win its prior. Now, facing the issues of eternity, Lorenzo sent for Savonarola as "the only honest friar" he knew. He wanted to make confession of three crimes. The spiritual adviser instead proposed three terms of shrift. The first was a confident trust in God's mercy. To this the dying man assented. The second was the restoration of his ill-gotten wealth. To this also assent was given. The third required that he give back to Florence her liberties. To this Lorenzo gave no response and turned his face to the wall. The priest passed out without giving absolution. The account as thus given is based upon the earliest lives of Savonarola, by Burlamacchi and Mirandola. A different account was given by Politian in a letter to Jacopo Antiquario. Politian makes no mention of the third condition and reports that Savonarola left the dying man after giving his blessing. This version is accepted by Roscoe, Creighton (*Popes*, iv. 172 sqq.), and Lucas (pp. 83–84). The version adopted here is accepted by Villari (i. 168–169), Hase (p. 20), Clark (p. 116); Pastor (*Popes*, v. 92) seems to proceed upon the theory of its truth. Ranke wavers, but declared he did not see his way clear to deny it. During the three years 1494–97, Savonarola's ascendency was at its height. According to Guicciardini, his influence was most extraordinary. During this period Charles VII. came into Italy, Lorenzo's son Piero and the Medicis were banished from Florence and a theocratic government was established in the city. Fra Girolamo thundered from the pulpit against the rule of the Medicis and pleaded for their expulsion. When Charles was encamped near Florence, Savonarola, by the appointment of the Florentine seignory, met him and made a deep impression upon the monarch. The French army, through the monk's appeals to the king and his threats, restrained themselves from their usual violence in Florence, and Charles left the city, and pursued "his onward journey without delay." On the king's return from Naples to upper Italy, Savonarola again communicated with him in five letters, bidding the sovereign grant her liberties to Florence, a city of which he said "God had chosen her and had determined to magnify her so that who dared to touch her, touched the apple of His eye." No city ever had a more ardent lover than Florence had in Savonarola.

6. The Florentine Theocracy.

The expulsion of the Medicis involved a reorganization of the state, and in this work Savonarola had a part of prime importance. He was called upon as the chief citizen of Florence by the seigniory to propose a new constitution. Reluctantly he set himself to the task and took the government of Venice as his model. The supreme official, the doge, was left out, that place being given to Jesus Christ. "The government of the one in Florence," so he cried out in the pulpit, "could result only in despotism." "God alone shall be thy king, O Florence, as He was king of Israel under the old covenant." Savonarola's government was a theocracy; "its new head shall be Jesus Christ" was the ringing cry with which he closed his sermons on Haggai. Depicting this time of crisis, Guicciardini called the prior of St. Mark's the savior of his country (cf. Villari, i. 268, 298). The whole social fabric of Florentine society seemed for the moment to have undergone a change, and a millennial reign of order and good-will seemed to be impending. Love to Christ seemed to have become the predominant impulse. Deadly foes fell upon each other's necks; property illegitimately acquired was returned; the churches overflowed; the convents were filled up; profane amusements ceased. Indeed, says a contemporary writer, "the people of Florence seem to have become fools for Christ's sake."

But while Savonarola's influence over the people maintained itself for several years, the ideal elements of his government exposed him easily to attack. In the latter part of the fifteenth century its provisions seemed to be most impracticable. Besides, the Medicis were pressing to return to Florence as their rightful heritage, and their party and other enemies found abundant opportunity in Savonarola's unworldly peculiarities to increase the disaffection in Florence.

7. Relations with Alexander VI.

Alexander VI. was the chief factor in the last stage of Savonarola's career. The contrast between these two men has been compared with the contrast between Christ and Herod and between St. Paul and Nero. Moved by representations, reaching him from Florence itself, and by appeals of the Medicean princes, the pope summoned Savonarola to Rome July 25, 1495, and promised to "welcome him with love and fraternal affection." Savonarola refused, alleging sickness and the dangers by the way. Then followed papal briefs, Sept. 8, Oct. 16, inhibiting him from preaching. For five months Savonarola refrained from preaching, but on Feb. 17, 1496, at the call of the seigniory he again ascended the pulpit. He took the bold position that the pope might err, and that when he spake as a man and erred no man was bound to obey him. He entered upon a course of severe denunciations upon the Church and its representatives in Rome. Alexander tried bribery and offered Savonarola the red hat if he would keep silence, but in vain. Savonarola stood in the pulpit and declared he would not have mitres nor a cardinal's hat but only the red hat of martyrdom which God gives to his saints. His wonderful influence with the people had illustration in the carnival season of 1494. Boys who had been brought under the new religious movement and were grouped in brigades went from house to house, calling upon the occupants to give up their cards, dice, erotic books, and articles of adornment. They marched up and down the streets singing hymns which Savonarola had composed. In 1497, similar scenes were enacted, and on the last day of carnival week a great bonfire was made on the public square, of a pyramid of such articles, the pile being sixty feet high with a base of 240 square feet. This was known as the "burning of the vanities." At these times, Florence seemed to be going altogether to religion. ... left their husbands and betook themselves to convents. Others, who were married, took the vow of continence, and Savonarola even dreamed the city might reach so perfect a condition that all marriage would cease. People took the communion daily. Fra Bartolomeo threw his studies of naked figures into the fire and for a time thought it sinful to use in painting hands which should be continually folded in prayer.

With the year 1497 the troubles thickened around the Florentine reformer. Insulting placards were posted on the walls of his convent and distributed through the city.

8. Turn of Sentiment Against Savonarola.

Assassins moved by political rancor and ambition gathered in the cathedral to take his life. Savonarola intensified his denunciations of the "fornications in Italy, France, Spain, and all other regions." Lust had made of the Church a shameless courtesan. Priests openly acknowledged their bastards as sons. Alexander was evidently aimed at, and such open arraignment the pope could not safely tolerate. On May 12, 1497, Alexander declared Savonarola excommunicate as "one suspected of heresy." The seigniory was still on Savonarola's side and espoused his cause in letters to the Apostolic See. On Christmas Day, 1497, the prior violated the papal curse and celebrated mass three times, and on Feb. 11, 1498, he stood again in the pulpit and preached to an immense concourse of people declaring that popes might err as Boniface VIII. had erred. The heat of his utterance increased, and frequently, from this time on, he appealed to heaven as his witness that he was willing to go into fire of hell, if his motives were not pure, or to be struck dead on the spot if he were not sincere. The pope had one more weapon, the interdict, and this he threatened to hurl against the disobedient city. The seigniory sought to negotiate, but its membership became divided and decided it expedient that Savonarola should keep silence and the good-will of the Apostolic See be retained with an eye to future favors. It, however, refused to deliver up Savonarola to Alexander as he had requested. Savonarola preached for the last time Mar. 18, 1498. He in turn now determined to secure, if possible, the adjudication of an ecumenical council. The letters to the kings of France, England, and other countries, appealing to them to convoke such a council, were written but never sent.

At this juncture a completely new turn was given to Savonarola's career. Florence was suddenly startled with the report that an ordeal of fire was impending to test the prophet's supernatural claims.

9. The End.

The Franciscan monk Francesco da Puglia, in a sermon in S. Croce, issued the challenge. Savonarola hesitated and declared that he did not depend upon a miracle to attest his claims. Righteous lives were the test. But the popular demand forced him to accept the challenge. Fra Domenico, his intimate friend and a monk of St. Mark's, offered himself for the ordeal as did also many others. The seigniory appointed a day and the two parties filed their statements with this tribunal. The place fixed was the public square, where two pyres seventy feet in length, of inflammable materials, were built. All Florence was present to witness the spectacle. The Franciscans and Dominicans marched in solemn processions to the spot. The ordeal was set for eleven o'clock, but there was delay. Objection was made to Domenico's going through the fire wearing his priestly garments, on suspicion that they had been bewitched. The Dominicans yielded. The second objection was made that Domenico should not carry a crucifix or the host with him. The parleying was protracted. Rain fell, the day was declining, and the Franciscan challenger did not appear. The seigniory declared the ordeal abrogated. The spell of Savonarola's influence was gone. The mob now treated him as a coward or an impostor. Florence was mad with anger. A few, like Landucci, were bowed with disappointment and sorrow. The next day St. Mark's was assaulted. The resistance offered by the monks, even with firearms, staved off the end at best for a few hours. Savonarola and two of his chief supporters, Fra Domenico and Fra Silvestro, were imprisoned. Their first trial was before the seigniory. Alexander wrote that they should be sent to Rome but, if not, they should be tried "with torture." The agonies of the torture induced Savonarola to make confessions of imposture and other ill-doing, which he denied as soon as the delirium of the pain wore off. It was hard to manufacture, against the monk, charges deserving death. Savonarola was no heretic. But a commission sent by the pope—Turriano, the Venetian Dominican general, and Bishop Francesco Romelino, afterward cardinal—were equal to the task of finding the prisoners guilty of rank heresy. Letters came to Florence stating that Alexander had declared Savonarola should "be put to death even if he were another John the Baptist." The garbled records of the trial make it uncertain what the exact process was. Romelino's letters to Alexander show that the prisoners were to be treated as pernicious heretics. The intervals between the applications of torture the prisoners spent in comparing expositions on Pss. li. and xxxi. The three friends met and prayed on the morning appointed for the execution, May 23, 1498. Their bearing, that of humble trust in Christ, was adapted to win universal sympathy. The sentence ran that they should be hanged and their bodies burned. Absolution was pronounced. The bishop of Vasona in pronouncing the sentence of deposition upon Savonarola said, "I separate thee from the Church triumphant and the Church militant." Savonarola replied, "Not from the Church triumphant. That is not in thy power to do." The ashes of the three monks were cast into the Arno.

10. His Character and Work. Savonarola will be judged by the righteousness of his message, the calm stability of his last hours, and the environment in which he was placed. He stands forth as the greatest master of pulpit eloquence Italy has furnished. In an age when the classical renaissance introduced or fostered moral corruption, he represented moral righteousness in private life and in civil government. Lacking the sagacity of the statesman, he was inspired with patriotism and the devotion of the religious reformer. In appealing from the decision of Alexander VI., he was taking the position which Julius II., in his bull *Cum tanto divino*, 1505, justified. That bull pronounced papal elections secured by bribery void. If the bull was retroactive then Alexander was no pope. He had secured his election by shameless bribery. The world was at once divided between admiration for, and condemnation of, Savonarola. Even within the Dominican order the monk's memory was for a long time disparaged, and the Dominican general Sisto Fabri of Lucca, 1585, issued an order forbidding monks and nuns of his order to mention his name or retain any relic or book that could remind them of him. But the feeling in the Dominican order has changed and a warm and persistent effort has been made by Dominicans to prepare the way for the canonization of their most eloquent preacher. Protestants are inclined to regard him as in a sense a precursor of the Reformation, a seer of a new era in the Church. So Luther regarded him, and wrote a preface to an edition of his Meditation on Pss. li. and xxxi. (1523). Rietschl included him in the monument at Worms commemorating the Reformation, and placed him in company with Wyclif and Huss as forerunners of that great movement. Savonarola's expositions of the two Psalms composed during his imprisonment show him as a member of the Church universal. Here he appeals as a sinner directly to God's mercy. But in his "Triumph of the Cross," he accepts the seven sacraments and the other distinctive marks of the medieval Church. Schnitzer, the leading contemporary authority on Savonarola in Germany, gives him unstinted admiration. Pastor joins in admiring the purity of his purpose but condemns him as an unfaithful Roman Catholic in refusing obedience to the Apostolic See. The general sentiment in the Roman Catholic Church is represented by the judgment of Hefele-Knöpfler (*Kirchengeschichte* p. 503), that Savonarola's execution was a judicial murder. Florence regards the memory of her adopted citizen with love and has made every attempt to offer reparation for his execution. In 1882 the seigniory placed Girolamo's statue in the Hall of the Five Hundred and again, 1901, honored him by placing a tablet on the spot of execution with a statement that there "by unrighteous sentence" he and his two companions "were hanged and burned." On the wall of his cell in St. Mark's a medallion has been placed containing a head of the prior, and opposite the place where he was seized another memorial has been erected which the visitor often finds hung with wreaths of fresh flowers.

(PHILIP SCHAFF†.) D. S. SCHAFF.

BIBLIOGRAPHY: On bibliography consult: A. Audin de Rians, *Bibliographia delle opere e dell' edizioni di fra J. Savonarola*, Florence, 1847; Potthast, *Wegweiser*, pp. 1564–66.

Sources for a life are: Savonarola's Latin and Italian writings, consisting of sermons, tracts, letters, and a few poems. The largest collection of MSS. and original editions is preserved in the Central National Library of Florence. Printed works are: *Epistolæ spirituales et asceticæ*, ed. Quétif, Paris, 1674, Eng. transl., *Spiritual and Ascetic Letters of Savonarola*, ed. B. W. Randolph, London, 1907, new ed., 1909; the sermons were collected by a friend, Lorenzo Vivoli, and published as they came fresh from the preacher's lips—best ed. *Sermoni e prediche*, Prato, 1846; also ed. G. Baccini, Florence, 1889; a selection ed. Villari and Casanova, *Scelta di prediche e scritti di G. Savonarola*, Florence, 1898; Germ. transl. of twelve sermons and of the poem *De ruina mundi* by H. Schettmüller, Berlin, 1901; A. Gherardi, *Nuovi documenti e studi intorno a G. Savonarola*, 2d ed., Florence, 1887. "The Triumph of the Cross," ed. in Lat. L. Ferretti, Siena, 1899, Milan, 1901, Eng. transl. from this ed. by J. Procter, London, 1901, St. Louis, 1902. "Exposition of Pss. li., xxxi.," Lat. text with Eng. transl. by E. H. Perowne, London, 1900; Savonarola's poetry, ed. C. Guasti, Florence, 1862; E. C. Bayonne, *Œuvres spirituelles choisies de Savonarola*, 3 vols., Paris, 1880.

An extended list of works is given in Potthast, *Wegweiser*, pp. 1564–66; other lists are noted in the literature given below. Basal accounts are: P. Burlamacchi (d. 1519), *Vita Hieronymi Savonarolæ* (founded on an older Latin life by an eye-witness), ed. Mansi, Lucca, 1761; G. F. Pica della Mirandola (nephew of the celebrated litterateur), completed 1520, published, Mirandola, 1530, ed. Quétif, 2 vols., Paris, 1674; J. Nardi (a contemporary), *Le Storie della citta di Firenze, 1494–1531*, Florence, 1584; Luca Landucci (an ardent admirer of Savonarola and a Florentine apothecary), *Diario Florentine, 1450–1516*, Florence, 1883.

Of later accounts the three biographies which have made notable advance are: F. K. Meier, Berlin, 1836; F. T. Perrens, 2 vols., Paris, 1852, 3d ed., 1859; P. Villari, Florence, 1859, 2d ed., 1887, Eng. transl., 2 vols., London, 1888, 1 vol., 1899 (combines results of previous study with new material); idem, *Studies Historical and Critical*, ib. 1907. Other biographies are: F. C. Bartoli, Florence, 1782; A. G. Rudelbach, Hamburg, 1835; K. Hase, *Neue Propheten*, Leipsic, 1851; F. T. Perrens, 2 vols., Paris and Turin, 1853, 3d ed., 1859; R. Madden, 2 vols., London, 1854; V. Marchese, Florence, 1855; B. Aquarone, 2 vols., Alexandria, 1857; S. de Rorari, 2d ed., Legnago, 1868; E. C. Bayonne, Paris, 1879 (worthy); E. Warren, London, 1879; W. R. Clark, Chicago, 1890; A. G. Haygood, *The Monk and the Prince*, Atlanta, 1895; J. L. O'Neil, Boston, 1898 (has extended bibliography); G. McHardy, Edinburgh, 1901, New York, 1902; E. L. S. Horsburgh, London, 1901; N. Howard, ib. 1904; H Lucas, ib., rev. ed., 1906 (has full bibliography); W. H. Crawford, Cincinnati, 1907; W. E. Oliphant, London, 1907; H. Bergmann, Stockholm, 1909.

Other discussions, not simply biographical, but taking up various phases, literary or critical, are: W. Roscoe, *Life of Lorenzo de' Medici*, London, 1795, new issue, 1885; L. von Ranke, *Historisch-biographische Studien*, pp. 183–257, Leipsic, 1877 (discusses the interrelations of the works by Burlamacchi and Pica della Mirandola); C. Sickinger, *Savonarola, sein Leben und seine Zeit*, Würzburg, 1877; E. Comba, *Storia della Riforma in Italia*, Florence, 1881; Margaret Oliphant, *Makers of Florence*, London, 1881; Pastor, *Popes*, vi. 3–54; idem, *Zur Beurtheilung Savonarolas*, Freiburg, 1898 (answers criticisms by Luotto and Feretti); P. Luotto, *Dello Studio di Scrittura sacra secondo G. Savonarola e Leon XIII.*, Turin, 1896; idem, *Il vero Savonarola ed il Savonarola di L. Pastor*, Florence, 1897; Feretti, *Per la causa di Fra G. Savonarola*, Milan, 1897; M. Glossner, *Savonarola als Apologet und Philosoph*, Paderborn, 1898; J. L. O'Neil, *Was Savonarola really excommunicated?* Boston, 1900; J. Schnitzer, *Quellen und Forschungen zur Geschichte Savonarolas*, vols. i.–iv., Leipsic, 1902–10; G. Biermann, *Kritische Studie zur Geschichte des Fra G. Savonarola*, Rostock, 1901; E. S. Godkin, *The Monastery of San Marco*, London, 1901; *Cambridge Modern History*, chap. v., New York, 1902; Creighton, *Papacy*, iv. 168 sqq. (discussion of the authorities, p. 351; the student should not omit study of this useful note); Schaff, *Church History*, v., 2 § 76 (good list of literature, pp. 660–661).

SAVOY CONFERENCE: A conference between twelve bishops and twelve Puritan divines, with nine assistants on each side, at the Savoy Palace, London, Apr. 15- [illegible] the object being to revise the [illegible] conference was necessitate [illegible] to the Restoration and [illegible] as with the servi[illegible] sentiment of the country was strongly royalist, and consequently the bishops were able to resist, in their reliance upon popular feeling, the attempts of the Puritans to do away with parts of the service and with observances which to them savored of Roman Catholicism, and the Conference had as a result only the continued use of the Prayer-Book. The proposals desired by the Puritans were embodied by Baxter in his hastily compiled liturgy, which never came into use, but was republished by C. W. Shields, Philadelphia, 1867, New York, 1880.

Bibliography: D. Neal, *History of the Puritans*, ed. J. Toulmin, part iv., chap. vi., Bath, 1793–97; W. H. Hutton, *The English Church 1625–1714*, pp. 185–186, London, 1903; F. Procter and W. H. Frere, *New Hist. of the Book of Common Prayer*, pp. 169–193 et passim, ib. 1905; J. H. Blunt, *Annotated Book of Common Prayer*, pp. 30, 32, 97–98, 183, New York, 1908.

SAVOY DECLARATION. See Congregationalists, III., § 1.

SAXON CONFEDERATION, LOWER. See Lower Saxon Confederation.

SAXONS, CONVERSION OF THE: Of all the German tribes the Saxons longest preserved both their independence and their national religion. It is true that there are records of attempts to introduce Christianity among them before the time of Charlemagne, but these are either legendary, as the account of the baptism of Saxon envoys by Bishop Faro of Meaux at the court of Lothair II., or else were frustrated by the disinclination of the Saxon people to accept Christianity, as was the case with the efforts of the Hewald brothers (see Hewald). St. Boniface (q.v.) obtained a letter of recommendation to the Saxons (*Epist.*, xxii.), but his biographers do not relate that he worked among them. It was only the Saxon wars of Charlemagne that rendered a conversion of the Saxons both possible and necessary. Whether Charlemagne intended to incorporate Saxony in the Frankish empire when he began his Saxon campaigns is doubtful, but at all events he followed this course after 776, and he was therefore forced at the same time to undertake the Christianization of the people because of the close connection between Church and State in his domains. In his very first campaign (772) the destruction of the Irmensul accompanied the capture of the Eresburg, whereupon the Saxons retorted by attacking a church in Fritzlar and destroying the church at Deventer. The religious question was first treated in the peace of 776, when the Saxons, probably as a proof of the sincerity of their subjection, agreed to accept baptism. In the following year Charlemagne assembled an imperial diet at Paderborn, in Saxon territory, and Saxony was divided into missionary districts which were assigned to various Frankish dioceses and monasteries. Cologne receiving the land of the Boructeri, Mainz the districts of southern Saxony, bordering on its own territory, Würzburg the region about Paderborn, Abbot Sturm of Fulda the districts on the Diemel, and the monastery of Amorbach in the Odenwald the region about Verden. West Frankish bishoprics, such as Reims and Châlons, seem also to have shared in this missionary activity.

Although the task thus systematically undertaken was impeded by ever-recurring revolts against foreign rule (778, 782, 783, 784), each new victory of the Franks became the occasion for wholesale baptisms. The most dangerous insurrection was that of 782, which threatened the very existence of the Saxon Church and was suppressed only through the victories won by Charlemagne at Detmold and on the Hase in 783. When, two years later, Widukind and Abbio were baptized, the pacification and Christianization of the land were regarded as assured. Charlemagne sent word to Rome that the Saxons were converted and sought by promulgating the *Capitulatio de partibus Saxoniæ* (probably in 787) to secure the position he had won. The punishment of death, decreed by the old Saxon laws against violators of the heathen sanctuaries, but a penalty unknown to Frankish law, was now adopted for the protection of the new faith, and this penalty was decreed not only for the murderers of ecclesiastics, but also for all who conspired against Christians, damaged churches, observed the heathen custom of burning the bodies of the dead, contemptuously broke the commandment of the Church concerning baptism, or avoided baptism. Each church received rich allotments from the lands of its parishioners, tithes from private and royal property, and also the right of Asylum (q.v.). Besides this, it was decreed that the death penalty might be remitted in case of voluntary confession of guilt, that children should be baptized before reaching the age of one year, that the Sabbath should be observed and mass attended, and that Christians should be buried in consecrated ground.

Nevertheless, a new revolt in 792 was followed by a relapse into heathenism, the destruction of churches, and the murder of many of the clergy. Alcuin, writing to Megenfrid in 795 (*Epist.*, lxix.), laid the blame, at least in part, on the execution of tithes and extreme legal penalties, even while doubting whether the Saxons had really been elected into faith (*Epist.* lxvii.), but finally Charlemagne succeeded in pacifying the land, largely by deporting thousands of Saxon families to various parts of Franconia and Swabia (795, 797–799, 804). At the same time the severity of the law was modified, and at the imperial diet of Aachen (Oct. 28, 797) the death penalty was abolished and replaced by the wergild of sixty soldi, usual among the Franks. By 802 the land was considered to be entirely Christianized. As early as 787 the missionary district of Willehad (q.v.) at the mouth of the Weser had been created a diocese, of which Willehad himself had been consecrated bishop; the dioceses of Verden and Minden seem to have been organized about the same time; the bishopric of Münster was formed between 802 and 805; toward the close of Charlemagne's reign the bishopric of Paderborn was erected, the first bishop being Hathumar, a Saxon educated at Würzburg; and the remaining dioceses, Osnabrück, Hildesheim, Halberstadt, and Hamburg, were formed in the reign of Louis the Pious. (A. Hauck.)

Bibliography: Original sources are: *Regesta historiæ Westfaliæ*, ed. H. A. Erhard, 2 vols., Münster, 1847–51; *Geschichtsquellen des Bisthums Münster* vols. i. and iv., ib. 1851 sqq. *Kaiserurkunden der Provinz Westfalen*, ed. R. Wilmans and F. Philippi, 2 vols., ib. 1867–81; *Bremisches Urkundenbuch*, ed. D. R. Ehmck and W. von Bippen, Bremen, 1873 sqq., F. A. Ogg, *Source Book of Mediæval History*, pp. 114–123, New York, 1908. Consult: C. Stuve, *Geschichte des Hochstifts Osnabrück*, Jena, 1853; B. Simson, *Jahrbücher des fränkischen Reichs unter Ludwig*, 2 vols., Leipsic, 1874–76; G. Dehio, *Geschichte des Erzbistums Hamburg-Bremen*, vol. i., Berlin, 1876; W. von Giesebrecht, *Geschichte der deutschen Kaiserzeit*, i. 110 sqq., Brunswick, 1881; S. Abel and B. Simson, *Jahrbücher des fränkischen Reichs unter Karl dem Grosse*, 2 vols., Leipsic, 1883–88; C. Ritter, *Karl der Grosse und die Sachsen*, 2 parts, Dessau, 1894–95; G. Hüffer, *Korveyer Studien*, Münster, 1898; Robinson, *European History*, i. 129 sqq., 150 sqq.; Rettberg, *KD*, vol. ii.; Hauck, *KD*, ii. 360 sqq.; the literature under Charlemagne.

SAXONY: A kingdom of Germany, bounded on the north and east by Prussia, on the south by Bohemia, and on the west by the Thuringian states, with two small exclaves, Ziegelheim and Liebschwitz; area 5,856 square miles; population (1900) 4,202,216. Of this there were 3,954,132 Lutherans; 16,080 Reformed; 197,005 Roman Catholics; 2,028 German Catholics; 1,260 Greek Catholics; 12,416 Jews, and 19,295 others, including members of the fourteen Irvingite and fourteen New Apostolic churches, as well as of the twelve Methodist and four Baptist congregations. In 1905, of a population of 4,508,601, there were 4,250,659 Lutherans, Reformed, and Unionists; 218,275 Roman Catholics; 266 Russian Orthodox; 1,331 Greek Catholics; 22,858 other Christians; and 14,697 Jews. In recent years there has been a notable increase of accessions from the Roman Catholic Church to the Lutheran, the number advancing from 508 in 1899 to 1,266 in 1903, while conversions from Lutheranism to Roman Catholicism increased from 41 to 52 respectively. The Roman Catholic Church increase is due almost entirely to the immigration of laborers from Bohemia, Poland, Italy, and other Roman Catholic countries. Roman Catholic districts are found only in Saxon Upper Lusatia, about the nunnery of Marienstern east of Kamens, and in the vicinity of the nunnery of Marienthal near Ostritz. On the increase is the influence of various sects not only in the vicinity of Zwickau (see Zwickau Prophets), a hotbed of sects since the Reformation, but over all the kingdom. Particularly aggressive in recent years has been the New Apostolic Church (Geyerites and Krebsites). Included in the statistics of the Methodist Episcopals are the *Albrechtsleute* (see Evangelical Association), whose chief attraction is their close fellowship.

The established Church of Saxony is Lutheran. So long as the royal house is Roman Catholic the four ministers of worship, justice, interior, and finance must be of the State Church. Since 1874 its control has been vested in the national consistory, composed of a judicial president and an equal number of theological and judicial councilors, with the first court preacher as vice-president, and with a number of extra members. Between this consistory and the individual congregations stands the "inspection," consisting of the superintendent (ephorus) of the diocese and the chief civic official of the district. Upper Lusatia, which has no superintendent, is controlled (subject to the national consistory) by the prefecture of Bautzen. Since 1868 the laity have been permitted to represent individual congregations, and quinquennial national synods have been held, the latter composed of 34 clergy and 43 laymen. In 1903 there were 1,469 clerical positions, 619 being under royal patronage, 832 controlled by private patrons, and 18 alternating in patronage. In 1903 the births of Evangelical parentage numbered 142,641 and the baptisms 138,606; in the same year there were 32,416 marriages, and 32,047 betrothals of wholly Evangelical pairs. By the law of Dec. 1, 1876, omission of baptism or betrothal involves loss of the right to be a godparent, or to have either an active or a passive vote in church affairs. The church attendance is, in general, satisfactory; and there is an increasing interest in missions and other forms of practical religion. On the other hand, the number of communicants is unmistakably declining. Besides the Evangelical Lutherans, official recognition has been accorded since 1818 to the Evangelical Reformed, represented by churches at Dresden and Leipsic.

The Roman Catholic Church in Saxony, which has enjoyed freedom of worship and complete civil equality with the Protestant denominations since 1807, has been controlled since 1763 by a vicar apostolic and by a Roman Catholic consistory under him. He resides in Dresden, but is at the same time dean of the chapter of Bautzen, and is a bishop *in partibus*. The State requires all measures, even those bearing simply on internal administration, to be submitted to itself; and such changes as touch in the remotest degree civil relations must be approved by the civil authorities. The Roman Catholics have in Saxony seventy-five places of worship and ninety-seven clergy. In Upper Lusatia are the two Cistercian nunneries already mentioned, but the foundation of additional religious houses is forbidden, and every religious order is prohibited from entering the country. The only exception to the latter restriction is that of the law of Aug. 23, 1876, which admits, after approval by, and under supervision of, the civil government, such sisters as belong to orders settled in the German Empire and devoting themselves exclusively to the care of children and of the sick. The German Catholic congregations in Dresden, Leipsic, Chemnitz, and Geleneau, recognized since 1848, are now controlled by the Landeskirchenvorstand in Dresden, which convenes a synod triennially, and by the elders of each congregation. They are rapidly declining because of their increasing tendency to free thought, and are so lax that, in case of conversions to the Lutheran Church, baptism is required. In case of change of confession among the recognized bodies, the person concerned must declare his intention to his clergyman, who must warn him of the seriousness of his proposed step. If, after four weeks, he still adheres to his resolve, he is furnished a certificate of dismissal, which is sent the clergymen of the confession to which he has become a convert, and without this he can not be received into any of the recognized churches. In case the conversion is to an unrecognized church, the name of the convert must be entered in the official register of dissenters. This latter provision, dating from 1870, renders the formation of new religious bodies possible. Advantage was taken of it in 1871 by the "Separate Lutherans" (see LUTHERANS, II.), who charged the State Church with lapse from the Lutheran confession. They now have six congregations in Dresden, Planitz, Chemnitz, Crimmitzschau, Frankenberg, and Grün, with a membership of 1,500. (F. W. DIBELIUS.)

BIBLIOGRAPHY: The best sources of information are the annuals—*Statistisches Jahrbuch für das Königreich Sachsen*, published at Dresden, and *Kirchliches Jahrbuch*, published at Gütersloh; and P. Drews, *Das kirchliche Leben der evangel.-lutherischen Landeskirche des Königreichs Sachsen*, Leipsic, 1902.

SAYBROOK PLATFORM. See CONGREGATIONALISTS, III., § 1.

SAYCE, sês, ARCHIBALD HENRY: Church of England, archeological scholar; b. at Shirehampton (4 m. n.w. of Bristol), Gloucestershire, Sept. 25, 1845. He was educated at Queen's College (B.A., 1869), and was ordered deacon in 1870 and ordained priest in the following year. He was elected fellow of Queen's College in 1869, where he was also tutor in 1870–79. He was deputy professor of comparative philology at Oxford (1876–1889), and since 1891 has been professor of Assyriology in the same university. He was a member of the Old-Testament Revision Company, and was Hibbert lecturer in 1887, Gifford lecturer in 1900–02, and Rhind lecturer in 1906. He is a member of very many learned societies.

He has edited G. Smith's *History of Babylonia* (London, 1877) and *Sennacherib* (1878); *Records of the Past*, second series (5 vols., 1888–92); the English translation of G. Maspero's *Histoire ancienne des peuples de l'orient classique* as *The Dawn of Civilization* (3 vols., 1894–1900); Murray's *Handbook to Upper Egypt* (1896); *The Aramaic Papyri Discovered at Assouan* (1906); and *The Tablet from Yuzgat in the Liverpool Institute of Archæology* (1907). Among his numerous independent writings, special mention may be made of his *Assyrian Grammar for Comparative Purposes* (London, 1872); *Principles of Comparative Philology* (1874); *Astronomy and Astrology of the Babylonians* (1874); *Elementary Assyrian Grammar* (1874); *Babylonian Literature* (1877); *Lectures on the Assyrian Language and Syllabary* (1877); *Introduction to the Science of Language* (2 vols., 1879); *The Monuments of the Hittites* (1881); *The ancient Empires of the East: Herodotus i.–iii* (1883); *Fresh Light from the Monuments: A Sketch of the most striking Confirmations of the Bible from recent Discoveries in Egypt, Assyria, Palestine, Babylonia, and Asia Minor* (1883); *Assyria, its Princes, Priests, and People* (1885); *An Introduction to the Books of Ezra, Nehemiah, and Esther* (1885; 5th ed., 1909); *Lectures on the Origin and Growth of Religion as illustrated by the Religion of the ancient Babylonians* (Hibbert lectures for 1887; 1887); *The Hittites: or, The Story of a Forgotten People* (1888); *The Races of the Old Testament* (1891); *Social Life among the Assyrians and Babylonians* (1893); *The "Higher Criticism" and the Verdict of the Monuments* (1894); *A Primer of Assyriology* (1894); *Patriarchal Palestine* (1895); *The Egypt of the Hebrews and Herodotus* (1895); *Early History of the Hebrews* (1897); *Israel and the Surrounding Nations* (1898); *Babylonians and Assyrians* (New York, 1899); *Genesis* in *The Temple Bible* (London, 1901); *The Religions of Ancient Egypt and Babylonia* (Gifford lectures; Edinburgh, 1902); *Tobit and the Babylonian Apocryphal Writings* in *The Temple Bible* (London, 1903); *Monuments, Facts, and Higher Critical Fancies* (1904); and *Archæology of the Cuneiform Inscriptions* (1907).

SCADDING, CHARLES: Protestant Episcopal bishop of Oregon; b. at Toronto, Canada, Nov. 25, 1861. He was graduated from Trinity College, Toronto (1885), and was ordered deacon in 1885 and priested in the following year. He was curate at St. George's, New York City (1886–90); rector of Christ Church, Middletown, N. Y. (1890–91); Trinity, Toledo, O. (1891–96); and Emmanuel, La Grange, Ill. (1896–1906). He was Deputation lecturer on "the Church in the United States" for the London Society for the Propagation of the Gospel, and has lectured extensively in the United States on similar topics. In 1906 he was consecrated third bishop of the diocese of Oregon. He has written *Direct Answers to Plain Questions for American Churchmen* (New York, 1901).

SCALIGER, scal'i-ger (**DE LA SCALA**), **JOSEPH JUSTUS:** Founder of scientific chronology and philologist; b. at Agen (73 m. s.e. of Bordeaux) Aug. 4, 1540; d. at Leyden Jan. 21, 1609. Son of the famous French scholar, Julius Cæsar Scaliger, he devoted himself to the study of classical and oriental languages at Paris, after 1558. He entered the Reformed church, 1562, and became one of its leading representatives; traveled in Italy, England, and Scotland, 1565–66; studied at Valence, 1570; fled from his native land after the massacre of St. Bartholomew; was professor at Geneva, 1572–1574; spent his time in traveling throughout France or residing at the castle of his friend, a French nobleman, Louis Chastaigner de la Rochepozay, 1574–93; and was professor and head of the University of Leyden from 1593. Scaliger is the leading philologist of France, and secured the scientific investigation of the classics and the adoption of the principles for the correction of ancient texts by his acute critical method. In the field of historical chronology, his *M. Manilii Astronomicon libri quinque* (1579) may be considered an introduction to his famous work *Opus novum de emendatione temporum* (Paris, 1583; best enlarged ed., Cologne, 1629). In this he takes the Julian period as the larger basis, upon which he calculates the time periods of the history of the peoples. This embraces the periods of 7,980 Julian years, and is therefore a union of the sun, moon, and indiction cycles. Here is to be mentioned also *Hippolyti canon paschalis* (Leyden, 1595). He wrote his *Elenchus trihæresii Nicolai Serarii* (Franeker, 1605), against the attempted refutation by the Jesuits of his denial of monasticism during the Apostolic period; and in this he set forth on scientific grounds, for the first time, that the representation of the "contemplative life" by Eusebius (*Hist. eccl.*, ii. 17) was untenable. The capstone of his work was the edition and restitution of the synchronistic Eusebian chronicon, *Thesaurus temporum Eusebii* (Leyden, 1606), which by its inestimable sources of pre-classic history, seemed to him best adapted as a foundation upon which to erect the treasure-house of the times. The principal results of his investigation appeared under the subtitle *Synagoge historion*, better known under the separate title *Olympiadon anagraphe* (Berlin, 1852), partly in the words of the original authors, partly in a free rendering. To this he appended *Isagogici chronologiæ canones* ("Main Points to the Introduction of Chronology") as his own. His *Epistolæ* appeared Leyden, 1627, while *Epistres françoises* to him was issued Harderwyck, 1624, and *Lettres françaises inédites*, Paris, 1879.

(G. Laubmann†.)

Bibliography: Sources are: D. Baudius, *Oratio funebris honori . . . J. J. Scaligeri*, Leyden, 1609; D. Heinsius, *In obitum . . . J. Scaligeri . . . orationes duæ*, Leyden, 1609; D. Gerdes, in *Miscellanea Duisburgensia*, vol. iv., 6 vols., Amsterdam, 1732–45. Consult further: C. Nisard, *Le Triumvirat littéraire au 16 siècle*, pp. 149–308, Paris, 1852; J. Bernays, *J. J. Scaliger*, Berlin, 1855; E. and É. Haag, *La France protestante*, vii. 1–26, Paris, 1857; C. Seitz, *Mémoire sur J. J. Scaliger et Genève*, Geneva, 1895.

SCANNELL, THOMAS BARTHOLOMEW: English Roman Catholic; b. at London July 8, 1854. After completing his education at St. Edmund's College, Ware, and the English College, Rome, he was ordained to the priesthood in 1878, and from that year until 1885 was professor of philosophy in St. Edmund's College. He was for several years an administrator of the Southwark Fund for Infirm Priests, and has served as missioner in Brighton, Norwood, Sheerness, Folkstone, and Weybridge. In 1896 he was appointed as one of the papal commissioners on the question of the validity of Anglican orders, and since 1908 has been one of the canons of Southwark Cathedral. In collaboration with J. Wilhelm he prepared a *Manual of Catholic Theology, based on Scheeben's "Dogmatik,"* vol. i. (London, 1890), and besides editing the fourth and following editions of the *Catholic Dictionary* of W. E. Addis and T. Arnold (London, 1893 sqq.), has written *The Priest's Studies* (London, 1908).

SCAPEGOAT. See Atonement, Day of; Azazel.

SCAPULAR: A small badge or token consisting of two little pieces of cloth joined by cords, and worn over the shoulders, whence the name. Confraternities connected with various religious orders received the privilege of wearing this small representative of the habit, in token of participation in prayer, good works, and spiritual privileges with the order. These confraternities are now very widespread, and the wearing of the scapular is an approved act of devotion in the Roman Catholic Church. The most famous of the different scapulars is the brown or Carmelite scapular, the history of which goes back to a vision supposed to have been vouchsafed by the Virgin Mary to St. Simon Stock (1164–1212) of the Carmelite order, in which she promised blessings to those who should devoutly wear this scapular. Others are the black scapular of the Servite order and the red of the Passionists.

SCAPULARY. See Vestments and Insignia, Ecclesiastical.

SCARBOROUGH, scär'bur-ō, **JOHN:** Protestant Episcopal bishop of New Jersey; b. at Castlewellan (25 m. s. of Belfast), County Down, Ireland, Apr. 25, 1831. He was educated at Trinity College Hartford (A.B., 1854), and at the General Theological Seminary, from which he was graduated in 1857. He was ordered deacon in the same year and was advanced to the priesthood in 1858. After being curate of St. Paul's, Troy, N. Y., from 1857 to 1860, he was rector of the Church of the Holy Comforter, Poughkeepsie, N. Y. (1860–67), and of Trinity, Pittsburg, Pa. (1867–75). In 1875 he was consecrated bishop of New Jersey.

Bibliography: W. S. Perry, *The Episcopate in America*, p. 235, New York, 1895.

SCHAEDER, shē'der, **ERICH**: German Protestant; b. at Clausthal (25 m. n.e. of Göttingen), Hanover, Dec. 22, 1861. He studied at the universities of Berlin and Greifswald from 1881 to 1886 (lic. theol., Greifswald, 1891); was inspector of the Tholuck Seminary at Halle (1887–89); privat-docent for New-Testament exegesis at Greifswald (1891); associate professor of the same subject at Königsberg (1894–95) and at Göttingen (1895–99). Since 1899 he has been professor of systematic theology at Kiel. In theology he is conservative, and has written *Die Bedeutung des lebendigen Christus für die Rechtfertigung nach Paulus* (Gütersloh, 1893); *Ueber das Wesen des Christentums und seinen modernen Darstellungen* (1904); *Die Christologie der Bekenntnisse und die moderne Theologie* (1905); *Christenstand und kirchliche Lehre* (Berlin, 1906); *Die Offenbarung Gottes in der Geschichte der christlichen Kirche* (Gross-Lichterfelde, 1907); *Der moderne Mensch und die Kirche* (Gütersloh, 1908); *Schriftglaube und Heilsgewissheit* (1908); and *Theozentrische Theologie, Eine Untersuchung zur dogmatischen Prinzipienlehre*, vol. i. (Leipsic, 1909).

SCHAEFER, shē'fer, **PHILIPP ALOYS**: German Roman Catholic bishop of Saxony; b. at Dingelstädt (10 m. n.n.w. of Mühlhausen), Saxony, May 2, 1853. He was educated at the universities of Prague (1873–74) and Würzburg (1874–78; D.D., 1878); was curate at Plauen and at the Hofkirche in Dresden (1879–81); professor of Biblical science at the Lyceum of Dillingen (1881–85); of New-Testament exegesis at the universities of Münster (1885–95), Breslau (1895–1903), and Strasburg (1903–06), being also dean of Münster in 1887–88 and 1892–93, of Breslau in 1895–96 and 1901–02, and of Strasburg in 1903–05, and rector of Münster in 1890–91. In 1906 he was consecrated bishop of Saxony, and is also vicar apostolic in the kingdom of Saxony, apostolic prefect of Meissen-Lausitz, and dean of the cathedral of Bautzen. He has written *Biblische Chronologie vom Auszuge aus Aegypten bis zum Beginn des babylonischen Exils mit Berücksichtigung der Resultate der Aegyptologie und Assyriologie* (Münster, 1879); *Die Gottesmutter in der heiligen Schrift* (1887); *Das Neue Testament erklärt* (4 vols., comprising Thessalonians, Galatians, Corinthians, Romans, and Hebrews; 1890–93); *Einleitung in das Neue Testament* (Paderborn, 1898); *Die Aufgaben der Exegese nach ihrer geschichtlichen Entwicklung* (Münster, 1900); *Die Kaisererlasse vom 4. Feb., 1900, und die akademisch gebildeten Klassen* (1901); and *Klerus und sociale Frage* (1902).

SCHAEFER, PHILIPP HEINRICH WILHELM THEODOR: German Lutheran; b. at Friedberg (15 m. n. of Frankfort), Hesse, Feb. 17, 1846. He was educated at the universities of Giessen, Erlangen, and Leipsic, and at the seminary for preachers at Friedberg. He was pastor of the German Lutheran church in Paris in 1869–70 and inspector of the Seegelmannsche Anstalt at Alsterdorf, near Hamburg, in 1871–72. Since 1872 he has been pastor and director of the institute for deaconesses at Altona. In theology he is an orthodox member of his denomination, and, in addition to editing *Korrespondenzblatt der Diakonissen-Anstalt in Altona* (Altona, 1873 sqq.); *Monatsschrift für innere Mission* (Gütersloh, 1877 sqq.); *Die innere Mission in Deutschland* (1878 sqq.); *Jahrbuch der Krüppelfürsorge* (Hamburg, 1899 sqq.); *Evangelisches Volkslexikon* (Bielefeld, 1900), and *Reden und Predigten vom Gebiet der Diakonie und inneren Mission* (5 vols., Leipsic, 1890), has written *Die Diakonissensache und die Diakonissenanstalt zu Altona* (Bredstedt, 1875); *Die weibliche Diakonie in ihrem ganzen Umfang dargestellt* (3 vols., Hamburg, 1879–83); *Leidfaden der inneren Mission* (1888); *Praktisches Christentum* (4 vols., Gütersloh, 1888–1901); *Diakonissen-Katechismus* (1895); *Die innere Mission in der Schule* (1895); *Agende für die Feste und Feiern der inneren Mission* (3 parts, Berlin, 1896); *Pariser Erinnerungen eines deutschen Pastors* (Gütersloh, 1897); *Kalender der inneren Mission* (1897); *Die innere Mission auf der Kanzel* (Munich, 1897); *Unsere Schwester, ein Wort über und für die Diakonissensache* (Potsdam, 1903); and *Johann Heinrich Wichern* (Gütersloh, 1908).

SCHAEFFER, CHARLES FREDERICK: Lutheran (General Council); b. at Germantown, Pa., Sept. 3, 1807; d. at Philadelphia Nov. 23, 1879. He was educated at the University of Pennsylvania and studied theology under private direction; was ordained in 1829; pastor at Carlisle, Pa., 1829–34; at Hagerstown, Md., 1834–39; professor of theology at Capitol University, Columbus, O., 1840–43; pastor at Lancaster, O., 1843–45; at Red Hook, N. Y., 1845–51; at Easton, Pa., 1851–55; professor of the German language at Pennsylvania College, Gettysburg, Pa., 1855–64; and professor of systematic theology and president at the new theological seminary at Mt. Airy, Philadelphia, 1864–79. He was a representative of the strictly conservative and confessional party in the Lutheran Church, taking a leading part in the organization of the General Council in 1867. Among his works are English translations, of G. V. Lechler's commentary on Acts (1869) in J. P. Lange's *Commentary on the Holy Scriptures* (New York, 1865–80); of Johann Arndt's *Wahre Christenthum* with title *True Christianity* (Philadelphia, 1869); and of J. H. Kurtz's *Church History* (1868).

Bibliography: The *Life* by B. M. Schmucker and W. J. Mann, Philadelphia, 1880; and H. E. Jacobs, in *American Church History Series*, passim, New York, 1903.

SCHAEFFER, CHARLES WILLIAM: Lutheran (General Council); b. at Hagerstown, Md., May 5, 1813; d. at Philadelphia Mar. 15, 1896. He graduated at the University of Pennsylvania, 1832, and at the Gettysburg Theological Seminary, 1835; was pastor in Montgomery County, Pa., 1835–41; at Harrisburg, Pa., 1841–49; Germantown, Pa., 1849–75; professor of ecclesiastical history in the theological seminary at Mt. Airy, Philadelphia, 1864–96; and a member of the board of trustees of the University of Pennsylvania from 1857. He was one of the leaders of the conservative confessional party in the Lutheran Church, in whose councils he stood high. He was an authority on the history of the development of the Lutheran

Church in America, and published *Early History of the Lutheran Church in America* (Philadelphia, 1857); *C. H. Bogatsky's Golden Treasury*, translated from the German (1858); *Family Prayer, a Book of Devotions* (1859); *Halle Reports*, translated from the German, with extensive historical, critical, and literary annotations (vol. i., 1880); *Wackernagel's Life of Luther*, translated (1883); and *Hans Sachs' Wittenberg Nightingale*, translated (1883).

Bibliography: H. E. Jacobs, in *American Church History Series*, iv. 269 et passim, New York, 1893; and literature under Lutherans.

SCHAFF, schâf, DAVID SCHLEY: Presbyterian; b. at Mercersburg, Pa., Oct. 17, 1852. He was graduated from Yale (A.B., 1873), and Union Theological Seminary (1876). He was pastor of the Presbyterian church at Hastings, Neb. (1877–1881); associate editor of the *Schaff-Herzog Encyclopædia* (1881–83); pastor of the First Presbyterian Church, Kansas City, Mo. (1883–89); and professor of church history in Lane Theological Seminary, Cincinnati, O. (1897–1903). Since 1903 he has held a similar professorship in Western Theological Seminary, Pittsburg, Pa. He contributed to the *Bible Dictionary* of his father, Philip Schaff (Philadelphia, 1880); has revised and abridged J. S. Howson and H. D. M. Spence's commentary on Acts for the *International Revision Commentary* (New York, 1892); has written *The Life of Philip Schaff* (1897); and has continued the *History of the Christian Church* by his father (vol. v. parts 1 and 2, 1907–10).

SCHAFF, PHILIP.

Philip Schaff, Biblical scholar and church historian, organizer and editor of the first edition of this *Encyclopedia*, was born at Chur, Switzerland, Jan. 1, 1819; d. in New York City Oct. 20, 1893. There are three well-defined periods in his life:

I. Preparatory Period, 1819–43: From the schools at Chur and Kornthal (Württemberg) he passed to the gymnasium in Stuttgart, and the universities of Tübingen, Halle, and Berlin (1837–40). At Tübingen he heard Ferdinand Christian Baur (q.v.) but came especially under the influence of the Biblical theologian, Christian Friedrich Schmid (q.v.). At Halle he was on very intimate terms with Julius Müller and Tholuck (qq.v.) living a part of the time under the latter's roof. There he made his first American acquaintance, George Lewis Prentiss (q.v.), afterward his lifelong friend and for many years his colleague in Union Theological Seminary. At Berlin he was especially attracted by Neander, whose amanuensis he was for a time. He then traveled through Italy and Sicily as tutor to Baron Kröcher. In 1842 he received the *venia legendi* at Berlin and began his career as privat-docent at that university. It was at this period that he came to know Godet and Theodore Monod (qq.v.) and wrote his treatises, *Die Sünde wider den heiligen Geist und die daraus gezogenen dogmatischen und ethischen Folgerungen. Eine exegetisch-dogmatische Abhandlung, nebst einer historischen Anhange über das Lebensende des Francesco Spiera* (Halle, 1841), and *Das Verhältniss des Jakobus, Bruders des Herrn, zu Jakobus Alphäi, aufs Neue exegetisch und historisch untersucht* (Berlin, 1842), the former being his licentiate of theology and the latter his habilitation theme.

II. Mercersburg Period, 1843–63: He emigrated to the United States in 1843 at the invitation of the German Reformed Church to occupy a chair in its theological seminary in Mercersburg, Pa., and showed himself eminently qualified for the position, adding to scholarly attainments and religious fervor wise theological judgment, a faculty of adapting himself to new conditions, and of entering heartily into the republican forms of the West. On his way to America he spent two months in England, studying the language and coming into contact with some of the leaders of the Oxford movement. Arriving in Mercersburg he found John Williamson Nevin (q.v.) in charge of the seminary, and as colleagues they brought out the so-called "Mercersburg Theology" (q.v.), known throughout the English-speaking world and also in Germany, and charged with a Rome-ward tendency, but which really signified, so far as there was anything peculiar in it, merely an application of the historical spirit to all problems of theology and a churchly regard for the ancient liturgical forms of the Church.

1. Election; Literary Activity.

Suspicion soon fell upon Dr. Schaff as an alleged advocate of a de-Protestantizing tendency, and his inaugural address on *Das Princip des Protestantismus* (Chambersburg, 1845, Eng. transl. with Introduction by Dr. Nevin, *The Principle of Protestantism, as related to the Present State of the Church*) called forth the charge of heresy, which was argued before the synod at York in 1845, but he was acquitted by a practically unanimous vote. This address elaborated the two principles of Protestantism and the two dangers to which Protestantism is exposed, sectarianism and rationalism. Dr. Schaff in subsequent years said that he never dreamt of advocating anything heretical when he prepared and delivered his inaugural. His kindly references to the Middle Ages and to the Oxford movement probably suggested the charge. The great interest which this address aroused was the beginning of a new movement in the German Reformed Church. In the seminary Dr. Schaff at one time or another taught all the departments, having only a single colleague. He became identified with all the movements in the denomination, especially with the liturgical movement, serving as chairman of the committee to prepare a liturgy (1857). He brought out a *Gesangbuch* (1859) which introduced a new era in congregational song among the German-speaking churches of the United States by substituting a book of merit for books in which rationalistic hymns were freely used; and for the three-hundredth anniversary of the Heidelberg Catechism an elaborate edition of that catechism (1863). He had already written a simple catechism for children in German and English (1861); while his preference for church history was shown by his history of the Apostolic Church, which appeared first in German at Mercersburg (1851, 2d ed., Leipsic, 1854; English transl. by E. D. Yeomans, New York, 1853; Dutch, Tiel, 1857). The work was favorably received on all sides, both in Germany and the United States.

The important problem was presented during this period to the Reformed Church and other churches of continental origin as to how far they should yield in the matter of language and other customs to the usages of the United States. The feeling was very strong among the emigrants of the first generation against any change as treason to their traditions. Dr. Schaff had been called to train ministers through the medium of the German tongue, and this he conscientiously attempted to do in the class-room until he was compelled by the demand of the majority of the students to resort to English. He became aware that it was unwise to attempt forcibly to perpetuate the use of German in this land. In his address, *Der Anglogermanismus* (English transl., *Anglo-Germanism, or the Significance of the German Nationality in the United States*, Chambersburg, 1846) he recognised the sure tendency of the second and third generations to abandon those churches of German origin which persisted in maintaining the German language and other customs unmodified. His views met with a storm of opposition and German papers denounced him as a traitor to his German training. He took the same attitude with reference to German theology and German books, and held that it was unwise, as it was impracticable, to introduce them unmodified into the United States, and that they should be reproduced "and adapted to the practical wants of the free church in a free state." But these views did not interfere with the warmest love for his native Switzerland or the continuance of the warmest friendships in Germany and his unabated esteem for the diligence, simplicity, and independence of German professorial life. In 1854 he went to Europe for a year to recuperate after his strenuous labors. He delivered lectures on America and its institutions (German original, Berlin, 1854; 3d ed., 1865; English transl. by E. D. Yeomans, New York, 1855; Dutch transl. by De Schryver, Rotterdam, 1855) in different cities. One outcome of the year was his *Germany, its Universities, Theology and Religion* (Philadelphia, 1857, the first book he issued in English himself), in which he gave information concerning German universities, their professors, and other leading German divines, from personal acquaintance, which was very welcome to the growing number of American and British students interested in German theology.

2. Relation to Use of German.

III. New York Period, 1863–93: In consequence of the ravages of the civil war the theological seminary at Mercersburg was closed for a while and so in 1863 Dr. Schaff became secretary of the Sabbath Committee in New York City, and held the position till 1870. He advocated the American view of Sunday observance as opposed to the continental, and gave himself up with characteristic energy and practical foresight to the work of arousing public opinion, enlisting the cooperation of the German-speaking clergy for the American Sunday and securing the enforcement of Sunday laws. In this interest he traveled east and west, issued tracts, made addresses, called mass meetings, and in other ways advanced the cause. Also in Germany he advocated a better observance of the day before meetings of Christian clergymen and laymen in different cities held during visits in 1865 and 1869. On these visits, as on others, he also advocated the idea of the American Sunday-school and organized the first of such schools in Stuttgart (1865). In 1870 he was made professor in Union Theological Seminary, New York City, holding first the chair of theological encyclopedia and Christian symbolism till 1873, of Hebrew and the cognate languages till 1874, of sacred literature till 1887, and finally of church history, till his death.

1. Varied Activities.

But his labors in the class-room represented only a part of his public services. Movements in which he became prominently identified were the Evangelical Alliance, the revision of the English Bible, and the Alliance of the Reformed Churches. In all of these he showed himself one of the most devoted as he certainly was one of the most distinguished advocates. As secretary of the American branch of the Evangelical Alliance he threw himself into the preparations for the great conference which met in New York in 1873, and by three visits to Europe succeeded in enlisting the cooperation of many prominent clergymen and scholars who probably but for him would not have come, and whose presence made the New York meeting so unique. He himself presented papers at all of the general conferences of the Evangelical Alliance down to 1891, although not able to attend the last, and in the same direction of unity strove for the closer union of the bodies representing the Reformed type of the Reformation, joining in the formation of the Alliance of the Reformed Churches in London in 1875 and delivering the opening address at the first council held in Edinburgh in 1877.

Dr. Schaff's connection with the revision of the English Bible began in 1870. By invitation of the British committee he selected a representative committee of American scholars. He was indefatigable in procuring a hearty and sympathetic cooperation between the British and American committees. He saw the completion of the Revised New Testament in 1881 and of the Old Testament in 1885, and to the end of his life predicted that though the Revised Version was by no means perfect it would be ultimately accepted by the churches as an improvement upon the Authorized Version.

2. Literary Work.

A work in which he was preeminent was as mediator between German theology and church life and the English-speaking public. He represented the Evangelical type of German theology, and his thorough acquaintance with all types of German thought and his personal intimacy with many of the leading German scholars enabled him to interpret German theology with authority. His mastery of both German and English and his clear style furthered his influence. By his visits and addresses in Germany and through publications he was also the chief interpreter of American thought to the German religious public. This intermediary relationship was recognized on both sides of the sea, and in the address presented to him by the theological faculty of Berlin in 1892, on the fiftieth anniversary of his activity as a teacher, he was compared to Martin Butzer, who had carried the learning of the continent to England in the time of the Reformation, and also to Jerome, who translated the Greek Scriptures into Latin, because of his services in the cause of Biblical scholarship. As a theological writer he was prolific. He wrote and edited numerous works in the departments of exegesis, the chief of which was the American edition of Lange's *Bibelwerk* (25 vols., New York); propædeutic; hymnology (*Christ in Song*, 1868; enlarged by his son, 2 vols., 1897); symbolics (*The Creeds of Christendom*, 3 vols., 1877); also *Through Bible Lands* (1878); *A Companion to the Greek Testament and the English Version* (1883); *The Teaching of the Twelve Apostles* (1885). Church history was his most fruitful study, and he followed his Apostolic Church with a history of the Church down to 1073, and passing over the intervening period brought out two rich volumes on the German and Swiss Reformation respectively. He originated the American Society of Church History (1888), and arranged for the authorship and publication by it of the *American Church History Series* (13 vols., 1893 sqq.). He edited the series of *Nicene and Post-Nicene Fathers* (28 vols). He edited the first edition of this *Encyclopedia* (3 vols., 1884) and its companion, afterward combined with it, *The Encyclopedia of Living Divines* (1886).

His last public appearance was in Chicago at the Parliament of Religions, Sept. 22, 1893. He sat upon the platform while his paper on Christian Union was being read. The inscription on his tombstone presents the salient features of his career: "A teacher of theology for fifty years. Historian of the Church. President of the American Committee of Bible Revision. He advocated the reunion of Christendom." His great learning was held in the service of piety. He regarded love as the central principle of theology; and with a tolerant mind, which sacrificed none of the fundamental tenets of his own Reformed faith, he labored for fellowship and cooperation among all classes of Christian believers, among the Greek and Roman Catholics as well as among the numerous communions of Protestants. His motto was *Christianus sum. Christiani nihil a me alienum puto;* and his last confession, "I am a sinner, and place my trust in my Savior who died for me." DAVID S. SCHAFF.

BIBLIOGRAPHY: D. S. Schaff, *The Life of Philip Schaff*, New York, 1897.

SCHAITBERGER, shait'bārʜ-er, **JOSEPH**: Leader of the Protestants driven from the valleys about Salzburg in the persecution instituted in 1683 by Archbishop Maximilian Gandolf (see SALZBURG, EVANGELICALS OF); b. at Dürnberg, near Hallein (9 m. s.s.e. of Salzburg), Mar. 19, 1658; d. at Nuremberg Oct. 2, 1733. Though a simple miner, he studied deeply Luther's and Canisius's catechisms and attained a rich spiritual life. It was he who drew up on the archbishop's requirement the confession of faith for his Protestant friends and neighbors because of which they were driven from their homes in the winter of 1685. With his wife Schaitberger found refuge in Nuremberg and supported himself there as wood-worker and wire-drawer. During his last years he was a pensioner of the Carthusian monastery. He made many journeys through the valleys about Salzburg at no small personal risk, exhorting and encouraging the Protestants who had remained behind, and he wrote for them a number of missives treating questions of Christian faith and life which (twenty-four in number) were ultimately collected and printed as *Evangelischer Sendbrief* (Nuremberg, 1702). The book soon became known throughout all Germany and is still read. A poem of his, written in his native dialect on occasion of his exile and beginning "A poor exile am I," expresses the longing for home with true pathos, yet breathes a joyous trust in God. It has found place in many hymnbooks. (HERMANN BECK.)

BIBLIOGRAPHY: J. G. Schellhorn, *De religionis evangelicæ in provincia Salzburgensi ortu et fatis*, Leipsic, 1732; J. Moser, *Salzburger Emigrationsakten*, Frankfort, 1732; C. F. Arnold, *Die Vertreibung der Salzburger Protestanten*, Leipsic, 1900; idem, *Die Ausrottung des Protestantismus in Salzburg*, Halle, 1900–01; C. Grosse, *Die alten Tröster*, Hermannsburg, 1900.

SCHALL, shāl, **JOHANN ADAM**: German astronomer and Jesuit; b. at Cologne 1591; d. in China Aug. 15, 1666. He was educated in the Collegium Germanicum in Rome; entered the order of the Jesuits, and was in 1628 sent as a missionary to China, where he remained to his death. He reformed the Chinese calendar, acquired the confidence of the Chinese government, and translated into Chinese many mathematical treatises, interlarded with religious and Christian discussions. He also wrote *Historica missionis societatis Jesu apud Chinenses* (Vienna, 1665). G. H. KLIPPEL†.

BIBLIOGRAPHY: A. and A. de Backer, *Bibliothèque de la compagnie de Jésus*, ed. C. Sommervogel, vii. 705 sqq., Paris, 1896; A. Kircher, *China monumentis . . . illustrata*, pp. 104 sqq., Amsterdam, 1667; *KL*, x. 1754–56.

SCHANZ, shānts, **PAUL VON**: German Roman Catholic; b. at Herb (20 m. s.w of Tübingen), Württemberg, Mar. 4, 1841; d. at Tübingen June 1, 1905. He was educated at the universities of Berlin and Tübingen (Ph.D., 1866) and at the theological seminary of Rottenburg (1865–66); was lecturer at the Wilhelmstift, Tübingen (1867–70); acting professor of mathematics and science at the gymnasium of Rottweil (1870–72); and full professor of the same subjects in that institution until 1876. After 1876 he was connected with the University of Tübingen, first as professor of New-Testament exegesis (1876–83) and later as professor of dogmatics and apologetics (since 1883). In addition to being joint editor of the *Theologische Quartalschrift* and editing M. von Aberle's *Einleitung in das Neue Testament* (Freiburg, 1877) and the fifth edition of J. A. Möhler's *Neue Untersuchungen der Lehrgegensätze zwischen den Katholiken und Prote-*

stanten (Regensburg, 1900), he wrote a commentary on the Gospels (4 vols., Freiburg, 1879–85); *Nicolaus von Cusa als Mathematiker* (Rottweil, 1872); *Die astronomischen Anschauungen des Nicolaus von Cusa und seiner Zeit* (1873); *Galileo Galilei und sein Prozess* (Würzburg, 1878); *Apologie des Christentums* (3 parts, Freiburg, 1887–88); *Die Lehre von den heiligen Sacramenten der katholischen Kirche* (1893); *Moderne Apologetik* (Frankfort, 1903).

SCHAPPELER, sha'pel-er, **CHRISTOPH**: Reformer in South Germany; b. at St. Gall (19 m. s.e. of Constance), Switzerland, in 1472; d. there Aug. 25, 1551. Nothing is known of his education, except that it followed the scholastic vogue. He was engaged at the Latin school at St. Gall, 1493–1513; became preacher at the chief church at Memmingen, Upper Swabia, 1513, where with rare eloquence and upright life he fearlessly set himself against the priesthood of the older faith, as well as against private and public evils. At the approach of the Reformation, he deliberately made his choice, and cast his lot with Zwingli and his colleagues, introducing the movement in his city. Laying stress upon the Bible as the source of faith and ordinances, he attacked the mass, the claims of the pope, and the orders of the Roman Catholic Church. The writings of the Reformers were spread abroad, along with copies of the Scriptures, especially the New Testament; but the council could not be prevailed upon to interfere, since the movement had caught hold of the imagination of the people. On Feb. 27, 1524, the bishop of Augsburg excommunicated Schappeler, with the result of the greatest public excitement at Memmingen. On Dec. 7, 1524, he administered holy communion in both species and celebrated baptism in the German language. Finally a public disputation was held, Jan. 2–7, 1525, in which Schappeler presented his profession in seven articles: he renounced (1) the oral confessional; (2) supplication to Mary and the saints; (3) the practise of tithes; (4) the sacrifice of the mass, which he regarded as a memorial; (5) purgatory; (6) he demanded the Eucharist in both kinds; (7) he proclaimed the universal priesthood of believers. He overwhelmed his adversaries with Scripture. Practical results followed. The council, after taking advice from other scholars in neighboring towns, approved the marriage of the clergy, permitted monks and nuns to abandon the cloisters, subjected the priests to taxation and civil jurisdiction, forbade the tithe of the laity, and abolished the mass. Schappeler attracted not only an enthusiastic following in the town but also among the peasants of the surrounding country, who were oppressed with economic and legal grievances. As the author of the famous twelve articles, he had a prominent part in the impending Peasants' War (q.v.).

His Swiss nature had asserted itself in his attitude on social and political affairs. From the beginning he spoke on behalf of the lower classes, and was wont to appeal over the heads of the council to the whole community of citizens. The council's admonition only made him more discreet. From the year 1523 he vigorously opposed the right of demanding tithes, but he warned the peasants repeatedly against resort to violence. He took no part, personally, in the peasant parliament of the delegates of the three groups of Algäu, Lake Constance, and Baltringen in 1525 at Memmingen, but from Schappeler proceeded undoubtedly the demand that in the new order of things, both ecclesiastical and civil, a basis must be sought in divine law. He thoroughly approved of peasant organization in order to carry out this theoretical demand. The proposal for a Christian union of peasants that his friend and follower, Sebastian Lotzer, unsuccessfully tried to carry out, thwarted by the Swabian League, may be regarded as a scheme of Schappeler's. The authorship of the twelve articles has been variously attributed, partly because Schappeler subsequently did not acknowledge them and partly because of the failure to notice the inner resemblance to the ten articles submitted by the Memmingen peasants to the council, Feb. 23–Mar. 3, 1525, of which the former seem an enlarged and more refined version. Nevertheless, the ten articles must be taken as a sublimation of the long-continued public instruction of Schappeler. When the parliament met, Mar. 6–30, the ten articles were taken as the basis for the Christian union, and they had to be revised and strengthened by the support of Scripture. Whether Schappeler performed this of his own accord or was prompted by Lotzer or other leaders remains uncertain. At any rate they appeared in print. Two elements were embodied; ecclesiastical freedom, and release from intolerable feudalistic burdens. Moreover, the Swabian League, under the implacable Leonhard von Ech, refused all discussion, and in the confusion it took advantage of a long-cherished desire for an armed invasion of the imperial city, under pretense that Memmingen was the breeding-place of disturbance and Schappeler the chief agitator, to be visited with a bloody penalty. The latter left the city secretly and took refuge at St. Gall. In 1532 the congregation sought his recall by the council in vain. After two years the council consented to the surrender of his library and to an indemnity of one hundred florins (about $45). Later he was preacher at Luisibühl and at St. Mang in St. Gall. (W. Vogt.)

Bibliography: F. Dobel, *Memmingen im Reformationsalter*, 5 parts, Augsburg, 1877–78 (part 1 deals with Schappeler); C. A. Cornelius, *Studien zur Geschichte des Bauernkrieges*, Munich, 1861; E. Rohling, *Die Reichsstadt Memmingen in der Zeit der evangelischen Volksbewegung*, ib., 1864; A. Stern, *Ueber die 12 Artikel der Bauern*, Leipsic, 1868; F. L. Baumann, *Die oberschwäbischen Bauern . . . und die 12 Artikel*, Kempten, 1871; W. Vogt, *Die bayrische Politik im Bauernkrieg*, Nördlingen, 1883; *Cambridge Modern History*, ii. 160, 177, 179; and the literature under Peasants' War.

SCHARLING, shār'ling, **CARL HENRIK**: Danish theologian; b. in Copenhagen May 3, 1836. He studied at the University of Copenhagen (candidate in theology, 1859); spent the years 1860–63 in extensive travel, a result of which was the publication of *Breve fra Holland* (1864); *Grækenland* (1866); and *En Pilgrimsfærd i det hellige Land* (1876); was editor of *Ugeblad for den danske Folkekirke* (1865–1868), and of *Dansk Tidsskrift for Kirke- og Folkeliv*,

Literatur og Kunst (1869–70); became docent in ethics in the university 1867, and professor 1870. In 1872–74 he published his most important work, *Menneskehed og Kristendom*, in two volumes, a philosophy of history. Other theological publications are *Jacob Böhmes Theosophie* (1879); *Den lutherske Dogmatik overfor Nutidens kirkelige og videnskabelige Krav* (1883), the address at the university celebration of the fourth centenary of Luther's birth; *Christelig Sædelære efter evangelisk-luthersk Opfattelse* (2 vols., 1884–86), a systematic treatment of ethics; *Religionens Stilling i det menneskelige Aands- og Sjæleliv* (1897); and *Det svundne og det Vundne, Tanker og Overvejelser ved Aarhundredskiftet* (1903). In theology Scharling is a confessional Lutheran, opposed to the Grundtvig school of theology, somewhat inclined to polemics, in the interest of which he has written several works, and is fearless in controversy. He has not confined his literary activities to theology. Thus he is the author (under the pseudonym of Nicolai) of *Ved Nytaarstid i Nöddebo Præstegaard* (1862; many Danish editions and translations into German, French, and English, *Nöddebo Parsonage*, 2 vols., London, 1867), characteristic of Danish thought and personality; he wrote also the novel *Uffe Hjelm og Palle Löves Bedrifter* (1866); the biography of Christian IX. and Queen Louise (1895–98). His *The Rivals, or, Love and War* (London, 1869), and *Nicolai's Marriage* (2 vols, London, 1876) are other works which have appeared in English. JOHN O. EVJEN.

SCHARTAU, shär'tau, **HENRIK**: Swedish preacher; b. at Malmö (16 m. e.s.s. of Copenhagen) Sept. 27, 1757; d. at Lund (24 m. e. of Copenhagen) Feb. 2, 1825. He was of German descent; studied theology at Lund, 1771–78; was ordained in 1780; was domestic preacher, and later assistant to a rural pastor; but, 1786, became diakonus at the cathedral at Lund; archdeacon in 1793, and, besides, district provost, 1800. In 1810 he was a representative of the clericals in the diet which chose the king. He steered clear of the rationalistic moralism on the one hand and the pietism of the Unity of the Brethren on the other, between representatives of which the pulpit was divided at that time; and while the former preached the abstract formulas of God the Father, and the latter indulged in the mystical contemplation of the Savior's blood and wounds, he chose and preached with earnestness and power the third article, of the work of sanctification, that is, the justification of the sinner before God. At the same time he no less earnestly carried on his catechetical work. (A. MICHELSEN†.)

BIBLIOGRAPHY: Biographies are by A. Lindeblad, Lund, 1837, Germ. transl., Leipsic, 1842; and H. M. Melin, Stockholm, 1838.

SCHAUFFLER, shôf'ler, **ADOLF FREDERICK**: Presbyterian; b. at Constantinople, Turkey, Mar. 7, 1845. He was educated at Williams College (A.B., 1867), Union Theological Seminary (1868–1869), and Andover Theological Seminary (1869–1871), and from 1872 to 1887 was pastor of Olivet Presbyterian Church, New York City. Since 1887 he has been superintendent, and since 1902 president, of the New York City Mission and Tract Society, and has also been chairman of the New York State Sunday-school Association since 1899 and secretary of the International Sunday-school Lesson Commission since 1902. In theology he is a conservative. He has written *Ways of Working* (Boston, 1891); *The Teacher, the Child, and the Book* (1900); *The Pastor as Leader of Sunday-school Forces* (Nashville, 1903); *Sparks from a Superintendent's Anvil; practical Helper for every Sunday-school Worker* (1909); and *Knowing and Teaching the Scholar* (1910).

SCHAUFFLER, ALBERT HENRY: Missionary, "Apostle to the Slavs of the United States," brother of the preceding, and son of William Gottlieb Schauffler; b. at Constantinople, Turkey, Sept. 4, 1837; d. at Cleveland, Ohio, Feb. 15, 1905. He came to America, Apr., 1855, to enter Williams College, and graduated therefrom in 1859. After completing a course in Andover Seminary (1861) he studied a year (1862) at Harvard Law School in preparation for teaching at Robert College, Constantinople. On his return to Turkey, he became professor of law for two years in that institution; but a preference for missionary work led to his ordination, on June 3, 1865, at Pera, Constantinople, and his employment by the American Board in that city until 1870. While he was in America on furlough (1872), the American Board induced him to open the Austrian mission field. He located at Prague for two years (1872–74) and then at Brünn, Moravia, for seven years (1874–81). He was influential in obtaining from the Emperor Francis Joseph a decree which gave to Protestant churches and to the Young Men's Christian Association a fair amount of religious freedom in the Austrian Empire.

Obliged by affliction to return to America (1881) he was persuaded to undertake mission work among Bohemians settled in Cleveland, Ohio. He began work in Olivet Chapel in 1882, and in 1883 was appointed superintendent of Slavic missions in the United States under the Congregational Home Missionary Society. He organized Bethlehem (Bohemian) Congregational Church, Cleveland, Ohio (1888); opened Bohemian missions at St. Louis, Mo., Iowa City, Ia., Crete, Neb., Milwaukee, Wis., and Silver Lake, Minn.; Slovak missions in Pittsburg and its suburbs; Polish missions at Cleveland, O., Detroit, Mich., and Bay City, Mich., besides furnishing inspiration, counsel, and workers to other denominations which desired to enter where Congregationalists could not undertake such work. To carry forward this Slavic work he founded two new institutions for the training of Slavic workers, the Slavic department of Oberlin College for the training of ministers, and the Bethlehem Bible and Missionary Training School for women, as Bible readers.

He consecrated to missionary service a rare ability. His vigorous constitution withstood peril, persecution, and incessant toil. His disciplined mind tolerated only methodic, exact work, which he performed with unusual despatch. He was resourceful and cautious, and where diplomacy of a high order was required, his honest, fearless, and broad grasp of the situation secured for him success and the lasting respect of his opponents. He served the interest of foreign and home missionary work, especially as a linguist. His mastery of languages enabled him to begin work at once in the Austrian field and later to meet the incoming foreigner to America with a greeting in his mother tongue. He had a warm, sympathetic, and generous heart, and a moral earnestness which befitted his stability of character and conscientiousness.

FRANCIS METHERALL WHITLOCK.

SCHAUFFLER, shauf'ler, **WILLIAM GOTTLIEB:** Missionary, father of the preceding; b. at Stuttgart, Württemberg, Aug. 22, 1798; d. at New York Jan. 26, 1883. In 1804 his father removed to Odessa, South Russia. In 1820 he resolved to devote himself to missionary work and in 1826 emigrated to America and studied at Andover, 1826–31. Under the care of the American Board, he went to Constantinople, where he resided and labored, 1831–74. He was particularly interested in the conversion of the Jews, and for their benefit revised and superintended the publication of the Old Testament in Hebrew-Spanish (at Vienna, 1839–42). But his great work was the translation of the whole Bible into Osmanli-Turkish, the language of the educated Turks. This occupied him eighteen years. For his services to the German colony at Constantinople he was decorated by King William of Prussia. After 1877 he lived in New York. He was a remarkable linguist, being familiar with nineteen languages and able to preach extemporaneously in German, Italian, French, English, Spanish, and Turkish. He published *Meditations on the Last Days of Christ* (Boston, 1837).

BIBLIOGRAPHY: His *Autobiography* was edited by his sons, with introduction by E. A. Park, New York, 1888.

SCHAUMBURG-LIPPE, shaum'burg-lip'pe: A German principality bounded by the Prussian provinces of Hanover and Westphalia; capital Bückeburg; area 131 square miles; population (1905) 45,000, most of whom are Lutherans. In its present extent the principality dates from 1640. Like Lippe (q.v.) the country was Christianized in the time of Charlemagne, and was under the influence of Rome during the Middle Ages. Owing to the fact that nearly all the counts of the house of Schaumburg held high positions in the Roman Church, the Reformation made its way into the country at a comparatively late date. However, in the decade following 1560 the country became Evangelical, and the Mecklenburg Church Order of 1552 was adopted. In 1614 Prince Ernest promulgated a new church order which was only mildly Lutheran. From 1636 the reigning family at Bückeburg has adhered to the Reformed faith, though the population as a whole has remained Lutheran. The Lutherans have eighteen parishes, under a superintendent and two district superintendents, and recently their consistorial constitution has been supplemented after the modern synodal plan. The Reformed Church, on the other hand, with a parish at Bückeburg and another at Stadthagen, has belonged to the federation of Reformed churches in Lower Saxony for two hundred years. The Roman Catholics likewise have two parishes with full parochial rights.

(F. H. BRANDES.)

SCHECHTER, shek'ter, **SOLOMON:** Anglo-American Hebrew scholar; b. at Fokshani (100 m. n.e. of Bucharest), Rumania, Dec. 7, 1847. He was educated in the Talmudical school of Vienna and at the universities of the same city and Berlin. In 1882 he went to England as tutor in rabbinics to Claude G. Montefiore and eight years later was appointed lecturer on the Talmud at the University of Cambridge, where he became reader in rabbinics in the following year. In 1893 he visited Italy and five years later went to Egypt and Palestine, discovering in Cairo the valuable Genizah collection of Hebrew manuscripts, including the Hebrew original of parts of Ecclesiasticus. In 1898 he was appointed external examiner in Victoria University, Manchester, and in 1899 became professor of Hebrew at University College, London. Since 1902 he has been president of the Jewish Theological Seminary of America, New York City. He has edited *Abot de Rabbi Natan* (Vienna, 1887); *The Wisdom of Ben Sira: Portions of the Book of Ecclesiasticus from Hebrew Manuscripts in the Cairo Genizah Collection* (in collaboration with C. Taylor (Cambridge, 1899); *Midrash hag-Gadol* (1902); and *Documents of Jewish Sectaries* (2 vols., Cambridge, 1910). He has written *Studies in Judaism* (two series, 1896–1908); and *Some Aspects of Rabbinic Theology* (1909). For a time he was Talmudical editor of *The Jewish Encyclopedia*.

SCHEEL, shēl, **JUERGEN OTTO EINAR IMMANUEL:** German Protestant; b. at Tondern (25 m. n.w. of Flensburg), Sleswick-Holstein, Mar. 7, 1876. He was educated at the universities of Halle (1895–97) and Kiel (1897–99; lic. theol., 1900), and was privat-docent for systematic theology at the latter institution from 1900 to 1905, when he was made titular professor. Since 1906 he has been associate professor of church history at the University of Tübingen. In theology he belongs to the modern historical and critical school, and has written: *Die Anschauung Augustin's von Christi Person und Werke* (Tübingen, 1901); *Luthers Stellung zur heiligen Schrift* (1902); *Wie erhalten wir das Erbe der Reformation in den geistigen Kämpfen der Gegenwart?* (Leipsic, 1904); *Die dogmatische Behandlung der Tauflehre in der modernen positiven Theologie* (Tübingen, 1906); *Individualismus und Gemeinschaftsleben in der Auseinandersetzung Luthers mit Karlstadt, 1524–25* (1907); and *Die moderne Religionspsychologie* (1908); besides editing the *Enchiridion* of St. Augustine (Tübingen, 1903), and the first two supplementary volumes to the Berlin edition of the works of Luther (Berlin, 1905).

SCHÉELE, shēl'e, **KNUT HENNING GEZELIUS VON:** Swedish Lutheran; b. at Stockholm, Sweden, May 31, 1838; graduated at Upsala; became privat-docent, 1865; provost, 1877; ordinary member of consistory, 1878; professor, 1879; inspector of the teachers' seminary, 1880; censor of the demission examinations in the Swedish upper schools, 1884; and in 1885 was appointed bishop of Wisby. He was member of the house of nobility in the Swedish parliament, 1865–66; and in 1901 represented his university and country at the Yale bicentennial. He is the author in Swedish of "The Ontological Evidence of the Existence of God" (Upsala, 1863); "The Preparations of the Theological Rationalism" (1868); "Church Catechising" (1869); "Theological Symbolics" (1877–79); "From the Court into the Sanctuary" (Stockholm, 1879), and "The Fight for the Peace" (1881).

SCHEFFER, shef′fer, **JACOB GYSBERT DE HOOP**: Dutch ecclesiastical historian and leader of the Mennonites in Holland; b. at The Hague Sept. 28, 1819; d. at Amsterdam Dec. 31, 1893. He studied theology at Amsterdam and Utrecht, intending to become a Mennonite preacher, but took a lively interest in literary questions, and was one of the founders in 1844 of the Vereeniging voor oude Nederlandsche letterkunde. His interest in art and letters was evident throughout his life, as when he edited *Navorscher* (the Dutch "Notes and Queries"). From 1848 to 1859 he was a Mennonite preacher at Hoorn, Groningen, and Amsterdam. Then he became professor in the seminary of the Algemeene Doopsgezinde Sociëteit. With the elevation in 1877 of the Amsterdam Athenæum to the rank of a university, he was appointed to the chair of Old-Testament exegesis and early Christian literature, while he continued to lecture on the history of the sect and practical theology in the Mennonite seminary. His most important work was done in the field of church history, in the interest of which he edited (1870–80) with Willem Moll the periodical *Studiën en Bijdragen*. In this first appeared his principal production, the *Geschiedenis der Kerkhervorming in Nederland van haar ontstaan tot 1531* (2 vols., Amsterdam, 1873), a definitive treatment of the beginnings of Dutch Protestantism. A number of studies in the history of the Mennonites, many of them appearing in the *Doopsgezinde Bijdragen*, which he edited from 1870 to 1893, showed remarkable industry and acuteness. A third department of his studies dealt with the Brownists, or English Independents settled in Holland, from whom came the "Pilgrim Fathers" (see Congregationalists), and Scheffer made important contributions to the history of these people (in the *Verslagen der Koninklijke Akademie*). Scheffer was next led to take up the history of baptism by immersion, which he treated in the *Verslagen* of 1882. His researches led to the abandonment of the old Baptist theory of an uninterrupted succession of the doctrine of immersion from the apostles, and their importance has been recognized by the best modern Baptist authors, such as Newman and Lehman. No one among the Mennonites was better known abroad than Scheffer, whose work brought him into correspondence with many foreign scholars. At home he occupied for thirty years a position of great influence among the members of his communion, whose activity he promoted in manifold ways. Throughout his life he was an adherent of the liberal theology of what was formerly known as the "Groningen School." Though devoted to his own religious body, he never assumed that this alone possessed the truth or forgot proper consideration and charity toward other churches. He was an admirable type of the liberal, highly educated, thoughtful Dutch Mennonite. S. Cramer.

Bibliography: Sketches of his life are by Rogge, in the "Yearbook" of the Dutch Royal Academy of Sciences for 1894; and by A. Winkler Prins, Leyden, 1894; cf. *Doopsgezinde Bijdragen*, 1895, pp. 1 sqq.

SCHEFFLER, shef′ler, **JOHANN (ANGELUS SILESIUS)**: German mystic and poet; b. at Breslau 1624; d. there July 9, 1677. He studied medicine at Strasburg (1643–44), in Holland (1644–47), and Padua (1647–48). In Holland he became acquainted with Jacob Boehme's theosophical and mystical writings, brought from Silesia by Abraham von Franckenberg. On his return (1649) he became physician to the zealous Lutheran count, Sylvius Nimrod von Württemberg-Oels, at Oels in Silesia. He was intimate with Franckenberg, which probably led to his dismissal. Upon the death of Franckenberg (1652), he wrote an elegy, *Ehrengedächtnis*, which contained, in the style of Boehme, the main ideas of all his later writings. In 1652 he went to Breslau, and became a member of the Roman Catholic Church, at the same time assuming the name Angelus, from a Spanish mystic of the sixteenth century. He gave the reasons for his conversion in his *Gründliche Ursachen* (Olmütz, 1653). In his desire for mystical union with God he was repelled by the Lutheran religion as represented in the court preacher at Oels, through its objection to the contemplative life and asceticism; and he thought to obtain freedom in the Roman Catholic Church, which stood for the communion of the saints and seemed to be the embodiment of the Holy Spirit. In Mar., 1654, he became court physician to Emperor Ferdinand III., an honorary office without duties or emoluments, but exempting him from difficulties in consequence of his change of confession. He lived quietly at Breslau, engaged in a comparative study of doctrines and the preparation of his literary publications. The only incident reported of this period was that he led a pilgrimage (1656) to the convent of Trebnitz, three miles distant.

In 1661 the brooding mystic suddenly issued forth as a fanatical controversialist against Protestantism. He entered the order of the Minorites and received ordination as a priest. He received strong support from Sebastian von Rostock, the vicar-general of the archdukes of Austria, who were successively bishops of Breslau. At the vicar's instigation, an imperial edict was issued for the restoration of the Corpus Christi procession, at the first occurrence of which Scheffler carried the monstrance. The impending peril from the Turks brought forth a tract, *Von den Ursachen der turkischen Ueberziehung und Zertretung des Volkes Gottes* (Neisse, 1664), in which he ascribed the danger to the divine judgment upon the apostasy of the Protestants. After the conclusion of peace he wrote *Christschrift von den herrlichen Kennzeichen des Volkes Gottes*, in which he claimed the defeat of the Turks as proof that only a Roman theocracy could help Christendom. Counterblasts came from Christian Chemnitz (q.v.) and Adam Scherzer, and a long and bitter polemical feud ensued. Scheffler was appointed court-marshal and councilor to Sebastian von Rostock, now bishop-prince and imperial supreme commander in Silesia. The consequence was that Scheffler's polemics of impassioned enmity acquired peculiar significance and were read all over Germany. Of these he issued fifty-five in twelve years; thirty-nine were selected by himself and published posthumously under the title *Ecclesiologia* (Neisse, 1677).

Scheffler attained more permanent fame as a poet. One of his two principal works was *Johannis Angeli Silesii Geistreiche Sinn- und Schlussreime* (Vienna, 1657). It contained in five books 1,410 epigrams with superscriptions, consisting of two, four, and rarely more Alexandrine verses. An appendix contained ten sonnets. These, with two poems of considerable length, five epigrams in quatrain, and 246 in couplets, form the sixth book of the second edition known as *Cherubinische Wandersmann* (Glatz, 1674). In this work Scheffler's theosophical and mystical wisdom of life is expressed in brief, terse sentences. Man's goal should be unity with God obtained by absorption in him; and God is love. Man experiences God not by thought but by becoming what God is, by renunciation, patience, humility, and love. The work is more metaphysical in character than ethical or dogmatic. Though it is obscure and not without self-contradiction in form, exposing the author to the charge of pantheism, yet much is contained that is truly profound. For many thoughts he makes acknowledgment to predecessors; namely, Augustine Bonaventura, Jan van Ruysbroeck (qq.v.), Heinrich Harpius, and especially Johann Tauler (q.v.), but he leaves out Valentine Weigel and Jakob Boehme, evidently because the book was issued under Roman Catholic censorship. His book of spiritual hymns is still more famous, *Heilige Seelenlust oder geistliche Hirtenlieder der in ihrem Jesum verliebten Psyche gesungen von Johann Angelo Silesio und von Herrn Georgio Josepho mit ausbundig schönen Melodien geziert* (Breslau, no date). It consisted of three books containing 143 hymns, each with a melody. It appeared in 1657, and the same year a fourth book with thirty-two hymns and melodies was added. A second edition (Breslau, 1668) appeared with 205 hymns. The subject matter of these hymns consists of love and yearning of the soul for Jesus and the worshipful wonder at his glory; and they are of the pietistic, personal kind, characteristic of the subjective dotage of the mystics. The various hymnals of the later seventeenth and early eighteenth centuries, especially that of the Unity of the Brethren, contained many selections, which disappeared during the period of rationalism. In the recent Evangelical hymn-book the best ones reappear; such as "*Ich will dich lieben meine Stärcke*" (1657), "*Liebe die du mich zum Bilde*" (1657), "*Mir nach spricht Christus unser Held*" (…8), "*Ach sagt mir nicht von Gold und Schätzen*" (…7), and "*Jesus ist der schönste Nam*" (1657). …her book of poems is the *Sinnliche Beschreib-…r vier letzten Dinge* (Schweidnitz, 1675). His … collected in two vols. by D. A. Rosenthal (Regensburg, 1862); and *Selections from his Rhymes* was published in English by P. Carus (Chicago, 1909).

From his hymns and poems many translations into English have been made, though rarely do these embrace more than parts of the originals. Noted among these are "Earth has nothing sweet or fair," by Miss Cox; "Make my heart a garden fair"; "Jesus is the highest name," by A. T. Russell; "Morning Star in darksome night," by Miss Winkworth; and "Where wilt thou go? since night draws near," by A. Crull. (Carl Bertheau.)

Bibliography: A. Kahlert, *Angelus Silesius, eine litterarhistorische Untersuchung*, Breslau, 1853 (best); J. J. Rambach, *Anthologie christlicher Gesänge*, iii. 90 sqq., Altona, 1819; W. Schrader, *Angelus Silesius und seine Mystik*, Halle, 1853; O. Schuster, in *ZHT*, 1857, pp. 427 sqq., F. Kern, *J. Schefflers Cherubinischer Wandersmann*, Leipsic, 1866; E. E. Koch, *Geschichte des Kirchenliedes*, iv. 3 sqq., Stuttgart, 1868; W. Lindemann, *Angelus Silesius, Bild eines Konvertiten, Dichters und Streittheologen*, Freiburg, 1876; A. Seltmann, *Angelus Silesius und seine Mystik*, Breslau, 1896; R. von Kralik von Meyerswalden, *Angelus Silesius und die christliche Mystik*, Frankfort, 1902; W. Nelle, *Geschichte des deutschen evangelischen Kirchenliedes*, pp. 141 sqq., Hamburg, 1904; idem, *Johann Scheffler*, ib. 1904; *ADB*, i. 453–456; Julian, *Hymnology*, pp. 1004–07; *KL*, x. 1765–67.

SCHEIBEL, shai'bel, **JOHANN GOTTFRIED**: German Lutheran; b. at Breslau Sept. 16, 1783; d. at Nuremberg Mar. 21, 1843. He was educated at the University of Halle (1801–04); became minister at Breslau 1804–18; and theological professor in the University of Breslau after 1818. Scheibel's open profession of the plenary inspiration of the Scriptures and of the doctrines of the Lutheran Church on justification, original sin, and the real presence of Christ in the Lord's Supper was quite unusual and occasioned no little antagonism; but though his mode of expression was involved and not popular, he gradually gathered a following of believing, positive Christians from all classes about himself. Religion seemed to him something ready-made, and not only what was revealed, but what was evident to him, seemed to him important and necessary. His faith was the certainty that the matter in question was contained in Scripture. His first publication, *Einige Worte über die Wahrheit der christlichen Religion* (1815), was an attack upon the rationalistic criticisms of the Bible and of the doctrines of creation and atonement. In his *Untersuchungen über Bibel und Kirchengeschichte* (1816) he pleaded especially for the authenticity of the Old-Testament books. He became a sturdy opponent, after 1814, of the movement for the union of the Lutheran and Reformed Churches in Prussia, mainly in his anxiety for the Lutheran view of the Eucharist. When the synod at Breslau began the consideration of a new church order, he felt constrained to make a closer study, the result of which was *Allgemeine Untersuchung der christlichen Verfassungs- und Dogmengeschichte* (Breslau, 1819). The pastoral epistles of Paul, he claimed, revealed a government of elders from the instructing and lay classes, which also, he thought, Luther contemplated. His severe strictures on the agenda of union of King Frederick Wilhelm III. led to his suspension in 1830. Forbidden to take any official position as well as to engage in any literary activity for the Lutheran Church, he removed to Dresden, 1832, from where, as headquarters, he continued the fight by means of numerous polemical tracts. In consequence of a polemical sermon, the same year, he was ordered to leave Dresden, and went to Hermsdorf, near by. Compelled to leave this place in 1836, he found asylum at Glauchau where he engaged again in public preaching. Driven thence he spent the rest of his life at Nuremberg in literary work. Just as the efforts for restoration to his professorship and pulpit at Breslau were being successfully completed, after the death of King Friedrich Wilhelm, he passed away. (G. Froböss.)

Bibliography: M. Vorbrugg, *Rede am Grabe Scheibels*, Nuremberg, 1843; *Lebenslauf Scheibels vom oberkirchenkollegium veröffentlicht*, Breslau, 1843; H. Steffens, *Was ich erlebte*, vol. ix., Breslau, 1844; T. Wangemann, *Sieben Bücher preussischer Kirchengeschichte*, Berlin, 1859; J. Nagel, *Die Kämpfe der evangelisch-lutherischen Kirche in Preussen*, Gütersloh, 1869; R. Rocholl, *Die Geschichte der evangelischen Kirche in Deutschland*, Leipsic, 1897; E. Ziemer, *Die Missionsthätigkeit der evangelisch-lutherischen Kirche in Preussen*, Elberfeld, 1904; G. Froböss, *Kurze Abwehr*, ib. 1905; *ADB*, xxx. 693–699.

SCHELHORN, shel'hōrn, **JOHANN GEORG:** Name of two Lutheran theologians.

1. Johann Georg the Elder: was born at Memmingen Dec. 8, 1694, and died there Mar. 31, 1773. He studied philosophy and philology at the University of Jena 1712–14 and after 1717; was librarian in his native town and co-rector at the school, 1725–32; pastor at Buxach and Hardt, near Memmingen, 1732–34, and in Memmingen after 1734; and also superintendent after 1753. His importance is that of a collector of valuable material and correspondence, first in *Amœnitates literariæ* (14 vols., Leipsic, 1721–31). For the celebration of the Augsburg Confession in 1730 he wrote *Kurzgefasste Reformationsgeschichte der Stadt Memmingen*, and the fate of the Salzburg Protestants occasioned the *De religionis evangelicæ in provincia Salisburgensi ortu* (Leipsic, 1732). A new collection appeared, *Amœnitates historiæ ecclesiasticæ et literariæ* (2 vols., 1737–40), after he came into possession of the literary remains and correspondence of his deceased friend, Zacharias Konrad of Uffenbach. Among his valuable works were, *De vita, fatis ac meritis Philippi Camerarii* (Nuremberg, 1740); *Commercii epistolaris Uffenbachii* (Memmingen, 1753–56); and *Ergötzlichkeiten aus der Kirchenhistorie und Literatur* (3 vols., Leipsic, 1761–64).

2. The Younger, son of the above; b. at Memmingen Dec. 4, 1733; d. there Nov. 22, 1802. He studied philology, history, and theology at Göttingen and Tübingen after 1750; was pastor at Buxach and Hardt after 1756; and became associate of his father in the pastorate at Memmingen, 1762, also city librarian there; and in 1793, superintendent of Memmingen. Among his works were: *Beiträge zur Erläuterung der Geschichte, besonders der Schwäbischen Kirchen- und Gelehrten-Geschichte* (Memmingen, 1772–75); and *Kleinere historische Schriften* (2 vols., 1789–90). (T. Kolde.)

Bibliography: F. Braun, *J. G. Schelhorn*, in *Beiträge zur bayerischen Kirchengeschichte*, vol. iv., Erlangen, 1898 (supersedes all earlier discussions); *ADB*, xxx. 756–759.

SCHELL, HERMAN: German Roman Catholic; b. at Freiburg Feb. 28, 1850; d. at Würzburg May 31, 1906. He was educated at the universities of Freiburg (1868–70) and Würzburg (1870–73), and at the College of the Anima, Rome (1879–81); and after 1885 was professor of apologetics, comparative religion, and the history of Christian art in the University of Würzburg, of which he was rector in 1896–97. He wrote *Die Einheit des Seelenlebens aus den Principien der aristotelischen Philosophie entwickelt* (Freiburg, 1873); *Das Wirken des dreieinigen Gottes* (2 vols., Mainz, 1885); *Katholische Dogmatik* (4 vols., Paderborn, 1889–93); *Gott und Geist* (2 vols., 1895–96); *Katholizismus als Prinzip des Fortschrittes* (Würzburg, 1897); *Das Problem des Geistes* (1897); *Neue Zeit und alter Glaube* (1898); *Apologie des Christentums* (2 vols., Paderborn, 1901–05; 3d ed., 1907); *Christus: das Evangelium und seine weltgeschichtliche Bedeutung* (Mainz, 1903); *Gottesglaube und naturwissenschaftliche Welterkenntnis* (Bamberg, 1904); and *Kleinere Schriften* (Paderborn, 1908).

SCHELLING, shel'ling, **FRIEDRICH WILHELM JOSEPH VON:** German philosopher; b. at Leonberg (8 m. w.n.w. of Stuttgart) Jan. 27, 1775; d. at Rogatz (30 m. s.e. of St. Gall), Switzerland, Aug. 20, 1854. He studied theology and philosophy at Tübingen from 1790, and science and mathematics at Leipsic, 1796–97. With the assistance of Fichte and Goethe, he became professor at Jena, 1798–1803, where a brilliant literary and academic career opened for him. Impelled by an ardent philosophic interest, during a creative period, he made it his work to incorporate with his own the elemental principles of others as he met them successively in his career, and the result was more a stimulating influence of his vast prospective views than the establishment of enduring fundamentals. Starting out originally with the absolute idealism of Fichte, his reading of Spinoza led him to supplement this by the philosophy of nature. This was also an unfolding, as unconscious intelligence, from the absolute. He conceived this to proceed by a synthetic process from the lower inorganic to the higher organic forms, issuing into conscious intelligence in man, and he based it on the assumption of a soul of the world as the organizing principle. Works of this period were, *Ideen zur Philosophie der Natur* (Leipsic, 1797); *Von der Weltseele* (Hamburg, 1798); and *Erster Entwurf eines Systems der Philosophie* (Jena, 1799). The contradiction between intellectual and natural philosophy is resolved by the *System des transzendentalen Idealismus* (Tübingen, 1800), in dependence upon the esthetic philosophy of Kant and in connection with the romanticism of Schiller and the two Schlegels, which aimed to reconcile philosophy and poesy. As unconscious intelligence has been shown to give rise in nature to the inorganic and to a series of organisms, at the apex of which is man, the organism of conscious intelligence, so transcendental idealism reverses the point of view and submits the objective as ideal representation, or conscious production. Its highest form is art, in which the harmony of subject and object is realized. The study of Spinoza and Giordano Bruno (qq.v.) prepared him to work this out into the philosophy of identity, which first emerged in *Zeitschrift für speculative Physik* in 1801 (a journal which he issued jointly with Hegel), but appears fused with Platonic idealism in *Bruno, oder über das göttliche und natürliche Princip der Dinge* (Berlin, 1802), and expanded in popular form in *Vorlesungen über die Methode des akademischen Studiums* (Tübingen, 1803), which has been pronounced a model of literary form. The absolute is defined as absolute reason or the total indifference of subject and object. The highest law of its existence is absolute identity, or undifferentiated unity. Everything that exists is this absolute itself. It is the universe itself, not the cause of it. It is present in everything as both subject and object, ideal and real, with a preponderance of either one over the other. Theology, as the science of the absolute and divine essence, is the highest synthesis of philosophical and historical knowledge. The antithesis of the real and ideal occurs in the contrast of Hellenism and Christianity. The former illustrates the unconscious identity of nature; the ideal lay concealed in visible gods and polytheism. This was followed by separation or fate at the close of the ancient world. Christianity, as the inception of the period of providence, follows with the reconciled unity, and with God revealed. The incarnation of God is from eternity. The ideas of Christianity symbolized in its dogmas have a speculative significance. The fundamental dogma of the Trinity means that the eternal Son of God, born of the essence of the Father of all things, is the finite itself as it exists in the eternal intuition of God, who at the culmination of his phenomenal manifestation in Christ as suffering God terminates the world of finiteness and opens that of the supremacy of the Spirit. The consummation of the process is the regeneration of esoteric Christianity and the proclamation of the absolute gospel, or the self-consciousness of the absolute in which subject and object disappear, or the becoming of God.

In consequence of his polemics Schelling left Jena, and was professor at Würzburg, 1803–16. Under leave of absence he lectured at Stuttgart in 1810. In the mean time he was given more and more to syncretism and mysticism. In his *Philosophie und Religion* (Tübingen, 1804), he betrays a neoplatonic influence in affirming that finiteness and corporeality are the products of a falling away from the absolute as the means of the perfect revelation of God. Theosophical are the views in *Untersuchungen über das Wesen der menschlichen Freiheit* (Landshut, 1809), under the influence of Jakob Boehme (q.v.). He distinguishes in God, according to the mystics, three degrees: indifference, the primordial basis or "abyss" of divine nature; differentiation of this into ground and existence; and the identity or reconciliation of the two. By this he explains the origin of evil. The first, which is only the beginning of the divine nature, without form or personality, is a dark, negative ground, the basis of reality; it is that which is in God, yet not God himself. This, which is described as a certain yearning for self-assertion, is the basis of the bare existence of all things. Man, who is immanent in God, is capable of freedom; i. e., of enlightenment. By virtue of the dark ground, he has a particular will; as gifted by understanding he is the organ of the universal will. The separation of the two is the occasion of evil or imperfection.

The feud with F. H. Jacobi (q.v.), president of the academy, who severely assailed these views, led to Schelling's departure from Munich in 1820. He lectured several semesters at Erlangen, and was ordinary professor of the new university at Munich, 1827–40. During this period, restive criticisms of the system of Hegel, who, though his senior yet his follower, had resolved his principle of absolute identity into a system of synthetic logic, began to appear. Lecturing at Berlin, 1840–46, he further develops the departure made in his treatise on freedom. God, he now acclaims, may indeed be conceived as the culmination of a process in thought, but not of an objective process. Therefore, he partly reverses his position and declares the philosophy of Hegel as well as his own pantheistic system to be merely negative, which he supplements with a positive philosophy. Falling back on Kant's criticism of the ontological argument, he finds God not immanent in thought, but transcendent; not at the end of the process, but absolute first. God creates by a free act of will; and in positive philosophy, the real universe thus created, as well as the real God viewed as an objective principle, are not subjects of the speculative reason, but of experience, guided by the documents of revelation. The products of the theoretical are merely preparatory, affording ideals as means to the positive. Schelling distinguishes in absolute Spirit possibility of being, pure being, and absolute free being, which in creation reveal themselves as the three potencies—unconscious will, or *causa materialis;* conscious will, or *causa efficiens;* and their union, *causa finalis*. They furnish the basis of the Trinity. In nature potencies, at the end of revelation, or creation, they are three perfect personalities in one God. The potencies which exist in man as God's image suffered separation by the fall. In consequence, the second was deprived of its divine reality and was degraded to a potency operating only in purely natural ways. It regains its total freedom in the consciousness of man, through the theogonic process; first in mythology and then in revelation. This was the subject of his philosophy of mythology and revelation, respectively, in his "Philosophy of Religion" (in *Sämtlichen Werke*, 14 vols., Stuttgart, 1856–61). Following the suggestion of Fichte, Schelling divides the Christian era into Petrine Christianity, or Catholicism; Pauline, or Protestantism; and the Johannean with its idea of the Logos, the Church of the Future. See IDEALISM, II., §§ 6, 8; PANTHEISM, § 7.

BIBLIOGRAPHY. Besides the works on the history of philosophy (e.g., by J. E. Erdmann, 3 vols., London, 1892–98; W. Windelband, New York, 1893; F. Ueberweg, ed. Heinze, 9th ed., Berlin, 1901–05) consult. F. Köppen, *Schelling's Lehre, oder das Ganze der Philosophie des absoluten Nichts*, Hamburg, 1803; F. Berg, *Sextus, oder über die absolute Erkenntniss von Schelling* Würzburg, 1804; J. C. Götz, *Anti-Sextus, oder über die absolute Erkenntniss von Schelling*, Heidelberg, 1807, S. T. Coleridge, *Biographia literaria*, London, 1817; J. Fries, *Reinhold, Fichte und Schelling*, in *Polemische Schriften*, vol. i., Halle, 1824;

J. T. Schwarz, *Schelling's alte und neue Philosophie*, Berlin, 1844; A. J. Matter, *Schelling, ou la philosophie de la nature*, Paris, 1845; A. Engels, *Schelling und die Offenbarung*, Leipsic, 1842; C. Kapp, *F. W. J. Schelling: ein Beitrag zur Geschichte des Tages*, Leipsic, 1843; P. Marheineke, *Zur Kritik der schellingschen Offenbarungsphilosophie*, Berlin, 1843; C. L. Michelet, *Entwickelungsgeschichte der neuesten deutschen Philosophie*, Berlin, 1843; C. Rosenkranz, *Schelling*, Danzig, 1843; C. A. Brandis, *Gedächtnissrede auf F. W. J. von Schelling*, Berlin, 1856; *Fichte's und Schelling's philosophischer Briefwechsel*, Stuttgart, 1856; J. E. Erdmann, *Ueber Schelling, namentlich seine negative Philosophie*, Halle, 1857; R. Haym, *Hegel und seine Zeit*, Berlin, 1857; A. Planck, *Schelling's nachgelassene Werke und ihre Bedeutung für Philosophie und Theologie*, Erlangen, 1858; H. Beckers, *Schelling's Geistesentwickelung in ihrem inneren Zusammenhang*, Munich, 1875; T. Hoppe, *Die Philosophie Schellings und ihr Verhältniss zum Christenthum*, Rostock, 1875; O. Pfleiderer, *F. W. J. Schelling: Gedächtnissrede*, Stuttgart, 1875; C. Frantz, *Schelling's positive Philosophie*, 3 parts, Cöthen, 1879–80; J. Watson, *Schelling's Transcendental Idealism*, Chicago, 1882; R. Gebel, *Schelling's Theorie vom Ich des All-Einen und deren Widerlegung*, Berlin, 1885; K. Groos, *Die reine Vernunftwissenschaft*, Heidelberg, 1889; E. O. Burman, *Die Transcendentalphilosophie Fichtes und Schellings*, Upsala, 1891; F. Schaper, *Schelling's Philosophie der Mythologie*, Nauen, 1893; idem, *Schelling's Philosophie der Offenbarung*, Nauen, 1894; E. von Hartmann, *Schelling's philosophisches System*, Leipsic, 1897; L. Roth, *Schelling und Spencer*, Bern, 1901; K. Fischer, *Geschichte der neueren Philosophie*, vol. vi., Heidelberg, 1894; idem, *Schellings Leben, Werke und Lehre*, 3d ed., ib. 1902; M. Adam, *Schellings Kunstphilosophie*, Leipsic, 1907; G. Niehlis, *Schelling's Geschichtsphilosophie in . . . 1799–1804*, Heidelberg, 1907.

SCHELWIG, shel'vig, SAMUEL: Lutheran theologian and opponent of the Pietists; b. at Lissa (54 m. n.n.w. of Breslau) Mar. 8, 1643; d. at Danzig Jan. 18, 1715. He was the son of a Silesian preacher, and studied at Breslau and at Wittenberg, where he became an adjunct in the philosophical faculty in 1667; he went to Thorn as associate rector of the gymnasium in 1668; to Danzig in 1673, where he was subsequently appointed pastor of Dreifaltigkeitskirche, and rector of the academical gymnasium in 1685. Rigorously orthodox, ambitious, and quarrelsome, he soon became involved in a variety of conflicts. In Danzig he fell into strife with one of his colleagues, Constantine Schütze, the contest taking literary form in tracts and being continued until the city magistracy stopped the dispute (1693). The conflict between Schelwig and Spener then began. What particularly increased and embittered the strife was a journey undertaken by Schelwig through Northern Germany, the purpose of which his opponents asserted to be the forming of a confederation against Pietism. His most comprehensive anti-Pietistic work bears the title *Die sektiererische Pietisterei* (Danzig, 1696–97), which called forth a number of replies. In Schelwig's *Synopsis controversiarum sub pietatis prætextu motarum* (1701, 1703, 1720) he sought to demonstrate 264 Pietistic errors, which evoked replies from J. W. Zierold, pastor at Stargard, and J. Lange. Among the many orthodox opposers of Pietism, Schelwig was one of the readiest in equipment, but his methods were bitter and unclerical. C. MIRBT.

BIBLIOGRAPHY: J. G. Walch, *Religionsstreitigkeiten der evangelisch-lutherischen Kirche*, i. 602–603, 739–746, v. 749–750, 849 et passim, Jena, 1733; E. Schnaase, *Geschichte der evangelischen Kirche Danzigs*, pp. 332–353, Danzig, 1863; S. Schmid, *Die Geschichte des Pietismus*, pp. 228–236, Nördlingen, 1863; E. Sachsse, *Ursprung und Wesen des Pietismus*, pp. 321–332 Wiesbaden, 1884; A. Ritschl, *Geschichte des Pietismus*, vol. ii. Bonn, 1884; P. Grünberg, *Philipp Jakob Spener*, i. 297–302, Göttingen, 1893; *ADB*, xxxi. 30–36.

SCHENCK, FERDINAND SCHUREMAN: Reformed (Dutch); b. in Ulster County, N. Y., Aug. 6, 1845. He was graduated from Princeton University (B.A., 1865; M.A., 1868), Albany Law School (LL.B., 1867), and New Brunswick Theological Seminary (1872); engaged in the practise of law, 1867–69; was licensed by the classis of Ulster, 1872; served as pastor at Clarkstown, N. Y., 1872–77, at Montgomery, 1877–90, at Hudson, 1890–97, and at University Heights, New York City, 1897–99; became professor of practical theology in the New Brunswick Theological Seminary, 1899, where he has since remained, serving also as acting professor of philosophy in Rutgers College, 1904–05, and acting professor of ethics and evidences of Christianity there, 1906–07, also as acting professor of homiletics in Princeton Theological Seminary since 1909. He is the author of *The Ten Commandments in the Nineteenth Century* (New York, 1889); *Bible Reader's Guide* (1896); *The Ten Commandments and the Lord's Prayer* (1902); *Modern Practical Theology* (1903); *Sociology of the Bible* (1909); and *Christian Evidences and Ethics* (1910).

SCHENK, JAKOB. See ANTINOMIANISM AND ANTINOMIAN CONTROVERSIES.

SCHENKEL, shenk'el, DANIEL: Evangelical theologian; b. at Dägerlen, near Winterthur (12 m. n.e. of Zurich), Dec. 21, 1813; d. at Heidelberg May 18, 1885. He bore arms for three years in the Basel war of 1831. In the study of theology he was greatly influenced by W. M. L. de Wette (q.v.), by whom he was convinced of the necessity of critical investigation. After a period of study of primitive Christianity and church history at Göttingen, he returned to Basel, where, in 1838, he habilitated with the thesis, *Dissertatio critica et historica de ecclesia Corinthia primæva factionibus turbata* (Basel, 1838). In the mean time he edited the *Baseler Zeitung* which opposed the ecclesiastical and political radicalism of the time. In 1841 he was called as head preacher to Schaffhausen. He made important changes in the church organization, and his sermons attracted wide attention, even in the university circle. Schenkel first obtained scientific recognition by the publication of his *Wesen des Protestantismus aus den Quellen des Reformationszeitalters dargestellt* (3 vols., Schaffhausen, 1846–51), which was supplemented with *Das Prinzip des Protestantismus* (1852). In 1850, he returned to Basel as professor, his inaugural address being on *Die Idee der Persönlichkeit* (1850). The following year he was called to Heidelberg where he remained until his death.

As university preacher and head of the theological seminary, Schenkel had noteworthy success. A series of events—open opposition to the Jesuit mission at Heidelberg, 1851, protest against the new liturgy of the former Durlach Conference adopted by the synod in 1855, the strife over the agenda in 1858, the transactions concerning the Concordat, 1859, which threatened a combination of the ministry of Stengel and the church régime of Baden—these resulted in open conflict, the consequence of which was the end of the old church régime, the failure of the Concordat, the fall of the Stengel ministry, and the construction and approval by the general synod, 1861, of a new church constitution. In the mean time Schenkel, who was a rapid and voluminous writer, published *Gesetzeskirche und Glaubenskirche* (Heidelberg, 1852); *Schutzpflicht des Staats gegen die Evangelische Kirche* (1852); and *Evangelische Zeugnisse von Christo* (1853–59). In these writings Schenkel's ecclesiastical liberalism and Protestant tendency come to the front. Speculative acuteness he did not brook; and his controversy with Kuno Fischer ended in the latter's dismissal. The theological antagonism was becoming more pronounced and Schenkel felt constrained to oppose the orthodox reaction. His *Für Bunsen, wider Stahl, die neuesten Bewegungen und Streitigkeiten auf dem kirchlichen Gebiet* (Darmstadt, 1856) has been said to mark the turning point in his theological development. His next work and the second in importance, *Die christliche Dogmatik vom Standpunkte des Gewissens* (2 vols., Wiesbaden, 1858–59) is more in accord with his earlier position. It challenged attention by its vindication of the conscience as arbiter in intellectual religious questions. There followed, *Die Reformatoren und die Reformation* (1856); *Union, Konfession, und evangelisches Christenthum* (Darmstadt, 1859); and *Erneuerung der deutschen evangelischen Kirche* (Heidelberg, 1861).

The publication of the much-discussed *Charakterbild Jesu* (Wiesbaden, 1864; 4th. ed. 1873; Eng. transl., *The Character of Jesus Portrayed*, Boston, 1866) alienated many who had remained loyal to Schenkel and subjected him to open attack. The basis adopted is the Gospel of Mark as furnishing the safest historical confines. The final conclusions of the book are by no means radical, but a storm of protest was aroused by certain passages, especially by the assumption that there was a change during Jesus' public career in his self-determination and self-consciousness. A demand was made by a part of the clergy of Baden for the author's dismissal, but schism was averted by the conciliatory tact of the superior church council. He became head of the Protestant Union organized in 1863. Two more important works were *Die Grundlehren des Christentums aus dem Bewusstsein des Glaubens dargestellt* (Leipsic, 1877), and *Das Christusbild der Apostel und der nachapostolischen Zeit* (1879). In the former of these the privilege and service of critical scientific rationalism is conceded, but it is also pointed out that as a self-originated philosophy, it has not produced a dogmatic on the basis of revelation in history. Christianity he represents as the absolute religion, both because it presupposes the unity of God and man intrinsic in personal life, and because it regards as its religious ethical object the actualization of this unity in humanity through the absolutely divine imbued man Jesus Christ. He edited and published *Allgemeine kirchliche Zeitschrift* (1860–72); and *Bibellexicon, Realwörterbuch zum Handgebrauch für Geistliche und Gemeindeglieder* (5 vols., Leipsic, 1869–75).

(W. GASS†.)

SCHENZ, shents, WILHELM: German Roman Catholic; b. at Niederrieden (a village near Memmingen, 43 m. s.w. of Augsburg), Bavaria, Mar. 7, 1845. He was educated at the University of Munich (D.D., 1869), and, after being incumbent of a benefice in the same city (1869–72), was called to his present position of professor of Old-Testament exegesis in the Lyceum of Regensburg, of which since 1895 he has also been rector. During his administration he has reorganised the lyceum and erected a new observatory for it. Besides translating Anselm's *Cur Deus Homo* (Regensburg, 1880), he has written *Historisch-kritische Abhandlung über das erste allgemeine Concil in Jerusalem* (1869); *Das Laien- und das himmlische Priestertum nach dem ersten Briefe des Apostels Petrus* (Freiburg, 1873); *Einleitung in die kanonischen Bücher des Alten Testaments* (Regensburg, 1887); *Priesterliche Tätigkeit des Messias nach Isaias* (1892); *Lebende Bilder zum Bischofsjubiläum Leos XIII.* (1893); *Leo XIII. als Bischof von Perugia und von Rom* (1893); *St. Wolfgang in der Poesie* (1894); and *Erklärung der Altarbilder in der Albertuskapelle zu Regensburg* (1900).

SCHERER, she"-rār', EDMOND HENRI ADOLPHE: French Protestant critic and theologian; b. at Paris Apr. 8, 1815; d. at Versailles Mar. 16, 1889. Scherer's paternal ancestors were Swiss from the canton of St. Gall, who emigrated to Paris in the first part of the eighteenth century; his mother was an Englishwoman. After a preliminary education at the Lycée Louis le Grand, he was sent to England, where he came under the influence of Thomas Loader, a clergyman in Monmouth. Up to that time he had shown no religious tendencies; he dated the epoch of his conversion from Christmas, 1832, during a revival movement characterised by a personal religion of pietistic emulation and devotion to prayer, combined with strict orthodoxy, and belief in literal inspiration, original sin, and the "foolishness" of Christianity in contrast with the rationalism of such as Victor Cousin, with little concern for the state church and liturgy and theological science. Returning to France, he studied law (1833–35) without, however, giving up his interest in theological and philosophical questions; and proceeding to Strasburg, he studied theology (1836–1839); and was ordained, 1840. His ordination sermon betrays a depreciation of human speculation, science, and wisdom, in contrast with the authority of the Bible and the efficacy of prayer. For five years he refused to accept any official position, living at Strasburg and Truttenhausen and devoting himself to literary and theological studies. He published two long essays, *De l'état actuel de l'église réformée en France* (Paris, 1844), and *Esquisse d'une théorie de l'église chrétienne* (1845), written in a Calvinistic spirit, in which he outlined a Church independent of the State with a Presbyterian constitution. Led by a strictly Scriptural and practical theology resting upon earnest investigation, the Church would soon be freed from indifference, unbelief, and schism. In consequence, Scherer was in 1846 called to the chair of church history in the free theological school founded at Geneva by Merle d'Aubigné, and a year later exchanged this for the professorship of Biblical exegesis. Then as now, this institution received older students from the practical vocations who had not matured at the university, and counted among its students many coming evangelists in Europe and Canada. Soon after occupying this position, Scherer seemed to become aware of a conflict between the emotional needs of the religious consciousness and the theoretical convictions of the reason, but he still believed in the possibility of a union between sound theology and sound piety. The natural man, he thought, can not conceive religious things; only the experience of the Christian, by faith in Christ and love to him, unlocks the mystery. Accounts of "visitations of Christ," arranged somewhat in the form of a diary, from the year 1848, show Scherer in the heights of religious moments and from the personal mystical side. His transition from history to exegesis became fatal to his belief; he had always fully accepted the theory of verbal inspiration, and had subscribed without reserve the *Consensus Helveticus* of 1655 on vowel points and punctuation, but with the insight that this position was untenable his faith and theology also were shaken. In June, 1849, Scherer's friends became acquainted with his dissatisfaction with his position, and before the end of the year he had resigned and taken farewell of his students. But he continued with a series of free lectures on matters of faith which were a great attraction, June, 1849, to Feb., 1850, and were summed up in a pamphlet, *La Critique et la foi* (1850). The repetitions, contradictions, inaccuracies, and the temporal contingency of Biblical writers were pointed out and the fact that they did not claim to be inspired. The personal authority of Christ and his Spirit in the disciples, the facts in the religious consciousness of sin and redemption remained for him the pillars of revelation and faith. At this time Scherer regarded himself as still a believing Christian, logically carrying on the thought of the Reformation, but did not linger long in this position. His *Mélanges de critique religieuse* (1860) show a progress in negation. He examined the problem of sin and freedom which led him on the causal side to the question of miracles. A proposition is not true because it comes from Christ; but because its truth is affirmed in ethical consciousness, it comes from Christ. So far he could justify himself by reference to Alexandre Vinet (q.v.), but his interest in seeking individual freedom according to his subjective perception of truth led him farther. Original sin is a limitation of freedom; not that God was the author of sin, but rather Scherer came to deny original sin and to declare the freedom of man to achieve victory by struggle over a sinful world. Evil was a lesser good, the shadow needful for the completion of the optimistic world harmony. In order to conserve the humility under the sense of sin and the consequent desire of salvation, the necessity of sin to human development was to be held theoretically from the view-point of the theodicy; but practically sin was to be regarded as something that should not be. A dualism resulted from this position of heart and head. From the maze of the problem of freedom he could not extricate himself. From the relativity of freedom he proceeded to the invariability of law in nature until even the supernatural could no longer be maintained. Finally, Scherer attached himself to the Hegelian philosophy with enthusiasm. With the last step, that there is no final truth but that there are only truths which prepare themselves by self-destruction, he had to break with even the prominent and advanced theologians. Scherer confined himself to mere textual explanation in his lectures on the Epistles, 1856–60, and moved to Versailles in 1860. A call to the newly established chair of religious science at the École des Hautes Études he declined; the columns of the *Revue des deux Mondes* were open to him, and his course was marked out. The fruit of his literary labors, remarkable for originality, psychological acuteness, and ethical earnestness, was collected in *Études critiques sur la littérature contemporaine* (10 vols., Paris, 1863–95; Eng. transl. of one volume, *Essays on English Literature*, and *History of German Literature*, 5 vols., London, 1891). He was also coeditor of the *Temps* since it was founded in 1860. He performed eminent political service as mediator between the provisional governments of the German occupation and the population and was made senator for life in 1872. Scherer was never a polemical opponent of Christianity. Faith he likened to poesy, striking root everywhere, rising ever anew from the dust, to survive as long as humanity shall draw breath. The crisis of his faith brought him great suffering which left him a sad heart. The flood of theological and ecclesiastical malediction and ridicule he met either with total silence or answered with calm composure and noble patience, knowing that his course was the only one left to an upright man. (E. PLATZHOFF-LEJEUNE.)

BIBLIOGRAPHY: O. Gérard, *E. Scherer*, 2d ed., Paris, 1891; J. F. Astié, *E. Scherer, ses disciples et ses adversaires*, Lausanne, 1854; idem, *Les Deux Théologies nouvelles*, ib. 1862; idem, *E. Scherer et la théologie indépendante*, ib. 1892; G. Frommel, *Esquisses contemporaines*, pp. 199–288, ib. 1891; E. Logos, *Essai sur E. Scherer théologien*, ib. 1891; E. Dowden, *New Studies in Literature*, Boston, 1895; Mary Fisher, in *McClury's Magazine*, 1897.

SCHERER, shî'rer, **JAMES AUGUSTIN BROWN**: Lutheran; b. at Salisbury, N. C., May 22, 1870. He was educated at Roanoke College, Va. (A.B., 1890), and Pennsylvania College (Ph.D., 1897). After being pastor of the Evangelical Lutheran church at Pulaski, Va., in 1890–91, he founded a mission of his denomination at Saga, Japan, where he remained until 1897, being also a teacher in a Japanese government school in 1892–96. He returned to the United States in 1897 for reasons of health, and held pastorates at Cameron, S. C., in 1897–98, and at Charlestown, S. C., in 1898–1904, being at the same time a professor in the Lutheran theological seminary in that city. Since 1904 he has been president of Newberry College, Newberry, S. C. In theology he holds that the Book of Concord is the "true and logical development of Christian faith in Reformation times" and that "the principle of historic continuity should determine any subsequent statement." He has written *Four Princes: or, The Growth of a Kingdom: The Story of the Christian Church centred around four Types* (Philadelphia, 1903); *Japan To-day*

(1904); *Young Japan: Story of the Japanese People, . . . especially . . . their Educational Development* (1905); *The Holy Grail: Six Kindred Addresses and Essays* (1906); and *What is Japanese Morality?* (1906).

SCHERESCHEWSKY, she''re-shev'ski, **SAMUEL ISAAC JOSEPH**: Protestant Episcopal missionary bishop of Shanghai, China; b., of Jewish parentage, at Tanroggen, Russian Lithuania, May 6, 1831; d. at Tokyo, Japan, Sept. 15, 1906. He was educated at the Talmud Torah of Zhitomir, Russia, and the University of Breslau, where he spent two years. In 1854 he went to the United States, where he accepted Christianity. He studied theology at the Western Theological Seminary (Presbyterian), Alleghany, Pa., in 1855–58, but in 1858 entered the Protestant Episcopal Church and studied for another year at the General Theological Seminary. He was ordered deacon in 1859 and priested in 1860. He then went to China as a missionary, and was stationed successively at Shanghai (1860–63) and Peking (1863–75). From 1875 to 1877 he was in the United States, and in 1877 was consecrated missionary bishop of Shanghai. In 1883 he retired on account of paralysis, with which he had been stricken in 1881. He continued his work, nevertheless, with marvellous perseverance despite his infirmities. From 1886 to 1895 he resided in the United States, preparing a revision of the Mandarin Bible which he had translated unaided many years before. He then went again to Shanghai, where for two years he devoted himself to transferring the Romanized text of this version into Chinese characters. From 1897 until his death he resided in Japan, preparing a reference Mandarin Bible and a translation of the Apocrypha, the latter left unfinished.

Bibliography: W. S. Perry, *Episcopate in America*, p. 251, New York, 1895.

SCHERMANN, shêr'man, **THEODOR FRANZ JOSEF**: German Roman Catholic; b. at Ellwangen (45 m. e.n.e. of Stuttgart), Württemberg, Jan. 19, 1878. He was educated at the University of Munich (D.D., 1901), and, after being catechist and curate at Munich in 1901–02, studied in Paris and Italy for two years (1902–04). Since 1904 he has been privat-docent for church history, patristics, and Christian archeology at the University of Munich. He has written *Die Gottheit des heiligen Geistes nach den griechischen Vätern des vierten Jahrhunderts* (Freiburg, 1901); *Die griechischen Quellen des heiligen Ambrosius in seinen drei Büchern vom heiligen Geiste* (Munich, 1902); *Eine Elfapostelmoral oder die X-Rezension der beiden Wege* (1903); *Geschichte der dogmatischen Florilegien vom v.–viii. Jahrhundert* (Leipsic, 1904); and has edited *Propheten- und Apostellegenden nebst Jüngerkatalogen des Dorotheus und Verwandter Texte* (in *TU*, 1907); *Prophetarum vitæ fabulosæ indices apostolorum discipulorumque* (Leipsic, 1907); and *Griechische Zauberpapyri und das Gemeinde- und Dankgebet im I Klemensbriefe*, in *TU*, xxxiv. 2b (1909).

SCHEURL, sheirl, **CHRISTOPH GOTTLIEB ADOLF, FREIHERR VON**: German Lutheran, authority on canon law; b. at Nuremberg Jan. 7, 1811; d. there Jan. 23, 1893. He came of an ancient family which had immigrated from Breslau in the fifteenth century; studied at Nuremberg, completing the local gymnasium course in 1827, at Erlangen 1827–28, and at Munich, where his object was jurisprudence, 1828–31; he qualified as lecturer at the University of Erlangen in 1836; became extraordinary professor in 1840; and, in 1845, professor of Roman and canon law, and retired to his ancestral home in 1881.

Scheurl's importance inheres both in his productive authorship and in his official service in behalf of the Church, alike in the legislative chamber and in the general synod. His studies began with the Roman law, themes from which were treated in his dissertation (1835), his academic induction thesis (1836), his essay on *Nexum* (1839); his *Dissertatio de usus et fructus discrimine* (1846), in a guide to the study of the Roman jurisprudence (1855), and especially in his text-book of the *Institutiones*, which appeared in eight editions. The course of his own development, however, drew him more and more into the sphere of canon law; and to this he subsequently devoted his main powers, though he won distinction in both civil and canon law. During the years 1845–49 he was a member of the chamber of delegates, where he found rich opportunity of turning to account his comprehensive lore and his judicial opinions. In the national diet of 1849 he was active in the direction which was to determine the proper focus of his later life in questions affecting the constitution of the Evangelical state church. Possibly in those years Scheurl discerned his peculiar vocation, and thenceforward his professional activity applied itself predominantly to canon law. It was but a step in this direction that in 1865 he was elected to the general synod, to which he belonged until 1884.

His official activity was closely conjoined with productive authorship. Herein he gave predominant attention to questions of church constitution. So early as 1853 and 1854 he published two treatises on the constitutional relation of the Lutheran Church in Bavaria. In an independent investigation, 1872, he enlarged upon the status of the Church to the civil power in Bavaria. The decree of the general synod of 1873 evoked a further publication. The Bavarian situation naturally prompted investigations of a general and fundamental cast. Hence he treated (1862) the doctrine of church government, the problem of freedom of conscience, concepts of confessional church and state church (1867, 1868), and the tasks of the Christian State (1885). In the year 1857 he answered a number of general questions in pamphlets which he styled *Fliegende Blätter für die kirchlichen Fragen der Gegenwart*. Numerous articles in *ZPK*, whose associate editor he was from 1858, and in *ZKR*, dealt with questions of the Evangelical constitution, while on all sides he so advocated the rights of the Evangelical church that one may justly accord him the honorable title of "syndic of the Lutheran Church." He also specialized in the modern development of the marriage law, and this led to his *Entwickelung des kirchlichen Eheschliessungsrecht* (Erlangen, 1877), interesting because it is Scheurl's one considerable effort in the domain of canon law at large. Even prior to that publication he had given his attention to Luther's marriage law, and he incorporated his *Luthers Eherechtsweisheit*, which first appeared in *ZPK*, in his *Sammlung kirchenrechtlicher Abhandlungen* (1873). An exhaustive summary is contributed by his very excellent *Das gemeine deutsche Eherecht und seine Umbildung durch das R.-G. vom 6. Februar, 1875* (1882). With Roman Catholic canon law he occupied himself but little, publishing in 1847 a survey of the Concordat and constitutional oath, and later a number of briefer studies in periodicals. His last work in canon law, *Staatsgesetzgebung und religiöse Kindererziehung*, was published in *Deutsche Zeitschrift für Kirchenrecht* (1891). E. Sehling.

Bibliography: A. von Stählin, *Zur Erinnerung an Christoph Gottlieb Adolf Freiherr von Scheurl*, Leipsic, 1893; *Das Glaubensbekenntnis eines Rechtslehrers aus unserer Zeit*, Carlsruhe, 1899.

SCHIAN, shī'ān, **MARTIN**: German Lutheran; b. at Liegnitz (40 m. w.n.w. of Breslau), Silesia, Aug. 10, 1869. He was educated at the universities of Greifswald, Breslau (lic. theol., 1896), Halle, and Leipsic (Ph.D., 1895), and at the preachers' seminary at Wittenberg. After being curate (1895–1896) and pastor (1896–1901) at Dalkau, Silesia, he was pastor in Görlitz until 1906; privat-docent for practical theology at the University of Breslau and pastor of the Bernhardingemeinde in the same city 1906–08; and since 1908 professor of the same subject at Giessen. In theology he adheres to the older Ritschlian school. Besides work as editor on the *Preussische Kirchenzeitung* since 1905 and on *Studien zur praktischen Theologie* since 1907, he has written *Die Scholastik im Zeitalter der Aufklärung* (Breslau, 1900); *Unser Christenglaube* (Freiburg, 1902, 2d ed., 1910); *Das kirchliche Leben der evangelischen Kirche der Provinz Schlesien* (Tübingen, 1903); *Der deutsche Roman seit Goethe* (Görlitz, 1904); *Die Predigt* (Göttingen, 1906); *Die evangelische Kirchengemeinde* (Giessen, 1907); *Zur Beurteilung der modernen positiven Theologie* (1907); and *Die moderne Gemeinschaftsbewegung* (Stuttgart, 1909).

SCHICKLER, FERNAND DE, BARON: French Protestant layman; b. at Paris Aug. 24, 1835; d. there Oct. 18, 1909. He early distinguished himself by his devotion to the cause of Protestantism in France, which his wealth enabled him materially to aid. He became president of the Société de l'histoire du protestantisme français, 1865; president of the Société biblique protestante de Paris, 1878; member of the Central Council of the Reformed Churches, 1879; and was president of the liberal delegation of the reformed churches of France, 1877. He contributed to the history of the Bible Society of Paris, *Notices biographiques* (1868); to the *Histoire de France dans les archives privées de la Grande Bretagne* (1879); and published *En Orient* (Paris, 1862); *Notice sur la Société de l'histoire du Protestantisme français 1852–78* (1874); and the very elaborate *Les Églises françaises du réfuge en Angleterre* (3 vols., 1892).

SCHIELE, shī'le, **FRIEDRICH MICHAEL**: Lutheran; b. at Zeitz (23 m. s.w. of Leipsic) Nov. 11, 1867. He received his education at the gymnasium at Naumburg and at the universities of Tübingen and Halle; taught in the gymnasium of Schlüchtern and Ottweiler, 1894–1900; on account of ill-health he then laid aside professional employment to devote himself to literary work in the departments of theology, philosophy, and pedagogics; in 1907 he again took up teaching, becoming privat-docent for church history in the University of Tübingen. He has had editorial relations with the *Philosophische Bibliothek*, *Die christliche Welt*, *Chronik der christlichen Welt*, *Religionsgeschichtliches Volksblatt*, and *Die Religion in Geschichte und Gegenwart;* and has issued *Kants Beweisgrund zu einer Demonstration des Daseins Gottes* (Leipsic, 1902); an edition of Schleiermacher's *Monologen* (1902); *Minnesang und Volkslied* (1904); *Sang und Spruch der Deutschen im 19. Jahrhundert* (1904); *Deutscher Glaube* (1904); *Religion und Schule* (1906); and *Reformation des Klosters Schlüchtern* (1907).

SCHIJN, shein, **HERMANNUS**: Dutch Mennonite; b. at Amsterdam in 1622; d. there 1727. He studied medicine at Leyden and Utrecht, practised his profession at Rotterdam and then at Amsterdam, serving at the same time as minister of the conservative Mennonite church, upholding its faith both in his sermons and in his writings, and issuing a catechism, *Kort Onderwijs des christelijken Geloofs* (1697, and often). In opposition to the "Lamistic" (i.e., subjective-pietistic Socinian) party of his church, he maintained the traditional Biblical orthodox theology, rejecting with all Mennonites predestination and satisfaction for sin by Christ, and opposed union with the Socinian Collegiants, though in his *Plenior deductio* (see below) he spoke with respect of the leaders of the opposite party. He united with all schools of his church in the charities instituted for the oppressed Mennonites in other countries. But his significance lies in his attempt to win respect for the Dutch Mennonites through his writings, showing that only in the matters of baptism, non-resistance, and the refusal of oaths did they differ from other Protestant bodies, that they had no connection or affiliation of feeling with such Anabaptists as John of Leyden (see Muenzer, Anabaptists of), but were descended from the Waldenses and thence from the apostolic church itself. His first apologetic work was *Korte Historie der protestante Christenen die men Mennoniten of Doopsgezinden noemt* (Amsterdam, 1711), which elicited from the *Acta eruditorum* (v., supplement pp. 85 sqq., Leipsic, 1713) praise of a high degree. It was extended in *Historia Christianorum qui . . . Mennonitæ appellantur* (1723); Dutch transl., 1723, 1727). His *Historiæ Mennonitorum plenior deductio* (1729) discusses the Mennonite background, confessions, and notable representatives; there is a revised edition of this and his *Uitvoeriger Verhandeling* (2 vols., 1744), completed by Gerardus Maatschoen of Amsterdam, together with a third volume extending the biographies. S. Cramer.

SCHINNER, shin'ner, **MATTHIAS**: Cardinal; b. at Mühlebach in upper Valais, Switzerland, in 1456; d. at Rome Sept. 30, 1522. He was educated at Zurich and Como, and became bishop of Sitten in 1500. Appointed by Pope Julius II., in 1509, as legate in Switzerland, he was successful in bringing about an alliance between the pope and the Union against France; but losing the favor of the Swiss and not being allowed to return to his bishopric, he was compelled to resort to Rome, and was made a cardinal in 1511. In 1514 he went as a legate to England to enlist Henry VIII. to join in the league against Francis I. At the battle of Marignano (1515), in which the French disastrously defeated the allies, Schinner led the Swiss in person. Francis I. recognized in him one of his strongest enemies in diplomacy and battle. Again, driven out upon attempting to return to his country and bishopric in 1518, he led a force of allies against the French in 1521, and drove them out of Milan. Zwingli in his account of the campaign of 1512 makes mention of the great impression the cardinal made on the soldiers (*Werke*, ed. Egli and Finsler i. 23–37). When the Reformation broke out in Switzerland, he seemed to be in perfect harmony with the movement. He offered Luther a place of refuge and support in 1519, and continued for a long time to befriend Zwingli; but later he turned against the Reformation. When Johannes Faber (q.v.) met him in Rome in 1521, he agreed with him that the Reformation should be suppressed by force.

BIBLIOGRAPHY: P. S. Furrer, *Geschichte des Wallis III.*, pp. 242 sqq., Sitten, 1850; W. Gisi, *Der Antheil der Eidgenossen an der europäischen Politik . . . 1512–1516*, Schaffhausen, 1866; Pastor, *Popes*, vols. vi.–vii.; *KL*, x., 1790–1792.

SCHISM: A term generally applied to the division that, either wholly or partly, suspends the outward unity of the Church; also, in Roman Catholic canon law, the offense of producing or attempting to produce such a division, and further, the deliberate withdrawal from the bond of the Church by a refusal of obedience to its authorities on the ground that their powers are not legitimate. But mere insubordination to particular rulings or commands of the authorities and simple resistance do not constitute schism.

Nature and Classification.

Where secession ensues from denying individual confessional doctrines of the Church, that is, where the offense of schism is concurrent with heresy, it is termed "heretical schism." On the other hand, in the case of separation, when, for instance, the papacy is acknowledged *per se* but the actual pope is declared not legally elected, the schism is named "pure schism." A further distinction is drawn between "particular" and "universal" schism, according as unity with the whole Church is ruptured directly, as by secession from the pope; or only indirectly, by separation from another ecclesiastical superior, particularly from the bishop. According to Roman Catholic canon law, schism constitutes an ecclesiastical offense chargeable before the spiritual tribunal, and is threatened with summary excommunication, forfeiture of office, suspension from holy orders, disqualification for church positions, infamy, and confiscation of property.

The most serious divisions in the Christian, as later in the Roman Church, were caused by differences in the apprehension of Christian doctrine. To this category belong those divisions which arose in the fourth century and after, coincidently with the closer definition and elaboration of Christian dogmas; further and preeminently, the final separation between the Western and Eastern Churches in 1054; the rupture of the Protestants with the Roman Church in the sixteenth century; and the withdrawal of the so-called Old Catholics from the Church of Rome, in consequence of the Vatican Council.

Earlier Examples.

Another class of church divisions was provoked through a double occupancy of the Roman episcopal see. During the period of the Roman Empire, when the emperors possessed the right of confirmation at the elections of the pope, a discordant election had no decisive influence over the Church at large, and was without essential significance to its unity. Likewise in the tenth century, and in the first half of the eleventh, such was the determining influence that the German emperors exercised on the papal election, and such the position which they generally occupied toward the Church, that particular attempts of the Roman factions to elevate their creatures as popes, or to maintain them in the papacy, were ineffectual, and could lead to no noteworthy divisions. But a change set in from the middle of the eleventh century, when the reform party which began to rule the policy of the Curia sought to wrest this influence from the imperial power and to subject that power to the sovereign dispensation of the papacy. The central status in the Church which the papacy had acquired through the patronage of the emperors moved the latter, in order to possess the advantage of papal prestige in the battle now in progress, repeatedly to set up anti-popes. Thus in opposition to Alexander II., in 1061, Henry IV. put forward Cadalus (Honorius II.); in 1080, Wibert (Clement III.), against Gregory VII.; and Henry V. opposed Gelasius II., in 1118, with Mauritius Burdinus (Gregory VIII.). The division of the Church necessarily consequent upon the strife between the two supreme heads of Western Christendom became embodied in the highest instance of the ecclesiastical organism. Again, the discordant elections in 1130 (Innocent II. and Anacletus II.), and in 1159 (Alexander III. and Victor IV.), were occasioned, notwithstanding the Concordat of Worms (1122), by the persistent breach between the papacy and the empire, with its concomitant division of the cardinals and the Curia into an imperial and a papal faction, and disrupted the unity of the Western Church for a considerable time; especially the latter election, forasmuch as the partisans of Frederick I., after the death of Victor IV., opposed Alexander III., with Paschal III., 1164, and Calixtus III., 1168–78. From the time of the papacy's positive victory over the empire such divisions no longer occurred; for the attempt of Louis the Bavarian to offset John XXII. with an anti-pope in the person of the Minorite Pietro Rainulducci, as Nicholas V., 1328–1330, miscarried.

Only once after this period did a papal schism occur in the Roman Church, and it agitated and shattered the Church as no other. Because of its long duration (1378–1429), it was styled the "great papal schism." After the death of Gregory XI., 1378, who had restored the papal residence to Rome, the sixteen cardinals then present in Rome elected, Apr. 8, Archbishop Bartholomew of Bari as Pope Urban VI. However, he had embittered some of the cardinals through gross harshness and indiscriminate censure of prevalent abuses in the college of cardinals and in the Curia. Therefore a quota of cardinals, thirteen in number, who had betaken themselves to Avignon, elected, Sept. 20, Cardinal Robert of Geneva as Pope Clement VII., affirming that the election of Urban VI. was invalid on account of the coercion brought to bear against them by the population of Rome. In Italy, nevertheless, public sentiment continued overwhelmingly in favor of Urban VI., while Germany, England, Denmark, and Sweden also sided with him. On the other hand, Clement VII. soon became acknowledged by France; and after he had transferred his residence to Avignon, French influence also contrived to draw Scotland, Savoy, and later, Castile, Aragon, and Navarre to his cause. Thus two popes were arrayed one against the other. Each had his own college of cardinals, thus affording a protraction of the schism by means of new papal elections. Urban VI. was followed by Boniface IX. (1389–1404); Innocent VIII. (1404–06); and Gregory XII. (1406–15). After Clement VII., in 1394, came Benedict XIII. The papacy having shown itself incapable of abating the schism, the only expedient was the convening of a general council. This assembled at Pisa, in 1408, and the delegates sat from the start in common accord. Though the council deposed both Gregory XII. and Benedict XIII., and elected in their place Alexander V., who was succeeded in 1410 by John XXIII., this procedure failed to stop the schism. The two former popes asserted themselves so that the Church now had three popes. The futility of the Council of Pisa led to the convocation of the Council of Constance (1414–18). In 1415 this declared that, as representative organ of the ecumenical Church, it possessed the supreme ecclesiastical authority, and every one, even the pope, must yield obedience. In the same year, accordingly, it deposed John XXIII., and again declared Benedict XIII. as a schismatic to have forfeited his right to the papal see. With the election of Martin V., which took place Nov. 11, 1417, by action of the duly appointed conciliar deputation, the schism was practically terminated, though not absolutely ended until 1429; for Benedict XIII., though almost wholly forsaken, defied the sentence of deposition as long as he lived (d. 1424); and Canon Ægidius Munoz of Barcelona, whom the few cardinals that lingered with Benedict elected as Clement VIII., did not relinquish his dignity until five years after.

The Great Schism.

The last schism in the Roman Church was provoked by the conflict of the Council of Basel with Pope Eugenius IV.; whom the council, after his deposition, opposed with an anti-pope in the person of Duke Amadeus of Savoy, Felix V. (1439–1444). This schism, however, was insignificant, because Felix V. was unable to win any appreciable following outside the council. The Vatican Council declared the pope to be absolute monarch in the Church, and the episcopate now constitutes only his advisory adjunct at the general council. But if such is the case, then the episcopate is no longer competent, apart from the pope, where his right is in question, to exercise its earlier judicial prerogatives; and he alone, as the supreme organ, is authorized to decide on the matter of his legitimacy. Hence the means appointed by the Council of Constance for abolishing a papal schism can be no longer applied in the present status of the papacy.

Last Schism.

E. Sehling.

Bibliography: T. Le Mesurier, *The Nature and Guilt of Schism . . . with particular Reference to the Principles of the Reformation*, London, 1808; I. H. von Wessenberg, *Die grossen Kirchenversammlungen des 15. und 16. Jahrhunderten*, ii. 353 sqq., Constance, 1840; T. Lindner, *Geschichte des deutschen Reichs . . . unter Konig Wenzel*, 4 vols., Brunswick, 1875–80; L. Gayet, *Le Grand Schisme d'occident*, Florence, 1889; F. J. Scheuffyen, *Beiträge zu der Geschichte des grossen Schismas*, Freiburg, 1889; G. B. Howard, *The Schism between the Oriental and Western Churches*, New York, 1892; N. Valois, *La France et le schisme d'occident*, 2 vols., Paris, 1896; C. Locke, *Age of the Great Western Schism*, New York, 1897; M. Souchon, *Die Papstwahlen in der Zeit des grossen Schismas, 1378–1417*, Brunswick, 1898; L. Salembier, *Le Grand Schisme d'occident 1378–1417*, Paris, 1902; F. P. Bliemetzrieder, *Das Generalkonzil im grossen abendländischen Schisma*, Paderborn, 1904; Pastor, *Popes*, vol. i.; *KL*, x. 1792–1805.

SCHLATTER, shlď'ter, **ADOLF:** German Protestant; b. at St. Gall (19 m. s.e. of Constance), Switzerland, Aug. 16, 1852. He was educated at the universities of Basel and Tübingen (1872–75), and in 1888 became privat-docent at Bern, where he was appointed associate professor in the same year. Within a few months he was called to Greifswald as full professor of New-Testament exegesis, where he remained until 1893, when he went to Berlin as professor of systematic theology. Since 1898 he has been professor of New-Testament exegesis in the University of Tübingen. He has been associate editor since 1897 of the *Beiträge zur Förderung der christlichen Theologie*, and has written: *Der Glaube im Neuen Testament* (Leyden, 1885); *Einleitung in die Bibel* (Calw, 1889); *Erläuterungen zum Neuen Testament* (11 vols., 1890–1910); *Jason von Cyrene* (Munich, 1891); *Zur Topographie und Geschichte Palästinas* (Calw, 1893); *Der Chronograph aus dem zehnten Jahre Antonius* (Leipsic, 1894); *Geschichte Israels von Alexander den Grossen bis Hadrian* (Calw, 1901); *Predigten in der Stiftskirche zu Tübingen gehalten* (8 vols., Tübingen, 1902–10); *Die Theologie des Neuen Testaments* (parts i.–ii., Calw and Stuttgart, 1909); *Die Theologie des Neuen Testaments und die Dogmatik* (Gütersloh, 1909); and *Die philosophische Arbeit seit Cartesius nach ihrem ethischen und religiösen Ertrag* (1910).

SCHLATTER, MICHAEL: Reformed (German) Church in the United States; b. at St. Gall (19 m. s.e. of Constance), Switzerland, July 14, 1716; d. at Chestnut Hill, near Philadelphia, Oct. 31, 1790. He studied in the gymnasium of his native town, and probably also at Helmstädt; was for some time a teacher in Holland, where he was ordained to the ministry; and in 1745 was vicar at Wigoldingen, Switzerland. In 1746 he was commissioned by the synods of Holland a missionary to the destitute German churches of Pennsylvania, with special directions to visit the scattered settlements, to organise pastoral charges, and, if possible, to form a coetus, or synod. Schlatter arrived in Philadelphia Sept. 6, 1746, and was installed pastor of the united Reformed churches at Philadelphia and Germantown, Jan. 1, 1747, and proceeded to prosecute his special mission with great vigor. He traveled (1747–51) a distance of not less than 8,000 miles, throughout parts of Pennsylvania, Maryland, New Jersey, and New York, and preached 635 times. He estimated that there were at this time 30,000 German Reformed people in Pennsylvania, with fifty-three small churches, and four settled pastors. Schlatter formed the congregations into pastoral charges; and Sept. 29, 1747, the pastors and delegated elders met, at his instance, at Philadelphia, and organised the German Reformed coetus, or synod (see REFORMED [GERMAN] CHURCH). In the mean time trouble arose in the church at Philadelphia; a faction opposed the discipline and close alliance with Holland and chose as pastor, in Schlatter's place, J. C. Steiner, a recent arrival from Switzerland. In 1751 Schlatter went to Europe at the instance of the synod, where he succeeded in reassuring the synods of Holland discouraged by reports of the strife, and in raising a fund of £12,000 for the destitute churches in America on the condition, however, that the coetus in America must be entirely subject to the Church in Holland. In 1752 he returned to America, accompanied by six young ministers, and bringing 700 large Bibles for distribution to churches and families. While in Europe, he published, in Dutch, a "Journal" (Amsterdam, 1751; Germ. transl., Frankfort, 1752) of his missionary labors, containing an earnest appeal in behalf of the Germans in America. A large sum of money, said to have been £20,000, was collected and placed in the hands of a Society for the Promotion of the Knowledge of God among the Germans. In 1755 Schlatter was induced to resign his church in Philadelphia, and to become superintendent of the proposed charity schools. The establishment of these English schools aroused strong opposition among the Germans, and his position became unpopular. Accordingly he resigned in 1757 and accepted a chaplaincy in the Royal American regiment. He accompanied the expedition to Louisburg and remained with the army till 1759. He subsequently lived in retirement at Chestnut Hill, near Philadelphia. During the American Revolution he was an earnest patriot, and was for some time imprisoned for refusing to continue his position as chaplain in the British army.

BIBLIOGRAPHY: H. Harbaugh, *The Life of Rev. Michael Schlatter*, Philadelphia, 1857; H. W. Smith, *Life and Correspondence of Rev. William Smith, D.D.*, vol. i., ib. 1879; J. H. Dubbs, *Founding of the German Churches of Pennsylvania*, ib. 1893; idem, in *American Church History Series*, viii. 278–289, New York, 1895; H. E. Jacobs, in the same, iv. 288–289, ib. 1893.

SCHLECHT, shlĕcht, JOSEF: German Roman Catholic; b. at Wending (37 m. n. of Augsburg), Bavaria, Jan. 20, 1857. He was educated at the gymnasium of Eichstätt and the University of Munich; was curate at Eichstätt (1885–89); a member of the clerical staff of the Campo Santo, Rome, and director of the historical institute of the Görresgesellschaft in the same city (1890–91); instructor in the Lyceum of Eichstätt (1892–93); associate professor at the Lyceum of Dillingen (1893–97); and since 1897 has been connected with the Lyceum of Freising, where he has been successively associate professor (1897–1902) and full professor (since 1902). Besides being associate editor of the second volume of *Die katholische Kirche unserer Zeit und ihre Diener in Wort und Bild* (Munich, 1900); *Eichstätts Kunst* (1901); *Kirchliches Handlexikon* (1904 sqq.); and *Kalender bayrischer und schwäbischer Kunst* (Munich, 1906); he has written *Poesie des Sozialismus* (Würzburg, 1883); *Zur Kunstgeschichte der Stadt Eichstätt* (Eichstätt, 1888); *Eichstätt im Schwedenkriege* (1889); *Die Pfalzgrafen Philipp und Heinrich als Bischöfe von Freising* (Freising, 1898); *Doctrina duodecim Apostolorum* (Freiburg, 1900); *Die Apostellehre in der Liturgie der katholischen Kirche* (1901); *Bayerns Kirchenprovinzen* (Munich, 1902); *Das Leben Jesu* (in collaboration with P. Schumacher; 1902); *Andrea Zamometič, i* (Paderborn, 1903); and edited Kilian Leib's *Briefwechsel und Diarien* (Münster, 1909).

SCHLEIERMACHER, shlai'er-mɑ̄H''er, FRIEDRICH DANIEL ERNST.

Friedrich Daniel Ernst Schleiermacher, whose name marks an epoch not only in Protestant theology, but also in the sciences of religion and ethics, was born at Breslau Nov. 21, 1768, and died at Berlin Feb. 12, 1834. His father was a Reformed army chaplain who had settled in Breslau, where his son was educated until he was ten years old. A fresh outbreak of hostilities then recalled his father to the field, and the boy and his family removed to Pless, where he studied, partly in school and partly under his parents' direction; when his father and mother came under strong Moravian influence, young Friedrich was placed in a school at Niesky. Here he found congeniality of piety, culture, and friendship, and in his enthusiasm entered the Moravian seminary at Barby in 1785 to prepare for the ministry. But his rising spirit of criticism and independence received scant satisfaction, and by Jan., 1787, he found himself unable to remain longer in Barby. He accordingly withdrew

1. Life to 1796.

from the Moravians, and entered the University of Halle, where he plunged into Kantian and Greek philosophy, though even at this time his lack of agreement with Kant's system was clear. In 1789 he was compelled, by lack of funds, to withdraw from Halle, and after a year of private study at Drossen, near Frankfort-on-the-Oder, he passed his first theological examination. He became a private tutor in the family of Count Dohna at Schlobitten in West Prussia, where he learned the ways of polite society. Here, too, in his fragment on the freedom of the will he argued skilfully on the deterministic side, while the sermons of this period stress Christianity as the source of lofty ethical life. After two and a half years, however, a dispute connected with his tutorial duties led to a friendly severance of his relations with Dohna. After another sojourn at Drossen, Schleiermacher, in the autumn of 1793, became a member of the Godike seminary at Berlin, and also taught at the Kornmesser orphan asylum; but in the following year he accepted the post of assistant pastor at Landsberg-on-the-Warthe, where he was ordained. Here, while diligently discharging his pastoral duties, he translated the sermons of Hugh Blair of Edinburgh and of the English preacher John Fawcett (qq.v.). In June, 1795, the senior pastor died, and Schleiermacher was appointed Reformed preacher at the Charité in Berlin.

2. First Berlin Period. Schleiermacher's six years (1796–1802) as preacher at the Charité were rich alike in inspiration and in struggle. Here in Berlin the Enlightenment (q.v.) was still in full tide, but with its increasing shallowness enthusiasm for Romanticism (q.v.) steadily gained. When, in 1797, Friedrich Schlegel visited Berlin, Schleiermacher made his acquaintance, and under his inspiration wrote his *Reden über die Religion* (anonymous, Berlin, 1799) and *Monologen* (1800). In Feb., 1799, his literary relations were interrupted by his sojourn at Potsdam as court chaplain, but on his return to Berlin in May he resumed his pen. The work which followed the *Monologen*—the *Vertraute Briefe über Schlegels Lucinde* (also anonymous; Lübeck, 1800)—was less happy than his former work, and even this plea in behalf of the much-blamed romanticist could not prevent the breach that was already threatening his friendship with Schlegel. At this juncture Schleiermacher's old patron, the court preacher Friedrich Samuel Gottfried Sack (q.v.), who had long been sorely troubled by the young preacher's eloquent defense of Spinozism, offered him a new position, and in 1802 he went into his "exile" as court preacher at Stolpe.

3. The Reden. In estimating the literary results of Schleiermacher's first years in Berlin, it is to be noted primarily that his *Reden über die Religion* shows the close relation of its author to the romantic movement. In opposition to the pedantic Enlightenment he pleaded for a freer and more comprehensive culture based on fantasy and feeling, although his philosophical studies are still in control. In the background stands Kant's definition of the scientific theory of the universe as the impulse to seek elsewhere the unity of the world and the harmony of man's spiritual life; and to this is added Spinoza's tenet that the finite is comprised in and sustained by the infinite. The influence of Leibnitz is visible in the declaration that the life of the universe is mirrored in each individual, and there is recognized Schelling's poetic and philosophic interpretation of nature. The first discourse treats of the necessity of a defense of religion and of the reasons why religion is despised, and the second develops the basal definitions of the essence of religion. This is neither metaphysical interpretation of the world, nor moralistic legislation, nor a union of the two, but "taste and feeling for the infinite," based on apperception and feeling. Apperception presents the universe as a sum of free objects, unfettered by any system, among which each religious person may choose what is best adapted to him; and feeling is religion as the consciousness of the inward change of the individual through such apperception. Only in religion are apperception and feeling united, and their separation shows that the climax of religious experience, the union of the soul with the universe, has been missed, although action does not immediately proceed from them, even while they serve as the permanent basal determination of all action. In the third discourse the author prophesies the speedy passing of the supremacy of the arid rationalism which impeded the development of religious feeling. In the fourth he set forth his theories of the Church. True religious fellowship knew no distinction between clergy and laity; and religion as a whole was realized only in all religions together. The great churches, with their rigid organization and their connection with the State, had fallen far short of this ideal, and were rather training-schools for those who truly sought religion than real associations of pious souls; and the invisible communions severed from the great Church stood nearest to the realization of the ideal. The fifth discourse considered the theory of religion in general. The multiplicity of religions is due to the infinite essence of religion and the finite nature of man, and true religion exists only in the form of a specific type of belief in which the religious life is individualized. So-called natural religion is a mere abstraction, and the differences between positive religions is qualitative, not based on the different quantities of their underlying conceptions. In each of these religions there is a definite theory of the universe which in each case alters the complexion of the whole. In Christianity the cardinal ideas are the corruption and the redemption of man, with history as the stage of action. At the same time, Christianity does not claim to be the final form of all religion, and could a better be found, Christianity would not oppose it.

The *Reden* exercised an influence more lasting than immediate, but ultimately modified nineteenth-century theology more profoundly than any other book. It sharply stressed the concept of autonomy in religion, and thus gave a certain steadiness of development amid the swiftly changing and mutually destructive tendencies of theology; but, on the other hand, the author failed entirely to vindicate the practical character of Christianity, and sadly underestimated its historic aspects.

The *Monologen* reveal the development of Schleiermacher's distinctive ethical theories. Kantian influence is much diminished here, and the "Monologues" form a hymn to higher humanity, whose elements are set forth as purity of will, superiority over fate, individual training, and devotion to mankind. During his two years' residence in Stolpe Schleiermacher had ample opportunity to practise the superiority over fate which he preached, and this period of relative isolation and deprivation of books was not lost in his development, especially as it was favorable to the translation of Plato which he had begun in Berlin; the first volume appeared in 1804, a year later than his *Grundlinien einer Kritik der bisherigen Sittenlehre*. This latter work supplements the ethical theory of the "Monologues" by establishing for the first time the triple division of ethics into the theories of duty, virtue, and good by the coordination of these classes, thus affording a glimpse of the distinctive foundation of Schleiermacher's ethics. At this period in his *Zwei unvorgreiflichen Gutachten in Sachen des protestantischen Kirchenwesens zunächst in Beziehung auf den preussischen Staat*, he advocated a closer union between Lutherans and Reformed, a freer form of worship, and an educational and social improvement of the clergy.

4. The "Monologues"; Stolpe Period.

In 1804 the government refused to sanction his call to the projected Protestant theological faculty of Würzburg, and appointed him instead to Halle as extraordinary professor, where he lectured on New-Testament exegesis, philosophical and theological ethics, introduction to theology, introduction to church history, and dogmatics. In 1806 he became full professor and university preacher. During this Halle period Schleiermacher published, besides two more volumes of his translation of Plato, his *Weihnachtsfeier* (1805) and his treatise on I Tim. in the form of a letter to Joachim Christian Gass (q.v.). The former treatise is a dialogue on the signification of Christ and his work of redemption. In the treatise on I Tim. Schleiermacher seeks to prove that the epistle is a compilation from the other two pastoral epistles, and the discussion opened the way to a strict study of the pastoral epistles. Meanwhile the fall of Jena and Napoleon's hatred of the German spirit of Halle had caused the suspension of lectures there. Schleiermacher seized the opportunity by his sermons to link the spirit of patriotism and the life of the Church. In the winter of 1807, however, he went to Berlin, where he had already lectured on Greek philosophy. Here, at the newly founded university, Schleiermacher lectured after Jan., 1808, on ethics and theological encyclopedia, and in the winter of 1808–09 on dogmatics and politics. His *Gelegentliche Gedanken über Universitäten im deutschen Sinn* (1808) gives his views on the functions of the university. In the spring of 1809 he became preacher at the Dreifaltigkeitskirche in Berlin, and in 1809–10 also lectured on Christian ethics and hermeneutics. When, in the autumn of 1810, the University of Berlin was formally opened, Schleiermacher became the first dean of the theological faculty. From 1810 to 1814 he was also a member of the department of public instruction in the ministry of the interior.

5. At Halle; Call to Berlin.

To the period here under consideration belongs what may be termed Schleiermacher's theological program—the *Kurze Darstellung des theologischen Studiums* (1811). According to this theology is a positive science, being directed to the solution of a practical problem. The real soul of theology is its interest in Christianity as it lives in the Church, and the theologian's ideal is the union of this living interest with the widest scientific spirit. Schleiermacher divides the domain of theological knowledge into philosophical, historical, and practical. The first, as apologetics, gives the basis of piety and Christianity, and the special characteristics of Protestantism; while as polemics it is directed against such internal evils as indifferentism and separatism. Historical theology he divides into exegesis, church history, dogmatics, and statistics. The new element in this system is the incorporation of dogmatics and ethics in the historical department, a result of Schleiermacher's view that dogma in itself is not knowledge. His new science of statistics seems only now to be receiving the attention which it deserves. This troubled period was a time of stress for Schleiermacher. In the matter of union of the Lutheran and Reformed churches he, not without good reason, mistrusted the practicability of the government's scheme of organization. Although the union of 1817 was forced on the churches instead of being an expression of their spontaneous religious convictions, he supported such union, and maintained this position through the period of controversy that ensued. One of these disputes evoked his *Ueber den eigentümlichen Wert und das bindende Aufsehen symbolischer Bücher*, in which he limited the authority of the creeds to those expressions of the Protestant spirit which set forth the religious experience of the period of the Reformation and separated Protestantism from other systems of belief. The controversies of these years, combined with his teaching, left him scant leisure for writing. Nevertheless, he published a third volume of sermons in 1814, and in 1817 his *Kritischer Versuch über die Schriften des Lukas*, in which he traced the tradition of the Gospels to the primitive Christian community and maintained that it developed through oral transmission and fragmentary notes to the form of definite compilation. In 1832 he returned to the problem, and in his *Ueber die Zeugnisse des Papias von unsern beiden ersten Evangelien* was the first to suggest that the Gospel of Matthew is a collection of apothegms.

6. Incidental Activities, 1811–32.

Since 1819 Schleiermacher's energy had been devoted to the preparation of his *Christlicher Glaube nach den Grundsätzen der evangelischen Kirche im Zusammenhang dargestellt* (1821–22). The introduction to this work seeks to determine the place occupied by Christian piety in the spiritual life of society and to fix the scientific formulation appropriate to its articles of belief. Ethics must determine the concept of the Church, the philosophy of religion the grades and varieties of religion, and apologetics the essence of Christianity, while the Church is defined as a community with respect to piety. Interpretation of the Christian faith is, therefore, dependent on the definition of piety, which is the feeling of general dependence, since man becomes aware that the whole world and his own freedom depend on God. Having this definition of the Church, Schleiermacher proceeds to determine what is peculiar to the Christian Church. In the lower grades of religion, such as Fetishism and Polytheism (qq.v.), there is but an approximation to the feeling of dependence, this being realized only at the monotheistic stage. Even here there are two tendencies: the esthetic, in which piety is predominantly emotional; and the teleological, in which it is primarily active. The purest realization of teleological monotheism is Christianity, which is the highest religion, though not the only true one. Revelation can not be claimed exclusively for Christianity, for revelation is only the sum total of the individual concept of God. Essential to the essence of Christianity is the fact that redemption has the central place, and that its realization is dependent on Jesus, who was specifically different from his followers in that he needed no redemption. The coming of the Redeemer is the eternal act of God, and his actual appearance was neither a new revelation nor the development of a factor originally given; the supernatural and the natural interpretations are two equally justified and equally necessary sides of the same fact. Union with Christ is possible only through religious faith, in other words, by trusting him with the satisfying of the need of redemption; and proofs based on miracles, prophecy, and inspired writings are unnecessary and devoid of cogency. The articles of Christian belief serve not as proofs, but as expressions furthering piety; they describe the functions of personal faith, not the objects of belief. The difference between Roman Catholicism and Protestantism is that the former makes the relation of the individual to Christ depend on his relation to the Church, while the latter makes the individual's relation to the Church depend on his relation to Christ. The differences between Lutheran and Reformed Protestantism are merely technical. In his division of dogmatic Schleiermacher discusses first religious consciousness without regard to sin and redemption, and then this consciousness as modified by these two factors. He distinguished three types of dogmatic affirmations: descriptions of human conditions of life, concepts of divine qualities, and statements regarding the world. Each of these expresses the whole content of Christian consciousness, but the first is basal, since it represents most immediately the life of the religious man, and by it must be measured whatever is purely religious in the other two types.

7. Introduction to the Glaubenslehre.

In the *Glaubenslehre* itself, it is maintained that there is no need of a formal proof of the existence of the deity; and since the universal consciousness of God is connected with a perception of the general coherence of nature, the concepts of the divine creation and preservation of the world are gained. Of these the latter is by far the most important, since it alone corresponds to experience; but preservation must be so construed as to cover both dependence on God and the coherence of nature. Since the latter must not be excluded in favor of the former, the idea of miracles is ignored. The doctrine of angels and the devil forms an appendix to the theory of creation, and they are abandoned to poetic and liturgical language. By reference of the absolute feeling of dependence to God are derived the divine attributes of omnipotence, eternity, omnipresence, and omniscience, the fundamental attribute being that first named. Schleiermacher taught that both the world and man were originally perfect; the organization of the world is adapted to awaken and sustain piety, while human nature permits a constant development of this feeling, especially by evolution of consciousness of self into consciousness of race. The second part of the *Glaubenslehre* is devoted to the relations between the antitheses of sin and grace. Sin is set forth as the struggle of the flesh against the spirit, and as a defect of human nature incapable of good except through redemption, and all evil is the punishment of sin; nevertheless Schleiermacher regarded sin as an unavoidable inequality of development and transformed it, as presupposing the need of redemption, into a stage of evolution toward goodness. Yet Schleiermacher gave the doctrine of original sin a better Biblical basis, and postulated the common deeds and guilt of the whole human race. The divine qualities which bear relation to human sin are holiness, which causes conscience to arise in man, and justice, which causes him to recognize the counterpart of his own imperfection in the world as evil.

8. Doctrine of God, the World, Sin, and Grace.

The central position in the *Glaubenslehre* is formed by the development of the consciousness of grace. To Schleiermacher redemption was the transit from restricted to unrestricted consciousness of God, this being realized in a new social life considered by the community to be divinely founded and based on the deeds of Christ. But in view of the eternity of God, this redemption is the realization of the creation, and the Redeemer is, therefore, the primal pattern of man as revealed in history. In Christ mankind became religiously perfect, and as the pattern he was perfect historically, though subject to the influences of time and nationality. Only in his inmost nature was he free from limitations of time, and for this reason Christ is the organ for the indwelling of God in all humanity, since he possesses the power of reproducing, in those like to himself, his own life filled with God in the same way as man influences man. The sole factor in the redemptive work of Christ, in the opinion of Schleiermacher, was his person; his supernatural birth, resurrection, ascension, and second advent were regarded as of little moment. The office of Christ was, accordingly, the extension of the being of God in him to its being in all mankind, so that his passion and death serve but to keep his mind and spirit in remembrance. There can be no idea of the effect of Christ on God, but in the working of Christ on man there are two sides: redemption, or the com-

9. Christology.

munication of the power of his consciousness of God; and atonement, or the communication of the blessedness of such consciousness. The result of the work of Christ in the faithful is regeneration. The new life becomes permanent and indestructible through sanctification, and when regeneration is declared by Schleiermacher to be indelible, he is influenced in his view by psychological and metaphysical presuppositions.

10. Election, Pneumatology, Inspiration.

In the forefront of Schleiermacher's theory stands his interpretation of election, the object of which is the new creature as a whole, its end salvation exclusively, while in choice or rejection of individuals and peoples by the divine governance of the world he sees no final judgment. The doctrine of the communication of the spirit is also closely connected with the theory of the Church, since Schleiermacher regarded the Holy Spirit as the spirit pervading the whole community founded by Christ. In the Church he distinguished between essential and immutable elements arising from its relation to Christ and the Holy Spirit, and transitory components based on its contact with the world. The former included, besides preaching and the sacraments, the power of the keys (i.e., of legislation and discipline) and prayer in the name of Jesus. His concept of preaching was modified by his rejection of the Old Testament and his tenet of the inspiration of persons rather than of writings. Schleiermacher denies that infant baptism has any certain connection with regeneration, and rejects both the sacramentarian and the rationalistic interpretations of the Lord's Supper. The union of the Church with the world gives rise to the distinction between the visible and invisible Church, the former being in error and division through the influence of the world, while the latter is one and infallible. Eschatology is discussed from the point of view of the perfection of the Church. The work of redemption reveals two other qualities of God: love, the principle of God's communication of himself; and wisdom, which regulates its activity. The work concludes with an attempt to define the Trinity, and lands the author in something closely akin to Sabellianism.

11. Schleiermacher's Philosophy and Psychology.

It is generally thought that Schleiermacher's theological attitude must be interpreted with the help of his philosophical views, but his own statements show that while he felt that his philosophy and his theology to some degree influenced and even approximated each other, he held that neither was dependent on the other, and he expressly denied that both could be reduced to the same formula, while with equal explicitness he disavowed the intention of creating a philosophical dogmatics. In harmony with this the *Glaubenslehre* shows only the formal influence of philosophy. The philosophical writings of Schleiermacher are all fragmentary sketches of drafts of lectures, and they show that their author's dogmatic system was already essentially formed when he sought to formulate his philosophy. To Schleiermacher philosophy was not a closed science, but a never-ending problem, so that one can not speak of philosophical results, but only of philosophical presuppositions and the determination of rules for dialectics, or the art of thought. The object of thought is knowledge, but this implies correspondence not only of thought with being but also equal conformity to law in the case of the connection of ideas. The harmony of all human thought with being implies a higher presupposition, for if thought is to become conviction, there must be a supreme unity which subsumes the antithetical terms of ideal and real. But since this unity can not itself be known, its recognition is simply faith, a basal conviction incapable of further demonstration; and the connotation of this supreme unity is the correlated ideas of God and the world. After 1818 Schleiermacher supplemented this train of thought by another, which paved the way for the *Glaubenslehre*. Unity of will is as necessary as unity of knowledge; knowledge is thought preceded by being, will is thought followed by being. Unless will is to be resultless, there must be a conviction that being is accessible, and since all can not speculate, this second way of gaining conviction concerning God is the more usual. Since, however, the concept of God is demanded both by knowledge and will, the home of this idea must be in that element of human consciousness which underlies both knowledge and will, or, in other words, in the feelings, which constitute the transition from thought to will and form the common basis of both. Accordingly, the consciousness of God is originally given in the feelings. God and the world are indissolubly connected. To imagine the world without God is to miss the bond of union; to imagine God without the world is to form an empty concept. Yet God and the world are not identical, for the world is the supreme unity inclusive of all antitheses, while God is the supreme unity exclusive of all antitheses. Both ideas, therefore, sustain a distinct relation to knowledge, God being the *terminus a quo* and the world the *terminus ad quem*. In his lectures on psychology Schleiermacher declined to proceed from such metaphysical concepts as spirit and matter, or soul and body, affirming that only the ego, as the nexus of body and soul, was immediately given. In psychical life there are, therefore, only relative antitheses, which imply the original unity and exclude all dualistic theories. But these functions appear only in various degrees of interaction, and the relative antitheses fall into the three categories of affective and effective activities, objective and subjective consciousness, and consciousness of the ego and of others. The three categories proceed from each other in the order named, and the supreme unity of all is reached in religious feeling, in which even the antithesis of nature and the ego disappears.

12. His Science of Ethics.

Side by side with his works on dogmatics and the psychology of religion, independent value attaches to Schleiermacher's system of ethics. He had early become dissatisfied with the theories of Kant, and in his *Monologen* had sought to set forth positive ethical ideals. At Stolpe he abandoned Schlegel's idea of an ethical revolution in favor of a critical reform of ethical theories, and he pursued this purpose in his lectures on ethics at

Halle as well in as a series of monographs presented before the Prussian Academy of Sciences. He collected sufficient material for his philosophical ethics to be edited by A. Schweizer (*Entwurf eines Systems der Sittenlehre*, Berlin, 1835) and in briefer and more scientific form by A. Twesten (*Grundriss der philosophischen Ethik*, 1841). Schleiermacher regarded ethics as the speculative science of reason, and as including the conceptual presentation of all influence of reason on nature so far as it falls within the sphere of human experience. In the widest sense it is the philosophy of history or of civilization, and is not imperative but descriptive. It is not limited to the practical, but finds activity of reason also in the acquisition of knowledge and the enrichment of the inner life. Ethics must, accordingly, describe the union of reason and nature through the agency of the former, its end being the realization of the union of reason and nature. The power through which reason works in nature is ethically termed virtue, and the mode in which virtue tends to produce ethical good is termed duty. Ethics can be adequately presented only by the combination of these three elements, but the most important is the doctrine of the good, which is summed up by the concept of the supreme good that includes all the products of the rational activity of man. The subject of the ethical process is man as a species; although a distinction may be drawn between individual and class morality, this difference is relative, since each person is at once both an individual and a member of the race. Again, the influence of reason on nature may be twofold: organizing, as making nature the tool, or symbolizing, as reproducing nature. The combination of the individual and class activity of reason with the organizing and symbolizing tendencies results in a fourfold form of moral activity, which is represented respectively by nation and State, family and society, school and Church. The theory of virtue and duty is discussed but briefly by Schleiermacher. While virtue, as the individualized power of reason, is a unity, it may be divided into four categories: wisdom, or inclination to knowledge; love, or inclination to manifestation; discretion, or readiness in knowledge; and steadfastness, or readiness in manifestation. The theory of duty is summarized by Schleiermacher as constant conduct so that all virtues act with reference to all good, though in concrete cases the claims of the various spheres must be duly weighed. Here the relative antitheses of appropriation and association on the one hand and of the universal and individual type on the other give rise to a fourfold classification: the duty of right, corresponding to the universal association; the duty of vocation, corresponding to the universal appropriation; the duty of love, corresponding to the individual association; and the duty of conscience, corresponding to the individual appropriation.

Both its terminology and its omission of the entire concept of obligation deprived this ethical theory of the power which otherwise it might have possessed. In avoiding the errors of Kant and Fichte, Schleiermacher went to the opposite extreme of regarding morality as originally present and as the inevitably developing content of life. In this way he created something midway between ethics and the philosophy of history, but without the loftiness and strength required by ethics, and without the observation of actual factors demanded by the philosophy of history. The only new element is that the Christian, in virtue of the special definiteness of his consciousness of self, does in a special way the same thing that general reason constrains others to do. While the theory that Christianity is a new development and a higher point of view is merely touched on, in reality the Christian determination of ethical conduct prevails and conditions both the direction of interest and the choice of material. The two forms of Christian activity are purification and extension. Purificatory activity is manifested in the Church either as the influence of the community on individual members (church discipline) or as the influence of individuals on the community (church reform), and from the Church this purificatory influence extends to the home, the State, and international relations. Extensive activity, proceeding from the union of the divine spirit with the nature of man, is manifested either as a state of mind or as talent, the former being characteristic of the Church and the latter of the State, while the Christian spirit works even beyond the bounds of the Church in education and missions. Manifestative activity is developed in the service of God. In the narrower sense of the term this service is public worship, and in its wider sense the free expression of Christian morality; and at the same time this manifestative activity contains an element of public morality and of social and intellectual life, to all of which it gives the stamp of purity, freedom, and perfect humanity.

13. Criticism of the Ethics.

The last fifteen years of Schleiermacher's life show him at the height of his activity. He exercised a profound influence both through his sermons and through his lectures, which covered the greater part of philosophy and the most of theology excepting the Old Testament. He began to be considered the head of a distinct school, but, on the other hand, he was involved in many of the controversies of the period and was the object of constant suspicion. In Jan., 1823, a formal charge was actually brought against him on the basis of certain expressions used by him in private correspondence, and he lived in continual uncertainty whether he would be permitted longer to reside in Prussia. To all this was added his participation in the agenda controversy; and it was only after the modified royal agenda had been adopted (see Agenda, § 5) that Schleiermacher again enjoyed the favor of the king. In the third decade of the century Schleiermacher was busy editing the Berlin hymnal and opposing the proposed creed for the united Lutherans and Reformed. He contributed a number of articles to the newly founded *Theologische Studien und Kritiken*, in one of which he vigorously opposed rationalistic depreciation of the creeds, at the same time advocating all the principles of theological progress. He visited England in 1828 and Sweden in 1833, but his health was failing, and in Feb., 1834, he died.

14. Schleiermacher's Last Years.

15. Character and Influence.

What is especially striking in Schleiermacher is his versatility. He was a preacher of rare effectiveness; he lectured well on a large number of philosophical subjects; and by his translation of Plato and such treatises as that on the art of translation he contributed not a little to classical learning. In addition to all this he was a sturdy patriot and preeminently a social being. His versatility is mirrored in his theological writings, in which he sought to prepare a way in which Christianity and the highest culture might walk together in harmony. In this he did not desire forcibly to unite elements essentially heterogeneous, but he was himself both Christian and humanist. His "Discourses" affirm that religion is the central point of spiritual life, and the fundamental basis of his *Glaubenslehre* is that the human is perfected in the Christian. Whatever may be lacking from his theology, it is at least self-evident that this theology was Schleiermacher's own life; and his piety was pure, honorable, and earnest. With breadth of view Schleiermacher combined an unusual degree of resolution. The deficiencies of his ethical theories find their explanation in his personal conditions. Yet his energy overcame these hindrances, among which ill-health was not the least, and for years, besides his preaching and his writing, he lectured three hours daily. He demanded of no one what he himself would not do, and he invariably remained true to himself. Nothing could induce him to surrender a conviction which he had once formed, and he clung to his position even against the well-meant plans of his king for the reform of his church simply because he firmly believed that these proposed changes were perilous. The influence of Schleiermacher still persists, though by no means restricted to the school of mediating theologians commonly traced back to him. The modern historical school, rejecting Kant and Ritschl, turns more and more to Schleiermacher, drawn especially by his philosophical theories, his stress on the individualistic character of the positive religions, and his assumption of the principle of the development of religion. The agencies of this influence have been primarily the *Reden*, the *Kurze Darstellung des theologischen Studiums*, the *Glaubenslehre*, and the *Ethik*. Of his posthumously published lectures only the *Erziehungslehre* (Berlin, 1849) and the *Praktische Theologie* attracted wide attention; the *Leben Jesu* (1864) was a failure. Among his posthumous sermons his homilies on the Gospel of John are of value for a knowledge of Schleiermacher's school, which so pronouncedly follows the Johannine type of thought; and a valuable supplement to the whole problem is promised by C. Clemen's proposed edition of Schleiermacher's lecture on theological encyclopedia.

(O. Kirn.)

Bibliography: The one practically complete collection of the *Werke* is in three divisions—theology, sermons, and philosophy, by various editors, 32 vols., Berlin, 1835–62, many individual volumes of which passed through many editions. The jubilee edition of the *Reden*, 1899, and a critical edition of the *Monologen*, 1902, are noteworthy; also: *Philosophische Sittenlehre*, ed. J. H. von Kirchmann, Berlin, 1870. In addition are to be noted *Schleiermachers Briefwechsel mit J. C. Gass*, ed. W. Gass, Berlin, 1852; his *Briefe an die Grafen zu Dohna*, ed. J. Jacobi, Halle, 1887; his correspondence with Twesten in Heinrici, *A. Twesten*, Berlin, 1889; *Schleiermachers Sendschreiben über seine Glaubenslehre*, ed. H. Mulert, Giessen, 1908; and J. Baur, *Ungedruckte Predigten Schleiermachers aus den Jahren 1820–1828*, Leipsic, 1909. In English there have appeared: *Critical Essay on the Gospel of St. Luke*, London, 1825; *Schleiermacher's Introductions to the Dialogues of Plato*, transl. by W. Dobson, Cambridge, 1836; *Selected Sermons of Schleiermacher*, transl. by Mary F. Wilson, London, 1890; *Christmas Eve; a Dialogue on the Celebration of Christmas*, transl. by W. Hastie, Edinburgh, 1890; *Religion: Speeches to its cultured Despisers*, (transl. of the *Reden*), London, 1893.

A very full list of works is given in Baldwin, *Dictionary*, iii. 1, pp. 459–462. As sources for a life, there are the correspondence (*Briefwechsel*) as noted above, and *Aus Schleiermachers Leben. In Briefen*, ed. L. Jonas and W. Dilthey, 4 vols., Berlin, 1858–63, Eng. transl. by F. Rowan, 2 vols., London, 1860. Consult further: L. F. O. Baumgarten-Crusius, *Ueber Dr. F. Schleiermacher, seine Denkart und sein Verdienst*, Jena, 1834; C. A. Auberlen, *Schleiermacher: ein Charakterbild*, Basel, 1859; R. Baxmann, *Schleiermacher: sein Leben und sein Wirken*, Elberfeld, 1863; M. Baumgarten, *Schleiermacher*, Berlin, 1868; D. Schenkel, *Frdr. Schleiermacher: ein Lebens- und Charakterbild*, Elberfeld, 1868; T. Hossbach, *Schleiermacher: sein Leben und Wirken*, Berlin, 1869; F. Zachler, *Fr. Schleiermacher: kurzer Abriss seines Lebens und Wirkens*, Breslau, 1869; W. Dilthey, *Leben Schleiermachers*, Berlin, 1870; E. Maier, *Friedrich Schleiermacher. Lichtstrahlen aus seinen Briefen und sämmtlichen Werken*, Leipsic, 1875; S. Brunner, *Die vier Grossmeister der Aufklärungs Theologie* (Herder, Paulus, Schleiermacher, Strauss), Paderborn, 1888; C. P. Fischer, *Schleiermacher*, Berlin, 1899; R. Munro, *Schleiermacher*, London, 1903; O. Gramzow, *Schleiermacher*, Charlottenburg, 1904.

On his theology consult: F. W. Gess, *Uebersicht über das theologische System Schleiermachers*, Reutlingen, 1837; G. Weissenborn, *Vorlesungen über Schleiermacher's Dialektik und Dogmatik*, Leipsic, 1847; C. Schwarz, *Schleiermacher: seine Persönlichkeit und seine Theologie*, Gotha, 1861; S. Lommatzsch, *Schleiermachers Lehre vom Wunder und vom Uebernatürlichen*, Berlin, 1872; A. Ritschl, *Schleiermachers Reden über die Religion und ihre Nachwirkungen auf die evangelische Kirche Deutschlands*, Bonn, 1874; O. Ritschl, *Schleiermachers Stellung zum Christenthum in seinen Reden über die Religion*, Gotha, 1888; E. Schrecker, *Der Religionsbegriff bei Schleiermacher und seinen namhaftesten Nachfolgern*, Jena, 1890; O. Pfleiderer, *Die protestantische Theologie seit Kant*, Berlin, 1891; idem, *Geschichte der Religionsphilosophie . . . bis auf die Gegenwart*, ib. 1893; H. Bleek, *Die Grundlagen der Christologie Schleiermachers*, Freiburg, 1898; E. Fuchs, *Schleiermachers Religionsbegriff*, Giessen, 1900; K. Thiele, *Schleiermachers Theologie und ihre Bedeutung für die Gegenwart*, Tübingen, 1903; L. Göbel, *Herder und Schleiermachers Reden über die Religion*, Gotha, 1904; C. Clemen, *Schleiermachers Glaubenslehre in ihrer Bedeutung für Vergangenheit und Zukunft*, Giessen, 1905; W. J. Aalders, *Schleiermachers Reden über die Religion als Proeve van Apologie*, Leyden, 1910.

On his philosophy and ethics consult: J. Gottschick, *Ueber Schleiermachers Verhältnis zu Kant*, Tübingen, 1875; K. Beth, *Die Grundanschauungen Schleiermachers in seinem ersten Entwurf der philosophischen Sittenlehre*, Berlin, 1898; G. Thimme, *Die religionsphilosophischen Prämissen der Schleiermacher'schen Glaubenslehre*, Hanover, 1901; T. Camerer, *Spinoza und Schleiermacher*, Stuttgart, 1903; H. Mulert, *Schleiermachers geschichtsphilosophische Ansichten in ihrer Bedeutung für seine Theologie*, Giessen, 1907; G. Wehrung, *Der geschichtsphilosophische Standpunkt Schleiermachers zur Zeit seiner Freundschaft mit den Romantikern*, Stuttgart, 1907; E. Cramaussel, *La Philosophie religieuse de F. Schleiermacher*, Geneva, 1909; H. Scholz, *Christentum und Wissenschaft in Schleiermachers Glaubenslehre*, Berlin, 1909; H. Süskind, *Der Einfluss Schellings auf die Entwicklung von Schleiermachers System*, Tübingen, 1909; *Entwurf eines Systems der Sittenlehre*, ed. A. Schweizer, Gotha, 1835; *Grundriss der philosophischen Ethik mit einleitender Vorrede*, ed. D. A. Twesten, Berlin, 1841; F. Vorländer, *Schleiermachers Sittenlehre*, Marburg, 1851; L. Jonas, *Christliche Sittenlehre aus Nachschriften*, Gotha, 1891; F. Bachmann, *Die Entwicklung der Ethik Schleiermachers nach den Grundlinien*, Leipsic, 1892.

For his relation to education and the pulpit consult: A. Petersen, *Schleiermacher als Reformator der deutschen Bildung*, Gotha, 1869; P. Diebow, *Die Pädagogik Schleiermachers*, Halle, 1894; O. Kirn, *Schleiermacher und die Romantik*, Basel, 1895; H. Keferstein, *Schleiermacher als Pädagoge*, Jena, 1899; R. Wickert, *Die Pädagogik Schleiermachers in ihrem Verhältnis zu seiner . . . Ethik*, Leipsic, 1907; A. Schweizer, *Schleiermachers Wirksamkeit als Prediger dargestellt*, Halle, 1834; J. Bauer, *Schleiermacher als Prediger*, Giessen, 1908.

SCHLEUSNER, shlois'ner, **JOHANN FRIEDRICH:** Lutheran theologian; b. at Leipsic Jan. 16, 1759; d. at Wittenberg, Feb. 21, 1831. He received his education in his native city, at the St. Thomas school, and at the university, 1775–80, where he devoted himself to Biblical philology. He became preacher at the University Church, 1780; instructor, 1781; associate professor of theology at Göttingen, 1784–90; and full professor, 1790–95; professor at the University and provost at the central church at Wittenberg from 1795; and with the abolition of the university, first director of the Homiletic Institute and second director of the Seminary at Wittenberg. His lectures were mainly in New-Testament exegesis, but treated also somewhat of Old-Testament exegesis, dogmatics, and homiletics. His two main works were, *Lexicon græco-latinum in Novum Testamentum* (Leipsic, 1792; 4th ed., 1819); and *Thesaurus seu lexicon in LXX* (1820–21). The latter contains all the vocabulary of the Greek Old Testament with the Hebrew equivalents.

(E. Reuss†.)

SCHLICHTING, JONAS. See Socinus, Faustus, Socinians, I., § 2.

SCHLOEGL, shlö'gl, **NIVARD JOHANN BAPTIST:** Austrian Cistercian; b. at Gaaden (a village near Mödling, 8 m. s.s.w. of Vienna), June 4, 1864. He was educated at the Cistercian abbey at Heiligenkreuz, near Vienna (1876–80), the Obergymnasium at Wiener Neustadt (1880–84), and again at the abbey and the University of Vienna (1885–1889; D.D., 1894). He was consecrated to the priesthood in 1889, when he became connected with the abbey of Heiligenkreuz, where he was professor of Greek in 1889–91, 1892–93, 1894, and 1902–03, and professor of Old-Testament and Semitics, 1896–1908; and since 1908 professor of oriental languages and Old-Testament exegesis at Vienna. He was master of the novices at Heiligenkreuz, 1890–1908, and festival-preacher in the abbey-church in 1893–1894, and 1895–96. In 1906 he succeeded B. Schäfer as editor of the Leo-Gesellschaft's *Kurzgefasster wissenschaftlicher Commentar zu den heiligen Schriften*, to which he has contributed Samuel, Kings, and Chronicles (Vienna, 1904, 1907). He has also edited the Hebrew text of Ecclesiasticus xxxix. 12–xlix. 16 (Vienna, 1901), of Canticles (1902), and Samuel (1905), and Kings and Chronicles (1909), and has written *Geist des heiligen Bernhard* (4 vols., Paderborn, 1898–99), and *De re metrica veterum Hebræorum* (Vienna, 1899).

SCHLOTTMANN, shlot'män, **CONSTANTIN:** German theologian; b. at Minden (60 m. e.n.e. of Münster) Mar. 7, 1819; d. at Halle Nov. 8, 1887. He studied at the University of Berlin, devoting himself especially to philology and philosophy, and then turned to theology, where he came under the lasting influence of A. Neander. He then studied the practical side of the work of the ministry at the Wittenberg Seminary, but returning to Berlin, 1842, was induced to enter the academic career. Supporting himself a while by private teaching he habilitated in the Old Testament in 1847. His commentary on the Book of Job (Berlin, 1851) was his first important work. For a time he served in Constantinople as chaplain of the embassy; there he became acquainted with modern Greek and Turkish, and traveled in the East adding to the range of his oriental scholarship. In 1855, he was called to Zurich, where he lectured not only on the Old but also on the New Testament, and on systematic theology. He was ordinary professor at Bonn, 1859–66, and at Halle, 1866–87. He was able to point out at all points the relations of Hebrew and Indo-Germanic culture as well as the connections of Hebrew writings and the monuments of classic antiquity, and brought to good service his first-hand knowledge of oriental life. For criticism he was disinclined, especially the newer criticism of the Old Testament, as he showed in his *Kompendium der Biblischen Theologie des alten und Neuen Testaments* (Leipsic, 1889–95). Besides numerous contributions on various Old-Testament antiquities, he published, *Die Inschrift Eschmunazars, König der Sidonier* (Halle, 1868), and *Die Siegessäule Mesa's, König der Moabiter* (1870). He lectured also on apologetics, from which grew his writings *David Strauss als Romantiker des Heidenthums* (1878), and *Die Osterbotschaft und Visionshypothese* (1886). He was a member and president of the commission for the revision of Luther's translation of the Bible after 1871, and appeared as an anxious antagonist of the rising ultramontanism, which gave rise to his *Erasmus redivivus* (1889).

(Ernst Kühn.)

Bibliography: *ADB*, xxxi. 561 sqq.; Brandt, in *Deutsch-evangelisches Blatt*, 1889, pp. 187 sqq.

SCHMALKALD, shmäl'käld, **ARTICLES:** A written instrument of Luther received into the symbolic books of the Lutheran Church and so named after 1553. After the insistent demands of the German estates during several decades and the renewed urging of the emperor, Paul III. issued a call for a council to meet at Mantua May 8, 1537. The question arose as to the attitude of the Evangelicals. Elector Johann Friedrich of Saxony, who took the most active interest, appeared at Wittenberg June 24, 1536, and through his chancellor submitted four articles for an opinion from the theologians and jurists, in order to forearm himself and confederates for the coming council. Two days later the elector submitted that the council be wholly declined inasmuch as a reception of the summons would imply the recognition of the pope as the head of the Church. After a session that closed Aug. 6, the opinion prepared by Melanchthon was returned that if the pope would summon the Protestant estates like the rest, he did not yet regard their princes as heretics, and that by giving audience to the papal nuncio no acknowledgment of papal power was implied, and so far the invitation was not to be de-

Origin.

clined. The elector, taking it that the theologians had been prevailed upon by the jurists, had Melanchthon translate a protest into Latin to the effect that in case of taking the invitation under advice, the council should be understood to be free and open and not bound by papal prejudices; and he again called for a meeting of the scholars for the submission of certain questions. At the same time Luther received a specially assigned task, and it seems that he was already employed upon articles of belief. The absence of Melanchthon retarded the reply of the scholars; and Dec. 1, the elector took occasion to renew his appeal, to emphasize the necessity of declining a papal council, to sound the sense at Wittenberg on the question of holding an opposing Evangelical council; and he reverted to the task requested of Luther, deeming it necessary that the latter should, at least by Jan. 25, 1537, prepare a document, the summary of all that he had taught, preached, and written, as a final testament. Luther was to indicate also on what articles, not essential, any compromise could be made; and the Wittenberg theologians were called upon to make sure in advance of their agreement or disagreement with the proposed articles, independent of Luther's authority, so that there might be no subsequent dissent. On Dec. 11, the Wittenberg scholars tendered their second and satisfactory opinion; but as Luther's articles had not yet appeared, the elector reminded him by writing and named particularly Nikolaus von Amsdorf and Johann Agricola (qq.v.) among those theologians who were to be brought secretly to Wittenberg from the territories of the elector and his brother, Johann Ernst, at the elector's expense, to give their approval to the articles or to hand in their objections in writing. Luther set to work to prepare his articles, which were submitted to his colleagues and adopted before the end of the year, Melanchthon attaching with his signature the statement that the papal supremacy be acknowledged for the freedom of the Gospel. The official copy was forwarded to the elector Jan. 3, 1537, who expressed great satisfaction at the agreement of the articles with the Augsburg Confession (q.v.) and the unanimity of his theologians; and he set his chancellor to secure the signatures of the leading pastors so that in the case of Luther's sudden death his views should stand without admixtures from them.

Content. The articles were arranged in three divisions. The first discusses briefly the undisputed majesty of God. In the second, on the office and work of Christ, or human redemption, the first and principal article represents that man, without any merit of his own, but by the redemptive work of Jesus Christ, is justified by faith alone. In the second article, the mass is condemned as contrary to Scripture, and, like its alleged progeny, or as varieties of idolatry, purgatory, offices of saints, pilgrimages, monastic brotherhoods, relics, and indulgences are denounced. The third article demands the devotion of monastic properties to the education of youth and the use of the churches, and the fourth attacks the pope as Antichrist. The best government for the Church is for all to live under one head, Christ; and for the bishops to cooperate earnestly in a common doctrine, faith, prayer, sacrament, and work of love. In the third division are included articles on which Luther may have hoped for some degree of conciliation at least on the part of the more enlightened Roman Catholics; such as doctrines of redemption, sin, law, and repentance, in strong contrast with the penance of the papal Church. In contrast with the law and its significance for the way of salvation, there rises in due prominence the counsel and help of God offered against sin in the Gospel in various ways: of oral preaching, principally; of baptism, the sacrament, power of the keys, and confession; to which are correlated the articles on the ban, consecration and vocation, on the Church, and on how to become just before God, as well as on monastic vows and human ordinances.

History. The elector's intention was to lay the articles of Luther before a convention "for unanimous agreement," to be held at Schmalkald on Candlemas, Feb. 2, 1537; and all the Evangelical estates were summoned to send one or two theologians. In the first session, the Chancellor Brück proposed the discussion of the articles in preparation of the approaching council. But Melanchthon, who had not been in entire agreement with Luther's articles on the attack on the papacy, now obstructed this by informing Philip of Hesse on the same day that Luther had altered, under the influence of J. P. Bugenhagen (q.v.), the original cast of the article on the Lord's Supper, so that it was now in conflict with the Concord of Wittenberg (q.v.). In consequence and in order to avert a division, it was decided by the cities (Feb. 11) to decline the Saxon proposition and abide by the confessions now in the hands of the emperor upon which unanimity had been reached. To this the princes agreed in general, with the provision that the scholars review again the Augsburg Confession and Apology and fortify them with new arguments from the Scriptures and the Fathers, but make no internal changes in them or the Concord except to denounce more positively the papacy. While, for want of books, approval was suspended for further proof, Melanchthon, during the severe illness of Luther, wrote his *Tractatus de potestate et primatu papæ*, which was finished Feb. 17, in which, under the influence of the ever-increasing anti-papal feeling, he wrote in more drastic terms than was his custom. He antagonized emphatically the assumption of divine right by the pope, who, as the protector of false doctrines and godless worship, was much rather to be resisted as Antichrist. In the second part he set forth the true view of the episcopacy and of Evangelical ordination; and the obligation of allegiance to the bishops subject to the pope, who enforce godless doctrine and false worship, was repudiated. This tract, after being considered and approved by the estates, was subscribed, in common with the Augsburg Confession and the Apology, by the attendant theologians.

Luther's articles were to be read before the convention Feb. 18; but, owing to his illness, this did not take place. Finally, when all the business had been transacted, Bugenhagen issued the invitation to sign Luther's articles; but as Martin Butzer (q.v.)

declined, not because he found anything objectionable but on the ground that he was not authorized, and others followed his example, the matter was dropped in the interest of peace. The theologians in attendance and later others affixed their signatures simply to give in writing their expression of individual concord, without thought, as the council was declined, of issuing a confessional document of the Schmalkaldic league. A year later Luther issued his document with longer preface and various amplifications of the articles and more acute deductions. Apparently not well-informed of what transpired at Schmalkald during his sickness, Luther regarded his articles as an official instrument. In the preface he represented them as adopted, known, and resolved by his party for a basis of defense in the council. This notice may have contributed to the result that, while Melanchthon's tract retreated more and more into the background, Luther's articles gained in estimation. First, they were placed on the same plane with the Augsburg Confession by the Hessian theologians, 1544. When the elector returned from captivity he remarked that all the dogmatic confusion could have been averted, if the agreement proposed at Schmalkald in 1537 had been adhered to. In the controversies of the fifth decade, it became more and more expedient to class them with the formal confessions, whereby, as the expression of the most genuine Lutheranism, to combat the real or supposed Philippist opinions (see PHILIPPISTS). Adopted in nearly all "bodies of doctrine" begining with Brunswick, 1563, it was understood that they received acknowledgment by the authors of the Formula of Concord (q.v.), while Melanchthon's tract, whose authorship seems to have been forgotten, was placed in the appendix of the Schmalkald articles in the Book of Concord. Luther's articles written in German were translated by the Danish Petrus Generanus into Latin, *Articuli a Reverendo D. Doctore Martino Luthero scripto, Anno 1538* (Wittenberg, 1541; improved ed., 1542). For Schmalkald League see PHILIP OF HESSE. (T. KOLDE.)

In the Book of Concord.

BIBLIOGRAPHY: G. L. Plitt, *De auctoritate articulorum Smalcaldicorum symbolica*, Erlangen, 1862; F. Sander, *Geschichtliche Einleitung zu den schmalkaldischen Artikeln*, in *Jahrbücher für deutsche Theologie*, xx (1875), 475 sqq.; H. Birck, *Zu den Beratungen der Protestanten über die Konzilsbulle vom 4. Juni 1536*, in *ZKG*, xiii (1892), 487 sqq.; H. E. Jacobs, *Book of Concord*, passim, 2 vols., Philadelphia, 1893; J. F. Hurst, *Hist. of the Christian Church*, ii. 509 and passim, New York, 1900; K. Thieme, *Luthers Testament wider Rom*, Leipsic, 1900; W. Rosenberg, *Der Kaiser und die Protestanten in den Jahren 1537-39*, Halle, 1903; *Cambridge Modern History*, ii. 26, 215 sqq., 232-243, 252-258, New York, 1904; Moeller, *Christian Church*, iii. 132; Schaff, *Creeds*, iii. 253-257; idem, *Christian Church*, vi. 706. Consult also the biographies of Luther.

SCHMALKALD LEAGUE. See PHILIP OF HESSE, § 4.

SCHMALZ, VALENTIN. See SOCINUS, FAUSTUS, SOCINIANS, I., § 2.

SCHMID, shmit, **ALOYS VON:** German Roman Catholic; b. at Zaumberg (a village near Immenstadt, 13 m. s.w. of Kempten), Bavaria, Dec. 22, 1825; d. at Munich May 16, 1910. He was educated at the University of Munich (1844-50); was professor in the gymnasium of Zweibrücken (1850-52); professor of philosophy in the Lyceum of Dillingen (1852-66); and after 1866 was professor of apologetics and dogmatics in the University of Munich. He wrote *Die Bistumssynode* (2 vols., Regensburg, 1850-51); *Entwicklungsgeschichte der Hegel'schen Logik* (1858); *Thomistische und scotistische Gewissheitslehre* (Dillingen, 1859); *Wissenschaftliche Richtungen auf dem Gebiet des Katholizismus* (Munich, 1862); *Wissenschaft und Autorität* (1868); *Untersuchungen über den letzten Grund des Offenbarungsglaubens* (1879); *Erkenntnislehre* (2 vols., Freiburg, 1890); and *Apologetik als spekulative Grundlage der Theologie* (1900).

SCHMID, ANDREAS: German Roman Catholic; b. at Zaumberg (a village near Immenstadt, 13 m. s.w. of Kempten), Bavaria, Jan. 9, 1840. He was educated at the University of Munich (D.D., 1866), became subdirector and director of the Georgianum, a seminary for priests at Munich (1865), professor of pastoral theology, homiletics, liturgics, and catechetics in the University of Munich since 1877, though he no longer lectures. He has written *Der christliche Altar und sein Schmuck* (Regensburg, 1871); *Dr. Valentin Thalhofer, Dompropst in Eichstätt, eine Lebensskizze* (Kempten, 1892); *Geschichte des Georgianums* (Regensburg, 1894); *Caerimoniale für Priester, Leviten und Ministranten zu den gewöhnlichen liturgischen Diensten* (Kempten, 1895; 3d ed., 1905); *Religiöse Sinnsprüche zu Inschriften auf Kirchengebäude und kirchliche Gegenstände in lateinischer und deutscher Sprache* (1899); *Der Kirchengesang nach den Liturgikern des Mittelalters* (1900); and *Christliche Symbole aus alter und neuer Zeit* (Freiburg, 1909).

SCHMID, CHRISTIAN FRIEDRICH: German Lutheran; b. at Bickelsberg, in Württemberg, in 1794; d. at Tübingen Mar. 28, 1852. Educated at Maulbronn and Tübingen, he became lecturer in practical theology at the latter university in 1819, associate professor in 1821, and full professor in 1826, holding this position until his death. Though a member of the committee for the Württemberg liturgy of 1840 and of the council for church organization in 1848, he took little part in administrative affairs, nor was he conspicuous as an author, his importance being due rather to his influence as a teacher and a man. Proceeding from the Tübingen supranaturalism of his time, he later labored successfully for the positive foundations of Lutheranism, maintaining the tendency which had been traditional since the time of Bengel. He lectured on practical, moral, and exegetical theology. He was the author of the posthumous *Vorlesungen über biblische Theologie des Neuen Testaments* (Gotha, 1853, new ed., 1888; Eng. transl., *Biblical Theology of the New Testament*, Edinburgh, 1871), and *Vorlesungen über christliche Sittenlehre* (1861). (C. WEIZSÄCKER†.)

BIBLIOGRAPHY. C. Weizsäcker, in *Schwäbischen Merkur*, June 6, 1852; *Blätter der Erinnerung an C. F. Schmid*, Tübingen, 1852.

SCHMID, HEINRICH FRIEDRICH FERDINAND: German Lutheran; b. at Harburg (30 m. n.n.w. of

Augsburg) July 31, 1811; d. at Erlangen Nov. 17, 1885. He was educated at the universities of Tübingen, Halle, Berlin, and Erlangen, and in 1833 was called to the newly founded seminary for preachers at Munich. Four years later he became a lecturer in the theological faculty at Erlangen, and during this period published his *Dogmatik der evangelisch-lutherischen Kirche* (Erlangen, 1843; Eng. transl., *Doctrinal Theology of the Lutheran Church*, Philadelphia, 1876). In 1846, when he became privat-docent at Erlangen, Schmid published his *Geschichte der synkretistischen Streitigkeiten in der Zeit des Georg Calixt* (1846). Two years later he was appointed associate professor, and in 1852 full professor, first of church history and systematic theology, and later of historical theology. For his lectures on church history he wrote his *Lehrbuch der Kirchengeschichte* (Nördlingen, 1851), later expanded into the *Handbuch der Kirchengeschichte* (2 vols., Erlangen, 1880–81). A similar purpose was served by his *Lehrbuch der Dogmengeschichte* (Nördlingen, 1860), after he had already published his *Theologie Semlers* (1858). From 1855 to 1876 Schmid was editor of the *Zeitschrift für Protestantismus und Kirche*, to which he contributed much. His attitude toward Lutheranism was shown by his *Kampf der lutherischen Kirche um Luthers Lehre vom Abendmahl in Reformationszeitalter* (Leipsic, 1868), and *Geschichte der katholischen Kirche Deutschlands von Mitte des achtzehnten Jahrhunderts bis in die Gegenwart* (Munich, 1874). In 1881 he retired from active life. (F. Frank†.)

SCHMID, KONRAD: 1. Leader of the Flagellants of the fourteenth century. See Flagellation, Flagellants, II., § 4.

2. Swiss Reformer; b. at Küssnacht (15 m. n.e. of Lucerne) 1476 or early in 1477; d. in the battle of Kappel Oct. 11, 1531. He was educated at Tübingen, and entered the Johannite monastery of his native town. In 1515–16 he resumed his theological studies at Basel, and was inducted to the parish of Seengen in Aargau on Apr. 21, 1517. On Mar. 10, 1519, he was chosen commander, and in this capacity exercised much influence on the development of the Reformation in Zurich. He soon came under the influence of Zwingli and devoted himself to the Bible, patristics, and Greek. Schmid was regarded as a learned man, and a powerful preacher. As early as the spring of 1522 he delivered a sermon at Lucerne in which he assailed Roman Catholic doctrines. In the first Kappel war he served as chaplain. Schmid was less inclined to violent action than was Zwingli, with whom he toured the country in harmony as official itinerant preacher to strengthen the cause of the Reformation. More important was Schmid's influence as the supporter of the authorities in momentous disputations. He took part in the disputation with the monks of the city in the summer of 1522, in the conferences concerning images and the mass in the spring of 1524, and in a number of controversies with Anabaptists, including Hübmaier himself. These Anabaptist controversies gave rise to Schmid's two pamphlets *Ein christliche Ermanung zur waren Hoffnung in Gott und Warnung* (1527) and *Verwerffen der Artickeln und Stucken*. Though not always unopposed, Schmid admirably administered the parishes, charitable institutions, and other institutions under his control. In 1525 he married. His entire harmony with Zwingli in his latter years was shown by his taking the place of his greater colleague while Zwingli was on his way to Marburg, and also by the tenor of his last pamphlet, *Ein christlicher Bericht des Herren Nachtmahls*, with its Zwinglian views of the Lord's Supper. Besides the three pamphlets already mentioned Schmid published his Lucerne sermon in 1522. (Emil Egli†.)

Bibliography: Sources are the "Works" and "Letters" of Zwingli; the early lives of that Reformer; and the "History of the Reformation" by H. Bullinger, ed. J. J. Hottinger and H. H. Vögeli, 6 vols., Frauenfeld, 1838–40. Consult further: H. Hess, in *Zürcher Chorherren* for New Year, 1825; S. Vögelin, Sr., in *Zürcher Taschenbuch*, 1862; C. Dändliker, in the same, 1897; and the literature under Reformation which deals with Switzerland.

SCHMIDT, shmit, CARL: German Protestant; b. at Hagenow (17 m. s.w. of Schwerin), Mecklenburg-Schwerin, Aug. 26, 1868. He was educated at the universities of Leipsic and Berlin (1887–94; Ph.D., 1892); in 1899 he became privat-docent for church history and titular professor at Berlin, and in 1910 assistant professor in church history. He is also an attaché of the Royal Prussian Academy of Sciences, engaged in the investigation of early Christian literature, particularly Coptic. He has been associate editor of *Texte und Untersuchungen* with A. Harnack since 1906, and has written *De codice Bruciano seu de libris gnosticis qui in lingua coptica extant commentatio* (Leipsic, 1892); *Gnostische Schriften in koptischer Sprache aus dem Codex Brucianus* (1892); *Plotins Stellung zum Gnostizismus und kirchlichen Christentum* (1901); *Fragmente einer Schrift des Märtyrerbischofs Petrus von Alexandrien* (1901); *Die alten Petrusakten* (1903); *Acta Pauli aus der Heidelberger Papyrushandschrift* (1904); *Koptisch-gnostische Schriften* (1905); *Der erste Clemensbrief in altkoptischer Uebersetzung* (1908); and *Altchristliche Texte* (1910; in collaboration with Schubert).

SCHMIDT, CHARLES GUILLAUME ADOLPHE: Evangelical church historian; b. at Strasburg June 20, 1812; d. there Mar. 11, 1895. Even in his earlier period of instruction, which was passed in the Protestant gymnasium of his native city, he manifested an unusual interest in national and local history, and also in botany and mineralogy. In 1828 he entered the Protestant Seminary, and his tendency grew into marked preference for church history. In 1833 on his travels he went to Geneva, where the sight of the manuscripts of the time of the Reformation, particularly of letters, directed his special attention to that period. After further travels in France, Switzerland, and Germany, he returned and took his examinations, receiving his doctorate after presenting as his thesis *Essai sur les mystiques du XIV. siècle* (Strasburg, 1836), a work which introduced him to a department which he later enriched. Within a few months he began to lecture in the Protestant Seminary of Strasburg; in 1839 he became professor of practical theology, although this department was not one in which his interest was supreme; in this capacity he served in the university 1848-64, when he received the chair of church history which was his first choice. He had, besides, the principal authority in the Protestant Gymnasium, 1849-59 and 1865-69. His strength was also drawn upon for numerous services in other directions to the advantage of the city.

Schmidt's literary works appeared now in the German and now in the French language. They fall into four groups, which represent four departments of church history. The first is that which deals with church history at large, in which may be placed *Essai historique sur la société civile dans le monde romain et sur sa transformation par le christianisme* (Strasburg, 1853; Eng. transl., *The Social Results of Early Christianity*, London, 1885), which was crowned by the French Academy; thirty years later he finished his literary labors with a work in this department, his *Précis de l'histoire de l'église d'occident pendant le moyen-âge* (1888). The second group is that which has to do with the Church of the Middle Ages, and contains a series of monographs devoted to the various sects and to the mystics of the period. Here belong his thesis for the doctorate already mentioned: *Meister Eckart* (1839); *Essai sur J. Gerson* (1839); *Johannes Tauler von Strassburg* (Hamburg, 1841); *Der Mystiker Heinrich Suso* (1843); *Essai sur le mysticisme allemand au XIV. siècle* (Strasburg, 1847); *Die Gottesfreunde im 14. Jahrhundert* (Jena, 1854); *Rulman Merswin, le fondateur de la maison de Saint-Jean de Strasbourg* (Strasburg, 1856); *Nicolaus von Basel und die Gottesfreunde* (1856); *Nicolaus von Basel, Leben und ausgewählte Schriften* (1866); and *Nicolaus von Basel, Bericht von der Bekehrung Taulers* (1875); in these there was steady progress and change in opinion, as the author was not averse to learning from his contemporaries. His chief work in this department was *Histoire et doctrine de la secte des Cathares ou Albigeois* (2 vols., Paris, 1849), in which he laid the basis for future expositions. A third group is related to the Reformation in Germany and France. Here are to be noted *Gérard Roussel, prédicateur de la reine Marguerite de Navarre* (Strasburg, 1845); *La Vie et les travaux de Jean Sturm* (1855); and three volumes contributed to the series on the founders and fathers of the Lutheran and Reformed churches—*Peter Martyr Vermigli* (Elberfeld, 1858); *Philipp Melanchthon* (1861); and *Wilhelm Farel and Peter Viret* (1861). Besides these and other writings, a noteworthy series of articles was contributed to the *Theologische Studien und Kritiken*. The fourth group dealt with local history, to which the last twenty-five years of his life were given. Here may be named *Histoire du chapitre de Saint-Thomas de Strasbourg pendant le moyen-âge* (Strasburg, 1860); *Histoire littéraire de l'Alsace à la fin du XV. et au commencement du XVI. siècle* (2 vols., Paris, 1879; crowned by the French Academy); *Michael Schütz genannt Toxites* (1888); and *Livres et bibliothèques à Strasbourg au moyen âge* (1893). Schmidt was engaged all his life, more or less, upon the gathering of other materials which he playfully designated as "hours with the muse," and these in the course of time grew into greater or lesser wholes. Such were his *Strassburger Gassen- und Häuser-Namen im Mittelalter* (2d ed., 1888); *Wörterbuch der Strassburger Mundart* (1896); and *Les Seigneurs, les paysans et la propriété rurale en Alsace au moyen âge* (1897), the last two posthumous.

The foregoing by no means exhausts Schmidt's literary productivity, not to mention his numerous reviews and other more or less ephemeral writings. Enough has been said to exhibit his exceedingly great diligence. Commensurate with this was his fulness of knowledge, the thoroughness which he displayed in research, and the reliability which was the result. There was also a strong personal reserve or modesty, and a dislike for the rhetorical. He also exhibited pronounced personal piety, a mild and tolerant personality, and a manly earnestness. His later years found him growing, as he more and more appreciated Lutheranism, in opposition to Rome and in antipathy to Zwinglian spiritism. He outgrew also his early partiality for Romanticism. With him departed the last representative of the early generation of Strasburg theologians who, before the Franco-Prussian War, acted as mediators between German and French theology, whose influence extended beyond the scene of their labors.

(P. Lobstein.)

Bibliography: A sketch of Schmidt's life was furnished by R. Reuss to the *Journal d'Alsace*, Mar., 1895, and reprinted separately, Strasburg, the same year. The same writer provided a preface drawn from Schmidt's remains to the *Wörterbuch*, ut sup., and further material was provided by Pfister prefatorially in *Les Seigneurs*, pp. v.-xxxv.

SCHMIDT, FREDERICK AUGUSTUS: Lutheran; b. at Leutenberg (68 m. s.w. of Leipsic), Germany, Jan. 3, 1837. He was brought as a child to the United States, and received his education at Concordia College, St. Louis (B.A., 1857); entered the Lutheran ministry as pastor of the German Congregation, Eden, N. Y., where he served, 1857-1859; was pastor of St. Peter's Lutheran Church, Baltimore, 1859-61; professor in the Luther College, Decorah, Ia., 1861-72; professor of theology at Concordia Seminary, St. Louis, 1872-76; at Madison, Wis., 1876-86, at Northfield, Minn., 1886-1890, and since 1890 at the Seminary of the United Norwegian Lutheran Church, Minneapolis; he also edited *The Lutheran Watchman*, 1865-66, *Altes und Neues*, 1880-85, and *Lutherske Vidnesbyrd*, 1882-88.

SCHMIDT, HERMANN CHRISTOPH: German Lutheran; b. at Frickenhofen (a village near Gaildorf, 31 m. n.e. of Stuttgart) Feb. 23, 1832; d. at Breslau Nov. 19, 1893. He was educated at Tübingen (1850-54), where, after having been vicar at Korb and private tutor at Berlin and Danzig, he was lecturer in 1858-61. He was then city vicar of Stuttgart until 1863, acting as general supply to the clergy, and in the latter year was called in a similar capacity to Calw, where he remained until 1869, sturdily opposing the local Pietism with the supranaturalism which characterized his theological position throughout his life, but unable to influence the people generally. From 1869 to 1881 he was attached to the Leonhardskirche at Breslau. Here he also took an active part in practical religious life, especially in the Innere Mission (q.v.), being president of the South German conference after 1869 and publishing at Hamburg in 1879 his *In-*

nere Mission in Württemberg. In 1881 Schmidt was called to Breslau as professor of systematic and practical theology and New-Testament exegesis, a position which he held until his death. After 1886 he was also a member of the Posen examining committee, and until his death he served as university preacher. His program was outlined in his *Die Kirche, ihre biblische Idee und die Formen ihrer geschichtlichen Erscheinung in ihrem Unterschiede vom Sekte und Häresie* (Leipsic, 1884), in which he held that the Church is a constant magnitude, while heresy destroys the fundamental distinction between the kingdom of God (or the Church) and the world, a gap which is bridged by sectarianism. All heresy is prefigured in Gnosticism, and all sectarianism in Ebionism and Montanism, while the phenomena of modern theology are closely akin to this prototype of heresy, which, like modern rationalism, has always rejected the concept of supranaturalistic revelation. He became, therefore, more and more an opponent of Ritschl and his school, but he was unable to carry out his intention of presenting his own doctrinal system in detail, although his contributions to theological periodicals and to the earlier editions of the original of this work make his position plain.

In addition to the works already noted, Schmidt was the author of a *Handbuch der Symbolik* (Berlin, 1890) and of a series of essays collected under the title *Zur Christologie* (1892). In 1891, after having repeatedly been the delegate of the faculty to the provincial synod of Posen, he was elected to the general synod. Constantly defending the independence of his communion, even to the last year of his life, he was rector of the university in 1891–92, but his struggle with the school-laws and the opposition of the majority of the faculty to his attitude impaired his health, which had already suffered from the death of his eldest son. (E. Schmidt.)

Bibliography: G. Weitbrecht, in *NKZ*, 1894, pp. 510–534.

SCHMIDT, NATHANIEL: Ethical culturist; b. at Hudiksvall (170 m. n.n.e. of Stockholm), Sweden, May 22, 1862. He was educated at the gymnasium of his native town, Colgate University (A.B., 1882; A.M., 1887), and the universities of Stockholm (1882–84) and Berlin (1890). From 1888 to 1896 he was connected with Colgate University, where he was successively associate professor of Semitic languages and Hellenistic Greek (1888–90) and professor of Semitic languages and literatures (1890–1896), and since 1896 has been professor of Semitic languages and literatures in Cornell University. He was director of the American School for Oriental Study and Research in Palestine (1904–05) and of the expedition for the exploration of the Dead Sea and Arabia Petra in 1905. In theology he belongs to the radical school, and has written *The Prophet of Nazareth* (New York, 1905); and *The Message of the Poets; the Book of Job and Canticles, and some minor Poems in the Old Testament* (1911); besides editing Ecclesiasticus for *The Temple Bible* (London, 1903).

SCHMIDT, PAUL WILHELM: Swiss Protestant; b. at Berlin Dec. 25, 1845. He was educated at the university of his native city, where he was privat-docent (1869–76); editor of the *Protestantische Kirchenzeitung* (1870–76); and general secretary of the Deutscher Protestantenverein (1874–76). Since 1876 he has been professor of New-Testament exegesis and dogmatics in the University of Basel. In addition to his activity as one of the collaborators on the New-Testament section of the *Protestanten-Bibel* (Leipsic, 1873; Eng. transl. by F. H. Jones, *A Short Protestant Commentary on the Books of the New Testament*, 3 vols., London, 1882–84), he has written *Spinoza und Schleiermacher* (Berlin, 1868); *Neutestamentliche Hyperkritik, an dem jüngsten Angriff gegen die Aechtheit des Philipperbriefes auf ihre Methode hin untersucht, nebst einer Erklärung des Briefes* (1880); *Der erste Thessalonicherbrief neu erklärt, nebst einem Excurs über den zweiten gleichnamigen Brief* (1885); *Christentum und Weltverneinung* (Basel, 1888); *Anmerkungen über die Komposition der Offenbarung Johannes* (Freiburg, 1891); and *Geschichte Jesu* (vol. i., Tübingen, 1900; 4th ed., 1904; vol. ii., 1904; popular ed., 1 vol., 1906).

SCHMIDT, WILHELM: German Protestant; b. at Erfurt June 6, 1839. He was educated at the universities of Marburg and Halle (Ph.D., Jena, 1863); was pastor at Schönstadt (1866), Henschleben (1866–74), and Cürtow (1874–94); being also chaplain in the army and in the hospital at Creuznach in 1870–71. Since 1894 he has been professor of systematic theology in the University of Breslau. His works include *Zur Inspirationsfrage* (Gotha, 1869); *Die göttliche Vorsehung und das Selbstleben der Welt* (Berlin, 1887); *Das Gewissen* (Leipsic, 1889); *Der alte Glaube und die Wahrheit des Christentums* (Berlin, 1891); *Christliche Dogmatik* (2 parts, Bonn, 1895–98); *Die Lehre des Apostels Paulus* (Gütersloh, 1898); *Der Kampf der Weltanschauungen* (Berlin, 1904); *Der Kampf um die sittliche Welt* (Gütersloh, 1906); *Die Forderung einer modernen positiven Theologie in kritischer Beleuchtung* (1906); *Moderne Theologie des alten Glaubens in kritischer Beleuchtung* (1906); *Der Kampf um den Sinn des Lebens von Dante bis Ibsen* (2 parts, Berlin, 1907); *Die verschiedenen Typen der religiösen Erfahrung und der Psychologie* (1908); and *Der Kampf um die Seele* (1909).

SCHMIDT, WOLDEMAR GOTTLOB: German Protestant theologian; b. at St. Afra in Meissen (14 m. n.w. of Dresden) June 2, 1836; d. at Leipsic Jan. 31, 1888. He studied at Leipsic and Göttingen, 1854–57; taught at the Gymnasia of Plauen, Zwickau, and St. Afra, 1858–66, when he became extraordinary professor in the University of Leipsic, full professor in 1876. His subjects covered mainly the New Testament, but he lectured also on theological encyclopedia and catechetics, also directing two catechetical societies. Owing to his multiplied academic activity, Schmidt found but little time for authorship. His most extensive work in this field is his *Lehrgehalt des Jacobus-Briefes* (Leipsic, 1869); he also edited Ephesians in the 5th edition of Meyer's Commentary. His lesser publications include a printed address on the dogma of the Incarnation (1865), and a Reformation anniversary program of 1882, on the narrative concerning Stephen in the Book of Acts. In these writings he evinced the thorough, incisive, and yet contained style of treatment that he showed in the professor's chair. C. T. Ficker.

SCHMIEDEL, shmî'del, PAUL WILHELM: German Protestant; b. at Zaukeroda (40½ m. s.w. of Dresden), Germany, Dec. 22, 1851. He was educated at the universities of Leipsic (1871–74) and Jena (1874–75; lic. theol., 1878), and in 1878 became privat-docent for theology at Jena, where he was appointed associate professor in 1890. Since 1893 he has been professor of New-Testament exegesis at the University of Zurich. In theology he is a moderate liberal, and has written *Quæ intercedat ratio inter doctrinam epistolæ ad Hebræos missæ et Pauli apostoli doctrinam* (Jena, 1878); *Briefe an die Thessalonier und Corinther* (Freiburg, 1891); *Johannesschriften des Neuen Testaments* (2 parts, Halle, 1906; Eng. transl., *The Johannine Writings*, London, 1908); and *Die Person Jesu im Streite der Meinungen der Gegenwart* (Berlin, 1906; Eng. transl., *Jesus in Modern Criticism*, London, 1907); has edited R. Seydel's *Religionsphilosophie* (1893); and has prepared a new edition of G. B. Winer's *Grammatik des neutestamentlichen Sprachidioms* (2 parts, Göttingen, 1894–98).

SCHMOLCK, shmolk (SCHMOLKE), BENJAMIN: German hymnist; b. at Brauchitschdorf, Liegnitz (38 m. w. of Breslau), Dec. 21, 1672; d. at Schweidnitz (32 m. s.w. of Breslau) Feb. 12, 1737. He studied at Leipsic, 1693–97; and, after acting as his father's assistant till 1702, spent the rest of his life in ministerial work at Schweibnitz, though suffering from paralysis after 1735. As a hymn-writer he was influenced by the Silesian school of poetry. He was fond of plays on words, and treated the Old Testament from the point of view of allegory. In meter and in rime he showed freedom and a light hand, but deep poetical feeling and thought were often lacking, and subjectivity characterizes his work. His literary production was large, his hymns alone number nearly 900. His compositions show the character of occasional versification, but some of the best of his hymns are still in use. Several of his hymns have been rendered into English; so his "Mein Jesu, wie du willst," Eng. transl. by Miss Borthwick, "My Jesus, as thou wilt"; "Was Gott thut das ist wohlgethan," Eng. transl. by J. Kelly, "Whatever God doth is well done."

(Hermann Beck.)

Bibliography: A 2d ed. of his *Lieder und Gebete*, ed. L. Grote, with a valuable biography, appeared Leipsic, 1860. Consult further: E. E. Koch, *Geschichte des Kirchenlieds*, v. 463 sqq., 3d ed., 6 vols., Stuttgart, 1866–80; S. W. Duffield, *English Hymns*, pp. 371–372 et passim, New York, 1886; H. Beck, *Die religiöse Volkslitteratur der evangelischen Kirche Deutschlands*, Gotha, 1891; C. Grosse, *Die alten Tröster*, Hermannsburg, 1900; W. Nelle, *Geschichte des deutschen Kirchenliedes*, pp. 533 sqq., Hamburg, 1904; Julian, *Hymnology*, pp. 1011–1014.

SCHMUCKER, shmuk'er, BEAL MELANCHTHON: Lutheran, son of Samuel Simon Schmucker (q.v.); b. at Gettysburg, Pa., Aug. 26, 1827; d. in Pottstown, Pa., Oct. 18, 1888. He was graduated from Pennsylvania College (1844), and the Theological Seminary of his native town (1847); and served the Lutheran congregations at Martinsburg and Shepherdstown, Va. (1848–51), Allentown, Pa., (1852–62), Easton (1862–67), Reading (1867–81), and Pottstown, Pa. (1881–88). It was particularly through his intimate friendship with Charles Porterfield Krauth (q.v.) that his theological convictions developed into the very opposite of those of his father. He became a strong defender of historic Lutheranism and was one of the pillars of the General Council. His attitude in the doctrinal controversies of the American Lutheran Church of his time is clearly set forth in the charge which he delivered to the professors at the installation of the first faculty of the Theological Seminary in Philadelphia Oct. 4, 1864: "The Confessions of the Evangelical Lutheran Church stand out prominently in the inner history of the Christian Church as the most full, clear, precisely defined, and harmoniously developed system of doctrine which, by the help of the Holy Ghost, men have yet builded upon the only foundation of the Apostles and Prophets, Jesus Christ himself being the Chief Cornerstone." His strength lay in the carefulness and thoroughness with which he labored in the various important interests committed to him, and the fine tact and parliamentary adroitness with which he represented them in ecclesiastical conventions. To the end of his life he served as secretary of the board of directors of the theological seminary, and as secretary of the board of foreign missions of the General Council. But he was most prominent in the field of liturgics. His knowledge of details in matters pertaining to the order of service, especially of the Lutheran Church of the sixteenth and seventeenth centuries, was unusually extensive and accurate, and the excellent *Church Book* of the General Council (1868) is greatly indebted to him. As secretary of the Church Book Committee he gradually collected for their work a liturgical library of inestimable value, which is now preserved in the Krauth Memorial Library of the Lutheran Seminary at Philadelphia. To him, more than to any other man, is due the success which has crowned the efforts to secure the common service for English Lutherans in America. He proposed the adoption of the principle that all important questions were to be decided according to the consensus of the Lutheran liturgies of the sixteenth century. Schmucker was also an indefatigable, painstaking, and thorough investigator in the field of local history of Lutheran Churches in America. For years he gathered much and valuable material in this line, and became assistant editor in the new edition of the *Halle'sche Nachrichten* by W. J. Mann and W. German. He made contributions to the theological magazines which are of permanent value to the historian and appeared also as separate pamphlets. The following deserve to be noted particularly: *The First Pennsylvania Liturgy, Adopted in 1748* (1882); *The Early History of the Tulpehocken Churches* (1882); *The Lutheran Church in Pottstown* (1882); *The Lutheran Church in Frederick, Maryland* (in *Quarterly Review*, 1883); *The Lutheran Church in the City of New York during the First Century of its History* (in *Church Review*, 1884–85);

The Lutheran Catechism. Its Translation into English (1886); *English Translations of the Augsburg Confession* (1887); *The Organization of the Lutheran Congregation in the Early Lutheran Church in America* (1887); *The Lutheran Church in York, Pa.* (1888). ADOLPH SPAETH.

BIBLIOGRAPHY: A memorial by A. Spaeth appeared in the *Lutheran Church Review* for 1889. Consult further: H. E. Jacobs, *American Church History Series*, vol. iv. passim, New York, 1893; A. Spaeth, *Charles Porterfield Krauth*, vol. i., ib. 1898.

SCHMUCKER, SAMUEL SIMON: Lutheran theologian; b. at Hagerstown, Md., Feb. 28, 1799; d. at Gettysburg, Pa., July 26, 1873. He studied at the academy at York, Pa., the University of Pennsylvania (B.A., 1817), and Princeton Theological Seminary. He was ordained by the synod of Maryland and Virginia in 1821, and served a parish in New Market, Va., and vicinity, up to the year 1826. When the General Synod, founded in 1821, established its theological seminary at Gettysburg, Pa., in 1825, he was called to the head of the institution and for four years was the only theological instructor. Subsequently Charles Philip Krauth and Charles Frederick Schaeffer (qq.v.) were associated with him. After nearly forty years of service he resigned in 1864. About 400 students received their training chiefly under his influence.

He was one of the most prolific writers of the American Lutheran Church, setting forth the standpoint which he represented as a teacher in the seminary, and endeavoring to disseminate its principles by a series of more or less popular writings, such as his *Elements of Popular Theology* (Andover, 1834, 9th ed., Philadelphia, 1860); *Psychology, or Elements of a New System of Mental Philosophy* (New York, 1842); *The Lutheran Manual on Scriptural Principles* (Philadelphia, 1855); *The Lutheran Symbols, or Vindication of American Lutheranism* (Baltimore, 1856), and dissertations, sermons, and articles in *The Lutheran Observer* and *The Evangelical Review*. He was particularly interested in the problem of a union of all Protestant denominations. As early as 1838 he issued an appeal to the American churches, with a plan for a general union. Later he took a prominent part in the organization of the Evangelical Alliance and was present at the first meeting in London, 1846. His last production, *The Unity of Christ's Church* (New York, 1870) was devoted to its interests, written in view of its approaching convention in New York, 1873.

Dr. Schmucker, on the one side, exerted a decided and positive influence toward holding together and organizing the Lutheran Church in this country. At the same time, he occupied a position foreign to and actually destructive of the true spirit of Lutheranism, if the fundamental question of the confession and its historical continuity be considered. At the time when he began his active labors the Lutheran Church in this country was threatened with disintegration. German rationalism and English deism had affected the Lutherans, though not to the same extent as other Protestant denominations. In New York the Lutherans fraternized with [illegible]nis with the Reformed. [illegible]he English language had arrived. But there was no English Lutheran literature, and no seminary where pastors could be educated to preach the Lutheran faith in the English tongue. At this point young Schmucker, with his unquestionable talent for organization and administration, put forth his most energetic efforts to secure for the Lutheran Church in America a continued existence and a respected place among the Protestant denominations of the country. The preservation of the General Synod, the founding of its educational institutions, the Theological Seminary and Pennsylvania College at Gettysburg, are owing chiefly to his self-sacrificing labors. And these institutions were meant to be of a conservative character, to construct and preserve Lutheranism in America. But, on the other hand, his influence as professor of theology tended to unsettle and invalidate the historic confessional basis of the Lutheran Church. According to his conviction it was the vocation of the American Lutheran Church to free herself from all respect "for the authority of the fathers, whether they be Nicene or Ante-Nicene, Roman or Protestant." He strove to eliminate everything distinctively Lutheran and to substitute the basis of the Evangelical Alliance for the Augsburg Confession and Luther's Catechism. These tendencies culminated in the *Definite Platform* which he published anonymously in 1855. It claimed to be an "American Recension of the Augsburg Confession," representing the standpoint of the General Synod. In this document twelve of the original twenty-one doctrinal articles of the Augsburg Confession were changed, mutilated, or entirely omitted. The seven articles on abuses (XXII. to XXVIII.) were all omitted. Dr. Schmucker's theological standpoint may be characterized as a peculiar mixture of Puritanism, Pietism, and shallow rationalism. His *Definite Platform* was never formally adopted by the General Synod, though many prominent men in it sympathized with its spirit. It rather paved the way to a reaction in favor of the Lutheran Confession. ADOLPH SPAETH.

BIBLIOGRAPHY: *Pennsylvania College Book*, ed. E. S. Breidenbach, Philadelphia, 1882; H. E. Jacobs, *American Church History Series*, vol. iv. passim, New York, 1893; A. Spaeth, *Charles Porterfield Krauth*, vol. i., ib. 1898.

SCHNECKENBURGER, shnek'en-bürg"er, **MATTHIAS:** German Swiss Protestant; b. at Thalheim, near Tuttlingen (55 m. s.s.w. of Stuttgart), Jan. 17, 1804; d. at Bern June 13, 1848. He was educated at the universities of Tübingen and Berlin, returning to the former university as theological lecturer in 1827. He became assistant pastor at Herrenberg, 1821, and professor of theology at the newly founded university of Bern in 1834, lecturing primarily on church history and systematic theology, and also on New-Testament exegesis. He also shared the chair in dogmatics with Gelpke and Lutz, his province being ecclesiastical dogmatics. Here he, essentially a Lutheran, had the delicate task of arranging his courses to meet the needs of Reformed students. He accordingly took as the basis of his lectures on dogmatics the second Helvetic Confession, comparing it with Lutheran theology and with modern dogmatic systems. At the same time, the Reformed atmosphere of Bern exercised a constantly increasing effect on Schneckenburger himself, especially as neither the political conditions nor the religious thought of the period at Bern were conducive to the one-sided intellectualism of German universities. Broadening the scope of his lectures, Schneckenburger dealt with apologetics, the philosophy of religion, the influence of philosophy on theology since the time of Descartes, and the conflict of modern thought with Christianity. In the latter subject Schneckenburger assumed a strongly theistic position and opposed Hegelianism. He likewise investigated with ever-increasing interest the divergencies between Lutheran and Reformed doctrine, as set forth in his lectures on symbolics. For the six last years of his life, inspired both by the rise of the Old Lutheran movement and by his position as a Lutheran teaching Reformed dogmatics, he devoted himself especially to a study of early Reformed theology and its various schools, developing his views in courses of lectures on comparative dogmatics. With all this activity Schneckenburger never lost interest in the practical work of the Church, and was for many years a director of the missionary society founded under his inspiration. Among his writings were: *Ueber Glauben, Tradition und Kirche* (Stuttgart, 1827); *Ueber das Alter der jüdischen Proselytentaufe und deren Zusammenhang mit dem johanneischen und christlichen Ritus* (Berlin, 1828); *Beiträge zur Einleitung ins Neue Testament* (1832); *Ueber das Evangelium der Aegypter* (Bern, 1834); *Ueber den Zweck der Apostelgeschichte* (1841); and *Die orthodoxe Lehre vom doppelten Stande Christi nach lutherischer und reformierter Fassung* (Pforzheim, 1848).

(C. B. Hundeshagen†.)

Bibliography: E. F. Gelpke, *Gedächtnissrede auf . . . Matth. Schneckenburger, gehalten . . . 16. Juni, 1848. Nebst der Grabrede von E. Wyss*, Bern, 1848.

SCHNEDERMANN, shnē'der-mān" **GEORG HERMANN**: German Lutheran; b. at Chemnitz (43 m. s.e. of Leipsic), Saxony, July 3, 1862. He was educated at the universities of Leipsic and Erlangen (1872–75; Ph.D., Leipsic, 1878), and after being a private tutor (1875–77), was attached to the theological seminary at Leipsic until 1879. In 1880 he became privat-docent for New-Testament exegesis at the University of Leipsic, and three years later (1883) went to Basel under the auspices of the Verein für christliche Wissenschaft as instructor in systematic theology. Returning to Leipsic in 1889 as instructor in New-Testament exegesis and systematic theology, he was appointed, in the following year, to his present position of associate professor of dogmatics and catechetics, being also director of the catechetical seminary and second university preacher. Besides editing F. Weber's *System der altsynagogalen palästinischen Theologie* (in collaboration with F. Delitzsch; Leipsic, 1880); and *Beiträge zur Vertiefung der kirchlichen Unterweisung* (in collaboration with M. Pache; 1903), he has written *Die Controverse des Ludovicus Capellus mit den Buxtorfen über das Alter der hebräischen Punctation* (1879); *De fidei notione ethica Paulina* (1880); *Das Judentum und die christliche Verkündigung in den Evangelien* (1884); *Die Briefe Pauli an die Thessalonicher, Galater, Korinther, Römer* (in O. Zöckler and H. Strack's *Kurzgefasster Kommentar;* Nördlingen, 1887); *Die Gefangenschaftsbriefe des Apostels Paulus* (in the same series, 1888); *Von dem Bestande unserer Gemeinschaft mit Gott durch Jesum Christum* (1888); *Ringet darnach, dass ihr stille seid* (3 sermons; 1889); *Das moderne Christentum, sein Recht und sein Unrecht* (Leipsic, 1889); *Der jüdische Hintergrund im Neuen Testament* (1890); *Frank und Ritschl* (1891); *Vorstellung vom Reiche Gottes* (2 parts, 1893); *Von rechter Verdeutschung der Evangelien* (1896); *Unzulänglichkeit der gegenwärtigen kirchlichen Unterweisung* (1897); *Der christliche Glaube im Sinne der gegenwärtigen evangelischen lutherischen Kirche* (1902); *Das Wort vom Kreuze, religionsgeschichtlich und dogmatisch beleuchtet* (Gütersloh, 1906); *Ohne des Gesetzes Werk. Eine Anleitung zu selbstständigen geschichtlichem Verständniss des Neuen Testaments* (1907); and *Die heilige Schrift im Religionsunterricht* (1909).

SCHNEPFF, shnepf, **ERHARD**: German Reformer; b. at Heilbronn (26 m. n. of Stuttgart) Nov. 1, 1495; d. in Jena Nov. 1, 1558. He studied at Erfurt and Heidelberg; taught in the latter city and possibly heard Luther's disputation there Apr. 26, 1518. When Œcolampadius resigned as preacher at Weinsberg in 1520, Schnepff accepted the post, but was expelled by the Austrian government because of his Evangelical preaching in 1522; under the protection of Dieterich von Gemmingen he preached at Guttenberg and Neckarmühlbach, and in 1523 in the little imperial town of Wimpfen. He avoided a call to act as field preacher for the peasants in 1525 by his hasty marriage with Margaretha Wurzelmann, daughter of the mayor of Wimpfen; the same year he signed the *Syngramma Suevicum* (of Brenz) directed against the Œcolampadian doctrine of the sacrament, and before the year ended he was summoned by Count Philip of Nassau to introduce the Reformation in Weilburg. In 1527 Landgrave Philip of Hesse called him to Marburg University, of which he was rector in 1532 and 1534, and took him to the diet at Speyer in 1529, and in 1530 to Augsburg, where he preached frequently till forbidden by the emperor, also taking part in the discussions. His course here was praised for its consistency by Baumgärtner, ambassador of Nuremberg, also for its courage. After Duke Ulrich of Württemberg won back his country in 1534, he called Schnepff together with Ambrosius Blaurer (q.v.) to lead the Reformation. Schnepff was appointed to the Hospital Church in Stuttgart, and successfully accomplished his work in the northern half of the country. While Schnepff and Blaurer agreed regarding the sacrament on the basis of the formula of Mar., 1529, there was no lack of friction and misunderstanding, which brought admonitions to be peaceful from the landgrave, Strasburg, and Melanchthon. On the Urach "idol day," Sept. 16, 1537, with Brenz Schnepff argued against Blaurer for the retention of such church pictures as gave no offense. He accompanied the duke to Vienna, where the latter took the oath to King Ferdinand, and on his return was charged with preparation of forms for church government, revised by Brenz and printed in 1536. In Sept., 1536, he was in Tübingen with Melanchthon, and in Schmalkalden in Feb., 1537, where he signed Luther's articles. In July, 1540, he was sent to a discussion at Hagenau, whence he went to Strasburg and on July 18 preached there in the cathedral. Later he visited Worms, and, in 1541, Regensburg. He joined several of the Württemberg theologians in pronouncing against the landgrave's bigamous marriage; meanwhile his position at court and with the government became insecure, so that in 1539 he was already thinking of going to Saxony. In 1544 he went to Tübingen and was honored with the doctorate, and in February began to act as superintendent of the theological seminary, where he lectured on the Old Testament and on Melanchthon's *Loci*, also preaching with acceptability. In 1546 he carried on a discussion with the Augustinian Johann Hofmeister at Regensburg. On the approach of the Spaniards in the Schmalkald War, Schnepff fled on Jan. 7, 1547, to Blaurer at Constance, but was soon able to return. He did not accept the Interim (q.v.), and said farewell to his flock in a sermon on Nov. 11, 1548, lamented by his people, who formed a procession on his departure, while the duke sent a present. Melanchthon invited him to Wittenberg, but a professorship was offered in the University of Jena, just then being founded, where he soon had a class of sixty students. He undertook the office of superintendent, and became one of the most influential theologians and churchmen in ducal Saxony. Under political pressure he joined in opposition to Melanchthon and broke with his former friends in Württemberg; in the colloquy at Worms the Ernestine theologians delighted the Roman Catholics by their enmity to Brenz and Melanchthon, which caused the breaking off of the colloquy. He avoided intercourse with Brenz, who was his son Dietrich's father-in-law, and with Jakob Andreä, who was formerly his favorite scholar; against Brenz he became violent. Although he took part with Strigel and Hügel (reluctantly) in the *Konfutationsbuch*, he endeavored to make peace between Strigel and Flacius.

A sermon on the wedding feast of the king was printed (Tübingen, 1578); also his *Gutachten für den schmalkaldischen Konvent* (1540); *Konfession etlicher Artikel des Glaubens* (1545); and *Refutatio Majorismi* (Jena, 1555). G. BOSSERT.

BIBLIOGRAPHY: J. Rosa, *Oratio de vita E. Schnepffi*, Leipsic, 1562; M. Adam, *Vitæ Germanorum theologorum*, pp. 320, 578, Heidelberg, 1620; L. M. Fischlin, *Memoria theologorum Wirtembergensium*, i. 9, supplement 8, Ulm, 1709–1710; N. G. Eickhoff, *Die Kirchen-Reformation in Nassau-Weilburg*, Weilburg, 1832; T. Pressel, *Ambrosius Blaurers Leben*, Stuttgart, 1861; J. Hartmann, *Erhard Schnepf, der Reformator*, Tübingen, 1870; J. Ficker, *Thesaurus Baumianus*, Strasburg, 1905; *Briefwechsel der Brüder . . . Blaurer, 1509–48*, ed. T. Schiess, 2 vols., Freiburg, 1908–1910; *ADB*, xxxii. 168 sqq.

SCHNITZER, shnit'zer, **JOSEF**: German Roman Catholic; b. at Lauingen (24 m. n.e. of Ulm), Bavaria, June 15, 1859. He studied at the universities of Munich and Vienna (1889–91); was associate professor of church history and canon law at the Lyceum of Dillingen (1893–1902); accepted, in 1902, the position of professor of the history of dogma, symbolics, and pedagogics at the University of Munich. In 1908, in consequence of his Modernism, he was suspended from exercising all ecclesiastical functions and was given leave of absence as professor. The intention was to transfer him to the philosophical faculty, but this has not yet been done. In addition to preparing the second edition of I. Silbernagl's *Verfassung und gegenwärtiger Bestand sämtlicher Kirchen des Orients* (Regensburg, 1904), he has written *Berengar von Tours, sein Leben und seine Lehre* (Munich, 1890); *Die Gesta Romanæ Ecclesiæ des Kardinals Beno und andere Streitschriften der schismatischen Kardinäle wider Gregor VII.* (Bamberg, 1892); *Katholisches Eherecht* (Freiburg, 1898); *Quellen und Forschungen zur Geschichte Savonarolas* (3 parts, Munich, 1902–1904); and *Hat Jesus das Papsttum gestiftet?* (1910).

SCHNUETGEN, shnüt'gen, **ALEX**: German Roman Catholic; b. at Steele (3 m. e. of Essen) Feb. 22, 1843. He studied at Münster, Tübingen, Louvain, and Mainz (1860–66), and since 1866 has been a member of the clergy staff of Cologne Cathedral, where he has been successively vicar (1866–87) and a member of the chapter (since 1887). He has likewise been honorary professor of Christian archeology at the University of Bonn. Besides editing the *Zeitschrift für christliche Kunst* since 1888, he has collaborated in preparing *Katalog seiner Sammlung von Geweben und Stickereien des Mittelalters und der Renaissance* (Cologne, 1876), and in editing the Ada manuscript of Treves (Leipsic, 1889).

SCHODDE, shod'de, **GEORG HENRY**: Lutheran; b. at Alleghany City, Pa., Apr. 15, 1854. He was graduated from Capital University, Columbus, O. (A.B., 1872), the theological seminary of the same institution (1874), and studied at the universities of Tübingen (1874–75) and Leipsic (Ph.D., 1876). After holding a pastorate in his denomination at Wheeling, W. Va. (1877–82), he was appointed to his present position of professor of Greek at Capital University, and has also been professor of New-Testament exegesis in the theological seminary attached to the same university since 1894. In theology he is a positive conservative Lutheran, and has written *The Protestant Church in Germany* (Philadelphia, 1903). He is editor of the *Theological Magazine* (Columbus, O.) and has translated from the Ethiopic the Book of Enoch (Andover, 1882) and the Book of Jubilees (Oberlin, 1888), and from the German Franz Delitzsch's *Day in Capernaum* (New York, 1887) and B. Weiss's *Religion of the New Testament* (1905) and *Commentary on the New Testament* (2 vols., 1906).

SCHOEBERLEIN, shö'ber-lain, **LUDWIG FRIEDRICH**: German Lutheran; b. at Kolmberg (28 m. w.s.w. of Nuremberg) Sept. 6, 1813; d. at Göttingen July 8, 1881. After studying at Munich and Erlangen, he was a private tutor at Bonn and city vicar at Munich. In 1841 he became theological lecturer and privat-docent at Erlangen, and in 1850 went to Heidelberg as associate professor of theology. From 1855 until his death he was full professor of the same subject at Göttingen, being also consistorial councilor after 1862 and abbot of Bursfelde after 1878. He also served as curator of the Göttingen orphan asylum and member of a liturgical committee and of a hymnal committee for Hanover. His chief writings, which mostly relate to liturgics, were as follows: *Die Grundlehren des Heils, entwickelt aus dem Prinzip der Liebe* (Stuttgart, 1848); *Der evangelische Gottesdienst* (Heidelberg, 1854); *Der evangelische Hauptgottesdienst in Formularen für das ganze Kirchenjahr* (1855); *Ueber den liturgischen Ausbau des Gemeindegottesdienstes in der deutschen evangelischen Kirche* (1859); *Schatz des liturgischen Chor- und Gemeindegesangs nebst den Altarweisen in der deutschen evangelischen Kirche* (3 vols., Göttingen, 1863–72); *Geheimnisse des Glaubens* (Heidelberg, 1872); and *Prinzip und System der Dogmatik* (1881). In 1876 he founded, together with M. Herold and E. Krüger, the periodical *Siona* for the advancement of liturgics and church music. (J. A. Wagenmann†.)

Bibliography: *Allgemeine evangelisch-lutherische Kirchenzeitung*, 1881, no. 29, pp. 688 sqq.; *Siona*, 1881, no. 8, pp. 101 sqq.

SCHOELL, shöl, CARL WILHELM: Lutheran; b. at Guglingen (23 m. n.n.w. of Stuttgart), Württemberg, Aug. 4, 1820; d. in London, May 13, 1899. He was educated at Tübingen; became, in 1846, assistant minister, and in 1859 pastor of the German Lutheran Church in the Savoy, now Cleveland Street, London. He was examiner in the German language and literature to the Military Education Division, War Office, London, from 1858; to the Civil Service Commission, London, from 1864; and in the University of London, 1872–75, and 1882–87. He was the author of *De ecclesiasticæ Britonum Scotorumque historiæ fontibus* (Berlin, 1851).

SCHOENFELDER, shön'fel-der, JOSEF MARIA: German Roman Catholic; b. at Forchheim (9 m. n. of Erlangen), Bavaria, June 8, 1838. He was educated at Bamberg, Erlangen, and Munich, and after being *sacellanus* at Bamberg (1861–65) and professor of theology at Hildesheim (1866–67), was vicar of St. Cajetan's, Munich (1867–71) and court-preacher at St. Michael's in the same city (1871–1874). Since 1869 he has also been connected with the University of Munich, where he has been successively privat-docent (1869–73), associate professor of theology (1873–74), and professor of Biblical oriental languages, Old-Testament introduction, and exegesis (since 1874; emeritus since 1903). He has likewise been canon of St. Cajetan's since 1886. He has written *Die Kirchengeschichte des Johannes von Ephesus* (Munich, 1862); *Salomonis Episcopi Bassorensis Liber Apis* (Bamberg, 1866); *Onkelos und Peschitto* (Munich, 1869); and *Die Klagelieder des Jeremias nach rabbinischer Auslegung* (1887).

SCHOENHERR, schön'her, JOHANN HEINRICH: Theosophist; b. at Memel (74 m. n.e. of Königsberg) Nov. 30, 1770; d. at Königsberg Oct. 15, 1826. After preliminary training at the city school of Angerburg, whither his parents had removed, he was sent to Königsberg for commercial training; but he was averse to this pursuit, and studied in the gymnasium of Königsberg and then entered the university, where he nominally studied law, though his strong liking was for philosophy with a theosophical trend. With but little money, in 1792 he traveled in Germany, visiting Rinteln and Leipsic to study philosophy. On his return he had reached such a degree of self-sufficiency that he felt able, without further study at the university, to expound his views in private. His extreme earnestness gained him friends and the means to propagate his system, and he became marked as a man apart from his contemporaries even in his appearance, for he allowed his beard and hair to grow in literal agreement with Lev. xix. 27. Königsberg was at that time in the throes of a decided rationalism, although nominally devoted to orthodox Lutheran doctrine, and the student body especially was devoted to rationalistic views. So the young theosophist, with a supreme confidence in his mission, expounded what he believed would inaugurate a new era in human knowledge. He conceived himself to be an inspired prophet, and his fundamental principles a new revelation; only the application of these principles to nature, history, and human life would be admit as subjects of discussion, together with the proof of them from the Bible. He gathered about him a circle of scholars, who were to be the seed from which should grow a society renewing humanity. Meetings were held twice a week, on Wednesday and Sunday evenings, for discussion and instruction, to which women were admitted, and a simple meal usually closed the session. In all this there was no thought of personal domination by Schönherr; his only object was the diffusion of his system of knowledge. Nor was there intention to form a sect, and he was himself a regular attendant upon divine service. Once he was threatened with prosecution, but influential interests prevented persecution.

Besides this circle gathered about Schönherr, there was a second which had as its center a gifted disciple named Johann Wilhelm Ebel (q.v.), who had adopted without reserve the teachings of his master. Ebel had become through this system a positive Biblical theologian, and after 1810 preached in Königsberg earnestly on the subjects of sin, grace, and redemption. Possessing a fine presence, great pulpit ability, and an unassuming address, he became the leader in the pulpit of the city. His following was from various circles, but principally from the higher and official classes—a contrast with the immediate following of Schönherr which included students and the humbler classes. The latter was in this environment also the supreme spiritual authority. The separation of the two circles came through the teacher's introduction of the principle of flagellation, based on Gal. v. 24; Ps. lxxxiv. 2; I Cor. xiii. 3; and Heb. xii. 4, which was the "pleasing sacrifice" of Rom. xii. 1. Were not this self-sacrifice offered, a martyr death or bloody sufferings would be required. Ebel opposed this extreme, and the personal friendship of the two came to an end, though Ebel still held to the teaching of his master. After a journey to St. Petersburg in 1823–24, Schönherr grew feeble; this feebleness was increased through self-inflicted castigations and his death soon followed.

His system united profound religious sensibility

to philosophic earnestness; yet in itself it was but a confused dualistic philosophy of nature which would have no enduring interest but for the judicial processes carried through 1835–41 (see EBEL, JOHANN WILHELM) at Königsberg, interest in which is by no means dead, especially in view of the secrecy which still covers the actual proceedings. Schönherr's thinking began with sheer dualism, as he posited two primitive potencies, one active and male, the other passive and female, both personal and possessing intellect, will, form, and color; these were named fire and water, or light and darkness. From the union of these originated the universe, including God—for the system is not merely a cosmogony, it is also a theogony. By an adaptive exegesis of the doctrine of the Trinity and of the Biblical account of creation he sought to justify his system as being in accord with revelation. The account of creation was followed by a most interesting chapter on the fall. Evil arose through the fall of Lucifer (Satan), a being of light created by God, who through envy led the first pair to disobey God; through eating of the fruit of the tree of knowledge there was introduced into the hitherto sinless nature of man the power of darkness; death and misery became man's lot, and as original sin was transmitted to his descendants. Sin made redemption necessary, and through this the harmony of the primitive potencies and of their methods of working is restored. This process was introduced by Jesus Christ, in whom the law of righteousness is embodied and the inworking of Lucifer is abolished, and so the world is released from evil. For the law of righteousness grounded in Christ proceeds from him and passes over into the "primal natures" (*Hauptnaturen*), who are made complete through the Holy Spirit, in whom also Christ is present; by their mediation this law passes over into the "secondary natures"; in the former light is dominant, in the latter, darkness, and this darkness must be striven against by means of fighting, fasting, watching, prayer, and wrestling, and in this way room is made for light. By this course of reasoning Schönherr fell upon a new righteousness of the law. Just as he partly included and partly ignored the simple facts of the life of Christ, so to the teaching of Paul concerning the righteousness which springs from faith he gave no place, reproducing redemption by way of knowledge in the fashion of the early Gnostics (see GNOSTICISM).

Eschatology had an important place in the system. The second coming of Christ was regarded as imminent, since the present is the seventh (and last) period of the development of the kingdom of God. To this theosophist the dreadful events following the outbreak of the French Revolution portended the end; Napoleon was Antichrist, the millennial kingdom was near, and Königsberg with its seven hills was the city of Rev. xvii. 9. With the parousia would come the fulfilling of the kingdom.

In the case of Ebel, in the pulpit the fundamentals of Evangelical Christianity were proclaimed; but in the narrower circle of his immediate disciples the cure of souls was based upon the anthropology of Schönherr. While this circle was small, it was influential. The doctrine of primal and secondary natures was especially stressed, together with emphasis upon knowledge. The secondary natures were to be led to self-consciousness; this was to be accomplished by the open expression of their most secret thoughts, especially of their sins, and this in turn enabled the foreordained ministers of souls to give the advice by which the process of redemption was to be furthered. Thus Ebel gained an unwonted power over souls. But this caused repulsion among certain of those who had at first listened, among whom was Hermann Olshausen (q.v.), opposition sprang up, and the judicial decision soon followed which is summed up in the article on Ebel (q.v.).

(PAUL TSCHACKERT.)

BIBLIOGRAPHY: The writings of Schönherr are the following: *Der Sieg der göttlichen Offenbarung, vorbereitet zum ersten Mal*, Königsberg, 1803; *Vom Siege der göttlichen Offenbarung. Der Erste Sieg* (1804); cf. *Grundzüge der Erkenntniss der Wahrheit aus Heinrich Schönherrs nachgelassenen philosophischen Blättern mit einigen Ergänzungen aus Schriften Anderer*, Leipsic, 1852. On the life and system consult: J. I. Mombert, *Faith Victorious, Being an Account of the Life and Times of the Venerable Dr. Johann Ebel*, pp. 258 sqq., New York, 1882 (contains a very full and useful bibliography of the subject); H. Olshausen, *Lehre und Leben des Königsberger Theosophen Johann Heinrich Schönherr*, Königsberg, 1834 (adverse); Von Wegnern, in *ZHT*, viii (1838), 106–233; E. von Hasenfeld, *Die religiöse Bewegung zu Königsberg*, Braunsberg, 1858; Ernst Graf von Kanitz, *Aufklärung nach Aktenquellen über den 1835–42 zu Königsberg . . . geführten Religionsprozess*, Basel, 1862; F. Zimmer, in *ZWT*, xliv (1901), 253–312; *ADB*, v. 519 sqq.

SCHOETTGEN, shöt'gen, **JOHANN CHRISTIAN**: German New-Testament scholar and philologist; b. at Wurzen (15 m. e. of Leipsic) Mar. 14, 1687; d. at Dresden Dec. 15, 1751. He studied at the Saxon state school at Pforta and at the University of Leipsic, where he also lectured. In 1716 he assumed the rectorship of the Latin school at Frankfort-on-the-Oder; in 1719 went to Stargard in Pomerania as rector professor of humane letters at the Gröningisches Kollegium and also as rector of another school there; and in 1728 to Dresden, as rector of the Kreuzschule. He was an exceedingly fruitful author, especially in New-Testament exegesis, in which he sought to utilize his rabbinic knowledge. He was a well-grounded philologist, and an authority on the local history of Upper Saxony. His chief work, displaying his abilities as an exegete and his profound rabbinic information, is *Horæ Hebraicæ et talmudicæ in universum N. T., quibus horæ I. Lightfooti in libris historicis supplentur, epistolæ et apocalypsis eodem modo illustrantur* (Dresden, 1733). In 1742 there appeared: *Horæ hebraicæ et talmudicæ in theologiam Judæorum dogmaticam antiquam et orthodoxam de Messia impensæ*. Of less importance was his *Novum lexicon Græco-Latinum in N. T.* (Leipsic, 1746; new ed. by J. F. Krebs, 1765; another by G. L. Spohr, 1790). His edition of the Greek New Testament (1744) is a recasting of the text of Gleditsch (1735) with peculiar text divisions and tabulated contents. The *Opuscula* issued by Grundig (1766) contain his outlines for local, school, and Reformation history. Schoetigen was a typical exponent of an age which has been designated as the cradle of the entire body of Old-Testament science along modern lines. GEORG MUELLER.

BIBLIOGRAPHY. K. Gautsch, in *Archiv für sächsische Geschichte*, new series, iv. 328–351; *ADB*, xxxii. 412–417.

SCHOLASTICISM.

I. Introduction: The term scholasticism is commonly used to designate the scientific theology of the Middle Ages, from the eleventh to the sixteenth century. As an index of the scope of this theology may be mentioned the notice by Johannes Pitseus in *De illustribus Angliæ scriptoribus* (Paris, 1619), who counts 160 English commentators upon the "Sentences" of Peter Lombard (q.v.); 152 commentaries were produced by the Dominicans, almost as many by the Minorites, not to speak of other works. Distinguished from exegetical, homiletical, and practical works, and heretical literature, the term scholasticism applies to what is now known as systematic theology, or dogmatics; and all the schoolmen of the varying tendencies represented orthodox church doctrine. By the reform theologians at the conclusion of the Middle Ages, the Humanists, and the Reformers, the prevalent dogmatics and its method was stigmatized as "school theology," and characterized as empty formalism, and untheological speculation, subtle and pedantic, in contrast with vital considerations held to be practical and religious, or a theology based on the Bible. From this point of view resulted its unjustified depreciation as well as the incorrect adverse parallelism of scholastic and mystical theology. Scholasticism and mysticism, however, represent a relation similar to that of dogmatics and religious contemplation. The latter also gives rise to theoretical explanations, as a rule referred to as "mystical"; yet, in the nature of the case, they qualify themselves as the descriptions of soul states, the antecedents of Christian ethics. Although they are in contrast with scholastic methods, they are not incompatible with them and their object was, with the aid of speculative inquiry, the analysis of church doctrine. The adverse judgment is also incompetent, because, instead of applying pure historical standards, it is pronounced from the point of view of present-day philosophy and the religious antithesis of the time of the Reformation. A correct judgment can arise only from a due historical appreciation of the religious, ecclesiastical, and scientific conditions from which scholasticism proceeded. Such a review will lead to the verdict that scholasticism fixed its vision firmly upon the loftiest goals of human knowledge, and that it strove for their attainment with a marvelous and untiring acumen, faithfully availing itself of all means at its command. That the religious and secular knowledge of the times imposed limitations is self-evident. And that in this work, many of its virtues cast their shadows, and that the spontaneous activity of its spirit gradually crystallized in forms and stagnated into fruitless exercises of a purely formal mental acuteness is not characteristic of scholasticism alone. Nay, rather at the climax of its movement was there such an abundance of strenuous earnest thinking and a measure of enthusiastic devotion as has not elsewhere appeared in all the ages of the history of theology, and its original thinkers in number and eminence have in all probability not since then been surpassed.

II. Preparation: The history antecedent to scholasticism is the whole theology of the earlier Middle Ages. This period took over Christianity in the shape of fixed formulated doctrines, and the representatives of these doctrines were at the same time the exponents of education and higher culture. The Church clothed its doctrines with divine authority. In accordance therewith the great theological teachers of the early Middle Ages would submit in their manuals only summaries of patristic theology and citations from the Fathers. Augustine and Gregory the Great (qq.v.) were the masters whose thoughts or even words were adopted bodily. Controversies were waged over the understanding of the authorities, not over the matter in question. Theology in the early Middle Ages may be described on the whole as traditionalism. But the vital development of church life demanded of theology new practical and ceremonial forms, and the interest to understand the traditional stuff made itself felt from an inner necessity. If the delivered doctrines were sacred and inviolable, only one form of their appropriation was possible; namely, the proof of their rationality and the recognition of their unity. Orthodox positiveness assumed a rationalistic character; the more so inasmuch as ancient philosophy and the doctrines of the Church had been handed down most closely combined. The proof of the rationality or tenability of church doctrine consistent with a systematic philosophy—this formed the program of an enormous intellectual task; it was the labor of scholasticism. Confined to a fixed group of "given" subjects, hemmed in by sacred tradition, and not without stumbling, with ever so many modifications, fresh departures,

1. Orthodoxy and Philosophy.

and concessions to the old, slowly and surely reason gained its position alongside of authority. Then, of a sudden, the silent development was precipitated by the wide-spread sensation caused by Berengar of Tours' (q.v.) impassioned criticism of the doctrine of the Eucharist, in which reason and dialectic alone were to be the arbiters of truth. The defense of authority itself employed such dialectic subtleties as the distinction between the permanent accidents of the bread and its temporary substance. The more and more flourishing school system of cathedral and cloister, the itinerant restlessness of scholars, the attraction of brilliant teachers—all combined speedily to disseminate scientific theology.

2. Anselm and Abelard. At this point two mighty spirits entered the current, creating two methods that governed scientific work for a long time to come. These were Anselm of Canterbury and Abelard (qq.v.). Anselm's method is marked by the following points: (1) he was a realist, i.e., the champion of the reality of the universal; of species and genus, of concept and idea. These universals are objective realities, not merely a *flatus vocis*, "blast of sound," or pure subjective images. Upon this hinged the battle throughout the Middle Ages. Upon its vindication depended the right and merit of speculation in theology; to inquire into the realities at the basis of church doctrine, and to create if necessary new formulas. Anselm's problems (2) arose from the consideration of the thing itself. They are of a practical, religious importance, and their solution aims at clear expression and forms intelligible to the times. Witness in *Cur deus homo?* the practical idea of God as the sovereign Lord and the work of Christ in forms derived from the sacrament of penance. The pious daring and religious tendency of Anselm's intellectual work betray the spirit of Augustine. From him also (3) descended Anselm's voluntarism. God's sovereign will rules the world and the nature of will is freedom. Anselm, with his maxim *Credo ut intelligam*, also (4) starts out from belief in the traditional doctrines. But this is only in order to gain *experientia* of the matter described by the formulas. The existence of God, the Trinity, and the incarnation can be proved by "reason alone." Anselm means that the positive faith of the Church is for him who obtains inner experience of its content the rational truth. The significance of Anselm is that he regenerated the formulas of Augustine in the spirit and mode of thought of the latter. In sharp contrast is the thought of Abelard. Starting with the contradictions in tradition, he held (1) that the task of science is to reconcile them by dialectic (in his work, *Sic et non*). He does not contemplate experience by himself of the truths of religion, but a rational formulation of the articles of belief. Thereby (2) he by no means aimed to shake the faith as handed down in the Athanasian formulas. He would only set limits to the belief in authority. That which was believed must [illegible] inwardly understood, and the truths of [illegible] must be made probable and clear to [illegible] The writings of the Fathers were [illegible] "with the necessity of believing," [illegible] liberty of judgment," or reason. ([illegible] authority of the Old and New Testament Scriptures consists in their inherent superiority. Abelard, believing that the substance of church doctrine was in harmony with the Bible, did not mean to attack it. (5) On the question of the reality of the universal, he combated the realism of his teacher William of Champeaux (q.v.), yet seemed to have represented a moderate realistic position himself. His interest was preoccupied by the dialectical treatment of theology, and therefore abstracted from an intimate interest in realism. Pure nominalism, on the other hand, would have reduced his dialectic to a mere word-battle, and, being already disreputable, it was little adapted to his mediating tendency, which sought the harmony of "authority and reason." (6) Abelard proved his constructive talent by reforming the Augustinian division of theology from faith, love, and hope, to faith, sacrament, and love, in correspondence with the historical situation in the Church of his time.

3. Influence of Anselm and Abelard. The method of Anselm was the more tedious; no one without speculative endowments could employ it. Abelard's method seemed made to order for scholastic practise. It afforded the use of the reason when the time was eager and ripe. It drove through the land like a storm-burst. It introduced to the scholars a mass of information and a formal discipline of thought, but in the final result it was fruitless. In the preparation of his Sentences (c. 1150), Peter Lombard (q.v.), prudent in judgment, moderate in the application of reason, fortunate in the classification of his materials, at once orthodox and scientific, followed the method of Abelard. The foundation for dogmatics which he laid and Abelard's method became through this text-book the standard for all the Middle Ages, just as his commentary on the Pauline Epistles made its way as a standard "glossary." Strict traditionalism still prevailed and impassioned attacks were made on the new theology by Bernard of Clairvaux, William of St. Thierry, John of Salisbury, Walter of St. Victor, and the brothers Gerhoh and Arno of Reichersberg (qq.v.); yet men like Gerhoh, from a genuine religious interest, began to deal with the substance of doctrine itself. The spiritual independence at the root of the dialectic of Abelard stirred also in the older orthodoxy. Rupert of Deutz (q.v.) worked out his themes in dependence upon Scripture. Honorius of Autun (q.v.) followed the footsteps of Anselm, his master in thought and method, in *Octo quæstiones* and in *Elucidarium*, in which he treated Christian theology entire. More important are the two works of Hugo of St. Victor (q.v.), *De sacramentis* and *Summa sententiarum*, in which he partly depended on Anselm, and made the sacraments his main topic. Although disavowing "reason" and "experience," yet professing to depend on Scripture, he betrays evidence of [illegible] thinking for himself. On the whole and indi[illegible]ly, although strict orthodox development [illegible] spirit and Abe[illegible] [illegible]odox continu[illegible] [illegible] the Fathers, [illegible] a new light. [illegible] the liberation of theology from the close of the eleventh century was the forerunner arrived with the middle of the twelfth. Intellectual activity, hitherto only ecclesiastical, now turns also to the nat-

4. Awakening of the Twelfth Century.

ural life and benefits. Laymen enter upon literature. The world picture becomes richer and broader, and insight into human life deeper. History supplants chronicle. Understanding makes place for the unity of development and for human individuality. Poets present real human characters; interest in nature awakens. The thirst for reality craves first-hand inquiry and knowledge. Free spirits with a daring criticism and independent judgment, even toward ecclesiastical offices and institutions, are to be found now in the Church. In the wider movement the question of the time was whether the former unity of the ecclesiastical and the secular philosophy could be longer maintained. To do this theology laid an extensive lien upon philosophy (Aristotle) in order to satisfy the new interests and perchance to win them to the confines of the ecclesiastical point of view. As of old, so now, with the rise of the universities, theology was to be the queen of the sciences. Monasticism undertook preaching and the advancement of science. A wealth of new material and a power of method were afforded by the study of Aristotle and his Arabian commentators. Then there was Augustine, rich in metaphysics and psychology, and versatile in his fine observations of life. His smoothly chiseled and opulent formulas, the spiritual vigor of which now first attained to appreciation, lured to imitation. A host of well-disciplined churchmen, of indefatigable industry and brilliant endowment, sprang up to make the Church supreme in every department as in no other era.

At first only Aristotle's writings used from antiquity were in evidence, as that on the categories and *De interpretatione* (*dialectica vetus*).

5. Revival of Aristotle.

Then, in the twelfth century the whole organon (*dialectica nova*) came into use, introduced by the translation of Boëthius (q.v.) and later by John of Venice (c. 1128). But it was through the Arabian philosophers that the rest became known, from the beginning of the thirteenth century. The Arabian commentaries and amplifications brought with them a plethora of problems, but many also in the pantheistic form of the Neoplatonists (see NEOPLATONISM) of the unity of the active intellect in humanity, the eternity of matter, and the denial of individual immortality, rendering the reconcilement of positive religion with secular philosophy ever more difficult and ultimately impossible. Although Avicenna and Averrhoes (qq.v.) had asserted that science did not abolish but rather sustained practical views of religion, yet orthodox theology had condemned it. In this occasion the tide of Eastern philosophy again set in, in the West. This had to coordinate itself on Western ground with church dogma and the Augustinian [illegible] in these, on the one hand, more flesh [illegible] than in the doctrines of the Koran; [illegible] the narrower limitations of ex- [illegible] gma. Besides, the new influ- [illegible] many starting-points in the dialectic spirit for the particular and the newly awakened interest in elementary problems, in the construction of cosmic views, and in the knowledge of nature. The consequence as a whole was the eager resort to the dialectic art of Aristotle, and gradually his methodical physics, psychology, metaphysics, and theory of knowledge adapted themselves. Of importance to this influx of Greek philosophy was the *De divisione philosophiæ* (c. 1150) of Dominicus Gundissalinus, including all those Aristotelian branches in the circle of necessary school studies. Wide theological circles, however, held themselves aloof from many articles of the new system. This is not surprising in view of the recurrence of the entire movement hostile to Abelard. A provincial synod at Paris (1210) condemned the writings of Amalric of Bena (q.v.), consigned those of David of Dinant (q.v.) to the flames, and prohibited the private or public reading of Aristotle's natural philosophy and the comments of Averrhoes thereon under threat of excommunication. The legate Robert forbade the reading of the metaphysics and natural philosophy and the comments on the same at the University of Paris in 1215; but as early as 1231, Pope Gregory IX. recommended expurgated copies, and twenty-four years later they were adopted by resolution of the faculty of arts, so rapidly did Aristotelian study make headway in science and purely formal interests. Theology, also, gradually followed. Indeed, the great theologians before Alexander and Albert regarded the intellectualism and the logical analysis of the concepts of Aristotle as profane. They held to the older theology of a realistic world of divine ideas, according to the Augustinian formulas, which would become manifest to spirit living in fellowship with God, which were illumined from above. The spirit of Anselm and Hugo rather than the method of Abelard guided theology till the middle of the thirteenth century. But its scientific character was to be maintained. The entering wedge was the admission of the method of Abelard, and led to farther advance in the direction of the particular. A negative result was frequently the wrangling over words and the art of confusing the subject by hair-splitting distinctions. Yet it served as a tutelage for method of thought and the minor work for the approach of the most complex problems with Aristotelianism and its new questions and tools. The signal of wavering is already apparent in the writings of the stanch orthodox William of Auvergne (bishop of Paris, after 1228); but pronounced is the dialectic practise and interest to solve everything in the *Summa aurea* of William of Auxerre (d. 1231 or 1237).

III. The Scholastic Period of the Thirteenth Century: 1. The Franciscan Advance: The originator of scholastic theology in the narrower sense of the term was the Franciscan, Alexander of Hales (q.v.), author of the *Summa universæ theologiæ*. This is neither a commentary nor a citation of Lombard, but a broadly outlined systematic work. A mass of material is collected which is arranged, criticized, and logically elaborated with untiring industry. The questions and problems raised by him and also many of his solutions became the prototypes for the dogmatics of the Middle Ages. Such are the *justitia originalis* and *donum superadditum* (original righteousness and superadded grace); *synderesis* (rudiment of conscience); the sharp distinction of *gratia gratis data* (preparatory grace freely given in particular effects) and *gratia gratum faciens* (grace as an abiding principle of character); of *meritum de congruo* (merit from the proper use of nature), and *meritum de condigno* (merit on the basis of supernatural grace); of *carentia justitiae originalis* as *culpa* (guilt) and *concupiscentia* as *poena* (punishment), in the doctrine of original sin. Also, the distinction of *attritio* and *contritio;* as repentance from servile fear and moral penitence. Alexander knew how to seize upon the inmost springs of the religious life of his day, to set them forth in clear apt statement, and with a sure skill to make the new philosophical knowledge and dialectic method subservient to dogma. Although much indebted to Aristotle and citing him continuously, he did not belong to the Aristotelians, but remained an Augustinian Platonist. He held fast to the realism of ideas and for him knowing maintained the religious character of illumination by means of "eternal ideas." Combination with the forms of Aristotelian metaphysics and psychology did not always redound to clearness and consistency. The work received highest recognition when Pope Alexander IV., in 1256, ordered it to be completed (the conclusion consisting of the last three sacraments and eschatology, and, in the third part, the doctrine on ethics were wanting). According to Roger Bacon (q.v.), as a result of Alexander's influence, academic study was reversed in placing the sentences first and Biblical interpretation second. Alexander gave the Church a thorough orthodox system with which to meet the intellectual movement of the time; in it Christianity was digested in thought and presented by means of all the newly acquired philosophical materials and motives.

1. Alexander of Hales.

In the Oxford school of theology, Robert Grosseteste (q.v.) gave impulses to theology decisive for the English Franciscans. He was a thoroughgoing realist; but, as in the view of Anselm, the knowledge of the universal realities must be appropriated in experience, which accounts also for his stress otherwise on scientific empiricism. Knowledge of nature he promoted together with mathematics, grammar, and practical philology. At one with this may have been his emphasis on the authority of the Bible for theology. Faith is essentially the "faith of those things which are believed by the authority of sacred Scripture." Faith in the truths of the Bible is redemptive. God is the will that works salvation, but good is realized only as it is done by human free will. The historical significance of this remarkable personage is in the noteworthy combination of empiricism with speculation—of interest in connection with the traditional authoritative conception and the religious consciousness. The influence of this combination which he inspired was the main reason for the tenacity with which the Franciscans held to the thought and method of the old Augustinian Anselmic theology.

2. The Oxford School.

3. The Dominican Advance: The theological movement of the thirteenth century, however, was brought to its eminence by a deeper conception and a stronger infusion of the system of Aristotle into theological discussion. This took place, in the first instance, through the Dominicans, Albert the Great (see ALBERTUS MAGNUS) and Thomas Aquinas (q.v.), his foremost pupil. Albert, inspired with a consummate passion for knowledge, collected all that was possible to human understanding, but did not advance beyond reproduction. Aristotle formed his framework, and the packing in of much Augustinian-Platonistic material naturally resulted in serious contradictions. To his world-philosophy were added the church dogmas which remained essentially unchanged, no matter how much Aristotelian material was introduced. Thomas, on the contrary, penetrating and clear in conception, equipped with a fresh insight into fundamentals, a great systematic talent, and a remarkable gift of presentation, was uniquely qualified to take in the Aristotelian philosophy as a whole, and, with a sure and skilful art, of incorporating all except the absolutely contradictory. Without relinquishing dogma at any point, he reestablished the same on the new philosophy like superstructure on foundation. The entire Greek position with regard to the soul is accepted. The supreme object of man is to know. Theology is a speculative science that leads to human blessedness, which is the perfect knowledge of God. Accordingly, the nature of man does not center in will but in cognition. The intellect impresses upon volition its spiritual character. In reason as the spiritual power of choice is the seat of "free will." Here the Augustinian point of view gives way to the Greek. Human reason, or philosophy, may of itself conceive only a few religious truths and these only imperfectly and slowly; revealed knowledge must amplify, confirm, and complete. Revelation is at hand in the inspired Scriptures. By them man becomes absolutely certain of the truth because God is their author. Therefore, the Bible is the only certain and absolutely binding authority. But revelation is doctrine, preeminently the doctrine of the "first truth," God. Doctrine is summed up in the Apostle's Creed, and guarded against heretical misinterpretation by the Nicene Creed, the conciliar decisions, and the Fathers. A *nova editio symboli* is in the power of the pope, who calls the council and confirms its sentence. Faith takes hold of the revealed truth. As the "reward of life eternal" is promised to faith, the will finds that which is believed agreeable. The effect of faith upon intellect for the acceptance of what is presented for belief can take place only by the infusion of a "divinely inspired disposition," inasmuch as the truths involved are supernatural. Through this "divinely inspired disposition" the intellect is adapted to believe; "an act of faith consists principally in cognition and therein is its perfection." The *fides informis* becomes *fides formata* by the addition of love. This is self-evident; faith in itself remains

1. Albert the Great; Thomas Aquinas.

what it is but the will invests it with a personal and meritorious character. What man first would and could not, he now can and will. The knowledge by faith is supernatural and can not be demonstrated by "human reason"; yet theology is to refute the opponents of faith and elucidate and make probable the articles of belief by the aid of philosophical thought. This affords "reasons," which are not really "demonstrable," but "certain arguments, showing that what is set forth in faith is not impossible." On the question of universals, Thomas represents generally the moderate realistic point of view prevailing also elsewhere in the thirteenth century. The universal, in the first place, appears as an image of the human mind, which conceives and abstracts the common elements within changing phenomena. Things exist only as particulars; the conception of universality exists only in the intellect. But nominalist he is not; the universal, manifest in particulars, may be taken as the form of the particulars. These forms exist as realities in God, in whom they may be said, with Plato, to be preexistent ideas or universals. Their existence is not therefore merely subjective (*post rem*), but objective (*ante rem* or *in re*). Thomas became the philosophical and theological authority, henceforth, of the Dominican order.

However, a vague restlessness as the sense of an innovation that was to be resisted made itself widely felt. The ideas of Averrhoes presuming to be Aristotelian were awakening suspicion.

2. Reaction Against Thomas.

That Thomas sharply rebuked the doctrines of Averrhoes, particularly that of the unity of the *intellectus agens* in all men, availed nothing. The Minorite John Peckham (q.v.), archbishop of Canterbury, opposed the advancement of the Thomistic doctrines over the order, taking exception specially to the view that the intellective soul was the only human form. A pro-Augustinian reaction set in. The Franciscan William of Mara published his *Summa contra Thomam* (1284), assisted probably by his friend Roger Bacon. As the consistency with dogma was irreproachable, objection was raised against the overreaching of the purely philosophical judgments in theology and the destruction of the older metaphysics with its purely religious knowledge.

3. Various Trends: The breach was not radical; the new philosophy and Aristotle were universally recognized; the representatives of the older schools studied Aristotle; and a mystic like Bonaventura (q.v.) cites him continually as authority.

1. Bonaventura.

Plato, however, is not to be abandoned, for he accords with Augustine. But the authority of Scripture as the authority of the Holy Spirit exceeds that of Augustine. Theology is the "knowledge of things eternal," or "a wisdom and knowledge of God according to piety." "Theology is an affective science and its knowledge is the grace of speculation, but principally that men may become good thereby." The natural "speculative intellect" is complemented by a *habitus* ("disposition") which is the "grace of contemplation." Granted that Aristotle is right with respect to natural cognition; theology, however, pertains to the knowledge of practical experience. Here Augustine is authoritative; and in God is conceived all knowledge of eternal ideas. In connection, the aim is the volitional activity of love, which is the supreme act of the soul; and by it blessedness is attained. This voluntarism is also from Augustine. In detail Bonaventura keeps close to Alexander; hence, his teaching is frequently more liberal or approximates Pelagianism more than that of Thomas, as is manifest in his *meritum de congruo*, *attritio*, and "to do that which is in himself." To Augustine is to be referred his symbolic explanation of the sacraments. The combination of universals, contemplation, and voluntarism is peculiar in itself; and Bonaventura's significance is that by him, in adherence to Augustine, the greatest authority of the West, is expressed the instinctive effort of the peculiar character of Christianity to maintain itself against the Hellenism of the Aristotelians.

The same contrast may be recalled also in the Sentence commentary and *Quodlibita* of Richard of Middleton (at Paris, 1228). This sober and clear mind affords an excellent glimpse into the Franciscan theology of the period, although not representing the Franciscan realism.

2. Henry of Ghent.

The zealous antagonist of the mendicants, Henry of Ghent (q.v.), opposed the older theology and applied the dialectic of Aristotle. On the question of universals, the essences of things are the "eternal ideas" in the divine intellect, which by a creative act of God are transposed into actual existence, and this is then conceived by the understanding as particular and universal. The things in a person's environment first produce *imaginationes* or *phasmata*, from which the *intellectus agens*, which is the "created light," abstracts the universal, or the concept, which is again reflexively referred to the cause which produced the "images." In this process Henry has in mind in addition to *intellectus agens*, a certain illumination by the uncreated light, which, given by the grace of God to whom he will, makes immediately evident from above the reality of things to the spirit. In dependence on Augustine and Anselm, he teaches the primacy of the will, lays stress on complete freedom, and disavows all dependence of will upon thought. In spite of this voluntarism he qualified theology as a speculative science. Like him, the theologians before Duns Scotus represented Augustine in general, laying main stress on the mystical speculation and relegating the voluntarism to second or third rank of importance. Bible and Church are to him the authorities of faith, which is the acceptance as true of the articles of belief. These can not possibly be proved; hence faith must be the gift of grace. Sin has weakened the energy of will and darkened the intellect. Grace as *gratia gratis data*, that is, *vocatio*, by the Word without or within enables man to *meritum congrui* and this leads to sacramental *gratia gratum faciens;* man is now "justified" and can deserve *meritum de condigno*. This in dogmatics is following the footsteps of Alexander and Bonaventura in outline, though deviating in some details.

These two tendencies, the old Augustinian theology and the modern Aristotelianizing, had in common the basic authority of Scripture and the dogma arising therefrom, which were to be expounded by means of the philosophy of Aristotle. The swing of the pendulum in the direction of philosophy bore results. Here and there dogmatic speculation rooted itself in strange soil; dialectic arts were called in to reconcile contradictory philosophic views. The Biblical studies of the past centuries retreat to the background; the interest in patristic literature is waning. Sentences in process of collection from the time of Abelard are deemed sufficient. Nowhere was the older theology so powerfully and peculiarly represented as at Oxford, in the tradition of Grosseteste (q.v.) and Adam Marsh. Roger Bacon's supreme valuation of empiricism and experimental science led him to demand a limitation and division of the sciences. Theology was to cease to amalgamate itself with philosophy; because, dominated thereby, it engages itself with a number of purely cosmological problems which do not concern it; purely theological questions resort to philosophical methods; and real Biblical study is relinquished amid foreign interests, such as "analysis employed by logicians, forced agreements such as the legalists use and the rhythmical harmonies of the rhetoricians." So it has become customary from the time of Albertus Magnus and Alexander of Hales (qq.v.), and even at Oxford from 1250, to read the Sentences *solemniter*. And all this notwithstanding the fact that all these men understood almost nothing of real philosophy, according to Roger Bacon, since they did not grasp Aristotle, and could not on account of the wretched translations. The peculiar task of theology should be "about the sacred text." Better than the collections would be to read the *Historica scholastica* (Peter Comester, q.v.), as was done before Alexander. Biblical interpretations interspersed with dogmatic expositions is the ideal before Bacon. Protests now arise from the spiritual-minded against the "curious and sterile science" or "questions" which have banished Biblical study. Perhaps the revival of Biblical study from the closing decades of the thirteenth century may be attributed to this attitude of the older theology. The order, which is to prevail for the fourteenth and fifteenth centuries, has now formed itself according to which theological study falls into three stages: cursory reading of the Scriptures, the explanation of the Sentences, and the *lectio ordinaria*, or master's minute Scripture interpretation. The first two are conducted by two *baccalaurei;* the third by the *magister regens*. Though always marking the high point in theology, yet Biblical study could be pursued only according to the dogmatic schematism, the Bible being used as a source-fund of speculative doctrines.

3. Biblical Conservatism; Roger Bacon

4. Duns Scotus (q.v.): An Oxford Franciscan, this greatest of the scholastics, enters the movement at the turning of the thirteenth to the fourteenth century. Versed in mathematics and physics, he also possessed a fine perception for the observation of the ac-[illegible] in psychology and religious life. He stood with [illegible]anciscan colleagues for the older theology on realism and voluntarism, sin and redemption, and on the symbolic explanation of the sacraments; but differed by abandoning the faltering attitude toward Aristotle. A close student and commentator of Aristotle, unequaled in his mastery of the dialectic method, with consummate energy he criticized the doctrines of the Platonic Augustinian system and their proofs, and created new formulas and new proofs. He exerted himself to give statement to the fact of the matter and not merely to well-modulated formulas. As a mere summary in passing he (1) sought to reestablish and advance the old realism with the new scientific means. (2) He carried through logically the primacy of the will with reference to God as well as to creature. (3) He grounded anew, and for the future, the particular doctrines of the Franciscans, overthrowing critically those to the contrary. After this follows (4) his ecclesiastical positivism. Theology is a positive science. The free will of God has revealed itself in free contingent acts and orders. This revelation is at hand in Scripture. Religious knowledge is not universal philosophical knowledge, but a practical understanding; it has to do with the "final end revealed by God and the attitude of human will which it conditions." In consequence the positive doctrines and ordinances of the Church are *a priori* the absolutely necessary means for the attainment of the ultimate end. Thereby, it is presupposed that church doctrine is Scripture doctrine; but the prescriptive authority is that of the Church. But this formula placed the dogma in the same relation as the positive statutes warranted by the right of the State. Both may be systematized, interpreted, and criticised, without being abolished in either case. An immediate consequence is (5) the disintegration of the unified world-philosophy of Thomas. On the one hand is the view of the natural in conformity with laws; on the other is the contingent activity of God presenting itself casually in acts, doctrines, orders, and institutions. The methods of knowledge are different in kind: there, are necessary truths of reason; here, contingent truths of history.

1. Critical Work.

Duns is significant not only in criticism or the judgment of the particular; he represents (6) also a general religious theory that adheres to Augustine and conforms with the basic tendencies of medieval piety. God is Will; man is will: the former "dominant," the latter "subject." The absolute free-will of God appoints, works, and organizes the whole; and all things are means for the attainment of the final end, the blessedness of the predestinated. From this point of view are to be understood the predestination of Christ to become man, the nature of man and sin, the validity of the work of Christ, the persuasive power of the Word which this conditions, the renewing divine efficacy in the sacraments, as well as merit and blessedness. On the other hand, man is represented to be absolutely free. Here are rooted all the Pelagianizing elements in the thought world of Duns. But the freedom of the creature obtains only for the immediate connection, of which man is in the act of becoming conscious; absolutely, man is wholly sub-

2. Theological Views; Regressive Results.

ject to the unity of the great objective plan. Though criticizing particular formulas and proofs, in substance and tendency Duns is at one with the old theology of the thirteenth century. His significance is therefore that alongside of the intellectualism of Thomas, the Augustinian voluntarism remained; that dialectic did not sweep out of existence the old problems of religious metaphysics; and that theology employed itself with realities and not merely formulas. Pelagian and disorganizing elements are not wanting, and continued powerfully in development. Although he strove for real things in theology, yet no one was as much responsible for the gradual deterioration of scholasticism into dialectic virtuosity, subtleties, and logomachy on the one hand, and a rigid positivism on the other. More remarkable is it that the last great protagonist of realism was the teacher of the man who disseminated nominalism in wide circles, William of Occam (q.v.). The increasing secularizing of the Church, the medieval traditionalism that became entangled in the chains of proof and forgot the substance, the rivalry of schools and orders anxious to uphold complete the doctrines of their masters, the critical tendency of Duns, using positivism as counterbalance and seal of certainty—all these contributed to reduce spirit to dulness and more and more to substitute the pursuit of formulas for that of knowledge.

IV. Decline of Scholasticism. **1. Divergent Schools of the Fourteenth Century:** Two systems now prevailed in the pursuit of theology; the Thomistic and the Scotist. The scientific development proceeded along two lines: First, the Scotist emphasis upon the active principle in knowing as well as the direction of the knowing faculty upon the particular, together with the increasing complication of the realities immanent in the thing to be realized, led to a break with realism and the revival of nominalism through Occam. The inordinate criticism of dogma secured the widest opportunity in the *potentia absoluta* of God, but was made harmless by positivism. In particular church doctrines the criticism and formulas of Duns were followed. Nothing hastened the downfall of scholasticism more rapidly than the trifling with possibilities, to set oneself at rest finally with the authoritative. Among nominalists were Adam Goddam, Robert Holcot, Jean Buridan (q.v.), Marsilius of Inghen, and later Pierre d'Ailly (q.v.), as also the last representative, Gabriel Biel (q.v.). Also the Dominican Durand of St. Pourçain (q.v.) departed from the doctrine of his order. Theological knowledge, according to him, is concerned only with supernatural redemptive truths of revelation as they occur in the Bible. Knowledge is possible only on the basis of empirical realization, and speculation and illumination of reason are to be rejected. As frequently among the nominalists, the authority of Aristotle is declined where he differs from the "truth of things." In like manner the authority of all human teachers including those of the order is not binding.

1. Crass Nominalism.

The second line of development was that represented by the two schools, in contrast with the rationalism and positivism of the nominalists, which in their way sought to connect with the mystical and Augustinian tendencies of the older theology.

2. The Averrhoistic.

The first of these, first represented by Petrus Aureolus (d. about 1345), John of Baconthorp (d. 1346), and Joannes de Jauduno (master at Paris after 1316), repudiated the Thomistic understanding of Aristotle and adhered to Averrhoes. Just as the things in the world known in themselves become fully realized by the light of the *intellectus agens*, so the objects of faith presented in the Bible may be conceived by means of a "disposition" of faith whose character consists in taking the Scripture as divine truth. This is the light of faith that operates to make thought cleave to the objects of faith so firmly as to possess a real knowledge of them (Baconthorp). Joannes de Jauduno declared all the Averrhoistic doctrines, such as the eternity of the world and the unity of the intellect, as rationally necessary, and preserved the idea of revelation as a means to salvation just as his master had in a practical religious interest with the Koran. In like manner the Paduan school of the fifteenth century assigned to the Averrhoistic ideas a similar position to that which they occupied in the peripatetic philosophy from the thirteenth.

3. The Ægidian.

More important was the *Schola Aegydiana* or theology of the Augustinian hermits. Ægidius de Columna (q.v.) wrote a commentary to the first three books of the Sentences. Jacob Capocci (d. 1308) followed him, then Augustinus Triumphus (q.v.), Gerhard of Siena, Prosper of Reggio, Simon Baringundus, and the German Heinrich von Freimar and Thomas of Strasburg (d. 1357). Ægidius considered in theology an affective "disposition" of knowledge which is akin to the speculative. God is not conceived "according to the mode of reason," but "according to the form of revelation." All sciences shall be subservient to theology, which, however, is not under the necessity of explaining its principles. Salvation is to be realized in life by "act of the will." The universal is *in ipsa re* as the *natura rei*, which is something different from the particular thing of sense; and as *ante rem* it subsists in God as eternal idea. Stress is laid upon the fact that God moves all creatures "to their activities" and that they are his "instruments and less than instruments." This natural operation of God is preliminary to the operation of grace. Preparation for the *gratia gratum faciens* is possible only as a divine calling and an inspiration of good reflections precedes. The sacraments, according to Thomas of Strasburg, are only means for the grace immediately wrought of God in the soul. Scotist and Thomistic elements mingle; on the whole the basis of the older theology is conserved without a thoroughgoing advance. An interesting and important advance was made by Gregory of Rimini (d. 1358), who regarded theology as an essentially practical science so far as it guides to eternal life, but containing also speculative principles, which it proves from Scripture. The principal authority for Gregory was Augustine; but it is remarkable that he professed nominalism and attempted to derive it from Augustine. Not "the lack of original righteousness" constitutes the nature of original sin, but "concupiscence itself is original sin." "Act of lust" is not here thought of, but the "carnality" arising from the generative desire of parents, which is a "real quality" in the human soul. "The works of unbelievers which seem virtuous and commendable are truly sinful and punishable, vicious, and morally evil." Children dying unbaptised shall be subject not only to the "punishment of the damned" [i.e., judgment of original sin], but also "to the punishment of pain." Turning sharply against the idea of a "general influence of God" by which sinners *de congruo* are capable of earning "first grace," he held that to be capable of good requires a "special aid of God"; of himself man may earn neither the *gratia gratum faciens* nor the dispersive *gratia gratis data*. The good in man is a direct act of God. The only cause of salvation is the divine predestination embracing in itself, as in Augustine, "calling" and "justification" and not being dependent on foreknowledge. Gregory was a genuine scholastic with a lively interest in philosophical problems and a delight in proofs, and also a man of not inconsiderable independence, shown by his going over to nominalism and by the energy with which he was able to think himself to an independent position amid the views of Augustine. Pelagianism is again reduced to a fundamental heresy, and contemporaneously Bradwardine (q.v.) completed his great anti-Pelagian work.

3. Culmination: The scientific activity of the thirteenth century had therefore been directed to satisfy the intellectual necessities raised by the twelfth, by means of unified philosophical theory in which was merged the dogma of the Church with the philosophy of Aristotle. The boldest and clearest attempt of Thomas Aquinas obtained only qualified approval.

4. Disintegration and the Reformation.

Duns Scotus split apart the two elements; with William of Occam (see OCCAM, WILLIAM OF), the unity became illusory. Nothing illustrates the situation better than the recall in the fourteenth century of the sentence of Averrhoes: a principle may be correct in philosophy but false in theology. Where there was a readiness to follow Thomas, it stopped short with the practical deductions; faith and incentive to his daring idealism failed. The increasing intellectual self-dependence afforded theology an uncapricious character, and criticism did not universally blunt itself as the nominalistic positivism. Again theologians arose, like Anselm of old, who approached theological problems with a striving for the truth of experience, and these cared more for the faith and a reformation of life than for "system." Such movements were not interrupted in the Franciscan order, and that Duns and Occam were members was not accidental. Characteristic of the time is it that, impelled by inmost experience, Thomas Bradwardine (q.v.) of Oxf[illegible] lied his age from Pelagianism to th[illegible] determinism of grace, and a man [illegible] Rimini so earnestly reverted to [illegible] came Wyclif (q.v.), anti-schol[illegible] realistic critic, without, how[illegible] cautions of the nomin[illegible] [illegible] naive credulity of Anselm. He was induced by practical motives and theology was the means to his ideas of reform. As realist he saw in it no mere contrivance of words but realities, which led to real consequences. His thought was controlled by two main principles: the Augustinian predestination and the Biblical discipleship of Jesus.

2. Restoration; Finality of Thomas.

But to the cry for reform in the fifteenth century was opposed, as usual, the counter-effort at restoration. In such cases, restoration allies itself with retrenchment, insisting only upon the main things. Yet such reduction is in danger of stagnation, unless new spiritual tendencies from fresh points of view set in. Thus the battle between the "old" and the "modern," realism and nominalism, continued, but the charge against and ridicule of scholastic practise in theology emanated not only from Humanists but from theologians as well. Slowly scholasticism turned into new channels. For example, the nominalist Pierre d'Ailly (see AILLY, PIERRE D') limited his Sentence commentary to what appeared to him practical, seemingly important problems. Likewise for Thomas Netter (q.v.) in his *Doctrinale antiquitatem* against Wyclif; the problem pertains to Church and institutions; the Bible and earlier Fathers furnish the proofs. Above all new problems are disavowed, and the older ones are to be reduced to main points and simplified, but the native power of the authors is dead. The recourse is to seek a *via media* among the opinions of the past, or at most adherence to a great master. By clearness, simplicity, thoughtfulness, and the elimination of paradoxes and extremes, no system of the past was so well adapted to this process as that of Thomas Aquinas. Besides, the practical theologians, the German mystics, followed him as their teacher and pure nominalism with its criticism and fruitless dialectic was more and more doubted, while realism rose again to power through Platonism in Niholas of Cusa (q.v.) and Averrhoism (the Paduan School). Johannes Capreolus (q.v.), the chief of Thomists, in his four books, *Defensiones theologiæ divi doctoris Thomæ* (5 vols., Turin, 1901–04) criticizes the other scholastic theories and recommends in all points a return to Thomas, thus introducing the Thomist reaction of the fifteenth century. Gradually, here and there, the theological *Summa* of Thomas became the basis of lectures instead of the Sentences of Lombard. Dionysius Rickel (see DIONYSIUS THE CARTHUSIAN) presented the scholastic theories clearly in his Sentence commentary, generally in adherence to Thomas. A comprehensive presentation by Gabriel Biel followed in most questions the views of Scotus and Occam. Soon after, Francis Lycketus prepared his commentary on the *Opus Oxoniense* of Duns, and Thomas del Vio wrote his commentary on the [illegible]*ma theologica*, and Franciscus de Silvestris Fer[illegible]nsis, on *Summa contra gentiles*, both by Thomas. [illegible] and more distinct became the return to the [illegible] and the recognition of Thomas [illegible]it of scholasticism. He formed [illegible]nt restoration of scholasti[illegible] [illegible]alamanca, took place in

Spain in the sixteenth century. Thomists were also the intellectual antagonists of Luther. Recently Pope Leo XIII. pronounced this the normal theology.

V. Characterization in Summary: As a rule the schoolmen present their teaching in the form of commentaries on the Sentences of Peter Lombard. The problems raised by him are resolved into an increasing multiplicity of questions, often so remote from the text that this is soon forgotten by the reader. The series of distinctions by Lombard remain as an outline for the accumulating material. To extract the basic ideas of the theologians is one of the gravest impediments to the modern understanding of the peculiarity of the scholastic systems. Another is the repeated differentiation of the material into new questions the basis for the opposite views of which are thoroughly established and thoroughly refuted. For instance, a distinction of Lombard is resolved into a number of *quæstiones* and each of these into a number of articles. Other subdivisions may follow: such as, *membra, principalia, partes, tractatus, dubia, ad finitum.* In detail each article is so treated as to raise a question; then citations for and against are quoted from the Church Fathers down to the scholastic masters. After the *quod non* or *quod sic* is concluded, follows the *responsio* of the author or the *corpus* of the article. Then follows the discussion in much detail of the views produced first for, then against, the question, not infrequently including the characteristic opinions of the author. Into this endlessly irksome mold, the explanation of every problem is dragged. But its great service was its vitalization of dialectic art and of logical categories for scholars and for the development of education to the present day. Easier and simpler was the presentation of Thomas, who parted from the scheme of Lombard and built his own system on the grand and simple outlines of (1) of God, (2) to God, (3) through Christ. He also possessed the art of setting forth perspicuously the essential and of expressing it in a form easily understood. Yet even here the endless analysis and monotonous dialectic are wearisome.

1. Method.

From the time of the famous introduction of V. Cousin to the works of Abelard (1839) it has become customary to trace the history of scholasticism by the thread of the conflict of rationalism and nominalism. But this division will not classify in theology and must be complemented by the further view-points of Augustinianism and Aristotelianism, voluntarism and intellectualism, positivism and rationalism, practical and theoretical knowledge, as has been done in the preceding sketch. The traditional and inviolable Biblical material authorized by the Church is to be interpreted and systematized. In addition it must be brought into harmonious relation with secular knowledge. In the example of Thomas, the philosophy of Aristotle takes its place beside church doctrine. Reason is not only the logical faculty, but also the organ of philosophic intuition. Hand in hand with revelation, it erects a grand system of religious philosophy. Revealed thoughts are not to be rationalized or proved in the sense but merely shown as probable and conformable to reason. As a result orthodoxy and rationalism are commuted, giving rise to a speculative theoretical knowledge as subject of theology. Exactly this entrance of the rational element called forth the protest of the older theology and the movement introduced by Duns Scotus. The older theology, though acceding to the entrance of the science of Aristotle, and adopting the dialectic, desired to see the religious character of theology preserved, partly by adherence to the religious speculation of Augustine and his doctrine of will, and partly by the retention of realism. This latter seems contrary to the purpose; yet realism derived its ideas as inherent in things from heaven; it touched the divine in everything that transpired; everything earthly was a medium revealing the heavenly, and knowledge assumed an immediate mystical character. To Duns philosophy and theology were distinct in object and kind. The latter was concerned with a purely practical knowledge. The will of God revealed itself to human will as its end and provided the means and ways for attainment. The Church with its dogmas and institutions is that way. Though dealing with subjects common to both, metaphysics deals with the truths necessary to the thought of being; theology with positive revelation. Theology and philosophy must part. This practical knowledge of theology, however, becomes scientific by the dialectical proof of the inner unity of revelation and its ecclesiastical institution. But instead of doing this Duns simply makes revelation equivalent to church doctrine and order, and instead of producing a new conception of faith correlative to a practical revelation he rests correspondingly with the intellectual assent of tradition. And instead of wholly severing the bond to Aristotle he weaves him entirely into theology from new points of view. The result is shown in the endless unrest suspended over his system of thought. With a sure eye for system he takes in hand the exposition of the particular doctrines; with a keen criticism of tradition he has paved the way, but he is impeded from attaining his aim of practical knowledge by the ready-made church doctrines, and, in part, by the Aristotelian dogma. Hence, the brilliant criticism of Duns proves to be in vain, and his characteristic tendency is ever deterred by the ecclesiastical positivism. So much more divergent is the inconsistency between aim and result as Duns, unlike Thomas, who follows a certain tendency of rationalizing faith, would conceive it only in its practical nature. But the undertaking of Thomas was also untenable because of the disparity of the religious faith and philosophic knowledge which he vainly aimed to unify. Faith as theoretical assent is the rock on which Duns splits and the fortress of Thomas; the relation of philosophy and theology is the stronghold of Duns, the weakness of Thomas. The latter founders on a false deduction; the former on the incapability of prosecuting a true one. The one was impeded by philosophy; the other by church doctrine.

2. Problem.

Hereby are distinguished the two methods of scholasticism. The one is the union of dogmatics with Aristotelian philosophy, as the ultimate conclusion of natural metaphysics; the other represents separation and theology as the purely practical religious knowledge of the way to God. Having the

3. Three Types.

inviolable formulas of the Church and the Aristotelian logic in common, the two methods frequently coincide, in part or whole, in presenting the same doctrine. Doctrinal reconstruction is precluded for both by their presuppositions. Thus adherence to the foundations and problems of Lombard for centuries is self-evident. Original observations and judgments occur but do not dare to brave the ban of church doctrine and practise. More radical in antagonism to the system of Thomas was the work of Occam. The aim of this was to expose the irrationality of dogma and with an unsparing criticism to show on every hand the antitheses to the church tenets as thinkable. It was customary to make excursions in the light of the *potentia absoluta*, how things might have been in the absence of reality; but in the sterile atmosphere of the day those possibilities soon dispersed and the church positivism remained. But historically considered this aspect of the matter was of the utmost significance. When confidence in single church doctrines was once attacked, the criticism of single dogma and doctrines became customary, and finally theology led quite barrenly to the consideration of the ecclesiastical doctrines and ordinances as mere empirical realities. Not without enhancing the natural element in church ordinances, this theology undertook the support of Pelagianism and the externalizing of grace in the institution of penance from an inner relationship of choice. The negative criticism of the materials of tradition and a rationalizing and naturalizing positivism within the limits of its power—these are the principles of nominalism. They are the distinguishing marks of the third type of scholastic theology. Following mainly the outline of Duns Scotus, it is distinguished from his system by the qualities characteristic of the mode of thought of the nominalistic theologians, namely, crassness of criticism, inner contempt of dogma, and the lack of a unified Christian philosophy.

The supreme tendency of the theology of the thirteenth century—to provide the new world in the act of self-realization with a self-consistent philosophy, which should render the kingdoms of the world

4. Surviving Influences.

subject to the pope and all secular knowledge a pillar to the arch of church doctrine—was reversed by nominalism. The older theology of the twelfth and thirteenth centuries which was instinctively disinclined to Aristotle prevailed. This right was justified by Duns and Occam, though otherwise than as those old theologians had anticipated. The practical situation which had occasioned the enormous labor of the thirteenth century continued. It is self-evident, then, that in the fourteenth century Thomism on the one hand and Augustinianism on the other took their places beside nominalism. The Thomists desired to enforce the primacy of the Church in learning and life, and became the bitterest foes of the Reformation; the Augustinians, not without being affected by nominalistic criticism, endeavored to rescue the primacy of religious life, and became the forerunners of the Reformation. A historical magnitude like scholasticism, lasting four centuries, was not without its permanent influence in philosophy and theology. Not only is this found in Roman Catholicism as already pointed out, but also in the influence of Duns upon Luther in favor of a practical religious doctrinal system setting forth the way of redemption as manifest in revelation. So also the influence of Thomas upon Melanchthon, who allowed philosophy as *ancilla theologiæ* to contribute the materials of natural knowledge to dogmatics. In principle, the older Protestant theology adhered to the rejection of scholasticism by the Reformation, and the Enlightenment (q.v.) was incapable of receiving a profound historical appreciation of scholasticism. This change did not occur until the revival of the historical sense by Romanticism (q.v.). From the time of F. C. Baur's great work on the Trinity, Protestant history of dogma has given more unbiased attention to scholasticism, especially after interest was stimulated by Albrecht Ritschl's inquiry into the persistence of scholastic thought within Protestantism. Yet no field presents so many unclaimed problems as the history of scholasticism. (R. SEEBERG.)

BIBLIOGRAPHY: W. L. G. von Eberstein, *Die natürliche Theologie der Scholastiker, nebst Zusätzen über die Freiheitslehre und den Begriff der Wahrheit bei denselben*, Leipsic, 1803; R. D. Hampden, *The Scholastic Philosophy Considered in its Relation to Christian Theology*, 2d ed., London, 1837; G. O. Marbach, *Lehrbuch der Geschichte der Philosophie*, part 2, Leipsic, 1838–41; X. Rousselot, *Études sur la philosophie dans le moyen âge*, Paris, 1840–1842; R. Hasse, *Anselm von Canterbury*, 2 parts, Leipsic, 1843, Eng. transl., London, 1850; A. Jourdain, *Recherches critiques sur l'âge et l'origine des traductions latines d'Aristote*, 2d ed., Paris, 1843; B. Hauréau, *De la philosophie scolastique*, 2 vols., ib. 1850; idem, *Histoire de la philosophie scolastique*, ib. 1872–80; idem, *Grégoire IX. et la philosophie d'Aristote*, ib. 1872; F. Morin, *Dictionnaire de philosophie et de théologie scolastiques*, 2 vols., ib. 1856; E. Plassmann, *Die Schule des heiligen Thomas von Aquino*, 5 vols., Münster, 1857–62; H. D. Köhler, *Realismus und Nominalismus in ihrem Einflusse auf die dogmatischen Systeme des Mittelalters*, Gotha, 1858; W. Kaulich, *Geschichte der scholastischen Philosophie*, part 1, *Von Joh. Scotus Erigena bis Abälard*, Prague, 1863; A. Stoeckl, *Geschichte der Philosophie des Mittelalters*, 3 vols., Mainz, 1864–66; idem, *Doctrine philosophique de S. Thomas d'Aquin*, Paris, 1893; C. S. Barach, *Zur Geschichte des Nominalismus vor Roscellin*, Vienna, 1866; L. Figuier, *Vies des savants illustres du moyen âge, avec l'appréciation sommaire de leurs travaux*, Paris, 1867; F. D. Maurice, *Mediæval Philosophy of the First Six Centuries*, new ed., London, 1870; M. Schneid, *Die scholastische Lehre von Materie und Form*, Eichstatt, 1873; J. Schwertschläger, *Die erste Entstehung der Organismen nach der Philosophie des Alterthums und des Mittelalters*, ib. 1873; J. Bach, *Die Dogmengeschichte des Mittelalters vom christologischen Standpunkte*, 2 parts, Vienna, 1873–75; A. Ebert, *Allgemeine Geschichte der Literatur des Mittelalters im Abendlande*, 3 vols., Leipsic, 1874; M. Schneid, *Aristoteles in der Scholastik. Ein Beitrag zur Geschichte der Philosophie im Mittelalter*, Halle, 1875; J. H. Loewe, *Der Kampf zwischen dem Realismus und Nominalismus im Mittelalter*, Prague, 1876; C. Werner, *Der Entwicklungsgang der mittelalterlichen Psychologie von Alcuin bis Albertus Magnus*, Vienna, 1876; idem, *Die Scholastik des späteren Mittelalters*, 4 vols., ib. 1881–87; idem, *Die* [illegible] *minalisirende Psychologie der Scholastik des späteren* [illegible] *ittelalters*, ib. 1882; N. Valois, *Guillaume d'Auvergne,* [illegible] *vie et ses ouvrages*, Paris, [illegible]; F. X. Pfeifer, *Harmoni-*

London, 1882; J. Schwane, *Dogmengeschichte der mittleren Zeit (787–1517)*, Freiburg, 1882; É. Guera, *Vrais principes de philosophie scolastique*, Paris, 1883; G. Runze, *Der ontologische Gottesbeweis. Kritische Darstellung seiner Geschichte seit Anselm bis auf die Gegenwart*, Halle, 1883; J. Astromhoff, *Introductio ad intelligendam doctrinam Angelici Doctoris*, Rome, 1884; R. L. Poole, *Illustrations of the History of Mediæval Thought*, London, 1884; C. M. Schneider, *Das Wissen Gottes nach der Lehre T. von Aquin*, 4 parts, Regensburg, 1884; F. Ehrle, *Bibliotheca theologiæ scholasticæ*, Paris, 1885; P. Nova, *Dictionnaire de terminologie scolastique*, Avignon, 1885; K. Prantl, *Geschichte der Logik im Abendlande*, 4 vols., 2d. ed., Leipsic, 1885; H. T. Simar, *Die Lehre vom Wesen des Gewissens in der Scholastik des 13. Jahrhunderts*, Freiburg, 1886; J. von der Aa, *Cursus compendiarius philosophiæ scolasticæ*, Louvain, 1887; A. Adeodatus, *Die Philosophie der Neuzeit und die Philosophie des heiligen Thomas von Aquino*, Bonn, 1887; H. von Eicken, *Geschichte und System der mittelalterlichen Weltanschauung*, Stuttgart, 1887; P. de Martigné, *La Scholastique et les traditions franciscaines*, Paris, 1888; É. Blanc, *Traité de philosophie scolastique*, 2 vols., Lyon, 1889; V. Lipperheide, *Thomas von Aquino und die platonische Ideenlehre*, Munich, 1890; H. Appel, *Die Lehre der Scholastiker von der Synteresis*, Rostock, 1891; C. Baeumker, *Beiträge zur Geschichte der Philosophie des Mittelalters*, 3 vols., Münster, 1891 sqq.; J. von Falke, *Geschichte des Geschmacks im Mittelalter*, Berlin, 1892; J. Gardair, *Corps et âme. Essais sur la philosophie de S. Thomas*, Paris, 1892; D. Nasmith, *Makers of Modern Thought, 1200–1699*, 2 vols., London, 1892; J. J. Berthier, *Tabula systematica totius summæ theologicæ*, Freiburg, 1893; E. Gebhardt, *L'Italie mystique; histoire de la renaissance religieuse au moyen âge*, 2d ed., Paris, 1893; A. Portmann, *Das System der theologischen Summe des heiligen Thomas von Aquin*, Lucerne, 1894; O. Willmann, *Geschichte des Idealismus*, vol. ii., 3 vols., Brunswick, 1894–1897; A. Mignon, *Les Origines de la scolastique et Hugues de Saint Victor*, 2 vols., Paris, 1895; M. C. J. Wulf, *Hist. de la philosophie scholastique dans les pays-bas*, Brussels, 1895, new ed., Louvain, 1900; idem, *Introduction à la philosophie néo-scolastique*, ib. 1904; idem, *Hist. de la philosophie médiévale*, ib. 1905, Eng. transl., *Scholasticism Old and New; an Introduction to scholastic Philosophy, medieval and modern*, New York, 1906; J. M. Littlejohn, *Political Theory of the Schoolmen*, New York, 1896; F. Picavet, *Roscelin philosophe et théologien*, Paris, 1896; idem, *Abélard et Alexandre de Hales créateurs de la methode scolastique*, ib. 1896; idem, *Esquisse d'une histoire des philosophies médiévales*, ib. 1905; G. Lefèvre, *Les Variations de Guillaume de Champeaux et la question des universaux*, Lille, 1898; T. F. Mandonnet, *Siger de Brabant et l'Averroisme latin au xiii. siècle*, Freiburg, 1899; C. Fraessen, *Scotus Academicus seu universa doctoris subtilis theologica dogmata*, Rome, 1900; A. Gardner, *Studies in John the Scot*, London, 1900; Jerome of Montefortino, *Duns Scoti Summa theologica*, Rome, 1900; R. Seeberg, *Die Theologie des Duns Scotus*, Leipsic, 1900; J. Draeseke, *Johannes Scotus Erigena*, ib. 1902; J. Guttmann, *Die Scholastik des 13. Jahrhunderts in ihren Beziehungen zum Judentum und zur jüdischen Litteratur*, Breslau, 1902; C. Alibert, *La Psychologie thomiste et les théories modernes*, Paris, 1903; H. Felder, *Geschichte der wissenschaftlichen Studien in Franziskanerorden bis Mitte des 13. Jahrhunderts*, Freiburg, 1904; K. Krogh-Tonning, *Der letzte Scholastiker, Dionysius de Leuwis de Rickel*, ib. 1904; P. Minges, *Duns Scotus Indeterminist?* Münster, 1905; J. Rickaby, *Scholasticism* (in *Philosophies, Ancient and Modern*), London, 1908; M. Grabmann, *Die Geschichte der scholastischen Methode*, vol. i. *Die scholastische Methode von ihren ersten Anfängen in der Väterlitteratur bis zum Beginn des 12. Jahrhunderts*, Freiburg, 1909; J. L. Perrier, *The Revival of Scholastic Philosophy in the Nineteenth Century*, New York, 1909; H. O. Taylor, *The Mediæval Mind*, 2 vols., New York, 1911; Schaff, *Christian Church*, V., 1, chaps. xii.–xiii.; the works on the history of philosophy by H. Ritter, Hamburg, 1844–45; E. Erdmann, 3 vols., London, 1893; W. Windelband, ib. 1893; and F. Ueberweg, ed. M. Heinze, 8th ed., vol. ii., Berlin, 1905; the litera[illegible] and that under individual [illegible] work, e.g., Abelard; Albertus [illegible]y, Raymond; Peter Lombard; [illegible]

SCHOLIA.

1. Character of Scholia. The patristic scholia on the Bible are distinguished from Biblical commentaries in that, instead of following the text continuously, they explain only such individual points as seem to require elucidation. The scholion thus resembles the gloss (see GLOSSES, BIBLICAL AND ECCLESIASTICAL), though in the medieval period "gloss" denotes a scholion which can not be ascribed to a definite author. In Greek philology, on the other hand, a gloss originally meant an obscure phrase or word, later being applied metaphorically to the interpretation of such a phrase or word. In such glosses the obscure words were replaced by intelligible ones, either on the margin of the text or above the words in question. Later still, the gloss comprised not only the interpretation of obscure words and phrases, but etymologies and elucidations of subject-matter in the text under consideration. Both the state of patristic exegesis and linguistic usage render it impossible to distinguish sharply between scholia and commentaries, especially as the individual notes of the commentaries possess a certain degree of independence and are thus akin to the scholion. Moreover the scholion is defined by Suidas and the *Etymologicum magnum* as a note placed beside the text during school instruction. It thus bore a distinctly informal character, was essentially characterized by the individuality and ability of the teacher, and was not necessarily intended for publication. The linguistic usage of patristic exegesis furnishes many examples of these meanings of the term scholion. Arethas (q.v.) terms his commentary on Revelation a "scholiastic synopsis," and the commentaries on Matthew and Mark in Cod. Laur. VI., 18 and Codex Vaticanus 1,445 are likewise designated as scholia. The author of the catena Laur. VI., 33, on the other hand, distinguishes sharply between scholion and commentary, and this distinction is still more marked in the catena on Paul in Vindobonensis 166. The catenas are the principal sources for excerpt scholia, these being notes drawn from commentaries or other writings and appended to the words of the text they elucidate. Besides these sources, the independent labor of scholiasts must be considered, in which the individuality of the author appears more prominently than in the notes proceeding from studies in schools. Such scholia are the notes and comments of a reader less intent on explaining his text than on marking and elucidating passages which especially attract his attention. The scholiast's freedom is restricted in texts regarded as sacred, of which an authoritative interpretation had early been given. In itself it is immaterial whether the scholiast made his annotations for purposes of instruction, or for himself. In Biblical scholia the latter was rarely the case.

One of the most interesting Biblical scholia is the Codex Marchallianus on the prophets, which was revised according to the Tetrapla of Origen. On its margins scholia record the critical labors of Origen, and also contain other pertinent matter of various periods. Especially instructive for scholia literature is the Athos manuscript Laura 184 B. 64 containing Acts and the Catholic and Pauline epistles. The scholia contain valuable critical notes, mostly with the citation of the authorities and works from which they are drawn. The principal sources are the *Stromata* and the commentaries of Origen, though Irenæus, Clement, and Basil are also used. The scholia are not invariably named, however, the anonymous ones apparently belonging to the original owner of the manuscript, which has been plausibly supposed to have come from the school of Arethas of Cæsarea. The character of the scholia of this manuscript clearly show that the interest of the writer was concentrated on the subject-matter and its problems, thus leading to a scientific revision of the entire manuscript. The Biblical scholia afford no certain data concerning the problem of their origin, since they for the most part presuppose the exegetical tradition of the commentary. The analogy of the scholia on the Church Fathers must accordingly be employed. Here the most important scholia are those on Clement of Alexandria, written by Baanes and Arethas, and the scholia on Gregory Nazianzen. The scholia of Baanes are primarily linguistic, though they also give notes on mythology and history. The interest of Arethas was primarily theological, though he cites the classics as well as the Bible or such Church Fathers as Athanasius, Gregory of Nyssa, and Gregory Nazianzen (qq.v.). He pays especial attention to allegorical exegesis, etymologies, definitions, figures, and similes, short rules of life, paronomasias, antitheses, and anecdotes from history and natural science. The objects of Elias of Crete, one of the scholiasts on Gregory Nazianzen, were to interpret theological, ethical, and scientific material, as well as the mythological and linguistic problems of his text.

2. Biblical and Patristic Scholia.

It may be assumed that similar interests and intentions led to the writing of scholia on the Bible; but if this be true, these scholia can rightly be judged only in connection with classical philology, the methods being identical, despite the divergence of matter and of aim. In the Hellenistic period criticism became an indispensable element of education to protect the sources of classical training and to guard their exegesis. Thus arose the classical commentaries, collections of scholia, florilegia, and lexicons. Even more attention, however, was directed to interpretation of the language and the matter than to criticism, and allegorical exegesis was carried far (see EXEGESIS OR HERMENEUTICS). This tendency to interpret and deepen authoritative tradition led, in ancient philology, to a special class of scholiastic literature, designed to reconcile the discrepant statements of an author. This latter type to harmonize difficulties forms an important class of Christian scholia, exemplified not only by frequent passages in the commentaries of Origen, but also by marginal notes on manuscripts of the Bible, as in Laur. VI., 33 and Cod. Coisl. 206. The earliest patristic collection of scholia is doubtless the *Hypotyposeis* of Clement, its sources being the original elders and Pantænus, the founder of the catechetical school at Alexandria, whose object was to deepen knowledge, investigation, and interpretation of the Bible. The work, as described by Photius (*Bibliotheca*, cix.), was a condensation and a summary, incomplete, allegorizing, and full of repetitions. Despite the unfavorable attitude of Photius, who was theologically opposed to Clement, it is clear that the latter's book was scholiastic in character. Origen is expressly said to have written scholia, besides his homilies and commentaries. Many of these scholia are preserved in the catenas, and Jerome mentions such comments on Leviticus, Isaiah, Psalms i.–xv., Ecclesiastes, and John. The Athos manuscript likewise cites Origen's scholia on Genesis, and mentions his *Stromata* as a source for its own scholia. The scholia of Origen are characterized by brevity and cogency. They contain notes on the text, pertinent interpretations, and information on the subject-matter, with relatively little allegorizing. The catenas contain numerous scholia of Theodore of Mopsuestia and other Antiochian theologians, while Theodoret is also occasionally mentioned as a scholiast.

3. Early Biblical Scholia.

The majority of the anonymous scholia are characterized by Byzantine orthodoxy, as is shown by the scholia of Hesychius on the Psalms. Whether the scholia of Johannes Hamartolus on the same book is of a like anti-Origenistic spirit is problematical, but at all events he furnished the sole source for the catena of Nicetas. Byzantine scholia are essentially of one type; dogmatic, ascetic, and allegorical interpretations prevail, rather than notes on geography, history, or subject-matter. Numerous examples of these scholia may be drawn from J. C. G. Ernesti's editions of the *Glossæ sacræ* of Hesychius (Leipsic, 1785) and Phavorinus (1786), as well as from C. F. de Matthæi's *Glossaria Græca minora* (2 vols., Riga, 1774–75) and J. Alberti's *Glossarium Græcum in sacros Novi Testamenti libros* (Leyden, 1735). The oldest treatise on Biblical difficulties is Philo's *Quæstiones et solutiones quæ sunt in Genesi et in Exodo*, translated from Armenian into Latin by J. B. Aucher (Venice, 1828), and from the Latin into English in Bohn's *Theological Library, Works of Philo*, iv. 284 sqq., London, 1855. Of the Church Fathers Eusebius wrote on the solution of discrepancies in the Gospels, those preserved (ed. A. Mai, *Nova collectio*, i. 1–60, 61–189, Rome, 1825) treating respectively of the genealogy and infancy of Christ, and of his passion. A comprehensive work of similar character was written by Theodoret (*MPG*, lxxx. 77–856), discussing the Octateuch, Kings, and Chronicles. In like manner, the "Collection of Problems and Solutions" ascribed to the presbyter Hesychius (*MPG*, xciii. 1391–1448), the 446 "Questions and Answers" of Anastasius of Sinai (*MPG*, lxxxix. 311–824), and the *Quæstiones ad Amphilochium* of Photius (Mai, *Nova collectio*, i.) contain chiefly exegetical difficulties side by side with dogmatic and ascetic problems. To the Western Church be-

4. Byzantine and Other Works.

long the *Quæstiones ex Vetere et Novo Testamento*, probably composed by Hilary. The manuscripts contain numerous collections on "difficulties," mostly anonymous. In Codex Vindobonensis XXIX. are the "Answers" of Severus of Antioch to Eupraxius, while in the Moscow manuscript of Arethas is a related work of similar form.

5. Editions. Comparatively few scholia have as yet been printed, though those of Clement, Origen, Eusebius, Athanasius, Cyril, and others have been excerpted from the catenas, and individual anonymous compositions have been edited. The tasks preliminary to a corpus of Biblical scholia are many and difficult, involving the determination of which scholia are excerpts, what is their relation to their sources, the deviations of their transmission, the problem as to which scholia are original and hence independent sources, the interests and tendencies revealed in the scholia, and the relation of the scholia to the text as either corrupting it or preserving it. The first attempt to make a comprehensive collection of patristic scholia was by J. Gregorius, in his posthumous *Scholia Gregoriana* (ed. J. E. Grabe, Oxford, 1703), the chief sources being Origen, Chrysostom, Theodore of Mopsuestia, Œcumenius, Theophylact, and Nicetas. A similar attempt was made by E. W. Grinfield's *Novum Testamentum Græcum* (4 vols., London, 1843–48), the first two volumes paralleling each verse with the Septuagint, and the latter two containing parallels from Philo, Josephus, the Apostolic Fathers, the New Testament Apocrypha, etc. The parallels in Wetstein's edition of the New Testament (2 vols., Amsterdam, 1752) also have the value of a collection of scholia. The patristic scholia, so far as they can be referred to specific authors, are contained in the great editions of the Church Fathers, and in the collections of Montfaucon (*Collectio nova patrum*, 2 vols., Paris, 1706), A. Mai (*Patrum nova bibliotheca*, 8 vols., Rome, 1844–1871), and J. B. Pitra (*Spicilegium Solesmense*, 4 vols., Paris, 1852–58, and *Analecta sacra*, Paris, 1876 sqq.). These are mostly fragments derived from catenas, and the same scholia are sometimes represented by different recensions, as the scholia of Eusebius on Luke, of which Mai gives three texts. The fragments of Hippolytus on the Pentateuch, the historical books, Psalms, Proverbs, Ecclesiastes, Isaiah, and Ezekiel are edited by H. Achelis in his edition of Hippolytus (I., ii. 1–194, Leipsic, 1897). The fragments of Origen on the Octateuch, Job, Psalms, Proverbs, Isaiah, Jeremiah, Ezekiel, and Daniel are given by Pitra in his *Analecta sacra* (ii. 349–350, iii. 1–364, 523–527, 538–551), and scholia of Origen and Eusebius on Psalms i.–cxviii (ib., 369–520); E. Klostermann has edited the scholia of Origen on Jeremiah, Lamentations, and Samuel in the third volume of his edition of Origen (Leipsic, 1901). Scholia of Eusebius on the Psalms are given by Montfaucon (ut sup., i. 1–2) and Mai (ut sup., IV., i. 65–66), scholia of Athanasius on Job and the Psalms by Pitra (*Analecta*, v. 3–27), scholia of Basil and Hilary on the Psalms by the same scholar (op. cit., 76–104, 141–144), and anonymous scholia on Psalms i.–xiii. by C. F. de Matthæi (*Lectiones Mosquenses*, ii. 41–52, Leipsic, 1779. Victor of Capua's collection of *Scholia veterum patrum* is edited by Pitra (*Spicilegium*, i. 265–276; the same volume [pp. 18–20] also containing anonymous scholia on Proverbs). Mai (ut sup., vii. 2) has given scholia from Origen, Didymus, Hippolytus, Apollinarius, and Polychronius on Proverbs, Isaiah, and Ezekiel, as well as the fragments of Cyril of Alexandria on Proverbs, the Song of Solomon, and Daniel (ii. 468–469, iii. 137–138). The scholia of Chrysostom on Kings, Job, Proverbs, Jeremiah, and Daniel are contained in *MPG*, lxiv. 193–194, 501–502. A special type of scholion is presented in the *Expositio interlinearis in Job* ascribed to Jerome (*MPL*, xxiv. 1475–76), in the *Quæstiones Hebraicæ in Genesin* (ib. 983–984), and *In libros Regum et Paralipomenōn* (ib. 1391–92).

6. Editions of N. T. Scholia. Among New Testament scholia mention should be made of the fragments of Clement's *Hypotyposeis* (ed. T. Zahn, *Supplementum Clementinum*, pp. 64–65, Erlangen, 1884), of Origen and Apollinarius on Luke (Mai, *Auctores classici*, x. 474–482, 495–499), of Hippolytus on Matthew (ib. 197–208), of Theodore of Mopsuestia on the Gospels and the Pauline epistles (ed. O. F. Fritzsche, Zurich, 1847), of Chrysostom on Romans and the Catholic epistles (*MPG*, lxiv. 1039–40), of the Athanasian homilies on Matthew and Luke (Montfaucon, ut sup., ii. 24–48; *MPG*, xxvii. 1391–1404), of Cyril of Alexandria on Matthew (Mai, *Nova collectio*, VII., ii. 142–148), Luke (Mai, *Auctores classici*, x. 1–407, 501–546, 605–613), and Hebrews (Mai, *Nova collectio*, VIII., ii. 142–148), and of Severus on Luke and Acts (idem, X., i. 408–457, 470–473, X., ii. 457–470). Of the anonymous scholia the *Scholia in quatuor evangelia*, first edited by Mai (*Auctores classici*, vi. 379–500, ix. 431–512; reprinted in *MPG*, cvi. 1077–1290), are especially important. These seem to be in the main excerpts. Those on Matthew and John correspond in content to Chrysostom, while the scholia on Mark and Luke are most nearly akin to the anonymous portions of Cramer's catena. The most extensive collection of anonymous scholia, however, is in C. F. Matthæi's major edition of the New Testament (Riga, 1782–88). Matthæi likewise published anonymous scholia on Revelation in his edition of Victor's commentary on Mark (pp. 210–224, Riga, 1775). In his edition of the catenas J. A. Cramer has made many addenda from manuscripts containing scholia, especially on Mark, Luke, Acts, and certain Pauline epistles (Oxford, 1838–44); and fragments of chiliastic scholia on Matthew have been edited by G. Mercati (*Studi e testi*, xi. 1–2). See CATENÆ and GLOSSES.

(G. HEINRICI.)

BIBLIOGRAPHY: H. F. von Soden, *Die Schriften des N. T.s in ihrer ältesten erreichbaren Textgestalt*, i. 293–294, Berlin, 1902; G. Karo and J. Lietzmann, in the *Nachrichten* of the Göttingen Royal Society of Sciences, philosophical-historical class, 1902, parts 1–3; J. E. Sandys, *Hist. of Classical Scholarship*, Cambridge, 1903.

SCHOLTEN, JAN HENDRIK: Dutch Protestant theologian; b. at Vleuten, near Utrecht, Aug. 17, 1811; d. at Leyden Apr. 10, 1885. He was educated at the University of Utrecht (1828–35), interrupting his studies in 1830 to serve in the campaign against Belgium. He was pastor at Meerkker for two years (1838–40), and professor at Franeker (1840–43). A few months later Scholten became associate professor of theology at Leyden, and full professor in 1845, retaining the latter position until his death, though after 1881 he was professor emeritus. Lecturing at first on natural theology and introduction, he began in 1845 to treat the Dutch creeds and the principles of the Reformed Church. Beginning with 1852 he added to his work an alternating course on Christian dogmatics and New-Testament theology, while with the change of the system of instruction in 1877 he took charge of the lectures on the philosophy of religion and the history of the concept of God. The writings of Scholten mark a steady evolution in his theological attitude, changing from conservatism to a full acceptance of the results of the critical school. This is exemplified by the difference between his *Historisch-kritische inleiding tot de schriften des Nieuwen Testaments* (Leyden, 1856) and his *Het evangelie naar Johannes* (1864). His dogmatic writings were *Dogmatices Christianæ initia* (1853–54), *Geschiedenis der christelijke godgeleerdheid gedurende het tijdperk des Nieuwen Testaments* (1856), and especially his *De leer der Hervormde Kerk in hare grondbeginselen* (1848–50). This latter work marked an epoch in the history of Dutch Protestantism, which had for several years approximated the Bible rather than Reformed standards. Scholten now became the leader of opposition to the Groningen school, which sought to return to the Gospel and the Arminian concept of the person of Christ, and in his work on the doctrines of his church he stoutly defended Calvinistic determinism. The position here held by Scholten was further developed in his *Geschiedenis van godsdienst en wijsbegeerte* (1853) and was still more elaborated in his *De vrije wil* (1859). The question of the day became the relation of man to Calvinistic predestination, and the relation of that doctrine to Christianity; so that Scholten saw himself compelled to become the protagonist of the determinists, and thus to be the leader of the "modernists." Some idea of his position may be gained from his rectoral address *De godgeleerdheid aan de Neederlandsche hoogescholen* (1876) and his monograph *Supranaturalisme in verband met Bijbel, Christendom en Protestantisme* (1867), and from other contributions.

As a delegate of the theological faculty of Leyden, Scholten was repeatedly a member of the synod and of the synodal committee of his church. In 1854 he was commissioned by the synod to prepare the translation of the Gospel and Epistles of John which appeared in 1868. (A. KUENEN†.)

BIBLIOGRAPHY: *Protestantische Kirchenzeitung*, 1884, pp. 789–794, 1885, pp. 380–385; A. Kuenen, in *Jaarboek der kon. Acad. von Wetenschappen*, 1885 (a memorial address).

SCHOLZ, scholts, **ANTON**: German Roman Catholic; b. at Schmachtenberg, Bavaria, Feb. 25, 1829; d. at Würzburg Sept. 30, 1908. He was educated at the Lyceum of Aschaffenburg (1849–1850) and at the universities of Munich and Würzburg (1850–53; D.D., Würzburg, 1856); was curate of Zell (1853–55); secretary of Bishop Anton von Stahl (1855–61); parish priest at Eisingen, near Würzburg (1861–72), being also district inspector of schools from 1863 to 1872. In 1872 he was appointed professor of Old-Testament exegesis and Biblical oriental languages in the University of Würzburg, of which he was rector in 1879–80 and 1892–93. In 1903 he retired from active life. After 1885 he defended the thesis that certain books of the Bible, such as Esther, Jonah, Judith, Tobit, Bel and the Dragon, and Susanna, are not historical, but are midrashic apocalypses. He was also a protagonist of Biblical criticism after 1895, and after long discussion, his views were recognised as justifiable by a papal decision in 1905. He wrote *De inhabitatione Spiritus Sancti* (Würzburg, 1872); *Der masorethische Text und die Septuaginta-Uebersetzung des Buches Jeremias* (Regensburg, 1875); *Kommentar zum Buche des Propheten Jeremias* (1880); *Die alexandrinische Uebersetzung des Buches Jesaias* (1880); *Kommentar zum Buche des Propheten Hoseas* (1882); *Kommentar zum Buche Joel* (1883); *Judith, eine Prophetie* (1885); *Kommentar zum Buche Judith* (1887); *Kommentar zum Buche Tobias* (1889); *Kommentar über das Buch Esther mit seinen Zusätzen und über Susanna* (1892); *Zeit und Ort der Entstehung der Bücher des Alten Testaments* (1893); *Kommentar über das Buch Judith und über Bel und Drache* (1896); *Kommentar über den Prediger* (Leipsic, 1901); and *Kommentar über das Hohelied* (1904).

SCHOOLMEN. See SCHOLASTICISM.

SCHOPENHAUER, shō'pen-hau"er, **ARTHUR**: German philosopher; b. in Danzig Feb. 22, 1788; d. in Frankfort-on-the-Main Sept. 21, 1860. He was son of a prosperous merchant who destined him to follow his own calling. After his father's death, his mother became a well-known novelist, member of the literary group at Weimar, drawn there by the fame of Goethe. His early life was one of vicissitude; he lived successively at Danzig and Hamburg, and in France, England, Italy. He tried his hand at commercial life, science and philosophy, studied at Göttingen, Berlin, and finally at Jena, where, in 1813, he received his degree with a dissertation *Ueber die vierfache Wurzel des Satzes vom zureichenden Grunde* (Rudolfstadt, 1813, 5th ed., 1891; Eng. transl., *The Fourfold Root of the Principle of Sufficient Reason*, New York, 1889). This contained the germ of his later thought. His chief works are, *Die Welt als Wille und Vorstellung* (Leipsic, 1819; Eng. transl., *The World as Will and Idea*, London, 1883); *Ueber den Willen in der Natur* (Frankfort, 1836, 5th ed., Leipsic, 1891; Eng. transl., *Will in Nature*, 1889, and in Bohn's *Philosophical Library*); *Die beiden Grundprobleme der Ethik* (Frankfort, 1841) *Parerga und Paralipomena* (Berlin, 1851). His *Sämmtliche Werke* were issued in 6 vols. (Leipsic, 1873–74; 3d ed., 2 vols., 1891). As a philosophical writer Schopenhauer is unexcelled unless by Plato in penetrating analysis, logical acumen, boldness of conception, subtlety of reasoning, picturesqueness of presentation, brilliancy and fascination of literary style.

According to Schopenhauer reality is characterised by a blind impulse which actualizes itself in the infinite variety of living forms in the world. The "will to live" describes this all-impelling force. Hence arises the fierce instinct of self-preservation by which every individual is ruled, and also the relentless warfare in which every individual both seeks to defend himself and to devour others. If in man the intelligence is more fully developed and the sensibilities more refined, this only deepens his consciousness not alone of actual but also of imagined and therefore of possible misery. The more complex the life, the more aggravated the wretchedness. Not joy, but unhappiness is life's positive content. Even freedom from pain results in ennui. Morality is impossible. The instinct of self-preservation becomes self-seeking, vanity, hypocrisy; and however the will may seem to be refined by culture, this is only apparent; it is hopelessly fettered and can not be changed by training. History but confirms the impression made by an analysis of man's nature. A hope of redemption appears to be offered by science, and especially by art, which opens the door to contemplation in which the intense struggle for existence is momentarily stilled. But even this promise is illusory; for the initiated it simply puts off the evil day, for all others it is wholly unavailing. The only sure path to emancipation lies in renouncing the will to live. He who beholds all others in this vast vortex and knows that for them as well as for himself deliverance can come only through supreme and final renunciation of the *principium individuationis*, will dedicate himself to asceticism, to disillusionment as to pleasure, to total abstention from sexual intercourse and ultimately from food. C. A. Beckwith.

Bibliography: English transls. other than those noted in the text are: *Select Essays*, Milwaukee, 1881; *Religion: a Dialogue, and other Essays*, London, 1889 (from *Parerga*). *The Wisdom of Life, being the First Part of . . . Aphorismen zur Lebensweisheit*, ib. 1890; *Counsels and Maxims: Being the second Part of . . . Aphorismen zur Lebensweisheit*, ib. 1890; *The Art of Controversy*, New York, 1890; *Selected Essays*, London, 1891 (in Bohn's *Philosophical Library*); *The Art of Literature*, London, 1891; *Studies in Pessimism*, ib. 1891, 7th ed., 1906; *On Human Nature*, London and New York, 1897, 3d ed., 1906; and *The Basis of Morality*, London, 1903.

As sources for a life use: *Briefwechsel zwischen Arthur Schopenhauer und Johann Aug. Becker*, ed. J. K. Becker, Leipsic, 1881; *Schopenhauer-Briefe*, ed. L. Schemann, ib. 1893; *Briefe an Becker, Frauenstadt, Von Doss, Lindner und Asher*, ed. Grisebach, Leipsic, 1895. On his life consult: J. Frauenstädt and E. O. Lindner, *Arthur Schopenhauer: von ihm, über ihn*, Berlin, 1863; W. Gwinner, *Schopenhauer und seine Freunde*, Leipsic, 1863; D. Asher, *Arthur Schopenhauer: Neues von ihm und über ihn*, Berlin, 1871; H. Frommann, *Arthur Schopenhauer*, Jena, 1872; W. Gwinner, *Arthur Schopenhauer aus persönlichem Umgange dargestellt*, Leipsic, 1878; K. Bähr, *Gespräche und Briefwechsel mit A. Schopenhauer*, Leipsic, 1894; *ADB*, xxxii. 333–346.

On his philosophy consult: F. Dorguth, *Schopenhauer in seiner Wahrheit*, Magdeburg, 1845; C. Bartholmess, *Histoire critique des doctrines religieuses de la philosophie moderne*, vol. ii., Strasburg, 1855; A. Cornill, *Arthur Schopenhauer als eine Uebergangsformation von einer idealistischen in eine realistische Weltanschauung*, Heidelberg, 1856; C. G. Bähr, *Die schopenhauer'sche Philosophie in ihren Grundzügen*, Dresden, 1857; R. Seydel, *Schopenhauers philosophisches System*, Leipsic, 1857; G. de Spiegel, *L'Esprit de la philosophie de Schopenhauer*, Darmstadt, 1863; R. Haym, *Arthur Schopenhauer*, Berlin, 1864; C. A. Thilo, *Schopenhauers ethischer Atheismus*, Leipsic, 1868; W. Scheffer, *Arthur Schopenhauer: die Philosophie van het Pessimisme*, Leyden, 1870; A. von Wurzbach, *Artur Schopenhauer*, Vienna, 1871; A. Taubert, *Der Pessimismus und seine Gegner*, Berlin, 1873; M. Venetianer, *Schopenhauer als Scholastiker*, ib. 1873; J. Huber, *Der Pessimismus*, Munich, 1876; T. Trautz, *Der Pessimismus: seine Begründung in der neueren Philosophie*, Carlsruhe, 1876; Helen Zimmern, *Arthur Schopenhauer: his Life and his Philosophy*, London, 1876; F. Bowen, *Modern Philosophy. From Descartes to Schopenhauer and Hartmann*, New York, 1877; E. Dühring, *Der Werth des Lebens*, 2d ed., Breslau, 1877; idem, *Kritische Geschichte der Philosophie*, Berlin, 3d ed., Leipsic, 1878; E. von Hartmann, *Neukantianismus, Schopenhauerianismus und Hegelianismus in ihrer Stellung zu den philosophischen Aufgaben der Gegenwart*, Berlin, 1877; E. Herrmann, *Woher und wohin? Schopenhauer's Antwort auf die letzten Lebensfragen*, Bonn, 1877; J. Sully, *Pessimism: a History and a Criticism*, London, 1877; L. von Golther, *Der moderne Pessimismus*, Leipsic, 1878; E. Caro, *Le Pessimisme au xix. siècle: Leopardi, Schopenhauer, Hartmann*, Paris, 1879; P. Mainländer, *Die Philosophie der Erlösung*, Berlin, 1879; L. Ducros, *Schopenhauer: les origines de sa métaphysique, ou les transformations de la "chose en soi" de Kant à Schopenhauer*, Paris, 1883; R. Koeber, *Die Philosophie Arthur Schopenhauers*, Heidelberg, 1888; O. Cramer, *A. Schopenhauers Lehre von der Schuld in ethischen Beziehungen*, ib. 1895; W. Caldwell, *Schopenhauer's System in its Philosophical Significance*, Edinburgh and New York, 1896; S. S. Colvin, *Schopenhauer's Doctrine of the Thing in Itself*, Strasburg, 1897; R. Böttger, *Das Grundproblem der schopenhauer'schen Philosophie*, Greifswald, 1898; O. Damm, *Schopenhauers Ethik*, Annaberg, 1898; M. Joseph, *Die psychologische Grundanschauung Schopenhauers*, ib. 1898; W. Deutschthümler, *Ueber Schopenhauer zu Kant*, Vienna, 1899; P. J. Möbius, *Ueber Schopenhauer*, Leipsic, 1899; S. Rappaport, *Spinoza und Schopenhauer*, Berlin, 1899; E. Clemens, *Schopenhauer und Spinoza*, Leipsic, 1900; R. Saitschick, *Genie und Charakter, Shakespeare, Lessing, Schopenhauer*, Berlin, 1900; J. Volkelt, *Arthur Schopenhauer*, Stuttgart, 1900; O. Damm, *Schopenhauer's Rechts- und Staatsphilosophie*, Halle, 1901; T. B. Saunders, *Schopenhauer*, London and New York, 1901; R. Schluter, *Schopenhauers Philosophie in seiner Briefen*, Leipsic, 1901; E. Hubbard, *Schopenhauer*, London, 1905; D. Irvine, *Defence of Pessimism*, ib. 1905; A. Kowalenski, *Arthur Schopenhauer und seine Weltanschauung*, Halle, 1908; T. Whittaker, *Schopenhauer*, ib. 1909; R. Basardjian, *Schopenhauer der Philosoph des Optimismus*, Leipsic, 1909; G. F. Wagner, *Encyklopädisches Register zu Schopenhauers Werken*, Carlsruhe, 1909; J. Mühlethaler, *Die Mystik bei Schopenhauer*, Berlin, 1910; G. Weng, *Schopenhauer, Darwin, Pessimismus oder Optimismus*, ib. 1910; the works on the history of philosophy by E. Zeller, Munich, 1873; J. E. Erdmann, London, 1898; W. Windelband, New York, 1893; and Ueberweg-Heinze, Berlin, 1905.

SCHORTINGHUIS, shēr''ting'hwis, **WILLEM**: Dutch Reformed poet and theologian; b. at Winschoten (21 m. e.s.e. of Groningen) Feb. 23, 1700; d. at Midwolda (18 m. e. of Groningen) Nov. 20, 1750. He was educated at the University of Groningen (1719–22), and early in 1723 became second preacher at Weener in East Frisia, where his antipathy to Pietism was changed to admiration by his senior, Henricus Klugkist. Through the exertions of the two, the pietistic movement spread widely in the province among Lutherans and Reformed alike, promoting both the inward and the outward prosperity of the church. In 1734 Schortinghuis was called to the pastorate of Midwolda, where he passed the remainder of his life, successfully promoting the cause of true piety. Though far from being a poet, Schortinghuis began his literary career by his *Geestelike gesangen* (1733), which was soon followed by his *Bevindelike gesangen*, hymns of edifying and didactic purport which long remained popular in conventicles. His *Nodige waarheden in 't herte van een Christen* (Groningen, 1738) was designed primarily for those who were about to make profession of their faith. His chief work was the *Het innige Christendom . . . voorgestelt in t' samenspraken tuschen een geoefende, begenadigde, kleingeloovige en onbegenadigde* (1740). In this work the author became the representative of Pietism in the Dutch Reformed Church of the eighteenth century, and gave a description of, and counsel for, a life of practical holiness. It caused a lively controversy because of its mystical trend, and its author secured the requisite approbation of the theological faculty of Groningen only with difficulty. Within the year a second edition appeared with the approbation of the classis to which Schortinghuis belonged, but his opponents secured from the Synod of Groningen the prohibition of a third edition until the doubts of the faculty should be satisfied. The strife was even carried outside his own synod. Despite all this, the *Het innige Christendom* exercised a wide influence.

(S. D. van Veen.)

Bibliography: H. van Berkum, *Schortinghuis en de vijf mésten*, Utrecht, 1859; J. C. Kromsigt, *Wilhelmus Schortinghuis*, Groningen, 1904.

SCHOTT, shot, HEINRICH AUGUST: German Lutheran; b. at Leipsic Dec. 5, 1780; d. at Jena Dec. 29, 1835. He was educated at the university of his native city (Ph.D., 1799); lectured there on theology and philology (1801–05), being morning university preacher after 1803; was associate professor in the philological faculty (1805–08); and in the theological faculty (1808–09); full professor and preacher at the castle church at Wittenberg (1809–1812); and at Jena from 1812. While at Leipsic Schott edited the *Ars rhetorica* of Dionysius of Halicarnassus (Leipsic, 1804), and the Greek text of the New Testament with a Latin translation (1805), and wrote his *Entwurf einer Theorie der Beredsamkeit mit besonderer Anwendung auf Kanzelberedsamkeit* (1807). At Wittenberg he composed his *Epitome theologiæ Christianæ* (1810). His chief work was *Theorie der Beredsamkeit, mit besonderer Anwendung auf die christliche Beredsamkeit* (3 parts, Leipsic, 1815–28). Special mention should be made of his *Isagoge historico-critica in libros Novi Fœderis sacros* (Jena, 1830) and his Latin commentary on Thessalonians and Galatians (Leipsic, 1834). His apologetic contributions, such as his *Briefe über Religion* (Jena, 1826), are of minor value. A number of briefer contributions from his pen were collected in his *Opuscula* (2 vols., 1817–18). (L. Pelt†.)

Bibliography: J. T. L. Danz, *Heinrich August Schott*, Leipsic, 1836.

SCHOTT, THEODOR FRIEDRICH: German Lutheran and historian; b. at Esslingen (17 m. e.s.e. of Stuttgart) Dec. 16, 1835; d. at Stuttgart Mar. 18, 1899. He was educated at the seminary of Blaubeuren and Tübingen (1853–57), and after being vicar for two years at Bopfingen and Köngen, was a teacher at Hofwyl near Bern from 1859 to 1861; then he studied the history of the French and Italian Reformation at Paris for three months, and, after a short term as vicar, he became teacher of religion at the Stuttgart gymnasium. He was next pastor at Berg, a suburb of Stuttgart, for six years (1867–73), and from 1873 until his death was librarian of the public library in Stuttgart. He was likewise a director of the Württemberg branch of the Gustav-Adolph-Verein and helped found the Verein für Reformationsgeschichte, and was also active in philanthropic work. After 1876 he was editor of the *Allgemeines Kirchenblatt für das evangelische Deutschland*, and, besides many briefer contributions, wrote *Hugenottengeschichten* (Stuttgart, 1869); *Die Aufhebung des Ediktes von Nantes* (Halle, 1886); and *Die Kirche der Wüste 1757–87* (1893).

(H. Hermelink.)

Bibliography: *Biographisches Jahrbuch*, ed. A. Bettelheim, iv (1899), 75–77.

SCHRADER, shrō'der, EBERHARD: German Protestant Orientalist; b. at Brunswick Jan. 5, 1836; d. at Berlin July 4, 1908. He was educated at the University of Göttingen (Ph.D., 1860), and 1862 became privat-docent at the University of Zurich, where he was appointed full professor of theology in 1863. In 1870 he was called to Giessen in a similar capacity, and thence to Jena in 1873. From 1875 until his final retirement, brought about by impaired health in 1899, he was professor of Semitic languages in the philosophical faculty of the University of Berlin. He was the pioneer of Assyriology in Germany. Besides editing the eighth edition of W. M. L. de Wette's *Lehrbuch der historisch-kritischen Einleitung in die kanonischen und apokryphischen Bücher des Alten Testaments* (Berlin, 1869) and the *Keilinschriftliche Bibliothek* (6 vols., 1889–1901), he wrote *De linguæ Æthiopicæ cum cognatis linguis comparatæ indole* (Göttingen, 1860); *Studien zur Kritik und Erklärung der biblischen Urgeschichte* (Stuttgart, 1863); *Die assyrisch-babylonischen Keilinschriften, kritische Untersuchung der Grundlagen ihrer Entzifferung* (Leipsic, 1872); *Die Keilinschriften und das Alte Testament* (Giessen, 1872; 3rd ed., entirely revised, by H. Zimmern and H. Winckler, Berlin, 1902; Eng. trans. of the second edition, *The Cuneiform Inscriptions and the Old Testament*, by O. C. Whitehouse, 2 vols., London, 1885–88); *Die Höllenfahrt der Istar* (Giessen, 1874); *Keilinschriften und Geschichtsforschung, ein Beitrag zur monumentalen Geographie, Geschichte und Chronologie der Assyrer* (1878); *Zur Kritik der Inschriften Tiglath-Pileser's II, des Asarhaddon und des Asurbanipal* (Berlin, 1880); *Zur Frage nach dem Ursprunge der altbabylonischen Cultur* (1884); and *Die Keilinschriften am Eingange der Quellgrotte des Sebeneh-Su* (1885).

Bibliography: C. Bezold, *Eberhard Schrader. Eine Lebensskizze*, Strasburg, 1909; E. Meyer, *Gedächtnisrede auf Eberhard Schrader*, Berlin, 1909; O. C. Whitehouse, in *Expository Times*, Dec., 1910, pp. 104–106.

SCHROECKH, shrök, JOHANN MATTHIAS: German Lutheran; b. at Vienna July 26, 1733; d. at Wittenberg Aug. 1, 1808. After completing his education at Göttingen, he spent a year at Leipsic in further study and assisting his uncle, Karl Andreas Bell, to edit the *Acta eruditorum* and *Leipziger Gelehrten Zeitungen*. Still continuing his editorial labors, he lectured at the university on parts of the New Testament, as well as on literary history and church history, and in 1761 was made associate professor. In 1767 he accepted a call to Wittenberg as professor of poetry, exchanging this chair in 1775 for that of history. Besides his *Lebensbeschreibungen berühmter Gelehrter* (Leipsic 1764–69), *Allgemeine Biographien* (Berlin, 1767–91), and *Christliche Kirchengeschichte* (see below), Schröckh revised four parts (on Italy, France, Holland, and England) of a German transl. of W. Guthrie and J. Gray's *General History of the World* (1770–76) and the fourth edition of L. Offerhaus's *Compendium historiæ universalis* (1778), and wrote his *Lehrbuch der allgemeinen Weltgeschichte* (1774), the fourth part (from 1750 to 1760) of the *Unparteiische Kirchengeschichte Alten und Neuen Testaments* (Jena, 1766), *Historia religionis et ecclesiæ Christianæ adumbrata in usum lectionum* (Berlin, 1777), and *Allgemeine Weltgeschichte für Kinder* (4 vols., Leipsic, 1779–84). By far his most important work, however, was his great *Christliche Kirchengeschichte* (45 vols., Leipsic, 1768–1812), the first thirty-five volumes extending to the Reformation, and the rest (of which the two final volumes were edited by H. G. Tzschirner after Schröckh's death) bearing the special title of *Kirchengeschichte seit der Reformation*. The work is still of distinct value.

The theological position of Schröckh was one of modified supranaturalism, and his method, with its excellences and its defects, was essentially that of the period in which he lived, the period of the "Enlightenment" (q.v.). (J. A. WAGENMANN†.)

BIBLIOGRAPHY: An autobiographic sketch is in J. R. G. Beier's *Allgemeine Magazin für Prediger*, v. 2, pp. 209–222, 12 vols., Leipsic, 1789–96. Consult further: K. H. Pölitz, *Leben J. M. Schröckhs*, Wittenberg, 1808; K. L. Nitzsch, *Ueber J. M. Schröckhs Studienweise und Maximen*, Weimar, 1809; H. G. Tzschirner, *Ueber J. M. Schröckhs Leben, Charakter, und Schriften*, Leipsic, 1812.

SCHROERS, shrörs, **JOHANN HEINRICH**: German Roman Catholic; b. at Krefeld (20 m. s.w. of Essen) Nov. 26, 1852. He was educated at the universities of Bonn, Würzburg, Innsbruck, and Munich (Ph.D., Würzburg, 1880); was engaged in parochial work in Munich (1880–85); became privatdocent for canon law at the University of Freiburg (1886), whence he was called in 1886 to his present position of professor of church history in Bonn. He has written *Der Streit über die Prädestination im neunten Jahrhundert* (Freiburg, 1880); *Hinkmar, Erzbischof von Reims, sein Leben und seine Schriften* (1884); and *Kirche und Wissenschaft* (Bonn, 1907).

SCHUBERT, shū'bert, **GOTTHILF HEINRICH VON**: German Lutheran and naturalist; b. at Hohenstein (40 m. s.s.e. of Leipsic), Saxony, Apr. 26, 1780; d. at Munich June 30, 1860. Though intended by his father for the ministry, the rationalism at Leipsic, where he began his theological studies, was so uncongenial to him that he devoted himself to medicine at Jena. For a time he was a physician at Altenburg, but feeling impelled to deeper study of the natural sciences, he went in 1805 to Freiburg, where he wrote the first part of his *Ahnungen einer allgemeinen Geschichte des Lebens* (Leipsic, 1806). In 1806 he removed to Dresden, and there completed the *Ahnungen* (1821), which was followed, a few years later, by the *Symbolik des Traumes* (Bamberg, 1814), and the *Ansichten von der Nachtseite der Natur* (Dresden, 1808). In 1809 he was made rector of the newly founded Realschule at Nuremberg. Here, too, through the influence of a master baker named Burger, Schubert again turned his thoughts to religion. For a time he was tutor to the children of the grand duke of Mecklenburg, Frederick Louis, and was also invited to become the director of a proposed normal school. The latter project fell through, however, because of the avowed intention of Schubert to give all his teaching a religious trend. He was, accordingly, glad to accept a call to Erlangen as professor of natural history, where he lectured not only on mineralogy, botany, and zoology, but also on forestry and mining. In 1820 he made a tour of Switzerland, and shortly after his return wrote the popular *Lehrbuch der Naturgeschichte für Schulen* (Erlangen, 1822), followed by the *Physiognomik der Natur* (1826). He then visited southern France and Italy, the results being embodied in a work of two volumes, and on his return accepted a call to the University of Munich. Here, despite some opposition, his lectures became immensely popular, and here he wrote his most important book, *Geschichte der Seele* (2 vols., Stuttgart, 1830). In 1836 he made a visit to Palestine, describing his experiences in a work of three volumes. Retiring from active life in 1853, Schubert devoted himself entirely to writing, the result being his *Die Krankheiten der menschlichen Seele* (Stuttgart, 1845); his autobiographical *Der Erwerb aus einem vergangenen und die Erwartungen von einem zukünftigen Leben* (3 vols., Erlangen, 1854–56); his *Erinnerungen aus dem Leben . . . Herzogin von Orleans* (Munich, 1860; Eng. transl., *Reminiscences of the Life of . . . the Late Duchess of Orleans*, Bath, 1862); and his *Geschichte von Bayern für Schulen* (1864). Among his very numerous other books, mention may be made of the *Altes und Neues aus dem Gebiete der inneren Seelenkunde* (Leipsic, 1817–44); *Geschichte der Natur* (Erlangen, 1830); *Züge aus Oberlins Leben* (4th ed., Nuremberg, 1832); and *Vermischte Schriften* (2 vols., Erlangen, 1857–60.)

(JULIUS HAMBERGER†.)

BIBLIOGRAPHY: Consult, besides the autobiographic *Der Erwerb*, ut sup.: M. Zeller, *Dr. Gotthilf Heinrich von Schubert's Jugendgeschichte*, Stuttgart, 1880; idem, *Gotthilf Heinrich von Schubert's Tagewerk und Feierabend*, ib. 1882.

SCHUBERT, HANS GEORG WILHELM VON: German Protestant; b. at Dresden Dec. 12, 1859. He was educated at the universities of Leipsic, Bonn, Strasburg, and Zurich (1878–83; Ph.D., Strasburg, 1884); was private tutor in Elberfeld (1883–84); studied theology at Tübingen and Halle (1884–86); was a teacher in the Rauhes Haus, Hamburg (1887–91); associate professor of church history at Strasburg (1891–92); professor of the same subject at the University of Kiel (1892–1906), and since 1906 at the University of Heidelberg, of which he was rector in 1910. Besides revising the second edition of the first volume of W. Möller's *Lehrbuch der Kirchengeschichte* (3 parts, Tübingen, 1897–1902), he has written *Die Unterwerfung der Alamannen unter die Franken* (Strasburg, 1884); *Roms Kampf um die Weltherrschaft* (Halle, 1888);

Die evangelische Trauung, ihre geschichtliche Entwicklung und gegenwärtige Bedeutung (Berlin, 1890); *Die Komposition des pseudopetrinischen Evangelien-Fragments* (1893); *Das Petrusevangelium, synoptische Tabelle, nebst Uebersetzung und kritischem Apparat* (1893; Eng. transl., "The Gospel of St. Peter," Edinburgh, 1893); *Die Entstehung der schleswig-holstein'schen Landeskirche* (Kiel, 1895); *Siebenbürgen* (Tübingen, 1900); *Ansgar und die Anfänge der schleswig-holstein'schen Kirchengeschichte* (Kiel, 1901); *Die heutige Auffassung und Behandlung der Kirchengeschichte* (Tübingen, 1902); *Der sogenannte Praedestinatus* (Leipsic, 1903); *Grundzüge der Kirchengeschichte* (Tübingen, 1904, 3d ed., 1906; Eng. transl., *Outlines of Church History*, London, 1907); *Hamburg, die Missionsmetropole des Nordens im Mittelalter* (1904); *Kurze Geschichte der christlichen Liebestätigkeit* (1905); *Kirchengeschichte Schleswig-Holsteins*, part 1 (1907); *Bündniss und Bekenntniss 1529–1530* (1908); *Beiträge zur Geschichte der evangelischen Bekenntnis- und Bündnissbildung* (1909); *Calvin. Rede* (1909); and *Bekenntnisbildung und Religionspolitik* (1910).

SCHUERER, shü'rer, **EMIL**: German Protestant; b. at Augsburg May 2, 1844; d. at Göttingen Apr. 30, 1910. He studied at the universities of Erlangen, Berlin, and Heidelberg (1862–66); Ph.D., Leipsic, 1868). He was privat-docent for theology at the University of Leipsic (1869–73); and associate professor of the same subject (1873–78); accepted a call to Giessen as full professor (1878); and at Kiel (1890); and professor of New-Testament exegesis at Göttingen after 1895. In theology he was an adherent of the moderate historical and critical school. He wrote: *Schleiermachers Religionsbegriff und die philosophischen Aussetzungen desselben* (Leipsic, 1868); *De controversiis paschalibus secundo post Christum natum saeculo exortis* (1869); *Lehrbuch der neutestamentlichen Zeitgeschichte* (1874), which in the later editions, entitled *Geschichte des jüdischen Volkes im Zeitalter Jesu Christi* (3 vols., 1886–90; 4th ed., 1909; Eng. transl. by J. Macpherson, S. Taylor, and P. Christie, *A History of the Jewish People in the Time of Jesus Christ*, 5 vols., Edinburgh, 1890–91), has become one of the leading authorities on its subject; *Die Gemeindeverfassung der Juden in Rom in der Kaiserzeit nach den Inschriften dargestellt* (Leipsic, 1879); *Die Predigt Jesu Christi in ihrem Verhältnis zum Alten Testament und zum Judentum* (Darmstadt, 1882); *Die ältesten Christengemeinden im römischen Reiche* (Kiel, 1894); and *Das messianische Selbstbewusstsein Jesu* (Göttingen, 1904).

SCHUERMANN, shür'män, **ANNA MARIA VON**: Patroness of Jean de Labadie (q.v.); b. at Cologne Nov. 5, 1607; d. at Wienwert (37 m. w.s.w. of Groningen) May 4, 1678. She early showed extraordinary mental capacity, especially for linguistics, and was celebrated for skill in music, drawing, painting, carving, wax-modeling, and etching. Her brother, Jan Gottschalk, who had become acquainted with Labadie in Geneva, and believed he was called to reform the Church, inspired her with the same conviction. She joined Labadie when he visited the Netherlands and became a member of his household in Amsterdam, a step that cost her all her old friends. She revoked all her former writings, wrote defenses of Labadie and his congregation, and supported him with her wealth. The relations between her and Labadie were of a mystical character; no word of accusation was ever made against her. Her *Eukleria* (part 1, Altona, 1673, part 2, Amsterdam, 1685) gives an account of her life and ideals. Her *Opuscula* appeared Leyden, 1648. (P. Tschackert.)

Bibliography: A report which will serve as a source for the life, probably based upon autobiographic communications, is found in G. Arnold, *Kirchen- und Ketzerhistorie*, vol. iv., addition, pp. 1339–60, Frankfort, 1729. Consult: P. Tschackert, *Anna Maria von Schürmann*, Gotha, 1876; M. Göbel, *Geschichte des christlichen Lebens in der rheinisch-westphälischen evangelischen Kirche*, ii. 180–299, Coblenz, 1852; and the literature under Labadie, Jean de, Labadists.

SCHULTENS, shul'tens, **ALBERT**: Celebrated Arabist and Hebrew scholar; b. at Groningen Aug. 22, 1686; d. at Leyden Jan. 26, 1750. In his fourteenth year he matriculated in theology at the University of Groningen, where he studied Aramaic, Syriac, and finally Arabic as necessary to an understanding of the other Semitic languages. In 1706 came his disputation *De utilitate linguæ Arabicæ in interpretanda Sacra Scriptura* (printed in his *Opera minora*). He then went to complete his studies at Leyden under Hadrian Reland, taking his doctorate in theology in 1709, continuing for two years the study of oriental manuscripts; [in 1711 he became pastor at Wassenær;] became professor of Hebrew at Franeker, 1713, serving also as university preacher in 1717; he went to Leyden as rector of the Collegium theologicum, became ordinary professor of oriental languages in the university there in 1732, and in 1740 professor of Hebrew antiquities. His reputation is due to the fact that he was the first to apply in comprehensive style Arabic to the elucidation of Hebrew; that he made mistakes is true, but this was to be expected of a pathfinder. His most renowned pupil was Nikolaus Wilhelm Schröder, author of the frequently reprinted *Institutiones ad fundamenta linguæ Hebraicæ* (Groningen, 1766). The principles advocated by Schultens have been newly applied and advanced by Justus Olshausen (q.v.) and Heinrich Leberecht Fleischer, while the grammars of Bernhard Stade, Wilhelm Gesenius, Eduard König, and Hermann Lebrecht Strack (qq. v.) are not uninfluenced by the work of Schultens.

His chief work was *Origines Hebrææ sive Hebrææ linguæ antiquissima natura et indoles ex Arabiæ penetralibus revocata* (2 vols., Franeker, 1724–38; 2d ed., Leyden, 1761). Other works are *Institutiones ad fundamenta linguæ Hebrææ* (Leyden, 1737); *Liber Jobi cum nova versione ad Hebræum fontem et commentario perpetuo* (2 vols., 1737); *Proverbia Salomonis* (1748); *Opera minora* (1769). He also edited the *Rudimenta linguæ Arabicæ* of Thomas Erpenius and added to it a *Clavis* (1733). (H. L. Strack.)

Bibliography: W. Gesenius, *Geschichte der hebräischen Sprache und Schrift*, pp. 126–129, Leipsic, 1815; F. Mühlau, in *Zeitschrift für lutherische Theologie und Kirche*, 1870, pp. 1–21; Lichtenberger, *ESR*, xi. 529–530.

SCHULTHESS, shul'thess, **JOHANNES:** Swiss Protestant theologian; b. at Zurich Sept. 28, 1763; d. there Nov. 10, 1836. He studied theology at the Carolinum in Zurich. His main interest in early life was the development of the public school system. His *Kinderbibel des Alten Testaments* (Zurich, 1813) and *Schweizerischer Kinderfreund* (1812–13) were long valued text-books. In 1796 he became professor of Greek and Latin, in 1816 of theology, with the title and position of canon of the cathedral. He worked with great industry at the exegesis of the New Testament and wrote *Exegetisch-theologische Forschungen* (3 vols., 1818–24), and a commentary on James (1824). In collaboration with J. K. von Orelli he published *Rationalismus und Supranaturalismus, Kanon, Tradition und Skription* (1822); and *Revision des kirchlichen Lehrbegriffs* (1826). For a time he edited the periodical *Annalen* founded by Wachler. His critical historical views appear most clearly in his last work, *Vorlesungen über das historische Christentum nach der wissenschaftlichen Ansicht des 19. Jahrhunderts* (1837).

Schulthess took part in the controversy that broke out in the second decade of the nineteenth century concerning the Lord's Supper, and wrote *Evangelische Lehre von dem freien Gnadenmahl, ein Beitrag zur Vereinigung der evangelischen Kirchen* (1818), and *Die evangelische Lehre vom heiligen Abendmahl* (1824). He regarded himself as the representative of the genuine Zwinglian doctrine and as such he opposed ultramontanism and "all mysticism and pietism." He wrote in 1815 *Das Unchristliche und Vernunftwidrige, geistig und sittlich Ungesunde mehrerer Büchlein, die seit einiger Zeit von der Traktatgesellschaft in Basel und ihren Freunden heimlich ausgestreut werden.* He was preeminently of a polemical nature, although in private intercourse a genial companion and tolerant of the opinions of others. In contrast with his theological liberalism and progressiveness was his political conservatism. After the establishment of the Zurich university in 1833, he was appointed extraordinary professor of New-Testament exegesis and catechetics. Among his great services to science and the Church was his editing and publishing, together with his friend Schuler, the works of Zwingli (11 parts with supplement, Zurich, 1828–61).

(P. Christ†.)

Bibliography: J. Schulthess (his son), *Denkschrift zur hundertjährigen Jubelfeier der Stiftung des schulthessschen Familienfonds*, Zurich, 1859; A. Schweizer, *Biographische Aufzeichnungen*, ed. P. Schweizer, ib. 1889.

SCHULTZ, shūlts, **FRIEDRICH WILHELM:** Protestant theologian; b. at Friesack (33 m. n.w. of Potsdam), Mark Brandenburg, Sept. 24, 1828; d. at Breslau, 1888. He studied at Berlin, 1847–51; became privat-docent there, 1853; professor extraordinary, 1856; and ordinary professor, 1864, at Breslau. He wrote *Das Deuteronomium erklärt* (Berlin, 1859); *Die Schöpfungsgeschichte nach Naturwissenschaft und Bibel* (Gotha, 1865); the comments on Ezra, Nehemiah, and Esther, in J. P. Lange's Commentary (Bielefeld, 1876); and with W. Strack prepared the commentary on Psalms and Proverbs (Munich, 1888) in *Kurzgefasstes Kommentar.*

SCHULTZ, HERMANN: German Lutheran; b. at Lüchow (37 m. s.e. of Lüneburg) Dec. 30, 1836; d. at Göttingen May 15, 1903. He was educated at the universities of Göttingen and Erlangen (1853–1856), and, after being a private tutor at Hamburg for two years, returned to Göttingen as a lecturer in theology, becoming privat-docent in 1861. In 1864 he was called to Basel as full professor, and in 1872 accepted a similar position at the reorganized University of Strasburg. In 1874–76 he was professor of theology at Heidelberg, but in the latter year was recalled to Göttingen, where he passed the remainder of his life. He was created a consistorial counselor in 1881 and abbot of Bursfelde in 1890, and was also first university preacher and director of the seminary for practical theology, although his lectures were on the Old Testament and all departments of systematic theology.

In 1863 Schultz published at Frankfort the second edition of H. A. C. Hävernick's *Vorlesungen über die Theologie des Alten Testaments*, but his most important contribution to this theme was his *Alttestamentliche Theologie* (2 vols., Frankfort, 1869; 5th ed., 1896; Eng. transl. from the 4th ed. by J. A. Paterson, Edinburgh, 1892), in the successive editions of which he passed from the position of Ewald to that of Graf. Problems of Biblical theology often led him to discuss questions in systematic theology, as is shown by his *Voraussetzungen der christlichen Lehre von der Unsterblichkeit* (Göttingen, 1861). The majority of the dogmatic studies of Schultz were connected with Christology and the cognate theme of the theory of the atonement, these investigations reaching their culmination in the *Lehre von der Gottheit Christi* (Gotha, 1881), the conclusions of which were in substantial accord with the *Communicatio idiomatum* (q.v.), while the whole work, though independent of Ritschl, was distinctly Ritschlian in spirit. Of the other dogmatic contributions of Schultz the most important was his *Studien und Kritiken zur Lehre vom heiligen Abendmahl* (Gotha, 1886), which was practically a defense of the old Lutheran position. The versatility and receptivity of his theology find an admirable exemplification in his *Grundriss der christlichen Apologetik* (Göttingen, 1894; Eng. transl., London, 1905), which followed his *Grundriss der evangelischen Dogmatik* (Göttingen, 1890) and *Grundriss der evangelischen Ethik* (1891). In these three works he sought to reach others than those who attended his lectures, and the same spirit of practical Christianity was manifested in his *Zu den kirchlichen Fragen der Gegenwart* (Frankfort, 1869), as well as in his volumes of sermons, *Predigten, gehalten in der Universitätskirche zu Göttingen* (Gotha, 1882) and *Aus dem Universitätsgottesdienst* (2 vols., Göttingen, 1902–03). He did not, however, establish a distinct school, although he never lacked pupils who gratefully acknowledged the debt which they owed him.

(Eberhard Vischer.)

Bibliography: *The Expository Times*, July, 1903; *Beweis des Glaubens*, Sept.–Oct., 1904.

SCHULTZE, shūlt'se, **AUGUSTUS:** Moravian; b. at Nowawes (a suburb of Potsdam), Prussia, Feb. 3, 1840. He was graduated from the Moravian college at Niesky (1858), and at the theological seminary at Gnadenfeld, Silesia (1861). He was then a teacher in the French Academy at Lausanne, Switzerland (1861–62), and classical instructor in the college at Niesky (1862–70). In 1870 he left Germany for the United States, and has since been connected with the Moravian College and Theological Seminary at Bethlehem, Pa., first as professor of exegesis and dogmatics until 1885, and then as president. From 1881 to 1893 he was one of the three members of the governing board of his denomination in America. Besides editing *Der Brüder Botschafter* for several years, he has written *History of the Widow's Society of Bethlehem* (Bethlehem, Pa., 1880); *Aarlig Dagbog* (1888); *Die Missionsfelder der erneuerten Brüderkirche* (1890); *Grammar and Vocabulary of the Eskimo Language of Northwestern Alaska* (1894); *The Theology of Peter and Paul* (1896); *Guide to the Old Moravian Cemetery at Bethlehem* (1898); *The Books of the Bible Analyzed* (1902); and *Christian Doctrine and Systematic Theology* (1909).

SCHULTZE, BENJAMIN: Missionary to India and Translator of the Bible. See INDIA, II., § 2.

SCHULTZ, MAXIMILIAN VIKTOR: German Lutheran; b. at Fürstenberg (a village near Corbach, 28 m. s.w. of Cassel), Waldeck, Dec. 13, 1851. He was educated at the universities of Basel, Jena, Strasburg, and Göttingen, and, after several years of study in Italy, became privat-docent at the University of Leipsic in 1879. In 1884 he was called to Greifswald as associate professor of church history and church archeology, where he has been professor of the same subject since 1888. He has written or edited *Die Katakomben von San Gennaro dei Poveri in Neapel* (Jena, 1877); *Archäologische Studien über altchristliche Monumente* (Vienna, 1880); *Die Katakomben, ihre Geschichte und ihre Monumente* (Leipsic, 1882); *Das evangelische Kirchengebäude, ein Ratgeber für Geistliche und Freunde kirchlicher Kunst* (1886); *Geschichte des Untergangs des griechisch-römischen Heidentums* (2 vols., Jena, 1887–92); *Das Kloster San Marco in Florenz* (Leipsic, 1888); *Die altchristlichen Bildwerke und die wissenschaftliche Forschung* (1889); *Archäologie der altchristlichen Kunst* (Munich, 1895); *Waldeckische Reformationsgeschichte* (Leipsic, 1903); *Codex Waldeccensis, unbekannte Fragmente einer griechisch-lateinischen Bibelhandschrift* (Munich, 1904); *Geschichts- und Kunstdenkmäler der königlichen Universität Greifswald* (1906); *Die altchristlichen Grabstätten Siciliens* (1907); *Philipp Nicolai* (1908); and *Waldeckische Landeskunde* (1909).

SCHULZ, shūlts, **ALPHONS:** German Roman Catholic; b. at Karchau (a village near Nimptsch, 29 m. s.w. of Breslau) Apr. 27, 1871. He studied at the lyceum of Braunsberg and the University of Münster (1891–97; D.D., Münster, 1897), and in Jerusalem (1897–98). He was privat-docent for Old-Testament exegesis at the Lyceum of Braunsberg (1900–04); professor in the gymnasium of the same city (1901–04); and since 1904 has been associate professor of Old-Testament exegesis in the Lyceum. He has written *De Psalmis gradualibus* (Münster, 1897); *Quellen zur Geschichte des Elias* (Braunsberg, 1906); *Göttliches und Menschliches im Alten Testament* (1906); and *Doppelberichte im Pentateuch* (Freiburg, 1908).

SCHULZ, DAVID: German Lutheran; b. at Pürben, near Freystadt (75 m. n.w. of Breslau), Nov. 29, 1779; d. at Breslau Feb. 17, 1854. He was educated at the University of Halle (Ph.D., 1806), where he became privat-docent in 1806. On the closing of the university, he took a like position at Leipsic, but when Halle was reopened in 1808, Schulz returned to his alma mater. In 1809 he was appointed associate professor of theology and philosophy, but in the same year accepted a call to Frankfort as full professor of theology. With the incorporation of the University of Frankfort with that of Breslau in 1811, Schulz went to Breslau, retaining his professorship until blindness forced him to retire from active life. Theologically he was a rationalist. His exegetical and critical writings are antiquated, though his polemic works still possess a certain historical interest. His principal works, which are prolix and repetitive, are: *Der Brief an die Hebräer* (Breslau, 1818); *Die christliche Lehre vom heiligen Abendmahl* (Leipsic, 1824); *Was heisst Glauben und wer sind die Ungläubigen?* (1830); and *Die Geistesgeben der ersten Christen* (Breslau, 1836). He edited the third edition of the first volume (containing the Gospels) of J. J. Griesbach's *Novum Testamentum Græce* (Berlin, 1827). (J. J. HERZOG†.)

SCHULZE, shūl'tse, **LUDWIG THEODOR:** German Lutheran; b. at Berlin Feb. 27, 1833. He was educated at the university of his native city (lic. theol., 1856; Ph.D., 1858), where he became privat-docent for New-Testament exegesis and Biblical theology in 1859. Four years later he was called to Königsberg as associate professor of theology, and was also chaplain of the house for deaconesses and a member of the committee on theological examinations. From 1866 to 1874 he was inspector of the Kloster unserer lieben Frauen at Magdeburg and head of the seminary for the training of teachers of religion at the gymnasium. Since 1874 he has been professor of dogmatic theology and ethics at Rostock; he was rector magnificus of the University of Rostock in 1894 and has repeatedly been dean of the theological faculty. In theology his position is essentially conservative. He has written *De fontibus ex quibus historia Hycsorum haurienda sit* (Berlin, 1858); *Ueber die Wunder Jesu Christi, mit besonderem Bezug auf Renan* (Königsberg, 1864); *Martha und Maria, zwei Lebensbilder nach der heiligen Schrift* (Gotha, 1865); *Passions- und Osterfeier* (sermons; 1866); *Vom Menschensohn und vom Logos* (1867); *Friede im Herrn* (sermons; 1871); *Philipp Wackernagel, ein Lebensbild* (Leipsic, 1879); *Friedrich Adolf Philippi, ein Lebensbild* (Gütersloh, 1883); *Luther und die evangelische Kirche* (Rostock, 1883); *August Neander, ein Lebensbild* (Leipsic, 1890); *Die Theologie der Offenbarung, ihr Wesen und ihre Aufgabe in der Gegenwart* (Rostock, 1894); *Die Irrtumslosigkeit Jesu* (Gütersloh, 1908); and *Unsere Quellen für das Leben Jesu Christi* (1909). He prepared the third edition of K. F. A. Wuttke's *Handbuch der christlichen Sittenlehre* (2 vols., Leipsic, 1874–75) and contributed the sections on the introduction to the New Testament, the New-Testament revelation of salvation, the history of the New-Testament period, and the life of Jesus and the apostolic Church to O. Zöckler's *Handbuch der theologischen Wissenschaften* (3 vols., Nördlingen, 1883–84).

SCHULZE, MARTIN: German Protestant; b. at See, Upper Lausanne, Switzerland, Jan. 26, 1866. He studied at the University of Halle (1889–93) and after being director of the Tholuck hall for theological students in the same city for a few months, became privat-docent for New-Testament exegesis and dogmatics at Breslau within the year, and was appointed associate professor in the same institution (1899), but since 1904 has been professor of systematic theology at the University of Königsberg. He has written *Zur Frage nach der Bedeutung der heiligen Schrift* (Halle, 1894); *Die Religion Jesu und der Glaube an Christus* (1897); *Das Wesen des Christentums* (1897); *Calvins Jenseits-Christentum in seinem Verhältnis zu den religiösen Schriften des Erasmus* (Görlitz, 1902); *Wert und Unwert der Beweise für das Dasein Gottes* (1905); and *Der persönliche Character des protestantischen Christentums* (Halle, 1909).

SCHUPP, shūp (**SCHUPPIUS**), **JOHANN BALTHASAR:** German preacher and satirist; b. at Giessen Mar., 1610; d. at Hamburg Oct. 26, 1661. He studied philosophy at Marburg, but becoming convinced of the uselessness of the current metaphysical subtleties, he turned to theology. After completing his triennium he undertook a pedestrian tour in accordance with the custom of the times, and finally stopped at Rostock where he took his master's degree in 1631, and began to give lectures. In 1634 he accompanied a young nobleman, Rudolf Rauw of Holtzhausen, on a journey to Holland, and on his return was made professor of history and oratory at Marburg. His vivacious manner and geniality made him extremely popular with the students. Meanwhile he devoted a great part of his time to the study of theology. In 1643 he was chosen preacher at the Elisabethkirche, a position he filled while performing the duties of his professorship, and in 1646 became court preacher and counselor of the consistory for Landgrave Johannes von Hesse-Braubach. The prince was so well pleased with Schupp that he sent him in 1647 as his ambassador to the peace convention at Münster and Osnabrück. He was about this time elected pastor of the Jacobikirche, at Hamburg, where he was extraordinarily successful, though his popularity aroused the jealousy of his brother clergymen.

Before this time Schupp had written only in Latin, excepting some small volumes of hymns. He now began to write in German, issuing in 1656 the famous sermon *Gedenk daran, Hamburg*—the only one of his sermons he published entire. He published a number of pieces in 1657 under assumed names (Antenor, Mellilambius). To one of his Latin writings, published at Copenhagen, he appended the so-called Psalm cli., and the supposed letter of Paul to the Laodiceans. At this, the wrath of his colleagues broke out. His offense consisted in lashing the sins of the time with wit and satire, but the special charge against him was that he published apocryphal writings. He was summoned before a commission appointed by the ministry and requested not to issue theological writings under assumed names, not to publish apocrypha, to submit to a censorship, and not to introduce fables, jokes, and humorous anecdotes, alongside the sayings and accounts of the Bible. He is said to have agreed to the first two conditions, and promised to keep within bounds on the other matters. But *Salomo oder Regentenspiegel* and *Freund in der Noth* were already in press, and their appearance caused another commotion with an appeal to the theological faculties of Wittenberg and Strasburg for advice on two hypothetical questions that described Schupp's offense. The clergy were advised to appeal to the state authorities, and the latter enjoined quiet upon both parties to the controversy (March, 1658). Schupp was now plunged in a complicated literary feud which continued until his early death at the age of fifty-two.

Schupp was an honest, pious man and a faithful Christian. His writings, especially the little German tracts, went through many editions, had a decided influence upon the people, and present an interesting picture of the manners of his time. His sermons were criticized for lack of dignity, but they were earnest, attractive, and wholesome in their influence. (CARL BERTHEAU.)

BIBLIOGRAPHY: P. Lambecius, *Programma in Schuppii obitum*, Hamburg, 1661; J. Möller, *Cimbria literata*, ii. 790–804, Copenhagen, 1744; C. Ziegra, *Sammlung von Urkunden . . . zur hamburgischen Kirchengeschichte*, ii. 249–338, Hamburg, 1764; A. Vial, *Johann Balthasar Schuppius, ein Vorläufer Speners*, Mainz, 1857; K. E. Bloch, in the *Jahresbericht über die königliche Realschule . . . zu Berlin*, Berlin, 1863; E. Oelze, *Balthasar Schuppe*, Hamburg, 1863; G. Baur, *Johann Balthasar Schupp als Prediger*, Leipsic, 1868; T. Bischoff, *Johann Balthasar Schupp*, Nuremberg, 1890; Paul Stötzner, *Beiträge zur Würdigung von Johann Balthasar Schuppe lehrreichen Schriften*, Leipsic, 1891; J. Lühmann, *Johann Balthasar Schupp*, Marburg, 1907; *ADB*, xxxiii. 67–77.

SCHWABACH, shvā'bāH, **ARTICLES:** A Protestant confession drawn up in 1528. They derive their name from being brought into connection with a meeting in that year in Schwabach regarding the Brandenburg visitation. They go back to the attempts at alliance resumed by the Evangelical Estates immediately after the protest at the Diet of Speyer (see SPEYER, DIET OF) in the spring of 1529. The preliminary agreement on Apr. 22, 1528, was between Saxony, Hesse, Nuremberg, Strasburg, and Ulm, and looked to the consideration of the Eucharistic problem in a meeting to take place at Rotach, in the Franconian mountains. The meeting was postponed till Aug. 24 and again till Oct. 16 as a result of a conference of the elector, Margrave George of Brandenburg, and Philip of Hesse at Saalfeld. The margrave desired a uniform creed, liturgy, and regulation of ecclesiastical affairs in the territories of the allies, and in this Elector John was in accord with him. Accordingly Luther, while at Marburg (apparently on Oct. 4), received a letter from the elector, dated Sept. 28, asking him, Melanchthon, and Jonas to confer with the elector, but on Oct. 7 Luther was directed to prepare the articles at once, and by Oct. 10 they were in the elector's hands.

The Articles are seventeen in number and, while closely following the Marburg Articles, lay special stress on the points wherein uniformity was necessary in order to secure political union. They likewise lay sharp stress on Luther's distinctive Eucharistic doctrines, and expressly assail the teachings of Zwingli. On Oct. 16, 1529, at the concluding of the alliance, they were laid before the conference held at Schwabach, and there rejected by the Upper Germans. Besides being employed in drawing up the Augsburg Confession, the Schwabach Articles were used by the elector in May, 1530, to prove his orthodoxy to the emperor, a wretched Latin translation being sent to Innsbruck. The original draft of the articles is lost, and they first appeared in print at Coburg about 1530 under the misleading title of *Die bekenntnus Martini Luthers auff den jtzigen angestellen Reichstag zu Augspurk einzulegen, In siebentzehen Artikel verfasset.* Shortly afterward Luther himself published the Articles with a preface of his own. (T. KOLDE.)

BIBLIOGRAPHY: H. E. Jacobs, *The Book of Concord*, i. 303–354, ii. 27–28, Philadelphia, 1893; J. J. Müller, *Historie von der evangelischen Stände*, Jena, 1705; T. Kolde, *Der Tag von Schleiz*, in *Beiträge zur Reformationsgeschichte J. Köstlin gewidmet*, pp. 84 sqq., Gotha, 1896; Schaff, *Creeds*, i. 228–229.

SCHWALLY, shväl'lî, FRIEDRICH: Orientalist; b. at Butzbach (11 m. s. of Giessen) Aug. 10, 1863. He received his education at the gymnasium at Darmstadt and at the universities of Giessen and Strasburg; he was called as privat-docent to Strasburg to teach Semitic languages, becoming extraordinary professor there in 1898, and going to Giessen in the same capacity in 1901, being promoted to ordinary professor in 1906. He has issued *Das Leben nach dem Tode. Nach den Vorstellungen der alten Israel und des Judentums einschliesslich des Volksglaubens im Zeitalter Christi* (Giessen, 1892); *Idioticon der christlich-palästinischen Aramäisch* (1893); *Kultur des alten Orients* (1896); *Ibraham ibn Muhammed el-Baihaqi Kitâb el Mahâsin val Masâwi* (3 parts, Leipsic, 1899–1902); assisted in putting forth a critical edition of the Hebrew text of the Book of Kings (1904); and edited the second edition of T. Nöldeke's *Geschichte des Qorans* (1909).

SCHWANE, shvä'ne, JOSEPH: German Roman Catholic; b. at Dorsten (35 m. s.w. of Münster), Westphalia, Apr. 2, 1824; d. at Münster June 6, 1892. He studied at Münster, 1843–48; at Bonn and Tübingen, 1848–50; became privat-docent in the theological faculty at Münster, 1853; professor extraordinary there, 1859; and ordinary professor, 1867. He was author of *Das göttliche Vorherwissen* (Münster, 1855); *De controversia inter Sanctum Stephanum et Sanctum Cyprianum* (1859); *Dogmengeschichte* (1862–90); *De operibus supererogatoriis* (1868); *Specielle Moraltheologie* (1871–1878); *Allgemeine Moraltheologie* (1885).

SCHWARTZ, shvärts, CHRISTIAN FRIEDRICH: German Protestant missionary; b. at Sonnenburg (19 m. n.e. of Frankfort-on-the-Oder), Prussia, Oct. 26, 1726; d. at Tanjore (170 m. s.s.w. of Madras), India, Feb. 13, 1798. He studied theology at Halle; and having made himself master of the Tamil language, was sent as missionary to Tranquebar in 1750 by the Danish Missionary Society in Copenhagen. Having entered the service of the Society for Promoting Christian Knowledge in London, in 1767, his station was in 1779 removed to Tanjore, where he remained to his death. He founded many congregations among the natives, exercised a most beneficial influence during the war of Hyder Ali, and contributed much to make the name and character of Europe respected and trusted in India.

BIBLIOGRAPHY: *Remains of . . . C. F. Schwartz, Missionary in India, consisting of his Letters and Journals; with a Sketch of his Life*, 3d ed., London, 1826; H. M. Pearson, *Memoirs of . . . C. F. Schwartz*, new ed., 2 vols., 1855; J. D. Jaenicke, *Memoirs of . . . Jaenicke . . . with . . . Letters and Notices of Schwartz*, ib. 1833; W. Germann, *Missionär C. F. Schwartz, sein Leben und Wirken*, Erlangen, 1870; W. P. Walsh, *Heroes of the Mission Field*, London, 1879; A. C. Thompson, *Protestant Missions, their Rise and Early Progress*, New York, 1894; Helen H. Holcomb, *Men of Might in Indian Missions*, ib. 1901; C. C. Creegan, *Pioneer Missionaries of the Church*, ib. 1903; H. C. Vedder, *Christian Epoch Makers*, Philadelphia, 1908.

SCHWARZ, shvärts, FRIEDRICH HEINRICH CHRISTIAN: German Lutheran; b. at Giessen May 30, 1766; d. at Heidelberg Apr. 3, 1837. After completing his education at the university of his native city, he assisted his father as pastor at Alsfeld, and was then pastor of Dexbach (1790–1796), Echzell (1796–98) and Münster, near Butzbach (1798–1804), where he developed conspicuous ability as a teacher, in addition to his clerical duties. From 1804 until his death he was professor of theology at Heidelberg, his special fields being pedagogics and systematic theology. His theological point of view was one of Biblical and practical supernaturalism, combined with a unionistic tendency. Besides issuing works on pedagogy, in which field he is perhaps better known than as a theologian, he edited for several years the *Theologische Annalen* (1824 sqq.), *Die Kirche* (1816–17), and also the pedagogical *Freimütige Jahrbücher.* His independent theological writings were *Sciagraphia dogmatices Christianæ in usum prælectionum* (Heidelberg, 1808; revised under the title of *Grundriss der kirchlichen protestantischen Dogmatik*, 1816); *Das Christentum in seiner Wahrheit und Göttlichkeit betrachtet, oder die Lehre des Evangeliums aus Urkunden dargestellt* (1808); and *Handbuch der evangelisch-christlichen Ethik für Theologen und gebildete Christen* (1821; revised in 1830 as *Die Sittenlehre des evangelischen Christentums als Wissenschaft*).

Schwarz was a zealous advocate of the union of the Lutheran and Reformed Churches in Baden, and after the union toiled with his colleague Daub to this end, also in preventing loose latitudinarianism and in giving proper validity to the creeds of both denominations. (C. B. HUNDESHAGEN†.)

SCHWARZ, JOHANN KARL EDUARD: German Lutheran; b. at Halle June 20, 1802; d. at Jena May 18, 1870. He was educated at the university of his native city (1822–24), and after being a teacher at Magdeburg for a year, was appointed, in 1826, pastor in the neighboring town of Altenweddingen. In 1829 he was called to Jena as chief pastor and superintendent, being at the same time honorary professor at the university. In 1844 he was appointed full professor, lecturing on homiletics, catechetics, and ethics, besides directing the homiletic and catechetic seminars, but in 1865 was compelled by illness to retire from active life. He was for many years theological editor of the *Jenaer allgemeine Litteraturzeitung*, was one of the founders of the *Protestantische Kirchenzeitung*, and in 1859 edited the *Weimarsches Kirchenblatt*. Besides writing a volume of sermons (Jena, 1837) and an unfinished biography of Nikolaus Amsdorf, he had charge of an *Evangelisches Kirchenbuch* (2 vols., Jena, 1860–63), of which he wrote vol. ii. (C. Pertz†.)

SCHWARZ, KARL HEINRICH WILHELM: German theologian and historian; b. at Wiek (21 m. n. of Stralsund), on the island of Rügen, Nov. 19, 1812; d. at Gotha Mar. 25, 1885. He attended the gymnasium at Greifswald, 1826–30; studied theology and philology under Gesenius and Tholuck at Halle; in 1831 went to Bonn; studied in Berlin, 1832–34; whence he returned to Greifswald. While under sentence of imprisonment at Wittenberg in 1837 for breach of academical regulations, he was allowed to attend the preachers' seminary conducted by Heubner and Rothe. In 1841 at Greifswald he became licentiate in theology and in 1842 licentiate at Halle, where he collaborated on the *Hallische Jahrbücher*. At Leipsic and Cöthen he attended the meetings of the "Protestant Friends" but their rationalism repelled him. The minister of public worship decreed his suspension and he was rehabilitated at Halle only in 1848. In his *Wesen der Religion* (Halle, 1847) he deals in the first part with the conception of religion as the realization of God and in the second part with the history of religion and the philosophic systems of Kant, Jacobi, Schleiermacher, Hegel, and Feuerbach. In 1849 he became extraordinary professor and in 1854 published *Lessing als Theolog*. His most important work is *Zur Geschichte der neuesten Theologie* (Leipsic, 1856), wherein he treats of the antithesis between rationalism and supernaturalism, which was overcome by Schleiermacher and Hegel. In contrast with them stands modern orthodoxy, typified by Hengstenberg, while Strauss's *Leben Jesu* characterizes the historical critical process. The third part describes the philosophic-dogmatic process, first the redemption theology of Strauss and Feuerbach, then the reaction against it and Schleiermacher's school, finally the transition to the free theology of the future for which he stood. In 1856 Duke Ernst II. of Coburg-Gotha called him to Gotha as court preacher. In 1858 he became head court preacher and member of the ministerial department for public instruction and worship, and in 1877 general superintendent of the state church of Gotha. In 1866 he published for the public schools of the duchy of Gotha a very popular *Leitfaden für den Religionsunterricht*. He was also active in matters affecting the organization of the church and in those which concerned Church and State. (G. Rudloff.)

SCHWEBEL, shvē'bel, JOHANN, AND THE REFORMATION IN PFALZ-ZWEIBRUECKEN: Johann Schwebel, or, as he styled himself, Schweblin, was born at Pforzheim (50 m. w.n.w. of Carlsruhe) in 1490; d. at Zweibrücken May 19, 1540. Thoroughly prepared in the excellent Latin school of his native town, he entered the University of Tübingen in 1508, that of Leipsic in 1509, and that of Heidelberg in 1511, taking his degree in canon law in 1513. Still earlier he had entered the Hospitallers' order of the Holy Ghost. Consecrated as priest at Strasburg on Apr. 15, 1514, he lived in his cloister at Pforzheim, where he contracted intimate relations with Melanchthon. From 1519 Schwebel preached in the hospital of his order in Evangelical fashion, and although he observed moderation, he roused the hostility of the "old believers" to such a degree that he deemed it advisable, in 1521, to leave the order and seek protection in Sickingen's castles, where, n communion with Sickingen, Hutten, Butzer, and others, he grew still more decided. Like Œcolampadius, Schwebel now read the mass in German, though he held no official post with Sickingen. He married in 1521, and in the autumn of 1522 returned to Pforzheim, where he again occupied his position in the hospital, at first unmolested. In a tract that appeared at Pforzheim Dec. 1, 1522, *Ermahnung zu dem Questionieren, abzustellen überflüssige Kosten*, Schwebel opposed the "farming" of the credulous common people in connection with collecting donations for hospitals and the poor. He is also perhaps the author of another work that soon appeared at the same place, *Liber vagatorum*, describing the artifices employed by the vagabonds of that age for swindling the people.

Education and Early Labors.

In the spring of 1523, Schwebel had to leave Pforzheim again. An invitation from Duke Ludwig II. of Pfalz-Zweibrücken then led him to Zweibrücken; where no later than April of 1523 he appears as preacher and forthwith developed a fruitful activity, to which Ludwig interposed no obstacle. In a series of sermons, Schwebel expounded Matthew, Romans, Galatians, and Corinthians. When in 1527 he preached on the Old Testament, he studied Hebrew so eagerly that his adversaries in ridicule styled him *Judaicus*. When Duke Ludwig published the Nuremberg edict of Mar. 6, 1523, and in 1526 put a new edge on the same, prohibiting preaching of the Gospel except as approved by the Church, Schwebel did not change his manner of preaching, and before long his influence began to spread over neighboring places. Early in 1524 Schwebel victoriously defended his doctrine against the arch-priest Nicholas Kaltenheuser of Bitsch, who denied his authorization to preach. Schwebel's first wife having died early, he married again, and justified the step in a special tract. In a sermon on I Cor. iii., delivered at the beginning of 1525, he expressed himself openly against purgatory. About this time Schwebel sent a brief presentation of his doctrine to a citizen of Metz, which was translated into French and printed at Strasburg. Another small tract of his, *Hauptstück*

Beginning of Work in Zweibrücken.

und Summa des gansen Evangeliums, dates from 1525. In 1526, when, previously to the Diet of Speyer, the bishops took measures against the Evangelical preachers, the bishop of Metz desired to call Schwebel to account. And although Jacob Schorr, an influential counselor of Duke Ludwig's, in a repeatedly printed *Radschlag über den Lutherischen handel auf Speyerischen Reychstag*, had as early as 1524 made spirited defense of the "invincibly authenticated" doctrine of Luther, Ludwig still entertained serious scruples, and Schwebel, for a time, discontinued the communion under both species. Through Ludwig's marriage with the Evangelical Elizabeth of Hesse (Sept., 1526), the friends of reform obtained powerful support, yet Ludwig did not side openly with the Evangelical cause. He did not refuse his protection to Evangelical preachers who were assailed by their bishop, and he also drew men of Evangelical sentiments into his circle; but, on the other hand, he left priests undisturbed who discharged their office in the traditional manner. When Ludwig died on Dec. 3, 1532, aged only thirty years, Ludwig's brother, Palsgrave Ruprecht, together with the widowed mother, assumed the regency in the name of his only son, Wolfgang, six years of age.

Palsgrave Ruprecht's Regency.

Ruprecht was originally destined to the spiritual career, and had early become a canon in Mainz and Strasburg. He was a zealous friend of the Reformation, and evinced full confidence in Schwebel. Immediately after assuming the regency, he summoned Schwebel to prepare a liturgy, which as early as Jan., 1533 (not 1529), obtained the regent's approbation, and was printed at Strasburg under the title: *Form und Mass, wie es von den Predigern des Fürstenthums Zweibrück in nachfolgenden Mängeln soll gehalten werden*. This liturgy treats in twelve articles of the life and official conduct of the clergy, the solemn observance of Sundays and festivals, week-day sermons, baptisms, communion and confession, visitation of the sick, burial, catechetical sermons, and prayer. The volume was sent to the clergy with the remark that whoever could not adhere to the same in good conscience should communicate his opinion to the ducal chancery. On May 5, 1533, when Pastor Meissenheimer of Zweibrücken resigned his office, Schwebel became his successor, and soon gained controlling influence upon the church administration. The liturgy was now gradually introduced throughout the principality. Ruprecht paid no heed to protests lodged against the same, on July 23, 1533, by Vicar-general Tettenleben of Mainz, by Archbishop Albrecht of Mainz, in Nov., 1533, and again early in 1534, and by the bishop of Speyer. Schwebel, in a statement rendered by Ruprecht's direction, declared it a duty of the civil authority to proceed against the scandalous living of the Roman Catholic clergy, concerning which everybody made complaint. The bishops tolerated that scandal, yet sought to punish something instituted by Christ himself. Though even Schorr counseled prudence, Schwebel influenced Ruprecht, early in 1535, to command all priests and monks who lived in concubinage to marry before Easter under penalty of expulsion. And though the bishop of Metz, Apr. 9, 1535, lodged complaint, and urgently entreated to "leave the priests in their ancient and customary manner of life according to the precepts of the Church," only reporting those who lived unseemly for chastisement, Ruprecht consistently enforced his mandate. With the reforms that Ruprecht devised, the great majority of the population stood thoroughly in harmony. The assertion of N. Paulus (*Historisch-politische Blätter*, cvii. 805), to the intent that their introduction was coercive and had been wrought contrary to the will of the people, has no support in the records. In 1533 Schwebel gained a like-minded fellow-laborer in his friend Kaspar Glaser, who was adopted as such by reason of his mediating position as the young Palsgrave Wolfgang's teacher. A second very able compatriot, Michael Zimmermann (Hilsbach), assisted him from the close of 1532 at first as schoolmaster and later as pastoral colleague.

Completion Of Reform Measures.

Schwebel's theological position was of a moderate tone. With Ruprecht's consent, he subscribed the Augsburg Confession and Apology. Of the Lord's Supper it is stated in the liturgy prepared by Schwebel, that, waiving subtle questions, one should set faithfully before Christians what the Evangelists write of the Lord's Supper, to the end that they may in faith receive what Christ offers them when he says, "Take, eat; this is my body"; and "Drink ye all of it. This cup is the new testament in my blood." Schwebel followed with interest the proceedings that led to the Wittenberg Concord, subscribed the same himself, and invited the remaining preachers of the duchy to subscribe. On occasion of a church visitation undertaken in the Lichtenberg jurisdiction, in 1538, a great diversity manifested itself both in doctrine and in practises. One priest continued to administer his office, quite to the displeasure of his congregation, in Roman Catholic fashion. Doubtless this helped to induce the most eminent of the duchy's clergy to convene in a kind of synod. The resolutions which, on May 21, 1539, this body submitted for approval aimed at a greater unity in doctrine, proposed the appointment of churchwardens to administer the church properties and Christian discipline. In the town of Zweibrücken, at the beginning of 1540, this "Church Discipline" was adopted. On occasion of a church visitation not long afterward in the jurisdiction of Veldenz this "Discipline" was introduced there as well. For sixteen years Schwebel labored in Zweibrücken. His death was probably caused by the pestilence. By that time the Reformation was diffused throughout the duchy. Glaser, his successor, continued the work in like spirit. Under the rule of Palsgrave Wolfgang, the process was completed through the introduction of the excellent liturgy of 1557.

JULIUS NEY.

BIBLIOGRAPHY: The "Works" of Schwebel were collected and issued by his son in three parts, 4 vols., Zweibrücken, 1597-98, though the work was badly done, but the charge is not proved that they were distorted in the Reformed interest. To the second part (the letters) a biography was prefixed which has been the one source of all later sketches. Additional letters were published by J. Schneider in *Zeit-*

schrift für Geschichte des Oberrheins, xxxiv (1882), 223 sqq. Later and more accessible sketches are in M. Adam, *Vitæ Germanorum theologorum*, pp. 62 sqq., Heidelberg, 1620; J. G. F. Pflüger, *Geschichte der Stadt Pforzheim*, pp. 305, 336 sqq., Pforzheim, 1861–62; F. Jung, *Johannes Schwebel, der Reformator von Zweibrücken*, Kaiserslautern, 1910; J. Ney, in *Zeitschrift für bayerische Kirchengeschichte*, 1910, pp. 174 sqq.

SCHWEGLER, shveg'ler, **FRIEDRICH CARL ALBERT**: Distinguished representative of the Tübingen School; b. at Michelbach, near Halle (35 m. n.e. of Stuttgart), Württemberg, Feb. 10, 1819; d. at Tübingen Jan. 5, 1857. He studied at the seminaries of Schönthal and Tübingen; devoted himself especially to the study of church history; was for nearly a year pastor at Bebenhausen; became docent in philosophy at Tübingen, 1843; professor of Roman literature and antiquities in 1848; and, shortly before his death, professor of ancient history. He distinguished himself greatly at the university, and studied with zeal the Hegelian philosophy. In 1841 appeared *Der Montanismus und die christliche Kirche des zweiten Jahrhunderts* (Tübingen, 1841). Through Strauss's *Leben Jesu* and other studies he found himself at variance with the teachings of the Church, and published *Das nachapostolische Zeitalter* (1846). It exaggerates the Baur hypothesis of the early Church, and dislocates the origin of the writings of the New Testament. The work asserts that early Christianity was pure Ebionism (see Ebionites) and builds up the history of the early Church on this foundation. He edited the *Clementinischen Homilien* (Stuttgart, 1847); and published *Die Metaphysik des Aristoteles*, text, translation, commentary, and exposition (4 vols., Tübingen, 1847–48); *Geschichte der Philosophie im Umriss* (Stuttgart, 1848; 16th ed., 1905; Eng. transl., New York, 1881); the *Historia ecclesiæ* of Eusebius (2 vols., Stuttgart, 1852); *Römische Geschichte* (3 vols., Tübingen, 1853–58); and *Geschichte der griechischen Philosophie* (1859).

SCHWEINFURTH, GEORGE JACOB. See Church Triumphant, I.

SCHWEINITZ, shvai'nits, **EDMUND ALEXANDER DE**: Bishop of the Unity of the Brethren; b. at Bethlehem, Pa., Mar. 20, 1825; d. at South Bethlehem, Pa., Dec. 18, 1887. He was graduated from the theological seminary of his denomination at Bethlehem in 1844; studied at Berlin, 1845; was pastor at Canal Dover, O., 1850; Lebanon, Pa., 1851–53; Philadelphia, 1853–60; Lititz, Pa., 1860–64; and Bethlehem, Pa., 1864–80; and was consecrated bishop in 1870. He was president of the provincial board—i.e., the governing board—of the American province of the Unity of the Brethren, and of the theological seminary, 1867–84. He was of a family that for more than a hundred years has furnished ministers in an unbroken line to the American branch of the Moravian Church, and was a great-great-grandson of Count Zinzendorf (q.v.). He was the author of *The Moravian Manual* (Philadelphia, 1859), *The Moravian Episcopate* (Bethlehem, 1865); *The Life and Times of David Zeisberger* (Philadelphia, 1870); *Some of the Fathers of the Moravian Church* (Bethlehem, 1881); and *The History of the Unitas Fratrum* (1885).

SCHWEITZER, shvait'ser, **ALBERT**: German Protestant; b. at Kaysersberg (39 m. s.w. of Strasburg) Jan. 14, 1875. He was educated at the universities of Strasburg, Paris, and Berlin (Ph.D., Strasburg, 1899), and since 1902 has been privat-docent for New-Testament exegesis at Strasburg. He has written *Die Religionsphilosophie Kants von der Kritik zur reinen Vernunft bis zur Religion innerhalb der Grenzen der blossen Vernunft* (Freiburg, 1899); *Das Abendmahl im Zusammenhang mit dem Leben Jesu und der Geschichte des Urchristentums* (2 parts, Tübingen, 1901); *Von Reimarus zu Wrede, eine Geschichte der Leben-Jesu-Forschung* (1906; Eng. transl., *The Quest for the Historical Jesus; a critical Study of its Progress from Reimarus to Wrede*, New York, 1910); and *Deutsche und französische Orgelbaukunst und Orgelkunst* (Leipsic, 1906).

SCHWEIZER, shvait'ser, **ALEXANDER**: Swiss Protestant theologian, follower of Schleiermacher; b. at Murten (15 m. w. of Bern) Mar. 14, 1808; d. at Zurich July 3, 1888. He studied at Zurich, Berlin, and Jena, and was ordained in 1831. While yet a student he wrote *Kritik des Gegensatzes zwischen Rationalismus und Supranaturalismus*, and *Darstellung der Versuchungsgeschichte* (published together, Zurich, 1833), in both of which his dependence on Schleiermacher is evinced. In 1833, while a student at Jena, he received a call as assistant preacher to the Reformed congregation at Leipsic. In 1834, he visited Berlin and saw Schleiermacher for the last time a few weeks before the latter's death, after which he wrote *Schleiermacher's Wirksamkeit als Prediger* (Halle, 1834). In 1834 he received a call from Zurich as instructor at the newly founded university, where he taught New-Testament exegesis and practical theology and acted as vicar at the cathedral. He became full professor in 1840. In the excitement attending the candidacy of Strauss for a position on the faculty at Zurich Schweizer condemned an unfair criticism of the former's *Leben Jesu*, but, while he recognized the greatness of that work, himself disputed some of the author's main positions, and attempted to prevent his call to Zurich, and, after this call had been given, protested against the action. In his *Evangelium Johannes für das Leben Jesu kritisch untersucht* (Leipsic, 1841) he attempted to show that the Fourth Gospel is composed of two parts, one Galilean, the other Judean, a hypothesis which he later gave up. Meanwhile he had issued *Leitfaden zum Unterricht in der christlichen Glaubenslehre* (Zurich, 1840), which was followed by *Die Glaubenslehre der evangelisch-reformierten Kirche* (1844–47), an apology for the Reformed doctrine, and supplemented by *Die protestantischen Centraldogmen in ihrer Entwicklung innerhalb der reformierten Kirche* (1854–56). In *Die christliche Glaubenslehre nach protestantischen Grundsätzen* (Leipsic, 1863–69) he betrays an eminently speculative spirit and a philosophically monistic point of view, and shows that modern dogmatics must go to the living Christian consciousness for its material. Schweizer paid much attention to ethics (although he issued no formal treatise upon it), especially as connected with threatening social problems. He is also recognized as a scientific organizer of the study of practical theology, in this interest writing *Ueber Begriff und Einteilung der praktischen Theologie* (Leipsic, 1836); *Homiletik der evangelisch-protestantischen Kirche* (1848); and *Pastoraltheorie; oder die Lehre von der Seelsorge des evangelischen Pfarrers* (1875). His own homiletic activity during thirty years of preaching in the cathedral illustrated the worth of his conceptions, and five volumes of his sermons were published between 1834 and 1862.

(P. Christ†.)

Bibliography: *Professor A. Schweizer. Biographische Aufzeichnungen, von ihm selbst entworfen,* ed. P. Schweizer, Zurich, 1889.

SCHWENCKFELD, shvenk'felt, VON OSSIG, CASPAR, SCHWENCKFELDIANS.

I. Biography: Caspar Schwenckfeld was born in Nov. or Dec., 1490, on the Ossig estate near Lüben (41 m. n.w. of Breslau), duchy of Liegnitz; d. at Ulm Dec. 10, 1561. Descended from an ancient aristocratic family, in consideration of an annuity, he later surrendered the ancestral estate to his younger brother.

1. Early Life.

After visiting the school at Liegnitz, he went to Cologne, in 1505, to pursue general study, though probably without matriculating; proceeded to Frankfort-on-the-Oder, 1507; and later, perhaps, to Erfurt. His university studies embraced the liberal arts, scholastic theology, and canon law. It does not appear that he came into close touch with Humanism (q.v.); nor did he acquire an acquaintance, during his period of study, with Hebrew and Greek. At the close of 1510, or beginning of 1511, he entered the court service, from which he withdrew in 1522 or 1523. Religiously his attitude, in the mean time, was one of indifference; and he first came under the influence of religion in the Evangelical sense when, after the protest of Luther against the traffic of indulgences, the latter's writings were circulated and reprinted in Silesia, which also suffered grievously from the practise. Notwithstanding his later antagonism to Luther, Schwenckfeld always acknowledged that he owed to him his conversion to the Gospel, and his adherence to the Reformation probably dates from the winter of 1517–18. He now committed himself to the study of Luther's writings and of the Holy Scriptures, of which, during 1519, he read four chapters daily, so as to complete their perusal within a year. When his sovereign decided in favor of the Reformation, he publicly espoused the transformation of ecclesiastical conditions in Liegnitz, and in Silesia at large, by allying himself with clericals and laymen of like views, foremost of whom was V. Crautwald, by means of letters and personal preaching, and by direct influence upon his sovereign prince and the church rulers.

Meanwhile, Schwenckfeld had formed personal connections with Wittenberg, where he had visited, Dec., 1521, or Feb., 1522. He became acquainted with Philipp Melanchthon, J. P. Bugenhagen, Justus Jonas, the Zwickau Prophets (qq.v.), and Carlstadt (see Draconites, Johannes). He did not meet Luther while at Wittenberg, although he shortly afterward entered into correspondence with him.

2. Reformer: Works.

Though Schwenckfeld continued to be especially associated with Carlstadt, yet, he by no means followed in all the latter's methods and those of the Zwickau enthusiasts. On the contrary, his course as a Reformer, despite his zeal, was, in that first period, conservative. Soon began a certain estrangement from Luther. The collapse of the former ecclesiastical relations with the concomitant decline of both morals and religion, the dearth of fruits from Luther's preaching, and the carnal conduct of many who loudly professed their adherence to the Reformation with their lips, only disquieted and saddened Schwenckfeld. As early as 1524, he wrote *Ermanung dess missbrauchs etlicher fürnempster Artikel des Evangelii, aus wölcher unverstandt der gemayn man in flayschliche Freyhayt und yrrung gefüret wirt.* Antagonism to Luther first set in when Schwenckfeld put forward his peculiar doctrine of the Lord's Supper in 1525. Schwenckfeld had studied the writings of both Zwingli and Luther, had taken a keen interest in the dispute on the communion, and now affirmed that he had received through special revelation a new understanding of the Lord's Supper and of the words of institution. These he submitted to Crautwald, who at first stood aloof, but then went over to Schwenckfeld's opinion, which he aided in establishing upon thoroughgoing premises. Schwenckfeld next referred his views, together with the deliverances of Crautwald, to the Wittenberg theologians, on the occasion, at the close of 1525, of a visit to Wittenberg. In successive interviews with Jonas, Bugenhagen, and Luther, both sides stood firm on this and other questions; and henceforth Luther and the Wittenberg theologians regarded Schwenckfeld as a dangerous heretic. The first consequence of this separation was an overture to Schwenckfeld from the Reformed theologians. Œcolampadius (q.v.) issued, with a friendly preface, Schwenckfeld's tract, *De cursu verbi Dei* (Basel, 1527); and in 1528 Zwingli fostered the printing (without Schwenckfeld's knowledge) of one of the circular letters of Schwenckfeld regarding the communion (Zwingli's *Opera*, iii. 563–588, Zurich, 1832). Losing the favor of King Ferdinand of Bohemia because of befriending the Anabaptists, Schwenckfeld left Silesia in 1529, never to return. He also departed from Strasburg, where he had taken refuge, in 1533 and 1534. During this period he repeatedly asserted himself in positive terms on the subject of the communion, collecting his utterances in the tract *Bekanntnus vom heiligen Sacrament des Leibs und Bluts Christi* (Strasburg, 1530). During the ensuing years, Schwenckfeld sojourned in various towns of Swabia. From 1538 new controversies arose, involving, beside his previous divergencies, now also his Christology. His treatment of this theme in a series of essays was followed in 1538–39 by the tracts *Von der göttlichen Kindschafft und Herrlichkeit des gantzen Sones Gottes,* and *Ermanunge zum waren und seelig machende Erkänntnis Christi (Der erste Theil der Christlichen orthodoxischen Bücher und Schriften*, pp. 486 sqq. and pp. 77 sqq., 1564–70). His chief opponent was Martin Frecht (q.v.) at Ulm, who brought about his departure in 1539, and his formal condemnation at the convention of Evangelical theologians at Schmalkald in 1540 led by Melanchthon. No less hostile were the Swiss theologians, mainly to his Christology; foremost of these was Vadianus at St. Gall (see WATT, JOACHIM VON). Schwenckfeld defended his view in numerous missives and tracts; among which the most comprehensive in substance was *Konfession und Erklärung vom Erkäntnus Christi und seiner Göttlichen Herrlichkeit* (1540; ut sup., pp. 91 sqq.). During the succeeding years he frequently changed his abode, though not without a successful propaganda of his doctrines among both theologians and laymen, the latter including various princes. His death was followed by a more favorable judgment of his life and greater esteem for his personality.

II. Characterization: Schwenckfeld's character was marked by a genuine piety and religious feeling, attested beyond question by a transformation from a state of religious and moral indifference—though, at its worst, not of a perverted type—to that of a man for whom religion came to be his one and all. Many passages in his writings bear witness of pure devoutness and profound Christian mysticism, which, however, did not render him guilty of indifference to morality or wholesome activity. In his personal life he laid stress on holiness; and those persons who without prejudice expressed judgment had a favorable, even a hallowed, impression of him. Even his worst enemies scarcely attribute any evil to him. His industry in matters of religion was enormous, and, as far as possible, in a personal way. He preferred to treat all subjects either by letter or oral discussion. The picture of a practical Pietist which he presents was not without its shady side. Devout and humble, he yet became quite often conscious of a feeling that he was not "as other men are." His polemics, compared with that of most of his antagonists, was more mild, leaving here and there, however, the impression of artificiality. He was inflexible in opinion; for, self-taught, he was so thoroughly imbued with self-discovered truths that no authority could make him waver. An aristocrat he continued to be all his life, refusing either to bow to another or to the multitude, but desiring to find a resonant echo in a small circle of like-minded associates. He had no appreciation of the necessity of larger associations, external ordinances, or anything statutory; and in this he was by nature a pure enthusiast. His intellectual powers, both of constructive thought and expression, were affluent; nor was he wanting in originality, though of restricted compass. In the course of years, he acquired a respectable knowledge of patristic and medieval theology, particularly on the mystical side, as well as an acquaintance with the current output. His own theology was not a finished system, but certain dominant and fundamental ideas repeatedly recur. Pertinent for review are those points which bear a historical significance; namely on the Word and the Spirit, the Lord's Supper, and Christology.

III. Theology: Central in Schwenckfeld's theology was his relative definition of the Word and the Spirit; or of historical revelation and present regeneration.

1. Word and Spirit. In the development of his thought, he shows contact with Augustine, German mysticism, especially with John Tauler (q.v.), and perhaps with the Bohemian, or Moravian, Brethren (see BOHEMIAN BRETHREN; UNITY OF THE BRETHREN). In addition he makes a series of independent deductions, and rounds off this aggregate complex, beside making skilful correlations with the teaching of Holy Scripture, on the one hand, and, on the other, with the doctrines of faith, regeneration, and justification. Taking issue vigorously with the Lutheran theology, he distinguishes himself from men like S. Franck (q.v.), in so far as he does not represent the innate theory of the inner Word, but is a strict supernaturalist; and has, besides, a far deeper apprehension of the corruption of human nature through sin, and places a higher valuation upon the importance of historical redemption through Jesus Christ. To this theme, indeed, Schwenckfeld more or less explicitly recurs in almost all his writings. His first connective presentation of the relation of the Word and the Spirit, though unfinished in outline and less sharply defined against the Lutheran view, was in the tract issued by Œcolampadius (ut sup.), a document of no great length, but rich in matter. What induced definiteness in both respects was the publication of a great number of tracts against Flacius. The principal of these, constituting also the chief sources for Schwenckfeld's doctrine of the Word and the Spirit, were the following: (1) *Vom underschaide des worts Gottes und der Heyligen Schrifft;* (2) *Von der hailigen Schrifft irem Innhalt / Ampt / rechtem Nutz / Brauch und Missbrauch* (Strasburg, 1594); (3) *Vom leerampt des newen Testaments. Das khein predicant der nicht from ist und Gottselig lebt / das Evangelium . . . khan seliglich mit frucht predigen* (1555); (4) *Confutatio und Ablainung des dritten Schmachbuchlins F. Illyrici;* (5) *Beschluss unnds Valete Auff Flaciy Illyrici letste zwai schmachbüchlin . . .* (1555); and (6) *Vom worte Gottes das khein ander wort Gottes sei / aigentlich zu reden, denn der Sun Gottes.* Schwenckfeld correlates the doctrine of the Word as a means of grace with that of the Scripture as revelation, and conditions one upon the other. He shares the ancient orthodox conception of inspiration, save that he contests the point that its direct product appears in the Bible; which, for him, has rather merely the value of a human, imperfect image and similitude of that which inspiration wrought in the hearts of the prophets and apostles. Accordingly, Scripture has no manner of significance as regards the inception of the religious life in man, but simply adverts to the same, and bears witness thereof. It is not the Scripture which brings the Spirit, but man filled with the Spirit brings this to the Scripture (*Vom Worte Gottes*, xxii.c). Without arriving at permanent and very closely defined ideas on this point, he valued the Scripture mainly as a trustworthy historical documentary source of Christian revelation (lxxi., xvi.); and, like Zwingli, as a normative guide for all inward revelations (ii.r sqq.). As not every one possesses, by nature, " his immanent living Word " (*Christlichen orthodoxischen Büchern*, p. 887) the renewing of man depends upon the immediate efficacy of Christ in the Holy Ghost; who, however, is intrinsically identical with the historic incarnated Christ (ut sup., pp. 566 sqq., p. 324; *Vom Worte Gottes*, li.r; *Von der heiligen Schrift*, cviii.). The main ground for separating the operations of Word and Spirit, and thereby ascribing regenerative grace exclusively to the immediate activity of the Spirit, lies for Schwenckfeld, as for the Reformed, in his distinctly expressed predestinarianism: God wills that all his gifts flow from the same celestial fountain into the hearts of the elect, through Jesus Christ, the head of the Church in the Holy Ghost; and that no external medium can be set up between them, not even as between the head and the body (*De cursu verbi Dei*, xiii.). Beyond these deductions, in the main, on the relation of the Word and the Spirit, no closer construction is warranted. Schwenckfeld may be said to have been the author of that mediating spiritualistic trend of thought after the Reformation (" middle way "), which, holding fast to the doctrine of grace and redemption, historically obtained by Christ, yet attributes the operation of that grace upon the predestinated to the immediate activity of the Spirit alone, allowing, however, a certain importance to Scripture and preaching.

2. Creed and Sacrament.

If Schwenckfeld did not concede religious significance, in the strict sense, to Holy Scripture, his valuation of the confessions must needs be yet slighter. When the matter came to a thorough test, he stood in accord with not a single doctrine of the Augsburg Confession. The whole Confession, and more so the obligatory subscription to the same, had its place, in his view, among the statutory measures for the founding of a Church; which measures he disputed as conflicting with the Spirit and freedom. His ideal of church organization was of separate congregations, which were to be brought together, at most, into a moral and holy fellowship by the creation of a proper jurisdiction. Not improbable is it that he inspired certain merely sporadic tendencies of Luther. On such grounds Schwenckfeld could not ascribe to the sacraments a real character as vehicles of grace. In the doctrine of baptism, he has been classed with the Anabaptists, but incorrectly; for, though he was at one with them in rejecting the baptism of infants (according to some of his utterances, he was willing to retain that practise as an outward ceremony), he nevertheless regarded the baptism of adults as equally unavailing. Schwenckfeld's doctrine of the Lord's Supper is rooted, first, in his general theory of the essence of the means of grace; then, in his construction of the meaning of the words of institution; and, finally, in his peculiar Christology. In his exposition of the words of institution, Schwenckfeld, resting upon a " visitation from on high," advanced the view that the words " This cup is the new testament " (cf. Luke xxii. 20) are not according to the original rendering by the Holy Spirit. The demonstrative *touto* is not an adjunct of the word for " cup "; but, being separated by the article, *to*, it is absolute, " This." Afterward Luke and Paul, by way of emendation, added the word " cup " or " drink." Accordingly, the Lord speaks of the character of his blood, saying: " This (drink) is the new covenant in my blood " (*Epistolar*, ii. 16). Complemented with John vi., the proper sense of the eucharistic words proved to be: " My body is this; namely, bread, in the signification of spiritual food. My blood is this; namely, drink, in the signification of spiritual drink for the soul." If Schwenckfeld not only dismisses from the very words of institution all manner of reference to any intimate, real connection of the elements with Christ's body and blood in the Roman Catholic or Lutheran sense, his Christology, or still more strictly, his theory of the relation between the divine and the earthly, debarred him from such an assumption. He combined, even more closely than the Lutherans, the humanity of Christ with his divinity; so that a conclusion for the physical ubiquity of Christ would not have been illogical, and so far the Philippists (q.v.) were correct in regarding him as the author of that doctrine; but, on the whole, he was unwilling to bring deity, including the deity enveloping the humanity of Christ, into closer relation with anything created. Forasmuch, then, as the divine never mediates itself through the created, the presence of Christ is certainly not mediated by the eucharistic elements; and their apprehension spiritually by faith is no longer impeded. Accordingly, Schwenckfeld's doctrine of the Lord's Supper is to be classified with the spiritualistic-dynamic; and, among the Reformation theories, is in closest affinity with Calvin's.

3. Christology.

Schwenckfeld's Christology grew out of his conception of the relation between the divine and the human in general. Everything human, whatever comes into being by creative process, stands in strong contrast with God: " All creatures are external to God, and God is external to all creatures " (*Epistolar*, ii. 105). Wherefore, if the relation of Christ to God is to be unique, that of perfect oneness with God, then a unique condition must underlie the origin of his human nature. Such is the fact; since his nature was not " created," but " begotten." God is the Father of Christ's humanity also (*Epistolar*, i. 612; *Christlichen orthodoxischen Büchern*, p. 521). Schwenckfeld is particularly intent upon the designation of Christ as the second Adam, through whom the creation of man first attained its consummation. This flesh of Christ, standing from the very beginning in a peculiar relation to God, came into the world, like his divinity, by the Virgin Mary. For the entire life of Christ, no less than for his birth, Schwenckfeld aims, so far as possible, at a mutual absorption of the human and the divine. The Lutheran formulas seemed to him insufficient; they still persistently savored of Nestorianism; on the other hand, he would fain retain the constant integrity of the two natures, and rejects all manner of reciprocal transformation (*Christlichen orthodoxischen Bücher*, pp. 218, 230). Schwenckfeld shared with the Lutherans the interest in the close union of Christ's humanity with his divinity and its endurance even after his exaltation. In his formal expression of this, he more nearly approximated Eutychianism (q.v.) and brought to view a number of paradoxical phrases rather than a clear representation of a state of reality. The work of Christ is considered as the winning of salvation through the historic Christ, and the dispensation of salvation through the glorified Christ. According to G. L. Hahn both propositions comprise: (1) redemption from the power of the devil; (2) purification of human nature from sin, or justification; and (3) emancipation from the state of the creature and adoption into the state of sonship, or regeneration; the entire emphasis falling upon the distributive activity of the exalted Christ, and the acceptance of the same by faith. And here, again, Schwenckfeld lays greater stress on moral and religious transformation, than on justification; though the latter is not altogether eliminated. This appears most evidently in the sentence: "God regards no one righteous in whom there is none of his essential righteousness" (*Epistolar*, i. 812). These conceptions, however, are not original with Schwenckfeld. Likewise in his mystical conception of faith and resignation, he no more than reflects medieval heritage.

IV. The Schwenckfeldians: Personally Schwenckfeld occupied a neutral position ("the middle way") between the great ecclesiastical and religious parties of his time; and he was desirous of gaining this neutral status for his adherents as well. These, therefore, withdrew quietly from the organized Church; adopting, at first, the designation "Confessors of the Glory of Christ," and after 1539 that of "Schwenckfeldians." They grouped themselves in individual congregations, and soon acquired the more or less distinct character of a sect. Congregations grew up most numerously in the two regions where Schwenckfeld had carried on his personal propaganda, Silesia and Swabia, and in the towns where he had sojourned. Beside these, Görlitz, Glatz, Goldberg, Löwenberg, Jauer, and Wohlau became permanent sites of considerable congregations. At a comparatively early date, the movement also took root in Prussia. Schwenckfeld had become personally acquainted with Duke Albrecht (see ALBRECHT OF PRUSSIA), and sought to win both him and the foremost theologians in Prussia; Paul Speratus (q.v.), for instance. Especially in southern Prussia, there was a strong favorable movement between 1530 and 1535; but it declined after a colloquy at Rastenburg in 1531, and after the leading theologians and the duke declared themselves more and more adversely. At the present stage of research, a prolonged, in main outline intelligible history of the Schwenckfeldians appears only, beside at Landau in the Rhenish Palatinate, in Württemberg and specially in Silesia. Duke Christopher of Württemberg issued a stern restriction against them in 1554, though some traces of them were still evident in the seventeenth century. In Silesia the congregations increased, toward the close of the sixteenth century, by receiving Anabaptists, and in the seventeenth century, through the accession of the adherents of Jakob Boehme (q.v.). But they retained the Schwenckfeldian type, as shown by confessions published at the beginning of the eighteenth century. During the entire seventeenth century, they flourished principally in the vicinity of Goldberg; but at the beginning of the eighteenth attention was drawn to them by means of an adverse tract. As a result a confession of faith was demanded of them, and in 1720 the Emperor Charles VI. despatched a Jesuit coercive mission against them, which, however, did not effect their extermination. A part of them emigrating into Saxony were denied tolerance and proceeded successively to Holland, England, and to eastern Pennsylvania in the United States. When Frederick the Great had taken possession of Silesia, he not only granted them tolerance, by an edict of 1742, but also restoration of their confiscated properties. Their congregations are famed for their earnest piety and sound morality. R. H. GRÜTZMACHER.

The Schwenckfeldians, or Schwenckfelders, are found in this country only in Pennsylvania. In 1734 some 200 of Schwenckfeld's followers emigrated to America and settled in Bucks, Berks, and contiguous counties in Pennsylvania. They have always been opposed to war, secret societies, and the judicial oath. Their doctrines are drawn from the Bible in the light of the indwelling Word. They hold that the higher nature of Christ was progressive, rising steadily from the human into the divine, and that faith, justification, and regeneration mean a positive change and that the constant aim in Christian life should be Christ-likeness. Discipline is strictly maintained. There are district conferences and a general conference in which all members without distinction of sex are entitled to sit. The Schwenckfeldians support missions at home and also, through other societies, in China, India, and Japan. There are 6 ministers, 8 churches, and 827 communicants. The number of churches has doubled, and the number of communicants more than doubled, since 1800. H. K. CARROLL.

BIBLIOGRAPHY: The full edition of the Works of Schwenckfeld has never been published, but one is projected under the editorship of C. D. Hartranft and others, see below, *Corpus Schwenckfeldianorum*. The *Schriften* as published, to which reference is made in the text, is the 4 folio-volumes edition, i. *Der erste Theil der christlichen orthodoxischen Bücher*, 1564; ii. *Epistolar*, 1st part, 1566; iii. *Epistolar*, 2d part, vol. i., 1570; iv. *Epistolar*, 2d part, vol. ii., 1520. Consult: J. Wigand, *De Schwenckfeldismo*, Leipsic, 1587; G. Arnold, *Kirchen- und Ketzerhistorie*, ii. 241 sqq., 4 vols., Frankfort, 1700–15; C. A. Salig, *Vollständige Historie der augspurgischen Konfession*, book XI., Halle, 1730; G. L. Hahn, *Schwenckfeldii sententia de Christi persona et opere*, Wratislaw, 1847; H. W. Erbkam, *Geschichte der protestantischen Sekten im Zeitalter der Reformation*, Gotha, 1848; O. Kadelbach, *Ausführliche Geschichte Schwenkfeldts und der Schwenkfeldtianer*, Lauban, 1861; Hampe, *Zur Biographie Kaspar von Schwenckfeld*, Jauer, 1882; F. Hoffmann, *Kaspar Schwenckfelds Leben und Lehren*, Berlin, 1897; R. H. Grützmacher, *Wort und Geist*, § 16, Leipsic, 1902; H. W. Kriebel, *The Schwenkfelders in Pennsylvania*, Lancaster, 1904; *Corpus Schwenckfeldianorum. Published under the Auspices of the Schwenckfelder Church, and the Hartford Theological Seminary*, vol. i., *A Study of the earliest Letters of Caspar Schwenckfeld v. Ossig*, ed. C. D. Hartranft, O. B. Schlutter, and E. E. Schultz Johnson, Leipsic, 1907; F. W. Loetscher, *Schwenckfeld's Participation in the Eucharistic Controversy of the 16th Century*, Philadelphia, 1907; A. A. Seipt, *Schwenckfelder Hymnology and the Sources of the First Schwenckfelder Hymn-book printed in America*, Philadelphia, 1909; *ADB*, xxxiii. 403–412.

SCHWERIN, shvê-rîn': A former German diocese, established in the second half of the twelfth century, and secularized about the middle of the seventeenth. It replaced the short-lived diocese of Mecklenburg, which had come to an abrupt end on the martyrdom of its bishop, Johannes Scotus, by the Wends in 1066. On Sept. 25, 1149, Archbishop Hartwich consecrated Emmehard bishop of Mecklenburg, but the opposition of Henry the Lion seems to have prevented him from ever entering his see, and in 1160 Henry conferred the bishopric on a Cistercian named Berno, then resident at Schwerin. Meanwhile this city had become the seat of a German count and the principal town of the Abodritians, and the new prelate accordingly made Schwerin his see city. The boundaries of the diocese were henceforth formed by a flat curve from the Bay of Wismar to the Elde on the west, the coast from the Bay of Wismar to the Greifswalder Bodden on the north, and by the diocese of Havelberg (q.v.) on the south. On the east the boundary was long uncertain, but in 1260 it was finally decided that the strip of territory between the Recknitz and the Trebel should belong to the diocese of Kammin (q.v.). (A. Hauck.)

Until the end of the episcopate of Brunward (1192–1238) the diocese of Schwerin suffered much from the hostility of the pagan Wends, but despite all obstacles the cause of Christianity triumphed. The bishops came to rank as princes of the empire, although subject to the archbishop of Bremen. In the administration of Magnus (1516–50), who was also duke of Mecklenburg, the Reformation practically put an end to the diocese, the bishop himself openly declaring for Lutheranism in 1553. His cousin and successor, Ulrich I. (1550–1603), whose election was never confirmed by the pope, was most contemptuous in his treatment of the ancient faith. The succeeding "administrators" of the diocese were insignificant, and in 1648, at the Peace of Westphalia, Duke Adolph Frederick of Mecklenburg-Schwerin received the bishopric as a hereditary principality in lieu of Wismar and other districts which Mecklenburg was obliged to cede to Sweden.

Bibliography: *Mecklenburgisches Urkundenbuch*, 12 vols., Schwerin, 1863 sqq.; A. Rudloff, *Geschichte Mecklenburgs*, pp. 54 sqq., Berlin, 1901; Hauck, *KD*, vols. iii.–iv.; Gams, *Series episcoporum*, p. 310.

SCIENCE, CHRISTIAN.

[Note: "I have examined this article, edited it, and now approve it."—Mary Baker G. Eddy.*]

I. The Official Statement: Christian Science, discovered and founded by the Rev. Mary Baker G. Eddy, is defined in the Standard Dictionary as "a system of moral and religious instruction, founded upon principles formulated by Rev. Mary Baker G. Eddy and combined with a method of treating diseases mentally. 'Christian Science is based on teachings of Scripture which it interprets, giving the Christ principle and rule in divine metaphysics, which heals the sick and sinner. It explains all cause and effect as mental, and shows the scientific relation of man to God.'" The full exposition of this Science is given in Mrs. Eddy's book, *Science and Health with Key to the Scriptures*, which was first published in 1875.

1. The Founder: The consideration of Mrs. Eddy's unique and extraordinary achievements as a religious reformer and as the founder and leader of a religious denomination, which in a comparatively short time has gained world-wide recognition and now commands the allegiance of a multitude of thinking people, naturally divides itself into four chronological periods: her early preparation for what was to be her lifework; her discovery of Christian Science in 1866 and her pioneer work in establishing it; her career as a teacher, and her crowning success as a leader.

1. Early Preparation. Mrs. Eddy was born in Bow, near Concord, N. H., July 16, 1821, and died at Chestnut Hill, Mass., Dec. 3, 1910. She came of Scotch-English stock and numbered among her ancestors Capt. John Lovewell of Dunstable, N. H., a famous Indian fighter and Gen. Henry Knox of Revolutionary fame. Her parents, Mark and Abigail Ambrose Baker, were earnest Christians. Her mother's father, Deacon Nathaniel Ambrose, founded the North Congregational Church of Concord, N. H., which was known as "Deacon Ambrose's church." The Baker family was also largely interested in the establishing of the Methodist Episcopal Church in the same city. Mrs. Eddy's great-grandfather, Captain Joseph Baker, was a member of the provincial congress and actively assisted the province to take its stand for the new republic. His sons, one of whom was Mrs. Eddy's grandfather, were all soldiers of the American Revolution. The early trend of Mrs. Eddy's thought was markedly spiritual and philosophical, as was shown by her girlhood choice

* This approval extends, of course, only to the first part of this article, which is printed as submitted, except for changes in matters of typography and paragraphing, and in the incorporation by the author of later figures and restatements made necessary by revised bases.

of such studies as natural science, logic, and moral philosophy. At an early age she wrote verses, which express thoughts akin to the teaching of Christian Science. Her inherent breadth of view was evidenced by the fact that when in her girlhood she joined the Congregational Church, she refused to subscribe to the doctrine of unconditional election or predestination. In addition to her academic education, Mrs. Eddy had the advantage of instruction from a number of private teachers, among whom was her brother Albert Baker, a graduate of Dartmouth College and a distinguished lawyer, Mr. Corser of Sanbornton Bridge Academy, and Professor Dyer H. Sanborn. Her careful training, supplemented by years of research and study, bore fruitage in her writings, which were voluminous before she began her labors as a Christian Scientist. During her residence in the South as the wife of Major George W. Glover of Charleston, S. C., she wrote much for southern magazines. No one can study her writings without being impressed by the thorough familiarity with the best in literature therein displayed. An important forerunner of her discovery of Christian Science was Mrs. Eddy's study of homeopathy, which she entered upon in her early womanhood mainly for the purpose of improving her health. Her aversion to the dissecting-room prevented her from obtaining an expert knowledge of surgery and from completing her course, but her experiments in homeopathy were valuable in directing her attention to the proposition that all causation is mental.

2. The Discovery of Christian Science.

Regarding her discovery of Christian Science, Mrs. Eddy says in her book, *Retrospection and Introspection:* "It was in Massachusetts in February, 1866, that I discovered the Science of divine metaphysical healing, which I afterwards named Christian Science. The discovery came to pass in this way. During twenty years prior to my discovery, I had been trying to trace all physical effects to a mental cause; and in the latter part of 1866 I gained the scientific certainty that all causation was mind and every effect a mental phenomenon. My immediate recovery from the effects of an injury caused by an accident, an injury that neither medicine nor surgery could reach, was the falling apple that led me to the discovery." Mrs. Eddy spent the next three years in retirement, studying the Bible and finding there the principle and rule of her healing. She then tested her healing system practically in every possible way, and finally in 1875, after nine years of preliminary work, wrote the Christian Science text-book, *Science and Health with Key to the Scriptures*. Her literary output after that was tremendous, comprising books, sermons, essays, polemics, poems, magazine articles, editorials. Her chief books in addition to *Science and Health* are: *Miscellaneous Writings* (1896); *Retrospection and Introspection* (1892); *Pulpit and Press* (1898); *Unity of Good* (1891); *Rudimental Divine Science* (1891); *No and Yes* (1891); *Christian Science versus Pantheism* (1898); *Christian Healing* (1886); *People's Idea of God* (1886); *Christ and Christmas* (1897); *Message to the Mother Church* (1900); *Our Leader's and Communion Messages* (1901).

X.—19

3. Organization of the Church of Christ, Scientist.

In 1879, Mrs. Eddy organized in Boston, Massachusetts, The First Church of Christ, Scientist, and was ordained as its pastor. This body was composed of twenty-six members. In 1895, sixteen years later, the church, to accommodate its increased membership, erected a handsome edifice on the corner of Falmouth and Norway Streets, Boston, at a cost of $200,000. This seats about 1,200 people. In June, 1906, a magnificent new structure, adjoining this and having a seating capacity of 5,000, was completed. It cost about $2,000,000. The First Church of Christ, Scientist, in Boston is known as the Mother Church of this denomination. The Christian Science denomination had, in Jan., 1911, 1,244 branch churches and societies, holding Sunday services. Chicago has nine large churches with five handsome edifices. Greater New York has twelve churches. In Greater New York there are eight church buildings, First Church edifice having cost over $1,150,000. Concord, N. H., has a strong organization and a beautiful granite church, a gift from Mrs. Eddy, which cost over $200,000. Mrs. Eddy located this church, bought the land, started the building, and paid for it, part of the money having been contributed to her for this especial purpose by Christian Scientists in all parts of the world, who wished to have a share in the work. There are influential Christian Science churches in San Francisco, Los Angeles, Oakland, San José, Minneapolis, Milwaukee, Brooklyn, Philadelphia, Washington, Cleveland, St. Louis, Buffalo, Pittsburg, Cincinnati, Atlanta, Providence, Toronto, and, it may be said, in all the large cities of the United States and Canada. There are firmly established churches in London, England, of which First has recently completed a fine edifice at Sloane Terrace, S. W. The organization in Manchester, England, has its own church edifice, as has that in Edinburgh, Scotland. There are organizations in Australia, Germany, France, Scandinavia, Holland, South Africa, South America, Mexico, Hawaii, The Philippines, and in many of the English Colonies.

4. Mrs. Eddy's Work as a Teacher.

The following incident, which occurred in Chicago, June 13, 1888, at the meeting of the National Christian Science Association, illustrates Mrs. Eddy's quality as a publicist and indicates the vital importance of the message entrusted to her. Mrs. Eddy had been invited to this gathering as a guest, and one of her stipulations on accepting the invitation had been that she should not be called upon to speak. The meeting was held in Central Music Hall, then the largest and best in the city. When Mrs. Eddy arrived at the hall, she not only found a great assembly, which occupied every seat and every foot of standing-room, extending out even into the corridors, but she was also astounded to learn that she was announced as the only speaker. Catching her theme as she walked from the entrance to the platform, she delivered extemporaneously the remarkable address, "Science and the Senses," which may be found in her *Miscellaneous Writings*. The effect of her words was so great that many authenticated cases of healing are recorded as having occurred in the audience. Modern thought, to which the term, "the effect of mind on the body," is a psychological and medical commonplace, finds it difficult to comprehend the crassly materialistic conditions which confronted Mrs. Eddy when, in 1867, she taught her first student the elements of the theory and practise of Christian Science. As she claimed, and as her followers firmly believe, her new light on the Bible and on the sayings and teachings of Jesus Christ came as a divine revelation, as a result of which she was able to demonstrate through spiritual means only the truth of Jesus' statement, "These signs shall follow them that believe," by healing the sick, reforming the sinner, and even raising those pronounced dead by reputable *materia medica* practitioners. She had formulated a new system of religion, philosophy, and medicine—a system which annihilated the accepted belief in the reality and substantiality of matter; and she stood before the whole world its sole advocate. As soon as she found one individual willing to learn of her discovery, she began teaching, and from this humble beginning developed the educational system, which has made Christian Science an international propaganda. "The motive of my earliest labors has never changed," writes Mrs. Eddy in *Retrospection and Introspection*. "It was to relieve the sufferings of humanity by a sanitary system that should include all moral and religious reform." In 1881, Mrs. Eddy obtained a charter from the Commonwealth of Massachusetts—the only one of the sort ever granted—and organized the Massachusetts Metaphysical College, in which during the eight succeeding years she taught over 4,000 persons. Many of these were indigent students, who received their tuition free. It was her custom to make it possible for all worthy applicants to avail themselves gratuitously of her personal instruction. In 1889, she closed the college, notwithstanding that hundreds of applicants were awaiting admission. Her purpose in doing this was to secure time to revise *Science and Health* and further to extend her field of labor. Later she established a board of education, based on the college, which board is now in active operation. Mrs. Eddy founded the *Christian Science Journal* in Apr., 1883, and was for many years its editor as well as its chief contributor. She founded the *Christian Science Quarterly* in 1890, the *Christian Science Sentinel* in 1898, *Der Christian Science Herold* (in German) in 1902, and *The Christian Science Monitor*, a daily newspaper, in 1908. She gave these periodicals to her church together with the plant of the Christian Science Publishing Society. For many years her only income was from the sale of her books and the interest on her investments. She healed the sick and the sinner without price. She contributed a large portion of her means to various charities and public enterprises. She was also public-spirited and took an interest in the affairs of her state and in matters pertaining to the betterment of her own city. She was simple in her tastes and habits, punctual and systematic in her work.

5. Mrs. Eddy as a Leader.

The organization, nature, constitution, and government of the Mother Church, its tenets, its church manual, and its special form of public service are all of Mrs. Eddy's devising. They are in most respects unique, without precedent in church economy, proofs of her wisdom, and evidence of her ability as a leader. While the business of the Church of Christ, Scientist, is conducted by a board of directors, the inspiration and fountain head of the series of remarkable steps, which have brought Christian Science to the fore so unswervingly and so rapidly, can be traced to this modest and unassuming, but strong and resourceful woman. It is impossible to investigate the far-reaching effects of the majority of her acts without coming to the inevitable conclusion that she was divinely directed. One can not study Mrs. Eddy's interpretation of the Lord's Prayer as it is given in "Science and Health" without being strongly impressed by the absolute absence of literalism in her exegesis of the Scripture, the spirituality, idealistic morality, and pure ethics of Christian Science. The First Church of Christ, Scientist, has no creed, but the fundamentals of Christian Science are stated in the form of church tenets, written by Mrs. Eddy, which every person joining the Mother Church is required to sign. These tenets are copyrighted and published in *Science and Health*, from which they are reprinted with Mrs. Eddy's permission:

1. As adherents of Truth, we take the inspired Word of the Bible as our sufficient guide to eternal Life.
2. We acknowledge and adore one supreme and infinite God. We acknowledge His son one Christ; the Holy Ghost or divine Comforter; and man as God's image and likeness.
3. We acknowledge God's forgiveness of sin in the destruction of sin and the spiritual understanding that casts out evil as unreal. But the belief in sin is punished, so long as the belief lasts.
4. We acknowledge Jesus' atonement as the evidence of divine, efficacious Love, unfolding man's unity with God through Christ Jesus the Wayshower; and we acknowledge that man is saved through Christ, through Truth, Life, and Love as demonstrated by the Galilean Prophet in the healing of the sick and overcoming of sin and death.
5. We acknowledge that the crucifixion of Jesus and his resurrection served to uplift faith and understanding to understand eternal life, even the allness of Soul, Spirit, and the nothingness of matter.
6. And we solemnly promise to watch and pray for that Mind to be in us which was also in Jesus Christ; to do unto others as we would have them do unto us; and to be merciful, just, and pure.

Christian Science churches have no pastors in the ordinary sense of the term and no personal preaching. In 1895, in order to secure uniformity in the statement of Christian Science, Mrs. Eddy ordained the Bible and *Science and Health* as the impersonal pastor of the denomination. The Sunday services are presided over by readers, usually chosen from among the members of the church, who serve a term of three years. These readers present a lesson-sermon, prepared by a committee appointed by the trustees of the Publishing Society, which consists of a compilation of Scriptural texts with correlative passages from the Christian Science text-book. In correspondence with the order in other churches, the remainder of the service includes Scripture-reading, hymns, prayer, and benediction. The Wednesday evening meeting is devoted to individual testimonies and experiences. The branch churches conform to requirements stated in the Manual of the Mother Church, but they have their separate congregational government. The readers, who conduct the services in branch churches, must be members in good standing of the Mother Church and are subject to its discipline. For the purpose of expounding Christian Science and bringing it to the attention of the public at large, Mrs. Eddy constituted through the Mother Church a body of qualified speakers called the Christian Science Board of Lectureship. The members are subject to the call of the various churches, which are required to give at least one lecture annually, to which the public is freely invited. The denomination also provides publication committees, the duty of which is to correct misstatements in the public press regarding Christian Science or Christian Scientists. It will be seen that although of comparatively recent development, the Christian Science denomination is completely organised down to details.

6. The Teaching of Christian Science. The Christian Science text-book sets forth Christian Science as a religious system based upon Scriptural teachings. It elucidates faithfully the great fact that God is the only cause and creator; that God made man in his own image and likeness; that "all is infinite Mind and its infinite manifestation." Christian Science affirms that God is Person in the infinite sense, but not in the humanly circumscribed sense; that the Holy Ghost, as taught in the Scriptures, is "the spirit of truth"; that Christ is the spiritual idea, the image of divine Mind which is one with the Father. By means of direct logical deductions from these premises, the Christian Science text-book teaches that sin, disease, and all the woes of mankind, though seemingly real to mortals, have no divine authority; that they are material, erring, mortal phenomena, must be so recognised and overcome by spiritual understanding of divine reality. This eternal verity gives hope and courage to those afflicted with disease by revealing to them the divine power, which heals and saves mankind. Christian Science has no kinship with pantheism, theosophy, spiritualism, Hinduism, or hypnotism. It holds that man is inseparable from Deity, being, as Scripture declares, the image, expression, or likeness of God, but denies that he is part of God as pantheism teaches. Christian Science recognises no mind apart from God. Its practise is in harmony with Jesus's declaration, "Not as I will, but as thou wilt." It therefore repudiates the action or influence of the human mind or will as employed in hypnotism. In the practise of Christian Science, human will is stilled and the divine will governs.

Healing the sick is not the prime mission of Christian Science. Its higher mission is to effect the triumph over all evil. Bodily improvement follows as the natural sequence of spiritual regeneration. It holds that the evil-doer is surely on the road to doom though he may not yet have realised this, while the well-doer is in the right path though he may not yet understand it, for "whatsoever a man soweth, that shall he also reap." Christian Science teaches that true and effectual prayer is the spiritual realization of divine Truth and Love and of God's infinitude and omnipotence, which lifts mortals above the power of sin and disease.

LEWIS C. STRANG.

II. Judicial Estimate of the System: The human soul was never so insistent as it is to-day on something adequate to rest upon. It wants to know experimentally and immediately that God is all in all. Orthodoxy is to some no longer satisfying; historic forms to an increasing number seem hopelessly inflexible. Coin current ages long in the soul's vocabulary has lost much of its luster and not a little of its acceptability. Meanwhile, prophets true and false are crying everywhere: "Repent ye: for the kingdom is at hand." One prophetic voice was heard above all others, the voice of Mrs. Eddy; and it gained a hearing both unexpected and phenomenal. Though there are at most not more perhaps than 70,000 actual members in the Christian Science organization, these are representative of a larger number of adherents. It is easy to account for the astounding growth of Christian Science. Materialism is a spent force. The world has given it fair trial and is turning definitely from it. Materialism has neither satisfied the deeper yearnings of the soul nor met the body's constant needs.

1. The Theological Situation.

2. Mrs. Eddy's Idealism. Mrs. Eddy was the first person in the modern world to proclaim the psychic kingdom so convincingly as to gain a respectable following and organise it into a compact cult not to be dismissed by smart criticism or unintelligent abuse. She did not, to be sure, think the psychic problem through. She knew neither the evolution of philosophy nor the content of psychology. She had reach but not grasp. With no sense of humor she could bear to quote in introduction to a book for which she claimed a more than "human origin" those well-known burlesque lines of Fichte's Idealism:

> "I, I, I, I itself, I,
> The inside and the outside, the what and the why,
> The when and the where, the low and the high,
> All I, I, I, I itself, I."

Mrs. Eddy was an idealist, but had no disposition to be one with other idealists. She would stand alone, associated not with man but God. Sometimes she so used language as to give the impression that her proper place was in the Trinity. These were her words in 1906: God is "divine Principle—as Life, represented by the Father; as Truth, represented by the Son; as Love, represented by the Mother." Sometimes, as a few years earlier, she allowed the reader's mind to drift another way in verse like this:

> "As in Blessed Palestine's hour, so in our age
> 'Tis the same hand unfolds His power and writes the page."

And the leader of the cult in New York City once wrote Mrs. Eddy thus: "They who refuse to accept you as God's messenger, or ignore the message which you bring, will not get up by some other way, but will come short of salvation."

However Mrs. Eddy might describe herself, she

acted as one having unique authority. Being unable to see that spirit can be both original and ultimate and yet for all practical purposes matter may have the character and composition which it appears for this earthly while to have subject to laws which must be obeyed, she ventured to explain not how God actually works but how He ought in her judgment to work, and stilled in advance all criticism of what might appear to some as presumption with the announcement that she is not "apart from God," she moved on to the assertion that God does work as she described, that evolution both in matter and in spirit is but the explication of her theory of life.

3. Her Teaching.

Historic Christianity she dismissed as summarily as science and philosophy. The Trinity was to Mrs. Eddy a variable and not a constant. Sometimes she assigned the third place in the Trinity to Christian Science; sometimes she kept it for herself. When she did not write that "the true Logos is demonstrably Christian Science" she was sure to say that "Jesus is the human man and Christ is the divine" and to allow one of her accredited teachers to teach that "Jesus of Nazareth is often mistaken for the real Christ." One of the Sacraments she abandoned altogether, putting in the place of the Lord's Supper a Galilean breakfast, and the other she evacuated of its historic meaning. Prayer she robbed of its petitional element and turned it into declaration of existing facts. To evil she denied all real existence and yet was obsessed habitually by what she called malicious animal magnetism which had all the attributes of the legendary devil except his horns and hoofs. In spite of these limitations and crudities, Mrs. Eddy won a following as obedient to her every wish as any modern army is to its commander. Convinced that Spirit is invincible and that "matter and mortal body are the illusions of human belief," she lived up to her convictions in the face of every jeer and joke. Insistent that "mind is all in all" and that "health is not a condition of matter but of mind," she would heal every ill that flesh is heir to by explaining to the seeming ill that things are not what they seem and—to quote one authorized to speak for her—"though the evidences of the senses may declare to the contrary we should still stick to the spiritual truth and should continue to denounce the false evidences." Broken bones and contagious diseases may appear a little stubborn because they have on their side a public opinion not yet permeated by the Christian Science spirit. Defer a while, said Mrs. Eddy, to public ill-informedness. The time will come when the limb lost in a railway accident may be replaced "as readily as the lobster's claw," and boards of health, she evidently thought, understand with her that contagion is "engendered solely by mortal belief."

Exactly what the therapeutic value of Christian Science is no one knows. The cures so widely advertised have never been subjected to any searching test which satisfies the trained pathologist. Judge Clifford P. Smith solemnly affirms that Christian Science has cured every kind of illness known to medicine, and Mrs. Eddy claimed to have added to the list the raising of the dead and the causing of an apple blossom to unfold in January. Although the full measure of the efficacy of Christian Science healing is not known it is known that the principle of suggestion underlies the cure in every Christian Science case as in every other case of mental healing. The disavowal of the principle is either ignorance or fatuous policy. In no other cult has auto-suggestion proved so powerful. Through the complete isolation of the patient from all alien influences the suggestion in many instances amounts to hypnotism, which is nothing but suggestion narrowed and in consequence profound. If Christian Science were to confine its therapeutic activity to diseases in which —as practically all psychologists and pathologists agree to-day—there is proper place for it, much criticism of its therapeutic methods would promptly disappear. It is only the Christian Science disregard of the distinction, which if not always evident yet is usually existent, between the organic and the functional in disease that causes disquiet and has led in some sections to active legislation to protect children, small and great, from the dangers existing in a rapidly advancing civilization, which often experiments first, sometimes with disastrous consequences, and later formulates its theories.

4. Suggestion as a Basis.

The life-story of the founder of Christian Science has been told both by unfriendly and friendly hands, and the result has been to minimize her claims to sanctity. If the public is not inclined to-day to take the attitude of those who love her best and, because they read no records save those she approves, know her least, it has no longer any disposition to deny that from the standpoint of achievement Mrs. Eddy stood alone among the women of the world. The mystery surrounding both the founder and the faith is gone. But the fact remains that Mrs. Eddy and her followers identified themselves as have no other people in the world with the religious and the philosophical revolt against materialism, and if as years go by they prove wise enough to eliminate the crass and the crude, the foolish and the dangerous, and to profit by the criticism, not all of which has been ill-natured or disrespectful, which they have of late received, Christian Science may become a blessing to the world.

5. Prospects.

Lyman P. Powell.

III. Critical View of the Doctrines: Christian Science, as a distinct cult, dates back to 1866, when Mrs. Mary Baker Grover Eddy formulated its teachings or principles into a system. In 1875 her book, *Science and Health, with Key to the Scriptures*, was published and since then has been the recognized text-book of Christian Science, and is given a place side by side with the Bible. Mrs. Eddy claimed that forty-odd years ago she discovered "the Christ Science," which she named "Christian Science," and also that her book came to her as a direct revelation from God. This latter claim is made in the book itself and in many utterances of Mrs. Eddy and her followers. How definite this claim is may be learned from the following quotation from *The Boston Herald*, of Dec. 2, 1900, which appeared in that paper over the signature of Mrs. Eddy: "I should blush to write of 'Science and Health, with Key to the Scriptures,' as I have were it of human origin, and I, apart from God, its author. But as I was only a scribe, echoing the harmonies of Heaven in divine metaphysics, I can not be super-modest in my estimate of the Christian Science text-book."

The present has to do with Christian Science only as a religious system; and with an authorized copy of *Science and Health, with Key to the Scriptures* in hand (74th ed., 1893, 103d ed., 1896), there can be no doubt as to the principles which constitute the system.

Any system of thought or philosophy, which claims to be a religious system, must be tested first by its idea of God. In this department

1. Doctrine of God.

Christian Science is a confused and confusing system. It is a strange mixture of pantheism and platonism, borrowing from both and differing from each. The pantheism of the East admitted the reality of the universe and taught that it is God. Christian Science denies the reality of matter (*Science and Health*, 103d ed., p. 173), teaches that mind is all and identifies mind with God (*Science and Health*, 103d ed., pp. 166, 171). This is the old monism, of which J. G. Fichte was the foremost apostle. He declared that God alone is and beside him is nothing. Christian Science says that "nothing possesses reality or existence except Mind, God" (103d ed., p. 226). The following sentences, found everywhere on the pages of *Science and Health*, give the belief of this system. "In Christian Science we learn that God is definitely individual, and not personal"; "An individual God rather than a personal God." This individuality is defined as "the infinite and divine principle." Again, "God is a spirit, and spirit is divine principle." And definitely is it stated, "God is divine principle." "God is Spirit, and Spirit is divine Principle" (103d ed., pp. 225–227). This is the answer given to the question, "What is God?" "God is divine Principle, supreme incorporeal being, Mind, Spirit, Soul, Life, Truth, Love" (103d ed., p. 461). On the same page it is declared that these terms are synonymous and that they are "intended to express the nature, essence, and wholeness of Deity." The system identifies the existence of God with the existence of man as a spiritual being. "God, without the image and likeness of himself, would be a nonentity, or Mind unexpressed" (103d ed., p. 199). "Man is coexistent with God" (103d ed., p. 473). According to this system God is Principle, is love, is Life, is Truth: but principle without personality, love without a lover, life without a living being, truth without any consciousness. Mrs. Eddy's favorite word for God is Principle, an absolute depersonalized term, one which does not admit of the ideas of consciousness, volition, or feeling. Mrs. Eddy says, "God is good, God is truth, God is love." But she says more than that and it is that addition which defines Christian Science; for she declares: "Good is God, truth is God, love is God." Thus Mrs. Eddy puts attributes of God in the place of God, and deifies the attributes. All admit that God is good, is truth, is love, but objection arises when it is said that good is God, truth is God, love is God. There are many detached sentences in *Science and Health* which any Bible student would accept as true expressions of the Biblical idea of God, but these sentences are offset by others which teach the very opposite ideas. Pres. William Herbert Perry Faunce, of Brown University, holds that "much of the success of Christian Science is due to the fact that its vague phraseology is equally acceptable to the evangelical Christian and to the atheist. The average Christian, approaching the Christian Science creed on one side, hears that God is 'spirit, omnipresent and eternal'; and at once accepts the teaching. The atheist, coming up on the other side, hears that God is 'principle, truth, harmony,' and he can accept it without the slightest change of position" (*Search-Lights on Christian Science*, New York, 1899).

A system is to be judged not by isolated sentences, but by its tone and tendency, its ultimate reach. The essential idea of God presented in Christian Science is that God is principle, not personality. As such the God of Christian Science has no existence apart from the mind or life that thinks God. President Faunce tells of a young man who had passed through Christian Science into atheism, who, when asked to describe the path he had traversed, answered: "The Christian Science teacher began by thoroughly persuading me that God is not personal, but is pure 'Principle.' After some months I accepted that; and then I said to myself: 'What is a principle? Does it have real existence? Is it an entity or reality?' I soon saw that a 'principle' is simply an idea of my own mind, and when the Scientist dissolved my God into 'principle' I ceased to believe in any God whatever. I now believe simply in myself."

This is the ultimate of the Christian Science idea of God, it teaches one to find the spiritual reality, the "divine principle," within himself. But this does not accord with Biblical teaching, which is that God is Spirit, distinct from nature which he has created: that he is a being who wills and loves, who is to be obeyed and loved; a real, substantive existence, a self-conscious, intelligent, voluntary agent; a being who can say "I am," and to whom we can say "Thou"; a being on whom men are dependent and to whom they are accountable. Christian Science denies all this in denying personality to God. Since the God of Christian Science is other and less than personal, he is other and less than the Christian's God, the Father of our Lord Jesus Christ and the Father of our spirits.

After defining God as Principle, the question is asked, "Is there more than one Principle?" (*Science and Health*, 103d ed., p. 461). And the answer is: "There is not. There is but one

2. Doctrine of the Trinity.

Life, one Truth, one Love; and this is God." On page 227 is this definite statement concerning the Trinity: "Life, Truth, and Love constitute the triune God, or triply divine Principle. They represent a trinity in unity, three in one—the same in essence, though multiform in office: God the Father; Christ the type of Sonship; Divine Science, or the Holy Comforter. These three express the threefold, essential nature of the Infinite." Such utterances as these are out of harmony with all that teaching of the Scriptures which represent the Eternal God as manifesting himself as Father, Son, and Spirit (Matt. xxviii. 19; I Cor. xii. 4–6; II Cor. xiii. 14; I Pet. i. 2, etc.).

3. Christology. The position of Christian Science concerning the person and work of Jesus Christ radically differs from that generally accepted. To begin with, Christian Science teaches that "Mary's conception of him (Jesus Christ) was spiritual" (*Science and Health*, 103d ed., p. 228). This is what Mrs. Eddy says of it: "The illumination of Mary's spiritual sense put to silence material law, and its order of generation, and brought forth her child by the revelation of Truth, demonstrating God (Principle) as the Father of men" (103d ed., p. 334). There is need to observe closely this claim of Christian Science. It claims to be the Holy Spirit, and as such to be the generating cause of Jesus. But if of Jesus, why not of other children? Mrs. Eddy meets the question by the statement: "The time cometh when the spiritual origin of man, the Science which ushered Jesus into human presence, will be understood and demonstrated"; but "until it is learned that generation rests on no sexual basis," Mrs. Eddy advises, "let marriage continue" (103d ed., p. 274). Of the existence of this tenet of Christian Science multitudes of the adherents of the system have no knowledge. But it is a fundamental element in the structure of the whole system and is essentially immoral. No accusation of immoral practise is brought against Christian Scientists, yet the accusation of immorality must be laid against this teaching of Christian Science. Though it is an absurd and preposterous teaching and might conceivably be laughed out of court, still it can not be merely laughed at as teaching what is subversive of the marriage relation. In her *Miscellaneous Writings* (p. 288) Mrs. Eddy asks the question, "Is marriage nearer right than celibacy?" and this is her answer: "Human knowledge indicates that it is, while science indicates that it is not."

In harmony with this notion concerning his conception Christian Science denies the actual incarnation of Christ, and so the reality of his person. Mary did not give birth to an actual body, but to a spiritual idea, an idea produced by her communion with the divine Principle. She gave birth to an ideal. But what Jesus said of himself is the opposite of this. He said: "A spirit hath not flesh and bones as ye see me have" (Luke xxiv. 39). In explanation of this utterance Mrs. Eddy says: "To accommodate himself to immature ideas of spiritual power—for spirituality was possessed only in a limited degree, even by his disciples—Jesus called the body, which by this power he raised from the grave, 'flesh and bones'" (103d ed., p. 209). In the theory of Christian Science flesh is an illusion, therefore Christ did not come in the flesh. There is a verse in St. John which may well be quoted in this connection: "Hereby know ye the Spirit of God: every spirit that confesseth that Jesus Christ is come in the flesh is of God; and every spirit that confesseth not that Jesus Christ is come in the flesh is not of God; and this is that spirit of anti-Christ, whereof ye have heard that it should come; and even now already is it in the world" (I John iv. 2–3).

4. Doctrine of Christ's Presence. Christian Science deals with Christ as a dual existence, the seen and the unseen, the Jesus and the Christ. Jesus is a mortal belief which has disappeared (*Science and Health*, 103d ed., p. 229). Christ is a principle, a spiritual idea, which continues "to exist in the eternal order of Divine (Christian) Science." According to this teaching the only Christ which humanity has to-day is Christian Science (103d ed., p. 293). That this is a legitimate inference from the teaching of Christian Science is sustained by the teaching in *Science and Health* that Christ is "Divine Science." Here is a sentence from that volume: "There is but one way to Heaven and harmony, and Christ, Divine Science, shows us that way." Another thing that sustains the inference that Christian Science is humanity's Christ, is the teaching that identifies the second coming of Christ with Christian Science (103d ed., pp. 43, 293). Mrs. Eddy says, "The second appearance of Jesus is unquestionably the spiritual advent of the advancing idea of God in Christian Science" (103d ed., p. 126). Adherents of Christian Science may not accept this teaching, but they readily fall into the habit of attributing to Christian Science the blessings which they receive and their praise is all of Christian Science. The leaders encourage this and they are consistent in doing so, for in their teaching, if not in their convictions, Christian Science is the Christ present and operative in human life. The acceptance of the Christology of Christian Science, as it is presented in *Science and Health*, may be considered the most effective way of destroying the soul's consciousness of the Christ of Christian thought and belief.

5. Doctrine of the Holy Spirit. Denying personality to God and to Christ, Christian Science likewise denies personality to the Holy Spirit. There is no Trinity, as it is generally understood. *Science and Health* affirms: "The theory of three persons in one God suggests heathen gods, rather than one ever present I Am" (103d ed., p. 152). Then, true to its idea of the impersonal deity, Christian Science teaches that "Life, Truth, and Love constitute the triune God, or triple divine principle. God the Father, Jesus the type of Sonship (not Sonship, only the type of sonship), and Divine Science, or the Holy Comforter" (103d ed., p. 227). It is here that Christian Science approaches the blasphemous by claiming to be the Holy Spirit. Mrs. Eddy very definitely says with reference to the Comforter whom Jesus promised, "This Comforter I understand to be Divine Science." The following quotations from *Science and Health* (103d ed.) establish this fact of the identifying of Christian Science with the Holy Spirit. "It (Christian Science) is a divine utterance, the Comforter which leadeth into all Truth" (p. 21). "John the Baptist prophesied the coming of the immaculate Jesus, and saw in those days the spiritual idea as the Messiah, who would baptize with the Holy Ghost—Divine Science" (p. 553). In the Glossary (p. 579) is this definition: "Holy

Ghost, Divine Science; the development of eternal Life, Truth, and Love."

Christian Science makes a distinction between "mortals" and "immortals." "Mortals," who are not created in God's image, are simply human beings, "material falsities, errors which must disappear to give place to the facts which belong to immortal man." The life of these mortals, or temporal life, is a false sense of existence. "To himself, mortal and material man seems to be substantial; but this is mere belief, or a false view of substance, and involves error." "Mortal man seems to himself to be substance, but he is 'image'" (*Science and Health*, 103d ed., p. 197). "Mortal body and material man are delusions which spiritual understanding and science destroy" (p. 198). "Mortals are material falsities" (p. 472). The "immortals" are the ideas or reflections of God, they always have been, never shall cease to be, and are absolutely perfect. According to this system the "immortal," the essential or spiritual man, "is coexistent and eternal with God" (pp. 231, 509), "has existed forever, and is always beyond and above the mortal illusion of any life, substance, and intelligence as existent in matter" (p. 198), has no separate existence apart from God (p. 257), "possesses no life, intelligence, or creative power of his own" (p. 471), "is perfect even as the Father is perfect" (p. 191), "can do no harm, for his thoughts are true thoughts, passing from God to man" (p. 283). The doctrine of man is stated in the paragraph on "Real Life" (p. 242): "When Being is understood, Life will be recognized as neither material nor finite, but as infinite—as God, universal Good; and the belief that life, or mind, was ever in a finite form, or good in evil, will be destroyed. Then it will be understood that Spirit never entered matter, and was therefore never raised from it."

6. Anthropology.

In its teaching on man Christian Science puts him on an equality with God in his origin, character, and eternity. It declares in unequivocal language that man never was formed from the dust of the earth, that God never breathed into his nostrils the breath of life, that in his case there is neither birth nor growth, maternity nor decay, that he is and always has been as perfect as the God whom he reveals and whose character he reflects. It is only necessary to compare this teaching with the Bible statements concerning man to see how widely Christian Science differs from the Bible on this subject. The Bible says: "God created man" (Gen. i. 27). That which is created can not be coexistent with its creator. The Bible represents man's life as a vapor appearing for a little time (James iv. 14), as a weaver's shuttle (Job vii. 6), as a hand-breadth (Ps. xxxix. 5), as a tale that is told (Ps. xc. 9). These and similar utterances do not accord with the idea that man is coexistent with and eternal like God. The Bible says that "death has passed upon all men" (Rom. v. 12), that "it is appointed unto man once to die" (Heb. ix. 27), that his years are three score and ten or four score (Ps. xc. 10). Such utterances contradict the Christian Science teaching that "man is incapable of death." The teaching of Christian Science that "man is perfect even as the Father is perfect," is denied in such passages as Job ix. 20; Ps. cxliii. 2; Isa. lxiv. 6; Ephes. ii. 1, and similar passages, all of which are in line with the general teaching of the Bible. It is impossible to accept the teaching of Christian Science on the creation and constitution of man and the teaching of the Bible on the same subject. If one is true the other is false. They are distinctly unlike and there is no possible compromise between the two.

7. Doctrine of Sin.

Long ago it was said that the sign-post at which true and false theology parts company is sin. Christian Science knows no such thing as sin. Dominated by the idea that man is coexistent with God and has no actual entity apart from God (*Science and Health*, 103d ed., p. 471), Christian Science affirms that sin is only a belief of mortal mind. Mrs. Eddy declares "man is incapable of sin, sickness, and death, inasmuch as he derives his essence from God, and does not possess a single original, or underived power. Hence the real man can not depart from holiness" (p. 471). The dictum of *Science and Health* is that "evil should de denied identity or power, because it has none of the divine hues" (p. 475), that "evil is but an illusion, and error has no real basis, it is a false belief" (p. 476), that "evil can only seem real, by giving reality to the unreal" (p. 466), that "evil is the awful deception and unreality of existence" (p. 103). All these utterances are condensed in this one: "Evil has no reality. It is neither person (hence there is no devil, the idea is 'pure delusion'; (p. 559), nor place (hence there is no hell), nor thing (hence there is no accountability), but is simply belief, an illusion of material self" (p. 237). Growing out of this doctrine of the unreality of evil, Christian Science teaches that sin has no existence, that it is not of the verity of being, and that it "exists only so long as the material illusion remains" (p. 207). The Christian Science principle of the "unreality of evil" plunges a dagger through the Bible doctrine of man's moral accountability and lets out the very heartblood of the distinctive teaching of the Scriptures. The Bible says: "The soul that sinneth, it shall die" (Ezek. xxviii. 4, 20); Christian Science says: "The soul can not sin." The Bible doctrine is: "If we say we have no sin, we deceive ourselves, and the truth is not in us" (I John i. 18); the doctrine of Christian Science is: "Man is incapable of sin." The Bible statement is: "He is just to forgive us our sins" (I John i. 9); Christian Science says: "To suppose that God forgives sin is to misunderstand Love." The Bible declares: "He that covereth his sins shall not prosper, but whoso confesseth and forsaketh them, shall find mercy" (Prov. xxviii. 13); Christian Science exhorts: Deny the reality of sin.

8. The Atonement.

Denying the reality of evil and the existence of sin, Christian Science denies the fact of the atonement. According to its teaching Christ did not suffer or die to deliver men from sin. In fact Christian Science denies altogether the reality of the suffering of Christ and calls his death "the great illusion." But Mrs. Eddy has difficulty in facing its historic reality and even at the cost of sacrificing consistency says: "Had wisdom characterized all the sayings of Jesus, he would not have prophesied his own death." In a paragraph on "Reconciliation" we read that "Jesus aided in reconciling man to God, only by giving man a truer sense of Love, the divine Principle of his teaching, which would redeem man from under the law of matter, by this explanation of the law of Spirit" (*Science and Health*, 103d ed., p. 324). Here we are taught not that Jesus reconciled man to God, but "aided in reconciling man to God," and that he did this "only by giving man a true sense of love." This certainly is not Pauline theology. "Reconciled to God by the death of his Son" (Rom. v. 10); "Reconciled us to himself by Jesus Christ" (II Cor. v. 18); "Reconcile both unto God in one body by the cross" (Eph. ii. 16); "Having made peace through the blood of his cross, by him to reconcile all things unto himself; . . . you that were sometimes alienated and enemies in your mind by wicked works, yet now hath he reconciled in the body of his flesh through death" (Col. i. 20–22). It is impossible to reconcile Paul's doctrine of the reconciliation with that of Christian Science. Paul presents reconciliation as fact accomplished by Christ through his death. Christian Science presents reconciliation as a process, in which Jesus aids by giving man a truer sense of Love. In a paragraph on "Substitution" we read: "One sacrifice, however great, is insufficient to pay the debt of sin. The atonement requires constant self-immolation on the sinner's part. That God's wrath should be vented upon his beloved Son is divinely unnatural. Such a theory is man-made. The atonement is a hard problem in theology; but its more reasonable explanation is, that suffering is an error of sinful sense, which Truth destroys, and that eventually both sin and suffering will fall at the feet of everlasting love" (*Science and Health*, 103d ed., p. 328). The statements of this paragraph are quite out of harmony with statements in the Bible. "One sacrifice, however great, is insufficient to pay the debt of sin," but the Bible says: "By his own blood he entered in once into the holy place, having obtained eternal redemption" (Heb. ix. 12); "once in the end of the world hath he appeared to put away sin by the sacrifice of himself" (Heb. ix. 26); "by the which we are sanctified through the offering of the body of Jesus Christ once" (Heb. x. 10); "this man after he had offered one sacrifice for sins forever" (Heb. x. 12). "The atonement requires constant self-immolation on the sinner's part." Then atonement is not made by Christ for the sinner, but by the sinner for himself. The Bible teaches that we do not atone for ourselves; that we "receive" the atonement, and that we receive it through our Lord Jesus Christ (Rom. v. 11). "That God's wrath should be vented upon his well-beloved Son is divinely unnatural. Such a theory is man-made." Yet the Bible says that he was "smitten of God," that "the Lord hath laid on him the iniquity of us all," that "it pleased the Lord to bruise him" (Isa. liii. 4, 6, 10); and "God spared not his own son, but delivered him up for us all" (Rom. viii. 32). In Christian Science there is no place for the atonement as generally understood by Christians. In this system salvation is not through a Savior sacrificing himself for man, but through an illumination of man's own mind. This is the way in which Christian Science defines salvation: "Explaining and demonstrating the way of Divine Science, he became the way of salvation to all who accepted his word, that mortals might learn of him and escape from evil. The true man being linked by Science to his Maker, mortals need only turn from sin, and lose sight of themselves, in order to find the real man and his relation to God, and recognize the divine sonship" (*Science and Health*, 103d ed., p. 211). According to this the medium of salvation is not a Savior, but Christian Science. So it is definitely stated. "Christ is the idea of Truth, and this idea comes to heal sickness and sin, through Christian Science, which denies corporeal power" (p. 469). This denies *in toto* the idea of a personal Savior. Of course, in a system which denies the reality of sin, as moral evil, there can be no place for atonement. One asks, "What becomes of the atonement when suffering which was not suffering (only a 'great illusion'), in a body which was not a body (only a 'mortal belief'), was offered in expiation for sin which was not sin?"

9. Doctrine of Prayer.

As prayer is generally understood it has no place in Christian Science. Prayer implies that God is a personal conscious Being. Christian Science denies this, declares that God is principle and hence inhibits prayer. Mrs. Eddy asks: "Who would stand before a blackboard and pray the principle of mathematics to work out the problem? The rule is already established, and it is our task to work out the solution. Shall we ask the Divine Principle of all goodness to do his own work? That work was finished long ago; and we have only to avail ourselves of God's rule, in order to receive the blessing" (*Science and Health*, 103d ed., p. 308). She also asserts that "Prayer to a personal God is a hindrance, it is a misapprehension of the source and manner of all good." The Christian Scientist may declare that he believes in prayer, but if pressed for his definition of prayer, provided he be well versed in the doctrines of his system, he will state that "prayer is the affirmation of principle." "A request," writes Mrs. Eddy, "that another may work for us never does our work. The habit of pleading with the divine Mind, as one pleads with a human being, perpetuates the belief in God as humanly circumscribed" (p. 308). Prayer is defined as "the habitual struggle to be always good" (p. 309). It is said that "the only beneficial effect of prayer for the sick is on the human mind, making it act more powerfully on the body, through a blind faith in God," and that "it is not Truth which does this" (p. 317), so Christian Science would eliminate all prayer for the sick, because the "common custom of praying for the recovery of the sick, finds help in blind belief; whereas help should come from the enlightened understanding" (p. 318). The idea of prayer, presented in Christian Science, is quite opposite to the whole idea and economy of prayer as presented in the Bible, understood and practised by Christians in all ages.

10. The Scriptures. Christian Science recognizes Mrs. Eddy's *Science and Health, with Key to the Scriptures* as of equal authority with the Bible. Great attachment for the Bible is declared, but any passage which contradicts any of the postulates of the system is rejected. Thus, Mrs. Eddy gives no explanation of Gen. ii. 7, "And the Lord God formed man of the dust of the ground and breathed into his nostrils the breath of life; and man became a living soul." Commenting on this verse, Mrs. Eddy asks: "How can the material organization become the basis of man? How can the non-intelligent become the medium of Mind, and error the enunciator of Truth? Is this truth? or is it a lie, concerning man and God?" And she answers: "It must be the latter, for God presently curses the ground" (*Science and Health*, 103d ed., p. 517). Adam has made a good deal of trouble for theologians of all schools. Mrs. Eddy met the difficulties and in her own way solved them by a display of philological skill. She holds that Adam is merely a name for the "matter" which opposes "mind." In order to prove this she says: "Divide the name Adam into two syllables, and it reads, a dam, or obstruction. This suggests the thought of something fluid, of mortal mind in solution" (p. 233). These two instances of exegesis are samples of the way in which the Bible is treated by this system. Such treatment utterly destroys its majesty and meaning. A comparison of the estimate which Christian Science puts on the Bible and on the text-book *Science and Health* shows the relative place of each in the system. The following parallel column exhibits these estimates. This column is made from sentences in *Science and Health* and the *Miscellaneous Writings:*

The Bible.	Science and Health.
(1) In parts composed of legends, metaphors, fables, allegories, and myths.	(1) Revealed truth, the perfect word of God.
(2) Full of mistakes.	(2) Uncontaminated truth.
(3) Full of thousands of errors.	(3) Truth without mixture of human error.
(4) A compilation of human documents.	(4) Divine teaching.
(5) Contains statements which are not true.	(5) Infallible teaching.

This comparison might be drawn out to great length, but these statements are sufficient to show the superior place which Christian Sciense assigns Mrs. Eddy's book.

11. Service. Christian Science centers thought on self and self as free from all maladies, from sin, suffering, and sorrow. If the reality of sickness and suffering be denied, the channels of sympathy and philanthropy dry up. If the reality of sin and death be denied, that act quenches all missionary ardor. Christian Science builds splendid temples of stone and adorns them with all the genius of architect and artist. But Christian Science builds no hospitals or orphanages, or schools; for sickness, which needs a hospital; want, which needs an orphanage; and ignorance, which needs a school, have no actual existence. They are only illusions of mortal mind.

Genuine Christianity builds churches, but does not lavish all its money on them, for there are hospitals and asylums and kindergartens and colleges to be built and to be built by the money of those who kneel at the cross of Christ and from him learn that the true economy of life is to minister even unto the least of the children of men.

J. F. Carson.

Bibliography: W. H. Holcombe, *Letters on Spiritual Subjects in Answer to Inquiring Souls*, Philadelphia, 1885; H. M. Tenney, *Christian Science: its Truths and Errors*, Cleveland, Ohio, 1888; E. P. Terhune, *Fallacy of Christian Science*, New York, 1890; J. M. Buckley, *Christian Science and Superstitions*, ib. 1899; R. H. Newton, *Christian Science: Truths of spiritual Healing and their Contribution to the Growth of Orthodoxy*, ib. 1898; J. H. Bates, *Christian Science and its Problems*, ib. 1898; W. P. McCorkle, *Christian Science*, Philadelphia, 1900; C. F. Winbigler, *Christian Science and Kindred Superstitions*, New York, 1901; M. W. Gifford, *Christian Science against itself*, Cincinnati, 1902; M. C. Sturge, *Truth and Error of Christian Science*, New York, 1903, new ed., 1908; C. G. Pease, *Exposé of Christian Science Methods and Teachings*, ib. 1905; E. A. Kimball, C. P. Smith, S. J. Hanna, *Christian Science and Legislation*, Boston, 1906; R. D. Kathrens, *Side Lights on Mary Baker Eddy Glover-Science Church Trustees Controversy*, Kansas City, 1907; L. P. Powell, *Christian Science, the Faith and its Founder*, New York, 1907; F. T. Brown, *The Truth and Error in so-called "Christian Science,"* New Haven, 1907; J. M. Gray, *The Antidote for Christian Science*, New York, 1907; R. C. Harker, *Christian Science*, Cincinnati, 1908; F. S. Hoffman, *The Sphere of Religion*, New York, 1908; L. A. Lambert, *Christian Science before the Bar of Reason*, ib. 1908; G. C. Mars, *The Interpretation of Life, in which is Shown the Relation of Modern Culture to Christian Science*, ib. 1908 (a defense of Christian Science); Sibyl Wilbur, *Life of Mary Baker Eddy*, Concord, 1908 (circulated by Christian Scientists); F. Ballard, *Eddyism "Christian Science" miscalled. A Delusion and a Snare*, London, 1909; I. M. Haldeman, *Christian Science in the Light of Holy Scripture*, New York, 1909; S. J. Hanna, *Christian Science: the Religion of the Bible*, Boston, 1909; *The Faith and Works of Christian Science*, New York, 1909; F. E. Marston, *The Mask of Christian Science*, ib. 1909; G. Milmine, *The Life of Mary Baker G. Eddy and the History of Christian Science*, ib. 1909 (critical and adverse); S. Paget, *Faith and Works of Christian Science*, ib. 1909 (thorough medical criticism of the system); F. Podmore, *Mesmerism and Christian Science. A Short History of Mental Healing*, London, 1909; C. R. Brown, *Faith and Health*, New York, 1910 (adverse, by a former Christian Scientist); B. O. Flower, *Christian Science as a Religious Belief and a Therapeutic Agent*, Boston, 1910 (critical; rejects the philosophy of Christian Science but admits numerous cures); F. E. Marsten, *The Mask of Christian Science: a History of the Rise and Growth of the System together with a Comparison of metaphysical Healing with Matters scientific*, New York, 1910; W. W. Walter, *Five Years in Christian Science*, Chicago, 1911; R. C. Armstrong, *Christian Science Exposed*, Fort Worth, Texas, 1911.

SCILLI, MARTYRS OF: Twelve Christians, seven men and five women, martyred on July 17, 180, either at Scilli, a city of the proconsular province of North Africa, or at Sila or Silli, two small cities of Numidia. The story goes that on July 17, 180, six Christians who were named Speratus (the spokesman), Nartzallus, Cittinus, Donata, Secunda, and Vestia, were brought before the proconsul Saturninus and repeatedly urged to swear by the genius of the emperor and thus to secure imperial clemency for their crime, which consisted in simple adherence to Christianity. This demand was steadfastly refused, and a respite of thirty days twice offered by the proconsul was as firmly declined. Saturninus thereupon condemned the six Christians and an equal number of absentees—the four men, Veturius, Felix, Aquilinus and Cælestinus, and the two women, Januaria and Generosa—to be beheaded. Until 1881 the martyrdom was known only from the Latin *Acta martorum Scillitanorum proconsularia* (ed. C. Baronius, *Annales ecclesiastici ad annum Christi 202*, 12 vols., Mainz, 1609); *Fragmentum de martyribus Scillitanis* (ed. J. Mabillon, *Vetera analecta*, vol. iv., part 3, Paris, 1723); a document edited by T. Ruinart (*Acta martyrum*, pp. 131–132, Regensburg, 1859); eight Latin manuscripts mentioned, though not published, by the Bollandist Cuperus (*ASB*, July, iv., 207–208); and a text edited by Aubé (*Les Chrétiens dans l'empire romain*, pp. 503–509, Paris, 1881). On the basis of these texts, the martyrdom was assigned to the year 200. In 1881, however, H. Usener edited in the list of lectures at Bonn a ninth-century Greek text of the passion discovered by him in the Bibliothèque Nationale, Paris. This text is not only far more correct than the Latin *Acta*, but apparently comes from an eye-witness or ear-witness who drew up the record shortly after the execution of the martyrs. Since this discovery the Latin versions themselves have been reedited by the Bollandists in the *Analecta Bollandiana* (viii. 5–8, Paris, 1889), and by J. A. Robinson in *Texts and Studies* (I., ii. 106 sqq., Cambridge, 1893), both unduly exalting the Latin versions at the expense of the Greek. There is, however, no martyrology which gives so purely and unfeignedly a true picture of early Christian life and death as the text published by Usener.

It is clear from the *Acta* that considerable hatred of the Christians was still possible in the early years of the reign of the third Antonine emperor, although the rigor of Marcus Aurelius had been much mitigated, as shown by the fact that Saturninus did not resort to torture, but repeatedly offered the Christians time to reconsider. It is also noteworthy that it would appear that the martyr Speratus made a distinction between the Pauline writings and the other books of the New Testament.

(Franz Görres.)

Bibliography: Consult the following works cited under Persecution of Christians: Keim, 1881, Neumann (i. 71–76, 284–286), and Allard (i. 436–439); and also: B. Aubé, *Les Chrétiens dans l'empire romain 180–249*, Paris, 1881; idem, *Étude sur un nouveau texte des Actes des martyrs scillitains*, ib. 1881; F. Görres, in *ZWT*, 1884, pp. 37–84, 1891, pp. 235–243; idem, in *Philologus*, 1884, pp. 134–140, 615–624; idem, in *JPT*, x. 228–268, 395–434; R. Hilgenfeld, in *ZWT*. xxiv. 3, pp. 291–331; *DCB*, iv. 592–593.

SCOT, MICHAEL: Scottish scholar; b. [in the county of Durham] England, c. 1190; [d. c. 1235, probably in Italy]. After studying natural science at Oxford, he went to Paris, the court of Emperor Frederick II. of Germany [in Sicily], Toledo, back to Frederick's court, and at a later period returned to England, where he is supposed to have held some office at the court of King Edward I. [He is said to have taken holy orders and to have enjoyed the favor of Honorius III. and Gregory IX., but never held an office in the Church, though once he was nominated archbishop of Cashel.] Scot owed his fame to his translations into Latin of Arabic works, those of Averroës among others. By commission of the emperor, he also translated Aristotle's "History of Animals" and his books *De cœlo et mundo*. His own writings did not attain to the merit of his translations. [A number of them are still in manuscript. To later times he was a necromancer and not a scientist, and as such Dante puts him in hell (*Inferno*, cant. xx.).]

Carl Mirbt.

Bibliography: Earlier works are in large part superseded by J. Wood Brown, *Life and Legend of Michael Scot (1175–1232)*, Edinburgh, 1897. Consult further: P. F. Tytler, *Lives of Scottish Worthies*, 3 vols., London, 1831–33; *Histoire littéraire de la France*, xx. 43 sqq.; A. Jourdain, *Recherches critiques sur l'âge et l'origine des traductions latines d'Aristote*, Paris, 1843; B. Hauréau, *De la philosophie scolastique*, i. 467 sqq., ib. 1850; L. Leclerc, *Hist. de la médecine Arabe*, ii. 451 sqq., Paris, 1876; *DNB*, li. 59–62; Bayle, *Dictionary*, v. 100.

SCOTCH CONFESSION OF FAITH: A confession drawn up by John Knox and five associates appointed by the Scotch Parliament which assembled at Edinburgh in August, 1560, after the death of the queen-regent, Mary of Guise, in June and at the close of the civil war. It consists of a preface and twenty-five articles on the chief doctrines of religion which are briefly, tersely, and vigorously stated. It agrees with the other Reformed confessions of the sixteenth century, but in some articles is more pronounced in its opposition to the Roman Catholic Church than most of them. These parts Mitchell (ut inf., p. 123) called the "unrestrained" portions. It was composed in four days, twice read, article by article, in Parliament, and adopted by the same as being "based upon the infallible Word of God." Only three temporal lords voted against it, for the reason that they believed as their forefathers believed. The Roman Catholic bishops were called upon to object and refute, but kept silence. Seven years later (1568), after the abdication of Queen Mary, the confession was readopted, and the Reformed Kirk of Scotland was formally acknowledged and established. In 1580 the confession was signed by King James II., and a supplementary confession (sometimes called the Second Scotch Confession) added to it. It was practically superseded by the Westminster Confession, which was adopted by the Scotch Assembly in 1648. The confession is printed in the Acts of the Scotch Parliament for 1560; in John Knox, *History of the Scotch Reformation* (ed. D. Laing, vol. ii., Edinburgh, 1895); in D. Calderwood, *History of the Kirk of Scotland* (Edinburgh, 1842); in W. Dunlop, *Collection of Scotch Confessions* (vol. ii., London, 1857); in H. A. Niemeyer, *Collectio confessionum Reformatarum* (Leipsic, 1840; Latin only); and in Schaff, *Creeds*, iii. 437–485 (English and Latin), cf. i. 680–696.

(Philip Schaff†.) D. S. Schaff.

Bibliography: J. Knox, *Hist. of the Reformation . . . in Scotland*, ed. C. Lennox, pp. 213–215, London, 1905· the literature under Knox, John, especially T. McCrie, and H. Cowan (pp. 222–234); W. M. Hetherington, *Hist. of the Church of Scotland*, pp. 50–54, New York, 1881; P. H. Brown, *John Knox*, i. 88–90, London, 1895; idem, *Hist. of Scotland*, ii. 70–72, Cambridge, 1902. A. F. Mitchell,

The Scottish Reformation, pp. 99, 123, Edinburgh, 1900; C. G. McCrie, *The Confessions of the Church of Scotland, their Evolution in History*, ib. 1907.

SCOTCH PARAPHRASES: A book of praise for church use made in Scotland in the eighteenth century. In May, 1742, the general assembly of the Church of Scotland appointed a committee to make or collect translations in verse of select passages of Scripture. Their work was sanctioned by the Assembly, 1751, and appeared as *Scripture Songs*, forty-five in number, and now rare. In 1775 another committee undertook the revision of these, adding twenty-two paraphrases and five hymns the precise authorship of which can not be determined in all cases. Some twenty were altered or rewritten from Watts, and three from Doddridge; one each was contributed by Thomas Blacklock, John Ogilvie, and Thomas Randall; three are by William Robertson (1742–51), and several by John Morrison (d. 1798). The name of William Cameron (d. 1811) appears chiefly as an improver of other men's verses. The most important share, both for quantity and quality, was taken from the manuscripts of Michael Bruce (1746–67). The *Paraphrases* are marked by a dry neatness and precision of style, which excludes whatever could offend the most sober taste, and leaves little room for lyrical or devotional fire. Their eminent respectability and long service have made them household words in Scotland, and they have been constantly and largely drawn upon by English and American hymnals.

Bibliography: Julian, *Hymnology*, pp. 1024–25, 1033–34.

SCOTLAND.

Scotland is the northern member of the United Kingdom of Great Britain and Ireland; area, nearly 30,000 square miles; population 4,579,223. In 1851 the population was eighty-four per cent. Presbyterian. While this high percentage has not been maintained during the increase from 2,888,742 (in 1851) to the figures given above, the population is still predominatingly Presbyterian.

I. The Presbyterian Church.—1. As a Whole: The struggle of the Reformation in Scotland was brief and decisive. It soon gave place to the contest for supremacy between Presbyterianism and Episcopalianism, which lasted over a century; with the revolution of 1688, Scotland became as overwhelmingly Presbyterian. The first presentation of Scotch Presbyterian doctrine was the confession formulated by John Knox (q.v.) in 1560 (see Scotch Confession of Faith). This was replaced in 1647 by the Westminster Standards (q.v.). This confession, together with the two catechisms of like name, has exercised a positive influence upon organization and worship, wherever Scottish Presbyterianism has spread.

1. History.

The Church in Scotland did not share in the political and industrial prosperity that followed the union with England (1707). Religious indifference which found expression in Deism (q.v.) made itself felt in Scotland. The question of clerical patronage became a stumbling block to the peaceful growth of the Church. The claim of the landed aristocracy and of the crown to the right of appointing clericals to office was incompatible with the unity and independence of the system of Scotch Presbyterian organization. The claim had been at various times abolished; but in 1712 the Tory majority in Parliament revived it, causing a profound state of dissatisfaction among the masses of the people bearing fruit in church divisions. The first of these, called "The Secession," occurred in 1733 under Ebenezer Erskine (q.v.). While this was the first formal and organized separation, the Covenanters (q.v.) had already separated and in 1743 organized as Reformed Presbyterians (see Presbyterians, I., 5). The opposition to the exercise of patronage grew to such an extent that ministers could be installed in office only with military aid. In 1752 arose a new separate body called the "Relief" (see Presbyterians, I., 2, § 3). In the course of a century the number of separatist organizations had grown to about 500 congregations and in 1847 they were combined as the United Presbyterian Church. With the beginning of the nineteenth century a reawakening took place in the Church of Scotland (see Presbyterians, I., 1) under the leadership of such men as Thomas Chalmers (q.v.), under which the church aligned itself more and more with the doctrinal viewpoint of the separatists. The patronage struggle, stimulated by the spiritual revival, was again resumed, with a view to restriction and correction of evils, and the general question of the spiritual independence of the Church came to the front. This led to the "Disruption" and the organization of the Free Church of Scotland (see Presbyterians, I., 2). In the next sixty years the Free Church doubled in membership. In 1874 the right of patronage was removed by parliament, the election of the clergy was granted to communicants and adherents, and the Established Church has consequently gained in popularity.

2. Separation and Union.

At the close of the last century there were, accordingly, three great Presbyterian churches in Scotland: the Established Church consisting of 1,377 congregations; the Free Church with 1,068 congregations; and the United Presbyterian Church with 593 congregations. The difference between them was principally involved in the relation of Church and State. The Established Church was in accord with the existing state of things. The Free Church theoretically favored State recognition and endowment, but entered increasing protest against the prevailing arrangements, which, in spite of the abolition of patronage, were felt to be identical with the former state of things. The United Presbyterians repudiated all connection between Church and State. All adhered to the Westminster Confession, but the United Church in 1879 and the Free Church in 1892 adopted a declaratory act, defining more closely their attitude, to the effect mainly of moderating ultra-Calvinistic points and not requiring total subscription from candidates to clerical office. Negotiations for union between the Free and United Churches opened in 1863, broken off in 1873 and resumed in 1896, resulted, Oct. 31, 1900, in the organization of the United Free Church of Scotland (see PRESBYTERIANS, I., 2). While this resolution for union was carried in the general assembly of the Free Church by a vote of 643 to 27, this small minority now declared itself to be the only true and legitimate Free Church and laid claim to all the property of the organization. For the resulting legal complications and the settlement see PRESBYTERIANS, I., 2-3. For a detailed history of the Presbyterian Church in Scotland in its several branches and for the present situation see PRESBYTERIANS, I.

3. Mode of Worship. The time of worship is in the morning and evening of the Sabbath. In the country, if the second service is held at all, it is usually in an adjoining chapel, school, or hall. Prayer is voluntary and extempore, no liturgy having been used from the time of Archbishop Laud (see LAUD, WILLIAM). Except in the Highlands singing is usually accompanied by a musical instrument, and the number of church organs is increasing rapidly in the cities. Some congregations sing metrical versions of the Psalms of the seventeenth century, but the great majority sing hymns also. The *Church Hymnary* published (1898) by the authority of the established church, the two parties in the present United Free, and the Irish Presbyterian Churches, has been widely adopted. The sermon, usually from twenty-five to thirty-five minutes in length, is the chief part of the service. Systematic exposition of the Scriptures, though still prominent, especially in the morning service, is on the wane. Baptism is performed in church as part of the public service, or at home. Communion is received by all at least twice a year; and by many, four times. There is no confirmation in the proper sense of the word, but the minister gives special instruction to the young people before their first communion. Weddings are usually at home, but there is a tendency to transfer them to the church, as in England. There is a service in the house of mourning; and at the grave, including a short prayer, but no address. The minister is expected to visit not only the sick but all the members of his congregation regularly. He is the superintendent of the Sunday-school and usually leads the highest or, so-called, Bible class at a special hour. Of late years there has been a very large growth of young people's societies called "gilds," associated with the church, and especially of the Young People's Society of Christian Endeavor. The organization of Scotch Presbyterianism is essentially alike in all the Churches. The church elders are chosen by all the communicants and bound by the confession, and, together with the minister, they constitute the

4. Constitution. church session and have authority over matters of church discipline. A number of congregations, varying between 10 and 200, each represented by an elder elected by the church session (one elder for every 400 communicants in the United Free Church), and the minister, constitute a presbytery, which has general oversight over the congregations. A group of presbyteries forms a synod to which the acts of the presbyteries may be appealed. The members of the general assembly are chosen annually by the presbyteries from the ministers and elders, and it is the court of final appeal (see POLITY, ECCLESIASTICAL; PRESBYTERIANS, X.). In the Established Church some of the members are chosen by the towns and the universities. Candidates for the ministry must have attended lectures on the classics, mathematics, and philosophy, at a university, for at least three semesters. Each candidate is then examined as to his moral and religious fitness by a presbytery, and then again on his university studies by a committee of the general assembly. Four more years of theological study follow.

2. Severally: The Established Church—officially, the Church of Scotland—is ideally independent neither in legislative nor administrative powers, since it did not decline the dispositions of the civil courts with which the decisions of the general assembly were in conflict prior to 1843. In addition, when the right of patronage was abolished and the privilege of creedal modification was obtained, these changes were not valid for the church before the approval of the State was given. Notwithstanding this Church is freest among the State churches. The king is in no sense its head. His representative, the lord high commissioner, has no vote in the general assembly. He may summon and dismiss it, in the name of the king, as may the moderator in the name of Jesus Christ. For the statistics and work of this church see PRESBYTERIANS, I., 1. The decision of the house of lords against the union of the Free and United Presbyterian Churches, instead of crushing the United Free Church, awoke an enthusiasm for it that had not previously existed. Clergy, missionaries, and students, with scarcely an exception, stood by it, and by 1904 the organization showed an actual increase in membership. As a consequence of the decree of the house of lords which pronounced the constitution of the Free Church unalterable, the committee representing the assembly between sessions raised, within ten days, the claim for the privilege of heeding the commands of Christ without the fear of legal consequences. This was reiterated by the general assembly of 1905 more formally and explicitly. The ancient Scotch doctrine of spiritual independence was restated, emphasizing that the Church and it alone possessed the right to alter its creed, and asserting the rule of majority in all church affairs, governing also the matter of property. For the statistics of this body see PRESBYTERIANS, I., 2. The Free and the United Presbyterian Churches had different methods for raising contributions for clerical support. In the Free Church contributions were made to a central fund which was proportionately divided among the ministers, each congregation usually having a parsonage and being allowed to add a bonus to its minister's compensation, after satisfying the central fund. In the United Church the congregations paid the ministers directly, but when the salaries did not come up to about $750 (generally with parsonage), the difference was made up from a reinforcement fund. The effort to coordinate these two methods met with difficulties.

The Free Church of Scotland is relatively strong only in the highland districts (see PRESBYTERIANS, I., 3), is rigidly conservative, especially insisting on the plenary inspiration of the Scriptures, and violently opposes the spirit of modern criticism. Its general assembly in 1905 rejected the declaratory act of 1892, and forbade the singing of "human songs" and the use of the organ in divine service. There are three other small Presbyterian churches in Scotland, remnants of minorities that refused to follow majorities in falling away from what they considered the truth. They are (1) the Free Presbyterian Church; (2) the Reformed Presbyterian; and (3) the Original Secession, properly called the "Old Light" (see for data and history of these churches PRESBYTERIANS, I., 4-6).

II. The Scotch Episcopal Church: This church was in former times the great rival of the Presbyterian Church. After the downfall of the Stuarts its service was forbidden and subjected to other restrictive measures, while the church itself was almost expelled from the country. In 1792 full toleration was again granted. Owing to English influence most of the aristocracy and the landed nobility belong to this Church. Its cause has gained also by thorough organization. The country is divided into seven dioceses: Moray, Aberdeen, Brechin, St. Andrews, Edinburgh, Glasgow, and Argyle. From 1876 an excellent system of lay representation has been organized, whose aim is the support of the bishops in all financial affairs. The attractiveness of the church service and the earnest and self-denying activity of the clergy have contributed to its rapid growth. In 1910 it reported 404 churches and mission stations, 335 clergymen, and 51,289 communicants, with contributions of about $100,000 for main purposes. On account of its alleged High-church proclivities, a small body forming nine parishes has separated, and claimed direct connection with the Church of England.

III. Congregationalists: There is no trace of a movement in Scotland simultaneous with that turbulent period in political life which gave rise to the Independents. However, in 1728 John Glas (q.v.), a minister of the Established Church, founded a body still represented by one or two small congregations. From the end of the eighteenth century an Independent movement has achieved notable results. It had its origin in the revival of the Christian ideal in which the brothers Robert and James Haldane (q.v.) took a part, which was no doubt reenforced, from England. The congregations formed joined the Congregational Union organized in 1863. A division in the Secession Church in 1841 resulted in the founding of the Evangelical Union. James Morison (q.v.) had been expelled from the old church for emphasizing the love of God without leaving room for election by grace. The denomination which he founded, often called the Morisonian church, preferred the Congregational to the Presbyterian government. In 1896 the Congregationalist and Evangelical Unions were united to form the present Congregational Union of Scotland. This body has a theological faculty at Edinburgh with three professors. It is distinguished for its zeal in mission and temperance organization. A minority of eight congregations and five ministers refused to follow the Evangelical Union in joining with the Congregationalists in 1896. The total of Congregationalists reported for Scotland at the end of 1909 was 207 ministers, 4 evangelists or lay pastors, 70 lay preachers, 213 congregations, 35,845 members, with Sunday-school teachers to the number of 2,744 and 26,194 scholars. The Baptist Union has existed in Scotland from 1750 (according to some only from 1765) when a renowned Baptist, Archibald Maclean, preached in Edinburgh. The movement doubtless received impetus with the acquisition of the Haldane brothers. The numbers of Baptists are comparatively small; their doctrine is Calvinistic; their worship simple; and their organization strictly congregational, although a Union and an interior mission have been provided for. Some of their preachers are laymen, and numerous congregations practise open communion. This church has a seminary with five instructors and fourteen students. It reports at the end of 1909 122 ministers, 156 local preachers, 155 congregations, 21,240 communicants, 2,127 Sunday-school teachers, and 18,969 scholars.

IV. Other Protestant Bodies: The Methodists are weakly represented in Scotland. There are two branches, the Wesleyans and the Primitive Methodists, which form parts of the English organizations of the same name. Wesley first visited Scotland in 1751, and in 1767 there were 468 members of his church. There are now forty-five circuits and missions with forty-five ministers. A powerful mission established in recent years in Edinburgh bears the outline of an institutional church, and wields great influence. The Primitive Methodists have eighteen circuits and twenty ministers. There are small representations of the Quakers, the Catholic Apostolic Church (Irvingites), Unitarians, and the New Jerusalem Church or Swedenborgians. Probably none of these consists of more than twelve congregations.

V. The Roman Catholic Church: This numbers considerably more than half a million. Most of them are of Irish descent, but about 30,000 are Scotch. This element is found among the Highlanders of Gaelic tongue and has been steadfastly loyal from primitive times. The Roman Catholic hierarchy was reorganized in 1878 into six dioceses; St. Andrew's and Edinburgh, Glasgow, Aberdeen, Dunkeld, Galloway, and Argyll, the first two of which are archbishoprics. At the close of 1909 there were about 250 parishes, 600 priests, 400 church buildings, 13 cloisters for men, and 51 for women. Week-day schools attended by thousands of children are conducted, partly supervised and supported by the State.

A glance finally is to be given at those who have drifted away from all church connections. It is calculated that they amount to 1,600,000 or thirty-seven and one-half per cent. of the total population. A number of institutions like the Bible and tract societies, the city missions, the schools for morally neglected children, the temperance societies, and others have been created by the Church as a whole for the elevation of all classes.

(JOHN CAIRNS.)

BIBLIOGRAPHY: For the early period the most important literature will be found under CELTIC CHURCH; for the Presbyterian churches under PRESBYTERIANS; other books of importance are under the articles on the worthies of Scotland, such as COLUMBA, JOHN KNOX, and others named in the text. For sources use: Haddan and Stubbs, *Councils*, vol. ii.; *Chronicon Anglo-Scoticum* (60 B.C.–1189 A.D.), ed. C. W. Bouterwek, Elberfeld, 1863, Eng. transl. in J. Stevenson's *Church Historians of England*, London, 1856; Thomas of Burton, *Chronica monasterii de Melsa*, ed. E. A. Bond in *Rolls Series*, no. 43, 3 vols., London, 1866–1868; *Chronica de Mailros* (731–1275), ed. J. Stevenson, Edinburgh, 1835, Eng. transl., *Chronicle of Melrose*, in J. Stevenson's *Church Historians of England*, London, 1856; A. Theiner, *Vetera monumenta Hibernorum et Scotorum historiam illustrantia, 1216–1547*, Rome, 1864; *Annales Angliæ et Scotiæ (1292–1300)*, ed. H. T. Riley in *Rolls Series*, No. 28, vol. ii., London, 1865; R. Hart, *Ecclesiastical Records of England . . . and Scotland to the Reformation*, 2d ed., Cambridge, 1846; J. F. S. Gordon, *Ecclesiastical Chronicle for Scotland*, 4 vols., Glasgow, 1867; M. E. C. Walcott, *Scoti-Monasticon, the Ancient Church of Scotland. Hist. of the Cathedrals, Conventual Foundations, and Hospitals*, London, 1874.

On the antiquities consult: T. S. Muir, *Ecclesiological Notes on the Islands of Scotland*, Edinburgh, 1885; W. F. Skene, *Celtic Scotland*, 3 vols., new ed., Edinburgh, 1886–1890; G. Chalmers, *Caledonia*, 8 vols., Paisley, 1887–1902; J. Robertson, *Scottish Abbeys and Cathedrals*, Aberdeen, 1891; H. C. Butler, *Scotland's Ruined Abbeys*, New York, 1899; M. E. L. Addis, *The Cathedrals and Abbeys of Scotland*, Philadelphia, 1901; D. Butler, *Scottish Cathedrals and Abbeys*, London, 1901; J. Anderson, *Early Christian Monuments of Scotland*, Edinburgh, 1903.

General works are: A. Stevenson, *Hist. of the Church and State of Scotland from the Accession of King Charles I. to . . . 1625*, 2d ed., Edinburgh, 1844; J. Lee, *Lectures on the Hist. of the Church of Scotland from the Reformation to the Revolution Settlement*, ed. W. Lee, 2 vols., Edinburgh, 1860; G. Grub, *Ecclesiastical History of Scotland from the Introduction of Christianity to the Present Time*, 4 vols., Edinburgh, 1861; W. Chambers and Others, *The Scottish Church from the Earliest Times to 1881*, Edinburgh and New York, 1881; J. Campbell, *Mediæval Scotland, 1093–1513*, Edinburgh, 1881; N. L. Walker, *Scottish Church Hist.*, Edinburgh, 1882; J. Cunningham, *The Church History of Scotland from the Commencement of the Christian Era*, 2 vols., 2d ed., Edinburgh, 1883; J. M. Ross, *Scottish Hist. to the Reformation*, Glasgow, 1884, J. Anderson, *Scotland in Early Christian Times*, 2 parts, Edinburgh, 1886; D. Keith, *A Hist. of Scotland, Civil and Ecclesiastical, . . . to . . . 1153*, 2 vols., Edinburgh, 1886; W. G. Blaikie, *The Preachers of Scotland, Past and Present*, 5 vols., Edinburgh, 1890–91; A. T. Innes, *Studies in Scottish History, Chiefly Ecclesiastical*, London, 1892; D. C. Edmonds, *The Early Scottish Church, its Doctrine and Discipline*, London, 1906; J. H. Shepherd, *Introduction to the Hist. of the Church of Scotland*, ib. 1906; G. W. T. McGown, *Scottish Heroes of the Faith*, ib. 1907; J. Watson, *The Scot of the 18th Century, his Religion and his Life*, ib. 1907; W. Beveridge, *Makers of the Scottish Church*, Edinburgh, 1908; R. C. Maclagan, *Religio Scotica. Its Nature as traceable in Scottish saintly Traditions*, ib. 1908; *Cambridge Modern History*, v. 279 sqq., New York, 1908; A. Macrae, *Scotland from the Treaty of Union with England to the Present Time (1707–1907)*, London, 1909; D. Macmillan, *The Aberdeen Doctors. A notable Group of Scottish Theologians of the first episcopal Period, 1610–38*, ib. 1909; C. W. Thomson, *Scotland's Work and Worth*, 2 vols., ib. 1910; P. H. Brown, *Hist. of Scotland*, 3 vols., ib. 1910; W. L. Mathieson, *The Awakening in Scotland; a History, 1747–97*, Glasgow, 1911.

For the period prior to the Reformation consult: C. Innes, *Scotland in the Middle Ages*, Edinburgh, 1860; T. McLaughlan, *The Early Scottish Church; Eccles. Hist. of Scotland from the first to the twelfth Century*, Edinburgh, 1864; Miss M. G. G. Kinloch, *Hist. of Scotland, chiefly in its ecclesiastical Aspect . . . to the Fall of the old Hierarchy*, Edinburgh, 1873; W. Lockhart, *The Church of Scotland in the Thirteenth Century: The Life and Times of David de Bernham of St. Andrew, 1239–53*, London, 1889; R. M. Stewart, *The Church of Scotland from the Time of Queen Margaret to the Reformation*, London, 1892; J. Dowden, *The Celtic Church in Scotland*, London, 1894; W. Cathcart, *The Ancient British and Irish Churches*, London, 1894; J. Paton, *Scottish Hist. and Life*, Glasgow, 1902; R. W. Billings, *The Baronial and Ecclesiastical Antiquities of Scotland*, London, 1909 sqq.

On the Roman Catholic Church in Scotland consult: J. Robertson, *Concilia Scotiæ*, Edinburgh, 1864; W. M. Brady, *Annals of the Catholic Hierarchy in England and Scotland*, London, 1883; W. Forbes-Leith, *Narratives o Scottish Catholics under Mary Stuart and James VI.*, Edinburgh, 1885; A. Bellesheim, *History of the Catholic Church in Scotland*, 4 vols., Edinburgh, 1887–90; W. Paterson, *Letters to my Countrymen*, 6 parts, Edinburgh, 1900; J. Forbes, *L'Église catholique en Écosse à la fin du xvi. siècle*, Paris, 1901; W. F. Leith, *Memoirs of Scottish Catholics during the 17th and 18th Centuries*, 2 vols., London, 1909.

On episcopacy in Scotland read: J. P. Lawson, *Hist. of the Episcopal Church of Scotland*, 3 vols., Edinburgh, 1844; J. B. Craven, *Hist. of the Episcopal Church in Orkney*, Kirkwall, 1883; H. M. Luckock, *The Church in Scotland*, London, 1893; H. D. Henderson, *The Episcopal Church in Scotland*, London, 1902; J. T. F. Farquhar, *The Visible Church in the Light of Reason and Hist.*, Aberdeen, 1904.

SCOTLAND, FREE CHURCH OF, FREE PRESBYTERIAN CHURCH OF, REFORMED PRESBYTERIAN CHURCH IN, UNITED PRESBYTERIAN CHURCH OF, UNITED ORIGINAL SECESSION CHURCH OF. See PRESBYTERIANS.

SCOTT, CHARLES ANDERSON: Presbyterian; b. in London May 30, 1859. He received his education at Uppingham School, at St. John's College, Cambridge (B.A., 1882; M.A., 1896; Hulsean prize, 1884), New College, Edinburgh, and the universities of Leipsic and Jena; was assistant minister of Queen's Cross Church, Aberdeen, 1887–89; minister at College Park, Willesden, 1892, and of St. John's, Kensington, 1898–1907, being also examiner in historical theology for the University of London, 1902–07; and Dunn professor of the New Testament in the Theological College of the Presbyterian Church of England at Cambridge since 1907. He has published: *Ulfilas, Apostle of the Goths* (London, 1885); *Evangelical Doctrine Bible Truth* (1901); *Making of a Christian* (1902); and contributed to the *Devotional and Practical Commentary* the volume on Revelation (1905), as well as the same volume in the *Century Bible* (1902); also the essay on "Jesus and Paul" in *Cambridge Biblical Essays* (1909).

SCOTT, HUGH McDONALD: Congregationalist; b. at Guysborough, Nova Scotia, Mar. 31, 1848; d. at Chicago Apr. 29, 1909. He was graduated from Dalhousie College, Halifax (A.B., 1870), and from the University of Edinburgh (1873). During the same year he studied at Berlin, and later (1878–81) at Leipsic. In 1874 he was ordained to the ministry, and for four years (1874–77) was pastor of the Presbyterian church at Merigomish, Nova Scotia. After 1881 he was professor of church history at the Chicago Theological Seminary. He wrote *The Nicene Theology* (Stone lectures; Chicago, 1896), while from 1883 to 1890 he contributed the section on church history to *Current Discussions in Theology*, published by the faculty of the divinity school.

SCOTT, ISAIAH BENJAMIN: Methodist Episcopal bishop; b. in Woodford County, Ky., Sept. 30, 1854. He received his education at Clark Seminary (now Clark College), Atlanta, Ga., and Central Tennessee College (now Walden University), Nashville (B.A., 1880; M.A., 1883); entered the Tennessee conference in 1881, and was transferred to the Texas conference, where he was professor in Prairie View State Normal and Industrial College, 1881, and served as pastor at Houston, Galveston, Austin, and Marshall, 1882–87; was presiding elder of the Marshall and Houston Districts, 1882–93; president of Wiley University, Marshall, Tex., 1893–96; editor of the *Southwestern Christian Advocate*, New Orleans, 1896–1904; was elected bishop for Africa, 1904.

SCOTT, ROBERT: Church of England; b. at Bondleigh, Devonshire, Jan. 26, 1811; d. at Rochester Dec. 2, 1887. He was educated at Christ Church, Oxford (B.A., 1833); was fellow and tutor of Balliol College, 1835–40 (M.A., 1836); rector of Duloe, Cornwall, 1840–50; prebendary of Exeter Cathedral, 1845–66; rector of South Luffenham, Rutland, 1850–54; select preacher at Oxford, 1853–54, 1874–75; master of Balliol, 1854–70; professor of Scripture exegesis, 1861–70; and dean of Rochester, 1870–87. He was a member of the New-Testament revision committee; author of *Twelve Sermons* (London, 1851); *University Sermons* (1860); and of a commentary on the Epistle of James (1881) in the *Bible Commentary* (1872–82). From 1836 to 1843 he labored together with H. G. Liddell in the preparation of the great *Greek-English Lexicon* (Oxford, 1843; 7th enlarged ed., 1883), upon which he was occupied all in all for forty-seven years.

BIBLIOGRAPHY: *The Guardian*, Dec. 14, 1887; E. Abbott and L. Campbell, *Benjamin Jowett*, 3 vols., London, 1897–1899; *DNB*, li. 65–66.

SCOTT, THOMAS: Church of England; b. at Braytoft, Lincolnshire, Feb. 4, 1747; d. at Aston Sandford (near Thames, 11 m. e. of Oxford), Buckinghamshire, Apr. 16, 1821. He was ordained priest in 1773, and in 1781 succeeded John Newton, who had converted him to Calvinism, as curate of Olney. In 1785 he became chaplain of the Lock Hospital, London; and in 1801, vicar of Aston Sandford. His first publication was *The Force of Truth* (London, 1779, and numerous editions), narrating his change from rationalistic Unitarianism to the highest type of Calvinistic fervor, a work regarded as one of the most impressive spiritual autobiographies ever written. His most important work was *The Holy Bible with Notes* (5 vols., 1788–1792; very many reissues and reprints). This has long been considered a model family Bible, and has been read more widely, perhaps, than any other. It speaks volumes for Scott's industry and perseverance that without early educational advantages, oppressed by poverty, and compelled for years before his ordination to earn his living as a farm-laborer, he yet was able to acquire considerable learning, and produce a work, published under the severest pecuniary straits, yet spoken of as the greatest theological performance of his age and country. J. H. Newman wrote of him as a man to whom he almost owed his soul. Scott's *Essays on the Most Important Subjects in Religion* were published in 1793, 15th ed., 1844; and his *Village Discourses* in 1825. His *Works* in ten vols., edited by his son, appeared 1823–25.

BIBLIOGRAPHY: A. C. Downer, *Thomas Scott the Commentator. A Memoir of his Life*, London, 1909; *The Life of . . . T. Scott . . . Including a Narrative Drawn up by himself*, ib. 1822; *The Life of . . . Thomas Scott*, in *Christian Biography*, ib. [1838?]; J. Stephen, *Essays in Ecclesiastical Biography*, pp. 413 sqq., 14th ed., ib. 1860; *DNB*, li. 73–75.

SCOTUS ERIGENA, JOHANNES.

Johannes Scotus Erigena stands out as one of the most distinguished figures not only of the ninth century but of the whole history of philosophy and theology. His early life, however, as well as his inner development, is hidden up to the time to which his writings bring us. The one fact which is clear is that his birthplace was Ireland; to this the name Scotus (or Scotigena) as well as Erigena testifies (both these titles in those times indicating Ireland), and there is the express statement of Prudentius, "Hibernia sent thee to Gaul" (*De prædicatione*, in *MPL*, cxv. 1194). It was probably in Ireland that he received his education, though in the Frankish kingdom he first comes into historical light, but as already a man of mature powers. From this last fact it would follow that he was born in the early years of the century. That he won the distinguished favor of Charles the Bald is clear from the dedication to the latter of numerous writings and from many passages in his poems. He became celebrated and was the acquaintance of the distinguished men of the times—Hincmar, Servatus Lupus, Usuardus, Ratramnus and others, not to omit Prudentius of Treves (qq.v.). As the last-named left the court in 847, Scotus must have arrived there before that. Here probably Scotus did his literary work, though not as an ecclesiastic; there is no trace of his being a monk, and it is doubtful whether he was a priest. But he entered into the theological controversies of the time.

1. Early Life.

His first essay in this direction was in the matter of the eucharistic controversy begun by Ratramnus concerning the change of the elements, though the writing long ascribed to Scotus is now known to be the *De Eucharistia* of Ratramnus (Laufs, in *TSK*, 1828, pp. 755–756). Yet Hincmar charged him with regarding the elements as symbols of the presence of Christ, though whether this view was put forth in Scotus' own writing is doubtful, in spite of the fact that his position must have been well known. More important for Scotus

2. Participation in Controversy.

was his entrance into the Gottschalk controversy concerning predestination (see GOTTSCHALK, 1). He was urged by Hincmar and Pardulus of Laon to take part in this, and wrote between 849 and 853 the *De divina prædestinatione*, in which he charged Gottschalk with heresy and ignorance, and expressed with great frankness his views on the being of God, the identity of foreknowledge and predestination, and good and evil. These views sounded so strange and blasphemous to his contemporaries that a very storm was aroused and synodical condemnation of some of his theses was evoked (Synod of Valence, 855). Hincmar pronounced against some of the positions of Scotus, though holding others. Pope Nicholas disapproved of Scotus in a letter to Charles (extant in C. Du Boulay, *Hist. universitatis Parisiensis*, i. 184, Paris, 1665), because the translation of the writings of Dionysius had not, as ecclesiastical custom demanded, been sent for approval, an offense aggravated by the fact that the translator was under suspicion in respect to matters of faith. He desired Charles to notify Scotus to appear before the pope or at least to remove him from his place at the head of the school in Paris.

The poems of Scotus permit the tracing of his life till the death of Charles in 877, and he seems to have lived even until 882, if an extant epigram may be attributed to Hincmar. But of the end of his life French sources give no information.

3. Reports of Later Life. This last is not surprising considering the confusion of the times and the fact that Scotus held no ecclesiastical preferment. There are reports of activity in England. Thus Asser, the biographer of Alfred the Great, speaks of a certain Johannes "of the race of old Saxons" called to England and made abbot of Athelney where he was assassinated by Gallic enemies (*Monumenta historica Britannica*, i. 493 sqq., ed. H. Petrie, J. Sharpe, and T. D. Hardy, London, 1848); but this can not have been John Scotus Erigena, who was not a Saxon. The same author (p. 489) mentions a "Johannes, a priest and monk, a man of acute intellect, skilled in letters and other arts," who may be identical with the one named above but is more likely another man, and he can not be Scotus since he is designated a monk. While there is no reason for holding, as has been maintained, that Alfred would not have invited Scotus to England because of the latter's unorthodoxy, the advanced age of Scotus at this time would be a real obstacle. Later reports like that of William of Malmesbury (*MPL*, clxxix. 10, 1653) rest upon inference from the statement of Asser and from a tradition about the murder of an abbot of Malmesbury, over whose grave a light appeared to show that he was a martyr and a saint. Tradition identified this abbot with Scotus, and possibly upon the basis of a combination of these different supposed data arose the medieval tradition and the making of a statue to "John Scotus who translated Dionysius from Greek into Latin." Little dependence can be placed upon this entire story. The most probable conclusion is that Scotus died in the Frankish kingdom.

Among his contemporaries he enjoyed a reputation for wonderful gifts and learning and great keenness and eloquence. Yet his writings do not show that he towered above the great men of his time.

4. His Learning. What seems to have made his reputation was his close knowledge of Greek, an acquirement rare and in that period usually elementary when it was known. While the extent of his knowledge of Greek authors is uncertain, since he cited many of them from Latin translation, his translation of Dionysius and of the difficult *Ambigua* of Maximus speaks for a real scholarship. With his knowledge of Greek went a high valuation of Greek ideas, evinced in various ways—in his manner of speaking of the Greeks, and in his regard for the formula regarding the procession of the Holy Spirit from the Father through the Son, though he held also that the *filioque* was justified. The knowledge of Greek mediated for him a freer handling of theological and philosophical questions. But the entire disposition of Scotus differed from that of his contemporaries by virtue of his aptness in handling philosophical and philosophical-theological questions, added to a certain ready facility. From Dionysius and Maximus he learned how to treat speculatively the doctrine of God and the problems related to this in a way strange to the western theological discussions of the period. He thus had the key to an understanding of the speculative elements so rich in such older theologians as Basil, the two Gregorys, Origen, Ambrose, and Augustine,—elements which went back to Neoplatonism or to Philo. It is suspected but not proved that Scotus knew and used the works of the Greek philosophers; he certainly had in hand Boethius, Macrobius, Marcianus Capella, and other mediators of ancient learning to the Middle Ages, and he gained from them a meaning different from the more literal and constrained results won by his contemporaries. He was the first Westerner of the Middle Ages to think comprehensively and philosophically and to attempt the construction of a system.

Scotus made no sharp distinction between philosophy and theology; rather they were both essential means by which to gain knowledge of truth. He never stopped to consider whether his system was more philosophy than theology. So, in the matter

5. Views on Reason and Authority. of reason and authority he would not have said that the first belonged to philosophy and the other to theology; for him both had their right in both regions and sprang from the same root —divine wisdom. Still, reason had the precedence, and authority had its origin from reason; reason, being in itself worthful and invariable, did not need the support of authority, while, on the other hand, authority appears feeble when not upheld by reason. Hence Scotus would employ authority for those who could not rightly use reason; yet he could advise: "Let no authority drive thee in terror from the conclusions suggested by right contemplation" (*De divisione naturæ*, i. 66). As contrasted with his times, he had a clear consciousness of what might be accomplished by means of human reasoning power. Yet he did not undervalue authority, though he emphasized reason where it led to clear results. The authority of Scripture he fully allowed. The involved meaning of Scripture was infinite, so that the exegesis of different commentators might all contain truth (iii. 24). With respect to the Fathers, he claimed the right in cases where they differed to follow the one who to him seemed to be right, though he disclaimed the purpose of deciding between them.

The philosophic-theological system of Scotus is set forth in his great work *De divisione naturæ* [ed. T. Gale, Oxford, 1681 (1685?) and C. B. Schlüter, Münster, 1838; Germ. transl., 2 vols., Berlin, 1870–76], which must be taken as the basis in an exposition of his ideas, though other works furnish confirmation and illustration. **6. His System.** It is in dialogue form, between a master and a pupil; and it has been well said in praise of the composition that both contribute to the development of the line of thought. By nature Scotus means everything with which thought has to do, existence and non-existence—the last, to be sure, in the special sense in which the author regards God as non-existent. Nature includes God and the world, even though neither has a predicate in common with the other. The word "nature" is not quite a fitting expression of what Scotus had in mind; it might be rendered by "the All." This he divided into four categories: that which creates but is not created; that which creates and is created; that which is created and does not create; and that which is not created and does not create. Uncreated creating nature is God, as is also uncreated and non-creating; the last is the world in its return to God [i.e., God as the end of all things]. The second and third categories are those of the ideal and the real world; the system thus leads from God through the ideal and the real back to God.

Book i. discusses the being of God in his self-existence, book ii. the first revelation of God in the world of ideas or original causes, books iii. and iv. discuss the real world, and book v. deals with the return of the world to God. **7. Doctrine of God.** Scotus' doctrine of God goes back to the kataphatic and apophatic ("affirming and denying") theology of Dionysius (i. 13). All positive predicates attributed to the mundane can be superlatively attributed to God as the transcendental or "super-being," but these predicates are positive in form only, in fact negative (by virtue of the "super"; iii. 20). Hence positive leads to negative, and in this way all predicates may be denied to deity, since deity is incomprehensible. His being is a "super-being," hence not in the category of being as applied to the mundane, and so can be called a "not-being." But this "not-being" is not to be understood as pure negation. Considering the self-existence of God, Scotus affirms that God can not grasp the entire fulness of his being; God knows that he is nothing of all that is in the world, but does not know what he is (by which Scotus means that even God can not comprehend and define himself as a certain definite something). The whole mundane existence is by God created and formed after his plan, and the realization of the world involves the self-consciousness of God, but this self-consciousness is not to be thought of as like that of man, since God is absolute and most complete unity (i. 12, 73). This conception of unity is for Scotus the highest, most comprehensive, and transcendental, its fulness unattainable by man; it means the absolute oneness of willing and knowing. It was Scotus' doctrine on this point which led him so bitterly to assail Gottschalk's doctrine of predestination. While on the one side Scotus regards God as altogether severed from the world, there is another side of the consideration according to which God and the world are identical (iii. 17); the reconciliation of these two sides is in the conception that the world is the revelation of God (i. 13). God creates himself in the world and is All in all; he is the substance of all things, the last unknowable basis of its existence as of its accidents; hence God is all and all is God, yet meanwhile he remains over all within himself, does not go forth into what he creates. The analogy employed is the relationship between human thought and speech; thought clothes itself in speech but does not go forth in the speech. While God's inner being remains unknown, yet there is knowledge of him according to the measure by which he reveals himself. Scotus borrows from Dionysius and Maximus the expression "theophany," which he uses in various senses. It may mean special divine appearances or visions to a creature, or the virtues which God works in a creature which then become the basis of a knowledge of God; or, finally, each creature is itself a theophany in so far as God is revealed in it. Consequently the knowledge a creature has of its own being is a knowledge of God proportionally as God is revealed in the creature.

The next category, which leads from the absolutely unknowable divine unity to the manifoldness of the world, is the creation of the ideal world or the totality of potencies which in turn **8. The Ideal World.** emits from itself the world of sense. Scotus knows as ideas divine predestinations, acts of will, original causes (ii. 2), which are the names he gives to goodness, essence, life, reason, intelligence, wisdom, virtue, blessedness, truth, eternity, greatness, love, peace, unity, perfection (ii. 36, iii. 1). But this is not a complete enumeration or arrangement of these ideas, which, in view of the divine unity in which they issue, is impossible. They are the radii of which the unity is the center, which can be indefinitely multiplied without changing the being of the circumference. The first step of the self-revealing God is taken in making himself accessible to the creature; the means of doing this is unknown; but it is affirmed that God is eternal, according to his eternal (not temporal) being. The unlimited fulness of the ideas is summed up in the divine Logos or Son of God; in him in whom they are created do they exist without change. To be known in a certain sense coincides with being; so one may say that one is in another when he is known by that other (ii. 8, iii. 4, iv. 9), and of God it is true that he becomes so far as he becomes known (i. 12). Hence the "invariable movement" taking place in the Trinity by which God is made accessible to knowledge is a real creation, and ideas become so far as they are made accessible to knowledge. Scotus conceived the primal causes as wholly enclosed in the divine being, yet as also proceeding thence and as having in a certain manner independent existence.

9. The World of Sense.

The third category of Scotus is the world in the usual sense of that term. The basis of this is the primal causes; it is therefore eternal in the same sense as those causes (v. 25). This eternity did not come about through constant repetition of a world cycle, as with the Stoics and Origen. The apparent contradiction involved in the conception of the world's return to God (the fourth category) is solved by the distinction of Scotus between the material or sensible existence and the purely spiritual existence of the world. At the head of the created world stood the angels, with spiritual bodies and free from all material qualities; at times these really appeared to men (v. 38). They were produced all at once from the primordial causes, were in nine classes, of which only those in the highest class were free from error. Their knowledge comes not from experience but from view of God in theophany and of their own being. The fallen angels, Satan at the head, fell immediately after their creation, they have material bodies which feel desire and will go out of existence with the world (v. 13, iv. 24). Next to the creation of these was that of the world of space and time. In considering space (cf. i. 21 sqq.) he regarded locality as limitation in space equivalent to definition or circumscription in logic; space is that in which matter is extended. Space and time are not prior to the world, but with it came into existence from the eternal basis. Geometrical relations Scotus distinguished from the figures which represented them (iv. 8), and they are reducible to absolute spacial unity. The monad is the principle of number (iii. 1, 12). Matter is not eternal (iii. 14), but came into existence in the course of creation by the concourse of immaterial principles, quantity and quality. Elsewhere (i. 56) it appears as the variability of variable things, i.e., that which lies at the basis of everything variable, the Aristotelian *hyle*. Distinction is to be made between matter and the physical world; a body comes to exist when the substantial form unites with matter, and these two are to be distinguished apart. The "form" is something constant, eternal, issues from the primordial causes, and returns thither; but constant change underlies matter. One can hardly explain how Scotus derived matter from quantity and quality, but his realism shows in his drawing the particular from the general.

10. Anthropology; Doctrine of Evil.

Scotus' anthropology is difficult because it is involved with his doctrine of evil and sin. He held that by divine appointment man had preeminent rank in the All. Man shares in the being of lower creatures that are without souls, in the life force of plants, in the physical life of animals, and in the intellectual life of angels (iv. 8, 14). He is the world's central point and the part which leads in the return to God. As to evil, the monistic conceptions of Scotus compelled him to think of evil as a necessary factor in evolution, which was, however, to be overcome. But this involved him in difficulties which he did not surmount. He sought to exclude evil from divine appointment, even from divine foreknowledge, since God knew only what he created; he did not create evil, therefore did not know it (ii. 28). Elsewhere Scotus was compelled to concede to God knowledge of evil, but he did not reconcile the disagreement. To do this he would have had to show a difference in the kind of divine knowledge, and that would have conflicted with his doctrine of unity. Even though God did not create evil, he included its existence or entrance in his world plan. If the basis of evil were sought, the answer was—it had none (v. 35); yet the instability of the will was noted by Scotus and the pride which made man and not God the end. If there were in Scotus' system a ground for evil, it was in formal creative freedom. Paradise was for Scotus man's original complete condition, to which he will again attain in the future (iv. 17 sqq.). Exactly in view of the fall it is said that the origin of man was so ordered that not all individuals at one time proceeded from the background of existence as did the angels (iv. 12, ii. 6). Originally man was, like the angels, in spite of the mass of individuals, intended to be a unity; but in consequence of sin the female sex was derived from the male (iv. 23). This conception can be held only by means of a fully spiritual interpretation of the history of creation, for which Origen furnished the pattern. Original sin is not purely a matter of inheritance but is to be brought into relation with man's origin. But how sin comes as an actuality in the life and soul Scotus does not explain. Nevertheless, according to this author, the present material condition is determined by human sin, though a clear presentation of the facts is not given.

11. Consummation of All Things.

The last division in the system of Scotus is the termination of the entire course of the world and the return of all things to God. Central in this process is the person of Christ, in whom are embraced all mankind and the whole world, who leads all back to God and frees man. This comes about through his death and resurrection, which last abolishes distinction of sex, the risen being neither male nor female (ii. 13, v. 20, 25). Following resurrection comes a double change; one affects all men, and is attainment of all knowledge suited for the creature; the other affects the most exalted clarified spirits, and is induction into the deepest secrets and into the transcendent absorption into the godhead. A development of the lower creature into the higher with continual progress to the highest is affirmed—after the elimination of sex distinctions earth and paradise will become one (v. 20), then paradise and heaven, the higher absorbing the lower. All unnatural distinctions will be abolished, all natures will return to their primordial causes and with these become one in God. Evil is nothing substantial, it had no place in primordial cause, it is only instability of will which is an accident attendant upon God-created natures. Since the changes outlined above produce a will fully sanctified and united with God, the will is in full accord with the divine will; there is then no cause of evil. The consequences of evil likewise vanish, since that which is only an accident can not assume the form of substance; at the end of world-history evil in every form is to be annihilated. This is the necessary consequence of the system of Scotus, to which he gave extended discussion. According to his system, it was impossible that a nature, something created by God, could suffer eternally. And he attempted to show how a vice could attach to a pure nature without corrupting it, also how it might be punished, though in itself nothing, otherwise than in the nature possessed by it; his demonstration, however, is unsatisfactory. How the bad will can continue to exist while the nature is completely pure is not made clear, and this difficulty is the greater because Scotus regarded the will not as an accident but as an essential. Yet Scotus has (x. 38) a sentence which should be noticed. He says that practically all authors agree that as many men attain to the heavenly kingdom as there are angels who have fallen, and remarks that, if that is correct, then must the number of men who eventually are born equal that of angels or else not all men attain to the purpose of their creation, which last is contrary to the reasons already given for the salvation of all men in Christ. In that case only demons and the devil are doomed to eternal condemnation. The system of Scotus in its consequences favors throughout the doctrine of Apocatastasis (q.v.).

The foregoing points have been the more thoroughly considered because in his general thinking this scholar was true to the teaching of the Church. Where he differed from it he seems to have concealed the fact even from himself. He used trinitarian formulas frequently; he assumed that the Father created in the Son—the Logos or intelligence—the primordial causes, while in the Holy Spirit he saw the active principle through which those causes issued in effects. The teaching of the Church on Christology he assumed in his system without regarding the deep-lying difficulties. Whether Scotus can be called "the father of scholasticism" is the more doubtful inasmuch as his interest was more philosophical than theological. His personal position is freer and more independent than that of later schoolmen. His relation to mysticism is peculiar; he can not be called a mystic, for the personal experiences of mystics were never his or at least never found expression; yet his system is full of mystical thought dialectically justified. Through this thought and by the translation of the Dionysian writings he exercised an uncommon influence upon mysticism. He also greatly affected medieval speculation, especially in the twelfth century; in the first part of the thirteenth century he had considerable vogue in Paris, ecclesiastical opposition to him found voice, and Honorius III. ordered the destruction of his *De divisione naturæ*. This worked forgetfulness of him so that he does not appear on the Tridentine index. A requirement of the present is a complete critical edition of his works, with an adequate investigation of his relation to his predecessors. (S. M. Deutsch†.)

12. His Position in General.

Bibliography: For the life consult: G. B. Schlüter, *Scotus Erigena*, Münster, 1838; F. Christlieb, *Leben und Lehre des Johannes Scotus Erigena*, Gotha, 1860; J. Huber, *Johannes Scotus Erigena*, Munich, 1861; O. Hermens, *Das Leben des Scotus Erigena*, Jena, 1868; L. Noack, *Ueber Leben und Schriften des Joh. Scotus Erigena: die Wissenschaft und Bildung seiner Zeit*, Leipsic, 1876; P. Hoffmann, *De Johannis Scoti Erigenæ vita et doctrina*, Halle, 1877; K. Werner, *Johannes Duns Scotus*, Vienna, 1880.

For his philosophy consult: P. Hjort, *Johann Scotus Erigena, oder von dem Ursprung einer christlichen Philosophie und ihrem heiligen Beruf*, Copenhagen, 1823; H. Schmidt, *Der Mysticismus des Mittelalters in seiner Entstehungsperiode*, Jena, 1824; F. C. Baur, *Die christliche Lehre von der Dreieinigkeit und Menschwerdung*, ii. 263–344, Tübingen, 1842; A. Helfferich, *Die christliche Mystik*, vol. ii., Gotha, 1842; St. René Taillandier, *Scot. Erigène et la philosophie scolastique*, Strasburg, 1843; N. Möller, *Joh. Scotus Erigena und seine Irrthümer*, Mainz, 1844; J. P. Hauréau, *De la philosophie scolastique*, Paris, 1850; idem, *Histoire de la philosophie scolastique*, ib. 1872; W. Kaulich, *Geschichte der scholastischen Philosophie*, Prague, 1863; A. Stöckl, *Geschichte der Philosophie und Theologie im Mittelalter*, i. 31–128, Mainz, 1864; idem, *De Joh. Scotus Erigena*, Münster, 1867; J. G. Boivin, *Philosophia quadripartiti Scoti*, 4 vols., Paris, 1868; H. Rähse, *Des Joh. Erigenas Stellung zur mittelalterlichen Scholastik und Mystik*, Rostock, 1874; F. J. Hoffmann, *Der Gottes- und Schöpfungsbegriff des Johannes Scotus Erigena*, Jena, 1876; G. Anders, *Darstellung und Kritik der Ansicht von Johannes Scotus Erigena, dass die Kategorien nicht auf Gott anwendbar seien*, Jena, 1877; G. Buchwald, *Der Logosbegriff des Johannes Scotus Erigena*, Leipsic, 1884; T. Wotschke, *Fichte und Erigena*, Halle, 1896; M. DeWulf, *Histoire de la philosophie médiévale*, Louvain, 1900; A. Gardner, *Studies in John the Scot (Erigena)*, London, 1900; J. Dräseke, *Johannes Scotus Erigena und dessen Gewährsmann*, Leipsic, 1902 (on the sources used by Scotus); the works on the history of philosophy by H. Ritter, Hamburg, 1844 (vii. 206–296); J. E. Erdmann, Eng. transl., 3 vols., London, 1892–98; W. Windelband, Eng. transl., New York, 1893; and F. Ueberweg, ed. Heinze, 9th ed., Berlin, 1901–05.

SCOTUS, JOHANNES DUNS. See Duns Scotus.

SCOULLER, skū'ler, JAMES BROWN: United Presbyterian; b. near Newville, Cumberland County, Pa., July 12, 1820; d. at Newville, Pa., 1899. He graduated at Dickinson College, Carlisle, Pa., 1839, and at the Associate Reformed Theological Seminary, Allegheny, Pa., 1842; was pastor of United Presbyterian churches in Philadelphia, 1844–46; Cuylerville, N. Y., 1847–52; Argyle, N. Y., 1852–62; and editor of *The Christian Instructor*, Philadelphia, 1862–63. He was the author of *A Manual of the United Presbyterian Church* (Pittsburg, 1881); and *Calvinism: its History and Influences* (1885).

SCOVEL, SYLVESTER FITHIAN: Presbyterian; b. at Harrison, O., Dec. 29, 1835; d. at Worcester, Ohio, Nov. 29, 1910. He was graduated from Hanover College, Hanover, O. (A.B., 1853), and New Albany Theological Seminary, New Albany, Ind. (1857). He then held pastorates at Jeffersonville, Ind. (1857–60), and the First Presbyterian churches of Springfield, O. (1861–66), and Pittsburg, Pa. (1866–83); he was president of the University of Wooster, Wooster, O. (1883–99); and after 1899 professor of morals and sociology in the same institution. In theology he was a conservative, and wrote *Centennial History of the First Presbyterian Church of Pittsburg* (Pittsburg, 1884).

SCRIBES: A term used, especially in the New Testament, to denote those skilled in the Mosaic law. The profession or calling came into being after the return from the exile (for mention of scribes in its more literal sense cf. Jer. viii. 8), when in place of the kingdom there was set up the dominion of the Mosaic statutes, which furnished the rule for

Meaning of Term.

the guidance of life in all its aspects among the Hebrews. The man who initiated this condition of things, Ezra, himself bore this designation (cf. Ezra vii. 6, 11, 12, 21; Neh. viii. 1, etc.), which was given to him probably on account of his [supposed] care for the law in respect to the making and distribution of its exemplars or manuscripts. The New-Testament word for "scribe" is often *grammateus* (Matt. ii. 4, v. 20, etc.); but two other sides of the activities of these men gave rise to the designation *nomikos*, "lawyer" (Matt. xxii. 35, etc.), and *nomodidaskalos*, "doctor of the law" (Luke v. 17; Acts v. 34; cf. the expression "interpreter of the Jewish laws," Josephus, *Ant.*, XVII., vi. 2).

Work on Hebrew Text.

The first task of these men was to preserve the text of the sacred books, particularly of the law of Moses (the Pentateuch), in a form suited to the maintenance of the Hebrew religion. This task they sought to perform through copies which guarded on the one side the essential content and on the other had regard for scruples which might be raised. Exact information of the means employed by the early scribes in carrying out these purposes is unfortunately not obtainable because of the sparseness and fragmentary character of the material at hand. Yet careful and critical use of this material as found in scattered notices leads to results quite worth while. Over the reading in public worship much care was exercised. According to the Mishna (*Megilla*, iv. 10) Gen. xxv. 32 and Ex. xxxii. 21–24 were read but not interpreted (see SYNAGOGUE); and according to the old tradition in *Megilla* 25b for expressions which might give offense or which might raise scruples euphemisms or other phrases were substituted. For the divine name *Yhwh* was substituted "Adonai," except that in the combination *Adonai Yhwh, Elohim* was substituted for *Yhwh* (see JEHOVAH; YAHWEH). There were changes too in the written text. Such a change is the one which results from the confusion which might come from Baal, meaning "lord" or "master," and Baal as the name of a heathen deity (cf. Hos. ii. 16–17); thus with the Ish-bosheth of II Sam. ii.–iv. cf. the Esh-baal of I Chron. viii. 33, in accordance with which the Chronicler replaces the earlier name (Merribbaal) for Mephibosheth; the other name of Gideon used in Judges vi.–ix., Jerubbaal, is replaced in II Sam. xi. 21 by Jerubbesheth; in II. Sam. v. 16 appears the form Eliada for which the older form was Beeliada (I Chron. xiv. 7). A testimony to this habit exists in the gloss found enclosed in Num. xxxii. 38, "(their names being changed)," referring to the mountains Nebo and Baal-meon [one of which is the name of a heathen deity Nebo, see BABYLONIA, VII., 2, § 11, and the other contains the element Baal]. In II Sam. vii. 23 a plural verb accompanies the plural form Elohim, but in the parallel I Chron. xvii. 21 a singular verb is employed, by which the unity of God is maintained. Especially important is the regarding as holy of the names Yah and Yahweh (note Lev. xxiv. 11: "And the Israelitish woman's son blasphemed the name," where "Yahweh" is not written in the text). In effect this has been treated above, but the practise further involved the inclusion of Yah as one word in "Hallelujah" in the psalms, and also in other expressions. Similarly the Jews put such expressions as "heaven," "name," and the like in place of a name for God. Moreover, before the introduction of the vowel sounds, the pronunciation of many words had been changed through the working of varied influences. The word *Molek* (Moloch, q.v.), formerly pronounced *Melek* (cf. Isa. xxx. 33) has received the vowels of *bosheth*, "shame," and the same is probably true of Ashtoreth and Tophet; in imitation of *shikkuz*, "monster," are vocalized *Chiun* and *sikkuth*, "tabernacle" (Amos v. 26). Milcom, the name of the god of the Ammonites, is to be restored in II Sam. xii. 30 in place of "their king's" (cf. Jer. xlix. 1–3, margin). An artificial distinction is made for the sake of theology in the word *'abbir* (the original pronunciation) as it applies to bulls as possessions of men and to the word in such passages as Isa. i. 24 and Isa. x. 13 (in the last passage a new reading is substituted in the keri; see KERI AND KETHIBH). Euphemistic expressions are substituted by a difference in the pointing of the original text in such passages as Deut. xxviii. 30; Gen. xxxiv. 2. In the Biblical Aramaic of the verb "to be" a lamedh is substituted for a yodh as preformative in the imperfect, probably in order to avoid producing a word which looks like the divine name *Yhwh* and so leading to accidental pronouncing of that name; in early Egyptian-Aramaic papyri the forms with yodh appear. In the study of the text one has to guard against both undervaluation of the text by the scribes as well as against overvaluation. For further discussion of these topics see BIBLE TEXT; and MASORAH.

Activities as Interpreters of the Law.

The Mosaic law was not what would according to modern conceptions be considered a systematic body of ecclesiastical law, still less a complete legal code. Yet after this law had gained its unique position, only those statutes and usages which had the sanction of long custom and had so become sacred could attain to the position of official law; a new code could not be created. As a result it became necessary so to explore and explain the written law that it should be found sufficient to meet the exigencies of everyday life. Of Ezra (Ezra vii. 10) it is said that he "prepared his heart to seek the law of the Lord, and to do it, and to teach in Israel statutes and judgments." When one recalls the condition under which the law existed (as just noted), also its nature, and that since Malachi the prophetic spirit had died out, and that the impulse which had come with the return from exile and its experiences had died out with the generation which had known them and had taken with it the stimulus to independent religious life, explanation is easy of the tendency to slavish observance of the letter of the law, and the way was opened for that scribal exposition of the law which "strained at a gnat and swallowed a camel" (Matt. xxiii. 24). One may compare Christ's proof of the resurrection which rests upon Ex. iii. 6 (Matt. xxii. 32) with that adduced in the Babylonian Talmud on Deut. xxxi. 16, where Gamaliel cites "thou shalt sleep with thy fathers, and this people will rise up," and may note that in thus quoting Gamaliel was supported by other rabbis almost as noted as he. By a certain method of exegesis this was regarded as justified. The exigencies of civil, legal, and ritual life occasioned ever new questions, and these called for progress in the science of interpretation of the law, and these interpretations came to codification in the Mishnah (see TALMUD). A supplement directed toward the insuring of observance of the law resulted from this scribal activity in the matter of study of its provisions. In order to forestall transgression, additional regulations or commands were provided which were hardly within the range of possibility to observe. Thus in *Pirke Aboth* i. 1 it is said "make a bridle about the law." The scribes were not so much theologians as jurists; and so they were members of the Sanhedrin (q.v.) and are mentioned constantly in that relationship.

Work as Teachers. If the Jews were to remain "the people of the law," the science of law being once obtained, it must be preserved for future generations. In carrying out this purpose, especially before the essential matter was reduced to writing, there was required of the scribes a teaching activity. The instruction was oral; only manuscripts of the Bible were at hand; the lectures and discussions were held generally in special places designated for that purpose, in Jerusalem halls and chambers in the forecourt of the Temple. Teacher and pupils sat, the teacher upon a platform somewhat elevated. The religious discourses of the sabbath and other occasions were in no small part delivered by the scribes. Many of them busied themselves with the Haggada, though the Halaka was their especial province (for Haggada and Halaka see MIDRASH). Most of the scribes naturally belonged to the party of the Pharisees (see PHARISEES AND SADDUCEES), and as a consequence were to be found mostly in Judea and especially in Jerusalem. Yet, inasmuch as the high priests were Sadducees, there must have been Sadducean scribes. For their judicial or professorial activity the scribes received no compensation. Many supported themselves by manual labor, and not a few were so well-to-do as to be able to live upon their income from property; but they might also receive entertainment so long as they continued their teaching activities. It was regarded as improper to make knowledge of the law a means of gain (*Pirke Aboth*, i. 13; *Baba bathra*, 8a). But there must have been many exceptions to this rule (cf. Mark xii. 40; Luke xx. 47, xvi. 14); and the circumstance that the scribes demanded an abnormally high degree of honor may be taken as proof that disinterestedness was not so general as Jewish sources seem to make it. (H. L. STRACK.)

BIBLIOGRAPHY. Discussions of the subject are to be found in the commentaries on the Gospels and on Acts, generally at the passages where mention of the scribes occurs, often in the works on the history of the Apostolic Age, in those on the life of Christ (e.g., Edersheim, i. 93 sqq.; Farrar, i. 255–256), and in works on the history of Israel (such as those of Jost, Grätz, and Ewald). For the English reader there is nothing better than § 25 of the Eng. transl. of Schürer's *Geschichte* (same section in the German). Consult further: T. C. Lilienthal, *De nomikois juris utriusque apud Hebraeos doctoribus privatis*, Halle, 1740; A. T. Hartmann, *Die enge Verbindung des Alten Testaments mit dem Neuen*, pp. 384–413, Hamburg, 1831; A. F. Gfrörer, *Das Jahrhundert des Heils*, i. 109–214, Stuttgart, 1838; W. Bacher, *Die Agada der babylonischen Amoräer, . . . der Tannaiten, . . . der palästinensischen Amoräer*, 6 vols., Strasburg, 1878–99; V. Ryssel, *Die Anfänge der jüdischen Schriftgelehrsamkeit*, in *TSK*, 1887, pp. 149–182; F. Weber, *Jüdische Theologie*, Leipsic, 1897; C. D. Ginsburg, *Introduction to the Hebrew Bible*, pp. 241 sqq., London, 1897; L. Blau, *Studien zum althebräischen Buchwesen*, vol. i., Strasburg, 1902; J. W. Lightley, *Les Scribes . . . leur origine chez les Israélites*, Cahors, 1905; *DB*, iv. 420–423; *EB*, iv. 4321–29; *JE*, xi. 123–126; *DCG*, ii. 582–584; and the literature under PHARISEES AND SADDUCEES.

SCRIPTORIS, scrip-tō'ris, PAUL: Scholastic theologian; b. at Weil (14 m. w. of Stuttgart) about 1450; d. at the monastery of Kaisersberg in Upper Alsace Oct. 21, 1505. At an early age he entered the order of the Minorites of the strict observance, and was educated at Paris, where he became a firm adherent of Scotistic realism. In this spirit he labored first, apparently, at Mainz and later at Tübingen, where he was guardian of the Franciscan monastery until 1501. Although not connected with the university, he lectured in his monastery on the "Sentences" of Duns Scotus, the throngs that came to hear him including Thomas Wyttenbach, Johann von Staupitz (qq.v.), and other leaders of nascent Protestantism. These lectures, entitled *Lectura fratris Pauli Scriptoris . . . quam edidit declarando subtilissimas doctoris subtilis sententias circa Magistrum in primo liber*, constituted the first book printed at Tübingen (1498), and amply prove that, while their author foresaw the coming of a new régime in which scholasticism should yield place to patristics, he was neither a humanist nor, as some have claimed, a "Reformer before the Reformation." Acquainted with Greek, although not employing his knowledge in Biblical studies, Scriptoris also lectured on the cosmography of Ptolemy and on Euclid. He was likewise active as a preacher in the vicinity of Reutlingen and Horb, but his merciless castigations exposed him to the censure of the Tübingen theologians, and complaints were lodged against him with his provincial, particularly as he was unpopular with his monks. In 1501 he was removed from office. Henceforth he was obliged to restrict himself to literary labors in the monastery at Basel, later being required to defend his views before his superiors at Zabern. He escaped, however, possible imprisonment and went to Rome to lay his cause before the Curia. Returning unmolested, he was directed by the Franciscan vicar general to teach theology in Toulouse, but died while on the way to take up his new office.

(H. HERMELINK.)

BIBLIOGRAPHY: N. Paulus, in *TQS*, 1893, pp. 289–311; J. J. Moser, *Vitae professorum Tubingensium*, pp. 60–68, Tübingen, 1718; *ADB*, xxxiii. 488–489.

SCRIPTURE, READING OF, IN WORSHIP. See PERICOPES.

SCRIVENER, scriv'ner, FREDERICK HENRY AMBROSE: Church of England, New-Testament scholar; b. at Bermondsey, London, Sept. 29, 1813; d. at Hendon (8 m. n.w. of London), Middlesex, Oct.

30, 1891. He was educated at Trinity College, Cambridge (B.A., 1835; M.A., 1838); became assistant master of King's School, Sherborne, 1835; was curate of Sandford Orcas, Somerset, 1838–1845; head master of Falmouth School, 1846–56; perpetual curate of Penwerris, Cornwall, 1846–61; became rector of St. Gerrans, Cornwall, 1861; prebendary of Exeter, 1874; and vicar of Hendon, 1876. He was a member of the New-Testament revision committee, 1872–80; received a pension of £100, in 1872, in recognition of his eminent Biblical services; and was the author of *A Supplement to the Authorized English Version of the New Testament* (London, 1845); *Collation of Twenty Greek Manuscripts of the Holy Gospel* (Cambridge, 1853); *Codex Augiensis, . . . (and) Fifty other Manuscripts*, Gk. and Lat. (1859); *Novum Testamentum Textus Stephanici* (1860; 7th ed., 1877); *Plain Introduction to the Criticism of the New Testament* (1861; 4th enlarged ed., 2 vols., 1894); *Collation of the Codex Sinaiticus* (1863; 2d rev. ed., 1867); *Bezæ Codex Cantabrigiensis*, Gr. and Lat. (1864); *Six Popular Lectures on the Text of the New Testament* (1875); and edited *The Cambridge Paragraph Bible* (1870–73), the introduction to which appeared in separate revised edition (1884); and *The New Testament in the Original Greek, according to the Text Followed in the Authorized Version together with the Variations Adopted in the Revised Version* (1881).

BIBLIOGRAPHY: P. Schaff, *Companion to the Greek Testament and the Revised Version*, New York, 1883; C. R. Gregory, *Canon and Text of the N. T.*, pp. 460–462, New York, 1907; *DNB*, li. 136.

SCRIVER, scrī'ver, **CHRISTIAN:** German Lutheran devotional writer; b. at Rendsburg (18 m. w. of Kiel) Jan. 2, 1629; d. at Quedlinburg (31 m. s.w. of Magdeburg) Apr. 5, 1693. He entered the University of Rostock in 1647, and in 1653 was appointed archdeacon at Stendal, whence he was called in 1667 to Magdeburg as pastor of St. James's. Here he remained twenty-three years, until in 1690 he was made chief court chaplain at Quedlinburg, a position which he held until his death. The friend of Spener, Scriver was one of those theologians of the latter part of the seventeenth century who opposed the formalism then besetting Lutheranism, and thus prepared the way for Pietism, even while himself maintaining strict orthodoxy. The writings of Scriver now most interesting were devotional, those including the *Gottholds vierhundert zufällige Andachten* (1667; last ed., Basel, 1893; Eng. transl., *Gotthold's Emblems: or, Invisible Things understood by Things that are made*, by R. Menzies, Edinburgh, 1857), a collection of 400 parables; *Gotthold's Siech- und Siegesbette* (1687; new ed., Stuttgart, 1870); and *Chrysologia Catechetica, Goldpredigten über die Hauptstücke des lutherischen Katechismus* (1687; new ed., Stuttgart, 1861). His most important work, however, was his *Seelenschatz* (5 parts, 1675–1692; new ed., 3 vols., Berlin, 1852–53), describing the progress of the soul from misery to eternal life and combining allegory, dogmatics, and ethics. Scriver was also a hymn-writer, though here he was but second-rate. Nevertheless, three of his compositions have been translated into English: "Auf, Seel, und danke deinem Herrn" as "To God, my soul, thank-offerings pay"; "Der lieben Sonne Licht und Pracht" (his best hymn), found in a number of renderings; and "Hier lieg ich nun, mein Gott, zu deinen Füssen" as "Here, O my God, I cast me at Thy feet." The collected works of Scriver have been edited by J. H. Heinrich and R. Stier (6 vols., Barmen, 1847–52). (HERMANN BECK.)

BIBLIOGRAPHY: To the funeral sermon by S. Calvisius, Helmstadt, 1694, there is added a sketch of Scriver's life. There are biographies by O. Weinschenk, Leipsic, 1729, and H. Krieg, Dresden, 1872. Consult further, H. Beck, *Die religiöse Volkslitteratur der evangelischen Kirche Deutschlands*, pp. 143 sqq., Gotha, 1891; C. Grosse, *Die alten Tröster*, Hermannsburg, 1900; Julian, *Hymnology*, pp. 1034–35.

SCUDAMORE, scud'a-mōr, **WILLIAM EDWARD:** Church of England; b. at Wye (24 m. s.e. of Rochester), Kent, July 24, 1813; d. at Ditchingham (12 m. s.e. of Norwich), Norfolk, Jan. 31, 1881. He was educated at St. John's College, Cambridge (B.A., 1835), of which he became a fellow in 1837. After teaching for a time, he was appointed, in 1839, rector of Ditchingham, a parish which he held until his death. Theologically he was distinctly a High-churchman, though not of the most advanced type. An admirable patristic and liturgical scholar, he was the author of *The Communion of the Laity* (London, 1855); *Litanies for Use at the various Seasons of the Christian Year, before and after the Holy Communion, and on other Occasions* (1860); *The North Side of the Table: An historical Enquiry* (1870); and *Notitia Eucharistia* (1872; a masterpiece in its field). In the sphere of polemics and church history he wrote *Letters to a Seceder from the Church of England* (London, 1851); *England and Rome: A Discussion of the Principal Points of Difference* (1855); and *The Diocesan Synods of the Earlier Church* (1878). He also gained a lasting reputation as a devotional writer, his works here being *Steps to the Altar: A Manual of Devotions for the Blessed Eucharist* (London, 1846, and constantly reprinted); *Words to Take with us: A Manual of Daily and Occasional Prayers* (1859); *The Hour of Prayer, being a Manual of Devotion for the Use of Families and Schools* (1873); and *Incense for the Altar: A Series of Devotions for . . . Communicants* (1874).

BIBLIOGRAPHY: A. Davenport, *Scudamore and Bickersteth; or "Steps to the Altar" and "The Devotions of the Reformers" compared*, Hobart Town, 1851; *DNB*, li. 157–158.

SCUDDER, scud'er, **HENRY MARTYN:** Missionary to India and Japan; b. at Panditeripo, Jaffna District, Ceylon, Feb. 5, 1822; d. at Winchester, Mass., June 4, 1895. He was the son of John Scudder (q.v.); was educated at New York University and Williams College, and graduated at the former, 1840; studied at Union Theological Seminary, New York, 1840–43; was missionary under the American Board at Madras, India, 1844–51; and, after exploring the Arcot district, was stationed there where he established a dispensary. His study of medicine gave him special facility for access to the people. In 1864, his health declined and he returned to America, becoming successively pastor of the Grand Street Reformed Church, Jersey City, N. J., 1864–65; the Howard Presbyterian Church, San Francisco, Cal., 1865–71; the Central Congregational Church, Brooklyn, N. Y., 1871–82; and the

Plymouth Congregational Church, Chicago, 1882–87. He joined his son and daughter in missionary service in Japan, 1887–90. He published in Tamil, *Liturgy of the Reformed Protestant Dutch Church* (Madras, 1862); *The Bazaar Book* (1865); *Sweet Savors of Divine Truth* (1868); and *Spiritual Teaching* (1870; Eng. transl., 1870).

SCUDDER, JOHN: Missionary of the Reformed (Dutch) Church; b. at Freehold, N. J., Sept. 13, 1793; d. at Wynberg (7 m. s.e. of Capetown), Southern Africa, Jan. 13, 1855. He was graduated at the College of New Jersey, 1811; and at the College of Physicians and Surgeons, New York, 1815; and practised medicine until 1819. While in professional attendance upon a lady, he took up a tract entitled *The Conversion of the World* and his religious sense of duty was so impressed that he gave his life to missionary labor. After being licensed by the New York classis, he proceeded, under the American Board, to Ceylon, where he arrived 1820; was ordained there, 1821; established a hospital at Jaffnapatam; was foremost in organizing a college there, 1822; had an extensive revival 1824; and in 1836 with Miron Winslow was transferred to Madras, in order that he might print Scriptures and tracts in Tamil. In the first year they printed six million pages. Scudder fixed his residence at Chintadrepettah, near Madras, and thus, under his attention, there grew up the Arcot mission, which was received under the care of the American Board in 1852, and of the Reformed (Dutch) Church the next year. He was in America, 1842–46, in the interest of foreign missions. In 1849 he was in the Madura mission, and with this exception all his energies were given to the Arcot mission. His health gave way in 1854, and he went to the Cape of Good Hope, where, upon the point of returning to India, he was stricken by apoplexy. He was incessant in his heroic labors, given much to Evangelistic itinerancy. It is remarkable that his eight sons, two grandsons, and two granddaughters have been members of the Arcot Mission. He published *Letters from the East* (Boston, 1833); *Letters to Pious Young Men* (1846); and *Provision for Passing over Jordan* (New York, 1852).

Bibliography: J. B. Waterbury, *Memoir of Rev. John Scudder . . . Thirty-six Years Missionary in India*, New York, 1870; W. B. Sprague, *Annals of the American Pulpit*, vol. ix., ib. 1873; E. T. Corwin, *Manual of the Reformed Church in America*, pp. 716–720, 4th ed., ib. 1902.

SCULLARD, scul'ard, **HERBERT HAYES:** Congregationalist; b. at Belper (7 m. n. of Derby), England, July 4, 1862. He received his education at Pembroke House School, Lytham, Lancashire, Lancashire Independent and Owen's Colleges, Manchester, St. John's College, Cambridge (B.A., 1888; M.A., 1891); and London University (B.A., 1883; M.A., 1885; B.D., 1904; D.D., 1907); was minister of York St. Congregational Church, Dublin, 1890–1896; and of Howard Congregational Church, Bedford, 1897–1907. Since 1907 he has been professor of church history, history of Christian ethics, and of religions in New and Hackney Colleges, London University. In theology he is an Evangelical. He has written: *St. Martin of Tours* (Manchester, 1891); *John Howard* (London, 1899); *Early Christian Ethics in the West* (1908); and contributed an essay to *Christ and Civilization*, issued by the National Free Church Council (1910).

SCULPTURE, CHRISTIAN USE OF.

In the artistic life of the Church and of Christianity Painting and Architecture (qq.v.) took precedence of sculpture.* In the Middle Ages the plastic arts were an adjunct of architecture; in the preceding epochs under the influence of the antique their position was freer but less independent. The Renaissance first set forth new views of art and gave to the other branches their equal rights. In the primitive Church and even in the Middle Ages the development of sculpture, especially in statuary, was hindered by its old association with idolatry. So in the early period, where the plastic art appears, it is limited to relief forms.

I. The Early Christian Period: Christian work of this sort in the early period worked most upon sarcophagus relief and ivory. The peculiar history of the sarcophagus began with the fourth century, when new forms of burial were sought. In the churches and the cemeteries above ground, then becoming more numerous, the stone coffin found its use, and numerous exemplars come from the central points of Rome, Ravenna, and Arles. On the front of the sarcophagus, seldom on the other sides, in high relief are portrayed Biblical events, generally in historical sequence, though sometimes freely arranged. Usually the series is arranged without pillars, trees, and the like separating the different scenes. Often, after the ancient fashion, the portrait of the deceased was worked into the fabric of the relief. Western art showed inclination for human figures, the Hellenist-oriental preferred animal and plant forms. While there was a general uniformity, individual tendencies showed themselves locally. Recent discovery has made clear in Hellenist-oriental work a commingling of Syrian and Egyptian elements in varying proportions; this field far surpasses in artistic worth the western-Latin sculpture on the sarcophagi. The leading position of Byzantine art appears particularly in ivory carving, emanating from Byzantium, Antioch, and Alexandria as the principal centers; facility in execution best shows itself in copies of work from the fourth to the sixth centuries. There is an inner connection with the antique; in conception, execution, and content, the graceful naturalness of Hellenistic art lived on in ornament. The variety of objects is large, these being found as diptychs, chests for sacramental or secular use, medallions for the adornment of episcopal chairs, figurines, and the like. For work in wood the relief on the door of the St.

* "Sculpture" and "plastic art" as used in this article include carving as well as works which ordinarily go under those terms.

Sabina Church in Rome is a fine example, so far as archeological purpose goes. Terra-cotta and the noble metals furnished material also, while the furniture of church and home provided other ground for work. Here the lamps were especially selected for ornamentation with cross, monogram, animals, plants, secular and sacred figures or scenes. A long list of clay and metal objects also offered a basis, while portals, pillars, railings, ambo, and other objects were enriched by ornaments of this kind. Of statuary proper, especially of a monumental character, little has come down, though there is literary testimony to a once abundant material. Among extant examples, the good shepherd takes the first place. While the brazen statue of St. Peter in the Vatican is of the thirteenth century, there is one of marble of early date, and the seated Hippolytus in the Lateran is of his own times, though modeled on antique lines.

II. The Middle Ages: As the spiritual life of the Carolingian period took its departure from classical tradition, so the plastic arts followed the same trend. While the Germanic tribes, as they came into the sphere and under the influence of the Roman culture, recognized and bowed to the imposing force of these forms, they yet retained their own genius which shone out with greater or less clearness. Sculpture was largely expressed in carving of ivory, and the lineage of the work was Roman, with a relatively high facility in execution. But there is often to be discovered the naive freshness of German genius. In lands like Ireland and England, where Roman influence was less direct, the native genius is still more in evidence. In France there were many centers for this class of productions, in Germany the Lower Rhine was the busiest workshop, though northern Germany had an artistic carver in Tuotilo of St. Gall. The eleventh-century architecture, developing out of the old Carolingian style, gave opportunity for the development of sculpture. On the outside the space over the portal was employed; while on the inside capital, baptismal stone, ambo, and the cultic objects formed the ground for this sort of adornment. The plastic arts took their place alongside of painting and served on the great surfaces to set forth the symbolism of Christendom. This is especially true of Germany (Hildesheim, 1015; Augsburg, 1060; and the doors for Novgorod, Gnesen, and of St. Zeno in Verona, all from German hands). The conception follows the trend of the architecture and is decorative in purpose, the pattern is antique with little tendency to novelty; in the carving of ivory (book covers, diptychs, chests, croziers, and the like) Carolingian influence often remains unbroken, while at times independent observation and execution are apparent, especially in a Saxon environment. Monks and the clergy were the principal artists of the eleventh and the twelfth centuries.

1. Influence of Early Models.

After a slow development in the twelfth century, under the stimulus of Gothic architecture, German plastic art of the Middle Ages reached its culmination in classic completeness and monumental creations, the Saxon countries being in the lead. Wechselburg, Freiburg, and Naumburg furnish the noblest and oldest expressions of the invention of this period. While in South Germany masterpieces are found, French influences, naturally, are stronger—indirect in Bamberg, direct in Strasburg. The tendency was to give way to individualistic expression in the concrete, though the means chosen were not always happy; there was moreover the effort after a harmony between the solemnity of place and of purpose and individual life. The ideal was more subjective and artistic, though the tradition of the twelfth century was not abandoned. France also in the twelfth century experienced a lively development in plastic art, in which the schools of Provence, Toulouse, and Burgundy were prominent, and this development was not uninfluential even in Spain. Roman traditions are in evidence still, with a fondness for adornment of entrances. The thirteenth century, that of the Gothic style of architecture, brought about a distinct revolution. The mighty structures which arose, especially in the central provinces of northern France, demanded, with their imposing doors and lofty and richly membered architecture, a wealth of statuary and relief work. With enthusiasm the plastic art took up its task and achieved the classical completeness of Christian imagery. Painting, equally zealous, followed the lead and limited itself no more to figures, scenes, and groups, but set forth the whole drama of salvation from the creation to the judgment. Fancy had full play, while the Bible, legend, popular and learned conceptions, history, and typology combined to furnish the subjects (cf., e.g., the cathedrals of Chartres and of Reims). Yet the call of architecture imposed its limits upon sculpture, within which there were a depth of sensibility and a fineness of observation which justifies comparison with the antique. The general effect was that of a more youthful and graceful style than obtained in Germany. Especially in the portrayal of the person of Christ this century surpassed all previous ones, and long stood in the lead. In this and in the figures of the apostles the Renaissance was anticipated. Hence French influence flowed out to the neighboring lands. So strong was this in Germany that connection with the past was practically broken. With this development came also application of this art to the cultic objects, even the most insignificant, and color was used to enhance the effect; additional to stone as materials were used wood, stucco, the precious metals, and enamel. The Netherlands felt even more forcibly than Germany the influence of France. In England native elements mingled with the French. In Italy during the eleventh and twelfth centuries there were mingled the various streams of Byzantine, Roman, and Lombardic art. In the thirteenth century Pisa led the way to a higher exposition through Niccolo Pisano, a man thoroughly and intelligently grounded in appreciation of the classical ideals of beauty, while his son Giovanni was even more influential. In the East, Christian art employed itself with architecture and painting, the early prejudice against the plastic continuing. Carving in ivory is the one branch of this art which reached eminence there.

2. Results of Gothic Development.

III. The Modern Period: In the fifteenth century

in Italy art released itself from the traditions of the Middle Ages, and in the process individualism, for which Humanism (q.v.) had victoriously fought, led the way back to nature as a source of inspiration and thence to an increasing richness of creations, in which the deep content of life was exhibited. As compared with Greek art, which drew from the same source, the Christian is distinguished by an effort to portray the inner life and not mere external beauty of form. Plastic art, recognizing its task, released itself from the limits imposed by architecture and then imparted some of the freedom thus gained to painting. The artists were encouraged, moreover, by native enthusiasm, the nobility, both secular and ecclesiastical, serving as patrons. Thus the Church offered no opposition, and plastic art was allowed free scope in the churches. Even mortuary monuments, which hitherto had followed the old style, joined the new movement. Monastic structures, in spite of conservative tendencies, followed on, and the workmen were now found among the laity. A higher idealism guided the hand of the artist, who conceived his work in the spirit of a holy service. While the artists were many, they were united in this conception of their province, though individuality was not submerged. While the most varied material was employed, marble was most highly regarded; there was also much use of many-colored terra-cotta, rendered durable by glazing or enameling. Florence was the leader, where Lorenzo Ghiberti (d. 1455) and Donatello worked, in whom the strength of invention and execution which characterised the new era unfolded itself. In the latter full yielding to nature and reality, elevation almost to harshness, grace even to delicacy flow together in the harmony of art. Portrayal of the human form was recognized as the highest result here; while the influence of the classical was felt, it was rather by assimilation of its ideals than by imitation. As Florence was the center in the early Renaissance, so Rome became the center in the "high Renaissance," containing, as it did, not merely the remains of antiquity but also the recollections of a great history. The incarnation of the ideals and powers of this later period were concentrated in Michelangelo Buonarotti. None had so great power in forcing the marble to express his will; he created a new era in the exaltation of the common forms into the gigantic, wherein nature was expressed but after the type of civilized man. Examples of his art are the Pietà, David, Moses, and the dying slave, each exemplifying a phase of his art which has its own excellencies and greatnesses. It was inevitable that such a man should influence not only his own time but also dominate largely the future through his inspiration of other artists.

1. The Renaissance in Italy.

2. New German Era.

In Germany not only the views but the social and especially the cultural organization of the Middle Ages still obtained, and where new motives and pictures came in, these were of a religious character. There were lacking the keen spirit, the generous patronage of the rich, and the immediately working influence of antiquity that were present in Italy. There was no attempt at the great and monumental; but in place of this, there was an appreciation of reality and of the truth of the phenomenal, without earnest effort after or concern for an ideal of beauty. The nude was not employed, the draperies of figures being heavy and abundant and in the fashion of the period. Yet there was earnestly sought the combination of internal and external truth, the expression of the personal, perception of the spiritual. Art is here the expression of common life and speaks a popular language, dwelling upon sacred history and the history of the saints; Mary was not the queen of heaven but rather the lovely virgin or the agonized mother. But these aims were sometimes marred by a repellent materialism. The sculptor and the painter united forces and together produced such works as altar-pieces and the like. The period between 1450 and 1530 is the second period of bloom in German plastic art. Everywhere were created great altar-pieces, the joint production of painting and sculpture, while the registers of corporations exhibit numerous names of artists, though there were no such prominent centers of influence as were Florence and Rome in Italy. As the center of the Frankish school, however, Nuremberg must be named. The carvings which came out of the workshop of Michael Wohlgemut show the first traces of the new movement, and in the work of his younger contemporary Veit Stoss this movement reached its culmination. The medium was wood, and the aim was sharp definition and a conception of reality. Examples of his work are the altar of Mary in Cracow, the greeting of the angels in the Church of St. Lorenz, and creations in the Jakobskirche in Nuremberg. With him should be mentioned as the master in stone work Adam Kraft (b. about 1450; d. 1509), who had an archaistic bent which he used in pieces that exhibit a devotional restfulness, as shown in his Seven Stations and his group of the crucifixion, while in the celebrated chapel of the sacrament in the Lorenzkirche a feeling for the decorative and mastery of technique are combined. A third name is that of Peter Vischer (b. about 1455; d. 1529), the author of numerous works, with whom his sons collaborated. He excelled both his contemporaries in largeness of conception and feeling for beauty, though between him and Adam Kraft significant relations existed. Toward the latter part of his life he came under the influence of the Renaissance, but retained his Teutonic traits, as is shown by his chief work, the memorial in the Sebalduskirche (completed 1519). A man held in highest honor was Tilmann Riemenschneider (d. 1531), artist in both stone and wood, and a great body of disciples attest his eminence. Swabia participated in this development of German art, although painting was there more favored. Ulm Jörg Syrlin, father and son, developed a significant activity; to the son was ascribed the high altar at Blaubeuren, one of the masterpieces in this line of Christian art, with which must be named the crucifix in the chief church at Nördlingen. The Tyrol produced in this period Michael Pacher, a man of high artistic capacity. On the Lower Rhine home production was stifled by the importation of art work from the Netherlands, and what work was done there was patterned after the models thus obtained. In North Germany Hans Brüggemann, though incited by Netherlandic art, through his own genius gave his work distinction, producing the great altar in the cathedral at Sleswick.

During the sixteenth century the Italian Renaissance began to diffuse its results over Germany with the result that the classicism then fashionable came in. In Italy at the end of this century the baroque style entered and prevailed. The creator here was the papal architect Lorenzo Bernini (d. 1680). This style ran to the pathetic and affecting; and since it needed for effectiveness the aid of painting, plastic art surrendered its independence to its sister art. Thus there came into being the theatrically composed portrayals of history of saints and martyrs characterized by unbalanced piety, frivolous sensualism, and repellent realism. While the Thirty Years' War shattered German art for the time, Prussia showed the first recovery, artists being imported. But the baroque stylist Andreas Schlüter (d. 1714) was of home growth, whose equestrian statue of the great elector is the most characteristic production, though his marble pulpit in the Marienkirche in Berlin is a graceful and decorative composition.

With the end of the eighteenth century the independence of art ceased. There began a *rechauffé* of all periods and styles which gave both to architecture and to sculpture a chaotic impress. Modern intercourse and expositions facilitated methods of reproduction, brought persons and schools of all lands together, and produced the great mixture of styles which is found in the present. At first, the antique was in fashion, represented by the Italian Antonio Canova (d. 1822) and the Dane Bertel Thorwaldsen (d. 1844). The latter lives through his great creation, now in the Vor-Frue-Kirke in Copenhagen, the Christ accompanied by his band of disciples, a work which vividly brings to mind Matt. xi. 28. Exaltation and gentleness envelop this form, fashioned in antique beauty. The most eminent representative of classicism in Germany was Christian Daniel Rauch (d. 1857), who, though his inclination was toward the secular, yet left in his praying Moses (in the Friedenskirche at Potsdam) evidence of perception of the needs of religious sculpture. In Ernst Rietschel there was completed an approach to realism. While his delicate Pietà in the Friedenskirche at Potsdam is based on ideal classicism, the Luther memorial at Worms has received the entire force of historical presentation. But in Germany classicism is worthily represented only by Adolf Hildebrand. For the rest, plastic art is showing all types from fantastic symbolism to the sharpest realism and the most bizarre impressionism. The same may be said of France, where August Rodin, following his predecessors François Rude and David d'Angers, has made a break with the classicistic past and introduced a thoroughgoing subjectivism, his figures showing emotionalism and the sensual. Yet the representative Frenchman of today is not Rodin but Albert Bartholomé, whose creations reveal lofty conception, harmony, and proportion, especially as exhibited in his Monument aux morts in the churchyard of Père la Chaise in Paris. In Belgium Konstantin Meunier (d. 1905) placed his great talents at the service of the social question, portraying the laboring classes with fidelity to life.

3. Recent Art.

As a whole the art of the present is eclectic, though originality is not lacking, while strong individuality is also a marked characteristic. Hellenism is still distinguishable in plastic form, and romantic and ecclesiastical traditions remain in force, especially in Roman Catholic art. But the tendency of art as a whole is to walk in the free paths of subjectivism, and it reflects, equally with literature, the spiritual, ethical, and religious incoherence which marks the times. Moreover, the close bonds, so evident in the Middle Ages, between architecture and sculpture have been severed. On the other hand, in the works of memorial character religious art has produced some memorable results, though even in these great dangers are manifest. In decorative work ecclesiastical art still leans upon the models presented by the Middle Ages.

(VICTOR SCHULTZE.)

BIBLIOGRAPHY: In general, much of the literature under ART AND CHURCH; CEMETERIES; and PAINTING has bearing on the subject, some of it is immediately pertinent, especially the works of Auguste, Didron, Lenoir, Hemans, Otte, Jameson, Schlosser, Kraus, Lowrie, Schultze, Garrucci, Burckhardt, Wölfflin, and Rosenberg. The reader is directed also to the series of monographs published as *Zur Kunstgeschichte*, Strasburg, 1900 sqq.; *Künstler-Monographien*, Bielefeld, 1901 sqq., and *Great Masters in Sculpture*, published by Bell, London, 1903 sqq. Also to H. Stegman, *Sculpture of the West*, London, 1907; and A. Kuhn, *Allgemeine Kunst-Geschichte*, Einsiedeln, 1908.

For the ancient period consult: W. Lübke, *Geschichte der Plastik*, Stuttgart, 1880; idem, *Grundriss der Kunstgeschichte*, ed. M. Semrau, 5 vols., ib. 1903–05; C. C. Perkins, *Historical Handbook of Italian Sculpture*, London, 1883; A. Bayersdorfer, *Klassischer Skulpturenschatz*, Munich, 1896; A. Springer, *Handbuch der Kunstgeschichte*, 2 vols., 4th ed., Leipsic, 1895; J. Ficker, *Die altchristlichen Bildwerke im christlichen Museum des Laterans*, Leipsic, 1890; G. Stuhlfauth, *Die altchristliche Elfenbeinplastik*, Freiburg, 1896; J. Wiegand, *Das altchristliche Hauptportal an der Kirche der heiligen Sabina zu Rom*, Treves, 1900; F. Freiherr Goeler von Ravensburg, *Grundriss der Kunstgeschichte*, ed. M. Schmid, Berlin, 1901–03; J. Strzygowski, *Koptische Kunst*, Vienna, 1904; K. M. Kaufmann, *Handbuch der christlichen Archäologie*, Paderborn, 1905; E. Redslob, *Das Kirchenportal*, Jena, 1909. A rich source of knowledge is Cabrol, *Dictionnaire*, e.g., the article "Agneau," i. 878 sqq.

For the pre-Reformation period consult: W. Bode, *Geschichte der deutschen Plastik*, Berlin, 1885; A. Schmarsow, *Donatello*, Leipsic, 1886; P. Clemen, *Merovingische und karolingische Plastik*, Bonn, 1892; E. von Flottwell, *Meisterwerk deutscher Bildnerei in Naumburg*, Magdeburg, 1892; E. Meyer, *Die Skulpturen des Strassburger Münsters*, Strasburg, 1894; W. Vöge, *Die Anfänge des monumentalen Stiles im Mittelalter*, ib. 1894; L. Gonse, *La Sculpture française depuis le xiv. siècle*, Paris, 1895; M. R. James, *The Sculptures in the Lady Chapel at Ely*, London, 1895; E. Stueckelberg, *Longobardische Plastik*, Zurich, 1896; A. Weese, *Die Bamberger Domskulpturen*, Strasburg, 1897; M. G. Zimmermann, *Oberitalienische Plastik im frühen und höhern Mittelalter*, Leipsic, 1897; S. Lami, *Dictionnaire des sculpteurs de l'école française du moyen âge*, Paris, 1898; E. Mâle, *L'Art religieux du xiii. siècle en France*, ib. 1898; K. Moriz-Eichhorn, *Der Skulpturencyklus in der Vorhalle des Freiburger Münsters*, Strasburg, 1899; J. Mantuani, *Tuotilo*, Strasburg, 1900; L. J. Freeman, *Italian Sculpture of the Renaissance*, New York, 1901; A. Venturi, *Storia dell' Arte Italiana*, Milan, 1901 sqq.; A. Goldschmidt, *Die Freiberger Goldene Pforte*, Berlin, 1902; A. Marignan, *Hist. de la sculpture en Languedoc du xii–xiii. siècle*, Paris, 1902; K. Franck, *Der Meister der Ecclesia und Synagoge am Strassburger Münster*, Düsseldorf, 1903; R. S. L. Gower, *Michael Angelo Buonarotti*, London, 1903; D. A. E. Lindsay, *Donatello*, ib. 1903; A. Brach, *Nicola und Giovanni Pisano und die Plastik des xiv. Jahrhunderts in Siena*, Strassburg, 1904; M. Sauerland, *Die Bildwerke des Giovanni Pisano*, Düsseldorf, 1904; A. Alexander, *Donatello*, Paris, 1905; H. Bergner, *Handbuch der kirchlichen Kunstaltertümer in Deutschland*, Leipsic, 1905.

For the modern period consult: A. Woltmann, *Die deutsche Kunst und die Reformation*, Berlin, 1867; A. Oppermann, *Ernst Rietschel*, Leipsic, 1873; F. and K. Eggers, *C. D. Rauch*, 5 vols., Berlin, 1873–91; C. Gurlitt, *Geschichte des Barock, Rokoko und Klassizismus*, Stuttgart, 1887–89; L. and E. L. de Taeye, *Études sur les arts plastiques en Belgique*, Brussels, 1891; A. Sach, *Hans Brüggemann*, Sleswick, 1896; B. Daun, *Adam Kraft*, Berlin, 1897; idem, *Veit Stoss und seine Schule*, Leipsic, 1903; A. R. Willard, *Hist. of Modern Art*, London, 1900; M. H. Spielmann, *British Sculpture and Sculptors of To-day*, ib. 1901; W. C. Brownell, *French Art*, Westminster, 1902; D. Christison, *The Carvings and Inscriptions on the Kirkyard Monuments of the Scottish Lowlands*, Edinburgh, 1902; E. Claris, *De l'impressionisme en sculpture*, Paris, 1902; H. Thode, *Michelangelo und das Ende der Renaissance*, 2 vols., Berlin, 1902–03; A. Heilmeyer, *Die moderne Plastik in Deutschland*, Leipsic, 1903; É. Humblot, *Documents sur la sculpture religieuse*, Saint-Disier, 1903; L. Taft, *The Hist. of American Sculpture*, New York, 1903; S. Trier, *Thorvaldsen*, Copenhagen, 1903; L. de Fourcaud, *François Rude*, Paris, 1904; C. Mauclair, *Auguste Rodin*, London, 1905; C. Meunier, *Constantin Meunier et son œuvre*, Paris, 1905; F. Bond, *Wood Carvings in English Churches*, London, 1910.

SCULTETUS, scul-ti'tus (**SCHULTETUS**), **ABRAHAM**: German Reformed; b. at Grüneberg (86 m. n.w. of Breslau) Aug. 24, 1566; d. at Emden (60 m. w.n.w. of Bremen) Oct. 24, 1624. Educated at the universities of Wittenberg (1588–90) and Heidelberg (1590–91), he was ordained in 1594 to the ministry of Schriesheim near Heidelberg, whence he was called, a few months later, to be court chaplain to the Elector Frederick IV. In 1598 he became pastor of the Franciscan church at Heidelberg, ecclesiastical councilor and inspector of pastors and schools in 1600, succeeded Pitiscus as court preacher on his death in 1614, and in 1618 was made professor of theology at the university. Meanwhile he had been employed in various missions of importance. He was called in 1614 to the court of Brandenburg to counsel the Reformed convert, Elector John Sigismund, in arranging the ecclesiastical affairs of the province; in 1618 was one of the Palatine delegates to the Synod of Dort; in 1619 he accompanied the electoral envoys to Frankfort to choose the new emperor, and in 1620 followed his elector, who had been offered the Bohemian crown, to Prague, where he was involved in the fatal events after the battle of Weissenberg (Nov. 8, 1620). Scultetus fled from Prague to Heidelberg, but further residence there was impossible, and he sought refuge with his adherents successively in Bretten and in Schorndorf in Württemberg, and was called, in 1622, to be pastor at Emden, where he passed the remainder of his life.

One of the most distinguished Reformed theologians of his period, Scultetus was a prominent figure in the irenic proposals steadily refused by the Lutherans. His chief works were the *Medulla theologiæ patrum syntagma* (4 parts, Heidelberg, 1598–1613), and the *Annalium evangelii passim per Europam quinto decimo salutis partæ seculo renovati decas prima et secunda ab anno 1516–36* (Heidelberg, 1618–20); to these may be added the posthumous *Narratio apologetica* (Emden, 1625).

(H. Mallet†.)

Bibliography: The funeral sermon by F. Salmuth was published, Emden, 1625. Consult: E. Meiners, *Oostvrieschlandts Kerkelijke Geschiedenisse*, ii. 439 sqq., Groningen, 1739; P. Bayle, *Dictionary*, v. 100–104; *ADB*, xxxiii. 492 sqq.

SCYTHIANS. See Gog and Magog.

SDRALEK, shrä'lek, **MAXIMILIAN LUKAS**: German Roman Catholic; b. at Woschczyts (a village near Sohraul, 57 m. s.e. of Oppeln), Upper Silesia, Oct. 11, 1855. He was educated at the universities of Breslau and Freiburg (D.D., 1880), and in 1882 became privat-docent for church history and canon law at the former institution. In 1884 he was called to Münster as professor of church history, but in 1896 returned to Breslau to accept his present position of professor of the same subject. He has also been resident canon of the Breslau Cathedral since 1900, and was rector of the university 1906–1907. Besides editing the *Kirchengeschichtliche Studien* and the *Kirchengeschichtliche Abhandlungen*, he has written *Hinkmars von Reims kanonistische Gutachten über die Ehescheidung des Königs Lothar II.* (Freiburg, 1881); *Die Streitschriften Altmanns von Passau und Wezilos von Mainz* (Paderborn, 1891); *Wolfenbüttler Fragmente, Analekten zur Kirchengeschichte* (Münster, 1891); and *Die Strassburger Diözesansynode* (Freiburg, 1894).

SEABURY, SAMUEL: First bishop of the Protestant Episcopal Church; b. at North Groton (now Ledyard), Conn., Nov. 30, 1729; d. at New London Feb. 25, 1796. He graduated at Yale College, 1748, and soon after began the study of medicine. In 1752, though he had already devoted himself to the clerical calling, he went to Edinburgh to complete his medical studies, and there became acquainted with a remnant of the ancient Church of Scotland. He was ordained deacon by the bishop of Lincoln, Dec. 21, 1753; and priest two days later at London; arrived at New Brunswick, N. J., as missionary, 1754; was rector at Jamaica, L. I., 1757–1767; and at Westchester, N. Y., from 1767. Deriving his support as missionary from the Church of England, and being under the oath of allegiance, he remained stanchly loyal, which brought him into disfavor with the patriots. He made himself particularly obnoxious by a series of pamphlets signed A. W. Farme and entitled, *Free Thoughts on the Proceedings of the Continental Congress* (Nov. 16, 1774); *The Congress Canvassed* (Nov. 26); and *A View of the Controversy between Great Britain and her Colonies* (Dec. 24). He was seized by an armed band, removed to Connecticut, and held prisoner at New Haven, for six weeks. Upon being passed through the British lines he retired to New York, where he supported himself in part by the practise of medicine, served as chaplain of the king's American regiment, and maintained his loyalty till the end of the war. In 1783 he was elected bishop by the clergy of Connecticut, and proceeded to England for ordination. This was refused by the archbishop of Canterbury, because certain complications with the civil oath of allegiance had not yet been resolved, and Seabury turned to Scotland, where he was consecrated in 1784 by three nonjuring prelates. He returned to Connecticut, 1785, where, resident as rector at New London, his episcopal jurisdiction was recognized, and was extended, by invitation, over Rhode Island. He was the first presiding bishop of the churches in the several states united under the general convention in 1789. He united with the three bishops subsequently consecrated in England in the formation of the new constitution rendering the American church independent and autonomous, in the joint consecration of the first bishop of Maryland, Thomas J. Claggett. Consequently no bishop has ever been consecrated without deriving his prerogatives both through the Scottish and Anglican lines of descent.

Seabury was fitted by his ecclesiastical knowledge and persistent devotion to his church system, exercised with remarkable prudence and patience, to render services making him a pioneer and founder of American Episcopalianism, fortunately resulting in guiding a free, valid, and regular succession through the crisis of American independence, and demonstrating that the episcopacy was adaptable in a free state. His permanent services include the securing, by amendment, of coordinate legislative functions for the house of bishops, and the restoration of the oblation and invocation to the communion office, according to his pledge to the Scotch Church which ordained him. His *Discourses on Several Subjects* was published (New York, 1793; 2 vols., Hudson, 1815).

Bibliography: E. E. Beardsley, *Life and Correspondence of Rev. S. Seabury*, Boston, 1881; W. B. Sprague, *Annals of the American Pulpit*, v. 149–153, New York, 1859; W. S. Perry, *Hist. of the American Episcopal Church*, passim, 2 vols., Boston, 1885; idem, *The Episcopate in America*, pp. 1–3, New York, 1885; C. C. Tiffany, in *American Church History Series*, vol. vii, passim, ib. 1895; S. D. McConnell, *Hist. of the American Episcopal Church*, passim, 7th ed., ib. 1897; W. J. Seabury, *Memoirs of Bishop Seabury*, ib. 1908; and in general the literature under Protestant Episcopal Church which deals with the early period.

SEABURY, WILLIAM JONES: Protestant Episcopalian; b. in New York City Jan. 25, 1837. He was educated at Columbia College, New York City (A.B., 1856), and, after practising law for a few years, entered the General Theological Seminary, from which he was graduated in 1866. He was ordered deacon and ordained to the priesthood in the same year. He was rector of the Church of the Annunciation, New York City (1868–98), and since 1873 has also been professor of ecclesiastical polity and law in the General Theological Seminary. Besides editing S. Seabury's *Memorial* (New York, 1874) and the same theologian's *Discourses on the Nature and Work of the Holy Spirit* (1874), he has written *Suggestions in Aid of Devotion and Holiness* (New York, 1878); *Manual for Choristers* (1878); *A Guide to the Observance of the Canons of the Church affecting those who are seeking Holy Orders* (1888); *Lectures on Apostolical Succession* (1893); *An Introduction to the Study of Ecclesiastical Polity* (1894); *Notes on the Constitution of 1901* (1902); and *Memoir of Rev. Samuel Seabury* (1908).

SEALS. See Dress and Ornament, Hebrew, § 6.

SEAMEN, MISSIONS TO.

I. In Great Britain: As early as the middle of the eighteenth century sermons were preached and printed on behalf of seamen by John Flavel (q.v., 1630–91). An organization named **The Bible Society** (see Bible Societies, I., 1) was organized in London in 1780 to supply English soldiers with the Holy Scriptures. Very soon its efforts were extended to embrace the seamen of the royal navy.

1. Work in the Navy.

The ill-fated "Royal George," sunk off Spithead, England, Aug. 29, 1782, was the first ship supplied with Bibles. The society's name was changed to **The Naval and Military Bible Society,** and it still continues its beneficent work of supplying the Scriptures to the army and navy of Great Britain. Incidentally, it helped to form the British and Foreign Bible Society (see Bible Societies, I., 2), which society in turn helped to call into existence the American Bible Society (see Bible Societies, III., 2). Seamen as a class, in those days, were devoid of scriptural knowledge, neglected by the Church at large, without Gospel ministrations or privileges, sea missionaries, or any special humanitarian effort on their behalf. When attempts were made to furnish seamen with church services and the Holy Scriptures, unchristian officers in the royal navy opposed with considerable spirit the new movement, but in the year 1828 the king was petitioned to abrogate an admiralty order, then issued, prohibiting the free distribution of tracts in the navy.

Outside of the navy a Methodist clergyman, George Charles Smith, established prayer-meetings for seamen on the Thames at London. The first recorded prayer-meeting was held on the brig "Friendship" on June 22, 1814. These prayer-meetings multiplied until on Mar. 23, 1817, the first bethel flag—indicating that divine service would be held on board ship—was unfurled by Captain Hindulph of South Shields, England.

2. Work in the Merchant Marine.

The Port of London Society, organized Mar. 18, 1818, was the first regular seamen's society in England formed for the specific purpose of preaching to seamen. Its first meeting-place was on a ship of three hundred tons and Smith was the first chaplain. Nov. 12, 1819, **The Bethel Union Society** was formed to establish unity of purpose and action between various seamen's societies in Great Britain, formed by the exertions of chaplain Smith. An amalgamation of these two societies produced the **British and Foreign Sailors' Society,** international and interdenominational in its plan.

he object of the society is the religious, intellectual, nd social elevation of British and foreign seamen. t is world-wide in its operations, having stations in he chief ports of the world, and is associated with 13 missions in 110 ports. In these ports there are 11 buildings, called palaces, bethels, institutes, iomes, rests, reading-rooms, or missionaries' quarers. For harbors, roadsteads, and rivers, there are orty-three floating bethels, steam launches, mission utters, sail and row boats; 1,191 Christian shipnasters, and 124 helpers, have joined, since 1866, ts Bethel Union Association, an association of Chrisian shipmasters who have a flag which they hoist n port, indicating their connection with the union and their willingness to hold or attend religious worship. In the service of the society there are 167 chaplains and missionaries.

3. Various Societies Operating.

The Missions to Seamen, the official society of the Church of England (headquarters 11 Buckingham Street, London, England), is the largest seamen's society in the world. It employs sixty-four chaplains and sixty-eight lay assistants, with twenty-six large and small boats in various parts of the world. **The Royal National Mission to Deep Sea Fishermen**, London, England, carries on a vigorous work on the North Sea (England), and in Labrador, Newfoundland, by means of its hospital work ashore and afloat. The society owns five large steam vessels, a number of luggers, and has been instrumental in destroying the iniquitous system whereby liquor and tobacco were sold to the fishermen at enormous profit, resulting in loss of life and character. Within the last five years its superintendent, Dr. Grenfell, has interested America in the work on the Labrador coast. Besides the larger national societies in England, there are a number of smaller missions to seamen independent in government and local in their operations, such as the **Glasgow Seamen's Friend Society** and the **Liverpool Seamen's Friend Society**. **The Seamen's Mission**, headquarters at the "The Queen Victoria's Sailors' Rest," Poplar, E., London, is associated with the Wesleyan Methodist Church of England and has for its primary object to minister to the spiritual wants of the thousands of seafaring men who frequent the port of London. **The Liverpool Seamen's Friend Society**, formerly known as the Liverpool Seamen and Emigrants' Friend Society and Bethel Union, having its headquarters at "Gordon Smith Institute for Seamen," Paradise Street, Liverpool, has for its object to promote the religious and social welfare of seamen, their families, and other persons connected with shipping, and of emigrants, by earnest endeavour to bring them under the power of the Gospel of Jesus Christ, and to encourage among them habits of temperance and frugality.

There are several other local societies of minor importance. The foregoing are singled out for notice because of their size and importance.

II. Continental Missions: Continental mission work for seamen is of a later date than that of Great Britain or America. The Scandinavian seamen's mission was begun by the Norwegian minister Storrjohann. In 1864 he founded the **Society for Promoting the Gospel Among Norwegian Seamen in Foreign Ports**, popularly known as the "Norwegian Seamen's Mission" with its headquarters in Bergen, Norway, and having forty-four stations abroad.

1. Scandinavian.

A similar organization was started in 1867 in Denmark, at Copenhagen, the **Society for the Preaching of the Gospel for Scandinavian Seamen in Foreign Ports**, with six stations in England and America. In 1869 the **Svenska Afdelningen af Föreningen för uppställande af skandinaviska Sjömanshem i utländska Hamnar**, a mission for the erection of Scandinavian sailors' homes, was established. These homes have nearly always a chaplain attached to them and an active missionary work is usually carried on, resulting in accessions to the regularly established Scandinavian churches in Sweden and abroad. The Scandinavian churches on the Pacific coast of the United States are largely the outgrowth of this movement which has preserved the Scandinavian element and given it remarkable solidarity in a part of America settled by emigration of mixed character.

2. German.

Germany's entry into missions for seamen is coincidental with her rise as a naval and maritime power in the decade from 1880 to 1890. Johann Heinrich Wichern (q.v.), the father of the Innere Mission (q.v.), became interested in the needs of seamen and made some suggestions as early as the year 1849. German Evangelical congregations in foreign countries, seeing the needs of their countrymen abroad, were the first to realise their obligations and to make efforts for the moral welfare of German seamen. The Rev. F. M. Harms, pastor of the German Evangelical congregation in Sunderland, organized the first congregation in Great Britain and in 1885 founded the **General Committee for General Evangelical Seamen's Mission in Great Britain.** The Central Board of the Innere Mission in Berlin awakened interest in the Fatherland which resulted in a quickened movement for seamen all over the world wherever Germans were located. The field of the General Committee is Great Britain, except the Bristol Channel, and it is active in forty-two ports with twenty missionaries, six sailors' homes, thirteen reading-rooms. The local committees are subsidized with 30,000 marks annually. The **German Lutheran Association for the Care of Seamen** began the work on the Bristol Channel in 1887 and sent the Rev. J. Fungclaussen as first German seamen's pastor to Cardiff, Wales. The association began work in 1891 at Hamburg, in 1896 on the lower Weser at Bremerhaven and Geestemünde, in 1906 in New York. A third organization was founded in 1895 by members of the Evangelical High-Consistory and the Central Board for Innere Mission in Berlin, to interest the old provinces of Prussia. This is the **Committee for German Evangelical Seamen's Mission.** The Baltic ports from Memel to Lübeck are under supervision of a special seamen's pastor. The chief ports connected with the committee's work are Antwerp, Rotterdam, Marseilles, Genoa, Constantinople, St. Petersburg, Copenhagen, Shanghai, Buenos Aires, Valparaiso, and Baltimore, Md.

There are now 175 ports where the work of the German Evangelical Seamen's Mission is carried on in some way. There are twenty-nine sailors' homes (with lodgings) and forty-four institutes (reading-rooms). For the welfare of sailors twenty seamen's pastors and forty missionaries (house-fathers, deacons) are at work in the field, besides about ninety who devote a part of their time to this service. The statistics for 1907 show that 13,800 men took lodging in the homes; the reading-rooms were visited by 160,000; 29,400 attended the religious services; more than 900,000 marks were deposited by sailors for safekeeping or to be sent home.

III. American Missions: The mission to seamen in America began in 1812, and was initiated by **The Boston Society for the Religious and Moral Improvement of Seamen.** As far as is known it had no direct visible relation to the movement in Britain, for the operations of the war between Great Britain and the United States created such difficulties that the work was suspended. In 1816 prayer-meetings were started in New York and in 1819 the first mariners' church ever erected was opened in Roosevelt Street, New York, by the **New York Port Society,** now in its ninety-second year. Bethel Unions or Marine Societies, as they were called then, were opened in Philadelphia, Baltimore, New Orleans, Charleston, S. C., Portland, Me., and New Bedford, Mass. In 1828, the year of the founding of the National Society for Seamen, the **American Seamen's Friend Society,** 76 Wall Street, New York City, unquestionably the most widely operative and efficient of existing missionary societies for seamen, came into being. Its first president was Hon. Smith Thompson, then secretary of the United States Navy; Rev. C. P. McIlvaine, afterward Protestant Episcopal bishop of Ohio, was its corresponding secretary; and Rev. Joshua Leavitt its general agent. Article II. of its constitution provides:

1. Beginnings; American Seamen's Friend Society.

"The object of this society shall be to improve the social and moral condition of seamen by uniting the efforts of the wise and good in their behalf, by promoting in every port boarding-houses of good character, savings-banks, register offices, libraries, museums, reading-rooms, and schools, and also the ministration of the gospel, and other religious blessings."

Its first foreign chaplain was Rev. David Abeel (q.v.), who reached his field of labor at Whampoa, the anchorage for ships trading at Canton, China, Feb. 16, 1830. In its fortieth year (1867–68) its laborers (chaplains and sailor missionaries) were stationed at twenty foreign and thirteen domestic seaports. The services rendered in the evangelization of the Hawaiian Islands by the American Seamen's Friend Society's chaplains, 1840–70, Rev. Titus M. Coan and Rev. S. C. Damon, popularly known as "Father Damon," are worthy of mention because of their association with the American Board of Commissioners for Foreign Missions, and with an almost forgotten chapter in American marine history, the whaling industry.

At the eightieth anniversary held in 1908 the society had seventeen foreign stations and sixteen domestic stations. In the United States of America: Brooklyn Navy Yard; Gloucester, Mass.; Norfolk, Newport News, Va.; Charleston, S. C.; Pensacola, Fla.; Savannah, Brunswick, Ga.; Mobile, Ala.; Galveston, Tex.; New Orleans, La.; Portland, Astoria, Oregon; Tacoma, Seattle, Wash.; San Francisco, Cal.

2. Stations and Operations.

In South America: Buenos Aires, Rosario, Argentine Republic; Montevideo, Uruguay; Valparaiso, Chile; Rio de Janeiro, Brazil.

In Europe: Stockholm, Gothenburg, Sweden; Copenhagen, Denmark; Rotterdam, Holland; Hamburg, Germany; Antwerp, Belgium; Genoa, Naples, Italy; Funchal, Madeira.

In Asia: Bombay, India; and Yokohama, Japan. At that time the society had shown a steady advance and decided increase in efficiency. From its beginning the national society had cared for the physical and mental needs of seamen along with its spiritual ministrations, and in its eightieth year the society opened the new institute, 507 West Street, New York, costing $325,000, the largest institution in the world for merchant seamen. In brief terms, the institute aimed to reach the whole ship and the whole man. Around the Bethel was grouped a hotel, club, and social features adapted to the steamship sailor's needs. So successful was the effort that in one year three or four new places modeled after it had been initiated. The loan library work began in an organized way in 1859, and became and has remained an important and regular feature of the society's operations, circulating since 1859 a grand total of 25,708 libraries, an average of 521 per year for fifty years. In the fifty-second year of the loan library work 3,000 libraries are in active use. These libraries contained 620,808 volumes of general matter, and 26,702 Bibles were sent in them, 12,000 manuals of worship for seamen, and 25,938 (estimated) hymn-books. 445,044 seamen have had access to the books by actual record, although more than one million seamen must have been reached by them. The number of books sent to sea by this system since its start in 1859 would nearly equal the present combined libraries of Princeton and Columbia universities. Public recognition of this work has been generous and frequent. In 1900 the Paris Exposition medal was granted the society for its literary work, and at the Jamestown Exposition, 1907, a diploma and bronze medal was awarded for the society's exhibit. When the explorer Peary went to the North Pole he had two of the American Seamen's Friend Society's Loan Libraries with him on the "Roosevelt."

Chief among the local societies unattached to the American Seamen's Friend Society are the following: Seamen's Church Institute, New York (Protestant Episcopal), with a sailors' home, a boat for work in the harbor of New York and a branch at Houston and West Streets; the New York Port Society with the Mariners' Church and reading-room, and a work among the Latin seamen; and the Boston Seamen's Friend Society (Congregational). Extra missionary effort on behalf of seamen which may legitimately be called "Missions to Seamen"

3. Auxiliary Movements.

is carried on by establishments known as sailors' homes. London, Liverpool, Glasgow, Newcastle-on-Tyne, Cardiff, Leith, Antwerp, Buenos Aires, Rosario, Sydney, Bombay, Karachi, Calcutta, New York, Boston, Philadelphia, Baltimore have such places supported by (1) the income from lodgers; (2) general subscriptions; (3) state subsidy, or city grant. Nearly all of them have resident chaplains, missionaries, or helpers who devote time to the spiritual and moral welfare of the seamen. Sailors' homes are no longer being built, the changed conditions of sea life rendering them obsolete, and seamen's institutes, adapted to modern conditions of sea life, are taking their place.

The papers published by the missionary societies laboring among seamen are an important factor in the work, helping to carry the Gospel afloat. The oldest paper in the world for seamen is the *Sailors' Magazine and Seamen's Friend*, in its eighty-second year, published by the American Seamen's Friend Society, 76 Wall Street, New York, which society also publishes the *Life Boat*, devoted to creating marine interests in the Sunday-schools of America. The *Chart and Compass* is published by the British and Foreign Sailors' Society, London England; *The Word on the Waters* is the organ of the English Church's society; *Sea Breeze* is issued in furthering the interests of the Boston Seamen's Friend Society, Boston, Mass.; *Toilers of the Deep* is sent out by Royal Missions to Deep Sea Fishermen, London, England; *Ashore and Afloat*, edited by Miss Weston of Portsmouth, England, is circulated in the British and American Navies. *Blätter für Seemans-Mission* is published at Berlin.

Since the Spanish-American War the Young Men's Christian Association in America has devoted considerable energy and money to promoting the standards and principles of that organization among the men of the United States navy, thus leaving the societies engaged in welfare work for seamen to concentrate their energies on the merchant marine, a class of men numbering three millions and a half of all nationalities.

The Seamen's Christian Brotherhood, an organization for Christian seamen, was started at an international conference of seamen's chaplains, held under the auspices of the American Seamen's Friend Society in 1908. In two years it spread into the ports of twelve different countries and promises to be of significance and spiritual worth to seamen. Its flag is a star, cross, and crown on a blue ground. Wherever a chapter of the organization is formed, ashore or afloat, the flag is hoisted on Sunday. The missionary movement on behalf of seamen held aloof from work of a social nature until the last decade when a healthy and conservative movement set in, recognizing the physical and social needs of seamen, resulting in a changed method of work which attracts all classes of seamen, the irreligious as well as the religious.

GEORGE MCPHERSON HUNTER.

BIBLIOGRAPHY: T. C. Garland, *Leaves from my Log of Christian Work among Sailors*, London, 1882; *The Word on the Waters. Quarterly Record of Mission Effort amongst Sailors*, London, 1859 sqq.; A. Gordon, *What Cheer O! The Mission to Deep Sea Fishermen*, London, 1890; T. S. Treanor, *The Log of a Sky Pilot*, London, 1893; S. G. Wintz, *Our Blue Jackets. Miss Weston's Life and Work*, London, 1894; M. Mac Lean, *Seafarers from the Land of the Rising Sun in London*, London, 1896; J. Slater, *The East in the West; or, Work among the Asiatics and Africans in London*, ib., 1896; H. Dalton, *Deutsche Seemannsmission*, Berlin, 1897; O. Strecker, *Die Geschichte der . . . verbundenen lutherischen Vereinen für innere Mission getriebenen kirchlichen Versorgung deutscher Seeleute*, Hanover, 1899; F. T. Bullen, *With Christ in Sailor Town*, London, 1901; idem, *With Christ at Sea*, New York, 1901; idem, *A Sailor Apostle*, ib. 1903; M. L. Walrond, *Launching out into the Deep. The Missions to Seamen*, London, 1904; N. Duncan, *Dr. Grenfell's Parish. The Deep Sea Fishermen*, London, 1905; R. Münchmeyer, *In d. Fremde. Einige Zeugnisse aus der Auslandsarbeit*, Marburg, 1905; and the *Reports* of the various societies named in the text.

SEARLE, sōrl, **JOHN PRESTON**: Reformed; b. at Schuylerville, N. Y., Sept. 12, 1854. He was graduated from Rutgers College (A.B., 1875) and New Brunswick Theological Seminary (1878); was ordained (1878), and after holding pastorates at Griggstown, N. J. (1878–81), and the First Reformed Church, Somerville, N. J. (1881–93), he was appointed in 1893 to his present position of professor of systematic theology at the New Brunswick Theological Seminary. He has also been president of the faculty of the same institution since 1902. He is vice-president of the Board of Foreign Missions of his denomination, and is the author of a number of sermons, addresses, and contributions to religious periodicals.

SEARS, sīrs, **BARNAS**: Baptist educator; b. at Sandisfield, Mass., Nov. 19, 1802; d. at Saratoga Springs, N. Y., July 6, 1880. He was graduated from Brown University in 1825; and from Newton Theological Seminary in 1828; was pastor at Hartford, Conn., 1829–31; professor of ancient languages in Hamilton (N. Y.) Literary and Theological Institution, now Madison University, 1831–33; and pastor at the same time at Hamilton. He studied at Halle, Leipsic, and Berlin, 1833–35, and in 1834 baptized J. G. Oncken and six others, forming the first German Baptist Church in communion with the Baptists of England and America. He returned to Hamilton in 1835; was professor of theology in Newton Theological Seminary, 1836–48; and president, 1837–48. For several years he was the editor of the *Christian Review*. He was president of Brown University, 1855–67; and general agent of the Peabody Educational Fund, with residence at Staunton, Va., 1867–80. He published a *Life of Luther* (Philadelphia, 1850), and an edition of P. M. Roget's *Thesaurus* (Boston, 1854).

SEARS, EDMUND HAMILTON: B. at Sandisfield, Mass., Apr. 6, 1810; d. at Weston, Mass., Jan. 14, 1876; was graduated from Union College, 1834; and from Cambridge Divinity School, 1837; was pastor of Unitarian societies at Wayland, Mass., 1839–40 and 1847–65; at Lancaster, Mass., 1840–47; and at Weston, 1865–76. Though connected with the Unitarian body, he held Swedenborgian opinions, and often professed his belief in the absolute divinity of Christ. He wrote largely for the *Monthly Religious Magazine*, of which he was joint-editor, 1859–71. He published *Regeneration* (Boston, 1853), *Pictures of the Olden Time* (1857), *Athanasia, or*

Foregleams of Immortality (1858), *The Fourth Gospel the Heart of Christ* (1872), and *Sermons and Songs* (1875). His writings are noted for their great spiritual power and beauty; he wrote also two exquisite Christmas-hymns, "Calm on the listening ear of night," and "It came upon the midnight clear" (1834 and 1849 or 1850).

Bibliography: S. W. Duffield, *English Hymns*, pp. 264–265, New York, 1886; Julian, *Hymnology*, p. 1036.

SEBA. See Table of the Nations, § 6.

SEBASTIAN, se-bas'ti-an or bast'yun: Saint and martyr; patron of archers, and formerly invoked to avert pestilence; martyred at Rome. Ambrose (*MPL,* xiv. 1497) states that Sebastian was born at Milan and suffered martyrdom at Rome; and it is also certain that he suffered martyrdom on Jan. 20 of an unknown year (305?). These few facts are all that are certainly known concerning him. The Acts of St. Sebastian (*ASB*, Jan., ii. 265–278) contains, besides many miracles and conversions, such a mass of historical inconsistencies that, even though probably written in the early part of the fifth century, they can not be regarded as original documents. Three data in the life of the saint, however, were from an early period regarded as authentic. His martyrdom was fixed in the first reign of Diocletian; he was an officer of the imperial bodyguard; and he was shot with arrows in the Colosseum. These three statements are derived from the forged Acts. That he fell a victim to the great Diocletian persecution of 303 sqq., as the Acts state, is merely a conjecture not wholly devoid of plausibility; but the so-called *Depositio martyrum* of the Chronicle of Liberius affirms that St. Sebastian was buried in the catacombs on Jan. 20, 354. Again, Roman criminal law did not prescribe execution by shooting with arrows as a death penalty for Christians, the punishments in question being decapitation, crucifixion, fighting with wild beasts, or death by burning or scourging.

A mosaic picture of the saint, dating from about 682, is preserved in the church of San Pietro in Vincoli. It represents St. Sebastian, not, as in Renaissance art, as naked and young, but as a bearded man of adult age, with a long mantle, the fine raiment of a courtier, a nimbus, and a diadem in his right hand. No representation of the martyrdom is known from the first six centuries; nor does even this earliest portrait contain any trace of an arrow to symbolize the supposed manner of St. Sebastian's death.

(Franz Görres.)

Bibliography: Documents other than the *Acta* are published in *MGH, Script.*, xv. 1 (1887), 379–391, 2 (1888), 771–773; *ASM*, iv. 1, pp. 383–410; and the fragment of the Sebastian saga by C. R. Unger in *Heilagra Manna Sögur*, ii. 228–235, Christiania, 1877. Consult further: J. C. F. Bähr, *Geschichte der römischen Literatur im karolingischen Zeitalter*, p. 259, Carlsruhe, 1840; P. J. Chapusot, *Notice sur la vie de S. Sébastien et sur la rélique . . . conservée dans l'église de Chalons*, Châlons-sur-Marne, 1863; J. M. Trichaud, *La Légende de S. Sébastien*, Marseilles, 1872; F. X. Kraus, *Roma Sotterranea*, pp. 119, 133,181, 518, Freiburg, 1879; F. Görres, in *ZWT*, xxiii (1880), 31–64, 165–197; idem, in *JPT*, xiii. 511–518; P. Allard, *La Persécution de Dioclétien*, i. 131–132, Paris, 1890; V. Cocchi, *Memorie di S. Sebastiano*, Frosinone, 1892; *DCB*, iv. 593.

SEBASTOS CYMINETES: Greek Orthodox theologian; b. at Cymina, near Trebizond, 1630; d. at Trebizond Sept. 6, 1702. He was apparently educated in his native country, and in 1671 became the head of the Greek patriarchal school in Constantinople. Later he assumed a like position at Trebizond, where he spent the remainder of his life. He energetically opposed the entrance of Western theology into the Greek Orthodox Church. Only a few of his many works have appeared in print, among them being the *Heortologion* (Bucharest, 1701) and especially the posthumous *Dogmatike didaskalia* (1703). The latter consists of three parts: "When the elements are changed into the body and blood of Christ; that the Virgin was subject to original sin; that the 'parts' are not changed into the body and blood of Christ." Some of the work was obviously not written by Sebastos, a portion being ascribed by Sathas to the patriarch Dositheos. In his work Sebastos maintains that the elements are transformed through the Epiklesis (q.v.), as the Orthodox liturgy teaches, but that the "parts" are not changed; he holds that the Virgin was born in sin, but was delivered from original sin through the annunciation, as Christians are freed through baptism.

Sebastos again discussed the Eucharistic controversy in a long letter to Chrysanthos, later patriarch of Jerusalem ("True Church," I., ii. 245 sqq., 253 sqq.; cf. viii. 92). His philosophical writings are devoted to the dissemination of ecclesiastical Aristotelianism.

(Philipp Meyer.)

Bibliography: Fabricius-Harles, *Bibliotheca Græca*, xi. 531, 634, Hamburg, 1808; F. Kattenbusch, *Lehrbuch der vergleichenden Confessionskunde*, ii. 413–414, Freiburg, 1892; É. Legrand, *Bibliographie hellénique*, iii. 47, 62, Paris, 1895.

SECESSION CHURCH. See Presbyterians, I., 2, 3, 6.

SECESSION CHURCH IN IRELAND. See Presbyterians, III., 3.

SECESSION CHURCH OF SCOTLAND, UNITED ORIGINAL. See Presbyterians I., § 6.

SECKENDORF, sek'en-dōrf, **VEIT LUDWIG VON:** German Lutheran statesman and scholar; b. at Herzogenaurach (6 m. s.w. of Erlangen) Dec. 20, 1626; d. at Halle Dec. 18, 1692. He was educated at the University of Strasburg (1642–45); after which he was appointed page to Duke Ernest the Pious, his duties being to supervise the library, to draw useful and interesting material from designated books, and to communicate the results to the duke, a task which laid the basis for his own writings. In 1648 Seckendorf was made gentleman of the bedchamber, and in 1652 court councilor and councilor of justice. Three years later as privy court councilor and councilor of the board of domains he rendered important service in regulating the finances of the country and in a number of diplomatic affairs. In 1664 Duke Ernest made him chancellor, but in the same year he entered the service of Maurice, duke of Saxony-Zeitz, as chancellor and president of the consistory. These positions he held, in spite of many jealous attacks, until the death of Maurice in 1681. Still retaining his position as district director at Altenburg, Seckendorf now found time and leisure to indulge his literary tastes. His interest became more and more concentrated on the problem of the value and essence of practical Christianity, and he thus became closely associated with such men as Philipp Jakob Spener, whom he had called to Dresden. Seckendorf could scarcely be called a Pietist, though he defended Spener in his *Bericht und Erinnerungen auf eine neulich im Druck lateinisch und deutsch ausgestreute Schrift Imago pietatis* (Halle, 1692), after having translated into Latin Spener's Frankfort sermons of 1677 under the title *Capita doctrinæ et praxis Christianæ insignia* (1689). The qualities of Pietism which attracted Seckendorf were its moral earnestness and its emphasis upon practical Christianity, though his critical nature kept him from sympathy with Pietistic mysticism. But in the evening of his life he was again drawn into the movement when, on Sept. 9, 1692, Elector Frederick III. of Brandenburg appointed him chancellor of the newly founded University of Halle. On Oct. 31 Seckendorf entered upon his duties, where the difficult task awaited him of reconciling the controversy between Francke and the clergy of Halle. A few weeks later he died.

Despite his manifold official activity, Seckendorf found time at Gotha for a series of writings, such as the *Justitia protectionis in civitate Erfurtensi* (1663), *Repetita et necessaria defensio justæ protectionis Saxonicæ in civitate Erfurtensi* (1664), and the *Compendium historiæ ecclesiasticæ . . . in usum gymnasii Gothani* (Leipsic, 1666). During this period he likewise wrote his *Teutscher Fürsten Stat* (Hanau, 1656), followed by the *Christen Stat* (1685). The latter work, influenced largely, especially in the first part, by the *Pensées* of Pascal, was partly an apologetic directed against atheism, and partly reformatory in purpose.

The work on which Seckendorf's fame rests, however, is his *Commentarius historicus et apologeticus de Lutheranismo seu de reformatione* (Leipsic, 1688–92). The work was essentially a refutation of the *Histoire du Luthéranisme* of the Jesuit L. Maimbourg (Paris, 1680), of which Seckendorf made a partial Latin translation, with a *Dissertatio historica et apologetica pro doctrina D. Lutheri de missa* to serve as a sort of preliminary work (Jena, 1686). For his *Commentarius* Seckendorf, as the trusted friend of all the Saxon princes, had access to original documents to a degree enjoyed by no later scholar, and a mass of sources, both manuscript and printed, hitherto unutilized, were also sent him, thus enhancing his wealth of material. His method is to give, paragraph by paragraph, Maimbourg's presentation in Latin translation, with a refutation from original sources, pertinent *additiones*, often of considerable length, being appended. The *Commentarius* is, therefore, not a uniform artistic presentation, but is still an indispensable source for every historian of the Reformation because of its wealth of material. (T. Kolde.)

Bibliography: The funeral sermon by J. J. Breithaupt was published at Zeitz, 1693, and a memorial address by C. Thomasius in his *Kleine Schriften*, no. XIII., p. 497 sqq., Halle, 1721. Consult further: R. Pahner, *Veit Ludwig von Seckendorf und seine Gedanken über Erziehung und Unterricht*, Leipsic, 1892; D. G. Schreber, *Historia . . . Viti Ludovici a Seckendorf*, ib. 1733; J. V. von Ludewig, *Oekonomische Anmerkungen über Seckendorfs Fürstenstaat*, Frankfort, 1753; A. Beck, *Ernst der Fromme*, 2 vols., Weimar, 1865; W. Schrader, *Geschichte der Friedrichs-Universität zu Halle*, vol. i., Berlin, 1894.

SECKER, seck'er, THOMAS: Church of England; b. at Sibthorpe, Nottinghamshire, 1693; d. at London, Aug. 3, 1768. He was graduated at Leyden (M.D., 1721); then entered Exeter College, Oxford; was ordained priest, 1723; rector of Houghton-le-Spring, 1724; of St. James's, Westminster, 1733; appointed chaplain to the king, 1732; consecrated bishop of Bristol, 1735; was transferred to Oxford, 1737; and in addition was installed dean of St. Paul's, 1750; and was archbishop of Canterbury, 1758–68. Secker was a remarkable instance of the orthodox eighteenth-century prelate, assumed a lively interest in the questions of his time, and possessed a fund of knowledge wide and deep. His *Works* were collected, twelve vols., London, 1770, with a *Review of his Life and Character* by B. Porteus.

Bibliography: Consult, besides the sketch by Porteus, ut sup.: J. H. Overton and F. Relton, *The English Church (1714–1800)*, passim, London, 1906; *DNB*, li. 170–173.

SECOND ADVENT.

The belief in the second coming of Christ can be understood only as presented in a coherent historical outline. The eschatology of the Old Testament and, in its main ideas, of the Jewish apocalyptical literature, is concerned with the confident assurance that God's rule must finally prevail. The concrete forms of this hope vary with the conception of the universe and the horizon of religious interests.

1. The Old Testament.

The prophetic hope, especially of the more remote period, casts its pictures on the background of this world, with the predominant interest in Jerusalem and Israel. The Day of Yahweh (see Day of the Lord) must come, which will free God's people from unjust oppression and bring judgment on the enemy (Ob. 15; Isa. xiii. 6 sqq.). At first this was not conceived as a single decisive epoch, but as a day of visitation upon a particular enemy, which might be multiplied (cf. Jer. xlvi. 10). The view was gradually extended so as to include not only the neighboring peoples but all nations. With this, real eschatological elements are approximated, with at least a suggestion of transcendental tendency. Only the righteous nation shall be saved, from whom sinners shall be separated, leaving only a "remnant" (Isa. i. 27, iv. 3). Whoever will call upon Yahweh shall be saved, and for this the grace of God provides beforehand (Mal. iii. 1 sqq.), in which the personal and eternal relation to God appears as the essential, working itself out of the historical situation. That the scene, however, is mundane shows itself in the narrower idea of the Messianic hope. The Messiah is never the judge of the world but the king awakened and enthroned by God, and he shall lead his people to victory and rule over them in justice and peace (Jer. xxx. 9; Isa. ix. 6-7). God shall be present with his people and sin and evil shall vanish. This shows a tendency toward transcendence, although Zion is yet in this world (Isa. ii. 2, iv. 5). There is to be no world cataclysm and renewal, although there shall be signs and wonders. No universal resurrection is implied, the passages so taken merely representing additions (Isa. xxvi. 19; Dan. xii. 2), as well as that expressing a unique expectation of a new heaven and a new earth (Isa. lxv. 17 sqq., lxvi. 22). The average consciousness in the Old Testament implies no dual theory, no dual world; hence no ground for a dual Messianic revelation.

2. Jewish Apocrypha and Apocalypses.

A decided change first appeared in the century before the birth of Christ. More and more distinctly the apocryphal and apocalyptical literature created a transcendent picture of the end of the world, until the rabbinical writings after Christ produced a finished system of eschatology. As the older earthly hopes for Israel and Jerusalem continue, an ellipse, so to speak, with two foci appears; one is the center of a group of Messianic expectations here, the other of more strictly deduced new transcendent and more individualistic ideas. This led ultimately to a double revelation, parallel to the Christian view. The judging of the nations appears according to the older prophetic style. The Messiah shall redeem Israel, and as judge shall punish, and be king after God's own heart. The New Jerusalem shall be created by God and transferred from preexistence into the world; yet it has a mundane character, and its inhabitants have not eternal but long and peaceful life. Above all this is erected a transcendent world, not only by the later apocalypses, which, surpassing the Book of Daniel, employed themselves with the background of an earthly history and the conflicts of a spirit world, not only at a later stage, by identifying the Messiah with the Son of Man of Daniel and regarding him as a preexistent Being; but in early times, the claims of an individual personality appear alongside of the national Messianic hope. The hope of a common blessedness in this world is transferred to another, after death, involving the individual resurrection of the just for life eternal. Two eons are recognized, separated by the day of Yahweh, which after a universal resurrection shall determine the deserving fate of the blessed and the damned. Beyond is a new heaven and a new earth. The individual interest, not content with the transcendent blessedness of the single personality, regains coalescence with history and totality. Yet the picture is variously shortened by particularisms: redemption is not universal like that of Joel and the New Testament; the saved are to be at most the Jews only "in this country"; the Messiah gains no universal significance and has no place in the final judgment, except in the Book of Enoch, where the Son of Man ascends the throne in glory and chooses among men. This, however, was the result of Christian influence. According to IV Esdras vii. 28 sqq. the Messiah dies, after reigning 400 years, together with all men. Then the new eon opens with resurrection and judgment, paradise and gehenna. The tendency was generally to restrict the function of the Messiah in this world and dilate upon the eon of the next world at the termination of the Messianic period, in which eon the Messiah has no longer any part.

It was otherwise in Christianity. The dual conception of the universe was assumed; the division between the "the present eon" and the "eon to come" is the inseparable assumption of Christian thought (Matt. xii. 32; Luke xvi. 8).

3. New Testament.

But the Old Testament's Messianic idea, which served to give value to the personality of Jesus, is employed in undiminished force with reference to the final goal beyond. The inheritance of the Old Testament is clothed in apocalyptic transcendental form. The Messiah does not perform an earthly work, which can not be transferred to the beyond, but reveals in his person the personality of the Father. The basis of salvation hence is not membership in the nation from which the Messiah is descended, but personal relationship to the Messiah, who gathers about him his nation of believers. The mother of the Christians is no longer an earthly Jerusalem, but that city above which is identical with the congregation of the perfect (Gal. iv. 26). The personality of Jesus acquires eternal significance; those who belong to him belong for time and eternity to God.

4. The Twofold Conception.

The central position of the personality of Christ leads to the conception of a double Messianic revelation, the end of which, however, is not, as in the Jewish apocalyptic system of thought, an exaltation of the kingdom of the Messiah, first established upon earth, into the heavenly world, but a return of Christ from the kingdom beyond into the midst of conceivable reality. For no earthly Messianic kingdom was established at the first coming of Christ. On the contrary, he was rejected by his people. If he is nevertheless to remain the Messiah, the basis of his kingdom must be a transcendent one, centering in himself as a personality secured in God, and conserving other personality with his own. Jesus himself certainly lays claim to an actual reign. He will come as the Son of Man in the clouds and will establish the kingdom which shall absolve all earthly kingdoms (Mark xiii. 26, xiv. 62). But the same title is used of him in expressions that declare that Jesus is homeless upon the earth, that he sows only for the future, that he suffers in order to rise hereafter, that he serves in order to give his life as a sacrifice for sin, that his authority upon the earth is to forgive sins, and that he has come to seek the lost (Mark ii. 10, viii. 31, x. 45). Thus the purely personal character of the Messiahship of Jesus is harmonized with the apocalyptic transcendental plan. Personalities constitute the materials of the transcendent structure of which the personality of Christ is the cornerstone (Mark xii. 10; Eph. ii. 20 sqq.). The resurrection of Jesus was not that coming again; for he appeared personally only to the disciples and later exists in spiritual continuity. For Israel and the world, there began another period of waiting, during which the words of his witnesses are at work bringing about repentance and faith.

Those that surrender themselves to him he includes in his unseen fellowship, so that, although they live in the flesh, they no longer essentially belong to the present world (Gal. i. 4). They are, by virtue of their membership in the body of the living Christ, though in the world not of the world, but translated into eternity (John xvii. 11, 14 sqq.; Eph. ii. 2, 5 sqq.). Such expressions as these are not meant figuratively in the New Testament, but serve to describe an unseen reality which is future in so far as it has not yet entered the domain of tangible appearance, but is present in so far as it exists behind the visible world and is accessible to faith. The only thing yet looked for is the episode transforming the mystical fellowship of the Head and members into the actual. This will result in Christ's return designated as *parousia* (Matt. xxiv. 3, 37, 39); or *erchetai*, "he cometh" (Mark xiii. 26; Rev. i. 7, xxii. 7, 20); but, from an earthly viewpoint better expressed as a "revelation," "coming," or "appearance" (Luke xvii. 30; I Cor. i. 7).

5. Compounded in the New Testament. As evidence how inseparably associated with New-Testament faith the expectation that Christ must, from his focus of the redemption of souls, carry it out to its utmost consequences, stands the fact that in all the varying doctrinal types of the New Testament, the blessing of salvation is everywhere described as present and future. The "salvation" of the primitive apostolic mode of expression is to be realized at the return of Christ, but for the "saved" (Acts ii. 47) it is a reality dominating present life, since it is guaranteed by the Spirit and by personal relation to the exalted Christ (ii. 38; I Pet. iii. 21). The Johannine "eternal life" is certainly a present possession, but instead of being conceived as immanent it is to await its perfection and reduction to form in the future (John xvii. 3, vi. 40). As certainly as Paul's experience of justification forms the present and actual basis of the Christian life of faith so certainly is it adapted to eschatological conception. "Justification" is awaited as an acquittal in the final judgment (Gal. v. 5; Rom. viii. 30). It is a "giving of life" (Gal. iii. 21), the operative assurance of the favorable outcome of the final judgment. Salvation is by hope (Rom. viii. 24); so also adoption is partly a future reality (Gal. iv. 5; Rom. viii. 15). The eschatological element comes forward no less in the thoughts of Jesus on the kingdom. However, he who accepts it in the present is received within its secure protection (Mark x. 15). The perfected kingdom is identical with the future world; it is a "kingdom of heaven." As the future world, according to the apocalyptic view, opens with the appearance of the Messiah, so also the kingdom of God on earth is at hand when the Messiah appears; the King is the kingdom. The force of Luke xvii. 20 is to rebuke the manner of judging by signs and seasons, and does not negate the main point of receiving the present revelation of the kingdom in order to gain admission to its complete future development. Already evidences appear. The power of Jesus over demons demonstrates that he has wrested the dominion of the world absolutely from Satan (Matt. xii. 28–29). His own are now concealed in the community of the kingdom (Col. i. 13); its complete realization is only a matter of time. The reign of God which shall come with power, contrasted with its first weak appearing (Mark ix. 1), is only its unfolding, just as Christ who as the Son of God was established with power seems, but was not, a contradiction of the Christ crucified (Rom. i. 4).

The significance of the parousia consists in finally bringing about this transformation; the surviving tension between center and circumference is removed. A complete termination of earthly history is expected. The Son of Man unrecognized on earth shall appear again unmistakably in a glory that shall bring terror to his enemies and perfect redemption to his faithful (Matt. xxiv. 27, 30). The offenses shall be removed from his kingdom, and the chosen shall be gathered and reunited into an eternal community of glory (Matt. xiii. 31, 40, 49 sqq.). History, however, must first be fulfilled to the extent that the Gospel shall be preached to all nations (Matt. xxiv. 14). The preaching of the Gospel serves only as a testimony; the final deliverance will appear no more as developing out of humanity than the first, but as an act of God entering from without. The coming of the Son of Man is cataclysmic. The human race of all periods of history shall be summoned for judgment. The belief in a general resurrection of the dead is implied with this expectation (John v. 29; Rev. xx. 11 sqq.). The appearance of Christ as judge of the world is a step beyond Jewish apocalyptic literature. In the New Testament he has become the representative of God on earth, not in an incidental matter but to actualize in history and person God's revelation of grace. Apart from all metaphysical statements, the "power" of Jesus is adequate to forgive sins, to establish the basis for the coming judgment (Mark ii. 10). Standing at the center of humanity whence access to God is only through him, the fate of every individual rests on him. Its consummation is postponed to the end of the world in agreement with the history of Christian faith, inseparable as it is from transcendence. If Jesus is the expression of the purpose of God in the history of revelation, then his personality as Savior and Judge must also stand at the goal of this history (Matt. xi. 27, xxvi. 64). The day of Yahweh becomes the day of Jesus Christ (I Cor. i. 8, v. 5), and Christ's seat of judgment is that of God (II Cor. v. 10; Rom. xiv. 10).

6. The Parousia.

For believers the significance of the parousia lies in the consummation of that which they already possess within themselves; after the salvation of the soul comes the complete salvation of the body (I Cor. xv. 43 sqq.). Even impersonal creation, as the scene of redeemed humanity, shares in the transformation. A new heaven and a new earth in which all contradiction between inner and outer is overcome appears in place of the old (Rev. xxi. 1). Not a nebulous ideal world is pictured, but the new Jerusalem coming down from heaven has all the characteristics of reality, though without the elements of the earthy (xxi. 2).

Whether these thoughts on the second advent necessarily fit together harmoniously from the given premises or are the result of wilful systematizing must be determined by the answer given to two questions: Did Jesus himself actually have in mind his coming again to judge the world? Is the hope for his return one of the inalienable elements of Christian faith? The literature of the New Testament appears without exception controlled by the apocalyptic eschatological expectation that Jesus as the Christ will some time terminate the history of the world, and open the new world of God for the reception of his followers. There appears, in place of the fantastic apocalyptic "watching," just as clearly the idea of a present fellowship with Christ which guarantees to faith the attainment of its goal. Who is the author of this grand conception? Jesus or Paul? Is this a theological speculation, or rather a comprehensive expression of the belief in the religiously understood and yet in reality world-ruling Messiahship of Jesus? If the latter, then the outcome of the historical judgment will depend upon the justification of this belief. Whoever does this will not assume that Jesus used the name of Messiah uncertainly and sustained himself inwardly in his sufferings with a vague hope of returning; but the religious Messianic faith of the New Testament, instead of indulging a meaningless return, involves the claim to the judgment of the world. W. Bousset's assertion, that the faith of the Church pushed the self-assumed position of Jesus as a witness in the divine judgment gradually forward to a world-judgment, rests merely upon an unproved presupposition that Jesus disavowed himself as the judge of the world. The prevailing critical assertion that a finished little apocalypse was inserted with the discourse of Jesus in Mark xiii. would be valid proof against the origin from Jesus of that apocalypse pertaining to the parousia. If, in addition, the authentic literature on the life of Jesus be restricted to the Gospel of Mark, it would be easy to interpret from the few remaining passages the consciousness of a mere witness in the divine judgment and the triumph of his person and kingdom in history (Mark viii. 38, xiv. 62 sqq.). However, the theory of a little apocalypse would also be of historical value only if Jewish origin could be assumed, but, in general, it is of a specifically Christian character, placing the figure of Jesus prominently at the center of the transcendent expectations. The decision of the matter lies deeper than with mere critical literary research. It appears that various critics would assent to only one side of the twofold problem they face, particularly those who would segregate, in the consciousness of Jesus, the eschatological elements from his person. Jesus would thereby be isolated in a position inconceivable to human perception; the Jewish and Christian contemporaneous literature would be filled with apocalyptic hopes, while the faith of Jesus without discriminating emphasis would have contented itself with the other world, resurrection, judgment, and the kingdom of God, in general. Similarly, but creating less disorder in the historical situation, is the theory of the "eschatological school" said to have been left behind by Jesus, which claims that every statement of the Evangelists concerning the presence of the kingdom is an intrusion of rabbinical representation. As to the truth of the matter itself, this is supposed, on many sides, to be resolved by the ignorance of Jesus concerning the nearness of the time. As truly as a change occurs in Paul's idea of the nearness (II Thess. iv. 17; II Cor. v. 2 sqq.), a historical view may not assume that Jesus announced his return in the following generation. No words are so well authenticated as the statement that he knew neither the day nor the hour (Mark xiii. 32). Is this to refer to the particular moment, while as the general extension, the immediate future is self-evidently fixed? But the events pronounced under the woes, particularly the appearing of many false messiahs, and the preaching of the Gospel to all the nations, necessarily imply a longer development and thoughts of a community of the kingdom on earth. This being so, then the words relating to a personal return of Jesus are to be taken as pointing to the destruction of Jerusalem (Matt. x. 23, xvi. 28). Even if the mistaken formulation of these words effected in the community a wide-spread belief in the near approach of the end (John xxi. 23; II Thess. ii. 2); and this belief gave rise, in the account, to the close temporal approximation of the judgment of the people of God and the universal judgment of the human race, although only inwardly associated by Jesus, yet the distinction of the two acts is unmistakably present throughout.

7. The Consciousness of Jesus.

For the positive estimation of the belief in the second coming no clear direction can be given. It all depends on the attitude taken with reference to the authority of Jesus and the personal needs seeking satisfaction in the truths of Christian faith. A mere regulative idea to act as an ethical incentive would be indifferent to eschatological hopes. This position, especially prominent from Kant to Schleiermacher and Ritschl, results more and more in the divergence of individual immortality and the consummation of society. The chief interest, according to Ritschl, accrues to the kingdom of God, unfolding upon an earthly basis, as the end or ideal common to God and his chosen religious community, which, rising above the natural limitations of ethnic distinctions, advances to the ethical unity of all the peoples. Whether this involves merely a constant ideal hovering before, or a real historical goal, is nowhere made distinct; but if the latter, there is no light thrown upon the relation in which the individuals departing previously from history stand with reference to the common goal. These projects rule the newer theology so far as it, not without candor, applies itself to a philosophy of the world, as well as to the religion of Jesus and the Apostles. For the modern attitude, resting on the basis of an empirical world, the acme of thought is a personal society, realized, with the conquest of purely natural motives, in ethical ends. Timidly and insecurely the consequence is scarcely ventured upon that this kingdom of God may be in full reality the goal of historical evolution subserved also by the natural world. The result is scarcely more than an idealistic self-reflection. In fact all ideas are enlisted in the scheme of the immovable con-

8. Practical Estimation.

trast of nature and spirit. Personal spiritual exertions have the value of preserving from absorption in mere nature, but not the promise of ever becoming reality in the historical sense. Individual postulates reaching over into transcendent realization are possible, but not a consistent, sustaining certainty. On the contrary the incomparable power of the unconstricted New-Testament faith which unites the apocalyptic assurance of actual consummation with the interest in personalities is assured in God and in their community. The combination of the certainty of the beyond with the positive worth of personality constitutes the sure ground of life for believers. This certainty is guaranteed through the purely personal activity and experience of Christ who possessed in this world, which rejected him, nothing but his personality assured in God, but departing with this possession inwardly triumphant to open the outward victory by the resurrection, to assemble his own to his exalted activity, and to raise them in unity with himself as head to God in the other world, and, finally, in his last revelation, to extend the ultimate consequences of the reign of God over the world and his society of the kingdom. The certainty of redemption includes this hope as an essential element, and the conviction that the disappearance of one would mean the loss of entire certainty of redemption engirdling real life, is proof that this subsists not on illusions. Meantime, a self-reliant faith has no occasion to indulge the utilization of phenomenal expressions presuming to be "realistic," the forms thence available for the description of transcendent realities being obtained from the hither world only. Most significant, however, for the ethical judgment of the world by the Christian and his attitude therein is an earnest belief in the return of Jesus and in the world-comprehending transcendent consummation of his kingdom. From the point of view of the kingdom of God as the "Father's house" for redeemed personalities assembled in eternity, the purely contingent state of life is judged as mere scenery, "for the fashion of this world passes away" (I Cor. vii. 31). Therefore the Christian emulates not things in the course of this life but persons, not culture but Evangelization. He also does not look for an uninterrupted ethical evolution; all attempts in this direction, which are to be prosecuted because the kingdom of God aims to comprehend all life as one, are ever doomed to violent interruption, so long as the world of sin will stand, in which a progressive revelation of light calls forth a corresponding revelation of darkness. No Church in its outward aspect and no Christian state is therefore an immediate vestibule of the perfect kingdom; on earth there can be only folds to guard the members of Christ mingling with other elements, until his appearing, and with him that of the saints hitherto scattered throughout all history, as the everlasting community.

(E. F. KARL MÜLLER.)

BIBLIOGRAPHY: For the doctrine as found in the Bible consult the literature in and under BIBLICAL THEOLOGY (especially the works by Duhm, Smend, Dillmann, Bennett, Davidson, Toy, and Schultz for the O. T.; and by Beyschlag, Adeney, Holtzmann, Stevens, and Gould for the N. T.); DAY OF THE LORD; and under ESCHATOLOGY. For the doctrine in the apocryphal and pseudepigraphi literature consult the works under MESSIAH, MESSIANISM (especially those by Briggs, Orelli, Stanton, and Woods), and under PSEUDEPIGRAPHA (especially those by Charles, and Drummond). Consult further: W. Burgh, *Lectures on the Second Advent of our Lord Jesus Christ*, 4th ed., London, 1845; D. Brown, *Christ's Second Coming; Will it be Premillennial?* ib. 1846; S. Lee, *Eschatology; or the Scripture Doctrine of the Coming of our Lord*, Boston, 1858; D. N. Lord, *The Coming and Reign of Christ*, New York, 1858; J. Berg, *The Second Advent of Jesus Christ not Premillennial*, Philadelphia, 1859; E. Luthardt, *Die Lehre von den letzten Dingen*, Leipsic, 1861; J. F. Demarest and W. R. Gordon, *Christocracy; or, Essays on the Coming and Kingdom of Christ*, New York, 1867; J. Grant, *The End of All Things; or, the Coming and Kingdom of Christ*, 3 series, London, 1866–67; W. Weiffenbach, *Der Wiederkunftsgedanke Jesu*, Leipsic, 1873; S. M. Merrill, *The Second Coming of Christ Considered in its Relation to the Millennium, the Resurrection, and Judgment*, Cincinnati, 1879; S. Davidson, *Doctrine of the Last Things*, London, 1882; G. N. H. Peters, *The Theocratic Kingdom of our Lord Jesus Christ, as covenanted in the O. T. and presented in the N. T.*, New York, 1885; J. C. Rankin, *The Coming of the Lord*, ib. 1885; R. N. Burns, *When will Christ Come?* Toronto, 1886; W. Kelly, *Lectures on the Second Coming and Kingdom of the Lord and Saviour Jesus Christ*, London, 1886; T. Kliefoth, *Christliche Eschatologie*, Leipsic, 1886; J. S. Russell, *The Parousia: a critical Inquiry into the New Testament Doctrine of our Lord's Second Coming*, London, 1887; N. West, *Studies in Eschatology; or, thousand Years in both Testaments*, New York, 1889; C. A. Briggs, *The Messiah of the Gospels*, New York, 1894; idem, *The Messiah of the Apostles*, ib. 1895; H. Dieckmann, *Die Parusie Christi*, Geestemünde, 1898; R. H. Charles, *Doctrine of a Future Life in Israel, in Judaism, and in Christianity*, London, 1899; J. Weiss, *Die Predigt Jesu vom Reiche Gottes*, Göttingen, 1900; E. Cremer, *Die Wiederkunft Christi und die Aufgabe der Kirche*, Gütersloh, 1902; P. Pols, *Jüdische Eschatologie*, Leipsic, 1903; W. Rheinland (F. W. Stuckert), *Das Kommen des Herrn*, 8th ed., Neumünster, 1904; W. Bousset, *Die Religion des Judentums im neutestamentlichen Zeitalter*, Berlin, 1906; S. Modalski, *Jesu Wiederkunft*, Breklum, 1907; M. Kähler, *Angewandte Dogmen*, pp. 487 sqq., Leipsic, 1908; F. Tillmann, *Die Wiederkunft Christi nach den paulinischen Briefen*, Freiburg, 1909; A. D. Fairbanks, *Christ's Second Coming*, Boston, 1910; Schürer, *Geschichte*, ii. 496 sqq., Eng. transl., II., i. 126 sqq. (gives a good list of literature); *DB*, i. 741–757. The subject is discussed also in the works on systematic theology (see DOGMA, DOGMATICS).

SECRECY OF THE CONFESSIONAL: When, in the early Middle Ages, the discipline of auricular confession prevailed in the Church, the obligation of absolute secrecy on the part of the confessor followed as a necessary consequence. The secret of the confessional partakes of the nature of the ordinary secret called professional, e.g., that of the lawyer with respect to his client, or of the physician toward his patient, and adds thereto a special religious obligation resulting from the sacramental character of the confession. This obligation, often referred to in the statutes of ecclesiastical law, and expressly formulated in the Fourth Lateran Council (1215), chap. xxi., admits of no exception or attenuation even though the life of the confessor were at stake (cf. Hefele, *Conciliengeschichte*, v. 888). It extends to all matter strictly pertaining to sacramental confession independently of the circumstance whether absolution be granted or not. Though primarily binding the confessor, the same obligation rests also on other persons whether lay or cleric who by accident or otherwise may have obtained knowledge of the confession. To induce this obligation the confession should be sacramental in character, i.e., it should be made in good faith and with the intention of receiving absolution. Thus if a penitent were to simulate confession by way of a joke, the confessor would incur only the natural obligation governing such matters, and likewise if the narration of one's sins were made merely in order to obtain counsel or consolation, the secret, though still of the professional kind, would not, however, entail the strict obligation of the sacramental seal. There are on record a few historic instances in which the secrecy of the confessional has been heroically defended. The most notable perhaps is that of St. John of Nepomuk (q.v)., who is honored as a martyr of the confessional. In 1377 he was chosen by the pious Johanna, wife of the Emperor Wenceslaus, to be her spiritual guide. The emperor, whose life was that of a dissolute tyrant, being jealous of his consort, endeavored first by cajolery and later by threats to obtain from the confessor a revelation of her confessions. John remained firm, and after much inhuman treatment he was ordered by the enraged Wenceslaus to be cast into the River Moldau. The order was carried out after nightfall on the vigil of the Ascension, May 16, 1383. JAMES F. DRISCOLL.

BIBLIOGRAPHY: J. P. Gury, *Compendium Theologiæ Moralis*, Paris, 1881; and in general writers on moral theology; F. Marne, *Vie de Saint Jean Népomucène*, Paris, 1741; A. Butler, *Lives of the Saints*, iv. 332.

SECRET, DISCIPLINE OF THE. See ARCANI DISCIPLINA.

SECRÉTAN, sec″rê-tān′, **CHARLES:** Swiss Protestant; b. at Lausanne Jan. 18, 1815; d. there Jan. 21, 1895. Educated at Lausanne and Munich, he became, in 1838, associate professor of philosophy at the Academy (after 1891 the University) of Lausanne, where he was promoted to a full professorship three years later. In 1845 he was one of the professors suspended by the radicals during the Vaud revolution, and accordingly delivered his lectures privately until, in 1850, he was called to the Academy of Neuchâtel. In 1866, however, he was recalled to Lausanne, where he spent the remainder of his life. His view of the universe, as revealed in his writings, was threefold; philosophically he passed from the position of Schelling and Baader to that of Kant; theologically he abandoned all positive speculation for a dogmatic of ethical consciousness based on Kantian philosophy; sociologically his position was original, though destined to exercise little influence.

Secrétan's *Philosophie de la liberté* (2 vols., Paris, 1849) postulates the identity of the principle of being with the Deity, which is free in self-limitation, and endowed with spirit and will. Man, free to make his own choice, preferred voluntary independence, which he used in favor of evil, this selection being explained by the theory of a preexistent fall. Instead of permitting evil to work itself out, however, the Creator planned a return to redemption, the primeval purpose of creation, by begetting a perfect type of humanity (the Son of God), whose sufferings, representing man's pain in consequence of sin, cause a reaction realized in Christian history, the end of which is the everlasting life of emancipated humanity. In the two subsequent editions of this work (1866, 1879) Secrétan sought to adapt his old text to his changing views, but the attempt was impossible and his ethical and religious concepts received their new form in his *Recherches de la méthode qui conduit à la vérité sur nos plus grands intérêts* (Neuchâtel, 1857), *La Raison et le christianisme* (Paris, 1863), *Discours laïques* (1877), *Religion et théologie* (1883), *La Civilisation et la croyance* (Lausanne, 1887), and the posthumous *Essais de philosophie et de littérature* (1896). But despite all his shifting of position, he steadily maintained the two principles of freedom and duty, though he surrendered all derivation of the cosmos from a single principle. To him religion was neither the uncritical acceptance of a sum of data, nor the observance of certain rites, nor poetic feeling, but obedience to the moral law in man's own heart, conceived as the operation of a personal force outside him. His attitude toward dogma, therefore, may be described as increasingly indifferent, especially in relation to man's moral position; and he utterly rejected the doctrines of plenary inspiration, the equal importance of all the books of the Bible, and the vicarious sacrifice in the death of Christ, giving this, like the resurrection and the ascension, a distinctly symbolic meaning. He likewise rejected the tenets of eternal punishment and the moral requirement of belief in miracles, and, in his humility, sometimes doubted personal immortality. Personally he preferred the free churches to those supported by the State, though he held that the Church failed to meet the demands of modern times, and advocated greater familiarity with modern culture on the part of ministers, with an intensification of practical work and less stress on purely theological problems.

Shortly after the publication of his second great work, the *Principe de la morale* (Lausanne, 1883), Secrétan turned his attention especially to sociology, his *Civilisation et la croyance*, already noted, treating its theme from the threefold point of view of philosophy, theology, and sociology, while the economic and political sides receive almost exclusive attention in his *Le Droit de la femme* (Paris, 1887), *Études sociales* (1899), *Les Droits de l'humanité* (1890), and *Mon Utopie* (1882). He sought, on the one hand, to secure for the masses that prosperity which the economic development of centuries had taken from them by unequal division of property and class favoritism; and on the other hand, here parting company with socialism, he emphasized the natural and inherent inequality of individuals, and their consequent rights to different degrees of wealth and wages. He strongly advocated cooperative labor, savings-banks, insurance against old age, accident, and loss of employment, as well as the emancipation of woman, for all which he strove with the technical knowledge of a political economist and the motives of an ethicist and friend of the people.

(E. C. PLATZHOFF-LEJEUNE.)

BIBLIOGRAPHY: G. Frommel, in *Esquisses contemporaines*, Lausanne, 1891; F. Pillon, *La Philosophie de Charles Secrétan*, Paris, 1897; J. Duproix, *Ch. Secrétan et la philosophie kantienne*, ib. 1900.

SECULARISM: An atheistic and materialistic movement established in England about the middle of the nineteenth century, at one time counting hundreds of thousands of adherents. The founder was George Jacob Holyoake [b. in Birmingham Apr. 13, 1817; d. at Brighton Jan. 22, 1906; received his education at the Mechanic's Institution in Birmingham, where he taught until he entered political and literary life; began lecturing in 1841 on Robert Owen's social philosophy, and directed his efforts to the uplift of the laboring classes; in 1842 he was imprisoned for blasphemy], who, in 1846, assisted in starting a periodical called *The Reasoner*, which soon became the chief organ of English freethought, a movement which was atheistic rather than theistic, but possessed of a marked tendency toward the formation of associations, and characterized by utilitarian aims in the sphere of morals. Although the followers of the school repudiated the designation "atheists" (see ATHEISM), and claimed to be simply "non-theists," they were soon termed "secularists" because of their avowed purpose of working "for the welfare of men in this world," ignoring altogether any hypothesis of a future life. The sole ethical principle of the school was utilitarian, and its dogmatic position was entirely negative, denying the justifiability of assuming the existence of God, the divine governance of the world, the reasonableness of prayer, the possibility of a future life, and the like. At the same time this position was primarily not one of absolute denial, but rather of extreme agnosticism, with the assumption that what can not be positively and indubitably known should be ignored, both in theory and in practical life.

Under the guidance of Holyoake secularism was a relatively tame movement, but with the early eighth decade of the nineteenth century its character changed under the leadership of the well-known Charles Bradlaugh (q.v.), and it became not only radical in politics, but bitterly hostile to all forms of religion, even while adopting a sort of religious ceremonial drawn up by Bradlaugh's friend, Austin Holyoake, and entitled *Rituale Holyoakense, sive hierurgia secularis*. In all this the more vulgar forms of secularism revealed a certain degree of affinity with Positivism (q.v.), while the more cultured adherents of the movement came to prefer to term themselves "agnostics" (see AGNOSTICISM). Since the closing decades of the nineteenth century secularism as a distinct sect seems more or less to have disappeared or to have been merged in such forms of modern anti-Christian radicalism as societies for ethical culture (see ETHICAL CULTURE, SOCIETIES FOR). (O. ZÖCKLER†.)

BIBLIOGRAPHY: J. Buchanan, *Faith in God and Modern Atheism*, ii. 233-291, London, 1857 (records the beginnings of the movement); M. Davies, *Heterodox London*, i. 364 sqq., ii. 116-200, ib. 1874 (gives the later development); C. Bradlaugh, *Autobiography*, ib. 1873; J. MacCann, *Secularism: unphilosophical, immoral, and antisocial*, ib. 1881; *Christianity and Secularism. A written Debate between Rev. G. Sexton and C. Watts*, ib. 1882; J. Foxley, *Secularism*, ib. 1882; R. G. Ingersoll, *Secular Lectures*, Manchester, 1882; W. G. Blaikie, *Christianity and Secularism Compared*, London, 1883; R. Potter, *Examination of Secularism*, Melbourne, 1883; S. H. Gem, *Christianity and Secularism*, London, 1890; W. H. Harris, *The Secularist Programme*, ib. 1891; M. Keibel, *Die Religion und ihr Recht gegenüber dem modernen Moralismus*, pp. 51 sqq., Halle, 1891; R. A. Armstrong, *Agnosticism and Theism in the 19th Century*, London, 1905; *DNB*, supplement, i. 248-250 (life of Bradlaugh).

SECULARIZATION.

By secularization is meant confiscation of church property by the State and the use of the revenues thus acquired for other than church purposes; or, in the narrower sense of the term, it denotes the transformation of spiritual domains into secular possessions, the first instance of this being the negotiations immediately preceding the Peace of Westphalia (q.v.), particularly in France.

1. Carolingian and Merovingian Action.

At the very beginning of the Carolingian period there was a comparatively extended secularization in France, and medieval tradition is essentially correct in declaring that Charles Martel deprived the Church of a great part of its estates for the benefit of his vassals. The reason for this course was the financial poverty of the State, especially in view of the exhaustion of the crown lands and the increasing danger of Saracen invasion, while Charles had in addition the personal motive of creating a vassal body rivaling that of his Merovingian predecessors. The estates thus confiscated were not restored under the sons of Charles Martel, but a legal form was devised which, while recognizing the spiritual quality of the confiscated estates and while laying a tax on the church institutions affected, protected the present incumbents, even while further use of church property by the State was rendered possible through new investiture in case of a change of incumbent. Under Henry II. the monasteries were the object of attack, while, following the traditions of his house, he regarded the episcopate as his surest defense against the secular lords. The emperor availed himself of the pretext of reforming the monasteries to appropriate a large portion of their property, with which he reimbursed both himself and his followers for his political generosity toward the episcopate. At the same time, whatever was necessary to the maintenance of the monastery itself was spared.

2. Tendencies at End of Middle Ages.

In the course of the Middle Ages half of the national estates of Germany had come under Mortmain (q.v.), and poverty-stricken peasants, in their blind fury, longed for the secularization of all church property—a desire ominously echoed in the hearts of many who elsewhere had no sympathy for the lower classes. Roman Catholic princes, the Archduke Ferdinand among them, vied with Protestants here, and as early as 1525 a general secularization was proposed, which was to be carried out by the Empire, not by the common people. Spiritual princes and prelates were to have so much as was sufficient to proper dignity, and canons were to retain their canonries, but prelacies and canonries were gradually to die out. A few nunneries were to be retained; and the income of the confiscated estates was to be devoted especially to the salary of parish priests, the maintenance of a bishop (stripped of all temporal power), and the erection of a high school in each district. Though the power of the spiritual princes was too strong to permit such drastic measures, it was the Roman Catholics themselves, with Austria to set the example, who commenced the abolition of monasteries. All this was the tendency of the day, but Luther warned his adherents that the property of the Church must be administered in the interests of the Church, and that the conditions of country pastors must first of all be improved, after which the residue might be devoted to benevolent institutions and to general interests. It was in this spirit that the Saxon visitation was conducted and that Melanchthon advised the council of Strasburg in 1538. At the same time, many secular authorities grasped the opportunity to turn to private advantage the course advocated by Luther and Melanchthon, and failed to make proper provision for preachers and schools, the care of the poor, and the advancement of education, so that the Schmalkald Convention of 1540, at the instance of Melanchthon, formally demanded reformation of church property rather than secularization, even while advocating the secularization of spiritual domains. In many lands, as in Hesse, large institutions, such as the strongly Protestant University of Marburg, were endowed from suppressed monasteries, while in 1525 Prussia was changed from a spiritual state to a secular archduchy.

3. Conditions under the Reformation.

The estates of the Church in the various territories at the rise of Protestantism fell into three categories, each of which underwent a separate development: the property and income of individual churches and benefices, the property of religious corporations (property of chapters, monasteries, etc.), and the property and income of ecclesiastical dignitaries (local bishops). The property and income of individual parishes remained practically unchanged, although there were minor losses, as in the case of Stole Fees (q.v.) and certain cases of enforced contribution, while instances of deliberate violation of the spirit of the new regulations were not unknown. In Württemberg Duke Christopher sought to offset the attempts of Ulrich to secure complete secularization by a specially administered "general church fund" which should permanently apply ecclesiastical property to the benefit of Protestantism. This fund was to provide for the endowment of new pastorates, the repair of pastors' residences, the support of aged pastors, and the like; but the destruction of the multifarious local legal persons which the ecclesiastical properties formed under Roman, canon, and common Protestant church law were a peril to Christopher's scheme, which finally suffered incameration in 1806. In many districts the estates of ecclesiastical corporations were undiminished, although their objects were changed, only hospitals, poorhouses, etc., retaining their original purposes. Much of the confiscated property was devoted to educational ends; in other cases the corporations survived, though they became benevolent institutions; while yet others, when their incumbents died or resigned, were given back to their patrons or founders. In Württemberg the monasteries were retained as schools; and this transformation of monasteries, rather than entire secularization, was the course pursued by Duke Ernest the Confessor of Lüneburg and Duchess Elizabeth of Calenburg-Göttingen, as well as by Duke Julius of Brunswick. The University of Helmstädt was endowed from suppressed monasteries, and educational and eleemosynary institutions were founded in similar fashion in Hanover, Hesse, Mecklenburg, and elsewhere.

4. Effects on the Princes of the Church.

The property and income of ecclesiastical dignitaries underwent a profound change with the rise of the new doctrine. Protestantism left no room for the union of temporal and spiritual lordship in the bishops which had hitherto prevailed, and some bishops, like those of Samland and Pomerania, voluntarily resigned their secular powers when they embraced the tenets of Luther. More than this, the entire episcopate vanished with the extension of the consistorial system, and as bishops died, they were not replaced. Members of the secular nobility were elected or appointed to administer the vacant sees, and the episcopal estates gradually became incorporated with the secular domains. In many religious foundations immediately dependent on the Empire the Reformation was similarly carried out, and in this way Protestantism gained control of the dioceses of Magdeburg, Bremen, Verden, Lübeck, Osnabrück, Ratzeburg, Halberstadt, and Minden, while for a time the Roman Catholics were threatened with the loss of Münster, Paderborn, Hildesheim, and Cologne, although the Counter-Reformation ultimately enabled them to retain possession of these sees. The Protestantized dioceses, on the other hand, went their course to secularization, such being the fate of Bremen, Verden, and Magdeburg, which became secular duchies, of Halberstadt, Minden, Camin, Schwerin, and Ratzeburg, which were changed into principalities, and of many lesser foundations. By the provisions of Jan. 1, 1624, the only unsecularized imperial diocese in Protestant hands was Lübeck, and the sole unsecularized monasteries were those of Gandersheim, Hervorden, and Quedlinburg; while the Protestants were now declared entitled to peaceful possession of all sequestrated and transformed ecclesiastical estates and foundations.

The suppression of the Jesuits in the eighteenth century gave secular lords wide pretexts for confiscation of church property, such sequestration following the banishment of the order from Portugal (1759), France (1764), Spain (1767), Naples, Malta, and Parma (1768). On the suppression of the order by Clement XIV. on July 21, 1773, the pope appointed a special congregation to decide concerning their property, and this congregation accordingly addressed a circular letter to the episcopate directing the bishops to take possession of Jesuit property and apply it to the purposes designated by the pope. Since, however, German law refused to recognize the papal supremacy which was thus implied, and since the bishops could not, by the provisions of the papal brief, take any independent action, the secular authorities everywhere seized the Jesuit estates, even though the imperial councilor deemed this property to be essentially that of the Church.

5. Consequences of the French Revolution.

The French Revolution was especially fateful for church property, for the financial needs of France were deemed too great to be satisfied by merely taxing such property. The excuse alleged by the revolutionists formed but the counterpart to the theory which gained supremacy in the Gallican Church, as well as among seventeenth-century Roman Catholic canonists in general, that the church property of the clergy consisted in their associations. This encountered Protestant opposition by its basal hierarchic identification of clergy and Church, and from the alleged usurpation of church property by the clergy the Encyclopedists (q.v.) argued that, since the clergy as a corporation was dependent on the State, the State could confiscate the estates of the clergy. The National Assembly declared, on Nov. 2, 1789, that all ecclesiastical property was at the disposal of the nation, at the same time guaranteeing the salaries of the clergy. The suppression of all monasteries soon followed, and in quick succession came the fall of the church organization and of the Church itself. Even on its restoration by the concordat of July 15, 1801, it was forced to submit to the sale of its property, although the government pledged itself to pay the clergy a suitable salary; and even when a portion of the Church's belongings were again returned to its own control, these were held to be not its property, but to appertain to the State and the communes. No less ominous for the possessions of the Roman Catholic Church were the consequences of the French Revolution in Germany. Here an important factor was the theory of " the law of nature," which had been evolved in the eighteenth century, largely on the basis of the legal tenet of eminent domain—a theory which by some writers was carried so far as to make the Church a mere society subserving the interests of the State. In the second half of the eighteenth century the idea of secularization was widespread, and was exemplified not only by Joseph II. of Austria and the elector of Mainz, but even by the course proposed by a Roman Catholic canon, Friedrich Karl von Moser, in 1787. By the secret provisions of the peace of Campo Formio (Oct. 17, 1797) the emperor agreed to cede to France the greater part of the region to the left of the Rhine, including Mainz. This implied not only the secularization of this region, but also, since Austria claimed compensation on the right bank of the Rhine, the devotion, and consequent secularization, of church estates in the empire. Only the quondam prince elector of Mainz (now electoral archchancellor) and the heads of the Maltese and Teutonic Knights remained spiritual estates; all other imperial spiritual principalities and dignities were declared secularized and apportioned among secular estates, chiefly Protestant.

6. Effect on the Papal Authority and Property.

The effect of these secularizations and the regulations accompanying them was so great as to involve the destruction of the organization of the Roman Catholic Church in Germany. The severest blows were struck at the authority of the pope, who was not even consulted in the matter, and with the suppression of the monasteries he lost a host of devoted adherents. The mingling of Protestant and Roman Catholic populations opened a way to Protestantization which was checked only by the infiltration of ultramontanism into the Roman Catholic laity and later into the clergy, and by the weakening of the State Church and the concessions of the government; while the erection of a German primacy fostered the schismatic tendency which characterised the German episcopate in the time of Joseph II. Against all this the Curia could only protest, and with so little effect at the time that the spiritual estates hitherto spared were quickly secularized. Far more perilous was the fact that the promised reorganisation of the dioceses and chapters was not realised, despite the exertions of the primate, Prince Dalberg. Pending this delay vacant sees remained unfilled, and the old bishops died one by one, until in 1814 there were but five bishops in Germany. The dioceses were administered by vicars general, and, as the number of suffragans was likewise diminished, the sacraments of confirmation and ordination could no longer be performed. Cathedral chapters were also unfilled, and countless parishes were empty or impoverished, while temporal dignitaries, on the basis of the estates they had received through sequestration, alleged the right of succession to the prerogatives of presentation and collation which had been granted to bishops and monasteries.

In this general trouble Protestantism also shared. In Württemberg the property of the Church was declared to belong to the State; and in Prussia war expenses led to the confiscation of the property of those monasteries and spiritual foundations which still survived, only the chapter of Brandenburg escaping suppression, while in Westphalia the secularisation even of Protestant foundations was accomplished within a few years.

7. Legal Aspects of the Process.

In considering the legal aspects of secularization in Germany a distinction must be drawn between the various reasons underlying it. The abolition of the temporal lordship of imperial dioceses and prelacies involved no invasion of church property, for this secular power was due to purely political, not religious, causes, and originated under the conditions in which the Church, as the great civilizing factor of the West in the Middle Ages, had been forced to discharge many purely secular functions if all the higher culture of the Greco-Roman world was not to disappear amid the wild struggles of the ruder northern nations. Thus the Church opposed to the factions of the secular State the marvelous ideal of the spiritual universal State. But the days had passed when kings must reign through their bishops because they could not reign through temporal princes, counts, and lords, and by the end of the thirteenth century the political states had passed their period of disability, having become able to dispense with ecclesiastical guardianship. As early as the fifteenth century the modern concept of the State had arisen, and with the abolition of the old confusion of public and private spheres of right the union of temporal sovereignty with spiritual dignity came to be regarded as anomalous, though for a considerable time it dragged out an ostensible existence in the constitution of Germany. The Curia demanded a restitution of the old status, including the restoration of the Holy Roman Empire, the reerection of the spiritual principalities, and the return of the property wrested from the Church, but all in vain. The sole consolation of the pope was his continued control of the States of the Church in Italy. Neither can the confiscation of royal fiefs and of Regalia (q.v.) be regarded as invasions of the rights of the Church, since they had been used distinctly for political ends. It is, however, a question what constituted a royal fief, some defining it as the temporal rights connected with an imperial bishopric or abbey, while others restrict it to specific estates and privileges. In the Frankish kingdom the royal monasteries were deemed the property of the king or of the treasury, while the king controlled, though in more restricted degree, the property of the dioceses. In Germany churches and their endowment were the possession of the laity who had established them, though after the twelfth century the Church succeeded in reducing this control to the mere right of Patronage (q.v.). From the end of the ninth century the great majority of German bishoprics, including all their estates and prerogatives, were the property of the Empire, so that the property belonging to a church really meant only the permanent usufruct of such estates and prerogatives. The object of Investiture (q.v.) was the bishopric and the episcopal office, or both temporal and spiritual functions, and it is clear that previous to the investiture controversy the king controlled the bishoprics, i.e., the temporal side. After 1111, however, the king not only restricted himself to the temporal aspect of the matter, but expressly granted that a part of the *temporalia*, such as church edifices and oblations, belonged unconditionally to the Church.

8. Legal Basis of Alienation of Property.

The diversion of the property of the estates of the Roman Catholic Church to Protestant uses in territories where the new doctrines were introduced was deduced from the reformatory rights of secular rulers as construed in the form which it assumed in the sixteenth century as distinct from the extinct positive law of the Middle Ages. Historic relations to the western Church and the necessity of control in the midst of confusion had placed the empire in jurisdiction, and this was transferred to the territorial rulers. Since Protestantism gained its legal basis through the help of temporal lords, its endowment was accomplished in legal form; and the church organizations arising from the Reformation were not due to the exit of Protestants from the Roman Catholic Church, but to the cleavage of the Western Church into Roman Catholic and Protestant. On the basis of their legal position as assured in the religious treaties of peace, the Protestants could claim that since their organization was no less a legitimate continuation of the pre-Reformation Church than Roman Catholicism, so the property which they received from this pre-Reformation body had not been decatholicised by the Reformation, and had consequently not been alienated from the Church to which it had been dedicated. On the other hand there was at least a formal injustice in the diversion of true church property for secular uses. It is true that many of the older secularizations represent a reaction against the excessive accumulations of property under mortmain, which disturbed the economic balance of society. But this plea can not be alleged in extenuation of the confiscation of church property in the early nineteenth century, nor is the excuse valid that many of the richer ecclesiastical corporations and institutions of recent centuries served the interests of the privileged classes rather than the ends of the Church. It must further be recognised that the false theories of the "law of nature," alleged in extenuation of the illegal confiscation of a great part of Roman Catholic and of no small portion of Protestant church property at the commencement of the nineteenth century, can not validate injustice. This holds true both of the theory of eminent domain and of the doctrine that the property of the Church is really the property of the State, and may be devoted to religious ends only so long as the State pleases. The modern theory of the State rejects the tenet of eminent domain [not, however, in the United States], and while recognising the supremacy of the State over private property, forbids such property to be devoted to mere political or economic needs of the State [in the United States the rights of eminent domain operate only upon just compensation to the owners of property]. Equally erroneous is any foundation of the State right of secularization on the alleged supremacy of society, for the right of the State to sequester the property of corporations is bound by precisely the same restrictions as its right to confiscate the property of individuals. False also is the theory that the power of the State absorbs all social and spiritual life, for religion, in particular, is no function of the State. The Church is a special organization for the promotion of the moral life and has its own justification; its property serves its special end, and is as exempt from the capricious control of the State as is any other private property. It is with justice, therefore, that modern legislation declares the property of the Church inviolable and expressly guarantees its security, although, as in the case of private property, it reserves the right of escheatage; nor does the mere fact that the property of a particular foundation is designed for spiritual ends of itself make the diocese, and eventually the Roman Catholic Church, the legal heir in case the foundation in question lapses. At the same time, a number of modern codes expressly enact that the property of individual foundations which can no longer be applied to their original ends may be used only for religious purposes.

The modern Roman Catholic theory that, although the religious corporations were suppressed, their property was reserved for religious and educational purposes, so that the Roman Catholic

Church has a permanent claim on the property in question, is legally untenable, and has been granted only by the Austrian concordat. Secularized property and the property of the Church are irreconcilable concepts, and only through rededication could property once sequestrated again come to belong to the Church. At the same time, the State is ethically bound, since it holds so large a portion of the possessions of the Church through its secularizations, to provide adequately for the needs of the two communions which all German states regard as corporations in public law. This has been carried out perhaps more favorably to the Roman Catholic than to the Protestant communion. And it should be noted that purchasers of secularized property, having a legal title from the State treasury, are the valid owners of such property, though Roman Catholic purchasers are in duty bound, according to canon law, to gain the approval of the pope to their purchase.

9. Modern Roman Catholic Theory Invalid.

The secularization of the States of the Church deserves special consideration. This "patrimony of Peter" (see PAPAL STATES) was regarded as the property of the Church, and every pontiff was required to pledge himself that none of it should be alienated—a fact which did not prevent Pius VI. from accepting the peace of Tolentino (1797), by which Avignon and Venaissin, together with Ancona and the legations of Bologna, Ferrara, and Romagna, were lost to the Church. Between the States of the Church and the concept of the modern secular State there was the widest discrepancy. The modern State is construed as an independent organization resting on its own ethical foundation, as the legitimate organization for the complete life of its people, in whose behalf all its energies are devoted. That the State should be in control of a subject beyond its own borders, which was the relation of the Roman Catholic Church to the States of the Church, is irreconcilable with the modern theory of the State; and though the States of the Church were incapable of the profound transformations undergone by secular powers, this very fact would ultimately have proved fatal. The States of the Church lacked, moreover, an organic national basis, and the whole trend of modern history was opposed to them. In 1798 the boundaries of the States of the Church were abolished, though restored, essentially undiminished, at the Congress of Vienna; but the temporal power of the pope over his states was possible only through repeated, and finally permanent, armed intervention of foreign powers, until, amid profound changes in Europe, the Italian revolutions of 1859–60 robbed the States of the Church of a great part of their possessions, while the overthrow of the French Empire in 1870 encouraged the Italians, after taking Rome on Sept. 20, 1870, to incorporate the remainder of the papal dominions in the kingdom of Italy. True to the principle that the continuance of the temporal power of the pope was essential, especially at that period, to the independence of the Roman Catholic Church and of her earthly head, Pius IX. placed all who had taken part in the act which he termed "robbery of God" under major excommunication. Meanwhile the kingdom of Italy, on May 13, 1871, promulgated its law concerning the Curia and the Roman Catholic Church. By this the pope was guaranteed the personal prerogatives of a sovereign, the Holy See was endowed with a yearly pension of 3,225,000 francs (corresponding to the former papal budget for apostolic palaces, the holy college, the congregations, the secretaryship of state, and diplomatic representation abroad), freedom was granted the pope in the discharge of his office in the governance of the Church, while on Italian soil he was granted free communication with his bishops and foreign governments, and the full immunity of diplomats was accorded his nuncios and legates to foreign courts as well as to the diplomats accredited to the Holy See.

10. The States of the Church.

Despite the loss of his temporal sovereignty, the pope still possesses a quasi-sovereignty in his relations, as a spiritual power, to sovereign states, as well as a still more real power which gives him, besides the honors rendered to his person, the right of embassy and of concluding quasi-international treaties. On the other hand, the essential differences of his quasi-sovereignty from the full sovereignty of temporal powers forbids any actual equality between the two. He can not, for example, wage war, since he has no state to form the object of attack. All this involves difficult and thus far unsolved problems of international law, which are only complicated by the Italian law of guaranty. Not only would Italy have to answer, by the law of nations, for any armed attack upon the pope, but, again by the law of nations, the Italian government must be responsible for any misuse of its guaranty to the pope of the privilege of legal immunity, even in the case of breaches of the peace which otherwise violate international law. On the other hand, considerations of practical policy justify recognition of a privileged and immune legal position of the pope in the international fellowship of Christian nations so long as the Roman Catholic Church maintains its quasi-state organization. This assures to the papacy the possibilities of such far-reaching political development that, recognizing that a double sovereignty of spiritual and temporal power over the same peoples is irreconcilable, the pope, since his loss of temporal sovereignty, has renewed with increased energy those ancient claims to spiritual universal monarchy which represent him as the one true sovereign over the national states, these being regarded by curialists as mere provinces of his world dominion, over which he is to exercise rule. The Roman Church is, in a word, both an institution of political power and a Christian body for the worship of God, and for this reason the relation of temporal states toward it can be governed only by individual rules, not by any general theory of the relation of the State to the Christian Church as a whole.

11. Anomalous Position of the Papacy.

On the secularization of churches, and especially of monasteries, in Italy see ITALY, I., §§ 1–2, and on the secularization in France, wrought by the law of separation of Dec. 9, 1905, see FRANCE, I.

(E. SEHLING.)

BIBLIOGRAPHY: A. Kleinschmidt, *Die Säkularisation vom 1803*, Berlin, 1878; F. A. Gasquet, *Henry VIII. and the English Monasteries*, rev. ed., London, 1899; M. Anglade, *De la sécularisation des biens de clergé sur la révolution*, Paris, 1901; M. Erzberger, *Die Säkularisation in Württemberg, 1802–10*, Stuttgart, 1902; H. Reimers, *Die Säkularisation der Klöster in Ostfriesland*, Aurich, 1906; K. Schornbaum, *Die Säkularisation des Klosters Heidenheim*, Neuendettelsau, 1906; F. Körholz, *Die Säkularisation und Organisation in den preussischen Entschädigungsländern . . . 1802–06*, Münster, 1907; M. Pfeiffer, *Beiträge zur Geschichte der Säcularisation in Bamberg*, Bamberg, 1907; A. M. Scheglmann, *Geschichte der Säkularisation im rechtsrheinischen Bayern*, 3 vols., Regensburg, 1903–08; *KL*, x. 1526–34.

SEDARIM, SEDAROTH. See PARASHAH.

SEDES VACANS: The ecclesiastical term for a "vacant see." For the principles and practise governing in case of vacancy of the papal see, see POPE, PAPACY, PAPAL SYSTEM. The cases here considered are those of actual and constructive vacancy in ordinary bishoprics.

An episcopal vacancy occurs through death, abdication, translation, deposition, and the like; and lasts till the occupancy has been regularly renewed. In such a case, the episcopal jurisdiction devolves upon the Chapter (q.v.), which [in the Roman Catholic Church], within eight days as reckoned from the moment of certified knowledge that the vacancy has begun, must appoint one or more stewards, and a capitulary vicar (see VICAR); the latter may be the former episcopal vicar general. In case the chapter is dilatory, or if no chapter attaches to the vacant church, the right of nomination devolves, in connection with a suffragan church, on the metropolitan; in the case of a metropolitan church, on the eldest suffragan bishop; in the case of an exempt church, on the bishop nearest. Where the vacant church has no chapter, if at the time the metropolitan church itself is without an archbishop, the nomination devolves on the metropolitan chapter. According to the Council of Trent the capitulary vicar is expected to be at least a doctor or licentiate in canon law. Where a suitable person is present in the chapter, selection must be made accordingly. The capitulary vicar exercises his vested rights independently, like the bishop, until the renewed occupancy of the episcopal see and may not by the chapter be deprived of his administration. In general, pending the election, episcopal rights which emanate from the "episcopal standing" or from papal delegation continue dormant, except as the Curia makes provision to the contrary or as the situation demands the summoning of a bishop from without. The principle prevails that during the interim no alteration may be undertaken of a nature prejudicial to the future bishop. In particular, the episcopal revenues for the interim period are not to be employed, except that the capitulary vicar's salary may be defrayed therefrom. The vacancy ceases with the new bishop's official occupancy.

A distinction is drawn between actual and constructive episcopal vacancy, as when the bishop is hindered from undertaking his incumbent administration. In case this obstruction is only partial, a coadjutor acts; but if it be absolute, a procedure then ensues parallel to the case of actual episcopal vacancy. But the situation is different where communication with the bishop is still possible; in that case his jurisdiction is not suspended so obviously, and his appointed vicar general may officiate. After the vicar general's death, the appointment of a new vicar general appertains to the pope, the chapter not being authorised to install a vicar.

E. SEHLING.

In the Anglican communion the arrangements for the administration of a vacant see and for filling the vacancy vary in different parts. In England the administration of the diocese falls during a vacancy largely to the Chapter (q.v.; which is supposed always to be the bishop's council), with certain prerogatives reserved to the metropolitan of the province. A bishop is of course called in to perform any distinctly episcopal function, but he has no jurisdiction or power beyond that which is distinctly committed to him for the occasion. The crown nominates a successor to the vacant see, but he must be elected by the chapter.

Where, as outside of England, the Church is not in any direct relations with the State, the successor is elected by representatives of the diocese, both clerical and lay, assembled in synod or council or convention. Such election needs confirmation by the bishops of the national church or of the province, and in America by representatives of other dioceses. During a vacancy the administration of the diocese in America belongs to the standing committee of the diocese, which corresponds in its functions to the chapter as the bishop's council, and in other national churches either to a similar representative body or to a vicar general as may be prescribed by local diocesan or provincial canons, subject to limitations like to those mentioned in the case of England.

A. C. A. HALL.

SEDGWICK, sej'wic, DANIEL: English hymnologist; b. at London Nov. 26, 1815; d. there Mar. 10, 1879. He was originally a shoemaker, became a dealer in second-hand books in 1837, and fell in with collectors, mainly of theological literature. In 1839 he united with the Baptists. Being fond of hymns, he bought the old books containing them, and about 1840 began the systematic collection and study of texts and editions, and, at the same time, taught himself writing. He gradually acquired a unique library, and a knowledge of the subject long unrivalled. The popularity of Roundell Palmer's *Book of Praise* (London, 1863) and the care Sedgwick had bestowed in making it a model of accuracy in texts, dates, and ascriptions of authorship, established his reputation; and thenceforth the compilers of nearly every prominent English hymnal availed themselves of his help. He published *Catalogue of Scarce Religious Poetry, containing a Choice Collection of Original Psalms, Hymns, and Poems* (London, 1859); a series entitled *English Hymn Writers; Reprinted Verbatim from the Originals, with Biographical Sketches*, including such names in single volumes as John Ryland, William Williams, and A. M. Toplady; and *Comprehensive Index of Names of Original Authors of Hymns* (1860).

BIBLIOGRAPHY: Julian, *Hymnology*, pp. 1036–37; *DNB*, li. 182.

SEDLNITZKI, sêdl-nit'ski, **LEOPOLD GRAF VON**: German prince bishop of Breslau and convert to Lutheranism; b. at the castle of Geppersdorf in Austrian Silesia, July 29, 1787; d. at Berlin Mar. 25, 1871. He was educated at the University of Breslau (1804–09), and in 1810 was ordained to the priesthood. His intention to devote himself to theological teaching was frustrated by illness, and in 1811 he accepted from the prince bishop of Breslau the posts of assessor and secretary in the vicariate which administered the spiritual affairs of the diocese. Even at this time he was by no means in full accord with the course pursued by the Roman Catholic Church. At the same time, he firmly maintained the external unity and the apostolic character of that church, regarding the Reformation as a break in the unity of the Church and as a disturbing factor in its divinely appointed development. Before long Sedlnitzki accepted an appointment in the royal service at Breslau, where he plunged into a multitude of new tasks concerning the Church and higher education. Discovering that the Protestant gymnasia were superior to the Roman Catholic, he considered it his duty to raise the standard of the schools of his church. He thus found himself obliged to consider more closely the relation of the Roman Catholic and the Protestant churches, and accordingly began a thorough study of Protestant symbolics. Nevertheless he still remained true to his church, though disapproving indulgences, the growth of adoration of saints and of pilgrimages. The conclusions thus reached could not be concealed, but despite his views, which now involved doubts of the unity and catholicity of the Roman Catholic Church, Sedlnitzki was unanimously elected bishop in 1835. He accepted with reluctance, and soon had to encounter serious opposition. Matters reached a climax in his refusal to obey the papal brief of Mar. 25, 1830, to the effect that mixed marriages could be blessed by the church only after the contracting parties had promised to bring up their children in the Roman Catholic faith. Sedlnitzki, preferring to obey the laws of the State rather than those of his church, offered to resign his see on June 10, 1839. King Frederick William IV. vainly sought to restrain him from this extreme step, and, on the acceptance by Rome of Sedlnitzki's resignation, appointed him in 1840 privy councilor at Berlin. For a short time the ex-bishop continued to celebrate mass on high festivals but soon became more and more imbued with Protestant ideas, and, on Apr. 12, 1868, he marked his complete break with his church by receiving Protestant communion.

Henceforth Sedlnitzki sought with all earnestness to advance the cause of Protestantism. As early as 1864 he had founded a Lutheran institution, the Paulinum, for the education of boys, especially of those intended for the Lutheran ministry and for higher education. He later founded at Berlin the Johanneum, where young Lutheran theological students might receive appropriate training. In his will he devoted a considerable portion for the foundation of a similar Johanneum at Breslau, and a like foundation was provided for Silesia in the Sedlnitzkische Vikariatsfond. In addition to all this a fund was created by him to provide theological works for the education of needy clergy.

(DAVID ERDMANN†.)

BIBLIOGRAPHY: Consult his *Selbstbiographie. Nach seinem Leben und seine Papieren herausgegeben mit Aktenstücken*, Berlin, 1872.

SEDULIUS, se-dū'li-us, **CŒLIUS**: Christian poet of the early fifth century. Almost nothing is known of his life, even the name Cœlius [or Circilius] is not assured, and it is only probable that he lived in Greece. His fame comes through his poems, especially his *Carmen paschale*, in 1,753 hexameters and five books, with a prologue of eight distichs, dedicated to a presbyter Macedonius. The poem deals with the miracles of Christ, the first book being an introduction discussing the miracles of the Old Testament, and the other four being based on the Gospels, particularly Matthew. The material is freely handled, and in form the poem belongs to the best of early Christian Latin literature. Sedulius later rendered his work into prose, to which he gave the title *Opus paschale*. In this the bombastic style contrasts strongly with the concise and compact diction of the poem. Sedulius left also two hymns. The first is an elegy in fifty-five distichs, which connects the events of the Old Testament with those of the New in the form of antetype to type. The structure is artificial, a hexameter on the Old Testament being succeeded by a pentameter dealing with the New Testament. The second hymn, a call to praise of Christ, is alphabetical in twenty-three strophes, the first lines of the strophes beginning with the letters of the alphabet in turn. Two parts of the composition have been used as church hymns, strophes A–G (as a Christmas hymn), and H, I, L, N (at the feast of Epiphany).

The cento *De verbi incarnatione* was formerly wrongly attributed to Sedulius. (G. KRÜGER.)

BIBLIOGRAPHY: The poems were edited by F. Arevalo, Rome, 1794 (with preface of value) and reproduced in *MPL*, xix.; J. Looshorn, Munich, 1870; and J. Huemer, in *CSEL*, vol. x., 1885. Two brief Eng. transls. are in D. J. Donahoe, *Early Christian Hymns*, pp. 67–68, New York, 1908. Consult: J. Huemer, *De Sedulii . . . vita et scriptis commentatio*, Vienna, 1878; C. L. Leimbach, *Ueber den christlichen Dichter Sedulius*, Goslar, 1879; G. Boissier, in *Journal des savants*, Sept., 1881; J. Kayser, *Beiträge zur Geschichte und Erklärung der ältesten Kirchenhymnen*, pp. 337–385, 1881; S. W. Duffield, *Latin Hymn Writers and their Hymns*, pp. 83–87, New York, 1889; A. Ebert, *Geschichte der Litteratur des Mittelalters im Abendlande*, i. 373–381, Leipsic, 1889; M. Manitius, *Geschichte der christlich-lateinischen Poesie*, pp. 303–312, Stuttgart, 1891; A. Baumgartner, *Die lateinische und griechische Litteratur der christlichen Völker*, pp. 195–198, Freiburg, 1905; Bardenhewer, *Patrologie*, p. 395, Eng. transl., St. Louis, 1908; *DCB*, iv. 598–600 (noteworthy); Julian, *Hymnology*, p. 1037.

SEDULIUS SCOTUS (SEDULIUS JUNIOR): Irish monk, probably to be identified with Siadhal Mac Feradach, who died abbot of Kildare 828. Of his life nothing is known, although some have identified him (probably incorrectly) with the "Sedulius, bishop of Britain of the race of the Scots," who was one of the signers of the decrees of a synod held at Rome in 721 (cf. Haddan and Stubbs, *Councils*, ii., part 1, p. 7). This prelate was almost certainly a Scotch diocesan, though his see (if he possessed one) is unknown. The writings of Sedulius, which are little more than compilations from the Fathers, especially Origen, are as follows: *Collectanea in omnes beati Pauli epistolas; Explanatiuncula de breviariorum et capitulorum canonumque differentia; Explanationes in præfationes sancti Hieronymi ad evangelia;* and *De rectoribus Christianis et conventientibus regulis quibus est respublica rite gubernanda* (all ed., most conveniently, in *MPL*, ciii. 1–351). Johannes Trithemius, who confuses Sedulius Scotus with his more distinguished namesake, as well as with Bishop Sedulius, ascribes to him (*De scriptoribus ecclesiasticis*, cap. cxlii.), in addition to the works already mentioned, *De miraculis Christi; Ad Theodosium imperatorem; In majus volumen Prisciani; In secundam editionem Donati; Exhortatorium ad fideles;* and *Epistolæ ad diversos.*

Bibliography: J. Healy, *Insula sanctorum et doctorum*, pp. 30–39, 574–576, Dublin, 1890; Lanigan, *Eccl. Hist.*, i. 17, iii. 255; *DCB*, iv. 600; *DNB*, li. 188–189; Ceillier, *Auteurs sacrés*, xii. 357–361.

SEEBERG, sé'berg, OSKAR THEODOR ALFRED: Russo-German Protestant; b. at Pedua, Esthonia, Russia, Sept. 24, 1863. He was educated at the universities of Dorpat (1884–89), Erlangen, and Leipsic (1891). In 1890 he was teacher of religion at the municipal school for girls in Dorpat, and in 1891, after his return from Germany, he resumed this position, being also chosen assistant pastor of St. Peter's, Dorpat. In the same year he became privat-docent at the University of Dorpat, where he was promoted to the rank of docent within a few months; in 1895 he was appointed associate professor of New-Testament exegesis, and 1897 full professor of the same subject; in 1908 he went to Rostock in the same capacity. In theology he belongs to the liberal school, and has written *Die Anbetung des Herrn bei Paulus* (Riga, 1891); *Der Tod Christi in seiner Bedeutung für die Erlösung* (Leipsic, 1895); *Der Katechismus der Urchristenheit* (1903); *Das Evangelium Christi* (1905); *Die Taufe im Neuen Testament* (Gross-Lichterfelde, 1905); *Die beiden Wege und das Aposteldekret* (Leipsic, 1906); *Die Leiden der Christen* (Barmen, 1906); *Die Didache des Judentums und der Urchristenheit* (Leipsic, 1908); and *Christi Person und Werk nach der Lehre seiner Jünger* (1910).

SEEBERG, REINHOLD: German Lutheran; b. at Pörrafer, Livonia, Apr. 5, 1859. He was educated at the universities of Dorpat (1878–82) and Erlangen (1882–84; mag. theol., Dorpat, 1884). In 1884 he became privat-docent for systematic theology at the former university, where he was appointed associate professor and second university preacher in the following year. In 1889 he was called to Erlangen as professor of church history and New-Testament exegesis, his chair being changed in 1894 to that of systematic theology. Since 1898 he has been professor of systematic theology at the University of Berlin. He has written *Der Begriff der christlichen Kirche*, i (Erlangen, 1885); *Der Apologet Aristides* (1894); *Lehrbuch der Dogmengeschichte* (2 vols., Leipsic, 1895–98, new ed., 1907–08); *Gewissen und Gewissensbildung* (Erlangen, 1896); *Die Kirche und die soziale Frage* (Leipsic, 1897); *Die Stellung Melanchthons in der Geschichte der Kirche und der Wissenschaft* (Erlangen, 1897); *Die Theologie des Duns Scotus* (Leipsic, 1900); *Grundriss der Dogmengeschichte* (1901; 3d ed., 1910); *An der Schwelle des zwanzigsten Jahrhunderts* (1901); *Luthers Stellung zu den sittlichen und sozialen Nöten seiner Zeit* (1901); *Die Grundwahrheiten der christlichen Religion* (1902; Eng. transl., *Fundamental Truths of the Christian Religion*, New York, 1908); *Luther und Luthertum in der neuesten katholischen Beleuchtung* (1904); *Das Abendmahl im Neuen Testament* (Gross-Lichterfelde, 1905); *Aus Religion und Geschichte* (2 vols., Leipsic, 1906–08); *Die kirchliche sociale Idee* (1907); *Offenbarung und Inspiration* (1908; Eng. transl., *Revelation and Inspiration*, New York, 1910); *Von Christus und von dem Christentum* (Berlin, 1908); *Sinnlichkeit und Sittlichkeit* (1909); *Adolf Stoecker* (1909); and *Alte und Neue Moral* (1910).

SEEBOHM, FREDERIC: Barrister and author; b. at Bradford, Yorkshire, 1833. He was called to the bar (Middle Temple) in 1856. His published works include: *The Facts of the Four Gospels* (London, 1861); *The Crisis of Emancipation in America; being the Review of the History of Emancipation from the Beginning of the American War to the Assassination of President Lincoln* (1865); *The Oxford Reformers of 1498: being a History of the Fellow-Work of John Colet, Erasmus and Thomas More* (1867); *The Era of the Protestant Revolution* (1874); *The English Village Community Examined in its Relations to the Manorial and Tribal Systems* (1883); *The Tribal System in Wales: being Part of an Inquiry into the Structure and Methods of tribal Society* (1895); *Travelling Impressions in, and Notes on, Peru* (1901); and *Tribal Custom in Anglo-Saxon Law* (1902).

SEEHOFER, sé'ho-fer, ARSACIUS: Bavarian Reformer; b. at Munich early in the sixteenth century; d. at Winnenden (20 m. n.e. of Stuttgart) 1542. He was educated at the universities of Ingolstadt and Wittenberg, at the latter place coming under the influence of Melanchthon. In the summer of 1523 he was charged with delivering exegetical lectures of Melanchthonian content, and, compromising documents being found in his residence, he was formally tried for heresy, seventeen articles drawn from his manuscript being deemed unsound. After a period of imprisonment, Seehofer recanted on Sept. 7, 1523, and was directed to retire to the monastery of Ettal. The affair caused great excitement, especially through publications by Argula von Stauff (q.v.), Luther, and a South German author, Martinus Reckenhofer of Clausen; whereupon the university resolved to demonstrate in a public disputation the justice of its course. Since, however, safe conduct was not granted to the opponents of the university, the disputation, which began on Apr. 11, 1524, and lasted several days, was without result. In some unknown way Seehofer escaped from his confinement, but nothing is known of his movements until 1528, when he was in Wittenberg, where Melanchthon recommended him as a teacher at Eisfeld. In 1530 he was in Prussia, and in 1532 in Augsburg, where internal ecclesiastical strife prevented him from accepting the deaconate offered him. In 1535 he again visited Augsburg, where he taught in a school. He was then reader at the monastery of St. George in Württemberg, after which he was a pastor in various places, including Leonberg. From 1537 until his death he was pastor at Winnenden, where he wrote his only work, *Enarrationes evangeliorum dominicalium* (Augsburg, 1539). (T. Kolde.)

Bibliography: T. Kolde, *Arsacius Seehofer und Argula von Grumbach*, in *Beiträge zur bayerischen Kirchengeschichte*, vol. xi., Erlangen, 1905; the literature under Melanchthon; and Stauff.

SEEKERS: A name used in the English revolutionary period, probably not designating a distinct religious body, but applied as a nickname to the Independents, the two names appearing in the same period. Robert Baillie (q.v.), author of *A Dissuasive from the Errours of the Time, . . . especially of the Independents* (London, 1645), speaks of the Seekers as people that are represented in "all the sects." Reggius (i.e., G. Horn, in *De statu ecclesiæ Britannicæ*, Danzig, 1647) heard that the Seekers believed the Apostle Paul still to be living and that he would in a short time appear. E. Pagit affirmed that "some of them" declared the Church to be "in the wilderness" and that they were "seeking" it. An *Anonymi epistola* (contained in the Whitsuntide program of the University of Göttingen, 1814) speaks of the "new sect of the Seekers or Inquirers, commonly called 'Seekers.'" Whenever the "Seekers" are compared with the Church, the Presbyterians are referred to as representing the latter, which seems to show that Seekers and Independents were one.

The *Epistola* gives the following as characteristics of the Seekers: (1) They deny the absolute authority of the Scriptures, because the original manuscripts have been lost; moreover, the Bible is declared to be unsuitable as a foundation of faith, because few men can read it in the original languages; (2) the Church's doctrine concerning God as a "thing most easy to understand" is questioned; (3) the limitation of the sacraments to two is not founded on Scripture; (4) with regard to baptism, they doubted whether only ministers of the Church could perform it; whether it was right to perform it only in churches; whether the baptism of children should be encouraged; whether the customary formula was proper, preferring the form "in the name of Christ" or "of the Lord Jesus"; (5) they criticized the celebration of the Lord's Supper, discussing whether women should participate, whether ministers only should distribute the bread and wine, and whether it should be administered only in the church; (6) they attacked the church doctrine of the sufficiency of faith, (7) the Church's mode of investiture in office; and (8) proclaimed the absolute religious freedom of all men.

It is improbable that any sect advocated these heterogeneous views and only these, though in general they accord with the Independents' position. The view that the Independents and Seekers are one is supported by a sentence from a letter of Cromwell's, of Oct. 25, 1646 (*Oliver Cromwell's Letters and Speeches*, ed. T. Carlyle, 3 vols., London, 1866): "to be a seeker is to be of the best sect next to a finder, and such an one shall every faithful humble seeker be at the end. Happy seeker, happy finder!" (F. Kattenbusch.)

The term is properly applicable not to a sect but to individuals who failed to find satisfaction in the doctrines and practises of any existing denomination, though they hoped by further study of the Scriptures or by special divine revelation to gain new light adequate for their guidance. Roger Williams (q.v.), after he had founded a church of immersed believers, reached the conviction that the ordinances had been lost in the great apostasy, and that no one had a right to restore them without a special revelation from God. A. H. N.

Bibliography: E. Pagitt, *Heresiography: or, a Description of the Hereticks and Sectaries of these latter Times*, London, 1645; H. Reggius (i.e., Georg Horn), *De statu ecclesiæ Britannicæ hodierno*, Danzig, 1647; *Reliquiæ Baxterianæ*, ed. M. Sylvester, p. 76, London, 1697.

SEELEY, SIR JOHN ROBERT: Man of letters; b. at London Sept. 10, 1834; d. at Cambridge Jan. 13, 1895. He graduated at Cambridge (B.A., 1857); became fellow of Christ's College, 1858; a master in City of London School, 1861; professor of Latin, University College, London, 1863; professor of modern history at Cambridge, 1869. He was the author of the very celebrated *Ecce Homo, a Survey of the Life and Work of Jesus Christ* (London, 1865; latest ed., 1908), which evoked among many others the reply of Joseph Parker, *Ecce Deus* (1867). Other works of theological interest were *Lectures and Essays* (1870); *Natural Religion* (1882). He wrote also a number of works in political history and in literature, including *The Growth of British Policy* (1895; contains a memoir by G. W. Prothero).

Bibliography: Besides the memoir by Prothero, ut sup., consult: *DNB*, li. 190–193; J. R. Tanner, in *English Historical Review*, x (1895), 507–514; M. Todhunter, in *Westminster Review*, cxlv (1896), 503 sqq.; H. A. L. Fisher, in *Fortnightly Review*, lxvi (1896), 183 sqq.

SEELYE, JULIUS HAWLEY: Congregationalist; b. at Bethel, Conn., Sept. 14, 1824; d. at Amherst, Mass., May 12, 1895. He was graduated from Amherst College, 1849; from Auburn Theological Seminary, 1852; and studied at Halle, Germany, 1852–53; became professor of moral philosophy and metaphysics, Amherst College, 1858; member of Congress, 1875; and was president of Amherst College, 1877–90. He translated Albert Schwegler's *History of Philosophy* (New York, 1856); and wrote *The Way, the Truth, and the Life, Lectures to Educated Hindus* (Bombay and Boston, 1873); and *Christian Missions* (New York, 1875).

SEGARELLI, GHERARDO. See Apostolic Brethren.

SEGNA, sên'yä, FRANCESCO: Cardinal; b. at Poggio Ginolfo (diocese of Marsi), Italy, Aug. 31, 1836. He was educated at the Roman Seminary and the College of the Sapienza, after which he was professor of dogmatics in the College of St. Apollinaris, Rome, and divisional director of Oriental affairs in the Propaganda. In 1881 he was appointed canonist of the Holy Penitentiary, as well as canon of Santa Maria in Trastevere. He was assistant secretary for extraordinary ecclesiastical affairs until 1884, when he accompanied Rampolla to Madrid as councilor of the nuncio. After his return to Italy, he became auditor of the Rota, director of the Penitentiary, secretary for extraordinary ecclesiastical affairs, and canon of St. Peter's. In 1894 he was created cardinal deacon of Santa Maria in Portico. He is also archivist of the Curia and prefect of the Index, and has taken a prominent part in the discussion concerning the validity of Anglican orders.

SEGNERI, sên-yê'rî, **PAOLO:** Italian Jesuit; b. at Nettuno (31 m. s.s.e. of Rome) Mar. 21, 1624; d. at Rome Dec. 6, 1694. He entered the Society of Jesus (1637); was ordained priest, 1652; and from then until 1665 he taught in a Jesuit school at Pestoia. From 1665 to 1692 he spent half of each year in retirement, and the rest in traveling as a missionary throughout northern Italy. He became the foremost preacher among the Jesuits in Italy, and has been styled the "restorer of Italian eloquence." His sermons were modeled upon Chrysostom's. When the Jesuits at Rome perceived that Quietism (see MOLINOS, MIGUEL DE) was slowly undermining Romanism, and particularly Jesuitism, they sent him "a bundle of Quietistic books with directions to prepare an antidote to them." So in 1680 he published at Florence a small volume with the title, *Concordia tra la fatica e la Quiete* ("harmony between effort and Quiet"), in which without naming Molinos, or disparaging the contemplative life, he endeavored to show that the successful prosecution of Quietism was possible only to a few. His book raised, however, a storm of opposition from the then powerful Quietists, and was put on the Index. He prudently remained away from Rome. In 1692 Pope Innocent XII. called him to Rome as his preacher-in-ordinary, and theologian of the penitentiary. His *Opere* appeared in Venice in 4 vols., 1712, and later; also Milan, 1845–47 (best edition). His best-known work is *Il Quaresimale* (thirty-four Lenten sermons, Florence, 1679; Eng. transl. by James Ford, *Sermons from the Quaresimale of . . . P. Segneri*, 3 vols., London, 1857–61, 4th ed., 1869, reprinted 2 vols., New York, 1872). Besides this, there have been translated: *The Devout Client of Mary Instructed* (London, 1724; 1857); *The Knowledge of Ourselves* (1848); *Father Segneri's Sentimenti; or, Lights in Prayer* (1876); *Panegyrics* (1877); *Manna of the Soul* (2 vols., 1879); *Practice of Interior Recollection with God* (1881).

BIBLIOGRAPHY: G. Massei, *Breve Ragguaglio della Vita del . . . P. Segneri*, Venice, 1701; E. P. Hood, *Lamps, Pitchers, and Trumpets*, vol. i., London, 1867; J. Bigelow, *Molinos the Quietist*, pp. 18–24, New York, 1882; *KL*, xi. 70–71.

SEGOND, sê'gon, **JACQUES JEAN LOUIS:** Swiss Protestant theologian; b. at Plainpalais, Geneva, Oct. 4, 1810; d. at Geneva June 18, 1885. He studied at the universities of Geneva, Strasburg, and Bonn; was pastor of the Geneva National Church at Chênes-Bourgeries, 1840–41; founded a society at Geneva for the exegetical study of the New Testament which lasted 1836–41, and [illegible] free lectures in the university on Old-Te[illegible] exegesis; lectured on Old-Testament [illegible] 1862–64; and was professor of Old-Test[illegible] gesis, 1872–85. His fame rests upon his [illegible] at the request of the Venerable Com[illegible] tors of Geneva, *La Sainte Bible; Ancien Testament* (2 vols., Geneva, 1874), *Le Nouveau Testament* (1880); reprinted by the University Press (Oxford, 1880). His other works include *Ruth* (Geneva, 1834); *L'Ecclésiaste* (1835); *De voce Scheol et notione Orci apud Hebraeos* (1835); *De la nature de l'inspiration chez les auteurs et dans les écrits du Nouveau Testament* (1836); *Traité élémentaire des accents hébreux* (1841); *Soirées chrétiennes* (2 ser., 1850; new ser., 1871); *Géographie de la terre sainte* (1851); *Récits bibliques à l'usage de la jeunesse* (1862); *Chrestomathie biblique* (1864); and *Le prophète Esaïe* (1866).

BIBLIOGRAPHY: Lichtenberger, *ERS*, xi. 196–197.

SEIDEMANN, sai'de-mân, **JOHANN KARL:** German Lutheran; b. at Dresden Apr. 10, 1807; d. there Aug. 5, 1879. He was educated at the University of Leipsic (1826–28), and, after teaching in his native city in various institutions, was called in 1834 to the pastorate of Eschdorf, not far from Pillnitz. Here he remained until his retirement from active life in 1871. The first noteworthy work of Seidemann was his *Eschdorf und Dittersbach* (Dresden, 1840), supplemented, twenty years later, by his *Ueberlieferungen zur Geschichte von Eschdorf, Dittersbach und Umgegend* (1860). His first book was quickly followed by a series of monographs on the history of the Reformation in Saxony: *Thomas Münzer* (Dresden, 1842); *Die Leipziger Disputation im Jahr 1519* (1843); *Karl von Miltiz* (1844); *Erläuterungen zur Reformationsgeschichte durch bisher unbekannte Urkunden* (1844); and *Beiträge zur Reformationsgeschichte* (2 parts, 1846–48).

After 1846 Seidemann became more and more interested in the writings of Luther. In 1856 he published at Berlin the completion of W. M. L. de Wette's edition of Luther's letters, and three years later he issued forty-one additional letters of the Reformer in his *Lutherbriefe* (Dresden, 1859). In 1872 he edited the diary of Anton Lauterbach, which had recently been discovered by F. Schnorr von Carolsfeld (Dresden, 1872); and three years later published *D. Jakob Schwenk, der vermeintliche Antinomer, Freibergs Reformator* (Leipsic, 1875). In 1874 he discovered, in the Dresden library, Luther's earliest lectures on the Psalms—an autograph—which he edited under the title of *Luther[illegible] erste und älteste Vorlesungen über die Psalmen a[illegible] den Jahren 1513–16* (Dresden, 1876), of which on[illegible] the first volume appeared. When he died, he ha[illegible] nearly completed the collection of material for critical edition of Luther's "Table-talk." He ma[illegible] be considered the founder of modern research co[illegible] cerning Luther, though he was a collector and i[illegible] vestigator rather than a historian.

(T. Kolde[illegible])

BIBLIOGR[illegible]

parents were Moravian, but he became a student in Pennsylvania College, Gettysburg, 1839–41, without graduating; and his theological study was mostly private. He became pastor at Martinsburg and Shepherdstown, Va., 1843; Cumberland, Md., 1847; Baltimore, Md., 1852; of St. John's, Philadelphia, 1858; and of Holy Communion, Philadelphia, 1874. He was one of the most eloquent preachers of the country, possessing a style that was clear, ornate, and forceful. He was one of the founders of the General Council, and one of the committee which made its *Church Book*. He edited *Prophetic Times*, a monthly, 1863–75; was joint editor of *The Lutheran*, 1860–61; of *The Lutheran and Missionary*, 1861–73; editor of the latter, 1873–79; and traveled in Europe and the East, 1864–65. He was the author of *Lectures on Epistles to the Hebrews* (Baltimore, 1846); *Baptist System Examined* (Philadelphia, 1854); *Digest of Christian Doctrine* (1855); *Last Times* (1856); *Holy Types* (1860); *Book of Forms* (1860); *Evangelical Psalmist* (1860); *Parable of the Ten Virgins* (1862); *Ecclesia Lutherana* (1867); *Plain Words*, sermons (1869); *Lectures on the Apocalypse* (3 vols., 1870–84; 6th ed., 1900); *The Javelin, by a Lutheran* (1871); *Uriel, Occasional Discourses* (1874); *Church Song* (1875–81); *Lectures on the Gospels* (2 vols., 1876); *A Miracle in Stone* (1877); *Recreation Songs* (1878); *Thirty-three Practical Sermons* (1879); *Voices from Babylon* (1879); *Blossoms of Faith*, sermons (1880); *The Golden Altar*, manual of private devotions (New York, 1882); *Gospel in the Stars* (Philadelphia, 1882); *Luther and the Reformation* (1883); *Lectures on the Epistles* (2 vols., 1885); *Right Life* (1886); *Letters of Jesus* (1889); *Beacon Lights* (1900); *The Christ and his Church* (1902); and *Recent Sermons* (1904).

SEITZ, saits, ANTON: German Roman Catholic; b. at Windsheim (30 m. s.e. of Würzburg), Bavaria, May 27, 1869. He was educated at the universities of Leipsic and Munich (1887–88), and then studied theology at Würzburg from 1888 to 1892, after which he was curate at Hammelsburg. From 1895 to 1897 he studied philosophy at Munich (Ph.D., 1897), and in 1902 became privat-docent at Würzburg. Since 1904 he has been professor of apologetics at the University of Munich. Among his works are: *Die Apologie des Christentums bei den Griechen des vierten und fünften Jahrhunderts in historisch-systematischer Darstellung* (Würzburg, 1895); *Die Willensfreiheit in der Philosophie des Christian August Crusius gegenüber dem Leibnitz-Wolffschen Determinismus in historisch-psychologischer Begründung und systematischen Zusammenhang* (1899); *Willensfreiheit und moderner psychologischer Determinismus* (Cologne, 1902); *Die Heilsnotwendigkeit der Kirche nach der altchristlichen Literatur bis zur Zeit des heiligen Augustinus* (Freiburg, 1903); *Christuszeugnisse aus dem klassischen Altertum von ungläubiger Seite* (Cologne, 1906); and *Das Evangelium vom Gottessohn. Eine Apologie der wesenhaften Gottessohnschaft gegenüber der Kritik der modernsten deutschen Theologie* (1908).

SELAH (SELA): The former capital of Edom (q.v.), mentioned II Kings xiv. 7 and Isa. xvi. 1. The name means "rock" (cf. Gk. *Petra*, and Judges i. 36; Isa. xlii. 11). It is situated sixty miles north of Elath and seventy miles south from the Dead Sea, in the Wadi Musa, a deep cleft of the Mount-Seir range, near the foot of Mount Hor. It is approached through a narrow defile on the east, a mile and a half long, called the *Sik* ("cleft") of Wadi Musa. The rock of red sandstone towers to a height of from 100 to 300 feet above the floor of the wadi, and in places the way is so narrow that the traveler can almost touch the sides on either hand. Once the way was paved, and bits of the pavement can be seen. Abruptly the traveler comes upon the so-called Khaznet Fir'aun ("treasury of Pharaoh"), really a temple cut from the living rock, with a façade eighty-five feet high, beautifully sculptured, and in remarkable preservation. Two hundred yards farther along the valley, which widens considerably at this point, is the amphitheater, also entirely from the rock, thirty-nine yards in diameter, and with thirty-three tiers of seats, accommodating from 3,000 to 4,000 spectators. Farther on there are curious tombs, some very elaborate, other temples, chief of which is the Kasr Fir'aun ("palace of Pharaoh"), a ruined basilica, and a triumphal arch.

Besides the Biblical passages noted above, reference to this place may perhaps be seen in the work "rock" in II Chron. xxv. 11, 12; Jer. xlix. 16–18; Ob. 3. Nothing definite is known of the history of the place before its capture by Amaziah (II Kings xiv. 7), who renamed it Joktheel. The Nabatæans conquered the region c. 300 B.C., and made Selah, under its Greek form Petra, their capital. The city rose into prominence, being upon the high-road between Arabia and Syria, and so important for the caravan trade. The Seleucidæ made vain attempts to take it. Pompey captured the whole region called by Greek writers Arabia Petræa, i.e., Arabia whose capital is Petra. In Petra, Hyrcanus II. and his son Herod, afterward Herod the Great, found a hiding-place (Joseph, *Ant.*, XIV., i. 4; *War*, I., vi., 2, xiii. 8). In the first Christian centuries Petra was the capital of a Roman province, and it is from this period that the ruins most in evidence date. It became an episcopal see, and its bishops are mentioned as late as 536 A.D. It was destroyed by the Mohammedans probably between 629 and 632, was lost to knowledge till rediscovered by the Egyptian rulers in the thirteenth century, and then again sank completely out of notice until Seetzen, in 1807, visited it, and gave the world the wondrous tale. It is now quite often visited by tourists and other travelers.

BIBLIOGRAPHY: K. Baedeker, *Palestine and Syria*, pp. 176–183, Leipsic, etc., 1906; J. L. Burckhardt, *Travels in Syria and the Holy Land*, London, 1822; L. de Leborde, *Journey through Arabia Petræa*, London, 1838; E. H. Palmer, *Desert of the Exodus*, pp. 366 sqq., 440 sqq., Cambridge, 1871; E. Hull, *Mount Seir, Sinai, and Western Palestine*, London, 1885; J. Barth, in *American Journal of Semitic Languages*, xiii (1896–97), 267–268; J. Lagrange, in *Revue biblique internationale*, vi (1897), 208–230, vii (1898), 165–182; T. Noldeke, in *ZA*, xii (1897), 1–7; M. de Vogué, in *Revue biblique internationale*, vi (1897), 231–238; *JBL* (1899), 132 sqq.; *DB*, iv. 430–431; *EB*, iv. 4344–45; and the literature under EDOM.

SELAH, sī'la: A musical or liturgical term which occurs seventy-four times in the Bible (seventy-one times in the Psalms, and in Hab. iii. 3, 9, 13). Its meaning is not known, and modern scholars are much divided over its interpretation. It has been supposed (1) to represent the Greek *psalle*, "play on the harp," or "staccato"; (2) to be an abbreviation; (3) to mean "pause"; (4) to mean "for ever" (so the Targum, Aquila, Theodotion); or (5) to be a direction to raise the voice, equivalent to the musical sign *forte*, or *fortissimo*.

BIBLIOGRAPHY: C. A. Briggs, in *JBL*, xviii (1899), 132–143, J. Parisot, in *Revue biblique internationale*, viii (1899), 573–581; Emilie G. Briggs, in *American Journal of Semitic Languages*, xvi (1899–1900), 1–29; *DB*, iv. 431–432; *EB*, iv. 4346–47; and the commentaries on the Psalms.

SELBIE, JOHN ALEXANDER: United Free Church of Scotland; b. at Maryculter (7 m. s.w. of Aberdeen), Kincardineshire, Feb. 4, 1856. He was educated at the University of Aberdeen (M.A., 1876), the University of Tübingen (1878), and Free Church College, Aberdeen (from which he was graduated in 1880). In 1882 he became minister of Birsay Free Church, Orkney, and in 1896 succeeded his father as minister at Maryculter. In 1905 he retired from the ministry to devote himself entirely to literary work. Since 1893 he has been the assistant of James Hastings in the preparation of the *Dictionary of the Bible* (5 vols., Edinburgh, 1898–1904), *Dictionary of Christ and the Gospels* (2 vols., 1906–07), the *Dictionary of Religion and Ethics* (1908 sqq.), and *Smaller Dictionary of the Bible* (1908). He is editor of the foreign department of *The Expository Times*, and has translated E. König's *Exiles' Book of Consolation* (Edinburgh, 1899). In theology he is an adherent of the school represented by Driver's *Introduction to the Literature of the Old Testament*, and is "generally in sympathy with all modern liberal currents of theological opinion."

BIBLIOGRAPHY: *Expository Times*, Feb., 1907, contains sketch and portrait.

SELBIE, WILLIAM BOOTHBY: Congregationalist; b. at Chesterfield (22 m. n. of Derby) Dec. 24, 1862. He received his education at Manchester Grammar School and Brasenose and Mansfield colleges, Oxford (M.A., Trinity Hall, Cambridge, 1904); was lecturer in Hebrew and Old Testament, Mansfield College, Oxford, 1889–90; minister of Highgate Congregational Church, London, 1890–1902, and of Emmanuel Congregational Church, Cambridge, 1902–09; became principal of Mansfield College, Oxford, 1909. He has written *Life and Teachings of Jesus* (London, 1908); and *Aspects of Christ* (New York, 1909).

SELBORNE, ROUNDELL PALMER, EARL OF: B. at Mixbury (55 m. n.w. of London), Oxfordshire, Nov. 27, 1812; d. at Blackmoor, Petersfield (50 m. s.w. of London), May 4, 1895. He was educated at Trinity College, Oxford (B.A., 1834; M.A., 1837); called to the bar, 1837; became a queen's counsel, 1849; member of parliament, 1847–52, 1853–57, 1861–82; solicitor-general, 1861; attorney-general, 1863–66; and lord chancellor of England, 1872–74, 1880–85. He was elected lord rector of the University of St. Andrew's, 1877; raised to the peerage, 1882; and was president of the first house of laymen of the Church of England, Westminster, Feb., 1886. His principal significance for theology lies in the fact that he edited *Book of Praise, from the Best English Hymn-Writers* (London, 1863 and often), marking one of the great advances in English praise books (see SEDGWICK, DANIEL).

BIBLIOGRAPHY: R. T. Davidson and W. Benham, *Life of Archibald Campbell Tait*, 2 vols., London, 1891; W. Ward, *William George Ward and the Oxford Movement*, ib., 1889; idem, *William George Ward and the Catholic Revival*, ib., 1893; *DNB*, xliii. 150–154; Julian, *Hymnology*, p. 1589.

SELBY, THOMAS GUNN: English Wesleyan, b. at New Radford (2 m. n. of Nottingham) June 5, 1846; d. at Bromley (8 m. s.e. of London) Dec. 12, 1910. His father was a silk merchant, and educated him first in private schools at Nottingham and Derby, then in the Wesleyan College at Richmond, but he did not study for a degree. He was missionary at Fatshan and Shin Chau Foo in Canton Province, China, from 1868 till 1881, after which time he traveled extensively in other provinces. On his return to England in 1883 he served as Wesleyan minister at different places. In 1898 he retired for literary work to Bromley. He wrote several good books on China, *The Chinaman in his own Stories* (London, 1895); *Chinamen at Home* (1900); *As the Chinese see us* (1901); he also wrote a life of Christ in Chinese and was active on the executive board of the Anti-Opium Society from 1883 to his death. But it is as a preacher that he will be longest remembered. He published many volumes of sermons, *The Imperfect Angel, and other Sermons* (1890, 4th ed., 1894); *The Lesson of a Dilemma, and other Sermons* (1893, 4th ed., 1899); *The Holy Spirit and Christian Privilege* (1894); *The Unheeding God, and other Sermons* (1st and 2d ed., 1899); *The God of the Frail* (1902); *The Alienated Crown* (1904); *A Strenuous Gospel* (1906); *The Divine Craftsman, and other Sermons* (1909). He delivered the Fernley lecture at Liverpool on *The Theology of Modern Fiction* (1896); contributed to the series of *Books for Bible Students* that on *The Ministry of the Lord Jesus* (1896); to *Clerical Life, Letters to Ministers* (1898); and to *The Cross and the Dice-box: Sermons and Addresses to Workingmen* (Manchester, 1903); and published independently *The God of the Patriarchs. Studies in the Early Scriptures of the Old Testament* (1904).

SELDEN, JOHN: English jurist, statesman, and archeologist; b. at Salvington, West Tarring (11 m. w. of Brighton), Sussex, Dec. 16, 1584; d. in London Nov. 30, 1654. Selden received his education at Chichester free school, and Hart Hall, Oxford, but did not graduate, leaving college to take up the study of law at Clifford Inn. In 1604 he was admitted to the Inner Temple, and was called to the bar in 1612. Influenced by Ben Jonson Camden, and especially by Robert Bruce Cotton, he turned to theoretical and historical juridical investigations resulting in *Analecton Anglo-Britannicon* (1607); *Jani Anglorum facies altera* (1610); *England's epinomis* (1610); and *De laudibus legum Angliæ* (1616). He first won fame with his *De dis*

Syris (1617; Eng. transl., *The Fabulous Gods Denounced in the Bible*, Philadelphia, 1881), which attracted attention and was reprinted on the continent, and was long regarded as authoritative, though later oriental studies have shown that it relied too implicitly upon rabbinical sources, and was of course dependent upon the earlier philology and exegesis. This work was followed by a large number of oriental studies, made possible by his access to the rich collections of the Bodleian and of Lambeth palace. His most important investigations were: *De successionibus in bona defunctorum ad leges Ebræorum* (London, 1631, with a supplement, *De successione in pontificatum Ebræorum*, Leyden, 1638); *De jure naturali et gentium juxta disciplinam Ebræorum* (London 1640); *De anno civili et calendario veteris ecclesiæ seu reipublicæ Judaicæ* (1644); *Uxor Ebraica, seu de nuptiis ed divortiis veterum Ebræorum* (1646); *De synedriis et præfecturis juridicis veterum Ebræorum* (1650–1655). These publications were characterized by great learning, and in them Selden introduced to the western world many matters of oriental culture and history, such as the Coptic-Arabic calendar notation.

His *Historie of Tithes* (1618), in which he sought to prove that tithes had been enjoined by "ecclesiastical and positive law," but not by the *jus divinum*, caused him to be brought before the court of high commission for trial. He was compelled to express regret for having published the book, which was suppressed and its author forbidden to answer his opponents.

Selden, in consequence of this act, entered politics and took a foremost part in the fight for individual liberty, being in parliament in 1623, 1626, and in 1628, and later, where he led the attack against the duke of Buckingham, Charles' minister, aided in the fight for the habeas-corpus act, and was repeatedly imprisoned. He took a prominent part in the ensuing conflicts against the clerical party. As a member of the Long Parliament and the Westminister Assembly he used his influence against the catholicizing State Church. In his *Table-Talk* (1689; reprint, Oxford, 1892) he took the position that the State was sovereign, but that Church and State should each manage its own affairs. Selden was accused of infidelity, a charge to which his friendship with Hobbes gave a pretext, but he opposed Hobbes' doctrines and believed to the end in the divine origin of the Christian religion.

In his later years he joined the Presbyterians but opposed the excesses that ended in the death of Charles. His name is honored for his integrity and versatile learning. His writings, which include many not mentioned above dealing with subjects in law and history, suffer from obscurity, prolixity, and an unsatisfactory method. They are distinguished by subtlety and fearless outspokenness. After the king's death he retired to scholarly private life. A large proportion of his books, manuscripts, and archeological treasures ultimately came into possession of the Bodleian library. His *Works* were collected by Dr. Wilkins (3 vols., London, 1726, with *Life* prefixed).

Bibliography: J. Aikin, *The Lives of J. Selden and Archbishop Usher*, London, 1812; the *Life* by Wilkins in the *Works*, ut sup.; a biography by Singer appears in the editions of the *Table Talk* after 1847; A. à Wood, *Athenæ Oxonienses*, ed. P. Bliss, vol. iv., London, 1817; *DNB*, li. 212–224.

SELEUCIDÆ, sel-iū'si-dī or ci-dê ("descendants of Seleucus"): The name given to the dynasty founded in Syria by Seleucus, one of the generals of Alexander, which ruled Syria either in whole or in part and more or less continuously from about 321 to 65 B.C. The history of the dynasty necessarily involves also that of the usurpers or contestants who succeeded in establishing themselves for longer or shorter times, sometimes in only a part of the territory, during this stormy period. The history is of interest to the student of theology for at least three reasons: (1) because of the nearly continuous contact with the Jews and the effects upon their fortunes, especially in the reign of Antiochus Epiphanes (see below); (2) because of the Hellenization of the region, preparing for the culture which was to be in no small part Christian; and (3) because of the development of the city of Antioch, which was to become a great seat of Christian learning and activities (see Antioch, School of; Antioch, Synods of).

Seleucus I. Nicator (306–281), the founder, was a Macedonian, and one of the generals of Alexander in his Asiatic campaigns. On the death of Alexander, and at the first distribution of the provinces, Seleucus did not at once receive a separate assignment of territory, but was attached as chiliarch to Perdiccas, the "protector of the kingdom." But in 321 he obtained Babylonia, whence, however, he was expelled in 316 by Antigonus, but with the help of Ptolemy regained it in 312, thus fixing the era of the Seleucids (Oct. 1). After the victory over Antigonus at Ipsus in 301, Syria also came to him as a part of his dominions and Antioch displaced Babylon as the capital. Meanwhile, between 311 and 302 he carried his arms victoriously as far as the Indus, and in 306 assumed the title of king. With this success, he was too good a strategist to attempt to hold territory so far away as the extreme east, and so for a valuable consideration (500 elephants) yielded to Chandragupta (Sandracotta) the northwestern provinces of India. In the allotment after the battle of Ipsus Ptolemy had received Cœle-Syria and Palestine, territory which Seleucus coveted, and in a momentary panic had withdrawn. Seleucus claimed this as forfeited, but Ptolemy again assumed control in spite of Seleucus' protests, and the regions became anew the source of strife for a century between Egypt and Syria (see Ptolemy). In the contests which continued between those who were striving for Alexander's empire, Seleucus made constant gains, and at the end of his life all of Asia Minor except the extreme northeastern portion bordering on Armenia came into his possession; but this was really a source of weakness rather than of strength, as the history of the following reigns demonstrates. Meanwhile he was constantly engaged in the organization of his kingdom and in attempts at cementing the unrelated parts. He was assassinated by Ptolemy Ceraunos, son of Ptolemy I., in 281. He was a good administrator, an able statesman, generous and open as a man, withal a patron of art, trade, and agriculture.

Antiochus I. Soter (281–261), son of Seleucus, found that instead of coming quietly into possession of his kingdom he would have to fight for it. One of the purposes of the assassination of Seleucus by the freebooting Ptolemy Ceraunos was the removal of the leading personage in the East and the affording thus of an opportunity for carving a kingdom for himself. The effect was to throw the entire Greek world into a turmoil, with the various Greek aspirants or monarchs attempting to make capital out of the situation. Antiochus I. had been trained both in war and in government. When his father was killed, he was at work in his province (Babylonia), and his hold upon the East was firm because of the loyalty of the inhabitants to one of their own race (his mother was an Iranian). Ptolemy was prevented from more than a half-hearted bid for the kingdom by troubles at home. The real seat of war was Asia Minor, and the situation there was complicated by the irruption of the Gauls—the ancestors of the Galatians to whom Paul carried the Gospel and wrote his epistle (cf. W. M. Ramsay, *Church in the Roman Empire*, p. 105 et passim, New York, 1893). In spite of some victories (Antiochus is said to have won his title of Soter by a defeat of the Gauls), Asia Minor was in part lost to Syria, and the Seleucid possessions there constantly dwindled under the attacks of Macedonians and Egyptians, the whole north of that region was also lost to the Armenians. War with Ptolemy Philadelphus also intervened, the theater being the eastern coast of the Mediterranean and southeastern Asia Minor.

Antiochus II. Theos (261–246) was the second son of Soter, the eldest son having been charged with conspiracy and executed. The war with Egypt continued with varying fortune until the marriage of Antiochus with Berenice, daughter of Ptolemy Philadelphus, when his former wife Laodice was formally divorced and banished. History does not give a very clear picture of this king. He is portrayed as sensuous and debauched, and was the object of the flattery which produced his name Theos ("God"). He seems to have practically deserted Berenice for Laodice, and died at Ephesus, possibly poisoned by Laodice, who feared for the succession of her son. His death brought new turmoil to the kingdom, the two queens striving for their offspring. Berenice proclaimed her infant son king in Antioch, and he was slain within a few days while she herself fell soon by an assassin. Laodice, in Ephesus, proclaimed her son.

Seleucus II. Callinicus (246–226). The assassination of Berenice and her son brought her brother Ptolemy III. from Egypt to avenge her death, and there resulted his famous march through Asia (see Ptolemy), as well as conquests in Asia Minor of Seleucid possessions there. The queen mother of Callinicus was holding portions of Asia Minor really for her younger son Antiochus Hierax, who rebelled against Callinicus while the latter was recovering a part of his eastern kingdom. Eventually Mithridates of Pontus intervened in Asia Minor against Callinicus, who was attempting to subdue his brother, and that region was virtually lost to the Seleucidæ; in the East Callinicus had only partially recovered his possessions, the kingdom of Parthia being established there, when he was killed by a fall from his horse.

Seleucus III. (Ceraunus) Soter (226–223), son of Callinicus, thus succeeded to a difficult position. He attempted to recover Asia Minor, and was warring there when he fell, probably a victim to conspirators in his own camp.

Antioch III. Magnus (223–187), younger son of Callinicus, was in Babylon when his predecessor fell. He was called at once into action to repel assaults upon his realm from foes without and to put down rebels from within, assailing the eastern portion of his kingdom. After succeeding there, he took advantage of the opportunity to gain the long-contested Cœle-Syria and Palestine offered by Theodotus, governor of Cœle-Syria, when Ptolemy Philopator had disregarded his merits and permitted court jealousies to influence him. Antiochus at once recovered parts of the Phenician littoral, which was but the beginning of a series of operations which was to win Egyptian possessions in Asia for Syria. Continued success attended him till, at the battle of Raphia in 217, he suffered a disastrous defeat, which, however, Ptolemy did not follow up. Antiochus used the respite to regain his strength, this time employing his forces in the recovery of central Asia Minor, which he accomplished by 213. Before undertaking the more distant parts of the work in his plans of campaign, he associated his son Antiochus with him in the government, so as to leave a ruler in the capital in case of accident. In 212 he turned to the East—to Armenia, eastern Iran, Parthia, and Bactria—and penetrated to northern India, subduing states that had revolted, making tributary those which were on the fringes of his empire, and binding the petty kings, whom he left on their thrones, to his interest either by matrimonial alliances or by indebtedness to his magnanimity. By these exploits, in which he manifested a moderation equalled only by his statesmanship as exemplified by his treatment of the once hostile kings, he won the title of Magnus. In the East he had practically reconstituted the empire of Alexander. One blot stands to his discredit in that he set the example, to be followed by several of his successors, of pillage of temples in his seizing of the treasure of the temple of Anaitis (Aine) at Ecbatana. This act was impolitic, raising against him the hatred of the worshipers, and the practise was to cause infinite trouble to his descendants. In 204 he returned to Syria proper, but not to rest. With the death of Ptolemy IV. Philopator and the accession of the infant Ptolemy V. Epiphanes in Egypt, the time seemed ripe to realize the long-halted ambitions of Syria for the possession of Palestine. This he achieved, making, however, a matrimonial alliance with Ptolemy by betrothing to the latter his daughter Cleopatra with the revenues of the conquered territory as dowry. He next attacked Asia Minor to enlarge his holdings there (199–198); at this moment the Egyptian-Greek general Scopas attempted to recover Palestine for the Ptolemies but was defeated in the decisive battle at Paneias which terminated Egyptian rule in Asia (198). The next year Antiochus carried further his assault upon Asia Minor by sea and land, recovering Ptolemaic territory nearly all the way along the southern and eastern coasts. He then challenged Rome by passing into Europe, his successes seeming to him as a Greek to give him the right to intervene in the constant struggle of the Grecian states in behalf of a reunited Greek world. This brought a protesting Roman embassy, demanding his retirement and the restriction of his operations to Asia. But he assumed to be the liberator of Greece from the Romans, despised the Roman power, entered upon the struggle less fully prepared than was his wont, and suffered defeat at Thermopylæ. The Romans carried the war into Asia, and Antiochus met a crushing defeat at Magnesia, after which he was compelled to give up all the territory north of the Taurus mountains, was fined 15,500 talents, and a large quantity of corn. In 188 Antiochus departed to the East, and the report was that he was killed while plundering or on his way to plunder the temple of Baal at Elymais (cf. Dan. xi. 19; I Macc. viii. 6).

Seleucus IV. Philopator (187–176), son of Antiochus the Great, succeeded to a difficult task, that of recovering the prestige lost by his father in the contest with the Romans, while at the same time he had to pay the indemnity imposed by the latter. He found an empty treasury (which his comparatively peaceful reign succeeded in filling) and a consequent advisability for cessation from the ceaseless wars in which his predecessors had engaged (cf. Dan. xi. 20). It is possible, however, that he was prevented from intervening in the wars of the Greek world by an embassy from the Romans. He is the king mentioned in II Macc. iii. as sending, to confiscate the money in the treasury of the Temple at Jerusalem, his minister Heliodorus who is reported to have entered the sanctuary and to have been prevented by a terrible apparition there from accomplishing his purpose. On his return, Heliodorus formed a conspiracy and murdered Seleucus, putting on the throne the infant son of Seleucus (intending thus to keep the power in his own hands), passing by the elder son Demetrius (a hostage at Rome), and disregarding Antiochus the brother of Philopator. But the plans of Heliodorus came to nothing when Antiochus forced his way to the throne.

Antiochus IV. Epiphanes (175–164), son of Antiochus III., grew up in Rome where he was a hostage; he accepted Greek citizenship at Athens and a magistracy. Interest in him for the student of Jewish and Christian history centers in his determined attack in behalf of Greek culture and religion upon Jewish nationality, religion, and Scriptures, provoking the uprising which resulted in the temporarily brilliant period of Maccabean rule (see HASMONEANS). That he is the focus of the Book of Daniel (q.v.) is now generally accepted, while his picture, also from a Jewish angle of vision, is in I and II Maccabees (for a brilliant analysis of his character from a more than usually sympathetic point of view consult E. R. Bevan, *House of Seleucus*, ii. 128 sqq., London, 1902). When the stroke of Heliodorus became known, Epiphanes left for Syria, aided by Eumenes and Attalus of Pergamene, and soon succeeded in seating himself on the throne, overcoming opposition, getting rid in the usual way of rivals, and reducing to quiescence those opposed to him. In 173 he sent an embassy to Rome to seek assurance of friendship, which was granted with some reserve, though amity was assured. War with Egypt was begun by the latter, the object being the annexation of the Seleucid empire to Egypt. But Antiochus made adequate preparation not only for defense but for aggressive action, associated his infant son with him so as to leave a ruler in case of accident, defeated the Egyptians near Pelusium, pushed on and seized that frontier fortress, captured Ptolemy Philometor, established Seleucid government at Memphis with Philometor as viceroy, and withdrew after unsuccessfully assailing Alexandria. But Philometor came to an agreement with his brother to reign jointly, and Epiphanes returned to Egypt to subdue it once more only to receive the Romans' curt order to withdraw (168). Meanwhile his forces had been making a conquest of Cyprus, whence the Romans compelled their withdrawal.

The regions of expansion for Antiochus were thus circumscribed by the great western power. But the peculiar mission to which he deemed himself called was still possible of exercise, and that was the advancement of Hellenic religion and culture in the regions which were acknowledged as his own. He was especially a devotee of Zeus, of whom it is probable that he thought himself an incarnation (hence his own title for himself—Theos Epiphanes, "God Manifest"). Among the Jews, through the favor of the Greek rulers of Egypt and Syria and under the constant pressure of contact and the pass to favor which a tendency to adopt Greek culture put in the hands of apostate Jews, the drift was almost away from their own national religion. Onias had been overthrown as high priest by Jesus (175), who changed his name to the Greek Jason, and was in turn outbid for the priesthood by another Jew with a Greek name, Menelaos. Greek sports and exercises had been introduced for Jewish youth, and some even were ashamed of Jewish parentage and sought to eliminate the marks of it. Of course the nation at large had not gone over to Hellenism, though there was a large drift and it might have come to that. But a report during the king's Egyptian campaign that Jerusalem had declared for Ptolemy led Antiochus to sate his vengeance for defeated plans upon the Jews. The fact that the Hellenism of Menelaos had led to this was probably fuel to the flame of his anger. He first punished Jerusalem as a rebellious city; later he determined upon making it a stronghold of his kingdom as an outpost against Egypt, and to make it safe it was to be Hellenized. The Jewish religion was to be blotted out, the Temple was plundered and converted into a sanctuary of Zeus Olympios, the worship of Dionysos was introduced, the Jews were to sacrifice to heathen deities and eat sacrificed swine, while their books were to be destroyed. These measures were enforced by frequent massacres. Such measures as these with a people like the

Jews, always ready to be aroused into fanaticism, cemented the party opposed to Hellenism, caused revolt in those who were wavering in their adherence to the national faith, and led by degrees from passive to the active resistance which culminated in the Maccabean revolt and later in deliverance and autonomy for the nation (see ISRAEL, HISTORY OF, I., § 11; HASMONEANS, § 1). Antiochus left the carrying-out of this policy to Lysias, one of his council and a general of his army, and in 166–165 started on what proved to be his last expedition to the East. That he was impelled to this by an empty treasury is almost certain. He had posed as a patron of Hellenism not only by the attempt to convert the Jews, but by his large expenditures for temples to Greek deities, and not less by his extension of the city of Antioch, and by the rebuilding and readornment of cities in the East. Thus he began the erection of an incomparably splendid temple of Zeus at Athens, which was not finished till the reign of Hadrian (130 A.D.). Indeed, his central thought along these lines was evidently to unify his kingdom by means of Greek culture (I Macc. i. 41). Besides these expenditures, he had spent large sums on Greek celebrations, and thus left an empty treasury where he had found a full one. The report as to his death is to the effect that he barely escaped with his life from an attempt to loot a temple of Anaitis, and that soon after he was seized with some sudden malady—epilepsy or apoplexy—and died at the Persian town of Taba 165–164 (II Macc. ix. 7).

Antioch V. Eupator (164–162) had been associated with his father in the government, but during his term Lysias was the real ruler. The first result of the death of Epiphanes was that in Palestine the proscription of the Jewish religion as such ceased, probably because Lysias had seen that by such means the people would best be reduced to quietness. In Dec., 164, the worship of Yahweh was renewed in the Temple. But the contest had entered upon a new phase in which not merely religion but nationalism was the issue. The Syrians were practically forced, by the excesses of the Jews in punishing apostates, to carry on the war; the Maccabees sustained a severe reverse in 163 at Beth-zur, and Jerusalem was besieged. An attempt by a certain Philip to seize the Syrian throne compelled Lysias to make terms with the Jews, leaving a Syrian guard in the citadel at Jerusalem. He hastened back to meet Philip, whom he defeated. Meanwhile Demetrius I. had escaped from Rome, seized the throne, and had both Eupator and Lysias beheaded.

Demetrius I. Soter (162–150), son of Seleucus IV. Philopator, attempted while still at Rome to secure the consent of the senate to his return and assumption of the throne. But the Romans preferred the weakness of a court cabal in the East (which would give opportunity for intervention) to control by a single hand which gave promise of firmness. Procrastination resulted, and Demetrius took the veiled hint of Polybius that action was better than diplomacy. Accordingly he escaped from Rome, relied upon the inherent loyalty of the East to his house as against the palace camarilla headed by Lysias, and was not disappointed. The army seized and at a hint slew Lysias and Eupator, and Syria proper acclaimed the new king. Rome was not pleased, however, and permitted a certain Timarchus to assume kingship over the Medes; but Demetrius soon disposed of Timarchus, and continued the process of making sure his control of those regions. In Judea strife was continuing between the Greek party and the nationalists, and the former appealed to Demetrius for support; the latter established Alcimus, the spokesman of the Greek party, as high priest, and sent Nicanor against the Maccabees. In the ensuing conflict Judas gained his last great victory over Nicanor, and followed this up by appealing to Rome. But while the embassy was on its way Demetrius sent Bacchides with a strong force, and he defeated and slew Judas, established a chain of forts to hold the Jews within bounds, including the Acra at Jerusalem, which long remained a menace to the city. Encouraged by his successes elsewhere, Demetrius intervened in Asia Minor, but at length was disastrously defeated. His opponents there retorted by putting forth Alexander Balas as a claimant to the throne (153), asserting that he was the second son of Antiochus. The new claimant won over the Roman senate, and during the subsequent conflict Demetrius fell and Alexander became king.

Alexander I. Balas (Theopator Euergetes; 150–145) was assisted in overthrowing Demetrius by Ptolemy Philometor, whose daughter Cleopatra he married. Alexander's purpose in gaining the crown seemed from the issue merely the opportunity for indulgence in sensual pleasure. Government was turned over to his minister Ammonius, whose crimes were legion and inflamed the people. Meanwhile the Jews under Jonathan and Simon were making capital out of the conditions and the rivalry of kings in Syria. While Balas and Demetrius were striving for the throne, both were bidding for the support of the Jews, and the latter accepted each of the concessions made by either of the parties. So it came about that Jonathan became high priest, the Hellenistic party in Judea became practically extinct, the garrisons from the border fortresses were withdrawn, though that in the Acra at Jerusalem still remained; while the Jews were more closely bound together by the newly recognised high-priestly status of the Hasmoneans. In 148–147 **Demetrius II. Nicator,** the son of Demetrius Soter, a boy of fourteen, was put forward as a claimant to the Syrian throne, and the Philistine cities declared for him. The Jews were, however, faithful to Alexander, defeated the army raised in the Philistine territory, and so protected Alexander's southern approaches. Ptolemy Philometor again intervened, this time in favor finally of Demetrius, occupied Antioch, and, himself rejecting the offer of the crown of Syria, conferred it upon Demetrius (145), Alexander and Philometor both losing their lives as a result of the later phases of the conflict.

From this time the story of Syria is that of a series of struggles for the throne on the part of those who had claims more or less direct, two and even three kinglets at a time exercising authority over parts of the realm or retiring to gather strength for a new essay at power. **Demetrius II. Nicator** (145–138, 128–124) was practically maintained on the throne by the Cretan mercenaries, of evil fame, who had assisted to place him there, who, with Jewish contingents, rioted in Antioch and boasted of the slaughter of the gentiles wrought there. **Tryphon,** one of the generals of Balas, disputed the reign of Nicator, setting up **Antiochus VI. Theos Epiphanes Dionysus** (145–?), son of Alexander Balas, in Antioch while Demetrius ruled in Seleucia. The gains of the Jews seemed dangerous to Tryphon, and he treacherously captured Jonathan the Maccabee and slew him, hoping thus to leave the Jews without a leader and at his mercy. This alienated the Jews under the unexpected leadership of Simon, who espoused the cause of Demetrius. About 143–142 Tryphon had the young Antiochus assassinated and himself aspired to the throne, hoping to found a new dynasty. About 140 Demetrius determined upon a campaign in the East to recover that region from the Parthians; but he was captured by them (138) and held a close prisoner. This seemed to leave Tryphon a clear field. But **Antiochus VII. Sidetes** (138–128), younger son of Demetrius I., had grown up in Side of Pamphylia. When his brother was captured in Parthia, he entered Seleucia as the rightful king, and in the presence of a Seleucid the backing of Tryphon fell away while he was himself captured and forced to commit suicide. During the reign of Sidetes the genius of the Seleucids shone out with a dying gleam. The gains of the Jews had been enormous through the bidding of rival claimants to the Syrian throne and their own seizure of opportunities. They had gained territory never before in possession of Hebrews. Sidetes demanded indemnity for their conquests, which Simon attempted to meet with commercial bargaining. In 134 Sidetes sent an army which besieged Jerusalem and put the Jews in a humbler frame of mind, yet without raising fanatical opposition. He then set out for Parthia to recover the East and release his brother. Successful at first, in the end he was defeated and slain. Meanwhile, in the earlier stages of the conflict the Parthian king had released Demetrius, and later attempted to recapture him. The latter, having regained Syria, attempted the conquest of Egypt to restore his mother-in-law Cleopatra against Ptolemy Euergetes. But he was checked at Pelusium, while Syria revolted against him as soon as he left, **Alexander Zabinas** (129–122) being put forth as a pretender by Euergetes; Demetrius was defeated, became a fugitive, and fell at Tyre. Under Cleopatra, daughter of Ptolemy Philopator, the struggle went on between the house of Seleucus and Alexander. **Seleucus V.** (125–124), son of Nicator, was assassinated, possibly by order of Cleopatra, while his brother, **Antiochus VIII. Grypos** (125–124–113; 111–96) defeated Zabinas and ended his reign. Cleopatra then attempted to poison him but was caught in her own device (121?). Grypos amused himself with feasts, until **Antiochus IX. Cyzicenus** (113–95), his half-brother, assailed him and compelled him temporarily to withdraw (113); but two years later he returned and recovered all but Cœle-Syria, which Cyzicenus held. The rival kings died within a year of each other, both probably by violent deaths; then the sons of Grypos (**Seleucus VI., Antiochus XI., Philip, Demetrius III. Eucarus,** and **Antiochus XII.**) fought with the son of Cyzicenus (**Antiochus X. Eusebes**). In the mêlée Tigranes of Armenia captured the kingdom and held it (83–69), but in 69 the Roman Lucullus permitted **Antiochus XIII. Asiaticus** to sit on the throne. In 65 Pompey made Syria a Roman province.

Geo. W. Gilmore.

Bibliography: As sources recourse should be had to *CIG* and *CIS;* C. Michel, *Recueil d'inscriptions grecques,* Paris, 1900; to the historical works of Polybius, Appian, Strabo, the younger Pliny (*Hist. naturalis*), Isidore (*Stathmoi Parthikoi*), the *Chronicorum libri duo* of Eusebius (which contains some sources otherwise lost); and from the Jewish side the *Antiquities* and *War* of Josephus, and I and II Maccabees. For the English reader a splendid work is available in E. R. Bevan, *House of Seleucus,* 2 vols., London, 1902. Of singular value for completeness and exactness are: J. G. Droysen, *Geschichte des Hellenismus,* 2 vols., Hamburg, 1836–43; B. Niese, *Geschichte der griechischen and makedonischen Staaten seit der Schlacht bei Chäronea,* 3 parts, Gotha, 1893–1903. Other literature bearing on the subject is: L. Flathe, *Geschichte Macedoniens und der Reiche welche von makedonischen Königen beherrscht wurden,* vol. ii., Leipsic, 1834; H. F. Clinton, *Fasti Hellenici,* pp. 310–350, Oxford, 1851; A. P. Stanley, *Hist. of the Jewish Church,* pp. 285–396, London, 1877; E. Babelon, *Catalogue des monnaies grecques. Les Rois de Syrie, d'Arménie, et de Commagene,* Paris, 1890; A. Kuhn, *Beiträge sur Geschichte der Seleukiden . . . 129–164,* Altkirch, 1891; F. Susemihl, *Geschichte der griechischen Litteratur in der Alexandrinerzeit,* 2 vols., Leipsic, 1891–92 (gives excellent sidelights); A. Holm, *Griechische Geschichte,* vol. iv., Berlin, 1894, Eng. transl., *Hist. of Greece,* vol. iv., London, 1898 (comprehensive); H. Willrich, *Juden und Griechen vor der makkabäischen Erhebung,* Göttingen, 1895; J. P. Mahaffy, *Greek Life and Thought,* London, 1896; S. Mathews, *Hist. of New Testament Times in Palestine,* chaps. i.–vi., new ed., New York, 1910; G. Hoelscher, *Palästina in der persischen und hellenistischen Zeit,* Berlin, 1903; P. Barry, in *JBL,* xxix (1910), 126–138; Schürer, *Geschichte,* i. 166 sqq., Eng. transl., I., i. 169 sqq. For the Jewish side use may be made of the literature on the period indicated under Ahab, and Israel, History of (some exact references will be found to this literature in C. F. Kent, *Hist. of Jewish People,* p. 367, New York, 1899); and of the later commentaries on Daniel and on I and II Maccabees. The history of Egypt and Syria so interlaced during this period that the literature given under Ptolemy will be found illuminative for the most part.

SELF-DEFENSE: A term of jurisprudence, politics, and ethics, requiring a different treatment in each. In law it is an act which has the outward form of a penal offense, but instead of being penal it is permissible and justifiable—a defense which is requisite in order to ward off an illegal attack of which there is immediate danger. The danger may be of loss of life, bodily injury, or injury to honor or property. The defense may go to the length of killing the aggressor, even without respect to the value of the good that is threatened; but excess beyond a reasonable measure of defense involves guilt, though not penal, in view of the alarm caused in the one threatened. In the political field the question of self-defense assumes importance in deciding the justification of war or revolution. In a thoughtful discussion of the question (*Ethik,* II., ii. 265 sqq.) Hans Lassen Martensen is inclined to justify revolutions of a national character, such as the revolt of the Low Countries against Spanish domination, as cases in which a nation is defending its life.

From the purely ethical standpoint, personal self-defense is not only a right but a duty, to be restricted to the defense of life or female honor (R. Rothe, *Ethik*, ii. § 894). If life is attacked in such a manner that it can not be defended by flight or by recourse to the protection of the State, and if no purpose is served by its sacrifice except the permission of a crime, then the one attacked has the duty of opposing not violence to violence, but right to violence. The individual is here fighting not for himself alone, but for social rights, and for moral principle. Martyrdom is a different case; here the duty of bearing witness to divine truth rises above the duty of self-preservation in the same measure as the value of the truth of God above the life of sense. The defense of other goods than life and the sexual honor is morally not so universal a duty, and the measures of self-defense should be proportionate to the value of the thing threatened. The Bible contains no prohibition of self-defense; Matt. v. 38–39 can not be adduced under the conditions here laid down, and Ex. xxii. 2, 3 is not a general moral precept but a regulation of the Mosaic law. The action of Peter in the garden of Gethsemane was from his point of view justifiable self-defense; the special reason for Christ's rebuke of it is obvious. Ethical and juridical constructions diverge on this matter. In all instances the moral sense must intensify the consciousness of duty. On the other hand, the law makes concessions in self-defense which are untenable in moral judgment.

(KARL BURGER†.)

SELF-DENIAL: A term, the exact adversative of Selfishness (q.v.), expressing the reference of human will and desire not to self but to the altruistic object (Matt. x. 38–39, xvi. 24–25; Mark viii. 34–35; Luke ix. 23–24). It represents a New-Testament idea (*arneisthai; aparneisthai*). Of self-denial in the sense in which Jesus enjoined it upon his followers the world before him was unconscious, and outside of him has no knowledge of it. Self-denial demands nothing less than the renunciation of the self and the deliverance of the will from the false egoistic center, thereby virtually abolishing or losing the natural life and gaining a new true life-center, by joining the will with the divine, or having one's life hid with Christ in God (Col. iii. 3), not living for self but Christ (II Cor. v. 15; cf. Gal. ii. 20). It involves the exercise of a lifetime. Its first appearance is in repentance. When the divine Spirit takes hold of man, he is thrown into self-conflict. An inclination to truth and righteousness in him awakens the desire or will to escape from the carnal self. This willing is as yet weak, but God permits the upright to conquer. Regeneration takes place, and self-denial becomes a daily exercise and enters into every contested act or step that makes for righteousness and holiness. It is thus the inner principle of Christian discipleship. With a daily self-abnegation and crucifying of the flesh, the new life in Christ grows, increases in strength, and reaches a more and more complete character. Self-denial becomes habitual. It is contrary to the spirit of the Gospel to prescribe a law to self-denial and convert it into a work of merit. As a product of the freedom of the regenerate it possesses ethical value, and is an important means to the promotion of Christian unity, in the suppression of all the motives that violate brotherly love, and the alternative advancement of the gentleness that overcomes an erring one, the humility that serves, and the fidelity that yields in order to win.

(KARL BURGER†.)

BIBLIOGRAPHY: H. Martensen, *Christian Ethics*, ii. 411, Edinburgh, 1882; I. A. Dorner, *System of Christian Ethics*, pp. 378 sqq., New York, 1887; J. Köstlin, *Christliche Ethik*, pp. 74, 119, 123, 197–198, Berlin, 1899; the literature under SELFISHNESS; and the lexicons under *ἀρνεῖσθαι*, *ἀπαρνεῖσθαι*.

SELFISHNESS: A term of late origin for a conception of great antiquity, which means, more appropriately than "egoism," the exclusive reference of human will and desire to self in contrast with the love and obedience by which man is obligated to God by virtue of his created character (cf. SELF-DENIAL). This abnormal tendency may be regarded dogmatically as the fundamental sin; ethically, as the root of sinful development, and as the concomitant and undercurrent of all natural morality. Man as a dual being, in his personality akin with God, and identified on the one side with the world, had the duty and privilege of maintaining fellowship with God by free grateful love, and first of consecrating himself to God, and then by faithful service of sustaining the world in obedience toward God and likewise sanctifying it for him. In the faithful pursuit of this mission, the image of God was to be realized in him, as the end of his life and development. How he departed from this original career set before him is a matter that pertains to the problem of the origin of evil. Attention is called here only to the difference between the idea that selfishness is the root of sin (J. Müller) and its alternative, that it originated from sense (R. Rothe). As by a false self-assertion man sought his own life and, independently of God, yielded to the temptations to be like God, he released the impulses of sensuousness within (Gen. iii.). Spiritual apostasy from God resulted in sensual inclination toward the world. Man who, by self-exaltation, seeks to force his own salvation instead of accepting it from above, brings upon himself the punishment of self-humiliation. He becomes a slave to carnality and appetite. The development springing from this perverse tendency of selfishness may assume either of two commutable and multitudinously intersecting directions—the passion of sensual indulgence and spiritual pride. The sensualist pursues happiness by seeking to conquer the world and finding satisfaction in its goods and joys. From this arises the so-called "battle for existence," offered as a hypothesis for the history of human development. The elements of truth in this are that selfishness recognizes no social obligation. Spiritual pride, on the other hand, feigns to despise selfishness, and aspires to satisfaction in an assumed spiritual perfection. Its motives are the conceit of knowledge and the passion to rule. The sensual man is not without pride, setting up his theory of self-justification; and spiritual pride frequently suffers most humiliating disasters when the suppressed and despised sensuality reasserts itself.

The coarse and common sins classify themselves under sensuality, the more refined and spiritual ones under pride. Self is in all instances central; love of God is in all its forms negated and excluded, while the morality based on egoism is atheistic. The effort to oppose a coarse selfishness to a "rational self-love" which places the benefits and advantages of self uppermost but concedes also something similar to others, may be taken as a disguise of its real nature and a dissembling of virtue. Its egoism is chiefly commercial. Live and let live is its maxim. In family-life selfishness ascends even as far as heroism or self-sacrifice. Parents deny themselves to accumulate for their offspring or provide for their education. In the aristocracy all is sacrificed to the maintenance of the name. Ambition in knowledge, art, and statesmanship is virtually self-seeking. Even piety is not inaccessible to it. Here it appears in both forms; passion of spiritual indulgence and self-righteousness. Not content with simple Biblical fare, it drags worldly affectations and modes into the religious life. Self-righteousness is the root of Pharisaism; and how ineradicably it is embedded in the human heart is illustrated in Christian history and human experience. In the last account, selfishness rewards its votaries with death. Seeking to save their lives they shall lose them. (KARL BURGER†.)

BIBLIOGRAPHY: R. Rothe, *Theologische Ethik*, vol. i., Wittenberg, 1867; A. Wuttke, *Christian Ethics*, i. 175, ii. 165, New York, 1876; J. Müller, *Lehre von der Sünde*, ii. 3–4, Breslau, 1839–44, Eng. transl., 2 vols., Edinburgh, 1877; I. A. Dorner, *Christliche Glaubenslehre*, ii. § 177, 2 vols., Berlin, 1886, Eng. transl., Edinburgh, 1880–82; idem, *System of Christian Ethics*, pp. 378 sqq., New York, 1887; A. H. Strong, *Philosophy and Religion*, pp. 450–457, ib. 1888; H. L. Martensen, *Ethik*, i. 132 sqq., Berlin, 1894, Eng. transl., London, 1881–82; J. Köstlin, *Christliche Ethik*, pp. 74, 93 sqq., 197 sqq., 393, 456 sqq., 532, 548 sqq., Berlin, 1899.

SELIGENSTADT, sē'lig-en-stāt": A small Hessian town on the Rhine (15 m. e.s.e. of Frankfort), at which Archbishop Aribo (Arno) of Mainz convened, probably on Aug. 12, 1023, one of the most important of the comparatively few German medieval provincial synods. It was attended by Bishops Burchard of Worms, Werner of Strasburg, Brun of Augsburg, Eberhard of Bamberg, and Meginhard of Würzburg, and the abbots of Fulda, Hersfeld, Lorsch, St. Maximin, Toley, St. Burchard in Würzburg, Schlüchtern, St. Alban, Klingenmünster, and Bleidenstadt. The decisions of the synod concern, among other matters, the observance of fasts before high feasts, the ember-day fasts, the prohibition of superstitious usages, synodal procedure in cases of adultery, the degrees of kinship, prohibition of a transfer of a church without the permission of the diocesan, and penance. There was also a prohibition against going to Rome without the consent of the bishop or his vicar; and it was likewise enacted that those charged with grave offenses should be obliged to perform the penances enjoined by their parish clergy before being permitted to go to Rome to seek absolution from the pope, such a visit being itself contingent upon the consent of their diocesans. The two latter requirements have by some been construed as attempts to reduce papal prerogatives to mere honorary privileges, but as a matter of fact they simply reaffirm usages which already existed. (A. HAUCK.)

BIBLIOGRAPHY: R. Müller, *Erzbischof Aribo von Mainz*, Berlin, 1881; W. Dersch, *Die Kirchenpolitik des Erzbischof Aribo von Mainz*, Marburg, 1899; Hauck, *KD*, iii. 534 sqq.; Hefele, *Conciliengeschichte*, iv. 671.

SELL, EDWARD: Church of England, orientalist; b. at Wantage (14 m. s.w. of Oxford) Jan. 24, 1839. He finished his education at the Church Missionary College, London, 1862, and was fellow of Madras University, 1874; was made deacon in 1862, and priest, 1867; was principal of the Harris High School for Mohammedans, Madras, India, 1865–81; became secretary of the Church Missionary Society for the dioceses of Madras and Travancore, 1881; examining chaplain to the bishop of Madras, 1899; and canon of St. George's Cathedral, Madras. He is one of the chief authorities on Mohammedanism, and in this interest has written *The Faith of Islam* (London, 1880, 3d ed., 1907); *The Historical Development of the Qur'an* (1897; 2d ed., 1909); *Essays on Islam* (1901); *Islam: its Rise and Progress* (1907); *The Religious Orders of Islam* (1908); *The Khulafa'r-Rashidun* (1909); *The Cult of Ali* (1909); *The Battles of Badr and Uhud* (1909); *Al-Qur'an* (1909); *Sufiism* (1910); *The Druses* (1910); *Ghazwas and Siriyas* (1911).

SELL, KARL: German Protestant; b. at Giessen Nov. 29, 1845. He studied at the universities of Halle, Göttingen, and Giessen (1863–70; Ph.D., Giessen, 1869); was curate at Darmstadt (1869–1871); pastor there (1871–82); supreme consistorial counselor and superintendent in the province of Starkenburg (1882–91), and since 1891 has been professor of church history in the University of Bonn. He has written *Das Christentum gegenüber den Angriffen von Strauss* (Heilbronn, 1877); *Aus Religions- und Kirchengeschichte* (Darmstadt, 1880); *Alice, Grossherzogin von Hesse* (1883); *Die geschichtliche Entwicklung der Kirche im neunzehnten Jahrhundert* (Giessen, 1887); *Aus der Geschichte des Christentums* (Darmstadt, 1889); *Philipp Melanchthon und die deutsche Reformation bis 1531* (Halle, 1897); *Die Entwicklung der katholischen Kirche im neunzehnten Jahrhundert* (Leipsic, 1898); *Goethes Stellung zur Religion und zum Christentum* (Freiburg, 1899); *Die Religion unserer Klassiker, Lessing, Herder, Schiller, Goethe* (Tübingen, 1904, 2d ed., 1910); *Katholizismus und Protestantismus in Geschichte, Religion, Politik, Kultur* (Leipsic, 1908); *Wilhelm von Humboldt in seinen Briefen* (1909); and *Christentum und Weltgeschichte bis zur Reformation* and *seit der Reformation* (2 parts, 1910).

SELLIN, ERNST FRIEDRICH MAX: Austrian Protestant; b. at Altschwerin (80 m. n.w. of Berlin), Mecklenburg, May 26, 1867. He was educated at the universities of Rostock, Erlangen, and Leipsic; taught in a gymnasium at Parchim (1891–94); was privat-docent for Old-Testament exegesis at Erlangen (1894–97); professor of Old-Testament exegesis and archeology in the Evangelical theological faculty of the University of Vienna (1897–

1908), during this period making important excavations in Palestine; and since 1908 professor at Rostock in Old-Testament exegesis. He has written *Beiträge zur israelitisch-jüdischen Religionsgeschichte* (2 vols., Leipsic, 1896–97); *Serubbabel, ein Beitrag zur Geschichte der messianischen Erwartung und der Entstehung des Judentums* (1898); *Studien zur Entstehungsgeschichte der jüdischen Gemeinde nach dem babylonischen Exil* (2 vols., 1900); *Tell-Ta'anek. Bericht über meine Ausgrabungen in Palästina* (1904); *Die alttestamentliche Religion im Rahmen der anderen altorientalischen* (1908); *Das Rätsel des deuterojesajanischen Buches* (1908); *Die israelitisch-jüdische Heilandserwartung* (in *Biblische Zeit- und Streitfragen;* Gross-Lichterfelde, 1909); and *Altes Testament* (Leipsic, 1909).

SELNECKER, NIKOLAUS: German Lutheran theologian, hymnist, and collaborator on the Formula of Concord; b. at Hersbruck (17 m. e.n.e. of Nuremberg) Dec 5. (or 6), 1530; d. at Leipsic May 24, 1592. He early manifested marked musical talent, but it was only after completing his course in law at the University of Wittenberg (1550–54) that he turned to the study of theology, mainly under the influence of Melanchthon, whose distinctly irenic type of theology he adopted. After lecturing for a time on philology, philosophy, and theology, he was recommended by Melanchthon, in 1557, as third court chaplain to Elector August of Saxony, and in Jan., 1558, he accordingly removed to Dresden. A year later he also took charge of the training of the choir in the court chapel, and for four years he was, in addition, tutor of the heir-apparent, Alexander (d. 1565). During this Dresden period he published exegeses of the Psalms, Wisdom of Solomon, and I John, as well as *Catalogus præcipuorum conciliorum œcumenicorum et nationalium a tempore apostolorum usque ad nostram ætatem* (2 parts, Frankfort, 1571) and such dogmatic and practical works as his *Libellus brevis et utilis de cœna Domini* (Leipsic, 1561) and *Pædagogia Christiana* (Frankfort, 1565). Meanwhile Melanchthon had died, and Selnecker came under the far from irenic influence of his father-in-law, Daniel Greiser, thus being transformed into a bitter polemist. The opponents whom he now created seized as a pretext his severe criticism, in one of his sermons, of the elector's inordinate fondness for hunting, and in 1564 Selnecker left Dresden. In the following year he accepted a call to Jena, but two years later he and his Philippistic colleagues (see PHILIPPISTS) were expelled from the country on the accession of Duke John William. He now turned to his former patron, Elector August, who appointed him, in 1568, professor in Leipsic, and also pastor of the Thomaskirche and superintendent. In 1570, securing from the elector leave of absence for two years, he accepted a call to Wolfenbüttel as court chaplain, ecclesiastical councilor, and supreme superintendent-general. Here, however, he became involved in most rancorous theological discord, accused by the Philippists of being an apostate to Flacianism, and by the Gnesio-Lutherans of being a friend of the despised Wittenberg theologians. Escape seemed impossible, and his only solace was in writing, this period, while he was residing at Gandersheim, witnessing the composition of his *Institutio religionis Christianæ* (Frankfort, 1572). In the summer of 1573 he worked for a few months at Oldenburg, where he sought to introduce a Lutheran church order, and was then recalled to his Leipsic professorship, resuming his superintendency and pastorate at the Thomaskirche in 1576.

This second Leipsic period was the most important, theologically, in the career of Selnecker, who found a task distinctly congenial to his irenic type of mind in the furtherance of the Formula of Concord (q.v.), even while becoming utterly estranged from his former friend Jakob Andreä (q.v.), who was bruskly dismissed from office by the elector. Selnecker's own time was, however, at hand. As long as August lived, his protégé was busily engaged in writing, making visitations of churches and schools, and in pastoral work, but with the accession of Christian I. in 1586 Philippism revived, and the second Crypto-Calvinistic controversy broke out. In 1589, unable conscientiously to refrain from criticizing Calvinism, Selnecker was suspended from office, although he still resided for a time at Leipsic. Within a few months, however, he fled, first to Halle and then to Magdeburg, and later secured the position of superintendent at Hildesheim. Late in 1591, on the sudden death of Christian, Selnecker was one of those invited to return to Leipsic and resume office. Despite serious illness, he accepted the call, but died almost immediately after his arrival.

The list of Selnecker's writings includes about 170 items, but of the collected edition which he planned, only four parts of his Latin works appeared (Leipsic, 1584–93). His writings are, in content, dogmatic and polemic, exegetic, historical, and devotional. The chief of these, apart from those already noted, are *Relationes aliquot: De consilio scripti Libri Concordiæ; De persona Christi et cœna Domini; De autoritate et sententia Confessionis Augustanæ; De autoritate Lutheri et Philippi; De controversiis nonnullis articulis* (Leipsic, 1581) and *Historie von der Augsburgischen Konfession* (1584).

A poet of some ability not only in Latin, but even in Greek, Selnecker occupies a prominent place among the hymnists of his period. He collected his hymns, together with those of other writers, in his *Fünfzig Psalmen des königlichen Propheten David ausgelegt* (Nuremberg, 1563); *Der ganze Psalter des königlichen Propheten David ausgelegt* (1565–66); *Tröstliche Sprüche und Grabschriften aus heiliger Schrift* (1567); *Psalter Davids mit kurzen Summarien und Gebetlein* (1572); and *Christliche Psalmen, Lieder und Kirchengesänge* (Leipsic, 1587). Many of his hymns mirror forth his personal experiences and events in his career, but they have preserved their popularity in Germany to the present day, while seven of them have been translated into English, the largest collection of the latter being in the Ohio *Evangelical Lutheran Hymnal* (Columbus, 1880). (F. W. DIBELIUS.)

BIBLIOGRAPHY: F. Dibelius, in *Beiträge zur sächsischen Kirchengeschichte*, part 4, 1888; Buchwald, in *Unsere Kirchenliederdichter*, iv (1905); G. J. Planck, *Geschichte des protestantischen Lehrbegriffs*, vol. v., 6 vols., Leipsic,

1781–1800; H. L. J. Heppe, *Geschichte des deutschen Protestantismus*, vols. iii.–iv., 4 vols., Marburg, 1853–59; K. F. Göschel, *Die Konkordienformel nach ihrer Geschichte*, Leipsic, 1858; G. Frank, *Geschichte der protestantischen Theologie*, vol. i., ib. 1862; R. Calinich, *Kampf und Untergang des Melanchthonismus in Kursachsen*, ib. 1866; Julian, *Hymnology*, pp. 1038–41.

SELWYN, sel′win, **GEORGE AUGUSTUS:** Church of England; b. at Church Row, Hampstead, London, Apr. 5, 1809; d. at Lichfield (15 m. n.n.e. of Birmingham) Apr. 11, 1878. He was educated at Eton and Cambridge (B.A., 1831; M.A., 1834). While curate at Windsor in 1841, he was appointed first bishop of the Anglican Church in New Zealand. At his farewell sermon before leaving England there was present John Coleridge Patteson (q.v.), then a youth of fourteen, later bishop of Melanesia. Besides ministering to the spiritual wants of his colonial diocese, he extended his operations to the South Sea Islands, navigating his own vessel, the "Southern Cross," for this purpose. He brought youths from Melanesia to New Zealand, who, after receiving instruction, returned to enlighten their countrymen. In 1861 this branch of work was entrusted to Bishop Patteson, who had assisted him from 1855. In 1854, in England, he obtained permission to subdivide his diocese of New Zealand and establish a general synod of self-government. Accordingly, upon his return four bishops were consecrated and a legal constitution went into effect. In 1868 he became bishop of Lichfield.

Bibliography: Mrs. E. A. Curteis, *In Memoriam. A Sketch of the Life of . . . G. A. Selwyn*, Newcastle, 1878; H. W. Tucker, *Memoir of the Life and Episcopate of George Augustus Selwyn . . .*, 2 vols., London, 1879; G. H. Curteis, *Bishop Selwyn of New Zealand, and of Lichfield*, ib. 1889; E. A. Bulley, *George Augustus Selwyn, First Bishop of New Zealand*, ib. 1909.

SELWYN, WILLIAM: Church of England; b. in London in 1806; d. at Cambridge Apr. 24, 1875. He was educated at St. Johns College, Cambridge (fellow, 1829; M.A., 1831; B.D., 1850; D.D., 1864), became deacon, 1829, and priest, 1831; rector of Branstone, 1831; canon of Ely, 1833; vicar of Melbourne, 1846; and Lady Margaret professor at Cambridge, 1855. Among his works are: *Principles of Cathedral Reform* (Cambridge, 1840); *Horæ Hebraicæ* (1848–60); *Testimonia patrum in veteres interpretes* (1859); and he edited *Origines contra Celsum*, books i.–iv (1877).

Bibliography: A sketch of the life by J. S. Wood is in Selwyn's *Pastoral Colloquies on the South Downs*, Cambridge, 1876, and another is in *DNB*, li. 233–234.

SEMI-ARIANS. See Arianism, I., 3, § 6.

SEMIPELAGIANISM: A synergistic view raised in opposition to Augustinian monergism. The origin and scope of the term in the history of dogma has not yet been clearly determined.

Augustine not Wholly Authoritative.

From a passage in the *Historia Pelagiana* (Padua, 1673) of Enrico Noris it is regarded as being created by the medieval scholastic theologians, but more probably Noris there traces back its origin to the post-Tridentine elaborators of the scholastic theology. Certainly it is not found in current usage as late as the sixteenth century. It appears isolated in the Lutheran Formula of Concord (*Epitome*, 581, 10) and by the year 1601 it is found in the records of the Congregatio de auxiliis in reference to an assailed thesis of Luis Molina (q.v.); and subsequently it became common. From this it appears probable that the term arose in the Molinist strife between the Dominican Thomists with the Jesuits. Its general acceptance may then have been occasioned by the public notice of the Molinist strife produced by the Jansenist controversy (see Jansen, Cornelius, Jansenism). Evidently the term was to represent that doctrine of sin and grace in which Prosper of Aquitaine (q.v.) opposed the Massilians, and was later represented by Faustus of Riez (q.v.), and in some points declared heretical by the Synod of Orange, 529. The Synod of Carthage (418) had adopted among the eight canons against the Pelagians (see Pelagius, Pelagian Controversies) that (1) Adam became mortal only by the fall; (2) infants must be baptized on account of original sin; (3) divine grace involves, besides forgiveness, the power to avoid sin; (4) sinless perfection is impossible on earth. The entire Augustinian doctrine of grace was, however, not approved in this. Two years later Augustine, in formulating the Pelagian heresy, goes beyond the judgment of the council in stating that Pelagians assume that the grace by which men are justified was not given *gratis* but "upon merit." Not all who approved the condemnation of Pelagius were in accord throughout with Augustine. The question whether the "grace of creation, remission, and doctrine" were sufficient to attain salvation or whether a "grace of inspiration" was inwardly essential in addition and for every act—the real point at issue—could be answered, as shown in Augustine's own thinking before 396, in the anti-Pelagian sense even where the Augustinian mode of thinking was not wholly followed. Once Augustine experienced this in the objection of a certain Carthaginian Vitalis, to whom he replied (c. 420), emphasizing grace "prevenient to human will." Again, upon the agitation occasioned by his doctrine of grace before merit and of predestination, in apparent contradiction with the merit of good works, among the monks of Hadrumetum, he forwarded to them for further enlightenment the *De gratia et libero arbitrio* teaching that the work of grace does not make freedom and merit nugatory, but is their only basis; he followed this with the *De correptione et gratia*, containing the doctrines of freedom by grace only, of perseverance, and the fixed number of the elect.

The last-named work stirred lukewarm friends to hostility in the monastic circles about Marseilles and Lerins, southern Gaul, including such men as

Objections in Southern Gaul.

Johannes Cassianus and Hilary, later bishop of Arles (qq.v.). The former held (*Collationes patrum*, xi.–xvii.) that man possessed a rudiment of good will, which the grace of inspiration even if prevenient served to reenforce. Man must be saved by grace but conditioned on his consent, and "all who perish do so contrary to the will of God." Reports of the disaffection reached Augustine in two letters from Prosper and another from

Hilary (428 or 429). With serious reverence for the piety of the Massilians, their objections are stated: (1) against the doctrine of predestination, involving human incapability of freely appropriating saving grace, on the ground that it is an innovation against the Fathers and subversive of the admonition and cure of souls of the Church. Moreover (2) the divine counsel of redemption contemplates all men; the choice of being saved or not is in the power of free will; and predestination (of which Rom. viii. 29–30 necessarily forced recognition) was based on the foreknown "merit of faith and perseverance." Augustine answered with *De prædestinatione sanctorum* on the "beginning of faith" and *De dono perseverantiæ* on persevering by grace alone. This was done in a fraternal spirit for the instruction of the Massilians, and Augustine therewith called attention to a similar former error on his part; but emphasizing, as these writings did, the most objectionable points, they naturally failed at conciliation. After Augustine's death (Aug. 28, 430), the polemics taken up by Prosper became more intense. The latter wrote *responsiones* to the Massilians (*MPL*, li. 155–174), and (li. 187–202) against an attack of Vincent of Lerins (q.v.); and then with Hilary resorted to Rome (432) for aid; but Celestine I. (q.v.) declined to take an open attitude. His letter to the bishops of southern Gaul to restrain the "presbyters" from menacing the unity of the Church by raising improper questions was vaguely non-committal. Prosper wrote his *De gratia dei et libero arbitrio* (li. 213–276) against the *Collationes* of Cassianus and removed to Rome (434) from the scene of conflict. The *Commonitorium pro catholicæ fidei antiquitate* (*MPL*, l.), which treats Augustine with silence, may be taken to indicate that Prosper abandoned a hopeless cause. The Massilians remained in possession of the field in southern Gaul. There the doctrine of predestination was regarded as a heresy about 450; the presbyter Lucidus who taught it was recalled, 473; and two synods (Arles and Lyons) authorized Bishop Faustus of Riez (q.v.) to present it anew in comparison with the right synodal doctrine. The result was his *Libri duo de gratia*, in which Pelagius and the "error of predestination" are alike denounced, without the conscious advancement of a special doctrine. More in line with Augustinian tradition were two anonymous writings of the fifth century, possibly from Gaul. *Libri duo de vocatione omnium gentium*, sometimes ascribed to the later Leo I., attempts to disguise the severity of the Augustine position by the conception of a *gratia* or *benignitas generalis* beside the *gratia specialis;* but basing the attainment of the "special grace," not in the human employment of *gratia generalis*, but purely in the divine will, makes the latter irrelevant. The *Hypomnesticon contra Pelagianos et Cœlestianos*, probably of the middle of the fifth century and apparently Gallic in origin, is remarkable for its reconstruction of the Augustinian doctrine of grace. It disavows the basing of predestination on "faith foreknown," but reckons also with a resistance to grace; the elect only are predestined, and "for those foreknown in evil works there may be said to be a predestined punishment." Rome seems to have assumed a similar attitude, though less outspoken. This is shown by an ancient but ungenuine appendix to the letter of Celestine I. cited above, a catalogue of orthodox guide-points on the doctrine of grace whose origin is unknown, although sometimes ascribed to the later Leo I. It is wholly Augustinian on total incapability, prevenient grace, and perseverance; but there is silence on irresistibility and predestination. That the writings of Faustus were included among the non-approved works at the close of the fifth century is quite possible.

The Controversy over Faustus; Synod of Orange.

The conflict was renewed in the sixth century from another point of departure. When in the controversy between the Scetic monks and the papal legates at Constantinople, 519, over the formula "one of the Trinity suffered in the flesh," a certain North African bishop, Possessor, tarrying there, extended his support to the legates by citing for authority Faustus of Ries. At this the monks declared Possessor and all those in accord with him to be Pelagians, and the controversy was opened concerning the orthodoxy of Faustus. The monks went to Rome (519) to secure the support of Pope Hormisdas and at the same time the disavowal of Faustus. The pope withheld decision at their departure after a stay of fourteen months, and, in reply to the motion of Possessor in 520, declared that Faustus, like all others not included among the Fathers, was incompetent to judge on dogmatic questions. The pope found error in the works of Faustus, but did not pronounce him heretical. Although Hormisdas appealed to the letters of Augustine (ut sup.) sent to Prosper and Hilary in behalf of the true doctrine on grace and free will, it does not follow that he recognized the ultra-predestinarian view as that of the Church. From Rome the Scetic monks had issued a written appeal to the African bishops living in exile in Sardinia, to support their Christological and anti-Pelagian views. One of them, Fulgentius of Ruspe (q.v.), responded in a thoroughgoing Augustinian manner in his *Ad Petrum diaconum de incarnatione et gratia* (*MPL*, lxv. 451–493), the seven books of *Contra Faustum* (now lost), *De veritatione prædestinationis* (603–671); and, with other bishops, *Epistula synodica* (435–442). The importance of this incident consists only in the revival of interest at Rome for the heritage of Augustine. In southern Gaul, Cæsarius of Arles (q.v.), a pupil at Lérins, and in certain respects esteeming Faustus, was, however, a representative of genuine Augustinianism, although from his sermons apparently unconcerned about the irresistible effect of grace. At the Synod of Valence (528 or 529) his doctrine was assailed in his absence. His counterstroke was a series of eight negative and seventeen positive canons adopted by the "authority and admonition of the apostolic seat" by the Synod of Orange taken from Prosper's theses of the *Sententiæ ex Augustino*. These not only negated all Pelagianism but partly the principles which had become dominant in southern Gaul a century before and were probably the opinion of a majority still. The resolutions affirmed the total moral inability of the natural man to do good, the dependence of all moral human activity upon grace, or *infusio et inspiratio Sancti Spiritus;* and the prevenience of grace to all merit and human choice and volition. Irresistibility is nowhere affirmed; the disconnection of baptism and the impartation of grace, which may be shown repeatedly in Augustine, is discarded and baptism is pronounced a vehicle of grace; and an anathema is declared upon those who maintain the predestination to evil, which is the only mention of that doctrine. Boniface II. approved these resolutions of Orange and they became the official disposition of the Semipelagian controversy for all time.

The View Defined. The Massilians held Pelagius to be a heretic and accepted the decision of the Synod of Carthage (418). They concurred in Augustine's doctrine of grace, including the thesis that man requires the inspiration of grace to do good. But they declined the Augustinian monergism; their synergistic view involved the decision on man's part, with reference to eternal life, whether by virtue of his freedom he assented, and therefore submitted to the operation of divine grace, or was indifferent to grace, therefore rejecting it. The Augustinian theses, that faith is purely an effect of grace; that grace is irresistible; that no human act (as *meritum*) is ever to be considered as a cause of the divine operation of grace; that salvation has its basis only in the divine election—these were unacceptable. This view has been designated as Semipelagian on the presupposition of the difference between Augustine referring the salvation of those who are saved to the grace of God alone, and Pelagius referring the same to the possible well-doing of man without the "grace of inspiration." Accordingly the synergism of the Massilians is correctly presumed to be "half" Pelagian, and the discovery by Augustine and Prosper of *reliquiæ* of Pelagianism is from their point of view well founded. But it is improper to make the doctrine of grace of Augustine, as a whole never recognized by the Church, the standard with which to compare a heresy. Semipelagian it was, for, in common with Pelagius, its thought was anti-Augustinian not only on points of Augustine never approved by the Church, but also on theses whose negation was later expressly condemned. But no Pelagian thought condemned by the Church of that time has ever been pointed out in it. Was Semipelagianism something other than the anti-Pelagian popular Catholicism of the time? The departures from Augustinian doctrine not censured at Orange should not be designated Semipelagian. From the point of view of the Church the material concept of Semipelagianism should be defined only by the standard of the later official doctrine, not by Augustinianism as such. As a censured heresy its distinctive marks are: (1) denial of prevenient grace; (2) refusal to recognize that "faith" was a "gift of God"; (3) refusal to regard the natural man as totally incapable of doing good, making the spontaneous cooperation of man a condition to the operation of grace; (4) presuming grace to be imparted in consequence of "some merit." A broader definition of the content and scope of the concept of Semipelagianism devolves upon a critical consideration of the development of the Roman Catholic Church. The attitude of the Roman Church to Augustine is untrue to fact. He is the *doctor ecclesiæ*, yet his doctrine of grace has never been officially sanctioned. The later development, even that which has official sanction, has drifted away in the direction characterized by Semipelagian thought. This untrue attitude arises from the obscure perplexities, which were to be left alone in the adjustment of the Semipelagian controversy. The decision of Orange is equivocal. Thorough Augustinianism may add to the sentence that "all the baptized should be able, if they will, to labor faithfully to become perfect," that of Augustine, "if God have compassion, we also exercise will." On the other hand, the idea of resistance to grace is not prohibited. This position appears already in the *Hypomnesticon*, antedating Semipelagianism. Here all the unbaptized, even the dying infants of Christians, remain subject to the uncertainty of predestination; merely the fact of their being non-elect is the reason why grace has never sought their rescue. But with reference to the baptized the anti-Augustinian tendency was triumphant. For even if the non-resistance of the elect was not taken as the ground of their election, yet the predestination to death of reprobates was grounded upon the foreseen demerit of their resistance, involving also the conditioning of election on the failure of the foreseen resistance. Augustine's doctrine was thus uprooted; for all the baptized the decision of eternal life rested upon free will. To such thought the revival of the predestination doctrine by Gottschalk (q.v.) seemed to be heresy. Therefore this view of the *Hypomnesticon* may be termed crypto-Semipelagianism. The Franciscan theology of the thirteenth century passed beyond this. With the aid of the distinction, coming down even from the fifth century, of *gratia generalis grata data* and saving grace, and *meritum de congruo*, and *meritum de condigno* (see SCHOLASTICISM, II., § 1), the Semipelagian representations appeared in new garbs. These views may be termed Neo-Semipelagianism. The two latter may justly be charged against the Roman Church of the present. (F. LOOFS.)

BIBLIOGRAPHY: T. Eleutherius, *Historiæ controversarium de divinæ gratiæ auxiliis*, Antwerp, 1705; C. W. F. Walch, *Historie der Ketzereien*, vol. v., Leipsic, 1770; J. Geffcken, *Historia Semipelagianismi antiquissima*, Göttingen, 1826; G. F. Wiggers, *Versuch einer pragmatischen Darstellung des Augustinismus und Pelagianismus nach ihrer geschichtlichen Entwickelung*, Hamburg, 1833; idem, in *ZHT*, xxiv (1854), 3–42, xxv (1855), 268–324, xxvii (1857), 163–263, xxix (1859), 471–591; P. Sublet, *Le Semipélagianisme des origines dans ses rapports avec Augustin, le pélagianisme et l'église*, Namur, 1897; F. Wörter, *Beiträge zur Dogmengeschichte des Semipelagianismus*, Paderborn, 1898; idem, in *Zur Dogmengeschichte des Semipelagianismus*, ed. Knöpfler et al., v. 2, Münster, 1899; M. Tacquin, in *Revue des sciences philosophiques et théologiques*, i (1907), 506–508 (on the date when "Semipelagianism" arose); Hefele, *Conciliengeschichte*, ii. 697 sqq., 724 sqq., Eng. transl., iv. 123 sqq., 152 sqq., Fr. transl., ii. 2, pp. 1053 sqq., 1085 sqq. (should be consulted for supplementary bibliography); Schaff, *Christian Church*, iii. 857–865; *KL*, xi. 121–126; and the literature under AUGUSTINE; CÆSARIUS; CASSIAN; FAUSTUS OF RIEZ; FULGENTIUS; HILARY OF ARLES; PELAGIUS, especially *NPNF*, 1 ser., vol. v., the "Introductory Essay"; PREDESTINATION; and PROSPER; and especially the works under DOCTRINE, HISTORY OF.

SEMITIC LANGUAGES.

I. Name: Up to the latter part of the eighteenth century, before Sanskrit was known to Europe, or attention had been directed to the Central and Eastern Asiatic tongues, or those of Africa (except Coptic), "Oriental languages" signified only Hebrew and its sister dialects: these alone, with the exception of Coptic, had been the object of scientific study. Up to this time all study of non-classical languages was connected with the Bible; Biblical students accomplished all that was done in Hebrew, Arabic, Ethiopic, and the related tongues, for the preceding 300 years. But when the linguistic circle began to widen, and attempts were made at classification, the need of special names for different linguistic groups was felt; and, for the more general divisions, recourse was naturally had to the genealogies in the table of nations in Gen. x. The credit, if such it be, of having originated the name "Semitic" (from Noah's son Sem, or Shem) for the Hebrew group, is to be given either to Schlözer or to Johann Gottfried Eichhorn (q.v.)—to which of the two is doubtful. The first known use of the term is in Schlözer's article on the Chaldeans, in Eichhorn's *Repertorium* (viii. 161, 1781), and he seems to claim the honor of its invention; but a similar claim is made by Eichhorn for himself, without mention of Schlözer, in his *Allgemeine Bibliothek*, vi. 772 (Leipsic, 1794), and Eichhorn appears to have been accepted as the author of the name. In a short while, however, it was everywhere adopted, and is now the recognised name of this group of languages. In Germany and France, and to some extent at least in England (so Coleridge, *Table-Talk*, 1827), the form "Semitic" was employed (after Septuagint and Latin Vulgate, and Luther's "Sem," instead of Hebrew "Shem"); while some English and American writers prefer the form "Shemitic," after the more accurate transliteration of the Hebrew. Between the two there is little to choose, but the shorter form, now the more common one, is preferable to the other, because it is shorter, and inasmuch as it is farther removed from genealogical misconception. The once popular but unscientific threefold division of all the languages of the world into Japhetic, Shemitic, and Hamitic, is now abandoned by scholars. "Shemitic" is misleading, in so far as it appears to restrict itself to the languages spoken by the peoples mentioned in the table of nations as descendants of Shem, while it in fact includes dialects, as the Phenician and the Philistine, which are assigned in the table to Ham. The form "Semitic" (in English, but not in German and French), as farther removed than "Shemitic" from "Shem," may, perhaps, be more easily treated as in itself meaningless, and made to accept such meaning as science may give it. On the other hand, as meaningless, it is felt by some to be objectionable; and other names, expressing a geographical, or ethnical, or linguistic differentia of the languages in question, have been sought, e.g., Western Asiatic, Arabian, Syro-Arabian: but none proposed has been definite and euphonic enough to gain general approbation, and it is likely that "Semitic" will retain its place for the present. If a new name is to be adopted some such term as "Triliteral" would be the most appropriate, since triliterality of stems is the most striking characteristic of this family of languages, and is found in no other family.

II. Territory: In ancient times (1,000 B.C.) the Semites occupied as their proper territory the southwestern corner of Asia; their boundaries, generally stated, being—on the east, the mountain range running south from about forty miles east of the Tigris River, and the Persian Gulf; on the south, the Indian Ocean; on the west, the Red Sea, Egypt, the Mediterranean Sea, and Cilicia; and on the north the Taurus or the Masius Mountains. The north and east lines are uncertain, from the absence of full data in the early Assyrian records. At least 1,500 years before the beginning of the Christian era, Semitic emigrants from Southern Arabia crossed the Strait of Bab-el-Mandeb, and occupied the part of Africa lying just south of Egypt, their territory being about that of the modern Abyssinia: these were the Gees ("emigrants," or possibly "freemen"), or Semitic Ethiopians. The main Semitic region thus lay between the tenth and thirty-eighth degrees of north latitude and the forty-fourth and sixtieth degrees of east longitude, with an area of over a million square miles. Semitic colonies established themselves early in Egypt (Phenicians in the Delta, and perhaps the Hyksos), and on the north coast of Africa (Carthage and other cities) and the south coast of France (Marseilles) and Spain, possibly (though this is uncertain) in Asia Minor and in Greece. In modern times Syrian Semites are found in Kurdistan, as far east as the western shore of Lake Urumiah (lat. 37° 30′ N.; long. 45° 30′ E.); but it is doubtful whether this region was Semitic before the beginning of the Christian era. A large part of Semitic territory was steppe or desert. Only those portions which skirt the banks of rivers and the shores of seas (with the exception of the city of Mecca and possibly one or two other small cities) were occupied by settled populations; the desert was traversed by tribes of nomads, whose life was largely predatory. Semitic speech is interesting, not from the size of the territory and population it represents, but from the controlling influence it has exerted on history through its religious ideas.

1. In Historical Times.

The original seat of the Semites is unknown. There must have been a primitive Semitic race (with a primitive Semitic language), which existed before the historical Semitic peoples and dialects had taken shape; but of this primitive race we can say no more than that it goes back to a remote antiquity, since of one of its daughters, the Babylonian people, there are traces in the fourth millennium B.C.

2. The Original Home. The attempt has been made to determine the habitat of the Semites, before they broke up into separate nations, from their traditions, and from the vocabulary of the primitive tongue made out by a comparison of the existing dialects; but no trustworthy result has been reached. The oldest accounts say nothing definite. Gen. xi. 2, for example, contains the statement that the whole body of the descendants of Noah journeyed "eastward" (so *mikkedhem* is to be rendered), that is, toward the Tigris-Euphrates region; but the starting-point is not given, nor is there here anything of a separate Semitic people. Again, in the same chapter, the assembled human race is said to have been scattered from the city Babel, without, however, any indication of the points to which the descendants of Noah's three sons severally went. At most, a dim feeling may be discerned here that the Semites had once lived together in the Tigris-Euphrates valley; but this might be referred to the fact that the Hebrews believed that they themselves had come from that region to Canaan. No other Semitic people has, so far as is known, any ancient tradition on this point. The evidence from the primitive Semitic vocabulary is equally vague. Its terms for land, mountains, rivers, seas, metals, grains, fruits, and animals, do not fix any particular spot in western Asia as the locality where such terms must have originated. Certain similarities between the Egyptian and Semitic languages have suggested the theory that the Semitic-Hamitic community, out of which came later the Semitic and Egyptian peoples, once dwelt in Africa near the Mediterranean shore, and split into sections, one remaining in Africa, the other passing into Asia; but the arguments for this view are not convincing (some scholars, it may be added, place the home of the primitive Semitic-Hamitic people in Arabia, q.v.). It is necessary, therefore, to regard as not established the hypotheses which make the mountains of Armenia, or the lower Tigris-Euphrates valley, or the Arabian Desert, or Africa the cradle of the Semitic race, and to leave the question at present unsolved. The choice is between Arabia and Africa, the preponderance of present opinion being doubtful.

The Semitic territory was enclosed by that of Indo-Europeans on the east and the west, and Egypt on the south. In ancient times, however, the language was little affected by foreign influence, except at one point.

3. Foreign Influence. According to the view now held by most Assyriologists, the Babylonian-Assyrians, conquering the non-Semitic Sumerians, who preceded them as occupants of the Tigris-Euphrates valley, in adopting the civilization of the conquered, adopted a number of their words. Hebrew made a few loans in early times from the Egyptian, and at a later period, possibly from the Indian, and then from the Persian, Greek, and Latin; and the ecclesiastical Aramaic was naturally greatly affected by Greek and Latin. The loanwords are easily recognized, except those which come from the Sumerian.

All the Semitic nationalities, except the Arabian and the Geez (Ethiopia), died out before the second century of the Christian era. The Babylonians and Assyrians disappeared as a political force in the sixth century B.C., and their language survived only a few centuries. The Phenicians lingered in Asia till the time of the Antonines, and their

4. Disappearance of Semitic Languages. language in Africa (Carthage) till toward the fifth century of the Christian era (mentioned by Augustine and Jerome). The Syrian Arameans lost their independence in the eighth century B.C., but continued to exist, and their dialect revived in the second century A.D. as a Christian language; and the Jewish Aramaic continued for some centuries (up to the eleventh century A.D.) to be the spoken and literary tongue of the Palestinian and Babylonian Jews. The Jewish people, broken up by the Romans in the first and second centuries A.D., and scattered over the world, have carried Hebrew with them as a learned, artificial tongue. The South Arabians (Minæans, Sabæans, and perhaps others), once a flourishing community, lingered till the Mohammedan conquest in the seventh century of the Christian era, and were then absorbed in the general Arabian mass. The North Arabians did not appear as a nation till the seventh century A.D., and their language is now widely spoken. Geez proper died out about the sixth century A.D., remaining, however, as the ecclesiastical and learned language; and the nationality is still in existence.

III. Divisions: The various Semitic dialects closely resemble one another, there being, for example, between no two of them such dissimilarity as exists between Greek and Latin; but the family is divided into two well-defined groups and several sub-groups, the difference between the two main groups, in vocabulary and forms, being considerably greater than that between any two

1. Grouping. members of the same group or sub-group. The relations of the dialects may be seen from the following table, which is designed to include all Semitic forms of speech that can lay claim to linguistic individuality, except a few modern jargons mentioned below.

- I. North Semitic.
  - 1. Eastern.
    - a. Babylonian.
    - b. Assyrian.
  - 2. Northern. Aramaic.
    - a. East Aramaic.
      - α. Syriac (Dialect of Edessa).
      - β. Mandean.
      - γ. Nabatæan.
    - b. West Aramaic.
      - α. Samaritan.
      - β. Jewish Aramaic (Daniel, Ezra, Targums, Talmud).
      - γ. Palmyrene.
      - δ. Egyptian Aramaic.
  - 3. Western.
    - a Phenician. Old Phenician. Late Phenician (Punic).
    - b. Hebrew.
    - c. Moabitish and other Canaanitish dialects.
- II. South Semitic.
  - 1. Northern. Arabic.
  - 2. Southern.
    - a. Sabæan, or Himyaritic; Minæan. Mahri. Hakili (Ehkili).
    - b. Geez, or Ethiopic.
      - α. Old Geez.
      - β. Tigrê.
      - γ. Tigriña.
      - δ. Amharic.
      - ε. Harari.

2. Use of Those Tongues.

From the cuneiform tablets discovered in 1887 at Tell el-Amarna (see AMARNA TABLETS) in Egypt, near Thebes, it appears that c. 1400 B.C. Babylonian was the official language in Canaan and the language of intercourse between the kings of Babylonia and Egypt. The Babylonians had before that time overrun and occupied Canaan and impressed their culture on the land, so that, though Egypt then held Canaan, the Egyptian governors of the cities (among them the governor of Jerusalem) wrote to the Egyptian royal government in Babylonian, and Egyptian youth at court studied Babylonian.

Of these dialects, the following are now spoken: (1) Aramaic, by the Nestorian and Jacobite Christians in Upper Mesopotamia, near Mosul, thence eastward to the western shore of Lake Urmi, and northward in the Kurdish Mountains (Nöldeke, *Grammatik der neusyrischen Sprache*, Leipsic, 1868); and by the remnant of the Mandeans in Lower Mesopotamia (Nöldeke, *Mandäische Grammatik*, Halle, 1874). West Aramaic is now spoken only in three small villages near Damascus. (2) Arabic is the only Semitic dialect that has now any real life. It is spoken in various sub-dialects—by the Bedouin of the Arabian Desert; in Egypt, and, as ecclesiastical language, in Turkey; in the Magreb (north coast of Africa); in Syria; in Malta, where the vernacular is a strange mixture, with Arabic as its basis, but with many Italian and other words; on the coast of Malabar (the Mapuli jargon). The Mozarabic, a Spanish-Arabic jargon formerly spoken in the south of Spain, became extinct in the last century. (3) Geez: the four dialects, Tigrē, Tigriña, Amharic, Harari, are still spoken in Abyssinia. (4) Hebrew at a comparatively early date began to be displaced by Aramaic, which became the common language of intercourse in the greater part of western Asia and so the vernacular of the Jews. The earliest notice of the use of Aramaic by Jews is found in the Aramaic papyri discovered in the island of Elephantine in the Nile opposite Assuan. Here as early as the sixth century B.C. dwelt a Jewish community possessing a temple and carrying on a regular Jewish worship; their commercial and other documents are all written in Aramaic. This language gradually took the place of Hebrew in Palestine, and maintained itself till some time after the Mohammedan conquest, when the Jews gradually adopted Arabic. In general the Jews speak the language of the people among whom they dwell, keeping up, however, to a greater or less extent, the knowledge of the old tongue. Hebrew is now studied by the Jews as a sacred language, and by a few of them, chiefly the older orthodox bodies in Germany, Austria, and Russia, is to some extent written and spoken. This spoken language contains a large admixture of modern European terms. The literary Hebrew of today occupies about the same position among the Jews as Latin among us. The so-called "Yiddish" (that is, German Jewish) is a Rhineland German speech, with admixture of Hebrew and Slavic words, now spoken by Jews in Russia, Austria, America, and elsewhere in the diaspora [and printed by them in the Jewish character].

Of languages which have been strongly affected by Semitic tongues may be mentioned the Iranian Husvaresh or Pahlavi (the language of the Bundehesh), which is greatly Aramaized; the Iranian Persian, whose vocabulary is largely Arabic, and even its syntax appears to have been somewhat Semitized; the Indian Hindustani, which, developed under Moslem influence, also contains a large number of Arabic words; and the Turkish, especially the literary and learned language of Constantinople, which in like manner, and for the same reason, has a large infusion of Arabic.

IV. Characteristics: These may be divided into formal (grammar), material (vocabulary), and stylistic (rhetoric and thought). The Semitic phonetic system has a marked individuality. It is probable that the original Semitic alphabet was nearly identical with that of the classical Arabic, containing

1. Grammar; Phonetics.

six gutturals (Alef, Ha, Ḥa, Ḫa, Ayin, Gayin), five uvulars (Ḳaf, Ṭa, Ẓa, Ṣad, Ḍad), two palatals (Kaf, Gam), two linguo-dentals (Ta, Dal), two labials (Pa, Ba), six liquids (Ra, Ya, Lam, Waw, and the nasals Mim, Nun), three sibilants (Sin, Śin, Zayin), and perhaps six spirants (Kaf, Gam, Ta, Dal, Pa, Ba). No existing dialect has all these letters, but there are traces of most of them in all. Thus, comparison of Assyrian and Arabic makes it probable that the former contained all these h-sounds (ḥa, ḫa, ha), though only one of them (ha) is now found in it. From Septuagint transliterations it appears that Hebrew possessed Gayin, as well as Ayin; the South Semitic group shows all the uvulars, and the Hebrew all the spirants. It may be, however, that the parent Semitic speech had fewer uvulars and spirants, and that the Southern group developed the former, and the Northern the latter. It is doubtful whether Hebrew Samek and Sin represent two different sounds. It is likely, also, that not all the sounds above mentioned are original, i.e., some of them may be merely modifications of earlier and simpler sounds; but here the concern is only with the consonantal material possessed by the primitive Semitic tongue, and not with the material out of which its alphabet may have been formed. The Semitic alphabet is thus seen to be characterized by fulness of guttural, uvular, and spirant consonants. In the several dialects the movement has been toward a diminution of the number of gutturals and uvulars, namely, by changing these into similar letters pronounced farther forward in the mouth. Assyrian, Galilean Jewish, Aramaic, and Mandean threw off the most of the gutturals; modern Arabic has diminished the number of its uvulars, and Geez the number of its uvulars and gutturals. This is a tendency, observable in all languages, to bring the consonants forward in the mouth and thus facilitate their pronunciation. The vowel material of the primitive Semitic was simple, consisting, probably, of the three vowels, a, i, u, with the corresponding long ā, ī, ū. These have been variously modified in the different dialects. Assyrian has ē; Aramaic, ē, ō; Hebrew, ā, ē, ĕ, ŏ, ō; modern Arabic, ā, ē, å (aw), ō; Geez, ē, ĕ, ō.

Morphologically, the Semitic languages belong to the class called inflecting, standing in this respect alongside of the Indo-European. Their most marked peculiarity is their triliteralism; most stems consist of three consonants, on which, by prefixes, affixes, infixes, and internal vowel-changes, all derived forms are made. The noun has gender (masculine and feminine), number and case. The verb has gender, number and person, but properly no distinction of tense (in the sense of time), instead of which there are two forms which denote respectively completedness and ingressiveness of action. The notions of reflection, intensity, causation, are expressed by derived verbal stems made by prefixes and infixes. The Semitic syntax is marked by great simplicity of articulation. The different clauses of the sentence are, for the most part, connected by the most general word "and"; there is little or no inversion and transposition for rhetorical effect; and there are no elaborate periods. The structure is commonly and properly described as monumental or lapidary. The most striking special peculiarity of the syntax is the phonetic abridgment of the noun (the construct state; [in Hebrew, where one word is limited by another, not the limiting but the limited word is changed in form to the "construct state," so that the Indo-European genitive relation is in a manner reversed]) to show that it is defined by the following word or clause. The absence of compounds (except in proper names) is another marked feature—an illustration of the isolating character of the thought. The whole conception of the sentence is detached, isolated, and picturesque. Of these general Semitic characteristics the Hebrew and Assyrian, which first produced literatures, show the most, and the Aramaic and Arabic, whose literary life began late, the least.

2. Morphology and Syntax.

The Semitic word-material differs greatly according to the periods and the circumstances of the various peoples. The pre-Christian literary remains are very scanty. From the Israelites there have come down only a few prophetical discourses, historical books, sacred hymns, and ethical works, together with several law books, no secular productions except the Song of Songs; from the Babylonians and the Assyrians, somewhat more—royal and commercial inscriptions, geographical, astronomical, grammatical, and religious works, and fragments of epic and other poems; from the Phenicians, a few short inscriptions; and from the others, nothing. The Hebrew vocabulary is full in terms relating to religious feelings and acts, scanty in philosophical and artistic terms and in names of things pertaining to common life; the Assyrian has more of the last, but is almost equally rich in the first. In later times, however, the Aramaic (classical and Jewish), and the Arabic under Greek influence, created larger vocabularies, and developed some power of philosophical expression. The Hebrew vocabulary is now being enlarged in this direction by the Jews. From the nature of the national culture, these languages, though their vocabularies are sometimes (the Arabic especially) very large, do not satisfy the needs of western life. They multiply words for objects and acts which we do not care to particularize, and are deficient in terms for those which we wish to express with precision. The above description of the vocabulary and syntax will serve to characterize the style and thought of the Semitic tongues. The highest artistic shape they have not, either in prose or in poetry. They do not readily lend themselves to philosophy proper or to art. But in the simple expression of emotion, and the condensation of practical wisdom into household words, they are not surpassed by the most highly developed Indo-European languages: in these respects the Bible has an acknowledged preeminence.

3. Vocabulary and Style.

V. Literary Products: It will be sufficient here to mention briefly the general characteristics of the literature of the Semitic languages. Of the different forms of poetry the Semites have produced little more than the lyric, as in the Old-Testament Psalms, the Syrian hymns, and the Arabian Kasidas. The old Babylonian inscriptions contain two cosmological poems of great interest, and the Gilgamesh (formerly written Izdubar) cycle of stories has an epic tone; but this cycle has not a definite literary unity like the Iliad, and it is uncertain how much of all the early poetical material is derived from a non-Semitic (that is, Sumerian) source; the rhythmic form is in part Semitic. The Semites have never produced a native drama. Neither the Book of Job nor the Song of Songs is a drama; the former is a colloquy of five men who make long argumentative speeches, and the question is summed up in a group of discourses by Yahweh; the latter is a collection of loosely connected wedding-songs, without plot or movement. The drama of the late poet Ezekiel has been regarded as an imitation of Greek models. The subjective character of the Semitic poetic thought is obvious: actions or phenomena in outward nature or in human life are generally described not for their own sake, but as a part of the feeling of the writer. As poetry it takes high rank. The Hebrew lyrics are sonorous and rhythmical; the Arabian are ingenious and lively; the Syrian, however, are tame. The metrical form of Hebrew poetry (see Hebrew Language and Literature, III.), and to some extent of Babylonian, is parallelism of members, and the rhythmic progression is by stress of voice, not by length and number of syllables—a member is defined as having two, three, or four beats; the Arabic, however, has a well-defined system of feet characterized by number and length of syllables. Rime appears first in Syriac Christian hymns, and is feebly represented in Arabic. The historical writing of the Semites has never attained a scientific or artistic form. It is either baldly annalistic (as parts of the Old-Testament Book of Kings, the Assyrian royal inscriptions, and the Arabic histories), or, when it attempts more connected presentation of the facts, it is subjective and pragmatic, arranging the historical facts so as to point a moral or support a theory. In one department, prophetic discourse, the Semitic literature is unrivaled; there is nothing in any other family of languages like the prophetic oratory of the Old Testament, or the declamation of the Koran. In other departments, as fiction and philosophy, the Semites have never been original, but always imitators (*Thousand and One Nights*, the Arabian philosophy;

the Persian Arabic is, of course, not to be considered here).

VI. Relation to Other Families of Languages: So far as present knowledge goes, it is doubtful whether the Semitic family is genetically connected with any other in the world except the Egyptian and Cushite groups. Various unsuccessful attempts have been made to show a relationship between it and the Indo-European. The case is different with the Egyptian, between whose stock of sounds, personal pronouns, numerals, and verbal forms, and the Semitic there is a remarkable resemblance; but the great differences between the two families in other respects make great caution necessary in comparing them. There is a similar resemblance between the structure of the Semitic verb and that of the Cushite group of languages (the Galla, Saho, and others, near Abyssinia), but nothing definite. At most, an original Semitic-Hamitic family may be conjectured out of which these two have grown; but in that case their separation took place so long ago, their paths since that time have been so different, and the traces of kinship have been so far obliterated, that little can be got from a comparison between them, except in the way of reconstructing the history of the original family. One main obstacle in the comparison of Semitic words with others is the triliteralism of stems of the former; and it has therefore been attempted to reduce these to biliterals, but hitherto with indifferent success. It need not be denied that this problem may hereafter be solved, and comparisons instituted between Semitic and other families that may be of service to all.

C. H. Toy.

Bibliography: General works are: E. Littré, *Comment dans deux situations historiques les sémites entrèrent en compétition avec les Aryens pour l'hégémonie du monde*, Paris, 1879; F. Delitzsch, *Wo lag das Paradies?* Leipsic, 1881; F. Hommel, *Die Semiten und ihre Bedeutung für die Kulturgeschichte der Menschheit*, Leipsic, 1881; idem, *Die semitischen Völker und Sprachen*, ib. 1881; F. Lenormant, *Les Origines de l'hist. d'après la Bible et les traditions des peuples orientaux*, 2 vols., Paris, 1880–82, Eng. transl. of vol. i., *Beginnings of Hist.*, New York, 1882; T. Nöldeke, *Sketches from Eastern History* ("Some Characteristics of the Semitic Race"), New York, 1892; G. A. Barton, *Sketch of Semitic Origins*, New York, 1902; and the publications of the Congress of Arts and Sciences (St. Louis Exposition), vol. iii., Boston, 1906.

On the science of language consult: H. Steinthal, *Charakteristik der hauptsächlichsten Typen des Sprachbaues*, Berlin, 1860; F. Max Müller, *Science of Language*, New York, 1865; W. D. Whitney, *Language and the Science of Language*, New York, 1873; F. W. Farrar, *Families of Speech*, London, 1870; A. Hovelacque, *La Linguistique*, Paris, 1876; A. H. Sayce, *Introduction to the Science of Language*, London, 1880; J. Byrne, *Principles of the Structure of Language*, London, 1885; H. Paul, *Principles of the Hist. of Language*, London, 1891.

On Semitic comparative grammar, lexicography, and language-history consult: T. Benfey, *Ueber das Verhältniss der ägyptischen Sprache zum semitischen Sprachstamm*, Leipsic, 1844; E. Renan, *Hist. générale et système comparé des langues sémitiques*, Paris, 1863; F. Müller, *Indogermanisch und semitisch*, Vienna, 1870; F. W. N. Philippi, *Status constructus im Hebräischen*, Weimar, 1871; E. Schrader, in *ZDMG*, xxvii. 3 (1873); A. Koch, *Der semitische Infinitiv*, Stuttgart, 1874; W. Wright, *Comparative Grammar of the Semitic Languages*, London and New York, 1890; T. Nöldeke, in *Encyclopædia Britannica*, xxi. 641–656; idem, *Beiträge zur semitischen Sprachwissenschaft*, Strasburg, 1904; idem, *Neue Beiträge zur semitischen Sprachwissenschaft*, ib. 1909; H. Ewald, *Abhandlung über die geschichtliche Folge der semitischen Sprachen*, Göttingen, 1871; C. Abel, *Sprachwissenschaftliche Abhandlungen*, Leipsic, 1884; A. H. Huizinga, *Analogy in the Semitic Languages*, Baltimore, 1891; J. Barth, *Die Nominalbildung in den semitischen Sprachen*, Leipsic, 1894; idem, *Sprachwissenschaftliche Untersuchungen*, ib. 1907; O. E. Lindberg, *Vergleichende Grammatik der semitischen Sprachen*, Gothenburg, 1897 sqq.; *A Glossary of Aramaic Inscriptions: a comprehensive Collection for the Study of Comparative Semitic Philology*, Cambridge, 1898; H. Zimmern, *Vergleichende Grammatik der semitischen Sprachen*, Berlin, 1898; E. König, *Hebräisch und Semitisch. Prolegomena und Grundlinien einer Geschichte der semitischen Sprachen*, Berlin, 1901; idem, *Hebräisches und aramäisches Wörterbuch zum Alten Testament mit Einschaltung und Analyse aller schwererkennbaren Formen. Deutung der Eigennamen sowie der massoretischen Randbemerkungen und einem deutsch-hebräischen Wortregister*, Leipsic, 1901–10; G. Dalman, *Grammatik des jüdischen palästinischen Aramäisch*, Leipsic, 1905; W. Gesenius, *Hebräisches und aramäisches Handwörterbuch*, 14th ed. by F. Buhl and H. Zimmern, Leipsic, 1905; H. L. Strack, *Grammatik des biblisch-aramäischen*, Leipsic, 1905; F. Brown, S. R. Driver, C. A. Briggs, *Hebrew and English Lexicon of the O. T.*, Boston, etc., 1906; C. Brockelmann, *Grundriss der vergleichenden Grammatik der semitischen Sprachen*, part I., Berlin and New York, 1908; idem, *Semitische Sprachwissenschaft*, Leipsic, 1910; L. Belleli, *An Independent Examination of the Assuan and Elephantine Aramaic Papyri with eleven Plates and two Appendices on sundry Items*, London, 1909; *Beiträge zur christlich-arabischen Literaturgeschichte*, Leipsic, 1909; M. van Berchem, *Arabische Inschriften*, ib. 1909; idem, *Materiaux pour un Corpus inscriptionum Arabicarum*, Paris, 1910; J. P. Alone, *Short Manual (with Vocabulary) of the Amharic Language*, London, 1910; E. H. Armbruster, *Initia Amharica. An Introduction to spoken Amharic*, ib. 1910; H. Bauer, *Die Tempora im Semitischen*, Leipsic, 1910; C. Bezold, *Verbalsuffixformen als Alterskriterien babylonisch-assyrischer Inschriften*, Heidelberg, 1910; Fabre d'Olivet, *La Langue hébraique restituée, et le véritable sense des mots hébreux rétabli et prouvé*, Paris, 1910; J. B. Chabot, *Les Langues et les littératures araméennes*, ib. 1910.

SEMLER, sem′ler or zem′ler, **JOHANN SALOMO:** Pioneer in Biblical criticism; b. at Saalfeld (66 m. s.w. of Leipsic) Dec. 18, 1725; d. at Halle Mar. 4, 1791. His father was archdeacon at Saalfeld, and introduced the son to the circles of Pietism (q.v.) in early youth. But young Semler, already a wide reader and possessed of a phenomenal memory, soon felt a profound disinclination toward all manner of Pietism, only by degrees, however, becoming conscious of his fundamental objection to this movement. At the University of Halle, which he visited in 1743, he was especially drawn toward Siegmund Jakob Baumgarten (q.v.), whose erudition appealed to him, and there took his master's degree in 1750. In the same year he became an unsalaried professor in the gymnasium at Coburg, where he gave instruction in the elements of Arabic, and was also editor of the Coburg *Staats- und Gelehrtenzeitung*. The year 1751 brought him the call of a professorship in history and Latin poetry at Altdorf. But in 1752, at the instance of Baumgarten, he was called to Halle as professor of theology, where there opened up for him a field of labor suitable to his talents. After Baumgarten's death (1757), he grew more free and spontaneous, and a few years later he was one of the most celebrated theologians of Germany.

Semler's critical investigation was directed first of all to the Scriptures. What he undertook was unheard of in German theology, yet there was no doubt of his right to make Scripture the object of scientific research. His Biblical investigations were concerned with the transmission and the nature of the text. He soon came to believe in various revisions of the New-Testament text, strove after more certain standards for fixing the value of particular manuscripts, and discerned the importance of patristic citations. This new attitude respecting the text involved the germinating principles for a new valuation of the canon. To this problem was devoted his *Abhandlung von der freien Untersuchung des Kanons, nebst Antwort auf die tübingische Vertheidigung der Apokalypsis* (4 parts, Halle, 1771–76). He came to recognise the fact that the canon of the Old Testament, like that of the New, underwent a historical development and grew up by degrees, and hence may not pass for "inspired" in the traditional sense and has not, therefore, the "authority" heretofore ascribed to it. This principle of the liberty of Christians to deal with the canon, involved the further task of gaining a criterion for gaging the value of the particular constituents of such a collection, offering as such the test of the presence in the books of the spirit of Christ. This led him to recognise in the Old Testament and the New two stages of religion, the Jewish national, and the universal religion of Christianity, and this showed the way to a wholly new explanation of Scripture. He established the point that the doctrine of Jesus and the apostles contains Jewish conceptions of only synchronous value. The problem of scientific exegesis is to determine what belongs to these "local" and "temporal" elements. So early as 1760, he gave expression to these maxims, and applied the same in *De dæmoniacis, quorum in evangeliis fit mentio* (Halle, 1760). Semler further developed the idea of utilising Talmud and Apocrypha in exegesis.

With Semler there began a new epoch in ecclesiastical history. His historical labors exhibit him both as editor (*Tertulliani opera*, 6 vols., Halle, 1769–76; *Apparatus ad libros symbolicos ecclesiæ Lutheranæ*, 1775), and as critic (*Commentarii historici de antiquo Christianorum statu*, 2 vols., 1771–1772; *Versuch eines fruchtbaren Auszuges der Kirchengeschichte des N. T.*, 3 vols., 1773–78). His guiding principles include constant return to the sources, the importation of purely natural factors in the history of the Church, employment of psychology to aid in the understanding of history, and recognition that development has taken place in the history of the Church. This new mode of survey showed its most pronounced reaction in the sphere of ecclesiastical dogma. One of Semler's most important theses was his distinction between theology and religion. By means of this distinction he created free course for his criticism and thereby liberated scientific research from the theological odium, his purpose being to grapple with the Christian faith itself. Another main idea of Semler's is that in all ages there has been a diversity of theological and religious views, and that this discrepancy exists of right. Consequently all doctrinal schemes are mere attempts to comprehend the truth, with the results that the practise of appraising the dogma of one's own church in distinction from that of other ecclesiastical fellowships was no longer to be upheld, the basis for a propaganda among adherents of an alien confession vanished away, and even the gap between Christianity and non-Christian religions became lessened by coordination of all into the divine cosmic plan. The task of defining the value and effective scope of the theology recognized by the Church, and the relation of this ecclesiastical doctrine to the asserted freedom of the individual, Semler sought to resolve by distinguishing public religion—i.e., Christian regulations in the way of external ordinances—from private religion, i.e., the particular Christian's religious convictions.

Semler excited great surprise among his contemporaries by his attitude toward the practical life of the Church. When the agitation over the "Wolfenbüttel Fragments" (q.v.) reached its height, Semler undertook to controvert the "Fragmentists" with keen polemics. Semler's attitude in various disputes was the necessary result of the fundamental thoughts of his theology. Yet he was no constructor, nor did he clearly define for himself the consequences of his own formal postulations. Indeed, he himself often fell far short of exercising the objectivity that he demanded abstractly; and his direct interest was much more pronounced than he personally admitted. He was far more accessible to conservative sentiments than could be expected, especially in his labors as critic. Similarly, the very heaviness of his style is due to his continual struggling with new material and to his inability to wait for publication until he had completely mastered the subject-matter. His real merit lay in assisting to pilot theology into a new phase of development by importing into theology the historical mode of contemplation. In its final decade, Semler's literary activity shows a change in his interests, as he busied himself with natural sciences, alchemy, mystical theosophy, and freemasonry (*Unpartheiische Sammlung zur Geschichte der Rosenkreuzer*, 4 parts, Leipsic, 1786–88). At the same time he did not abandon theology (*Letztes Glaubensbekenntnis*, 1792).

CARL MIRBT.

BIBLIOGRAPHY: Semler's autobiography was published in two parts, Halle, 1781–82. Consult further: J. G. Eichhorn, *Allgemeine Bibliothek der biblischen Literatur*, v. 1–201, Leipsic, 1793; Diestel, in *Jahrbücher für deutsche Theologie*, xii (1867), 471–498; P. Gastrow, *Johann Salomo Semler in seiner Bedeutung für die Theologie mit besonderer Berücksichtigung seines Streites mit G. E. Lessing*, Giessen, 1905; the work by G. Karo with the same title, Berlin, 1905; H. Hoffmann, *Die Theologie Semlers*, Leipsic, 1905; L. Zscharnack, *Lessing und Semler. Ein Beitrag zur Entstehungsgeschichte des Rationalismus und der kritischen Theologie*, Giessen, 1905; F. Huber, *Johann Salomo Semler, seine Bedeutung für die Theologie*, Berlin, 1906; *ADB*, xxxiii. 698–704.

SEMPRINGHAM, ORDER OF. See GILBERT, SAINT, OF SEMPRINGHAM.

SEN, KESHAV CHANDRA: Hindu Theist; b. at Calcutta Nov. 19, 1838; d. there Jan. 8, 1884. As a boy he was imperious in character and self-willed, not especially religious in spirit, but amid the low moral condition of the times he stood out as a pure-minded boy, shy but self-contained. As he passed into youth he became austere in his habits, a vegetarian, showing an antipathy toward all frivolities, and absorbed in philosophical and religious subjects. It was at this time that Christian literature began to make its deep impression on his mind.

As an outlet to his feelings he started the Goodwill Fraternity, where those of like minds met for prayer and the expression of a deepening religious spirit. Devendranath Tagore (see Tagore, Devendranath), then leader of the Brahmo Somaj, attended on one occasion a meeting of this society, and this formed the first step in the later friendship between the two. At this time (1858) the family *guru* came to perform rites of religious initiation, precipitating a severe mental struggle for Keshav; in the face of the family pressure he stood out against idolatrous rites, and his victory brought him into still closer sympathy with Devendranath Tagore, who had been watching his struggles.

In Apr., 1859, in the establishment of the Brahmo School Keshav appeared in the rôle of an enthusiastic teacher of theism. Devendranath Tagore joined hands with Keshav in this new enterprise. Keshav lectured on the philosophy of theism, and Devendranath on the doctrine and theology of the Brahmo Somaj. In 1860 his first publication appeared, a tract entitled *Young Bengal. This is for You*, and was followed by twelve others, embodying the substance of his lectures before the Brahmo School. In Aug., 1861, he began publication of *The Indian Mirror* for the propagation of his ideas. In 1862 he was formally appointed a minister of the Brahmo Somaj, and into its development he threw his whole nature.

In Aug., 1862, the first intercaste marriage according to Brahmo rites took place, encouraged by Keshav, but disapproved by Devendranath. And as such marriages increased in number, the constitutional difference of opinion between the two leaders became emphasized. Devendranath was a conservative and drew his inspiration more and more from the *Upanishads*, while Keshav drew his from Christian sources. Though close friends, their radically different attitude to social reform finally created a cleavage that grew wider with every strain. In Feb., 1864, Keshav began his first tour over India, visiting Bombay, Poona, Calicut, and Madras. The welcome he received everywhere, and the apparent ripeness for his theistic message suggested the idea of a Brahmo Somaj for India.

On his returning to Calcutta both leaders became conscious that their differences were irreconcilable. And in 1866 Keshav and his radical followers seceded from the Somaj to found the Brahmo Somaj of India. Devendranath continued the old Calcutta Brahmo Somaj under the name of the Adi Brahmo Somaj. In the midst of these troublous times, Keshav felt his separation from his old friend keenly, and, driven to seek comfort somewhere, found it for a time in retirement, spent largely in the study of the life of Christ. The lecture he soon after delivered on *Jesus Christ, Europe and Asia* created a sensation, separating him still more from Brahmos of the older party. His explanation five months later in a lecture on *Great Men* brought him little comfort, as it opened him to charges of recantation on the one side and of egotism on the other. On Jan. 24, 1868, the foundation of the Brahmo Mandir was laid. In Mar., 1868, he began his second missionary journey over India, ending it at Monghyr on the banks of the Ganges. Here Keshav was received with the utmost enthusiasm, while people prostrated themselves before him calling him "Lord," "Master," and "Savior." His failure to rebuke this brought unfortunate consequences. On Aug. 22, 1869, the Brahmo Mandir was formally opened with imposing ceremonies. In Sept., 1872, he founded the Bharat Ashram, where Brahmos lived a communistic life, which continued for seven years but finally broke up because of internal discord and the gross misbehavior of some inmates. From 1875 to 1878 he developed an ascetic life, cultivated the *Bhakti* spirit characterised by singing and violent dancing, which aroused the disgust of many and the suspicion of others. In 1878 occurred the "Cuch Behar marriage" of his daughter under fourteen years of age to the Maharaja of Cuch Behar yet under sixteen years of age, according to Hindu idolatrous rites. This marriage was severely criticized as a lapse from Brahmo principles. The confidence of many in his leadership was shaken, and they withdrew to found the Sadharan Brahmo Somaj. In 1881 Keshav formally announced the name "New Dispensation" as the name of his church, and himself as its prophet, and demanded immunity from all criticism, since he declared that he was guided by the direct commandment of God. This abnormal estimation of himself as an avenue of truth brought its unfortunate fruit in the worship of some, the disaffection of others, and discord in the Somaj. See India, III.

Justin E. Abbott.

Bibliography: The most noted of the writings of Keshav Chandra Sen are: *The Brahmo Samaj; Lectures and Tracts*, 2 series, London, 1870; *The Brahmo Samaj; Keshub Chunder Sen in England*, 2 vols., Calcutta, 1881; and his *Diary in England*, Calcutta, 1886. For his life and activities consult: P. C. Mozoomdar, *Life and Teachings of Chunder Sen*, Calcutta, 1887; J. F. B. Tinling, *An Evangelist's Tour round India, with Account of Keshub Chunder Sen and the Modern Hindu Reformers*, London, 1870; S. D. Collet, *Keshub Chunder Sen's English Visit*, ib. 1871 (contains some of his speeches); Ramachandra Vasu, *Brahmoism . . . with . . . Account of Keshub Chunder Sen's Connection with the Movement*, New York, 1884; T. E. Slater, *Keshab Chandra Sen and the Brahmo Samaj*, Madras, 1884; and the literature under Brahmo Somaj.

SENDOMIR, CONSENSUS OF: An agreement drawn up in 1570 between the Lutherans, the Reformed, and the Bohemian Brethren at Sendomir, a town in what was formerly Little Poland (125 m. s. of Warsaw). While the state of affairs at the time rendered some agreement between these religious bodies desirable, it was decided that small preliminary conferences should be held, as between the Lutherans and Reformed at Vilna on Mar. 2, 1570, and between the Lutherans and Bohemian Brethren at Posen on Feb. 13, 1570, while the Sendomir Synod itself was held Apr. 9–15, 1570, its object being the organization of a Polish Protestant Church. The nobility, desiring to oppose a solid front to Roman Catholicism, earnestly advocated union, and the Reformed passed lightly over doctrines which disturbed the more scrupulous Lutherans. The Bohemian Brethren took a middle ground, thus having the balance of power between the Lutherans and the Reformed, the representatives of the latter being the most numerous, and also being favored by the nobility. The nobles, indeed, tacitly assumed that the conference was a Reformed synod, and they had plainly come prepared to declare the Second Helvetic Confession the national creed of Poland. The Bohemian Brethren, while regarding the Helvetic Confession as in agreement with their own, saw no reason to surrender the creed of their own communion; and the Lutherans, declining to abandon the Augsburg Confession, and at the same time far from insisting that it be made the formal creed of the synod, proposed the joint formulation of a new and distinctly Polish confession. It was accordingly resolved that the preparation of such a creed should be taken up by the next synod, scheduled to meet at Warsaw at Whitsuntide. Since, however, some expression of the unanimity already attained was desired, two ministers were delegated to draw up an agreement. This was submitted to the synod on Apr. 13, whereupon a Lutheran representative requested the addition of a statement on the Eucharist, as well as the adoption of an entire article from the Saxon Confession of 1551. This request was granted, but the Eucharistic doctrine was so modified as to represent essentially the position of Melanchthon, so that those Lutherans who, in the Formula of Concord, proscribed Philippism, rejected the Consensus of Sendomir.

The Consensus sought to provide a defense against Roman Catholics, sectarians, and foes of the Gospel, and also to obviate all strife and enmity. Each of the sects represented might conduct the worship and administer the sacraments of the other; each Church concerned might retain its liturgy and usages, except when these should interfere with purity of doctrine; and all weighty matters of religion in Poland, Lithuania, and Samogitia were to be considered in joint council. The proposed preparation of a distinct Polish confession was never realized, but, on May 20, 1570, a conference of Lutherans and Bohemian Brethren was held at Posen, where a number of resolutions were adopted which may be regarded as supplementing the Consensus of Sendomir. After considerable debate, it was decided that the Eucharistic teaching should be in accord with the Consensus of Sendomir and the Saxon Confession; each sect should retain its own usages, and where the same place had a congregation of each, the minister of either might, in case of necessity, represent the other; all polemics must be avoided, and proselyting was forbidden; mutual conferences for the furtherance of the union were to be held when necessary; no pastor should admit to the Lord's Supper the adherents of the other sect without the consent of the pastor of the persons concerned, except on the occasion of diets, general synods, and journeys; those excommunicated in one sect should not be admitted to the Lord's Supper in the other, and a similar rule should apply to the clergy in case of deposition; all rites of the Roman Catholic Church were gradually to be abolished; and in case it should prove impossible peaceably to correct any eventual error in teaching or liturgy in either sect, the matter was to be brought for final adjudication before the general synod of Great and Little Poland.

(H. W. Erbkam†.)

Bibliography: The Consensus was first printed 1583, and reprinted Thorn, 1592, 1596, Heidelberg, 1605, Geneva, 1612, 1654, Frankfort, 1704; in D. E. Jablonski's *Historia consensus Sendomiriensis*, Berlin, 1731; in H. A. Niemeyer's *Collectio confessionum*, pp. 551–591, Leipsic, 1840; and in German in C. J. Nitzsch, *Urkundenbuch der evangelischen Union*, pp. 72 sqq., Bonn, 1853. Consult the pertinent literature under Poland; the work of Jablonski named above; Schaff, *Creeds*, i. 586–588; J. G. Walch, *Historische . . . Einleitung in die Religionsstreitigkeiten*, iii. 1043, 10 vols., Jena, 1733–39, and Nitzsch, ut sup., p. lxx.

SENECA, sen'e-ca, **LUCIUS ANNÆUS**: Roman philosopher and author; b. in Corduba (Cordova), Spain, c. 8 B.C.; d. near Rome 65 A.D., being forced to commit suicide. As a prodigy in versification and rhetoric he soon rose to eminence, and entered the senate. Exiled to Corsica at the accession of Claudius, 41 A.D., he returned in 49 to become the educator and counselor of young Nero. His great talents were undoubtedly used to commend or screen the criminal ambition of Agrippina and the parricide committed by Nero. Seneca was early attracted by Pythagoreanism, and, while he became a devotee of this cult, his erudition for his time was almost universal. In the bitter analysis of the non-spiritual strivings of actual mankind Seneca has outstripped all his predecessors. Stoic pride as well as a curious aspiration after spiritual rest, submission to fatal mechanism, as well as a striving after personal immortality, may be observed in his brilliant essays, among which the *epistulæ morales* are the last and greatest. There is in him also an unmistakable drift and trend away from the pantheism of his school toward a theistic conception of soul-happiness and soul-obligations. The motto "know thyself" as applied to conscience and motive has been more vigorously put into play by Seneca than by any former philosophical writer of classical antiquity ("Perchance, if you search diligently, you will find within your own bosom the vice of which you ask"; *De beneficiis*, VII., xxviii. 3). In the frank admission of essential moral weakness coupled with the assertion of the highest obligation of moral conduct, Seneca not rarely reminds his readers of the New Testament. Still, in his philosophy of freedom he emphasizes everywhere the right and privilege of suicide. The historian who was most like him, Tacitus, treats him with striking coolness and reserve. The "correspondence" of Seneca and St. Paul (their death was close together) is a transparent fiction. E. G. Sihler.

Bibliography: Recent Eng. transls. of some of Seneca's works are: *Morals: a Selection*, by W. Clode, London, 1888; *Minor Dialogues*, by A. Stewart, ib. 1889; *On Benefits*, by T. Lodge, ib. 1899; *Tranquillity of Mind* and *Providence*, by W. B. Langsdorf, New York, 1900; *Ten Tragedies* . . . , by W. Bradshaw, London, 1902, and *Tragedies*, . . . by F. J. Miller, Chicago, 1907; *Morals*, New York, 1904; *Select Essays* and *Satire on the Deification of Claudius*, by A. P. Ball, ib. 1908; *Tragedies, in English Verse*, by F. J. Miller, London, 1908; *Three Tragedies: Hercules Furens, Troades, Medea*, . . . by H. M. Kingery, London and New York, 1908; *Quæstiones Naturales*, by J. Clarke, New York, 1910; *Select Letters*, by W. C. Summers, ib. 1910. On Seneca's life and activities consult: E. G. Sihler, *Testimonium animæ*, chap. 18, New York, 1908; A. Fleury, *S. Paul et Sénèque*, 2 vols., Paris, 1853; C. Aubertin, *Étude critique sur les rapports supposés entre Sénèque et Paul*, Paris, 1857; F. C. Baur, *Drei Abhandlungen zur Geschichte der alten Philosophie*, pp. 377–430, Leipsic, 1876; J. B. Lightfoot, Essay on

Paul and Seneca in his commentary on Philippians, 4th ed., London, 1878; F. W. Farrar, *Seekers after God*, Philadelphia, 1883; J. Kreyberr, *L. Annæus Seneca und seine Beziehungen zum Christenthum*, Berlin, 1887; S. Rubin, *Die Ethik Senecas*, Munich, 1901; R. Waltz, *Vie de Sénèque*, Paris, 1909; the literature under NERO; and the works on the history of philosophy.

SENNACHERIB. See ASSYRIA, VI., 3, § 12.

SEPARATE BAPTISTS. See BAPTISTS, II., 4 (f).

SEPARATED BRITISH METHODISTS. See METHODISTS, I., 2.

SEPARATES: An American Calvinistic Methodist sect, composed of Whitefield's followers, which sprang up in 1750 under the name of "New Lights." They were, however, subsequently organized into separate societies by Shubal Stearne, and then took the name "Separates." Stearne became a Baptist in 1751, and many of the Separates followed him into that church; and the sect died out. "The distinctive doctrine of the sect was, that believers are guided by the immediate teachings of the Holy Spirit, such supernatural indications of the divine will being regarded by them as partaking of the nature of inspiration, and above, though not contrary to, reason." See METHODISTS, I., 2.

SEPARATISTS, THE. See COMMUNISM, II., 9.

SEPHARVAIM sef"ār-vē'im (SIPPAR). See BABYLONIA, IV., § 11.

SEPP, CHRISTIAAN: Dutch Mennonite theologian and historian; b. at Amsterdam 1820; d. at Wijk aan Zee (15 m. n. of Haarlem) 1890. His longest period of active labor was spent as a preacher for his denomination at Leyden (1854–82). But his work as a preacher was only a small part of his activities; he edited the theological review *Godgeleerde Bijdragen* (1855–70); and was the author of a series of historical works which embodied the fruits of diligent research in the history of Dutch Protestant theology and biography, orthodox and sectarian, including the Anabaptists. Of these works the following may here be noticed: *Pragmatische Geschiedenis der Theologie in Nederland 1787–1860* (Leyden, 1860); *Johannes Stinstra en zijn Tijd; eene Bijdrage tot de Geschiedenis der Kerk en School in de 18de eeuw* (Amsterdam, 1865–66); *Het Godgeleerd Onderwijs in Nederland gedurende de 16. en 17. eeuw* (2 parts, Leyden, 1873–74); *Bibliotheek van Nederlandsche Kerkgeschiedschrijvers* (1886); *Verboden Lectuur. Een drietal Indices librorum prohibitorum* (1889). Many of his studies on men and books are collected in *Geschiedkundige Nasporingen* (3 parts, 1872–75); and *Kerkhistorische Studien* (1885). S. CRAMER.

SEPP, JOHANN NEPOMUK: Roman Catholic church-historian; b. at Tölz (26 m. s. of Munich), Bavaria, Aug. 7, 1816; d. at Munich June 5, 1909. He studied at Munich; traveled in the East, 1845–1846; became professor of history at Munich, 1846; was deposed and expelled from the city, 1847, for his political opinions; reinstated, 1850; retired, 1867. He had considerable influence in politics. Among his works are: *Das Leben Jesu Christi* (5 vols., Regensburg, 1842–46; 4th ed., with Daniel Haneberg, Munich, 1898–1902); *Das Heidenthum und dessen Bedeutung für das Christenthum* (1853); *Jerusalem und das Heilige Land* (Schaffhausen, 1862–63); *Thaten und Lehren Jesu mit ihrer weltgeschichtlichen Beglaubigung* (1864); *Geschichte des Apostel vom Tod Jesu bis zur Zerstörung Jerusalems* (1865); *Kritische Reformentwürfe beginnend mit der Revision des Bibelkanons* (Munich, 1870); *Das Hebräer Evangelium* (1870); *Deutschland und der Vatikan* (1872); *Görres und seine Zeitgenossen* (Nördlingen, 1877); *Meerfahrt nach Tyrus zur Ausgrabung der Kathedrale mit Barbarossas Grab* (Leipsic, 1879); *Kritische Beiträge zum Leben Jesu und zur neuesten Topographie von Jerusalem* (Munich, 1890); *Die Religion der alten Deutschen und ihr Fortbestand in Volkssagen* (1890); *Die Geheime Offenbarung Johannis* (1902); and *Orient und Occident; 100 Kapitel über der Nachtseite der Natur Zauberwerk und Hexenwesen in alter und neuer Zeit* (Berlin, 1903).

SEPTIMIUS SEVERUS, sî-vī'rus: Roman emperor 193–211; b. at Leptis (62 m. s.e. of Carthage), on the north coast of Africa, Apr. 11, 146; d. at Eboracum (York), England, Feb. 4, 211. His family was of equestrian rank, and in 172 he seems to have been made a senator by Marcus Aurelius. In 190 he became consul, and in the following year received from Commodus the command of the German legions in Pannonia. On the murder of Pertinax by the troops in 193, they proclaimed Septimius emperor, whereupon he hurried to Italy and took possession of Rome without opposition. The legionaries of Syria, however, proclaimed Pescennius Niger emperor and those of Britain, Albinus; and only after bloody wars was Septimius able to make himself master of the Roman world. With Septimius Severus begins the series of military emperors and the motto of his life was his dying exhortation to his sons, "let us work!" His entire reign was devoted to the welfare of the empire, and he finally succumbed to overexertion in a campaign against the Caledonians. Stern, wise, and energetic, Septimius restored peace to the empire after the misrule of Commodus and the civil wars. No emperor before Constantine was so important for the development of Roman law.

It is generally assumed that Septimius was friendly to the Christians until 202, when, for some unknown reason, he became their enemy and persecutor. This rests upon an incorrect interpretation of the words of his biographer Spartianus: "In his journey [through Palestine in 202] he established very many laws for the Palestinians; he forbade the Jews to be placed under heavy punishment, but sanctioned this in the case of Christians." This was really no new law, but only a reemphasizing of laws already existing, and was designed to check the Christian propaganda rather than to set on foot a general persecution. Nor was there any wide persecution, and there are many evidences that not only was the emperor not personally hostile to the Christians, but he even protected them against the populace. There were doubtless Christians in his own household, and in his reign the church at Rome had almost absolute peace. On the other hand, individual officials availed themselves of the laws to proceed with rigor against the Christians. Naturally the emperor, with his strict conception of law, did not hinder such partial persecution, which took place in Egypt and the Thebaid, as well as in proconsular Africa and the East. Christian martyrs were numerous in Alexandria (cf. Clement, *Strom.*, ii. 20; Eusebius, *Hist. eccl.*, V., xxvi., VI., i. sqq.). No less severe were the persecutions in Africa, which seem to have begun in 197 or 198 (cf. Tertullian's *Ad martyres*), and included the Christians known in the Roman martyrology as the martyrs of Madaura. Probably in 202 or 203 Felicitas and Perpetua (q.v.) suffered for their faith. Persecution again raged for a short time under the proconsul Scapula in 211, especially in Numidia and Mauritania. Later accounts of a Gallic persecution, especially at Lyons, are legendary. In general it may thus be said that the position of the Christians under Septimius Severus was the same as under the Antonines; but the law of this emperor at least shows clearly that the rescript of Trajan had failed to execute its purpose. (A. HAUCK.)

BIBLIOGRAPHY: Sources are: The history of Dio Cassius, chaps. lxxiv.–lxxvi., lxxx.; the work on Severus by Spartianus; Lapridius's Alexander Severus; and Herodian, *Historia*, books v.–vi. Consult further: C. Fuchs, *Geschichte des Kaisers L. Septimius Severus*, Vienna, 1884; Gibbon, *Decline and Fall*, chaps. v.–vi.; G. Uhlhorn, *Der Kampf des Christenthums*, pp. 284 sqq., Stuttgart, 1875; B. Aubé, *Hist. des persécutions de l'église*, pp. 53 sqq., Paris, 1875; H. Schiller, *Geschichte der römischen Kaiserzeit*, i. 2, pp. 705 sqq., Gotha, 1883; J. Reville, *La Religion à Rome sous les Sévères*, Paris, 1885; P. Allard, *Hist. des persécutions pendant la première moitié du iii. siècle*, ib. 1888; K. J. Neumann, *Der römische Staat und die allgemeine Kirche*, i. 95 sqq., Leipsic, 1890; A. Linsenmayer, *Die Bekämpfung des Christentums durch den römischen Staat*, 109 sqq., 117 sqq., Munich, 1905.

SEPTUAGESIMA. See CHURCH YEAR; and LENT.

SEPTUAGINT. See BIBLE VERSIONS, A, I., 1.

SEPULCHER, HOLY. See HOLY SEPULCHER.

SEQUENCE: A hymn or chant sung on certain days in the mass after the gradual and before the Gospel. The term was originally a musical one, applied to the series of tones sung after (hence its name) the last syllable of the Hallelujah belonging to the versicle between the epistle and the Gospel, and it probably translated the Greek *akolouthia*, the word by which Byzantine writers on music denoted the *heirmos* ("melody"). For the Hallelujah see LITURGICS, III. The melodies of the sequences, the oldest extant choir-books of which date from the tenth century, gave rise to one of the most important discoveries both for religious and for secular song and poetry. Notker (q.v.), a monk of St. Gall, was inspired to reduce these melodies to a system by a West-Frankish antiphonary, brought from Jumièges (near Rouen) when the Normans devastated that monastery (apparently in 862). In this antiphonary some verses were modulated in accordance with the sequences, and they possessed sufficient charm for him to imitate them, and he succeeded in producing regular sequences with double versicles of equal length, though the simple sequences without the response are the older form. In all this acquaintance with Greek hymnody was also undoubtedly a factor. Greek hymns had been translated into Latin during the reign of Charlemagne, and traces of such work have been preserved at St. Gall. But although Notker was unquestionably the discoverer of the sequence, the extent of his activity is entirely unknown. In France the composition of sequences proceeded along the lines laid down at St. Gall. Side by side with the old ways that admitted of no alteration, other hallelujah melodies and musical *motifs* gave rise to new sequence melodies. Rhythm became a conscious aim, and the words were adapted to the melody, syllable for syllable. The sequences of Limoges differed from those of St. Gall by the final assonance of the versicles in *-a* (under the influence of the word hallelujah); rhythm within the verse made steady progress; and finally the old verses of most unequal length developed into rhythmical and riming lines, from which, in the twelfth century, Adam of St. Victor made a selection, which he combined in strophes and thus helped to become predominant over the rest. In the St. Gall sequences the syllabic system is, in general, strictly followed, and elision is rare, while the lines are of unequal length; in Adam of St. Victor all this is changed, and melody and text are entirely independent. The spirit in which sequences were composed is indicated by Gottschalk of Limpurg, who declared that he drew his words from Jerome (the Bible) and his melody from Gregory (the Sacramentary).

Origin and Development.

Though in liturgical books the sequences are usually given without their authors' names, a number of such composers are known: besides Notker and Adam, Ekkehart I. and II., Fulbert (author of the "Sonent regi nato"), Waltramm, Berno, Hermannus Contractus, Henricus Monachus (author of the "Ave præclara maris stella"), Wipo (author of the "Victimæ paschali"), Gottschalk of Limpurg, Innocent III. (author of the "Veni Sancte Spiritus"), and Thomas Aquinas (author of the "Lauda Sion salvatorem"). Later the sequence lost many of its characteristic features, especially under the influence of the hymn, from which it always differed, however, in that its melody was continuous, even though its strophes might be metrically or rhythmically equal. The text frequently contained a refrain, due to the fact that the same cadence was repeated at the close of the versicles. In the older manuscripts the melodies are denoted by "neumes," which passed through various stages of development until they were superseded by the system of staff notation. The older sequence melodies also have distinct names, many of which are of uncertain meaning. Here belong the beginning of the hallelujah Psalm verse generally sung on a particular feast, as the "Dies sanctificatus" for Christmas; names of musical instruments, *Organa, Fidicula, Symphonia, Tuba;* loan-words or translations from the Greek, *Græca, Hypodiaconissa, Romana, Hieronyma;* and probably allusions to older melodies, *Puella turbata, Planctus sterilis, Berta vetula, Vaga*, etc.

Names of Composers and Sequences.

The composition of sequences reached its climax with Adam of St. Victor (q.v.). He, like Notker, probably adopted to some extent popular melodies of the period; but after Adam new sequences were with few exceptions, mere imitations of earlier forms and melodies. Many of these melodies were such favorites that new texts were given them; and to this category belong Notker's melodies *Mater*, *Occidentana*, and *Justus ut palma major* and *minor*, Wipo's Easter hymn, Gottschalk's *Laus tibi, Christe, qui es*, the sequence of the Virgin (*Ave præclara*), the Easter sequence (*Mane prima sabbati*), and some of Adam's, while the *Lætabundus exultet*, by an unknown author, proved the most popular of all. In the oldest period the texts and, in part, the melodies of sequences were restricted in territory, so that a distinction may be drawn between German (St. Gall), Upper Italian (Verona, Nonantula), French (Limoges), and English (Winchester) sequences; but when the riming sequence was developed, some were used largely throughout the Roman Church, as the *Natus ante sæcula* for Christmas, the *Sancti Spiritus adsit* for Whitsuntide, the *Clare sanctorum* for feasts of the apostles, and the *Sancti baptistæ* for John the Baptist. On the other hand, despite the approval of Nicolas I. and Innocent III., Rome generally, as well as many dioceses and orders, declined officially to welcome the sequence. The Cistercians and Carthusians rejected it altogether, and the Cluniac monks reluctantly permitted it only on four feasts. In France and Germany, on the other hand, sequences were always popular, many sequentiaries containing more than a hundred texts. The melodies were mostly transmitted orally, the Neumenal collections being intended only for the choirmasters. The singing of the sequence was restricted to the clergy and choir, the congregation being forbidden to take part. The introduction and the concluding passage were usually sung by the entire choir, while the double strophes were sung antiphonally, with musical accompaniment.

Culmination.

Soon after the rise of sequence composition, vernacular sequences were written in France (the Eulalia sequence). In Germany translations appeared more tardily, the favorite here being the *Ave præclara maris stella*, as in Sebastian Brant's *Ave durchlüchte stern des meres*. The sequence form influenced medieval Latin poetry, encouraging it to abandon the old forms and to create many new strophes, this influence ultimately extending to the vernacular. With the increase in the calendar of saints the number of sequences became enormous, some 5,000 texts with between 500 and 600 melodies. Many of these were poetically valueless, and after several synods had sought to reform conditions, the Council of Trent finally succeeded. The missal of Paul V. (1570) contains only four: *Victimæ paschali*, *Veni Sancte Spiritus*, *Lauda, Sion, salvatorem*, and *Dies iræ*, to which was later added the *Stabat mater*, generally ascribed to Jacopone da Todi, or to Innocent III. (qq.v.). The Reformers were hostile to the sequence, and in the Lutheran Church, after long efforts, it was replaced by a congregational hymn. In France sequences of late date were stubbornly maintained, only to disappear ultimately when the unity of the Roman Catholic liturgy became an accomplished fact. The custom of singing the *Lætabundus* at the Easter dinner given by the pope seems to have given rise to parodies of the sequence, such as the *Vinum bonum et suave*, or the *Victimæ novali cinke ses*, while Johann Nass composed in derision of Luther the *Invicti Martini laudes intonant Christiani*. [In many Anglican churches the sequence is represented by a hymn sung by the choir between the epistle and Gospel (C. Walker, *Ritual "Reason Why,"* 2d ed. T. I. Ball, pp. 166–167, Milwaukee, 1908]. (J. Werner.)

Decline.

Bibliography: Collections, examples, or translations of sequences are to be sought in: H. A. Daniel, *Thesaurus hymnologicus*, vol. ii., Halle, 1843; F. J. Mone, *Lateinische Hymnen des Mittelalters*, 3 vols., Freiburg, 1853–55; R. C. Trench, *Sacred Latin Poetry*, London, 1864; C. E. P. Wackernagel, *Das deutsche Kirchenlied*, vol. ii., 5 vols., Leipsic, 1864–77; G. Morel, *Lateinische Hymnen des Mittelalters*, 2 vols., Einsiedeln, 1867 (a rich collection); J. M. Neale, *Mediæval Hymns and Sequences*, 3d ed., London, 1867; *Seven Great Hymns*, New York, 1867; W. Christ and M. Paranikas, *Anthologia Græca carminum Christianorum*, Leipsic, 1871; D. T. Morgan, *Hymns of the Latin Church*, London, 1871; C. B. Pearson, *Sequences from the Sarum Missal*, ib. 1871; J. Kehrein, *Lateinische Sequenzen des Mittelalters*, Mainz, 1873 (most complete collection); F. A. March, *Latin Hymns*, New York, 1874; H. M. MacGill, *Songs of Christian Creed and Life*, London, 1876; C. Blume and G. M. Dreves, *Analecta Hymnica*, vols. viii.–x., xxxvii., xxxix., xl., xlii., xliv., Leipsic, 1886 sqq.; S. W. Duffield, *Latin Hymn-Writers and their Hymns*, New York, 1889; W. H. J. Weale, *Analecta liturgica*, Bruges, 1889 sqq. (supplements Kehrein, above); G. M. Dreves, *Prosarium Lemovicense*, Leipsic, 1890; U. Chevalier, *Bibliothèque liturgique*, vols. vii., ix., Paris, 1900–01; W. A. Merrill, *Latin Hymns*, Boston, 1904; C. E. W. Brainerd, *Great Hymns of the Middle Ages*, New York, 1909; C. Blume and H. Bannister, *Liturgische Prosen erster Epoche aus den Sequenzenschulen des Abendlandes, insbesondere die dem Notkerus Balberus zugeschriebenen, nebst Skizze über den Ursprung der Sequenz*, Leipsic, 1911.

Consult: F. Wolf, *Ueber die Lais, Sequenzen und Leiche*, Frankfort, 1841; F. Clément, *Hist. générale de la musique religieuse*, Paris, 1860; K. Bartsch, *Die lateinischen Sequenzen des Mittelalters*, Rostock, 1868; *Verzeichniss der Handschriften der Stiftsbibliothek von St. Gallen*, pp. 509–530, Halle, 1875 (indexes the sequences); J. Pothier, *Les Melodies grégoriennes*, Tournay, 1881; D. S. Wrangham, *The Liturgical Poetry of Adam of St. Victor*, 3 vols., London, 1881; A. Reiners, *Die Tropen-, Prosen-, und Präfationsgesänge des feierlichen Hochamtes des Mittelalters*, Luxemburg, 1884; L. Gautier, *Hist. de la poésie liturgique*, Paris, 1886; idem, *La Poésie religieuse dans les cloîtres des ix.–xi. siècles*, ib. 1887; M. Manitius, *Geschichte der christlich-lateinischen Poesie bis zur Mitte des 8. Jahrhunderts*, Stuttgart, 1891; O. Fleischer, *Neumen-Studien*, Leipsic, 1893 sqq.; W. H. Frere, *The Winchester Tropes*, London, 1894; A. Dechevrens, *Du rhythme dans l'hymnographie latine*, 1895; N. Gihr, *Die Sequenzen des römischen Messbuches*, Freiburg, 1896; C. Blume and G. M. Dreves, *Hymnologische Beiträge*, Leipsic, 1897 sqq.; P. Wagner, *Ursprung und Entwickelung der liturgischen Gesangsformen*, Freiburg in Switzerland, 1901; idem, *Normenkunde*, ib. 1905; J. Werner, *Notkers Sequenzen*, Aarau, 1901; J. Thibaut, *Origine byzantine de la notation neumatique de l'église latine*, Paris, 1907; S. M. Jackson, *The Source of Jerusalem the Golden*, Chicago, 1910; Julian, *Hymnology*, pp. 1041–53, 1700–01 (lists first lines, and gives the use).

SERAPH. See Angel, I., § 4.

SERAPION, se-ra'pi-on or se-rē'pi-on: The name of sixteen (or seventeen) persons more or less known to early Christian history, of whom the following may be noted.

1. Bishop of Antioch probably 190 or 191 to 211 or 212, successor of Maximinus and predecessor of Asclepiades. He was the author of a writing to a certain Domninus who had fallen away to Judaism;

of another to Pontius and Caricus regarding Montanism; of a treatise warning the church at Rhossus against a Gospel of Peter see (PETER THE APOSTLE, III.); and of other writings to various persons (Eusebius, *Hist. eccl.*, V., xix., VI., xii.; Jerome, *De vir. ill.*, xli.; Socrates, *Hist. eccl.*, III., vii.).

2–4. Three men of the name were known in the Alexandrian church of the third century. The first was a martyr under Decius, celebrated Nov. 14. The second of the name in the same persecution sacrificed, but repented and received the sacrament on his death-bed. The third is named by Philip of Side among the leaders in the Alexandrian catechetical school, but his identity can not be more closely determined.

5. Bishop of Thmuis in Lower Egypt, a friend of St. Anthony and also of Athanasius, who directed to him four letters concerned with a form of the Macedonian heresy. The year of his death is unknown. At the Synod of Seleucia, 359, Ptolemæus took part as bishop of Thmuis. The treatise against Manicheanism belonging to him, intruded in part into the work of Titus of Bostra, has been edited by Brinkmann (in *SBA*, 1894, pp. 479–491). Mai edited two letters to Bishop Eudoxius and to a monk (reproduced in *MPG*, xl. 923–942). Pitra has edited some fragments (in *Analecta sacra*, ii. pp. xl., 27–28, iv. 214, 443–444); while some prayers in MS. 149 of the monastery on Mt. Athos are attributed to him (nos. 1, 15), and others (16, 17) are probably his (Wobbermin in *TU*, xvii. 3b, 1898). An addition to this, an appendix to the same collection in the form of letters "On the Father and the Son," may safely be attributed to him.

6. A monk of the Scetic desert, leader of the anthropomorphite monks (see ORIGENISTIC CONTROVERSIES).

7. Serapion Sindonetes, so called from the linen or cotton clothing which he wore. He is one of the heroes of the *Historia Lausiaca*, who experienced many adventures in his journeys to Greece and Rome. Nau sees in him the hero of the story of Thais. Leontius of Naples reports in the life of Johannes Eleemon that this Serapion sold his garments and his copy of the Gospels in order to be able to give alms.

8. Bishop of Heraclea. Chrysostom of Constantinople ordained to the diaconate a person named Serapion and assigned him the duties of archdeacon. He supported the bishop in his disciplinary measures, and by his severity widened the breach between bishop and clergy. While Chrysostom was at Ephesus, he entrusted to Serapion the administration of the diocese; at this time Severian of Gabala was at the capital intriguing against Chrysostom, and Serapion had him expelled. After his return from his first exile, Chrysostom had his supporter made bishop of Heraclea in Thrace. In the subsequent misfortunes of Chrysostom Serapion shared, was deprived of his bishopric and deported to Egypt.

(G. KRÜGER.)

BIBLIOGRAPHY: All of the men named are discussed in *DCB*, iv. 612–615. Consult further, on 1: Tillemont, *Mémoires*, iii. 168, § 9; Krüger, *History*, passim; Harnack, *Litteratur*, ii. 1, pp. 211 sqq.; Bardenhewer, *Patrologie*, p. 112, Eng. transl., St. Louis, 1908; and V. de Buck in the ed. of the *Acta Sanctorum* published Paris, 1883, Oct., xiii. 248–252. On 5: Bardenhewer, ut sup., pp. 234–235 (where bibliographical matter is furnished confirmatory of that given in the text. On 7: note Nau, in *Hist. de Thaïs, Annales du Musée Guimet*, xxx (1903), 51.

SERGIUS, ser'ji-us: The name of four popes.

Sergius I.: Pope 687–701. Of Syrian ancestry, he himself was born at Palermo, and, coming to Rome in the pontificate of Adeodatus (q.v.), was ordained to the priesthood in 682 or 683. On the death of Conon in 687, he became the candidate of the municipal authorities, the militia, and a large part of the clergy of Rome, with a view to ending the rivalry of the archdeacon Paschalis and the archpriest Theodore, each of whom had seized a portion of the Lateran without being able to dislodge his antagonist. When Sergius entered the Lateran, Theodore at once renounced his claims, but Paschalis, though compelled to do likewise, summoned his patron, John, exarch of Ravenna, to Rome. When the latter arrived, he recognized the validity of the election of Sergius, though extorting from him the hundred pounds of gold which Paschalis had promised in return for the exarch's assistance. Enthroned on Dec. 15, 687, Sergius sought not only to defend the authority of the Curia in the East, but to strengthen relations with the Anglo-Saxon church in the West, and to secure connection with the Anglo-Saxon missions to the continent. Both in Britain and with Pippin (see WILLIBRORD, SAINT) he was completely successful. He baptized Cædwalla, king of Wessex, at Rome in 689, and a few years later reinstated the deposed Wilfrid of York, but the statement of the *Liber pontificalis*, that he consecrated Brihtwald, eighth archbishop of Canterbury, probably confuses the sending of the pallium with the consecration, which, according to Bede (*Hist. eccl.*, v. 8), was performed by the French Metropolitan Goduin, or Godwin. The pope's attitude toward the East was determined by his decided rejection of the decisions of the Trullan Synod of 692 (see TRULLAN SYNODS), and on his emphatic refusal to subscribe to them, Justinian II. sent the Protospathary Zacharias to bring the pontiff to Rome. But Italy rallied to the pope's defense, and Zacharias escaped death only by throwing himself upon the protection of Sergius, who thus emerged victorious, even while deepening the gulf already existing between the Eastern and the Western Church. The death of Sergius took place Sept. 8, 701, and he is commemorated on that day in the Roman "Martyrology." (A. HAUCK.)

BIBLIOGRAPHY: *Liber pontificalis*, ed. L. Duchesne, i. 244, Paris, 1886, ed. T. Mommsen, in *MGH*, *Gest. pont. Rom.*, i (1898), 210 sqq.; R. Baxmann, *Die Politik der Päpste*, i. 188, Elberfeld, 1868; M. Heimbucher, *Die Papstwahlen unter den Karolingern*, pp. 15 sqq., Augsburg, 1889; Hefele, *Conciliengeschichte*, iii. 345 sqq., Eng. transl., v. 239 sqq., Fr. transl., iii. 1, pp. 578–591; Bower, *Popes*, i. 492–496; *Platina*, Popes, i. 168–172; *DCB*, iv. 618–620; *ASB*, Sept., iii. 425–445; Ceillier, *Auteurs sacrés*, xii. 964.

Sergius II.: Pope 844–74. By birth he was a Roman noble, and was educated at the papal court, finally being made archpriest by Gregory IV. On the death of this pontiff, in Jan., 844, a deacon named John was put forward as a candidate for the papal throne by the populace, only to succumb to the nominee of the nobles, Sergius, whose intervention alone saved his rival from death. His enthronement without the consent of the Emperor Lothair was, however, regarded by the latter as an infringement of imperial prerogatives, and in the summer of 844 an army, under the command of Lothair's son, Louis, invaded Roman territory; but the pope received the prince with all honor, though not avoiding a stormy interview with the bishops and princes in Louis's train. It is clear, nevertheless, that the pope retained his position and successfully debarred the hostile army from Rome; but, on the other hand, the Romans were obliged to take the oath of allegiance to the emperor, while Sergius crowned Louis king of the Lombards and appointed Drogo of Metz papal vicar north of the Alps. At the same time, Sergius maintained an unfavorable attitude toward Ebo of Reims (see Ebo) and Bartholomew of Narbonne, who had been suspended because of their sympathy with Lothair, though later, at the instance of the emperor, he sided with Ebo against Hincmar of Reims (q.v.). During this pontificate the city of Rome was sacked, and the churches of St. Peter and St. Paul were plundered by the Saracens in Aug., 846, the pope dying shortly afterward, Jan. 27, 847.

(A. Hauck.)

Bibliography: *Liber pontificalis*, ed. L. Duchesne, ii. 86 sqq., Paris, 1894; Jaffé, *Regesta*, pp. 327–328; R. Baxmann, *Die Politik der Päpste*, i. 349, Elberfeld, 1868; A. von Reumont, *Geschichte der Stadt Rom*, ii. 196, Berlin, 1868; M. Heimbucher, *Die Papstwahlen unter den Karolingern*, pp. 149 sqq., Augsburg, 1889; Götz, in *ZKG*, xv (1890), 342 sqq.; J. Langen, *Geschichte der römischen Kirche*, ii. 822, Bonn, 1885; F. Gregorovius, *Hist. of the City of Rome*, ii. 180–183, 190, iii. 83–85, 91, London, 1894–95; Bower, *Popes*, ii. 215–216; Platina, *Popes*, i. 218–220; Milman, *Latin Christianity*, iii. 16; Hauck, *KD*. ii. 512–513; and especially Mann, *Popes*, ii. 232–257; Ceillier, *Auteurs sacrés*, xii. 406.

Sergius III.: Pope 904–911. On the death of Theodore II., in 897, he was, although only in deacon's orders, the candidate of a faction of the populace for the papal throne, but, being forced to yield to John IX. (q.v.), he took refuge with the Margrave Adalbert in Tuscany, where he remained until the deposition of Christophorus (q.v.) in 904, when he returned to Rome, being enthroned probably Jan. 29 of the same year. He rebuilt the Lateran, which had been destroyed by an earthquake, and condemned the validity of all ordinations by Formosus (q.v.). His death occurred in May, 911.

(A. Hauck.)

Bibliography. *Liber pontificalis*, ed. L. Duchesne, ii. 236, Paris, 1892; Jaffé, *Regesta*, p. 445; J. M. Watterich, *Romanorum pontificum . . . vitæ*, i. 32, 37, 85, 660 sqq., Leipsic, 1862; Mann, *Popes*, iv. 119–142; A. von Reumont, *Geschichte der Stadt Rom*, ii. 227, Berlin, 1868; R. Baxmann, *Die Politik der Päpste*, ii. 78, Elberfeld, 1869; J. Langen, *Geschichte der römischen Kirche*, iii. 313, Bonn, 1892; F. Gregorovius, *Hist. of the City of Rome*, iii. 217, 220, 231–248, London, 1895; Hefele, *Conciliengeschichte*, iv. 574; Bower, *Popes*, ii. 306–307; Platina, *Popes*, i. 243–244; Milman, *Latin Christianity*, iii. 155–158; Ceillier, *Auteurs sacrés*, xii. 741–743.

Sergius IV.: Pope 1009–1012. He was a Roman by birth, and after having been bishop of Albano, was raised to the papal throne in July, 1009. The sole traces of his brief pontificate, which was ended by his death in June, 1012, are a number of privileges to monasteries. He is especially noteworthy as the first pope to adopt a new name on election, his original name having been Peter. (A. Hauck.)

Bibliography: *Liber pontificalis*, ed. L. Duchesne, ii. 267, Paris, 1892; Jaffé, *Regesta*, p. 504; J. M. Watterich, *Romanorum pontificum . . . vitæ*, i. 69–99, 700, Leipsic, 1862; A. von Reumont, *Geschichte der Stadt Rom*, ii. 227, Berlin, 1868; J. Langen, *Geschichte der römischen Kirche*, iii. 403; Mann, *Popes*, v. 142–154; Gregorovius, *Hist. of the City of Rome*, iv. 11–13, London, 1896; Bower, *Popes*, ii. 334–335; Platina, *Popes*, i. 266–267; Milman, *Latin Christianity*, iii. 222; Ceillier, *Auteurs sacrés*, xiii. 64, 189–190.

SERGIUS AND BACCHUS: Two Syrian martyrs of the early fourth century. According to the *Acta* and *Passio* (see bibliography) Sergius and Bacchus were two officers in the service of Emperor Maximinus Daja of Syria (305–313), and were so trusted by him that they were accorded his complete confidence and high rank at the palace. But they were denounced to the emperor by jealous enemies as Christians. He then ordered them to betake themselves to the temple of Jupiter, and upon their refusal had them dressed in women's garments and led through the streets of the city, and afterward sent them to Antiochus, prefect of Barbalissus (Beth Balash). After vain attempts to detach them from their faith, Bacchus was beaten to death with thongs, while Sergius was compelled to put on sandals through the soles of which nails had been driven, and was led to Resaph in Commagene and there beheaded. The fame of the martyrs spread very early, and a church in Eastern Syria is said to have been dedicated in their honor as soon as 354 (P. Le Bas and W. H. Waddington, *Voyage archéologique en Grèce et en Asie Mineure*, vol. iii., no. 2124, Paris, 1847), while in 512 another was dedicated to them and to Leontius in 512. To one of the churches dedicated to Sergius Justinian's consort Theodore presented a jeweled cross, afterward carried away by the Persians and restored to Gregory of Antioch by Chosroes of Persia in 593. The repute of the martyrs spread into the West. At Rome there was an oratorium on the north side of the Vatican basilica (*Römische Quartalschrift*, 1896, p. 243), and still another memorial to both martyrs in Rome is attested by the *Liber pontificalis* (ed. Duchesne, i. 512, Paris, 1886). In France and elsewhere their names were honored, as by a cloister at Angers and a church at Chartres (E. Le Blant, *Inscriptions chrétiennes de la Gaule*, i. 305, Paris, 1856). In Christian art they are represented in armor with palm branches. Their day in both the Eastern and the Western churches is Oct. 7.

Bibliography. Sources are the anonymous *Acta* and the account by Simeon Metaphrastes, with commentary in *ASB*, Oct., iii. 833–883, partly also in *MPL*, cxv. 1005 sqq.; cf. the *Acta martyrum et sanctorum* of P. Bedjan, iii. 283 sqq., Paris, 1892; the Greek *Passio* in *Analecta Bollandiana*, xiv (1895), 373 sqq.; and the "Hymn" of Walafrid Strabo in *MGH*, *Poet. Lat. ævi Car.*, ii (1884), 418–419. Consult further, J. Wolf, *Die heiligen Märtyrer Sergius und Bacchus Kirchenpatronen zu Kreuzeber*, Göttingen, 1823; *KL*, xi. 192–193; *DCB*, iv. 616–617.

SERGIUS CONFESSOR: Mentioned by Photius as the author of a history of the political and ecclesiastical events during the first eight years of the

Emperor Michael II. Balbus (820–829), with a glance at the "shameful" deeds of the Emperor Constantine Copronymus (751–774). The history was marked by simplicity, clearness, and beauty of exposition. Unfortunately the work is utterly lost. The title of confessor indicates that the bearer was a champion of images in the controversy over the subject (see IMAGES AND IMAGE WORSHIP, II.), and, as applied by Photius to this man, tends to identify the latter with the confessor of that name celebrated May 13 in the Greek Church, who was exiled under Leo III. (813–820) and seems to have died during the reign of Theophilus (829–842). (G. KRÜGER.)

BIBLIOGRAPHY: Nikodemus Hagiorites, *Synaxaristês tôn dôdeka mênôn tou eniautou*, iii. 37, Zanthe, 1868; *KL*, ii. 193; Basil, *Menologium*, *MPG*, cxvii. 454; Ceillier, *Auteurs sacrés*, xii. 428.

SERGIUS OF CONSTANTINOPLE: Patriarch of that city 610–638. He is noteworthy as the author of a very celebrated Greek hymn, known as the *Akathistos* from the fact that it was sung standing (given in *MPG*, xcii. 1335–1348; and in Pitra, *Analecta sacra*, i. 250–262, Paris, 1876). He seems to have paid considerable attention to the development of the liturgy. For further information concerning him see MONOTHELITES. (G. KRÜGER.)

BIBLIOGRAPHY: Krumbacher, *Geschichte*, pp. 671–672; *DCB*, iv. 617–618.

SERMON. See HOMILETICS.

SERPENT IN WORSHIP, MYTHOLOGY, AND SYMBOLISM.

I. In the Bible.
Name and Conceptions (§ 1).
Mythology (§ 2).
The Brazen Serpent; "Nehushtan." (§ 3).
Origin and Significance (§ 4).
The Probable Solution (§ 5).
II. In Worship.
The Basis (§ 1).
In the Greek World (§ 2).
Ancestor Cults and the Mysteries (§ 3).
Rome and Babylonia (§ 4).
Syria and Egypt (§ 5).
India (§ 6).
Other Countries (§ 7).
III. In Mythology.
Greece (§ 1).
Babylonia and Egypt (§ 2).
IV. In Symbolism.
General (§ 1).
Egyptian, Mithraic, and Indian Art (§ 2).
In Other Lands (§ 3).
V. In Folk-lore.

I. In the Bible: In the Old and New Testaments ten (or eleven) words or expressions are found which in the English versions are rendered by "serpent" or some equivalent (note that *kippoz*, Isa. xxxiv. 15, is by some rendered "serpent" rather than "owl," reference being made to the Arabic *kaffas*, *kaffaza* as favoring this meaning), though in but few cases can identification of the species be made. The number of terms employed is not coextensive with the number of species of serpents found in Palestine and the neighboring regions, of which thirty-three are known. Of these several are poisonous, including the Egyptian cobra, the horned viper, and the sand viper. In the Bible many of the notions concerning the reptile appear which are common to most early peoples, including some of those pertaining to mythology. Its traits are described and its names or epithets are applied, in prose and poetry, to tribes, classes, individuals, and personifications. Thus it is a subtile beast, more cunning than any other (Gen. iii. 1); Dan (the tribe) is a (treacherous and dangerous) serpent in the way, a (biting) adder in the path (Gen. xlix. 17); the wicked secrete and infuse a poison like that of the serpent and are not subject to charms which prevent their doing harm (Ps. lviii. 4); so scribes and Pharisees (Matt. xxiii. 33), Pharisees and Sadducees (Matt. iii. 7), and Pharisees alone (Matt. xii. 34) are called serpents and offspring of vipers; wickedness, even though crushed, engenders a serpent as does a serpent's egg (Isa. lix. 5); and the effects of wine are like a serpent's bite or the sting of an adder; the disciples of Jesus Christ are to be so immune from harm that they may take up or tread upon serpents without injury to themselves (Mark xvi. 18; Luke x. 19; cf. Acts xxviii. 3); the serpent's habit of lurking in walls is referred to, so that he who would trespass (Eccles. x. 8) or carelessly leans on the wall (Amos v. 19) is bitten; the serpent's method of locomotion is one of mystery and wonder (Prov. xxx. 19); it is one of the creatures of Hebrew mythology, Leviathan being the swift or gliding or crooked serpent (Job xxvi. 13; Isa. xxvii. 1); and in Revelation Satan, the devil, is a serpent (xii. 9, xx. 2), and as a dragon or serpent he figures in apocalyptic events (xii. 14–15). In Gen. iii. (J; embodying primitive conceptions) the serpent is a sentient creature endowed with speech, contradicting the utterance of Yahweh, and leading man to disobedience. It is conceived as once having had a different means of locomotion, its present method being a punishment for its part in the fall (verse 14; interesting in this relation are the conceptions of the winged serpent—see below IV., § 2—and the four-footed reptile, as well as of the dragon, which combines both features). The hostility that has become instinctive between the race of man and that of the serpent is also traced to this cause, and it is noteworthy that in accordance with the assumed former parity in intercourse there appears in verse 1 no shrinking of the woman from the serpent as it approaches to accomplish its purpose. Similarly in verse 14 there is expressed a quite common primitive idea that dust is the serpent's food. The exegesis which sees Satan in this living thing is read into the passage in the light of a much later and more highly developed demonology (cf. Rev. xii. 9, xx. 2), for the conception of the serpent here is that of an animal only.

1. Names and Conceptions.

What little the purified Hebrew mythology has to say of the serpent is doubtless to be explained on the basis of common Semitic notions regarding the animal. The mythological references in the Old Testament are few: Job iii. 8 (R. V. and A. V. margin) and xxvi. 13, by most commentators referred to the dragon which enfolds the sun in its coils (a common oriental explanation of the sun's eclipse); and Isa. xxvii. 1, where the reference is almost certainly to the animal depicted in Babylonian cosmological myths. It is to be noted that the term "Leviathan" stands for several conceptions: in Job xli.; Ps. lxxiv. 14; and Ezek. xxix. 3 the context points to the crocodile; Ps. civ. 26 refers evidently to some inhabitant of the sea (the whale, G. E. Post, in *DB*, iii. 102); and the mythical dragon or perhaps the serpent of chaos and of the deep waters, as above (see DRAGON).

2. Mythology.

Of serpent-worship almost nothing appears in the Old Testament. Reference to the one clear case is given in II. Kings xviii. 4, where in addition to the stereotyped formula by the Deuteronomic editor of the book, customary as the summing up of a king's reign, there is added the somewhat cryptic remark: "and brake in pieces the brazen serpent that Moses had made; for unto those days the children of Israel did burn incense to it; and he called it Nehushtan." The marginal readings in the English versions attempt an interpretation of "Nehushtan," while the R. V. margin shows that the subject of the verb "called" is in doubt—whether that subject is Hezekiah, or whether it is impersonal, "one called" (i.e., "it was called"). It is recognized that the verb may be pointed as a plural written defectively, "they called" (so the Septuagint [codex L] *kai ekalesan*), and may continue in thought the plural of the preceding clause. And this rendering in turn submits to three interpretations which affect the sense of the passage: Nehushtan might have been the ordinary name applied in honor while it existed by the worshipers (see below); or a name applied to it by worshipers after it was broken and in contempt for it; or by the authorities to wean away respect for it and to prevent sedition or discontent. Besides this, the name "Nehushtan" is also difficult, both as to meaning and as to derivation. It has been taken by many commentators into connection with the *neḥosheth*, "brazen," of the first part of the verse, and this is indicated by the marginal readings in A. V. In this case either of two interpretations would satisfy the meaning: the term might be one of contempt: "a mere bit of brass"—or it might as well be a title of honor: "the work of brass par excellence," the "noted image made of brass." Another derivation has been proposed which lies quite near at hand, viz., from *naḥash*, "serpent." The difficulty then is to account for the termination *tan*, for which a South Arabian origin is to be sought, and the entire word is then to be explained as a loan word from the Arabic.

3. The Brazen Serpent; "Nehushtan."

The text does not state when the cult of the object began, although the object itself is asserted to be identical with that the origin and purpose of which are stated in Num. xxi. 4-9. That such a worship could have begun under the eye of Moses is out of the question, assuming for a moment the identity of Nehushtan with the image made by Moses. The continuance of the cult till the time of Hezekiah is the one fact clearly expressed. The method of dealing with the narrative in the critical school is that which takes account of the attempts customary in religious history to accredit with a high antiquity practises either already in use or those which it is desired to install. It is then held as a corollary that the account in Numbers is etiological. That is to say, it is held that the attribution of a Mosaic origin to the brazen serpent was to accredit the cult by those who followed or introduced it, and that this in turn gave rise to the (late) narrative in Numbers. Thus Cheyne (e.g., in *EB*, iii. 3338) holds that Nehushtan was one of the objects introduced into the Temple from the East (Babylonia). This hypothesis, while not impossible, is not susceptible of verification. His question regarding the primitive character ascribed to the object is pertinent, however, especially in view of the fact that the worship could not have arisen in the time of Moses. A serpent deity Ẓiru appears to have had a place in the temple of Marduk, where its function was that of a watcher or guardian against foes (Schrader, *KAT*, pp. 503-505), so that a basis exists for Cheyne's hypothesis. But another explanation exists nearer at hand in direct derivation from the Canaanites, even though ultimate reference to Babylonian usage be asserted. No longer regarded as tenable is the explanation of William Robertson Smith (*Journal of Philology*, ix. 99), who, assuming the Temple as the locus of the cult, considers the object a totem image belonging to the clan of David. To support this names in the Davidic family are adduced which are related to *naḥash*, "serpent,"—Naḥshon (Ruth iv. 40), and Abigail daughter of Nahash (II Sam. xvii. 25), as well as the fact that Adonijah sacrificed at "the stone of the serpent" ("of Zoheleth," I Kings i. 9). And no more likely is another hypothesis (Stade's) that it may represent the mythological serpent or dragon in heaven or perhaps an ancestor cult. Much the more likely is the suggestion that the worship was taken up from Canaanitic sources (K. Marti, *Geschichte der israelitischen Religion*, p. 101, Strasburg, 1903). Whether the cult had any more significance than as a "remainder" taken over from the Canaanites or even brought into Canaan by the Hebrews is unknown. The connection with Numbers suggests a relationship with the healing powers ascribed to the serpent, but this is pure hypothesis.

4. Origin and Significance.

From the fact that in II Kings xviii. 4 it is said that Hezekiah cut down "the Asherah" (in the singular, cf. R. V.; the A. V. plural "groves" is wrong), although it is known that the Asheroth were numerous (see ASHERAH), it is plausibly argued by commentators that the reference is to the Asherah in the Temple at Jerusalem, and that consequently the Nehushtan was there. But this reasoning is not conclusive, for probably the "high places" which were "removed" were not all in the Temple (see HIGH PLACES). The reference of the object to the time of Moses may mean no more than that it was very old, and the narrative in Num. xxi. would serve as the basis for such a report provided it or its elements were in existence at the time. The followers of the cult would doubtless attempt to justify it by some such claim (cf.

5. The Probable Solution.

the remark of Jeroboam I. when he set up the golden calves, I Kings xii. 28). There is reason to believe that the worship of the snake was not confined to Jerusalem. Altogether aside from the great part played by the serpent in the mythology of the surrounding peoples and the certainty that this influenced the Hebrews, there is direct evidence in a small bronze serpent which was found at Gezer. The question of the relationship between Num. xxi. 4 sqq., to II Kings xviii. 4 is by some regarded as close, the former being considered as built upon the latter. This is quite in accordance with the mythopœic genius, and Numbers is, on the critical hypothesis, the later. Such a passage as Deut. viii. 15 and the fact of the comparative abundance of serpents in the Arabian desert would assist, especially in the case of the attribution of the origin of the brazen serpent to Mosaic times. In the passage in Numbers it is on the surface of the narrative that merely looking on the image brought healing. There is no suggestion that the brazen serpent is a divine figure, nor, on the other hand, is there a hint that it called for the exercise of faith in a peculiar degree; the healing was accomplished for those who looked on the image because it was the means appointed by Yahweh for that end. It became a mere sign to serve that purpose (cf. the symbolism in John iii. 14).

II. In Worship: From the standpoint of animistic primitive religion there is little cause for wonder in the diffused cult of the serpent, whether that cult rise to the height of actual worship or be but the lower degree of veneration, totemic regard and immunity from destruction, or mere symbolism.

1. The Basis.

The reptile's peculiar form and often its remarkable beauty and striking marking, its mysterious and sometimes exceedingly rapid mode of progression, its staring gaze and power to charm (as exercised on birds and the smaller animals), its ability apparently to renew its youth and certainly its beauty by the shedding of its skin, the insidious character of its attack and the deadly character of its bite as exhibited in some species—all these and other characteristics have combined to make it one of the most admired and most dreaded of animals, and to give it a double repute for wisdom and power to heal, as well as for unrelenting hostility and demonic hatred for the race of men (cf. Gen. iii. 15). So that it is not remarkable that in religious symbolism the serpent should figure so largely, that nations celebrated for wisdom should make it an accompaniment of their gods, heroes, and kings, and that in mythology and folk-lore its rôle should be so extensive. And the spell of the serpent is not yet loosed, so that in few departments of comparative religion is there greater need of more careful scrutiny of statements of fact and especially of inferences current in the books on the subject. It is usual to assume that every effigy or representation of a serpent, as also the use of it in rites, is proof of serpent-worship in that locus or connection. Thus it is commonly held that the use of the snake in the snake-dances of the North American Indians involves worship. Yet it is probable that the true explanation in this instance is the supposed connection of the serpent in folk-lore with rain and thus with agricultural fertility, so that the snake-dance belongs in the realm of sympathetic magic ritual to induce rain and consequently bountiful harvests (see below on the connection of serpents with springs). Similarly the sculptures, etc., of the cobra with three, five, or seven heads, which is so often figured shadowing with its inflated hood this or that deity in India, no more warrant conclusion as to serpent-worship in that relation than does the fact that deities are represented as seated on a lotus prove worship of the lotus. Its function there is merely that of an attendant upon the deity, an enhancement of whose powers is implied by the attendance of the deadly beast. In this connection its presence is in line with the efforts of a crude religious art, which, under the form of four- or six-handed beings with distorted shape and outré accompaniments, seeks to express the attribution to the gods of power and wisdom vastly superior to those qualities as seen in human beings.

It must not be concluded from the foregoing, however, that serpent-worship is or ever has been a rare phenomenon. It is both a priori probable that animistic peoples would worship an animal so uncanny as the serpent, and demonstrable that such worship was actual and continued beyond the animistic stage. But it is important to remember in this connection that when the stage of anthropomorphic religion was reached, there would be a natural tendency to cover up the traces of animal-worship as being less noble, and so those traces would easily become lost. Such a course would especially be followed in the literary religions. This does not involve the absolute extinction of the cult, however, for the worship often continued as a rural cult, or, perhaps, *sub rosa*, after the more aristocratic worship of the anthropomorphized deity had taken its place. Much of the evidence to be cited from Greece in all probability comes from this conservative stratum of the population.

Some of the most cogent proofs of serpent-worship in the ancient world come from the Greek area, especially in connection with (1) the submerged pre-Homeric religion, and (2) the later "folk-religion" and the renascence of the mysteries (see TRIBAL AND CULTIC MYSTERIES) in the century preceding and following the Christian era.

2. In the Greek World.

The evidence is largely monumental, and is established under circumstances which make it evident that, e.g., Zeus superseded a deified snake, installing himself instead as the object of worship, and adopting its rites and sacrifices. Thus a huge bearded snake is figured on a Hymettus marble which was taken to Berlin in 1879, and is inscribed "to Zeus Meilichios" ("Meilichios," here used euphemistically, meaning "kind"). A votive tablet is known, also figuring a bearded snake. Another from Eteonos in Bœotia shows a serpent emerging from a cave while a worshiper and his daughter stand in front, the former in the act of worship. The supplanting by Zeus Meilichios of the snake is clearly exhibited by a figure that is human in form, the snake being reduced to normal size (in the former cases it is gigantic) and located beneath the throne, while the sacrifice is the pig (offered to the chthonic deities, not to those of the heavens, as was Zeus), and the seated deity is identified with Zeus Meilichios, the deity of the snake tablet just described (Jane Ellen Harrison, *Prolegomena*, pp. 17–28, Cambridge, 1908). On another tablet the huge snake, this time not bearded, is figured with worshipers, and this, too, is inscribed "to Zeus Meilichios." It will be recalled that Æsculapius (Asklepios) is usually represented as carrying a staff on which a snake is twined. A votive tablet found in the Asklepieion and now in the Athens museum shows the god standing in front of a huge serpent, while worshipers, apparently a single family, bring a lamb as sacrifice. Here the anthropomorphic transition is already made, but the snake still remains. In other votive offerings the snake is present, but greatly reduced in size. In sanctuaries in other cities evidently belonging to a god of healing, probably Æsculapius, representations of snakes are commonly the votive offerings. According to Pausanias (II., xi. 8), serpents of Æsculapius were fed at Sicyon, and the same author (III., xxiii. 7) reports that at Epidaurus the statue of Æsculapius holds its hand over a serpent and (II., xxviii. 1) a yellow serpent is sacred to him, while the legend of Sicyon (II., x. 3) is to the effect that he came to that city in the form of a serpent. Epidaurus Limera was built, according to the tradition (Pausanias, III., xxiii. 7), where a serpent brought from Epidaurus disappeared in the earth (which the oracle had foretold as the omen by which to found the city), and altars to the god of healing are there, while the same story is told of the founding of Sosipolis (VI., xx. 5). The connection of the snake with Æsculapius is indirectly confirmed by the narratives of cures on the steles found at Epidaurus. In several cases the beneficiaries of the healing shrine dreamed of snakes (Mary Hamilton, *Incubation*, p. 22, no. 17, p. 26, no. 38, p. 27, no. 40, London, 1906), and snakes were often sent from Epidaurus to be the agents of healing elsewhere (ib. pp. 30–31), as is shown by the satirical *Ploutos* of Aristophanes (ib., p. 35). The cases of Zeus and Æsculapius make it probable that in other instances, at least in Greek environment (and the general law suggests the same among other peoples), where the serpent accompanies the representation of the deity, worship of the animal lies in the background.

3. Ancestor Cults and the Mysteries.

Other examples in the Grecian world worthy of notice are that at Hierapolis the serpent was a god and was employed in the mysteries of Leto and Kora. This animal figured in the Bacchic orgies, also in the Mithraic (see below). Serpents were sacred to Trophonius (Pausanias, IX., xxxix. 3). It will be recalled that the serpents which slew Laocoon retired to the temple of Pallas, while at Athens a huge snake was supposed to have its den on the Acropolis in the temple of Pallas, guardian of the city. The relation of the snakes to the dead and the very probable association with ancestor-worship are established by a series of representations referred to in Harrison's *Prolegomena* (ut sup., pp. 326–331, 349–354). The dead hero is in one case shown inhabiting his tomb, while on an altar to the hero Aristeandros snakes were carved. This may have to be related to ancestor-worship also. There will occur to the reader here the instance of Æneas sacrificing to his father's manes (*Æneid*, v. 84), when a snake appeared and the worshipers were uncertain whether this were the "genius of the place" or an "attendant" (*famulus*) of Anchises. The advanced thought of the time transmuted the primitive reincarnation of the dead in a snake (see on folk-lore, below) into this more advanced form. The Ophites (q.v.) kept a tame snake which they induced to encircle the bread of the sacrament and worshiped as the king of heaven (Epiphanius, *Haer.*, xxxvii.; Tertullian, *Haer.*, ii., *ANF*, iii. 650).

4. Rome and Babylonia.

At Rome the instances of well-attested serpent-worship are few, and this accords with the less fanciful, more restrained, and sharper legal turn of mind of the Romans. The cult seems to have been established there in 462 A. U. C. (291 B.C.), if one may follow the indications in Ovid, *Metamorphoses*, xv. 5. At Lanuvium (16 m. s. of Rome) there was a temple of Juno and a great cave, in which was a huge snake to which worship was offered. The animal was used as an oracle also, maidens being taken there to prove their virginity, which was regarded as established if the snake received the offerings presented. Similarly, testimony which makes for serpent-worship in Babylonia is present. On Babylonian seals, serpent gods are figured, the lower parts consisting of serpent coils, with worshipers in front. Sometimes the serpent-deity is represented introducing the devotee to the god to whom worship is to be offered. The name of this deity is given as Ningishzida (cf. W. H. Ward, *Seal Cylinders of Western Asia*, chap. xviii., Washington, 1910). In the Marduk temple E-sagil at Babylon an image of a horned serpent was kept (Schrader, *KAT*, p. 504; cf. the references there, e.g., to the Ninib hymn II Rawlinson, 19, no. 2); for the Babylonian snake-deity Ẓiru cf. Schrader, ut sup., pp. 504–505, this god being known as "Lord of life." Such a title is ambiguous; it is applied in India to the cobra because of its deadly power; it might also mean the giver or source of life with reference to the frequent connection of the snake with water and fertility. Diodorus Siculus (ii. 70) affirms that in the temple of Bel (Marduk) at Babylon there was an image of "the goddess Rhea, . . . at her knees two lions, and near her very large serpents of silver, . . . also an image of Juno, holding in her hand the head of a serpent." This probably indicates the remains of adoration of the animal.

5. Syria and Egypt.

For Phenicia and Syria Macrobius (*Saturnaliorum conviviorum libri VII.*, i. 9) affirms that the Tyrians worshiped Janus under the figure of a serpent with its tail in its mouth, and there is good reason to believe that they employed also a serpent encircling a disc (see under symbolism, below). It seems probable that the serpent was sacred to the Phenician deity Esmun, who was in all probability a god of healing since he is identified with Æsculapius (Baudissin, *ZDMG*, lix., 1905, pp. 459

sqq.). Elagabalus is said as priest at Emesa to have imported and worshiped serpents from Egypt of the Agathodemon variety (Strabo, *Geographikē*, xvi. 756). While no country is richer than Egypt in snake symbolism, explicit evidence of worship is somewhat scarce. Apophis was the serpent of the underworld, and Set or Typhon is identified with him; Kneph is also represented as a hawk-headed serpent; Isis and Nephthys were both identified with the uræus goddess Uatchet, and a center of the uræus worship in predynastic times was the town in the Delta known as Per-Uatchet. In the cases of Apophis and Set, if there was actual worship it was probably of the type known as avertive, which derives its stimulus from fear. Serpents were kept, apparently as objects of devotion, at Thebes (Herodotus, ii. 74), and the cerastes has often been found embalmed there. The asp was sacred to a goddess Ranno, was a companion of Kneph, and the representative of Agathadæmon (which name may have had a euphemistic origin). Ælian (*De animalibus*, xvi. 39) tells of a large snake kept at the Æsculapium at Alexandria, and of one kept and fed at the temple at Metele in the Delta (*Vana historia*, xi. 17). Montfaucon (*Diarium Italicum*, vol. ii., plate 46) figures a marble, possibly from Egypt, found at Rome on which there is the portrayal of a worshiper before an idol the head of which consists of a triple serpent head. The deceased human might by the use of magic formulas become the serpent Sata, which proclaimed "I died daily and am born again each day" (E. A. W. Budge, *Gods of the Egyptians*, ii. 377, 2 vols., London, 1904).

6. India.

In India the worship of the serpent is a present and indubitable fact, especially in the rural districts. That this is an inheritance from the past is as little open to question. The evidence for past adoration is to be found not alone in the ever present representation of the animal in religious symbolism, which may often be accounted for on other grounds, but also diffusively in the references in the literature, as in the *Mahabharata*, in which nag (serpent) stories abound and involve the existence of the cult. In the Punjab the animal is a tutelary household divinity to which sacrifice is offered, and protection is assured by belief in penalties which will be incurred by killing the animal, such as subsequent barrenness of the wife (with which may be compared the Teutonic belief that the consequence is the death of a child). On the upper Ganges the Agarwalas are known to others by the name of snake-worshipers, and their chief deity is Astika Muni, a nephew of the mythological serpent Vasuki. In Malabar most house enclosures have the animal's effigy on stone, the live snakes are fed, while "snake groves" are maintained for the performance of rites. In most villages of the Deccan the nag is one of the village deities, and elsewhere in the peninsula sacrifices of hair are offered in behalf of children. Similarly, in Kashmir effigies of the creature abound before which offerings are placed. The worship exists largely in Sivaite connections, and the so-called naga tribes are continuing testimony to the existence of the cult.

In other parts of the world the evidence of this worship can be substantiated, though only illustrative examples will here be cited. In Africa the advance of civilization is destroying the cult, but it is known that in Dahomey, for instance, the earth serpent was once a great deity served by virgin priestesses, and on the slave coast the cult of the snake was all but dominant (J. B. Schlegel, *Schlüssel zur Ewe-Sprache*, p. xiv., Stuttgart, 1857). In Japan, outside of the regard for the mythical dragon, the still current animism includes the serpent as an object of prayer, and the gods of the water are often served under that form (W. G. Aston, *Shinto*, pp. 63–64, London, 1905). The Polynesian Ramahavaly is a deity of healing, and his messengers are snakes (W. Ellis, *Polynesian Researches*, 3d ed., London, 1854), possibly a case parallel to that of Æsculapius in Greece. In Sweden in the sixteenth century, snakes were household deities held immune from harm (Olaus Magnus, xxi. 47–48, Copenhagen, 1650), and in Prussia the same regard long survived (C. Hartknoch, *Alt und Neues Preussen*, i. 143, 162, Frankfort, 1684). In America, Mexico and Peru are richest in evidences of this cult, the Aztec Tezcatlipoca being the male and his consort Cohuacohuatl the female serpent. Quetzalcoatl was the feathered serpent, lawgiver and civilizer (J. G. Müller, *Geschichte der americanischen Urreligionen*, pp. 62, 585, Basel 1855; and the works of Prescott), while temples, the portals of which were built to resemble serpents' heads, were known and impress the fact of serpent-worship. In North America Hopi altars are decorated with figures of snakes, and the Kickapoo Indians reverence the mythical rain serpent above other deities. The so-called dracontia (temples of earth or mounds built in serpentine form) are known in this region. The cases claimed in England and France (Carnac in Brittany, Abury in Wiltshire and Stanton Drew in Somersetshire, England; cf. J. B. Deane, *Worship of the Serpent*, chap. viii., London, 1833) are by Fergusson (see bibliography) declared to be imaginary. But in Scotland the sacred character of the snakes pictured on stones is established (John Stuart, *Sculptured Stones in Scotland*, ii., p. lxxiv., Aberdeen, 1856), and there seems to be a dracontium in Argyllshire several hundred feet long.

7. Other Countries.

III. In Mythology: Greece presents perhaps the richest, at any rate the best known, aggregation of myths in which the serpent figures. The Titans in their battles with Zeus are represented as either wholly or partly serpentine, while Boreas has tails of snakes instead of feet (Pausanias, V., xix. 1). Typhon, a monster partly snake-like in figure, was struck by the lightning of Zeus and buried beneath Mt. Etna (Pindar, *Python*). According to another story (Strabo, xvi. 756) the channel of the Orontes in Syria was caused by the writhings of the monster in his agony. The serpentine horrors of the Gorgons, Furies, and Cerberus come naturally to mind; and in early times the Ægis of Athena was a cloak with scales and a fringe of serpents. This deity, when she won Athens from Poseidon, made the serpent Erechthonius guardian of the olive-tree which she planted (Pausanias, I., xxiv. 7). So serpents or dragons guarded the golden fleece and the golden apple in the garden

1. Greece.

of the Hesperides (ib. VI., xix. 8). Thetis transformed herself into a snake to escape from Peleus (ib. V., xviii. 5), and the existence of the winged snake is a belief of Greece as well as of Egypt and Arabia. The serpent Pytho guarded the oracle at Delphi and was killed by Apollo, who assumed the oracle (Hyginus, *Fabula*, cxl.; here original snake-worship is indicated). Hercules strangled two serpents sent against him by Hera, fought the Lernæan Hydra, and was the progenitor by the serpent Echidna of the snake-worshiping Scythians (Herodotus, iv. 9). Cadmus fought and killed a dragon and sowed its teeth, and he and his wife were transformed into serpents. Cecrops, first king of Attica, and Erechtheus of Athens (*Iliad*, ii. 547) were half serpents, and it is worth noting that Homer (*Iliad*, xi. 38) gives to Agamemnon the insignium of a three-headed snake.

2. Babylonia and Egypt.

Several cycles of myths in Babylonia contain allusions to this animal, always hostile to gods and men. In the Gilgamesh epic the hero loses through a hostile serpent the herb which was to renew the youth of the aged; the Etana myth has to do with one of these animals which plucked the wings of the eagle that was to carry Etana to heaven; in the fragment of the Labbu myth a water serpent is one of the plotters against man; and the animal is brought into relation with the creation myth and chaos, the monster Tiamat appearing in some of the representations to be not the griffin-like beast but a serpent (W. H. Ward, in *Bibliotheca Sacra*, xxxviii., 1891, 209–253), while Tiamat gave birth to serpents and dragons, terrible and irresistible until Marduk arose as the champion of the gods. Babylonians had the conception of a huge snake which engirdled the world, as well as of another which lay in the depths of the sea and is reflected in Hebrew cosmogony. The origin of the Orontes in Syria has already received mention. In Egypt mere reference is needed to Apophis, the great serpent of the underworld, enemy of Horus, Ra, and Osiris, as well as of the dead, and the personification of evil. Set was the snake which endured forever and punished wicked souls in hell (Budge, ut sup., i. 23–24, ii. 376–377). The text of Unas (fifth dynasty) gives sets of magical formulas by which to overcome the brood of serpents of the underworld (Budge, ut sup., i. 23). A huge snake thirty cubits long was believed to live in the "mountain of the sunrise." The myth of the winged serpent was widely current in Egypt and Arabia (cf. the conception of the feathered serpent of Mexico and Peru). So through the myths of other peoples runs the trail of the serpent. In India the sky snake Vritra or Ahi keeps away the rain that would break the drought, and is slain by the arrows of Indra; Rudra is the destroyer of serpents; Devi assumed this form to carry Vishnu through the deluge. The Scandinavian myth of the Midgard serpent which girdled the earth with its tail in its mouth comes readily to the memory (*Prose Edda*, 410 sqq.). For the Druid myth of the egg secreted by a writhing mass of snakes see DRUIDS. Among Mexicans the first woman's husband was a great male snake (see above under "Worship").

IV. In Symbolism:

1. General.

In religious art this animal has an important place throughout the world. With its tail in its mouth, sometimes combining the disc, probably uniting two ways of representing eternity or endless time, it appears among the most unrelated nations—in Egypt, Persia, India, China, and Mexico. This disc is sometimes interpreted as the solar disc, sometimes as the world-egg, and is often figured, either winged or plain, with the serpent (or two serpents) issuing from it, passing through it or around it, or facing it. The employment of an effigy or representation of the animal to designate a deity or sovereign as sacred is common in both Egypt and India, and Persius (*Satire*, i. 113) notes that the sign of two serpents indicates a sanctuary. This symbolism is carried out even in the New World, as illustrated by the altars of the Guiana Indians, of the Moquis (among whom the snake signifies lightning, and they incise or paint it on the wands and kilts worn in the snake-dance), of the Natchez, and even of the Indians who inhabited Mexico and Peru at the time of the conquest (Prescott, *Works*, passim).

2. Egyptian, Mithraic, and Indian Art.

No country employed the emblem more consistently and abundantly than Egypt, where it appears in the head-dress or crown or about the person elsewhere of gods and monarchs, apparently only to emphasize deity and kingship. Gods crowned with the disc and uræus are Amen-Ra, Ra-Heru-Khuti, Nut, and Tefnut; the uræus appears in the crown or head-dress of Bast, Sebeknit, Haru-Ur, Ptah-Seker, Sebek-Ra, Isis, Horus, Ptah, Menthu, and Ba-Neb-Ṭaṭau, while Renmut is uræus-headed. Especially abundant is the use of the serpent in the "Book of that which is in the Underworld" (cf. Budge, ut sup., i. 204–262), and the eleventh hour is well worth studying for the elaborateness of serpent symbolism and forms. Here the solar disc and serpent from the prow guide Ra's boat, twelve gods carry the serpent Meḥen to the East, preceded by two cobras carrying crowns, while the four-footed serpent (cf. Gen. iii. 14; note also the dragon of China and Japan) with wings is a prominent feature; in the sixth hour a serpent with one snake head and four human heads is seen, and the seven-headed snake is also known (Budge, ut sup., i. 267, who gives on ii. 64 one of the finest reproductions of the winged serpent). Mithraic art employs this animal extensively, especially with its figure of Kronos. Thus this symbol is represented at Modena in the folds of a serpent (*Revue archéologique*, 1902, i. 1); another found at Rome in the sixteenth century is entwined with a serpent, the head of which passes over the head of the statue and enters its mouth. The Mithraic bas-relief of Apulum, Dacia, shows on the bottom border the serpent which surrounds the world (F. Cumont, *Textes et monuments*, p. 309, 2 vols., Brussels, 1896–99). A Mithraic cameo shows on the reverse two serpents twined about wands, a third forming the wood of a bow, and a fourth forming the string, and on the obverse two snakes extended. A Mithraic leontocephalous Kronos has about him a number of serpents, and in another found at Florence the head of the enfolding serpent rests on the head of the Kronos. The plaques of the bull-slaying Mithra show snakes in various positions (cf. F. Cumont, *Mysteries of Mithra*, pp. 21, 22, 23, 39, 55, 105, 106, 108, 110, 117, 124, 139, 151, 176, 222, Chicago, 1903). Cumont interprets the serpent in the Kronos figures as typifying the tortuous course of the sun in the ecliptic; but as Kronos typifies time, it is better to take the presence of the serpent as merely intensive and suggesting unending time. In India the spectacled cobra is naturally most frequently represented, especially as an attendant upon deities. In this relation the animal is usually pictured with three, five, seven, or nine heads, the hood being inflated, and generally shielding the head of the deity. The god may, however, simply repose on the coils of the animal, or may be enfolded within them; or the serpent may form the adornment as necklace, armlet, or girdle, or may be held in the hand. Not merely are Brahman and Hindu gods represented as protected by the snake, but also the Jina (see JAINISM) and the Buddha (see BUDDHISM). In some of the great temples almost every architectural possibility is seized for decoration with this figure, and this holds true not only for India, but for Burma, Java, and Ceylon, also for China and Japan, if the dragon be taken into account, while in similar situations in Mexico and Peru the same is found.

3. In Other Lands.

The connection of the serpent with the tree of life, already suggested by its presence in the garden of the Hesperides and with the golden fleece, is illustrated in Babylonia, and the connection of this cycle with the serpent in Gen. iii. has been too often exploited to need more than mention here. In this region it also appeared among the decorations of the approaches to temples and palaces (H. Gunkel, *Schöpfung und Chaos*, p. 154, Göttingen, 1895), while it is striking that the caduceus (a staff wound with two snakes) is carried by Ishtar (cf. W. H. Ward, *American Antiquarian*, xx., 1898, p. 215), and this same serpent-staff appears on a vase of Gudea (H. Gressmann, *Altorientalische Texte und Bilder*, ii. 92, Tübingen, 1909). There come readily to mind the caduceus of Hermes in Greece, and the staff of Æsculapius twined with a single serpent. At Gournia in Crete the modern excavations have brought to light a goddess' image with serpents coiled about her; one at Cnossos is in the embrace of three, while a fourth projects its head above her tiara, and at Palaikastro a goddess holds a threefold serpent in her arms. It is but natural that the animal should appear on the coins of many cities. Thus a Tyrian coin carries a tree between two pillars or mazzeboth, and a snake twines about the tree; another coin bears the caduceus and also an altar, from the front corners of which snakes emerge; still another represents the Tyrian Hercules contending with the serpent; a coin of Berytus has a nude man (or god) between two snakes which form a single coil; and numerous coins bear designs which are but variants of these. Among cities which employed this animal on their coins, Pella and Adramyttium are representative.

V. In Folk-lore: No better illustration of the right of folk-lore as a handmaiden to the study of religion is furnished than in the body of common notions which gather about the serpent. This branch points the way to an understanding of many of the features already exhibited in the foregoing discussion of worship, mythology, and symbolism. The qualities ascribed to this animal by the common understanding may be grouped in five classes, viz., wisdom (including powers of healing), guardianship and protection, paternity or transmigration, the command over fertility, and hostility. These several ideas may be contemporaneously current in the same region; that is, it may be conceived that the serpent is both the protector and the enemy of man at the same time and place. Yet it must not be forgotten that often one or the other ideas either of benefaction or of maleficence may be dominant. As an illustration of the wisdom of the serpent (cf. Gen. iii.; it there is not only the most cunning of animals, it knows the qualities of the fruit of the tree) it serves in part to note that it was associated with Athene, Apollo, and Hermes, in Egypt with Kneph, in India with Siva (patron of the learned Brahmans), with Buddha, who is said to have communicated his complete system only to the Nagas, a supposed snake-like tribe, and with Vishnu, while in Tibet one of the sacred books was popularly supposed to have been derived from the Nagas. In its capacity as a healer in Greece it was associated with Æsculapius, in Egypt with Isis, Harpocrates, and Serapis, with Rudra in India, and with Ramahavaly in Polynesia. Ainus pray to it for a woman in labor, and for help against ague. It is often regarded as knowing and applying the properties of healing herbs. Pliny (xxv. 14) tells that Tylon was fatally bitten by a serpent, that his sister Moirē induced a giant to kill the animal, but that its mate brought a plant with which it touched the mouth of the dead snake and so revived it, and that Moirē learned the lesson and restored her brother to life by the same means; similarly Appollodorus (*Bibliothēkē*, III., iii. 1) asserts that Polyidus in the same way gave life back to Glaucus; other examples are noted in Pausanias, iii. 65 sqq. In India the same belief obtains, also that in its nests it preserves a stone which is a remedy for its own bite. In Calabar one means of ordeal is the fang of a snake introduced beneath the eyelid (T. J. Hutchinson, *Impressions of West Africa*, London, 1858). The part of the snake as guardian of the tree of life in widely variant cycles has already been noted—of this the garden of the Hesperides is but one case; in India it is regarded also as the guardian of hidden treasure, and Kipling makes use of this in his *Jungle Book*. It is supposed to secrete in its own head a valuable jewel, and even has one which it worships. The belief in it as protector of the household existed not only in Egypt (cf. E. W. Lane, *Manners and Customs of the Modern Egyptians*, i. 289, London, 1836), but in India, Korea, China, and Japan, while to kill one is unlucky. The idea of the connection of the serpent with fertility is world-wide. Sometimes, as in India, its action is adverse, and it restrains the showers till killed or forced by a god to release them. It is accredited with power over wind and rain, and in Chile was held to have caused the deluge. Yet in the Deccan offerings and prayers for rain are made to the nag in spring and autumn; Semites generally bring it into relation with springs. It is at times the protector of persons of sanctity or eminence, as when Scipio Africanus and Nero were believed to have been watched over by a snake, or when two are reported to have observed the first purification of Confucius, or when one shielded the Buddha from the sun's rays. On the other hand, it may be regarded as malevolent, as when the Hurons see in it the cause of disease, Australian tribes regard it as bringing death into the world, and the Puma Indians as the source of kidney and stomach troubles in children. So St. Patrick drives it from Ireland, Rudra is its destroyer in India, Buddha in infancy strangles one, as does Krishna, while Hercules kills two. In the Troad there was a tribe sprung from a serpent (Strabo, xiii. 1, 14), Ælian (*De animalibus*, xii. 39) tells of a race in Phrygia (Ophiogenæ) who were sprung from a woman and a serpent; Alexander was credited with serpent paternity (Plutarch, "Life of Alexander," ii.), and the Natchez, Linni Lenape, Huron, and Menominee Indians claim ancestry from it as one of their totems, as do some African tribes. The reverse relation is held as true, and after death a man's soul may inhabit the body of a snake (for cases among the Africans consult E. B. Tylor, *Primitive Culture*, ii. 8, 239-242, 310, 347, London, 1903)—the case of Æneas has already been noted. It was constantly associated with tombs, and thence doubtless with the underworld, with which in part may be connected its repute for wisdom. In the Japanese *Nihongi* a hero is made to reappear in serpent form to take vengeance upon his murderers.

GEO. W. GILMORE.

BIBLIOGRAPHY: On the serpent in the Bible consult: J. Buxtorf, *Exercitationes ad historiam*, pp. 458-492, Basil, 1659; G. Menken, *Schriften*, vi. 349-411, Bremen, 1858; P. Scholz, *Gotzendienst und Zauberwesen bei den alten Hebräern*, pp. 101-104, Regensburg, 1877; W. R. Smith, *Journal of Philology*, ix (1880), 99-100; W. Sharpe, *Humanity and the Serpent of Genesis*, Boston, 1886; J. P. Val d'Eremas, *The Serpent of Eden*, London, 1888; W. H. Ward, *American Antiquarian*, xx (1898), 162-165; J. G. Frazer, *Golden Bough*, ii. 426-427, London, 1900; V. Zapletal, *Der Totemismus und die Religion Israel*, pp. 68-69, Freiburg and Switzerland, 1901; *DB*, iii. 510-511; *EB*, iii. 3387-88; *JE*, ix. 212-213; R. G. Murison, in *American Journal of Semitic Language and Literature*, xxi. 115-130; and the commentaries on the passages adduced in the text.

On the worship, etc., outside of Biblical mention consult: J. B. Deane, *The Worship of the Serpent Traced throughout the World*, London, 1833 (most later books cite Deane, but his work is to be used with the greatest caution); H. R. Schoolcraft, *Notes on the Iroquois: Antiquities and general Hist. of Western New York*, 1846; W. H. Prescott, *History of the Conquest of Mexico*, New York, 1843; idem, *Hist. of the Conquest of Peru*, ib. 1847 (both of these works are standard, and exist in almost numberless cheap reprints); E. G. Squier, *The Serpent Symbol and the Worship of the Reciprocal Principles of Nature in North America*, New York, 1851 (of little value); J. C. M. Boudin, *Études anthropologiques*, Paris, 1864; J. Fergusson, *Tree and Serpent Worship*, London, 1869 (one of the best); W. R. Cooper, *The Serpent Myths o Ancient Egypt*, London, 1873; C. Schoebel, *Le Mythe de la femme et du serpent*, Paris, 1876; H. Clarke and C. S. Wake, *Serpent and Siva Worship in America, Africa, Asia*, London, 1877 (to be used with caution); H. Jennings, *The Rosicrucians, with a Chapter on Serpent-Worshippers*, new ed., London, 1879; W. H. Ward, in *Bibliotheca Sacra*, xxxviii (1881), 209-253; J. G. Bourke, *The Snake Dance of the Moquis of Arizona*, New York, 1884; A. Reville, *Native Religions of Mexico and Peru*, London, 1884; C. W. King, *The Gnostics and their Remains*, ib. 1887; C. S. Wake, *Serpent Worship and Other Essays*, London, 1887; idem, *Serpent Worship and Totemism*, ib. 1888; *Ophiolatreia: an Account of . . . Serpent Worship*, privately printed, 1889 (connects serpent-worship and phallicism); C. F. Oldham, in *Royal Asiatic Society's Journal*, 1891, pp. 361-392, 1901, pp. 461-473 (on worship in India); F. T. Elworthy, *The Evil Eye*, London, 1895; J. W. Fewkes, *Comparison of Sia and Tusayan Snake Ceremonials*, Washington, 1895; J. B. Ambrosetti, *El Simbolo de la Serpiente en la alfareria funeraria de la region calchaqui*, Buenos Aires, 1896; D. G. Brinton, *Myths of the New World*, Philadelphia, 1896; J. W. Fewkes in *Reports of* the Bureau of American Ethnology, xvi (1897), 267-312, xix (1900), 957-1011; Pausanias, ed. Fraser, 6 vols., London and New York, 1898; A. Wilder, *Serpent as a Symbol*, in *Metaphysical Magazine*, xv (1901), 1-20; E. Crawley, *Mystic Rose*, pp. 192 sqq., New York, 1902; H. R. Voth, *The Oraibi Summer Snake Ceremony*, Chicago, 1903; S. Reinach in *Gazette des beaux-arts*, III., xxxii (1904), 13-23 (on finds in Crete); L. Frobenius, *Das Zeitalter des Sonnengottes*, vol. i., Berlin, 1904; H. E. Sampson, *The Message of the Sun, and the Cult of the Cross and Serpent*, London, 1904; C. F. Oldham, *The Sun and the Serpent: a Contribution to the History of Serpent Worship*, London, 1905; E. Amélineau, *Du rôle des serpents dans le croyances religieuses de l'Égypte*, in *RHR*, li (1905), 335-360, lii (1905), 1-32; R. M. Burrows, *The Discoveries in Crete*, pp. 137-138 et passim, New York, 1907; J. Harrison, *Prolegomena to the Study of Greek Religion*, 2d ed., London and New York, 1908 (important); J. Meier, in *Anthropos*, iii (1908), 1005-1029 (New Pomerania); S. Reinach, *Orpheus*, passim, New York, 1909; C. Spiess, *Die Joholn-Gottheit und ihr Schlangenkult*, Brunswick, 1910; G. A. J. Hasen, in *Bijdragen tot de taal-lan den volkenkunde van Nederlandsch-Indie*, xxxix. 175-204; A. Kemp-Welch, *The Woman-headed Serpent in Art*, in *19th Century and After*, lii. 983-991; L. Stieda, in *Globus*, lxxv. 160-163; and, in general, works on travels in various countries, as well as those on the different religions of the world.

SERVATIUS, ser-vē'shi-us, **SAINT:** Gallic bishop of the fourth century. He is mentioned as one of those present at the Synod of Sardica in 347, and is apparently identical with one of the envoys from Magnentius to Constantius in 350, as well as with the Servatio, bishop of Tongres, who bravely defended Athanasian orthodoxy at the Synod of Rimini in 359. It is, on the other hand, doubtful whether he attended a provincial synod said to have been held at Cologne in 346. According to Gregory of Tours (*Historia Francorum*, ii. 5; cf. *De gloria confessorum*, lxxi.), a Servatius or Arvatius (the latter the better reading) was bishop of Tongres about the time of the Hun invasions under Attila. Learning of the approach of the barbarians, he made pilgrimages to Rome to avert, if possible, by prayers at the tomb of St. Peter the destruction which threatened Tongres, only to receive the divine command to return to his doomed city. He obeyed, and removed to Maestricht, where he died in 450, a year before Tongres was sacked by the Huns. It would seem, however, that the Hun invasion has here been confused with some earlier barbarian inroad.

A very ancient tradition of the Church at Maestricht gives May 13, 384, as the date of the death of Servatius of Tongres, and his grave soon became a favorite place of pilgrimage, so that in 562 his remains were removed to a church erected in his honor. In 726, after the victory of Charles Martel over the Saracens on St. Servatius' day, the bones of the saint found their final resting-place, though relics found their way to various places, as Duisburg, Worms, and especially Quedlinburg. In medieval art St. Servatius is represented as overshadowed by an eagle soaring above him, or as lying in a grave with three wooden shoes, the traditional instruments of his martyrdom. (O. ZÖCKLER†.)

BIBLIOGRAPHY: An early *Vita* is given in the volume of Kurth noted below, and with other material in *Analecta Bollandiana*, i (1882), 85–111; similar early material is edited in *MGH*, *Script.*, vii (1846), 172 sqq. and xii (1856); *ASB*, May, iii. 215 sqq. (with commentary from pp. 209 sqq.); and B. Krusch's ed. of *Passiones vitaeque ævi Merovingici* in *MGH*, *Script. rer. Merov.*, iii (1896), 83 (on which cf. G. Kurth in *Analecta Bollandiana*, 1897, pp. 164–172). Consult further: G. Kurth, *Deux biographies inédites de St. Servais*, Liége, 1881; idem, *Nouvelles recherches sur S. Servais*, ib. 1884; P. F. X. de Ram, *Notice sur S. Servais, premier évêque de Tongres*, 2d ed., Brussels, 1847; Corton, in *De Katholiek*, 1884; J. Branckem, *St. Servatius-Legende*, Maastricht, 1884; A. Prost, *Saint Servais*, Paris, 1891; F. Görres, in *ZWT*, 1898, pp. 78–83; F. Wilhelm, *Sanct Servatius oder wie das erste Reis in deutscher Zunge geimpft wurde*, Munich, 1910; Tillemont, *Mémoires*, viii. 639 sqq.; Rettberg, *KD*, i. 204 sqq.; Friedrich, *KD*, i. 300 sqq.; Hauck, *KD*, i. 33–34, 51–52; *DCB*, iv. 823.

SERVETUS, ser-vī'tus, MICHAEL (MIGUEL SERVETO).

Michael Servetus, famous as an antitrinitarian and an opponent of Calvin, was b., probably at Tudela (52 m. n.w. of Saragossa), Spain, Sept. 29, 1511, and was executed at Geneva Oct. 27, 1553. Expected to become a jurist, he first studied at Saragossa, and in 1525 was made amanuensis to the royal chaplain, Juan de Quintana, whom he accompanied to Toulouse in 1528. Here he continued his legal studies, and also became interested in the Bible, holding private readings with some of his fellow students and likewise plunging into the writings of Melanchthon and Paul of Burgos. In Feb., 1530, he attended the coronation of Charles V. at Bologna with Quintana, and then accompanied his patron, who had meanwhile become confessor to the king, to Germany. While there is no real basis for the story that he met Luther personally, it is not impossible that he went with Butzer to Basel in the autumn of 1530, although the only demonstrable fact is that he met Œcolampadius in October of the same year. By this time the antitrinitarianism of Servetus had been fully evolved, and finally arousing the opposition even of the kindly Œcolampadius, he went to Strasburg, where he was received by Capito and Butzer. When, in 1531, he printed at Hagenau his *De Trinitatis erroribus libri septem*, Œcolampadius sought to have the writings of Servetus officially suppressed, while Zwingli issued an earnest warning against the tenets of the Spanish teacher. In his *Dialogorum de Trinitate libri duo*, with its appendix, *De justicia regni Christi et de caritate capitula quatuor* (Hagenau, 1532) he now sought to obviate the unfavorable impression of his previous work by making certain formal concessions, though maintaining that neither the ancient Church nor the Reformers understood the Bible, and declaring himself unable either to agree or to disagree entirely with either party.

1. Early Life and Wanderings.

Disappointed in his far-reaching schemes, Servetus left Germany, and, dropping his theological pursuits for the nonce, devoted himself to the study of medicine at Paris, taking the name of Villanovanus from his father's native city of Villanueva in Aragon. In 1534 he left Paris and lived for some years at Lyons, where he gained partial support by proof-reading, and then published a new edition of Ptolemy (Lyons, 1535); but in 1537 he returned to Paris and gained distinction as a physician, writing his *Syruporum universa ratio, ad Galeni censuram diligenter expolita. Cui post integram de concoctione disceptionem praescripta est vera purgandi methodus, cum expositione aphorismi: concocta medicari* (Paris, 1537). His views on the juridical value of astrology, however, as expressed in his *Apologetica disceptatio de astrologia* (Paris, 1538), drew upon him such grave charges from the University of Paris that he was forced to leave the capital for Charlieu, where he practised medicine for the short time that he was permitted to remain. He then lived peacefully at Vienne for a number of years, and during this period issued an entirely revamped edition of Sanctes Pagninus' Latin translation of the Bible (see BIBLE VERSIONS, A, II., 3). During these years, moreover, Servetus had been gradually formulating a work to prove that primitive Christianity had been corrupted by the early ecumenical councils. He then began correspondence with Calvin, apparently to gain the requisite approval for the publication of his conclusions; but the impudent tone assumed by Servetus finally angered the Genevan, who, on Feb. 13, 1546, wrote Farel: "If he [Servetus] comes [to Geneva], I shall never let him go out alive if my authority has weight." Servetus now entered upon negotiations with other Genevan preachers and with Viret, fully recognizing the personal peril in which he stood; and in 1553 he secretly printed at Vienne his *Christianismi restitutio* (reprint Nuremberg, 1791; Germ. transl., 3 vols., Wiesbaden, 1892–96), a book repeating with increased emphasis his old attacks on the doctrine of the Trinity, which he declared had arisen with the corruption of the Church.

2. Physician and Classical Scholar.

The positive tenets of Servetus' *Restitutio* are equally difficult to deduce and to summarize. While rejecting the Trinity in essence, he maintained a Trinity of revelation in his theory of the twofold revelation of God, in the first of which the Word was present as a divine primal light, and in the second the Spirit as a divine primal power. After the creation the Word was prefigured in Adam, the theophanies, etc., until it became incarnate in Christ; and through the exalted Christ, now Jehovah himself, the Spirit, formerly existent only as the world-soul, the power of life, the natural apperception of the divine, and the Law, realizes its fulness as the principle of regeneration and immortality inherent in man. Such was the weight laid by Servetus on these problems that his system had room for faith only as the recognition of the divinity of Christ. Consciousness of sin was almost

3. Theological System.

entirely lacking, and he even denied that one could sin, strictly speaking, before one had reached the age of twenty. His stress on intellectuality naturally had no place for infant baptism, and for this very reason he stressed the importance of adult baptism as the conferring of the Spirit, the Lord's Supper as the food of the Spirit, and good works, especially asceticism, as the exercise of the Spirit. Eschatologically he maintained that the Christian is completely freed from the dross of earthly life by a purifying fire.

As the physician-in-ordinary of the archbishop of Vienne, Servetus naturally endeavored to keep his authorship of the *Restitutio* secret, but Calvin recognized the source as soon as he became aware of the book, and at once assailed it as a most dangerous attempt to discredit and destroy nascent French Protestantism.

4. Tried by the Inquisition.

It would seem that Calvin's first information was gained from a letter of a Protestant refugee named Guillaume Trie, then residing at Geneva, to a Roman Catholic kinsman, Antoine Arneys, at Lyons, mocking at the ancient Church for harboring a heretic like Servetus. Arneys, many allege at the indirect instance of Calvin, denounced Servetus to the Inquisiton. At the first trial Servetus denied all knowledge of the *Restitutio*, whereupon, at the instance of the Inquisitor Ory, Arneys wrote Trie asking for a complete copy of the work. This was no longer accessible, but instead Trie submitted as documents twenty-four letters of Servetus to Calvin, the Genevan theologian meanwhile seeking to avoid any suggestion that he might be a party to a trial before the Holy Office, deeply regretting that his plan of suppressing Servetus necessitated his formal cooperation, and later expressly denying that he had any part whatever in the proceedings. On Apr. 4, 1533, Servetus was arrested at Vienne and examined on the two days following, when he denied that he was Servetus, claimed to have adopted the name of that scholar that he might measure himself with Calvin in dialectics, and offered to make complete retractation. On Apr. 7 he was permitted to escape, either to guard the archbishop and other noted friends of Servetus against further embarrassment, or to save the Inquisition from being made a catspaw for Calvin. The trial, however, continued, and on June 17 Servetus was condemned to the stake, his books and his effigy being burned in his stead.

Meanwhile Servetus, being unsuccessful in reaching the Spanish line, sought to go to Italy by way of Switzerland, his route taking him through Geneva. Learning that his enemy was in the city, Calvin had him arrested on Sunday, Aug. 13, and

5. Before the Court at Geneva.

had his secretary, Nicolas de la Fontaine, take the legally requisite duty of plaintiff, the charge being the circulation of dangerous heresies, for which the defendant, a fugitive from justice, had already been imprisoned. Calvin drew up for De la Fontaine thirty-eight counts against Servetus, the special charges being antitrinitarianism and anabaptism. On Aug. 15 Servetus was brought to trial. As to the Trinity, he admitted that he used the term "Person" in a different sense from his contemporaries; he declared himself ready to retr his views on infant baptism; but he maintai that Calvin was guilty of grave errors of d trine. Calvin now found himself obliged to c forward as the plaintiff, and on Aug. 17 the two ponents came for the first time face to face. In beginning Servetus proved himself more th match for Calvin, but so strong were his panthe expressions that the Council, feeling that the come would prove a tragedy, determined to further information from Vienne. During the of waiting which ensued, Calvin wrote Farel (A 20) that he hoped Servetus would be sentenced capital punishment, though not by a painful death while Servetus (Aug. 22) vainly protested to the Council against being treated as a criminal, contrary to the tenets of the Apostles and the early Church. On Aug. 24 the prosecutor-general, Claude Rigot, presented a list of thirty charges which, ignoring the differences between Servetus and Calvin, and laying little stress on the Trinitarian problems, attacked primarily the basal ideas of the *Restitutio* that all Christianity which had previously existed was corrupt, that the Reformation was un-Christian, and that all who differed from Servetus were damned, likewise casting suspicion on the private life of the accused. In reply the latter maintained that his intention was good, that he had the highest veneration for the Scriptures, and that he must consider his tenets to be true until they were proved to be false. On Aug. 31 an answer was received from Vienne with a request for the surrender of the fugitive; but Servetus, when offered his choice, preferred to stand trial at Geneva, especially as Calvin was already involved in his struggle with the Libertines. Exhausted by hearing a theological debate between the two principals on Sept. 1, the council determined that the remainder of the controversy should be carried on in writing, and on the following day Calvin declared that the Geneva preachers were ready to prove thirty-eight passages from Servetus to be either heretical, or blasphemous, or contrary to the Word of God and the teaching of the Church. Evidently learning of Calvin's dispute with Philibert Berthelier (see CALVIN, JOHN, § 13), Servetus changed his tone to one of more boldness. The council hesitated to condemn him, and on Sept. 19 determined to send the minutes of the proceedings to Bern, Basel, Zurich, and Schaffhausen, and to ask the advice of both the theologians and the councils of these four cities. At this juncture Servetus formally charged Calvin with deliberate suppression of Christian truth and the like, and demanded that the Geneva theologian be banished and his property confiscated in behalf of the plaintiff, requests which were naturally refused.

On Oct. 19 answers were received from the four Swiss cities unanimously condemning the doctrines of Servetus and urging the obviation of a peril which threatened the entire Reformed Church, though without direct allusion to the death penalty. The Geneva council now proceeded to final action, and on Oct. 26 Servetus was condemned, not to a merciful death, as Calvin and the other Genevan ministers had wished, but to the stake. The antitrinitarian implored pity from Calvin, who replied that he had never been actuated by vindictiveness, and urged him to seek the divine forgiveness and mercy. On the following day the sentence was carried out, since Farel, whom Calvin summoned to accompany the condemned, was unable to induce Servetus to retract. The execution of Michael Servetus involved Calvin in obloquy in his own and in succeeding generations, an obloquy partly merited and partly undeserved. Almost immediately after the event, in Feb., 1554, Calvin published his *Defensio orthodoxæ fidei de sacra trinitate*, which was followed by Beza's *De hæreticis a civili magistratu puniendis*, issued in September of the same year; while the dissatisfaction with the execution was voiced by the writings of Sebastianus Castellio (q.v.). On the 350th anniversary of the burning of Servetus an "expiatory monument" was erected near the scene of his execution. [A monument to Servetus was erected at Annemasse (4 m. from Geneva), on the French border. It represents Servetus in prison and has on it an extract from one of his prison letters. Professor Odhner of the Swedenborgian Seminary at Bryn Athyn, Pa., has discovered that Servetus in a remarkable manner anticipated the teachings of Swedenborg.]

6. The Execution and Opinions Regarding it.

(EUGEN LACHENMANN.)

BIBLIOGRAPHY: Sources are Calvin's *Opera*, ed. Baum et al., viii. 453–872, xiv. 58 sqq., and xxvi.; T. Beza, *Calvini Vita*, Geneva, 1554; the "Acts" of the trial at Vienne, ed. D'Artigny, Paris, 1749; and the "Acts" of the trial at Geneva, ed. J. H. A. Rilliet, Geneva, 1844. Besides the literature on Calvin, much of which discusses at length the relations of Servetus and Calvin and the execution of Servetus, consult: F. Trechsel, *Michael Servet und seine Vorgänger*, Heidelberg, 1839; W. K. Tweedie, *Servetus and Calvin*, London, 1846; F. C. Baur, *Die christliche Lehre von der Dreieinigkeit und Menschwerdung Gottes*, iii. 54–103, Tübingen, 1843; I. A. Dorner, *Lehre von der Person Christi*, ii. 649–660, Berlin, 1853; E. Saisset, *Mélanges d'histoire*, pp. 117–227, Paris, 1859; K. Brunnemann, *Michael Servet*, Berlin, 1865; A. Chauvet, *Étude sur le système théologique de Servet*, Strasburg, 1867; H. G. N. Tollin, *Luther und Servet*, Berlin, 1875; idem, *Melanchton und Servet*, ib. 1876; idem, *Charakterbild Michael Servets*, ib. 1876; idem, *Das Lehrsystem Michael Servets*, 3 vols., Gütersloh, 1876–78; idem, *Michael Servet und Martin Butzer*, Berlin, 1880; G. C. B. Pünjer, *De M. Serveti doctrina*, Jena, 1876; M. M. Pelayo, *Hist. de las Heterodoxos Espanjoles*, ii. 249–313, Madrid, 1877; A. Roget, *Hist. du peuple de Genève*, vol. iv., Geneva, 1877; R. Willis, *Servetus and Calvin*, London, 1877 (the classic work); A. von der Linde, *Michael Servet, een Brandoffer der Gereformeerde Inquisitie*, Groningen, 1891 (hostile to Calvin); F. Buisson, *S. Castellion, sa vie et son œuvre*, 2 vols., Paris, 1892; J. E. Choisy, *La Theocratie à Genève au temps de Calvin*, Geneva, 1901; idem, in *Revue chrétienne*, 1903; L. Monod, in *Revue chrétienne*, 1903; A. Dide, *Michel Servet et Calvin*, Paris, 1908; W. Osler, *Michael Servetus*, London and New York, 1909; C. T. Odhner, *Michael Servetus; his Life and Teachings*, Philadelphia, 1910; Schaff, *Christian Church*, vol. vii., chap. xvi (where a discriminating list of literature, with notes, is supplied); and in general the works on the church history of the period.

SERVIA: A kingdom (after 1879) situated in the Balkan peninsula, in southeastern Europe, between Austria-Hungary on the north and Turkey on the south; area (estimated) 18,757 square miles; population (1905) 2,683,025, belonging mainly to the eastern Orthodox Church. This, according to art. 3 of the constitution of 1901, has the same dogmas as the Eastern Ecumenical Church, but is independent and autocephalous. The Eastern Orthodox confession is the religion of the State, which the king and his children must profess (§ 7). By the terms of art. 33, proselyting is forbidden as an offense to the state religion; yet, according to the same paragraph, complete tolerance is practised, since it is stated that freedom of conscience shall be unrestricted. All recognized religious societies are legally protected, so far as their religious exercises do not violate public order and morality. According to § 98, all foreign religious societies may conduct themselves according to their own tenets, with the stipulation only that no manner of correspondence may be carried on between the church authorities of such religious societies and those abroad, without permission of the minister of worship. In like manner, no act of such foreign church authorities may be published in the kingdom without the same consent. It is thus not difficult for the officiating minister of worship to construe his power against communications between the pope and the Servian Roman Catholic clergy.

The independence and autonomy of the State Church grew up by degrees. The first foundation was granted by the sultan in Constantinople; when, in 1766, he created a vladika, or superior bishop, in Belgrade and abolished the former patriarchate of the Servian population in Turkey, previously located at Ipek in northern Albania. The vladika being a Phanariot, however, was amenable to the patriarch of the capital, and through him also to the sultan. Yet it was a form of church rule with its seat at Belgrade, and as such it might have asserted itself longer, had not the bribery and oppression of the Phanariot party proved too irritating; for the Greek metropolitans pursuing their own interests placed themselves actually in opposition to the efforts of the Servians for independence from Turkish despotism. In consequence, after many acts of violence by the Servian Prince Milosh, there resulted in 1852 the recognition of an independent metropolitan by the patriarchate; the latter only requiring the approval of the metropolitan by the patriarch, who was also to be regularly remembered in the prayers of the Church, and the recognition of the episcopal oversight of the patriarch by the annual contribution to him of 1,200 dinars ($234). But with the establishment of the Servian kingdom, all this was annulled.

The metropolitan and bishop of Belgrade now rules the State Church independently, which has a well-defined representative constitution; for the degrees of its order are in its representative bodies. The highest is the archihierarchical synod conducted and represented by the metropolitan. To this belong the other two bishops; namely, of Nish and Schitscha (a cloister near the Ibar, though the bishop resides at Tschatschak), also the two archimandrites (abbots), and the archpriests, one for each of the twenty-one eparchies (civil districts). It elects the metropolitan, subject to royal approval, and the archimandrites (priors of the cloisters), and is the bishops' court of justice. The intermediate ecclesiastical court is the appellate consistory, whose members are proposed by the metropolitan from the total body of clergy to the minister of worship, and require royal approval. The measures and resolutions passed in the eparchies are subject to the acceptance of their synodical convention, which also takes cognizance of appeals. The eparchical consistories are composed of five popes (or Greek parish priests) and monks, under the bishop's direction. Their function is to promote religion among the people, to care for the church property, to settle matrimonial disputes, and to exercise discipline over the clergy. The clergy comprises the regular monastic clericals, from among whom the bishops are taken, and the married priests, or popes. Many of the latter, however, are qualified merely to assist at mass and to dispense a few sacraments. The bishops appoint all the priests independent of the State, which does not contribute for their support, but only a certain part for the bishops and the archpriests. The fifty-two to fifty-four cloisters have sufficiently affluent revenues to discharge the pastoral duties even without state assistance. The training of the clergy requires four years in the gymnasium and four years in the seminary. For the people education was made obligatory in 1882, and there are thirty-eight intermediate schools. The Roman Catholic Church numbers about 24,000, mostly inhabiting the banks of the Save and the Danube, with more than 6,000 in Belgrade. They are under the Croatian bishop of Djakovar, who also bears the title of bishop of Belgrade and Semendria. The Evangelical congregation is inconspicuous and small in numbers; and has placed itself under the superior church council of Berlin.

WILHELM GÖTZ.

BIBLIOGRAPHY: P. Coquelle, *Le Royaume de Serbie*, Paris, 1894; W. Miller, *The Balkans*, London and New York, 1896; N. Ružičić, *Das kirchlich-religiöse Leben bei den Serben*, Göttingen, 1896; H. Vivian, *Servia, the Poor Man's Paradise*, London, 1897; E. Lazard and J. Hogge, *La Serbie d'aujourd'hui*, Brussels, 1901; M. E. Durham, *Through the Lands of the Serb*, London, 1904; F. Kanitz, *Das Königreich Serbien und das Serbenvolk*, 2 vols., Leipsic, 1904–09; Prince and Princess Lazarovich-Hrebelianovich, *The Servian People: their past Glory and their Destiny*, 2 vols., New York, 1910.

SERVIAN ORTHODOX CHURCHES IN AMERICA: These churches are administering to the spiritual needs of the Servian immigrants from Dalmatia, Austria proper, Servia, Montenegro, Bosnia, and Herzegovina, who ecclesiastically are under the jurisdiction of the primate of the Servian Church in Austria, the metropolitan of the Orthodox Church of Dalmatia, the Holy Synod of Servia, and the metropolitan of Montenegro. The earliest immigration to the United States was that of the seafaring Dalmatians, whom the gold fever of 1849 brought to California, and the early "Austrian" colonies in New Orleans, Mobile, and San Francisco were doubtless theirs. Servians at present are to be found throughout the United States and Alaska. The first Servian church was built in Jackson, Cal., 1894, by the Archimandrite Sebastian Dabovitch, who later, in 1905, established his headquarters in Chicago as the administrator of the Servian Orthodox Church in North America, under the jurisdiction of the Russian archbishop of New York City. There are, according to moderate calculations, about 80,000 Servians in the United States, their clergy consisting of one archimandrite and nine priests, and they have churches at Chicago and So[uth] Chicago, Ill.; MacKeesport, Wilmering, So[uth] Pittsburg, and Steelton, Pa.; Jackson and [Los] Angeles, Cal.; Kansas City, Kansas; St. Lo[uis], Mo.; also in Douglas, Alaska; Butte, Mont.; [Bar]berton, Ohio; and Bisbee, Ariz., in care of visit[ing] priests, and those at Pueblo, Cal., and Buffalo [N.] Y., in charge of Russian priests.

The Supreme Council of the Servian Ortho[dox] Society with a membership of 6,500 has its h[ead]quarters in Pittsburg, and there exists also the [Ser]vian Federation "Sloga," the aim of which i[s to] consolidate the various Servian organization[s in] this country.

A. A. STAMOCK[...]

SERVICE, JOHN: Church of Scotland; b. [at] Campsie (10 m. n. of Glasgow) Feb. 26, 1833; d. [at] Glasgow Mar. 15, 1884. He studied at the Uni[ver]sity of Glasgow irregularly from 1858 to 1862; was engaged in editorial work, 1857–62; became minister at Hamilton 1862; but resigned after ten months, on account of ill-health, and retired to Melbourne, Australia, 1864–66; was minister at Hobart Town, Tasmania, 1866–70; returned home, 1870, and was minister of the parish of Inch, Wigtownshire, 1872–1879; and of Hyndland Church, Glasgow, 1879–84. He wrote a novel which appeared in *Good Words* under the title *Novantia*, and was published as *Lady Hetty* (3 vols., London, 1875); *Salvation Here and Hereafter* (1877), which caused a sensation in Scotland on account of its Broad-church views; *Sermons* (1884); and *Prayers for Public Worship* (1885).

BIBLIOGRAPHY: A biographical notice is prefixed to the volume of *Sermons*, 1884; *DNB*, li. 259.

SERVITES (*Servi beatæ Mariæ Virginis*): A Roman Catholic order devoted to the glorification and service of the Virgin through prayer and asceticism. On the feast of the ascension of the Virgin (Aug. 15), 1233, seven leading citizens of Florence, who had previously belonged to a society for her praise, were filled with a desire to devote themselves entirely to her service. The names of the seven were Bonfiglio Monaldi, Bonagiunta Manetti, Manetto dell' Antella, Amideo Amadei, Ricuere Lippi Ugoccioni, Gerardo Sostegni, and Allessio Falconieri. With Monaldi as their head, they lived first at the Campo Marzo near Florence, and then (about 1236) on Monte Senario. Their habit then consisted of an ash-gray cloak and a haircloth shirt. In 1239 the cardinal legate Gottfried of Castiglione gave them a milder Augustinian rule and the name of Brothers of the Passion of Jesus. Their habit was now changed to a white mantle, black hood and scapular, and leathern girdle. The order was confirmed by Alexander IV. in 1255, and was extended to France (where the habit was a white mantle and white clothing), and to Holland and Germany (1267–85). Innocent V. (1276) forbade them to receive novices but Honorius IV. (1285–87) gave them many privileges to which Martin V. (1424) added those of the mendicant orders. Later they spread to Poland and Hungary, and in 1567 were in importance the fifth mendicant order. In 1411 Antonio of Sienna founded the Observantine Servites, who became extinct in 1568. In 1593 Bernardino de Ricciolini founded the congregation of Hermit Servites, which spread in Italy and in Germany. The Servite monks possess houses in Italy (Rome, San Marcello, Bologna, Florence, Naples, and Palermo), in Austria (nine monasteries in the Tyrol province and eight in the Austro-Hungarian), England (especially London), and the United States (two in Chicago and one in Milwaukee).

Servite nuns, or "Black Sisters," were founded by Benizi, and were especially numerous in Italy and southern Germany; while tertiary Servite nuns were established by Juliana Falconieri (d. 1341) at Florence, were confirmed by Martin V. in 1420, and were spread throughout Germany by the Archduchess Anna Juliana Catharine (d. 1622). Paul V. made these German Tertiaries a separate congregation. (O. Zöckler†.)

Bibliography: The most important sources are in course of preparation under the care of P. M. Soulier and A. Morini, *Monumenta ordinis Servorum S. Mariæ*, Brussels, 1897 sqq. Consult further: M. Poccianti, *Chronicon rerum totius sacri ordinis Servorum beatæ Mariæ*, Florence, 1616; A. Giani, *Annales sacri ordinis Servorum beatæ Mariæ*, Florence, 1618, extended by A. M. Garbi and P. Bonfrisseri, 3 parts, Paris, 1719–25; P. Florentini, *Dialogus de origine ordinis Servorum*, in I. Lami, *Deliciæ eruditorum*, vol. i., Florence, 1736; P. Tonini, *Il Santuario della santissima Annunziata di Firenze*, Florence, 1876; *Hist. de l'ordre des Servites de Marie, . . . 1230–1310, par un ami des Servites*, 2 vols., Paris, 1886; P. M. Soulier, *Vie de S. Philippe Benizi, propagateur de l'ordre des Servites*, ib. 1886; idem, *Life of St. Juliana Falconieri, Foundress of the . . . Religious of the Third Order of Servites*, London, 1898; B. M. Spörr, *Lebensbilder aus dem Servitenorden*, 4 vols., Innsbruck, 1891–95; Heimbucher, *Orden und Kongregationen*, ii. 218–231; *KL*, xi. 204–212.

SESSION: The lowest court in the Presbyterian Church, composed of the pastor and elders. See Presbyterians, X., 1, § 2 (6).

SESSUMS, DAVIS: Protestant Episcopal bishop of Louisiana; b. at Houston, Tex., July 7, 1858. He was educated at the University of the South, Sewanee, Tenn. (M.A., 1878), and at the theological department of the same institution. He was ordered deacon and priested in 1882, and, after a few months as curate of Grace Church, Galveston, Tex., in 1883, was successively curate and rector of Calvary, Memphis, Tenn. (1883–87); rector of Christ Church, New Orleans (1887–91); and was consecrated bishop coadjutor of Louisiana (1891); within the year, on the death of Bishop J. N. Galleher, he succeeded to the full administration of the diocese.

SETH, SETHITES.

By Sethites are meant the ten patriarchs named in Gen. v., namely: Adam, Seth, Enos, Cainan, Mahalaleel, Jared, Enoch, Methuselah, Lamech, and Noah.

I. Relation of the List to Non-Israelitic Tradition: An Indo-Germanic origin has been mistakenly supposed, Noah being equated with -nysos in Dionysos on account of Noah's relation to the vineyard (P. K. Buttmann, *Mythologus*, i. 173, Berlin, 1828); also with the Sanscrit *nâvaka* (*nâvika*, "seaman"; J. Grill, *Erzväter der Menschheit*, pp. 41 sqq., Leipsic, 1875); also with the Egyptian *Menes*, Greek *Minos*, on the basis of a supposed form *Manoah* (S. Lefmann, *Proceedings* of the International Congress of Orientalists, p. 3, 1903). These are untenable hypotheses. F. Delitzsch (*Babel und Bibel*, p. 32, Leipsic, 1902) relates the list with the ten antediluvian Babylonian kings. But a comparison of the names in each series (the Babylonian as given by Eusebius, *Chronicon*, ed. A. Schöne, i. 7 sqq., Berlin, 1866, from Berosus) shows practically no etymological or graphic resemblance. But it is claimed that by transformation and abbreviation and by translation the earlier could give rise to the later. F. Hommel (*PSBA*, 1892–93, pp. 243 sqq.; *Expository Times*, 1899–1900, p. 343, 1902–03, pp. 103 sqq.) reasons that *Alorus*, = Babylonian *Aruru*, wife of Ea, creator of man, is to be equated with Adam = "mankind"; the third in the Babylonian series, Amelon, Babylonian *amelu*, "mankind," = Enos, "mankind," and so on. The comparison, however, gives no real results; e.g., in the first case creator and created are paralleled. But it is pointed out that in each list there is a series of ten antediluvians, the last of whom is the hero of the flood; that in both lists the individuals are credited with exceedingly long lives; and that some relations may be traced by transformation or otherwise between the individual names—as when Ammenon (the fourth, corresponding to Cainan) is made to mean "master workman." It may be granted that in three or four cases the Hebrew might arise by translation, as in the case of Amelon and Enos; yet even this does not prove priority for the Babylonian; rather one should affirm that the Babylonian tradition supports the view that the names of the ten kings show a Babylonising of neutral material. The method in which the regnal years of the Babylonian kings are reckoned (the cycle of 3,600 years) speaks for this supposition; the number ten is itself against a pure Babylonian origin. Among Hebrews ten figures frequently (cf. the tenfold occurrence of "and God said" in Gen. i. 3–29; see for further illustrations Numbers, Sacred). On the contrary, among Babylonians the decimal system had no fundamental position, sixty (five times twelve) being the basis of their cosmic system. F. Lenormant (*Les Origines de l'histoire*, i. 217 sqq., Paris, 1880) would secure an Egyptian origin for Seth through the mediation of Hittites and Hyksos. E. Meyer (*Set-Typhon*, Leipsic, 1875) claims that the god Set had a primitive and pure Egyptian origin, his name meaning "the dark destructive night," that equalizing him with Baal as a sun-deity came about through Canaanitic influence (cf. Wiedemann, in *DB*, extra vol., 195), that the Hyksos identified Set with their Baal, and consequently the Hittite Baal took the name Set. Hommel incorrectly assumes a relationship of Seth with the Egyptian Set (*Die altorientalischen Denkmäler*, pp. 53, 56, Berlin, 1903), stating that "according to the restored oldest text of Gen. v. Seth corresponds to Adapa; the Egyptians have obscured this, making Set the brother and opponent of Osiris." Nor can the Sethite tradition be traced to Canaanitic-Phenician origins. Rather should one claim that the Cainite genealogy (Gen. iv. 17–24) so corresponds to the narrative of the Phenician cosmogony as given by Eusebius that it must be credited with a Palestinian-Phenician basis. But there is the statement of Philo Byblius (in Eusebius, *Præparatio evangelica*, I., x. 5 sqq.) that *Aiōn* (Time) had the care of trees, while the descendants of Aiōn, viz., Phōs, Pur, and Phlox (Light, Fire, and Flame), discovered fire and its uses, and their descendants were Casius, Lebanon, and Antilebanon, while their mother had commerce with those whom she met. Resemblance between this statement and Gen. iv. 17–24 is only in the general idea of giving the beginnings of inventions; reference is closest to the Greek myth of the discovery of fire, and the report of the shamelessness of woman reminds rather of Babylonian temple prostitution than of Gen. vi. 1–4, where the part of the women is innocent. The use by Philo Byblius of the name Jao does not prove Hebrew origin, as J. Lagrange supposes (*Études sur les religions sémitiques*, pp. 411–412, Paris, 1905), since that name is very old. Positive indications of Canaanitic-Phenician origin of the patriarchs' names lacks specific foundation.

II. Relationship of the Sethite Series to the Cainite Series: In J only the Cainite series is complete (Gen. iv. 17–24), the Sethite is fragmentary (Gen. iv. 25–26); the complete Sethite series comes from P. It is noteworthy that the names of Cainites are the same or similar to the Sethites'. Buttmann's remark (*Mythologus*, i. 171) that the same list appears twice with small variations in order and form has been often echoed (e.g., *EB*, iv. 4411); on the other hand, the independence of the lists is maintained (Driver, on Genesis, p. 80, London, 1905), and Zimmern (in Schrader, *KAT*, p. 542) affirms both to be very old. Probably Israelitic tradition had report of two lines of Adamic descendants.

III. The General Idea of the Sethite Line: While Ewald long held that the conception of the patriarchs among the ancestors of the Israelites was practically that of demigods (*Geschichte des Volkes Israel*, i. 383, Göttingen, 1865), R. Brown (cf. *Beweis des Glaubens*, 1893, pp. 353–354) attributed to the patriarchs an astronomical significance in relation to the zodiac; Hommel (*Expository Times*, 1902–03, p. 105) remarks that the Chaldeans related the last seven [Babylonian] patriarchs to the seven planets, and the Babylonians distributed them among the ten months of the world year; and Zimmern (Schrader, *KAT*, p. 541) thinks that the Biblical ten patriarchs were originally heroes of the months of the first world year. But no trace is left [in the Bible] of this deification of the Sethites. For the statement that Seth is a divine name F. Ulmer (*Die semitischen Eigennamen*, p. 26, 1901) gives no proof. If the mythological view-point fails, ethnography is not more shadowed forth in the list. Lenormant (ut sup., i. 208 sqq.) would have the oldest races divided by these lists into the nomadic and the settled, or the yellow and the white. But the Old Testament makes the distinction rest upon religious-moral grounds. Over against the impious Cainites were the relatively better Sethites. In J are preserved in the Sethite genealogy the relatively good descendants of Adam by whom mankind is carried through the flood. J did not intend to say that the worship of Yahweh began with Sethites (Gen. iv. 26b). If there were grounds for thinking that J had intended to bring the Cainite genealogy into proportionate connection with that of Seth, his intention failed in that he inserted the birth of Enos. In Gen. iv. 25–26 J laid his basis in the Sethite line, from which was to come he who, because of his relative rightness of relations with God, should lead mankind through the judgment to a better period of history. It was from the religious-moral view-point in the earliest Israelitic tradition that antediluvian man was divided into two lines, and so interpreters have generally understood it. If, as seems to be proved, the Hebrew narrative of primitive times is relatively independent, the question arises as to the meaning of the duality of series of patriarchs. Then the following considerations arise. (1) The religious-ethical superiority attributed to the Sethites is only relative. (2) From Sethites, not from Cainites, was derived the ancestor of postdiluvian mankind; the "comfort" (Gen. v. 29) expected from Noah was based in part upon immunity from a cursing of the earth on account of sin as in the case of Adam (Gen. viii. 21–22), it can not rest wholly upon the planting of the vineyard (as Budde thinks, *Urgeschichte*, pp. 306–309). The curse of Yahweh was not to be averted by human action. (3) While the Masoretic text brings only one Sethite down to the flood, the Samaritan brings three; but the former appears to be the original conception. (4) The Sethite genealogy of J can not be considered entirely independent of the Cainite. The double line in Hebrew tradition arose not in the fact that Adam had two sons (Budde, us sup., p. 184) but because the early tradition distinguished between two lines ethically distinct. On this ethical distinction was based, probably, the long period of life awarded to the antediluvians.

IV. The Significance of the Individual Sethite Names: It seems that Seth, so far as he emerged in Hebrew tradition, was the substitute for Abel, who had perished in an outbreak of sinful power. But it remains questionable whether P (as Dillmann, in his commentary, on Gen. v. 3, and Budde, *Urgeschichte*, p. 163, think) intended to make Seth Adam's first son. The narrator's silence regarding the relation of Seth to preceding children of Adam does not involve that he presupposed in his readers ignorance of that relation; according to analogy in the rest of the chapter, Seth is thought of as the first of Adam's children. Yet it can not be said with assurance that the narrator presupposed his readers' knowledge of Cain and Abel, nor does the fact that the name Enos means "mankind" involve for Seth restriction to the meaning "sprout." It can not be decided whether Cainan means "creature" or "worker in metals." Mahalaleel is "praise of God." Jared is regarded by Friedrich Delitzsch as meaning "offspring" (*Wo lag das Paradies*, p. 149. Leipsic, 1881); but it may mean "servant" or "descent" [i.e., to a place]. Enoch means "consecration" and then "the consecrated one." Methuselah means "man of the javelin," and Lamech "warrior" or "conqueror." Noah means "rest." Whether these patriarchal names along with the assured or probable significance included each a special conception depends upon the answer to the question whether the Hebrews attached to each the idea of a step in human development. Such a series of meanings has been sought by F. Böttcher, *Exegetisch-kritische Aehrenlese zum alten Testament* (Leipsic, 1849); but the series breaks down upon examination. Budde supposes that the latter half of the series embodies such a conception; here again, however, the facts do not afford support—thus, the succession Jared-Enoch marks no progression either in significance of name or of activity. Moreover, Hebrew antiquity did not connect the beginning of reverence of Yahweh with Mahalaleel ("praise of God"), but with Enos. The Bible puts real significance into the existence and name of Noah, through whose mediation a condition of "rest" was attained in removing the feeling of distance of humanity from God as well as the fear of divine punishment, bringing about a new harmony; in his planting of the vineyard is not to be seen the rescue of the earth from the curse pronounced upon it.

V. Postcanonical Ideas of Seth and the Sethites: Jewish writers attributed to individual Sethites important places in religious and general development. Seth was rapt away to heaven for forty days and learned of the angels the basal precepts of the moral law; he also initiated the art of writing, named the five planets, discovered the division of time into months, weeks, and years (note the order), and knew of the appearance of the "star in the east." Knowing of the coming double destruction of the earth by fire and water, his descendants preserved the knowledge gained through their ancestor by two pillars of clay and of stone, the latter of which "exists till this day in the land of Siris" (Nile) (Josephus, *Ant.*, I., ii. 3. Josephus seems here to reflect Manetho as preserved by Syncellus). Jews, Samaritans, and Gnostic Christians professed to possess writings of Seth, as did Mohammedans (cf. Fabricius, *Codex pseudepigraphus*, i. 141–147, ii. 49–55, Hamburg, 1722–23; and E. Kautzsch, *Apokryphen und Pseudepigraphen*, ii. 538, Tübingen, 1900). Later men knew the name of his wife, Asura (Jubilees, iv. 11), Horaia according to the Sethites (Epiphanius, *Hær.*, xxxix. 5), from which probably came Norea (Irenæus, *Hær.*, i. 34). Enos wrote about religion and how to pray (Fabricius, ut sup., i. 157–158; Kautzsch, ut sup., i. 467, ii. 46, 73, 258). Alexander wrote about the grave of Cainan, who married his sister Mualelet, but before the flood wandered away from his family (Fabricius, ut sup., i. 159–160). "Jared" was rendered so as to show that in his time the "watchers" [i.e., angel guardians of the nations] "came down" to earth to train men in uprightness (Jubilees, iv. 15; cf. however Enoch, vi. 5–6); or his name conveyed the information that his sons began to transgress the commands he gave and to mingle with the impure Cainites (Book of Adam). Methuselah, who married his father's sister Edna (Kautzsch, ut sup., ii. 536), founded a court of justice and a school where the law of nature was taught. For Enoch and Noah see the articles. Many other details are narrated in pseudepigraphic books.

VI. Relation of Sethites to the "Sons of God," Gen. vi. 1–4: By "sons of God" can not be meant Sethites. The word *ha'adham* (E. V., "men") in Gen. vi. 1 has the article and must mean the whole race; the same must then be true of the word in verse 2 (this in spite of Strack's argument in his commentary on Genesis, pp. 26–27, Munich, 1905, where he reasons from Judges xix. 30 that a word may be used in its general sense and then in its narrower; he also argues against the general sense in verse 1). Moreover, "sons of God" is a common designation for angels. It is in the highest degree probable that to the mingling of supermundane and mundane beings would be attributed the origin of giants (see COMPARATIVE RELIGION, VI., 1 § 7). As the Sethites are not the "sons of God," so they are also not the "children of Sheth" (Num. xxiv. 17). (E. KÖNIG.)

BIBLIOGRAPHY: Of first importance are the commentaries on Genesis (noted under HEXATEUCH), in particular those of H. Gunkel, Göttingen, 1901; S. R. Driver, London, 1904; J. Böhmer, Stuttgart, 1905; H. L. Strack, Munich, 1905; and J. Skinner, Edinburgh and New York, 1910. The subject is often treated in works on the history of Israel—special attention may be called to those of H. Guthe, Tübingen, 1904, and S. Oettli, Stuttgart, 1905. Other works are: P. Buttmann, *Mythologus*, ii. 1–27, Berlin, 1829; H. Lüken, *Die Traditionen des Menschengeschlechts*, pp. 146–188, Münster, 1869; K. Budde, *Die biblische Urgeschichte*, Giessen, 1883; A. H. Sayce, *Races of the Old Testament*, London, 1891; idem, *The 'Higher Criticism' and the Monuments*, ib. 1894; idem, *Patriarchal Palestine*, ib. 1895; H. E. Ryle, *The Early Narratives of Genesis*, ib. 1892 (of high value); F. Hommel, in *PSBA*, xv (1893), 243–246; idem, *Die altisraelitische Ueberlieferung in inschriftlicher Beleuchtung*, pp. 308–309, Munich, 1897, Eng. transl., *Ancient Hebrew Traditions as Illustrated by the Monuments*, London, 1897; H. Gunkel, *The Legends of Genesis*, Chicago, 1901; E. Worcester, *The Book of Genesis in the Light of Modern Knowledge*, London, 1901; H. Zimmern, *Biblische und babylonische Urgeschichte*, Leipsic, 1901, Eng. transl., *The Babylonian and the Hebrew Genesis*, London, 1901; H. Greenwood, *The Book of Genesis Treated as an Authentic Record*, 2 vols., ib. 1903–04; R. Kittel, *Die babylonische und die biblische Urgeschichte*, Leipsic, 1903, Eng. transl., *Babylonian Excavations and Early Bible History*, London, 1903; J. Nickel, *Genesis und Keilschriftforschung*, pp. 164 sqq., Freiburg, 1903; T. G. Pinches, *The O. T. in the Light of the Historical Records of Assyria and Babylonia*, London, 1903; A. Jeremias, *Das A. T. im Lichte des alten Orients*, Leipsic, 1904; J. Meinhold, *Die biblische Urgeschichte*, Bonn, 1904; J. Böhmer, *Das erste Buch Mose*, Stuttgart, 1905; A. R. Gordon, *The Early Traditions of Genesis*, Edinburgh, 1907; Schrader, *KAT*, pp. 539 sqq., and *COT*; Bertheau, in *Jahrbücher für deutsche Theologie*, xxiii. 657 sqq.; Klostermann, in *NKZ*, v. 208 sqq.; *DB*, iv. 470; *EB*, iv. 4410–17; *JE*, xi. 207.

SETHIANS. See OPHITES.

SETON, sē'tun, ELIZABETH ANN: Roman Catholic, founder of the Sisters of Charity; b. at New York Aug. 28, 1774; d. at Emmittsburg, Md., Jan. 4, 1821. She was the daughter of Richard Bayley, a physician, and married William Seton. After his death, 1803, she entered the Roman Catholic Church, Mar. 14, 1805. In order to support herself and children, she taught school at Baltimore, 1806–08; but, after taking the veil with her sisters-in-law, Harriet and Cecilia Seton, on a gift of $8,000 she founded near Emmittsburg in 1809 a congregation of women for the care of children and orphans, which was placed under the rules and constitution (modified) of Vincent de Paul (q.v.) in 1811, thus becoming a religious order, and designated as the Sisters of Charity in the United States. In 1812 the order had increased to twenty members, with Mother Seton as superior-general, and at her death it numbered fifty. In 1814 the order took charge of an orphan-asylum in Philadelphia, and in 1817 of one in New York, and in the same year was incorporated by the legislature of Maryland. At the time of her death more than twenty communities had charge of free schools, orphanages, boarding-schools, and hospitals in a number of states.

Bibliography: Her *Memoir, Letters, and Journal* were edited by her grandson, W. Seton, New York, 1869. Consult further: *Memoirs of Mrs. Seton, Written by herself*, Elisabethtown, N. J., 1817; C. I. White, *Life of Mrs. Seton*, 7th ed., New York, 1856; Mme. de Barberey, *Vie de Madame Elizabeth Seton*, 2 vols., Paris, 1872; Heimbucher, *Orden und Kongregationen*, iii. 536-537; *KL*, xi. 214-215.

SEVEN DOLORS OF THE VIRGIN MARY, FEAST OF THE. See Mary, Mother of Jesus Christ, III.

SEVEN, THE SACRED NUMBER.

The number seven was regarded as sacred by most ancient Oriental peoples and by the Greeks and Romans. Among the Chinese the empire was divided into seven provinces; the emperor made offerings on seven altars to seven chief classes of spirits, was placed in his coffin on the seventh day after death, and was buried in the seventh month.

1. Among Ancient Non-Hebraic Peoples. In India the Rig Veda knows of seven Adityas, seven *rishis* as the progenitors of the seven great Brahmanical castes, seven divisions of the earth, seven rivers of Hindustan, and seven celestial mountains. The Iranians had seven Amshaspands and certain festivals of seven days each, while the seven gates of Mithra were important in Mithraism. In early Teutonic belief periods of seven days and of seven years were known and the early Celts had numerous sacred Heptads. The number seven occurs constantly in the mythology of the Greeks, while among the Romans the hills of the city of Rome formed a heptad. Still more important was the sanctity of the number seven among the Assyrians and the Babylonians. At a very early period the latter people had a hebdomadal division of the month, they regarded the number of the planets as seven. The designation of the seven days of the week based on this planetary system was apparently unknown to the early Babylonians; nor was the view that the seventh, fourteenth, twenty-first, and twenty-eighth days of each month were *dies nefasti* so wide-spread in effect on Babylonian theory and practise as the kindred Sabbath among the Jews. That the sanctity of the number reaches back to the oldest development of religion and culture along the banks of the Euphrates is shown by the seven gates of Hades in the Ishtar legend, the seven Igigi, the frequent representation of groups of seven deities, seven altars, and the like.

In both the Old and the New Testament the number seven is important. Labor on the seventh day is forbidden (Ex. xx. 8-11; Deut. v. 12-15; and see Sabbath); and the Passover and the Feast of Tabernacles were seven-day festivals. The consecration of priests lasted seven days; the seventh month was marked by the celebration of the Feast of Tabernacles, of the day of atonement, and Rosh ha-Shanah; the sabbatical year was celebrated

2. In the Old Testament. every seven years, and the year of jubilee every seven times seven years. The court of the tabernacle had eight times seven pillars, the candlestick had seven branches, and the sacred ell was seven handbreadths. The number was important in taking oaths, as the verb *nishba'*, "to swear" (cf. *shebha'*, "seven"), shows, and was also a factor in matters pertaining to satisfaction and punishment (cf. Gen. iv. 24; Ex. vii. 25; Lev. xxvi. 18 sqq.; Deut. xxviii. 7 sqq.; Prov. vi. 31). It also occurred in various ceremonies of purification (Lev. xiv. 51; see Defilement and Purification, Ceremonial). In concluding covenants and in expiatory sacrifices this number figured: as in sprinkling the sacrificial blood seven times in sin offerings (Lev. iv. 6, 17, xvi. 14 sqq.), and in sevenfold sacrifices. Seven entered into proverbial expressions of daily life (e.g., Isa. iv. 1, xi. 15, xxx. 26; Jer. xv. 9; Micah v. 5; Prov. vi. 16, ix. 1, xxvi. 16, 25; Psalms xii. 6; Job. v. 19). Heptads are not uncommon in the history of the Jewish people, as the seven sons of Japheth (Gen. x. 2), Saul (II Sam. xxi. 9), Jehoshaphat (II Chron. xxi. 2), Job (Job i. 2), and the mother of the Maccabees (II Macc. vii.). Jacob served seven years for each of the daughters of Laban (Gen. xxix.) and bowed seven times to Esau (Gen. xxxiii. 4). Pharaoh's dream foreboded seven years of plenty and seven years of famine (Gen. xli.); David was offered his choice between seven years of famine, three months of exile and peril, or three days of pestilence (II Sam. xxiv. 13); and Solomon took seven years to build the temple. For multiples of seven it may be noted that the household of Jacob numbered seventy (Gen. xlvi. 27), there were seventy elders (Num. xi. 24), and seventy sons of Jerubbaal (Judges viii. 30), and allusions are frequent to periods of seventy years (Ps. xc. 10; Isa. xxiii. 15; Jer. xxv. 11, etc.); while the phrase "seventy and sevenfold" occurs in the Song of Lamech (Gen. iv. 24).

In the Gospels and Acts groups of seven persons are mentioned. Christ manifested himself after his resurrection to seven of his disciples (John xxi. 2);

3. In the New Testament. seven brothers and their wife figure in the quibble of the Sadducees (Mark xii. 20 sqq.); there were seven appointed to office in the church at Jerusalem (Acts vi. 5) and seven sons of Sceva (Acts xix. 14); a multiple of the number is found in the seventy disciples of Jesus in Luke x. 1. Reference is made to periods of seven days in Matt. xvii. 1-2; Acts xx. 6, xxi. 4, 27, xxviii. 14; and seven occurs in proverbial phrases in Matt. xii. 45 (Luke xi. 26), xviii. 21 sqq. (note also the augmentative "seventy times seven"), and Luke viii. 2 (seven devils cast out of Mary Magdalene). Latent heptads, like those of the sevenfold designation of the spirit of God in Isa. xi. 2, the seven penitential Psalms, and the seven petitions in Solomon's prayer at the dedication of the Temple (I Kings viii. 29-53), occur with relative frequency in the New Testament. To this category belong the seven petitions of the Lord's Prayer according to Matthew

(vi. 9–13), the seven parables (Matt. xiii.), and the seven woes (Matt. xxiii). The apostolic epistles contain the following noteworthy heptads: seven afflictions and seven gifts (Rom. viii. 35, xii. 6–8); seven qualities of heavenly wisdom (James iii. 17); and seven virtues proceeding from faith (II Pet. i. 5–8). The Apocalypse is especially rich in heptads, not only latent (e.g., v. 12, vi. 15, vii. 12, xix. 18, xxi. 8), but explicit, as seven churches (ii.–iii.), seven seals (v. 1 sqq.), seven trumpets (viii. 2 sqq.), seven thunders (x. 3–4), seven angels (xv. 1 sqq.), and seven vials of wrath (xvi. 1 sqq.); the apocalyptic beast has seven heads and seven diadems (xii. 3, xiii. 1, xvii. 7 sqq.); there are seven spirits before the throne of God (i. 4, iii. 1, iv. 5, v. 6).

4. In Christian Theology and Liturgics.

The Church Fathers dealt largely with the number seven, basing their theories largely on Judeo-Christian and Neo-Platonic writers. Many of them regarded seven simply as the symbol of perfection and of cosmic completion (Ambrose, Augustine, Jerome, Gregory the Great, and Chrysostom). Others sought more esoteric meaning and exegesis, as Cyprian (*De exhortatione martyrii*, xi.), who regarded seven as composed of three, to symbolise the creative Trinity, plus four, to typify the four elements of creation; or Gregory the Great (*Moralia*, xxx. 16), who, in Philonic fashion, made the microcosm man a heptad consisting of three spiritual and four corporeal qualities. To the heptads thus evolved the Middle Ages added, drawing especially from the latent heptads of the Old and New Testaments, and from the explicit heptads of the Apocalypse. The heptad of the seven mortal sins was definitely formulated by Gregory the Great and Isidore of Seville. Analogies were formed after the eleventh century in the seven cardinal virtues (first definitely fixed by Hugo of St. Victor and Peter the Lombard), the seven gifts of the Spirit (on the basis of Isa. xi. 2), the seven beatitudes (instead of the eight of Matt. v. 3 sqq.), the seven words on the cross, the seven sacraments, the seven joys and the seven dolors of the Virgin, the seven works of bodily mercy (based on Matt. xxv. 31 sqq.), and the seven works of spiritual mercy. Liturgics also developed heptads, especially as the ritual of the Old Testament furnished an abundance of precedents and motives. At an early date the seven canonical hours were introduced on the basis of Psalms cxix. 164, combined with Psalms lv. 17 and Dan. vi. 10; and the sevenfold orders of the clergy are ancient. Here, too, belong the seven salutations of the people by the priest at the mass, the reckoning of the Sundays in Lent as seven, the seven deacons at pontifical mass, and the like. A number of groups of seven saints in the calendar are medieval in origin, but some go back to an early date, as the Seven Sleepers of Ephesus (q.v.), and probably the twice seven "Helpers in Need" (q.v.).

Speculative philosophy long continued to operate with the number seven, especially in the realm of natural philosophy, borrowing much from the Talmud and the Cabala (qq.v.) as late as the seventeenth century. Here belong the names of Agrippa of Nettesheim, Paracelsus, V. Weigel, Jakob Böhme, and von Helmont, as in the seven "elemental spirits" of Paracelsus: elementary body, Archeus or Mumia siderial man or Evestrum, animal spirit, intelligent soul, spirit-ocean, and man of the New Olympus. Similar juggling with heptads is not uncommon in modern theosophical treatises with their frequent dependence on the concepts of the Cabala.

(O. Zöckler†.)

Bibliography: On the ethnic use of the number note: R. von Ihering, *Evolution of the Aryan*, p. 113, London, 1897; F. von Andrian, in *Mitteilungen der anthropologischen Gesellschaft in Wien*, xxxi (1901), pp. 225–274; W. H. Roscher, in *Philologus*, 1901, pp. 260–273 (on the number among the Greeks); idem, in the *Abhandlungen* of the Saxon Academy, xxi. no. 4, and xxiv. For the Biblical usage consult in general the commentaries on the passages, as the works on Biblical theology; also: K. C. W. F. Bähr, *Symbolik des mosaischen Cultus*, i. 119–208, Heidelberg, 1837; C. Auber, *Hist. et théorie du symbolisme religieux*, i. 97–155, Paris, 1870; J. A. Martigny, *Dictionnaire des antiquités chrétiennes*, pp. 503–504, Paris, 1877; R. Samuel, *Seven, the Sacred Number*, London, 1887 (not reliable); H. Gunkel, *Zum religionsgeschichtlichen Verständniss des N. T.'s*, Göttingen, 1903; T. K. Cheyne, *Bible Problems and the New Material for their Solution*, pp. 57 sqq., London, 1904; E. Schürer, in *ZNTW*, 1905, pp. 1–66; *DB*, iii. 562–563, 565; *EB*, iii. 3436–37; *JE*, ix. 349; Vigouroux, *Dictionnaire*, fasc. xxviii., cols. 1677–97. On the number in post-Christian times consult: G. M. Dursch, *Der symbolische Charakter des christlichen Religion*, ii. 536, Schaffhausen, 1859; R. Cruel, *Geschichte der deutschen Predigt im Mittelalter*, pp. 522 sqq., Detmold, 1879; C. Kiesewetter, *Geschichte der neueren Occultismus*, ii. 16 sqq., 59 sqq., Leipsic, 1891; J. Sauer, *Symbolik des Kirchengebäudes*, pp. 61–78, Freiburg, 1902; O. Zöckler, *Die Tugendlehre des Christentums*, pp. 99 sqq., 243 sqq., Gütersloh, 1904; and the literature under Numbers, Sacred.

SEVEN SLEEPERS OF EPHESUS, ef'e-sus: According to Gregory of Tours (*De gloria martyrum*, xciv.), whose account is based upon an old Syrian version of the legend, seven Christian youths at Ephesus, during the persecution under Decius (250), took refuge in a cave just outside the city. At the emperor's command the heathen sealed up the cave. Instead, however, of perishing the youths fell into a sleep, from which they awakened nearly two hundred years later, when some of the stones happened to be removed from the entrance. In the presence of Theodosius II. and Bishop Maximus they reaffirmed their Christian faith and then expired, to sleep till the end of the world.

In its details the legend varies considerably. The supposed duration of the sleep ranges from 175 to 197 years, while the date of the miracle is given as Aug. 4, or Oct. 22, by the Greeks, and June 27, or July 27, by the Latins. Also the names of the sleepers differ in the Greek, Latin, and Ethiopic versions, and some accounts make the number of sleepers eight. According to occidental tradition their names were, Maximianus, Malchus, Martinianus, Dionysius, Johannes, Serapion, and Constantinus. Recent attempts to trace the legend to its source have not led to any consensus of opinion. It has been regarded (1) as purely Christian in its origin (Baronius, Cuypers, Stadler); (2) as developed from a pre-Christian and heathen nucleus, modified by the death of certain Christians in a cave during the Decian persecution (Koch, Bernoulli); (3) as a modification of the Hellenic myth of Endymion, united with an original Syrian legend (Clermont-Ganneau); (4) as pre-Christian, but purely Jewish, in its origin (Cassel). (O. Zöckler†.)

BIBLIOGRAPHY: The *Passio septem Dormientium*, ed. B. Krusch, is in *MGH*, *Script. rer. Merov.*, i (1885), 848–853; and, with a preface, in *Analecta Bollandiana*, xii. 371–387, Paris, 1893; in Migne, *MPL*, lxxi. 1105–18; also, with comment by Cuypers and the *Acta*, in *ASB*, July, vi. 375–397. Consult: C. Baronius, *Martyrologium Romanum*, Cologne, 1610; A. Reinbrecht, *Die Legende von den sieben Schläfern*, Göttingen, 1880; J. Koch, *Die Siebenschläferlegende*, Leipsic, 1883; I. Guidi, *Testi orientali sopra i Setti Dormienti di Efeso*, Rome, 1885; P. Cassel, *Harmageddon*, Berlin, 1890; J. Clermont-Ganneau, in *Comptes rendus de l'academie des Sciences*, 4th ser., xxvi. 564–576, Paris, 1899 (cf. *Analecta Bollandiana*, 1900, pp. 356–357); C. A. Bernoulli, *Die Heiligen der Merovinger*, pp. 160–169, Tübingen, 1900; Gibbon, *Decline and Fall*, iii. 412–413; *DCB*, ii. 136; *KL*, xi. 278–279; *Catholic Encyclopedia*, v. 496–497.

SEVENTH-DAY ADVENTISTS. See ADVENTISTS, 2.

SEVENTH-DAY BAPTISTS. See BAPTISTS, II., 4, b.

SEVENTH-DAY BAPTISTS, GERMAN. See COMMUNISM, II., 5.

SEVERIANS. See OPHITES.

SEVERIANUS, se-vi″ri-ê′nus: Bishop of Gabala in Syria; d. after 408. He is of importance for the history of ecclesiastical politics at Constantinople in the time of Chrysostom. Socrates (*Hist. eccl.*, VI., xi.; Eng. transl., *NPNF*, 2d series, ii. 145–147) relates that he was led by the success of Antiochus of Ptolemais in preaching at the capital to do the same, and also achieved success, though he was not perfect in Greek; he also won the friendship of Chrysostom. But he employed himself during the absence of Chrysostom in intriguing against him; Serapion, the supporter of the bishop, reported the activity of Severianus, and Chrysostom had him expelled from the city. The Empress Eudoxia, however, had him recalled, and Severianus continued his intrigues, and in further developments appears to little advantage. Palladius blames him for the removal of Chrysostom from Cucusus to Pityus. Gennadius (*De vir. ill.*, xxi.) calls him a man learned in the Scriptures and an excellent orator, and read a commentary of his on Galatians and a *Libellus gratissimus de baptismate et epiphaniæ sollemnitate*, possibly to be identified with a *Logos eis ta theophania* (*MPG*, lxv. 15–26). Of the former there seems to be extant only what is contained in citations in catenæ and like works. Of his homilies there remain fifteen in Armenian translation (ed. J. B. Aucher, 1827), two of these also are contained in Greek in the works of Chrysostom (*MPG*, lvi. 553–564), and one among the homilies of Basil the Great (*MPG*, xxxi.). Another homily "On peace" (ed. A. Papadopulos-Kerameus, in *Analecta*, i. 15–26, St. Petersburg, 1891), two fragments of a homily in Sahidic (ed. J. Leipoldt, in *Aegyptische Urkunden der königlichen Museen zu Berlin*, *Koptische Urkunden*, i. 6, pp. 425–428, Berlin, 1904), a small fragment of a writing against Novatian (in Gelasius, *De duabus naturis*), and various sermons in Coptic translation (cf. W. E. Crum, *Catalogue of the Coptic MSS. in the British Museum*, London, 1905) are extant. Ascribed to him also are homilies on the brazen serpent, on "The Seals of the Books," and one against the Jews (among Chrysostom's works in *MPG*, lvi. 499–516, lxiii. 531–544, lxi. 793–802). The fragment in *MPG*, lxv. 27–28, *De pythonibus et maleficiis*, ascribed by Mai to Severianus, is the work of Peter Chrysologus (see CHRYSOLOGUS; cf. F. Liveriani, *Spicilegium Liberianum*, i. 192–193, Florence, 1863). (G. KRÜGER.)

BIBLIOGRAPHY: Besides the sources in Socrates, ut sup., and Sozomen, *Hist. eccl.*, VIII., x., Eng. transl., in *NPNF*, 2 ser., ii. 405, consult: Fabricius-Harles, *Bibliotheca Græca*, x. 507–510, Hamburg, 1807; O. Bardenhewer, *Patrologie*, p. 306, Eng. transl., St. Louis, 1908; idem, in *KL*, xi. 215 sqq.; *DCB*, iv. 625–626 (exceptionally good); Ceillier, *Auteurs sacrés*, vii. 4–5, 121, 205–209, 343, x. 8.

SEVERINUS, se″ve-rî′nus: Pope 638–640. On the death of Honorius I. (Oct. 12, 638), a mutiny broke out in Rome, and though the Roman Severinus was chosen to succeed him, the army, filled with greed for the new pope's alleged wealth and aided by the populace, surrounded the Lateran. Three days later the leader of the mutineers, the chartularius Mauritius, helped seal the treasures of the Church, while at his instigation the exarch of Ravenna, Isaac, banished the leading clergy and seized the treasury. Under these conditions Severinus could not be enthroned, especially as the imperial confirmation, then necessary, was lacking. It was not until May 28, 640, that the pope was enthroned, and on Aug. 2 of the same year he died. He is important only as having defended the doctrine of two energies and two wills in Christ, thus reversing the monothelite *ekthesis* and the course of his predecessor. (A. HAUCK.)

BIBLIOGRAPHY: *Liber pontificalis*, ed. Mommsen in *MGH*, *Gest. pont. Rom.*, i (1898), 175–176; Jaffé, *Regesta*, p. 227; R. Baxmann, *Die Politik der Päpste*, i. 170, Elberfeld, 1868; J. Langen, *Geschichte der römischen Kirche*, i. 516, Bonn, 1881; Bower, *Popes*, i. 436–437; Platina, *Popes*, i. 149–150; Milman, *Latin Christianity*, ii. 71; *DCB*, iv. 628.

SEVERINUS, SAINT: One of the chief agents in the conversion of Noricum (the modern Carinthia) to Christianity; b. in Italy, probably early in the fifth century; d. in Noricum Jan. 8, 482. Of his early life nothing is known except that he resided for a time among the monks of the East. Shortly after the death of Attila in 453, he went to northern Noricum, where he lived a life of rigid asceticism, while later pupils gathered around him, so that he was able to found monasteries at Favianæ and Passau. His influence was directed primarily toward religious and ethical elevation, and not only did he enjoy the support of the clergy, but the people regarded him as a prophet; and at the same time, orthodox though he was, he was highly esteemed by the Arians and by the Germans generally.

The biography of Severinus by Eugippius (ed. H. Sauppe, *MGH*, *Auct. ant.*, i. part 2, 1877; P. Knoell, *CSEL*, viii. 2, Vienna, 1886) gives the first details of the religious conditions in Noricum since the entry of Christianity into the land soon after the close of the third century, except for the allusions of Athanasius to Norican bishops. In the biography the conversion of the land to Christianity is represented as complete, though pagan sacrifices were still occasionally offered in secret. There were dioceses at least of Lauriacum (Lorch) and Tiburnia (on the site of the modern Lurnfeld), and possibly of Celeia (Cilli) and Virunum (in Zollfeld, near

Klagenfurt); while churches existed not only at Lauriacum, but at Salzburg, Astura (near Klosterneuburg), Comagena (near Tulln), Cucullæ (Kuchel), Quintana (Plattling or Künzing), Boiodurum (Boitro), and Passau. The clergy were numerous, and the bishops were chosen by the people. Monasteries, on the other hand, do not seem to have existed before the coming of Severinus.

While Christianity was thus flourishing, political conditions were in an evil way. The power of the Huns was indeed broken, but the German tribes were steadily pressing the Romans back—the Alemanni from the west, the Thuringians and Rugians from the north, and the Goths from the east, the latter as formidable to the other Germanic tribes as to the Romans. Under such conditions Severinus labored, without the prestige of ecclesiastical or official position, solely through the power of his personality. Foreseeing that the Romans could not continue to hold the country, he begged that his body might rest in Italian soil. Accordingly, when Odoacer, in 488, drove the Roman power from Noricum, the body of the saint was interred first at Monte Feltri, near Naples, whence it was removed, four years later, to the monastery of Lucullanum, near the same city, which had been established for the exiled monks. (A. Hauck.)

Bibliography: The principal source, the *Vita* by Eugippius, ut sup., is also to be found, with commentary, in *ASB*, Jan., i. 483–499. For MSS. and other editions cf. Potthast, *Wegweiser*, pp. 1572–73. The *Translatio* is in *MGH*, *Script. rer. Langob.*, i (1878), 452–459, and *ASB*, Jan., i. 1098–1103. Consult further: J. Freiherr von Hormayr, *Wiens Geschichte und seine Denkwürdigkeiten*, i. 56–78, Vienna, 1823; J. L. Reitmayr, *Der heilige Severin der Einsiedler*, Regensburg, 1829; J. G. Waitzmann, *Lebensgeschichte des heiligen Severin*, Augsburg, 1834; J. F. von Patruban, *Lichter und Schatten*, pp. 1–15, Vienna, 1852; R. Pallmann, *Geschichte der Völkerwanderung*, ii. 393–413, Weimar, 1864; J. Leitner, *Leben und Wirken des heiligen Severin*, Passau, 1868; J. Jung, *Römer und Romanen in den Donauländern*, Innsbruck, 1877; idem, *Die romanischen Landschaften des römischen Reichs*, ib. 1881; G. Kaufmann, *Deutsche Geschichte*, ii. 23–27, Leipsic, 1881; A. D. Sembera, *Wien der Wohnsitz und Sterbeort des heiligen Severin*, Vienna, 1882; A. Ebert, *Allgemeine Geschichte der Literatur des Mittelalters*, i. 452–454, Leipsic, 1889; C. A. Bernoulli, *Die Heiligen der Merovinger*, pp. 47 sqq., Tübingen, 1900; Wattenbach, *DGQ*, i (1904), 50 sqq.; A. Baudrillart, *Saint Severin, apôtre du Norique (453–482)*, Paris, 1908; Tillemont, *Mémoires*, xvi. 168–181; Friedrich, *KD*, i. 358–383; Hauck, *KD*, i. 361 sqq.; Rettberg, *KD*, i. 226–245; *DCB*, iv. 627–628.

SEVERUS, sî-vî'rus: Bishop of Antioch; b. in Sozopolis of Pisidia; d. at Xois, on the Sebennitic arm of the Nile, Egypt, Feb. 8, 538. His grandfather had been bishop in Sozopolis, and took part in the Council of Ephesus (431) which condemned Nestorius. He was sent by his mother, after his father's death, to Alexandria for his education, where he came into connection with a pietistic circle, the Philoponoi, where he met his biographer Zacharias. After a period of diligent study he settled at Berytus Beirut), possibly in the autumn of 486, whither Zacharias followed him a year later to find him weaned away from the study of grammar and rhetoric and practise of law to the study of religion and theology, in which he requested the guidance of the newcomer. He was led to a study of the Church Fathers, particularly of Chrysostom and Cyril, and their influence and that of Evagrius was strongly felt, while he acquired rapidly a reputation for learning. As a first specimen of his rhetorical studies applied to Christianity he issued a panegyric of the Apostle Paul. Evagrius urged him to be baptized, from which he at first shrank; moreover, Zacharias refused to baptize him there, as he himself would not commune with the clerics of Berytus, being a Monophysite. Severus, however, went to Tripolis, where he was received into the Church, and then returned to Berytus.

This began a new period in his life. His asceticism was extreme, and he passed not only the evenings but part of the nights at prayer in the church. While Severus had declared that he would not be made to become a monk, it needed only a spur to bring this about, which was found in the death of Peter the Iberian. Evagrius urged him to put himself under the guidance of Peter's successor, and himself set the example. After visiting Tripolis, Emesa, and Jerusalem to pray over the subject, he entered the convent of St. Peter. There, however, the asceticism was not sufficiently pronounced for him, and he took up the hermit's life in the desert of Eleutheropolis, where his ascetic practises drew the attention of the abbot (Mamas?) of the monastery of Romanus, who offered him a home there. This he declined, and gave himself to solitude in a cell at Majuma, whither he attracted others, for whom he built a monastery with individual cells, using the remainder of his patrimony. He was made a priest by Epiphanius of Magydum, just then abiding in Palestine. This was the time of the appearance among the Palestinian monks of Nephelius, who had changed from being a heated opponent of the Chalcedonian creed to become its partizan, and was denouncing the monks of Majuma and Gaza, who, as followers of Peter the Iberian, opposed the findings of the synod. These were driven out, Severus became their advocate, and with a large number (200 or 396, according to different authorities) went to Constantinople, where he won his spurs as an ecclesiastical politician. He had part in the events which led to the fall of the Patriarch Macedonius, and his attitude was that of one who seemed to favor in turn this party and now that. He was even mentioned for the patriarchate; but failing in that, he became a friend of Timotheus, who was chosen. But he yielded to the desire to renew his life in the desert, and returned thither, and the monks at Majuma took up undisturbed their old manner of life. While at Constantinople he wrote a *Philalethes* directed against the "Nestorians," i.e., the Chalcedonians. For the imperial chancellor Zacharias Rhetor he answered a series of dogmatic questions in his *Apokriseis pros Eupraxion koubikoularion.*

The success of Severus at Constantinople had put new thoughts into his mind; he was the hero of the monks, whose influence upon public affairs was becoming ever greater. Flavian, patriarch of Antioch, was driven out and Severus was designated his successor, Nov. 6, 512, and on Nov. 25 he delivered his first sermon. His inaugural he sent to the other patriarchs; John III. of Alexandria and Timotheus of Constantinople recognised him, Elias of Jerusalem ignored the document. In his own diocese opposition arose. Julian of Bostra and Epiphanius of Tyre set themselves against him and urged that his see be taken away, and the Isaurian and other bishops refused recognition. His chief writing of this period was the three books *Kata Ioannou grammatikou tou Kaisareias*. Correspondence with the grammarian Sergius on the doctrine of the two natures is extant in the Syriac. Whether the "Apology for the Philalethes," the writing against the *Kodikilloi* of an Alexander, and the books "On the Two Natures" belong to this period is uncertain. In the correspondence Severus shows himself a prelate of parts, strong, just, circumspect, clever, plain, and not unlovable. As patriarch he remained true to ascetic ideals. He was faithful in his episcopal visitations, and was always ready to preach; while his sermons are described as being appreciated like rain on thirsty ground.

The ascent to the throne of Justin in 518 changed the situation in the ecclesiastical sphere. He drove out all the bishops, monks, and nuns in the diocese of Antioch who were tainted with monophysitism. Severus fled to Alexandria, where he is said to have arrived Sept. 29, 518. Timothy IV. received the refugees kindly, and for the time Severus was in retirement. Still in this period falls the dogmatic controversy with Julian of Halicarnassus (q.v.); and he corresponded with his supporters in Syria. The reign of Justinian and the influence of Theodora seemed to offer opportunities of success for his opposition to Chalcedonism, and in 535 he started toward Constantinople, but the overthrow of Anthimus destroyed his prospects. He was with other Monophysites excommunicated at the synod of 536, while the edict of Aug. 6 forbade him the capital. He returned to Egypt, and took up his lonely residence in the desert south of Alexandria. His death gave rise to legends concerning the events which attended it, and to his body was accredited the power of healing all infirmities; still the hatred of his opponents followed him and aspersed his memory a hundred years later. (G. KRÜGER.)

BIBLIOGRAPHY: Many of the works of Severus remain inedited in MSS. in the great libraries (cf. e.g., W. Wright, *Catalogue of the Syriac MSS. in the British Museum*, general index, pp. 1322 sqq., London, 1872). A list of writings attributed to him is found in B. de Montfaucon, *Bibliotheca Coisliniana*, pp. 53–57, Paris, 1715, cf. Fabricius-Harles, *Bibliotheca Græca*, x. 614–623, Hamburg, 1807. Fragments have been printed in Mai, *Nova collectio*, vii., 8 sqq., 71–73, ix. 725–759, in the same author's *Classici auctores*, x. 408–473, and in his *Spicilegium Romanum*, x. 202–205, 212–220; in *MPG*, lxxxvi. 1, cols. 1841–49; in R. L. Bensly, *Fourth Book of Maccabees and Kindred Documents in Syriac*, pp. xxvii.–xxix., 75–102, Cambridge, 1895; and in *MPG*, xlvi. 627–652 (there attributed to Gregory of Nyssa; cf. M. A. Kugener, in *Revue de l'orient chrétien*, iii. 1898, pp. 435–451). Letters of his are published in the *Sixth Book of the Select Letters of Severus, . . . ed. and transl.*, *E. W. Brooks*, 2 vols., London, 1902–04. And extracts from a baptismal liturgy are given by A. Resch, *Agrapha*, in *TU*, v. 4 (1889), 361–372.

For the life all prior editions of the two sources are rendered obsolete through the ed. by M. A. Kugener of the "Lives" by Zacharias the Scholastic and Johannes bar Aphthoma, both in *Patrologia orientalis*, ed. R. Graffin and F. Nau, vol. ii., parts 1 and 3, Paris, 1903–05. J. Eustratios has a monograph on Severus, written in Greek, Leipsic, 1894; the commentary on the "Church History" of Zacharias Rhetor, edited in Germ. transl. by K. Ahrens and G. Krüger, Leipsic, 1899, corrections to which are furnished in *Revue orientale chrétienne*, v (1900), 201 sqq., 461 sqq.; M. Peisker, *Severus von Antiochen*, Halle, 1903; B. Evetts, *Hist. of the Patriarchs of the Coptic Church of Alexandria*, in Graffin's *Patrologia orientalis*, ut sup., i. parts 2 and 4, Paris, 1904–06; *DCB*, iv. 637–641 (valuable); *KL*, xi. 222–223; Ceillier, *Auteurs sacrés*, xi. 106–109 et passim; and literature on MONOPHYSITES. On his theology consult: J. C. L. Gieseler, *Commentatio qua Monophysitarum . . . opiniones illustrantur*, 2 parts, Göttingen, 1835–38; I. A. Dorner, *Lehre von der Person Christi*, ii. 164 sqq., Berlin, 1853, Eng. transl., *Hist. of the Development of the Doctrine of the Person of Christ*, 5 vols., Edinburgh, 1861–63; F. Loofs, in *TU*, iii. 1–2 (1888); Harnack, *Dogma*, vol. iv. passim.

SEVERUS, SEPTIMIUS. See SEPTIMIUS SEVERUS.

SEVERUS, SULPICIUS: Ecclesiastical historian; b. in Aquitania about 360; d. there after the year 420. He received an excellent education, devoted himself to the law, and won fame as an advocate. His good fortune seemed sealed when he married the rich daughter of a consular family; but he lost his wife early, and turned away from the world to the ascetic life, following the example of his friend Paulinus of Nola (q.v.), and inspired by Martin of Tours (q.v.), with whom he lived till the latter's death, regarding him as his spiritual father and a God-sent prophet and apostle. Gennadius (*De vir. ill.*, xix.; Eng. transl. in *NPNF*, 2 ser., iii. 389–390) says that Severus became a priest, but no record exists of his employment in priestly duties. The same authority says also that Severus was led away by the Pelagians, recognized his error, and imposed upon himself the penalty of silence till death.

As scholar and author Severus took high rank in his generation. He is a noble representative of the formal culture which existed in South France in the fourth and fifth centuries, for he had been a diligent student of classical writers. Hence his "Chronicle" has the flavor of such authors as Sallust and Tacitus, Velleius and Curtius, while the "Dialogues," though specifically Christian, smack of Cicero. Infelicities are few, barbarisms and novelties do not appear; and withal the Frankish genius shines out in stylistic refinements and elegant turns of expression. As a critic he surpassed his time; especially worthy of notice is this trait in his investigation of the story of Judith. Of the "lesser works" mentioned by Gennadius there are extant only the letters to various persons (his sister, Paulinus, and others). Of some of these doubt has been expressed, but they may well be genuine, since one can not expect the same qualities of style in such writings as in works that are formally literary and designed for an educated public. Besides these, Severus has left three concededly genuine works, in which his aim was to commend to the educated world, especially to Aquitania, historical Christianity and the Christian ascetic life. His "Chronicles" is a working-up of Biblical material into a historical book for reading; his "Life" of Martin of Tours is a brilliant and edifying memoir of that saint. The third is his "Dialogues." The first has come down in only one manuscript of the eleventh century; of the second there are many manuscripts, the oldest of which, of the seventh century, is a copy of a sixth-century exemplar (dated 519). The "Chronicles" fails in interest, partly because it is a deliberate making over, and its popularity was limited perhaps by the diffusion of the Bible itself. But the "Life" was a book of edification and interest of the first rank for its times, not because of the atmosphere of classicism which enfolds it, rather because through that atmosphere the type of Christianity shines out which the next millennium recognized as its own.

The "Chronicles," in two books, given out not before the year 403, begins with creation and holds to the usual reckoning of 6,000 years, yet not without critical remark. Its purpose is to communicate comprehensively and briefly the history in both Testaments, and the preface justifies the continuation till the then present time. It was an attempt to clothe the Bible in what was then modern dress. It has been called a felicitous attempt to weld together Biblical and classical studies and it displays a sober and critical sense, a rejection of typology and allegory, a free and earnest judgment of the relations of the times treated in connection with both Church and State, and at the same time discusses luminously Hebrew jurisprudence which is made intelligible in the language of Roman law. In that part which deals with post-Biblical history the work is of special value for its light upon Priscillianism (ii. 46–51, cf. "Dialogues," iii. 11–13), being a source of the first rank; the impartiality here displayed assures the author honorable remembrance. Of value is the work also for the history of Arianism, and it throws light also upon oriental history, especially where other authorities are lacking. Thus in the history of the fall of Jerusalem the source used by Severus was the lost account by Tacitus, with which the account by Josephus is at variance (cf. Schürer, *Geschichte*, i. 631–632 note, Eng. transl. I., ii. 244 sqq. note).

Entirely different in character from the "Chronicles" are the "Life of St. Martin" and the "Dialogues," with which may be placed three genuine letters which are concerned with Martin. The "Life" was written before Martin's death, but not issued till after that occurred; the two (not three) "Dialogues" belong to 405 or later. The "Life" is cast in complete accord with the contemporaneous belief in the miraculous, though passages of historical character are not entirely lacking. The critical faculty of the author is laid aside, and the work is another witness of the defenselessness of Roman culture against the barbarism which a pious faith and the fantasies of asceticism were bringing in. The wits of Aquitania and the frivolous priests were attracted not by the reconciliation of Christianity with culture, but with the stories of the saints which were to become in the dark ages the only reflectors of light. Yet the biography by Severus differed widely from those by his contemporaries in the absence of the erotic. For the conditions in Gaul in the second half of the fourth century the work is of very great value. The opposition between the monks and the secular clergy is so graphically portrayed that, with the exception of the Letters of Jerome, no other source exists which gives so clearly the difficulties and enmities which attended the naturalization of monasticism in the West. These two related works reveal monasticism as undertaking the Christianizing of the peasants. Severus shows the secular clergy as equally earnest in their opposition to Priscillianism and to monasticism. This especially comes out in the "Dialogues," which, calling the clergy Pharisees, attempts to hold up the mirror to their offensiveness. Yet the main purpose is to glorify Martin and to win Gallic Christianity for asceticism. Martin is compared with the Egyptian monks and shown not only to equal but to surpass them in saintliness and miraculous power. The comparison with these monks gives occasion for notable bits of information: regarding Christianity in the Cyrenaica (i. 3–4); concerning Origen (i. 6–7) and Jerome (i. 8, 21); about the different conditions of monasticism in the East and in Gaul; concerning the Gallic clergy (i. 21), and other like matters. It seems that some one had charged Severus with lying in his life of Martin, and so new details concerning him are related, in which the miraculous still abounds. In the second dialogue are the parts which deal with the Priscillianists, and the last chapter shows Martin as the greatest Christian ascetic, whose deeds were to be recorded and heralded both in the East and in the West.

(A. Harnack.)

Bibliography: The critical edition of the *Opera* is by C. Halm in *CSEL*, Vienna, 1866. The best earlier edition was by H. de Prato, 2 vols., Verona, 1741–54. The editio princeps of the "Chronicle" was by Flacius, Basel, 1556, but the *Vita Martini* and the "Dialogues" appeared in print as early as 1500. The *Opera* are also in *MPL*, xx. 95–248. The one indispensable discussion is by J. Bernays, *Ueber die Chronik des Sulpicius Severus*, Berlin, 1861. Consult further: *Hist. littéraire de la France*, ii. 104 sqq., 742–743; Tillemont, *Mémoires*, vol. ii.; W. S. Gilly, *Vigilantius and his Times*, pp. 35–63, London, 1844; M. Herbert, *Œuvres de Sulpice Sévère*, Paris, 1847 (Fr. transl. with notes); C. Halm, in the *Sitzungsberichte* of the Bavarian Academy, 1865, ii. 37–64; J. H. Reinkens, *Martin von Tours*, pp. 258–274, Breslau, 1866; J. J. Ampère, *Hist. littéraire de la France avant Charlemagne*, i. 196 sqq., Paris, 1867; W. Gundlach, in *NA*, xi (1886), 291–309; A. Ebert, *Allgemeine Geschichte der Literatur des Mittelalters*, i. 327–336, Leipsic, 1889; M. Manitius, in *NA*, xiv (1889), 165–170, xv (1890), 184–186; W. S. Teuffel, *Geschichte der römischen Literatur*, pp. 1136–39, Leipsic, 1890; Bardenhewer, *Patrologie*, pp. 396–397, Eng. transl., St. Louis, 1908; Ceillier, *Auteurs sacrés*, viii. 110–126; *DCB*, iv. 634–635; *KL*, xi. 225–227.

SEWALL, siū'al, **FRANK**: Swedenborgian; b. at Bath, Me., Sept. 24, 1837. He was educated at Bowdoin College (A.B., 1858; A.M., 1862) and the universities of Tübingen, Berlin, and the Sorbonne. He was pastor of a church of his denomination at Glendale, O. (1863–69); president of Urbana University, Urbana, O. (a Swedenborgian institution), and also pastor of the Swedenborgian church in the same town (1869–86). He was then pastor of the church of his denomination in Glasgow, Scotland (1886–89); and since 1889 has been pastor of the New Church, Washington, D. C. He has likewise been general pastor of the Maryland Association of the New Jerusalem since 1893. In theology he describes himself as "a devout believer in the theological writings of Emanuel Swedenborg as containing the heavenly doctrines of the New Church signified by the New Jerusalem in the Revelation; . . . also a believer in the philosophical and scientific works of Swedenborg as containing the germs and the guiding rational principles of all the true science of the future." Among his writings, those of theological interest are the following: *The Christian Hymnal* (Philadelphia, 1867); *The New-Churchman's Prayer-Book and Hymnal* (1867); *The Pillow of Stones: Divine Allegories in their Spiritual Meaning* (1876); *The Hem of his Garments: Spiritual Studies in the New Testament* (1876); *The New Metaphysics: or, The Law of End, Cause, and Effect* (London, 1888); *The Ethics of Service: or, the Moral Law of Use* (New York, 1888); *Dante and Swedenborg, with other Essays in the New Renaissance* (London, 1893); *Swedenborg and Modern Idealism: A Retrospect of Philosophy from Kant to the present Time* (1902); *The Pulpit and Modern Thought* (Boston, 1906); *Reason in Belief: or, Faith for the Age of Science* (London, 1906); and *Swedenborg and the Sapientia Angelica* (1910). He has translated Swedenborg's *De Anima* under the title *The Soul or Rational Psychology* (New York, 1886) and edited, with introduction and notes, Kant's *Dreams of a Spirit Seer* (London, 1899).

SEWALL, JOHN SMITH: Congregationalist; b. at New Castle, Me., Mar. 20, 1830. He was educated at Bowdoin College (A.B., 1850), and, after being commander's clerk in the United States Navy in China and Japan in 1850-54, entered Bangor Theological Seminary, from which he was graduated in 1858. He was pastor at Wenham, Mass. (1859-67); chaplain of the Eighth Massachusetts Volunteers in 1864; professor of rhetoric and oratory in Bowdoin College (1867-75); and professor of sacred rhetoric in Bangor Theological Seminary from 1875 until his retirement as professor emeritus in 1903. He has written *The Logbook of the Captain's Clerk* (Bangor, 1905).

SEWEL, WILLEM (WILLIAM SEWELL): Dutch Friend; b. at Amsterdam of English parentage, 1650; d. about 1725. He served his time as a weaver, but acquired Greek, Latin, English, French, and High Dutch. He is known as the author of *Histori van de Opkomste, Aanwas, en Voortgang der Christenen, bekend by den naam van Quakers* (Amsterdam, 1717; Eng. transl., by himself, *The History of the Rise, Increase, and Progress of the Christian People Called Quakers*, London, 1722; Philadelphia, 1855). One of his objects was to correct the "misrepresentations" in Gerard Croese's *Historia Quakeriana* (3 books, Amsterdam, 1695-1704).

SEXAGESIMA. See Church Year; and Lent.

SEXT: The service for the "sixth hour" in the Breviary (q.v.), recited normally at noon, to which the invariable hymn refers. Its structure is the same as that of Terce and None (qq.v.). In monastic houses it precedes the community mass on ordinary days and simple feasts, and follows it on Sundays and higher feasts.

SEYERLEN, sai'er-len, **KARL RUDOLF:** German Protestant; b. at Stuttgart Nov. 18, 1831; d. at Jena Mar. 28, 1906. He was educated at the University of Tübingen (Ph.D., 1854); was curate at Giengen, near Geisslingen (1854-55); studied for a year in Paris; was then a teacher of religion at the gymnasium of Ulm (1857-59); lecturer at Tübingen (1859-61); deacon at Crailsheim (1862-69); deacon (1869-72), and archdeacon (1872-75) at Tübingen. After 1875 he was professor of homiletics and catechetics at Jena. He was associate editor of the *Zeitschrift für praktische Theologie* (1879-91) and wrote *Entstehung und erste Schicksale der Christengemeinde in Rom* (Tübingen, 1874); *Friedrich Rohmers Leben und wissenschaftlicher Entwicklungsgang nach dem Entwurfe Bluntschlis* (2 vols., Munich, 1892); and *Beziehungen zwischen abendländischem und morgenländischem Wissen mit Rücksicht auf Salomon ibn Gebirol* (Leipsic, 1900). He also edited J. K. Bluntschli's *Denkwürdigkeiten aus meinem Leben* (3 vols., Nördlingen, 1884) and F. Rohmer's *Wissenschaft vom Menschen* (2 vols., 1885).

SEYMOUR, sî'mōr, **GEORGE FRANKLIN:** Protestant Episcopal bishop of Springfield, Ill.; b. in New York City Jan. 5, 1829; d. at Springfield, Ill., Dec. 8, 1906. He was graduated from Columbia College (A.B., 1850) and the General Theological Seminary (1854). He was ordered deacon in 1854 and was priested in 1855. From that year until 1861 he was rector of Holy Innocents, Annandale, N. Y. (1855-61), where he founded St. Stephen's College, of which he was the first warden. He was then rector at St. Mary's, Manhattanville, New York City (1861-62), Christ Church, Hudson, N. Y. (1862-63), and St. John's, Brooklyn (1863-67). In 1865 he was appointed professor of ecclesiastical history in the General Theological Seminary, of which he was chosen dean in 1875 and there he remained until 1879. In 1878 he was consecrated bishop of Springfield. Theologically he described himself as "an American Catholic bishop in the One, Holy, Catholic, and Apostolic Church of Christ." He was a deputy from the American Church to the Old Catholic Congress at Vienna in 1897. He wrote *Some Considerations why the Name of the Protestant Episcopal Church should be changed* (Milwaukee, 1888); *What is modern Romanism?* (1885); *Amusements in their Relation to Religion* (Lima, Ind., 1890); *An Open Letter to Bishop Doane in Reference to the Consecration of Bishop Brooks* (Milwaukee, 1892); *The Transfiguration: The Place of the Feast of the Transfiguration* (in collaboration with J. H. Egar; New York, 1893); *Marriage and Divorce* (Milwaukee, 1893); *The Church Idea of the Family* (Springfield, Ill., 1899); and *The Sacrament of Baptism, Related Ordinances, and the Creed* (New York, 1903).

Bibliography: W. S. Perry, *The Episcopate in America*, p. 257, New York, 1895.

SHAFTESBURY, shafts'bur-i, **ANTHONY ASHLEY COOPER, THIRD EARL OF.** See Deism, I., § 8.

SHAFTESBURY, ANTHONY ASHLEY COOPER, SEVENTH EARL OF: English philanthropist; b. in London Apr. 28, 1801; d. at Folkestone (60 m. s.e. of London) Oct. 1, 1885. He was educated at Harrow and at Christ Church, Oxford (M.A., 1832; D.C.L., 1841); entered parliament in 1831 and sat as a commoner 1830-31, 1833-46, and 1847-51, in that year taking his seat in the house of lords by succession to his father. His rank, connections, and abilities entitled him to a high place in government, but in the interest of his philanthropic enterprises he preferred to remain unhampered by the requirements of office and of strict adherence to party politics. His first humanitarian activity was directed to the alleviation of the situation of lunatics, the result of which was not only parliamentary regulation of the care of a class badly treated but the directing of the attention of medical men to sounder methods. He also secured legislation limiting the hours during which employees in mills and factories should be kept at work, and agitation covering over ten years was necessary to obtain the relief which finally came. Conditions in collieries and mines also attracted his attention, the awful conditions under which women and even tender children worked for eighteen hours being by him brought to the notice of parliament with the result that legislation eliminated the worst of the evils. The apprentices of the chimney sweeps labored under quite similar harsh conditions, and their situation was alleviated. The "ragged schools" were also benefited by his championship, and he was chairman of the Ragged School Union for thirty-nine years. Under the stimulus of his exposure of lodging-house and other evils, conditions in these institutions and in the tenement houses were made much better. Besides the interests already mentioned, he was active in the counsels of the British and Foreign Bible Society, of which he was long president, in the London City Mission, in the Church Missionary Society, and in the Young Men's Christian Association. He was a faithful attendant of the Church of England, but his sympathies were with evangelicalism wherever found.

Bibliography: E. Hodder, *Life and Work of the Seventh Earl of Shaftesbury*, 3 vols., London, 1886; G. H. Pike, *Shaftesbury, His Life and Work*, ib. 1894; *The Good Earl: Career of the Seventh Lord Shaftesbury*, ib. 1886; *DNB*, xii. 133–137.

SHAHAN, THOMAS JOSEPH: Roman Catholic; b. at Manchester, N. H., Sept. 11, 1857. He was educated at Montreal College, Montreal (1872–78), the American College, Rome (1878–82; D.D., College of the Propaganda, Rome, 1882), the University of Berlin (1889–91), the New Sorbonne and the Institut Catholique, Paris (1891). Ordained to the priesthood in 1882, he was chancellor and secretary of the diocese of Hartford, Conn. (1883–88), and since 1891 has been professor of church history and patristics at the Catholic University of America, Washington, D. C., also president since 1909. He likewise lectured on the history of education in the Catholic University Institute of Pedagogy, New York City, in 1902–03, and since 1895 has been editor of the *Catholic University Bulletin*. Besides being one of the editors of the *Catholic Encyclopedia*, he has written *The Blessed Virgin in the Catacombs* (Baltimore, 1892); *Giovanni Battista de Rossi* (New York, 1900); *The Beginnings of Christianity* (1903); *The Middle Ages* (1903); and *The House of God, and other Addresses and Studies* (1905).

SHAKERS. See Communism, II., 10.

SHALLUM, shal'lum: Fifteenth king of Israel, successor of Zachariah whom he slew, thus ending the dynasty of Jehu. He reigned only a month, probably in the year 740 B.C. (though the old chronology placed him in 771), when he was himself slain by Menahem (q.v.), who seized the throne (II Kings xv. 10–15). A reference to this unsettled period is seen by several commentators in Zech. xi. 8 (cf. J. F. McCurdy, *History, Prophecy and the Monuments*, i. 357, New York, 1894).

SHALMANESER. See Assyria, VI., 3, §§ 3, 7, 10.

SHAMANISM, shā'man-izm: The name for a complex of practises and beliefs connected in some parts of the world with an animistic stage of culture. "Shaman" is of Hindu-Persian origin, and denotes "idolater." The term is much in need of redefinition, being used loosely and applied vaguely to usages which are properly placed under other heads. Shamanism is often defined as the "religion" of certain tribes, mainly Mongolian or Finno-Tataric, in northern Asia. The area thus indicated must be extended to America, where the medicine-man of the Indians has in great part the same functions and beliefs and follows the same practises as the shaman of Asia. Shamanism is not a religion; the term, used properly, represents certain religious concomitants and practises, just as do the terms "magic" and "taboo" (see Comparative Religion, VI., 1, a, § 5, c). The shaman is a functionary who is in part displaced by the priest and the doctor in more advanced stages of culture. Other of his functions than those included under the priestly and the medicinal fall into desuetude with advancing culture. In part, also, the functions of the shaman are exercised by the fetish doctor under fetishism. While the shaman may be described as priest and doctor in embryo, the chief characteristic of shamanism is discerned in distinguishing between shaman and priest. The priest beseeches favor of gods (or spirits), the shaman believes himself able to command spirits, and is not seldom spirit embodied. The connection with animism is shown in the idea of disease entertained by shamans, this being regarded as the work of spirits who must be mastered.

The functions of the shaman are summed up in the securing of good for those who retain his services and the averting of evil from them. This includes the direction of ceremonial, arrangement of dances and feasts, healing of the sick, guarding from sorcery, securing rainfall, and divining. In these various performances ecstasy is often employed by the shaman, and is induced either by narcotics or by self-hypnotism. The means by which these various functions are performed are held to be mysterious, known only to the user, or if known to another yet dangerous for him to employ. In the healing of the sick there are often combined an empirical herbarium and the supposed control of spirits. Deception of the patient and identity of means employed characterize the operations of shamans in the old world and the new, where they frequently diagnose illness as caused by foreign substances introduced into the body by spirits or sorcerers, and these substances they pretend to remove by manipulation and suction, having previously "palmed" or otherwise concealed them about their own persons. Knowledge they pretend to gain by sending forth the "dream spirit" (one of four spirits possessed by them) on a search for the cause of ill or means of good. The compulsion of spirits is accomplished by the "word of power"—incantations consisting of unintelligible formulas and often of mere gibberish, in which, however, the shaman has full confidence. As with the fetish priests, some shamans are specialists, confining their activities to particular domains, as the healing of cattle. A belief in sympathetic magic (see COMPARATIVE RELIGION, VI., 1, a, § 5) is a normal accompaniment of shamanism.

The shaman may come to his powers either by prenatal endowment derived from an ancestor, by gift from a favoring spirit, especially one seen in the puberty watch, or from training by an experienced practitioner. Upon the shaman his profession entails a crude morality, since the control of the spirits is not easy and imposes rules of conduct which the shaman must observe. These frequently include a sort of asceticism, anticipating that principle in the religious development of a later stage of culture.

GEO. W. GILMORE.

BIBLIOGRAPHY: For the western continent a thesaurus of materials is found in the *Reports of the Bureau of American Ethnology*, an annual published by the Smithsonian Institution, Washington, D. C. Consult further: G. Roskoff, *Das Religionswesen der rohesten Naturvölker*, Leipsic, 1880; W. Radloff, *Das Schamanentum und sein Kultus*, ib. 1885; Priklonskij, *Das Schamanentum der Jakuten*, Vienna, 1888; T. Achelis, *Moderne Völkerkunde*, Stuttgart, 1896; Anthropological Institute of Great Britain and Ireland, *Journal*, xxxi (1901); J. Stadling, *Through Siberia*, London, 1901; C. Lumholtz, *Unknown Mexico*, New York, 1902; J. Sheepshanks, *My Life in Mongolia and Siberia*, London, 1903.

SHAMMAI, sham'mê or sham'a-ai: Jewish rabbi of the first century B.C., contemporary and opponent of Hillel (q.v.). He appears to have been a Palestinian, a man of somewhat violent temper who yet realized his shortcoming, but also of great modesty. His religious views were strict even to severity. He founded a school antithetical to that of Hillel, and the proverb arose, "Hillel looses what Shammai binds."

BIBLIOGRAPHY: H. Graetz, *Geschichte der Juden*, iii. 213–214, 256, Leipsic, 1888; Z. Frankel, *Hodegetica in Mischnam*, pp. 39–40, ib. 1859; *JE*, xi. 230.

SHANAHAN, EDMUND THOMAS: Roman Catholic; b. in Boston, Mass., Nov. 22, 1868. He was educated at Boston College (A.B., 1888), the Roman Academy and Seminary and the College of the Propaganda, Rome (S.T.D., 1893), and the University of Louvain (1895). In 1894 he was instructor in philosophy and theology in the American College, Rome; associate professor of theology in the Catholic University of America, Washington, D. C. (1895–98). Since the latter year he has been Shakespeare-Caldwell professor of theology in the same institution, where he has also been dean of the faculty of theology since 1901. He was a lecturer before the American University Extension Society, Philadelphia, in 1897, and lecturer in philosophy at the University of Pennsylvania in 1898-99.

SHARP, GRANVILLE: English philanthropist; b. at Durham Nov. 10, 1735 (old style); d. at Fulham, London, July 6, 1813. Disapproving of the government action relating to the American colonies he resigned his position in the ordnance office, July, 31, 1776, and devoted himself to study. Before this he became famous for his course in befriending and successfully defending the negro slave James Somersett from his master, which finally led to the momentous decision "that as soon as any slave sets his foot upon English territory, he becomes free." He thenceforth devoted himself to the overthrow of slavery and the slave-trade. He conceived the idea of a colony for the liberated slaves, 1783, which afterward materialized in the settlement of Sierra Leone. During the last years of his life he took a prominent part in the founding of the British and Foreign Bible Society and was identified with a number of promotive societies. He was a good linguist and a pious man. He wrote, *A Representation of the Injustice of Private Property in the Persons of Men* (London, 1769), followed by an *Appendix* (1772); *A Declaration of the People's Natural Right to a Share in the Legislature* (1774), in behalf of the American Colonies; and his chief later work, *Remarks on the Uses of the Definitive Article in the Greek Text of the New Testament* (Durham, 1798).

BIBLIOGRAPHY: P. Hoare, *Memoirs of Granville Sharp*, London, 1820; J. Nichols, *Literary Anecdotes of the 18th Century*, 9 vols., ib. 1812–15; J. Stephen, *Essays in Ecclesiastical Biography*, 2 vols., 4th ed., London, 1860; *DNB*, li. 401–404.

SHARP, JAMES: Archbishop of St. Andrews; b. in the castle of Banff (40 m. n.n.w. of Aberdeen) May, 1618; assassinated on Magus Muir, near St. Andrews (31 m. n.e. of Edinburgh), May 3, 1679. He was educated at Aberdeen (M.A., 1637); in 1649 was professor of philosophy in St. Leonard's College, St. Andrews; presented to the Church of Crail, 1648; was made a prisoner by Cromwell's forces and confined in the Tower, 1651–52; was chosen to plead the Presbyterian cause before the Protector, 1657; and when George Monk marched upon London, 1660, he was sent over to Charles II. at Breda, to secure the royal confirmation of "the government of the Church of Scotland, as it is settled by law, without violation," as well as of the act of the resolutioners. The former, of course, was understood in the Presbyterian sense. Sharp, being of the party of resolutioners and selected for his mediating position between Charles and the Presbyterians, was charged with duplicity and with finally betraying the latter for his own interests. At any rate, in 1661, the Scottish parliament annulled all the parliaments held since 1633, with all their proceedings, and thus totally abolished all the laws made in favor of the Presbyterian Church. The "Church of Scotland" thus became the old Episcopal Church; and Sharp, in Dec. 12, 1661, was in London consecrated archbishop of St. Andrews. With the zeal of a convert he persecuted his former allies. Invested with the title and style of primate of Scotland, he re-erected the court of high commission in 1664, which severely punished, some even with death, those who in any way interfered with the prelatical designs, and executed nine persons after the king had required the persecutions to cease. His perfidy and cruelty led to his assassination by a band of Covenanters who encountered the prelate's carriage while lying in wait for his chief agent, Carmichael.

BIBLIOGRAPHY: *Life of James Sharp, Archbishop of St. Andrews . . . first printed in 1678, to which is added, an Account of his Death, by an Eye-Witness*, Edinburgh, 1719; *The Life of Mr. James Sharp . . . to his Instalment in the Archbishopprick of St. Andrews*, ib. 1719; *A True Account of the Life of . . . James Sharp*, London, 1723; T. Stephen, *Life and Times of Archbishop Sharp*, ib. 1839; R. Keith, *Historical Catalogue of the Scottish*

Bishops, new ed., Edinburgh, 1824; W. M. Hetherington, *Hist. of the Church of Scotland*, passim, New York, 1881; W. Beveridge, *Makers of the Scottish Church*, passim, 1908; *DNB*, li. 404–407.

SHARP, JOHN: Church of England archbishop of York; b. at Bradford (8 m. w. of Leeds), Yorkshire, Feb. 16, 1644–45; d. at Bath Feb. 2, 1714. His father was a puritan, his mother an ardent member of the Church of England, and from both he derived corresponding elements of character. He received his education at Christ's College, Cambridge (B.A., 1663; M.A., 1667); was made deacon and priest, 1667, and soon after became tutor in the family of Sir Heneage Finch at Kensington House, in 1673 being made archdeacon of Berkshire on Finch's nomination; in 1675 he became prebendary of Norwich and incumbent of St. Bartholomew's Exchange, London, and in 1679 lecturer at St. Lawrence, Jewry, in 1675 exchanging the incumbency for the rectorship of St. Giles's-in-the-Fields; in addition, in 1681 he was made dean of Norwich; named in 1686 chaplain in ordinary to King James II., he was provoked by attempts of Roman Catholics to convert his parishioners, preached two sermons which were construed as reflecting upon the king, and his chaplaincy was not allowed until 1687; further evidence of his independent spirit was shown by his refusal to read the declaration of indulgence of 1688, and by his prayers for King James before the prince of Orange in 1689; he became dean of Canterbury in 1689; declined to receive any of the sees of the Nonjurors (q.v.), but in 1691 became archbishop of York. In this position he showed himself an able and diligent administrator; he investigated the history and rights of the see, leaving the work in manuscript; he was active in repairing the minster after the fire of 1711, dealt with his clergy kindly but firmly, insisted upon sound and instructive preaching, and aimed to eliminate polemics against dissenters. Under Queen Anne he became still more influential, acted as her almoner, and was her counselor, showing great wisdom in this unofficial position. He was interested in the continental dispute between Lutherans and Calvinists, in this cause corresponding with Daniel Ernst Jablonski (q.v.), and the correspondence appeared in French translation and in the appendix to the *Life* (see below). Archbishop Sharp left the impression of being one of the great men of the Church of England, independent in opinion, straightforward in action, kindly in disposition, liberal in education and tastes, with numismatics as his diversion, leaving a collection of coins and a manuscript on the coinage of England as evidences. He left in print a large number of occasional sermons, as well as *Fifteen Sermons Preached on Several Occasions* (London, 1700; several editions). His *Works* appeared in 7 vols. (1754) and in 5 vols. (Oxford, 1829).

Bibliography: His *Life* was written by his son Thomas, but was not printed till 1825, when it was edited by T. Newcome, and is founded upon the diary of the archbishop. Consult further: C. J. Abbey, *The English Church and its Bishops, 1700–1800*, i. 103–105, London, 1887; J. H. Overton, *The Church in England*, vol. ii., passim, ib. 1897; W. H. Hutton, *The English Church (1625–1714)*, ib. 1903; A. Plummer, *English Church History, from the Death of Charles I. to the Death of William III.*, Edinburgh, 1907; *DNB*, li. 408–411.

SHARPE, SAMUEL: Egyptologist and Biblical translator; b. at London Mar. 8, 1799; d. there July 28, 1881. He was a banker, 1814–61; and, upon retirement from business, devoted himself, without university training, to Biblical study, 1861–81. In 1821 he turned from the Established to the Unitarian Church. He early became interested in Egyptology, and published *Egyptian Inscriptions* (1st and 2d series, London, 1836–56); *History of Egypt from the Earliest Times till A.D. 640* (1846; 6th ed., 2 vols., 1876). To Biblical literature he contributed *The New Testament*, a translation from J. J. Griesbach's text, with notes (1840; 5th ed., 1862); *The Hebrew Scriptures*, a revision of the authorised version of the Old Testament (3 vols., 1865); *The Holy Bible* (1881), a revision of the authorized English translation; and *History of the Hebrew Nation, and Literature* (1869).

Bibliography: P. W. Clayden, *Samuel Sharpe, Egyptologist and Translator of the Bible*, London, 1883; *DNB*, li. 425–427.

SHAW, JOHN BALCOM: Presbyterian; b. at Bellport, N. Y., May 12, 1860. He received his education at Lafayette College (B.A., 1885; M.A., 1888) and Union Theological Seminary, New York City (graduated 1888); was ordained to the ministry 1888, and was pastor of the West End Presbyterian Church, New York City, 1888–1904; and has been in charge of the Second Presbyterian Church in Chicago since 1904. He has also been president of the Presbyterian Council of the Brotherhood of Andrew and Philip since 1895, besides serving on the boards of various educational institutions. He has written *The Difficult Life* (Chicago, 1904); *Life that follows Life* (1907); and *Vision and Service* (1907; sermons).

SHAW, WILLIAM ISAAC: Wesleyan Methodist; b. at Kingston, Canada, Apr. 6, 1841; was graduated from Victoria University, Cobourg, Canada (A.B., 1861; LL.B., 1864), at McGill University, Montreal (M.A., 1880); engaged in the ministry of the Wesleyan Methodist Church of Canada, 1864–77; and in 1877 became professor of exegesis and church history in the Wesleyan Theological College, Montreal, of which he is principal. He is the author of *Discussion on Retribution* (Toronto, 1884); *Digest of the Doctrinal Standards of the Methodist Church* (1895).

SHEBA. See Arabia, III.; and Table of the Nations, § 6.

SHEBNA (SHEBNAH): A high official in the palace of Hezekiah, mentioned in Isa. xxii. 15–25, xxxvi. 3, 11, 22, xxxvii. 2; II Kings xviii. 18, 26, 37, xix. 2, and made the object of Isaiah's severe prophetic menace in the passage first mentioned. These eleven verses all refer to Shebna, as nearly all commentators agree; but though the text is free from corruption and the language is relatively clear, the passage is not without obscurity. While Isa. xxii. 20 sqq. refers to Eliakim, in verse 25 the prophet probably returns to Shebna. The place to be given Eliakim as Shebna's successor was plainly one of high rank, and Shebna himself was "over the house" (verse 15; cf. Gen. xli. 40; I Kings xviii. 3 sqq.), thus being, as it were, a major-domo. He is marked as an upstart by the triple "here" in verse 16, as well as by the omission of his father's name; and in the account of the siege of Jerusalem by Sennacherib in 701 B.C. (Isa. xxxvi. 3, 11, 22, xxxvii. 2; II Kings xviii. 18, 26, 37, xix. 2) he appears in the subordinate position of an official scribe or mere minister, while Eliakim occupies the rank of the highest state official. There is no reason for surprise that the very Shebna whom the prophet had threatened with dismissal and death in exile (Isa. xxii. 17–19) should accompany his superior, Eliakim, to treat with the Assyrian envoys at Hezekiah's command, and should even request the intercession of Isaiah (Isa. xxxvii. 2; II Kings xix. 2); and as it is improbable that there were two high officials during the reign of Hezekiah both of whom bore the name of Shebna, this same man is doubtless to be understood throughout. While it is evident from such passages as Jer. xviii. 7 sqq. that Isaiah's menacing words, which did not in the least constitute a formal prophecy, did not require a literal fulfilment, there is no doubt that they were essentially realized in Shebna's degradation and his replacement by Eliakim.

Since, in Isa. xxii. 20–21, Eliakim is described as a servant of the Lord, and as destined to be "a father to the inhabitants of Jerusalem, and to the house of Judah," it would appear, by implication, that Shebna was lacking in the fear of God and guilty of gross oppression, thus abusing his official position; and even were this the fault of his favorites, the evil influence of his band of parasites would necessarily end on his downfall. An erroneous exegesis assumes that Isaiah accuses Eliakim of nepotism and threatens his overthrow at the very moment of his rise to power; but, rightly understood, the phrase "in that day," in verses 20, 25, implies the simultaneous nature of Eliakim's elevation and Shebna's fall. In describing the prestige which Shebna was to confer upon his family, Isaiah compares him to a "nail in a sure place" (verses 23–24), likening the subordinate members of his house to various earthen vessels, which would be shattered if the nail should break. It has been maintained by B. L. Duhm (*Das Buch Jesaia übersetzt und erklärt*, Göttingen, 1892, *ad loc.*) that only Isa. xxii. 15–18 are genuine, the remainder of the passage in question being added later, 19–23 by a friend of Eliakim, and 24–25 by one of his enemies; but the truth is that the whole passage is a genuine prophecy of Isaiah, who branded the powerful functionary at the head of the reigning house as its disgrace (verse 18), probably on the occasion of viewing the magnificent tomb which Shebna had built for himself.

A. KAMPHAUSEN.

BIBLIOGRAPHY: The full discussion of the subject is by A. Kamphausen in *Zeitschrift für Pastoral Theologie*, xxiv. 557–573, 631–640, Eng. transl. in *AJT*, 1901, pp. 43–74; E. König, in *NKZ*, 1902, pp. 621–631.

SHEDD, JOHN HASKELL: Missionary to Persia; b. at Mt. Gilead, Ohio, July 9, 1833; d. at Urumia, Persia, Apr. 12, 1895. He was the son of the Rev. Henry Shedd, one of the pioneer home missionaries in Ohio; was graduated from Marietta College (1856) and from Andover Theological Seminary (1859), was ordained Aug. 3, 1859, and sailed the same month on his way to Persia as a missionary of the American Board in the Nestorian Mission. He served as a missionary from 1859 to 1870 under the American Board and from 1878 to 1895 under the Presbyterian Board, to which in 1870 the work for the Nestorians was transferred. From 1872 to 1878 he was a professor in Biddle University, Charlotte, N. C. Urumia, Persia, where he died, was his home during the whole of his missionary work.

Dr. Shedd's missionary work deserves special record along four lines. On his arrival on the field as a young missionary of unusual energy and ability he was restive at the limitation of the work to the Nestorians and he sought hard to have it extended to the Armenian and Moslem population of the field. Only the sudden break-down of another missionary prevented his opening a new station at Van, Turkey. These efforts, though not successful at the time, were among the influences that prepared for the later wide extension of the work, which has made the mission to the Nestorians a mission to Persia and given it a wider scope than yet belongs to any other of the missions to the oriental churches. Although his own work was confined mainly to the Nestorians, he always planned and worked with the larger field in view. A second line was the effort to evangelize the mountain Nestorian tribes. No more difficult missionary field exists than the mountain region bounded by lines connecting Urumia, Van, Jezireh, and Mosul. Dr. Shedd was a worthy successor of Dr. Asahel Grant and the Rev. S. A. Rhea in this work. Between 1860 and 1870 he made no less than eighteen journeys through this wild and dangerous region, preaching, organizing, and planning. It would be unjust to say that these efforts resulted in failure, but the success was small. Another line of work in which Dr. Shedd's memory and influence will be lasting was the training of native workers. He always conceived of this as the primary purpose of missionary educational work, and largely for this reason he gave himself with energy from 1878 till his death to the work of Urumia College. The love and respect of his pupils for him were great and abiding. But the chief service he rendered the cause of missions was in the organization of the native Syrian Evangelical Church. In his plans and principles in this work he was ahead of his time. When a young missionary he criticized severely the policy of the mission in not placing responsibility on the natives. While averse to any violent break with the old Nestorian Church and never giving up hope of its revival, he thoroughly believed in an organized Evangelical body; and the organization of the Evangelical church provides for its complete ecclesiastical autonomy with an adapted Presbyterian government. It also provides for organized cooperation of the native church and the foreign missionaries in the work of all settled preachers and all village schools. This is carried on by executive boards of the native church, which control the work concurrently with the mission.

W. A. SHEDD.

SHEDD, WILLIAM GREENOUGH THAYER: Presbyterian; b. at Acton, Mass., June 21, 1820; d. at New York Nov. 17, 1894. He was graduated from the University of Vermont, 1839; and from

Andover Theological Seminary, 1843; became Congregational pastor at Brandon, Vt., 1844; professor of English literature, University of Vermont, 1845; of sacred rhetoric in Auburn (Presbyterian) Theological Seminary, 1852; of church history in Andover (Congregational) Theological Seminary, 1853; associate pastor of the Brick (Presbyterian) Church, New York City, 1862; professor of Biblical literature in Union Theological Seminary, New York, 1863–74; and of systematic theology, 1874–90, where he was known for the rigid logic and close compactness of his system, embodied in his *Dogmatic Theology* (vols. i.–ii., Worcester, 1889; vol. iii., New York, 1894). He translated from the German of Francis Theremin, *Eloquence a Virtue* (New York, 1850), and H. E. F. Guericke's *Manual of Church History* (2 vols., Andover, 1860–70); and wrote *A History of Christian Doctrine* (2 vols., New York, 1865); *Homiletics and Pastoral Theology* (1867); *Sermons to the Natural Man* (1871); *Theological Essays* (1877); *Commentary on Romans* (1879); *Sermons to the Spiritual Man* (1884); *The Doctrine of Endless Punishment* (1886); and *Orthodoxy and Heterodoxy* (New York, 1893).

Bibliography: J. De Witt, in *Presbyterian and Reformed Review*, vi (1895), 295–322.

SHEEHAN, PATRICK AUGUSTINE: Irish Roman Catholic; b. at Mallow (17 m. n.n.w. of Cork), County Cork, Mar. 17, 1852. He was educated at St. Colman's College, Fermoy, and at Maynooth College, and after being ordained in 1875 and being for two years attached to the mission in Exeter, was successively curate in Mallow (1877–81, 1889–95) and Queenstown (1881–89). Since 1895 he has been parish priest of Doneraile, and also canon of Cloyne since 1903. He is the author of *Under the Cedars and the Stars* (London, 1903) and its companion volume, *Parerga* (1908); *Mariæ Corona, Chapters on the Mother of God and her Saints* (2d ed., Dublin, 1902); and *Early Essays and Addresses* (London, 1906); also of several novels dealing with religious themes, among them *The Triumph of Failure* (London, 1899), *My new Curate* (1900), and *Luke Delmege* (1902).

SHEEP. See Pastoral Life, Hebrew.

SHEEPSHANKS, JOHN: Church of England retired bishop; b. in London Feb. 23, 1834. He was educated at Christ's College, Cambridge (B.A., 1856, in the 2d class of the theological tripos), and was ordered deacon 1857 and ordained priest in the following year. He was curate of Leeds (1857–59); rector of New Westminster, B. C., and chaplain to the bishop of Columbia (1859–67); vicar of Bilton, Yorkshire (1868–73); vicar of St. Margaret Anfield, Walton-on-the Hill, Liverpool (1873–93). In 1893 he was consecrated bishop of Norwich. He resigned his see in 1909. While in British Columbia, he did much missionary work among the Indians, particularly at Cariboo, and is also noteworthy as being the only English clergyman who has ever preached in the Mormon Tabernacle in Salt Lake City. He has traveled extensively in Siberia and Tibet, and at Urga saw the adoration of the Llama of Mongolia. He has writted *Confirmation and Unction of the Sick* (London, 1889); *Eucharist and Confession* (1902); *My Life in Mongolia and Siberia* (1903); and *The Pastor in his Parish* (1908).

Bibliography: D. W. Duthie, *A Bishop in the Rough*, London, 1909 (relates his experiences in British Columbia).

SHEKINAH, she-kai'na (Talmudic Hebr., "abiding [of the divine presence]"): A post-Biblical term to express the relation of Yahweh to the world, and especially to Israel. The concept, based on the Old Testament, arose among the Palestinian and Babylonian Jews, who stressed the immanent activity of God, as opposed to the Alexandrine doctrine of a supramundane and extramundane deity. In the Targums the expressions "shekinah of Yahweh," "glory of Yahweh," and "word of Yahweh" are synonymous, and "shekinah," "glory," and "word" come to be designations of Yahweh himself. The shekinah itself is generally regarded as "resting" or "dwelling," so that the Targum of Onkelos interprets "God shall dwell in the tents of Shem" (Gen. ix. 27) as "God shall make his shekinah to dwell in the tents of Shem" (cf. the Targum on Ex. xxv. 8, xxix. 45; Num. v. 3, xi. 20, xiv. 14, xvi. 3, xxxv. 34; Deut. i. 42, xxxii. 10; Ps. xvi. 8, xliv. 10, lxxiv. 2; Hag. i. 8); but it is also said "to depart" (as in the Targum on Ex. xxxiii. 3, 5; Job xxxiv. 29; Ps. xxii. 25, xxvii. 91, xxxix. 47), "to pass by" (Ex. xxxiv. 6), "to walk" (Deut. xxiii. 14), and "to be" or "not to be" (Ex. xvii. 7; Num. xiv. 42; Deut. iv. 39). In all these passages "shekinah" stands for "Yahweh," but in other places it represents "name" (Deut. xii. 5, 11, 21), "face" (Num. vi. 25; Deut. xxxi. 17–18), and "hand" (Ex. xvii. 16). It is clear, moreover, that Onkelos did not regard the shekinah as an independent entity between Yahweh and Israel but as a name for Yahweh himself (cf. his Targum on Ex. xxxiii. 14–16, xxxiv. 9).

Talmudic and Midrashic literature gives far more material on the activity of the shekinah than does the Targum, though in all the concept of the shekinah is the same. From the day of the erection of the tabernacle, the shekinah dwelt within, this concept of its descending and abiding doubtless being derived from the Babylonian idea of a divinity enthroned in the adytum, thus taking up its abode there for adoration, but returning, if angered, to the sky, a trait also assigned to the shekinah. After the conquest of Canaan the shekinah moved wherever the tabernacle went, finally abiding in the temple built by David and Solomon, in which it rested at the east end. At the exile it went, according to some, with the deported Jews, but according to others, returned to heaven; at all events, like the ark of the covenant, the Urim and Thummim, etc., it was not in the second temple. Nevertheless, its immanent activity in the world did not cease, so that such scholars as Ishmael ben Elisha (first century) and Hoshaiah Rabbah (early third century) could say that "the shekinah is in every place."

While the interrelation of the shekinah and mankind is represented in manifold ways, it may be said, in general, that the impious make the shekinah withdraw from earth, but the pious secure its return. Prayer, piety, worship, study of the law, perfect administration of justice, practise of virtue, and blameless joyousness bring the shekinah near, but it flees from sorrow, idleness, laughter, frivolity, jesting, pride, and things of no account. On the other hand, it abides with the sick and with those happily wedded. The shekinah, which is symbolized by the lighting of the perpetual lamp, is regarded as possessed of wings, so that "Moses was, from his birth, under the wings of the shekinah." This would apparently imply a figure somewhat like that of the cherubim and genii, and a face and radiance are also ascribed to the shekinah.

Later Midrashic literature makes the shekinah an independent entity standing between God and the world, so that the shekinah can even be said to "go to the presence of God," a view frequently expressed in Cabalistic literature, as well as by Maimonides and his school. The view of Maimonides, however, that the shekinah, like the "glory" and the "word," was a fiery created being which communicates the divine activity to the world, was combated by Naḥmanides. Among the pseudo-Messiahs of the Jews, Shabbethai Ẓebi declared himself to be the incarnate shekinah. In the New Testament the shekinah is not mentioned, although Christ may be identified with it in Matt. xviii. 20.

(August Wünsche.)

Bibliography: A. F. Gfrörer, *Geschichte des Urchristenthums*, i. 272–352, Stuttgart, 1838; J. Langen, *Judenthum in Palästina zur Zeit Christi*, pp. 201 sqq., Freiburg, 1866; S. Maybaum, *Anthropomorphien und Anthropopathien*, Breslau, 1870; C. C. W. F. Bähr, *Symbolik des mosaischen Cultus*, i. 471 sqq., Heidelberg, 1874; F. Weber, *Jüdische Theologie*, Leipsic, 1897; G. Dalman, *Die Worte Jesu*, vol. i., Leipsic, 1898; W. Bousset, *Religion des Judenthums im neutestamentlichen Zeitalter*, pp. 309 sqq., 340, Berlin, 1903; A. B. Davidson, *Old Testament Prophecy*, pp. 148, 220, Edinburgh, 1903; *DB*, iv. 487–489; *JE*, xi. 258–260.

SHELDON, CHARLES MONROE: Congregationalist; b. at Wellsville, N. Y., Feb. 26, 1857. He was graduated from Brown University (A.B., 1883) and Andover Theological Seminary (1886). He was pastor of the Congregational Church at Waterbury, Vt. (1886–89); and since 1889 has been pastor of the Central Congregational Church, Topeka, Kan. He states that practically his whole theological position centers about the attempt to put into practise the creed of Christ. He has written *Richard Bruce: or, The Life that now is* (Boston, 1892); *Robert Hardy's Seven Days* (1893); *The Twentieth Door* (1893); *The Crucifixion of Philip Strong* (Chicago, 1894); *John King's Question Class* (1894); *His Brother's Keeper: or Christian Stewardship* (Boston, 1895); *In His Steps* (Chicago, 1896); *Malcolm Kirk* (1897); *Lend a Hand* (1899); *The Redemption of Freetown* (1898); *The Miracle at Markham* (1898); *One of the Two* (1898); *For Christ and the Church* (1899); *Edward Blake* (1899); *Born to Serve* (1900); *The Reformer* (1902); *The Heart of the World* (1905); and *Paul Douglas, Journalist* (1909).

SHELDON, GILBERT: Church of England archbishop of Canterbury; b. at Ashbourn (13 m. n.w. of Derby) July 19, 1598; d. at Lambeth Nov. 9, 1677; He studied at Trinity College, Oxford (B.A., 1617; M.A., 1620; fellow of All Souls', 1622; B.D., 1628 D.D., 1634); was ordained in 1622, almost immediately becoming domestic chaplain to Thomas, Lord Coventry; was made prebendary of Gloucester, 1632; vicar of Hackney, 1633; rector of Oddington, Oxford, and of Ickford, Buckingham, 1636; rector of Newington, Oxford, 1639, having been meanwhile warden of All Souls' College since 1626, of which he was in 1634 and 1640 pro-vicechancellor. He was a strong anti-Puritan, and was ejected from his wardenship by the Parliamentary visitors in 1648, being imprisoned for resisting the attempt to take his lodgings, but recovered the office in 1659. During the exile of Charles II., Sheldon was constant in his efforts in favor of Charles, and on the Restoration was naturally in high favor. In 1660 he was made bishop of London, and the Savoy Conference (q.v.) was held at his lodging; in 1663 he became archbishop of Canterbury. Although he was elected chancellor of Oxford University in 1667, he was not installed, and resigned 1669. He built and endowed the Sheldonian theater at Oxford. His career as bishop was one of great fidelity to duty. Most marked were his benefactions, both to the poor and in behalf of public interests, as in the case of his subscription to the rebuilding of St. Paul's after the fire of London. His total benefactions were said to have exceeded £72,000—an enormous sum for those times. He was devoted to the antiquities of the university, and in particular was a patron of the historian of Oxford, Anthony à Wood. The only published work left by him is a sermon before the king June 20, 1660, though a considerable body of manuscripts is extant.

Bibliography: A. à Wood, *Athenæ Oxonienses*, ed. P. Bliss, vol. iv., London, 1820; M. Burrows, *Worthies of All Souls*, London, 1874; G. C. Brodrick, *Memorials of Merton College*, Oxford, 1885; W. H. Hutton, *The English Church (1625–1714)*, pp. 197–198 et passim, London, 1903; A. Plummer, *English Church History (1649–1702)*, pp. 64, 70–71, Edinburgh, 1907; *DNB*, lii. 24–26.

SHELDON, HENRY CLAY: Methodist Episcopalian; b. at Martinsburg, N. Y., Mar. 12, 1845. He was graduated from Yale (A.B., 1867), and the Theological School of Boston University (1871). After studying at Leipsic in 1874–75, he was professor of historical theology in Boston University until 1895, when he was transferred to his present position of professor of systematic theology. In theology he inclines toward evangelical Arminianism, as opposed both to strict Calvinism and to liberalism. He has written *History of Christian Doctrine* (2 vols., New York, 1886); *History of the Christian Church* (5 vols., 1894); *System of Christian Doctrine* (1903); *Unbelief in the Nineteenth Century* (1907); *Sacerdotalism in the Nineteenth Century* (1909); and *New Testament Theology* (1911).

SHEM, SHEMITES. See Table of the Nations.

SHEMAIAH, she-mê'yā or shem''a-ai'ā: A name of frequent occurrence in the Old Testament. The most important men who bore it were:

1. A prophet of the time of Rehoboam (I Kings xii. 21–24), who forbade that king to enter upon a war with the ten tribes who had established the northern kingdom. The passage belongs to a late stratum of the Books of Kings, and the parallel (II Chron. xi.–xii.) adds midrashic material concerning Shemaiah in which the prophet regards the attack of Shishak as a consequence of the sins of Judah. To this prophet is attributed a history of the reign of Rehoboam (II Chron. xii. 15), upon

which presumably the Chronicler drew. The statement is not improbable, and the author of the Books of Kings notes the existence of such books as materials from which he drew; the possibility of the existence and activity of such a person in the time of Rehoboam is granted, and much of the material dealing with the end of the period of the Judges and with the beginning of the kingdom goes back to this time.

2. An opponent of Jeremiah living among the exiles, who sent a letter to Zephaniah the priest at Jerusalem blaming Jeremiah for advising the exiles to prepare for a considerable stay in Babylonia (Jer. xxix. 24 sqq.). Jeremiah declared Shemaiah to be a lying prophet and predicted his punishment and the destruction of his house.

3. An opponent of Nehemiah (Neh. vi. 10 sqq.), also a prophet and an associate of Sanballat (q.v.). He attempted to lead Nehemiah into a cowardly course so as to discredit him with the people.

(R. Kittel.)

SHEOL. See Hades.

SHEPARD, THOMAS: Puritan; b. at Towcester (59 m. n.w. of London), Northampton, Eng., Nov. 5, 1604; d. at Cambridge, Mass., Aug. 25, 1649. He graduated at Emmanuel College, Oxford (B.A., 1623; M.A., 1627); was lecturer at Earl's Coln, 1627–30; was silenced for non-conformity by Laud, Dec. 16, 1630; became lecturer at Towcester; was employed as chaplain and tutor in the family of Sir Richard Darly, Buttercrambe, Yorkshire, for a year; was pastor at Heddon, Northumberland, another year, but was again silenced, 1633; and sailed for America, Dec., 1634, but was compelled by a storm to put back. He had to hide himself lest he should be taken, but finally, July, 1635, got away, and landed at Boston, on Oct. 3, and became minister at Cambridge, Feb., 1636, till his death. He took an active part in founding Harvard College and secured its location at Cambridge, and was prominent in the synod at Cambridge which ended the Antinomian controversy. In learning, piety, spiritual insight, and practical force he takes a first rank among Puritan divines; especially exemplified in his treatise, *The Parable of the Ten Virgins Opened and Applied* (1659; reprinted Aberdeen, 1838 and 1853, with biographical preface by J. Foote). In all he is said to have written 382 books and pamphlets, among which were *New Englands Lamentation for Old Englands Present Errours and Divisions* (1645); *Certain Select Cases Resolved* (1648); *The Clear Sunshine of the Gospel Breaking Forth upon the Indians in New England* (1646; reprinted, New York, 1865); and *Theses Sabbaticæ* (1649). A collective edition of his works, with memoir by J. A. Albro (originally published Boston, 1847, reproduced in *Lives of the Chief Fathers of New England*, vol. iv., Boston, 1870), was published (3 vols., Boston, 1853). His *Autobiography* was published in Alexander Young's *Chronicles of the First Planters of Massachusetts Bay* (Boston, 1846).

Bibliography: Besides the *Autobiography* and the memoir by Albro, ut sup., consult: A. Whyte, *Thomas Shepard; Pilgrim Father and Founder of Harvard. His Spiritual Experience and Experimental Preaching*, Edinburgh, 1909; Cotton Mather, *Magnalia*, i. 380 sqq., Hartford, 1855; W. B. Sprague, *Annals of the American Pulpit*, i. 59–68, New York, 1859; W. Walker, *Creeds and Platforms of Congregationalism*, ib. 1893; idem, *Ten New England Leaders*, ib. 1901; A. E. Dunning, *Congregationalists in America*, ib. 1894; *DNB*, lii. 50–51.

SHEPHERD OF HERMAS. See Hermas.

SHEPHERDS. See Pastoral Life, Hebrew, III.

SHERATON, JAMES PATERSON: Canadian Anglican; b. at St. John, N. B., Nov. 29, 1841; d. in Toronto Jan. 24, 1906. He was educated at the University of New Brunswick (A.B., 1862), and received his theological training at the University of King's College, Windsor, N. S., and privately with the bishop of Fredericton. He was ordered deacon in 1864 and ordained priest in the following year. After being a missionary at Weldford, Shediac, and Petersville, N. B., successively (1865–73), he was rector of St. James', Pictou, N. S. (1874–77). From 1877 till his death he was principal and professor of Biblical and systematic theology in Wycliffe College, Toronto, and after 1889 honorary canon of St. Alban's Cathedral, Toronto.

SHERLOCK, RICHARD: Church of England; b. at Oxton, a township on the peninsula of Wirral (s.w. of Liverpool), Cheshire, Nov. 11, 1612; d. at Winwick (17 m. e. of Liverpool), Lancashire, June 20, 1689. He was educated at Magdalen Hall, Oxford, and Trinity College, Dublin (M.A., 1633). Until 1641 he was minister of small parishes in Ireland; and proceeded to Oxford where he was chaplain of the garrison and of New College, 1644–48. He was expelled thence, 1648, and ejected from the curacy of Cassington, 1652, owing to his stanch Anglican loyalism; became private chaplain, 1652–1662; and, with the Restoration, rector of Winwick, 1662–89. In controversy with the Friends he published *The Quakers Wilde Questions Objected against the Ministers of the Gospel and many Sacred Gifts and Offices of Religion, with Brief Answers thereto. Together with a Discourse of the Holy Spirit, his Impressions and Workings on the Souls of Men* (London, 1854). His main work was *Mercurius Christianus; the Practical Christian, a Treatise Explaining the Duty of Self-Examination* (1673 and often; the 6th ed., including a biography by his nephew, Thomas Wilson, 1713; 7th ed., 2 vols., Oxford, 1841–44).

Bibliography: Consult, besides the life by Wilson, ut sup.: T. D. Whitaker, *History of Richmondshire*, 2 vols., London, 1823; J. H. Overton, *The Church in England*, 2 vols., ib. 1897; *DNB*, lii. 92–93.

SHERLOCK, THOMAS: Church of England, son of William Sherlock; b. at London in 1678; d. there July 18, 1761. He was educated at Cambridge (B.A., 1697; M.A., 1701); was master of the Temple, 1704–53; became prebendary of St. Paul's, 1713; was master of St. Catherine's Hall, 1714–19; became dean of Chichester, 1715; canon of Norwich, 1719; bishop of Bangor, 1727; of Salisbury, 1734; and of London, 1748. *The Use and Intent of Prophecy* (London, 1725) was a compendium of six sermons against the Deists; his most famous work was *The Tryal of the Witnesses of the Resurrection of Jesus* (1729, and often). Besides this may be noted his *Discourses Preached at Temple Church* (4 vols., 1754–97; 6th ed., 5 vols., 1772–75).

BIBLIOGRAPHY: S. Nicolls, *A Sermon Preached . . . on the Death of Dr. T. Sherlock*, London, 1762; D. S. Wayland, *A Biographical Sketch of Bishop Sherlock*, Derby, 1823; L. Stephen, *Hist. of English Thought in the 18th Century*, passim, 2 vols., New York, 1881 (very full and worth consulting); J. H. Overton, *The Church in England*, 2 vols., London, 1897; J. H. Overton and F. Relton, *The English Church (1714–1800)*, ib. 1906; *DNB*, lii. 93–95.

SHERLOCK, WILLIAM: Church of England; b. at Southwark, London, about 1641; d. at Hampstead, London, June 19, 1707. He was educated at Peterhouse, Cambridge (B.A., 1660; M.A., 1663); became rector of St. George's, Botolph Lane, London, 1669, where he gained fame as a preacher and attracted attention by his opposition to the Puritans and their theology. In 1681 he became prebendary at St. Paul's; was lecturer at St. Dunstan's-in-the-West; became master of the Temple in 1685; dean of St. Paul's, 1691; and rector of Therfield, Hertfordshire, 1698. Contending under James II. for the doctrine of the divine right and passive obedience, *Case of Resistance* (London, 1684), he at first refused the oath at the Revolution, but desisted from non-juring, 1690. His most popular work was *A Practical Discourse concerning Death* (1689; 28th ed., 1767). With *A Vindication of the Doctrine of the Holy and Ever-blessed Trinity* (1690), he plunged into the Socinian controversy of the time. His position, that in the three persons of the Trinity there was what may be called "a mutual self-consciousness, a consciousness common to the three," and that therefore the three are essentially and numerically one, brought upon him the irony and invective of Robert South (q.v.), and the charge of tritheism from the Socinians. Among his numerous other publications, practical and controversial, the most frequently republished are, *A Discourse concerning a Future Judgment* (1692), and *A Discourse concerning the Divine Providence* (1694). The *British Museum Catalogue* devotes over eight pages to his works and the editions of them, and to the replies, satires, and controversial pamphlets they evoked.

BIBLIOGRAPHY: R. Wallace, *Antitrinitarian Biography*, i. 214–215, London, 1850; J. Hunt, *Religious Thought in England*, 3 vols., ib. 1870–73; J. H. Overton, *The Church in England*, 2 vols., ib. 1897; W. H. Hutton, *The English Church (1625–1714)*, ib. 1903; J. H. Overton and F. Relton, *The English Church (1714–1800)*, ib. 1906; *DNB*, lii. 95–97.

SHERWOOD, JAMES MANNING: Presbyterian; b. at Fishkill, N. Y., Sept. 29, 1814; d. at Brooklyn, N. Y., Oct. 22, 1890. He was educated mainly by private tutors; was pastor at New Windsor, N. Y., 1835–40; Mendon, N. Y., 1840–45; Bloomfield, N. J., 1852–58; editor of *National Preacher*, 1846–49; *Biblical Repository*, 1847–51; *Eclectic Magazine*, 1864–71; founder and editor of *Hours at Home*, 1865–69; editor *Presbyterian Review*, 1863–71; *Presbyterian Quarterly and Princeton Review*, 1872–1878; *Homiletic Review*, from Sept., 1883; also of the *Missionary Review*. He was extensively engaged as a reader of manuscripts for publishing houses, and critically noticed for the press several thousand volumes, chiefly in the reviews of the country. He was the author of *Plea for the Old Foundations* (New York, 1856); *The Lamb in the Midst of the Throne* (1883); editor of *Memoirs*, and two volumes of *Sermons* of Ichabod Spencer (1855); David Brainerd's *Memoirs*, with notes and estimation of his life and character (1884).

SHIELDS, CHARLES WOODRUFF: Educator and author; b. at New Albany, Ind., Apr. 4, 1825; d. at Newport, R. I., Apr. 26, 1904. He was graduated from the College of New Jersey, 1844; and from Princeton Theological Seminary, 1847; became pastor at Hempstead, Long Island, 1849; of Second Church, Philadelphia, 1850; professor of harmony of science and revealed religion in the College of New Jersey, 1866; and, in addition, professor of modern history, 1871, which professorship he soon resigned. His appointment to the professorship of the harmony of science and religion, the first of its kind, was occasioned by the publication of *Philosophia Ultima* (see below), in which he expounded an academic scheme of irenical studies for the reconciliation of religion and science. In his lectures and writings he stood for the restoration of theology, as a science of religion, to its true philosophical position in a university system of culture, as distinguished from the clerical or sectarian system of education, and the placing of philosophy as an umpire between science and religion as embracing without invading their distinct provinces. This view was set forth in *Religion and Science in their Relation to Philosophy* (New York, 1875). The final philosophy, or science of sciences to come, is to be reached inductively from the collective intelligence of men working through successive generations, *Philosophia Ultima* (Philadelphia, 1861; rev. and enlarged ed., vol. i., *Historical and Critical Introduction on the Final Philosophy as Issuing from the Harmony of Science and Religion;* vol. ii., *History of the Sciences and the Logic of the Sciences;* vol. iii., *Scientific Problems of Religion and the Christian Evidences of the Physical and Psychical Sciences*, New York, 1905). As a Presbyterian he was an earnest advocate of the restoration of the Presbyterian prayer-book of 1661 for optional use by ministers and congregations, and published *The Book of Common Prayer as Amended by the Presbyterian Divines* (Philadelphia, 1864), with an appendix entitled *Liturgia Expurgata* (1864). His irenicism also contemplated a church unity on a liturgical basis, looking toward an ultimate organic reunion of Presbyterianism, Congregationalism, and Episcopalianism in what he termed the American Protestant Catholic Church. His writings on this theme created intense interest: *Essays on Christian Unity* (1885); *The Historic Episcopate* (New York, 1894); *The United Church of the United States* (1895); and *Church Unity* (1896). In 1898 he took orders in the Protestant Episcopal Church.

SHINAR. See BABYLONIA, I.

SHINTO. See JAPAN, II., 1.

SHIPLEY, ORBY: Roman Catholic; b. at Twyford House (9 m. n.e. of Southampton) July 1, 1832. He received his education at Jesus College, Cambridge (B.A., 1854; M.A., 1857); entered the ministry of the Church of England, in which he remained until 1878, when he was received into the Roman Catholic Church. He has been a prolific literary worker, being especially interested in devotional literature and in religious poetry. Thus he has edited Luis of Granada's *Counsels on Holiness of Life* (London, 1862); J. B. E. Avrillon's *Eucharistic Meditations for a Month* (1862) and *Avrillon on the Holy Spirit* (1866); D. Bourdaloue's *Spiritual Exercises* (1868); A. de Guevara's *Mysteries of Mount Calvary* (1868); A. Stafford's *Life of the Blessed Virgin* (1869); Ignatius of Loyola's *Spiritual Exercises* (1870); and T. Carre's *Sweet Thoughts of Jesus and Mary* (1889). Of liturgical works he has edited, among others, *Eucharistic Litanies, from Ancient Sources* (1860), *The Daily Sacrifice* (1861), and *The Divine Liturgy* (1863), combining these in one (1868); *The Liturgies of 1549 and 1662* (1868); and *The Ritual of the Altar* (1870). In religious poetry he has edited *Lyra Eucharistica* (1863); *Lyra Messianica* (1864); *Lyra Mystica* (1865); *Annus Sanctus* (1884); and *Carmina Mariana* (2 vols., 1893–1902). In the way of collections of essays he has put forth *The Church and the World* (3 vols., 1866–68); *Tracts for the Day* (1867); *A Glossary of Ecclesiastical Terms* (1872); *Ecclesiastical Reform* (1873); *Studies in Modern Problems* (1874); and *Truthfulness and Ritualism* (1879–80). Independently he has published *Six Short Sermons on Sin* (1867); *Four Cardinal Virtues* (1871); *Secular Judgments in Spiritual Matters* (1871); *A Theory about Sin in Relation to Some Facts of Daily Life* (1875); and *Principles of the Faith* (1879).

SHIPP, ALBERT MICAJAH: Methodist Episcopal (South); b. in Stokes County, N. C., Jan. 15, 1819; d. at his home in Marlboro County, S. C., near Cheraw, June 27, 1887. He was graduated from the University of North Carolina, 1840; entered the ministry, 1841; became president of Greenborough Female College, N. C., 1847; professor of history and French in the University of North Carolina, 1849; president of Wofford College, Spartanburg Court-House, S. C., 1859; professor of exegetical and Biblical theology in Vanderbilt University, Nashville, Tenn., 1874; and dean of the theological faculty, and vice-chancellor of the university, 1882. He originated the policy of Biblical chairs for teaching the Bible to the whole body of students in all Methodist institutions of learning, and was one of the first advocates of Biblical institutes for the education of preachers for the Methodist Episcopal Church (South). He wrote *The History of Methodism in South Carolina* (Nashville, 1882).

SHISHAK. See EGYPT, I. 3, § 3; JEROBOAM; and REHOBOAM.

SHORE, THOMAS TEIGNMOUTH: Church of England; b. at Dublin Dec. 28, 1841. He was educated at Trinity College, Dublin (B.A., 1861), and was ordered deacon in 1865 and ordained priest in 1866. He was curate of St. Jude's, Chelsea (1865–1867), St. Paul's, Kensington (1867–69), and St. Peter's, Vere Street, London (1869–70), and incumbent of St. Mildred's, Lee (1870–73), and of Berkeley Chapel, Mayfair, London (1873–90). Since 1901 he has been canon of Worcester Cathedral. He was honorary chaplain to the Queen in 1878–81 and chaplain in ordinary in 1881–1901, and since 1901 he has been chaplain in ordinary to the king. He was religious instructor to the three daughters of King Edward VII. In theology he is a Broad churchman of the type of Maurice (whose curate he was at St. Peter's) and Kingsley. He has written *Some Difficulties of Belief* (London, 1877); *The Life of the World to Come* (1878); *St. George for England* (1882); *Worcester Cathedral* (1899); and *Auricular Confession and the Church of England* (1899), besides preparing the volume on I Corinthians for Bishop Ellicott's *Commentary* (1883) and on *Prayer* for the series of *Helps to Belief* (1886), of which he is the editor.

SHORTHAND AND CHURCH HISTORY. See STENOGRAPHY.

SHOWBREAD. See TEMPLE.

SHUCKFORD, SAMUEL: Church of England; b. at Norwich about 1694; d. at London July 14, 1754. He was educated at Caius College, Cambridge (B.A., 1716; M.A., 1720); was curate of Shelton, Norfolk, 1722–46; prebendary of Canterbury, from 1738; and rector of Allhallows, Lombard Street, London. He was the author of the famous work, *The Sacred and Profane History of the World Connected from the Creation of the World to the Dissolution of the Assyrian Empire at the Death of Sardanapalus, and to the Declension of the Kingdoms of Judah and Israel under the Reigns of Ahaz and Pekah* (2 vols., 1727; rev. ed. by J. T. Wheeler, 2 vols., London, 1858). This was intended to supplement Humphrey Prideaux's *Connection*, but was finished only to the death of Joshua.

BIBLIOGRAPHY: *DNB*, lii. 168, where references are given to scattered notices.

SHUEY, shū'ī, WILLIAM JOHN: United Brethren in Christ; b. at Miamisburg, O., Feb. 9, 1827. He was educated at the academy, Springfield, O.; was pastor at Lewisburg, O., 1849–51, Cincinnati, 1851–59; Dayton, O., 1860–62; presiding elder, 1862–64; and a member of the publishing house at Dayton, O., 1864–97, retiring in the last-named year. In 1855 he was engaged in the planting of a mission near Freetown, Sierra Leone, on the West Coast of Africa.

SHUSHAN: The Biblical name for the place now known as Sus or Shush in southwest Persia, anciently the capital of Elam, east of Babylonia. The Septuagint form of the name is *Sousa*, agreeing with the ordinary name Susa, Elamitic *Shushun*, Assyr. *Shushan*. The Greeks called the country of which it is the capital Susiana, and in the time of Herodotus (Rawlinson's *Herodotus*, i. 679, New York, 1875) it was called Kissia. Descendants, apparently of the inhabitants of Shushan, who had been transported to Samaria by the Assyrian king, are spoken of as Susanchites (Ezra iv. 19). The city is said to have been situated either on the river Ulæus (Dan. viii. 2; cf. Pliny vi. 27) or the Choaspes or Kherka (Herodotus, v. 49). Disputes about the location with reference to these rivers would probably be solved were the canal system of the early period well known. The Choaspes forked twenty miles above Susa, but connecting canals probably ran so as to make reconcilable the variant accounts of its location. The ruins which mark the site are located in 49° 48′ east longitude and 32° 10′ north latitude.

Mention of the city possibly appears as early as c. 2400 B.C. under the name Sas, Sisa, or Susun (probably meaning "the old" city, which suggests that it was already a place of considerable antiquity). In 2275 (if the report of Asshurbanipal be accepted) its king Kudur-nanḫundi invaded Babylon and carried away from Erech a statue of the goddess Nana (Ishtar; see BABYLONIA, VI., 1, § 1). In the period of their era of conquests the Assyrians repeatedly invaded Elam, and about 640 Asshurbanipal captured the city, recovered the image which (as he says) was carried away 1,635 years earlier, removed an immense treasure, and transplanted some of the people to Samaria. Under the Persian rule it became the winter residence, perhaps the chief capital, of the Achæmenides (cf. Xenophon, *Cyropædia*, VIII., vi. 22; Herodotus, iii. 30, 65, 70). The plot of the book of Esther is laid there in this period, and the story implies the presence of large numbers of Jews. Alexander took the city in 330, and is said to have found gold and silver amounting in value to sixty million dollars, together with great treasures in art, including the Praxitelean bronze statues of Harmodius and Aristogiton, liberators of Athens. Under the Seleucidæ (q.v.) the city lost importance, which it regained to some extent during the later reigns of the Arsacidæ down to 226 A.D. Then it declined, and was taken by the Mohammedans in 640. It practically disappeared from history after this and was heard of only at intervals.

The era of exploration was opened by W. K. Loftus in 1852, when trenches were dug, trilingual inscriptions of Artaxerxes Mnemon found at the base of certain columns bearing the names of three kings named Artaxerxes, and of Darius, as well as the divine names Ahuramazda, Anaitis, and Mithra. Marcel Dieulafoy in 1885 was enabled to reopen excavations there through the aid of a French physician at the Persian court and under the protection of the French government. This series of exploration resulted in the uncovering of part of the palace and other structures, and in settling the topographical details of the city. Other results were the recovery of features of art and architecture of great beauty and uniqueness, including the pillars with capitals of bulls' heads, three great porticoes and the hall of columns, the frieze of lions, and that of archers now in the Louvre. The still later exploration under J. de Morgan resulted (1901–02) in the discovery of the now famous Code of Hammurabi (see HAMMURABI AND HIS CODE).

BIBLIOGRAPHY: W. K. Loftus, *Travels and Researches in Chaldea and Susiana*, pp. 343 sqq., London and New York, 1857; F. Delitzsch, *Wo lag das Paradies?* Leipsic, 1881; Mme. Jane Dieulafoy, *La Perse, la Chaldée, et la Susiane*, Paris, 1887; M. Dieulafoy, *L'Art antique de la Perse*, Paris, 1889; idem, *L'Acropole de la Suse*, ib. 1890; J. F. McCurdy, *History, Prophecy and the Monuments*, i. 125–126, ii. 371–372, 385, New York, 1896; J. de Morgan, *Delegation en Perse*, vol. ii., Paris, 1901; B. T. Evetts, *New Light on the Bible and the Holy Land*, chap. ix., New York, n. d.; and Rawlinson's *Herodotus* (consult the Index).

SIAM AND LAOS: The kingdom of Siam includes an irregular stretch of territory in southeastern Asia, bounded by British Burma on the west, the French colonies of Cambodia, Anam, and Tonking on the northeast, and extending through more than half of the Malay peninsula to the south. The area is estimated at about 195,000 square miles, and the general physical features of the country include a rough upland in the north and two river valleys between high mountain ranges extending toward the south. The rainfall is abundant, and in their lower portions the rivers traverse immense alluvial plains which are to a considerable degree overflowed during a portion of the year, resulting in great fertility of the soil. The streams are only measurably navigable inasmuch as they are frequently broken by rapids. The climate is tropical, though less torrid than that of South India, and the year is divided into two seasons of about equal length, the rainy season extending from May to October, and the dry season covering the rest of the year.

The population is estimated at about 6,686,846, and belongs chiefly to the Shan race, about 1,000,000 being Chinese, Burmese, and others. The Shan population again is divided between the Siamese, occupying the southern portion of the kingdom, and the Laos, who are found in the north or hill country. The Siamese are the more polished and agreeable in manners, the Laos the more uncultured, but more sturdy and virile. The government is an absolute monarchy, although under the late king, Chulalongkorn, it became noted for its liberality and sympathy with aggressive modern improvements. Like other Asiatic countries, Siam has suffered from the aggression of European powers. The western coast was surrendered to the Burmese and subsequently to England. The French colonies on the east encroached gradually upon the territory of the Mekong river until it became a question whether the kingdom would continue intact. At present the entire kingdom is practically divided up between England and France, in so-called spheres of influence, England holding the general control of the northern Malay peninsula of the territory bordering on Burma, while France claims a corresponding influence along the whole valley of the Mekong.

There are few cities of importance, Bankok, the capital, being practically the only one widely known. The dominant religion, especially in the southern section, is Buddhism, and it is claimed to be the purest form of that faith except perhaps that in Ceylon. In no other country is it so completely identified with the life of the people. There is scarcely a family but is represented by at least one member in the priesthood, and not only its ceremonies but the social life and pleasures are under the control or auspices of the temples, while monasteries and pagodas with their vast number of priests are in evidence on every hand. In a measurable degree throughout Siam proper, and especially in the hill country to the north, demon worship is prevalent, a form of the Shamanism which is found throughout Asia and Africa. While brutal, especially in its terrifying power and in its relation to disease, it is not as fatal to vigor of life and thought as the Buddhism of the southern portion, and is more easily overcome by Christian influences, particularly as they approach it through the medium of medical aid.

The first missionary effort in Siam was in 1828, when Dr. Karl Friedrich August Gutzlaff (d. 1851) of the Netherlands Missionary Society visited Bankok with the special purpose of seeking an entrance to China. Through his representations, David Abeel of the American Board came to that city in 1830, but the first effective work was done by Dr. Daniel Beach Bradley, Rev. Jesse Caswell of the American Board, and Rev. William Dean of the American Baptist Missionary Union. Dean's work, chiefly among the Chinese, Dr. Bradley's medical work, and particularly the influence of Mr. Caswell, who was appointed by the king as tutor of his son, the late king of Siam, laid the foundation of the successful labors of succeeding years when the Presbyterian Board in 1848 entered the country and the American Board withdrew, preferring to put its strength into other fields. The early work was not productive of specific results, and it was not until 1859 that the first convert was baptized. Three years later a new station was opened to the south at Petchaburee, and shortly after a tour of exploration into the Laos states resulted in the establishment, in 1867, of mission work at Chieng Mai on the river MePing, about 500 miles north of Bankok. From the beginning this work gave promise of great success, and numerous stations have been established. Medical work was begun in 1875, and three years later a boarding-school for girls was opened, and one for boys in 1888. As the work among the distinctively Siamese Laos tribes has progressed, there has come to be a feeling that through them the Shan tribes to the east and north might probably be reached. Under French law no missionary effort can be carried on in the province of Tonking, but the members of the Laos churches, as they cross the border for business, are constantly coming into relations with the people and are carrying the Gospel in much the same way as the Christians did in the first century. Of late years the work in Siam proper has taken a new start and has met with greater success. A considerable amount of shore work is done by means of a vessel that touches at the different ports on the extended coast line, and from these points into the interior the influences are rapidly spreading.

One peculiarity of the mission work in this kingdom is that it is entirely under the care of one organization, the Board of Foreign Missions of the Presbyterian Church in the United States of America. There is thus not only a unity which is lacking in other fields, but a freedom from intervention and disintegrating influences. The statistics of the work for the year 1908–09 are as follows: Siam: Stations, 7; missionaries, 37 (10 ordained, 6 medical, 1 lay, 14 married women, 6 single women); native helpers, 41 (1 ordained preacher); churches, 9; communicants, 580; schools, 8; pupils, 660; in Sunday-schools, 805; contributions, $24,225. Laos: stations, 5; missionaries, 47 (16 ordained, 7 medical, 20 married women, 4 single women); native helpers, 92 (5 ordained preachers); churches, 18; communicants, 3,494; schools, 27; pupils, 781; in Sunday-schools, 2,843; contributions (incomplete), $11,369. Total: stations, 12; missionaries, 84; native helpers, 133; churches, 27; communicants, 4,074; schools, 35; pupils, 1,441; in Sunday-schools, 3,648; contributions, $35,594. EDWIN M. BLISS.

Modern exploration shows that the Shan race has spread in China in the province of Yunnan northward as far as 25° north latitude, westward as far as the Selwin River, and as far eastward as the province of Kwantung. So that over an area of 400,000 square miles the predominant element of the population is Laos. This involves the fact that on a most conservative estimate five millions of Laos are living in southern China, and raises the total of the race to about twelve millions using the Laos language. This fact is of importance for the diffusion of Christian literature in that tongue.

BIBLIOGRAPHY: E. Young, *The Kingdom of the Yellow Robe: Sketches of the domestic and religious Rites of the Siamese*, London, 1898; P. A. Thompson, *Lotus Land; Account of the Country and the People of Southern Siam*, ib. 1906; C. Gutzlaff, *Ausführlicher Bericht von seinem dreijährigen Aufenthalt in Siam*, Elberfeld, 1838; J. B. Pallegoix, *Description du royaume Thai ou Siam*, 2 vols., Paris, 1854; Sir John Bowring, *Kingdom and People of Siam*, 2 vols., London, 1857; Mrs. F. R. Feudge, *Eastern Side; or, missionary Life in Siam*, Philadelphia, 1871; B. Taylor, *Siam*, New York, 1881; *Siam and Laos as Seen by our American Missionaries*, Philadelphia, 1884; A. R. Colquhoun, *Among the Shans*, London, 1885; Miss M. L. Cort, *Siam*, New York, 1886; H. W. Smith, *Five Years in Siam, 1891–96*, 2 vols., ib. 1898; J. G. D. Campbell, *Siam in the 20th Century*, London, 1902; Lillian J. Curtis, *Laos of North Siam*, Philadelphia, 1903; A. Wright and O. T. Breakspear, *Twentieth Century Impressions of Siam. Its History, People, Commerce, Industries and Resources*, London, 1909; J. H. Freeman, *An Oriental Land of the Free; or Life and Mission Work among the Laos of Siam, Burma, China, and Indo China*, Philadelphia, 1910; P. A. Thompson, *Siam; an Account of the Country and the People*, Boston, 1911.

SIBBES, sibz (**SIBBS, SIBS**), **RICHARD**: Puritan; b. at Tostock (33 m. e. of Cambridge), Suffolk, 1577; d. at Gray's Inn, London, July 5, 1635. He was successively student and fellow of St. John's College, and lecturer of Trinity Church, Cambridge (B.A., 1599; M.A., 1602; B.D., 1610); preacher of Gray's Inn, London, 1617–26; master of Catharine Hall, Cambridge, from 1626; and perpetual curate of Holy Trinity, Cambridge, from 1633. His best-known works are, *The Bruised Reede and Smoaking Flax* (London, 1630), to which Richard Baxter owed his conversion; *The Soul's Conflict* (1635); *The Returning Backslider* (1639); and *A Learned Commentary upon the First Chapter of the Second Epistle of St. Paul to the Corinthians*, ed. Thomas Manton (1655). His literary activity was, however, much more extensive than this, thirty-three titles of books and sermons being known. His *Complete Works* were published with memoir by A. B. Grosart (6 vols., 1862–63).

BIBLIOGRAPHY: Besides the principal memoir by Grosart, the reader may consult the *Life* by E. Middleton, in 9th ed. of *The Bruised Reede*, London, 1808; that in a new ed. of Sibbes's *Divine Meditations*, Newport, 1799 (ed. G. Burder); and one by S. Clarke in *The Soules Conflict*, Glasgow, 1768. Also: T. Fuller, *Hist. of the Worthies of England*, ed. J. Fuller, 4 parts, London, 1662; Samuel Clark, *Lives of Thirty-two English Divines*, 3d ed., ib. 1670; B. Brooke, *Lives of the Puritans*, ii. 416 sqq., ib. 1813; *DNB*, lii. 182–184.

SIBEL, sai'bel, **KASPAR**: Dutch Reformed; b. at Unterbarmen (a part of Barmen, 26 m. n. of

Cologne) June 9, 1590; d. at Deventer, Holland, Jan. 1, 1658. He was educated at Herborn, Siegen, and Leyden, and, after preaching to various congregations, was called, in 1609, to be minister of the churches of Randerath and Geilenkirchen in the principality of Jülich, the oversight of the church at Linnich soon being added to his duties. Sibel met with extraordinary success at Randerath, where he labored exposed to considerable personal peril from the attempts of Roman Catholics to regain their position. He was a delegate to the Reformed convention at Düren (Aug. 17, 1610) to organize the first general synod of the lower Rhine (see REFORMED [DUTCH] CHURCH); and later was deputized to attend the other synods. He accepted in 1611 a call to Jülich, where, in addition to his regular duties, he had to minister to the Protestants in the surrounding district, while during an outbreak of the plague he proved himself a true pastor in the face of death. In 1617, on his return from a journey to Holland, he accepted a call to Deventer, especially as he realized that the strife then raging in Jülich-Cleve-Berg was but the prelude to the long civil war which was to devastate Germany. At Deventer he found himself in his element, and his influence quickly spread beyond the limits of the city. He took part in the preparations for the Synod of Dort, to which he was a deputy; and at his instance the estates of Overyssel approved the canons of Dort and rejected the five Arminian articles. Still more important was his activity as a member of the committee for the new Dutch translation of the Bible proposed by the Synod of Dort. As one of the revisers, he was chosen vice-secretary of the board of revision, which sat for eleven months in Leyden, and for three years he essentially furthered the work. He was active also in providing capable teachers for the school in Deventer, but at the same time maintained close relations with his native country, inducing the states general to threaten reprisals against any interference with Protestant services in Jülich-Berg, and otherwise aiding his coreligionists.

In 1647 a stroke of apoplexy forced Sibel to retire from active life. As a preacher he enjoyed high reputation, being known as the Chrysostom of his locality, and his sermons up to 1644 were collected under the title of *Caspari Sibelii opera theologica* (5 parts, Amsterdam, 1644). In homiletics, while he paid due regard to form and arrangement, he was especially concerned with the subject matter. He was also much given to exposition of a passage in a sermon series. Among his other works, special mention may be made of his *Meditationes catecheticæ* (4 parts, Amsterdam, 1646–50) and of his autobiographical *Historica narratio de curriculo totius vitæ et peregrinationis meæ*, of which two manuscript volumes are preserved in the Deventer library (the part before 1609 ed. L. Scheibe, in *Festschrift zur Feier des dreihundertjährigen Bestehens der . . . lateinischen Schule zu Elberfeld*, Elberfeld, 1893).

(EDUARD SIMONS.)

BIBLIOGRAPHY: Besides the autobiographical *Historica narratio*, ut sup., consult *ADB*, vol. xxxiv.; *Zeitschrift des Berg. Geschichtsvereins*, vol. xxviii (by W. Harless, on *Elberfelder Kirchen*) and also vol. iv (by Bouterwek, on *Die Reformation in Wupperthal*).

SIBYL, SIBYLLINE BOOKS.

Among the productions of late Jewish and early Christian literature the Sibylline Oracles have special interest because of their manifold relations with the Roman-Greek system of oracles. The sibyls of Greek and Roman antiquity were prophetesses who, now here, now there, uttered their denunciatory predictions, of which what remains, however, is but the dying echoes of the former activity. There were possibly in Greece in the eighth and seventh centuries B.C. Cassandra-like figures uttering from city to city their dread prophecies to the terror of men; the home of this art seems to have been Asia Minor, the earliest reports implying Erythrea and Samos as the centers. Later reports know of a Delphian sibyl, a sister of Apollo named Artemis. In Rome the sibyl came only at the end of the regal period from the Greek colonies of southern Italy. The oriental sibyls become known first after Alexander, mainly in Asia Minor, where East and West met and women's part in religion was prominent. But all knowledge of these characters is dim and vague; they appear as prophetesses, not as personalities, and gave their name to a large pseudonymous literature in the apocalyptic period of Jewish development.

1. The Greek Sibyls.

The earliest writer to give the names of a series of sibyls is Heraclides Ponticus (cited by Clement of Alexandria, *Strom.*, I., xxi., *ANF*, ii. 325), who speaks of a Phrygian-Delphian sibyl Artemis and a Heraclean called Herophile. Later the list of sibyls grows, and they are known at Delphi, Erythrea, Sardis, and Cumæ, while Clement of Alexandria (ut sup.) speaks of an Egyptian and a Roman sibyl; Suidas knows of nine; Varro notes ten: a Persian, a Libyan, a Delphian, a Cimmerian (in Italy), the Erythrean, the Samian, the Cumæan (Amalthea), the Hellespontian, the Phrygian, and the Tiburtine named Albunea. To this Varronian catalogue there are a number of witnesses, e.g., Lactantius (*Institutes*, I., vi., *ANF*, vii. 15–16; worth consulting) and Isidore of Seville (in his *Originum . . . libri*, VIII., viii.), as well as a series of later authorities. Some of the lists contain variations, however, notably that by an anonymous writer who composed an introduction to the collection of the Jewish-Christian Sibylline Books (i.–viii.) and that in a series of excerpts of the fifth century known as the "Tübingen Theosophy." The report of Pausanias regarding the sibyls (X., xii.) has especial interest, representing an attempt to reduce the number of these prophetesses to four, viz., the Libyan, Herophile (to whom he refers all reports regarding the Greek sibyls), the Cumæan whom he names Demo, and the Hebrew-Babylonian-Egyptian whom he names

2. Lists of Sibyls.

Sabbe. But of all those mentioned in these lists, most of whom are hardly anything more than literary fictions, the oldest and best attested is the Erythrean, for whose existence Varro cites the testimony of the chronographer Apollodorus. The grotto of the sibyl mentioned by Pausanias was rediscovered in 1891, in which an inscription dealing with the sibyl tells of her wonderful birth, of her delivery of oracles immediately thereafter, and of her age as already 900 years. Eusebius in his Chronicle places her appearance in the ninth olympiad; an old tradition is known which places her origin in the eighth pre-Christian century. Next to her the sibyl of Samos is best attested, according to Varro, by Eratosthenes, who found mention of her in the Samian annals, while Eusebius places her in the first year of the seventeenth olympiad (711 B.C.). According to early testimony the Cumæan sibyl was, so to speak, a branch of the Erythrean; and this is supported by the name given in the Varro-Lactantius list (ut sup.). Belief in the Cumæan sibyl at Rome goes back to the end of the kingly period, when her oracles had importance for the State. After the destruction of the collection of oracles by the burning of the temple of Jupiter in 83 B.C., a new collection was sought, particularly from Erythrea. The author of the Pseudo-Justinian *Cohortatio* (chap. xxxvii.) has left an interesting description of the grotto of the Cumæan sibyl, who was identified with the river and oracle deity Carmenta. Another sibyl had her sanctuary near the Tiber on the Anio, and under her proper name of Albunea was called the Tiburtine sibyl. Concerning the Babylonian sibyl Pausanias reports (X., xii.) that there was a "Hebrew" sibyl named Sabbe, daughter of Berosus and Erymanthe. The *Cohortatio* (x.) identifies her with the Cumæan prophetess. Moses of Chorene (q.v.; in *Historiæ Armeniacæ*, i. 5) speaks of a more highly credited Berosian sibyl; the Veronian catalogue mentions a Persian prophetess of whom Nicanor, Alexander's biographer, speaks; later reports seem to regard these as the same, and the original source of Varro probably rightly brought together the three—Babylonian, Persian, and the Hebrew, the last the daughter of Noah—and the process of shortening the list went on in the anonymous introduction to the Sibylline Books already named and in the "Tübingen Theosophy." The age of the foundation of these reports is not sure, but they may go back to Alexander Polyhistor (early in the first century B.C.). The so-called Babylonian sibyl in these notices is no other than the assumed Hebrew sibyl; but this does not account for her name, Sambethe or Sabbe, nor for the report that she was the daughter of Berosus, nor for her designation as Babylonian. An inscription (in *CIG*, 3509) seems to refer to an oracle-sanctuary of the Chaldean Sambethe. If a Chaldean (Babylonian) Sambethe-sanctuary is proved, the tradition of such a sibyl seems to have history behind it; such a prophetess would naturally be Hellenistic and would write in Greek, and would not unnaturally be connected with Berosus the historian.

This was the ground in which grew the crop of Jewish sibylline poetry. In Egypt began the great Jewish diaspora mission; there the Jews appropriated Greek culture, philosophy, and the forms of Greek literature, and sought through them to recommend Jewish culture to the Greeks. Jewish chronographers attempted to show a greater antiquity for their race; Jews first sought and then fabricated testimony of Greeks to prove the latter indebted to Moses for the best of their wisdom, and used the sibylline literature as a means, putting in the sibyl's mouth utterances regarding the Jewish people, the Jewish deity, the conversion of the gentiles, and the coming golden age. And the Christians imitated them, but with less success. The Church Fathers accepted these writings at their face value (so Justin, Athenagoras, Theophilus, Clement of Alexandria, Lactantius, and Augustine). With the downfall of heathendom, these were less used, but were still employed till late in the Middle Ages. The most of this literature was collected by diligent hands and has survived, and into it a sort of unity has been worked. Two or three groups of collections stand out, presenting types of text. One group (designated as Φ) consists of books i.–viii. 485; a second (Ψ) has viii. and i.–vii.; a third (Ω) has vi., vii. 1, viii. 218–428 numbered ix., iv. numbered x., and then xi.–xiv., the whole a continuation of the existing collection of eight books. The date of these collections is probably between the beginning of the fourth and the middle of the fifth century. Of printed editions the older ones may be mentioned—Xystus Betuleius (1545), S. Castalio (1555), Opsopœus (1599), Gallæus (1689), Gallandi (*Bibliotheca veterum patrum*, vol. i., Venice, 1788), and Friedlieb (Leipsic, 1852). Of abiding value is the great edition of C. Alexandre (*Oracula sibyllina*, 2 vols., Paris, 1841–56); A. Rzach's *Oracula sibyllina* (Vienna, 1891) uses the manuscripts for a modern reconstruction of the text; but much better is J. Geffcken's edition (Leipsic, 1902).

3. Jewish-Christian Sibylline Writings.

Of all these writings the oldest, most important, and richest in contents is iii. 97–829, falling into three divisions, 97–294, 295–488, 489–795 (796–829 being merely concluding remarks). The first deals with the building of the tower of Babel, the wars of the sons of Saturn and the Titans, a brief review of world history, prediction of the Solomonic realm till the emergence of the Romans, and the seventh king of Egypt, and a noteworthy description of Israel from Moses till the return from exile. The second part is a series of oracles on the nations: Babylon, Egypt, Ethiopia, Libya, the West, a number of cities, Macedonia, Asia, Phrygia, Ilium (and a polemic against Homer); then a cento of mingled predictions. The third contains a preaching of repentance to the Greeks humiliated by the Romans, the story of the coming fortunes of the Jews, judgment to come on the outer world, the Messianic kingdom and the vain war against it, preaching of repentance again, and a picture of the future blessedness. Three times the seventh kingdom (king) of Egypt appears (192–193, 314–318, 608–615), construed as referring to Ptolemy VII. Physcon, and doubt is expressed whether this is to be dated 170–164 or 145–117; many date the book c. 140 B.C. But account must be taken of the

4. Book iii.

possibility of the inclusion of earlier pieces, the correct apprehension of which makes possible another dating, dependent upon a different interpretation of certain intruded parts. But at any rate, this part must have arisen in the Maccabean period, for the condition described is that of the independent Jewish state while the preaching is directed against the Romans who have subjected Hellenism. Yet a late part of the Maccabean time is indicated, since 470 sqq. points to Sulla and his Asian campaign, and 350 sqq. deals with the war against Mithridates c. 88 B.C., quoting an oracle on the affair. Since the author uses these documents, he must have written after 88 B.C., probably in the time of Queen Alexandra. He worked, as did the apocalyptical writers, only in part with his own material, for the most part taking over existing matter. Probably his own composition is to be found in iii. 211–294, which describes the Jewish people, of which 271–272 especially fits the Jewish diaspora of Alexandra's period. This part is, however, closely related to the passage 520–795, which accordingly also may be regarded as the Jewish writer's own. Whether the sermon to the Greeks belongs here is doubtful, as it fits equally well with the times of Sulla and of the Mithridatic war, the one indication of a later date being its advanced eschatology. Probably to the same author are to be ascribed lines 162–166, 194–210, 295–336, 489–519—all of them introductions to longer sections, — and with some probability the entire conclusion; also in general 156–166, 196–294, 489–795 except 608–615.

5. Use of Older Material.

There are also older pieces from the time of Ptolemy VII. worked into the composition of the whole—so 167–195, 314–318, 608–615. This writer has also taken into his work a series of heathen oracles, a process which he deemed suitable to impress the non-Jewish world. There is express testimony from heathen sources (Varro, Bocchus, and Pausanias) to a tradition that the Erythrean (Delphian) sibyl foretold the fall of Ilium and charged Homer with lies and plagiarism of her verses (cf. iii. 414–432 of the present collection); the preceding oracle concerning Phrygia makes the impression of being derived from a heathen source, as does 381–387, there being testimony that the Persian (Chaldean) sibyl spoke concerning Alexander; similarly the oracle against Rome (350 sqq.) is not in the style of the present writer, but is heathen and of great political interest; so the early sibylline characteristics shine out of lines 337–349, 433–438. In these passages oracles of various heathen sources seem to have been collected and arranged in artistic fashion. Such a borrowing appears in the early part of this book—105–154 is unmistakably gentile; in Lactantius (*Institutes*, I., xiv. 2) there is a parallel to the Euhemeristic turn of thought in the conflict between the Kronides and Titans. But this passage is in close connection with that concerning the tower of Babel, and the speaker as sibyl identifies herself with the older sibyl (iii. 809 sqq.); it would be expected almost that this speaker would use earlier prophecies; and Alexander Polyhistor (Eusebius, *Chronicon*, I., xxiii.), Josephus (*Ant.*, I., iv. 3), and Abydenus (Eusebius, *Chronicon*, I., xxxiii.–xxxiv.) cite an oracle in heathen form on this subject. The original sibyl may have derived the story from Hebrew tradition or from folklore. This book then seems to come from the time of Queen Alexandra, and uses older fragments of Jewish origin, and of heathen origin from the Erythrean and other Greek oracles. The lines 211–294 and 520–795 are valuable for the religious situation at the end of the Maccabean period.

6. Introduction to Book iii.

In iii. 1–95 two hands are apparent, 46–62 and 63–92 showing distinct differences. The first belongs in the period of the first triumvirate, according to the usual dating; but in 46–50 a Christian seems to speak. With 46–62 may possible be placed 1–45, a Christian editing of c. 70 A.D. The passage 63–92 is more difficult to date, but may belong to c. 25 B.C., since Sebaste is to be the source of Antichrist. But it might refer to Simon Magus, and so be as late as the second half of the first century. The mention of the widow has been especially puzzling, since it can no longer be taken to mean Cleopatra. The first and second books must be taken into account in fixing the date; they were the first to assume a unity and then to form two books; this appears in the manuscripts of Φ, which call books i. and ii. "the first *logos*," of which book iii. was "the second." Books i.–ii. are outlined in i. 1–323, and were to set forth the fortune of the world in ten families, of which only seven appear, the last three being removed in the working over. This part, generally recognized as of Jewish origin, was separated into two parts by an editor of expressly Christian character. But the dates of these separate editings are not easy to determine; estimates vary from the beginning of the Christian era till the third Christian century, the later dating being based upon the doubtful datum of the existence of the masculine cæsura. Other indications adduced are equally elusive. The ruin predicted in the third book at the beginning agrees with the origin of the basal writing of books i.–ii. Book i. handles the theme which in all probability was treated in the part broken off when iii. was added—viz., creation and the flood; in i. there are echoes of the Babylonian version of the flood (lines 230–260), showing that the report of the flood from book i. was once at least in book iii., and, like iii. 96–154, depended upon the Babylonian Sambethe. The manuscripts indicate 1,034 lines for book iii., of which only 829 (895) are extant, an indication which shows the extent of the piece broken off from the beginning of book iii.

7. Books i.–ii.

It is probable that iii. 46–62 and 63–92 were introduced subsequent to the compilation of the rest of the book; if then 46–92 belongs to the period c. 70 A.D., the destruction of the beginning of book iii. and the rise of the basis of books i.–ii. are prior to that date. The section ii. 167–176 is a part of the Christian redaction. In which the theme is the return of the twelve tribes from the East to take vengeance upon the "Assyrian prince." This theme is a favorite in the late Jewish apocalyptic writings, as in IV Esdras, the Syriac Baruch, and other writings dating from the end of the first Christian century into the third century. In this third-century apologetic the prediction of the Antichrist Beliar is prominent. The "Assyrian prince" who persecuted the Jews can scarcely be any other than Odenatus, king of Palmyra, against whom the predictions of book xiii. are directed, who also in the Apocalypse of Elias appears as the chief Antichrist opposed to Judaism. This places the redaction of books i.–ii. in the second half of the third century. But iii. 63–92 is related to ii. 167 sqq., and the editor of book ii. and writer of iii. 63 sqq. must have been the same person or have belonged to the same environment; the widow of iii. 77–78 must be Zenobia of Palmyra, who reigned after Odenatus. To this same environment belongs book viii., which is a conglomerate of pieces of varied character. Lines 1-216 are early, before the death of Marcus Aurelius, the last part much edited, however; 217–250 is an acrostic (on the Greek *Iesous Chreistos theou huios soter stauros*), and is followed by a Christological section 251–323, and this by a medley, the whole style of which recalls the editor of books i.–ii., whole series of lines being repeated from the one in the other, especially as dealing with the destruction of the world by fire, the purification by the same means, etc. If the editors of these parts are not the same, their methods and the time in which they worked were close together. Possibly this editor wrote viii. 169–177. The editor of books i.–ii., the author of iii. 63–92, and the compiler of book viii. in its present form are (is) to be placed in the time of Odenatus and Zenobia or immediately after Zenobia's death.

8. Books iv., v., viii.

A second group of connected pieces is composed of books iv., v., and the oldest part of book viii., and in situation this group builds around book iv., which is Jewish. The fact that temple and sacrificial offerings are past (lines 27–28) is explained by the fact that after the fall of the Temple the Jews soon lost the idea of sacrifice. In consequence of the fall of Jerusalem, the writer hates Rome and Italy, and must have written soon after 79 A.D., and looks for the return of Nero for revenge on Rome, thus giving the earliest testimony for the Nero saga. In 49–114 the compiler has used an older and probably Greek oracle—97-98 is attested by Strabo. The ten families (ut sup.) reappear here, and this section may be pre-Christian. Toward the end the burning of the world reappears, with the resurrection of the dead. Book v. is difficult, though critics agree that the basis is Jewish, while there is question as to its origin from one hand. The section 1–51, a tedious and uninteresting enumeration of the Roman emperors till Hadrian, by its character demands a different authorship from the rest. Three sections, 137–178, 214–285, 361–446, seem to be closely related to each other, and present three themes—the returning Nero, threats against Rome, and the New Jerusalem. A fourth section is found in 93–110, the subject of which is also Nero and his return. These all seem to have arisen out of practically the same situation, and the author's anger against Rome is roused by his experience in the destruction of the Temple, while he looks for a New Jerusalem with its new Temple. The varying character of the picture of Nero, now human now ghostly, may come from the changing moods of the author, who was influenced also by the heathen oracles which he has embodied; he lived within a generation after the fall of Jerusalem. Out of a similar situation (or the same) arose Rev. xvii.–xviii., xxi. In the rest of book v. are sayings which betray the Egyptian type. Especially characteristic is the section 484–510, which undoubtedly points to the Jewish temple in Leontopolis (see LEONTOPOLIS); the conception in this part, that a great temple is in the future to be built in Egypt, is intelligible when it is remembered that the Leontopolis temple stood until 73 A.D. An Egyptian Jew expected its reconstruction, and its destruction in the last period before the great judgment. Whether the remaining pieces, to be characterized broadly as Egyptian, are by the author of the Nero pieces is not to be decided categorically; he may have been the first to incorporate them in a work, and he may have imitated the older portions. The book looks like the work of one redactor, begun in the reign of Marcus Aurelius, with interpolations by a Christian. In this same connection belongs viii.1–216, dealing with the returning Nero, the author of which was a Christian who wrote near the end of Marcus Aurelius' reign and took into his work a number of older sayings, though the form has in some cases been considerably changed.

9. Books vi., vii., xi.–xiv.

Books vi. and vii. belong together. Both are by Christian authors, but their type is apocryphal or heretical. Book vi. is anti-Jewish, is written in praise of the Son of God, is adoptionistic, and stresses the baptism of Jesus. Its date is doubtful, but it may have been known to the editor of books i.–ii. The author of book vii. was probably born a Jew, wrote in imitation of earlier sibylline writers, and where he is independent is quite interesting (e.g., 64–95, 118–162). His Christology is heretical in color, but he adheres to the logos type of Christology; he may have been a Jewish-Christian Gnostic, and possibly wrote c. 150 A.D. Books xi.–xiv. have a certain unity. Book xi. is the oldest, Jewish in origin, and has been regarded as edited in the third Christian century, though that seems too late as his work would have little meaning for that time. He pictures the age of Cleopatra and the end of the Egyptian kingdom, but his prophecies are worthless; more likely he belongs to Augustan times. Book xii., picturing in quiet narrative the Roman emperors from Augustus to Alexander Severus, can not have emanated from a Christian, but must be by a Jew, loyal to the empire, not orthodox, but cosmopolitan, living after Alexander Severus. As an oriental regarding the empire, he is often interesting in his views. But lines 28–34 must have been adapted by a Christian who dealt with the birth of Christ. Book xiii., starting in where xii. leaves off, is exceedingly interesting. It carries on the story from Alexander Severus to Gallienus. Possibly recognizable forms are Gordian I., and III., Philip the Arabian and his son, Gallius, Æmilius Æmilianus, Aurelian, and Gallienus. Odenatus is the savior who is born of the sun, and is the lion who slays the Persian shepherd and the Roman usurpers. It has been suspected that the interpolator of book xii. is the editor of xiii.; in that case he worked over xi.–xii. with his own collection. In this time originated the Hebrew and probably the basis of the Coptic Elijah apocalypse, while it was also the period of the editor of books i., ii., and viii. of Commodian's *Carmen apologeticum*, and the apocalyptic sayings of Lactantius (ut sup.). The Christian sibyllist makes a hero of Odenatus, the Jewish Apocalyptist makes him an antimessiah. Book xiv. is by an ignorant man who essays to give a sketch of Roman imperial history but is hopelessly confused; possibly he wrote in the awful times which swept over Egypt [*sic*] after the time of the death of Odenatus and Zenobia, and he was hardly a Jew. His work is a polemic against evil, rapacious, and godless kings. The "holy nation" of line 360 refers not to the Jews but to Christians.

Theophilus of Antioch (*Ad Autolycum*, ii. 36; Eng. transl. in *ANF*, ii. 109) gives two citations from a beginning of the sibylline books which exalt the true God and chide idolatry. The general view is that Theophilus has quoted from the early introduction to book iii., but Geffcken (ut sup.) sees in the fragments an elaboration of the present introduction to iii., and would derive them from an anthology from verses devoted to an apologetic purpose, supporting this by the facts that in the following chapter Theophilus is dependent upon such a work and that Clement of Alexandria cites some verses of this fragment (*Strom.*, V., xiv.), derived from an anthology (Elter, *De gnomologiorum Græcorum historia atque origine*, Bonn, 1894-95; university program). There are facts against this conclusion, however, such as the one that Lactantius must have regarded these verses as belonging to the proem of book iii. And, in spite of Geffcken's claim that they are of Christian origin, there is nothing which goes against a Jewish derivation, though not from the author of book iii. Under the name of the Tiburtine sibyl is a confused mass of sayings from the Middle Ages which has been again and again subjected to the process of editing. The development of this body of material has been worked out well by E. Sackur (*Sibyllinische Text und Forschungen*, Halle, 1898), the source of the Tiburtine sibyl being traced to a nucleus dating soon after the death of Constantius I. (361 A.D.). But a further history is suggested by R. Basset (*Les Apocryphes éthiopiens*, vol. x., *La Sagesse de Sibylle*, Paris, 1899), who makes it evident that the material which he publishes and the Tiburtine sibyl go back to a common source, dealing with nine ages of the world. The Arabic-Ethiopian sibyl is known also in a redaction of the period of Harun al-Rashid. The basal document may go back to the end of the third century, the period when metrical sibylline oracles passed over into prose. Even in the Middle Ages the sibyl remained a popular figure, cf. the opening lines of the poem *Dies iræ, dies illa, solvet sæclum in favilla, teste David cum Sibylla*. On Byzantine and medieval sibylline literature cf. F. Kampers, *Die deutsche Kaiseridee in Prophetie und Sage*, Munich, 1896. (W. Bousset.)

10. Other Collections.

Bibliography. The principal texts are noted in § 3 above. Add. P. Heitz's ed., after a MS. of St. Gall, Strasburg, 1903, with *Einleitung* by W. L. Schreiber; and the Eng. transl. in blank verse by M. S. Terry, New York, 1890.

For questions of introduction and exegesis consult: Bleek, in *Theologische Zeitschrift*, i (1819), 120-246, ii (1820), 172-239; G. Besançon, *De l'emploi que les pères de l'église ont fait des oracles sibyllins*, Paris, 1851; A. Hilgenfeld, *Die jüdische Apokalyptik in ihrer geschichtlichen Entwickelung*, pp. 51-90, Jena, 1857; H. Ewald, *Abhandlung über Entstehung . . . der sibyllinischen Bücher*, Göttingen, 1858; J. Langen, *Das Judenthum in Palästina zur Zeit Christi*, pp. 169-174, Freiburg, 1866; B. Badt, *De oraculis Sibyllinis*, Breslau, 1869; idem, *Ursprung, Inhalt, und Text des vierten Buches der sibyllinischen Orakel*, ib. 1878; H. Dechent, *Ueber das erste, zweite und elfte Buch der sibyllinischen Weissagungen*, Frankfort, 1873; M. Vernes, *Hist. des idées messianiques*, pp. 43 sqq., Paris, 1874; J. Drummond, *Jewish Messiah*, pp. 14 sqq., London, 1877; A. C. Bang, *Voluspà und die sibyllinischen Orakel*, Vienna, 1880; A. Bouché-Leclerc, *Hist. de la divination dans l'antiquité*, ii. 199-214, Paris, 1880; V. H. Stanton, *The Jewish and the Christian Messiah*, Edinburgh, 1886; T. Zahn, in *TKW*, 1886, pp. 32-45, 77-87; K. Buresch, *Klaros*, Leipsic, 1889; H. Diels, *Sibyllinische Blätter*, Berlin, 1890; S. A. Hirsch, in *JQR*, ii (1890), 406-429; W. J. Deane, *Pseudepigrapha*, 276 sqq., Edinburgh, 1891; J. E. H. Thompson, *Books which Influenced our Lord and his Apostles*, pp. 167-169, ib. 1891; E. Fehr, *Studia in oracula Sibyllina*, Upsala, 1893; M. Friedländer, in *REJ*, xxix (1894), 183-196; idem, *Geschichte der jüdischen Apologetik*, pp. 31-54, Zurich, 1903; W. Bousset, *Der Antichrist*, pp. 59-63 et passim, Göttingen, 1895; idem, in *ZNTW*, 1902, pp. 23 sqq.; E. Rohde, *Psyche*, pp. 62-69, 2d ed., Freiburg, 1898; E. Kautzsch, *Die Apokryphen und Pseudepigraphen*, ii. 177 sqq., Tübingen, 1900 (Germ. transl. with introduction and notes); O. Zöckler, *Die Apokryphen des A. Ts.*, pp. 477-484, Munich, 1901; J. Geffcken, *Komposition und Entstehungszeit des Oracula Sibyllina*, Leipsic, 1902; idem, in *TU*, viii. 1 (1903); E. Oldenburger, *De oraculorum Sibyllinorum elocutione*, Rostock, 1903; E. Hennecke, *Handbuch der neutestamentlichen Apokryphen*, pp. 339-350, Tübingen, 1904; M. Monteiro, "*As David and the Sibyls say*," *a Sketch of the Sibyls and the Sibylline Oracles*, London, 1905; A. Rzach, *Analekta zur Kritik und Exegese der sibyllinischen Orakel*, Vienna, 1907; J. Schleifer, *Die Erzählung der Sibylle. Eine Apocryphische, nach den karschunischen, arabischen und äthiopischen Handschriften zu London*, ib. 1908; Schürer, *Geschichte*, iii. 421-450, Eng. transl., II., iii. 271-291 (excellent list of literature at end of German text); Harnack, *Litteratur*, i. 861-863, ii. 581-589; *DB*, i. 743, iii. 227, extra vol., pp. 66-68; *EB*, i. 245-250; *JE*, xi. 319-323.

SICARII, si-kē'ri-ai or si-ca'ri-ī (Lat. "Assassins"): The term applied to Jewish zealots before and during the Jewish war, whose aim was to drive the Romans from the country. The name comes from *sica*, "a small dagger," which they concealed under their cloaks, using it during assemblies or pilgrimages to kill their enemies, including Jews who were friendly to the Romans (Josephus, *Ant.*, XX., viii. 10; *War*, II., xiii. 3). The most prominent of their victims was the high priest Jonathan, said to have been slain at the instigation of Felix the governor of Judea.

Bibliography: Schürer, *Geschichte*, i. 574 sqq., 584, Eng. transl., 178 sqq., 189.

SICKENBERGER, sik'en-berн"-er, **JOSEPH:** German Roman Catholic; b. at Kempten (81 m. s.w. of Munich) Mar. 19, 1872. He was educated at the University of Munich (D.D., 1900) and also studied in Italy, Vienna, and Paris. In 1902 he became privat-docent at Munich, where he was appointed associate professor of patrology and Christian archeology in the following year. In 1905 he was called to Würzburg as full professor of the same subject, and since 1906 has been professor of New-Testament exegesis and theology at Breslau. He has written *Titus von Bostra, Studien zu dessen*

Lukashomilien (Leipsic, 1901); *Die Lukaskatene des Niketas von Herakleia* (1902); and has edited *Fragmente und Homilien des Cyrill von Alexandrien zum Lukasevangelium*, in *TU*, 1909; besides being New-Testament editor of the *Biblische Zeitschrift*.

SICKINGEN, FRANZ VON: Knight of the German Empire, and protector of the Reformers; b. in the castle of Ebernburg, near Kreuznach (21 m. s.w. of Mainz), May 1, 1481; d. in the castle of Landstuhl, near Zweibrücken (60 m. s.w. of Heidelberg), May 7, 1523. He was a picturesque representative of the "robber knights" who recognized no superior but their monarch, and enjoyed no occupation so much as that of private warfare. These knights had serious grievances in the early part of the sixteenth century. Growth of commerce and wealth in the cities had been accompanied by agricultural depression, and the knights found their estates becoming valueless and their incomes reduced to almost nothing. They were free to renounce the station and prestige of the order of knighthood and as common civilians and soldiers to enter the service of the emperor; the alternative was wholesale brigandage. Sickingen chose the alternative. Desirous of serving the emperor as with independent authority, this order was opposed to any approximation to orderly government, and considered the territorial princes its sworn enemies. The reforms of the national government, which through the Reichskammergericht (supreme court of the empire) forbade private warfare and installed Roman law in the place of the old feudal customs, endangered this calling, and in 1522 the general discontent broke out, under the leadership of Sickingen, into open repudiation of the actions and authority of the Reichskammergericht.

In Sickingen the revolters recognized an experienced and energetic leader. He had in 1516 made a raid upon the city of Worms, and for five years, in the face of a decree of banishment issued against him, had harassed and ravaged the country around the city; he had been in the service of Francis I. of France in 1516, and in 1517 had entered that of the German Empire; he had carried on operations against the imperial city of Metz, and against Landgrave Philip of Hesse; and with Ulrich von Hutten (q.v.) he had thrown himself into the cause of Charles V. of Spain. He had proffered aid to Reuchlin in his controversy, and with Hutten had frankly declared his approval of Luther, to whom he pledged his assistance. Butzer (q.v.) lived in his castle, the Ebernburg, where Œcolampadius (q.v.) served as chaplain from Apr. to Nov., 1522, and Johann Schwebel (q.v.) was another Reformer who found refuge with him.

Hutten and Sickingen regarded as urgent and necessary a restriction upon and partitioning of church property (see SECULARIZATION), and they counted on the help of part of the aristocracy, who eyed with growing disfavor the increase of wealth and the display of it in the cloisters and abbeys. Sickingen, favored by Luther, and directly incited against the unregenerate priests, declared hostilities against the pope and the lords of the church. The attack, combining secular and religious interests, was directed against the ecclesiastical princes and restricted to them; for it was their worldly possessions that aroused the Lutheran divines, their jurisdiction that offended the cities, and their territorial powers that opposed knightly liberties. Sickingen, with his attempt to overthrow the constitution of the empire, as a champion of the poorer people, a Gospel pioneer, and a leader of the "Fraternal League" organized at Landau Aug. 13, 1522, for the protection of the nobility, opened the first war of religion to be declared on German soil. Doubtless thoughts of personal advancement served to inspire him in this cause, for he was moved by an inordinate ambition that embraced the electorate of Treves.

On Aug. 27, 1522, Sickingen issued a declaration of war against Richard von Greiffenklau zu Vollraths, archbishop of Treves, who, as one of Luther's most powerful enemies and an enemy of the Gospel, received the first fury of the attack. After receiving consecration in the principality of Schaumburg, Sickingen appeared before Treves Sept. 8. When ordered by the imperial council to withdraw, he replied that he was as much a servant of the emperor as the council, and that he was moving against the archbishop in the conviction that the emperor would sanction the punishment of this priest. He intended to better the action of the council by establishing a regular system of law, and to win for himself a peaceful life as ruler of Treves. But the archbishop repulsed his assaults with such success that on Sept. 14 the siege was raised. On Oct. 10 he and his associates were laid under the ban of the empire for violating the peace of the country. With absolute indifference he broke into the Palatinate and plundered the town of Kaiserlautern. He had friends in the imperial council and in the Palatinate, and troops were levied for him in the Sundgau, Alsace, Breisgau, and Bavaria. But the princes of Treves, Hesse, and the Palatinate had in September of 1522 pledged themselves to destroy the "robber knights," and on Apr. 29, 1523, they besieged his stronghold of Landstuhl. He still looked for strong reenforcements from Germany and France, and for a simultaneous uprising in the dominions of the three princes, but he was fatally disappointed. His friends were restrained by the superior power of the princes and the Swabian League; he was mortally wounded on the third day of the siege, and on May 6 the garrison capitulated. D. PERCY GILMORE.

BIBLIOGRAPHY: H. Ulmann, *Franz von Sickingen*, Leipsic, 1872; F. P. Bremer, *Franz von Sickingen's Fehde gegen Trier*, Strassburg, 1885; P. M. Rade, *Hutten und Sickingen*, Barmen, 1887; J. Janssen, *Hist. of the German People*, iii. 276-308, St. Louis, 1900; J. Köstlin, *Martin Luther*, Berlin, 1903; *Cambridge Modern History*, ii. 41, 43, 154 sqq., New York, 1904.

SIDON. See PHENICIA, PHENICIANS, I., § 5.

SIDONIUS, si-dō'ni-us, APOLLINARIS, CAIUS SOLLIUS MODESTUS: Gallic Roman poet, bishop of Clermont, and saint; b. at Lyons Nov. 5 of some year between 430 and 433; buried at Clermont Aug. 21, 479 (482 or 484). He came of a noble family, his grandfather having held high office and being the first Christian in the family; his father also was "prefect in the pretorium of the Gauls." He received his education in the yet flourishing schools of grammar and rhetoric of his native region, devoting his attention to the acquisition of facility and perfection in writing prose and poetry in Latin.

Early Life.

He had in view fame as a writer and in the service of the State, and among his instructors were Claudianus Mamertus (q.v.) and other noted teachers. His marriage with Papianilla, daughter of Avitus, one of the prominent men of Auvergne, made him at home in what was to be a sort of fatherland to him; his wife brought to him possessions and a happy family life which fitted him for the rôle of a poet of home life and home blessings. But his ambition, fostered by the combination of wealth and culture, rendered him not content to lead the life of an obscure countryman. The raising of Avitus to imperial dignity influenced the muse of Sidonius in the direction of the panegyric. Sidonius accompanied his father-in-law to Rome and issued there his poem of praise (in which the Christian note is altogether absent), which was regarded as so remarkable that it secured for the author a place, marked by a bronze statue, among the celebrated authors thus honored in the Trajan basilica. But the reign of Avitus was short, Ricimer bringing about his overthrow after seventeen months. After the fall of Lyons, Sidonius turned his poetry to the praise of the victor in a composition which has historic value for its portrayal of the Franks (lines 238–254). The period of retirement which succeeded left traces in the epistles of Sidonius, and these are valuable in that they give pictures of the culture of the time (*Epist.*, ii. 2) as well as of historic events. During the reign of Theodoric II., Sidonius seems to have lived in retirement; and under Anthemius (467–472) he went to Rome at the command of the emperor in order to represent the people of Auvergne. There he came into close contact with the two most prominent senators, and followed their counsel to dedicate to the new emperor a new panegyric. This is the latest of his dated *carmina*, which resulted in an appointment as prefect of senate and city; it is of historical value for its description of the Huns, its mention of Geiserich, and the description of the situation of the East Goths about 467. An epistle of Sidonius of about 470 (v. 13) has historical worth also because of its dealing with the Governor Seronatus; and near this in point of time is the remarkable letter (ii. 1) which narrates the choice presented him of becoming a bishop or losing his Roman rights—as a matter of fact the nobility saved their rights through the hierarchy.

Soon after, Sidonius became bishop of Clermont, which belonged to the archdiocese of Bourges. As

Sidonius as Bishop.

bishop Sidonius gave up the writing of secular poetry, but in the exercise of his office he was drawn into the political arena. His brother-in-law Ecdicius was the refuge of the Roman party, while Clermont, the last firm stronghold of the Romans in Aquitania, threatened to fall before the Goths. Sidonius appealed for help near and far, and among the appeals is a letter (vii. 6) against Eurich. The ecclesiastical situation was lamentable; nine sees were vacant, and even the memory of ecclesiastical discipline had ceased. With the strife of Burgundians and Goths the land seemed about to be torn apart; all efforts were to be directed to the end that Eurich permit bishops to be consecrated in order that the people of Gaul might be held in the faith. The cause for the sad condition was attributed by Sidonius to the heads of the diocese of Arles, and Bishop Græcus heard bitter reproaches. Still the condition was not so bad as it seemed to Sidonius; Clermont was not destroyed, and the Gothic court was not so hostile to culture. In Toulouse the most influential man after the king was Leo of Narbonne, the teacher of oratory to Marcus Aurelius. Into this period falls the most celebrated of all the letters of Sidonius (viii. 9); it contains a poem, doubtless intended for the king's ear, describing the world-power of the ruler of the Visigoths, and this may well be called Sidonius' fourth panegyric. Sidonius, who had left his see, was able after some time to return and exercise his office.

As a writer Mommsen (*Reden*, p. 139, Berlin, 1905) estimated Sidonius as far above any other of his times; yet, in spite of the sententious, satirical, and graceful passages which are found, his poetry has

His Writings.

less esthetic value than that of Ausonius. Still, his significance from a literary-historical standpoint is high. In matter of form, he bridges the transition to the medieval poetry by frequency in employment of rime, alliteration, and like artistic devices; his poetry shows also what was the fashion in his time; he serves to illustrate, as well, what forms the classical myths took during the downfall of the old order of things in Gaul. For church history the letters are more valuable than the *carmina*. Sidonius was not original, but he could well set forth the situation of things in language that was fitting and expressive. The nine books of letters are edited in groups. The first, written for the most part about 469 in Rome, begins with a dedication to Constantius, a cleric of Lyons, to whom a life of Bishop Germanus of Auxerre (q.v.) is ascribed. The letters of book ii. appear to have been issued about the middle of 472, though they are probably of earlier date, since they do not reflect the clerical situation, and the thought is not Christian. These two books (twenty-five letters) were the first edited. The next group, books iii.–vii. (seventy letters), reveals a different situation. It begins with the statement that the writer has unworthily been chosen bishop of Clermont. A section of this group (vi. 1–vii. 11) contains letters directed to bishops. Later, at the wish of friends, Sidonius gathered the remains of his correspondence for an eighth book, and not long after added a ninth, "after the pattern of Pliny." Chronology is not observed in the arrangement, although a certain general sequence is preserved. The letters, 147 in number, have great historical value for the reason that they exhibit as does no other document the style of the Latin school of rhetoric just before its downfall; from this point of view each separate letter is worthful, even though its substance is of little value. Among the persons addressed are the African Domnulus, two Spanish rhetoricians, a Frank who was named "Count Arbogastes of the Treveri," who received also a letter from Bishop Auspicius of Toul (himself a correspondent of Sidonius), and Firminus of Arles, the friend of Cæsarius (q.v.). About a third of the letters are addressed to ecclesiastics, thirty-six of them to bishops, and the sees of thirty-one of these are known. Perpetuus of Tours, a city which was still Roman, was a correspondent of Sidonius; there are letters to the bishops of Sens, Auxerre, Orléans, and to Lupus of Treves. Though passing by the bishop of Arles, Sidonius was in frequent correspondence with the suffragans of that see, the bishops of Orange, Vaison, and Marseilles; as a native of Lyons, he had a patriotic interest in it. There are letters to the suffragans at Autun and Langres, to the metropolitan of Aix and his suffragan at Ries, to Reims, Toul, and Geneva. His letters set the style for the circle of rhetoricians and the school of which he was a part, as is seen by the letters and writings of Ruricius, and of Alcimus Avitus and Ennodius (qq.v.); in a later period the interest in him arose anew, such men as Flodoard, Sigbert of Gembloux, Vincent of Beauvais, Peter the Venerable, Peter of Poitiers, and John of Salisbury (qq.v.) reading and admiring him. He was not without influence upon Petrarch.

His Significance.

So far as the poems of Sidonius go, they might all have been written by one not a Christian; on the other hand, heathen mythology is for him but a means of adornment, monotheistic thoughts appear in noble form, and he set more store by prayer than by the aid of the physician. However, the Christian writings do not seem to be of sufficiently high value to him, possibly because of his enforced service to the external organization of the Church. He had a sort of contempt for the lower classes who "spoke bad Latin," though he always displayed a kindliness of disposition toward them. As a preacher and saver of souls his repute was not high. His knowledge of the Scriptures, and his dogmatics were alike weak; he spoke, for instance, of the Holy Ghost becoming flesh in Christ. He had little knowledge of and as little interest in the dogmatic controversies of his times. He was urged to apply his pen to the writing of history, but wisely estimated his powers and declined. His service to the better part of the nobility of Gaul is summed up in his advice to the effect that since the Roman state was breaking up, it were better for them to save their nobility in the hierarchy and to carry over their Roman heritage to church offices. And yet he himself failed in large measure to achieve the end he thus set before them, not realizing the opportunity to fill the rhetoric of the schools with a Christian spirit. (F. ARNOLD.)

BIBLIOGRAPHY: Late editions of the works of Sidonius are: that of J. F. Grégoire and F. Z. Collombet, 3 vols., Paris, 1836; in *MPL*, lviii. 443–748, with the notes of Sirmondi; E. Barret, Paris, 1879, with valuable introduction and dissertations, though typographical errors are numerous; ed. C. Luetjohann in *MGH*, *Auct. ant.*, viii (1887), 1–264; ed. P. Mohr, Leipsic, 1895; cf. E. Geisler, *Loci similes auctorum Sidonio anteriorum*, Berlin, 1887. There is a Fr. transl. by E. Barret, Paris, 1888.

Sources for a life are Gennadius, *De vir. ill.*, xcii.; Gregory of Tours, *Hist. Francorum*, ii. 21 sqq. Consult: P. Allard, *Saint Sidoine Apollinaire*, Paris, 1909; M. Fertig, *Sidonius und seine Zeit*, 3 vols., Würzburg and Passau, 1845–48 (with valuable essays, and includes some translations); G. Kaufmann, *Die Werke des . . . Sidonius als ein Quelle für die Geschichte seiner Zeit*, Göttingen, 1864; idem, in *Neues schweizerisches Museum*, pp. 1–28, Basel, 1865; idem, in *GGA*, 1868, pp. 1001–1021; idem, in *Historisches Taschenbuch*, 1869, pp. 30–40; L. A. Chaix, *S. Sidoine Apollinaire et son siècle*, 2 vols., Clermont, 1866 (the fullest and most detailed account); F. Ozanan, *Hist. of Civilization in the 5th Century*, London, 1868; F. Dahn, *Könige der Germanen*, v. 82–101, Würzburg, 1870; P. Mohr, *In Apollinaris Sidonii epistulas et carmina observationes criticae*, Sondershausen, 1877; idem, *Zu Sidonius carmina*, Laubach, 1881; M. Budinger, *Apollinaris Sidonius als Politiker*, Vienna, 1881; T. Hodgkin, *Italy and her Invaders*, book iii., vol. ii., 4 vols., Oxford, 1880–85; L. Sandret, in *Revue des questions historiques*, xxxii (1882), 210–224; A. Esmein, *Sur quelques lettres de Sidoine Apollinaire*, Paris, 1885; T. Mommsen, *De vita Sidonii*, in *MGH*, *Auct. ant.*, viii (1887), pp. xliv.–liii.; idem, in *SBA*, 1885, pp. 215–223; L. Duval-Arnould, *Études d'hist. du droit romain . . . d'après les lettres . . . de Sidoine Apollinaire*, Paris, 1888; M. Müller, *De Apollinaris Sidonii latinitate*, Halle, 1888; A. Ebert, *Allgemeine Geschichte der Litteratur des Mittelalters*, i. 419–448, Leipsic, 1889; W. Smith, *Dictionary of Greek and Roman Biography*, iii. 817–819, London, 1890; W. S. Teuffel, *Geschichte der römischen Litteratur*, pp. 1194–1200, Leipsic, 1890; M. Manitius, *Geschichte der christlichen lateinischen Poesie*, pp. 218–225, Stuttgart, 1891; E. Bracmann, *Sidoniana et Boethiana*, Utrecht, 1904; Wattenbach, *DGQ*, i (1894), 97–98; R. Holland, *Studia Sidoniana*, Leipsic, 1905; Tillemont, *Mémoires*, xvi. 195–284; Gibbon, *Decline and Fall*, chap. xxxvi (important); Hauck, *KD*, i. 79 sqq., 83 sqq.; *DCB*, iv. 649–661 (detailed and thorough, but follows Chaix, ut sup.); *ASB*, Aug., iv. 597–624.

SIDONIUS, MICHAEL: Bishop of Merseburg. See HELDING, MICHAEL.

SIEFFERT, sî'fert, FRIEDRICH ANTON EMIL: German Reformed; b. at Königsberg, Prussia, Dec. 24, 1843. He was educated at the universities of Königsberg, Halle, and Berlin (lic. theol., Königsberg, 1867), and, after being privat-docent at the university of his native city (1867–71), was inspector of the theological seminary at Bonn (1871–73); associate professor at the university of the same city (1873–78); professor of Reformed theology at Erlangen (1878–89); and since 1889 professor of systematic theology and New-Testament exegesis in the Protestant theological faculty of the University of Bonn. He has written *Nonnulla ad apocryphi libri Henochi originem pertinentia* (Königsberg, 1867); *Ueber den socialen Gegensatz im Neuen Testament* (Erlangen, 1888); *Die neuesten theologischen Forschungen über Busse und Glaube* (Berlin, 1896); *Das Recht im Neuen Testament* (Göttingen, 1900); *Offenbarung und heilige Schrift* (Langensalza, 1905); *Die Heidenbekehrung im Alten Testament und im Judentum* (1908); and *Johann Calvins religiöse Entwicklung und sittliche Grundrichtung* (Leipsic, 1909); besides preparing the sixth, seventh, eighth, and ninth editions of H. A. W. Meyer's commentary on Galatians (Göttingen, 1880–99).

SIEFFERT, FRIEDRICH LUDWIG: German theologian and Biblical scholar; b. at Elbing (32 m. s.w. of Königsberg) Feb. 1, 1803; d. at Bonn Dec. 2, 1877. He prepared for the university at the Gymnasium of Elbing; entered in 1821 the University of Königsberg, where he studied under Herbart, and also under August Hahn, with whom he collaborated in issuing *Chrestomathia syriaca* (Leipsic, 1825), taking there his doctorate. He then went to Berlin for the study of theology, particularly under Neander. In the summer of 1825 he interrupted his sojourn at Berlin for a journey to Vienna to examine a manuscript in the Vienna library containing the commentary of Theodore, bishop of Mopsuestia, on the Minor Prophets. He returned to Berlin, where he was graduated licentiate in theology in 1826; and then went to Königsberg, where he became privat-docent at the university in 1827, having published in that year *Theodorus Mopsuestiensis Veteris Testamenti sobrie interpretandi vindex*, the fruit of his research in Vienna; he was appointed extraordinary professor in 1828. Soon afterward appeared his treatise *Ueber den Ursprung des ersten kanonischen Evangeliums* (1832), a work of high importance, showing that the first Gospel is a Greek recasting of the original composition by Matthew the apostle in Aramaic. It evoked a number of works in the domain of Gospel criticism, mostly approving his position. In due season, however, Sieffert took a pronounced stand against radical criticism, as in his *De librorum sacrorum auctoritate canonica* (1836), the publication of which attended his promotion to a regular professorship, in 1834. Meanwhile, he had also prosecuted his studies respecting Theodore of Mopsuestia (q.v.), and prepared a larger work on his life and writings. In the year 1837, there suddenly developed a disease of the eyes, which ultimately led to nearly total blindness. This moved him to the thought of combining his academic activity with some practical avocation, less taxing to the eyes. Accordingly, in 1839, he accepted a court preacher's office for the German Reformed congregation of the castle church; in 1841 he took office as assessor, in 1842 as councilor, in the consistory of the province of Prussia. Thenceforth, indeed, and for many years, he administered these three offices, in all evincing the same conscientiousness. But the increasing malady finally obliged him to relinquish one after the other of his official positions. Later, in the evening of his life, he ventured one more composition, dictating and publishing *Die apologetische Fundamentirung der christlichen Glaubenswissenschaft* (Gütersloh, 1871), in which he insisted on the central fact of the entire and personal phenomenon of Christ. In 1873, when released from all his official charges, he removed to Bonn, where he died.

F. SIEFFERT.

BIBLIOGRAPHY F. Sieffert, *F. L. Sieffert, Eine Skizze seines Lebens*, Königsberg, 1880.

SIEGFRIED, sig'frid, **KARL ADOLF**: German Lutheran; b. at Magdeburg Jan. 22, 1830; d. at Jena Jan. 9, 1903. He was educated at the universities of Halle (1849–51, 1851–52; Ph.D., 1859) and Bonn (1851), and taught in the Gymnasium zum Kloster Unserer lieben Frauen in Magdeburg (1856–1858), where he was likewise a member of the seminary for theological candidates, as well as in the gymnasium at Guben (1858–60) and the Domgymnasium of his native city (1860–65). From 1865 to 1875 he was professor and second pastor at the royal school at Pforta, and in the latter year published at Jena his *Philo von Alexandria als Ausleger des Alten Testaments*, which, valuable to the theologian, the philosopher, and the classical student alike, led to his call to Jena as professor of Old-Testament theology, a position which he filled from 1875 until his death. He overtaxed his strength, however, and from 1878 to 1880 was necessarily relieved of his duties, while in 1901 the final failure of his health compelled him to cease lecturing. The first large work which Siegfried issued after his appointment at Jena was the *Lehrbuch der neuhebräischen Sprache und Literatur* (in collaboration with H. L. Strack; Carlsruhe, 1884), and he then collaborated with B. Stade in preparing a *Hebräisches Wörterbuch zum Alten Testament* (Leipsic, 1893). His remaining publications of major importance were devoted to the Old Testament: the critical text of Job for *SBOT* (Baltimore 1893); the translation of Ezekiel for E. Kautzsch's new German translation of the Bible (Freiburg, 1894); and of the Wisdom of Solomon for the same scholar's *Apokryphen und Pseudepigraphen des Alten Testaments* (1900); and commentaries on Ecclesiastes, the Song of Solomon, Ezra, Nehemiah, and Esther for W. G. H. Nowack's *Handkommentar zum Alten Testament* (Göttingen, 1898–1901). He likewise collaborated with H. Gelzer in editing *Eusebii canonum epitome ex Dionysii Telmaharensis chronico petita* (Leipsic, 1884), and also issued a translation from the Syriac, entitled *Buch der Erkenntnis der Wahrheit*, by his deceased friend C. Kayser (Strasburg, 1893). Besides all this, Siegfried wrote a large number of magazine articles on the Old Testament, Hebrew grammar and lexicography, exegesis, Philo and Hellenism, and Judaism and Jewish literature, as well as on more miscellaneous topics, in addition to many articles in various works of reference. He was, moreover, a peculiarly able reviewer, and for nineteen years (1871–89) recorded the literature on the Old Testament and problems of Oriental philology appertaining to it for the *Theologischer Jahresbericht*. While in no sense a partizan, he was practically an adherent of the historico-critical school of Reuss, Graf, Kayser, and Wellhausen. He was appointed an ecclesiastical councilor in 1885 and privy ecclesiastical councilor in 1892.

(B. BÄNTSCH†.)

BIBLIOGRAPHY: B. Bäntsch, in *ZWT*, xlvi (1903), 580–588.

SIENA, SYNOD OF (1423–24): On June 22, 1423, the Synod of Pavia (q.v.) resolved upon removal to Siena, where on July 21 of the same year it was opened under the same presiding officers as at Pavia. The decrees of the second session, published Nov. 8, 1423, repeated the condemnation of Wyclif, Huss (qq.v.), and Peter of Luna, and discussed union with the Greeks and the extinction of heresies. After that the question of the reformation of the Church was opened, and the French proposed that, in accordance with the Council of Constance, cardinals should be chosen from all parts of Christendom and that they should number eighteen, or twenty-four at the most, nomination to be national, while the pope was to have only the right of confirmation. These propositions met with violent opposition from the papal legates. Divisions arose, and it was seen that nothing could be accomplished there, so the whole reform was left to a new synod, and Basel was decided upon as the seat of the next synod. On Mar. 7, 1424, the papal legates left

Siena, and the council was dissolved against the protests of the French participants.

(PAUL TSCHACKERT.)

BIBLIOGRAPHY: The best source is John of Ragusa, *Initium et prosecutio Basiliensis Concilii*, in *Monumenta conciliorum generalium saeculi XV.*, i. 12 sqq., Vienna, 1857. Consult further: Mansi, *Concilia*, vol. xxviii.; Hefele, *Conciliengeschichte*, vii. 392–409; the chronicle of Francesco di Tommaso, in Muratori, *Scriptores*, vol. xx.; Pastor, *Popes*, i. 238–239; Creighton, *Papacy*, ii. 145–150; Milman, *Latin Christianity*, vii. 535; *KL*, xi. 290 sqq.; and the literature under MARTIN V.

SIEVEKING, AMALIE WILHELMINE: German Protestant philanthropist and founder of the Hamburg Weiblicher Verein für Armen- und Krankenpflege; b. at Hamburg July 25, 1794; d. there Apr. 1, 1859. Orphaned at the age of fifteen, she lived with Fräulein Dimpfel, the daughter-in-law of the poet Klopstock, and there, in instructing the nieces of her patroness, she began a career as a teacher which continued, with only brief interruptions, until her death. Here, too, her rationalistic and skeptical attitude toward Christianity began to be modified, until later, after the death of a brother, and under the influence of the works of Thomas à Kempis and A. H. Francke, she attained to a deep and abiding faith in the Bible and in prayer. After a brief residence with a widowed aunt in Neumühlen, Amalie Sieveking was requested, in 1811, by a widowed relative of her mother's, Frau Brunnemann, to assist her in taking care of a sick son, and though the latter soon died, the home thus gained was kept until the death of Frau Brunnemann in 1839. Meanwhile she always had a class of young girls, and likewise taught in a free private school for poor girls. During this time her efforts to clear up for herself certain passages of the Bible seem to have led her to compose her *Betrachtungen über einzelne Stellen der heiligen Schrift*, which, in the hope that it might help others in that period of the revival of religious life, she published anonymously at Hamburg in 1823. About this same time, moreover, she formed the plan of establishing a Lutheran order of deaconesses (q.v.), but since she did not feel herself divinely called to do this in person, the realization of the concept was left for Theodor Fliedner (q.v.). Nevertheless, she discussed the entire matter with C. F. A. Hartmann (librarian and professor of history at Hamburg) and with J. Gossner (q.v.), the latter confirming her in her attitude of prudent hesitation. In 1827 she published at Hamburg (again anonymously) her *Beschäftigungen mit der heiligen Schrift*, and her circle of noteworthy acquaintances increased, while her girls' classes still continued with great success.

When, in 1831, cholera broke out in Hamburg, Amalie Sieveking deemed that the time had come to carry out her plan, and since none answered her call to unite with her in Christian care of the sick, she volunteered her own services, which were accepted when the first woman to fall a victim to the plague was brought to the hospital erected for such cases. Regarded at first as a mere enthusiast, her judgment and devotion soon won such recognition that she was appointed inspectress of all the nurses. Even after the completion of her work at the hospital, she realized that conditions were not yet favorable for her order of deaconesses, but in its stead she gradually formed the somewhat similar idea of founding a "Women's Society for the Care of the Poor and Sick." This she established early in 1832, the movement spreading from Hamburg to many other German cities. At the initial conference (May 23) she delivered an address (reprinted in *Bericht über die Leistungen des weiblichen Vereins für Armen- und Krankenpflege*, x. 56–68), in which she emphasized the necessity of devoted Christian faith and love in the care of the sick and indigent. The sick should be visited personally, and the poor should be given work, if possible, rather than money, while every effort should be made in behalf of religious training and life. All the details of the undertaking, which was mainly dependent on voluntary subscription, were most carefully regulated, these including not only the visiting of the poor and sick, but also the distribution of food, assignment of work in various trades, care of the raw materials, sale of the finished products, and the administration of the poorhouses and the childrens' hospital later founded by the society. While the members of the society, who rapidly increased in number, were naturally exposed to occasional gross deception by their wards, and though they were frequently charged with fostering hypocrisy, yet, on the whole, the movement must be characterized as most admirably adapted to its purpose, and as affording spiritual and physical aid in countless cases where a single individual would not have been able to render assistance. Toward the end of her life, besides having edited the annual *Bericht über die Leistungen des weiblichen Vereins für Armen- und Krankenpflege* (26 vols., Hamburg, 1833–58), she wrote *Unterhaltungen über einzelne Abschnitte der heiligen Schrift* (Leipsic, 1855), while a compilation from her writings was translated into English anonymously under the title *The Principles of Charitable Work—Love, Truth, and Order—as set forth in the Writings of A. W. Sieveking* (London, 1863).

(CARL BERTHEAU.)

BIBLIOGRAPHY: *Denkwürdigkeiten aus dem Leben von Amalie Sieveking*, Hamburg, 1860, Eng. transl., ed. C. Winkworth, *Life of A. W. Sieveking*, London, 1863; J. H. Höck, *Bilder aus der Geschichte der hamburgischen Kirche seit der Reformation*, pp. 353 sqq., Hamburg, 1900; *ADB*, xxxiv. 217 sqq.

SIGEBERT OF GEMBLOUX: A versatile and productive writer of the early Middle Ages, especially noteworthy as historian; b. probably in the neighborhood of Gembloux (10 m. n.w. of Namur, Belgium) about 1035; d. at Gembloux Nov. 5, 1112. He was educated in the abbey of Gembloux, became a monk there, and spent his mature life as teacher, first in the school of the abbey of St. Vincent at Metz, then (from c. 1070) at Gembloux. As teacher he was highly esteemed, and in general he is to be commended as a good example of the capable and learned Benedictine monk of the older time, filled with genuine piety but disinclined to all ascetic excesses, an earnest seeker after truth, a highly lovable and attractive personality. His best-known book is a world chronicle, *Decennalis liber*, continuing Jerome's translation of Eusebius' chronicle, covering the period 381–1111. Sigebert was nearly seventy when he began the work and he wrote it with reference to the similar chronicle of Marianus Scotus. Like the latter he makes the year of the incarnation the basis of his chronological system. The book can hardly be called history, being a bare list of events, among which naturally in the later time notices of the German empire and Sigebert's Belgian home predominate. The accounts of the years from 1105 to 1111 are the most extended and were probably expanded after the first completion of the chronicle. An introduction, explaining the purpose, use, and system of the book, is lost with the exception of some lines. Sigebert's chronicle was often revised and continued and became the source of very many later historical works. The best [almost ideal] edition is by L. C. Bethmann in *MGH*, *Script.*, vi (1844), 300–374, but the treatment of the sources here is wholly inadequate. After the chronicle Sigebert wrote a book on writers and their works supplementing the *De vir. ill.* of Jerome and Gennadius (ed. J. A. Fabricius, *Bibliotheca ecclesiastica*, pp. 93–116, Hamburg, 1718), which is his second important work for the present time. Sigebert took the side of the secular rulers in the contest with the popes which filled the greater part of his life. To a letter addressed by Gregory VII. to Bishop Hermann of Metz in 1081, seeking to prove that popes have the right to excommunicate kings, he wrote an answer which is apparently lost, although Bethmann (cf. *MGH*, *Lib. de lite*, i. 454–460, 1890) and A. Cauchie (*La Querelle des investitures dans les diocèses de Liège et de Cambrai*, i. pp. 66–99, Louvain, 1890) claim to have discovered it. A defense of masses said by married priests, however, is extant, written against Gregory VII. (ed. E. Sackur, *MGH*, *Lib. de lite*, ii. 436–448, 1892); and also a very able and sharp reply for the diocese of Liége to Paschal II., who in 1103 urged Count Robert II. of Flanders to punish the clergy and people of Liége for their adherence to the Emperor Henry IV. and to make war on the emperor (ed. E. Sackur, *MGH*, *Lib. de lite*, ii. 449–464, 1892). Sigebert's other writings were lives or eulogies of personages connected in tradition or history with Metz and Gembloux. Some are in verse, of which one especially, a long *Passio sanctorum Thebeorum*, written when Sigebert was forty-four years of age, attests real poetic gifts. Many of his writings are reprinted from earlier editions in *MPL*, clx.; cf. also lxxxvii. 303–314, and E. Dümmler in *Abhandlungen der Berliner Akademie*, pp. 1–125, 1893.

(O. Holder-Egger.)

Bibliography: For an extensive bibliography of editions consult Potthast, *Wegweiser*, pp. 1016–18, and cf. Wattenbach, *DGQ*, ii (1894), 155–162. Almost the only sources for the life and writings of Sigebert are a chapter of the *Gesta abbatum Gemblacensium* by Godescalc and the last chapter of Sigebert's *Scriptores ecclesiastici*, in which he gives a list of his writings, probably in substantially chronological order. Godescalc was a pupil of Sigebert and his work is a continuation of an earlier one by the latter. Consult further: S. Hirsch, *De vita et scriptis Sigeberti monachi Gemblacensis*, Berlin, 1841; the prolegomena of Bethmann in *MGH*, *Script.*, vi (1844), 268–299; H. E. Bonnell, *Die Anfänge des karolingischen Hauses*, Berlin, 1866; L. Demaison, *Étude critique sur la vie de S. Sigebert . . . par Sigebert de Gembloux*, in *Travaux de l'académie nationale de Reims*, lxiv (1880); Huyghens, *Sur la valeur de la chronique historique de Sigebert de Mons*, Ghent, 1880; A. Cauchie, *La Querelle des investitures dans . . . Liège et Cambrai*, 2 parts, Louvain, 1890.

SIGISMUND, sî'gis-mûnt", JOHANN: Elector of Brandenburg 1608–19; b. at Halle Nov. 8 (18), 1572; d. at Brandenburg Dec. 23, 1619. During the sixteenth century there were various changes in the religious situation at Brandenburg, depending upon the attitude of the ruling elector. Joachim I. (1499–1535) was a strict Roman Catholic; under Joachim II. the Reformation of Luther entered the country. The period of Johann Georg (1571–98) was the time of undisputed sway of strict Lutheranism, but his son Joachim Friedrich was inclined toward the Calvinistic doctrine. Johann Sigismund, the son of Joachim Friedrich, was educated as a strict Lutheran, according to the directions of his grandfather, by Simon Gedicke, at that time court preacher in Halle; but in 1588 his father sent him, together with his brother, Johann Georg, to the University of Strasburg, where both princes were favorably impressed by Calvinism. In 1605 he was in Heidelberg, where he became a close friend of Count Palatine Friedrich IV., and his wife, the daughter of William of Orange. His personal intercourse with Reformed princes and theologians led him to become a decided opponent of the Formula of Concord. For some time he tried to keep his change of convictions secret, but in 1613, on Ascension Day, a Reformed church service was held in the court chapel on the occasion of a visit of Landgrave Maurice, to the great vexation of the Lutheran clergy. On another occasion Martin Füssel, superintendent of Zerbst, administered the Lord's Supper after the Reformed rite. Simon Gedicke, provost of the cathedral, protested against the infringement of the parochial rights of Brandenburg and published a treatise, *Von den Ceremonien bei dem heiligen Abendmahl* (1613), against the Calvinists, especially against Salomo Finck, a court preacher newly called from Königsberg, who showed himself a decided Calvinist. A committee of the estates requested Christoph Pelargus, general superintendent of the Mark and professor of theology in Frankfort-on-the-Oder, to proceed officially against the court preacher; his refusal made him also a suspect of Calvinism. Before the elector was now placed the alternative either to take measures against Finck and Pelargus or to make his statement of adherence to the Reformed faith. He chose the latter, and on Dec. 18, 1613, announced to the clergy that he did not claim control over the consciences of his subjects, and similarly no one might dictate in the matter to him. He forbade untimely outbreaks from the pulpit, and permitted communion in the Reformed manner. He justified himself by appealing to the amended Augsburg Confession (*Augustana variata*) which, he said, was admitted in the Saxon kingdom. In an edict of Feb. 24, 1614, he again forbade invective from the pulpit and proclaimed as a basis of doctrine for all preachers "the doctrine of the divine Word according to the four chief symbols (including the Chalcedonian), the amended Augsburg Confession, and the Apology." On Feb. 21, 1614, there was designed a complete plan for subjecting the whole country to the Reformed faith. Strict Lutherans like Gedicke and Willich, archdeacon of St.

Peter, were forced to flee, and the elector called Abraham Scultetus (q.v.) to carry out the new plan. At his advice there was published on May 10 a "Confession of the Reformed Churches of Germany," the preface of which tried to show that even after the Reformation there were still left many Romanistic errors in the new faith, and that it was necessary to reform the church of Brandenburg anew in order to equate it with other Evangelical churches. This confession was a reprint of one first published at Heidelberg in 1562. In the same year the elector issued his own confession of faith, *Confessio Sigismundi*. It is not a complete confession, but touches merely the points of controversy. The elector again acknowledges the chief symbols and the emended Augsburg Confession as the basis of doctrine while he condemns all other writings "conceived by men," meaning principally the Formula of Concord. He rejects the doctrine of ubiquity and the Lutheran doctrine of the *Communicatio Idiomatum* (q.v.); in baptism he rejects the ceremony of exorcism; in the Lord's Supper bread and wine are visible symbols of invisible grace. The bread must be real unleavened bread, and the breaking of the bread must be preserved according to the example of Christ. He adopts the doctrine of election. The *Confessio Sigismundi* became authoritative among the Reformed in the eastern parts of Brandenburg-Prussia. Although the elector declared his intention not to interfere with the faith of his people, he continued the "reformation" of his country, by constituting a church council which was to take care of the interests of the Reformed faith. On Oct. 3 a disputation between Reformed and Lutherans was to take place, but the latter were so timid in the assertion of their rights that the elector himself broke off the colloquy and obliged every one present to observe the edict of Feb. 24. The hope of the clergy rested now upon the interference of the estates. In 1615 the estates seriously complained that preachers of doubtful standing were forced upon them, demanded the appointment of Lutherans in the schools and at the university, refused to acknowledge Pelargus as general superintendent, and asked the elector for the renewal and confirmation of his former pledges for the protection of Lutheranism. After they had made their demands a fourth time, the elector found it advisable to yield and declared now that "everybody in his country who desired, might adhere to the doctrine of Luther and the unchanged Augsburg Confession, also to the Book of Concord." Nevertheless, the propaganda in behalf of the Reformed confession was continued. The church council continued its activity; the state university and college were supplied with Reformed teachers; Reformed preachers presided over Lutheran congregations, and Pelargus in his love of peace ordained also Reformed clergymen. But after 1616 the opposition against the renovations became so strong and general both among the clergy and laity, that in 1618 the church council had to be dissolved, and thus the "work of the Reformation" in the Mark of Brandenburg came to an end. The Lutheran Church was preserved, the elector standing almost alone with his change of confession. His wife together with her daughters adhered faithfully to the Lutheran creed. His change of confession involved the elector in difficulties with the duchy of Prussia, of which he was feudal lord. The Prussian estates uttered the reproach that by adopting the Reformed confession Sigismund had violated the fundamental laws of the duchy. His theologians, Pelargus and J. Bergius, refused to accept an invitation to the Synod of Dort (1618), and its decisions acquired no authority in Brandenburg. The events in Brandenburg occasioned the issue of a great mass of polemical literature. Between 1613 and 1619 there appeared 231 treatises, among the contributors, on the Lutheran side, being Leonhard Hutter, Hoë von Hoënegg (qq.v.), and Friedrich Balduin; the treatises advocating the Reformed faith were mostly anonymous.

(G. Kawerau.)

Bibliography: L. Keller, *Die Gegenreformation in Westfalen und am Niederrhein*, iii. 219 sqq., Leipsic, 1895; A. Chroust, in *Forschungen zur brandenburgischen und preussischen Geschichte*, ix (1897), 12 sqq.; J. C. Beemann, *Oratio secularis in memoriam a . . . Johanne Sigismundo . . . introductæ reformatæ religionis*, Frankfort, 1713; D. H. Hering, *Historische Nachricht von dem ersten Anfang der evangelisch-reformierten Kirche in Brandenburg und Preussen*, Halle, 1778; idem, *Beiträge zur Geschichte der evangelisch-reformierten Kirche in den preussisch-brandenburgischen Ländern*, Breslau, 1784; W. Möller, in *Deutsche Zeitschrift für christliche Wissenschaft*, 1858, pp. 189 sqq.; Wangemann, *Johann Sigismund und Paul Gerhardt*, Berlin, 1884; E. Clausnitzer, *Die märkischen Stände unter Johann Sigismund*, Halle, 1895; F. Dittrich, in *Zeitschrift für die Geschichte der Altertumskunde Ermlands*, xiii (1900), 72 sqq.; *ADB*, xiv. 169 sqq., cf. xxv. 328 sqq. For the *Confessio Sigismundi* consult: K. Müller, *Die Bekenntnisschriften der reformierten Kirche*, pp. lvi. sqq., 835 sqq., Leipsic, 1903, cf. O. Hegar, *Zur Confessio Sigismundi*, Berlin, 1899.

SIHLER, sí'ler, **EDWARD WILHELM ALEXANDER**: Lutheran (Missouri Synod); b. at Bernstadt, Silesia (22 m. e. of Breslau), Nov. 12, 1801; d. at Fort Wayne, Ind., Oct. 27, 1885. From the gymnasium at Schweidnitz he entered the army, was a lieutenant of the line in 1819, in 1823 a student of the military academy in Berlin (with Von Moltke and Von Roon), but in 1826 left the service and became a student under Schleiermacher in Berlin (Ph.D., Jena, 1829). In 1830 he became an instructor in the famous Blochmann's Institute in Dresden, in 1838 a private tutor on the Livonian island of Oesel, and in 1840 the same at Riga. About 1835 he was converted and in 1843 came to the United States to labor among the Germans, who were then so destitute of religious teachers. His first charge was in Pomeroy, O., his second and only other charge at Fort Wayne from 1845 till his death. He was one of the organizers of the movement started in his study in 1846 out of which came the powerful Missouri Synod (see Lutherans, III., 5, § 1). He was its first vice-president and the first president of the middle district of his synod. He organized the Practical Seminary at Fort Wayne in 1845, and in it taught exegesis and dogmatics till 1861. He was a prominent preacher among the Germans of the Middle West and also an organizer of churches. He wrote in German several books, including an autobiography (down to 1843, St. Louis, Mo., 1879) and many articles.

SIHLER, ERNEST GOTTLIEB: Lutheran layman and classical scholar; b. at Fort Wayne,

Ind., Jan. 2, 1853. He was educated at Concordia College, Fort Wayne (A.B., 1869), Concordia Lutheran Divinity School, St. Louis (from which he was graduated in 1872), the universities of Berlin and Leipsic (1872–75), and Johns Hopkins (Ph.D., 1878). He was a classical instructor in New York City (1879–91); professor of classics at Concordia College, Milwaukee (1891–92); and since 1892 has been professor of Latin in New York University. In theology he "holds to the historical position of recorded Christianity, is a conservative in the full acceptance of Gospels and Epistles," and "believes that the spiritual failure of classical civilization is a profound argument for Christianity." He is the author of a number of editions of classics and of *Testimonium Animæ: or, Greek and Roman before Jesus Christ* (New York, 1908), a series of essays and sketches dealing with the spiritual elements in classical civilization; and *Annals of Cæsar; critical Biography, with a Survey of the Sources* (1910).

SIKHS, siks, SIKHISM.

I. History of the Sikhs.
Background and Sources (§ 1).
Life of the Founder (§ 2).
The Other Gurus (§ 3).
History from 1708 (§ 4).
II. The Religion.
The Granth (§ 1).
Belief and Practise (§ 2).

Sikh is the name accepted by a people in India found almost exclusively in the Punjab, who are bound together not by tribal affiliations but by a religious bond. The term, meaning "disciple," is the correlative of guru, "teacher," a common noun appropriated as the title of the founder of the religion and transmitted to the nine men who succeeded him as religious heads of the faith. The fact that "Sikh" came to have a semi-national significance is not an essential of the system, but merely a consequence of the political conditions at the breaking up of the Mohammedan power in northwest India during the eighteenth century.

I. History of the Sikhs: While the religion was founded and developed by a series of ten teachers who were called Gurus, the beginnings of their faith are traced by themselves to a man named Kabir, who, as so often in India, was regarded as an incarnation of deity. His birth date is variously given as 1398 and about 1500. He is said to have been miraculously conceived and born in or near Benares, to have grown up a religious reformer, and to have composed hymns which are received among the sacred writings of the Sikhs. His revolt was against all distinctions of caste and religion, against the Puranas and Shastras of Hinduism, and, necessarily, against the assumptions of the Brahmans, and no less against the bigotry fostered by the Koran. A number of sects, it is claimed, sprang from his teachings, the last of whom were the Sikhs. All these sects exemplify the tendency of Indian teaching to combine elevated ideals and noble reforms with gross superstition and foolish observances. The sources of knowledge of the Sikh religion and its founders and leaders are the following. The principal work and the sacred book of the Sikhs is the Adi Granth or Granth Sahib (see below), a work in an obscure dialect of the Panjabi called Gurmukhi, which includes compositions by the Gurus and also by Bhagats (Indian saints) who preceded the Gurus. Hymns are found also in Prakrit, Hindi, Marathi, Multani, and a number of local dialects. For the lives of the Gurus there is a series of works embodying accounts of their lives, teachings, and miracles, in various languages, principally Panjabi and Hindi, claiming to be by adherents of the faith who were in especially close relations with one or another of the Gurus. One manuscript of the earliest of these lives dealing with Guru Nanak bears the date of 1588, and was therefore written during the lifetime of a certain Bhai Budha, a venerable Sikh, who is admitted to have been a young contemporary and disciple of Nanak and to have lived to a great age, actually linking by his life the leadership of the first six Gurus. This would be of importance were it not for the fact that the life under discussion, and all later works of the kind, abound in the legendary, and have been besides extensively corrupted by the admixture of characteristic Hindu material which vitiates them for critical use. Two of the most extensive of these works, the *Nanak Parkash*, dealing with the life and teachings of Nanak, was written in 1823, and by the same author the *Suraj Parkash*, in 6 volumes, was written between that year and 1843. A great number of schismatic (for Sikhism had its schisms) and what may be called apocryphal works exist, all of which teem with the miraculous, while they are sparing of data which submit to verification.

1. Background and Sources.

The Gurus were ten in number, each of the nine last of whom became leader on the death (or retirement) of his predecessor. Their names and dates are as follows: Nanak (1469–1538), Angad (1504–52), Amar Das (1479–1574), Ram Das (1534–81), Arjan (1563–1606), Har Gobind (1595–1645), Har Rai (1630–1661), Har Krishan (1656–64), Teg Bahadur (1622–75), and Gobind Rai or Gobind Singh (1666–1708). The important names here are Nanak, Ram Das, Arjan, Har Gobind, Teg Bahadur, and Gobind Singh. The narrative, in brief, of the life of Nanak will give the flavor of all of these Indian lives. He was born in Apr.-May, 1469, at or near Talwandi (a small town 30 m. s.w. of Lahore), and died at Kartarpur (62 m. e. of Lahore) in 1538. His father was an accountant and agriculturist, consequently Nanak came not of priestly but of lay lineage. This fact is significant both for the character of the religion and for the tongue in which the literature is cast—the vernacular and not the Sanskrit. His home was away from the centers of Mohammedan influence and fanaticism, and this accounts for the impetus the religion secured before encountering opposition. According to reports, the astrologer who was called in at his birth foretold his greatness—some records affirm the presence of the gods; at the age of five he began to meditate on heavenly themes; when at the age of seven he went to school, the master wrote for him the alphabet, and he immediately composed an acrostic on the alphabet and speedily excelled

2. Life of the Founder.

aster in knowledge; this experience was re-
l when he went to study Persian at the age
en; while a youth engaged in herding cattle,
meditated the cattle trespassed on a grain-
o the wrath of the owner, yet on examina-
; was found that not a single shoot had been
led; once while he was sleeping under a tree,
adow remained fixed and protected him from
n, and at another time a cobra spread its hood
haded him (cf. SERPENT IN WORSHIP, etc.,
2). Apart from such tales, what may be
ed of his life is that he early reached con-
ns condemning the religious customs, both
and Mohammedan, current about him, em-
l himself in composing verses in the vernacu-
nbodying instruction on man's duty to God
an and expressive of revolt against the teach-
nd practises of the two dominant religions.
fused as a youth to put on the sacred thread
o declare himself a Hindu, confounding in
ent the Brahman who was to perform the
ony.

ak was married at fourteen, but could not
duced to take up an occupation, gaining
putation of a madman. At length he took
under the governor of Sultanpur, spent the
praising the Creator, and gave all but a pit-
of his wages to fakirs. Having retired into
ilderness, he was gone three days, during
he thought he had a vision of the Supreme,
nectar in the presence, and was pronounced
ue Guru. On his return he uttered a cryptic
ce condemning Hindus and Mohammedans,
ook up the life of a wanderer and religious
r, and began to make disciples. Like Socrates,
nd the themes for his teachings in the daily
out him, a question, a chance saying, or an
ence giving him the text for a discourse in
Manifesting a supreme disregard for rank
nity, he rebuked or taught with equal ardor,
y, or gentleness, as the case seemed to him
uire, all who met him or listened to him, ad-
g as on terms of equality ascetics, fakirs,
Brahmans, nobles, princes, and kings, all of
are said to have acknowledged the divine
of his teachings. He overcame the tempta-
f the devil who sought to buy him with the
of the earth from the accomplishment of his
ng mission. He is said to have traversed
and South India and to have visited Mecca
Iedina. During his life the organization of
ch church had begun by the founding of socie-
d the Guru's hymns were committed to mem-
sacred scriptures. At the end of his life he
urated the practise followed by the other
(except the tenth) and appointed his succes-
this case Angad. Just before his death Mo-
edans and Hindus contested for the honor
osing of his remains, but in the morning the
had disappeared—his supreme miracle. The
ds of Nanak were often exceedingly apt and
cing. Thus to a man who had acquired great
and ostentatiously displayed it he gave a
with the injunction to retain it carefully
t should be required of him in the next world.
an took it with the injunction to his wife, who declared the Guru mad and told him to return it to the giver. The latter then asked, if so small a thing as a needle could not be taken into the next world, how so great wealth could accompany the rich. On being asked how to take it there he replied: "Give some of thy wealth in God's name, feed the poor, and thy wealth shall accompany thee" (Macauliffe, i. 130).

3. The Other Gurus.

The name of the second Guru, Angad, embodies the theory respecting the person of the Guru. His name was Lahina, but this was changed to a word which included the word for "body," the idea being that the Guru for the time being was the embodiment of the first Guru, and that indeed all the Gurus were not ten but one, the spirit of the first descending to the second. A consequence of this is that the compositions of the Gurus all carry the pen name Nanak. Angad abandoned the wandering mode of life, settled at a place called Khadur, whither the Sikhs came for instruction and to bring their free-will offerings. His leadership was marked by the first Sikh schism, a part of the followers of Nanak choosing Sri Chand, oldest son of Nanak, as Guru, and this sect received the name of Udasis ("solitaries"). The period of the third Guru, Amar Das, was marked by a second attempt at schism, since Datu, the son of Angad, tried to set himelf up in opposition, but was not recognized by the Sikhs. Amar Das inaugurated the custom for the Sikhs of visiting the Guru three times a year for instruction in religion. It was he who began the work of building the sacred tank or pool. His period is marked also by formal complaints to the Mohammedan emperor against the faith, but Akbar dismissed these and showed favor to the Guru. He formulated the rules of the religion and created a sort of regulation of life. By the fourth Guru, Ram Das, the work of dissemination of the religion was undertaken by the despatch of missionaries, part of whose work was the collection of offerings for the completion of the sacred tank. The importance of this structure is great, since it gave the Sikhs a center and a home, the environs of the pool being built up and becoming the sacred city Amritsar, now the goal of the Sikh pilgrimage. The compositions of this Guru and of his predecessor were quite numerous. The fifth Guru, Arjan, youngest son of Ram Das, completed the erection of the tank and also the building of a temple in the middle of it, also beginning the erection of the city of Kartarpur. His oldest brother attempted to seize the leadership and created a second schism, giving rise to the Mina sect. This fact emphasized a growing tendency to diversity of faith and practise and the rise of rival scriptures. Accordingly he conceived and carried through the collection of the body of scriptures called the Adi ("first") Granth (see below), which was completed in 1604 (or within about fifty years of the death of the first Guru) and deposited it in the newly built temple. The importance of this for the Sikhs can not be overestimated, guaranteeing as it did the perpetuity of the sect. His period is marked by increased stress from the Mohammedans. Already under the previous Guru there had been armed conflict, which in Arjan's time became serious; there was now demand made that hymns in the Granth hostile to Mohammedanism be destroyed. Arjan was taken prisoner by the emperor and tortured to death ostensibly for refusal to become a Mohammedan, possibly, however, for giving aid to a revolting son of the emperor. Har Gobind, the sixth Guru, was the son of Arjan. Probably because of the increasing pressure of Moslem opposition, he instituted a standing army for the Sikhs, and militarism becomes more pronounced from this time on. Hostilities were frequent, the Guru was himself imprisoned, but the Sikhs were welded together by their trials. The next two Gurus were insignificant. The ninth, Teg Bahadur, youngest son of Har Gobind, took up again the practise of travel, but the military establishment was maintained. He is represented as going to the court at Delhi practically as a sacrifice for his people, where he was beheaded. The tenth Guru, Gobind Rai, afterward Gobind Singh, was the son of Teg Bahadur. He was engaged in conflict with the hill rajahs for almost his whole guruship, and fighting with Mohammedans was also practically constant. His significance for the religion is great. He abolished for the Sikh conformity to the Hindu customs of cutting the hair and shaving the head, instituted fivefold baptism with water stirred with a sword after which each Sikh took the name Singh (" lion "), forbade intermarriage of Sikhs with Mohammedans, confirmed tithes as the substitute for free-will offerings, completed the Granth and made it better suited to the changed conditions, and finally refused to appoint a successor, directing Sikhs to obey the Granth as " the visible body of the Guru." This left religious direction in the hands of the official " reader of the Granth."

4. History from 1708.

After the death of Gobind Singh in 1708, the history of the Sikhs is obscure till 1800. It is known that they were persecuted, and that a price of from five to twenty-five rupees was for a time offered by the Mohammedan ruler of the Punjab for each Sikh head. But as Mohammedan power declined in the region during the eighteenth century, there was organization of minor Sikh confederacies in the Punjab under elected leaders. Ranjit Singh (b. 1780, governor of Lahore 1800, d. 1839) conceived the plan of utilizing Sikh military fanaticism and religious zeal to create a kingdom with Lahore as the capital, and extended the realm to the Sutlej, then the border of British rule. During his life the relations between the British and the Sikhs was friendly. After his death the Sikhs crossed the frontier into British territory, and the dominion of the latter was gravely threatened. The Sikhs fought with their wonted bravery and were beaten back only after inflicting great losses and winning the respect of their foes. The second Sikh war in 1848 resulted in the same way, and the British then took over the administration of the Punjab. The Sikhs entered in numbers the British army in India, in which they still constitute a large and most loyal element. Th[illegible] proved their worth and loyalty first in the [illegible] Mutiny of 1857. Their numbers, as giv[illegible] census of 1901, are 2,195,339, all but [illegible] Punjab, and of these two-thirds are [illegible] Provinces and Kashmir. Religiously they fall into two great divisions and many sects. The divisions are the Sahijdharis and the Singhs, the former rejecting the baptism of Gobind Singh. Besides the schismatic Udasis and Minas referred to above, there are the Handalis, named after a convert of Amar Das, but not arising till about 1640. Their descendants, a small community, have their headquarters at Jandiala in the Punjab, where they are known as Niranjanie. As a religious sect the Sikhs are being absorbed by the dominant Hinduism, have lost almost entirely the language of their sacred book, and are in many respects forgetting the distinguishing practises which under their Gurus marked them as apart from the Hindus.

II. The Religion: The religious tenets of the Sikhs are exhibited in the Adi Granth (or Granth Sahib), consisting of the poetic utterances of the Gurus and of some Indian saints whose sayings the Gurus approved.

1. The Granth.

According to common conceptions, the Gurus were incarnations of deity, and, consequently, the book is inspired. In its present arrangement the Granth serves the purpose of a bible and a liturgy. It is in six parts: (1) an introduction by Nanak; (2) extracts from two of the " rags " (see below) used in devotions at eventide; (3) a devotional chapter composed of extracts from one of the rags; (4) a chapter of extracts from three of the rags used as a prayer before retiring; (5) the Granth proper, of compositions in meter arranged under thirty-one rags (musical measures to which the hymns were sung or chanted—the result is much like a hymn-book with the hymns arranged under the different meters, short, long, common, etc.); (6) a concluding portion by various authors, including Indian saints and fakirs. The extent is indicated by the fact that Trumpp's translation and notes (see bibliography) make a small quarto of 715 pages. The language of the Granth is obscure both as a dialect and because of the educational limitations of the Gurus. It was intended for the understanding of the common people, and was therefore in the vernacular; on this account the Brahmans remonstrated with the Gurus for putting in the common speech what the former contended should not be imparted to the populace, such knowledge being too high for them. But the Gurus were aiming at the very evil of retaining the knowledge of religion within the command of a few, and desired therefore not only that their own people should have this knowledge in their own language (not the Sanskrit), but that other nations should learn of it, and so hoped for the translation of their works into many languages. Of its contents varying estimates exist; the literature of the East rarely appeals to the mind of the West, and it is hardly strange that a book which so abounds in figures, which reflects a life and ordinary conceptions so different from those of the western world, and which is more or less repetitious should not appeal to those who have not [illegible]athed the inspiration of the East. Sir Lepel [illegible]y of the Punjab govern[illegible] it is scarcely possible to [illegible], being struck with the [illegible] figures and with the enlightened devotion of its language (in H. A. Giles and others, *Great Religions of the World*, New York, 1901). This book, like other sacred books, had its period of persecution at the hands of enemies of the religion. While the founder of the religion and writer of a considerable part of the Granth disclaimed special sanctity, he asserted his authority in matters of faith and practise.

Sikh theology is naturally based on established and current Hindu conceptions. Thus the reason for the existence of the Sikh religion is that which explains the avatars of Vishnu—when the world needs it, God vouchsafes a new revelation. The new worship is based on the old Hindu idea of the efficacy of repeating devotionally the name of God. God is one, but in the Hindu-pantheistic sense. He alone is real, all the world is unreal. He is formless, yet diffused throughout creation. God and his worshiper are in some sense one; yet the Hindu distinction between paramatman (supreme soul) and jivatman (individual soul) is maintained, the latter being an emanation of the former. Attempts have been made to show the influence of Christianity upon Sikh concepts and teachings. Many of the ideas are very similar and may possibly be of Christian origin; yet it must be said that all can be paralleled from pre-Christian Hindu or Buddhistic sources. How similar these ideas are to Christian teaching may be shown by a few examples. Nanak resisted the temptation of the devil who offered him the wealth of the world to abandon his mission (cf. Matt. iv. 8–10). He used to complain because when he was silent the Brahmans called him an idiot, and when he talked they said he chattered (cf. Matt. xi. 18–19). Among the figures he used was the disparity between the size of the seed of the Indian fig-tree and the tree itself (cf. Matt. xiii. 31–32). The incident of the needle related above (I., § 2) reminds of Matt. xix. 21. Angad made the purity and simplicity of children the quality of believers which endeared them to the Creator. However, the thoroughly Hindu foundation is unmistakable. The doctrines of reincarnation and of karma are held in their entirety; constantly in the teachings of the Gurus inequality of fortune to desert is explained as the result of deeds done in a former incarnation. Belief in Nirvana is a tenet of the faith, and the word is used in the twofold sense familiar to students of Buddhism—absorption into the Absolute with resultant loss of personality, and a sense cognate with that of "paradise." The sacred number is that of the Hindus—five, and true Sikhs are distinguished by reception of fivefold baptism and by the wearing of five articles—long hair, comb, sword, short drawers, and steel bracelet. The essentials of Sikh practise are abstention from Hindu pilgrimages, from idolatry and from offerings to idols, from wine and tobacco; women are not to be secluded nor is infanticide to be practised; the denunciation of suttee (concremation of a widow) is emphatic; observance of the caste system with its load of defilements and purifications is prohibited; and the duty of earning one's living is enforced. Stress is laid upon the virtues of truth, honesty, loyalty to the Guru and the religion, gratitude, charity to members of the faith, evenhanded justice, filial duty, humility, patience, distrust of self, freedom from superstition, and the recompensing of good for evil. Most of the Granth is taken up with metrical homilies upon these subjects and on the duty of avoiding the corresponding vices. The Sikh is to rise before day, to bathe, repeat part of the scriptures, and meditate on the divine name. He is to bear in mind that true sacrifice consists in being charitable to those who repeat God's name and practise humility. His ordinary acts are to become acts of devotion, and he is to pray for the extension of the religion.

2. Belief and Practise.

GEO. W. GILMORE.

BIBLIOGRAPHY: As a source incomparably the best work is M. A. Macauliffe, *The Sikh Religion; its Gurus, sacred Writings and Authors*, 6 vols., Oxford, 1908 (this translates the Granth, placing the separate compositions after the accounts of the Gurus to whom they are credited. In the lives of the Gurus the author has used the native sources, and the flavor of the originals is preserved; unfortunately, the matter is rather poorly arranged. The point of view is sympathetic to the religion). Next best is *Adi Granth, transl. by E. Trumpp*, London, 1877 (the transl. is inferior in its English—the translator was a German—and is said to be inadequate from the point of view of fidelity to the original; its value is that it translates consecutively; the introduction is extensive and has value). For the history of the Sikhs consult: J. D. Cunningham, *A Hist. of the Sikhs from the Origin of the Nation to the Battles of the Sutlej*, London, 1849; L. Griffin, *The Rajahs of the Punjab*, ib. 1873; idem, *Ranjit Singh*, ib. 1892; E. Trumpp, *Nanak der Stifter der Sikh Religion*, Munich, 1876. On the religion consult: H. H. Wilson, *Religious Sects of the Hindus*, Calcutta, 1846; *Sakhi Namah. Sakhee Book, or the Description of Gooroo Gobind Singh's Religion and Doctrines, transl. . . . by Sirdar Attar Singh*, Benares, 1873; A. Barth, *Religions of India*, pp. 242 sqq., London, 1881; E. Trumpp, *Die Religion der Sikhs nach der Quellen*, Leipsic, 1881; F. Pincott, in *Religious Systems of the World*, London and New York, 1893; A. S. Geden, *Studies in Eastern Religions*, London, 1900 (excellent); P. D. Chantepie de la Saussaye, *Religionsgeschichte*, ii. 155–157, Tübingen, 1905. Some magazine literature is indicated in Richardson, *Encyclopædia*, p. 1013.

SILOAM INSCRIPTION: An inscription found in the conduit in Jerusalem leading from the Virgin's Fount (or Virgin's Spring or Fountain of Steps) to the Pool of Siloam (see JERUSALEM, II.). The inscription was incised in the right-hand wall of the conduit as one enters from the pool, and about nineteen feet from the entrance. It occupied the lower part of an artificial niche so hewed as to form a rectangular cartouche, and the upper part of this niche was left vacant. The inscription was discovered in the summer of 1880 by two boys. Dr. Schick, a German architect then resident in Jerusalem, having heard of the find, examined it, and had the water lowered in order to make a copy of the inscription. His efforts were not very successful, owing in part to his lack of skill as an archeologist, and in part to the fact that there was a deposit of lime over the place, and further because of confusion made by chance marks or cracks in the rock. Dr. A. H. Sayce of Oxford made the next copy in Feb., 1881, which was more nearly correct. In April of the same year a correct copy was secured by Dr. Hermann Guthe, who removed the lime deposits by chemical means, made a cast from which squeezes were taken, and in this way removed all doubts as to the actual contents of the inscription.

This inscription is in six lines, written in the early script very closely resembling that of the Moabite Stone (q.v.) and of the current Phenician inscriptions. The first line is mutilated at the end, and a small break intrudes in lines two to four. The language is idiomatic Hebrew, the text is unpointed, and the orthography is, in the technical sense, "defective" in that the letters Waw and Yod, used as vowels, are often omitted where in later Hebrew they are written to aid in the pronunciation. An attempt was made to steal the inscription, and in the process it was broken; the fragments are now in the museum at Constantinople. The casts, squeezes, and the original in full light combine to make possible a nearly complete translation of the oldest Israelitish inscription known of any considerable length. Its date is by most scholars put not later than the reign of Hezekiah (714-686?), and it is placed in connection with II Kings xx. 20, where it is stated that Hezekiah "made a pool, and a conduit," and with II Chron. xxxii. 30, R. V., "Hezekiah stopped the upper spring of the waters of Gihon, and brought them straight down on the west side of the city of David." The following is the translation of Dr. S. R. Driver (*Notes on the Hebrew Text of . . . Samuel*, p. xvi., Oxford, 1890).

1. [Behold] the piercing through! And this was the manner of the piercing through. Whilst yet [the miners were lifting up]

2. the pick each towards his fellow, and whilst yet there were three cubits to be [cut through, there was heard] the voice of each call-

3. ing to his fellow, for there was a fissure (?) in the rock on the right hand . . . And on the day of the

4. piercing through, the miners (lit. hewers) smote each so as to meet his fellow, pick against pick; and there flowed

5. the water from the source to the pool, 1200 cubits; and one hun-

6. dred cubits was the height of the rock over the head of the miners. GEO. W. GILMORE.

BIBLIOGRAPHY: H. Guthe, in *ZDMG*, 1882, pp. 725-750 (the original publication by this scholar), and in *ZDPV*, xiii (1890), 203-204, 286-288; C. R. Conder, in PEF, *Quarterly Statement*, 1882, pp. 122 sqq.; P. Berger, in *Journal des débats*, Apr. 16, 1882; *Records of the Past*, new series, i. 168-175, London, 1889; W. F. Birch, in PEF, *Quarterly Statement*, 1890, pp. 208-210; S. R. Driver, ut sup., pp. xiv.-xvi., xxxii., xxxv.; C. Clermont-Ganneau, *Les Tombeaux de David et des rois de Juda et le tunnel-aqueduc de Siloe*, Paris, 1897; E. J. Pilcher, in *PSBA*, xix (1897), 165-182, xx (1898), 213-222, and PEF, *Quarterly Statement*, 1898, pp. 56-60; M. Lidzbarski, *Handbuch der nordsemitischen Epigraphik*, Weimar, 1898; A. Socin, *Die Siloah Inschrift*, Freiburg, 1899; T. H. Weir, *Short Hist. of the Text of the O. T.*, London, 1899; G. A. Cooke, *Text-Book of North-Semitic Inscriptions*, ib. 1903; *DB*, iv. 515-516; *JE*, xi. 339-341.

SILVERIUS, sil-vī'ri-us: Pope 536-537. The pontificate of Silverius, who was the son of Pope Hormisdas, fell during the period of the struggle between the Goths and the eastern Empire and of the discussion as to the value of the Chalcedonian decrees. According to the *Liber pontificalis*, he owed his elevation to the favor, won by money, of Theodatus, the Gothic king, and there was no formal election, his enthronement taking place June 8, 536. The speedy success of Belisarius in Italy made difficult the position of Silverius as the protégé of the Gothic king. By agreement Belisarius occupied Rome Dec. 9, 536; but the agreement was short-lived, for Silverius incurred the hostility of Empress Theodora by siding with the deposed Patriarch Anthimus. The pope soon renewed his relations with the Goths, and he was charged with purposing to admit them to Rome; this seems not improbable, in spite of the denial of his biographer, for from the Goths Silverius had most to expect. In Mar., 537, Belisarius deposed Silverius and banished him as a monk to Patara in Lycia. His successor was Vigilius, whose subserviency in dogmatic matters secured the favor of Theodora. The case against Silverius was reopened, and he was brought back to Italy, only to be banished to the island of Ponza in the Tyrrhenian Sea, where he died at a date unknown. (A. HAUCK.)

BIBLIOGRAPHY: *Liber pontificalis*, ed. Mommsen in *MGH, Gest. pont. Rom.*, i (1898), 144; Jaffé, *Regesta*, i. 115; Procopius, *De bello Gothico*, i. 25, printed in Muratori, *Scriptores*, i. 1, pp. 247-369; J. Langen, *Geschichte der römischen Kirche*, ii. 341 sqq., Bonn, 1885; F. Gregorovius, *Hist. of the City of Rome*, i. 369, 395-398, London, 1894; Bower, *Popes*, i. 344-347; Milman, *Latin Christianity*, i. 461; Hefele, *Conciliengeschichte*, ii. 571, Fr. transl., ii. 2, p. 873.

SILVESTER: The name of two popes and two antipopes.

Silvester I.: Pope 314-335. The important events falling during the pontificate of this pope were the conversion of Constantine [and the alleged "donation" of that emperor] and the beginning of the Arian and the Donatistic controversies, though in neither of them had he direct participation. Eusebius (*Vita Constantini*, III., vii.) reports that he was represented at the Council of Nicæa and also at the Synod of Arles, the latter of which sent its canons to him. The period of his pontificate is given by the Catalogus Liberianus.

(A. HAUCK.)

BIBLIOGRAPHY: *Liber pontificalis*, ed. Mommsen in *MGH, Gest. pont. Rom.*, i (1898), 47; Jaffé, *Regesta*, i. 28-29; R. A. Lipsius, *Chronologie der römischen Bischöfe*, p. 259, Kiel, 1869; Bower, *Popes*, i. 45-54; Milman, *Latin Christianity*, i. 94-95.

Silvester II. (Gerbert): Pope 999-1003. Gerbert was possibly a native of Aurillac in Auvergne, and his birth-year probably falls between 940 and 950; his education he received at the monastery of Aurillac, remaining in connection with the Abbot Gerald and his successor Raymond, and there manifesting his talent. Later he went to Spain and studied mathematics, astronomy, and music under Bishop Hatto of Vich in Catalonia, with whom in 970 he went to Rome, where his accomplishments led John XIII. to recommend him to Otto the Great. From Rome (c. 972) he went to Reims to receive instruction in dialectics from a celebrated archdeacon of that place, where he came into relations with Archbishop Adalbero, a man of great eminence in political as well as in ecclesiastical life. The archbishop stimulated Gerbert to teach as well as to learn; this he did, dealing with the "Introduction" of Porphyry, the "Categories" of Aristotle, and with writings of Cicero and Boethius. His pupils read the poets, and received training in the conduct of discussions. The course led up to the study of arithmetic, music, astronomy, and geometry, and the teacher became celebrated in France, Germany, and Italy. Some time during this period he held from Otto II. the abbey of Bobbio near Pavia, not later than the beginning of 983. As such he had a high position and took part in politics. Yet his position as abbot was rendered unpleasant by the possessions of the abbey, which made many his enemies. At the death of Otto II., he left the abbey, seeming to see decadence in Church and State, and went to Reims, intending to take up again his beloved studies. He again began to teach, having assembled a rich library; but he desired ecclesiastical activity, and became secretary of Adalbero and so participator in political affairs. The archbishop was engaged heartily in the service of protecting and safeguarding the interests of Otto III., in which he was ably assisted by Gerbert. Adalbero was interested also in France; and in the elevation of Hugh Capet to the throne, after the death of Louis V., the influence of the archbishop and of Gerbert was seen. After the death of Adalbero, Gerbert naturally expected to be chosen to the see of Reims, but was passed over in favor of Arnulf, who soon became a partisan of the Lothringians, which led to the accusation of treason being lodged against Arnulf and his trial before a synod, where the question was raised concerning the jurisdiction of a synod over a bishop. Eventually Arnulf resigned his see and Gerbert was elected in his place. After this event, Gerbert became pronouncedly anti-papal, turning against the pope the saying "man must obey God rather than man," and declaring that if the pope sinned against a brother and did not listen to the Church, he is to be regarded as a heathen and a publican. Gerbert did not abide by his principles, however. In 991 John XV. sent as his representative to France and Germany Abbot Leo of St. Boniface in Rome, that he might investigate the affairs of the see of Reims. At a synod called by Leo, June 2, 995, only four German bishops were present, and the French bishops held aloof. The apology delivered here by Gerbert marks the beginning of his backward tendency, and attempted to show that part of the trouble arose through Rome's delay in answering. Gerbert was prohibited from exercising the duties of his office until decision was made. At a new synod of July 1, 995, Gerbert was sure of French support and therefore was bolder; but no decision was reached, and Gerbert thought things favorable to himself and went to Rome to carry out his plan of defense. Meanwhile John had died and Gregory V. had taken his place, and was engrossed with the idea of reform of the Church. The prospect was therefore not altogether favorable to Gerbert, and in France his support had grown lukewarm. But Gerbert was in close relations with Otto III., who admired his learning and valued his services and was admired and praised by Gerbert for his character and power.

The favor of Otto was used with the pope in Gerbert's interests, and the latter was made archbishop of Ravenna, 998, where he appeared as the furtherer of Gregory's plans for reform, taking part in synods concerned with that business. The death of Gregory in Feb., 999, led to the elevation of Gerbert to the papal chair as Silvester II., through the favor of Otto. Gerbert turned his back upon his past, recognized Arnulf as archbishop of Reims, assisted the emperor in carrying out his plans for reconstituting his kingdom, plans which were essentially anti-German. Yet pope and emperor were not entirely at one, Rome was committed to neither, and the death of Otto, Jan. 23, 1002, broke the prospects of realization of Silvester's plans and his further hopes of greatness. The next year the latter also died.

Silvester's writings included the subjects of dialectics, mathematics, and theology. His *De corpore et sanguine Domini* inquires whether the Eucharist and the historical body of Christ are identical. Silvester's reputation was principally for great learning, which was so great that he was accounted a sorcerer. He was not creative, however. He was an idealist in politics, and this gave an air of insincerity to his attempts, while self-seeking is not to be eliminated from the motives which ruled his action. As a consequence his pontificate is memorable for nothing of achievement in Church or State.

(A. HAUCK.)

BIBLIOGRAPHY: The *Opera* were edited by J. B. Masson, Paris, 1611; by A. Duchesne, in *Historiæ Francorum scriptores*, ii. 789–844, 5 vols., Paris, 1636–49, whence they went into *MPL*, cxxxix. 201–268; the *Œuvres* with life, by A. Olleris, Clermont, 1867; the "Letters," with introduction, by J. Havet, Paris, 1889 (best); earlier ed. in Bouquet, *Recueil*, vols. ix.–x.; the *Opera mathematica* by N. Bubnov, Berlin, 1899. Bibliographies are to be found in: U. Chevalier, *Répertoire des sources historiques du moyen âge*, Paris, 1877; F. Cerroti, *Bibliografia di Roma*, Rome, 1893; and Potthast, *Wegweiser*, pp. 501–502.

The primary source for a life are his "letters"—note eds. above in *Opera* and *Œuvres*. Consult. Mann, *Popes*, v. 1–120 (with a critical list of literature); C. F. Hock, *Gerbert oder Papst Sylvester II.*, Vienna, 1837 (best); M. M. Büdinger, *Ueber Gerberts wissenschaftliche und politische Stellung*, Marburg, 1851; C. Prantl, *Geschichte der Logik im Abendlande*, ii. 53–57, Leipsic, 1856; F. Lausser, *Gerbert, étude historique sur le x. siècle*, Aurillac, 1866 (uses fresh material); E. de Barthélemy, *Gerbert, étude sur sa vie et ses ouvrages*, Paris, 1868; C. Quéant, *Gerbert, ou Sylvestre II. et le siècle de fer*, Paris, 1868; A. von Reumont, *Geschichte der Stadt Rom*, vol. ii., Berlin, 1868; R. Baxmann, *Politik der Päpste*, vol. ii., Elberfeld, 1869; M. Sepet, in *Revue des questions historiques*, vii (1869), 440–523, viii (1870), 122–169; H. Reuter, *Geschichte der religiösen Aufklärung im Mittelalter*, i. 78–84, Berlin, 1875; K. Werner, *Gerbert von Aurillac. Die Kirche und Wissenschaft seiner Zeit*, Vienna, 1879; H. Weissenborn, *Gerbert, Beitrag zur Kenntniss der Mathematik des Mittelalters*, Berlin, 1888; K. Schultheiss, *Papst Sylvester II. als Lehrer und Staatsmann*, Hamburg, 1891; idem, *Die Sagen über Silvester II.*, ib. 1893; R. Allen, in *English Historical Review*, vii (1892), 625–668 (a prize essay); T. K. Schlockwerder, *Untersuchungen zur Chronologie der Briefe Gerberts*, Halle, 1893; F. Gregorovius, *Hist. of the City of Rome*, iii. 466 sqq., London, 1895; F. J. Picavet, *Gerbert, un pape philosophe*, Paris, 1897; J. Lair, *Études critiques*, i. 94 sqq., Paris, 1899; C. P., *Les Papes français*, Tours, 1901; E. Duchesne, *Le Domostroi du pape Silvestre*, Paris, 1904; *Histoire littéraire de la France*, vi. 559–614; Ceillier, *Auteurs sacrés*, ii. 901–911; Schaff, *Christian Church*, iv. 777–782; Hefele, *Conciliengeschichte*, vol. iv.; Bower, *Popes*, iii. 331–333; Milman, *Latin Christianity*, iii. 202 sqq.

Silvester III.: Antipope 1044–46. See BENEDICT IX.

Silvester IV.: Antipope 1102. See PASCHAL II.

SILVIA AQUITANA: The name under which is known a pilgrim of the fourth century to the Holy Land, who has left a record of her travels. The trend toward pilgrimages became almost a craze in the fourth century, against which, e.g., Gregory of Nyssa protested (*MPG*, xlvi. 1016–24), though Jerome favored it (*Epist.*, xlvi., Eng. transl., in *NPNF*, 2 ser., vi. 60–65). A sort of guide-book made on a journey c. 333 A.D. exists in the *Itinerarium Burdigalense* ("The Bordeaux Pilgrim"), but it is not a journal of travel like that which exists in the *Peregrinatio S. Silviæ*, discovered in 1884 by G. F. Gamurrini at Arezzo in Tuscany and consisting of a letter describing her experiences written to the nuns of a cloister at her native place. The manuscript is not complete, lacks both beginning and end, and also a part from the middle of the narrative. Fortunately, the omissions are practically supplied by Peter the Deacon, who used the narrative, as did Bede. The date may be set between 379–387, with 394 as the latest date possible; in that year the bones of the Apostle Thomas were translated to the chief church at Edessa, which the pilgrim distinguished from the Martyrium which she visited. Recently, however, Meister (see bibliography) has proposed 533–540 as the date of the pilgrimage, and many have accepted his arguments. Gamurrini sought to identify the pilgrim with the traveler named by Palladius in the "Lausiac History," but Férotin (see bibliography) has with greater probability suggested the Spanish nun Eucheria, and at any rate "St. Silvia of Aquitania" is "a purely mythical personage." That the pilgrim was a person of consequence appears from the attentions which were showered upon her by clerics, monks, and bishops, and even by the military, escorts being furnished at times. She traveled in comfort and with a considerable retinue.

Peter the Deacon states that she made Jerusalem her headquarters, visited Bethlehem, Hebron, and the other cities celebrated in patriarchal history; covered all Palestine in her travels—Tabor, Carmel, Nazareth, Nain, Tiberias, Capernaum; then went to Egypt and back to Jerusalem, and then to Sinai and other sites in the Mosaic history, where the extant manuscript takes up the story. At Sinai she was shown the sacred sites, the thorn-bush and the like, went to Paran and Clysma, Rameses in Goshen, Tanis, and then to Jerusalem by way of Pelusium; then visited Nebo and the grave of Job in the Hauran by way of Aenon; next to Antioch, Hierapolis, Edessa, and Harran, her farthest point east. Her return led via Constantinople through Asia Minor, and in Seleucia she read the Acts of Thecla, while in Chalcedon she visited the grave of St. Euphemia.

The narrative is interesting, faithful, and sincere. Her notice of the worship of the Jerusalem community is important, being the only one covering that period; she attended such services as those of Christmas, Easter, Ascension Day, and Pentecost, and describes baptism and the instruction leading to it. Far behind this in worth are such books as Eucherius' *De situ Hierosolymitanæ urbis* (a compilation from oral and written sources), the *Breviarius de Hierosolyma* of the sixth century, Bede's *De locis sanctis*, and the work of Peter the Deacon (q.v.). Of independent worth is Theodosius' *De situ terræ sanctæ* (middle of the sixth century); the reports of the Gallic bishop Arculphus rest upon an *Itinerarium* of c. 580 and one of Adamnan. (G. Krüger.)

Bibliography: The editio princeps, by G. F. Gamurrini, the discoverer of the document, was issued at Rome, 1887, 2d ed., 1888, with the account of Peter the deacon and other matter, Italian transl., Milan, 1890. The best ed. is that of P. Geyer, in *CSEL*, xxxix., Vienna, 1898. Other texts are those of J. Pomialowsky, St. Petersburg, 1889; J. H. Bernard, for Palestine Pilgrims Text Society, with Eng. transl., introduction and notes, London, 1896; E. A. Bechtel, Chicago, 1902; and a fragment by E. von Dobschütz, in *TU*, 1899, pp. 167 sqq. Consult: L. Delisle, in *Bibliothèque de l'école des chartes*, xlvii (1877), 342–346; T. Mommsen, in *SBA*, 1887, pp. 357–364; E. Wölfflin, in *Archiv für lateinische Lexicographie und Grammatik*, iv (1887), 259–277; C. Weyman, in *TQS*, lxx (1888), 38–50; L. de Saint-Aignan, *Le Pèlerinage de S. Sylvie . . . en 385*, Orléans, 1889; E. Ebert, *Allgemeine Geschichte der Literatur des Mittelalters*, i. 345–347, Leipsic, 1889; G. Krüger, in *Preussische Jahrbücher*, lxvi (1890), 491–505; P. Geyer, *Kritische Bemerkungen zu S. Silviæ . . . peregrinatio*, Augsburg, 1890; F. Cabrol, *Étude sur la Peregrinatio Silviæ. Les Églises de Jérusalem, la discipline et la liturgie au iv. siècle*, Paris, 1895; J. von der Vliet, in *TSK*, xiv (1896), 1–29; M. Férotin, *Le Véritable Auteur de la Peregrinatio Sylviæ*, Paris, 1903; A. Bludau, in *Der Katholik*, lxxxiv. 2 (1904), 61–74, 81–98; J. Anglade, *De latinitate libelli qui inscriptus est Peregrinatio . . .*, Paris, 1905; C. Meister, in *Rheinisches Museum*, lxiv (1909), 337–392.

SIMEON, sim'e-on: Second bishop of Jerusalem and cousin of Jesus; d. c. 107. His father was Cleophas or Clopas (see Alphæus), who, according to Hegesippus (Eusebius, *Hist. eccl.*, III., xi. 2), was a brother of Joseph. His mother may have been the Mary mentioned in John xix. 25, who is designated as the wife of Cleophas. Owing to his family connections, Simeon was chosen successor of James the Just in the leadership of the Jerusalem congregation. He is said to have held his office a long time, and to have attained an age of 120 years. As successor of James, Simeon was the head not only of the congregation of Jerusalem but of all other congregations in Palestine. Since the congregation of Jerusalem left the city before the catastrophe of the year 70 and went to Pella, the seat of the activity of Simeon must have been there. Tradition also says that under Emperor Trajan and Governor Atticus he was denounced by the Jews as a Davidite and Christian, a pretender to the crown. At the order of Atticus he was for many days tortured and finally crucified. (H. Achelis.)

Bibliography: The sources are Eusebius, *Hist eccl.*, III., xi., xxii., xxxii., xxxv., IV., xxii. 4, Eng. transl. in *NPNF*, vol. i., passim; and the same author's "Chronicle" for the year 107. Consult further: Tillemont, *Mémoires*, ii. 186 sqq.; J. B. Lightfoot, *Apostolic Fathers*, part II., i. 15, 21–22, 39, 58, 60, 66, ii. 443–449, London, 1885; E. Löning, *Gemeindeverfassung des Urchristentums*, pp. 107–114, Halle, 1888; A. C. McGiffert, *Apostolic Age*, pp. 564–565, New York, 1897; T. Zahn, *Forschungen zur Geschichte des neutestamentlichen Kanons*, vi. 282 sqq., Leipsic, 1900; R. Knopf, *Nachapostolisches Zeitalter*, pp. 1 sqq., Tübingen, 1905; Harnack, *Litteratur*, i. 223 sqq.; *DCB*, iv. 677–678; *KL*, xi. 307–308.

SIMEON METAPHRASTES, met-a-fras'tiz: Byzantine hagiographer; flourished probably in the second half of the tenth century. Of his life scarcely a detail is known; even the younger Psellos' encomium and office for Simeon's day, Nov. 28 (now combined with St. Theoktiste's day, Nov. 9) (*MPG*, cxiv. 183–208), gives little information. It would seem, however, that Simeon was born at Constantinople, where he studied philosophy and rhetoric and attained high rank, although the only office which he is expressly said to have filled was that of logothete. The one concrete statement of Psellos, that Simeon took part in a naval expedition, is, however, incorrect. This error is due to the misunderstanding of a passage in Simeon's revision of Niketas Magister's life of St. Theoktiste, which really states that Niketas, not Simeon, served on the expedition of Himerios against Crete in 902. To the information thus gained Markos Eugenikos (d. 1443) adds that Simeon held a disputation with a Persian (Mohammedan?), and that, toward the end of his life, he became a monk and was buried in the Church of the Mother of God at Hodigi. Beginning with the time of Psellos (eleventh century), manuscripts of Simeon Metaphrastes are numerous, and he is mentioned with great frequency. A monastic record of 1196 ascribes to Simeon the authorship of a life of St. Paul of Mount Latros (d. Dec. 15, 956). It would seem, however, that this life was written soon after the reign of Nikephoros Phokas, or, still more probably, about 991; and it may well be doubted whether it really belongs to Simeon, especially as it is lacking in his collection and is assigned to him by only a single document. At the same time, it must be remembered that Simeon may have written encomiums which he did not include in his hagiography. It is clear, moreover, that the original collection includes the festal sermon of Emperor Constantine on the translation of the Edessa picture of Christ, delivered Aug. 16, 944, and incorporated by Simeon almost without change, thus definitely placing the compilation in the second half of the tenth century. Again, in the life of St. Samson, evidently written by Simeon, a miracle is recorded as happening to the Protospathary Bardas, the close friend of Romanos II., though the event in question may perhaps better be referred to the reign of Romanos' son, Basil (976–1025), while the life contains other allusions to the reign of John Tzimiskes (969–976). The theory of many scholars that the Logothete Simeon Magister to whom is ascribed a *Chronicon* (ed. *CSHB*, xxxi. 1838) is to be identified with Simeon Metaphrastes would prove that the author was a close associate of Romanos I. (920–944), although he wrote in the reign of Nikephoros Phokas (963–969); but the problem of the authorship of the chronicle is too unsettled to permit its use in determining the date of Simeon Metaphrastes. To the Logothete Simeon Magister is also ascribed a collection of canons (ed. *MPG*, cxiv. 235–292), which form the basis of the commentary of Alexios Aristenos (about 1130); and it is not impossible that this canonist was identical with the Logothete Simeon Magister who, according to the *Practica* of Eustathios Romanos (lxiv. 1), was an elderly member of the imperial court of justice about 1000, and even with the patrician and first secretary Simeon, who prepared two *novellæ* of Nikephoros Phokas in 964 and 967. The Arab historian Yahya ibn Said of Antioch, who continued the annals of Eutychius to 1026, sets the activity of "Simon, secretary and logothete who has written the accounts of the saints and their festivals," in the early part of the reign of Basil II. (976–1025), a statement borne out by the express declaration of Markos Eugenikos that Simeon's official career was during the reigns of Phokas, John (Tzimiskes), and Basil II. Nine letters are also ascribed to Simeon (*MPG*, cxiv. 227–236), and some others are preserved in manuscript, but none of these contain any data establishing their authorship. He is likewise the putative author of some prayers (*MPG*, cxiv. 219–224), iambics on the Eucharist (ib.), verses on Christ and the apostles (unedited), a series of "moral alphabets" (*MPG*, cxiv. 131–136; penitential prayers in alphabetical form), twenty-four "Ethical Discourses" excerpted from the writings of Basil the Great (*MPG*, xxxii. 1115–1382), 150 chapters on the fifty orations of Macarius the Egyptian (ib., xxxiv. 841–965; see MACARIUS, 1), and possibly three necrological poems (ed. L. Sternbach, in *Eos*, v. 7–21). Only a thorough stylistic study, combined with the establishment of the manuscript transmission, can determine which of these writings belong to Simeon Metaphrastes, whose name was used to give prestige to many works by other hands, not only for edifying literature in general, beginning with the thirteenth century, but also for an anonymous account of the building of St. Sophia (ed. T. Preger, *Scriptores originum Constantinopolitanarum*, i. 74–108, Leipsic, 1901). Older scholars ascribed to him a commentary on Luke on the basis of citations in the *Catena* of Niketas, although these passages are really quoted from his lives of the saints, as well as a work *De moribus ecclesiæ* (N. C. Papadopoli, *Prænotationes mystagogicæ*, Padua, 1697, p. 398), of which nothing more is known.

Life, Date, and Writings.

Simeon Metaphrastes owes his fame to his collection of the legends of the saints, which has won him the deep admiration not only of his own communion, but also of many Roman Catholic theologians. The extent, significance, and value of the work have all been matters of much debate, the cause being the concentration on individual texts rather than on the collection as a whole. It had already been observed by Leo Allatius (in his *De Symeonum scriptis diatriba*, Paris, 1664) that a certain complex of lives recurred in many manuscripts, while the transmission of the remaining lives was extremely discrepant. Working along this line, H. Delehaye and A. Ehrhard have carried the problem much nearer solution, the latter scholar determining the genuine lives in the hagiography of Simeon to be 149. These lives are preserved with remarkable uniformity in the various manuscripts, while the rest present the widest divergencies. The most of the genuine lives still need critical editing, and the Greek text of twenty-four is extant as yet only in manuscript. Nevertheless, the material already accessible is sufficient for a correct estimate of Simeon's mode of work, although complete knowledge would involve acquaintance with all his predecessors. This alone would serve to determine the independence of Simeon in the choice of his texts, which in calendrical order diverge sharply from other menologies and are surprisingly close to the Constantinople Synaxarion.

His Hagiography.

It is certain that Simeon created no new legends; he was, as the epithet given him implies, a metaphrast, reproducing the old legends in the style demanded by the literary taste of his time, and at the same time occasionally making alterations in the matter and connecting traditions which originally were distinct. The legends which he incorporated in his collection, and for the credibility of which he was in no way responsible, were themselves later revampings of the original acts of martyrs; and many offenses against good taste must be ascribed to his sources and to the requirements of his age rather than to Simeon himself, who was evidently a man of culture, taste, and talent. It should be noted, at the same time, that he did not stand entirely alone. A number of his contemporaries were working in the same spirit; men like Nikephoros Chumnos followed his example in the style of the thirteenth century, and in the fourteenth Konstantinos Akropolites gained the title of "the new Metaphrastes." In comparison with these imitators Simeon distinctly gains, and he was, so far as a tenth-century Byzantine could be, natural and simple in diction. (E. VON DOBSCHÜTZ.)

BIBLIOGRAPHY: The collected works are in *MPG*, cxiv.-cxvi. Cf. also *Analecta Bollandiana*, viii. 308-316, and Delehaye, in Griffin and Nau's *Patrologia orientalis*, ii. 4, pp. 546-557, Paris, 1907. Consult: L. Allatius, *De Symeonum Scriptis diatriba*, Paris, 1664; C. Oudin, *Commentarius de scriptoribus ecclesiæ antiquis*, ii. 1300-83, Frankfort, 1722; Fabricius-Harles, *Bibliotheca Græca*, viii. 29, x. 180-345, xi. 295-334, Hamburg, 1802-08; E. E. Kunik, in P. Krug's *Forschungen in der älteren Geschichte Russlands*, ii. 785-807, St. Petersburg, 1848; A. Rambaud, *L'Empire grec au x. siècle*, pp. 92-104, Paris, 1870; F. Hirsch, *Byzantinische Studien*, pp. 52 sqq., 303-355, Leipsic, 1876; R. Nicolai, *Geschichte der griechischen Literatur*, iii. 70, 100, 104, 107-109, Magdeburg, 1878; H. Delehaye, in *Revue des questions historiques*, x (1893), 49-85; *Analecta Bollandiana*, xvi (1897), 312-329, xvii (1898), 448-452; C. de Boor, in *Byzantinische Zeitschrift*, vi (1897), 233-284, x (1901), 70-90; A. Ehrhard, in *Festschrift zum elfhundertjährigen Jubiläum des deutschen Campo Santo in Rom*, pp. 46-82, Rome, 1897; N. Kondatoff, in *ZWT*, xlvi (1903), 434 sqq.; Krumbacher, *Geschichte*, pp. 178 sqq., 200 sqq., 358 sqq., 718-719, et passim.

SIMEON THE NEW THEOLOGIAN: Mystic of the Eastern Church; b. in the village of Galate in Paphlagonia c. 965; d. in a monastery not far from Chrysopolis, near Chalcedon in Bithynia, Asia Minor, between 1032 and 1041. He was sent to Constantinople for his education, but showed no interest in the rhetorical and philosophical studies which were to fit him for the service of the State for which he was intended, nor in the life at court which he tasted as a page. Simeon the Studite (q.v.) had already confirmed his desire for a religious life, and became his spiritual guide after he entered the monastery of Studion, where his mystical bent developed. Being expelled for maintaining an exclusive friendship with his teacher, a thing forbidden by the rules, he went to the monastery of Mamas, near by, of which he became the head and received priesthood. He raised the monastery out of its demoralized condition and established his fame as theologian by his extensive literary activity. During this period Simeon does not seem to have been molested because of his individual views. It was only after he had laid down his office (c. 1017), in order to live in retirement, that he was involved in a conflict with the highest spiritual authority. Stephanos, the syncellus of the patriarch, a canonist of fame and an acute dogmatician, attacked Simeon because he had permitted his namesake Simeon the Studite to be adored after his death in the monastery of Mamas. The syncellus demanded the abolition of this worship; since Simeon persistently refused to give up the worship of his spiritual father, he was banished from Constantinople by a synodical decree to the neighborhood of Chrysopolis. The adherents of Simeon compelled the patriarch to rehabilitate him formally, but he remained in exile and built a new monastery, where he died.

The theology of Simeon connects itself with a development of practical mysticism which may be traced to the end of the fourth century. Its characteristic element was the belief that in certain specially elevated moments there was possible a vision of the divinity as a supernatural light. Simeon was guided and taught by his confessor to consider the vision of the light as the aim of religious struggle. There is nothing novel in the religious experience around which the thoughts of Simeon moved, but the power with which he invested his experiences earned for him the title "new theologian." The vision of the light which was granted to him, Simeon understood as a revelation of God through which he was assured of grace and had personal intercourse with God. These experiences became for him the key for the interpretation of the New Testament, which he read with other eyes since he himself had come in contact with the realities of which the Scriptures testify. As the greatness of the Christian ideal in the New Testament became plainer to him, the more clearly he seemed to see that personal relation with divinity is the indispensable condition for an earnest Christian life, since only from a personally experienced grace flows the power for a life in the spirit. Simeon recognized that it is grace alone that elevates and renews man; no Greek has repeated so often and so emphatically the Pauline antithesis—from grace, not from works. Such principles involved a polemic against the spirit of his church; this inevitably raised opposition to him, but the opposition could not prevent the formation of a school around him or the penetration of his principles into monasticism. The Hesychasts (q.v.) stood entirely upon his shoulders. In the line of Greek mysticism that from Clement and Origen, by way of Gregory of Nyssa and Dionysius the Areopagite, finally leads to the Hesychasts, Simeon represents the culminating point. (K. HOLL.)

BIBLIOGRAPHY: The "Works" are in *MPG*, cxx., and an edition in modern Greek by Dionysios Zagoraios appeared Venice, 1790. A *Vita* by Simeon's pupil Nicetas Stethatos is still in manuscript, but its publication by L. Petit is soon to be expected. Consult: K. Holl, *Enthusiasmus und Bussgewalt. Eine Studie zu Symeon dem neuen Theologen*, Leipsic, 1898; Krumbacher, *Geschichte*, pp. 152-154; Fabricius-Harles, *Bibliotheca Græca*, xi. 302 sqq., Hamburg, 1808; *KL*, xi. 1070.

SIMEON THE STUDITE: Monk in the monastery of Studion at Constantinople, and teacher of Simeon the New Theologian (q.v.); flourished about 975. Exact knowledge of his life is lacking, what is known coming from Nicetas Stethatos, a monk of the same monastery in the middle of the eleventh century. According to Nicetas Simeon wrote *Biblon holēn ōpheleias ousan pneumatikēs agrammatos ōn* (*MPG*, clii. 266 sqq.), perhaps the same as "Thirty-two Ascetic Sermons" attributed to "Simeon the Monastic."

BIBLIOGRAPHY: Leo Allatius, *De Symeonum scriptis*, Paris, 1664; Krumbacher, *Geschichte*, pp. 140, 152–154.

SIMEON STYLITES. See STYLITES.

SIMEON OF THESSALONICA: Archbishop of that city in the early fifteenth century; d. probably in the latter part of 1428. Of his life almost nothing is known, except that he had become archbishop of Thessalonica before 1423, when the city was purchased from the Despot Andronikos Palaiologos by the Venetians, to whom Simeon remained loyal, despite the efforts of Murad II. to induce the Greeks to surrender Thessalonica to the Turks. As a theological writer Simeon exercised a wide influence, being used, and even copied, by many later authors. His works were first edited by Dositheos of Jerusalem (q.v.; Jassy, 1683), and were then reprinted in *MPG*, clv., which also gives the pagination of Dositheos. One of the chief mystagogic theologians of the later Greek Church, he lays far less stress on doctrine than on participation in the divine mysteries, which alone give salvation; and as a polemist his critique of the Bogomiles and his defense of the Hesychasts have the value of original sources. His chief work was the dialogue "Against all Heresies, and on the One Faith of our Lord and God and Savior Jesus Christ, the Holy Rites, and all Mysteries of the Church." The first part, which is much the briefer, is doctrinal, its special themes being the Trinity and Christology, but it also includes polemics against the Jews, Bogomiles, and Mohammedans, and declares that, while it is impossible to convert all men, the Christian should ever be ready to profess his faith. The second part of the dialogue, a mystagogic introduction to the liturgy, begins with the doctrine of baptism and chrism; while the Eucharist affords an opportunity for a most minute discussion of the entire ritual connected with it, the vestments, the sanctuary, etc. Ordination and the various orders of the clergy are then discussed, as well as confession, marriage, and extreme unction, with an appendix on prayer, the daily services, the hymns, the Trisagion (q.v.), and the benedictions.

The dialogue just analyzed (ed. Dositheos, pp. 1–270) is followed by a number of briefer writings. First among these is the treatise "On the Holy Temple" (pp. 271–291), mystagogic like the dialogue. This is followed by three expositions of the Nicene Creed: the "Synoptic Interpretation" (pp. 292–312); the "Most Necessary Exposition" (pp. 313–319; repeated almost word for word in the *Chronicon*, iv. 22, of Georgios Phrantzes, who may indeed have been, as he claimed to be, the author of the treatise, rather than Simeon); and the "Direct Interpretation" (pp. 319–322; incorporated in the first reply of the Patriarch Jeremias II., q.v., to the Wittenberg theologians, and likewise of dubious authorship). Unlike these last two treatises, there is no reason to doubt the authenticity of the "Answers to the Bishop" (pp. 323–370), the prelate in question perhaps being the Metropolitan Gabriel of Pentapolis. This contains information on liturgy and such problems as the origin of evil, life after death, and the angels. The last treatise in the edition of Dositheos imparts the theory of the priesthood to a monk intending to become a priest, a strong tendency toward symbolism being a marked characteristic of the treatise. A number of works as yet unedited are also ascribed to Simeon of Thessalonica, among them a treatise on the exit of the soul from the body and on "The Similar Triodia of Passion Week" (both preserved in manuscript at Jerusalem), as well as a number of letters contained in an Athos manuscript. (PHILIPP MEYER.)

BIBLIOGRAPHY: Leo Allatius, *De Symeonum scriptis*, pp. 185–194, Paris, 1664; C. Oudin, *Commentarius de scriptoribus ecclesiæ*, iii. 2242 sqq., Leipsic, 1722; M. Le Quien, *Oriens Christianus*, ii. 58–59, ib. 1740; W. Cave, *Scriptorum ecclesiasticorum hist. literaria*, ii., appendix, pp. 113–114, Oxford, 1743; Fabricius-Harles, *Bibliotheca Græca*, xi. 328–334, Hamburg, 1808; Ersch and Gruber, *Encyklopädie*, I., lxxxvi. 87 sqq.; Krumbacher, *Geschichte*, pp. 112–113; *KL*, xi. 1073–74.

SIMEON, CHARLES: Church of England; b. at Reading Sept. 24, 1759; d. there Nov. 13, 1836. He was educated at King's College, Cambridge, became fellow in 1782, and in 1783 incumbent of Holy Trinity Church in the same city. He may be considered the founder of the Low-church party. His "evangelical" preaching at first encountered opposition; but eventually he made many converts, and exerted a wide influence. He became interested in missions, and Henry Martyn's work is traceable to him in part. He established a society for purchasing advowsons, and thereby was able to put his sympathizers at strategic points. He published a translation of Claude's *Essay on the Composition of a Sermon* (London, 1801), to which he added notes and a hundred sermon-skeletons, and subsequently published such outlines (2,536 in number) upon the entire Bible (*Horæ Homileticæ*, 17 vols., London, 1819–28; new ed., with addition of remaining works, 21 vols., 1840); *Memorial Sketches of Rev. David Brown, with a Selection of his Sermons Preached at Calcutta* (1831); and a large number of occasional sermons.

BIBLIOGRAPHY: W. Carus, *Memoirs of the Life of Charles Simeon . . . with a Selection from his Writings and Correspondence*, London, 1847; F. Close, *Brief Sketch of the Character and Last Days of C. Simeon*, ib. 1836; J. Williamson, *Brief Memoir of the Rev. C. Simeon*, ib. 1848; H. C. G. Moule, *Charles Simeon*, ib. 1895.

SIMLER, JOSIAS: Swiss Protestant; b. at Cappel (15 m. s. of Zurich) Nov. 6, 1530; d. at Zurich July 2, 1576. He was educated at Basel and Strasburg, and, after completing his studies at Zurich in 1549, was for a few years a teacher and a ministerial supply. In 1552, however, he was made professor of New-Testament exegesis at Zurich, being also minister of the village of Zollikon, near Zurich, until 1557, and deacon of St. Peter's, Zurich, from 1557 to 1560. At Zurich he came into contact with such refugees from the Roman Catholic reaction under Queen Mary of England as John Jewel (q.v.) and John Parkhurst (later bishop of Norwich). In 1560 Simler succeeded Theodor Bibliander (q.v.), and, retiring entirely from ministerial work, divided the lectures on theology with Peter Martyr (q.v.), at whose death, in 1562, he took charge of the entire New-Testament department, which he controlled until he died.

Simler was a most prolific author. He began by translating into Latin a number of the works of Bullinger and other Protestant theologians, and by editing a portion of Peter Martyr's writings, although his projected edition of the collected works of the latter was never realized. He was himself deeply interested in problems of dogmatic theology, particularly in view of the attacks of Italian antitrinitarians upon Reformed tenets. First assailing the teaching of Francesco Stancaro (q.v.), that Christ was a mediator only in virtue of his human nature, in his *Responsio ad maledictum Francisci Stancari Mantuani librum adversus Tigurinæ ecclesiæ ministros de Trinitate et mediatore nostro Jesu Christo* (Zurich, 1563), he likewise wrote, in defense of orthodox Christology, his *De æterno Dei filio Domino et Servatore nostro Jesu Christo et de Spiritu Sancto, adversus veteres et novos antitrinitarios, id est Arianos, Tritheistas, Samosatenianos et Pneumatomachos libri quatuor* (Zurich, 1568); *Assertio orthodoxæ doctrinæ de duabus naturis Christi opposita blasphemiis et sophismatibus Simonis Budnæi* (1575); *Scripta veterum Latina de una persona et duabus naturis Christi adversus Nestorium, Eutychen et Acephalos olim edita* (1571); *De vera Christi secundum humanam naturam in his terris præsentia orthodoxa expositio* (1574); and the anonymous *Ministrorum ecclesiæ Tigurinæ ad confutationem Jacobi Andreæ apologia* (1575). His *Commentarii in Exodum* were published posthumously in 1584; and he was the author of *Oratio de vita et obitu . . . Petri Martyris Vermilii* (Zurich, 1563; Eng. transl. in A. Marten's version of the "Common Places" of Peter Martyr, London, 1583) and *De ortu, vita et obitu . . . Heinrici Bullingeri* (1575). Besides the works already enumerated, Simler wrote on astronomy, the history of literature, geography, and history, the latter category including his *De republica Helvetiorum* (Zurich, 1576), which went through repeated editions until the middle of the eighteenth century, and was translated into German, French, and Dutch. His manuscript historical material, collected by his grandson, is preserved in the municipal library of Zurich. (G. Meyer von Knonau.)

Bibliography: J. G. Stuki, *Vita Josiæ Simleri*, Zurich, 1577; W. A. B. Coolidge, *Josias Simler et les origines de l'Alpinisme jusqu'en 1600*, Grenoble, 1904; G. Meyer von Knonau, in *Jahrbuch des Schweiser Alpenklub*, xxxii. 217–235; *ADB*, xxxiv. 355–358.

SIMON, sai'mōn (SIMEON), BEN YOHAI: Rabbi of the second Christian century, to whom the authorship of the Zohar (see Cabala, § 17) is attributed. He was a favorite pupil of Akiba (q.v.), and was of the party opposed to the Romans. Tradition reports that he was compelled to remain in hiding in a cave for twelve years, until the death of the emperor (Hadrian), the cause being an outspoken condemnation of the Romans and their laws. An event which is better placed late in his life was his mission to Rome to obtain for his coreligionists greater freedom in worship and teaching, and in this mission he succeeded. During his hermit life is placed the composition of the Zohar, the basis of the tradition probably being that he combined a certain mysticism in his teaching. Yet his teaching, prevailingly halachic in type, was rationalistic in so far as he sought always the underlying reason for a Biblical injunction.

Bibliography: L. Lewin, *Rabbi Simon ben Jochai*, Frankfort, 1893; *JE*, xi. 359–363 (gives further literature, mostly in Hebrew).

SIMON THE MACCABEE. See Hasmoneans, § 2.

SIMON MAGUS.

In the Book of Acts (§ 1).
In the Apocrypha and Justin Martyr (§ 2).
His System According to Later Heresiologists (§ 3).
Untenable Theories Concerning Simon Magus (§ 4).
A Sorcerer Syncretized with the Sun (§ 5).
The Twofold Simonian System (§ 6).

1. In the Book of Acts.

One of the most difficult and interesting problems of apostolic and post-apostolic history is presented by Simon Magus, a Samaritan, who is described at once as a Christian, a Jew, and a pagan, a magician and a sorcerer, a Christian religious philosopher and an archheretic, a pseudo-apostle and a pseudo-Messiah, the founder of a religion and an incarnation of God. The earliest source concerning him is Acts viii. 5–24, where he appears as a sorcerer who had "bewitched the people of Samaria, giving out that himself was some great one," yet becoming an adherent of the Apostle Philip and marveling at "the miracles and signs which were done" (verses 5–13). In verses 14–19, on the other hand, he seeks from Peter and John, not (as one would expect in the case of a sorcerer) the power of working miracles like Philip's, but the gift of conferring the Holy Ghost by the laying on of hands, only to have his request refused because of the unworthy motives which had prompted it. It is held by some critics that this entire account was based by a redactor of Acts on some "Acts of Peter," this redactor substituting Philip for Peter in verses 5, 6, 12, 13, adding allusions to John in verses 18b, 19a, 24, interpolating verse 10, and adding verses 14–18a and 19b. It should also be noted, in this connection, that neither the extant Acts of Peter nor the Church Fathers mention Philip and John in their accounts of Simon Magus.

2. In the Apocrypha and Justin Martyr.

The record of Acts is continued by the various recensions of the apocryphal Acts of Peter and kindred literature (cf. Clement of Alexandria, *Strom.*, vii. 17; Hippolytus, *Philosophumena*, vi. 20; Eusebius, *Hist. eccl.*, ii. 14–15; Arnobius, *Adv. gentes*, ii. 12; Philostorgius, *Hær.*, xxix.; Epiphanius, *Hær.*, xxi. 4; etc.), all of which deal with the conflict between Simon Peter and Simon Magus. The scene is Samaria in the *Acta Vercellenses* only, the other sources substituting Judea (or Jerusalem and Cæsarea) and, most frequently, Rome. The time is the reign of Nero or (in the *Acta Vercellenses*) Claudius, but the only new trait ascribed to the characters is the pseudo-Messiahship of Simon Magus, which is shown, for instance, in his attempted ascension (frustrated by the prayer of Peter) and in the epithet: "He that hath stood." An entirely different picture is given by the heresiologists of the early Church. The fragments of Justin Martyr's lost work on heresies state that Simon Magus was born in the Samaritan village of Gitta, and went to Rome in the reign of Claudius. There he is described as honored by a statue on an island in the Tiber, this statue bearing the inscription *Simoni sancto deo* ("To Simon, the holy god"). This latter statement seems, however, to be due to confusion with a statue actually set up on the island in question in honor of the Sabine deity Semo Sancus, with an inscription including the words *Semoni Sanco deo*. At the same time, the tradition of Simon's residence at Rome in the reign of Claudius was evidently wide-spread, and Justin also states that nearly all the Samaritans honored Simon Magus "as the first god, above all power, authority, and might," and as accompanied by a certain ex-courtezan Helena, designated "the first understanding from himself" (*Apol.*, i. 26; *Trypho*, cxx.).

A valuable supplement to this information is given by a Roman heresiology written before 175 and incorporated by Irenæus in his *Hær.*, i. 23, also being used, in all probability, by Celsus, Tertullian, Hippolytus, and the pseudo-Tertullian.

3. His System According to Later Heresiologists. Here Simon Magus appears in an essentially Gnostic garb, being, on the one hand, the "highest God" (or "Father"), and, on the other, "the most sublime power of God"; while Helena (here brought into connection with Tyre) is represented as "the first conception of his [Simon's] mind," "the mother of all," "wisdom," "the Holy Spirit," etc. Emanating from the Father, she descended to the realms beneath, where, in conformity to his will, she created the angelic powers which, without knowing the Father, created the world and man. Unwilling to be considered creatures, the angels imprisoned her in a female body, and she is the lost sheep for whose salvation the Father (Simon) appeared, to rescue both her and mankind from the slavery of the cosmic angelic powers. To deceive these powers, he was manifested to mankind as man, as the Father to the Samaritans and the Son to the Jews, suffering docetic passion. To this Irenæus erroneously adds that Simon was supposed to have appeared as the Holy Ghost to the gentiles; and both he and Epiphanius give a number of further details which, while not impossible, can not definitely be ascribed to the system. An entirely different presentation of Simon's teaching is implied by Clement and Origen, and is further developed in the *Philosophumena* (vi. 7-18, x. 12; *ANF*, v. 74-81, 143). Here Helena ("Mind") is unknown, and Simon is given his self-designation—"He that hath stood"; but Clement adds practically no new material, and Origen little beyond the statement that Simon regarded idolatry as a matter of no concern (*Contra Celsum*, vi. 11). A similar ignorance of Helena and a like emphasis on Simon as "He that hath stood" are shown by the *Philosophumena*. Here the center of all being is "boundless power," which is both supramundane (inconceivable holy Silence) and intramundane (the "Father," "He that hath stood, that standeth, and is to stand," an androgynous power with neither beginning nor end, and essentially unitary). While remaining distinct as a seventh power, the Father causes to emanate three syzygies of cosmic powers, which in their spiritual aspect are "Mind," "Intelligence, "Voice," "Name," "Ratiocination," and "Reflection," and in their physical aspect are "Heaven," "Earth," "Sun," "Moon," "Air," and "Water." The Father is, moreover, "He that hath stood" in relation to premundane existence; "He that standeth" in relation to present being; and "He that shall stand" in relation to the final consummation. Man is simply the realization of "boundless power," the ultimate end of the cosmic process in which the godhead attains self-consciousness. All this material is recapitulated, with some additional data, by the pseudo-Clementine Homilies and Recognitions. Simon Magus is here described as a necromancer driven by Peter from Cæsarea to Antioch, and finally to Rome, everywhere shown to be an impostor, though declaring himself to be Christ, and overcome by divine miracles. Helena again appears, this time as "Wisdom," "the All-Mother," and "Lady," sending forth two angels (who seize power over her), one to create the world, and the other to give the Law. The pseudo-Clementine sources also add that Simon Magus was the son of Antonius and Rachel, that he was educated in Greek learning at Alexandria, and that, after being received among the thirty disciples of John the Baptist, he became head of the sect after the death of his teacher. He is likewise described, though without plausibility, as the representative of Samaritan worship on Mount Gerizim who expounded the Law allegorically and denied the resurrection of the dead, as the representative of pagan philosophy (especially of astrological fatalism), and even as the defender of Marcion's antithesis of the good and righteous God.

In some passages in these writings Simon Magus wears the mask of Paul, and attacks are made on Pauline teachings under the guise of polemics in favor of the Petrine theology against the tenets of Simon Magus.

4. Untenable Theories Concerning Simon Magus. There is, however, no basis for the theory that the picture of Simon Magus in the Clementine literature is deliberately designed to be a caricature of Paul inspired by the hatred of the Judaizing school, or for seeing in the struggle between Peter and Simon the victory of Petrine over Pauline Christianity. All the traits of Simon in this literature reveal him as only a magician or pseudo-Messiah, later given not merely Pauline, but also pagan and Marcionistic, characteristics; so that both in the apocryphal Acts and in the pseudo-Clementine literature Simon Magus was primarily not a pseudo-Paul, but a pseudo-Christ, and therefore the antithesis of Peter. Equally improbable is the hypothesis which identifies Simon Magus with the beast of Rev. xiii. 11-17, although it is not impossible that the Beliar which the Sibylline Books, iii. 63 sqq., describe as destined to come "from the Sebastenes" (Samaritans) represented Simon. It has likewise been maintained that Simon Magus is to be identified with the heresiarch Simon of Gitta, who should, on this hypothesis, be dated in the early part of the second century, but for this theory there is not the slightest ground, especially in view of the testimony of Acts, Clement of Alexandria, and Justin. It is, on the other hand, not improbable that Simon Magus is to be identified with a Jewish magician named Simon who acted as a go-between for the procurator Felix of Judea. This Simon is described by Josephus (*Ant.*, XX., vii. 2) as a Cypriot, but this statement probably rests upon a confusion of the Cyprian capital, Cittium (Hebr. *Kittim*), with the obscure Samaritan village of Gitta (Hebr. *Gittim*).

5. A Sorcerer Syncretized with the Sun.

All evidence goes to prove that Simon was what his epithet Magus implies—a sorcerer. This was the motive for his association with the apostles in Samaria, but while it would seem that he pretended to be, in the pagan sense, a god in human form (cf. Justin, *Apol.*, i. 26), there is no indication that either Acts or Justin regarded him as a pseudo-Messiah; and even the apocryphal Acts and the pseudo-Clementine literature characterize him as a false Christ merely on the ground that he was the first-born of Satan (cf. Ignatius, *Epist. ad Trallenses*, longer version, xi.). It is true that the heresiologists describe him as the supreme God and even as the Redeemer, but a careful study of the sources, particularly of the extant fragments of his "Great Announcement" (preserved by Hippolytus, *Philosophumena*, vi. 6 sqq.), shows that Simon himself made no claim to Messiahship, this being attributed to him by his disciples. With this falls the theory that Simon Magus was the founder of a universal religion intended to rival Christianity; and he was not even the founder of a sect in the sense that such heresiarchs as Marcion were. The very fact that Simon himself became the subject of Gnostic speculation shows that he was not the founder of Gnosticism, nor do the earlier sources so represent him; it was only his followers who made this claim for him. Historically, then, Simon was but a sorcerer who asserted that he was a god. This assertion, aided by the high fame which he enjoyed throughout Samaria (cf. Acts viii.), reached its culmination in his identification with the Semitic sun-god Shamash, whose cult was united with that of the moon-goddess Astarte. This is confirmed by Simon's companion, Helena, who is unknown to Acts, the apocryphal Acts, the Alexandrine heresiologists, or the "Great Announcement," but whose name ("Moon"), combined with the immoral past ascribed her and her Tyrian home, obviously points to the Tyrian moon-goddess with her licentious rites. How long this cult of Simon Magus, which had evidently arisen long before the time of Justin, persisted in Samaria and other regions is unknown, but in the days of Origen the "Simonians" were exceedingly few in number in Palestine and the neighboring countries (*Contra Celsum*, i. 57), and by the time of Epiphanius (*Hær.*, xxii. 2) they had become extinct. On the other hand, they had spread widely in the West before 200, and there long maintained themselves (cf. Hippolytus, *Philosophumena*, vi. 15). They seem to have developed a sect essentially occult and libertine in character, worshiping Simon (cf. Irenæus, *Hær.* I., xxiii. 4), and finally giving rise to two systems, that of the "Great Announcement" and that described by the heresiologists who based their writings upon Justin.

6. The Twofold Simonian System.

The authenticity of the "Great Announcement" has been assailed both because of its similarity to other Gnostic systems recorded by Hippolytus and on account of its divergence from Simon's teachings as described by other heresiologists. Neither of these arguments, however, is sufficient to prove the document spurious, especially in view of the confirmation of Hippolytus by other heresiologists; and the true explanation of the divergencies between the *Philosophumena* and Justin lies in the fact that there were two Simonian systems, one influenced by Alexandria and the other by Syria. The former influence is especially evident in the doctrine of the Godhead as "He that hath stood," which finds a close parallelism in the Philonian system, and is also perceptible in the purely allegorical method of Biblical exegesis adopted by the "Great Announcement" (cf. also the account in the pseudo-Clementine Homilies, ii. 22 sqq.). It is uncertain whether the "Great Announcement" was written in Alexandria, but at all events its citation of non-Samaritan prophets and of Proverbs shows that it was composed neither by Simon nor by any of his Samaritan followers. The account given by Justin and those who drew upon him, on the other hand, indicates that the second Simonian system was evolved in Syria, its elements being a syncretism of Babylonian mythology and Hellenistic allegory (for the latter cf. Irenæus, *Hær.*, I., xxiii. 4; Epiphanius, *Hær.*, xxi.). Both the Alexandrine and the Syrian form of Simonianism are unique in the history of Gnosticism in that they make a historic personage the supreme God, and, although destitute of any real Christian spirit, both show Christian influence, the Alexandrian "Great Announcement" using written Gospels and the Petrine and Pauline epistles, and the Syrian system comparing Helena with the lost sheep of Matt. xviii. 12 and Luke xv. 6. (Hans Waitz.)

In St. Peter's in Rome in the west division of the left aisle is an oil painting on slate by Francesco Vanni, "The punishment of Simon Magus," representing Simon Magus's fall from the skies at the prayer of St. Peter.

Bibliography: As an indirect source may be taken into account the excerpts from the *Apophasis* in Hippolytus, *Hær.*, VI., vii.-xviii (Eng. transl. in *ANF*, v. 76-81), on which cf. H. Stähelin, in *TU*, vi (1891). The most of the sources are named in the text, but the principal ones may be summarised here for convenience: Acts viii. 5-24; Justin Martyr, *I Apol.*, xxvi., lvi., and *Trypho*, cxx., both in *ANF*, vol. i.; Hegesippus, in Eusebius, *Hist. eccl.*, IV., xxii. 5, in *NPNF*, 2 ser., vol. i.; Irenæus, *Hær.*, I. xxiii. 1-4, in *ANF*, vol. i.; Clement of Alexandria, *Strom.*, II., xi. 52, VII., xvii. 107-108, in *ANF*, vol. ii.; Origen, *Contr. Celsum*, i. 57, vi. 11, in *ANF*, vol. iv.; the Clementina; Eusebius, *Hist. eccl.*, II., i. 12-15, in *NPNF*, 2 ser., vol. i.; Gregory Nazianzen, *Oratio*, xxiii. 18, xliv. Consult: F. C. Baur, in *Tübinger Zeitschrift für Theologie*, 1831, pp. 114-136; idem, *Paulus*, pp. 85 sqq., 218 sqq., Tübingen, 1845; H. Simson, in *ZHT*, xi (1841), 15-79; A. Schliemann, *Die Clementinen*, Hamburg, 1844; A. Hilgenfeld, *Die clementinischen Recognitionen und Homilien*, pp. 317 sqq., Jena, 1848; idem, in *ZWT*, xi (1868), 357-396, xlvii (1904), 545-567, xlix (1906), 66-133; J. Grimm, *Die Samariter*, pp. 125-175, Munich, 1854; E. Zeller, *Apostelgeschichte*, pp. 158 sqq., Stuttgart, 1854, Eng. transl., *Contents and Origin of the Acts of the Apostles*, i. 250 sqq., London, 1875; G. Volkmar, in *Tübinger theologische Jahrbücher*, 1856; R. A. Lipsius, *Quellen der römischen Petrussage*, pp. 13-46, Kiel, 1872; idem, *Die apokryphen Apostelgeschichte*, ii. 1, pp. 28-69 et passim, Brunswick, 1884; J. Delitzsch, in *TSK*, xlvii (1874); Dieterlen, *L'Apôtre Paul et Simon le Magicien*, Nancy, 1878; T. Zahn, *Cyprian von Antiochien und die deutsche Faustsage*, Erlangen, 1882; C. Bigg, in *Studia Biblica*, ii (1890), 157-193; F. Spitta, *Die Apostelgeschichte, ihre Quellen*, pp. 145 sqq., Halle, 1891; C. Clemen, *Chronologie der paulinischen Briefe*, Halle, 1893; M. Krenkel, *Josephus und Lucas*, pp. 178-190, Leipsic, 1894; A. C. McGiffert, *Apostolic Age*, pp. 99-100, New York, 1897; J. Kreyenbuhl, *Das Evangelium der Wahrheit*, i. 174-265, ii. 100 sqq., Berlin, 1900-05; P. Lugano, in *Nuovo Bulletino di archeologia cristiana*, vi (1900); J. F. A. Hort, *Notes Introductory to the Study of the Clementine Recognitions*, London, 1901; R. Liechtenhan, *Die Offenbarung im Gnosticismus*, pp. 5 sqq., 56-57, Göttingen, 1901; H. U. Mayboom, *De Clemens-Roman*, parts i.-ii., Groningen, 1902-04; H. Waitz, in *ZNTW*, v (1904), 121-143; idem, in *TU*, xxv. 4 (1904), 170 sqq., 202 sqq., et passim; Harnack, *Litteratur*, i. 153 sqq., ii. 2, pp. 518-540; Schaff, *Christian Church*, i. 257-258; Neander, *Christian Church*, vols. i-ii. passim; and, in general, histories of the apostolic age: *DB*, iv. 520-527; *EB*, iv. 4536-60; *JE*, xi. 371-373; *DCB*, iv. 681-688; the literature under CLEMENTINA; and GNOSTICISM; and the principal commentaries on the Acts of the Apostles.

SIMON (SIMEON) STOCK, SAINT: Carmelite and general of the order; b. in Kent, England, c. 1165; d. at Bordeaux, France, May 16, 1265. Tradition makes him take up the hermit's life at the age of twelve, entering the Carmelite order in 1201, and studying afterward at Oxford; he became vicar-general for the West, 1215, was in Palestine in 1237, went to England in 1244, and became general in 1245. His chief claim to fame is as propagator of the Scapular (q.v.).

BIBLIOGRAPHY: *ASB*, May, iii. 653-654, 762, vii. 790; the *Leben* by A. Monbrun, Regensburg, 1888; *DNB*, lii. 255; *KL*, xi. 319-320.

SIMON OF TOURNAI, tūr″nē′: Teacher at the Sorbonne about 1200. Of his life scarcely a detail is known, but if he may be identified with the Simon recommended to the archbishop of Reims by Stephen of Tournai (*MPL*, ccxi. 353), he would seem to have been born at Tournai (48 m. s. by w. of Ghent). According to Matthew Paris (*Chron. majora*, on the year 1201), who claimed to have his account from an eye-witness, Simon in one lecture alleged many objections to the doctrine of the Trinity, only to refute them in the following lecture. The applause which this won him filled him with such vanity that he blasphemously congratulated the Savior on the aid that his dialectic skill had given the Christian cause, though insuperable objections might have been brought against Christianity had the lecturer really been opposing it. Thereupon, Matthew records, Simon lost both speech and memory, and took two years to relearn the alphabet. A younger contemporary, the Dominican Thomas Cantipratanus (d. 1263), makes Simon declare Moses, Jesus, and Mohammed to be three impostors (*Bonum universale de apibus*, ii. 48; cf. IMPOSTORIBUS, DE TRIBUS), and then suffer loss of speech and memory; but Henry of Ghent (q.v.) merely states that Simon, being too ardent an Aristotelian, was regarded by many as a heretic (*De script. eccl.*, xxiv.). The entire account is explained by some as a legendary accretion, inspired by orthodox dread of the theological consequences of dialectic philosophy, about some catastrophe which befell Simon in the midst of a distinguished academic career.

(FERDINAND COHRS.)

BIBLIOGRAPHY: *Histoire littéraire de la France*, xvi. 394; B. Hauréau, *Hist. de la philosophie scholastique*, ii. 1, pp. 58 sqq., Paris, 1880; H. Denifle, *Chartularium Universitatis Parisiensis*, i. 45, 71, ib. 1890; Neander, *Christian Church*, iv. 418; *KL*, xi. 320-321.

SIMON ZELOTES, ze-lō′tēz: One of the twelve apostles. He is mentioned in all the New-Testament lists (Matt. x. 4; Mark iii. 18; Luke vi. 15; Acts i. 13). But with Luke alone, he bears the surname Zelotes; whereas in Matthew and Mark, as correctly read, he is termed the Cananite, a designation which appears to be derived from a corresponding local name. The correct explanation of the term "Zelotes" is supplied by Luke, with his translation "Zealot," "man of ardor." The origin of this surname might rest in Simon's personal characteristics or in his individual labors rather than on the basis of some supposed connection with the revolutionary Galilean faction of Zealots (q.v.).

Identification of Simon Zelotes with the Simon who is named among the brethren of Jesus (Matt. xiii. 55; Mark vi. 3), together with the cognate assumption that the latter was a brother of James the son of Alphæus, is quite unfounded (see JAMES, I., 3), as are the reports of a later activity of the apostle in Egypt and in Britain (Nicephorus Callistus, II., xl.), or in Persia and Babylonia (Abdias, *Hist.*, VI., vii.-viii.).

F. SIEFFERT.

BIBLIOGRAPHY: Besides the commentaries on the passages noted in the text, and the articles in the Bible dictionaries, consult: A. Edersheim, *Life and Times of Jesus the Messiah*, i. 251, 522, ii. 603, New York, 1896; T. Zahn, *Forschungen zur Geschichte des neutestamentlichen Kanons*, vi. 293, 321, 361, Leipsic, 1900.

SIMON, DAVID WORTHINGTON: English Congregationalist; b. at Hazel Grove (8 m. s.e. of Manchester), Cheshire, Apr. 28, 1830; d. at Dresden Jan. 17, 1909. He was educated at Lancastershire Independent College, Manchester (1848-54), and the universities of Halle and Heidelberg (1854-55, 1857-1858), and at Tübingen (Ph.D., 1863), residing for a time at Darmstadt. After holding Congregational pastorates at Royston, Herts (1856), and Rusholme, Manchester (1858), and after the completion of his studies in Germany, he was Berlin agent of the British and Foreign Bible Society (1863-69); principal and professor of general theology and philosophy at Spring Hill College, Birmingham (now Mansfield College, Oxford), until 1884; principal and professor of systematic theology and church history in the Theological Hall of the Scottish Congregational Church, Edinburgh (1884-93); and became in 1893 principal of the Yorkshire United Independent College, Bradford, Yorkshire. He translated E. W. Hengstenberg's "Commentary on Ecclesiastes" (in collaboration with W. L. Alexander; Edinburgh, 1860); I. A. Dorner's *History of the Development of the Doctrine of the Person of Christ* (5 vols., 1861–63); H. Cremer's *Biblico-Theological Lexicon of New Testament Greek* (in collaboration with W. Urwick; 1872); and L. Stählin's *Kant, Lotze, Ritschl* (1889); and wrote *The Bible an Outgrowth of Theocratic Life* (Edinburgh, 1886); *The Redemption of Man* (1886); *Reconciliation by Incarnation* (1898); *Some Bible Problems* (London, 1898); and *The Making of a Preacher* (1907).

SIMON, JOHN SMITH: Wesleyan Methodist; b. in Glasgow June 25, 1843. He was educated at Elisabeth College, Guernsey, and Victoria College, Jersey, and, after being a lawyer's assistant for four years, entered the Wesleyan ministry in 1863. He has served on many of the most important committees of his denomination, and in 1895 became one of the members of its Legal Conference. He was a delegate to the Methodist Ecumenical conferences of 1891 (Washington) and 1901 (London), and in 1907 was president of the Wesleyan conference. Since 1901 he has been governor of the Wesleyan Methodist Theological College at Didsbury, and is the author of *Manual of Instruction and Advice for Class Leaders* (London, 1892); *Summary of Methodist Law and Discipline* (1897); and *The Revival of Religion in England in the Eighteenth Century* (1907).

SIMON, RICHARD: French Roman Catholic and the real founder of Biblical criticism; b. at Dieppe (33 m. n. of Rouen) May 13, 1638; d. there Apr. 11, 1712. In 1658 he became a novice of the Oratorians, and, after withdrawing, returned in 1662 on receiving permission to continue his studies during his novitiate. He was ordained to the priesthood in Sept., 1670, but on May 21, 1678, was expelled from the Oratorians because of the publication of his *Histoire critique du Vieux Testament* (Paris, 1678, and often; Eng. transl. by R. Hampden, *Critical History of the Old Testament*, 4 parts, London, 1682). He then retired to the parish of Bolleville in Normandy, which he had received in 1676, and later lived at Dieppe, Rouen, and Paris. Before his expulsion from the Oratorians he was for a time professor of philosophy at Juilly, though he found a more congenial task in cataloguing the oriental manuscripts of the library and in Biblical, rabbinical, and patristic studies. Rationalistic in temperament, and quarrelsome in disposition, the fresh knowledge which he acquired involved him in countless controversies, the most famous being that which centered about the *Histoire critique* just mentioned. This work, after seven years of preparation, had been passed by the censor and was in print, with the exception of the title and the dedication to the king, when the preface and table of contents fell into the hands of Bossuet. The heading of the fifth chapter, "Moses can not be the author of all the books attributed to him," was enough to cause Bossuet to interfere, and on June 19, 1678, the copies of the work, with a few exceptions, were destroyed. From one of those which escaped Daniel Elzevir prepared an incorrect edition (Amsterdam, 1680), and in 1685 Simon himself published another edition at Rotterdam with a preface as if from a Protestant and notes referring to Simon in the third person. The work was vehemently attacked, but the New-Testament portions were so increased in size that they were issued in separate parts under the titles of *Histoire critique du texte du Nouveau Testament* (Rotterdam, 1689; Eng. transl., 2 parts, London, 1689), *Histoire critique des versions du Nouveau Testament* (Rotterdam, 1690; Eng. transl., London, 1692), and *Histoire critique des principaux commentateurs du Nouveau Testament* (2 parts, Rotterdam, 1693), these being followed by the *Nouvelles observations sur le texte et les versions du Nouveau Testament* (Paris, 1695) and by an anonymous French translation of the Vulgate (4 vols., Trévoux, 1702). This version was also attacked by Bossuet, and although Simon printed slips bearing changes in translation and explanations to be pasted over his first text, the book was prohibited. Toward the end of his life Simon printed *Lettres choisies de M. Simon* (Amsterdam, 1700) and, under the pseudonym of M. de Sainjore, *Bibliothèque critique, ou recueil de diverses pièces* (4 parts, Paris and Amsterdam, 1708–10). After his death his *Nouvelle bibliothèque choisie* appeared (2 vols., 1714), and among his other writings special mention may be made of his *Histoire critique des dogmes, des controverses, des coutumes et des cérémonies des Chrétiens orientaux* (Trévoux, 1711; Eng. transl. by A. Lovell, London, 1685).

Richard Simon was the first to attempt to write a history of the Bible as a piece of literature, an astounding innovation considering the intellectual conditions of his time. He did not, however, direct his attention to the contents of the Bible or to the development of religious concepts, but rather to the text, the versions, and the commentaries. Disregarding the traditional and dogmatic presuppositions of the age, he critically discussed the Septuagint and the Vulgate, and defended the translation of the Bible into the vernacular. He regarded the Masoretic text as representing a good tradition, but postulated the late origin of the Hebrew vowel-points and square script. In New-Testament criticism he defended the Hellenistic idiom against the purists. In regard to the origin of the Old Testament, he maintained that there were in Israel, from the time of Moses, public scribes whose duty it was to record all matters pertaining to religion and the State, and also, in their capacity of public orators, to give directions to the people, these addresses being published from time to time, and after the Exile giving rise to the Old Testament in its present form. The verdict of succeeding generations was most unfavorable to Simon, nor was it until the rise of Johann Salomo Semler (q.v.) that the true merits of Simon, with all his shortcomings, received full recognition.

E. NESTLE.

BIBLIOGRAPHY: A. Bernus, *Richard Simon et son Hist. critique du Vieux Testament*, Lausanne, 1869; idem, *Notice bibliographique sur Richard Simon*, Basel, 1882; L. Diestel, *Geschichte des Alten Testaments in der christlichen Kirche*, Jena, 1869; C. H. Wright, *Introduction to the Old Testament*, London, 1891 (the first part contains a history of criticism); H. Margival, in *Revue d'hist. et littérature religieuses*, i (1896), 159, ii (1897), 17, 223, 525, iii (1898), 117, 138, 508, iv (1899), 122, 192, 310, 435; A. Bludau, in *Der Katholik*, 1904, i. 29–422, ii. 114–122; A. Duff, *Hist. of O. T. Criticism*, New York, 1910.

SIMONS, MENNO.

I. First Statement: Menno Simons, Dutch Anabaptist, was born at Witmarsum (5 m. s.e. of Haringen), Holland, 1492, and died near Oldesloe (25 m. n.e. of Hamburg), Germany, Jan. 13, 1559. Though the Mennonites (q.v.) bear his name, he was not their founder, for they existed in Holland seven years before he became a convert; but he was one of their most influential leaders and by far their most important author.

1. Early Life and Views.

Many details of his life are uncertain, for his biography remained unwritten both in his own and in the following generation, so that it must be gleaned from scanty allusions in his writings and in the works of his contemporaries. In 1515 or 1516 he held an ecclesiastical office at Pingjum, a short distance from his birthplace. In 1532 he became pastor at Witmarsum, where, as he confessed in later years, he preached from motives of ambition rather than conviction. Much of his self-accusation, however, may be due to the morbid severity with which, like Bunyan and other converts, he judged himself, for no suspicion of reprehensibility seems to have attached to his name at any time, unless it be charged against him that he remained in the priesthood for twenty years despite his doubts. In the very first years of his parochial activity he became skeptical of the doctrine of transubstantiation, and found support for his views on baptism in the New Testament and the writings of Billican, who, with some other Protestants, permitted parents to choose between infant and adult baptism for their children. This and the execution of the Anabaptist Sicke Snijder at Leeuwarden in 1531 led to renewed study of the Bible and the works of the Reformers, with the result that Menno practically became an Evangelical preacher, though he had not yet broken openly with the Church. When he entered upon his new parish of Witmarsum, he seems already to have sympathized with Anabaptist views.

2. Paideutic Objective.

Menno's attention was less directed, however, against Roman Catholic teaching than against errors which had recently sprung up in Anabaptism, such as the doctrines of earthly power, sword, king, and the plurality of wives. In this spirit he wrote his first book, *Een gantsch duydelycke end klaer bewys uyt die H. S. dat Jesus Christus is de rechte beloofde David inn den geest . . . tegen de grouwelicke ende grootste blasphemie van Jan van Leyden*, although it was not printed until 1627. Menno's ambiguous position received a rude shock in Apr., 1535, when 300 Anabaptists were defeated at Bolsward by the imperial troops, 130 falling in battle, while the remainder, including his own brother, were made prisoners and drowned. He felt himself responsible in a sense for their fate, since he had not taught them the true way, and he also became convinced that his priestly office rendered it impossible for him to gain their confidence, so that on Jan. 12, 1536, he resigned his parish. This "conversion," or "rebirth," as Menno termed it, was characteristically Anabaptist, in that it was based less on a conviction of the grace of God through Christ in consequence of a sense of sin and repentance than on moral earnestness, renunciation, and devotion to divine truth, whether contained in the Bible or in the human heart. It was, therefore, the conversion of a layman rather than of a theologian or a priest. Yet Menno was not uneducated, for he wrote Latin fluently, was somewhat acquainted with Greek, and had a certain familiarity with the writings of his contemporaries (especially Erasmus) and the Church Fathers.

3. Later Life; Literary Activity.

After his withdrawal from the priesthood and the Roman Catholic Church, Menno remained for a time in Friesland, where all who should harbor him were threatened with death in Oct., 1536. Two months later, at the earnest petition of a number of those who agreed with him in faith and life, he received the laying on of hands from Obbe Philips, and became an elder (bishop) of the community. Where Menno passed the first years after he left the church is uncertain, but it is not improbable that he lived in East Friesland, baptizing both there and in Groningen in 1537. He seems to have lived in East Friesland until 1541; in Amsterdam and North Holland from 1541 to 1543; again in East Friesland from 1543 to 1545; in and near Cologne and Limburg from 1545 to 1547; and after this latter year in or near Lübeck, with the exception of a short residence at Wismar in 1553–54. His life during these years may be best traced by his writings, his first publications being the most important. To this category belong his *Van de ware nieuwe geboorte; Veele goede . . . leringhen op den 25. Psalm*, perhaps the best work of its author; *Van het rechte Christengeloove;* and *Van de geestelicke verrijsenisse*. The most important of all his works, however, was the *Fondamentboek* (c. 1539), in which he sought to prove the truth of his doctrines and urged the authorities to test the purity of the lives of the Anabaptists, thus ending the persecution and showing their wide divergence from the fanatics of Münster. In this book, moreover, Menno defines belief as trust in the grace of God and the promises revealed to man in the words and life of Christ, bringing sorrow for sin, yet comforting the heart and strengthening it in conformity to the divine pattern. The substitution of adult for infant baptism is based by him on the commandment of Christ and on apostolic usage, as well as on the doctrine of regeneration, of which baptism should be the seal. The true mark of the Christian was regeneration, not baptism, while the Lord's Supper was regarded not as a sacrament but as a memorial service. The *Fondamentboek* was also designed to warn his followers against errors which might be construed as morally reprehensible, such as the doctrine of David Joris that external acts were indifferent, provided the intention was good.

4. Theological Controversies.

The *Fondamentboek* was supplemented by the *Lieffelijcke vermaninge . . . hoe dat een Christen sal geschickt zijn en van het schouwen ofte afsnijden der valscher broederen en susteren* (1541); *Kindertucht* (Antwerp, 1543); *Verclaringhe des doopsels* (1544); *Oorsaecke waerom dat ik Menno Simons niet af en laate te leeren* (1544); and a book, now lost, directed against David Joris (1545), which was answered by Joris' son-in-law, Nikolaas Blesdijk, in *Verantwoording*, in 1546. During these years Menno resided for a time in North Holland, and in 1547 he was one of the three elders who took part in the conference with Blesdijk in Lübeck, where the views of Joris were utterly refuted. Meanwhile Menno became involved in the one great theological controversy of his life, the doctrine of the Incarnation. Several years after his conversion he became acquainted with the teaching of Melchior Hoffmann that the body of Christ was born in, not of, the Virgin Mary, so that the Son of God transformed himself into the nature of man, rather than took it upon him, also holding that this human being was formed by God without any cooperation of the mother. Although Menno laid little stress upon the acceptance of this doctrine, he was challenged to a disputation in 1543 by the East Frisian superintendent Johannes a Lasco (q.v.). They met in the following January, and Menno promised to send his opponent the reasons for his belief, writing them in Latin, but publishing them in Dutch under the title: *Een corte ende clare belijdinghe . . . van der menschwordinge enzv.* Lasco replied in his *Defensio incarnationis Christi* (1545), and his opponent responded in his turn with his *Eyne clare bekentenisse dat de gheheele Christus Jesus Godes eygen Sone is*, although it was not printed until 1554, when the controversy was renewed. Menno's insistence on this doctrine after 1547 is to be ascribed neither to obstinacy nor to an excessive regard for it, although he believed his dualistic theory more reasonable than the orthodox teaching. To his mind a Christ who was at the same time God and man was unthinkable, and he accordingly believed that he was created by God alone, without any intervention on the part of father or mother, and that in his earthly incarnation he was nothing but a man into whom the Word had been transformed. While the Church taught that we are brethren of Christ in that he took our flesh upon him, Menno held that only the regenerate are the brethren of Christ, and then simply because they, like him, are begotten of God. From this teaching, however, some drew the deduction that Christ was not consubstantial with the Father, but was merely one with him in will and intent, thus denying the Trinity. The assembly of elders accordingly convened at Goch in 1547 and excommunicated their colleague Adam Pastor, one of the foremost advocates of this doctrine. Menno, who was present, wrote a rather feeble refutation of Pastor, entitled *Belijdinghe van den drieenigen Godt*, although he did not break off all association with him.

5. Final Activities.

During his residence on the Lower Rhine in 1545–47 and after he had settled in Holstein in 1549, Menno made frequent journeys to confer with his fellow elders, and between 1552 and 1554 he published from his own press a number of writings, chiefly apologetic in character. One of these, the *Beantwoordinghe over eene schrift Gelii Fabri*, is the longest work of its author, and almost the only one which gives any information concerning his life and the conditions of his time. It treats, among other subjects, of the doctrine of the Incarnation, on which Menno disputed with Micronius at Wismar on Feb. 6 and 15, 1554. In the following year Micronius published the minutes of this disputation, to which his opponent replied in 1556, following it with another refutation in 1557. These are not the most felicitous of the products of Menno's pen; they are not at all free from personalities and wearisome repetitions. The closing years of his life were saddened by the controversies among his followers concerning excommunication. As early as 1551 Menno had ruled that the faithful should avoid all association with their fellow believers of unseemly life, unless these should prove responsive to admonition. In the course of the development of the community, however, many problems were evolved regarding excommunication. In 1550 Menno decided, in his *Klaer bericht van de excommunicatie*, that this avoidance should be extended to secular life as well, but not in cases where assistance might be rendered; he mitigated also the severity of the banishment as far as possible. The elders Leenaert Bouwens and Gillis van Aachen, on the other hand, demanded that excommunication be declared in the majority of cases without previous warning, and that, if one of a married pair had fallen under the ban, the other should avoid him or her. These measures aroused the deep resentment of the Anabaptists living along the Lower Rhine, and they accordingly sent their teachers Zylis and Lemmeken to Menno in 1556, whereupon, in the following year, he went to Franeker and Harlingen to win his fellow elders to a milder mood and restore peace. The reverse was the result, however, and Menno himself was threatened with excommunication. In his fear that he might have conceded too much to human weakness, he published his *Grondelic bericht* in 1558, declaring openly that he had formerly erred and presenting the strictest views. Zylis and Lemmeken replied, only to be answered by Menno in a book couched in no very measured tones, though written just before his death. As he lay dying, however, he lamented this temporary severity and warned his followers not to be servants of men, as he had been.

Menno's character was a mixture of humility, warmth of heart, pessimism with regard to the world and life, spiritual piety, loyalty and love to the "community," and obstinacy, while he was deeply conscious of his responsibility as elder of the people of God. None of his Dutch con-

6. Characterization.

temporaries surpassed him in ability to write in a popular and edifying vein, or in ease of composition. Through his toil, his books and letters, and the love which he bore his followers, with which he inspired them in their turn, he enabled the community to increase in numbers and to hold fast to their lofty morality. Every trace of the excesses of Münster and Joris had vanished, and henceforth the community was to remain true to the teachings of the New Testament as their sole rule of faith. Thus the followers of Menno reverenced him deeply, though only as one of their pious teachers. Gradually all his works were printed, not only as a source of appeal in the controversies over excommunication and the doctrine of the Incarnation, but also for edification. The pietistic element among the Anabaptists called themselves by his name, as their opponents had done since 1544. In Upper Germany and along the Rhine, on the other hand, the Anabaptists of the sixteenth century were estranged from him on account of their controversies [due to his insistence on his doctrine of the incarnation and marital avoidance in case one of the married pair was under discipline. Cf. A. H. Newman, *Hist. of Antipedobaptism*, pp. 309–312, Philadelphia, 1897], but in the seventeenth and eighteenth centuries his name and writings won their esteem as the representative of their separatistic life and their opposition to the established church.

The works of Menno, still preserved (so far as extant) in their original editions at Amsterdam, were written in colloquial Low German and translated into Dutch after his death. The first edition of a small collection appeared in 1562, followed by larger collections in 1601, 1646, and 1681, the latter being almost complete. A German edition of all his writings was published at Elkhart, Ind., in 1876, and Eng. transl., in 1871. Although there are several portraits of Menno, none of them were taken from life, and only one, which is preserved at Utrecht, seems to have come from a circle which knew him personally. In his later years he was a cripple. S. Cramer.

II. Second Statement: Menno Simons and his coworkers differed from the more prominent reformers of the sixteenth century in rejecting the doctrinal system of Predestination (q.v.). Prior to Jacobus Arminius (q.v.) they taught the freedom of the will. Of the doctrine that freedom of choice is not granted man, and yet he is held responsible and punished for sin, Menno speaks as "an abomination above all abominations" (Menno Simons, *Complete Works*, ii. 94, i. 221, Elkhart, Ind., 1871). John Calvin, in turn, who had evidently never acquired a first-hand knowledge of Menno's teachings, speaks of Menno in most contemptuous terms.

While, according to the leading German reformers, "what is not against Scripture is for Scripture and Scripture is for it" (Luther), Menno held that, as concerns Christian doctrine and ceremonies, nothing can be rightly maintained that is not expressly taught and authorized in the New Testament. Needless to say that he attributed to the opinion of neither pope—whom he considered Antichrist—nor Church Fathers any authoritative

1. Views of Scripture.

weight. On the relation of the Old Testament to the New-Testament Scriptures he differed fundamentally from Luther, Zwingli, and Calvin. Menno, as well as the Swiss Brethren and Huterites (see Mennonites), held that "Christ alone is our law-giver." The Old-Testament precepts were largely intended for premessianic times and have been restated by Christ and the apostles so far as they are to be applied to the Christian Church. The Old-Testament Scriptures are indeed a part of the Word of God, they are the foundation and groundwork for the New, while the latter is the fulfilment of the Old; but in matters of Christian worship, practise, and life, the New-Testament Scriptures are the only authority. While the Reformers Luther, Zwingli, and Calvin justified, on Old-Testament authority, a union of Church and State, war, capital punishment, the oath, and in part also ritualism, Menno rejected the same on New-Testament authority. Of the doctrine of the inner light, as held by Hans Denk (q.v.) and a few other Anabaptists and later by the Quakers, not a trace is found in his writings.

On original sin Menno teaches that through the fall all men inherit a sinful nature. Christ, the second Adam, has atoned for the guilt of

2. Sin; Justification by Faith.

original sin, hence no one will be condemned for the sin of Adam. All infants are saved through the atonement of Christ, according to his express promise. Condemnation awaits those who reject the means of salvation offered them. The doctrine of justification by faith is given great prominence in Menno's system. Luther's teaching on the sacraments (baptismal regeneration and forgiveness of sin through the observation of the Lord's Supper) he rejects as inconsistent with this doctrine. "To teach and believe," says Menno, "that regeneration is the result of baptism, my brethren, is terrible idolatry and blasphemy against the blood of Christ. For there is neither in heaven nor on earth any other remedy for our sins, be they inherited evil propensities or transgressions, than the blood of Christ alone, as we have often shown in our first writings" (*Works*, ii. 200). "The blood of Christ is and will ever be the only and eternally valid means of our reconciliation, and not works, baptism, or Lord's Supper" (i. 158). The statement that "Christ is the only means of grace" is found oftentimes in Menno's writings; all the riches of grace may be obtained through faith in Christ—by no means through works and ceremonies.

Probably no contemporary of Menno Simons insists with more emphasis on the inseparable connection of an obedient, holy life with

3. Holy Living; the Ordinances.

true faith. "Behold, beloved reader," says Menno, "thus true faith begets love and love begets obedience to the commandments of God" (*Works*, ii. 246). "For this can never fail, where there is true Christian faith, there is also dying to sin, a new creature, true repentance, a sincere regenerated, unblamable Christian" (i. 118). "True faith which avails before God is a living and saving power which is, through the preaching of the holy Word, wrought of God in the heart, renewing, changing and regenerating it to newness of mind" (i. 59). On the Christian ordinances Menno says: "All the rites ordained of God, both in the Old and New Testament, have been instituted that our faith may be exercised and our obedience proven" (i. 34). The baptism of infants is invalid. Incidentally baptism is spoken of as the reception of "a handful of water" (i. 38, i. 124). Menno also observes that "the poor world has hitherto believed the new birth to consist in immersion in the water while the words are said, I baptize thee," etc. (ii. 215). He did not hold that believers' baptism to be valid must be administered by a representative of a church that is entirely orthodox. On the Lord's Supper his teaching concurs with that of Zwingli; he disapproves of "open" communion.

4. The Church.

Menno defines the Church as the assembly of those "who hear, believe, accept, and rightly fulfil" the teachings of God's Word (ii. 345), hence a true Christian church is necessarily established on the voluntary principle. He says: "Faith is the gift of God, therefore it can not be forced upon any one by worldly authorities or by the sword." "Tell me, kind reader, where have you in all the days of your life read in the apostolic Scriptures that Christ or the apostles called upon the power of the magistracy against those who would not hear their doctrine and obey their word?" (ii. 71). "Behold how haughtily and how wickedly the princes assume, without any awe or fear, the authority of God and the office of the Holy Ghost" (i. 186). Toleration, accordingly, means the rejection of all persecution. Menno would have taken it as an insult had he been charged with advancing the modern idea that false doctrine is, on the ground of Christian love and forbearance, to be tolerated in the Church. The government of the Church was administered by the elders. Questions of faith and practise were not to be referred to individual congregations. The idea that among the early Mennonites "every church was a law unto itself" is erroneous. Menno and his colaborers withdrew from congregations that sanctioned what they believed to be unscriptural doctrine. The great missionary commission of Christ was held by Menno to have been given to the Church; he was in fact preeminently a missionary. With emphasis he insists on the duty of the Church to care for needy and destitute members. He testifies that notwithstanding the relentless, bloody persecution which had left in their care numerous widows and orphans, and in which many had lost their possessions, no one of the church which he represented, nor their children, had been known or would have been permitted to beg (ii. 309). The Church, according to Menno, is the "communion of saints" in deed and in truth. nevertheless there is always a possibility of those having a form of godliness and denying the power thereof being found in it. In his writings he referred to the fact that there was a hypocrite even among the apostles, but insists that neither offensive sin and transgression nor false doctrine must be tolerated in the Church. Of church discipline he says: "In short, as a vineyard without a fence or inclosure, or a city without walls or gates, so is a church without discipline and the excommunication." Members of the church were not permitted to eat or do business with those who had been excluded, except in cases of emergency (I Cor. v. 11; II Thess. iii. 14). On this point both Menno and Dirk Philips wrote treatises against the Swiss Brethren who disapproved of the "avoidance" of the excommunicated. The interesting history of this practise and the reasons why Menno advocated it can not be stated in a few sentences. That on his death-bed he expressed regrets for the stand which he had taken in this matter, as was believed by the "Waterlanders," who were of one mind with the Swiss, is evidently a fable. In the last weeks of his life he wrote a little book which was published after his death, insisting on "avoidance" as stringently as ever.

The swearing of oaths he believed to be forbidden by Christ. Of war he speaks as a "wicked, abominable business" (i. 137). Capital punishment he considered incompatible with Christian principles; he suggests confinement for life in its stead (ii. 407). Frequently he denounced the "houses of intemperance," "the accursed drunken taverns." He was an advocate of "the simple life"; church-members who permitted themselves to drift into worldliness were strictly disciplined by the church. Menno believed the coming of Christ near, not, however, to inaugurate the millennium, but for judgment.

5. Christology.

The old accusation of some of Menno's opponents that he denied the divine nature in Christ, an insinuation which was vigorously repudiated by him, must be placed in the same category as other slanders, such as that he upheld communism and was the head of a revolutionary sect. He held a peculiar doctrine on the Incarnation: "The whole Christ, God and man, man and God, is God's son and is of heaven" (ii. 151, Elkhart, Ind., 1871). Not only was he truly God from eternity, but his human nature was also of heaven and was not the result of a creation. Of Mary's body he partook not otherwise than as a seed of grain partakes of the field in which it is planted (ii. 337). To assert that he could in that case not be truly human is to deny God's omnipotence. Had he, as regards his humanity, "been of the impure, sinful flesh of Adam, he would be guilty also, through the eternal justice of God, of judgment and death. And if he himself owed a debt, how could he pay ours?" That this doctrine has a tendency toward the denial of Christ's divinity was indignantly denied by Menno. His opinion was, on the contrary, that what is generally considered the orthodox view of the incarnation dishonors Christ's divinity, representing him as a creature as concerns his body. "If the man [human nature of] Christ was of the flesh and blood of Mary, it is manifest that he was not God's son but a created being" (ii. 158). "That I have ever said this [that the Word was changed into flesh and blood] no one will, I believe, ever be able to prove; nevertheless they have the effrontery to say and write such of us. I have spoken of this as the eminent apostle has taught me, namely, that the Word was made flesh " (ii. 159). " As he is the only and true Son of God, he must also have the nature of the one of whom he is, this is too plain to be controverted " (ii. 392). " Although he humbled himself and laid down his divine splendor, privileges, and glory, nevertheless he was God and God's Word " (ii. 164). Menno states that " there are many among us " who have never " heard or asked a word " concerning the question of the origin of Jesus' body, and also testifies that he never refers to this doctrine in his sermons, " but I teach simply and plainly that Christ Jesus is truly God and man, a Son of God and a Son of man, conceived of the Holy Ghost and born of the pure virgin Mary " (ii. 332). The said doctrine of the incarnation was held by the Obbenites (see MENNONITES) before Menno identified himself with them, and it was, according to his own confession, only after severe and prolonged mental struggles that he arrived at the conclusion that it is entirely Scriptual (ii. 330).

6. Relation to Rationalism.

The supposition that the teachings of Menno and his coworkers were tinged with rationalism is without foundation. His faithful colaborer, Dirk Philips, of whom he observes that " Dirk and I are entirely of the same mind " and whose extant writings fill a stately volume—an English translation is now in press—occupied the same position toward rationalism as Menno, and the same is true of the Swiss Brethren. The Dutch historian Brandt asserted that the excommunication of Adam Pastor (q.v.) for denying the deity of Christ was the work of Dirk Philips. Others have opined that Menno was at variance with Dirk in this matter. From Pastor's *Underscheit tusschen rechte leer unde valsche leer* (published in vol. v. of *Bibliotheca Reformatoria Neerlandica*), it is clear that he held Menno responsible for his excommunication, and the latter testifies that Pastor was no longer of their number (ii. 96; the English translation of the passage is inaccurate, see *Menno Symons' Wercken*, p. 312, Amsterdam, 1681). In his refutation of Pastor, Menno speaks of the denial of the eternal preexistence of Christ as " a terrible blasphemy, curse, and abomination " (ii. 184). The hymn of Ludwig Haetzer (q.v.), expressing antitrinitarian sentiments, is not found in the hymn-books of Swiss and South German Anabaptists, nor of the Mennonites. It is doubtful whether its author was rebaptized or baptized others, although he agreed with the Anabaptists in their opposition to state-churchism and on a few other points (cf. F. Roth, *Augsburgs Reformationsgeschichte*, pp. 221–222, 232, Munich, 1901; Heberle in *TSK*, 1858, p. 845). His friend Hans Denk, unlike Haetzer, a man of unimpeachable character, was an advocate of liberalistic sentiments although not an antitrinitarian, and became the leader of an Anabaptist party called " Denkians," but before his death retracted his former teaching on the necessity of rebaptism. Unfortunately Menno and the Mennonites have sometimes been judged from the writings of such men, with whom in fact they had nothing to do.

7. Relation to the Reformers.

Touching the position of Menno and his friends with respect to the leading Reformers, it is to be noted that Menno's personal estimate of Luther was congenial and appreciative, far more so than the opinion entertained by Luther concerning any Anabaptists. Menno freely acknowledges that " the Lord has effected much good through Luther's first writings " (*Works*, i. 29). He severely criticizes Luther for permitting himself to lose sight of the principle of toleration which he had originally advocated. The Reformation, so far as it was identified with state-churchism, was in Menno's opinion quite superficial: it has, says Menno, not brought a change in the life of the people and its foundations were not laid along Scriptural lines. In the Lutheran states of central and northern Germany the priests were given orders to accept the new standards of faith and practise prescribed by the heads of the State. The priests, as a rule, accepted the new order of things and the populace followed them (no other creed being tolerated by the civil authorities) with the exception of those who accepted Anabaptist teachings. If we may believe Menno's testimony, both shepherds and flock continued " with few exceptions " in their old inconsistent life. There can be no doubt that Menno was eye-witness of much that must give him an unfavorable opinion of State-Church Reformation. It is interesting to notice his evident surprise upon forming the acquaintance of Johannes a Lasco (q.v.), that a man of his piety was a representative of Zwinglianism. Menno addresses him in one of his books as his " beloved, holy brother." In his view it was an inconsistency that while the pope was held to be antichrist, his ordination was accepted as valid. " The little gods of Babylon," says Menno, had been abandoned, but that which was in fact responsible for prevailing superficiality and inconsistencies had been left untouched.

8. Relation to the Swiss Brethren.

Menno, in his extant writings, never mentions or even alludes to any of the great leaders of the Swiss Brethren. Was he not informed of the history of the Swiss and South German Anabaptists? Is there a historical connection between the Swiss and the Melchiorites and Obbenites, and if such is the case, did Menno know of it? In vain is an answer to these questions sought in Menno's writings. Of Melchior Hoffmann it is known that he purposely ignored the Swiss and South German Anabaptists, it is doubtful whether he was ever connected with them. The Obbenites had, with the exception of the doctrine of the incarnation, discarded those teachings which had separated the Melchiorites from the Swiss Brethren, and Menno's insistence on the " avoidance " of the excommunicated was, as has been stated, not approved by the Swiss. He was well acquainted with the teachings of the Swiss and South German Anabaptists. It is evident from his writings that there is no direct historical connection between his people and certain medieval sects, but this, it may be observed, does not exclude the supposition that such a connection existed between the Swiss Brethren and older sects although Menno was clearly not aware of it. He says, "Soon after the death of the apostles, through the influence of the unenlightened bishops, trust in outward works was permitted to take the place of trust in Jesus Christ" (*Wercken*, p. 51, Amsterdam, 1681). "The understanding of the holy gospel, which was lost for many centuries, has been found again." "May the holy city and temple which lay desolate for many centuries, be again rebuilt," etc. Menno never mentions the Waldenses. Dirk Philips makes mention of them in his *Enchiridion*, but his observations show that he was not well informed concerning their teachings.

Concerning Menno Simons' relation to the Münsterites (see MUENSTER, ANABAPTISTS IN) it is first of all to be noted that not all Anabaptists of the Netherlands who disregarded the principle of non-resistance were followers of John of Leyden (see ANABAPTISTS; MUENSTER, ANABAPTISTS IN). Of his own brother, who in many historical works figures as a Münsterite, Menno says: "My poor brother has erred only in this, that he undertook to defend his faith with the fist and to oppose violence by violence" (*Works*, ii. 101). It must be remembered that an unprecedented persecution was waged against the dissenters. The law of the empire demanded that all who had submitted to rebaptism and were unwilling to recant must die, and this law dates from the year 1529—about four years prior to the rise of the Münsterites. Very many had lost their lives. The Anabaptists were in continuous danger of death and under temptation to take the sword in self-defense. While Menno was yet a priest a large number of dissenters, among them his brother, sought refuge in the "Old Cloister" near Bolsward and defended it against a contingent of troops. "The poor erring flock," says Menno, "which erred because they had no true shepherds, after many severe edicts, killing and slaughter, came together near my place of residence, in a place called Old Cloister, and, alas, through the godless doctrine of Münster, contrary to Christ's spirit, word, and example, drew the sword to defend themselves, which the Lord commanded Peter to put up into the sheath" (i. 4). Although these people followed the Münsterites to the extent of taking the sword, they must not be held responsible for the highly offensive practises originated by "King" John of Leyden at Münster; in fact even many of those who had accepted the latter's leadership and had gone to Münster were loath to follow him all the way. When John, after long and persistent effort, had persuaded Bernhard Rothmann and the other preachers in Münster (see MUENSTER, ANABAPTISTS IN) that polygamy was the Scriptural course for the "New Israel," a rebellion occurred among his followers within the walls of the besieged city. Mollenhecke, the leader of the resisting party, and his adherents were mercilessly put to the sword by "King" John. Of Münsterite teaching and practise Menno speaks invariably in severest terms of condemnation. He denounced John of Leyden as a blasphemer, seducer, and worthless character, notwithstanding his unusual gifts as a leader. He says of the Münsterites: "Their seditious abominations, such as choosing a king and what they taught concerning the kingdom, the sword, polygamy, worldly conformity, and the like abominations and infamy we reject and hate with all our soul" (i. 197). "So it is in your instance, O ye mad ones," he addresses them, "(forgive me, for it is the truth that I write). The prophets you read according to Jewish understanding, the doctrine of Christ and the apostles, you say, is all fulfilled and pretend that there is now another dispensation," etc. (i. 97). "They have justified open adultery under the cloak of the custom of the Jewish fathers, together with other infamy of which a true Christian must be appalled and ashamed" (i. 227). "Is it not a grievous error that you suffer yourselves to be so wretchedly bewitched by such worthless men, and so lamentably misled from one corrupt sect into another; first Münsterite, then of Batenburg, now Davidist [followers of Jan David Joris (q.v.)], and thus from Beelzebub to Lucifer and from Belial to Behemoth" (i. 94). "How many innocent hearts have they deceived! How many poor souls have they seduced! What great shame have they brought upon God's Word! What abominations have some of them committed under a pious appearance! How great cause have they given to the poor, blind magistrates who have, alas! no understanding of the holy word, to shed innocent blood" (i. 96).

9. Relation to Münster Anabaptists.

After Menno's renunciation of Romanism and his identification with the religious body which he so well represented, it was impossible for him to labor in public. He was an outlaw and a fugitive although, through the leniency of local authorities, he found it possible to sojourn comparatively long in a few places. Had, however, any appointment for a meeting in which he or one of his friends was to appear been publicly announced, he would unfailingly have been apprehended at the appointed place. In a number of instances the local authorities would apparently have tolerated him and his friends, had they not feared the vengeance of the provincial or imperial government. Menno knew full well that only as long as such magistrates could urge the excuse that they did not know of his whereabouts would they refrain from putting forth efforts to have him apprehended. He had a few private discussions with Zwinglian theologians, such as Johannes a Lasco, Martinus Micronius (qq.v.), and Gellius Faber, who had obligated themselves to observe strict silence concerning these conferences. In several of his books Menno asks his Protestant friends to arrange for a public debate with him, obtaining for him a safe conduct from the government, but this desire was never granted him. Even Count von Ahlefeldt, who permitted him to live on his estate at Wüstenfelde in Holstein (where Menno died in peace), would in all probability, had the matter been brought to the attention of the imperial authorities, not have admitted that he knowingly gave shelter to this "heresiarch." Toleration for Menno and his people prevailed neither on Roman Catholic nor Protestant territory. He complains bitterly that "not only among Papists and Turks, but among those who boast of the holy word" and "in their first writings said

10. Victim of Intolerance.

much of faith, that it is the gift of God and that it must not be forced upon any one by the sword of iron" (i. 196) whoever refused to accept the creed of the State was relentlessly persecuted. Even the ruler of Saxony and sovereign of Luther, Elector John Frederick, treated "Anabaptism" as a capital crime. In 1536 a number of Anabaptists were beheaded at Jena in Saxony, upon Melanchthon's advice, for no other cause than error in doctrine. Menno says: "I seek . . . the praise of the Lord and my salvation and the salvation of many souls. For this I, my poor feeble wife and little children have for eighteen years endured extreme anxiety, oppression, affliction, misery, and persecution, and wherever we sojourned, we were in fear and danger of life. Yea, when the preachers [of the state churches] repose on easy beds and downy pillows, we generally must hide ourselves in secluded corners . . . and when the dogs bark, it may mean that the catch polls are upon us here. Whilst they are gloriously rewarded for their services with large incomes and easy times, our recompense and portion must be fire, sword, and death" (i. 7).

The writings of Menno Simons and Dirk (Theodor) Philips are the principal sources for the study of the principles and aims of the most prominent dissenting party of the Netherlands, Germany, and Switzerland of Reformation times. Not only were these men the spokesmen of their immediate followers, but the Swiss Brethren were of one mind with them on all vital points of doctrine and practise. A view of the Reformation which fails to take due account of the great body of Christians which attempted, with unexcelled devotion to principle—the Reformed historian Ernst Müller speaks of them as "a church of martyrs"—the restoration of the Church to its primitive purity and power; which, at variance with the leading Reformers, insisted on the voluntary principle and separation of Church and State, must necessarily be inadequate.

JOHN HORSCH.

BIBLIOGRAPHY: Biographies have been written by A. M. Cramer, Amsterdam, 1837 (still the best); C. Harder, Königsberg, 1846; B. C. Roosen, Leipsic, 1848; Browne, Philadelphia, 1853; F. Bastian, Strasburg, 1857; and C. Fleischer, Amsterdam, 1892. See also the literature under MENNONITES.

SIMONS, WALTHER EDUARD: German Protestant; b. at Elberfeld May 27, 1855. He was educated at the universities of Bonn, Strasburg (lic. theol., 1880), Zurich, Berlin, and Göttingen, and after holding pastorates at Rheinfelden, near Basel (1881–83), and Leipsic (1883–92), became, in 1892, privat-docent for practical theology at Bonn, where he was appointed professor three years later. Since 1902 he has been professor of the same subject at Berlin, and also director of the catechetical seminar of the same university. In theology he belongs to the liberal school. He has written *Hat der dritte Evangelist den kanonischen Matthäus benutzt?* (Bonn, 1880); *Eine altkölnische Seelsorgegemeinde als Vorbild für die Gegenwart* (Berlin, 1894); *Die älteste evangelische Gemeindearmenpflege am Niederrhein* (Bonn, 1894); *Freikirche, Volkskirche, Landeskirche* (Freiburg, 1895); *Niederrheinisches Synodal- und Gemeindeleben "unter dem Kreuz"* (1897); *Konfirmation und Konfirmandenunterricht* (Tübingen, 1900); *Kölnische Konsistorialbeschlüsse* (Bonn, 1905); *Matthes Weyer, ein Mystiker aus der Reformationszeit* (Tübingen, 1907); *Ein Vermächtniss Calvins an die deutsch-evangelischen Kirchen* (1909); *Urkundenbuch zur rheinischen Kirchengeschichte*, i. *Synodalbuch* (1909; in collaboration with others); and *Die Konfirmation* (1909).

SIMONY: A term defined by Thomas Aquinas as "the deliberate will to buy and sell spiritual things [privileges and rights] and their appurtenances." The primitive Church regarded this offense as the gravest among those exclusively within the province of ecclesiastic legal ruling, it being conceived as a sin against the Holy Ghost in that it assumed to engage the offices of the Holy Ghost in consideration of money or its equivalent. The name has its origin, according to the narrative in Acts viii. 18 sqq., in the sacrilege of Simon Magus (q.v.), who desired to buy from the Apostle Peter the power to impart the Holy Ghost to whom he would. Especially the sale or purchase of ordination for money or its equivalent must, from this account, have been viewed as simony, seeing that (even as early as the fourth century) the theory had grown up that by means of ordination, through the laying on of a bishop's hands, the Holy Ghost is received, and with it the power to forgive and to retain sins. By degrees the concept reached the expanded form expressed by Thomas Aquinas, ut sup. In the main, however, simony was held to be traffic in spiritual offices. The viciousness of simony in this peculiar sense of the term was purposely emphasized by the popes in opposition to the emperors during the investiture strife (see INVESTITURE), and was employed as chief weapon in that conflict. The Evangelical conception of ordination involves the consideration of simony as the bestowal and procurement of spiritual offices for money.

It is directly consonant with the primitive concept of simony, that to give and to take money or its equivalent not simply for the sacrament itself, but also for the administration of sacraments and sacramental acts, came generally to be viewed as simony. Nevertheless, it soon grew clear that a voluntary gift in token of gratitude for such dispensations and their acceptance ought not to be so branded; indeed, where a fixed custom had grown up of showing oneself thankful by means of suitable presents, not to recognize the favor came to be regarded as reprehensible. In that way the Stole Fees (q.v.) came into being. A special kind of simony, which can occur only in the Roman Catholic Church, is the granting or obtaining of admission into a spiritual order for money or its equivalent.

An extension of the idea is found when the Church treats as simony the selling and buying of the right of patronage on its own account. According to canon law, certified simony involves in the Roman Catholic Church for all the guilty parties excommunication from which the pope alone can give absolution. If the act has remained secret, however, the bishops can absolve it. In connection with ordination, simony subjects the ordained offender to suspension from the received rites of consecration, and to the construction of irregularity. Likewise the ordainer becomes suspended from his pontifical prerogatives. All provisory transactions wherein simony has been committed are invalid. Whoever has procured a benefice through simony, becomes irregular, deposed from office, and incapable of obtaining another appointment. Forfeiture of the benefice ensues even for the one who has obtained it through an act of simony wrought by others without his accessory knowledge, counsel, or approval, only he may recover such benefice by dispensation, unless in case of a simoniacal election. The inmate of a cloister who is guilty of simony in connection with admission to the cloister is visited with suspension from all capitulary offices, and from all rights of jurisdiction. The latest regulations are found in *Constitutiones Pii IX., Apostolicæ sedis*, Oct. 12, 1869.

In the Protestant church, as well, all transactions affecting official appointments wherein simony has occurred are accounted void, so that any resulting grant of office becomes canceled. In the case of patrons the act is punished by withdrawal of personal right of presentation. Simony was also occasionally subjected to fine and imprisonment. Nowadays it is classed as a criminal offense, and so is liable to civil correction. Wherefore all cognizance in the matter devolves exclusively on the temporal courts. From the present standpoint of the Roman Catholic Church, simony is matter for ecclesiastical discipline and the disciplinary province of the church authorities. E. Sehling.

Bibliography: N. A. Weber, *A Hist. of Simony in the Christian Church*, Baltimore, 1909 (goes down to the 9th century); Bingham, *Origines*, IV., iii. 14, XVI., vi. 28–30; G. Phillips, *Lehrbuch des Kirchenrechts*, § 193, 7 vols., Regensburg, 1845–72; N. München, *Das kanonische Strafrecht*, ii. 274 sqq., Cologne, 1866; P. Hinschius, *Kirchenrecht*, v. 161 sqq., Berlin, 1893; A. Leinz, *Die Simonie. Eine kanonistische Studie*, Freiburg, 1902; Hirsch, in *Archiv für katholisches Kirchenrecht*, lxxxvi (1906), 3–19; D. Barry, in *Ecclesiastical Review*, Sept., 1906, pp. 234–245; J. Drehmann, *Papst Leo IX. und die Simonie. Ein Beitrag zur Untersuchung der Vorgeschichte des Investiturstreites*, Leipsic, 1908; *DCA*, ii. 1900–01; *KL*, xi. 321–324; Schaff, *Christian Church*, vol. 1, passim. Documents relating to the subject are given in Reich, *Documents*, pp. 152, 198.

SIMPLICIUS, sim-plish'i-us: Pope 468–483. According to the *Liber pontificalis* he came from Tibur (20 m. n.e. of Rome), and was consecrated as the successor of Hilary possibly on Mar. 3, 468. His importance arises from his participation in the Monophysitic controversy (see Monophysites, §§ 5–7), in which he was second only to Leo the Great and Hilary. He made Bishop Zeno of Seville apostolic vicar in Spain. His biography names four churches at Rome which were dedicated by him, the establishment of a *hebdomarius* for baptism and penitence, and the offering of costly church vessels. His death, according to Duchesne (*Liber pontificalis*), occurred on Mar. 10, 483 (not Mar. 2).

(A. Hauck.)

Bibliography: Sources are, *Liber pontificalis*, ed. Mommsen in *MGH, Gest. pont. Rom.*, i (1898), 112–113; Jaffé, *Regesta*, i. 77 sqq.; *Epistolæ Romanorum pontificum genuinæ*, ed. A. Thiel, i. 174 sqq., Braunsberg, 1867 (the letters of Simplicius); *MPL*, lxviii. 1019 sqq.; and Evagrius, *Hist. eccl.*, III., iv. sqq. Consult further: J. Langen, *Geschichte der römischen Kirche*, ii. 126 sqq., Bonn, 1885; Hefele, *Conciliengeschichte*, ii. 602 sqq., Eng. transl., iv. 26 sqq., Fr. transl., ii. 2, pp. 9, 15 sqq.; Bower, *Popes*, i. 257–271; Milman, *Latin Christianity*, i. 314, 326–327; *DCB*, iv. 690–695 (full discussion); and the relevant literature under Monophysites.

SIMPSON, ALBERT B: Presbyterian; b. at Cavendish, Prince Edward Island, Dec. 15, 1844. He was graduated at Knox College, Toronto, in 1865, and also received his theological education there. He was pastor of Knox Church, Hamilton, Ont., 1865–74, Broadway Tabernacle, Louisville, Ky., 1874–80, Thirteenth Street Presbyterian Church, New York, 1880–81; since 1881, of the Gospel Tabernacle in the same city. He has been president of the Christian and Missionary Alliance since 1887, and in theology holds "the Evangelical faith in a conservative rather than liberal sense," also believing in adult baptism by immersion, though not a Baptist. Besides editing the *Christian and Missionary Alliance* since 1887 and *Living Truths* since 1903, he has written *The Gospel of Healing* (New York, 1884); *Divine Problems in Genesis and Exodus* (1890); *The Land of Promise* (1892); *The Gospel of the Kingdom* (1893); *Jesus in the Psalms* (1895); *Heart Messages for Sabbaths at Home* (1897); *Larger Outlooks on Missionary Lands* (1897); *The Holy Spirit; or, Power from on High* (2 vols., 1899); *Days of Heaven upon Earth* (1900); *Discovery of Divine Healing* (1902); *Christ in the Bible* (a Bible commentary; 24 vols., 1902–1907); *Echoes of the New Creation* (1903); and collaborated with M. Wilson in *Henry Wilson, One of God's Best* (1909).

SIMPSON, JAMES GILLILAND: Church of England; b. at London Oct. 16, 1865. He was educated at Trinity College, Oxford (B.A., 1888), and was ordained to the priesthood in 1891. He was successively curate of Leeds parish church (1889–1893), curate of Edinburgh Cathedral and vice-principal of Edinburgh Theological College (1893–1894), rector of St. Paul's, Dundee (1895–1900), and principal of Leeds Clergy School and lecturer at Leeds parish church (1900–10), besides being chaplain to the bishop of Brechin (1896–1900), and select preacher at Oxford (1909). Since 1910 he has been a canon of Manchester. He has written *Christian Ideals* (London, 1908), *Fact and Faith* (1908), and *Christus Crucifixus* (1909).

SIMPSON, MATTHEW: Methodist Episcopal bishop; b. at Cadiz, O., June 21, 1811; d. in Philadelphia, Pa., June 17, 1884. He was educated at Madison College (subsequently merged into Alleghany College, Meadville, Pa.), where he was tutor in 1829; studied and practised medicine, 1829–35; was ordained deacon in the Methodist Episcopal Church 1835, and elder in 1837; was vice-president and professor of natural science in Alleghany College, 1837–39; president of Indiana Asbury University, Greencastle, Ind., 1839–48; editor of *The Western Christian Advocate*, Cincinnati, O., 1848–1852; and was elected bishop 1852. He changed his residence in 1859 from Pittsburg, Pa., to Evanston, Ill., and became president of the Garrett Biblical Institute in the latter place. He was the acknowledged prince of Methodist preachers, and his eloquent addresses did good service for the Union cause during the Civil War, enjoying, as he did, the personal friendship of President Lincoln. He was the author of *Hundred Years of Methodism*, New York, 1876; *Cyclopædia of Methodism*, Philadelphia, 1878; *Lectures on Preaching*, New York, 1879; and *Sermons* (posthumous, ed. G. R. Crooks, 1885).

BIBLIOGRAPHY: G. R. Crooks, *Life of Bishop Matthew Simpson*, New York, 1890.

SIMPSON, SAMUEL: Congregationalist; b. at Centreville, Mich., Nov. 24, 1868. He was educated at Olivet College, Olivet, Mich. (A.B., 1891), and Oberlin Theological Seminary (graduated 1894). He also studied at Hartford Theological Seminary (1896–98) and the University of Berlin (1900–01). He held Congregational pastorates at Garner, O. (1894–96), and Chardon, O. (1898–1900), and was associate professor of American Church history in Hartford Theological Seminary (1902–1909). He has written *The Life of Ulrich Zwingli, Swiss Patriot and Reformer* (New York, 1902).

SIMSON, JOHN: Scotch theologian; b. at Renfrew (6 m. n.w. of Glasgow) about 1668; d. at Edinburgh Feb. 2, 1740. He received his education at Edinburgh University (M.A., 1692); and appears to have studied theology at least under the advice of John Marck of Leyden, as he acknowledged receiving instruction from him; he is known to have been librarian at Glasgow College in 1696; he was licensed by the presbytery of Paisley in 1698, but, possibly owing to infirmity in health, did not receive a charge until 1705, when he was called to Troqueer, Kircudbrightshire; he became professor of divinity in the University of Glasgow, 1708. In this last place he was exceedingly influential, the presbyteries of the west of Scotland and north of Ireland receiving a considerable number of ministers from the men who studied under him, and yet his position was frequently assailed, and it was believed that he was untrue to the standards. In part this was due to his fundamental position that reason was the basis of theology and to his effort to make orthodoxy understandable. In Mar., 1714, charges were brought against him in the presbytery of Edinburgh, to which charges he made answer in 1715, and the answer was referred to a committee; the next assembly passed the matter over, and, in 1717, a qualified censure of certain opinions and expressions was passed. In his later teaching, after combating the Semi-arianism of Samuel Clarke (q.v.), he assailed Sabellianism; and in 1726 charges were once more brought against him, this time in the presbytery of Glasgow. The next year he was suspended by the general assembly, a committee being appointed to carry the case through. But in 1728 Simson's account of himself was regarded as establishing the orthodoxy of his belief, though his statements in teaching were not approved, and suspension followed till the presbyteries could be heard from; the suspension finally occurred and was confirmed in 1729. The emoluments of the chair were left to him, but he was deberred from teaching.

His only publications were those connected with his ecclesiastical trials: *The Case of Mr. John Simson* (Glasgow, 1715); and *Continuation of the Second Edition of the Case of Mr. John Simson* (Edinburgh, 1727–29).

BIBLIOGRAPHY: In the *British Museum Catalogue*, s.v., a column is devoted to titles of pamphlets, records, etc., dealing with the orthodoxy and trial of Professor Simson. Consult further: *Correspondence of Rev. R. Wodrow*, ed. T. MacCrie, 3 vols., Edinburgh, 1842–43; Hew Scott, *Fasti ecclesiæ Scoticanæ*, 5 parts, London, 1871; W. M. Hetherington, *Hist. of the Church of Scotland*, pp. 337, 340, 348, New York, 1881; H. F. Henderson, *Religious Controversies of Scotland*, pp. 5, 8, 11–17, Edinburgh, 1905; W. Beveridge, *Makers of the Scottish Church*, p. 174, Edinburgh, 1908; *DNB*, lii. 286–287.

SIMULTANEUM (Lat., "simultaneous [exercise of religion]"): A term formerly used in the German Empire to denote the authorization of more than one religious body to hold services side by side in the same territory, so that the worship of the comparatively weaker communion should be more than the right of mere household devotion. The term also connoted, as it still does, the simultaneous right of two congregations of different confessions to the same ecclesiastical foundation, especially to the same church building, or the same churchyard. Such simultaneous conditions repeatedly arose in Germany, notably in the West and Southwest during the period between the religious peace of Augsburg and the Peace of Westphalia. The chief causes of this were the Protestant confiscation of a large amount of church property after the Peace of Augsburg, followed by its restitution, during the Counter-Reformation, in accordance with the edict of Mar. 6, 1629; as well as the changes, in the course of the Thirty Years' War, in the status of the religious bodies in the various territories; the frequent conversions of ruling princes (especially from Protestantism to Roman Catholicism); and the legal establishment of the joint rights of Roman Catholics to Protestant churches. The legal theory of the simultaneous use of ecclesiastical institutions (especially church buildings) is, however, only scantily developed and is much contested, since regulation by law is almost entirely lacking, except in Prussia and Bavaria. The legal basis for the simultaneous use of a church may arise from joint ownership of the building by both congregations, although it is also possible that the church in question may belong solely to one of the congregations, so that the title of the other religious body is merely one of prescription, the exact determination of conditions requiring a knowledge of the origin of the simultaneum in each specific case. In these instances there are always two distinct congregations, conceived as separate legal entities, the view being untenable which maintains that the communions in question must be regarded, so far as the simultaneous church is concerned, not as distinct corporate bodies, but as a single congregation which still retains fellowship and unity of faith. Legal recognition of actual joint use is equivalent to a title to such right, and a legal simultaneum is also created in case one of the communions concerned cedes the privilege of joint use at the petition of the other party, while retaining the right of revoking such permission at any time. On the other hand, even right prescriptive can not create a simultaneum in case sufferance of joint use has been forcibly extorted from the party legally entitled to sole possession. Provision is thus made for cases in which the legal rights of the parties concerned can not be determined, the presumption being that the privilege of that party which was the later to receive permission of joint use was granted in response to petition and is revocable; while if the status of joint use can not definitely be determined, both communions are held to have equal rights.

The simultaneum is subject to great variation both in kind and in degree. One congregation may have the nave while the other has the chancel; separate hours may be appointed for the religious services of each communion; one of the parties may have the right to use the church only on special occasions, as for baptism; and in sporadic instances the two congregations may even worship together. Expenses, especially those for maintenance, must be defrayed according to any agreements previously drawn up, or, if occasion demands, from the common funds of the church. If such funds are lacking or are inadequate, both congregations, if possessed of simultaneous privileges, must contribute. When, however, one of the communions concerned has the exclusive right of possession, the other having only a right of use, the former must bear all charges legally incumbent on the owner, while the latter is required to contribute only in proportion to its rights of use. Any new creation of simultaneous rights in churches is precluded, from the standpoint of the Roman Catholic Church, by the rule that Roman Catholic churches must not be used for other than Roman Catholic services, and though Protestants may consistently grant the use of their church buildings to other religious bodies, as has been done repeatedly at the request of the Old Catholics, such action can scarcely give rise to obligations of a legal nature.

A simultaneum may be dissolved either by the union of the two congregations concerned (with the requisite sanction of their ecclesiastical superiors); or by surrender of rights by one of the parties in question, although this party is not thereby released from its possible obligations. It is a moot question whether one party may demand a settlement with reference to the simultaneous church and its joint property without the consent of the party of the second part, even though proper compensation be offered. This right is generally denied where the simultaneum has been created by legal enactments, as by the Peace of Westphalia; but if the simultaneum is based on a private contract, such a demand is legal as coming within the scope of private law. The principles of the modern State forbid it to use either administrative or legislative measures to compel churches to adopt a simultaneum. If, however, the parties to a simultaneum become involved in a controversy or dispute which disturbs the public peace, the authorities (especially the police) have the right to interfere. In case of severe breaches of the peace, the simultaneum may be temporarily suspended; but the attitude of the State toward religious communities forbids the permanent quashing of a simultaneum without the consent of the parties concerned.

In the case of cemeteries, however, the right of enforcing a limited or contingent simultaneum is reserved by the State in connection with its claim to jurisdiction over burial. The Peace of Westphalia enacted that if one of the recognized confessions possessed no cemetery of its own, its members might be interred in the churchyard of the other. This principle, with a number of modifications and amplifications, is still in force; but while it is recognised by the German Protestants as well as by the majority of the German States, the Roman Catholic Church rejects it except when absolutely compelled to do otherwise, in the latter contingency forbidding Protestant ministers to officiate at the burial, and also endeavoring, wherever possible, to set apart a special portion of the churchyard for non-Catholics.

The only modern possibility of the necessity of creating additional simultaneous conditions is the cleavage of a communion by differences evolved within itself. This contingency was realized in Germany by the Old Catholic movement. Both in Baden and in Prussia State law permits Old Catholic congregations, under specified circumstances, to have simultaneous use of Roman Catholic churches and churchyards, etc., but this has failed to give rise to a true simultaneum, since the Curia has forbidden Roman Catholics to worship in church buildings given by the government to Old Catholics.

E. SEHLING.

BIBLIOGRAPHY: P. S. von der Aurach, *Die kirchlichen Simultanverhältnisse in der Pfalz am Rhein*, Mannheim, 1866; M. J. Hartung, *Das kirchliche Recht der Protestanten im vormaligen Herzogthum Sulzbach*, Erlangen, 1872; E. Köhler, *Simultankirchen im Herzogtum Hesse*, Darmstadt, 1889; W. Wagner, *Untersuchung über die rysswicksche Religionsklausel*, Berlin, 1889; W. Kraje, *Kirchliche Simultanverhältnisse*, Würzburg, 1890; E. Sehling, *Über kirchliche Simultanverhältnisse*, Freiburg, 1891; idem, in *NKZ*, ii (1891), 777 sqq.; T. Lauter, *Die Entstehung der kirchlichen Simultaneen*, Würzburg, 1894; Waller, *Beitrag zum Recht der Simultaneen* (disputation at Erlangen, 1905); Stolz, *Das Simultaneum in Reppendorf* (dissertation at Würzburg, 1905). Further references to literature on German ecclesiastical law are given in Hauck-Herzog, *RE*, xviii. 374.

SIN.

In religious terminology sin is the name for evil. Practical philosophy [in the Kantian sense] deals with a contradiction between what is and what should be in human life, and, in its most intense moral form, with a "radical evil." The criminal code knows of misdemeanor, felony, crime. Moral judgment in common parlance speaks of want of character, violations of duty, and vice. As sin, evil is conceived in a religious philosophy only as it is judged remiss in its duty to deity with its precepts of life. The concept sin involves a peculiar modification of that of evil: (1) its heinousness is more serious for a religious person, because it is a transgression not only of a human but of a divine order; (2) the scope of this religious condemnation extends to offenses which do not occasion the censure or even the notice of human authority; (3) with the idea of evil understood as sin, there is combined the represen-

1. Nature.

tation of a permanent state of the human person transcending the individual act, which disturbs the relation to deity. The word sin involves a religious and a moral judgment of acts and of persons. The two are more or less inseparable. Natural religion considers as sins transgressions of the cult and the religious customs. In the ethical religions the positive standard appears as a sacred legal order, and sin assumes the character of legalistic violation. In the highest ethical religions, which, with H. Siebeck, may be called religions of salvation, there emerges, with an inward perception of the ethical life, the consciousness of a more intimate relation with deity. God leads his people with fatherly long-suffering and faithfulness, and expects in return not only obedience, but also gratitude and trust. He gives norms of religious life in the community, which transcend the ordinances of law, and aim at the mutual exercise of mercy and love. Where God's will is recognized, there the comprehensive norm of the good is disclosed. Where this standard is transgressed, God's personal will is violated and fellowship with him is interrupted. Christianity, the perfected ethical faith, understands by sin apostasy from God, which at the same time is inseparably the violation of the absolute ethical norm of his will. Both phases condition the nature of the Christian consciousness of sin, the first its permanent activity, the second its seriousness.

The Jewish faith attained a vitality and depth in the consciousness of sin not met with in any other pre-Christian religion. The general Semitic conception of sin as revolt against the divinity is not only followed to its issue, but also modified.

2. In the Old Testament. Offense to the will of God obtains a significance not exhausted in the consequent results of disaster. In the Babylonian penitential psalms, it is the external stress that awakens the thought of sin, followed by the cry for help and forgiveness. This coalescing of the stress of salvation with natural eudemonistic motives of an elementary religiousness is also manifest in the Psalms of the Old Testament (vi., x., lxxxviii., cii., cvii.); but in the upper stages of Israelitic piety the religious-ethical idea gains due prominence (xxxii., li.), and the certainty of the nearness of God overshadows the outer event (lxxiii. 23 sqq.). Hence by the time of the prophets it came to be recognized that the favor of Yahweh could not be secured by cultic zeal (I Sam. xv. 22; Hos. vi. 6). Among sins are reckoned, besides worship of idols (Hos. ii. 13; Isa. ii. 8; Ezek. vi. 13) and magic (Deut. xviii. 10–11), unbelief in Yahweh's power (Isa. vii. 9), trust in human help (Isa. xxii. 8 sqq.), unrighteousness in judgment and conduct (II Sam. xii. 9 sqq.), avarice (Isa. v. 8 sqq.), and extravagance (Amos vi. 4 sqq.). Yahweh's will is conceived as moral, and the requirements of his will as law, but this is presently exceeded. Insensibility to God's love (Hosea), ingratitude (Isa. v.; Jer. ii. 5), and hard-heartedness (Isa. xlvi. 12; Deut. ix. 6, 13) are conceived to be sins. The ceremonial law of the post-exilic period produced a change which affected rather the content than the intensity of the sense of sin. Attention is mainly directed to particular precepts for the maintenance of the obedience and purity of the pious. Ceremonial shortcomings are sinful (Ezek. xxii. 26). However, the sense of sin did not lose in subjective keenness, if it did in ethical depth. The strictness of the positive prescriptions impelled to supplication for grace. The consciousness of sin became superficial with the period of the Wisdom literature. Although the presumption remained that sin is against God (Prov. iii. 32–34), yet the idea is more current that it is offense against the wisdom of life, and on this account leads to misfortune (i. 24 sqq.). These tones reverberate in the post-canonical literature, until the belief in the future life, judgment, and reward afford a deeper insight. The Old Testament treats sin as universal in a great many instances. Often it is the correlate of human weakness and frailty (Job iv. 18). There are just ones who walk with God like Enoch and Noah, but such are models of piety, not of sinlessness. The latter vanishes in the light of God's majesty (Job ix. 2). The prophets called of God are not excepted (Isa. vi. 5). The law distinguishes between thoughtless sins (Lev. iv. 2), which may be atoned for by sacrifice, and presumptuous sins dishonoring Yahweh and entailing destruction (Num. xv. 30). As thoughtless may be reckoned the sins of youth (Job xiii. 26) and the unconscious errors of man (Ps. xix. 12); but they, too, oppress a tender conscience and cause a craving for forgiveness, if fellowship with God is not to be forfeited (Ps. xc. 8, xxxii. 6). Only those may be comforted by the presence of God, who are of a broken heart and a contrite spirit (Ps. xxxiv. 18). Thought on the universality of sin led to the conclusion of the inclination to evil in every man. The doctrine of an evil tendency is in the later Jewish literature, but analogous conceptions are found in the canonical Old Testament. Sin lies in wait for man (Gen. iv. 7); man's heart is naturally evil (Jer. xvii. 9). More frequently is there mention of individual responsibility for the sin of the community. Pre-exilic prophets speak of the common guilt of the people (Isa. i. 3–4; Mic. vii. 1 sqq.). In earlier times the individual shared the burden of the sin of the environment (Gen. xix. 15); later generations are punished for the sin of the earlier (Ex. xx. 5). Later this was to be reconciled with the consciousness of the independence and the worth of the individual. As it had become the rule not to inflict punishment on the children for the offenses of their fathers (Deut. xxiv. 16), it became recognized as the divine norm that each was to suffer for his own sin (Jer. xxxi. 29 sqq.). However, the theory of individual earthly requital encountered great difficulties in the face of the facts, due not only to the limitation of view to an external and temporal course of events, but to the overlooking of the moral solidarity. How torturing and hopeless the problem proved to be is shown not only in Ps. lxxiii. and the book of Job, but also in the attempt of late Judaism at an equation of sins and merits, and in this way to understand man's earthly destiny, without the aid of the later Jewish foreglimpse of the other world. For a long time Israel did not feel called upon to investigate the origin of sin. That it lay in the common nature of mankind seemed patent, and there was a general conviction of the power of the will to resist it (Gen. iv. 7). Where an evil act seemed inexplicable or fatal, it was supposed to have been ordained of God (Judges ix. 23; I Sam. xxvi. 19). Later Judaism treated such as due to evil spirits. Sin is not regarded as historically inherited (Isa. xliii. 27), but as the common attribute of one generation after another (Job xiv. 4). The account in Gen. iii. was not intended to explain the origin of sin but to show that death and other evils originated through it. Its influence, beside that of Gen. vi. 1 sqq., on the conception of sin is first marked in later Judaism (Eccles. ii. 24; Sirach xxv. 32). To Adam was then charged in part evil and in part an enhanced proneness to sin in humanity. In the first case, Adam's fall was said to have injured the state of man by bringing on evil and death (Baruch), yet each one was to be morally responsible for himself. But it is further asserted that Adam's sin increased man's inclination to evil (IV Esdras iii. 20 sqq.). But at the same place there was ascribed to Adam a root of evil; hence the historical explanation of sin was not consistently carried out. Least of all does the figure of the serpent offer a satisfactory explanation of the origin of evil. Identified later with Satan (see SERPENT IN WORSHIP, I., § 1), it served only to symbolize temptation. The Old Testament offers the thought of the generation of sin in its actual manifestation as well as a deep consciousness of guilt and consequent disaster, arousing the desire for deliverance; but it furnishes little for the solution of the theoretical problem.

3. In the New Testament.

The testimony of Jesus against sin is intimately associated with the prophetical preaching. Sin is resistance to the promotive leadership of God, hence with indifference to moral requirements (*anomia*, Matt. vii. 23), contempt of grace (xi. 20 sqq.), and denial of recognised truth (Matt. xii. 31 sqq.). It is treated as guilt deserving punishment (vi. 7). Its universality is assumed; all are called to repentance (iv. 17); and are called evil (vii. 11). The obligation of mercy Jesus bases on the general need of forgiveness (xviii. 11 sqq.); his contemporaries he calls an evil and adulterous generation (xii. 39). The victims of particular catastrophes are not sinners beyond others, but meet a judgment that all can avoid only through penitence (Luke xiii. 2–5). The human world is so much under the dominion of sin that offenses are unavoidable (Matt. xviii. 7 sqq.). Although he mentions the righteous whom he did not come to call to repentance (Mark ii. 17), yet their righteousness is questionable. The Pharisees who claim it are hypocrites (Matt. xv. 7). Even others who assume it like the rich young man are not sufficiently earnest in self-denial (xix. 16 sqq.). He who looks upon sin in his brother instead of in himself is worse (vii. 3–5). Jesus carries sin from its outer appearance back to its inner origin (v. 21–25, xv. 19), and sees in it a persistent tendency (vii. 16 sqq., xii. 35). Proportions of sin and guilt vary; there are tempters worthy of the severest penalty, relative innocents misled by seducers (xviii. 6), and there is an unpardonable sin (xii. 31 sqq.). The greater the possible knowledge of the divine command, the greater the responsibility (Luke xii. 47–48); where the revelation of grace receives no penitent response is the maximum guilt (Matt. xi. 20). Finally, the human attitude of acceptance or rejection is decisive, when the divine call to salvation is nigh (xxiii. 37). Jesus, like the prophets, does not explain the origin of sin; the fall is not mentioned in the Synoptics. From the practical point of view Jesus ascribes the present source of sin to the evil heart (Matt. xv. 19) and to the world's offenses (xviii. 7). As a further source is mentioned, repeatedly, the temptation of the wicked one (xiii. 19); but the subject is not treated theoretically. The reference serves to lay stress upon the infectious and far-reaching power of evil (v. 37; Luke xxii. 31). The thought of the kingdom of Satan involves a close relation of sin and evil (xii. 25 sqq.); their connection is illustrated (ix. 2–6), although to point out their proportion in individuals is not permissible (Luke xiii. 2–5). That God judges and punishes sin lies at the root of the teaching of Jesus throughout. Hence, there is no salvation without forgiveness (Matt. vi. 12, xviii. 23 sqq.); no way of accepting it but by confession of sins (Luke xviii. 13–14) and repentance (Luke xiii. 5). The new in the teaching of Jesus is the height of his religious-moral ideas (Matt. v. 48), in the light of which appear as sins what had been previously looked upon as excusable defects, and the way of salvation was revealed in his person (Matt. xx. 28). In connection with the contrast drawn between the salvation in Christ and the world without, Paul takes occasion to present a total picture of the nature and life of sin. It is not an individualised acting against the divine will, but a dominating power, a general tendency, and a total state (Rom. vi. 12, 14). It is personified, winning men to its service and compensating them (vi. 17, 23). Jews and gentiles are under its sway (iii. 9); so all, with the exception of Christ (II Cor. v. 21) and those whom he frees from the law of sin (Rom. viii. 3). Experience shows the universality of sin (i. 24–31), as do the Scriptures (iii. 9–20). In the last analysis, the death of Christ would have been dispensable, if there had been any other way to overcome sin (Gal. ii. 21). Therefore, the universality of sin is of divine ordinance (Rom. xi. 32); the only way of escape was to ensue, that opened by grace and faith (iii. 24–26), so that no person might glory (iv. 2). Slavery to sin leaves nothing to man but the experience of his impotence and the futility of his moral efforts (vii. 18 sqq.). The religious reference of sin as a contradiction against God is ever expressly emphasized and forms the background of Paul's statements. It is disregard of divine revelation, ingratitude for God's gifts (i. 19–21, 25), alienation from God (Eph. iv. 18), enmity toward God (Rom. viii. 7), the unethical tendency of living for self (II Cor. v. 15); and leads in social life to envy, hatred, strife (Gal. v. 20). It lays weight on earthly things (Col. iii. 2), and especially yields to carnal desires (Rom. i. 24). Therefore uncleanness and unbridled sensuality hold sway over mankind (Gal. v. 19–21), especially over the heathen world (Rom. i. 24 sqq.), while the Jews are more directly exposed to the danger of self-deception and self-righteousness (x. 3). But notwithstanding all moral differences (ii. 14), there is essentially no difference among men in God's sight (iii. 23). All are fallen under his judgment (iii. 19), and have forfeited the future glory (iii. 23). The gradations of sin are determined by the progress of divine revelation; the heathen perish without law (ii. 12); revelation of the law brings responsibility, the curse, wrath (iv. 15; Gal. iii. 10). Pre-Christian sins are treated by God with long-suffering (Rom. iii. 25); in view of Christian revelation, there is either grace (iii. 24) or judgment (II Cor. v. 10), either life or death (ii. 16). The connection of sin with the kingdom of Satan seldom occurs; only, deception and temptation are treated as his work (II Cor. iv. 4; Eph. ii. 2). Peculiar to Paul and original with him is his connection of sin with the flesh. He can not mean the identification of the flesh with sense, for sins of a purely spiritual nature he designates as works of the flesh (Gal. v. 16 sqq.). The whole man is represented as *sarx*, so far as he may be conceived in a religious-ethical sense (Rom. vii. 18). The distinction is formed from the standpoint that the spirit of Christ first makes man what he is by the divine will intended to be (II Cor. iii. 17). Flesh is man who dispenses with the divine Spirit or shuts himself against his influence. Paul is thus enabled to designate the entire pre-Christian development as the carnal or psychic (I Cor. xv. 45 sqq.). But this scheme gains its evident completion by another thought series of which Paul is unmistakably conscious. The flesh is the source of lusts which oppose God's commands (Gal. v. 16; Eph. ii. 3); and in this lies its positive significance for the origin of a bias of life against God. The pneumatic law which declares war on the lusts meets with opposition from the other (Rom. vii. 8, 14), which is called the "law in the members" (vii. 23). It is always the Christian's duty after he has been made free to withdraw his members from the service of sin (vi. 18–19). These statements can scarcely be reconciled unless it be assumed that in the flesh Paul saw the gateway for the entrance of sin into the human organism. The natural man is therefore flesh in the twofold sense that he is without the divine Spirit, and so long as this continues the desires of the flesh have the upper hand. A stronger influence on the development of Christian doctrine than the preceding line of thought has been wrought by the Pauline teaching of the deed of Adam and its consequences (Rom. v. 12 sqq.). The object of the passage is to elucidate the power of Christ's obedience by the adverse parallel of the disobedience of Adam with a commensurate significance. As by disobedience death entered the world, by obedience came life. Physical death is meant, but possibly the contrast with the life of Christ gave it a wider significance. The origin and dissemination of sin can not be deduced from the passage; it only states that Adam's transgression was the first sin, not that he produced the condition of sinning. It is to be admitted that in vii. the same is said of the individual's confronting a commandment as of the progenitor in v. The effect of the act of Adam appears different according as the variously interpreted clause "for that all have sinned" (v. 12) is understood; either as an additional circumstance, or, what seems more likely, as a reference to Adam's act, which would then be designated as a total act of humanity. According to the former, Adam would be only the leader; according to the latter, the totally valid representative or even the type of the human race. Questions are raised rather than answered. What it certainly implies, that Adam's act entailed a continuous judgment on mankind realized in death, does not exceed the view of Gen. iii. represented in late Jewish circles. These thoughts obtained a further expansion by Paul's noted parallelism, which occasioned a further extension of the comparison than the passage immediately had in view.

A striking completion of the Pauline doctrine of sin is contained in the Johannine writings. The totality of sinful life is more prominent. Sin is the rebellious refusal to accept the divine revelation of truth and love (John v. 40); it is essentially unbelief (xvi. 9); love of darkness (iii. 19); guilty blindness (ix. 41); contradiction of the divine standard of life (I John iii. 4). It constitutes a sphere of life, contrary to divine light and life (*kosmos*), and is attached to things that abide not (ii. 15 sqq.). The enemies of truth in it combine under the prince of this world (John xii. 31), hating the children of light and the light itself (xv. 19) but unable to sustain themselves under the condemnation of the light of Christ (iii. 19). Belief and unbelief originate a certain character, transcending time, so that one born of God seems incapable of sinning (I John v. 18), and one having known the truth who, by denying the same, has backslidden shall not be saved (probably sin unto death, v. 16). Constant need of forgiveness is recognized for the Christian life (i. 8). The Epistle to the Hebrews regards sin as a besetting, impeding power, causing man to stumble (xii. 1); polluting his conscience (ix. 14); separating him from God (xii. 14). Degrees in sin are discriminated as in the Old Testament; such as unintentional errors (ix. 7) and wilful sins (x. 26), among which is apostasy, for which there is no forgiveness (vi. 4–6). The Epistle of James emphasizes that God does not tempt to evil, but sin is conceived as lust, and brings forth death (i. 13–15).

4. Ancient and Medieval View.

The church doctrine is a continuation of the development of the Biblical only to a very limited extent. The principal thing in Scripture, the determination of evil according to experience by the norm of the revealed divine will, becomes subordinate; the first sin, its connection with extra-human evil powers, and its penal consequences upon the human race come to the front. A background of the original state has arisen having little foundation in Scripture. For a fuller presentation of the doctrine of sin in the early Church see AUGUSTINE, II.; PELAGIUS, PELAGIANISM; and SEMIPELAGIANISM. The Eastern Church regarded sin as a weakening of the intellect and of the freedom of the will, and integrates it with the fall, from which it derived universal death. It is uncertain, however, whether the fall represents a becoming stationary at a lower level or a sinking from a higher one. In case of the latter the loss of the image of God could be thought of as brought upon the race by Adam. Human free-will is preserved, already in antagonism to the physicism of Gnosticism. A more serious conception of sin arises in the West. But a strong sensuous admixture is already introduced by Tertullian with his combination of the physical unity of the generations from Stoicism, and the aversion to procreation of asceticism. In his presentation of sin Augustine starts from the will. Only after the fall, sin acquired the character of a tendency to evil imposed upon nature. This produces in the human race, as the "mass of perdition," moral depravity, which is incapable of good motives, though of apparently good actions. Freedom was retained but the good was beyond its power. Adam appears occasionally as the representative of humanity; predominantly, however, he is considered as its physical head. The transmission of sin takes place by the propagation of "corrupted nature." Sin is reproduced in "concupiscence," not without involving a divine judgment. This "original sin" deserves by itself eternal damnation; even children who have not actually sinned are subject to this damnation, although in the mildest degree, unless they have been baptized. The demoralization of sin, Augustine thus considers not alike in all. In the Greek conception there was only an inherited evil; to Augustine both an original sin and an original guilt. Augustinianism was opposed by Pelagianism which, as an ascetic moralism, to preserve moral self-development, held aloof from all physical representations of sin and hyper-physical ideas of grace. It denied that sin could be inherited; held that sin was disseminated by the force of example, and asserted that sin could be avoided, although admitting a habit of sinning as a moral impediment. Baptism it could not conceive as a means of grace against original sin. Grace is rather pardon and moral direction than an inner impartation of power. Semipelagianism gives man in the state of sin the capacity of acceding to grace, and of affording it an inner relation. Moderate Augustinianism was continued in medieval scholasticism. Without abandoning the formulas of Augustine a rational conception arose alongside of the religious, by which it was gradually supplanted. In the original state, no longer held as the normal, the lower powers were subordinate to reason, and reason subject to God (Thomas Aquinas). This "original righteousness" was a "superadded gift," not to be reckoned with human nature. The fall deprived man of the supernatural gift; still his reason and freedom remained. Original sin, according to Thomas, is formally a "defect of original righteousness"; materially it is "concupiscence." The last is not a natural factor, for "it exceeds the limits of reason"; it is "contrary to nature," an "injury to nature." Original sin is thus a corruption of human nature (*habitus corruptus*). Duns Scotus contests the sinful character of *concupiscentia*, and reduces original sin to the absence of a long-lost good.

The Reformation reasserted the religious character of sin, as a power fatal to the higher life. Art. 2 of the Augsburg Confession represents sin as the deficiency of the fear of God and trust in him, and concupiscence is subordinated as the consequence of this abnormity. Melanchthon follows Luther in regarding unbelief as the essential element in sin. Original sin is not a mere passive heritage but the active power of a life contrary to God, and dominates the personal will. Adam is not only the remote ancestor but the type of every one; and the race participates in his sin. In the ideal picture of the original state "original righteousness" is not a "superadded gift," but the natural perfection of man. The fall resulted in the corruption of human nature, which is propagated in the race. Only Zwingli broke radically with the Augustinian doctrine. Without denying that Adam brought universal corruption upon humanity he would admit guilt only where the inclination to evil is appropriated by an act of will. Outside of this it is an infirmity or disease. The Formula of Concord (q.v.) maintained the total corruption of human nature, and the spiritual death of the natural man. Human cooperation in salvation, or synergism, is wholly excluded. On the other hand, the somewhat Manichean Flacian expressions of a substantial reality of original sin is excluded and the idea of the capability of *justitia civilis* belonging to universal reason, taught by Melanchthon, is acknowledged. The older Protestant dogmatics elaborated these views into a system, taking in all the reconcilable materials of tradition. As an illuminated background of the doctrine of sin is drawn a broad representation of the excellence of the original state, which was of the highest religious, moral, and natural perfection. The fall was a plunge to fearful depths, to be explained only by Satanic deception. The result was pride, ambition, and inordinate desire. The sinful act subjects man to divine disfavor. He becomes guilty and worthy of punishment. The penalty is death, i.e., physical death and spiritual death or deprivation of the original perfection, which is damnation. Original sin is fundamentally threefold; inherited sinfulness, inherited guilt, and inherited desert of punishment. The descent of sin and its consequences from Adam upon his progeny takes place naturally by propagation as well as legally by imputation. To escape the harshness of the latter there was brought forward the *imputatio mediata*, according to which the descendants' own sin was to subject them to this judgment of guilt and punishment. This device, however, led to no clear results. Adam is moral as well as natural head of the race, and his sin is justly imputed to all (Quenstedt). His sin becomes that of his descendants by propagation and the inherent original sin justifies the divine imputation. This parallelism continued only so long as the distinction between the inherited condition and the personal act was not drawn. Where sinfulness did not arrive at action, as in deceased unbaptized infants, the inconsistency became apparent. As manifest in the race, original sin is represented as blindness of reason, of a will devoted to evil, and as a riotous life of impulse. This "corrupt state" is the fruitful soil of actual sins. Previous to their commission the judgment of God by virtue of imputation overhangs humanity. As second nature this state is propagated, forming the substratum of the development of the natural life, never wholly disappearing.

5. Doctrine of the Reformation.

Baptism removes the "formal guilt" or original sin, but not the desire to evil or *concupiscentia*. This disposition is not lost until the departure of the soul from the body. In degree it is total moral inability, at least in the spiritual sense.

The insuperable difficulties of this view consist in the speculative elements which are to be complemented by the empirical conception. The doctrine of the original estate makes the origin of sin inconceivable and is an inadequate support for its determination; for according to it the fall appears as a transformation prepared by nothing, which threatens the continuity of person and the possibility of imputation. The relation of Adam to his descendants is now of an individual to others, and again of a genus to its members. Sin, guilt, and punishment are inextricably confused. Most defiant is the inconsistency of individual responsibility with the summary fate of the race, including those who know nothing of Adam. Safer ground is offered by psychological and religious-ethical determinations, except for a closer distinction of the ethical and religious. A special defect is the oversight of sin as a social power. In considering the relation of Adam and the individual that of man and his fellow beings is overlooked. Only a powerful ecclesiastical authority could keep religious reflection in those grooves. The doctrine of original sin became one of the first objects of prey for the Enlightenment (q.v.), after the example of the Arminians. Kant astonished the rationalists by discussing a "radical evil" in human nature, a fundamental inclination to evil, rooted in will, preceding all empirical acts, involving guilt, and ineradicable by human power. True, this was not original sin, as Kant rejected historical origin and physical inheritance and insisted that evil was inexplicable. With Schleiermacher sin is the afflicting sense of impotence in the consciousness of God. It transcends the personal life, being in each the work of all and in all the work of each. It consists in the total incapability of good. Judged by the highest type of humanity realized in Christ, it is a disturbance of nature; in view of salvation to come and the consciousness of God involved it may be taken as ordered by God himself. The defect of this theory is the neglect of the ethical standard, and of sin as a transgression of will, in behalf of a metaphysical bias, threatening to make of sin only a certain necessary moment of development. This idea is distinctly represented by Hegel. Sin is the inevitable transition-point of the finite spirit that emerges from the conditioned state of nature to freedom. Richard Rothe designates the object of human life as an integral part of a speculative plot of a world drama. Matter is the basis of the earthly sphere; it is created by God, yet his opposite. Man continues God's creation, by overcoming with progressive spiritualization the material inanity present in himself as sensuousness. Sin is that motive of life which antagonizes the normal development by reverting to matter or nonentity. Yet not the determination of man by selfish and sensuous impulses constitutes actual sin but positive assent contrary to the moral law; not the natural egoism but egoism assumed as a principle. As contradiction of the divine cosmic order sin obtains religious significance also in the degrees of alienation from God and inimical opposition to him. The almost antipodal results are reached by Julius Müller. Sin originates not from natural conditions but from the self-determination of the creature. Its principle is selfishness, a primary life tendency based on freedom using sense as a medium of expression. It takes its departure from a primitive extra-temporal decision involving the character of freedom, of which the fall is the first revelation. The theory aims to preserve the universality of sin without abridgment of its guilty character, but only succeeds in basing personal responsibility on an artificially conceived presumption and in diverting the attention from the racial unity and its importance for the life of sin. A. Ritschl lays stress upon the social effect of sin, bringing into evidence a long-neglected Biblical element. The kingdom of God has its antithesis in a kingdom of sin, in which every sinful individual is actively and passively involved, receiving and imparting influences of evil. He properly refers for support to the New-Testament doctrine of the stumbling-block (*skandalon*).

6. Post-Reformation Views.

The assumption of a primitive state of perfection as well as of a fall permanently affecting the destiny of mankind has been irremediably shattered for dogmatics by historical and ethical criticism. The account of Genesis is to be understood as didactic narrative to be employed as illuminated by other Biblical statements. The original state is the condition of untested innocence, and Adam is the type of the race according to its created disposition and its empirical demeanor. His act is the type of the human racial sin, which in the successive generations and social intercourse continues progressively so far as it is not counteracted by moral forces. Universality of sin is the presupposition for the need of universal redemption and the universal validity of the work of Christ. A truth is thus stated accessible to every maturer experience and attested at all times by witnesses unbiased by dogma. It may be termed original sin; for, although an ethical quality of will, and as obstinacy to God to be conceived of only in personal life, yet in the testimony of experience it becomes organic disorder. As such it can be propagated. With the doctrine of the heredity of acquired characteristics modern thought is more apt to overestimate than depreciate heredity and thus neglect the guilty character of sin. The idea of guilt attaches to the conduct of the individual person and its presupposed freedom. The history of the doctrine shows that the Christian judgment always adhered to two points: the recognition of the comprehensive racial reality of sin, and the personal contingency of guilt. As to the latter, the Augustinian doctrine could never satisfy the ethical consideration. Hence a sharper distinction between sin and personal guilt is to be followed. Sin is all action against the norm of the divine will, irrespective whether this contradiction to God's will is known or willed by the individual or not. Guilt is only the conscious resistance to this norm within the limits and powers of per-

7. Criticism of the Doctrine.

sonal life. Thus the New Testament attests that the individual is not accountable for the sin of the race as such, but only for his conscious participation of the same (Luke xii. 37; Matt. xxv. 42), and forgiveness is not of original sin, but individual sins (Matt. vi. 12, ix. 2). Guilt is always individual. It may be said that the greater the spiritual maturity of a man the more his sin has become his guilt, and the further his influence extends the more the sin of the community establishes his personal guilt. Likewise the traditional view of eternal damnation as the universal punishment of sin is not to be maintained. That the sin of man, awakened by divine revelation to his life mission, is at the same time guilt that estranges from God and must be removed by forgiveness is the irrelinquishable conviction of every Christian. It does not follow, however, that the punishment must be absolute and alike for all sins. Eternal damnation as a general punishment of original sin is inadequate to God's offended righteousness. The New Testament suggests an individualizing on the part of God's righteousness (Matt. xi. 24; Rom. ii. 2 sqq.). The Christian faith maintains, (1) without forgiveness of sins, no salvation; (2) every one that persists in unbelief will receive just punishment in proportion to his guilt known only to God. Religiously sin is unbelief, and as such simply godlessness, admitting of no degrees; ethically, it is a deviation from the moral standard, varying in extent, principle, and persistence. God judges according to the impartial standard of just ethical estimation. Only his pardon follows the higher norm of grace not conceivable on the principle of adequate requital, but immanent in him in the total idea of the moral world order.

8. Theory of Sin.

The problem of the origin of sin offers no difficulties exclusively in the light of punishable sin. The basis of this is in the conscious practise of freedom on the part of the personal creature. More difficult is the inquiry how formal human freedom acquired a content contradicting the divine will. Reference to the total life and original sin only defers the problem. That God willed sin or imposed it on man through his nature or law of development is repulsive to Christian judgment, and would be inconsistent with the divine judgment of sin. Neither is the evil will creative, but limited to the choice of alternative conduct. Neither could an extra-human power contrary to God possess a creative power beside him to originate evil. Attempts at solution in this direction have resulted in holding evil to be the mere negation of the good, which is unsatisfactory to the Christian conscience. The only solution remains that the content of the evil will comes from God; but so far as this is true such content is not yet evil, but mere imperfection. This involves not only the sensuous character of the beginning of human life, but also the naive egoism which obligates man to self-preservation. Both advance to the valuation of spiritual and common good in the course of ethical development. With this, imperfection is transmuted into sin. God intends this imperfection to be removed by man's own moral self-determination; man wants to retain it against the known requirement of God. Imperfection becomes sin when approved and asserted by the alienated will as the state adapted to the subject. A derivation of sin does not contemplate at the same time establishing the basis of its religious and moral judgment. The latter approves itself by the revealed will of God; the former may be attempted only on the basis of coherent reflection upon the facts of experience. If the preceding explanation should lead to an apology for sin, it were better to abandon all attempt and assert the inconceivability of sin. Paul assumes this deduction of sin; the Church in its teaching abandoned his view by exaggerating the original state. If the first state was one of innocency and imperfection, then the latter became sin as soon as the human will refused the divine law of life that prescribed conquest. That it refused is an act of free will not further explainable, yet always to be determined as avoidable.

9. The Court of Conscience; Forgiveness.

Christian faith can neither admit that God causes sin as such, nor can it escape the conviction that he is eternally aware of it and subjects it to his world-dominion. How an act in time may be subject of eternal cognizance is inconceivable to finite mind. The fact itself is attested by the revelation of salvation through the death of Jesus Christ on account of sin. How God permits room for sin in the world is to be seen in fact. The judgment of sin is concomitant with its unfolding in that its promised success proves itself as deception and its expected freedom as servitude. Servitude is punishment for the sinful deed. The bondage of the will, however, consists less in a confinement of the field of its activity than in the contraction of its horizon of vision and in the determinism of its motives, both of which are characteristic of the natural man. Many other evils are attendant penalties of sin which manifest their contradiction to the divine order and may only be referred to the personal conscience for experience and proof. The same holds true of Death (q.v.). A revealing and intensifying judgment of sin takes place in conscience, which reckons it as guilt to the sinner; this happens to a certain extent in consequence of the moral law, and more extensively in consequence of the moral message of divinely sent prophets (Rom. v. 20). That God consents to the unfolding of sin and sustains humanity in spite of it receives full explanation in the manifestation of his holy love for human redemption. This is a progressive abolition of sin proceeding from within outward. Beginning with the forgiveness of the debt, it continues with a renewal of the will, and culminates in the removal of evil. Such a redemption must have a historical act of God as its starting-point, attesting the divine disapproval of sin as well as love for the sinner. The Gospel of such an act is essentially one of forgiveness. In the Vedas and the Babylonian prayers this appears rather as the removal of the penal consequences than the restoration of the personal fellowship with God, as in the New Testament (Matt. ix. 5–6; Rom. v. 2). In the forgiveness of sin, the interference of this with the central relation of life to God is annulled, hence within the conception of sin there is no wider contrast than that of unforgiven and forgiven sins. The former abolishes life in the highest sense; the latter gives it anew. This contrast has been employed for the classification of sin as pardonable and unpardonable; such as sins of oversight and rebellion in the Old Testament, and venial and mortal in the Roman Catholic Church. [The Roman Catholic distinction between mortal (or deadly) sin and venial sin is that the former deprives the sinner of habitual grace and of spiritual life, while venial sin does not. The names of the seven deadly sins will effectually illustrate their character: pride, covetousness, lust, anger, envy, gluttony, and sloth; and it is readily apparent that these sins, deliberately persisted in, will drive from the soul all state of grace. But if such deliberation is lacking, or if the sin be committed through an ignorance which the sinner has no means of avoiding, or if, again, the matter of the sin be of a less grave nature, then the sin committed is venial, i.e., "the all-just and all-holy God does not see in it such depravity as deserves to be punished by eternal torment" (Hunter, *Outlines of Dogmatic Theology*, 3d ed., iii. 40, New York, n.d.). It is, however, not always possible for man to know whether a given unlawful act is really sin, or whether, if sin, it is mortal or venial; this can certainly be known only by God; all that man can do is to have a more or less confident judgment in the matter. Venial sin does not cause even partial loss of habitual grace, since, if that were so, venial sin multiplied would amount to mortal sin, which is a contradiction. At the same time, venial sin hinders the operation of actual grace (i.e., grace which is the result of distinct divine acts). By the Decrees of the Council of Trent (Sess. xiv., cap. 5) it is obligatory to confess all mortal sins; it is not absolutely required to confess venial sins, although it is undoubtedly best to do so.] But the correctness of these distinctions is questionable. Both betray a confusion of legalistic and religious-ethical standards. Also the opinion of A. Ritschl that pardonable sins are sins of ignorance raises doubts. In accordance with the New Testament pardon is to be attributed purely to God's unlimited grace, Christ's atoning work, and man's contrite faith, and not conditioned by the minor importance of a certain category of sins. The unpardonable sin (Matt. xii. 31–32) is one that, as obstinate rejection and contemptuous debasement of the recognized truth, bars the return to repentance and faith. As pardon effects access to God, it translates into the kingdom where the divine will is supreme. This involves the renewed transformation of the whole life tendency, described by Paul as the becoming of a "new creature" (II Cor. v. 17) and by church doctrine as Regeneration (q.v.) or, with special emphasis on moral change, as Sanctification (q.v.). In the former sin does not disappear instantaneously and permanently (Rom. vi. 12 sqq.; Phil. iii. 12; I John i. 8, ii. 2); yet it is in a vanishing process and no longer capable of striking fresh root, the obverse side of which is cleaving to God through Christ, the unremittent battle against the remains of sin, and the practise of perfection. Like the individual, the Church may assume a purifying process against the common evil resident in itself, and the more its energies are rallied to its great ideals of the new life the further is its purification enhanced. (O. Kirn.)

Bibliography: For expositions of the Scriptural doctrine of sin the reader is referred first of all to the works cited in and under Biblical Theology, particularly those by Schultz, Beyschlag, Oehler, Duhm, Smend, Schlottmann, Noack, Duff, Piepenbring, Dillmann, Holtzmann, Stevens, Gould, Estes, and Bovon. Consult further: J. Taylor, *The Scripture Doctrine of Original Sin*, London, 1738, 4th ed., Newcastle, 1845; L. Ernesti, *Vom Ursprung der Sünde nach paulinischem Lehrgehalt*, Göttingen, 1855–62; G. M. Straffen, *Sin as set forth in Holy Scripture*, London, 1875; E. Ménégoz, *Le Péché et la redemption d'après St. Paul*, Paris, 1882; L. Lemme, *Die Sünde wider den heiligen Geist*, Breslau, 1883; J. S. Candlish, *The Biblical Doctrine of Sin*, Edinburgh, 1893; J. Köberle, *Sünde und Gnade im religiösen Leben des Volks Israel*, Munich, 1905; W. Staerk, *Sünde und Gnade nach der Vorstellung des älteren Judentums*, Tübingen, 1905; F. Bennewitz, *Die Sünde im alten Israel*, Leipsic, 1907 (1906); *DB*, iv. 528–536; *DCG*, ii. 630–635.

As a subject in systematic divinity sin is treated by all the great dogmaticians, and discussions are to be looked for in the works named in and under Dogma, Dogmatics. Special works which may be cited from the large literature on the topic are: A. Burgess, *A Treatise of Original Sin*, London, 1658; G. Tomline, *Refutation of Calvinism; in which the Doctrines of Original Sin, Grace . . . are explained*, London, 1811; G. Payne, *The Doctrine of Original Sin; or, native State and Character of Man unfolded*, London, 1845; M. P. Squier, *The Problem Solved; or, Sin not of God*, New York, 1855; E. Girard, *Lehre von der Sünde*, Strasburg, 1861; J. Müller, *Die christliche Lehre von der Sünde*, 2 vols., 5th ed., Breslau, 1867, Eng. transl., *The Christian Doctrine of Sin*, 2 vols., Edinburgh, 1868; E. Naville, *Le Problème du mal*, Paris, 1868, Eng. transl., *The Problem of Evil*, Edinburgh, 1871; J. B. Brown, *The Divine Mysteries: the divine Treatment of Sin, and the divine Mystery of Peace*, London and New York, 1869; W. G. T. Shedd, *Theological Essays*, pp. 211–264, New York, 1877; J. Tulloch, *The Christian Doctrine of Sin*, Edinburgh, 1877; G. Heinrici, *Die Sünde nach Wesen und Ursprung*, Frankfort, 1878; G. P. Fisher, *Discussions in History and Theology*, New York, 1880; A. Ritschl, *Rechtfertigung und Versöhnung*, vol. iii., 40–43, 2d ed., Bonn, 1882–83; R. W. Landis, *Doctrine of Original Sin as Received and Taught by the Churches of the Reformation*, Richmond, 1885; M. Dix, *The Seven Deadly Sins*, New York, 1888; S. Kierkegaard, *Zur Psychologie der Sünde*, Leipsic, 1890; J. Martineau, *Seat of Authority in Religion*, pp. 450–461, London, 1890; D. Gracey, *Sin and the Unfolding of Salvation*, London, 1894; R. Harris, *Is Sin a Necessity*, London, 1896; R. C. Horner, *Original and Inbred Sin*, Ottawa, 1896; C. Clemen, *Die christliche Lehre von der Sünde*, Göttingen, 1897; J. Royce, *Studies of Good and Evil*, New York, 1898; E. W. Cook, *The Origin of Sin and its Relations to God*, ib., 1899; F. R. Tennant, *Origin and Propagation of Sin*, London, 1902, 2d ed., 1906; idem, *The Sources of the Doctrine of the Fall and Original Sin*, ib. 1903; J. Turmel, *Hist. du dogme du péché originel*, Macon, 1904; J. N. Espenberger, *Die Elemente der Erbsünde nach Augustin*, Mainz, 1905; N. R. Wood, *The Witness of Sin*, New York, 1905; H. V. S. Eck, *Sin*, New York, 1907; N. W. Stroup, *The Fact of Sin Viewed Historically and Doctrinally*, Cincinnati, 1908; H. Windisch, *Taufe und Sünde im ältesten Christentum bis auf Origines. Ein Beitrag zur altchristlichen Dogmengeschichte*, Tübingen, 1908; M. L. Burton, *The Problem of Evil: a Criticism of the Augustinian Point of View*, Chicago, 1909; J. H. Busch, *Das Wesen der Erbsünde nach Bellarmin und Suarez. Eine dogmengeschichtliche Studie*, Paderborn, 1909; W. D. Hyde, *Sin and its Forgiveness*, Boston, 1909; W. E. Orchard, *Modern Theories of Sin*, London, 1909; F. J. Hall, *Evolution and the Fall*, New York, 1910; Vigouroux, *Dictionnaire*, fasc. xxxi. 7–16.

SIN: The name of a place in Egypt named in Ezek. xxx. 14–16. Trouble has been caused for exegetes and investigators by what is clearly a wrong arrangement of the verses; a correct division shows four pairs of names, thus: Pathros and Zoan; No and Sin; No and Sin; No and Noph. Of these pairs the first always belongs to Upper Egypt, the second to Lower Egypt. According, therefore, to the accepted Hebrew text, which is to be preferred, the correct view is, that Sin is a place in Lower Egypt. Ebers' surmise that it was in Upper Egypt because it appears to derive from the ancient *Sun*, which resembles the Greek *Syene*, overlooks the fact that this place existed in Hebrew times, and is mentioned by Ezekiel as Seveneh (xxx. 6). The Zoan that bears a relation to Sin in Ezek. xxx. 14–16, was probably known to the Hebrews under the name of Rameses (Gen. xlvii. 11). The Sin of Ezekiel is thought of as one of the most important places in Lower Egypt, being twice paralleled with Thebes (No); it could not therefore have been an unimportant place in the east of Lower Egypt (contrary to W. M. Müller, *EB*, iv. 4629). As "the fortress of Egypt," however, it protected during the course of history the town of Pelusium, which lay on the east arm of the Nile. To the east of this town a high boundary wall was erected (Diodorus Siculus, i. 57) and the town itself was surrounded by a wall twenty stadia long. The armies of invasion from the East could not ignore this arsenal and key to Egypt. As in strategic importance, so also in general significance Sin and Pelusium may be identical, as when Strabo alludes to the marshy surroundings of the town as Pelusium. But what was Sin-Pelusium called by the ancient Egyptians? Brugsch, in the appendix to his *Dictionnaire géographique*, accepted the view of Dümichen, the noted Egyptologist, in his *Geschichte des alten Aegyptens* (pp. 74, 263, 1878), according to which the capital of the nineteenth province of Lower Egypt was Am, named after the two eyebrows of Osiris, which were preserved as sacred relics in the temple of the town. W. M. Müller calls it *Ame(t)*, "Prince of Lower Egypt" (*EB*, iv. 4628). In ancient Egyptian the word *am* (Coptic, *ome*) signifies morass. Whether the ancient Egyptians, who loved to play on words, placed a double meaning on the word "Am," the "town of the two eyebrows," is uncertain; there was a temptation to play on the word as the city was surrounded by marshes. At the present day, an ancient ruined castle, northwest of the ruins of ancient Pelusium, is called Tineh ("clay," or "mud"), an evidence that Sin was an appellation of Pelusium.

(E. König.)

According to the best recent conclusions in Egyptology Sin is either an unknown city or (more probably) is to be identified with the Seveneh of Ezek. xxix. 10, xxx. 6 (R. V.). J. F. M.

Bibliography: Consult the commentaries on Ezekiel by Smend, Leipsic, 1880; Orelli, Munich, 1896; Bertholet, Tübingen, 1897; Kraetzschmar, Göttingen, 1900; G. Jahn, Leipsic, 1905; C. H. Cornill, *Das Buch des Propheten Ezechiel*, ib. 1886; and the articles in the Bible dictionaries.

SIN, DESERT OF. See Wandering in the Desert.

SIN OFFERINGS. See Sacrifice.

SINAI, sai'nai or sai'na-ai: The mountain on which, according to the Pentateuch, Moses gave the greater part of the Law to the Israelites; identified for a millennium and a half with a peak of the range which forms the center of the peninsula of Sinai, between the two northern arms of the Red Sea. The range in question consists of Jabal al-Dair (6,472 ft.), Jabal Musa (7,363 ft.), and Jabal Katarin (8,536 ft.), but it is extremely difficult of access, being off all the main routes, and surrounded by barren wastes, especially to the north.

Topography of the Traditional Sinai.

The central group of these mountains is bounded by valleys on three sides, but continues without deep indentation on the south. Jabal al-Dair throws out a triangular spur toward the north and is bounded on the east by the Wadi al-Sadad, called Wadi al-Saba'iyah further south. On the northwest of Jabal al-Dair is the Wadi al-Shaikh, which turns northward; and on the southwest is the short Wadi al-Dair, the upper part of which is called Wadi Shu'aib ("Valley of Jethro"), and which debouches into the Wadi al-Shaikh. The other side of the Wadi al-Dair is enclosed by the declivities of the second lofty peak, the southeast summit of which is called Jabal Musa ("the Mountain of Moses"), and the northwest summit Ras al-Ẓafẓaf ("Mountain of the Willow"; 6,540 ft.), the northwest slopes of the latter running parallel with those of Jabal al-Dair to the Wadi al-Shaikh, which continues to the southwest to the steep Wadi al-Laja, which soon turns to the southeast and leads to the abandoned Dair al-Arba'in ("Monastery of the Forty [martyrs slain by the Mohammedans]"). South of Jabal Musa and the monastery rises Jabal Katarin, the highest peak of the whole group, the foothills of which connect with Jabal Musa. On the northeast slope of the latter mountain is the Monastery of St. Catharine, behind the apse of the church of which is the Chapel of the Burning Bush, which is honored by the removal of the shoes of all who enter (cf. Ex. iii. 5). The summit of Jabal Musa may be reached in an hour and a half from the Monastery of St. Catherine. On the way a little spring is passed where Moses is said to have tended Jethro's flock (Ex. ii. 15 sqq.); at a height of 6,900 feet is the small chapel of Elijah (cf. I Kings xix. 11 sqq.); and on the summit are another chapel and a small mosque, beside which are the ruins of a church. [Beneath this mosque is a grotto, supposed to be that in which Moses stood when Yahweh passed by (Ex. xxxiii. 22).] The other summit is hard to climb. It takes its name, Ras al-Ẓafẓaf, from a willow (Arab. *ẓafẓaf*) from the wood of which Moses is supposed to have cut his miraculous rod (Ex. iv. 2). On the road which passes through the Wadi al-Dair into the Wadi al-Laja and past the Dair al-Arba'in, is the Ḥajar Musa ("Rock of Moses"), a block of reddish-brown granite about eleven feet nine inches high, identified with that from which Moses brought the water (Num. xx. 8 sqq.), and this water is said to have returned here after having accompanied the Children of Israel in their wanderings (cf. I Cor. x. 4). Near the junction of the Wadi al-Laja, Wadi al-Dair, and Wadi al-Shaikh is the traditional spot where the earth swallowed up Korah and his followers (Num. xvi.), while a small hole in the rock is shown as the mold of the golden calf (Ex. xxxii.). The plain of Wadi al-Raḥa, northwest of the junction of the three wadis just mentioned, is held by many to be the camping-place of the Children of Israel (Ex. xix. 2, 17).

According to tradition, Jabal Musa is the mountain where Yahweh first revealed himself to Moses (Ex. iii.), where he descended with fire and cloud and gave the Decalogue (Ex. xix., xx.; Deut. v.), and where Moses abode forty days and forty nights (Ex. xxiv. 18; Deut. ix. 9). If the arid Wadi al-Raḥa be taken as the camping-place of the Israelites, Ras al-Ẓafẓaf would be Sinai, since the peaks of Jabal Musa are invisible from Wadi al-Raḥa (cf. Ex. xix. 17, xxiv. 17). Since, however, the craggy and perilous summit of Ras al-Ẓafẓaf would be ill-adapted for the sojourn of Moses with Yahweh, it was assumed that Jabal Musa was Sinai. This theory led to the supposition that the place of assembly of Ex. xix. 17 was the Wadi al-Saba'iyah, which bounds Jabal Musa on the east; but this stony, arid, and narrow valley does not fit the topography required by the Bible. Sinai has also been identified with Jabal Sarbal (6,730 ft.), south of the Wadi Firan. This portion of the peninsula was evidently once densely populated; the city of Pharan is mentioned by Ptolemy (V., xvii. 3); and it was the seat of a bishop in the fourth century and of an archbishop in the fifth century, until, in the time of Justinian, the orthodox monks removed from Jabal Sarbal to Jabal Musa. This identification is, however, rendered impossible by the statement of the "Pilgrimage" of Silvia of Aquitaine that Faran was thirty-five (Roman) miles from the "mount of God," a distance which agrees with that between the oasis of Firan and the Sinaitic monastery, but is several times too large for that between the oasis and Jabal Sarbal. It would appear, therefore, that in the days of Silvia (about 385) Sinai was identified with Jabal Musa, and it is equally obvious that Ras al-Ẓafẓaf was held to represent Horeb.

Attempted Identifications in the Sinaitic Peninsula.

The Old Testament gives two different names to the "mount of God," Sinai and Horeb; and, while it was formerly held that Horeb was the general name of the region, and that Sinai was the name of the specific mountain, it is now maintained that Horeb is peculiar to E and D, and Sinai to J and P. Two possibilities thus arise, either that, like Hermon (q.v.), the same mountain had two names, or that the sources really designate two different places. The location of Horeb seems to be best indicated by Deuteronomy, which indicates (i. 2) that the mountain was west of Kadesh-barnea, and also states (i. 6–7, 19–20) that the Israelites went from Horeb to Kadesh-barnea "through all that great and terrible wilderness, which ye saw by the way of the mountain of the Amorites." In Ex. iv. 27, Aaron goes from Egypt into the wilderness to meet Moses, whom he finds at "the mount of God," or Horeb (cf. Ex. iii. 1), which would thus again seem to be located on the road running from Egypt eastward to Kadesh-barnea. J gives the name Sinai to the mountain on which Yahweh spoke with Moses (Ex. xix. 11, 18, 20, 23, xxxiv. 4), while P (Num. x. 12) locates the wilderness of Paran (q.v.) near the wilderness of Sinai, which obviously derived its name from Mount Sinai and is often mentioned (Ex. xix. 1; Num. i. 1, 19, iii. 4, etc.). This would apparently locate Sinai not far from Kadesh-barnea, in the desert lying north of the peninsula proper. The Song of Deborah (Judges v. 4–5) states that Yahweh rose up from Sinai to help the Israelites against the Canaanites, and that he came from Seir and the "field of Edom." Since, however, Sinai can not be sought in Edom, Seir and the "field of Edom" must designate the southern boundary of Canaan or of the mountain districts of the Amorites. This is borne out by Deut. xxxiii. 2–3, where Sinai is paralleled by Seir and Paran, while the goal was Kadesh-barnea (reading *Ḳadhesh* for *ḳodhesh*), these places all pointing to the southern boundary of Canaan toward Edom. These passages, therefore, like Hab. iii. 3, locate Sinai in the southern (or rather southeastern) vicinity of Kadesh-barnea; but while this may easily be reconciled with P, J and, still more clearly, E and D refer to the western neighborhood of Kadesh-barnea. If the Sinai of J be identified with the Sinai of Judges v. 4–5, and if the "three days' journey into the wilderness" of Ex. iii. 18, v. 3, viii. 27, be taken as having Sinai as the goal, the real distance must have been much minimized (cf. the daily marches recorded in Num. xxi. 12–20); but if these days' journeys be taken strictly, the statements of J, E, and D practically coincide and indicate that Sinai and Horeb were two names of the same mountain, or at least designated two mountains close together. Judges iv. 4–5 indubitably locates Sinai further east than is implied by any combination of the statements of the Pentateuch. The Old Testament thus gives divergent data regarding the location of the mountain on which the Law was given; but while it would seem that Judges v. 4–5 best represents actual tradition, the region is still too imperfectly explored to permit of identification of Sinai. The attempt has also been made to identify Sinai with Jabal Barghir, or Jabal al-Nur, four or five hours northeast of 'Aḳaba; and others, on account of the association of Moses with Midian (Ex. ii. 15, 22, iii. 1), have located Sinai in Midian (q.v.), southeast of Edom. This theory is, however, irreconcilable with Judges v. 4–5. The hypothesis has likewise been advanced that the theophany recorded in Ex. 16, 18; Deut. iv. 11, ix. 15 indicates that Sinai was regarded as a volcano, so that it has been supposed to be represented by one of the extinct craters of northwestern Arabia, southeast of Midian, in the region between Tabuk and Mecca. While some of the volcanoes in the Hauran, east of Damascus, may have been active within historic times, there is no certain evidence that the Israelites were acquainted with them, nor do the data of the Old Testament necessitate such a hypothesis. (H. GUTHE.)

Critical View.

BIBLIOGRAPHY: C. W. Wilson and H. S. Palmer, *Ordnance Survey of the Peninsula of Sinai*, 5 vols., Southampton, 1869–72; C. R. Lepsius, *Reise von Theben nach der Halbinsel Sinai*, Berlin, 1846, Eng. transl., *A Tour from Thebes to the Peninsula of Sinai*, London, 1846; idem, *Briefe aus Aegypten, Aethiopien, und der Halbinsel des Sinai*, Berlin, 1852, Eng. transl., *Letters from Egypt, Ethiopia, and the Peninsula of Sinai*, London, 1853; J.

Hamilton, *Sinai, the Hedjas, and Soudan*, London, 1857; W. H. Bartlett, *Forty Days in the Desert on the Track of the Israelites*, London, new ed., 1867; E. H. Palmer, *The Desert of the Exodus*, 2 vols., London, 1871; C. Beke, *Discoveries of Sinai in Arabia, and of Midian*, London, 1878; S. C. Bartlett, *From Egypt to Palestine through Sinai, the Wilderness, and the South Country*, New York, 1879; R. F. Burton, *The Land of Midian Revisited*, i. 144 sqq., 235–236, London, 1879; G. Ebers, *Durch Gosen zum Sinai*, Leipsic, 1881; A. P. Stanley, *Sinai and Palestine in Connection with their History*, new ed., New York, 1883; G. Ebers and H. Guthe, *Palästina in Bild und Wort*, ii. 255 sqq., Stuttgart, 1884; E. Hull, *Mount Seir, Sinai, and Western Palestine*, London, 1885; H. S. Palmer, *Sinai, from the Fourth Egyptian Dynasty*, London, 1892; R. L. Bensly, *Our Journey to Sinai*, London, 1896; A. Freiherr von Gall, *Altisraelitische Kultstätten*, pp. 1 sqq., Giessen, 1898; W. H. Hume, *Rift Valleys and Geology of Eastern Sinai*, London, 1901; E. Meyer, in *SBA*, xxxi (1905), 640 sqq.; idem, *Die Israeliten und ihre Nachbarstämme*, pp. 67 sqq., Halle, 1906; W. M. F. Petrie, *Researches in Sinai*, New York, 1906; E. Hornby, *Sinai and Petra*, London, 1907; Robinson, *Researches*, i. 90 sqq., 119 sqq., 140, 158, 176–177; *DB*, iv. 536–538; *EB*, iv. 4629–43; *JE*, xi. 381–383.

SINAITA. See JOHANNES CLIMACUS.

SINCLAIR, WILLIAM MACDONALD: Church of England; b. at Leeds June 3, 1850. He was educated at Balliol College, Oxford (B.A., 1873), and after being ordained to the priesthood in 1874 was successively curate of Tortworth, Gloucestershire (1874–75), assistant minister of Quebec Chapel, London, and evening lecturer in logic at King's College, London (1875–76), and vicar of St. Stephen's, Westminster (1880–89), besides being chaplain to the bishop of London (1877–83), assistant examining chaplain to Bishop Jackson of London (1883–85), examining chaplain to Bishop Temple of London (1885–97) and Bishop Creighton of the same diocese (1897–1901), honorary chaplain to the queen (1889–95) and chaplain in ordinary (1895–1901), honorary chaplain to King Edward after 1901, grand chaplain of England after 1894, and chaplain to the order of St. John of Jerusalem after 1900. Since 1889 he has been archdeacon of London and canon of St. Paul's, and has written, in addition to several volumes of sermons, *The Psalms, the Authorised Version in the Original Rhythm* (London, 1879); *Commentary on the Epistles of St. John* (1880); *Lessons on the Gospel of St. John* (1886); *The Christian's Influence* (1892); *Christ and our Times* (1893); *Words to the Laity on Subjects of Ecclesiastical Controversy* (1895); *Leaders of Thought in the English Church* (1896); *Points at Issue between the Church of England and the Church of Rome* (1896); *The Churches of the East* (1898); and *Memorials of St. Paul's Cathedral* (1909).

SINECURE (*sine cura*): A prebend whose enjoyment is not bound by services rendered, and is therefore to be distinguished from simple "Benefice" (q.v.), to which certain duties are attached, and from "cure," or the charge of souls. But where the incumbent of a benefice has authorization to sojourn at a distance from his place of office and to have his office discharged by a vicar, his benefice becomes a sinecure. While sinecures occur but seldom in the Roman Catholic Church, they still frequently appear in the Evangelical Church (of Germany). This is explained by the fact that, although in consequence of the Reformation foundations and cloisters were usually abolished and their properties applied in behalf of churches and schools or incorporated in the exchequer of the State, yet certain cloistral and endowed positions were perpetuated, and the Protestant endowment and cloistral prebends became sinecures which ceased to have any real ecclesiastical affinity.

But far more numerous than in Germany are the court, state, and church positions that are sinecures in England [these being often used as means for the advancement of learning by being given to scholars engaged in special tasks or investigations].

(E. SEHLING.)

SINGER, ISIDORE: Austro-American Jewish editor; b. at Weisskirchen (160 m. s.e. of Prague), Moravia, Nov. 10, 1859. He was educated at the universities of Vienna and Berlin (Ph.D., Vienna, 1884), and after founding, editing, and publishing the *Allgemeine österreichische Literaturzeitung* (Vienna) from 1884 to 1887, accepted the post of secretary and librarian to Count Alexandre Foucher de Careil, late French ambassador at Vienna. Going to Paris with the count, he became a member of the staff of the press bureau of the French Foreign Office. In 1894–95, after residing for a time at Rome, he founded and edited at Paris *La Vraie Parole* to counteract Edouard Drumont's anti-Semitic *La Libre Parole*. In 1895 he left Paris for the United States to publish *The Encyclopedia of the History and Mental Evolution of the Jewish Race*, which became *The Jewish Encyclopedia* (12 vols., New York, 1901–05), of which he was managing editor. He has written *Berlin, Wien und der Antisemitismus* (Vienna, 1882); *Presse und Judentum* (1882); *Sollen die Juden Christen werden?* (1884); *Briefe berühmter christlicher Zeitgenossen über die Judenfrage* (1885); *Auf dem Grabe meiner Mutter* (Prague, 1888); *Le Prestige de la France en Europe* (Paris, 1889); *La Question juive* (1893); *Anarchie et antisémitisme* (1894); *Der Juden Kampf ums Recht* (New York, 1902); and *Russia at the Bar of the American People* (1904).

SINGLENESS OF HEART: Perhaps the most adequate rendering of the Greek *haplotēs*, a word which occurs seven times in the New Testament and is variously translated in the English versions (Rom. xii. 8; II Cor. viii. 2, ix. 11, 13, xi. 3; Eph. vi. 5; and Col. iii. 22). The adjective *haplous* occurs Matt. vi. 22 and Luke xi. 34, and the adverb *haplōs* James i. 5.

As a Biblical-theological conception, *haplotēs* denotes a mood or condition of the religious-ethical life which in natural life is near the idea expressed by *naïveté*, but is, however, a matter of moral self-determination (Matt. xviii. 3). The New-Testament conception approaches very closely the classical use, but its use in the New Testament is to be explained from the fact that it served in Jewish Greek (Septuagint) as the translation of the Hebrew *yosher* and *tom*. The conception finds its real explanation in the fundamental view of the Evangelical announcement that the kingdom of God is the only highest good in such a way that all double-heartedness is excluded (Matt. vi. 33, 24, viii. 22,

x. 37–39; Luke xi. 23; etc.). Thus singleness of heart stands in contrast with a condition of heart in which different tendencies exist side by side, the religious-ethical disposition being interwoven with tendencies of the natural ego and thus obscured in its purity and deprived of its value which lies in its oneness and singularity (Matt. xxii. 37; II Cor. vi. 14 sqq.). Excluding the intermingling of different currents or tendencies, which destroy the compact unity of Christian character, singleness of heart in the religious sense denotes the entire uprightness, straightforwardness, and determination of the heart which in undivided receptivity accepts the grace of God as he offers it (Ps. cxix., cxxx.). In the ethical sense, singleness of heart denotes purity, soundness, and soberness of disposition by means of which the ethical action is the spontaneous outgrowth of love from faith. Self-preservation in singleness of heart is a duty of the justified who will not fall back into the error of self-redemption.

In dogmatics the conception has found its place under the conception of sanctification because of the peculiar constitution of the religious-ethical consciousness, which must cling to the human cooperation with grace in order that the progress of the state of grace according to the essence of the Kingdom of God may take place in an ascending line.

(L. Lemme.)

SINIM: The name of a region or a people mentioned in Isa. xlix. 12. The prophet announces in the context that Yahweh is about to gather his still scattered people from the places of their imprisonment. He then closes with the statement: "Behold, these shall come from far: and, lo, these from the north and from the west [Hebr. *miyyam*, "from the sea"]; and these from the land of Sinim." Divergent views exist as to the interpretation of the thrice-occurring "these." On first sight the meaning seems to be "these . . . , others . . . , and still others . . . ," i.e., three categories seem to be embraced. In that case, Nägelsbach's suggestion that the first "these" is general and is distributed by the second and third "these" does not comport with the text. It is to be noted that before the first and second cases comes the Hebrew word *hinneh* (rendered in the A. V. "Behold . . . lo," in the R. V. more correctly "Lo . . . lo"). It can not be supposed that a third "lo" has fallen out and that consequently the general statement "from far" is explained by the designation of special localities in what follows. Duhm and Marti propose to strike out the clause "from the north" and to substitute the sentence "and those from the ends of the earth," making four categories. But the junction in the text of "from the north and from the west" makes of this clause a joint description of one class of exiles—i.e., those in the northwest, the land of Phenicia in its whole extent, Syria, Asia Minor, and the "isles" (Isa. xlix. 1), where since the sixth century prisoners had been sold (cf. Obad. 20). The prophet does not intend to name here four regions (for a case where four are mentioned cf. Isa. xliii. 5–6), but three, and to this threefold partition Greek and Aramaic translations, and so the best Jewish tradition, testify. Nor is Cheyne justified in making *miyyam* here mean as an exception "from the South" (*Prophecies of Isaiah*, ii. 16, London, 1884).

In defining the expression "from far," one must realize that the spiritual center for the dispersed Israelites as well as the center of reference of the author of Isa. xl. sqq. was Palestine (cf. Isa. xl. 9, xlix. 14, lii. 7). As compared with Assyria and Babylonia, the northwestern regions of Phenicia and Syria were relatively near. Since the transportation of captives from Israel and Judah were to the Tigris and Euphrates (II Kings xvii. 6, xxiv. 15; Tobit i. 10, 14), when one spoke of exiles the Hebrews in those regions came naturally to mind. The expression "from far" would naturally refer, therefore, to those regions. But the collocation of words in the text does not relate "from far" and "from the land of Sinim," which latter therefore did not lie in the most distant east or south. In locating Sinim one must remember the law of prophecy: prophets whose date can be surely fixed reveal a parallelism between prediction and history, and they name only such lands or peoples as are within the ken of those whom they address. Accordingly Sinim must refer to the inhabitants of Sin (q.v.), viz., the inhabitants of the region about Pelusium, of which Sin was the frontier fortress, the key, the entrance, and the emblem. To note the importance to the Hebrews of the region of which Sin was the beginning one need but remember Jer. xliii. 1 sqq. Moreover, it is to be remarked that expressions such as "the land of . . ." designate always a small district (Isa. ix. 1). With this interpretation agrees the construction of the Targum, Jerome, Rashi, David Kimchi, Ibn Ezra, Bochart, Ewald, and Bunsen. One may not correct the text and read *Sewenim* (with A. Klostermann in *Deuterojesaia*, Munich, 1893; T. K. Cheyne, *Introduction to Isaiah*, London, 1895; K. Marti, commentary on Isaiah, Tübingen, 1900, and others), since *Swnh* (Ezek. xxix. 10) and *Syn* (Sin) (Ezek. xxx. 15) are different places in Egypt. [See remark under Sin, following signature.]

In accordance with the law of prophecy enunciated above, Sinim might refer to the Sinites of the Phenician coast (Gen. x. 17), only that these would be already included in the *miyyam* in the preceding clause. It would be possible also to think of the Kurdish clan Sin in the district of Kerkuk in the province of Bagdad suggested by Egli, provided the stock is really old enough and had significance for the bearers or readers of this prophecy; but in that case it would be natural to hear something of the exiles in that place, and the silence needs explanation. But this very law of prophecy does not encourage one to think of China. When this prediction was written there had been no emigration of Jews to China, and it was, in general, impossible for the author of the passage in question to have meant by Sinim the inhabitants of the Middle Kingdom. Authorities do not claim a settlement of Jews in China before the third century before Christ (*EB*, iv. 4644; *JE*, iv. 33–34), and the tradition of the Chinese Jews carries their history in the country back to the Han dynasty (206 B.C. to 201 A.D.). Finally, were the region of China referred to in the passage, etymological considerations would lead one to look for a sibilant different from the one which is found in the Hebrew word.

(E. König.)

Bibliography: Discussions of the subject are to be found principally in the commentaries on Isaiah (see the bibliography under that article), especially those of Delitzsch (3d ed., 1879, 4th ed., 1889), Gesenius, Hitzig, Ewald, Nägelsbach, Cheyne, König, Von Orelli (2d ed., 1904), Dillmann, Condamin, Marti (Tübingen, 1900), and Duhm (2d ed., Göttingen, 1892). Also the Hebrew dictionaries, especially Gesenius, *Thesaurus*, pp. 948–950, and Brown-Briggs-Driver, p. 696. Consult further: F. von Richthofen, *China*, i. 436–437, 504, Berlin, 1877, cf. Yule in *Academy*, xiii. 339; Egli, in *ZWT*, vi (1863), 400–410; T. K. Cheyne, *Introduction to the Book of Isaiah*, p. 275, London, 1895; idem, *Isaiah*, in *SBOT*; *DB*, iv. 538; *EB*, iv. 4643–44; *JE*, iv. 33; Jacobus, *SBD*, p. 817; G. P. von Möllendorf, *Das Land Sinim*, in *Monatsschrift für Geschichte und Wissenschaft des Judenthums*, xxxviii (1893), 8–9; E. König, *Hebr. und aram. Wörterbuch*, p. 300, Leipsic, 1910.

SINKER, ROBERT: Church of England; b. at Liverpool July 17, 1838. He was educated at Trinity College, Cambridge (B.A., 1862; M.A., 1865), where he was chaplain from 1865 to 1871, having been curate of Coton, Cambridgeshire, in 1863–66, and librarian since 1871. He has edited *Testamenta duodecim patriarcharum* on the basis of the Cambridge and Oxford manuscripts (Cambridge, 1869), together with an appendix giving a collation of the Roman and Patmos codices (1879), and has translated the same document for *The Ante-Nicene Library* (Edinburgh, 1872), besides editing Bishop Pearson's *Exposition of the Creed* (Cambridge, 1882). He has written *The Characteristic Differences between the Books of the New Testament and the immediately Preceding Jewish and the immediately Succeeding Christian Literature considered as an Evidence of the Divine Authority of the New Testament* (Cambridge, 1865); *Catalogue of Fifteenth Century Printed Books in the Library of Trinity College* (1876); *Catalogue of English Books Printed before 1601 in the Library of Trinity College* (1885); *Memorials of the Hon. Ian Keith-Falconer* (London, 1888; new ed., 1903); *The Psalm of Habakkuk: A revised Translation with exegetical and critical Notes on the Hebrew and Greek Texts* (Cambridge, 1890); *The Library of Trinity College, Cambridge* (1891); *Hezekiah and his Age* (London, 1897); *Higher Criticism: What is it?* (1899); *Essays and Studies* (Cambridge, 1900); and *Saul and the Hebrew Monarchy* (London, 1904).

SIRACH, WISDOM OF JESUS, SON OF. See Apocrypha, A, IV., 12.

SIRICIUS, si-rish'ius: Pope 384–398. He was a Roman, and was chosen, in succession to Damasus, Dec., 384, or Jan., 385. His pontificate has little historical significance, except for the development of the papacy. He regarded seriously his rights and duties as overseer of the Church, demanded that his decisions be preserved, and so prepared the way for Innocent I. and Leo I. His first letter, Feb. 10, 385 (to Bishop Himerius of Tarragona in Spain), dealt with the matter of converted Arians and the observance of the early times for baptism, Easter, and Whitsuntide, with various classes in the Church, such as penitents, undisciplined monks, married priests, and the like; a synod held at Rome Jan. 6, 386, dealt with matters of like purport. He also insisted upon compliance with canonical prescriptions in reference to filling bishoprics and admission to the ranks of the clergy. In regard to Illyria he fostered its relations to Thessalonia, intending through Illyria to hold open for himself a door to the East. In 390 or 392 he held a synod which excommunicated Jovinian and eight associates.

(A. Hauck.)

Bibliography: The *Epistolæ* and *Decreta* are in A. Gallandi, *Bibliotheca veterum patrum*, vol. vii., 14 vols., Venice, 1765–81; in *MPL*, xiii.; and F. C. P. Hinschius, *Decretales Pseudo Isidorianæ*, pp. 520 sqq., Leipsic, 1863. Consult: *Liber pontificalis*, ed. Mommsen, in *MGH*, *Gest. pont. Rom.*, i (1898), 85–86; Jaffé, *Regesta*, i. 40 sqq., P. Hinschius, *Kirchenrecht*, iii. 683, Berlin, 1882; G. Rauschen, *Jahrbücher der christlichen Kirche unter Theodosius*, p. 197 et passim, Freiburg, 1897; Mirbt, *Quellen*, pp. 50–51; Hefele, *Conciliengeschichte*, ii. 45 sqq., Eng. transl., ii. 385–388, Fr. transl., ii. 1, pp. 68–75; Bower, *Popes*, i. 107–138; Platina, *Popes*, i. 88–92; Milman, *Latin Christianity*, i. 119.

SIRMOND, sir'men, **JACQUES:** French Jesuit and one of the most noted of French Roman Catholic scholars; b. at Riom (8 m. n. by e. of Clermont-Ferrand) Oct. 12, 1559; d. at Paris Oct. 16, 1651. He entered the Society of Jesus in 1576, and, after completing his studies and teaching for five years, was called, in 1590, to Rome, where for sixteen years he was secretary to the Jesuit general, Aquaviva, at the same time pursuing studies which enabled him to give great assistance to Baronius in the preparation of his *Annales*. In 1608 he returned to France, and on Feb. 22, 1612, was one of the Jesuits who declared themselves ready to follow the Sorbonne with reference to Gallicanism. He took part in the condemnation of Suarez, and in 1617 became rector of the Collège Clermont at Paris, where he had already been for five years. After 1637 he was confessor to Louis XIII., and in 1615 and 1645 revisited Rome to take part in the election of new generals of his order.

As an editor Sirmond was indefatigable, his work here including editions of *Goffridi abbatis Vindocinensis epistolæ, opuscula, sermones* (Paris, 1610); Ennodius (1611; the standard for more than two centuries); *Flodoardi historia ecclesiæ Remensis* (1611); *Fulgentius de veritate prædestinationis et gratiæ* (1612) and *Librorum contra Fabianum excerpta* (1643); *Valeriani episcopi homiliæ viginti* (1612); *Petri Cellensis epistolæ* (1613); Apollinaris Sidonius (1614); Paschasius Radbertus (1618); *Idatii chronicon et fasti consulares* (1619); *Marcellini comitis Illyriciani chronicon* (1619); *Anastasii bibliothecarii collectanea* (1620); *Facundus episcopus Hermianensis pro defensione trium capitulorum* (1629); *Sancti Augustini novi sermones quadraginta* (1631); Theodoret (4 vols., 1642); Alcimus Avitus (1643; also a standard for over two hundred years); Hincmar of Reims (1645); and Theodulf of Orléans (1646). Among his more independent works special mention may be made of the following: *Prædestinatus* (Paris, 1643) and *Historia Prædestinatiana* (1648); *Appendix codicis Theodosiani novis constitutionibus cumulatior* (1631; best ed. by G. Hänel, Bonn, 1844); *Concilia antiqua Galliæ, cum epistolis pontificum, principum constitutionibus, et aliis Gallicanæ rei ecclesiasticæ monimentis* (3 vols.,

1629; supplementary volume by P. Delalande, 1666); *Antirrheticus de canone Arausicano* (2 parts, 1633–34); and the *Historia pœnitentiæ publicæ, item disquisitio de azymo* (1651). His collected works were edited by J. de la Baune under the title *Opera varia nunc primum collecta* (5 vols., Paris, 1696; enlarged ed., 5 vols., Venice, 1728).

(G. LAUBMANN†.)

BIBLIOGRAPHY: The funeral oration by H. Valesius and a short sketch of the life are included in vol. i. of the *Opera*. Consult further: A. de Backer and C. Sommervogel, *Bibliothèque de la compagnie de Jésus*, vii. 1237–61; Lichtenberger, *ESR*, xi. 619–622.

SISEBUT, si'sê-but: Successor of Gundemar (Gunthemar) as king of the Visigoths; d. in 620. He ascended the throne in 612, and was an excellent ruler in most respects, clement, just, and of a glowing religious devotion, distinguished also as an author and as a hero in war. He nevertheless won a dismal reputation as the first Spanish persecutor of the Jews.

Since the earlier periods of the Roman empire the Jews had been numerous in the Iberian peninsula, and were highly respected on account of their wealth. The Visigoths, tolerant as they were, maintained the public rights of the Jews during the entire Arian epoch. Recared the Catholic was the first to impose restrictions upon them, promulgating the prohibition against the circumcision of Christian slaves and the acquisition of them either by purchase or donation (*Leges Visigothorum*, XII., 2, no. 12, ed. K. Zeumer in *MGH*, *Leg. nationum Germ.*, i. 305, Hanover, 1902). On these provisions Sisebut based his two notorious laws concerning the Jews, starting his anti-Semitic campaign at the beginning of his reign (*Leges Visigothorum*, XII., 2, 13–14, pp. 305–309). As rightly interpreted by Dahn, his orders prescribe that Christian bondsmen of Jews should become Roman citizens and free by law, as should runaway Jewish servants who were willing to accept Christianity. Jews were not allowed to have as servants hired free men. Marriages between Jews and Christians were declared null and void. Isidore in his *Historia Gothorum* (issued in 624), while appreciating the pious intentions of his royal friend, objected to the mode of conversion employed. In fact, Sisebut's persecution went far beyond those restrictions. That there were many compulsory baptisms of Jews, there is no doubt, and so the third edict conjectured by Jost—presumably without justification—compelling them to choose between exile and baptism, is not necessary to explain the numerous departures of Jews from the country. Many sought refuge among the Franks.

With such a zealous ruler on the throne the Church was able to display far-reaching activity, especially as to synodal matters. But with all his religious enthusiasm Sisebut was no "parsons' king," sometimes rather sharply taking the episcopate to task. In 615 he inaugurated the war of extermination against the Byzantines which he carried to a successful end. As a victor he proved humane enough to set the captured Byzantines free and to dismiss them to their home country. (FRANZ GÖRRES.)

BIBLIOGRAPHY: Sources are. The *Chronica* of Isidore of Seville, ed. Mommsen in *MGH*, *Auct. ant.*, xi (1894), 479–480, and his *Historia Gothorum*, in the same, pp. 291 sqq.; the letters of Sisebut to Patricius Cæsarius, ed. W. Gundlach in *MGH*, *Epist.*, iii (1892), 662–675; his hexameters, ed. G. Goetz, *Index scholarum Jenensium*, Jena, 1887–88; the "Chronicle" of Fredegar, ed. B. Krusch in *MGH*, *Script. rer. Merov.*, ii (1888), 133; and the *Leges Visigothorum antiquiorum*, ed. K. Zeumer, pp. 305–309, Hanover, 1894. Consult: F. Dahn, *Die Könige der Germanen*, vols. v.–vi. passim, Leipsic, 1885; F. Görres, in *ZWT*, xl. 284–296, xli. 105–111, xliii. 270–322, 442–450, xlv. 41–72. Also: J. M. Jost, *Geschichte der Israeliten*, v. 110–120, Berlin, 1825; J. Aschbach, *Die Geschichte der Westgoten*, pp. 236–241, Frankfort, 1827; A. Helfferich, *Westgoten-Recht*, pp. 68–71, Berlin, 1858; P. B. Gams, *Kirchengeschichte Spaniens*, ii. 2, pp. 78–80, 85–90, 101, 3 vols., Regensburg, 1862–79; K. Zeumer, in *NA*, xxvii (1902), 409–444; Gibbon, *Decline and Fall*, chap. xxxvii.; *ADB*, xxxiv. 418–421; *DCB*, iv. 703–704; and the literature on the Jews in Spain and Portugal under ISRAEL, HISTORY OF.

SISERA. See DEBORAH, 2.

SISINNIUS, si-sin'ni-us: The name of several persons of note in church history.

1. **Pope,** Jan. 18–Feb. 8 (7?), 708. He was a Syrian, and was ill when elected to the papal chair; and all recorded of him is that he made preparations for the restoration of the city wall.

2. **The Novatian:** Novatian bishop of Constantinople. He studied with Julian under the philosopher Maximus; became a reader in the Novatian community, and in 395 bishop. Socrates (*Hist. eccl.*, V., x., xxi., VI., xxi., Eng. transl., *NPNF*, 2 ser., ii. 123, 129, 152, 156) notes his literary activity, especially in his work on penitence against Chrysostom, and one against the Messalians.

3. **Sisinnius of Constantinople:** Orthodox bishop of that city 426–427. He is mentioned by Socrates (*Hist. eccl.*, VII., xxviii., Eng. transl., *NPNF*, 2 ser., ii. 168–169).

4. **Patriarch of Constantinople,** 995–999. He wrote on the marriage law, and also an encyclical for the eastern bishops on the procession of the Holy Spirit.

(A. HAUCK.)

BIBLIOGRAPHY: On 1: Mann, *Popes*, i. 124–126; Bower, *Popes*, ii. 14; Platina, *Popes*, i. 175. On 2–4: *DCB*, iv. 704–705.

SISTERHOODS. See DEACONESS, III., 2; MONASTICISM; WOMEN, CONGREGATIONS OF; and WOMEN'S WORK IN THE CHURCH.

SISTERS OF CHARITY. See CHARITY, SISTERS OF.

SISTERS OF MERCY. See MERCY, SISTERS OF.

SIX ARTICLES, ACT OF THE: An act of the English parliament, dated June 28, 1539, marking a departure from Protestant principles. It imposed upon the English people the doctrines of transubstantiation under penalty of death by burning and confiscation of goods; depravation of the sacrament subjected to the same penalty; claims in behalf of communion in both kinds, and breaking of the vows of celibacy were felonies punishable with death; clerical marriages were dissolved; and special commissions were to be issued quarterly for the enforcement of the provisions of the act. The measure was in part political, aiming to prevent action against the king, Henry VIII., on the part of continental Roman Catholic powers. While the law was severe, executions were few under it. It was modified in 1544 and repealed in 1547. The text is given in Gee and Hardy, *Documents*, pp. 313–320.

BIBLIOGRAPHY: J. H. Overton, *The Church in England*, i. 390, 395, London, 1897; J. Gairdner, *The English Church in the 16th Century*, passim, ib. 1903; A. Plummer, *English Church History (1509–75)*, pp. 80–81, 84, 805, Edinburgh, 1905.

SIX-PRINCIPLES BAPTISTS. See BAPTISTS, II., 4 (a).

SIXTUS: The name of five popes.

Sixtus I.: Pope in the reign of Hadrian (Liberian Catalogue) and successor of Alexander (according to the papal lists). But the monarchical constitution of the Church was not introduced into Rome before the middle of the second century, therefore Sixtus must be regarded as a presbyter whose name went on the records because he was a martyr. (A. HAUCK.)

BIBLIOGRAPHY: *Liber pontificalis*, ed. Mommsen in *MGH*, *Gest. pont. Rom.*, i (1898), 96–100; Bower, *Popes*, i. 11; Platina, *Popes*, i. 22–24; Milman, *Latin Christianity*, i. 250.

Sixtus II.: Pope 257–258. He restored the communion between the Roman and African churches which had been broken off in the pontificate of his predecessor, Stephen I. (q.v.), in the strife over the baptism of heretics. He fell a martyr in the Valerian persecution, Aug. 6, 258. The later reports are mingled with legendary elements. The length of his pontificate is differently given in different sources. Harnack (*TU*, xiii. 1) regards him as the author of the pseudo-Cyprianic writing *Ad Novatianum*, though his view has not found general acceptance. He is right, however, if the question is concerning the authorship of a composition written at Rome, 253–258, for no other person of the period is likely as author. (A. HAUCK.)

BIBLIOGRAPHY: R. A. Lipsius, *Chronologie der römischen Bischöfe*, p. 213, Leipsic, 1869; J. Langen, *Geschichte der römischen Kirche*, i. 347, Bonn, 1881; Harnack, *TU*, xiii. 1 (1895), 1 sqq., xx. (1901), 116 sqq.; idem, *Litteratur*, ii. 2, pp. 190 sqq., 387 sqq.; Bower, *Popes*, i. 34–35; Platina, *Popes*, i. 53–55.

Sixtus III.: Pope 432–440. He was consecrated July 31, 432; was in office during the Nestorian and Pelagian controversies, but had little interest in Christological questions, and was concerned chiefly in restoring peace between Cyril and the Syrians. In reference to Pelagianism he was opposed to Julian of Eclanum. He maintained the rights of the pope over Illyria and the position of the archbishop of Thessalonica as head of the Illyrian church. His biography mentions the building (enlargement) of the churches of St. Lorenzo and of St. Maria Maggiore and of rich gifts secured for both churches and for St. Peter's and the Lateran basilica. (A. HAUCK.)

BIBLIOGRAPHY: *Liber pontificalis*, ed. Mommsen in *MGH*, *Gest. pont. Rom.*, i (1898), 96, ed. L. Duchesne, i. p. cxxvi., Paris, 1886; Jaffé, *Regesta*, i. 57; J. Langen, *Geschichte der römischen Kirche*, i. 387, Bonn, 1881; F. Gregorovius, *Hist. of the City of Rome*, i. 184–185, London, 1894; Bower, *Popes*, i. 186–189; *Platina*, *Popes*, i. 103–105.

Sixtus IV. (Francesco della Rovere): Pope 1471–1484. He was born in the vicinity of Savona (23 m. w. of Genoa) in 1414; entered the Franciscan order; studied in Pavia and Bologna, and obtained the doctor's degree at Padua. In 1464 he became general of his order; in 1467, cardinal, with the title of S. Pietro in Vincoli. He passed not only for a learned theologian, but was also an unscrupulous autocrat, never embarrassed on the score of means. When he ascended the papal throne in 1471, he first rewarded Cardinals Orsini and Borgia, to whom he owed his election; and then endowed his nephews with dignities and benefices. The one, Giuliano, obtained bishoprics, prebends, and the cardinal's rank, in quick succession. The other, Pietro Riario, was endowed still more affluently, and became noted for his prodigality with the wealth of the Church. After Pietro's death in 1474, the pope diverted his favors to Pietro's brother, Girolamo; and in 1480 appointed him "captain general" of the Church, and made two other nephews cardinals.

The existing situation laid a double task on the pope: on the one side, the adjustment of affairs in the East and protection against the Turks; on the other side, the strengthening of the papal political power. Sixtus discharged the first of these tasks piecemeal, sending auxiliary funds to the Venetians. In the other direction, he made effectual use of his nephews, weakening the feudal lords of the Papal States, while he kept creating new complications in the territorial policy of the Italian states and thus extended his own power (cf. F. Gregorovius, *History of the City of Rome*, book xiii. 3, London, 1900). A typical instance of his procedure appears in the conspiracy set afoot, with his acquiescence, by the Pazzi in Florence against Lorenzo the Magnificent in 1478. The assassins overpowered and killed their victim, Giuliano de' Medici, at high mass, but Lorenzo escaped. The news of the miscarriage of the plot put Sixtus in a rage and he sequestered all Florentine possessions in the Papal States of the Church, and declared war on the republic; peace was concluded only in view of the new Turkish war, 1480. On the death of Mohammed II. in the following year, his intrigues turned upon Italy again, in order to widen the dominion of Girolamo, whose portion already embraced Imola and Forli, by the addition of Ferrara. This fell through, but a bloody war with the barons in the Papal States ensued. Sixtus died Aug. 12, 1484, before matters were concluded. K. BENRATH.

BIBLIOGRAPHY: Pastor, *Popes*, iv. 197 sqq. (exhaustive); Creighton, *Papacy*, iv. 64–134; Muratori, *Scriptores*, ii., p. iii., cols. 1071 sqq.; W. Roscoe, *Life of Lorenzo the Magnificent*, 2 vols., new ed., London, 1876; J. Burchard, *Diarium*, ed. L. Thuasne, i. 1–16, Paris, 1883, Eng. transl., *Diary of John Burchard*, pp. 1–15, London, 1910; S. Infessura, *Diario della Città di Roma*, ed. Tommassini, pp. 75–283, Rome, 1890; J. Burckhardt, *Geschichte der Renaissance in Italien*, ed. H. Holtzinger, Stuttgart, 1904; Bower, *Popes*, iii. 238–254; Schaff, *Christian Church*, v. 2, § 52.

Sixtus V. (Felice Peretti): Pope 1585–1590. He was born at Grottamare (1 m. s. of Ancona) Dec. 13, 1521; received his education at the neighboring Franciscan cloister in Montalto; and soon became a favorite preacher. During the times of Julius III. he was in Rome, and won the attachment of Philip Neri (q.v.) and of Michele Ghislieri, afterward Pope Pius V. After he had been regent of his order's cloisters in Siena, Naples, and Venice, where he also represented the holy office before the senate, he was recalled to Rome as the order's procurator-general. Pius V. made him bishop of Fermo, and created him a cardinal in 1570. But the succeeding pope, Gregory XIII., kept him remote from affairs. During this period the increase of his collection of books was his absorbing pursuit in the beautiful villa on the Esquiline, which he exchanged in 1585 for the papal palace. When the election was settled, he surprised the constituency of the Church by showing himself the ruler born.

In the first place, Sixtus restored personal security and order in the Papal States. Within two years he exterminated brigandage, suppressing it with stern hand and by frequent executions. He also gave attention to the ordering of the civil administration and finances, terminated wastefulness and peculation, and within three years deposited three million crowns in Castle Saint Angelo as a prudential fund in event of need. Ultimately, however, he expended the sums acquired upon imposing public structures. Thus he had massive creations in stone achieved by the ingenious architect Domenico Fontana; whence the Rococo style came to dominate in Roman architecture for more than 100 years. His principal achievements in this line were the Via Sistina, and the Square of the Lateran. Moreover, Rome owes to this pope the restoration of one of the great aqueducts (named after him, Aqua Felice). Sixtus also left his footprints in the domain of ecclesiastical organization and administration; he found already in operation the still effective division of the governing boards as "congregations," whose number he increased to fifteen. Since the appointment of cardinals as members or as chairmen of the congregations had to emanate exclusively from the pope, the matter was duly provided that no opinions or decisions should be put forth which might contradict the general trend of papal policy. The administration of the city of Rome Sixtus concentrated in his own grasp, except for some few remnants of communal independence. Things took the same course in the remaining cities of the Papal States, and it was carefully provided that all significant positions came into the hands of ecclesiastics.

It is remarkable how Sixtus, who was inflexible in his own ecclesiastical and political policy, showed diplomatic pliancy even to the extent of wavering and indecision in dealing with other states. Thus Venice was able to enforce collection of tithes from the orders, as from the secular clergy. With Spain, despite the pope's yielding in the question of his feudal claims to Sicily, the situation came to open rupture because Sixtus declined to pay the 700,000 crowns promised toward equipment of the Great Armada on the ground that no landing was made on the English coast. So with Henry IV., the pope's continual changes so angered the king that he threatened openly to retract his obedience. Prior to a decision, Sixtus was overtaken by death, Aug. 27, 1590. K. Benrath.

Bibliography: The sources are illuminatingly discussed in Ranke, *Popes*, iii. 200-257, including the lives by G. Leti, 2 vols., Lausanne, 1669, and C. Tempesti, Rome, 1755, and a considerable number of documents. The account by Ranke, *Popes*, i. 34 sqq., is the best for the reader of English. The *British Museum Catalogue* has an interesting list of documents under "Rome, Church of, Popes, Sixtus V." Consult further, J. Dumesnil, *Hist. de Sixte-Quint*, Paris, 1869, J. A. Hübner, *Sixte-Quint*, 3 vols., ib. 1870; A. von Reumont, *Geschichte der Stadt Rom.*, iii. 584 sqq., Berlin, 1878; G. Gozzadini, *G. Pepoli e Sisto V.*, Bologna, 1879; M. Brosch, *Geschichte des Kirchenstaates*, vol. i., chap. vii., Gotha, 1880; L. Capranica, *Papa Sisto*, 3 vols., Milan, 1884; I. Raulich, in *Nuovo Archivio Veneto*, iv (1892); Bower, *Popes*, iii. 322-325.

SKALSKY, GUSTAV ADOLF: Austrian-Hungarian theologian; b. at Opatovice near Czaslau (45 m. e.s.e. of Prague), Bohemia, Mar. 13, 1857. He received his education at the gymnasium in Teschen, the University of Vienna under the Protestant Evangelical Faculty (D.D., 1898), and the University of Erlangen; served as pastor in Klimov, Bohemia, and Lhota in Moravia, till 1896, when he became a member of the Protestant Evangelical Theological Faculty in the University of Vienna, lecturing on pastoral theology and Austrian Protestant church law. He has been active not only in the lines of his teaching work, but in labors for the benefit of the Czechs and Slovacs in Vienna and also in connection with the organization of the Young Men's Christian Association in Austria. His theological standpoint is that of the New Lutheran Erlangen school, so far as its position is applicable to conditions in Austria. Besides a considerable number of works in the Czech language, he has issued *Zur Geschichte der evangelischen Kirchenverfassung in Oesterreich bis zum Toleranzpatente* (Vienna, 1898); *Zur Reform des oesterreichischen Eherechts* (1906); *Der oesterreichische Staat und die evangelische Kirche im Oesterreich in ihrem wechselseitigen Verhältnis 1848-61* (1908); and *J. A. Comenius als Reformator der Erziehung und der Schule* (1908); and has edited a number of important papers bearing on the early history of the Unity of the Brethren.

SKEAT, skit, WALTER WILLIAM: Church of England; b. at London Nov. 21, 1835. He was educated at Christ's College, Cambridge (B.A., 1858; M.A., 1861), and was curate at East Dereham, Norfolk (1860-62), and Godalming, Surrey (1863-64). He was mathematical lecturer at Christ's College (1863-71), and English lecturer (1867-83), while since 1878 he has been Elrington and Bosworth professor of Anglo-Saxon in the University of Cambridge. In 1873 he founded the English Dialect Society, and was its president till 1896. He is best known as an editor of Anglo-Saxon and Early English Texts, and among his works those of theological interest include his editions of Langland's *Piers Plowman* (2 vols., London, 1867-84); *Joseph of Arimathæa* (1871); *The Four Gospels in Anglo-Saxon and Northumbrian* (4 vols., Cambridge, 1871-1887); *Wycliffe's New Testament* (Oxford, 1879); Ælfric's *Lives of the Saints* (4 vols., London, 1881-1900); *The Gospel of St. Mark in Gothic* (Oxford, 1882); *The Complete Works of Geoffrey Chaucer* (London, 6 vols., 1894); and the *Proverbs of Alfred* (1907).

SKINNER, JOHN: The name of two Scotch divines.

1. Scotch Episcopal; b. at Longside (27 m. n. of Aberdeen), Scotland, May 17, 1744; d. at Aberdeen July 18, 1816. He received his higher education at Marischal College, Aberdeen; served as private tutor, 1761-63; was ordained deacon, 1763, and priest, 1764; took charge of the congregations of

Ellon and Udny, Aberdeenshire, 1764; was appointed to the Longacre congregation, Aberdeen, 1775; was consecrated coadjutor to the bishop of Aberdeen, 1782, succeeding to the bishopric, 1786, and being elected primus, 1788. His significance rests on two facts: (1) he was active in the transmission of the Scotch episcopal succession in America, having part in the consecration of Samuel Seabury (q.v.; also see PROTESTANT EPISCOPALIANS, I., § 2); (2) also in the ending of the non-juring Scotch schism. He presided at the synod at Aberdeen April 24, 1788, which resolved to pray for George III. as king, and later visited London in the interest of his church. He published *A Course of Lectures* (Aberdeen, 1786); *A Layman's Account of his Faith* (Edinburgh, 1801); and *Primitive Truth and Order Vindicated* (Aberdeen, 1803).

2. English Presbyterian; b. at Inverurie (14 m. n.w. of Aberdeen), Aberdeenshire, Scotland, July 18, 1851. He was educated at the University of Aberdeen (M.A., 1876), Free Church College, Aberdeen (1876–77), New College, Edinburgh (1877–80), and the universities of Leipsic (1876) and Göttingen (1877). He was Hebrew tutor at New College, Edinburgh (1879–80); held Free Church ministries at St. Fergus, Banffshire (1880–86), and Kelso, Roxburghshire (1886–90); and since 1890 has been professor of Hebrew and apologetics in Westminster College (the theological college of the Presbyterian Church of England), Cambridge, England. He has written *Historical Connection between the Old and New Testaments* (Edinburgh, 1899); and has edited Ezekiel for *The Expositor's Bible* (London, 1895); Isaiah for *The Cambridge Bible for Schools* (2 vols., Cambridge, 1896–98); and Genesis for the *International Critical Commentary* (1910).

SKINNER, THOMAS HARVEY: Presbyterian pastor and educator; b. near Harvey's Neck, N. C., Mar. 7, 1791; d. at New York Feb. 1, 1871. He was graduated from Princeton College, 1812; was copastor of the Second Presbyterian Church, Philadelphia, 1812–16; then pastor of the Arch Street Church, same city, 1816–32; professor of sacred rhetoric at Andover, 1832–35; pastor of the Mercer Street Presbyterian Church, New York, 1835–40; and professor of sacred rhetoric and pastoral theology in Union Theological Seminary, New York, 1848–71. He wrote *Aids to Preaching and Hearing* (1839), *Hints to Christians* (1841), *Life of Francis Markoe* (1849), *Discussions in Theology* (1868); he also translated and edited Vinet's *Pastoral Theology and Homiletics* (1854). Dr. Skinner was a leader in the New School branch of the Presbyterian Church, a preacher of great spiritual power, an able theologian, and a pattern of saintly goodness.

BIBLIOGRAPHY: G. L. Prentiss, *A Discourse in Memory of T. H. Skinner*, New York, 1871; idem, *The Union Theological Seminary in the City of New York: historical and biographical Sketches of its first fifty Years*, ib. 1889; idem, *The Union Theological Seminary in the City of New York, its Design and another Decade of its History*, ib. 1899.

SKOPTZI. See RUSSIA, II., § 5.

SKREFSRUD, skrefs'rūd, **LARS OLSEN:** Norwegian missionary to India; b. at Faaberg (84 m. n. of Christiania), Norway, Feb. 4, 1840; d. at Benagaria, near Ebenzer, India, Dec. 11, 1910. On account of poverty he was unable to attend the gymnasium, but by application he acquired a remarkable education, being gifted with the ability to use about forty-five languages. He attended Prochnow's missionary training-school in Berlin, graduating after a period of brilliant achievements; he was then sent by the Gossner society to Purulia, India, but friction arose with the German members of the mission, and Skrefsrud sundered his connection and established in 1867 the Santhal mission, which became in many ways a model. In the interest of the mission he several times visited Europe, first in 1873–74, when his lectures resulted in the formation of the first European Santhal mission committees; in 1881–83, when he was ordained by the Church of Norway; and in 1894–95, this time also visiting America. His contributions to linguistics were notable and numerous; among them may be mentioned *A Grammar of the Santhal Language* (Benares, 1873); *Santhal-English and English-Santhal Lexicon* (material completed in 1904 after a period of preparation covering thirty-five years); and a translation of the Bible into Santhal—one of the most difficult languages known. JOHN O. EVJEN.

SLATER, WILLIAM FLETCHER: English Methodist; b. at Uttoxeter (30 m. n. of Birmingham), Staffordshire, Aug. 25, 1831. He was educated at Wesleyan College, Didsbury (graduated 1855), and the University of Cambridge (B.A., 1875), and held successive pastorates in his denomination at Allendale (1855–58), Newcastle-on-Tyne (1858–60), Glossop (1860–63), Sunderland (1863–66), Harrogate (1866–69), Barnsley (1869–72), Cambridge (1872–1875), Leeds (1875–78), Edinburgh (1878–81), Liverpool (1881–84), and London (1884–87). From 1887 to 1903, when he retired from active life, he was professor of Biblical languages in Wesleyan College, Didsbury. In theology he is an Evangelical Arminian, and has written: *Religious Opportunities of the Heathen before Christ* (Sunderland, 1866); *Methodism in the Light of the Early Church* (Fernley lecture; London, 1885); *Faith and Life in the Early Church* (1892); the Gospel of Matthew in *The Century Bible* (1900); and *Limitations, Divine and Human* (1906).

SLATTERY, CHARLES LEWIS: Protestant Episcopal; b. at Pittsburg Dec. 9, 1867. He received his education at Harvard University (B.A., 1891) and the Episcopal Theological School, Cambridge, Mass. (B.D., 1894); was made deacon, 1894, and priest, 1895; was master of Groton School and rector of St. Andrew's, Ayer, Mass., 1894–96; dean of the cathedral of Our Merciful Savior, Faribault, Minn., 1896–1907; rector of Christ Church, Springfield, Mass., 1907–10; and became rector of Grace Church, New York City, 1910. He was also lecturer in Seabury Divinity School, Faribault, Minn., 1905–07, and in Berkeley Divinity School, 1909–10. He is the author of *Felix Reville Brunot* (New York, 1901); *Edward Lincoln Atkinson* (1904); *The Master of the World: a Study of Christ* (1906); *Life Beyond Life; a Study of Immortality* (1907); *The Historic Ministry and the Present Christ; an Appeal for Unity* (1908); and *Present-Day Preaching* (1909).

SLAVERY.

I. Slavery Among the Hebrews: Slavery existed among the Jews throughout their national life, although this servitude was one neither of debasement nor of cruelty. In patriarchal times the servants, together with the cattle, formed a portion of the estate of the head of the family or tribe (Gen. xxiv. 35, xxvi. 14; Job. i. 3), and there was, accordingly, a traffic in slaves (Gen. xxxvii. 28), which was actively carried on by the Phenicians.

1. Status of Hebrew Slaves.

The rich nomad chiefs owned numerous slaves, Abraham having 318 that were "born in his house," i.e., hereditary property (Gen. xiv. 14); and slaves were also purchased (Gen. xvii. 23, 27). The female servants seem to have been the especial property of the wife or daughter, and to have been given as concubines to the husband (Gen. xvi. 1 sqq., xxix. 24, etc.). The slaves "born in the house" were, in general, devoted to the family, and some had the entire confidence of their masters (cf. Gen. xv. 2–3). Even in the nomad period these servants were not mere chattels, and the fact that the rite of circumcision was performed on servants born in the house, as well as on those obtained by purchase, indicates that they were received as members of the same race, and as such had religious rights and duties. In the national period the traditional legal principles were observed, as in the Babylonian code of Hammurabi, although the latter lacked to some degree the ethical and religious spirit that, from the time of Moses, exercised its more humane influence on the Jewish law. The Mosaic idea that the whole Israelitish race had been in slavery in Egypt, and, being freed from the house of bondage by Yahweh (e.g., Ex. xx. 2; Deut. v. 6), had now become his servants and property, led to the inference that, being his own, they would never again become the servants of a stranger (Lev. xxv. 42, 55, xxvi. 13); while the recollection of their harsh treatment in slavery taught them to be considerate and humane to their servants (Deut. v. 15, xv. 15). With the development of national consciousness, however, the law distinguished between bondservants of Israelitish stock and aliens (cf. Lev. xxv. 39–46), though practise may have been less rigorous than theory.

2. Sources of Supply.

Slavery was, throughout Jewish history, one of the consequences of war, and as warriors were more apt to be killed than taken prisoners, the majority of captives were women, especially virgins, who were the prize booty of military and predatory expeditions (Gen. xiv. 12; Judges v. 30; II Kings v. 2; Deut. xx. 14, xxi. 10 sqq.; etc.). Many prisoners of war were sold in foreign lands (Joel iii. 4, 6; Amos i. 6), and many were bought by the Israelites from traveling Phenician merchants. Alien settlers in the land were also liable to come into bondage, and the Canaanitish population gradually became the slaves of the Hebrews, especially in the regal period. After the exodus, slaves of foreign stock were employed in lower menial capacities in the camp and in the sanctuary, thus ultimately giving rise to the Nethinim (see Levi, Levites, § 3). Both David and Solomon employed non-Israelitic slaves in public works, the latter monarch having 153,600 of these bondsmen (I Kings ix. 20 sqq.; II Chron. ii. 17–18). It was a capital crime unlawfully to deprive a man of his liberty and to sell him (Ex. xxi. 16; Deut. xxiv. 7; cf. the Code of Hammurabi, § 14). On the other hand, a thief caught in the act was to be sold into slavery unless he could make restitution (Ex. xxii., 3). Tradition forbade, however, the selling of a thief into foreign slavery, so that Herod's law requiring such sale (Josephus, *Ant.*, XVI., i. 1) was a serious infringement of hereditary legal custom. It was usually abject poverty and insolvency that entailed the loss of freedom (cf. Lev. xxv. 39, 47 sqq.), and in such a case a man might sell his own daughter. The regulations of the Book of the Covenant (Ex. xxi. 7–11) apply only to a daughter sold to be the concubine or wife of the buyer or his son, and expressly protect her rights as a member of the family; but Deut. xv. 12 sqq. distinctly refers to female slaves. The law does not specify whether a father may sell his son, but he doubtless did so, in case of poverty, rather than sacrifice his own freedom. A Jewish creditor might seize both the family and the person of his debtor, and sell him (Amos ii. 6, viii. 6; II Kings iv. 1; cf. Isa. l. 1; Neh. v. 5; Matt. xviii. 25), though this was not sanctioned in the Pentateuch.

3. Value of Slaves; Duration of Servitude.

A slave's value depended on sex, age, health, capacity for work, and the relation between supply and demand. Thirty silver shekels was the average damages for the death of a slave, whether male or female (Ex. xxi. 32), and some indication of the value of slaves may perhaps be gained from the scale given in Lev. xxvii. 2 sqq. for those desiring to be released from their vows to serve in the sanctuary: for a boy between one month and five years old, five shekels, and for a girl three shekels; for a male between five and twenty years old, twenty shekels, and for a female ten; for a man between twenty and sixty years old, fifty shekels, and for a woman thirty; for a man over sixty years old, fifteen shekels, and for a woman ten. The price for captive Jews, 120 drachmas a head, is almost the same average (Josephus, *Ant.*, XII., ii. 3). The duration of bondage was limited only in the case of Israelitish slaves, who were never absolutely to lose their freedom, unless they definitely refused to accept it (Ex. xxi. 1–11;

Deut. xv. 12–18; Lev. xxv. 39–55). An Israelite could buy a fellow Hebrew, whether male or female, for six years only, and in the seventh year must let the slave go free, a rule which probably applied also to those sold into slavery for theft (cf. Josephus, *Ant.*, XVI., i. 1). On the other hand, a gentile woman given to such a slave as a wife had no claim to freedom, and the offspring of the pair were also held in bondage. In the year of jubilee an Israelite slave was to be set free, together with his children (Lev. xxv. 39 sqq.), but if these were born of a gentile mother, they, like her, must remain in slavery (Ex. xxi. 4). The Hebrew slave of a gentile master should also be freed in the year of jubilee, although he should previously be redeemed, if possible, by his family or kindred, his price being reckoned according to Lev. xxv. 50 sqq.

Bondservants were better treated by the Hebrews than were those of ancient Greece and Rome, or even Phenicia and Babylonia. At the same time Mosaic law made a distinction between Hebrew slaves and those of alien birth, priestly legislation especially considering a Hebrew bondman not as a "bond-servant," but as a "hired servant" (Lev. xxv. 39–40, 46). While he was not to be compelled to do work that was too severe, or unworthy of a man, this falling to the lot of the alien, all slaves, without exception, benefited by the Sabbath law. Furthermore, both those slaves who had been born in bondage and also, as a rule, those who were acquired by purchase were circumcised, thus being received among the people of Yahweh, and so possessing the privilege of sharing in the religious feasts, especially in the Passover (Ex. xii. 44; Deut. xii. 12, 18, xvi. 11, 14). If a slave had been circumcised, he could never be sold to a gentile. While it was permissible to discipline a slave (cf. Prov. xxix. 19, 21; Ecclus. xxxiii. 24 sqq.), cruelty to slaves was punished, not simply by compensating the master for injury done to his slave, as in Babylonia (cf. Code of Hammurabi, §§ 199, 219), but by enacting that a master who seriously injured his slave, whether male or female, must manumit the slave in question without receiving compensation (Ex. xxi. 26–27). A master had no power over the life of his servant, and if he struck his slave with a rod and he died under his hand the servant should be avenged (Ex. xxi. 20–21); but if the slave survived his punishment for a day or two, no notice was taken, the money loss caused his master by his death being deemed a sufficient penalty. However, according to tradition, if the master used a deadly instrument in chastisement he incurred the death penalty, even though the slave did not die for some time; and tradition likewise held that, should a third person kill or wound a slave, he should be punished as though he had injured a freeman. The status of Israelitish female slaves who were to become part of the immediate family is set forth in Ex. xxi. 7–11; and it is also provided that a gentile prisoner of war should have a month to mourn her kinsfolk before being married to her captor (Deut. xxi. 10–14). Respect for the rights of a slave was considered a divine ordinance from very early times (Job xxxi. 13–15), and to the present day the lot of the slaves of the Semitic Mohammedans is a very tolerable one. In ancient Judaism, however, the Essenes and Therapeutæ alone rejected all slavery, since they regarded the system as irreconcilable with the brotherhood of all mankind, and consequently as unnatural. (C. von Orelli.)

4. Legal Position and Rights.

II. Slavery and Christianity: The problem of the influence of Christianity on slavery has been profoundly modified by the researches of economic history concerning the origin, nature, extent, character, and abolition of bondage, so that, rejecting the older view that the suppression of slavery was caused entirely by Christianity, many now hold that this abolition was a purely economic process in which religion had no part. Equally problematical is the precise state of affairs confronting Christianity when it came to confront slavery, for the extent of the system in antiquity is now underrated as much as it was formerly exaggerated. In Greece the climax was reached at the close of the Persian wars, when a single rich Athenian could lease a thousand slaves for the Thracian mines; and in Rome the system was most flourishing at the close of the Republic and the beginning of the Empire, when at Delos, the chief market, tens of thousands of slaves were sold daily. The majority of these were employed in agriculture and manufacturing, although the Romans availed themselves of household slaves to a greater extent than the Greeks, who preferred financial gain to luxury. At the same time, the freeman was never entirely superseded by the slave, least of all in the provinces (cf. for Palestine, Matt. xx. 1 sqq.; Mark i. 20; Luke xv. 17), even though cheapness made slave labor predominant in estates, mines, quarries, factories, and the handicrafts and trades of the great cities.

1. Extent of Greco-Roman Slavery.

The status and the treatment of slaves varied at different times and places as greatly as their numbers. In the patriarchal conditions of the earliest times the slave, generally a prisoner of war, belonged to the family and was treated accordingly. In Greece slaves enjoyed much liberty even later, especially at Athens; but in Rome rigid severity was the rule, particularly in large establishments where cruel overseers, mostly belonging originally to the servile class, intervened between master and slave (cf. Matt. xxiv. 49). While, moreover, the slaves seldom worked in fetters, punishments to insure obedience and to prevent escape were so cruel as to cause terrible insurrections. It is true that many slaves fared better than freemen, but even here any day might bring a change of masters, and though the slave had many safeguards, he was still, legally speaking, only a chattel, exposed to every caprice of his owner. His possession of moral qualities was ignored; he might at any time be torn from his family; and he could give testimony only under torture; yet in religious matters he seems to have enjoyed liberty. The ancient world never escaped the antinomy of regarding the slave as at once a person and a thing. Plato considered him a creature of a lower order of being, only semi-rational, this view perhaps being colored by the fact that most slaves

2. Status and Treatment of Greco-Roman Slaves.

were barbarians; while Cato reckoned slaves as farm implements. Toward the end of the Roman Republic the status and treatment of slaves changed partly under the influence of Greece and the superior culture of the Greek slaves, and partly through the Stoic doctrine of the equality of all men. Hadrian deprived the master of the right to put his slave to death and allowed him to be tried (as he always had been at Athens) in the courts; and Marcus Aurelius even permitted slaves to lodge complaints against their masters in certain cases, while manumission was made increasingly easy. In all this, however, there is no demonstrable trace of either Christian or Jewish influence, the real operative force being that of Greece. At the same time, the ancient world never dreamed of a society without slaves, except as a sort of Utopia or as a reminiscence of the golden age, which the Roman Saturnalia and similar slave festivals in Athens, Cydonia, etc., sought to typify, and the Essenes, Therapeutæ, and such Gnostic sects as that of the Carpocratian Epiphanes to realize.

With such tendencies as these Christianity had nothing in common. It simply accepted slavery as a necessary constituent of ancient civilization, nor is there the slightest evidence that it either condemned slavery as a principle or sought to abolish it. In his parables Christ presupposed the natural relations of master and slave (Matt. xviii. 23 sqq., xxv. 14 sqq.; Mark xiii. 34; Luke xii. 42 sqq., xvii. 7 sqq.); and Paul expressly declared that Christianity made no change in existing conditions, and that he who was a slave ought to remain one, even were freedom offered him (I Cor. vii. 21; cf. also the attitude assumed toward Onesimus in Philemon 16). All the gentile Christian communities contained large numbers of slaves (cf. Rom. xvi. 10–11; I Cor. i. 11; Phil. iv. 22), although these communities were far from consisting predominantly of bondmen. There were also Christian masters, as is clear from the admonitions in Eph. vi. 9; Col. iv. 1; I Tim. vi. 2 (cf. Clement of Alexandria, *Pædagogus*, III., iv. 26, xi. 73, xii. 84; Chrysostom, *Hom.* on I Cor. xl. 6). Of the conditions in Judeo-Christian households little is known (cf. Acts xii. 13). The Apostolic Constitutions (ii. 62) enumerate the purchase of a slave among the necessities of life which justify a Christian in visiting the marketplace; the *Acts of Thomas* represent the apostle as the slave whom Christ sells to a king of India; and Ignatius (*Epist. ad Polycarpum*, iv. 3) discourages the ransom of slaves at the expense of the community (cf. Salvianus, *Ad eccl.*, iii. 7), which seems to have intervened only when a slave's Christianity was endanged. On the other hand, wealthy Christians appear to have bought Christian slaves to manumit them (cf. Hermas, *Shepherd*, "Similitudes," i. 8; Apostolic Constitutions, iv. 9), and cases are also recorded in which Christians voluntarily sold themselves into slavery to aid the poor with their price (cf. I Clement, lv.). But despite external continuity, there was a change of spirit, kindness of masters and fidelity of slaves becoming a matter of Christian principle, instead of personal character, as in paganism (cf. Eph. vi. 5 sqq.; Col. iii. 22 sqq., iv. 1; I Tim. vi. 1–2; Tit. ii. 9–10; Philemon 16; I Pet. ii. 18 sqq; Didache iv. 10–11; Apostolic Constitutions, iv. 12), while Augustine, commenting on Ps. cxxv. 7 (*NPNF*, 1st series, viii. 602), expressly declares: "He (Christ) hath not made men free from being servants, but good servants from bad servants" (cf. *Conf.*, IX., viii. 17). Christians sought, moreover, to save the souls of slaves (Acts. xvi. 16 sqq.; Aristides, *Apol.*, xv.; Augustine, *De sermone Domini in monte*, i. 59). Christianity did even more than this—it gave the slave the status of a man (I Cor. xii. 13; Gal. iii. 28; Col. iii. 11; cf. Irenæus, *Hær.*, IV., xxi. 3; Origen, *Contra Celsum*, iii. 54; Lactantius, *Institutio*, v. 15). It is true that a slave required his master's permission before he could be baptized (Hippolytus, *Canones*, x. 63), but even if this were refused, he could still be an associate member of the congregation; and if he were baptized, he enjoyed the same rights as a freeman. Slaves might take orders, and some, as Calixtus I., even became popes, while many slaves were venerated as martyrs, among them Blandina and Potamiæna (qq.v.). Not only were Christian slaves forbidden to sacrifice for their masters, whether pagan or Christian (Tertullian, *De idolatria*, xvii.; Peter of Alexandria, *Canones*, vi.-vii.), but the new faith energetically combated the vices to which slaves of both sexes had been compelled to minister, besides doing away with execution by crucifixion and the branding of fugitive slaves.

3. Slavery and the Early Church.

The Christian Church, interested only in the faith of the slave, and leaving his legal position entirely to the State, made no attempt to abolish slavery. With the increasing secularization of religious life, the social cleavage between bond and free became wider still, and only the monasteries clung to the concept, based on a commingling of classic Stoicism and early Christianity, of the equal rights and the human status of the slave. It was from the monasteries, indeed, that the revolution with regard to slavery was destined to come. During the imperial period of Rome the importation of slaves had decreased, and they had largely been replaced by *coloni*, or serfs, whose number might include slaves, and more often free peasants. This system, aided by the subjection of the conquered peoples in the new German Empire, persisted in places as late as the eighteenth century; and though the Church took little part in all this, and though she frequently protected the oppressed and even recruited her clergy from the serfs, she herself exercised seigniorial rights and proved unable to exercise a moral influence sufficient to alter conditions. There were, moreover, actual slaves until late in the Middle Ages. Even the Church owned them and vigorously asserted her rights over them; but though the slave might still be bought and sold, and required his master's permission in the most important and personal decisions of life, he enjoyed (as in Greek and later Roman legislation) a limited freedom in regard to rights and property, as well as the protection of the wergild. The Church took these rights under her protection, afforded asylum to those seeking refuge, insisted on humane treatment of slaves, sought to make masters responsible for the morality of their slaves, for-

4. The Medieval Church and Slavery.

bade concubinage with slaves, and secured the freedman against capricious revocation of his liberty, while each parish exercised the right of protection over the freedmen within it. The manumission of slaves, very frequent in pagan time, was carried to an extreme after the conversion of the rich and great in the fourth century. It is clear, however, from the apocryphal acts (e.g., Acts of Peter and Andrew, xx.) that this was not regarded as a Christian duty in behalf of the slaves, but as an act of asceticism on a par with renunciation of property, later coming to form a preliminary to entrance on the monastic life (cf. Augustine, *Sermones*, ccclvi. 3, 6, 7). Manumission was usually formally declared in the church (Sozomen, *Hist. eccl.*, I., ix. 6; *Codex Theodosianus*, iv. 7), and the classic legal fiction of sale or gift to a divinity or temple was also observed by Christians.

5. European Slavery in the Middle Ages.

Unlike the Church, which maintained existing conditions, monasticism assailed slavery and finally, as already implied, overthrew it, the two positions being combined in Gregory the Great, who as a monk praised manumission as a good work, and as pope demanded the most rigid discipline from the slaves belonging to the Church (cf. *Epist.* vi. 12 with ix. 200). Canons of councils, as that held at Agde in 506, forbade bishops or abbots to diminish the property of the Church by manumitting slaves; and in many ways, as by the prohibition against ordaining a slave or receiving him in a monastery without his master's consent, it was clearly shown that slavery was accepted as an institution, the council of Elvira, by its eightieth canon, even excluding the freedmen [of pagans] from holy orders. The monasteries, on the other hand, received slaves as readily as freemen, and, unlike the churches, were not expected to own bondmen. Since, as already noted, the Church was more interested in the slave's Christianity than in the slave himself, frequent prohibitions were enacted, beginning with Constantine, against ownership of Christian slaves by Jews; and the laws against the exportation of slaves from the various Christian lands were closely connected with the prohibition against selling Christian slaves to pagans. Nevertheless, the Jews of Lyons imported large numbers of Christian slaves to Spain and Africa in the reign of Louis the Pious; the Venetians had an equally evil notoriety; and Rome itself was a center of the traffic. The slave-trade increased after the Slavic wars and the Tatar inroads, those sold into bondage being chiefly heathens.

It was only in the twelfth and thirteenth centuries that real slavery disappeared from northwestern Europe, although the system of serfdom long continued. In 1031 Conrad II. forbade all traffic in slaves, and a synod held at London in 1102 repeated the prohibition. In southern Europe, on the other hand, slavery still persisted, aided not only by the constant wars with the Mohammedans, but also by pirate raids. Slavery was made by custom to include Christians, despite the protests of the Church, which herself legalized the system as a punishment for heretics and enemies of the Curia, and made bondmen of the offspring of priests. Latin Crusaders did not hesitate to enslave Christian Greeks, and the revival of Roman law and the reverence in which scholasticism held Aristotle alike combined to maintain the system. At late as 1548 Paul III. confirmed the right of the clergy and laity to hold slaves, although their number was no longer large in Italy. In Spain, on the other hand, there was a regular system of slavery in the old Roman sense until the sixteenth century, the bondmen here being thousands of Moors; while the Portuguese imported negroes direct from Africa after 1441. On the other hand, Christians frequently became slaves of unbelievers, and, the redemption of captives being esteemed a good work from the earliest times (cf. Neh. v. 8; Socrates, *Hist. eccl.*, vii. 21), not only were funds of the Church devoted to this purpose by the council held at Châlons in the middle of the seventh century, but the Order of Mercy (see Nolasco, St. Peter) and Trinitarians (q.v.) were founded with this special object in view.

(E. von Dobschütz.)

6. Slavery in America.

Personal slavery having diminished in Europe in the fourteenth and following centuries (ut sup.), it was revived upon a gigantic scale on this continent shortly after the discovery of America. The scarcity of labor in the New World, and the necessity for it, seem to have overcome all objections to the system, whether founded upon motives of Christian duty or upon economic considerations. All the European nations, Roman Catholic and Protestant, which had colonies in America, engaged in transporting slaves from the coast of Africa to this continent. The result was that more than five millions of human beings were carried from Africa to America between 1579 and 1807, where they and their descendants became slaves. For more than two centuries and a half no voice, either in the Church or out of it, was heard against the slave-trade and its consequences.

7. The Philosophical Attack on Slavery.

About the middle of the eighteenth century, however, two distinct movements arose, one based on philosophical, and the other on Christian, grounds, one confined to France and the other to England. Upon one or the other of them, modern opinion and legislation in regard to negro slavery have been based. The philosophical basis is found in that portion of the celebrated work of Rousseau, *Émile*, called *Profession de foi d'un vicaire savoyard*. The views there laid down made a profound impression upon all writers on the theory of government during the remainder of the century. According to Rousseau, man is a being by nature good, loving justice and order. In an ideal state of society each member would be free, and the equal of every other. These doctrines and the vast system which grew out of them were, for various reasons, embraced with the utmost enthusiasm in France. But the first public official document in which these opinions are clearly set forth was the Declaration of Independence; though in France, the first article of "The Declaration of the Rights of Man and of the Citizen," adopted in 1789 at the beginning of the Revolution, asserts, "Men are born free and equal, and have the same rights." And as a logical result of this declaration, based upon the teaching of Rousseau, the French Convention (Feb. 4, 1794) decreed that negro slavery should be abolished in all the French colonies, and that all men therein should have the rights of French citizens. This was the first act by which any nation in Europe decreed the abolition of slavery.

By the side of these attacks of the French philosophers on slavery as a violation of natural rights, a movement arose about the same time, chiefly in England and in the United States, having the same object in view, but founded upon convictions of Christian duty. Conscience was the impulse to action, and the result was earnest, persistent, and personal work. The African slave-trade was at first the main point of attack by the abolitionists.

8. The Christian Attack; Abolition of Slave-Trade.

In 1772 Granville Sharp urged its suppression on religious grounds. Just before the Revolution, Virginia petitioned that no more African slaves be sent into the colony; a few years later, Thomas Clarkson (q.v.) devoted his life to convincing his countrymen that they should prohibit the slave-trade by law, as violating every principle of Christian humanity. Among the religious denominations which as a body took an active part in this work were the Quakers, who presented to the house of commons a petition for the abolition of the slave-trade in 1784; the Methodists and Presbyterians (see below); [and the Baptists. In 1789 the General Association of the Baptists of Virginia resolved: "That slavery is a violent deprivation of the rights of nature, and inconsistent with a republican government, and (we) therefore recommend to our brethren to make use of every legal measure to extirpate this horrid evil from the land." A. H. N.] By incessant work, and constant agitation of the subject in the press and at public meetings, the little band of abolitionists gained the support of many prominent public men in England, Wilberforce, Pitt, Fox, and Burke among the rest. Such was the feeling roused by the discussion of the subject, and especially the general conviction of the violation of Christian duty in maintaining the traffic, that, forced at last by the outcry of the public conscience, Parliament abolished the slave-trade in 1807. In the United States the foreign slave-trade was prohibited in 1808. Shortly afterward, all the maritime nations of Europe followed the example of England and of this country; and the work was crowned by the declaration of the European Congress of Vienna in 1815, engaging all the powers to discourage the traffic, as one "reproved by the law of religion and of nature"; thus recognizing the two forces, religion and philosophy, which had combined to bring about the result.

In this country the testimony of the Quakers, as a religious body, against slavery had been uniform from the beginning. In 1688 the German Friends residing in Germantown, Pa., petitioned the yearly meeting to take measures against slaveholding. From 1696 to 1776, the society nearly every year declared "the importing, purchase, or sale of slaves" by its members to be a "disownable offense." John Woolman and Anthony Benezet, illustrious as Quaker philanthropists, were the pioneer abolitionists of modern times.

9. Attitude of Religious Bodies.

In 1776 the holding of slaves was prohibited by the discipline of the Society of Friends, and since that time its members have been conspicuous in supporting anti slavery opinions and legislation. The highest judicatory of the Presbyterian Church in this country made formal declaration in favor of the abolition of slavery no less than six times between 1787 and 1836. In 1845 and in 1849 the General Assembly (Old School) in its action, without avowing any change of opinion as to the sinfulness of slavery, dwelt more particularly upon the formidable obstacles to the practical work of emancipation. In 1864, during the Civil War, that body proclaimed openly "the evil and guilt of slavery," and its earnest desire for its extirpation. The Methodist-Episcopal Church has been opposed to slavery from the beginning. At the organization of the general conference in 1784, a general rule of its discipline was adopted, declaring slavery contrary "to the golden law of God and the inalienable rights of mankind," and directing that preachers holding slaves should be expelled. Nevertheless, after 1808 slaveholding among the private members of the society was not made a subject of discipline, though the old rule affirming slavery to be a great evil, and that slaveholding should be a bar to office in the Church, was still unrepealed. The aggressive antislavery sentiment at the North was always very powerful among the Methodists; and in the general conference of 1844 it was strong enough to effect the passage of a resolution by which Bishop Andrew, who had come into the possession of certain slaves in right of his wife, was requested to suspend the exercise of all episcopal functions until the slaves were freed. This led to the disruption of the conference, and the formation of two Methodist-Episcopal churches in this country,—one at the North, and the other at the South. See Methodists, IV., 1, § 5.

Before the war there were, in the northern states, multitudes of Christians of thoroughly antislavery sentiments who took no active part in the abolition movement, because they were restrained by conscientious convictions as to their duties as citizens; but when slavery was made the pretext of rebellion and war against the government, and an attempt was made to found an empire the corner-stone of which was slavery, and especially when the national government had decreed the emancipation of the slaves, every motive for its further toleration was removed. By the victory of the North in the Civil War, the abolition of slavery in the United States was made complete. See Negro Education and Evangelization. C. J. Stillé†.

Bibliography: On slavery in the Bible consult: J. L. Saalschütz, *Archäologie der Hebräer*, ii. 236 sqq., Berlin, 1856; A. Barnes, *An Inquiry into the Scriptural Views of Slavery*, Philadelphia, 1857; M. Mielziner, *Die Verhältnisse der Sklaven bei den alten Hebräer*, Leipsic, 1859, Eng. transl., in *Evangelical Review*, 1862, pp. 311–355; P. Schaff, *Slavery and the Bible*, Mercersburg, 1860; M. J. Raphall, *Bible View of Slavery*, New York, 1861; M. Z. Zahn, *L'Esclavage selon la Bible et le Talmud*, Paris, 1867; P. Kleinert, *Das Deuteronomium und der Deuteronomiker*, pp. 55 sqq., Bielefeld, 1872; A. Grünfeld, *Die Stellung der Sklaven bei den Juden*, Jena, 1886; M. Mandl, *Das Sklavenrecht des*

A. T., Hamburg, 1886; J. Winter, *Die Stellung der Sklaven bei den Juden*, Halle, 1886; J. B. Lightfoot, in his commentary on Philemon, the introduction, 3d ed., London, 1890; T. André, *L'Esclavage chez les anciens Hébreux*, Paris, 1892; A. Bertholet, *Die Stellung der Israeliten und der Juden zu den Fremden*, Freiburg, 1896; J. F. McCurdy, *History, Prophecy, and the Monuments*, ii. 168 sqq., New York, 1896; Benzinger, *Archäologie*, pp. 123–127; *DB*, iv. 461–469; *EB*, iv. 4653–58; *DCG*, ii. 641–642; *JE*, xi. 403–408.

On slavery in Greece and Rome consult: H. Wallon, *Hist. de l'esclavage dans l'antiquité*, new ed., 3 vols., Paris, 1879; J. Marquardt, *Privatleben der Römer*, pp. 135 sqq., 175 sqq., Leipsic, 1886; W. Richter, *Die Sklaverei im griechischen Altertume*, Breslau, 1886; L. Halkin, *Les Esclaves publics chez les romains*, Liége, 1897; M. Schneidewin, *Antike Humanität*, pp. 206 sqq., Berlin, 1897; P. Guiraud, *La Main d'œuvre industrielle dans l'ancienne Grèce*, Paris, 1900.

On the general history of slavery employ: T. Clarkson, *Hist. of the Slave Trade*, London, 1849; É. Levasseur, *Hist. des classes ouvrières en France . . . jusqu'à la révolution*, 2 vols., Paris, 1859; A. Cochin, *L'Abolition de l'esclavage*, 2 vols., Paris, 1862, Eng. transl., *The Results of Slavery*, Boston, 1863, and *The Results of Emancipation*, ib. 1863; J. E. Cairnes, *The Slave Power; its Character, Career, and Probable Designs*, London, 1863; H. Wiskemann, *Die Sklaverei*, Leyden, 1866 (a crowned essay); H. Wilson, *Hist. of the Rise and Fall of the Slave-Power*, 3 vols., Boston, 1872–77; A. Tourmagne, *Hist. de l'esclavage ancien et moderne*, Paris, 1880; A. Ebeling, *Die Sklaverei*, Paderborn, 1889; C. D. Michael, *The Slave and his Champions: Granville Sharp, Thomas Clarkson, W. Wilberforce, Sir Thomas Folwell Buxton*, London, 1891; W. R. B. Brownlow, *Lectures on Slavery and Serfdom in Europe*, London, 1892; J. K. Ingram, *Hist. of Slavery and Serfdom*, London, 1895; C. J. M. Letourneau, *L'Évolution de l'esclavage*, Paris, 1897; H. J. Nieboer, *Slavery as an Industrial System*, The Hague, 1900; W. H. Smith, *A Political Hist. of Slavery*, 2 vols., New York, 1903; W. Stevens, *The Slave in History*, London, 1904.

On the relation of Christianity to slavery consult: E. Biot, *L'Abolition de l'esclavage dans l'occident*, Paris, 1840; J. A. Möhler, in *Gesammelte Schriften*, ii. 54 sqq., Regensburg, 1840; C. Schmidt, *Essay historique sur la société civile dans le monde romain, et sur sa transformation par le christianisme*, Strasburg, 1854; K. J. Hefele, *Beiträge zur Kirchengeschichte*, i. 212 sqq., Tübingen, 1864; A. Rivière, *L'Église et l'esclavage*, Paris, 1864; Overbeck, *Studien zur Geschichte der alten Kirche*, i. 158–230, Schloss Chemnitz, 1875 (on the relation of the early Church to slavery); P. Allard, *Les Esclaves chrétiens depuis les premiers temps de l'église jusqu'à la fin de la domination romaine en occident*, Paris, 1876; W. E. H. Lecky, *Hist. of European Morals*, ii. 66–90, 3d ed., London, 1877; V. Lechler, *Sklaverei und Christenthum*, Leipsic, 1877–78; T. Zahn, *Sklaverei und Christenthum in der alten Welt*, Heidelberg, 1879; idem, *Skizzen aus dem Leben der alten Kirche*, pp. 116–159, Leipsic, 1898; C. L. Brace, *Gesta Christi; or, a Hist. of Human Progress under Christianity*, London and New York, 1882; G. Uhlhorn, *Christian Charity in the Early Church*, Edinburgh, 1883; A. Roettscher, *Die Aufhebung der Sklaverei durch das Christentum*, Frankfort, 1887; R. Knopf, *Das nachapostolische Zeitalter*, pp. 67 sqq., Tübingen, 1905; A. Harnack, *Expansion of Christianity*, new ed., London, 1908; Schaff, *Christian Church*, i. 444–448, ii. 347–354.

On slavery in America consult: A. T. Bledsoe, *An Essay on Liberty and Slavery*, Philadelphia, 1857; G. Haven, *National Sermons*, Boston, 1869; A. G. Haygood, *Our Brother in Black; his Freedom and his Future*, New York, 1881; L. C. Matlack, *Anti-Slavery Struggle and Triumph in the M. E. Church*, New York, 1881; G. W. Williams, *Hist. of the Negro Race in America*, New York, 1882; A. Willey, *Anti-Slavery in State and Nation*, Portland, Me., 1886; J. R. Brackett, *The Negro in Maryland*, Baltimore, 1889; J. S. Bassett, *Slavery and Servitude in . . . North Carolina*, 2 parts, Baltimore, 1896–97; M. S. Locke, *Anti-Slavery in America, 1619–1808*, Cambridge, 1901; J. C. Ballagh, *Hist. of Slavery in Virginia*, Baltimore, 1902.

SLAVIC MISSIONS IN THE UNITED STATES: Missions founded in the interests of evangelism among the Bohemians who had emigrated to the United States, and later extended to include Poles and Hungarian Slovaks. There are already in this country nearly three millions of these people, many of them contiguous, accessible, and responsive to missionary effort. On coming to America multitudes of the Slavic race abandoned the formal adherence which in Europe they had preserved to the Roman Catholic Church, and, finding here unrestricted religious liberty, drifted from religious indifference into every phase of unbelief. The danger to the body politic from the existence of an element of the population with these tendencies, awakened the attention of the thoughtful and religious. The founder of the first mission was Charles Terry Collins (d. Dec. 21, 1883), pastor of Plymouth Congregational Church, Cleveland, Ohio, adjacent to whose parish were living, in 1880, 25,000 of the 250,000 Bohemians then in the United States. He took counsel with Dr. Albert Henry Schauffler (q.v.), then recently returned from service in Bohemia and Moravia, who undertook the conduct of the mission in 1882. Dr. Schauffler's pioneer work in Bohemia, his mastery of the language and of kindred dialects, and his passion for souls amply qualified him to organize and develop this new and important field. He was, moreover, the only American Protestant missionary linguistically qualified to carry on the work. Olivet Chapel, of which he accepted the pastorate, was at first made the center of his labors, but soon proved too distant from the chief Bohemian colony and a new location was secured. The Congregational Churches of the city were interested, and in June, 1883, adopted the work as their own, made an appropriation, and enlisted the aid of the denominational Home Missionary Society. The Bohemian Mission Board of Cleveland, Ohio, was incorporated Mar. 22, 1884, with representatives from each Congregational Church in the city which chose to elect such representatives. Meanwhile, in 1883, Dr. Schauffler had been commissioned by the Home Missionary Society superintendent of Slavic Missions in the United States, and among his duties was included that of surveying the centers of Slavic colonization in the United States with a view to future evangelization. The local mission in Cleveland was carried on in a place secured for it, and services were conducted in Bohemian and English, while a Sunday-school was also instituted. Interdenominational help was secured for the purchase of a lot and the erection of a church on Broadway, in the center of the colony; the building was dedicated Jan. 1, 1885, and was named "Bethlehem" after the church in which John Huss preached in Prague. A church was organized with fifty-nine members on Mar. 28, 1888—the first Bohemian Congregational church in the United States, from which three missions or branches have since been formed, Cyril Mission (1890), Immanuel Mission (1904), and Mizpah (1908), all in Cleveland. This church carries on a dual work with separate membership, pastorate, and services in Bohemian and English.

In accordance with the general duties of the superintendent mentioned above, Chicago was visited, the claims of the fifty thousand Bohemians of that city and vicinity were presented, and a mission organization was effected in 1884 with the assistance of Professor Samuel Ives Curtiss and Deacon C. F. Gates. The Rev. Edwin A. Adams, who had been an associate with Dr. Schauffler in Bohemia, was placed in charge of the Bohemian Mission in Chicago. The result is a church reporting about 200 members, with a Sunday-school having an average attendance of 500. Farther extension of this work appears in the opening of missions to this people at St. Louis (1889), Silver Lake, Minn. (1890), Milwaukee, Wis. (1890), Crete, Neb. (1895), St. Paul, Minn. (1895), and Vining, Iowa (1899). The Presbyterians have missions for the Bohemians at Pittsburg, Pa., and at Wisconsin, South Dakota.

Outside of Cleveland and Chicago, the first Slavic mission was the outgrowth of Polish Sunday-school work maintained chiefly by the First Congregational Church at Detroit, Mich., where in May, 1892, there was formed the first Protestant Polish church in the United States. The second Polish mission was undertaken in a large community contiguous to Bethlehem, Cleveland, Ohio, where Mizpah Chapel was erected in 1893 and work carried on with the concurrent use of four languages, Polish, Bohemian, German, and English. Under Congregational direction Polish missions have been attempted in Toledo, Ohio, Bay City, Mich., and in the states of Massachusetts and Connecticut. Work has also been done by the Baptists at Buffalo, by the Methodists at Baltimore and Detroit, and by the United Presbyterians at Pittsburg. Another interesting and successful work was begun Aug., 1890, at Braddock, Pa., among the Hungarian Slovaks—a Slavic people resident in Hungary prior to the advent of the Magyar—which resulted in 1896 in the organisation of a church with 119 members, and in the rapid extension of Slovak mission work to all the suburbs of Pittsburg, Pa.

Such expansion required additional workers, trained and educated in the Slavic and English languages, for thus far the converts had but a meager education. The Slavic Department of Oberlin Seminary was instituted in 1885, and has since been amply endowed, to educate a sufficient ministerial force; and also The Schauffler Missionary Training School of Cleveland, Ohio, was established (1886)—also endowed—for the training of Slavic women as missionaries and Bible-readers, through whom the homes of the foreign population may be reached, as can not be prudently done by men.

The estimated force (1911) of trained missionary workers is 125, occupying sixty church buildings, in thirteen different states, and working for five different denominations. There are, also, religious papers, published weekly and widely circulated, in Bohemian and Polish. It is everywhere confessed, by those who are opposed, as well as by friends of this work, that these missions have exerted a great and uplifting influence for good morals, good citizenship, and a high ideal of religious life, wherever established. FRANCIS METHERALL WHITLOCK.

BIBLIOGRAPHY: Consult the reports of Dr. Schauffler in *The Home Missionary Magazine*, New York; and the *Reports* of the Congregational Home Missionary Society, 1884 sqq.

SLAVS, CONVERSION OF THE. See CYRIL AND METHODIUS; MIECZYSLAW; and WENZEL, SAINT.

SLEIDANUS, slai-dē'nus, **JOHANNES**: Historiographer of the German Reformation; b. at Schleiden (35 m. s.w. of Cologne) probably in 1506; d. at Strasburg Oct. 31, 1556. His family name was Philippi. He was educated at Liége and apparently at Cologne and Louvain, and by 1530 was an Erasmian humanist, although professing deep admiration for Melanchthon. In 1533 he took up his residence in France, where he occupied a number of positions which brought him into contact with the anti-Hapsburg policy of Francis I., who sought alliance with German Protestantism. During this same period Sleidanus received from the works and personal letters of Calvin an influence which modified his entire outlook on life, and he became deeply interested in the importance of modern history for the statesman. In 1537 he published at Paris his epitome of Froissart's chronicle under the title *Frossardi . . . historiarum opus omne, jam primum et breviter collectum, et Latino sermone redditum* (Eng. transl. by P. Golding, London, 1608), and three years later was secretly commissioned to watch a delegate sent to the diet of Hagenau to prevent an alliance of the Schmalkald League, especially Philip of Hesse, with Charles V. On his return he wrote, under the pseudonym of Baptista Lasdenus, an attack upon the pope entitled *Oration . . . von des Bapstumbs auffkomen und abnemen* (Strasburg [?], 1541), following this with two similar "orations" (Augsburg [?], 1542; Strasburg, 1544). In 1541 Sleidanus was sent as interpreter on a second fruitless mission, this time directly to the leaders of the Schmalkald League. His position was then complicated by the repression of French Protestantism by Francis I., but though he spent some time in Germany, he returned to France, whence, after accompanying Cardinal Jean du Bellay in a vain effort to attend the Diet of Speier in 1544, he was apparently sent on a secret mission to Germany to win the Schmalkald League to alliance with France, thenceforth residing at Strasburg.

Butzer, whose shorter catechism Sleidanus had translated into Latin in 1544, now urged Landgrave Philip to appoint the statesman historiographer of the Reformation, for which he had long been gathering material. The work was delayed, however, by the French war, and in the mean while Sleidanus prepared a Latin translation of Philippe de Comines' chronicle under the title *De rebus gestis Ludovici . . . undecimi, Galliarum regis, et Caroli Burgundiæ ducis* (Strasburg, 1545). In 1545 he was sent on another fruitless mission to England, and this interruption was followed by another French war, but in 1551 he was promised an annual pension by Edward VI. and Cranmer. From the autumn of 1551 to Apr., 1552, he was an envoy at Trent, and took part in an embassy to Henry II., while in May, 1554, he was the representative of Strasburg at a conference held at Naumburg. During all this time he had labored on his history, despite poverty and scanty material, and in 1555 it appeared at Strasburg under the title *De statu religionis et reipublicæ, Carolo Quinto Cæsare, commentarii* (Eng. transl. by J. Daus, *A Famouse Chronicle of oure Time, Called Sleidanes Commentaries*, London, 1560, and E. Bohun, *The General History of the Reforma-*

tion of the Church from the Errors and Corruptions of the Church of Rome, ib., 1689). Storms of protest arose against it on every side, both Roman Catholic and Protestant, and Melanchthon declared that its revelation of Protestant folly and pettiness was such as to render it unfit to be placed in the hands of impressionable youth (*CR*, viii. 483).

The tenure of office of Sleidanus, who had taken an active part in school administration in Strasburg since 1553, expired in June, 1556, and such was the odium excited by his book that no one would now employ him. When, however, a university was founded at Duisburg, his name was proposed for the professorship of history, but before any action could be taken he was dead. A few months before his death he published his *De quatuor summis imperiis, Babylonico, Persico, Græco et Romano, libri tres* (Eng. transl., London, 1627), which ran through repeated editions and translations, being used as late as the eighteenth century. A number of his writings, including the one just mentioned, were collected in his opuscula (ed. H. Putschius, Hanover, 1608), and his correspondence has been edited by H. Baumgarten (*Sleidan's Briefwechsel*, Strasburg, 1881). (G. Kawerau.)

Bibliography: Earlier works are rendered passé by H. Baumgarten's *Ueber Sleidans Leben und Briefwechsel*, Strasburg, 1878, and the *Briefwechsel* of Sleidanus, ib. 1881. Consult further: J. G. Müller, *Aus den Eifelbergen*, Langenberg, 1887; Bourilly, *Jean Sleidan et le Cardinal du Bellay*, in *Bulletin historique et littéraire*, pp. 225 sqq., Paris, 1901; idem, *Guillaume du Bellay*, Paris, 1904; A. Hasenclever, *Sleidan-Studien*, Bonn, 1905; *ADB*, xxxiv. 354 sqq.

SMALLEY, smāl'li, JOHN: Congregationalist; b. in Columbia, Conn., June 4, 1734; d. in New Britain, Conn., June 1, 1820. He was graduated from Yale College, 1756, where he experienced what he described sometimes as his actual, sometimes as his second, conversion, his first having occurred during childhood. This later conversion he attributed to his reading of Edwards' treatise on the Will. Through this he became a leader in the contest against the enthusiasm of the Separates, against the Half-way Covenant, and in defense of the New-England Theology (q.v.).

Having pursued his theological studies with Dr. Joseph Bellamy, he was ordained Apr. 19, 1758, over the Congregational Church in New Britain, Conn. He remained in this pastorate more than fifty-five years, and the marked success of his pastorate is a matter of historical interest. His success as a theological instructor was yet more remarkable. Among his pupils may be named Nathanael Emmons, and Ebenezer Porter (qq.v.), who, as a professor at Andover, exerted a formative influence on the seminary. Four of Smalley's sermons were of great importance. Two were on *The Consistency of the Sinner's Inability* (Hartford, 1769; republished in England). Two were entitled *Justification through Christ an Act of Free Grace*, and *None but Believers saved through the All-Sufficient Satisfaction of Christ* (1786, 1787; repeatedly republished). He also issued two volumes of *Discourses* (1803, 1814).

Bibliography: W. B. Sprague, *Annals of the American Pulpit*, i. 559–565, New York, 1859; W. Walker, in *American Church History Series*, vol. iii. passim, ib. 1894; F. H. Foster, *Genetic Hist. of the New England Theology*, pp. 190–200, 221, Chicago, 1907.

SMARAGDUS, sma-rŏg'dus: The name of several medieval monastic authors.

1. Abbot of St. Mihiel, in the diocese of Verdun, and one of the most distinguished representatives of Frankish theology in the Carolingian period. In 810 he was one of Charlemagne's envoys to bear the resolution of the Synod of Aachen to Leo III., and was secretary in the ensuing negotiations regarding the procession of the Holy Ghost and the liturgical use of the Nicene Creed. Louis the Pious not only gave him many gifts and privileges for his monastery but also made him one of the arbitrators in the controversy between Ismundus, bishop of Milan, and his monks. His works, most of which are collected in *MPL*, cii., reveal considerable patristic learning and much practical piety, but are almost wholly devoid of originality. His chief exegetical work, *Commentarius, sive collectiones in evangelia et epistolas quæ per circuitum anni in templis leguntur*, is a compilation for homiletic use; but his *Expositio, sive commentarii in regulam Sancti Benedicti* reveals him as an adherent of the strict reforms of his contemporary, Benedict of Aniane (q.v.); and a similar tendency is discernible in his compilation of ascetic rules, chiefly from Cassian and Gregory the Great, entitled *Diadema monachorum*. The latter treatise was abridged by Smaragdus for the use of Louis the Pious, the strictly monastic sections being omitted, and the remainder expanded or curtailed as the special theme of this new *Via regia* demanded. He likewise wrote the *Acta collationis Romanæ* and collaborated in the *Epistola Frotharii et Smaragdi ad Ludovicum Augustum*, while he is also held to be the author of the *Epistola Caroli Magni ad Leonem Tertium Pontificem de processu Spiritus Sancti* (*MPL*, xcviii. 923). His *Commentarius in Prophetas* and *Historia Monasterii Sancti Michaelis* are still unedited, but a few fragments of his *Grammatica major, sive commentarius in Donatum* have been published by J. Mabillon (*Vetera analecta*, Paris, 1723, pp. 358–359). This was evidently the earliest of his works, probably written while he was still master of the monastery school (between 800 and 805). [His *Carmina*, ed. E. Dümmler, are in *MGH*, *Poet. Lat ævi Car.*, i. (1881), 607–619, ii. (1884), 698; cf. M. Manitius in *NA*, xi. (1886), 563.]

2. Biographer and successor of Benedict of Aniane; b. 783; d. at Aniane (16 m. w.n.w. of Montpellier) Mar. 7, 843. His real name was Ardo. His *Vita* of his predecessor, an admirable bit of biographical writing, has repeatedly been edited (*ASB*, Feb., ii. 106–620; *MPL*, ciii. 354 sqq.; *MGH*, *Script.*, xv. 098–220, Hanover, 1887).

3. Abbot of a monastery at Lüneburg, Saxony; flourished about 1000. He has been regarded, though without sufficient evidence, as the author of the *Grammatica major* noted above. (O. Zöckler†.)

Bibliography: The prolegomena in *MGH*, *Poet. Lat.*, ut sup., i. 604–607; *Histoire littéraire de la France*, iv. 439–447, 708; B. Hauréau, *Singularités historiques et littéraires*, pp. 100 sqq., Paris, 1861; K. Werner, *Alkuin und sein Jahrhundert*, pp. 25, 317–318, Vienna, 1876; A. Ebert, *Geschichte der Literatur des Mittelalters*, ii. 108–112, Leipsic, 1880; Wattenbach, *DGQ*, i (1893), 326; Werminghoff, in *Historische Zeitschrift*, 1902, pp. 193-213; O. Zöckler, *Die Tugendlehre des Christentums*, pp. 133–134, Gütersloh, 1903; Hauck, *KD*, ii. 113–114, 592–594 et passim; *DCB*, iv. 708–709; *ASB*, sec. iv., i. 589–590; *KL*, xi. 427–428.

SMECTYMNUUS. See CALAMY, 1.

SMEND, schmendt, **JULIUS:** German Protestant; b. at Lengerich (18 m. n.e. of Münster) May 10, 1857. He studied at the universities of Bonn, Halle, and Göttingen from 1876 to 1879 (lic. theol., Bonn, 1884); was assistant pastor at Paderborn (1879–81), Bonn (1882–85), and Siegen (1885); and pastor at Seelscheid (1885–91). He was then professor of practical theology at the seminary for preachers at Friedberg, Hesse (1891–93); and since 1893 has occupied a similar position at the University of Strasburg, where he was rector in 1906–07. In theology he describes himself as a "pupil of Albrecht Ritschl, but does not belong to any party and, with decidedly liberal theological convictions, is devoted as a preacher and teacher to the promotion of ecclesiastical piety." He has been associate editor (with F. Spitta) of the *Monatschrift für Gottesdienst und kirchliche Kunst* since 1897, and has written *Deutsches Liederbuch* (Dortmund, 1892); *Feierstunden* (Göttingen, 1892); *Der erziehliche Wert der Musik* (Dortmund, 1894); *Die evangelischen deutschen Messen bis zu Luthers deutscher Messe* (Göttingen, 1896); *Der erste evangelische Gottesdienst in Strassburg* (Strasburg, 1897); *Der Wert der Todeserinnerung für das innere Leben* (1897); *Kelchversagung und Kelchspendung in der abendländischen Kirche* (Göttingen, 1898); *Das Wesen der evangelischen Frömmigkeit* (Strasburg, 1899); *Feierstunden, neue Folge* (Göttingen, 1901); *Zur Frage der Kultusrede* (Freiburg, 1902); *Der evangelische Gottesdienst, eine Liturgik nach evangelischen Grundsätzen* (Göttingen, 1904); *Kirchenbuch für evangelische Gemeinden* (2 vols., Strasburg, 1906–08); *Schleiermachers politische Predigt* (1906); *Festpredigten* (1908); *Evangelische Predigten* (1910); and *Dem Volke muss die Religion erhalten Werden* (1911).

SMEND, RUDOLF: German Protestant; b. at Lengerich (18 m. n.e. of Münster) Nov. 5, 1851. He was educated at the universities of Göttingen, Berlin, and Bonn (Ph.D. Bonn, 1874), became privat-docent at Halle, 1875; associate professor 1880; professor of theology at Basel, 1881; professor of Old-Testament exegesis in the philosophical faculty of the University of Göttingen, 1889. He has written *Der Prophet Ezekiel Erklärt* (Leipsic, 1880); *Die Inschrift des Königs Mesa von Moab* (Freiburg, 1886; in collaboration with A. Socin); *Lehrbuch der alttestamentlichen Religionswissenschaft* (Freiburg, 1893); *Weisheit des Jesus Sirach, Text und Erklärung* (1906); *Griechisch-syrisch-hebräischer Index zur Weisheit des Jesus Sirach* (Berlin, 1907); and *Alter und Herkunft des Achikar-Romans und sein Verhältniss zu Aesop* (Giessen, 1908).

SMET, smet or smê, **PIERRE JEAN DE:** Jesuit missionary; b. at Termonde (20 m. s.w. of Antwerp), Belgium, Jan. 30, 1801; d. in St. Louis, Mo., May 23, 1873. He left Belgium for the United States at the age of twenty and became a Jesuit novice at Whitemarsh, Md., but in 1823 a new Jesuit settlement was established at Florissant, near St. Louis, whither De Smet went. His influence with the Indians became so strong that he was requested by the United States Government to allay threatened uprisings in Oregon and Washington (1858). Again in 1862 and 1867 he visited hostile tribes, but steadily refused to have any association with American military measures against the Indians. In 1868 he was the prime mover of the treaty of peace signed by Sitting Bull between the Sioux and the United States Government, and two years later he made another visit to the same important tribe. He was unceasing in his efforts to protect the Indians against the encroachments of the Americans, and his religious zeal and piety were commensurate with his humanitarian endeavors. His control over the Indians was marvellous, and in his efforts for the amelioration of their condition he crossed the ocean nineteen times, pleading their cause everywhere. Among his workers special mention may be made of his *Letters and Sketches, with a Narrative of a Year's Residence among the Indian Tribes of the Rocky Mountains* (Philadelphia, 1843); *Oregon Missions and Travels over the Rocky Mountains in 1845–46* (New York, 1847); *Voyage au grand désert en 1851* (Brussels, 1853); *Western Missions and Missionaries* (a series of letters; New York, 1863); and *New Indian Sketches* (1865).

BIBLIOGRAPHY: F. Deynoodt, *P. J. de Smet, missionaire belge aux États Unis*, Brussels, 1878; H. M. Chittenden and A. T. Richardson, *Life, Letters, and Travels of Pierre Jean de Smet, S. J.*, 4 vols., New York, 1905.

SMITH, ALEXANDER COKE: Methodist Episcopal, South, bishop; b. in Sumter Co., S. C., Sept. 16, 1849. He was educated at Wofford College, Spartanburg, S. C. (A.B., 1872), and, after holding various pastorates in his denomination, was professor of mental and moral philosophy in the same institution (1886–90); and of practical theology in Vanderbilt University, Nashville, Tenn. (1890–92), after which he again took up ministerial duties. In 1902 he was elected bishop.

SMITH, ARTHUR HENDERSON: Congregationalist; b. at Vernon, Conn., July 18, 1845. He was educated at Beloit College (A.B., 1867), Andover Theological Seminary (1867–69), Union Theological Seminary, New York (graduated 1870), and the College of Physicians and Surgeons, New York City (1870–71). In 1871–72 he was a missionary at Chicago and Clifton, Ill.; was stationed at Tientsin, China (1872–80) under the auspices of the American Board of Commissioners for Foreign Missions; was at P'ang Chuang, Shantung (1880–90), although in 1886–87 he was acting pastor of the First Congregational Church, Pasadena, Cal. He was in Peking during the siege of the city in 1900, and was then stated supply of Union Church, Tientsin, in 1900–01, after which he returned to P'ang Chuang for four years (1901–05). Since 1906 he has been a "missionary at large" in China, except for a brief visit to the United States, and is now engaged in literary work, speaking and traveling extensively in the interest of missions. In theology he is a liberal conservative, and, besides his work as associate editor of *The Missionary Review of the World*, has written *The Proverbs and Common Sayings of the Chinese* (Shanghai, 1888); *Chinese Characteristics* (Chicago, 1890); *Village Life in China* (1899); *China in Convulsion* (1901); *Rex Christus: An outline Study of China* (New York, 1903); *China and America Today: Study of Conditions and Relations* (1907); and *Uplift of China* (1907).

SMITH, BENJAMIN MOSBY: Presbyterian; b. at Montrose, Powhatan County, Va., June 30, 1811; d. at Petersburg, Va., Mar. 14, 1893. He was graduated at Hampden-Sidney College, Prince Edward County, Va., 1829, and at Union Theological Seminary, Va., 1834; was tutor there, 1834–36; pastor at Danville, Va., 1838–40; at Tinkling Spring and Waynesborough, 1840–45; and at Staunton, 1845–54; and then became professor of oriental and Biblical literature in Union Seminary. From 1858 to 1874 he was with Dr. Dabney pastor of the Hampden-Sidney College Church. He published *A Commentary on the Psalms and Proverbs* (Glasgow, 1859; 3d ed. Knoxville, Tenn., 1883); *Family Religion* (Philadelphia, 1859); *Questions on the Gospels* (vol. i., Richmond, 1868).

SMITH, CHARLES SPENCER: African Methodist Episcopal bishop; b. at Colborne, Ont., Mar. 16, 1852. He was ordained to the ministry of his denomination at the age of twenty; and was a member of the Alabama House of Representatives (1874–76). He then pursued a course of study at Meharry Medical College, Nashville, Tenn. (graduated 1880). In 1882 he founded the Sunday-school Union of the African Methodist Episcopal Church, of which he was secretary and treasurer until 1900, when he was elected bishop. He is presiding bishop of the missions of his denomination in South Africa, having visited the western and southwestern coast of that continent in 1894. He has written *Glimpses of Africa, West and Southwest Coast* (Nashville, 1895).

SMITH, CHARLES WILLIAM: Methodist Episcopal bishop; b. in Jefferson township, Fayette Co., Pa., Jan. 30, 1840. He was educated in the public schools and privately. For twenty-one years (1859–80) he held pastorates in the Centreville circuit, Somerset Co., Pa., Carmichaels, Pa., Bridgeport, Pa., Carson Street, Pittsburg, Uniontown, Pa., Arch Street, Alleghany, Pa., First Church, Canton, O., Smithfield Church, Pittsburg, and First Church, McKeesport, Pa. He was presiding elder of the Pittsburg district, 1880–84, and from 1884 until 1908, when he was elected bishop, was editor of the *Pittsburg Christian Advocate*. He was vice-chairman of the committee that framed the present constitution of his denomination and a member of that which compiled the present hymnal of the Methodist Episcopal Church and the Methodist Episcopal Church, South; and that assisted in organizing the Methodist Church in Japan.

SMITH, DAVID: Presbyterian; b. at Carluke (28 m. s.w. of Edinburgh), Lanarkshire, Scotland, May 21, 1866. He received his education at the academy at Rothesay, Isle of Bute, Glasgow University (M.A., 1887; D.D., 1908), and the Free Church College, Glasgow; was Geo. A. Clark scholar and lecturer in Glasgow University; minister of the United Free Church, Tulliollan, 1894–1907, and of St. Andrew's United Free Church, Blairgowrie, 1907–10; Bruce lecturer in Glasgow United Free College, 1909–10; and was appointed professor of theology in Magee College, Londonderry, 1910. He has written: *The Days of his Flesh: the earthly Life of our Lord and Saviour Jesus Christ* (London, 1905; 8th ed., 1910); *The Pilgrim's Hospice: a little Book on the Holy Communion* (1906); the volume on Matthew's Gospel in *The Westminster New Testament* (1908); *The Face of Jesus* (1908); *A Legend of Bethlehem* (1909); *Man's Need of God* (1910); *A Legend of Jerusalem* (1910); and the Epistles of John in *The Expositor's Greek Testament* (1910).

SMITH, ELI: American missionary and Biblical translator; b. at Northford, Conn., Sept. 15, 1801; d. at Beirut, Syria, Jan. 11, 1857. He was graduated from Yale College, 1821, and from Andover Seminary in 1826, and in May of the same year embarked as a missionary of the American Board to Malta. In 1827 he went to Beirut, and in March, 1830, undertook with Harrison Gray Otis Dwight, under directions from the American Board, a journey through Persia, to get information concerning the Nestorian Christians. The expedition, which lasted a year, resulted in the establishment of a mission among that people. In 1838 he accompanied Edward Robinson in exploring the desert of Sinai. He accompanied the same scholar on his journey in 1852, and contributed materially to the accuracy and discoveries of Robinson's *Researches*. In 1846 he began his translation of the Bible into Arabic, and finished a translation of the entire New Testament, and the Pentateuch, historical books, Isaiah, Jeremiah, and other portions of the Old Testament. He possessed eminent attainments in Arabic, and has a distinguished place in the annals of the American mission at Beirut. He published *Researches of . . . Eli Smith and . . . H. G. O. Dwight in Armenia: including a Journey through Asia Minor and into Georgia and Persia, with a Visit to the Nestorian and Chaldean Christians of Oormiah and Salmas* (2 vols., Boston, 1833; London, 1834).

Bibliography: *Missionary Herald*, 1857, pp. 224–229.

SMITH, GEORGE: Assyriologist; b. at Chelsea (4 m. s.w. of St. Paul's), England, Mar. 26, 1840; d. at Aleppo, Turkey, Aug. 19, 1876. He began life as an engraver; taught himself the oriental languages, and first came into prominence in 1866 by a contribution to the London *Athenæum*, upon the *Tribute of Jehu*, which revealed his studies, assiduously carried on at leisure moments, of the Ninevite sculptures in the British Museum. In 1867 he entered upon his official life at the British Museum, and in 1870 was appointed a senior assistant of the lower section in the department of Egyptian and Oriental antiquities, and from that time stood in the first rank of Assyrian scholars. He made expeditions to Nineveh in 1873 at the expense of the London *Daily Telegraph*, and in 1874 and 1875 on behalf of the British Museum, and obtained immense treasures in cuneiform inscriptions (see ASSYRIA, III., § 7, for his explorations). He published *The Phonetic Values of the Cuneiform Characters* (London, 1871); *The Chaldean Account of the Deluge . . . Reprinted from the Transactions of the Society of Biblical Archæology* (1873); *Assyrian Discoveries; an Account of Explorations and Discoveries on the Site of Nineveh, during 1873 and 1874 . . . with Illustrations* (1875); *The Assyrian Eponym Canon, Containing Translations of the Documents, and an Account of the Evidence, on the Comparative Chronology of the Assyrian and Jewish Kingdoms, from the Death of Solomon to Nebuchadnezzar* (1875); *Ancient History from the Monuments, I., Assyria, II., Babylonia* (2 vols., 1875–77); *The Chaldean Account of Genesis, Containing the Description of the Creation, the Fall of Man, the Deluge, the Tower of Babel, the Times of the Patriarchs, and Nimrod; Babylonian Fables, and Legends of the Gods; from the Cuneiform Inscriptions. With Illustrations* (1876); *History of Sennacherib* (1878). See ASSYRIA, III., § 7.

BIBLIOGRAPHY: A. H. Sayce, in *Nature*, Sept. 14, 1876; *TSBA*, vols. i.–v.; R. W. Rogers, *Hist. of Babylonia and Assyria*, vol. i., New York, 1900; H. V. Hilprecht, *Explorations in Bible Lands*, Philadelphia, 1903; *DNB*, liii. 39–41.

SMITH, GEORGE ADAM: United Free Church of Scotland; b. at Calcutta, India, Oct. 19, 1856. He was educated at Edinburgh University (1873–1875; M.A., 1875) and New College, Edinburgh (1875–78), and the universities of Tübingen (1876) and Leipsic (1877). He then traveled in Egypt and Syria, and in 1880 became assistant minister at the West Free Church, Brechin, also being tutor in Hebrew in the Free Church College at Aberdeen in 1880–82. From 1882 to 1892 he was minister of Queen's Cross Free Church, Aberdeen; became professor of Old-Testament language, literature, and theology in the United Free Church College, Glasgow, in 1892; and principal of Aberdeen University in 1909. He has traveled extensively in Palestine, and was Percy Turnbull Lecturer on Hebrew poetry at Johns Hopkins in 1896, Lyman Beecher Lecturer at Yale in 1899, and Jowett Lecturer in London in 1900. He has written *Book of Isaiah* (2 vols., London, 1888–90); *The Preaching of the Old Testament to the Age* (1893); *Historical Geography of the Holy Land* (1894); *Book of the Twelve Prophets, commonly Called the Minor* (2 vols., 1896–97); *Life of Henry Drummond* (1898); *Modern Criticism and the Preaching of the Old Testament* (Lyman Beecher lectures; 1901); *Forgiveness of Sins, and Other Sermons* (1904); and *Jerusalem: The Topography, Economics, and History from the Earliest Times to A.D. 70* (2 vols., 1908).

SMITH, GEORGE VANCE: English Unitarian; b. at Portarlington (40 m. w.s.w. of Dublin), Ireland, June 13, 1816; d. at Bowdon (25 m. e. of Liverpool), England, Feb. 28, 1902. He was educated in Manchester New College, York, 1836–41, and London University (B.A., 1841); was minister at Bradford, Yorkshire, 1841–43, and Macclesfield, 1843–46; theological tutor in Manchester New College, Manchester and London, 1846–57; minister at York, 1858–1875; at the Upper Chapel, Sheffield, 1875–76; and from 1876 was principal of Carmarthen Presbyterian College, Wales. He was one of the New Testament revisers from the formation of the committee in 1870. A "liberal Christian," unfettered by subscription to theological creeds, he was the author of *The Prophecies Relating to Nineveh and the Assyrians, Translated from the Hebrew, with Historical Introductions and Notes, Exhibiting the Principal Results of the Recent Discoveries* (London, 1857); *Eternal Punishment, a Tract for the Times: with Remarks on Dr. Pusey's Defence of the Doctrine* (1865); *The Bible and Popular Theology: A Re-statement of Truths and Principles, with special Reference to recent Works of Dr. Liddon, Lord Hatherley, the Right Hon. W. E. Gladstone, and Others* (1871); *The Spirit and the Word of Christ, and Their Permanent Lessons* (1874); *The Prophets and Their Interpreters* (1878); *Texts and Margins of the Revised New Testament Affecting Theological Doctrine briefly Reviewed* (1881); *The Bible and its Theology as popularly Taught* (1892); and one of the authors of *The Holy Scriptures of the Old Covenant, in a New Translation* (1859).

SMITH, HASKETT: Church of England; b. in London July 16, 1847; d. at Chorley Wood (20 m. s.e. of Hertford), Hertfordshire, Jan. 12, 1906. He was educated at Christ's College, Cambridge (B.A., 1870); was ordered deacon in 1870 and ordained priest in the following year; was curate of Canwick in 1870–72; and of St. Mary Magdalene, Lincoln, 1872–75; second master of Lincoln Grammar School, 1870–75; and rector of Brauncewell-cum-Anwick, Lincolnshire, 1875–99, although he resided for several years on Mount Carmel and traveled extensively, spending also two years in the United States, when he was in charge of All Saints', Pasadena, Cal., 1898–1900. In 1900 he took charge of Ballarat Cathedral, Australia. In theology he was a Broad-churchman. He wrote *The Divine Epiphany, in Ten Progressive Scenes* (London, 1878); *The Lord's Prayer: A Series of short meditative Addresses* (1885); *For God and Humanity: A Romance of Mount Carmel* (3 vols., Edinburgh, 1891); *Handbook for Travellers in Syria and Palestine* (London, 1892); *Guide to the Mediterranean* (1900); and *Patrollers of Palestine* (1906).

SMITH, HENRY: Puritan; b. at Withcote (12 m. e. of Leicester) c. 1550; d. at Husbands Bosworth (13 m. s.s.e. of Leicester), buried there July 4, 1591. His father was wealthy and his connections were aristocratic. His education was received at Oxford (B.A., 1578–79), and he became a Puritan while an undergraduate. He had conscientious scruples against taking a pastoral charge and so ministered in other ways, first in Husbands Bosworth, and from 1587 to 1590 in London where he was "lecturer" at St. Clement Danes. Ill-health compelled his resignation and he returned to the country to die. He made a great reputation for himself as a preacher, winning the sobriquet of "silver-tongued." His sermons were taken down in shorthand and printed at first without his knowledge, but before his death he made a collection of them and gave them his revision. They passed through at least seventeen editions, but the modern reader finds them less interesting than he expects. They are, however, good reading. Perhaps enough are given in *The Sermons of Henry Smith, the Silver-Tongued Preacher*, a selection edited by John Brown, London, 1909. He wrote also Latin poetry, and some has been translated.

Bibliography: There is a *Memoir* by Thomas Fuller in an edition of *Sermons*, London, 1675, new ed., 2 vols., 1866. Consult further *DNB*, liii. 48–49, where references are given to scattering notices.

SMITH, HENRY BOYNTON: American theologian; b. in Portland, Me., Nov. 21, 1815; d. in New York Feb. 7, 1877. He was graduated from Bowdoin College in 1834; studied theology at Andover and Bangor, and then spent a year as tutor in Greek and as librarian at Bowdoin. Late in 1837 he went abroad on account of ill-health, and passed the winter in Paris, hearing lectures at the Sorbonne, at the Institute, and at the Royal Academy. The next two years were spent chiefly at Halle and Berlin. After a short visit to England, he returned home in the summer of 1840, and was at once licensed to preach. But his health again gave way, delaying his settlement until the close of 1842, when he was ordained as pastor of the Congregational Church at West Amesbury, Mass. Here he labored four years, supplying also during two winters the chair of Hebrew at Andover. In 1847 he became professor of mental and moral philosophy in Amherst College, and in 1850 of church history in Union Theological Seminary, New York City. Three years later he was transferred to the chair of systematic theology. In both departments he wrought with the hand of a master, and, alike by his teaching and his writings, won a commanding position as one of the foremost scholars and divines of the country. His influence was soon felt throughout the Presbyterian Church and was especially powerful in shaping opinion in the New School branch of it, to which he belonged. He was sole editor of *The New-York Evangelist*, and joint editor of *The American Theological Review*, *The American Presbyterian and Theological Review*, and, later, *The Presbyterian Quarterly and Princeton Review*. In 1859 he published *Tables of Church History*, a work embodying the results of vast labor. He took a leading part in the memorable Union Convention at Philadelphia in 1867. During the war he wrote very ably in support of the national cause. In 1859 he revisited Europe, also in 1866, and again in 1869; the latter visit, lasting a year and a half, included a journey to the East. After his return he resumed his labors in the seminary, but with health so greatly enfeebled that early in 1874 he resigned his chair and was made professor emeritus.

Whether regarded as a theologian, as a philosophical thinker, or as a general scholar and critic, Smith was one of the most accomplished men of his time. He was specially gifted as a theological teacher, arousing enthusiasm in his students, inspiring them with reverence for the Holy Scriptures, fostering in them a devout, earnest, catholic spirit, dealing gently and wisely with their doubts, and impressing upon them continually, alike by example and instruction, the sovereign claims of their Redeemer, the glory of his kingdom, and the blessedness of a life consecrated to him. His services to the Union Theological Seminary were varied and inestimable. The Presbyterian Church in the United States also owes him a lasting debt of gratitude. He has been called "the hero of re-union," and no man better merited the praise. Most of his essays and reviews are embraced in his *Faith and Philosophy* (ed. G. L. Prentiss, New York, 1877); his *Lectures on Apologetics* (ed. W. S. Karr) appeared in 1882, New York. He was also the author of *Introduction to Christian Theology: 1: A general Introduction; 2: The special Introduction; or, the Prolegomena of systematic Theology* (ed. W. S. Karr, 1883); and *System of Christian Theology* (ed. W. S. Karr, 1884).

Bibliography: Mrs. H. B. Smith, *Henry Boynton Smith, his Life and his Work*, New York, 1880; L. F. Stearns, *Henry Boynton Smith*, Boston, 1892; G. L. Prentiss, *Union Theological Seminary in . . . New York; historical and biographical Sketches*, New York, 1889; idem, *Union Theological Seminary, . . . Another Decade of its History*, Asbury Park, 1899.

SMITH, HENRY GOODWIN: Presbyterian, son of the preceding; b. in New York City Jan. 8, 1860. He was educated at Amherst College (A.B., 1881) and at Union Theological Seminary, New York (1884). He was pastor of the Presbyterian church at Freehold, N. J. (1886–96), and, after studying in Europe in 1896–97, was appointed professor of systematic theology in Lane Theological Seminary, Cincinnati, O., a position which he retained until 1903, when he retired from active life.

SMITH, HENRY PRESERVED: Congregationalist; b. at Troy, O., Oct. 23, 1847. He was educated at Marietta College, Amherst College (A.B., 1869), Lane Theological Seminary (1872), and the universities of Berlin (1872–74) and Leipsic (1876–1877). He was instructor in church history at Lane Theological Seminary (1874–75), and in Hebrew (1875–76); professor of Hebrew and Old-Testament exegesis in the same institution (1877–93). From 1898 to 1906 he was professor of Biblical literature at Amherst College (1898–1906); and professor of Hebrew language and literature at Meadville Theological School, Meadville, Pa., since 1907. In theology he affirms his "belief in religion as the life of God in the human soul, and in the Christian religion as the fullest measure of that life, mediated through Jesus Christ." In 1875 he was ordained to the Presbyterian ministry, but was suspended for alleged "heretical" teaching by the Presbytery of Cincinnati in 1893. Six years later he was received into the Congregational ministry by the Hampshire Association. He has written *Biblical Scholarship and Inspiration* (in collaboration with L. J. Evans; Cincinnati, 1891); *Inspiration and Inerrancy* (1893); *The Bible and Islam* (New York, 1896); *Critical Commentary on the Books of Samuel* (1899); and *Old-Testament History* (1904).

SMITH, ISAAC GREGORY: Church of England; b. at Manchester Nov. 21, 1826. He was educated at Trinity College, Oxford (B.A., 1849), and was fellow of Brasenose College, Oxford, from 1850 to 1855. He was ordered deacon in 1853 and ordained priest in the following year. He was rector of Tedstone-Delamere (1854–72); vicar of Great Malvern (1872–96), and rector of Great Shefford (1896–1904), when he retired from active life. He was prebendary of Pratum Minus in Hereford Cathedral (1870–87), rural dean of Powick (1882–96), examining chaplain to the bishop of St. David's (1882–97), and honorary canon of Worcester (1887–96), and Bampton lecturer in 1873. He has written *Life of Our Blessed Saviour* (London, 1864); *Faith and Philosophy* (1867); *The Characteristics of Christianity* (Bampton lectures; 1873); *History of the Diocese of Worcester* (in collaboration with P. Onslow; 1883); *History of Christian Monasticism* (1892); *Boniface* (1896); *The Holy Days* (poems; 1900); *The Athanasian Creed* (1902); *What is Truth?* (1905); and *Thoughts on Religion* (2 series, 1909).

SMITH, JAMES ALLAN: Church of England; b. at Pyecombe, Sussex, Aug. 2, 1841. He was educated at Wadham College, Oxford (B.A., 1863), and was ordered deacon in 1864 and ordained priest in 1865. He was curate of Holy Trinity, Marylebone, 1864–66; lecturer of Boston, Lincolnshire, 1866–70; vicar of Holy Trinity, Nottingham, 1870–84; and vicar of Swansea in 1884–1902 and of Hay in 1902–1903; prebendary of Sanctæ Crucis in Lincoln Cathedral in 1875–97, and chancellor and canon residentiary of St. David's Cathedral in 1897–1903; became dean 1903; chaplain to the bishop of St. David's, 1897.

SMITH, JOHN: Founder of the General Baptists. See SMYTH, JOHN.

SMITH, JOHN: One of the leaders of the school of seventeenth-century philosophers known as the "Cambridge Platonists" (q.v.); b. at Achurch (14 m. s.w. of Peterborough), Northamptonshire, 1616; d. at Cambridge Aug. 7, 1652. He studied at Emmanuel College, Cambridge (B.A., 1640; M.A., 1644, in which year he was chosen fellow of Queen's). He seems to have shown something of Whichcote's marvellous power as a teacher, and to have been of pure and lofty character; but he left behind him nothing except the *Select Discourses* (ed., with *Memoir*, J. Worthington, London, 1660), which are animated by the breath of a high, divine reason, and show a logic almost as keen and direct as Chillingworth's, and an imagination as rich as Jeremy Taylor's. Taken together, they form the first part of a scheme of thought which Smith did not live to finish. The opening discourse, "Of the True Way or Method of Attaining to Divine Knowledge," gives the keynote of his system, and shows how he attempted to draw up a scheme of speculative, and Platonic, philosophy. Having defined the mode of attaining the divine, and distinguished it from atheism on one side and superstition on the other, he proceeds to expound its main principles, immortality and God, to which he intended to add "the communication of God to mankind through Christ.

BIBLIOGRAPHY. Besides the memoir in the *Select Discourses*, ut sup., consult: W. M. Metcalfe, *Natural Truth of Christianity*, Paisley, 1880; J. Tulloch, *Rational Theology and Christian Philosophy in England in the 17th Century*, ii. 117–192, Edinburgh, 1882; E. T. Campagnac, *The Cambridge Platonists*, Oxford, 1901; E. George, *Seventeenth Century Men of Latitude: Forerunners of the New Theology*, New York, 1908; *DNB*, liii. 74–75; and in general the literature under CAMBRIDGE PLATONISTS.

SMITH, JOHN PYE: English Independent; b. at Sheffield May 25, 1774; d. at Guildford (17 m. s.w. of London) Feb. 5, 1851. He had no regular schooling, but read omnivorously in his father's book-shop, and in 1796, on the expiration of his apprenticeship, studied theology at Rotherham Academy until 1800, when he was appointed resident tutor at Homerton College, London. Six years later he was promoted to a theological tutorship, which he retained until shortly before his death. As tutor he lectured on the New Testament, Hebrew grammar, logic, rhetoric, mathematics, and, in his later years, on science. He was essentially a man of industry, versatility, and piety rather than of brilliancy or depth, yet he made a profound impression on the theological thought of his time by his *Scripture Testimony to the Messiah* (2 vols., London, 1818–21; a valuable defense of Trinitarianism against Unitarianism) and *Relation between the Holy Scripture and some Parts of Geological Science* (1839). He was likewise the author, among other works, of *The Reasons of the Protestant Religion* (London, 1815); *Four Discourses on the Sacrifice and Priesthood of Jesus Christ, and on Atonement and Redemption* (1828); *On the Principles of Interpretation as applied to the Prophecies of Holy Scripture* (1829); *Scripture and Theology* (1839); and the posthumous *First Lines of Christian Theology* (1854).

BIBLIOGRAPHY: J. Medway, *Memoirs of the Life and Writings of John Pye Smith*, London, 1853; *DNB*, liii. 86–87.

SMITH, JOHN TALBOT: Roman Catholic; b. at Saratoga, N. Y., Sept. 22, 1855. He was educated at the Cathedral School, Albany, N. Y., and at St. Michael's College, Toronto (1874–81). After being a missionary in the Adirondacks from 1881 to 1889, he was editor of the *New York Catholic Review* from 1889 to 1892. Since 1900 he has been a trustee of the Catholic Summer School, and president since 1905. He has written *A Woman of Culture* (New York, 1881); *Solitary Island* (1884); *His Honor, the Mayor* (1891); *Saranac* (1893); *The Training of a Priest* (1896); *The Chaplain's Sermons* (1896); *Brother Azarias* (1897); *Lenten Sermons* (1899); *The Man who Vanished* (1902); *The Closed Road* (1904); and *History of the Catholics of New York* (3 vols., 1905).

SMITH, JOSEPH. See MORMONS.

SMITH, JOSEPH FIELDING: Mormon; b. at Far West, Mo., Nov. 13, 1838. At the age of ten, he went to Salt Lake with the other Mormons expelled from Nauvoo, and for six years (1848–54) was a herdsman, harvester, and woodsman in Utah. In 1854 he was sent as a Mormon missionary to Hawaii, where he remained until 1858, returning to be sergeant at arms of the territorial legislature (1858–59). In 1858 he was made a high priest and a member of the high council, and in 1860 was a missionary to England, also visiting Denmark and Paris in 1862. He again visited Hawaii in 1864, where he was in charge of the Mormon missionaries, but was recalled and was associated with the church historian's office, and engaged in home missionary work, until 1866, when he was ordained an apostle, being also elected a member of the city council of Salt Lake City and of the territorial legislature in the same year. In 1867 he was made one of the council of twelve, but in 1868 removed to Provo, Utah, returning, however, to resume his work in the historian's office. Appointed director of all the Mormon missions in Europe, he made a tour of England, Scandinavia, Germany, France, and Switzerland in 1874, and again visited Europe in 1877. He was recalled by the death of Brigham Young, but made a short mission to the eastern states in the same year, after which he was in charge of the endowment house at Salt Lake City until it was closed in 1884. In 1880 he was appointed second counselor to President John Taylor, and in 1882 was also president of the council of the Utah legislature, as well as president of the Utah constitutional convention. He was continued in his position of second counselor by President Wilford Woodruff, and, on the death of Lorenzo Snow in 1901, succeeded him as president of the Mormon Church, which dignity he still holds.

SMITH, JUDSON: Congregationalist; b. at Middlefield, Mass., June 28, 1837; d. at Roxbury, Mass., June 29, 1906. He was graduated from Amherst College (A.B., 1859) and from Oberlin Theological Seminary, Oberlin, O. (1863). He was tutor in Latin and Greek in Oberlin College (1862–1864); instructor in mathematics and metaphysics at Williston Seminary, Easthampton, Mass. (1864–1866), and was ordained to the ministry (1866). He was professor of Latin in Oberlin College (1866–70), and of ecclesiastical history and positive institutions in the Oberlin Theological Seminary (1870–84), also serving as dean of the faculty; lecturer in modern history at Oberlin College (1875–84), as well as at the Lake Erie Female Seminary, Painesville, O. (1870–84); and lecturer on foreign missions in the Hartford Theological Seminary from 1884 till his death. He was acting pastor at the Second Congregational Church at Oberlin in 1874–75 and again in 1882–84. In 1883–84 he was editor of *Bibliotheca Sacra*, on which he continued to serve as associate editor. After 1884 he was foreign secretary of the American Board of Commissioners for Foreign Missions. His theological standpoint was that of the New England theology, holding fast to the historic faith of Christendom, but welcoming all new light that broke forth from the Word of God. He was the author of *Lectures in Church History and the History of Doctrine from the Beginning of the Christian Era to 1648* (Oberlin, O., 1881), and *Lectures in Modern History* (1881).

SMITH, RODNEY ("GIPSY SMITH"): Methodist evangelist; b. at Wanstead (6 m. n.e. of London), Essex, England, Mar. 31, 1860. He is of Gipsy parentage, and was converted at the age of sixteen. In 1877 he became an evangelist under the auspices of the Christian Mission of London, and preached successfully in various places, particularly at Whitby, Sheffield, Bolton, Chatham, Hull, Derby, and Hanley. Meanwhile, the Christian Mission had developed into the Salvation Army (q.v.), and in 1882 Smith was dismissed for a technical breach of discipline. He continued to preach in Hanley, however, but in 1883, after conducting evangelistic services for a time at Hull, made a brief visit to Sweden. Returning to Hanley, he remained there until 1886 when he resigned to resume evangelistic work, being engaged in these labors until the end of 1888. Early in 1889 he visited the United States, conducting services in various cities, returning to England later in the same year and becoming connected with the Manchester Mission. In 1891 he again visited the United States. In 1892 he conducted services in Edinburgh, and from this grew the Gipsy Gospel Wagon Mission, devoted to evangelistic work among his own people. He visited America for the third time in 1893. After a five months' revival in Glasgow in 1893–94, Smith went to Australia, preaching at Adelaide, Melbourne, and Sydney, after which he returned to England by way of the United States. In 1895 he preached in London, Manchester, Edinburgh, as well as in many smaller cities, and in 1896 paid his fifth visit to America, returning to England and conducting brief evangelistic campaigns until 1897, when he became first missioner of the National Free Church Council. This position he still retains, and in this capacity he has conducted revivals throughout England, besides paying still another visit to the United States in 1907.

Bibliography: *Gipsy Smith, his Life and Work* (autobiography), new ed., New York, 1907.

SMITH, SAMUEL FRANCIS: American Baptist; b. in Boston, Mass., Oct. 21, 1808; d. there Nov. 16, 1895. He attended the Boston Latin School 1820–25; was graduated from Harvard University, Cambridge, Mass., 1829, and from Andover Theological Seminary, Mass., 1832; was pastor of the First Baptist Church, Waterville, Me., 1834–42, and during the same period professor of modern languages in Waterville College; pastor of the First Baptist Church, Newton, Mass., 1842–54; and editor of *The Christian Review*, Boston, 1842–48, and of the publications of the American Baptist Missionary Union, 1854–69. Though his fame rests upon the authorship of the hymn "My country, 'tis of thee" (written at Andover, Mass., in Feb., 1832, while a student in the theological seminary), and the missionary hymn "The morning light is breaking" (written in the same year and place), he wrote many other hymns. Most of the pieces included in Lowell Mason's *Juvenile Lyre* (Boston, 1832), the first book of children's music, were his translations from the German. He edited *Lyric Gems*, being selections of poetry, with several original pieces (Boston, 1843); and in collaboration with Baron Stow *The Psalmist* (1843) which contained twenty-seven of his own hymns, and is the most creditable and influential of the American Baptist collections of its period; also *Rock of Ages*, being selections of poetry, with some original pieces (1866); and he was the author of *Life of Rev. Joseph Grafton* (1848); *Missionary Sketches* (1879); *History of Newton, Mass., Town and City from its Earliest Settlement to the Present Time* (1880); and *Rambles in Mission-fields* (1884).

Bibliography: S. W. Duffield, *English Hymns*, p. 380, New York, 1886; Julian, *Hymnology*, pp. 1063–64.

SMITH, SAMUEL STANHOPE: American Presbyterian; b. at Pequea, Lancaster County, Pa., Mar. 16, 1750; d. at Princeton, N. J., Aug. 21, 1819. He was graduated from Princeton College, 1767;

was tutor there, 1770-73; first president of Hampden Sidney College, 1775; became professor of moral philosophy at Princeton College in 1779; and was president, 1794-1812. In 1786 he was a member of the committee which drew up the *Form of Government* of the Presbyterian Church. He had a high reputation as a pulpit orator and college president. He published *Sermons* (Newark, N. J., 1799); *Lectures on the Evidences of the Christian Religion*, (Philadelphia, 1809); *Lectures . . . on . . . Moral and Political Philosophy* (Trenton, N. J., 1812); *Principles of Natural and Revealed Religion* (New Brunswick, N. J., 1815); (posthumous) *Sermons*, with *Memoir* (2 vols., Philadelphia, 1821).

BIBLIOGRAPHY: W. B. Sprague, *Annals of the American Pulpit*, iii. 335-345, New York, 1858; I. W. Riley, *American Philosophy; the early Schools*, pp. 497-509, ib. 1907.

SMITH, SYDNEY: Church of England; b. at Woodford (7 m. n.e. of Charing Cross), London, June 3, 1771; d. in London Feb. 22, 1845. He was graduated from Oxford, 1792; took holy orders, 1794; was minister of Charlotte Episcopal chapel, Edinburgh, 1797-1802; canon of Bristol, 1828; and canon residentiary of St. Paul's, 1831. He was one of the most famous of English wits; but he was also a forcible, earnest preacher, and a sagacious critic and reviewer. He was the real founder of *The Edinburgh Review* (1802 sqq.) and wrote for it some eighty articles which are among the best that appeared during the first twenty-five years of its publication. Besides his *Sermons* (2 vols., London, 1809) he published *Peter Plumley's Letters, and Selected Essays* (1886), which did much to promote Roman Catholic emancipation; *Sermons Preached at St. Paul's Cathedral, The Foundling Hospital, and Several Churches in London, together with Others Addressed to a Country Congregation* (1846); *Elementary Sketches of Moral Philosophy* (1850); and in 1848 appeared the fourth edition of his works in 3 vols.

BIBLIOGRAPHY: Lady Holland (his daughter), *A Memoir of the Rev. Sydney Smith. With a Selection from his Letters*, ed. Mrs. Austin, London, 1855; S. J. Reid, *Sketch of the Life and Times of . . . Sydney Smith*, ib. 1884; A. Chevrillon, *Sydney Smith et la renaissance des idées libérales en Angleterre au xix. siècle*, Paris, 1894; *DNB*, liii. 119-123.

SMITH, THOMAS: Free Church of Scotland; b. at Symington (31 m. s.e. of Glasgow), Lanarkshire, July 8, 1817; d. at Edinburgh May 23, 1906. He was educated at the University of Edinburgh, and in 1839 was ordained a missionary to Calcutta. Until 1858 he was engaged chiefly in teaching in the General Assembly's Institution and after 1843, when he joined the Free Church, in the institute of the latter denomination. He was long an associate editor of the *Calcutta Christian Observer*, and for ten years edited the *Calcutta Review*. For a short time during the Mutiny he was chaplain of the Black Watch, and it is especially noteworthy that he was the first to organize the system of zenana missions in India. In 1858 he returned to Scotland; was minister of Cowgatehead Free Church, Edinburgh (1859-80); and professor of evangelistic theology in New College, Edinburgh (1880-93). He wrote *Mediæval Missions* (Edinburgh, 1880); *Anselm of Canterbury* (1882); *Alexander Duff* (London, 1883); *Memoirs of James Begg* (2 vols., Edinburgh, 1885-88); and *Euclid, his Life and System* (1902); translated the Clementine Recognitions for the *Ante-Nicene Fathers* (Edinburgh, 1867) and G. Warneck's *Modern Missions and Culture* (1883); and edited the letters of S. Rutherford (1881).

SMITH, WILLIAM ANDREW: Methodist Episcopal, South; b. at Fredericksburg, Va., Nov. 29, 1802; d. at Richmond, Va., Mar. 1, 1870. He professed religion at seventeen years of age, prepared for the ministry, and was admitted into the Virginia Conference in 1825. In 1833 he was appointed agent for Randolph-Macon College, then in its infancy. He then filled many of the most important stations in his conference until 1846, when he was called to the presidency of Randolph-Macon College. This position, as well as that of professor of mental and moral philosophy, he filled with great acceptability and efficiency until 1866, when he moved to St. Louis, Mo. After serving here as pastor of Centenary Church for two years, he became president of Central College, located at Fayette in that state. At the eventful general conference of 1844 he took a specially prominent part; and in the celebrated appeal of Rev. Francis A. Harding, and in the extra-judicial trial of Bishop James Osgood Andrew, he won a national reputation for deliberative and forensic eloquence and for rare powers of argument and debate. He was a hard student and an earnest thinker. The vigor and clearness of his intellect, his candor, independence, energy, and unquestioned ability, caused him to stand in the front rank of the leading minds in the Methodist-Episcopal Church, South. His *Philosophy and Practice of Slavery* (Nashville, 1857) attracted wide attention as one of the ablest presentations of the southern side of the slavery question ever published.

BIBLIOGRAPHY: A biographical sketch by Bishop J. C. Granbery is embodied in the *Minutes* of the denomination for 1870.

SMITH, WILLIAM ROBERTSON: English critical theologian and Semitic scholar; b. at New Farm, near Keig (22 m. n.w. of Aberdeen), Aberdeenshire, Nov. 8, 1846; d. at Cambridge Mar. 31, 1894. He was educated by his father and at Aberdeen

Life.

University (1861-65), New College (the Free Church theological hall), Edinburgh (1866-70), and the universities of Bonn and Göttingen (summers of 1867 and 1869), while in 1868-70 he was also assistant to the professor of natural philosophy in Edinburgh University. In 1870 he was appointed professor of oriental languages and Old-Testament exegesis in the Free Church College at Aberdeen, and five years later he became a member of the Old-Testament revision company. It was during this period that a crisis occurred in Smith's career when he was invited to prepare articles on Old-Testament criticism for the ninth edition of the *Encyclopædia Britannica*. The very first articles ("Angel" and "Bible") aroused a storm of protest, and on the unfavorable report of an investigating committee, in 1877, Smith demanded formal trial. His activity as a teacher practically ended in the following year; his entire series of articles for the encyclopedia were held to impair belief in the inspiration of the Scriptures; and in 1881 he was suspended from his professorship. He had meanwhile delivered at Edinburgh and Glasgow two series of lectures which were published as *The Old Testament in the Jewish Church* (Edinburgh, 1881) and *The Prophets of Israel* (1882). In 1881 he was invited to become editor in chief of the *Encyclopædia Britannica*, to which he had continued to contribute, and for which, besides his editorial duties, he now prepared a series of additional articles. He did not, however, permit his Semitic studies to languish, but spent the winter of 1879–80 in Egypt (also visiting Syria and Palestine) and the following year in Egypt and Arabia. In 1883 he was appointed to the Lord Almoner's professorship of Arabic at Cambridge, where he was elected a fellow of Christ's College in 1885, and in 1886–89 he was chief librarian of the university. In the latter year he was chosen Adams professor of Arabic, a dignity which he held until his death. In 1888–91 he had been Burnett Lecturer in Aberdeen, the three courses being the religious institutions of the Semites, their religious beliefs, and the historic significance and influence of their religion. Failing health, however, forbade him to publish more than the first series, *Lectures on the Religion of the Semites: Fundamental Institutions* (Edinburgh, 1889).

Smith maintained that Semitic religious concepts were common to all primitive peoples, and that these concepts were to be deduced from the data of known popular religions, the outworking of this theory being best seen in his *Kinship and Marriage in Early Arabia* (Cambridge, 1885) and in his *Religion of the Semites*. It was, indeed, in these two books that his scientific work reached its acme. His study of primitive Arab life, both as recorded in literature and as observed at the present day, led him to identify it, in all essentials, with that of the early Semites as a whole. As the basis of the most primitive Arab social organization he assumed matriarchy, with exogamous polyandry and a totemistic clan system, and for this he sought parallels among the Hebrews and Arameans. His underlying ethnological theories, however, need much investigation and revision, and his comparative method, operating with analogies, often gives his hypotheses only the support of phenomena first recorded at a late period. Nevertheless, the *Kinship and Marriage* represents an amalgamation of scattered data into a system of culture-history never before attained in Semitic science. In the *Religion of the Semites* Smith sought to ascertain the original significance of the earliest religious institutions, maintaining that the history of ancient religions must be based essentially on ritual, sacrifice, and religious law, and thus seeking to prove that religion was the common possession of the prehistoric Semitic race. Here again, however, the precautions already noted must be observed. He held that the conserver of religion was the tribe united by the consanguinity of all its members, personality being merged in communism. At this period there is an animism which makes little distinction between beings and things. The tribal god is considered the physical source of the tribe, and thus a member of it. To the earlier matriarchy corresponds a mother goddess, beside whom arises a father god with the development of patriarchy. As the tribe expands in power, the tribal god gains prestige and is regarded as king. With the rise of kingship comes an exaltation of law, the king often being the source of law and being in duty bound to safeguard it. The concept of the tribal god thus receives an ethical content, that of justice. This ancient tribal religion was crystallized in fixed institutions, particularly in sacrifice, and its cardinal concept was "sanctuary," which Smith compared with the Polynesian taboo and regarded as especially affecting sacred places. Side by side with this religion of the nomadic Semites Smith posited the Baal-cult of the agricultural Semitic peoples, Baal being, according to him, essentially a fertility deity. This double system was reflected by the Semitic sacrifices, those to Baal being a tribute of the products of the field, and those to the tribal god being an animal victim which was eaten (its blood being devoted to the deity), thus renewing and strengthening, by eating the same sacrificial victim, the blood kinship within the tribe as well as between the tribe and the tribal deity. This kinship, however, could be secured only if the sacrificial victim was itself akin to the tribe, so that the victim was the totem of the tribe, which might be killed only for the sacrificial meal. From such a meal Smith deduced his theory of sacrifice. Gradually the communal meal and the offering became blended, and the sacrifice even became (notably in India) a means of actually controlling the deity. On the other hand, his theory of the basis of human sacrifice is untenable, nor can all the phenomena of Semitic religion be derived, as he fancied, from a single source; while it is also problematical whether all the concepts of a primitive religion can be coordinated in a fixed system.

Theory of Semitic Religion.

(RUDOLF STÜBE.)

BIBLIOGRAPHY: *DNB*, liii. 160–162. In the *British Museum Catalogue*, s.v., are entries of pamphlets concerning the trial and the views of Smith, but they are controversial and add little to knowledge of his life. Consult on the trial H. W. Moncrieff, *Hist. of the Case of Professor W. Robertson Smith*, Edinburgh, 1881; H. F. Henderson, *The Religious Controversies of Scotland*, chap. xi., Edinburgh, 1905.

SMYRNA. See ASIA MINOR, IV.

SMYTH smaith (**SMITH**), **JOHN:** English Separatist, generally considered the founder of the General Baptists; d. in Amsterdam Aug., 1612 (buried Sept. 1). He studied at Christ's College (he is identified by the principal authorities with a John Smith who was graduated B.A., 1576; M.A., 1579). He was cited before the university authorities for preaching on Ash Wednesday, 1586, in favor of a strict observance of the Sabbath; was preacher or lecturer at Lincoln, 1603–05; after nine months of consideration and perplexity he left the Church of England, and became pastor of a Separatist congregation in Gainsborough, 1606. For further notice of his work see BAPTISTS, I., 1.

Smyth's publications were *A True Description out of the Word of God of the Visible Church* (1589; several times reprinted); *The Bright Morning Star, or the Resolution and Exposition of the twenty-second Psalm, Preached publicly in Four Sermons at Lincoln* (Cambridge, 1603; the only known copy is in the library of Emmanuel College, Cambridge); *A Pattern of True Prayer, a Learned and Comfortable Exposition or Commentary upon the Lord's Prayer* (London, 1605 and 1624; apparently the first edition has disappeared); *The Differences of the Churches of the Separation* (n.p., n.d., probably 1608 or 1609; it called forth a reply from Ainsworth, 1609); *Parallels, Censures, Observations* (1609; a reply to Richard Bernard and Ainsworth); *The Character of the Beast* (1609; in controversy with Richard Clifton on infant baptism); *A Reply to Mr. R. Clifton's 'Christian Plea'* (1610). The library of York Minster possesses a unique tract which contains (1) *An Epistle to the Reader by T. P.* [Thomas Piggott]; (2) *The Last Book of John Smith, Called the Retraction of his Errors and the Confirmation of the Truth;* (3) *Propositions and Conclusions concerning True Christian Religion, Containing a Confession of Faith of Certain English People, Living at Amsterdam, in 100 Propositions;* (4) *The Life and Death of John Smith* (reprinted in Robert Barclay's *Inner Life of the Religious Societies of the Commonwealth*, pp. i.–xvi., following p. 117, London, 1876).

BIBLIOGRAPHY: Edward Arber, *The Story of the Pilgrim Fathers*, pp. 131–140, London, 1897; T. Crosby, *Hist. of the English Baptists*, i. 91–99, 265–271, ib. 1738; J. Ivimey, *Hist. of the English Baptists*, i. 113–122, ii. 503–505, ib. 1811–30; J. Clifford, *The English Baptists*, app. x., xiii., London, 1881; H. M. Dexter, *The True Story of John Smyth, the Se-baptist*, Boston, 1881; A. H. Newman, *Hist. of Antipedobaptism*, pp. 376–393, Philadelphia, 1897; *DNB*, liii. 68–70.

SMYTH, JOHN PATERSON: Church of Ireland; b. at Killarney (44 m. w.n.w. of Cork), County Kerry, Feb. 2, 1852. He was educated at Trinity College, Dublin (B.A., 1880), and was ordered deacon in 1880 and advanced to the priesthood in the following year. He was curate of Lisburn Cathedral (1881–1883), and of Harold's Cross, Dublin (1883–88); and incumbent of Christ Church, Kingstown, until 1902. Since 1902 he has been vicar of St. Ann's, Dublin. He has also been chaplain to the Lord Lieutenant of Ireland since 1889 and professor of pastoral theology in Trinity College since 1902. He has written *How we got our Bible* (London, 1886; 18th ed., 1906); *The Old Documents and the New Bible* (1890); *How God Inspired the Bible* (1892); *The Divine Library: Suggestions how to Read the Bible* (1896); *The Bible for the Young* (3 vols., comprising Genesis, Exodus, Joshua, Judges, Prophets and Kings, and Matthew; 1901–08); *The Preacher and his Sermon* (1907); and *Gospel of the Hereafter* (1910).

SMYTH, SAMUEL PHILLIPS NEWMAN: Congregationalist; b. at Brunswick, Me., June 25, 1843. He was educated at Bowdoin College (A.B., 1863) and at Andover Theological Seminary (graduated, 1867). In 1863 he was an assistant teacher in the Naval Academy at Newport, R. I., and in 1864–65 was lieutenant in the Sixteenth Maine Volunteers. From 1867 to 1870 he was acting pastor of the Harrison Street Chapel (now Pilgrim Church), Providence, R. I., after which he was pastor of the First Congregational Church, Bangor, Me. (1870–75), and of the First Presbyterian Church, Quincy, Ill. (1876–82). In 1882 he became pastor of the First Congregational Church, New Haven, Conn., becoming pastor emeritus in 1908. He has written *The Religious Feeling: A Study for Faith* (New York, 1877); *Old Faiths in New Lights* (1879); *The Orthodox Theology of To-day* (1881); *The Reality of Faith* (sermons; 1884); *Christian Facts and Forces* (1887); *Personal Creeds* (1890); *Christian Ethics* (1892); *The Place of Death in Evolution* (1897); *Through Science to Faith* (1902); *Light in Dark Places* (1903); *Passing Protestantism and Coming Catholicism* (1908); and *Modern Belief in Immortality* (1910).

SNAPE, ANDREW: Participant in the Bangorian controversy (see HOADLY, BENJAMIN); b. at Hampton Court (13 m. s.w. of London) in 1675; d. at Windsor Castle Dec. 30, 1742. He was educated at Eton and at King's College, Cambridge (B.A., 1693; M.A., 1697; D.D., 1705); became lecturer at St. Martin's, London, and chaplain to the sixth duke of Somerset, by whom he was made rector of St. Mary-at-Hill and St. Andrew Hubbard in 1706; he became chaplain to Queen Anne and afterward to King George I.; then headmaster of Eton in 1711, in this period attacking Benjamin Hoadly, one of his *Letters to the Bishop of Bangor* (1717) passing through many editions; his part in the controversy caused the loss of the king's favor and the position of chaplain; he was made provost of King's College, Cambridge, 1719, and was vice-chancellor of the university, 1723–24; became rector of Knebworth, Hertfordshire, 1737, and the same year changed to West Ildesley, Berkshire, holding this position till his death. His sermons were collected, *Forty-five Sermons on Several Subjects* (3 vols., London, 1745); he also edited the *Sermons* of Dean Robert Moss (1732).

BIBLIOGRAPHY: *DNB*, liii. 203, where references to scattering notices are found.

SNETHEN, NICHOLAS: Methodist Protestant; b. at Fresh Pond (now Glen Cove), Long Island, Nov. 15, 1769; d. on a journey from Cincinnati May 30, 1845. In 1794 he entered the ministry of the Methodist Episcopal Church, and served for four years in Connecticut, Vermont, and Maine; preached in Charleston, S. C., 1798–99; and during 1800 was traveling companion of Bishop Asbury (q.v.); he was secretary of the general conference of 1800, and a member of the conferences of 1804 and 1812, taking a prominent part in the measures for the limitation of the prerogatives of bishops; he retired to his farm at Linganore, Md., 1806, but in 1809 reentered the ministry, serving in Baltimore, Georgetown, and Alexandria, and acting also part of the time as chaplain of the house of representatives; in 1829 he removed to Indiana, and, when the Methodist Protestant Church (see METHODISTS, IV., 3) was organized, united with it, preaching and traveling in behalf of it till his death; he became one of the editorial staff of *The Methodist Protestant* in 1834; in 1836 took charge of the college of the denomination which was founded in New York City, which enterprise, however, was a failure; in 1837 he returned to the west to take charge of the Manual Labor Ministerial College started at Lawrenceburg, Ind., which also failed, and he then took up his residence in Cincinnati, where he continued to live. His principal publications were *A Reply to O'Kelly's Apology* (1800), and *Answer to O'Kelly's Rejoinder* (1801); *Lectures on Preaching* (1822); *Essays on*

Lay Representation (1835); *Lectures on Biblical Subjects* (1836), and a volume of sermons (1846; ed. W. G. Snethen).

BIBLIOGRAPHY: References to him will be found in the literature on the early Methodists, e.g., J. M. Buckley, in *American Church History Series*, v. 341, 364, 366, 533, 599, New York, 1896.

SNOWDEN, JAMES HENRY: Presbyterian; b. at Hookstown, Pa., Oct. 18, 1852. He was educated at Washington and Jefferson College (A.B., 1875) and Western Theological Seminary, Alleghany, Pa. (graduated, 1878). He has held pastorates at Huron, O. (1879–83), First Presbyterian Church, Sharon, Pa. (1883–86), and Second Presbyterian Church, Washington, Pa. (since 1886). From 1893 to 1898 he was also adjunct professor of political economy and ethics in Washington and Jefferson College, and since 1898 has been editor-in-chief of *The Presbyterian Banner* (Pittsburg). He favored the revision of the Presbyterian Confession of Faith in 1901–03 and union with the Cumberland Presbyterian Church in 1904–06, and in theology belongs to the progressive wing of his denomination. He has written *Scenes and Sayings in the Life of Christ* (Chicago, 1903); and *Summer across the Sea* (New York, 1909).

SOCIAL BRETHREN: A denomination of Christians holding to the general doctrines of orthodox Christianity, formed in 1867 by an association of persons who had been members of various churches but disagreed with their former brethren on certain points of doctrine and usage. The leading points of their faith are belief (1) in the Trinity as united into one godhead; (2) in the Scriptures as containing all things necessary to salvation; (3) in Christ as the only mediator between God and man; (4) in the visible Church as the congregation of the faithful who have been redeemed through Christ, among whom the pure Word of God is preached and to whom the sacraments are duly administered; (5) in redemption, regeneration, sanctification, and salvation through Christ as enduring to the end, yet with a possibility of apostasy; (6) in baptism—by sprinkling, pouring, or immersion—and the Lord's Supper as ordinances of Jesus Christ appointed in the Church, of which true believers are proper subjects, to which all such have right to be admitted; (7) in suffrage and free speech in the Church as the right of all lay members; and (8) that ministers are called of God to preach the Gospel and that only.

The churches are principally in Illinois and Missouri. They are grouped into associations of the ordained ministers, licensed preachers, exhorters, and delegates of the societies of a covenant body of three or more churches; the associations possess appellate jurisdiction over the churches. The associations are affiliated in a general assembly composed of the ordained ministers, licensed preachers, exhorters, general superintendent of schools, and delegates of two or more associations, and this assembly has appellate jurisdiction over the associations. The associations meet annually, the general assembly every second year.

The *United States Census Bulletin* for 1910 gives them for 1906: 17 organizations, 15 ministers, 1,262 communicants, 15 church buildings with two rented halls, and church property valued at $13,800.

SOCIAL SERVICE OF THE CHURCH.

I. General Survey of Philanthropy. The pre-Christian world possessed no philanthropical institutions. The Old Testament demands mercy and charity and contains individual ordinances for the care of the poor (tithes, Deut. xiv. 28, 29, xxvi. 12 sqq.), but there was no organized philanthropy in Israel. There was no need of institutions because economic conditions prevented poverty on a large scale. Post-exilic Judaism laid great stress upon almsgiving and there was much mutual aid among the Jews, especially in the Diaspora. Likewise there was no organized charity in Greece and Rome. The aid of needy citizens in Athens as well as the distribution of corn in Rome were not acts of philanthropy, but of a political character. The idea of Christian philanthropy is approached most closely in the so-called *collegia* of the Romans, which aided their members by defraying funeral expenses, by distributing bread, wine, or money, and by giving financial aid in cases of sickness, journeys, and other eventualities.

1. Among Hebrews and Orientals.

A real activity of charity developed first in the Christian congregations; but here, too, there were no institutions for the reason that they were not needed. The members of the small congregations were able to fulfil their mutual duties without institutions, and the poor who were mostly slaves were provided for by their masters. These conditions changed with the fourth century in consequence of the entrance of the people generally into the Church and the economic decline of the empire with its resultant pauperism. The foundation of philanthropical institutions was one of the results of meeting larger needs with larger means. They originated in the Orient not earlier than the middle of the fourth century. Basil founded near Cæsarea a large institution for the sick, and especially for lepers and strangers; and, according to his letters, poorhouses at various points in his diocese, which were administered by rural bishops. At Antioch, during Chrysostom's activity (c. 380), there existed a hospital for the sick and a house for the poor before the city for those who, suffering from elephantiasis and cancer, were forbidden to enter the city. In Constantinople under Theodosius I. existed hospitals of the churches. Chrysostom mentions an inn for strangers, the necessary expenses for which were defrayed by the church. The assumption that the number of such institutions increased in the fifth and sixth centuries is undoubtedly correct, owing not only to their recognized value, but doubtless also to the expansion of monasticism, and Johannes Cassianus reports that the oriental monastical societies regularly supported xenodochia (houses for strangers); but there is no positive proof. With the growing number of institutions there naturally took place a division of labor. The foundation of Basil was at the same time an asylum for strangers, an institution for the poor, a place of occupation, a hospital, and a home for incurables. This combination was impossible for any length of time; and according to the rich terminology of the Codex of Justinian there was a differentiation into poorhouses, foundling-hospitals, orphanages, and homes for the aged.

2. In the Eastern Christian Church.

The Occident followed the example of the East somewhat later. Here philanthropical institutions seem to have been unknown until toward the end of the fourth century. Ambrose does not mention them and Augustine, in preaching of hospitality, clearly betrays that the reception of strangers in private houses was still necessary; but he, through one of his presbyters, erected a xenodochium. About Rome the first foundations proceeded from the circle of men and women influenced by Jerome. Later establishments are ascribed in the book of the popes to Pope Symmachus, to Belisarius, the general of Justinian, and Pelagius II. In the letters of Gregory I. xenodochia are mentioned several times. Beside those, Gregory the Great knows also of smaller institutions of the same kind, called deaconries, i.e., houses in which deacons cared for the poor of their district. He mentions such in Rome, Pesaro, and Naples. In Gaul Sulpicius Severus is the first to be known to have founded a philanthropical institution by transforming his own house into a *hospitium domus*. The early institutions were founded and supported by the churches or by private individuals. The Church undoubtedly gathered the means of support from its members. It is not improbable that in the beginning the State for a time participated in the support; but it is certain that as early as 390, the xenodochia and kindred institutions were left entirely to the care and administration of the Church, and the State restricted its power to protect and advance them. It approved the principles of organization, complemented them with norms of administration, and granted privileges which the Church then incorporated in legislation. The Roman emperors on the whole approved the episcopal administration of the philanthropical institutions, as well as of the other estates of the churches, and invested the bishops with the duty as well as the right over the acquired bequests. Roman law considered philanthropical establishments as ecclesiastical institutions and granted them and their administrators the same rights and privileges which the Church possessed in general. Concerning the inner arrangement and especially the personnel of the xenodochia there is only incomplete information. Their administration was in the hands of officers appointed by the bishop. In the hospitals there were physicians and a great number of servants partly remunerated, such as probably the Alexandrine Parabolanoi (q.v.). More frequently the nurses seem to have been taken from the circles of ascetics. They lived after the manner of the monks. This seems to have been the case especially in the Occident. Gregory the Great ordered that only *religiosi* should be elected deacons in Sardinia. The conceptions of *monasterium* and *xenodochium* seem to merge together. During the political disturbances from the second half of the fourth century, which finally led to the destruction of the Roman Empire, a great number of philanthropical institutions perished; but the institution as such continued in the East and the West. The number of xenodochia in medieval Constantinople, according to C. du Cange, amounted to thirty-five. Under Gothic rule the hospital of Cæsarius of Arles was founded and the three hospitals of Symmachus were built while Theodoric the Great governed Rome. In the Frankish Empire Childebert and his wife Ulthrogota founded a large xenodochium at Lyons; the one mentioned by Gregory I. was built by Queen Brunchilde and Bishop Syagrius at Autun. Besides large institutions like these there can not have been wanting xenodochia in the country; for the Synods at Orléans (549) and at Chalon-sur-Saône (after 644) protected their possessions in the same way as that of churches and monasteries. Gregory of Tours mentions an asylum for lepers at Chalon-sur-Saône; such are also said to have been at Verdun, Metz, and Maestricht (636), besides many other institutions at various places. Most widely dispersed throughout the Frankish Empire were the small poorhouses (*matriculæ*) in the different churches. In the course of time these *matriculæ* developed into brotherhoods of lower church servants, probably brought about by requiring of their inmates, if capable of work, small church services

3. The Occident.

in return for the alms received. The *matriculæ* of the Frankish period seem originally to have belonged regularly to churches or monasteries. From the Rule of Chrodegang it is evident that episcopal churches possessed *matriculæ* also in the country. The development of the law of church property in the Frankish period made it possible for individual *matriculæ* to develop into independent institutions under administrative heads. They were allowed to acquire their own property and to dispose of it, subject to the will of the bishop. Male adult paupers seem to have been cared for in the *matriculæ*, sofar as may be determined.

4. Decline in the Middle Ages. Although the philanthropical institutions transmitted from the ancient Church continued in the Frankish Empire, and their number, perhaps, even increased, yet after the migration of nations the period of the institutions closed owing to the economical transformation of Europe. Commerce was interrupted, change of population ceased, industry was paralyzed, and cities emptied themselves into the agricultural districts; hence, the need of such institutions ceased with the exception of asylums for lepers and hospices on the mountain-passes. From the time of Charles Martel and his sons and the alienation of ecclesiastical property the independent xenodochium almost entirely disappeared, except in Italy. They existed in the passes of the Alps for the reception of pilgrims, also in the bishoprics of Modena, Arezzo, Aquileia, partly the possession of the bishoprics and partly of the king or the landed nobility. Although their purpose was still the care of the poor and the reception of strangers, the revenues were frequently not used for that purpose, or the institutions had fallen into decay; and the efforts on the part of the nobles for their restoration and the application of their means to their original object were in vain. Thus in Italy the historical continuity was almost though not quite broken; the hospital of the Middle Ages linked itself with the xenodochium of the early Church. North of the Alps, it is evident that the xenodochia as institutions became quite extinct, and in Britain the name does not occur. Into the gap, however, advanced the rising monastic philanthropy. This is already indicated in the rules of Benedict, and the restoration of monastical philanthropy was included in the reform of the monasteries under Charlemagne and Louis the Pious in the ninth century, succeeding that of decay. It is true, the monasteries again greatly degenerated in the latter times of the Carolingians, but the efforts of Charlemagne were not entirely futile. The statutes of Corbie, the property-list of Prüm, and other sources indicate monasteries here and there in which strangers and poor people found refuge and assistance. But its very limited extent goes to show that institutional philanthropy at the beginning of the Middle Ages had lost its importance. The practise of hospitality in the monasteries indeed was more extensive, but this was in the least degree beneficent.

The further reform of the monasteries in the tenth and eleventh centuries and the foundation of the new orders had, no doubt, an influence upon the growth of monastical philanthropy.

5. Rise of Monastic and Cathedral Hospitals. In every well-arranged monastery there was now an infirmary for the monks, a hospital (*hospitale pauperum, eleemosynaria*) in which a number of paupers were continuously supported and needy travelers received refreshment, while well-to-do strangers were cared for in a special hospice for clericals and monks. But the support fell mainly to transients and beggars and the aid to the permanently dependent was negligible. Ulrich of Zell reports that in the Lent season of 1085, at Cluny, 1,700 poor were fed, but at the same time, the number of permanently aided people in the *eleemosynaria* of this extraordinarily rich monastery amounted only to eighteen. To the hospitals of the monasteries were then added those of the cathedrals. Canon 141 of the rule of Aix-la-Chapelle expressly prescribed that every cathedral should have also a hospital for the poor. The necessary expenses were to be provided from the property of the churches, and the canons had to contribute a tithe of their revenues. Although these ordinances may not have been followed strictly by all cathedral churches, yet from that time in many of them an asylum for the poor and numerous city hospitals existed. The work in these hospitals was done in the beginning by members of the monastery or the cathedral, or at least taken in charge by them; at a later time by the laymen of minor brotherhoods and sisterhoods who crowded the monasteries and cathedrals in great numbers. These formed a convent by themselves and developed in the course of time into an order by adopting a rule, most frequently the so-called rule of Augustine, and receiving a master or mistress. Thus there developed from the monastical hospital the house of the hospital brotherhood. Many of these hospitals remained in the possession and under the supervision of the monastery or cathedral to which they belonged, others acquired independence and became again mother-houses of new hospitals which were consolidated with them. There arose hospital orders, or monastical societies, the chief task of which was the hospital service. The most famous hospital orders are those of the knighthood. When hospital service among the knights gradually receded behind the service of arms and was left to the half lay brethren and half sisters of the third estate of the order, the common hospital orders took up their work. The largest among them were the Orders of the Cross who had settled chiefly in Italy, the Knights of the Cross with the Red Star in Bohemia and Silesia (see CROSS, ORDERS OF), the Knights of St. Anthony (see ANTHONY, SAINT, ORDERS OF), and the Order of the Holy Spirit.

The houses of the hospital orders and brotherhoods constituted the transition from the ecclesiastical to the municipal hospitals, whereby only these institutions again acquired a more general significance for the promotion of social conditions. Municipal became most of the "Holy Spirit hospitals," which since the thirteenth century were founded in different places in Germany; they were the fruit of either private or municipal initiative, to meet the emergent needs of the rapidly growing cities, but were in the least degree hospitals according to the later sense. The administration and care of inmates were as a rule in the hands of a corporation like an order, while others were under the direct administration of the municipal council which installed the hospital officers and in every case guarded the administration of the property. The inmates bought a place in these institutions for old age or were received through the favors of those having charge of the funds. Besides these, strangers, travelers, paupers, and the sick found in them a temporary refuge. Hospitals in the real sense there were none. Many cities beside the hospitals provided also a house for lepers before the gates. In France in 1225 there were 2,000 houses for lepers, in England 115. A special order was organized, the Order of the Brethren of the House of Lepers of St. Lazarus in Jerusalem, or, as it called itself at a later time, the Knighthood of St. Lazarus (see LAZARISTS). After the thirteenth century there were numerous houses for the support and burial of destitute pilgrims, and Alpine hospices, and orphans and foundlings were received in hospitals. Foundling-hospitals were numerous in Romance countries, but rare in Germany. The Elsingspittel in London was designed for the blind; in Paris Louis the Pious founded an institution for 300 blind people. Insane asylums are met with only toward the end of the Middle Ages, but they were penitentiaries rather than sanitariums. Fallen girls found refuge in the houses of the Order of St. Mary Magdalen and the Sisters of Penitence. The tendency toward municipal control increased until in the fifteenth century the appearance of civil, communal poor-relief, which took place first in the hospitals. Local councils proceeded from the control of purely municipal foundations to that of the ecclesiastical, made necessary by their decline. The members of the hospital orders had become rich lords and the funds for the poor had become diverted to their luxury or to ecclesiastical objects, frequently not without fraud; as a result of which the cities took over the hospitals for their reform and administration.

6. Municipal Hospitals.

At first the Reformation seems to have had a destructive rather than constructive influence upon philanthropy and philanthropical institutions, because of a sudden the old motives of almsgiving ceased before the appearance of the new of spontaneous benevolence (ut sup.). With the new stimulus the Lutheran Reformation revived the aim of communal poor-relief. The institutional for the time retired into the background. The process of secularizing was to be carried out everywhere, the older hospitals were to be reorganized or incorporated with the communal poor-relief, or new ones, essentially asylums for the sick, were to be erected. In spite of the renewed motive, the abundant charitable activity, and the wide multiplication of institutions, the worthy aim of the Reformation, which was the sufficient care of communal poor and the suppression of mendicancy, fell short of realization and went down in the Thirty-Years' War. More, however, was accomplished in the Reformed Church. In Zurich and Geneva, poor-relief was turned over wholly to the municipalities. By the restoration of the office of deacons the Reformed churches in the Netherlands and in France succeeded in calling to life a philanthropy that was in many respects exemplary; especially the excellently managed orphanages in the former, which had a great influence upon charitable work in Germany, in particular upon August Hermann Francke and in the nineteenth century upon Theodor Fliedner (qq.v.). In England medieval ecclesiastical philanthropy was replaced by the parish care of the poor under the authorization of the State. The principle of the "work-house" (ut sup.) established in England is still in force, but it has been supplemented by the foundation of special institutions; especially, for poor children (the district and parochial schools) and for the destitute sick (the infirmaries and convalescent homes). In the Roman Catholic Church, the Council of Trent commended the medieval type of the institutions to the special care of the bishops, but communal poor-relief was not restored, and philanthropy continued preeminently institutional. It is to the credit of that Church that after the Reformation great service has been rendered; new institutions and new orders have been added, especially in France, Italy, and Spain. The main defects to be pointed out are the diversion of funds to prelates and nobles, and the want of systematic efficiency and unity. The Lutheran Church received a new impetus from Pietism. The orphans' home in Halle, the great work of Francke, gave rise to many similar foundations; but the zeal soon slackened contemporaneously with State assumption of the entire sphere of poor-relief. By an edict of July, 1774, the government of Prussia was entrusted with the supervision of the pious bodies and all benevolent institutions, especially hospitals, orphanages, and poorhouses. Consequently numerous philanthropical institutions of the Church were secularized.

7. The Reformation.

The humanism of the Enlightenment presented the first idea of a rational philanthropy, revolutionizing the same not only in Protestantism but caught up as the keynote also in Roman Catholic domains. The interest aroused by an abundant humanistic current literature toward the close of the eighteenth century resulted in numerous establishments, beginning with the general charitable institution at Hamburg in 1788. Orthodox Christianity was stimulated by the influence and began to develop a more strenuous activity. The Society of Christianity of Basel, founded in 1780, cultivated not only the distribution of Bibles and tracts, but also the care of the poor and sick, training-institutions, and the like. The distress on account of the wars of French conquest and liberation called to life institutions of various kinds for the alleviation of pain and distress, and with the reawakening of the Christian sense, with the gradual invigoration of churchly life, there went hand in hand a revival of philanthropy which called into existence a multitude of

8. Humanism and Modern Philanthropy.

institutions of all kinds; especially houses for the education of male and female workers in the sphere of philanthropy (deacons and deaconesses), houses of refuge, Magdalen asylums, asylums for drunkards, colonies for workingmen, hospitals, infirmaries, institutions for the blind, the deaf and dumb, epileptics, and others. The Innere Mission reports for 1907 18,200 deaconesses of the Kaiserswerth Federation and others, and in all 25,000 sisters engaged in charitable relief; and likewise German brotherhoods with a membership of 2,645. There are no statistics for philanthropical institutions in Germany. Those for Prussia contained in *Statistisches Handbuch für den preussischen Staat*, i. 409 (1893), indicate 1,441 general institutions for the sick alone, with 75,224 beds, besides equally numerous institutions covering the other departments of philanthropy. A surprising feature of philanthropy in Germany is the preponderance of municipal institutions over those of the State, the Church, and private foundations. Here the idea of the Reformation is fully realized. The importance which philanthropical institutions on the whole have for the care of the poor is shown by the statistics of the German Empire for 1885 (*Statistik des Deutschen Reichs*, xxix.), according to which 270,038 persons in institutions and 616,533 persons outside of institutions were supported. Thus almost one-third of all the beneficiaries in the empire was supported in institutions, which warrants the inference that the philanthropic institution has become the permanent basis for public charity and is destined to advance along this line.

(A. Hauck.)

II. Philanthrophy in Great Britain: The history of the relation of Christianity toward eleemosynary activities in England and the other portions of the United Kingdom extends over a period of thirteen centuries divisible into three distinct epochs. The first of these covers the interval between the introduction of Christianity into England in 597 A.D., and the dissolution of the monasteries in that country which was practically completed by 1540. In Scotland they were put down, and in many cases destroyed by the mob, about twenty years later. More than, perhaps, in any portion of western and southern Europe, Christianity had appeared in England as a civilizing as well as a moralizing agency, and its functions resembled those of modern missions to the barbarous tribes of Africa and Polynesia rather than those of missions planted in the midst of the venerable civilizations of India and China. Throughout this period of nearly one thousand years, the framework of society was predominantly military. In such an atmosphere of continual contention the care of the sick, the relief of the needy, and even the instruction of youth, were possible only under the supernatural sanction claimed by the Church, and for the most part all three were in the hands of the monastic orders. The transition from paganism to Christianity among the masses of the population was a far slower process than was the nominal acceptance of that faith by the chiefs of the petty kingdoms forming the Saxon Octarchy. Speaking particularly of the Northumbrians, J. R. Green observes, "With Teutonic indifference, they yielded to their thegns in nominally accepting the new Christianity as these had yielded to the king. But they retained their old superstitions side by side with the new worship." With this view E. A. Freeman agrees. Such religious zeal and humane impulses as the Dark Ages produced found their expression mainly in the cloistered life. When, in the comparative enlightenment of the thirteenth century, the great preaching orders of itinerant friars sprang up, those who adopted the rule of Francis of Assisi (q.v.) were charged by their great founder to minister to the sick in the lazar-houses whose occupants leprosy and kindred diseases had doomed to isolation from their fellows. The oldest existing hospital in London, St. Bartholomew's, originated in a monastery dating from the twelfth century. Institutions set apart for the treatment of the sick as such were hardly known until the sixteenth century.

1. To Downfall of Monasteries.

With the downfall of the monasteries ends the first period. The next century and a half constitutes the second epoch. During it, philanthropy was dependent on the means and conscience of the individual citizen, except so far as the State supervened under the Elizabethan poor law. Toward the end of the seventeenth century forms of associated benevolence begin to appear. This phase constitutes the third stage in its evolution.

2. To End of Seventeenth Century.

It is easy to understand why the abrupt suppression of these ecclesiastical institutions in both England and Scotland should leave a chasm in the lives of the poor. The situation is brought vividly before the eye in the following passage from a report by the commissioners charged with receiving the surrender of Beaulieu Abbey in Hampshire (the original spelling is retained):

"Ther be Sayntuary men here for dett, felony, and murder, xxxii; many of them aged some very seke. They have all, within (except?) iiii wyves and childern, and dwellynge houses and ground wherby the lyve with their famylies, whiche beynge all assembled before hus, and the Kinges Highnes pleasure opened to them, they have verye lamentable declared that if they be nowe send to other Saynturyes, not onlie they but their wyves and childern also shal be utterly undon."

The law which dissolved the monasteries did indeed transfer the liability to perform the accustomed services for the poor to the shoulders of the new owners of the confiscated property, but it was a duty easily evaded. Though not the only cause, the alienation of monastic property—and there were 645 monasteries whose aggregate revenues were estimated at $8,000,000—was one of the principal causes of the great distress chronicled by Bishop Latimer and other contemporary writers. Himself no friend of the old order, that prelate breaks forth against the lax morality of the new in the following vehement passage from one of his sermons: "In times past men were full of pity and compassion, but now there is no pity. . . . Now charity is waxen cold, none helpeth the scholar nor yet the poor." For two generations there appears to have been an interregnum in the general provision made by society for its less fortunate members from the extinction of the religious orders to the passing of the first poor law, only partially filled by the custom of placing in the churches boxes for the receipt of alms for the poor. Instances also are recorded of poor men received into wealthier persons' households. Gradually benevolent private citizens came forward who were liberal in their bequests of property for maintaining schools and alms-houses. Perhaps the majority of the older towns of England contain grammar-schools dating their foundation to one of the Tudor sovereigns. It may be doubted whether, in many of these instances, the monarch for the time being had any real share in establishing them. Henry VIII.'s school at Coventry, for example, was so named in order to win his protection, but it was endowed by John Hales, a private citizen.

3. Sporadic Efforts for Relief of Need.

During the period which elapsed between the final severance from Rome and the accession of the House of Orange in 1688, the sympathies of the benevolent discovered further scope in founding loan charities for assisting deserving tradesmen to start in business, in dowries for portionless maidens, in ransoming the Christian captives of the Mohammedan despots on the North African littoral, in providing work for the unemployed poor, and in gifts and bequests to ameliorate the lot of the sick and of debtors and other prisoners. The late Rev. B. Kirkman Gray, in his standard work *A History of English Philanthropy* (London, 1905), mentions "forty-six bequests for setting the poor on work between 1572 and 1692." The express injunctions contained in the Gospels had always given to the relief of the sick and of prisoners an especial sanction, and the frequently recurrent visitations of the plague and other epidemics, as well as the harshness of the criminal law, offered abundant opportunity. The Rev. J. Bamford, rector of St. Olaves, Southwark, was a shining example of fidelity to one's post. During the plague year of 1603, he incurred considerable unpopularity among his flock by urging on them the unfamiliar practise of isolating patients under proper guardianship, instead of thronging round them or deserting them as pity or panic got the upper hand. Another remarkable example is that of Nicholas Ferrar (q.v.). This gentleman, who in early life had been secretary to the Virginia Company, removed from London during the plague year of 1625, and collected round him at Little Gidding, a sequestered village in Huntingdonshire, a band of persons of both sexes numbering at one time, including his own family, as many as forty, into a kind of religious community having for its object joint prayer, almsgiving, and acts of personal charity, such as teaching school, preparing cordials, dressing wounds, and otherwise tending the sick.

Unfortunately, these efforts, however creditable to those who made them, were but sporadic, inadequate to the needs of the time, and of uncertain duration. The community of Little Gidding survived its founder's death only to be dispersed in the unquiet times of the Civil War. This last event, by impoverishing the propertied classes, cut off a principal source of the flow of material charity,

4. Legislative and Other Relief Measures.

although the Puritan majority in the Long Parliament are entitled to credit for passing enactments conceived in the interest of the masses, such, for instance, as those in relief of poor debtors and for the reform of prison abuses. Dishonest trustees too often intercepted and misapplied the funds dedicated to endowments confided to their administration. Again, the philanthropist of the seventeenth century was handicapped at every turn by his want of practical knowledge. His art was in its infancy. The reserve of past experience on which he could draw was small. He had to make his own experiments, and to grope his way by the light of his own blunders. John Evelyn (d. 1706), a stanch churchman of the period, was one of four commissioners appointed by Charles II. in 1664 to undertake the care of the sick, wounded, and prisoners in the then pending war with the Dutch. His own district took in the coastline of Kent and Sussex, and he seems to have extended his attention to the families of the slain, for he notes in his diary under date of May 16, 1665, "To London to consider of the poore orphans and widows made by this bloudy beginning." He reckoned the expenses of his mission at $5,000 a week and subsequently at double that sum, and had the greatest difficulty in extorting it from the government of the day, as may be judged from the following passage from a letter to the lord treasurer's secretary: "One fortnight has made me feele the utmost of miseries that can befall a person in my station and with my affections: To have 25,000 prisoners, and 1,500 sick and wounded men to take care of, without one peny of money, and above £2,000 ($10,000) indebted. It is true I am but newly acquainted with buisinesse . . . learning that at once which others get by degrees." He proceeds to speak of his desire of serving God "in anything which I hope He may accept, for I sweare to you no other consideration should tempt me a second time to this trouble."

5. Rise of Corporate Philanthropy.

The closing years of the seventeenth century saw, as Kirkman Gray has pointed out, the extension of individual into corporate philanthropy. The leaders in this new departure included men like Robert Nelson (d. 1715) who had made the grand tour of France and Italy, for the older countries of the continent were at that time somewhat in advance of the English in this respect. The influx of Huguenot refugees consequent upon the revocation of the Edict of Nantes also lent a stimulus to the movement. With Nelson was associated Anthony Horneck (d. 1697), a German settled in England who had taken orders in the Established Church. Evelyn describes him as "a most pathetic preacher, a person of a saint-like life." Both Nelson and Horneck were authors of numerous theological works. They joined in forming associations for the reformation of manners and morals which sprang up during the last quarter of the century as a reaction against the license prevalent during Charles the Second's reign. Nelson was one of the founders of the Society for Promoting

Christian Knowledge (see TRACT SOCIETIES, III., 2) in 1698 and the Society for the Propagation of the Gospel in 1701. He was also a member of the commission appointed by the house of commons to add fifty new churches to the metropolis, then rapidly extending its boundaries. A great object of both the societies above named was, in the first instance, to extend religious teaching to portions of Great Britain and her dependencies which were untouched by the parochial system of the Church of England. Thus, regions so far apart as the Scottish Highlands and the American plantations became objects of their efforts. A cooperator in the same field was Thomas Bray, commissary to the governor of Maryland. The Society for the Promotion of Christian Knowledge had its headquarters in London, but had correspondents throughout the country. A great feature of its work was the establishment of "charity schools." These were originally day-schools imparting rudimentary instruction in reading and writing and, generally, also in arithmetic and some simple manual occupation. Religious instruction was insisted upon in all the schools. In the absence of any uniform or national system of education, the society did a great work, although the total number of children in attendance all over the country appears never to have exceeded 30,000 at any one time. The system continued to be actively carried out through the greater part of the eighteenth century. Toward the end of this period Miss Hannah Ball (d. 1792), an early disciple of John Wesley, started a Sunday-school at High Wycombe. Another was set on foot in Gloucester by Miss Cooke, also a Methodist, for the benefit of the children engaged in her uncle's pin-factory. From such small beginnings the movement was spread largely through the sympathy of the editor of the influential *Gloucester Journal*, the well-known Robert Raikes, (q.v.). In 1801 a conservative estimate computed these schools at 1,516, with an average exceeding 100 children in each, in London alone (see SUNDAY-SCHOOLS).

6. Hospitals; Care of Insane; Nursing.

The eighteenth century witnessed the spread, and indeed almost the genesis, of the modern hospital system. Until then, the only hospitals, even in London, had been adapted from the medieval monastic establishments of St. Bartholomew's and St. Thomas's. Bedlam was rather a house of detention than a curative institution for the insane. While the care of the sick, in its early stages, was intimately connected with the afflatus of Christianity, the forward movement of the period above mentioned appears to have owed its origin mainly to the humane instincts of leading medical practitioners combined with an entirely legitimate desire in the profession to utilise the institutional care of the sick in the study and advancement of the science and practise of the healing art. From these considerations it would seem that, so far as the extension of the hospital system at this date was a branch of philanthropy, it falls outside the title and scope of the present section. An exception should perhaps be made in the case of the new and more humane treatment of the insane inaugurated in 1791 at York by William Tuke (d. 1822), a tea-merchant of that city and a member of the Society of Friends. In the Tuke family, as in the sect to which it adhered, philanthropy has been hereditary. William Tuke's great grandson, James Hack Tuke (d. 1896), twice traveled in Ireland to administer relief during the famine year of 1847, and again during the distress of 1881. He also journeyed to Paris during the Commune of 1871 to distribute $100,000 raised by his denomination to relieve the sufferings arising from the siege of the preceding winter. A further exception with regard to the late Miss Florence Nightingale (q.v.), who first established a training-school for sick-nurses, and had herself in early life been a disciple of Elizabeth Fry (q.v.), should also, perhaps, be made.

7. Anti-Slavery and Prison-Reform.

Conversely, the Methodist movement of the same century (see METHODISTS, I.) was too exclusively concerned with the Evangelical revival to rank among directly philanthropic or social agencies, though John Wesley himself wrote against Slavery (q.v.). With the founders of the so-called "Clapham Sect," however, the association of the agitation against the slave-trade, and ultimately against slavery itself, was close and intimate. As early, indeed, as 1727, the Society of Friends at its annual meeting had taken up the position that "the importing of negroes from their native country and relations by Friends is not a commendable nor allowed practise." From these two bodies were drawn most of the champions of the crusade. The historian Lecky remarks that the activity of the philanthropic spirit "has been largely stimulated by the Evangelical Revival." The Society for the Abolition of the Slave Trade founded by Granville Sharp (d. 1813) in 1787 was largely composed of Quakers. William Wilberforce (q.v.) was a leading member of the Low-church or Evangelical colony settled round Clapham Common, and was besides an influential member of parliament and a friend of William Pitt, the prime minister. Thus he constituted a link between the religious and the political worlds. Thomas Clarkson (d. 1846) was already in deacon's orders in the Church of England when he took up the question, and actually refrained from taking priest's orders lest that profession should interfere with his prosecution of the cause, to which he felt so strong a call that he writes, "At length I yielded, not because I saw any reasonable prospect of success in my new undertaking (for all cool-headed and cool-hearted men would have pronounced against it) but in obedience I believe to a higher Power." Again, the era of Prison Reform (q.v.) was inaugurated by John Howard (q.v.). Of Non-conformist training and strong religious sentiments, his duties as high sheriff of Bedfordshire brought him into contact with the harsh treatment of prisoners in his native land. The horrors of jail fever were equaled by those of the miscellaneous herding together of the novice or perhaps the innocent with the most depraved. His end came in the course of prosecuting his investigations in the prisons of South Russia. His endeavors were directed toward the reform of the system; those of Elizabeth Fry who, like the Tukes, came of a prominent Quaker family, aimed at the reform of the individual prisoner. Their memories have been perpetuated and their work continued by societies bearing their names.

Inspired also by the Evangelical sentiment, and one of the foremost pillars of that branch of the Church of England throughout the middle half of last century, was Anthony Ashley Cooper, seventh earl of Shaftesbury (q.v.), of whom Professor Blaikie has remarked, "The lives of Howard, Mrs. Fry, Wilberforce, and other great philanthropists are associated mainly with a single cause—Shaftesbury's with half a score." Like Wilberforce, he stood for the ideal of philanthropy in the stormy cross-seas of politics. His sympathies for the suffering were first attracted to the insane by an inquiry instituted in parliament into the condition and treatment of that unfortunate class. Thenceforward he continued throughout his life a member of a permanent commission charged with the supervision of asylums for lunatics. In 1833 he proceeded to engage in the amelioration of the lot of industrial workers, particularly of women and children, at that time employed not only in factories but also in collieries. Not content with knowledge at second hand, he ascertained the conditions under which they worked by personal visitation. And here it seems permissible to observe that the charity of one generation is apt to become the oppression of its successors. One of the abuses against which Shaftesbury strove was the exploitation of young children in the textile trades. Yet this very practise had been fostered, if not inaugurated, in those schools for imparting instruction in manual crafts as well as in book-learning and conduct, set up by the Society for Promoting Christian Knowledge, and carried still further in schools connected with the workhouses of those days. Of course there was always this marked difference that the factories were run for private profit, while the receipts from the school-children's handiwork went to support the schools, and not into the pockets of the managers.

To return to Lord Shaftesbury. In the "hungry forties" he took up the cause of the uncared-for boys in the streets, and promoted the organization of the so-called Ragged Schools for their benefit—another of those charitable movements directly traceable to religious impulse. Rather than oppose, in common with the land-owning class as a whole, the repeal of the Corn Laws, he vacated his seat in the house of commons. By this time he had acquired a definite influence among the working classes, who were beginning to appreciate his disinterested efforts on their behalf. When the wave of discontent, which had been gathering mass and moment through a long series of years, threatened in 1848 to catch infection from Paris and to break forth into active revolt, he was besought to exercise that influence in favor of peace and order, and afterward received the thanks of the home secretary for his efforts in that direction. Another cause which enlisted his aid was that of the improvement of working-class dwellings. Lord Shaftesbury was also a supporter of the Young Men's Christian Association (see YOUNG PEOPLE'S SOCIETIES). This society was set on foot in 1844 with the primary object of evangelizing the masses of young men engaged in trade and business in the metropolis, many of them living at a distance from their families and friends, and left to their own resources to avoid or to succumb to the varied temptations surrounding them in so vast a city. In time it added to its original program by establishing libraries and reading-rooms, classes in various branches of study, and employment bureaus. Sir George Williams (q.v.), himself head of a large drapery firm in St. Paul's Churchyard, was identified with this effort from its commencement, and was its treasurer until his death, when the association included 7,229 branches scattered throughout the United States as well as the British Empire. A sister society for young women followed in 1855. Reference has been made to the Ragged School movement. Connected with it as regards the class to be benefited was the Reformatory and Refuge Union, founded in 1856 to supply a center of information and encouragement for the already numerous local and isolated efforts to meet the needs of the various classes of delinquents—e.g., youthful offenders, unfortunate women, and discharged prisoners.

8. Ragged Schools; Young People's Societies.

It has been pointed out above that the last two centuries have been the age of associated benevolence. But this is not to say that individual beneficence has been superseded. On the contrary, during the past half-century, as much at least as during any earlier period, schemes of the greatest magnitude have been the outcome of the initiative of a single person. Even the method of three centuries ago of bequeathing money for pensions or almshouses is not extinct. But the ideal of personal service is higher, and the chief benefactors have in their lifetime drawn together bands of sympathisers who act under their leadership and can continue their work. The great mission carried on by the late Dr. Thomas John Barnardo (d. 1905) had its modest beginning in his compassionate observation of the city arab class while himself a medical student. At the date of his death 60,000 children were computed to have passed through the various institutions he had founded, 16,000 having been placed in British colonies. Of these it is said that only 300, or less than two per cent, have failed to do well. Another great organization in the same field is the Church of England Society for Waifs and Strays. With its establishment the Rev. Edward de Montjoie Rudolf has been especially connected. The Society for the Prevention of Cruelty to Children, which holds a quasi-official position, and has had 144,234 children under its notice during the twenty-five years of its existence, was the creation of Benjamin Waugh, a Congregationalist minister. As an example of what individual inspiration can effect, it would be hard to find a more conspicuous example than that of the Salvation Army (q.v.), the creation of the evangelizing zeal of the Rev. William Booth (q.v.), and his wife Catherine Mumford Booth (q.v.). To plan an organization designed for home mission work upon a military framework must have demanded great originating power in the first instance. To extend it

9. Movements under Personal Initiative.

so as to meet multiform distress in many lands and races demanded obviously great organizing power. When General Booth issued his scheme of social reform *In Darkest England* (London, 1890), the Army had already officers and others engaged wholly in the work to the number of 4,506 in the United Kingdom and 4,910 in the United States and the rest of the world, and it possessed Shelters, Rescue Homes, a Prison Gate Mission, and other institutions. The Church Army is a somewhat similar organization founded in 1882 by the Rev. Wilson Carlile (q.v.), a Church of England clergyman, rector of St. Mary-at-Hill in London.

10. Movements in Scotland.

As stated above, the monastic system came to an end in Scotland about twenty years after its overthrow in England. In John Knox's work on ecclesiastical government, entitled *The Book of Discipline*, it is recommended that the revenues of the old Church should be applied among other things to the maintenance of education in the parish and burgh schools, and to the relief of the aged and infirm poor. The able-bodied poor were, according to his scheme, to be compelled to work. In 1562, the General Assembly of the Kirk petitioned for provision to be made for the poor. Practical effect, however, was not given to Knox's recommendations respecting education until an Act, passed in 1696, stipulated for the maintenance of a school in every parish at the cost of the heritors, or landowners. Nearly three centuries after Knox, another great divine of the Scottish Presbyterian church led the van in the reform of poor-relief, which took place in Scotland as in England, though not upon identical lines, in the first half of last century. This was Thomas Chalmers (q.v.), a man of wide interests who had added to his professional training in theology the study of natural science and of political economy. Placed in charge successively of the large parishes of Tron and St. John in the city of Glasgow, then rapidly growing into the commercial capital of Scotland, he organized, with the help of a number of zealous lay coadjutors, the administration of relief to the poor of the parish on such lines that, while the total expenditure was reduced from \$8,000 to \$1,400, "this result," according to Professor Blaikie, one of his biographers, "was accompanied not by a diminution but an increase of comfort and morality. Drunkenness decreased, and parents took an increased interest in the welfare of their children." The influence of Chalmers' experience and teaching in this department of philanthropy was wide-spread, and its fruits may still be seen in the extensive ramifications of the charity organization system on both sides of the Atlantic and of the Pacific.

11. Total Abstinence.

The movement in favor of Total Abstinence (q.v.) found in Ireland one of its earliest champions. This was Theobald Mathew (q.v.), a Franciscan friar in Cork. Visiting much among the poor, he became impressed with the evils of intemperance, and, having taken the pledge himself at the instance of some Non-conformist friends, he proceeded to preach what he already practised. Possessed of an engaging personality, his influence was immense with his fellow countrymen. Judges on assize commented on the diminution in crime. The exchequer officials had to comment upon the diminution in revenue, for the receipts from the excise on spirits fell by one-third. Unfortunately the famine diverted his energies to raising funds for the sufferers. He visited New York and Washington, and prosecuted his campaign there between 1849 and 1851.

12. The Colonies.

Enjoying ample land-room with general prosperity, the over-seas self-governing countries of the empire have so far escaped the necessity of discovering new solutions for distress in their midst. Local adaptations of machinery originated in older countries—the societies founded by St. Vincent de Paul (q.v.) from France, the Salvation Army and the Young Men's and Young Women's Christian Associations from England, and the Women's Christian Temperance Union from the United States—appear to have proved adequate hitherto to supplement the governmental activities of a democratic régime. A great deal of quiet benevolence and neighborliness is exhibited in the ready adoption of orphans and destitute children into private families.

Within the last forty years the desire for social reform in Great Britain has taken three new shapes, those, namely, of charity organization, of tenement reform, and, through reform of tenements, the reformation of the tenants, and of settlement work. While great public spirit and much genuine human sympathy have been displayed in these movements, and while, in all three, zealous clergymen and other church-members may be found taking a share, they, in common with the earlier hospital movement, have been too little the product of ecclesiastical or definitely religious leadership to come within the scope of the present treatment.

13. Prospects.

It may be that philanthropy is on the verge of passing into a further stage. From causes which were glanced at in the opening paragraphs, law, state-craft and diplomacy, medicine and literature, as well as education, were once subordinate but almost exclusive domains of the Church. To be able to read was proof presumptive that a man was a priest, or at least in minor orders. The four first pursuits have, of course, long since passed into the hands of the laity, and education is passing now. At the present moment, departments which hitherto have formed the realm of philanthropy are in process of annexation by the State itself. Already school-children are fed, septuagenarians pensioned, and employment bureaus and relief works subsidized at the public cost. Proposals embodying a drastic alteration of the poor law are being actively urged. If they are carried out in their entirety the drain on private resources will react first of all on the funds available for purposes of voluntary charity, while at the same time few departments of benevolence will remain outside the control of the State or of municipalities. The transference of power from the classes supplying benefactors to the classes supplying beneficiaries, already to a great extent effected, is likely to accelerate this process, of which the attendant dangers are obvious. It can only be hoped that the motives which have hitherto inspired philanthropic action will in the future inspire the conscientious and sympathetic discharge of their new duties on the part of the central and local administrations and their officials. In this connection the influence of the Christian Social Union, a body under the guidance of Bishop Gore of Birmingham, Canon Scott Holland, and other distinguished Anglicans both lay and clerical, which studies social and economic problems and seeks to control industrial and commercial relations in accordance with the principles enunciated in the New Testament and by the Church, may have a great future open to it.

C. H. d'E. Leppington.

III. Philanthropy in America: The development of philanthropy in the modern western world is illustrated by the parable of the seed growing secretly, "First the blade, then the ear, then the full corn in the ear." In the pioneer communities there is little poverty and no pauperism; the few who need assistance are cared for by their neighbors; organized charity is not needed. The churches in the early New England colonies included practically the whole population, and any of their members who were in need or in suffering were relieved by the voluntary compassion of the brotherhood. As the communities grew older, and families decayed, and the number of the defective and the decrepit and the helpless multiplied, some communal provision was made for the care of the poor; each town contracted with some citizen for the keeping of its dependents. Later, poorhouses were erected and yearly appropriations were made, at the town meetings, for the support of the poor. In these poorhouses the hopelessly insane were also confined, no provision yet being made for restorative treatment. Outside of New England the county was generally charged with the care of the poor; the almshouses and infirmaries were county institutions. Thus it will be seen that the tendency pointed out above (I., § 7) as prevailing among the Lutheran and Reformed churches at the time of the Reformation was active in the American communities. The care of the poor was turned over to the public authorities. When the town and the church were practically one this was of no importance; but when the standing order was disestablished, and the secular community was discriminated from the religious community, this virtual abandonment by the church of one of its primary functions was a serious matter for the church and perhaps for the poor.

1. Colonial Practise.

At the present day, therefore, the American churches do not consider themselves wholly responsible for the care of the poor of the community. The same thing is true of Great Britain. This work has been largely taken over by the civic authorities—by the town or the parish or the city or the county. The churches do, however, find work of this kind to do. Many churches have in their own membership those who, from misfortune or accident, are in want, and something is done for the relief of these, though, even here, the ministry often lacks much of being all that could be desired. The churches, also, through mission Sunday-schools and other such agencies, extend their acquaintance among the poor and the unfortunate, and thus the rich and the poor are brought together and want is supplied and sorrow comforted. Services of this nature are not noised abroad, but it is probable that the amount of help thus quietly extended to needy persons is considerable. A great variety of voluntary philanthropies are also maintained in every populous town or city. Hospitals, homes for the aged, orphanages, crèches, Magdalen asylums, societies for the relief of the poor in their homes, free dispensaries, diet kitchens, convalescent homes, district-nursing organizations, social settlements, and many other such organized methods of compassion and friendship are everywhere in operation. By these voluntary philanthropies a large part of the charity of the community is administered. These are, in good part, the inspiration of the churches; most of the workers in them are church-members. Generally these voluntary charities are undenominational; representatives of all the churches unite in maintaining them; they furnish a grateful occasion for the manifestation of Christian unity.

2. Church and Voluntary Philanthropies.

The administration of this voluntary philanthropy by the churches and the various charitable organizations, is apt to be defective in two ways; there is, first, much overlapping, and unscrupulous mendicants are often able to secure aid from several different sources at the same time; and, secondly, the relief is apt to be rendered without adequate investigation, and upon sentimental and emotional, rather than practical, considerations, so that habits of mendicancy are encouraged and the character of the recipients is damaged. For these reasons the organization of the voluntary charities has been found necessary, so that cooperation might be secured and relief be administered by more rational and conservative methods. The "Charity Organization Societies" or "Associated Charities" have been, for the last quarter of a century, effective agencies in the improvement of the methods of charitable relief. They have not always been able to secure so large a degree of cooperation as they have sought, for there are many sentimental persons in the churches and the charitable societies who have but dim comprehension of the amount of harm that may be done by fostering mendicancy, and who are more disturbed by a tale of physical discomfort than by the spectacle of a ruined character. But the principle of the charity organization societies, "Not alms but a friend," is the sound Christian principle; the aim is to stimulate self-respect, self-reliance, industry, and frugality; to give temporary relief when that is needed, but, above all, to help the poor to help themselves. Much criticism has been bestowed on this work by those who view the matter superficially; these organizations have sometimes been called "societies for the prevention of charity." It is quite probable that the repressive features of the work

3. Defects Remedied by Organization.

have sometimes been over-emphasized, but the need of such discriminations and restraints can not be gainsaid, and the efficiency of our voluntary charities largely depends on such cooperation and regulation as the charity organization societies seek to secure.

4. Public Administration of Aid.

The greater part of philanthropic work, however, is done by public agencies. The Christian religion has filled modern society with what Benjamin Kidd calls "a great fund of altruistic feeling," which finds expression in a variety of public philanthropies. To that extent the State has been Christianized. "All-of-us," cooperating through civil institutions and public agencies, are seeking to care for the poor and the sick and the unfortunate. Let it not be forgotten that it is the enforcement of the teachings of Jesus Christ by his Church that has brought this to pass. Such results are not visible in non-Christian countries. The public philanthropies are largely institutional. Hospitals, almshouses and infirmaries, asylums for the insane, the blind, the deaf, the feeble-minded, the epileptic, homes for orphan children, sanatoriums for the victims of tuberculosis—all such institutions are provided for the most part gratuitously for the helpless poor and the unfortunate. Much of this work is of such a character that it could not well be left to voluntary agencies; the burden of it ought to be borne by the entire community. That the community is willing to bear it—that public opinion requires the imposition of this charge upon the public treasury is a signal triumph of Christian civilization.

The legitimacy and necessity of what is technically called indoor relief are thus apparent. But the State also undertakes to administer relief to the poor in their own homes, and for this service it is ill qualified. If, indeed, such conditions as prevail in the German cities could be secured—if the municipality could enlist a large force of its most intelligent and competent men and women to serve as visitors, this work might be done by the public with the best results. In Berlin more than 3,000 visitors of the poor are appointed by the city. They are selected with great care, are men of character, and are compelled to serve. The districts are small and the service is not onerous, but it is not optional; the penalty of refusal or neglect is disfranchisement. With such a force of visitors the city can dispense relief intelligently. But it is doubtful whether any such service as this could be secured by an American city; the investigating force is always absurdly inadequate and generally incompetent; the officials charged with this duty are frequently careless and sometimes corrupt; the funds are used for political purposes, and, as a rule, the needy are neglected and impostors get the lion's share. For this reason some American cities have abolished public outdoor relief and leave the care of the people in their own homes to voluntary charity, sometimes employing the associated charities or other voluntary organizations to do the work of investigation, and granting relief upon their recommendation.

5. Principles of Work.

It thus becomes evident that the conditions of philanthropic work in America at the present time are somewhat chaotic; the work is not well systematized; there is much conflict of jurisdictions and much confusion of methods; there is great need of some revision of the entire program of charitable relief. The principles which should govern this administration have been somewhat roughly indicated in this survey. (1) It is important that the State should more clearly define its own philanthropic function; that it should determine how much it can wisely undertake in behalf of the dependent classes. The institutional work in which it is now widely engaged should, for the most part, be carried forward. If public outdoor relief is to be attempted this relief should be given in such a way as not to demoralize the recipients. The work to be done in such cases is largely the repair or the rebuilding of damaged character. It ought to be in the hands of those who have some skill in the restoration of souls. If the State can not furnish officials who know how to save men and women, it would better leave this work to be done by others. But it will still be necessary that the law stand near to help the volunteer workers. There is many a broken family the wreck of which is caused by the brutality and dissipation of the husband and father, and the wisest help will fail to lift the family out of misery unless he can be separated from them and subjected to a discipline in which he may recover his manhood. He ought also to be kept at productive labor and his net earnings turned over to his family. Charity workers are constantly meeting complications of this sort in which the power of the State must be invoked for the protection of the weak and the enforcement of conjugal or parental responsibility. If, therefore, such cooperation as this between the State and the volunteer workers is to continue, the terms upon which it is carried on should be explicitly defined by law. (2) It is also needful that the churches should come to a clear understanding of their relation to this entire problem of philanthropy. If they have inspired the commonwealth to undertake these works of compassion they have done well, but their work is not yet done; it is hardly conceivable that an institution which represents Jesus Christ in the world should ever be able to discharge itself from responsibility for the poor, the sick, and the unfortunate. It has no business on its hands more urgent than this; it can never convince the world of the genuineness of its commission unless it is addressing itself intelligently and efficiently to this task. (3) The churches of every town or city should recognize their joint responsibility for the care of all the poor and the miserable and the unfortunate of their community. If the State has taken over some portion of it, still the churches are responsible for seeing that the work of the State is humanely done. This is a work that can not be done by the churches without systematic cooperation. If there were no other reason for the union of the churches of the community, this would be reason enough. The Christian people of every city are confronted by poverty, sickness, distress, and misfortune. They can not count themselves disciples of Jesus Christ if they are indifferent to this call. And they can not meet this responsibility unless they unite. This is the summons to the organization of the municipal church, which must include all who call themselves Christians. Something which might thus be described ought to exist in every Christian community. The responsibility of this body for the care of the needy and the helpless can not be gainsaid. No creed is needed for such an organization; it should be simply "the union of all who love in the service of all who suffer." (4) In many communities the nucleus of such an organization already exists. There is a "Federation of the Churches," or a "United Brotherhood," which holds occasional union meetings, but sometimes finds it hard to justify its existence. Let it envisage this task. Let it assume the responsibility for the philanthropies of the city. (5) When it is manifest that the churches are united for this purpose, it will not be difficult to bring the local charities into cooperation. Most of the workers in these local charities are members of the churches and they will recognize the right of the municipal church to take charge of this business. Thus the entire field would be covered, every section of the city would be supervised, and the work would be so divided among the churches and the other organizations that there would be no overlapping, and no failure to reach and relieve cases of real need. (6) The administration of outdoor relief would thus be made intelligent and adequate; the churches by uniting would recover for themselves that sacred and vital function which through their divisions they have so largely permitted to lapse, and they would regain the opportunity of exercising that friendship which is the primary reason for their existence. How greatly this would strengthen their hold upon those portions of the community which are now largely alienated from them needs not to be said. The financial burden, if all the churches shared it, would be very light; the actual amount of money needed for the relief of want in American communities is not large; the help that is needed is moral, rather than material. Every poor family needs a friend, and in the majority of cases the less there is of financial assistance the better for all concerned. (7) This municipal church would also put itself into closest sympathetic relations with all the voluntary philanthropic institutions of the city which are studying these problems, and seeking to make their service more intelligent and efficient. All these institutions are dependent on the churches, and there is great need that their relation to the churches be made more vital and organic. The municipal church would have a committee in charge of the interests of each one of them, watching its work, giving sympathetic counsel and support, and reporting its needs to the churches. (8) The municipal church would also establish helpful relations with the municipal charitable and reformatory institutions, with hospitals, children's homes, work-houses, juvenile courts, jails, and prisons. Over all the unfortunate in these places it would exercise a watchful care. There would be an efficient committee over each of them observing the conditions, studying the problems, and keeping the Christian community thoroughly informed respecting them. It is not to be assumed that this supervision of public institutions would be necessarily critical or inquisitorial; it would normally be sympathetic and helpful; it would only seek to bring the good-will of the Christian community into close and practical relations with some of its neediest members.

It is a deplorable fact that the organizations which represent Jesus Christ in our modern communities have no methods of keeping themselves in touch with the inmates of these public charitable and correctional institutions. They have passed all that business over to the State, and have divested themselves of responsibility for it. It is a faithless performance. In that impressive parable of the judgment the Son of man arraigns those who are brought before him, because, as he says, "I was sick and in prison and ye visited me not. . . . Inasmuch as ye did it not to one of these my brethren, even these least, ye did it not to me." Until the Christian Church in every city or town has put itself into relations of practical friendship with all these classes, it is resting under a heavy condemnation.

Such are some of the pathological phases of the philanthropy which the Christian Church in the modern community may be expected to practise.

6. The Church's Higher Duties.

But the true philanthropy is not merely remedial. It seeks to discover and remove the causes of misery. And the Christian Church has, for society as well as for the individual, not only a message of redemption but also a message of regeneration. It must cleanse the sources from which want and sickness and vice are flowing. It is futile to go on relieving all these social maladies and leave untouched the causes which constantly produce them. And the municipal church, when it has once fairly grappled with its great tasks, will feel that its most important work, after all, is to give us a new heaven and a new earth wherein dwelleth righteousness. (1) It will discover that the sickness and physical debility to which it is trying to minister are in considerable part the result of bad housing-conditions, of unsanitary tenements and overcrowding, and it will turn the light on these conditions and stir up a public sentiment which shall abolish nuisances and pestilence-breeders, and secure healthy habitations for the people. (2) It will bring home to the Christian conscience of the community the fact that in most of our cities multitudes of children have no accessible playgrounds but the streets, and that the conditions there surrounding them are unfavorable to the development of sound character. Abundant evidence shows that the streets are the seminaries of vice and crime. Little that is normal in the life of a child is permitted in them; the tendency of the associations of the street is toward that which is abnormal and criminal. Safe and well-regulated playgrounds are a vital need of city boys and girls and far less costly than the reform schools to which so many of them are later sent. A few intelligent men and women have discovered the importance of this provision and are working to secure it, but the churches are primarily responsible for the welfare of these boys and girls, whether they belong to their Sunday-schools or not, and it is their business to educate the community upon this vital matter. (3) It is hardly needful to dwell upon the devastations of the drink evil (see TOTAL ABSTINENCE); nor to point out how large a share of our philanthropic labors and sacrifices are made necessary by this destructive vice. The municipal church will be wide awake to this evil, and may be depended on to do what it can to abate the injuries of which the saloons are the source. It is to be hoped, also, that it may discover the importance of meeting that bad influence by counter-attractions, and providing safe places of social resort for the multitude of homeless young men and women. The terrible ravages of the social evil will also challenge the faith and courage of the municipal church. For much of the poverty, the disease, the crime, the wreckage of homes is due to this cause. Competent observers of social conditions assure us that the damage done by the saloons is trivial compared with this. To whom may people look for an intelligent, thorough, adequate treatment of this social malady, if not to the Christian Church? Is it possible that the institution which is charged with the moral education of society can venture to ignore this responsibility? (4) Much of the poverty and sickness to which we are called to minister is due to the devitalized condition of the laborers, and this, in many cases, is the result of child labor in earlier years. When the municipal church begins to deal with the causes of the ills it is trying to cure, it will find here some serious work to do. (5) Unemployment is an ungainly word, but it describes an ugly thing. Much of it is due to shiftless men or inefficiency, but by no means all. Two-thirds of the families which apply in good times to the charity organization societies for aid are in need because they are out of work. To this tremendous problem the municipal church must address itself sympathetically and intelligently. This is the gravest of misfortunes, the sorest of troubles. If any man deserves a friend it is the man who is in need and is willing to work. Such a man ought never to be in doubt that there is one great friend to whom he can go, and that is the Christian Church. Such men generally do go to the ministers; there is a constant procession of them to the doors of the study, but it is hardly possible for the minister to find work for many of them; if the municipal church were properly organized it would have an employment bureau. (6) Not a little of the unemployment and the consequent poverty which taxes philanthropy is caused by industrial wars. Very destructive and disastrous to the fortunes and the characters of employers and employed are these bitter conflicts; the municipal church ought to be able to put an end to some of them. It is the representative of the Prince of Peace, and it has no more sacred function than that of the peace-maker.

These are not the only ways in which the municipal church could exert its influence in removing the causes of those ills to which it is called to minister. But enough has been said to make it clear that when the Christian Church comes to itself and realizes its opportunity and its responsibility it will find a mighty task upon its hands and a reason for being of which it has as yet hardly seemed to be aware. Not only in relieving existing want and suffering, but in attacking and removing their causes, it will rise to its full stature and fulfil its high calling. It will not be needful to explain to any one whose church it is; in its life the life of the Son of man will be reflected. Such a church will justify its own existence; it will be evident that its most vital function has been fully restored to it, and it will recover the credit it has lost, not only among the less fortunate classes, but also among all earnest men and women to whom the common welfare is a serious concern.

7. Conclusion.

WASHINGTON GLADDEN.

IV. Poor-Relief, General Survey: Pre-Christian times afford no evidence of a systematic relief of the poor. In the heathen world there were some approaches to it; such as at Athens the care of those incapacitated for work and in Rome the distributions of corn and, from Nerva's reign, the alimentations. Liberality and personal benevolence were customary in Israel. An organized poor-relief, however, was first provided by Christianity. The beginnings of the care of the poor in the congregation are noted in the New Testament; and by the second century the organization was complete. The means were collected by free gifts; partly through monthly contribution to the parish treasury, and partly through the oblations made at the celebration of the Lord's Supper, consisting principally of natural products. Compulsion to give, direct or indirect, was excluded (II Cor. ix. 7). The administration of these means and the general superintendence of poor-relief were vested in the bishop, who was assisted by several deacons. The discipline of the Church was a sufficient safeguard against the careless diversion of such means to the unworthy. The Church has at no other time more strongly emphasized the duty of the care for the poor and unfortunate, and at no other time has it more positively insisted that everything be done freely from the motive of love. Assistance was chiefly in kind, and the limited size of the parishes also made possible an effort to help each one according to his particular need. Above all, it was sought to make the poor economically independent by procuring for them employment and tools. A poor-list, in which the circumstances of the needy were described, prevented any being overlooked. Widows and orphans were special objects of attention, the education of the latter being entrusted to the bishop. The sick were attended, and strangers received the privileges of hospitality. By means of letters of introduction any stranger coming in Christ's name was kindly welcomed; and, before examination as to being a true brother, he was provided with rest and refreshment. He was cared for but two or three days at the expense of the Church; thereafter he must work [cf. Didache, xi. 5, ed. P. Schaff., p. 200 and note, New York, 1890]. The individual parishes also mutually aided one another. In this period

1. The Ante-Nicene Church.

poor-relief actually attained its end, and there was no want within the Christian communities.

2. The Post-Nicene Church. The triumph of the Church under Constantine, placing as it did large means at its disposal, at first tended to improve the condition of the poor. Freedom to receive bequests attached the ever-increasing idea that almsgiving had a penitential efficacy and opened an abundantly increasing source of revenue. These means enabled the Church to extend its poor-relief to meet the growing need attending the economic decline of the empire. The poor-lists of the metropolitan churches now numbered thousands of names. At Antioch 3,000 widows and young women, and at Alexandria, in the time of Johannes Eleemon (q.v.), 7,500 poor were regularly cared for. At the same time there were poorhouses, orphan-asylums, hospitals, and guest-houses for pilgrims and strangers. All the great bishops of the period were true guardians of the poor. Yet with the expansion of the Church, the relief of the poor was more and more transferred from the parishes to the Church at large, or to institutions. The oblations in increasing measure lost their significance, the larger part of the funds being supplied by the Church estates. Gradually the deacons, on account of the complicated administration of Church estates, made way for stewards as mediaries between them and the bishop. A considerable part of the work attended to previously by the parishes was transferred to the institutions, and the care of the poor lapsed into a wholesale almsgiving. Christian *charitas* came to be very like the Roman *liberalitas;* the bishops took the place of the emperor as the great purveyors of alms. The organized poor-relief of primitive days ceased, and begging became more and more prevalent.

3. The Middle Ages. The conditions amidst which the new Frankish kingdom came into being excluded the poor-relief of the congregation in the early times. This required a higher economic basis and higher development of the cities. Instead of administration of money there was a return to the distribution of natural products. The unsuccessful attempt at the restoration of primitive poor-relief disappears with the dissolution of the Frankish Church. Charlemagne had not only enjoined the Church to bestow on the poor a portion of its tithes, but promulgated laws compelling landed proprietors in case of need to support their vassals. In the famine year of 779 he levied a formal poor-tax. Begging was expressly prohibited. No landed proprietor was to suffer the poor to go begging on his domains. No one was to give to beggars who would not work. But after Charlemagne's death this scheme of poor-relief quickly fell to pieces. During the ensuing Dark Ages there was no organized poor-relief by either Church or State. The dictum that the property of the Church was the possession of the poor under the influence of the feudal system lost its meaning. It was not the parishes that exercised benevolence, but isolated individuals or associations in asylums and cloisters. The fundamental reason why there was no organized poor-relief in the Dark Ages was that benevolence was primarily not to help the poor, but to secure one's own personal salvation. There was abundant almsgiving in individual cases and beneficiary funds of all sorts were established; there were institutions, orders, and associations; but no effort was made to reduce the whole to a well-ordered system, and there was neither coherency nor at bottom the primary aim to help the poor. The result was general mendicancy, which was looked upon not as a disgrace but as a kind of profession. There were gilds and brotherhoods of beggars, and towns levied a tax on the beggar gild as they did on others. The *Liber vagatorum* (Eng. transl., *The Book of Vagabonds and Beggars*, London, 1860) which Luther republished, with an introduction, shows that frauds of every sort were associated with begging. Steps had to be taken against this state of things, though it would have been contrary to medieval views altogether to forbid it. Attempts were at least made to introduce some sort of order, to determine who might beg and how. These laws became numerous in the fifteenth century; and as these regulations of beggars precede the later administration of the poor, so they mark the first advent in the fifteenth century of communal poor-relief. This appears first as associational. Already the ancient work associations involved the duty of mutual aid. But now in the towns, independently of the gilds, which assisted their own poor when necessary, associations of citizens were formed for the care of the poor. At first these had no connection with the local government, which, from the fourteenth century, however, came to administer their affairs, and the associational relief became the communal. There had arisen, besides, a municipal poor-relief, an income being derived for that purpose from funds deposited by citizens with the authorities. As this work increased, special officers were appointed to superintend it.

4. The Reformation Period. These were, however, but beginnings. The Reformation awakened fresh motives of active charity, and set up new aims. By the doctrine of justification by faith, it struck at the motive of the merit of good works and replaced the same by that of loving gratitude. The new aim was not to secure personal salvation but primarily to relieve the poor. A new poor-relief was developed, the outlines of which had appeared in Luther's *An den Christlichen Adel deutscher Nation* (Wittenberg, 1520). Begging was to be abolished not merely by prohibition but by local provisions for all the poor. All who could work were to do so, and relief was restricted to the necessaries of life. It was in effect the old parish poor-relief of the primitive churches. In place of ordinances regarding beggary, poor-laws were passed; first, that of Augsburg (Mar. 21, 1522), more important that of Nuremberg (July 23, 1522). After the Peasants' War the poor-relief was reorganized with the reconstitution of the Church-system. Funds were collected in part through charitable endowments and in part through collections taken either in the churches or in house-to-house visitation. Contributions were voluntary and the funds were administered by overseers known as treasurers or deacons authorized by the congregations or civil governments; and they were governed by strict regulations. Excellent as the system was in theory, it did not succeed in practise. The income from endowments was not what had at first been anticipated; and, after the first enthusiasm had subsided, the collections declined. But, even more important, the overseers were inexperienced and incompetent. In the Reformed congregations of Germany, France, and particularly Holland, the aim toward a considerate, personal, and individual treatment of the poor was successfully worked out to the smallest details. In the Roman Catholic countries and districts voluntary poor-relief has continued through the various orders and establishments, though not by parish relief; and a work has been done to which Protestantism offers no parallel.

Fundamental are three great types of poor-relief, of which all others are modifications: namely, the English, French, and Dutch. Foremost is the English. The law of Elizabeth of 1601 has remained to this day as the basis of poor-relief. In every parish from two to four citizens in good standing were appointed overseers of the poor, and to them was confided the duty of providing work for all who were without means of support and had no settled employment. They had the right of taxing the members of the parish for means of supplying material for the employment of those capable of work, and for supporting those who were incapable. The emphasis upon setting to work the able-bodied led to the rise of workhouses (at first called "the industrial house"), the first of which was opened in 1679. In 1713 an act authorized such workhouses, and any pauper who refused assistance at one was denied it elsewhere. There then arose a distinction between assistance given in an institution (indoor relief) and that given outside (outdoor relief). By the Gilbert act of 1782 and the act of 1796, outdoor relief was legalized and became the rule. The "allowance" system was started, by which the difference between actual earnings and a minimum scale based on market prices and the size of the family was paid by the State. Pauperism vastly increased. In 1834 reforms were introduced. Outdoor relief was limited. Poor-associations, called unions, were formed, each with a board of guardians, composed of the justices of the peace and selected members of the parish, to distribute relief. A central board of commissioners, the poor-law board, was established, which from 1872 has been subordinated to the local government board. This system is now entirely a matter of civil administration; its aim is, by indoor strictness and hard labor, to diminish the numbers of outdoor paupers. It is lacking in the element of training and promotion, not providing suitably for the sick, the weak, or the unfortunate by accident. The civil poor-relief confines itself only to the immediate necessities and leaves the rest to benevolent initiative, and nowhere else have societies and institutions of free beneficence multiplied as in England.

5. Three Modern Types.

In France the constitution of July 4, 1793, proclaimed that public poor-relief was a sacred obligation. It was proposed by a decree of July 7, 1794, to acquire the hospitals and other private institutions. Workshops were to be opened for those who could work, and a yearly pension given to those who could not. Of this scheme the only part put into execution was that connected with the destruction of the old system. After the Revolution benevolent institutions so far as possible were restored to the Church, and Napoleon I. reestablished the orders of relief and granted every sort of State recognition and support. The old orders and congregations increased and new ones were gradually added; and relief rests mainly upon the voluntary aid of these. By a decree of Nov. 27, 1796, local boards (bureaux de bienfaisance) were established in the ecclesiastical communes, to render house-relief; but these are not in conflict with the institutions. These boards were not, however, made compulsory, and in 1897 existed in less than one-half of the communes. They have no power to levy assessments. The State has, however, taken over the care of the young and the insane and assigned them to the poor regulations of the departments.

The Thirty-Years' War almost put an end to poor-relief in Germany. After the war numerous regulations were adopted, but rather to prevent begging than to aid the poor. Toward the end of the seventeenth century workhouses and houses of correction were established. The Pietist movement, by its free impulse toward charity, and the Enlightenment (q.v.), by its humanism, contributed toward the progress of poor-relief. For the first time a comprehensive literature on poor-relief sprang up and from 1870 there has been an earnest effort for reform. A general institution for poor-relief was established at Hamburg, and widely copied. The basis for the care of the poor was really laid, however, by the general law of June 6, 1870, on the principle adopted in Prussia Dec. 31, 1842, and gradually extended to include all of the empire excepting Bavaria and Alsace-Lorraine. According to this the former home-relief was replaced by that of dependent residence, qualification for which was established by two-years' standing in the parish or lost by a two-years' absence. Whoever has no dependent residence is called "land poor." Whenever any one within this privilege happens to be in want the local charity must take cognizance of the same. The work is in general in charge of poor-associations, and its character and scope are determined by the laws of the different states, to which imperial legislation has entrusted all details. The Elberfeld system has been extensively and successfully introduced. The essential characteristic of this is the principle that to the individual overseer only a very small number of dependents (not more than four) are assigned with the largest freedom of adaptation, limited only by general directions. The theoretical result of the evolution of poor-relief is summed up in the phrase, promotion of self-support; and the practical result was voiced in the expression of the charity congress of 1857 at Frankfort—the organic cooperation of the civic authorities, the church offices, and voluntary associations. The Church fulfils an intermediate function between the private relief of individuals and associations, and the civic relief, being voluntary like the former and organised like the latter. The Church fosters the motive of voluntary charity and has regard in the distribution for the religious-moral welfare of the beneficiaries, especially of the young. The State acts in regard to its own safety, is impartial to all, and thus has the advantage of strict and just discrimination, systematic administration, and enforced contribution. The legitimate sphere of the charity of the Church is in the congregation, which is concurrent with that of the municipality and the State. See CHARITY. (G. UHLHORN†.)

1. Early Practise.

V. Poor-Relief in the United States: Two general methods of poor-relief exist in the United States; outdoor relief, and indoor (or institutional) relief. Each of these classes is subdivided into private and public relief. Public relief is relief given wholly or in part from public funds (state, county, or municipal). Private relief is relief given from funds administered by private organizations or societies receiving their funds from voluntary contributions, endowments, and the like. The basis of public poor-relief in the United States is the almshouse or poorhouse, the terms being synonymous. In early American life, inmates of poorhouses were let out to the lowest bidder, a system obviously unjust to the pauper. Poorhouses in the early nineteenth century were, so to speak, a human refuse heap for the dependent and defective classes. Abuses were frequent and the conditions of subsistence and existence of the inmates were anything but satisfactory. In the early middle period of the nineteenth century, special institutions began to be established for special classes of dependents and defectives. To-day in many parts of the country children under two years of age, the insane, the epileptic, and the more markedly feeble-minded have been removed from the poorhouse and placed in special institutions, generally under the State authorities. The residue of the poorhouse is composed largely of the aged and infirm. Most poorhouses shelter temporarily the tramp and vagrant classes, thereby perpetuating the existence of vagabonds, who are able-bodied but live in idleness. In many modern poorhouses the cottage system of construction and classification is in vogue. In New England and in the Middle Atlantic States the poorhouses are generally under township management; in other parts of the country they are under county management. However, in over one-half of the counties in the United States there are no poorhouses. Instead, paupers are maintained by so-called public relief or "boarding-out" under the supervision of overseers or similar officials, comparable to the English "relieving officer." The boarding-out system has its advocates on the ground of economy. While efforts are made with increasing frequency to control tendencies to pauperism and special aid through poor-relief, it must still be said that much of the public outdoor relief given to American dependents is misdirected or palliative, in that the relief results, at the best, in the perpetuation or reduction of pauperism in the individual case, but does not prevent the pauperism of others.

American poor-laws are based largely on English poor-laws. Settlement with the subsequent right to poor-relief is obtained through residence, the time necessary to acquire settlement differing in the various States from several months to several years. Much of the difficulty in wisely administering poor-relief in the United States arises from the temporary character of the appointments to office of the overseers of the poor, and their consequent lack of training in the best principles of charitable relief; partly also from the migratory nature of many of the families and individuals in receipt of poor-relief. Vagrancy laws are lax and indifferently enforced. The "passing-on system" of relieving the community of a considerable part of the burden of poor-relief is so frequent as to be a subject of much serious discussion among progressive charity workers.

2. Modern Conditions and Methods.

The United States is rich in certain forms of benevolent institutions. The special census report of benevolent institutions in 1905 shows 4,207 institutions of all kinds, 2,166 of which were known to have been in existence in 1890, 2,004 having been founded between 1890 and 1903 inclusive. Of these there were 1,075 orphanages and children's homes, 1,493 hospitals, 753 permanent homes for adults and children, 449 temporary homes for adults and children, 166 nurseries, 156 dispensaries, 61 schools and homes for the deaf, 39 schools and homes for the blind, 15 schools and homes for the deaf and blind. The total population Dec. 31, 1904, was 284,362; inmates admitted during 1904, exclusive of dispensaries and nurseries, 204,372. Cost of maintenance, 1903, $55,577,633, of which the annual subsidy from public funds was $6,089,226. This enumeration omits all almshouses, public and private hospitals for the insane, and schools for the feeble-minded, as well as institutional activities of an occasional character. Special census reports on the above-named institutions show the following:

	Dec. 31, 1903.	Admitted during 1904.
Insane in hospitals	150,151	49,622
Feeble-minded in institutions	14,347	2,599
Paupers in almshouses	81,764	81,412
	246,262	133,633.
Total for 1904		379,895

An article in *The Metropolitan Magazine* for Oct., 1909, estimates as follows New York State's charitable expenditures for 1907:

Institutions reporting to the State Board of Charity	$23,898,013
Institutions and organisations not reporting to board	17,000,000
Hospitals for insane, etc.	5,927,000
Churches	3,000,000
Individuals	15,179,770
	$65,004,783

The same article estimates that $260,019,132, or over a quarter of a billion, annually is expended for charity in the United States.

In about 200 cities in the United States there are charity organizations or similar private societies, the fundamental principles of which are the relief of the poor in their homes, registration of cases, cooperation with other charitable societies, careful investigation of applications for relief, or other aid. In some cities, notably New York, no public outdoor relief is given by the city; the private charitable societies alone caring for the poor in their homes. In most cities the charitable organizations and the public poor-officials work more or less in harmony in the administration of poor-relief. In general, institutions for special classes of the dependent and physically or mentally defective are under state or other governmental management. Almost every state has a public supervisory body, generally appointed by the governor to inspect and advise, and, in some states, to administer state charitable institutions. Generalizing, it may be said that poor-relief in the nineteenth century saw three general stages of development. The first, the development of institutions for the care of the various classes of the poor; secondly, the development of the system of the care of the poor in their homes in which the relief of the individual family was the goal. The third stage developed from about 1895, and is marked by increasing efforts to *prevent* pauperism.

The doctrine of prevention has become practically a gospel in charitable work. The most prominent movements to-day in preventive charity are tenement-house reform, warfare against tuberculosis, against child labor, the movement for parks and playgrounds, the movement for the reduction of congestion of population, for prison reform, for better health, and many other like movements. The problem of poor-relief in the United States is becoming a national problem of the reduction of poverty. The public press, periodicals, magazines, etc., are laying special emphasis upon charitable and correctional problems. Charity workers are emphasizing the prominence of heredity and environment as causes of poverty, and take the standpoint that with the reduction or removal of preventable conditions, due to heredity and environment, poverty will be reduced. O. F. Lewis.

Bibliography: On the history the standard work is G. Uhlhorn, *Die christliche Liebesthätigkeit*, 3 vols., Stuttgart, 1882–90, Eng. transl. of vol. i., *Christian Charity in the Ancient Church*, New York, 1883. Consult further on the history: E. L. Chastel, *Études historiques sur l'influence de la charité durant les prémiers siècles*, Paris, 1853; A. Emminghaus, *Das Armenwesen und die Armengesetzgebung der europäischen Staaten*, Berlin, 1870; A. Thijm, *De Gestichten van Liefdadigheid in Belgie van Karel d. Gr. tot aan de xvi. eeuw*, in *Mémoirs couronnés* of the Royal Academy, vol. xlv., Brussels, 1883; idem, *Les Hospitaux en Belgique en moyen-âge*, Löwen, 1883; B. Riggenbach, *Das Armenwesen der Reformation*, Basel, 1883; G. Ratzinger, *Geschichte der kirchlichen Armenpflege*, Freiburg, 1884; C. J. R. Turner, *Hist. of Vagrants and Vagrancy*, London, 1887; D. Tourbie, *Dänisches Armenrecht*, Berlin, 1888; F. H. Wines, *Report on the Defective, Dependent, and Delinquent Classes*, U. S. census, Washington, 1888; H. G. Willink, *Dutch Home Labour Colonies*, London, 1889; R. P. Lamond, *The Scottish Poor Laws*, Glasgow, 1892; L. A. Rubbrecht, *Remèdes contre le pauperisme*, Brussels, 1892; B. H. Dahlberg, *Bidrag tell Svenska Fattiglagstiftningens Historia*, Upsala, 1893; E. Chevallier, *La Loi des pauvres et la société anglaise*, Paris, 1895; J. Cummings, *Poor-Laws of Massachusetts and New York*, Baltimore, 1895; W. G. Lumley, *Union Assessment Acts and the Poor Rate Act*, London, 1895; A. Loth, *La Charité catholique en France avant le révolution*, Tours, 1896; Sir G. Nicholls, *A Hist. of the English Poor Law*, 2 vols., London, 1898; E. Mischler, *Die Armenpflege und Wohlthätigkeit in Oesterreich*, Vienna, 1899; E. M. Leonard, *Early Hist. of English Poor Relief*, Cambridge, 1900; O. B. P. G. de Cléron, *Assistance publique et bienfaisance privée*, Paris, 1901; W. H. Diemsday, *Hadden's Overseers' Handbook*, London, 1901; J. B. Little, *The Poor Law Statutes*, 3 vols., London, 1901; P. F. Aschrott, *The English Poor Law System*, London, 1902; H. S. Brown, *American Philanthropy in the 19th Century*, 2 vols., New York, 1902; A. Hoffmann and H. Simon, *Wohlfahrtspflege in Rheinland und Westfalen*, Düsseldorf, 1902; L. Lallemand, *Hist. de la charité*, 4 vols., Paris, 1902–10; J. J. Esser, *De pauperum cura apud Romanos*, Campis (?), 1902; C. A. Ellwood, *Public Relief and Private Charity in England*, Columbia, Mo., 1903; B. Kuske, *Das Schuldenwesen der deutschen Städte im Mittelalter*, Tübingen, 1904; E. Marescont du Thilleul, *L'Assistance publique à Paris*, 2 vols., Paris, 1904; E. Sellers, *The Danish Poor Relief System*, London, 1904; K. Singer, *Sociale Fürsorge*, Munich, 1904; B. K. Gray, *Hist. of English Philanthropy*, London, 1905 (important); E. W. Capen, *Historical Development of the Poor Law of Connecticut*, New York, 1905; J. E. Graham, *The Law Relating to the Poor*, Edinburgh, 1905 (deals with Scotland); E. von Müller, *Die Elendenbrüderschaften. Ein Beitrag zur Geschichte der Fremdenfürsorge im Mittelalter*, Leipsic, 1906; F. Appleton, *Church Philanthropy in New York*, New York, 1907; M. Fluegel, *The Humanity, Benevolence and Charity Legislation of the Pentateuch and the Talmud; in Parallel with the Laws of Hammurabi, the Doctrine of Egypt, the Roman Twelve Tables, and modern Codes*, Baltimore, 1908; M. Godbey, *The Bible and the Problem of Poverty*, New York, 1908; E. C. Rayner, *Story of the Christian Community, 1685–1909. A notable Record of Christian Labour in London Workhouses and Lodging Houses*, London, 1909; J. J. Walsh, *The Thirteenth, Greatest of Centuries*, New York, 1909; R. M. Berry, *Germany of the Germans*, ib. 1910 (deals with poor laws); Schaff, *Christian Church*, vol. v., part 2, § 79; the *Proceedings* of the national, state, and municipal Conferences on Charities and Corrections and the *Annual Reports* of the boards of charities, etc., of the various states and cities.

On the theory and practise in various countries consult: A. Baron, *Le Pauperisme*, Paris, 1882; J. Platt, *Poverty*, London, 1884; C. V. Bohmert, *Das Armenwesen in 77 deutschen Städten*, 3 parts, Dresden, 1880–88; W. Booth, *In Darkest England and the Way out*, London, 1890; E. G. Balch, *Public Assistance of the Poor in France*, London, 1893; H. G. Borgesius, *Het Vraagstuk der Armenzorging*, Amsterdam, 1895; J. A. Hobson, *The Problem of the Unemployed*, London, 1896; B. Gewin, *Arbeidsbeurzen*, Utrecht, 1898; W. C. and R. C. Glen, *General Orders of the Poor Law Commissioners and the Local Government Board Relating to the Poor Law*, London, 1898; E. T. Devine, *Practice of Charity*, New York, 1901; idem, *Essentials of a Relief Policy*, New York, 1903; idem, *Principles of Relief*, ib. 1904; idem, *Misery and its Causes*, ib. 1909; C. R. Henderson, *Introduction to the Study of the Dependent and Defective Classes and of their Treatment*, 2d ed., Boston, 1901; idem, *Modern Methods of Charity: the Systems of Relief . . . in the principal Countries having modern Methods*, New York, 1904; T. Mackay, *Public Relief of the Poor*, London, 1901; H. Albrecht, *Handbuch der sozialen Wohlfahrtspflege in Deutschland*, 2 parts, Berlin, 1902; *Beiträge zur Armenstatistik*, Jena, 1902; P. C. J. A. Boeles, *Armengoederen en Armenbesturen in Friesland*, Leeuwarden, 1902; T. B. Chilcott, *Law Relating to the Administration of Charities*, London, 1902; J. A. Riis, *The Battle with the Slum*, New York, 1902; J. Sutter, *Britain's Next Campaign*, London, 1903; R. Hunter, *Poverty*, New York, 1904; M. Higgs, *How to Deal with the Unemployed*, London, 1904; J. Ladoff, *American Pauperism and the Abolition of Poverty*, Chicago, 1904; C. S. Loch, *Methods of Social Advance*, London, 1904; E. U. Pasini, *La Difesa del Povero*, Perugia, 1904; C. F. Rogers, *Charitable Relief*, London, 1904; P. Alden, *The Unemployed*, London, 1905; Y. E. de Froment, *L'Assistance légale et la lutte contre le paupérisme en Angleterre*, Paris, 1905; A. Niceforo, *Les Classes pauvres*, Paris, 1905; W. Reason, *Our Industrial Outcasts*, London, 1905; A. G. Warner, *American Charities*, revised ed., Boston, 1908; H. M

Conyngton, *How to Help. A Manual of Practical Charity*, London, 1910; W. Cunningham, *Christianity and Social Questions*, New York, 1910; C. S. Loeb, *Charity and Social Life. A short Study of Religious and Social Thought in Relation to Charitable Methods and Institutions*, London and New York, 1910; H. F. Ward, *Social Ministry; an Introduction to the Study and Practice of Social Service*, New York, 1910; J. W. Harper, *The Church and Social Betterment*, Glasgow, 1910; W. J. Tucker, *The Function of the Church in Modern Society*, Boston, 1911.

SOCIALISM.

I. Definition: The term Socialism, derived from the Latin, *socialis*, from *socius*, "a companion," came into general use in 1835. It has passed through many changes of definition. It implies administration in the interests of society as a whole, so as to afford equal individual opportunity. This may be accomplished by the voluntary association of some of the individuals in a community, or of all the persons within a definite region. When extended over a national territory, it has been termed nationalism. As most frequently employed, the term, socialism, denotes control by organized society of land and capital, of industrial production, and of the distribution of the income therefrom. Political socialists ordinarily demand State ownership of land and of the instruments of production. Under the fire of criticism there has been a tendency to abandon this extreme position. The abler socialistic writers show themselves ready to accept experimentation, advancing toward the theoretic goal only so far as may be proved practicable. The platforms of political parties, however, which alone can be accepted as authoritative utterances, have in no respect relinquished the full nationalist program.

II. Communism: The extreme form of socialism is termed Communism (q.v.), which, in strict application, is the ownership in common of all possessions, public control and rearing of children, and the abolition of the marriage tie. In consequence of the universal odium felt toward the communists of Paris because of the atrocities of 1871, the word is now rarely used by socialistic writers. As a working system, communism, even when the right of separate families is respected, has not exhibited elements of permanence. Ancient and modern instances have been short-lived, showing greatest persistence when cemented by a common religious conviction. The monastic establishments of the Middle Ages, purely communistic in organization, separated the sexes; and similar to these were the Brethren of the Common Life (see Common Life, Brethren of the). The Libertines (q.v., 3) and the Familists (q.v.) were well-known communists of the Reformation period. John Ball, the Wycliffite priest, who instigated the Wat Tyler rebellion, was a medieval socialist, claiming that the people had been robbed of their proprietorship in the common land.

III. Ancient and Medieval Socialism: Socialistic features were found in the constitutions of Athens and Sparta, combined with slavery. Of the theoretic systems the more noted were Plato's "Republic," More's *Utopia* (Louvain, 1516), Campanella's "City of the Sun" (Frankfort, 1623), and James Harrington's *Common-Wealth of Oceana* (London, 1656), which last advocated a limited monarchy, having its revenue from public lands.

IV. Modern Socialism: The Socialism of to-day springs from three national sources: France contributed the doctrine of personal liberty and equality, England demonstrated the value of cooperation, Germany presented the ideal of the socialistic state.

1. The Preparation: The preparation for modern socialism came from the French philosophic literature of the eighteenth century. The chief writers were Voltaire, Rousseau (qq.v.), De Mably, Morelly, De Warville, Boissel, and Mabeuf. These writers gave direction to the popular unrest of France, and laid the theoretic foundation for a socialistic state marked by liberty, equality, and mediocrity, in which the inefficient, the indolent, and the unfortunate would find provision, and the refinements of civilization would take their chances. It was Jean Pierre Brissot de Warville who wrote *La propriété exclusive est un vol*, which trenchant sentence supplied to Proudhon his famous *La propriété c'est le vol*, "proprietorship is robbery." These men aimed at the subversion of the existing system in France, some of them taking part in the Revolution of 1789. Their writings prepared for the work of their successors in the following century. In England during this period Adam Smith published *The Wealth of Nations* in 1776. Contemporaneous with this literary movement was the development of the factory system, the adoption of steam power, and of the machinery at that time invented. The resultant evils called forth the first Peel factory legislation in 1802; and with Robert Owen's report to the parliamentary committee on the poor laws in 1817 began the English contribution to modern socialism. In that report Owen recommended segregating workers in communities of 1,200, where they should live in one building, and work and its products should be in common. Experiments attempted in England and America met with only temporary success.

Modern Socialism may be treated in two periods: the first extending from 1817 to the middle of the century, the second from that time to the present.

2. The First Period: When the Reform Bill of 1832 extended the franchise to the middle classes in **England**, the wage-earners regarded themselves as betrayed, and there resulted a movement known as Chartism, which demanded universal manhood suffrage. In 1848 the excitement became acute, and the cause was espoused by certain philanthropists, terming themselves Christian Socialists, among whom Frederick Denison Maurice, Charles Kingsley (qq.v.), and Ludlow were the leaders. They encouraged the wage-earners to form cooperative associations, the value of which approved itself widely; and the movement, merging with that of cooperation, disappeared from public view (see CHRISTIAN SOCIALISM). The pioneer in **France** was Saint Simon (q.v.), whose writings founded socialism on the teachings of Christ, stripped of traditional additions. His noble aim was defeated by the sensual mysticism of his followers. Fourier advocated communities of 1,800 persons, living in a great building a community life with free affinity instead of marriage. Experiments in France and America failed. Louis Blanc favored workshops under State rules, with superintendents elected by the operatives, and equal wages for all. The experiments by the provisional government of 1848, though failures, were not determinative of the value of the scheme. Proudhon opposed the immorality of the earlier socialists and advocated equality of wages and the confiscation of private property. His famous saying derived from De Warville, "Proprietorship is robbery," underlies the present socialist demand for the confiscation of all property employed in production. He expected a high moral development in society, under which government should become unnecessary because of human excellence. The stern repression of the socialists by the government in June, 1848, and the apparent prosperity of the second empire put an end to socialistic agitation until the rise of the present republic. **German** socialism begins with Johann Karl Rodbertus (1805–1875), whom many regard as the founder of so-called scientific socialism. He based his doctrine on the assertion that labor is the source and measure of all value, and demanded nationalization of land and capital for the purpose of abolishing the commercial crises which deprive men of work. He attacked the individualistic system as productive of such crises, and called for a gradual change without revolution.

3. The Second Period: As with Rodbertus, the activity of other distinguished socialists, overlapping the middle of the century, falls chiefly in the second period. Ferdinand Lassalle advocated a new political party, devoted to the interest of the wage-earner. He claimed that the wage-earners received a compensation sufficient to provide merely a bare existence, which statement has been called the "iron law of wages." He argued for productive cooperation by associations aided by State loans. Two names, Karl Marx and Friedrich Engels, are closely associated as the founders of the revolutionary school of so-called scientific socialism, which may be dated from the manifesto of the communist party in 1848. This was a somewhat incoherent defense of the abolition of private property, closing with an appeal to the socialists of all nations to unite. In 1867 the masterpiece of **Marx**, *Das Kapital*, set forth his economic theory of surplus value, which was virtually Lassalle's "iron law of wages," asserting that the wage-earner in industry received a bare subsistence and that the surplus of his product went to the capitalist. He advocated governmental ownership and control of land, capital, and all productive and distributive industry, remuneration of workers by certificates representing hours of labor, and payment for all workers regardless of quantity and quality solely according to the number of work-hours. Organized in 1862, the offspring of previous associations, the International Association of Working Men, better known as "The International," held world congresses until 1873. Beginning with the recommendation of cooperative societies, these bodies later demanded nationalization of the means of communication, mines, forests, and land, the abolition of rent, interest, profit, and all remuneration to capital. The International opposed itself to war, but lauded the communists of Paris in 1871 as martyrs to the cause of the wage-earners. In the congress of 1872 the Russian anarchists aroused serious strife which resulted in the death of the organization in the following year. In 1889, however, and frequently since then, international congresses have been held, notably one in London in 1896, disturbed by anarchists, who were thereupon excluded. The socialist movement in Germany advanced in two parallel lines, the aim of the one being socialization through the state, and that of the other the establishment of a cooperative system independent of state interference and gradually absorbing all industry. By a fusing of existing parties in 1875 was formed the present Socialistic Working Men's Party, which aims to convert "private property in the means of production into social property," and to conduct all production and distribution under social control.

1. In Germany.

2. In France, Italy, England, and Russia.

For some time succeeding the fall of the Paris commune **French** socialism was under a shadow, and suffered from differences which were reconciled and ended in 1905 by the formation of a united party, declaring for the transformation "of the capitalistic organization of society into a collectivist or communal organization." In 1892 the socialists of **Italy** separated from anarchism, but have since suffered from dissension, and have shown their activity chiefly in municipal work, in strikes, and in cooperation. After the wane of the Owen and the Christian socialist movements in **England**, though some Englishmen took part in the International, socialism evidently lost influence among the people. In 1884 two organizations came into existence, the Social Democratic Federation in politics and the Fabian Society in educational activity. The strength of the trade-unions and the native conservatism of the English workman have hindered the acceptance of socialistic principles. The great dock strike of 1888 aroused a new interest which issued in the organization of the Independent Labor Party. The socialistic vote in parliament presents a steadily increasing influence. In 1908 the conference of the labor party of Great Britain, formerly conservative, declared for State control of production. The Russian Socialists, generally known as Anarchists, except in methods differ little from those of other nations. Their chief aim is the abolition of the central despotism and the establishment of free federation of free associations, that is to say, the universal adoption of the Mir or Russian communal village government.

8. In the United States. In the United States, after the early community experiments, organized socialism dates from 1868 with the founding of the German Labor Association which became a section of the International. In 1874 was organized the body which became the Socialist Labor Party of North America. In 1897 a rival socialist party was organized, which, on receiving large accessions from the older party in 1899, took as its title the Socialist Party. In 1908 the Socialist Party polled 420,464 votes.

V. Demands of Organized Socialists: Socialistic parties are agreed on the principle of collective ownership and administration of the factors of production, the means of transportation and communication, and the method of distribution. In regard to the application of the details socialists are widely at variance. Whether all land, all machinery, all wage-paying shall be controlled by government are matters on which are held diverse views, though the political programs generally demand complete nationalization. While desiring to abolish rent paid to landowners, socialists expect rent to be paid to the State. Interest on loans and dividends on stock are regarded as unearned income which should be abolished. As the State cares for the individual, socialists demand that inheritance be denied, the savings of all passing to the State on their death. The immediate demands of the European socialistic parties call for little more than the freedom and protection enjoyed by the American citizen. The Russian desires the abolition of the central government; the German, of the paternal State; the French desire the State to assume the entire industrial direction. The control of industry by restriction, direction, and publicity, exercised by the state and federal governments as it is administered in this land, inasmuch as it is exercised collectively, is socialism as far as it extends. In the multitudinous duties of the factory inspector, in protective labor laws, in the limitation of the labor of women and children, and in the control of corporations by commission, the American state employs a direction of industry which is socialistic.

VI. Socialism Untried: The socialistic state or cooperative commonwealth of thorough-going socialism has never proved itself by experiment. What has been tried, has been the socialistic community within the competitive state. A few such communities, founded on strong religious sentiment, have survived a century. The majority, exhibiting a purely economic socialism, have been short-lived. Whether, therefore, an economic organization, possessing the materials and conducting the production of all economic goods, could be made successful, is a question purely theoretical. Cooperative societies for production and distribution have maintained themselves successfully in the presence of competition, especially in Belgium and England; but these enjoy the stimulus of competition. The claims made by socialistic writers are, therefore, based merely on conjecture, a condition to be remembered in estimating the advantages claimed for the system.

VII. Advantages Claimed: The chief claims of advantage over the competitive system may be thus stated: (1) The saving of the capital wasted in duplicating productive agencies, as parallel railways and light, telephone and telegraph systems on the same territory, etc. (2) The saving of competitive advertising, trade solicitation, and the like. (3) Scientific adjustment of production to consumption, thus avoiding economic crises. (4) The guaranty of a comfortable living to all men. (5) The abolition of the middle-man in disposal of goods. (6) The development of unselfishness throughout society. (7) The abolition of litigation concerning property. (8) The termination of trade disputes and strikes.

VIII. The Claims Considered: An examination of these claims reveals their weakness. It is evident that State socialism involves a radical overturning of the economic basis of society. To approve itself to calm judgment, it must be shown not only that State socialism must be more effective than the present system, but also that it would be better than any possible modification of the present system. Over against the above claims, considered in order, may be stated the following: (1) Duplication is not necessarily waste. Parallel railways often prove their value by developing new regions for increased market supply. The operation of the economic law of combination tends to the elimination of unnecessary duplication, while by government regulation unwise duplication may be checked. (2) Under socialism a large amount of advertising would still be necessary to inform the public of the usefulness of State products. Combination and agreement have the tendency to reduce wasteful competitive advertising. All the necessary saving might be had apart from socialism. (3) It has always been to the interest of producers to make a scientific adjustment of production to consumption. Thus far there is no known method sufficient for the task. It remains to be proved that human foresight can prevent economic crises. The socialist claim is sheer assumption. It must be shown in what way and by what wisdom this adjustment can be made, and also that it would be impossible under the individualist system. (4) By discouragement of the captains of industry, demoralization of the most thrifty and skilful workers, and denial of adequate rewards to stimulate invention, socialism would disastrously impair the productivity of society. All would be approximately on the same level, which would be a condition of general poverty. (5) The present middle-men would be largely replaced by officials required to manage the distribution of the products. Even under competition there is a tendency to eliminate the middle-men. The claim remains to be proved. (6) Far from developing a spirit of unselfishness, socialism, by its denial of just reward to skill and diligence, would produce a spirit of discontent on the part of the most able in society, who would be tempted to reduce their production to the meager output of the least valuable workers. (7) As personal property would still exist and rights would be established in connection with rentals, there would still be large room for invasion of rights and consequent litigation, especially if the right of gift and of inheritance were maintained. Industrial differences would require judicial adjustment in more instances than under the present system in which there is so much of negotiation between the interested persons. (8) Socialism does not remove the cause or the occasion of strikes, it merely shifts the basis; the contention, instead of being between private or corporate employer and employed, will be between the government and the employed. Complaints that some workers receive an undue proportion of the wealth produced, will doubtless be submitted to arbitration; but strikes would follow that arbitration as frequently as now. It is only on the Marxian basis of time payment regardless of quantity and quality of output that strikes would disappear; and, if that system were established, there soon would be a revolt of the more efficient workers.

IX. Criticism: In addition to these categorical strictures other objections of greater force may be presented: (1) Socialism would largely terminate individual opportunity. The individual would no longer be free to choose that work for which he is best fitted. All would be required to accept what the government indicated. What is unfortunately true of some to-day, would become the rule for all. (2) The demand for the nationalization of the soil may have some ground of reason in Europe where the toiler is excluded from the land held by great estates. It is foundationless in this country where it is difficult to obtain a sufficient number of persons to till the soil. (3) The doctrine of the increasing misery of the wage-earners, prominent in the Manifesto of 1848, is still held by some socialists, though abandoned by the more intelligent, who substitute the claim that the difference in the economic comfort of rich and poor is increasing. The latter claim is unsubstantiated, the former demonstrably false. (4) The tyranny of socialism would necessarily result in arrest of the general progress. The advance of civilization has come of individual initiative; socialism removes opportunity by suppressing individual production. Some socialists claim that the industrial phase of government would be conducted by the same men who are now industrial leaders. They fail to show how the most able are to be discovered and advanced to leadership. Under the competitive system the man who has the best machine or method of management passes the less progressive. Under socialism the men who are in control will not look with favor on the inventive person whose success would involve their retirement. Society will thus be robbed of the elements of progress which competition supplies. (5) The claim that the ablest will be the leaders is, however, without foundation. The highest talent can not be enlisted by a system which robs it of its adequate rewards; and, if coerced by stern necessity, will not have the spirit to give its best work. Furthermore, the structure of the industrial system will be political, not economic. The men in office will be the plausible and the talkative, not the thinkers and organizers. Such men will rigorously exclude from office the men who might achieve for society. (6) This absorption of all power by the political demagogue would be impregnably fortified by the absolute control and censorship of the press by the government which would suppress all external publication. As the government could not publish everything offered, it would be necessary to have a body to determine what books and what newspaper or magazine articles should be published. All articles and books seeking to expose government corruption would be sternly suppressed, and the one method of informing the public would thus be closed to all reformers. Under these conditions the arrest of general progress would be complete. (7) Although the more intelligent socialists, recognizing the share in production of inventive and organizing genius, the grades of skill, the participation of insurance, interest, and provision for replacement, have abandoned the Marxian doctrine of equal payment for all workers, manual and mental, according to the number of work-hours; nevertheless, the mass of socialists cling to the doctrine and proclaim it as their aim. This would be the robbery of the skilled in favor of the unskilled, robbery of the head-worker to enrich the hand-worker, an exploitation as unjust as any wrong of which socialists complain in the present system. (8) Socialists perceive that the institution of the family within the socialistic system threatens the prosperity and permanence of the system, as it constitutes an interest more engrossing than the body politic. This has been the defect in those experiments which have perished. Attack is, therefore, made upon the family by suggesting the separate support of the mother while she cares for her children, the public rearing and care of children, and even free and terminable marriages. Another attack on the family appears in the desire to abolish inheritance, first openly stated in the manifesto of 1848. This strikes at the right and duty of the father to support his children, fully recognized in both Jewish and Christian ethics. In application it would be undisguised legal robbery. (9) The confiscation of land and the factors of production without compensation to the owners, as advocated by the Fabian Society and others, would be robbery by legislation, as would also the repudiation of the national debt demanded by the English Social Democrats. It becomes evident from what precedes that, instead of developing a high brotherly regard for others, socialism exalts greed and indolence and the disposition to profit by the exploitation of others. In a word, socialism claims a right to do that which it condemns in the competitive system.

X. Improvements Needed: It may justly be admitted that improvements are needed and possible in the competitive system. For American industrial society the chief improvements needed may be grouped under three topics: (1) The relation between employer and employed. (2) The condition of the unskilled. (3) The equalization of production and consumption. Experiments in meeting these needs are in progress, some of which promise as satisfactory adjustment as socialism could effect.

XI. The Relation of the Church: The Christian Church has not been in favor with socialists because in their minds it is associated with oppression, in Europe with the oppression of the Roman Catholic Church, in America with the oppression of capitalists. The Church in America has not hitherto succeeded in disabusing the minds of the masses of their error, but recent activities and utterances of various branches of the Church, especially the establishment of labor departments, have been directed more efficiently to this end, and have been attended with marked success. Not a few socialists are found in the Church in England and America. The Christian Socialists in the United States have formed several organizations for conference and cooperation, notably the Christian Socialist Federation which declares for the cooperative commonwealth. Far more numerous in the Church are those who see the need of wise measures to modify the present economic system in the interest of the least paid, and of the activity of the Church as the messenger of Christ to persuade all classes to Christian brotherhood, that the change may be peaceful and permanent. Socialism, stirred by the withholding of his due from the wage-earner, attempts a solution by withholding his due from the economical and from the skilled. There is needed something more than a mere economic change; there is needed the spirit of Christ. It is the mission of the Church to teach men that spirit; and she must become the most potent agent in accomplishing that which socialism inadequately plans, the winning of the world to live in the spirit of the Redeemer.

JAMES CARTER.

BIBLIOGRAPHY: Consult the literature under Christian Socialism, and Communism, especially the works of Noyes, Nordhoff, and Hinds. Also: Morelly, *Code de la nature*, Paris, 1755; F. M. C. Fourier, *Théorie des quatre mouvements*, Paris, 1808; idem, *Le Nouveau Monde industriel*, ib. 1829; C. H. St. Simon, *L'Industrie*, Paris, 1817; idem, *L'Organisation*, ib. 1819; idem, *Du système industriel*, 3 vols., ib. 1821–22; idem, *Le Nouveau Christianisme*, ib. 1825, Eng. transl., *The New Christianity*, London, 1834; J. J. L. Blanc, *Organisation du travail*, Paris, 1840, Eng. transl., *Organisation of Labor*, London, 1848; É. Cabet, *Voyage en Icarie*, Paris, 1840; J. Ruskin, *Unto This Last*, London, 1862; K. Marx, *Das Kapital*, Hamburg, 1867, new ed., 3 vols., 1906, Eng. transl., *Capital*, 12th ed., London, 1908; T. Woolsey, *Communism and Socialism*, New York, 1880; E. Bellamy, *Looking Backward*, Boston, 1888; idem, *Equality*, London, 1897; A. Schaeffle, *The Quintessence of Socialism*, ib. 1889; Fabian Society, *Essays in Socialism*, London, 1890; F. Engels, *Socialism, Utopian and Scientific*, ib. 1892; R. T. Ely, *Socialism: its Nature, Strength, and Weakness*, ib. 1894; J. Jaurès, *Studies in Socialism*, ib. 1906; T. Kirkup, *History of Socialism*, 3d ed., New York, 1907; idem, *An Inquiry into Socialism*, 3d ed., ib. 1907; R. C. K. Ensor, *Modern Socialism*, 2d ed., New York, 1907; H. G. Wells, *New Worlds for Old*, Edinburgh, 1908; idem, *Socialism and the Family*, Boston, 1908; P. Leroy-Beaulieu, *Collectivism*, New York, 1908; W. R. Hunter, *Socialists at Work*, ib. 1908; *The Case against Socialism*, New York, 1908; G. M. Bell, *Social Service*, ib. 1908; M. Hillquit, *Socialism in Theory and Practice*, ib. 1908; idem, *Hist. of Socialism in the United States*, new ed., ib. 1910; W. Rauschenbusch, *Christianity and the Social Crisis*, ib. 1908; E. P. Tenney, *Contrasts in Social Progress*, ib. 1908; C. B. Thompson, *The Churches and the Wage Earners*, ib. 1908; W. E. Chadwick, *Social Work*, ib. 1909; idem, *Social Relationship in the Light of Christianity*, London, 1910; A. St. Ledger, *Australian Socialism; . . . its Origin and Development*, New York, 1909; E. Hammacher, *Das philosophisch-okonomische System des Marxismus*, Leipsic, 1909; J. Spargo, *Socialism*, New York, 1909; J. J. Ming, *The Morality of Modern Socialism*, ib. 1909; T. C. Hall, *Social Solutions in the Light of Christian Ethics*, ib. 1910; Jane T. Stoddart, *The New Socialism*, New York, 1910; H. Jones, *The Working Faith of the Social Reformer*, London, 1910; Y. Guyot, *Socialistic Fallacies*, New York, 1910; W. L. Wilson, *The Menace of Socialism*, Philadelphia, n. d.

SOCIÉTÉ ÉVANGÉLIQUE DE GENÈVE. See EVANGELICAL SOCIETY OF GENEVA.

SOCIETY OF MARY: 1. Marist Fathers: A religious order founded in 1816 uniting the work of education with that of missions. The founder was Jean Claude Marie Colin (b. at Saint Bonnet-le-Troncy, in the diocese of Lyons, Aug. 7, 1790; d. at Notre-Dame-de-la-Neylière, in the department of Rhône, Feb. 28, 1875), who persuaded his brother and some others to join in the organization of an order under provisional rules drawn up by him. He received the approbation of Pius VII. in 1818, and the members took up the task of preaching in the neglected parts of the diocese, and in 1829, having greatly increased in numbers, assumed charge of the ecclesiastical seminary of Belley. In 1835 the attention of the Holy See was turned to the South Sea Islands and the need for workers there; the Marists were asked to undertake missions in those regions, and accepted the invitation, upon which Gregory XVI. approved the Society of Mary in the brief *Omnium gentium* of Apr. 29, 1836, final sanction being given by Pius IX., Feb. 28, 1873. The mother house is at Lyons, but the order has spread until it consists of six provinces, two in France, one in the British Isles, one in the United States, one in New Zealand, and one in Oceania. In the United States the order has an archbishop, 105 priests, 75 novices, 5 lay brothers, 2 training-houses, 4 colleges, and 18 parishes besides missions. The government is under a superior general, with four assistants, a general procurator, a procurator apud sanctum sedem, and the first alone is elected for life; the official residence of the general officers is Rome.

2. Society of Mary of Paris: A society founded in 1817 by William Joseph Chaminade, the primary purpose of which is the salvation of its own members, and then all works of zeal. The formation of the society was stimulated by a desire to strengthen the church after the losses occasioned by the French Revolution, and various sodalities were formed, the culmination of which was the society under discussion. One of the peculiarities of this organization is the inclusion of both clerical and lay members, bound together by the vows of poverty, celibacy, obedience, and stability in the service of the Virgin, and employed in various works of mercy and service. Since the expulsion of the order from France in 1903, the headquarters are at Nivelles, Belgium, where the superior general resides. The order comprises seven provinces, and has houses in the principal countries of Europe outside Great Britain, also in Africa, China, Japan, the Hawaiian Islands, Canada, Mexico, and the United States. In the last the society settled in 1849, and it reports there 2 normal schools, 4 colleges, 3 high schools, and 44 parochial schools, principally in the Middle West.

Bibliography: On 1: The *Constitutions* were published at Lyons, 1873, and the *Statuta capitulorum generalium* in the same place, 1907. Consult: *Life of Venerable Fr. Colin*, St. Louis, 1909; *Père Colin*, Lyons, 1898; *Père Colin*, ib. 1900; Mangeret, *Les Origines de la foi catholique en Nouvelle-Zélande*, ib. 1892; C. Egremont, *L'Année de l'église 1900*, Paris, 1901; Baunard, *Un siècle de l'église de France*, ib. 1902; Hervier, *Les Missions maristes*, ib. 1902; Heimbucher, *Orden und Kongregationen*, iii. 339–343.

SOCIETY FOR PROMOTING CHRISTIAN KNOWLEDGE. See Tract Societies, III., 2.

SOCIETY FOR THE PROPAGATION OF THE GOSPEL IN FOREIGN PARTS. See Missions to the Heathen, B, II., 4, § 4.

SOCINUS, so-sai'nus, FAUSTUS, SOCINIANS.

I. History.
   Faustus Socinus (§ 1).
   Early Socinian Movement (§ 2).
   The Dispersion (§ 3).
II. Doctrines of the Socinians, or Older Unitarians.
   Scripture (§ 1).
   God (§ 2).
   Creation; Man (§ 3).
   Christology (§ 4).
   Work of Christ (§ 5).
   Soteriology; the Church; Eschatology (§ 6).

1. Faustus Socinus.

I. History: As a radical by-product of the Reformation appeared the antitrinitarian movement. At first it was represented by such individuals as the Anabaptists Hans Denk, Ludwig Haetzer, and Jakob Kautz (qq.v.), and by Michael Servetus (q.v.) and his followers (G. V. Gentile, Georgius Blandrata; qq.v.), but there was as yet no unity of organization. To it belonged also Laelius Socinus (q.v.); but the founder of the antitrinitarians as a sect was his nephew, Faustus Socinus (Fausto Sozzini; b. at Siena 1539; d. at Luclawice, near Cracow, Mar. 3, 1604). He was early left an orphan, and his education was defective. He devoted himself to the study of law like his relatives, specially Laelius, by correspondence with whom he derived anti-Roman religious and theological instruction. He lived at Lyons, 1559–62, and at Zurich, 1562, where he was absorbed in the study of the literary fragments of his uncle, and began his literary activity with *Explicatio primæ partis primi capitis Evangelii Johannis* (Rakow, 1562), a sort of program of antitrinitarianism. During 1562–74 he, decked with honors, held official positions at the court of Francesco de Medici at Florence, and indulged in the diversions of the period. At Basel, 1574–78, he elaborated his system, originating two of his most important works: *De Jesu Christo servatore* (Basel, 1594) against the French Reformed clergyman J. Covet, and *De statu primi hominis ante lapsum* (Rakow, 1610) against F. Pucci of Florence. He accepted an invitation of Georgius Blandrata (q.v.) to Transylvania, unsuccessfully aiding the latter in attempting to dissuade Franciscus Davidis (q.v.) from his non-adorant views. The theological turmoil, together with the outbreak of the pest, caused him to leave Transylvania, 1579, and proceed to Poland, where the name Socinus had acquired fame from his uncle's two sojourns (1556 and 1558), and where the Unitarian movement was gaining in political influence. Here (1579–1604) he made an earnest effort to unite the divergent parties into one organization. In Cracow, 1579–83, he endeavored in vain to join with the Polish Brethren, a society of Unitarians, but was hindered by his refusal to be rebaptized.

In common with the Anabaptists, the Unitarians strongly objected to the holding of political office, resorting to the civil courts, and military service. Theological differences also existed among Arians on the preexistence of Christ, on chiliasm, and the non-adoration of Christ (see Davidis, Franciscus, §§ 4–5); but by disputations in synods, by special discussions, and a number of literary works, Socinus finally succeeded in bringing about harmony and the acceptance of his own views. His idea of baptism (see below) prevailed over the Anabaptist at the Synod of Rakow, 1603. In 1583 he left Cracow from fear of the persecution of King Stephen Bathory and settled at Pawlikowice, a village near Cracow. He returned to Cracow, 1585–87, attending the Synod of Brzesc in Lithuania in 1588, where, by the brilliant success of his theological disputations, he permanently confirmed his influence over the Unitarians. Several times he was ill-treated; thus, in 1594, by a troop of soldiers, and on Ascension day, 1598, when students of Cracow, incited by Roman priests, threw him out of his sick-bed, carried him half-naked through the streets, and inflicted bloody injuries. Only by the mediation of Martin Vadovita, a professor of the university, did he escape death by drowning. During the assault all the papers, manuscripts, and books found in his house were burned on the market-place. He next lived at Luclawice, 1598–1604. His works, exegetical, polemical, and dogmatic, appeared in vols. i.–ii., *Bibliotheca fratrum Polonorum*, edited by his grandson, Andreas Wissowaty (Irenopolis [Amsterdam], 1656 and after); also under the special title, *Fausti Socini Senensis opera omnia*. The most important dogmatic works are, *Prælectiones theologicæ* (Rakow, 1609); *Christianæ religionis brevissima institutio per interrogationes et responsiones, quam catechismum vulgo vocant* (1608); and *Fragmentum catechismi prioris F. L. S., qui periit in Cracoviensi rerum ejus direptione*. Immediately after the death of Socinus appeared the Racovian Catechism, the chief symbol of the Socinians. The work of revising the catechism of 1574 was assigned to Socinus and another Unitarian, Statorius. Both worked independently; the *Institutio* of Socinus was left unfinished at his death; and after the death subsequently of Statorius the work was completed on the basis of the manuscripts of Socinus by Valentin Schmalz, Hieronymus Moskorzowski, and Johann Völkel (published in Polish, 1605; larger German ed., 1608; in Lat., *Catechesis ecclesiarum*, ed. and enlarged by Moskorzowski and dedicated to James I. of England, and briefly cited as *Catechismus Racoviensis*, 1609; another Latin ed. with emendations and additions by Johann Crell and Johann Schlichting, furnished probably by Wiszowaty and Joachim Stegman, Jr., Amsterdam, 1665; with much added matter, 1684; Eng. transl., by Thomas Rees, London, 1818).

Until the death of Socinus Unitarianism was in

the ascendency in Poland. Many small congregations were composed almost entirely of the nobility distinguished by humanistic culture.

2. Early Socinian Movement. The most important society was at Rakow (55 m. n.e. of Cracow), a city founded by the Reformed Johannes Sieninski in 1569, which soon became a colonial center for a free-thinking spiritual life, specially after the accession to Socinianism of the younger Sieninski. Its excellent school was attended at one time by 1,000 students. Philosophy and theology were taught; and associated with it was a publishing-house transferred from Cracow. Rakow was also the meeting-place of the annual general synod. The prosperity of Socinianism was mainly due to the influence of its great ministers, theologians, and scholars, proceeding from its academic center at Rakow. Valentin Schmalz (b. in Gotha 1572; d. at Rakow 1622) was won to Unitarianism while studying at Strasburg, 1591; came to Poland and was rebaptized; was rector of the school at Szmigel; became preacher at Lublin, 1598; and teacher and preacher at Rakow, 1605. He made many journeys in the interest of Unitarianism, and left fifty-two writings of a vehement polemical nature. Johann Völkel (b. at Grimma, 17 m. s.e. of Leipsic; d. 1618) became a Socinian in 1585, after the completion of his studies at Wittenberg; was rector of the school in Wengrow; and later preacher in Poland. His chief work, *De vera religione* (Rakow, 1630), was a systematic presentation of the Socinian doctrine and was authoritative. Christoph Ostorodt (b. at Goslar, 40 m. s.e. of Hanover; d. at Buskow, near Danzig, 1611) studied at Königsberg; became rector of the school at Luchow in Pomerania; entered the Unitarian society, 1585; fled to Poland and became preacher at Rakow. He was strongly Anabaptist, and warfare, public office, litigation, the oath, and riches were repugnant to him. His most popular work was *Unterrichtung von den vornehmsten Hauptpunkten der christlichen Religion* (Rakow, 1604). Hieronymus Moskorzowski (d. 1625) founded the Unitarian congregation in the town of Czarkow; and wrote polemical works beside an "Apology of the Socinians." In the following generation Johann Crell (b. at Helmersheim, in Franconia, 1590; d. at Rakow 1631), by his eminent endowments, thorough culture, and tireless energy, takes first rank. He was educated at Nuremberg and Altdorf; was converted to Unitarianism partly by Ernst Soner at Altdorf; fled to Poland, 1612; became professor of the Greek language in Rakow, 1613; rector of the school, 1616; and preacher at Rakow, 1621–31. Crell was an extremely prolific writer, producing commentaries on the New Testament; two books, *De uno Deo patre*, a very sharp attack by a Socinian upon the orthodox doctrine of the Trinity; and *Ad librum H. Grotii, quem de satisfactione Christi adversus Faustum Socinum Senensem scripsit, responsio.* All the works of Crell are published in *Bibliotheca fratrum Polonorum*, vols. iii. and iv. (ut sup.). Jonas Schlichting (b. at Bukowice, near Strasburg-on-the-Drewenz, 80 m. s.s.e. of Danzig, 1592; d. at Selchow, near Teltow, 11 m. s.w. of Berlin, 1661) studied at Rakow and at the University of Altdorf; became preacher at Rakow; went to Transylvania, 1638, to settle the controversy of the *Non-adorantes*, but without success; was outlawed by the diet which burned his confession of faith, 1647; and left Poland, 1658. He left commentaries on most of the books of the New Testament (*Bibliotheca*, vol. iv.); the *Confessio fidei christianæ* (1642), translated into Polish, German, French, and Dutch; and *De trinitate, de moralibus Veteris et Novi Testamenti* (1637). Johann Ludwig von Wolzogen (b. at Neuhäusel or Ersek-Ujvar, 50 m. n.w. of Budapest, 1599; d. 1661) was a distinguished exegete, and, besides his commentaries, wrote a *Compendium religionis Christianæ* and a severe criticism of the doctrine of the Trinity (*Bibliotheca*, vols. viii.–ix.). Samuel Przypkowski (b. 1592; d. in Brandenburg 1670) studied at Altdorf (1614–16); was compelled to flee from Poland; and wrote *Vita Fausti Socini* (1636); and a comparison of the Apostles Creed with the symbols of his day. Andreas Wiszowaty (b. 1608; d. at Amsterdam 1678) was a grandson of F. Socinus; educated at Rakow, Leyden, and Amsterdam; pastor of various congregations in Poland; expelled by the edict of 1657; lived at Mannheim, 1661–66, as pastor of the Socinian exiles; and subsequently at Amsterdam. The most important of his sixty-two writings was *Religio rationalis*. Stanislaus Lubienik or Lubienicki, the younger (b. at Rakow 1623; d. at Hamburg 1675), was the author of the *Historia Reformationis Polonicæ* (Amsterdam, 1685). Peter Morskowski was the author of *Politia ecclesiastica* or Socinian agenda, written at the order of a convention at Darwie, 1646 (3 books, Leipsic, 1745).

Socinianism, which had flourished during the first decades of the seventeenth century, succumbed to the Roman Catholic reaction started under Sigismund III. At the instigation of the Jesuits, the church at Lublin was destroyed, 1627.

3. The Dispersion. Under Ladislaus IV., by act of the senate at Warsaw (1638), the school at Rakow was suppressed, the Socinians were deprived of their church and printing-establishment, and their preachers and teachers were proscribed. Under John Casimir (1648–68) the final blows fell upon the remaining Unitarian congregations. The Swedish invasion occasioned a respite, and some resorted to the party in favor of the Swedish king, hoping for relief. In consequence they were accused of treason and suffered indescribable afflictions. After the withdrawal of the Swedes (1638) the Diet of Warsaw prohibited the confession and promotion of "Arianism" on pain of death. Many migrated to other lands, many joined the Roman Catholics, and others remained, secretly protected by Roman Catholics and Protestants. A new edict (1661) decreed a stricter enforcement of the laws against the Socinians. Soon the same fate befell the other Protestants, and the Jesuit reaction reached its climax with the massacre of Thorn, 1724. Socinianism secured an influential promoter in Germany in Ernst Soner (b. at Nuremberg 1572; d. at Altdorf 1612). He studied at Leyden, 1597–1598, where Ostorodt and Woidowski converted him to Socinianism. As professor of medicine and physics at Altdorf he clandestinely labored in the

interest of Socinianism and attracted a great number of Socinian students from Transylvania, Hungary, and Poland. Some time after his death this hearthstone of Socinianism in Altdorf was discovered. Some of the students recanted, others were banished, the Poles were expelled, and the Socinian writings were burned. Meanwhile some Polish exiles found a refuge in Oppeln and Ratibor, Silesia, and in the territory of the duke of Brieg. There, at Kreuzburg, they held two synods, in 1661 and 1663. Also Elector Karl Ludwig of the Palatinate allowed them to settle at Mannheim, but owing to their proselytizing tendencies they were compelled to leave in 1666 and scattered in Holland, Prussia, Silesia, and Brandenburg, forming local congregations. The pastor at Königswalde was Samuel Crell (b. 1660; d. at Amsterdam 1747), grandson of Johann Crell (ut sup.). Under the pseudonym Artemonius he published a treatise *Initium Evangelii Sancti Johanni* (Amsterdam, 1726), in which he sought to prove the corruption of the text of the prologue of the Fourth Gospel. He maintained that the ante-Nicene view of the Trinity differed from the post-Nicene. He wrote also a dogmatical treatise, based on Rom. v. 12 sqq., *Cogitationes novæ de primo et secundo Adamo* (Amsterdam, 1700). After his death Unitarianism disappeared from Brandenburg but not from the other territories of the Prussian monarchy. Toward the end of the sixteenth century Socinian congregations had sprung up near Danzig, Buskow, and Straszin. In 1640 Elector Georg Wilhelm, urged by the Prussian estates, enjoined vigilance for the expulsion of the Antitrinitarians, Socinians, and Photinians. Frederick William of Brandenburg, the "Great Elector," seconded by his deputy in Prussia, Prince Boguslav Radziwil, seeking to make his land an asylum for Protestant refugees, pursued the principle of toleration. Socinians consequently settled in the districts of Lyck, Rhein, and Johannisburg, without the privilege of owning land. In 1670 the estates secured a rescript for their expulsion. Upon the intercession of the elector and the king of Poland the storm was allayed; but in 1679, 1721, and 1729 the estates repeated their demands under Frederick William I. The Socinians maintained themselves in wretched conditions and in small numbers until the nineteenth century. In the Netherlands antitrinitarian ideas appeared simultaneously with Anabaptist views, and at first frequently combined with them. In 1597 and 1598 Ostorodt and Woidowski found many adherents in Amsterdam and Leyden. In 1599 the states-general ordered the burning of the Socinian writings and the expulsion of those two men. Nevertheless, the movement spread so as to call forth appeals for restriction from the synods (1628–53), until finally the states-general laid an edict of prohibition upon Socinianism. This was not strictly enforced, however, and many refugees from the contemporaneous Polish repression found asylum in Holland. Among those of special importance were Jeremias Felbinger (b. at Brieg in Silesia, 27 m. s.e. of Breslau, 1616), who was preacher in Straszin, and lived afterward in Poland, Prussia, and at Amsterdam, 1687. He was Arminian on the doctrine of redemption and taught the resurrection of the wicked to judgment. Christoph Sand, the younger (b. at Königsberg Oct. 12, 1644; d. at Amsterdam Nov. 30, 1680), was educated at Königsberg; went to Amsterdam, 1668; and was author of *Bibliotheca antitrinitariorum* (Freystadt, 1684). Daniel Zwicker (b. at Danzig 1612; d. at Amsterdam 1678) was compelled to leave his native city, 1643; lived after 1657 in the Netherlands; and wrote *Irenicum Irenicorum* (1658), which caused a great sensation. Reason, the correctly interpreted Scriptures, and true tradition are presented as the three fundamental norms. Socinianism in the Netherlands was ultimately absorbed by the Remonstrants, Anabaptists, and Collegiants (qq.v.).

In Transylvania, Unitarianism spread at the same time as in Poland, owing to the activity of Blandrata (q.v.), alternating between the two countries, and the influence of Franciscus Davidis (q.v.). In 1568, by resolution of the Diet at Thorenburg, the Unitarian confession was recognized, and, toward the end of the reign of Zapolya II., it promised to become the prevailing religion of the country; but the division caused by Davidis' non-adorantism was used by the Catholic opponents to their advantage. The *non-adorantes* were suppressed and excluded (1638) by the Unitarians; at the same time occurred the suppression of the Sabbatarian element; but a succeeding period of persecutions reduced the Unitarians themselves during the seventeenth and eighteenth centuries. The German and Polish elements disappeared completely after the eighteenth century, leaving only the Magyar. A theological representative of later Transylvanian Unitarianism was Bishop Sentabrahami (Michael St. Abraham), 1737–1758, author of a *Summa universæ theologiæ christianæ secundum Unitarios* (Klausenburg, 1787). From 1821 the Unitarianism of Transylvania entered into closer relations with that of England, and from 1834 with that of North America, a step which furthered its material and spiritual promotion. The Unitarians in Transylvania, inclusive of about 1,000 Hungarian Unitarians, may be estimated at nearly 60,000.

II. Doctrines of the Socinians or Older Unitarians: Early Socinianism is presented in its main sources, which are the works of Faustus Socinus, the Racovian Catechism, and the writings of the foremost Socinian theologians until about the middle of the seventeenth century contained in the *Bibliotheca Fratrum Polonorum*, vols. iii.–iv.

1. Scripture. It adheres throughout to the authority of Scripture, and is decidedly supernaturalistic. The Christian religion is the way revealed by God for the pursuit of eternal life. The Mosaic religion was incapable of breaking the power of the flesh, since it did not announce the hope of immortality, but limited itself to the prophecy of earthly happiness. Christianity is a perfected Mosaism, superseding the ceremonial and juridical laws, retaining and refining more sharply the ethical, and kindling by higher rewards the love of man to God. Though inspired, the Old Testament is practically superfluous and of only historical value. According to Socinus the sacred writers were inspired in respect to the content of religious truth only; in secondary matters even the apostles might err. His two criteria for the critical elimination of the ungenuine and for judging what is of divine content are (1) accordance with reason, and (2) moral significance and utility. The tendency was ever toward a more rationalistic faith.

The doctrine of God is divided into the ideas of the essence of God and of his will. The being of God undistinguished from his existence is not considered in the abstract metaphysical sense, but in the concrete relation to the world of finite being, more positively in relation to man.

2. God. Being and sovereignty are identical in God. He possesses absolute (*ex se ipso*) determination of will in the sense of the Scotist Scholasticism (q.v.). His existence, nature, and attributes are subjects of positive revelation; therefore involved with the proofs of the authority of Scripture. With respect to the divine attributes the canon holds that they are inseparable in understanding. Socinianism was occupied mainly with that of omniscience. God's foreknowledge is limited to the necessary, and does not apply to the possible; otherwise there would be no human freedom. Special attention is given to the attribute of divine unity, which coincides with the divine aseity, even the conception of God itself. The knowledge of the unity of God is necessary for salvation, because otherwise man would be uncertain as to who had revealed to him salvation. It is also profitable for salvation to know that God is only one person. Here is the nexus of the polemical battle with orthodoxy. The doctrine of the Trinity is represented as contrary to Scripture. That the Holy Spirit is anywhere in Scripture called God is denied. The passages in which Father, Son, and Spirit are represented, according to orthodoxy, to be coordinate, are invalidated. This is followed by the proof of reason against the Trinity, consisting in pointing out the inconsistencies and irrelevancies in the dogmatic formula and emphasizing the omission from Scripture of such terms as "substance," "person," "eternal generation of the Son," and "preexistence." Thus, the thesis of Socinus was sought to be established: "Plurality of persons in one divine essence is impossible." The creation out of nothing is denied by the Socinians and there is posited a preexisting matter from which God formed the world. *Ex nihilo* according to II Maccabees vii. 28 is identical with the *ex informi materia* (formless matter) of Eccles. xi. 17, or the *tohu wabhohu* (Gen. i. 2) which is not said in Scripture to have been created.

3. Creation; Man. Here appears the dualism that governs the whole system. The divine image in man consists essentially in his dominion over nature, including mind and reason; from these the likeness to God is derived. Man, created mortal, has by nature nothing of immortality, and therefore did not lose this virtue by the fall. Man was not created perfect or originally endowed with a high measure of wisdom. He had a negative or possible free will, not a positive actual freedom. The fall was due to a weak understanding and an inexperienced will, so that sensuality blinded the reason and incited to transgression. Inner nature merely asserted itself; yet Socinianism aimed to conceive sin as an act of freedom, in which it was not altogether consistent. Through sin Adam and his descendants have not lost free choice. In so far as original sin is the denial of this freedom, Socinianism disputes it most emphatically. Original sin as depravity of the choice of the good and as a penalty impending over man contradicts Scripture, which in its admonitions to repentance everywhere presupposes the freedom of man, and the doctrine not less emphatically contradicts reason. Lust and inclination to sin, in which original sin is said to consist, are possible in all but not shown to be in all. Granted that there is such a doom over all, that it is the result of Adam's sin would not follow. If this were so, original sin would cease to be sin; for there is no sin where there is no guilt. Hence there is no original sin as such. Inconsistently, however, the general mortality of the human race is traced to the sin of Adam; after the fall man, mortal by nature, was abandoned to his natural mortality because of the sin of Adam. With this assumption there is connected that of a certain sinful disposition produced by the continuous sinning of all generations. Accordingly, the freedom of man is weakened; but with the aid of God man may appropriate salvation. This divine reenforcement is needed to avoid gross and violent sins, contrary to reason; and those over which reason affords no mastery require specially potent and lofty promises of grace, and these are the promises in Jesus Christ.

The doctrine of salvation contemplates only a select part and has been characterized as ethico-aristocratic. The Gospel effects a total change in the spiritual nature of man.

4. Christology. Christ came, not to restore man to the original state before Adam, but to lift him to a more exalted one. The Christian is more than the truly human. Is then Christ also more than human? Socinianism answers that he was, on the one side, truly mortal man; on the other, more than mere man, a man with unusual endowments, imbued with immeasurable wisdom, and exalted by God to unlimited power and immortality. Christ was bound to be of like nature with man, because the goal of religion was immortality mediated by his resurrection, and if, on the other hand, his advantage above all men was in his divinity, he could not die. The Catechism expressly teaches that the Scripture denies to Christ the divine nature, in so far as it testifies to his humanity. Here lies the second great polemical center of Socinianism. Other human beings are called sons of God (Hos. i. 10; Rom. ix. 26). "Only begotten son of God" means "favorite and most beloved" (cf. Heb. xi. 17; Prov. iv. 3). "Equal with God" (John v. 18; Phil. ii. 6) refers to unity of power and work; and the statement "I and my Father are one" (John x. 30) is to be understood in the sense that the disciples are to be in accord as he and the Father are one (John xvii., 11, 22). Against the doctrine of preexistence it is maintained that the "beginning" (John i. 1) is the beginning of the Gospel (cf. xv. 27, xvi. 4). The creation of the world by the Word meant either the reformation of the human race, or the future eon of immortality. "The Word was made flesh" (i. 14) should be "was flesh," meaning that he through whom God revealed his will was subject to all human misery and death. The kenosis (Phil. ii. 6) can not possibly refer to divine nature. From John iii. 13, 31 and vi. 38, 62, it is concluded that Christ was caught up into heaven for a season like Paul. Contrary arguments of reason are added: (1) Two absolutely different substances can not unite in one person, because mortality and immortality, variability and invariability are irreconcilable; (2) if the union of the two natures be inseparable, then Christ could not have died; (3) the height of absurdity was the *communicatio idiomatum* of Lutheran doctrine. On the other hand, Socinians expressly asserted that Christ was "more" than all other human beings, superior in endowments but not in nature. He was conceived of a virgin, is perfectly holy, and has power to reign over all things. Just as dominion over the earth constitutes in man the inherent image of God, so the absolute power conferred by God upon Christ constitutes his divinity. In this sense he is truly God (I John v. 20) and is to be worshiped, next to the Father. Socinus calls the *non-adorantes* non-Christians, because they have not Christ.

5. Work of Christ.

The work of Christ in redemption is concentrated in his prophetic and kingly offices. For the prophetic office he was qualified by the instruction received during his sojourn in heaven (ut sup.). The content of revelation is essentially composed of "precepts and promises." The Lord's Supper is a ceremonial precept, supplementing the law of the Old Testament. Great emphasis is laid upon the symbolic idea of immersion and the breaking of bread. The Lord's Supper is taught as a memorial of Christ's death after the view of Zwingli, and the term sacrament is spurned. Baptism was deprecated as not of permanent validity, but only as a primitive rite of confession for Jewish and pagan converts. For those born of Christian parents it is unessential. It is not commanded and not designed for infants, who are incapable of confession, and those of Christian parentage are holy by virtue of descent (I Cor. vii. 14). Among promises, on the other hand, are (1) eternal life, characteristic of the New, absent from the Old Testament; (2) the Holy Spirit, not as a person but a power or divine activity, manifest visibly in the early Church and invisibly later as the spirit of revelation and faith. The essential element in the prophetic office is the death of Christ. The new revelation was attested (1) by the sinlessness of Jesus, (2) by his holy life, and (3) by his miracles and death. The doctrine of satisfaction is disputed in the manner of Scotist scholasticism. Christ's death was necessary to attest, first, the great love of God for human redemption; and, secondly, the resurrection to eternal life on the condition of obedience. The kingly office of Christ consists in the exaltation to the right hand of God to reign in his stead, power over his enemies, and the eternal reign and protection of the just, and begins with the ascension. The high-priestly office is an adjunct of the kingly, and means that he will, and actually does, come to the succor of man, which is styled a sacrifice. Its seat is in heaven, since on earth Christ is not high priest and has no tabernacle fit for the high-priesthood.

6. Soteriology; the Church; Eschatology.

The soteriological doctrine shows an essentially Pelagian form. Presupposing human autonomy, it conceives the divine will as manifest in revelations, to which the human obedience with divine reenforcement responds. On justification it is taught that that article of faith involves three elements: assent to the teaching of Jesus as true, trust in God through Christ, and obedience to the divine commandments. In effecting this, faith is justifying and saving. All imputation is repudiated. The true Church is "the company of those who hold and profess sound doctrine." The Church is one with a school of the true knowledge of God. In government it is an ecclesiastical democracy, subject only to Christ the head. The offices are those of pastor, elders, and deacons, of whom the first is elected by the synod. Church discipline is strictly insisted upon. Interference by the state is refused, even in case of heresy. The Christian is obligated to endure passively all that the civil power imposes, but active obedience is due only where there is no conflict with God's Word. "Rather to suffer than to commit injustice" is practised in private life; fellow church-members are to be prosecuted in civil courts only in urgent cases; and on the same principle military service is renounced, except that with weapons one is permitted to make a feint upon an enemy. Socinus and a majority of theologians approved of holding civic office as not in conflict with the law of Christ; but, in practise, this was impossible in view of the foregoing. In eschatology, the resurrection of the flesh is repudiated. The real substance of man or spirit will be retained, and identity of person clothed in a spiritual body (I Cor. xv.). The ungodly, with the devil and his angels, shall be annihilated. Thus the end like the beginning of the Socinian doctrine is immortality. (O. Zöckler†.)

Bibliography: On the life and teaching of Socinus consult: J. Crell, *Beschrijvinghe van Godt en zijne eygenschappen . . . Hier is by Ghevoeght F. Socini leven en daden*, Rakow, 1650 (?); S. Przykowski, *Vita Fausti Socino*, Cracow, 1636, Eng. transl., *The Life of that Incomparable Man Faustus Socinus*, London, 1653; G. Ashwell, *De Socino et Socinianismo*, Oxford, 1680; A. Calovius, *Scripta Antisociniana*, 3 vols., Ulm, 1684; J. Toulmin, *Memoirs of the Life, Character, Sentiments and Writings of F. Socinus*, London, 1777; G. F. Illgen, *Symbola ad vitam et doctrina Fausti Socini*, 3 parts, Leipsic, 1826–40; E. Tagart, *Sketches of the Lives and Characters of the Leading Reformers of the 16th Century*, London, 1843; P. Lecler, *Fauste Socin. Biographique et critique*, Geneva, 1885; Bayle, *Dictionary*, v. 168–180.

For the history of Socinianism consult: *Bibliotheca Fratrum Polonorum*, 6 vols., Amsterdam, 1626; B. Lamy, *Hist. du Socinianisme*, Paris, 1723; S. F. Lauterbach, *Ariano-Socinianismus olim in Polonia*, Leipsic, 1725; M. Maimbourg, *The Hist. of Arianism, . . . with Account of the . . . Socinian and Arian Controversies*, 2 vols., London, 1728–29; F. S. Bock, *Hist. Antitrinitariorum, maxime Socinianorum*, 2 vols., Königsberg, 1774–84; T. Lindsey, *Historical View of the State of the Unitarian Doctrine and Worship from the Reformation*, London, 1783; A. Fuller, *The Calvinistic and Socinian Systems Examined and Compared*, Edinburgh, 1815; F. Trechsel, *Die protestantischen Antitrinitarier vor Faustus Socinus*, 2 parts, Heidelberg, 1839–44; O. Fock, *Der Socinianismus nach seiner Stellung in der Gesammtentwickelung des christlichen Geistes*, i. 121–

283, Kiel, 1847; R. Wallace, *Antitrinitarian Biography*, 3 vols., London, 1850; W. Cunningham, *Historical Theology*, vol. ii., Edinburgh, 1862; E. L. T. Henke, *Vorlesungen über neuere Kirchengeschichte*, i. 453 sqq., Halle, 1874; J. Ferencz, *Kleiner Unitarierspiegel*, Vienna, 1879; J. H. Allen, in *American Church History Series*, x. 49–96, New York, 1894; H. Dalton, *Lasciana*, Berlin, 1898; W. J. van Douwen, in *TAT*, 1898, parts 1–3; J. F. Hurst, *Hist. of Rationalism*, revised ed., New York, 1901; O. Koniecki, *Geschichte der Reformation in Polen*, pp. 198–220, Breslau, 1901; G. Krause, *Reformation und Gegenreformation im . . . Polen*, Posen, 1901; A. C. McGiffert, *Protestant Thought before Kant*, pp. 107–118, New York, 1911; the works on the history of doctrine, e.g., Harnack, *Dogma*, v.–vii., especially vii. 119–167.

SOCINUS, LAELIUS (LELIO SOZZINI): Antitrinitarian, and uncle of Faustus Socinus (q.v.); b. at Siena in 1525; d. at Zurich May 16, 1562. One of the Italian free inquirers, he left Italy about 1544 to escape the Inquisition, and, going to Switzerland, found a home in Zurich. His candid intelligence and pleasant manner were the cause of much homage from the leading German and Swiss Reformers. Later on, though he did not expressly deny the doctrine of the Trinity, suspicion arose against him, and he needed the assistance of Bullinger to appease Calvin, and to turn aside the doubt as to his belief. Thereafter he abstained from controversy, and kept his opinions more to himself. At the time of his visit to Italy in 1560, on the occasion of his father's death, his correspondence brought upon his house the ill repute of heresy, so that the family estate was confiscated to the Inquisition, and he returned to Zurich to spend there the last two years of his life in poverty, and yet in peace and prestige due to the friendship of Sigismund II. of Poland. He published *De hæreticis, an sint persequendi . . . doctorum virorum . . . sententiæ* (Magdeburg [Basel], 1554); and *De sacramentis dissertatio* (Freistadt, Holland, 1654).

Bibliography: J. C. F. Hoefer, *Nouvelle biographie générale*, s.v., 46 vols., Paris, 1855–66; J. H. Allen, in *American Church History Series*, x. 49–56, New York, 1894; and the literature under Socinus, Faustus.

SOCRATES, sec'ra-tiz: Greek church historian; b. at Constantinople c. 380.

I. Life: Even in ancient times nothing seems to have been known of the life of Socrates except what was gathered from notices in his "Church History." His birth and education are related in V., xxiv. 9; his teachers were the grammarian Helladius and Ammonius, who came to Constantinople from Alexandria, where they had been heathen priests (V., xvi. 9). A revolt, accompanied by an attack upon the heathen temples, had forced them to flee. This revolt is dated about 390 (cf. the annotations of Reading and Hussey to V., xvi. 1). That Socrates later profited by the teaching of the sophist Troilus, is not proven; no certainty exists as to his precise vocation, although it may be inferred from his work that he was a layman. On the title-page of his history, he is designated as a *scholasticus* (lawyer). In later years Socrates traveled and visited among other places Paphlagonia and Cyprus (cf. *Hist. eccl.*, I., xii. 8, II., xxxviii. 30).

II. His "Church History": Socrates' work on church history was first edited in Greek by R. Stephen, on the basis of Codex Regius 1443 (Paris, 1544); a translation into Latin by Johannes Christophorson (1612) is important for its various readings. The fundamental edition, however, was produced by Valesius (Paris, 1668), who used Codex Regius, a Codex Vaticanus, and a Codex Florentinus, and also employed the indirect tradition of Theodorus Lector (*Codex Leonis Allatii*). The history covers the years 305–439, and was finished about 439, in any case during the lifetime of Emperor Theodosius, i.e., before 450 (cf. VII., xxii. 1; fuller details in Jeep, *Quellenuntersuchungen zu den griechischen Kirchenhistorikern* in *Neue Jahrbücher für Philologie und Pädagogik*, xiv. 137 sqq). The purpose of the history is to give a continuation of the work of Eusebius (I., i.). It relates in simple language and without panegyric what the Church has experienced from the days of Constantine to the writer's time. Ecclesiastical dissensions occupy the foreground; for when the Church is at peace there is nothing for the church historian to relate (VII., xlviii. 7). The fact that, besides treating of the Church, the work also deals with Arianism and with political events is defended in the preface to book V. Socrates seems to have owed the impulse to write his work to a certain Theodorus, who is alluded to in the proemium to bk. II. as "a holy man of God" and seems therefore to have been a monk or one of the higher clergy.

Period, Purpose, Scope.

The history in its present form is not a first edition. This is shown in the opening of the second book, where Socrates relates that he has thoroughly revised books I.–II. He has done this because in these books he had originally followed Rufinus, and in books III.–VII. he had drawn partly from Rufinus and partly from other sources. Then, from the works of Athanasius and the letters of prominent men of his time, he learned that Rufinus was not trustworthy, and was therefore induced to revise his work, and add the numerous documents scattered through the first two books. That the revision was not confined to these two books, but extended to the following ones, is shown by the erasure of the repetition at the end of the sixth book in the second Florentine manuscript. This passage proves also that the first edition was not only prepared but published. An attempt to state the sources used by Socrates was first made in a thorough manner by Jeep. It was shown that Socrates usually makes express mention of the source of his information. Geppert (see bibliography) offers a systematic analysis of these sources as follows: (1) Rufinus is often transcribed (I., xii., xv., II., i.; etc.), often quoted without acknowledgment from the Greek translation by Gelasius of Cæsarea; (2) Eusebius, *De vita Constantini*, cited in I., i., viii., xvi.; etc.; (3) Athanasius, *De synodis*, cited II., xxxvii.; and above all the *Apologia contra Arianos* (cf. the preface to book II.); (4) the collections of the acts of the councils by the Macedonian Sabinus, cited I., viii., II., xv.; etc.; (5) Eutropius, who is nowhere cited, although the comparison of Socrates II., xv. with Eutropius X., ix. shows the use of this author; (6) the Fasti, to whom Socrates is indebted for his political and semi-political data. Formally,

Sources.

Socrates is sometimes in accord with Idatius, sometimes with the *Chronicon paschale*, and occasionally with Marcellinus Comes. It is surprising that all the Olympiads are incorrectly stated by two years; (7) the list of the bishops of Constantinople, Alexandria, Antioch, and probably also of Rome and Jerusalem. For Constantinople, the bishops of the Arian and Novatian parties are also noted. Jeep believes that other sources have been used, for instance, Philostorgios, Eunapius, Auxanon, and the letters of Constantine. Harnack and Geppert conjecture the use of biographies of the emperors. This is not proven and seems especially improbable for the time of Constantine, since Socrates expressly states in the preface to book V. that he was unable to obtain data concerning the political events of that time and observes that henceforth he would write what he himself saw or what he had been able to learn from eye-witnesses. The composition of the "History" is not seldom mechanical. Socrates often cites Eusebius and Athanasius literally (ii. 37) and it not infrequently happens that he copies his sources almost word for word. Yet criticism of the sources is not lacking, as in the fact that recognition of the untrustworthiness of Rufinus induced Socrates to rewrite his work.

Author's Limitations and Relationships.

Socrates was one of the most celebrated men of his time, and could fully appreciate Hellenic discipline, of which he says that Christ and his disciples looked upon it as neither harmful nor divine, therefore every individual should be allowed to take the stand he pleases, either for or against it. Moreover, although the Holy Scriptures reveal divine dogmas to us and revive our piety—the real life and faith—nevertheless, they do not give training in logic, by the aid of which we must meet the adversaries of the truth; this, however, is essential, since the enemy is best combated with his own weapons. Socrates did not possess real learning; he relates simply, rarely cutting the thread of his descriptions by reflections, as, for instance, in III., vii., xvi. He had also little interest in mere theology. For him, the principal factor in Christianity was the doctrine of the Trinity, but he did not feel the need of conceiving this distinctly and intelligently and of formulating it. He essentially agrees with his citation from Evagrius' *Monachicum* (III., vii. 23): "We must bow down in silence before the unutterable." This indifference of Socrates to theology, perhaps also an inborn mildness of temperament, determined his attitude toward the ecclesiastical disputes of his time; he was opposed to the use of force against heretics (VII., xli., cf. xxix.). He does not judge harshly even the Arians, although he regarded them as notorious heretics (I., viii. 1–2). His attitude toward the Novatians was especially friendly; he reproaches Celestine with having persecuted the Roman Novatians (VII., xi.), and considers seriously whether the hard fate that befell John Chrysostom was not a punishment for his having destroyed Novatian churches (VI., xix. 7). He often alludes to the Novatians specifically (I., x., II., xxxviii.; etc.), and is remarkably well informed regarding their history. These facts have been explained by the assertion that Socrates himself was a Novatian, but this is incorrect, at least for the time when he wrote his "History." In V., xx. 1, he speaks of the Novatians in the same way as of the Arians, the Macedonians, and the Eunomians. The personal relations of Socrates with Auxanon, who had been present at the Nicene council and lived up to the time of the younger Theodosius (i. 13; cf. i. 10; Auxanon, whether of the same faith or not, could therefore give valuable information), and, on the other hand, the importance of the Novatian communities in Constantinople, explain his interest in this sect. It is self-evident, in spite of his good will, that no great work could be expected from a writer like Socrates. He was well qualified to relate personal experiences, but was not able to write history. This was the judgment of Valesius and it is confirmed by the later commentators. His reports are not reliable, and, in cases not a few, wrong. However, the later books, especially the sixth and seventh, contain much valuable information.

(G. Loeschcke.)

Bibliography: Other editions than those mentioned in the text are by G. Reading, Cambridge, 1720, reproduced in *MPG*, lxvii.; R. Hussey, Oxford, 1853, reproduced by W. Bright, ib. 1878. Eng. transls. are in Bohn's *Ecclesiastical Library*, London, 1851, and in *NPNF*, 2 ser., vol. ii.

On the life of Socrates consult the introductions to the editions as given in the text and above; Fabricius-Harles, *Bibliotheca Græca*, vii. 423 sqq., Hamburg, 1801; Ceillier, *Auteurs sacrés*, viii. 514–525; Bardenhewer, *Patrologie*, pp. 332–333, Eng. transl., St. Louis, 1908; Schaff, *Christian Church*, iii. 880–881; *DCB*, iv. 709–711; *KL*, xi. 473–476. On his work consult the essay of Jeep mentioned in the text, and the introductions in the editions of the text; F. A. Holzhausen, *De fontibus, quibus Socrates, Sozomenus, ac Theodoretus in scribenda historia sacra usi sunt*, Göttingen, 1825; J. G. Dowling, *Introduction to the Critical Study of Ecclesiastical Hist.*, pp. 34 sqq., London, 1838; H. M. Gwatkin, *Studies of Arianism*, p. 97, Cambridge, 1882; Batiffol, *Quæstiones Philostorgianæ*, Paris, 1891; Rauschen, in *Jahrbuch der christlichen Kirche*, 1897, pp. 2 sqq.; F. Geppert, *Die Quellen des Kirchenhistorikers Socrates Scholasticus*, Leipsic, 1898.

SOCRATES: Greek philosopher and teacher; b. in Pæania (on the east of Mt. Hymettus, near the modern Liopesi, 8 m. s.e. of Athens) 469 B.C.; d. at Athens in May or June, 399. As a youth he was a sculptor, but he later devoted his manhood, even till old age, to the assiduous practise of bringing to birth the thoughts and characters of his youthful countrymen, humorously likening his occupation to that of a midwife. In three battles—at Potidæa, at Delium, and at Amphipolis—he proved himself a brave and efficient citizen-soldier. At the age of sixty, as a senator—the only instance in which he accepted office—he showed his moral and political heroism by withstanding alone the excited passions, and for the time thwarting the perverse and vindictive purpose, of the people in their popular assembly. He also in 406 opposed the illegal disposition of the trial of eight generals by a single vote. At the age of seventy he was accused of corrupting the youth, and not worshiping the gods of his country, tried before the popular dicastery, condemned by a small majority of votes, and sentenced to death by drinking hemlock.

The philosophy of Socrates is not so much a system of doctrines as a spirit of inquiry and a method of search for the truth. That method, the method of question and answer, was so characteristic of Socrates, and at the same time so full of life and power that it was adopted more or less by all his disciples and has ever since been known as the Socratic method. It is seen in its perfection in the "Dialogues" of Plato, which are the idealized conversations of the idealized Socrates. The subject-matter of the Socratic philosophy is ethics in contradistinction to physics; its aim is practical to the exclusion of barren speculation; and conscious ignorance, modesty, moderation, and pure and high morality are among its most marked characteristics.

The chief good, our being's end and aim, according to the Socratic ethics, is happiness, that well-being which results from well-doing in obedience to the will of God and with the blessing of Heaven. Xenophon and Plato agree in making Socrates teach that he who knows justice is just, and the man who understands virtue is virtuous: in other words, he resolves all virtue into knowledge. But it is plain from both these writers that he used knowledge in a high and comprehensive sense unusual in ethical treatises, but strikingly analogous to that in which it is used in the Scriptures. He makes knowledge identical with wisdom, and ignorance with folly and sin, just as in the Bible piety is wisdom, and sin is folly: the wicked have no knowledge, while the righteous know all things.

Socrates believed in the existence of one supreme Divinity, the creator and disposer of the universe, all-powerful, omniscient, and omnipresent, perfectly wise and just and good. His method of demonstrating the existence of such a being was strictly Baconian, the same argument as Paley used in his *Natural Theology*. And what Xenophon records of his master of those unwritten laws in the soul of man which execute themselves, and make it impossible for any man to be unjust, or impure, or licentious, without paying the penalty (which proves a greater and better than any human lawgiver), recalls Bishop Butler himself. Socrates believed himself to be under the constant guidance of a divine voice, which always warned him when he was in danger of going or doing wrong, and thus, indirectly, always led him in the right way; and he taught that every man might have the same divine guidance. He held the doctrine of the immortality of the soul and the future life as strenuously as Plato did, but without those dreams and chimeras of its preexistence and successive transmigrations by which the creed of the latter was disfigured. It was the beauty and glory of Socrates' character, that his doctrine of providence and prayer and a future state was the controlling principle of his life, and he believed that death was not an evil, but the highest good and the richest blessing. His teachings, illustrated by a conscientious, unselfish, heroic, missionary life, and sealed by a martyr's death, are the main secret of his power, and these exhibit him in his true relation to Christianity.

D. PERCY GILMORE.

BIBLIOGRAPHY: Sources are the "Memorabilia" and "Symposium" of Xenophon, Plato's "Apology," "Symposium," "Crito," and "*Phaedo*," Plutarch's *De genio Socratis*, and Diogenes Laertius, "Lives of Philosophers." To be taken into account are the works on the history of philosophy by H. Ritter, 4 vols., Oxford, 1838–46; W. A. Butler, 2 vols., Cambridge, 1855; G. H. Lewes, 4 vols., London, 1857; J. B. Mayor, *Ancient Philosophy*, Cambridge, 1881; A. Schwegler, 3d ed., Freiburg, 1882; W. Windelband, New York, 1893; J. E. Erdmann, vol. i., London, 1892; E. Zeller, 2 vols., 1897; F. Ueberweg, ed. Heinze, 9th ed., Berlin, 1901–05, Eng. transl., of earlier edition, vol. i., London, 1875. Consult further: F. Charpentier, *La Vie de Socrate*, 3d ed., Paris, 1699, Eng. transl., London, 1758; R. Nares, *An Essay on the Demon or Divination of Socrates*, London, 1782; J. W. Hanne, *Socrates als Genius der Humanität*, Brunswick, 1841; J. P. Potter, *The Religion of Socrates*, London, 1831; idem, *Characteristics of the Greek Philosophers, Socrates and Plato*, ib. 1845; E. M. Goulburn, *Socrates*, London, 1858; E. Goguel, *Aristophane et Socrate*, Strasburg, 1859; H. Schmidt, *Sokrates*, Halle, 1866; A. Garnier, *Histoire de la morale*, Paris, 1865; A. Chaignet, *La Vie de Socrate*, Paris, 1868; E. Alberti, *Sokrates: ein Versuch über ihn nach den Quellen*, Göttingen, 1869; P. Montée, *La Philosophie de Socrate*, Arras, 1869; J. S. Blackie, *Four Phases of Morals*, London, 1871; H. E. Manning, *The Dæmon of Socrates*, London, 1872; A. Fouillée, *La Philosophie de Socrate*, 2 vols., Paris, 1874; C. Charaux, *L'Ombre de Socrate*, Paris, 1878; A. W. Benn, *The Greek Philosophers*, 2 vols., London, 1882; idem, *The Philosophy of Greece*, ib. 1898; A. B. Moss, *Socrates, Buddha, and Jesus*, London, 1885; C. du Prel, *Die Mystik der alten Griechen*, Leipsic, 1888; F. Dümmler, *Akademika*, Giessen, 1889; R. M. Wenley, *Socrates and Christ*, London, 1889; A. Döring, *Die Lehre des Sokrates als sociales Reformsystem*, Munich, 1895; R. W. Emerson, *Two Unpublished Essays*, Boston, 1896; A. D. Godley, *Socrates and Athenian Society in his Day*, London, 1896; E. Pfleiderer, *Sokrates, Plato und ihre Schüler*, Tübingen, 1896; J. T. Forbes, *Socrates*, Edinburgh, 1905; E. Lange, *Sokrates*, Gütersloh, 1906.

SODEN, HANS KARL HERMANN, FREIHERR VON: German Protestant; b. at Cincinnati, O., Aug. 16, 1852. He was educated at Esslingen, Urach, and the theological institute of Tübingen, and was then curate at Wildbad, near Stuttgart (1875–80), pastor at Dresden-Striesen (1881–82), and archdeacon at Chemnitz (1883–86). Since 1887 he has been pastor of the Jerusalemkirche, Berlin, and in 1889 became privat-docent for New-Testament exegesis at the university of the same city, where he has been associate professor since 1893. In theology he belongs to the liberal school, and has written *Der Brief des Apostels Paulus an die Philipper* (Freiburg, 1889); the volumes on Hebrews, the Epistles of Peter, James, and Jude, Colossians, Ephesians, Philemon for the *Handkommentar zum Neuen Testament* (2 vols., 1890–91); *Reisebriefe aus Palästina* (Berlin, 1898); *Palästina und seine Geschichte* (Leipsic, 1899); *Die Schriften des Neuen Testaments in ihrer ältesten erreichbaren Textgestalt* (Berlin, 1902 sqq.); *Die wichtigsten Fragen im Leben Jesu* (1904); and *Urchristliche Literaturgeschichte* (1905).

SODOM. See PALESTINE, II., § 10.

SOERENSEN, ANDERS HERMAN VILHELM: Danish clergyman; b. at Randers (a town of Jutland, 118 m. n.w. of Copenhagen) June 27, 1840. He was graduated from the Randers Latin School (1858), and from the University of Copenhagen (candidate in theology, 1865); with his wife he conducted in Copenhagen a school for girls, 1865–1874; in 1869 he was made chaplain at Frederiksberg (a suburb of Copenhagen), in 1876 pastor in Taanum-Hornbök (Viborg), and in 1890 pastor at Husby (Funen), his present charge. He is regarded as Denmark's greatest living authority on foreign

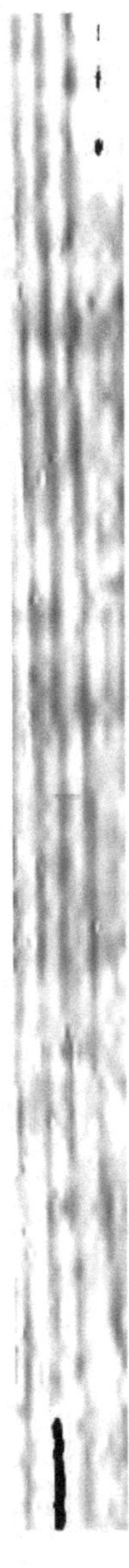

himself in the city during the reign of Solomon. It is thus evident that while Solomon held the kingdom together, it was not without difficulty or even without some diminution of territory. Possibly, however, Solomon attached less importance to protecting his frontiers than to strengthening Israel within. He built strong fortifications, prepared material of war, and kept his supplies in the best possible condition. Above all, he was successful in introducing the horse for cavalry and chariots.

Solomon seems to have possessed high talents for organization and finance, and his justice became proverbial. The entire land of Israel was divided into twelve administrative districts, each required to pay the expenses of the royal court for a month. There likewise seemed to have been special districts for public works, one of the chief officials of the kingdom being Adoniram, master of the levy. Hand in hand with this organization doubtless went the final absorption of the Canaanites, whom Solomon compelled to share in the levies and taxes of the Israelites. Besides introducing the horse into Israel, Solomon extended his commercial relations to the Sabeans of South Arabia and to Ophir (q.v.).

Solomon's financial talents seem to have been exhausted in acquiring vast wealth. He was even obliged, toward the end of his reign, to pawn twenty cities, while taxation was so heavy that discontent appeared in the revolt against his successor. Solomon had never learned in the stern school of his father. He grew up as a rich heir in the splendor of a royal court, inheriting certain despotic tendencies and weaknesses, and inclined to prodigality, display, and sensuality. In addition to the fortresses and the luxurious court, which included 700 wives and 300 concubines, his palaces and the Temple (q.v.) required an immense outlay. With the help of Syrian artists he transformed a large part of the hill of Zion in the eastern part of Jerusalem into a sort of city of palaces. Like his riches, the wisdom of Solomon was proverbial (cf. I Kings iv. 29 sqq.); 3,000 proverbs and more than 1,000 songs were ascribed to him; and he was said to be the author of Ps. lxxii. and cxxvii., as well as of the book of Proverbs (q.v.). (R. KITTEL.)

BIBLIOGRAPHY: The sources are I Kings i.–xi. and I Chron. xxix. 22–II Chron. i.–ix. Consult further: The works on the history of Israel by Milman, Stanley, F. Newman, Ewald, Stade, Köhler, Klostermann, Cornill, Kittel, McCurdy, Kent, and others named under AHAB or ISRAEL, HISTORY OF; G. Weil, *The Bible, the Koran, and the Talmud, or, Biblical Legends of the Musulmans*, pp. 200–248, London, 1846; G. Meignan, *Salomon; son regne, ses écrits*, Paris, 1890; M. Grünbaum, *Neue Beiträge zur semitischen Sagenkunde*, pp. 190 sqq., Berlin, 1893; idem, *Gesammelte Aufsätze zur Sprach- und Sagenkunde*, pp. 22 sqq., 167 sqq., ib. 1901; F. Vigouroux, *La Bible et les découvertes modernes*, iii. 253–405, 6th ed., Paris, 1896; B. W. Bacon, *Solomon in Tradition and Fact*, in *New World*, 1898, pp. 212 sqq.; R. Färber, *König Salomon in der Tradition*, Vienna, 1902; C. F. Kent, *Student's Old Testament*, ii. 14–16, 165–199, New York, 1905; G. Beer, *Saul, David, Salomo*, Tübingen, 1906; *DB*, iv. 559–569; *EB*, ii. 2235–38, iv. 4680–90; *JE*, xi. 436–448; Vigouroux, *Dictionnaire*, fasc. xxxv. 1382–96.

SOLOMON BAR ISAAC. See RASHI.

SOLOMON, ODES OF: The Odes of Solomon, which, until recently, were, except for certain fragments and quotations, altogether lost, were commonly connected in the tradition of Christian literature with the Psalms of Solomon (see PSEUDEPIGRAPHA, II., 1). In this grouping of material, the ancient stichometries gave them a place, more or less honorable, among the subcanonical literature. How near they came to actual ecclesiastical acceptance could only be guessed by analogy, from the companion volume to which they were attached. The stichometries, however, gave a rough idea of the compass of the book, from the point of view of a librarian or bookseller, from which it was easy to infer that a lost book of nearly the same compass as the Psalms of Solomon was once in circulation in Christian churches. In the next place, quotations professing to come from the missing book were recovered from two quarters: first, there was a passage relating to the birth of Christ from a virgin, quoted by Lactantius (*De div. inst.*, iv. 12; Eng. transl., *ANF*, vii. 110), which he said was from the nineteenth ode of Solomon. Second, there was a series of Odes of Solomon quoted in a Coptic book, a chief monument of Gnostic literature, which goes under the name of *Pistis Sophia*. These odes and fragments of odes were turned back into Greek and published by Ryle and James at the close of their edition of the Psalms of Solomon.

The book itself, so long lost, was recovered by J. Rendel Harris in a Syriac version, Jan. 4, 1909; it had been reposing along with a number of other Syriac fragments on his bookshelves, apparently for a couple of years or more, the manuscript in question having come from the neighborhood of the Tigris. When the identification was made, it appeared that the manuscript, a late paper one of no extrinsic value, contained both the Odes and the Psalms of Solomon; it was slightly mutilated at the beginning, so that odes one and two and a part of ode three were missing; at the other end the eighteenth of the Psalms of Solomon was gone and part of the seventeenth. The nineteenth ode contained the quotation which Lactantius gives in a Latin translation; all the matter quoted by the *Pistis Sophia* was also identified, and in addition a part of the first ode was also with some probability detected in the Coptic text. So that, with a very slight deduction for the imperfection of the manuscript, the complete book was recovered and restored to its place in Christian literature. The forty-two odes thus recovered are of rare beauty and spirituality; with possibly an exception or two, they come from a single hand, and represent a hitherto unknown department of early Christian literature. They were produced in the latter part of the first century or the early part of the second. The writer was a person of Gentile extraction, who had become attached to a Church of Judeo-Christians, probably in Palestine. He did not, however, accept circumcision or keep the Sabbath, occupying exactly the position which Justin Martyr did on those points, which he says he learned from an ancient Christian to whom he owed his conversion. So far as can be judged from the hints in the odes (it must be remembered that a psalter is not the easiest place from which to extract history), he knew Jesus as the Messiah or Christ, but did not know the Synoptic tradition about him. Whether he knew the Fourth Gospel, with which he has many ideas and expressions in common, is one of the points that are still in debate. He has occasional points of contact with the Pauline epistles, and even more with the Apocalypse, though it is difficult to establish quotations. His real Gospel appears to have been one of the lost Hebrew or Nazarene Gospels, perhaps the same as that of which Jerome found a copy in Tiberias. To this he owed some details in reference to the baptism, and perhaps one or two sayings of Jesus. It is curious that he has no eschatology, and no day of judgment; immortality is not innate, but acquired. On the ethical side the most important feature is that the book appears to contain the first Christian prohibition of the purchase of slaves.

The church orders and ritual are almost absent; it is not certain that baptism is alluded to, still less are there traces of a Christian eucharist, as commonly known. The only reference to the officials are an allusion: (1) to blessed deacons who carry the water of life, (2) to a priesthood in spiritual things which the writer says he possesses, which is carefully defined as not being of a carnal nature, but consisting of truth and purity in the inmost parts.

The writer shows a strong attachment to the Jewish religion on many sides: he has an affection for the sanctuary at Jerusalem, which must be assumed to have fallen before the time when he was writing; he holds fast to the Old Testament, allegorises (as do all early Christians) the story in Genesis, imitates the Psalms, and makes evangelical doctrine out of Isaiah (e.g., chap. xxxv.).

Though there is much that is still uncertain, as to the place, time, and character of the writer, enough is known to place him as a worthy representative of the first or second generation after the apostles; and the new hymns will exert a wide influence upon the thought of the Church.

J. RENDEL HARRIS.

BIBLIOGRAPHY: *The Odes and Psalms of Solomon*, edited from the Syriac by J. Rendel Harris, Cambridge, 1909 (*editio princeps*); J. Rendel Harris, *An early Christian Psalter*, London, 1909; *Ein jüdisch-christliches Psalmbuch aus dem ersten Jahrhundert. Aus dem Syrischen übersetzt von J. Flemming*, ed. A. Harnack, Leipsic, 1910; *Literarisches Zentralblatt*, 1910, no. 24, cols. 777–781.

SOLOMON, PSALMS OF. See PSEUDEPIGRAPHA, O. T., II., 1.

SOLOMON, WISDOM OF. See APOCRYPHA, A, iv., 13.

SOM, KONRAD. See SAM.

SOMASCHIANS, so-mas′ki-ans ("Regular Clerks of St. Majolus"): One of the most important monastic congregations evoked by the Counter-Reformation. They derive their name from the Italian village of Somascho (between Milan and Bergamo), where their founder, Girolamo Miani (or Emiliani), wrote the first rule for them. Miani, who was of senatorial rank, was born at Venice in 1481, and, entering the army, was recognized as a brave but dissolute officer. Captured at the storming of Castelnuovo, near Treviso, in 1508, he was led during his imprisonment to repentance for his past career, and on his liberation (according to many, through the miraculous aid of the Virgin) he devoted himself to asceticism, prayer, and the care of the sick and poor. At Venice he took orders, being ordained priest in 1518, and manifested the utmost self-denial and bravery, especially during the famine and plague of 1528. He now made absolute renunciation of his wealth, and, in the habit of a mendicant friar, gave himself to the care, education, and conversion of orphans and fallen women. Within the year he established an orphan asylum in Venice, which was imitated at Bergamo, Verona, and Brescia, and in 1532 he opened a home for fallen women in his native city. In 1532 or 1533 Miani established his congregation for the care of these institutions and the training of pupils for the same purpose; and Clement VII. gave him the mother house at Somascho, where Miani died Feb. 8, 1537, after having established daughter houses at Pavia and Milan. He was beatified by Benedict XIV., and canonized in 1761 by Clement XIII., his day being July 20.

Miani's successor, Angelo Marco Gambarana, secured from Pius V., in 1568, the formal constitution of the congregation under the Augustinian rule, their name being now taken from the church of St. Majolus at Pavia, given them by St. Carlo Borromeo (q.v.). The Somaschians, who were united with the Theatines from 1546 to 1555, and with the French Fathers of Christian Doctrine from 1616 to 1647, exercised deep influence on education through their many colleges, especially the Clementinum, founded at Rome in 1595; while they so increased in numbers that they were divided into the Lombard, Venetian, and Roman provinces, to which was later added the French. The Roman province is now the most important.

The constitutions of the congregation, gradually developed from the autograph draft of the founder, collected by the procurator-general Antonio Paulino in 1626, and confirmed by Urban VIII., have remained practically unchanged to the present day. They prescribe a habit precisely like that of the other regular clerks, strict simplicity of food and furniture, numerous prayers by day and night, fasts and self-castigation, and occupation with manual labor, care of the sick and orphans, and teaching.

(O. ZÖCKLER†.)

BIBLIOGRAPHY: The "Life" of the founder is given with commentary in *ASB*, Feb., ii. 217–274, Ital. transl. by A. Piegadi, Venice, 1865. Other lives are by S. Albani, Milan, 1600; A. Stella, Venice, 1605; P. G. de' Ferrari, ib. 1676; an anonymous one, ib. 1767; F. Caccia, ib. 1822; C. de Rossi-Borgogno, Rome, 1867; and W. E. Hubert, Mainz, 1895. Consult further, on the order: L. Holstenius, *Codex regularum monasticarum*, ed. M. Brockie, iii. 199–292, Augsburg, 1759; G. Giucci, *Iconografia istorica degli ordini religiosi*, vii. 160 sqq., Rome, 1847; E. Gothein, *Ignaz von Loyola und die Gegenreformation*, pp. 193–198, Halle, 1895; Helyot, *Ordres monastiques*, iv. 223 sqq.; Heimbucher, *Orden und Kongregationen*, iii. 275–278; *KL*, xi. 486–487; Ranke, *Popes*, i. 133–134.

SON OF GOD: A phrase standing for several different meanings in the New Testament. (1) It refers to the divine origination of J-
Spirit (Luke i. 35). (2) In the of
the Son. He is like the Father, i

to him, and thus reflects the Father's will. By reason of the fellowship of love, the Father is perfectly disclosed to him, and the depths of his own inner life are comprehended by the Father alone (Matt. xi. 27; John v. 17-21, 30, vii. 16-18, xii. 44-50, xiv. 7-11). (3) From the ethical oneness with the Father sprang the consciousness of the messianic or official sonship—the social aspect of his consciousness (Mark i. 11; cf. the baptismal formula, Matt. xxviii. 19; *Didache*, vii.). These two aspects—the individual and the social—may be distinguished but they can not be sharply separated. The messianic sonship points backward (I Sam. x. 1; Ps. ii. 7) and forward (Mark xiv. 61). In him the royal hopes of Israel are fulfilled; he founds the world-kingdom of God (John xvii. 18; cf. Matt. xxviii. 19; John xx. 21); his universal sovereignty is won through suffering (Matt. xix. 20-28). (4) Metaphysical sonship is also affirmed of him. As Logos he is the only begotten Son of God (John i. 14, iii. 16, v. 18; Rom. viii. 32). He is the image of the invisible God, first-born of all creation, mediator of all existence, through whom all things find their principle and progressively realise their divine end (I Cor. viii. 6; Col. i. 15-17; John i. 3, 10; Heb. i. 2-3). His pre-earthly existence was exchanged for humiliation and death here below (II Cor. viii. 9; Phil. ii. 5-7; cf. Rom. viii. 3; Gal. iv. 4; and see JESUS CHRIST, TWOFOLD STATE OF). Accordingly he was God's own son, the archetypal son of God; all others become sons of God through him (John i. 12). Yet all that belongs to him is a gift of God (Matt. xxviii. 18; John iii. 35, v. 22, xiii. 3; Acts ii. 36; Phil. ii. 9-10; Heb. i. 2, ii. 7-8; cf. also I Cor. xv. 24-28).

In historical theology the Son of God as pre-existent is the second person of the Trinity, consubstantial with the Father, and is described as only-begotten, the Word; as incarnate he took upon him human nature yet without sin; and existed in two whole, perfect, and distinct natures inseparably joined together in one person without conversion, composition, or confusion; very God and very man, one Christ, the only mediator between God and man (see CHRISTOLOGY, IV., VII.; MEDIATOR). Ritschl, following Schleiermacher, took the doctrine of the sonship of Christ out of metaphysics and planted it in the field of ethics and the religious life. As Son, Christ stands to the Father in a relation of incomparable fellowship; his will is identical with that of the Father in the establishment of the kingdom of God; moreover, he sustains a unique relation to the Christian community and to the world. While for man the Son as pre-existent is hidden, yet for God he exists eternally "as he is revealed to us in temporal limitation." Only for God himself, however, is the eternal Godhead of the Son intelligible as an object of the divine mind and will (A. Ritschl, *The Christian Doctrine of Justification and Reconciliation*, §§ 47-49, New York, 1900).

C. A. BECKWITH.

BIBLIOGRAPHY: The subject is treated best in the works on New-Testament theology (see under BIBLICAL THEOLOGY), and in those on systematic theology (see under DOGMA, DOGMATICS). Much of the literature given under CHRISTOLOGY is pertinent, also that under SON OF MAN. Consult further: K. F. Nösgen, *Christus der Menschen- und Gottessohn*, Gotha, 1869; J. Stalker, *Christology of Jesus*, London, 1879; A. Harnack, *What is Christianity?* ib. 1901; R. C. Moberly, *Atonement and Personality*, pp. 185 sqq., 211-215, ib. 1901; W. Lütgert, *Gottes Sohn und Gottes Geist*, Leipsic, 1905; M. Lepin, *Christ and the Gospel; or Jesus the Messiah and Son of God*, Philadelphia, 1911; *DB*, iv. 570-579; *DCG*, ii. 654-659; *EB*, iv. 4690-4704.

END OF VOLUME X.

Stanford University Libraries
3 6105 008 424 389

Zeitfracht Medien GmbH
Ferdinand-Jühlke-Straße 7
99095 Erfurt, Deutschland
produktsicherheit@kolibri360.de